KU-778-402

The
HUTCHINSON
DICTIONARY
of
ideas

Helicon

Copyright © Helicon Publishing Ltd 1994

First published 1994
Revised paperback edition 1995
Reprinted 1997

All rights reserved

Helicon Publishing Ltd
42 Hythe Bridge Street
Oxford OX1 2EP

Typeset by TechType

Printed and bound in Great Britain by
The Bath Press Ltd, Bath.

ISBN 1–85986–050–8

British Cataloguing in Publication Data

A catalogue record for this book is available
from the British Library

Contents

Contributors

Owen Adikibi PhD
Bernard Balleine PhD
Elizabeth Breuilly
Celia E. Deane-Drummond PhD
Denis Derbyshire PhD
Ian Derbyshire PhD
Mawil Izzi Dien PhD
Eric Farge
Graham Ley MPhil
Chris Murray
Martin Palmer
Roy Porter
Richard Prime
P M Rowntree
Joe Staines
Calum Storrie
Chris Stringer
Catherine Thompson
Colin Tudge

Editorial Team

Editor
Anne-Lucie Norton
Consultant Editor
Joe Staines
Coordinating and Index Editor
Paul Davis
Text Editors
Jane Anson
Elizabeth Clarke
Paul Davis
Ingrid von Essen
Gian Douglas Home
Louise Jones
Frances Lass
Edith Summerhayes
Proofreader
Hazel Clarke
Paperback Editor
Avril Cridlan

Production
Tony Ballsdon

Note on the paperback edition

This edition contains over one hundred revisions, including new and many substantially extended entries. We have also added dates of death where known.

Introduction

What does the book contain?

What are 'ideas'? Most people would recognize such examples as existentialism, the free market, glasnost and nationalism. There is, however, underpinning these theories another kind of human imagining that can be called concepts. Examples of these would be justice, evil, the supernatural, gravity. It seemed to the editors when compiling *The Dictionary of Ideas* that what was wanted was both the theories and concepts as well their visible (and invisible) manifestations. We also believed that the reader would value having, in *one volume*, both the people (biographical entries) who gave us these concepts and beliefs along with the ideas themselves (subject entries).

So what can the reader expect to find in *The Dictionary of Ideas?* There are more than 4000 entries cutting across 21 distinct disciplines. People and concepts from philosophy, religion, economics, psychology, mathematics, computing science, chemistry, political theory, life sciences, education and the women's movement are all included.

The audience

The book is not aimed at the specialist, nor is it for anyone requiring detailed information within their own discipline. Although some of the entries deal with ideas which are by definition difficult, they have been written with the general reader in mind. The average length of an entry is about fifty words, giving a basic definition and the most important facts.

What is in, what is out

The key to good reference book publishing is *selection*. It was extremely difficult to decide what to bring in and what to leave out given the deliberately inclusive nature of the *Dictionary*. The main criteria were to include major thinkers as well as important figures from the world stage, both past and present, along with the concepts, institutions, theories, beliefs, movements and even attributes they inspired. While -isms and -ologies clearly had a place in the book, what about mythological figures or political groups? Should we have included all scientists when they were responsible for inventing something or only if they discovered a principle?

In all of the disciplines listed above the reader will find the basic principles included. For those subjects that are clearly central to the history of ideas such as philosophy, religion, psychology, sociology, political and economic theory there is a much wider range of entries.

And why

Historical figures are included when they have been associated with great movements,. e.g. Mikhail Gorbachev, Napoleon, Bismark, Cromwell and F D Roosevelt, even if they themselves were not responsible for the theories upon which they based their actions. F D Roosevelt did not create the economic theories upon which The New Deal was built, but he is forever linked with it and earns a place in the book.

It was much more difficult to decide which literary and artistic figures to include. Our criterion was to include those who are so identified with a trend or movement that they have come to personify it for most people, such as Pablo Picasso for Cubism, Arnold Schoenberg for twelve-tone music, George Bernard Shaw for progressive thinking and pamphlet-writing. Others are in not just because they were esteemed practitioners of their art, but because they were highly regarded critics as well, for example, Filippo Brunelleschi (architecture), T S Eliot (writer) and Wassily Kandinsky (artist).

Cultural terms if they are strictly literary or artistic in application, for example *bel canto, Sturm und Drang*, Pointillism are not in. When, however, a term covers many fields of endeavour and has a wider resonance in society, such as structuralism or Postmodernism, then it is in.

Mythological figures when noted for a concept they inspired, for example Narcissus for narcissism, Pandora and her box are included, as are those represented over many centuries in artistic and creative activity such as Thor, Isis and Ra.

We have included a wide range of scientists if they invented something (Andrei Markov), developed something (Alexander Fleming) or won a Nobel Prize (Marie Curie).

International in scope

Many entries in the *Dictionary* were commissioned specifically for their non-Western content. There are hundreds of entries on aspects of Hinduism, Buddhism, ancient religions, native American religion and much more.

Special features

Quotes There are over 350 specially selected quotes included. The quotes are of two sorts: one type is a direct quote as spoken or written by the individual whose entry features; the second kind is a thematic quotation relating to the concept or belief given. Examples are aggression, faith, love, war.

Feature Articles In the *Dictionary* there are 21 specially written pieces which address a major issue or controversy in science, the arts or ethics. The range is wide and includes 'Animal Rights and Vivisection', 'Romanticism: An Idea and its Legacy' and 'Urban Design in the Twentieth Century: The City of Tomorrow?'

The features have been placed as near as possible to relevant entries in the *Dictionary* as the following list shows:

Headword	*Title of feature*
abortion	ABORTION: NO MORAL CONSENSUS
animal liberation	ANIMAL RIGHTS AND VIVISECTION
conservation	THE RACE TO PREVENT MASS EXTINCTION
Enlightenment	THE ENLIGHTENMENT
euthanasia	EUTHANASIA
evil	MORAL EVIL AND HUMAN NATURE
evolution	'OUT OF AFRICA' AND THE EVE HYPOTHESIS
humours, the four	ILLNESS: HEALTH, DISEASE AND THE HUMOURS
individualism	PERSONAL HAPPINESS AND THE CULT OF THE INDIVIDUAL
love	LOVE
madness	MADNESS
medical ethics	MEDICAL ETHICS: THE CROSSROADS REACHED?
mind body problem	MIND-BODY DUALISM AND THE RIDDLE OF HUMAN CONSCIOUSNESS
patronage	PATRONAGE: STILL ALIVE AND WELL?
politics	POLITICAL POWER: DOES IT INEVITABLY CORRUPT?
post-modernism	POST-MODERNISM: THE BEGINNING OF THE END?
progress	PROGRESS AND THE IDEA OF PERFECTABILITY
religion	SCIENCE AND RELIGION: ENEMIES OR PARTNERS?
romanticism	ROMANTICISM: AN IDEA AND ITS LEGACY
town planning	URBAN DESIGN IN THE TWENTIETH CENTURY: THE CITY OF TOMORROW?
utopianism	THE CITY AND UTOPIA

Tables, Chronologies and Boxes The *Dictionary* has 27 useful listings of information across many subject areas. Examples are: the Books of the Bible; Major Debtor Nations; Islamic calendar; Main Language Groups (and Number of Speakers); Major Political Thinkers and Patron Saints.

Indexes There are 33 pages of indexes, organized in two ways, one of all the subjects in the book and one of the individuals.

Cross References These are shown by a symbol immediately preceding the reference. Cross-referencing is selective: a cross reference is shown when another entry contains material that is relevant to the subject matter of an entry, and which the reader might not otherwise think of consulting. There are no cross-references in the feature articles, since to include them would have meant, in most cases, several symbols per line of text.

Anne-Lucie Norton

List of Feature Articles

List of Tables, Chronologies, and Boxes

Aaron c. 13th century BC. In the Old Testament, the elder brother of Moses and co-leader of the ◊Hebrews in their march from Egypt to the Promised Land of Canaan. He made the Golden Calf for the Hebrews to worship when they despaired of Moses' return from Mount Sinai, but he was allowed to continue as high priest. All his descendants are hereditary high priests, called the *cohanim*, or cohens, and maintain a special place in worship and ceremony in the synagogue. See also ◊Levite.

abbey in the Christian church, a monastery (of monks) or a nunnery or convent (of nuns), all dedicated to a life of celibacy and religious seclusion, governed by an abbot or abbess respectively. The word is also applied to a building that was once the church of an abbey, for example, Westminster Abbey, London.

The first abbeys, as established in Syria or Egypt, were mere collections of huts, but later massive and extensive building complexes were constructed throughout Europe. St Benedict's Abbey at Monte Cassino in Italy and Citeaux and Cluny in France set the pattern. In England many abbeys were closed by Henry VIII, who turned from the Roman Catholic Church. In other countries many were closed in the 18th and 19th centuries as a result of political revolutions.

abduction in philosophy and logic, a form of probable inference. Aristotle uses the term to refer to a weak ◊syllogism that fails to carry certainty. For US philosopher C S Peirce, it is the process of generating hypotheses.

Abel John Jacob 1857–1938. US biochemist, discoverer of adrenaline. He studied the chemical composition of body tissues, and this led, in 1898, to the discovery of adrenaline, the first hormone to be identified, which Abel called epinephrine. He later became the first to isolate amino acids from blood.

Abel Niels Henrik 1802–1829. Norwegian mathematician. He demonstrated that the general quintic equation

$$ax^5 + bx^4 + cx^3 + dx^2 + ex + f = 0$$

could not be solved algebraically. Subsequent work covered elliptic functions, integral equations, infinite series, and the binomial theorem.

He lived a life of poverty and ill health, dying of tuberculosis shortly before the arrival of an offer of a position at the University of Berlin.

Abelard Peter 1079–1142. French scholastic philosopher who worked on logic and theology. He opposed realism in the debate over ◊universals, and propounded 'conceptualism' whereby universal terms have only a mental existence. He asserted the imporance of reason in religious belief, and his skillful application of logic and dialectic to such doctrines as the Trinity and atonement, though controversial, gave theology a new breadth. His views were condemned by St ◊Bernard of Clairvaux. His romantic liaison with his pupil Héloïse caused a medieval scandal. Details of his controversial life are contained in the autobiographical *Historia Calamitatum Mearum/The History of My Misfortunes* and his correspondence with Héloïse.

Abelard, born near Nantes, became canon of Notre Dame in Paris and master of the cathedral school 1115. When his secret marriage to Héloïse became known, she entered a convent and he was castrated at the instigation of her uncle Canon Fulbert, and became a monk.

Resuming teaching a year later, he was cited for heresy and became a hermit at Nogent, and later abbot of a monastery in Brittany.

Insofar as reason is hidden, let us be content with authority.

Peter Abelard
Medieval Thought: St Augustine to Ockham
G Leff

Abercrombie Leslie Patrick 1879–1957. English architect, a pioneer of British town planning. He is known for his work replanning British cities after damage in World War II (such as the Greater London Plan, 1944) and for the ◊ new town policy.

ablution washing for a religious purpose. Hindus wash before praying, preferably in running water, and washing in certain rivers, especially the Ganges, is believed to give spiritual benefit. Muslims wash themselves (*wudu*) before prayers, but this is seen as a mark of respect for God and a preparation for prayer rather than conferring any benefit in itself.

abnormality feature or an occurrence that is not normal; an aberration or irregularity; also the state of being abnormal. The term is widely used in a medical context and in psychology.

In statistics, it denotes variance from the norm; in psychology, it is a term less widely used today because of disagreement about defining 'normalness', and other terms are preferred: deviant, maladjusted, etc. *Abnormal psychology* concerns itself with unusual or deviant behaviour, with mental disorders, and with unusual experiences reported by normal individuals. Several approaches are employed – biological, physiological, behavioural, psychodynamic, and sociological – and the subject area overlaps with that of psychiatry, clinical psychology, and parapsychology. Many of the phenomena are relevant to general psychology and are studied under its various headings.

Bibl. McDougall, William *An Outline of Abnormal Psychology* (London, 1926)

abolitionism in UK and US history, a movement culminating in the late 18th and early 19th centuries that aimed first to end the slave trade, and then to abolish the institution of ◊slavery and emancipate slaves.

In the USA, slavery was officially abolished by the ◊Emancipation Proclamation 1863 of President Abraham Lincoln, but it could not be enforced until 1865 after the Union victory in the Civil War. The question of whether newly admitted states would allow slavery had been a major issue in the break-up of the Union.

In the UK, the leading abolitionist was William ◊Wilberforce, who secured passage of a bill abolishing the slave trade in 1807.

abominable snowman or *yeti* legendary creature, said to resemble a human, with long arms and a thickset body covered with reddish-grey hair. Reports of its existence in the Himalayas have been made since 1832, and they gained substance from a published photograph of a huge footprint in the snow in 1951. No further 'evidence' has been found.

abortion ending of a pregnancy before the fetus is developed sufficiently to survive outside the uterus. Loss of a fetus at a later gestational age is termed premature stillbirth. Abortion may be accidental (miscarriage) or deliberate (termination of pregnancy).

Methods of deliberate abortion vary according to the gestational age of the fetus. Up to 12 weeks, the cervix is dilated and a suction curette passed into the uterus to remove its contents (*D and C*). Over 12 weeks, a prostaglandin pessary is introduced into the vagina, which induces labour, producing a miscarriage.

Worldwide, an estimated 150,000 unwanted pregnancies are terminated each day by induced abortion. One-third of these abortions are performed outside the law in unsafe conditions, resulting in about 500 deaths a day.

In 1989 an anti-progesterone pill was introduced in France, under the name RU 486; in 1991 it was licensed in the UK, known as mefipristone. Within 24 hours of ingestion, it leads to the expulsion of the fetus from the uterus, and can be used at an earlier stage in pregnancy. The pill is also an effective contraceptive when taken up to 72 hours after intercourse.

Abortion as a means of birth control has long been the subject of controversy. The argument centres largely upon whether a woman should legally be permitted to have an abortion and, that being so, under what circumstances. Another aspect is whether, and to what extent, the law should protect the fetus. Those who oppose abortion generally believe that human life begins at the moment of conception, when a sperm fertilizes an egg. This is the view held, for example, by the Roman Catholic Church. Those who support unrestricted legal abortion may believe in a woman's right to choose whether she wants a child, and may take into account the large numbers of deaths and injuries from back-street abortions that are thus avoided. Others approve abortion for specific reasons. For example, if a woman's life or health is jeopardized, abortion may be recommended; and if there is a strong likelihood that the child will be born with severe mental or physical handicap. Other grounds for abortion include pregnancy resulting from sexual assault such as rape or incest.

In the UK an abortion must be carried out under the terms of the 1967 Abortion Act, which states that two doctors must agree that termination of the pregnancy is necessary, and the operation must be performed on approved premises.

The legal cut-off point for therapeutic abortion – in Britain 24 weeks – is largely arbitrary. Techniques have been developed to sustain

Abortion: No Moral Consensus

Spontaneous abortion is common in pregnancy and raises no serious moral or philosophical issues. Induced abortion is a different matter. In earlier centuries, as now, deliberately procured termination of pregnancy was fraught with religious, legal, moral, and philosophical consequences. Traditionally, however, the destructive act of greatest concern was infanticide. Although many earlier societies tolerated or even encouraged the killing or abandonment of the newly born to keep the population down, within Christendom infanticide was always reckoned sinful, as every live-born human was believed to have a soul. In Britain, severe punishments were enforced from the early seventeenth century against mothers guilty of infanticide.

Abortion criminalized

Induced abortion was long judged immoral and/or sinful. In the Hippocratic Oath physicians swore not to procure abortions (though initially chiefly to uphold professional status). There was widespread suspicion in pre-industrial times of 'wise women' for allegedly using abortifacient herbs, such as pennyroyal, and many quack remedies were in fact disguised abortifacients. Specific legislation against abortion was rare, however, before the nineteenth century. In Britain, the first Act came in 1803. In the USA, Connecticut criminalized abortion in 1821; other states followed. By 1868 thirty-six states had anti-abortion statutes, such legislation remaining on the statute book till the 1960s.

A British act of 1861 further criminalized abortion unless performed by a licensed doctor on medical grounds. Comparable legislation was passed in Europe. Its effect was to create a growing trade in 'back street' abortions, often conducted illegally but lucratively by the medical profession. As the desire to limit families grew, and in the absence of safe, legal and cheap contraception, abortion became the most popular method of family limitation in Germany and Russia, and perhaps Britain and the United States till the 1930s.

In Britain, the 1861 Act remained in force until the Abortion Act of 1967, which legalized abortion where advised by a physician on medical grounds. The medical profession (and Parliament) adamantly rejected 'abortion on demand' or abortion as a woman's right – though in practice the 1967 Act quickly brought about abortion on demand. Since then, various attempts have been made (on religious or anti-permissive grounds) to tighten the Act. Campaigners argue for the rights of the unborn child.

Between 1967 and early 1973 a dozen states in the USA adopted abortion laws permitting abortion when performed by a licensed physician who judged that there was a substantial risk that continuance of pregnancy would gravely impair the physical or mental health of the mother, that the child would be born with serious defects, or when pregnancy resulted from rape or incest. The right to abortion was more firmly established in 1973, when the Supreme Court ruled (in *Roe* v. *Wade*) that the constitutional right to privacy (Fourteenth Amendment to the Constitution) gave the full right to abortion during the first three months of pregnancy. During the second trimester, abortion would be legal if required for maternal health. Once the fetus became viable (the beginning of the third trimester), it was lawful to prohibit abortion, depending on exceptions relating to the protection of the woman's life or health. *Roe* v. *Wade* thus invalidated the laws restricting abortion in almost every state. Anti-abortion pressure groups continue to campaign against the judgment.

Against God's law?

Nowadays, opposition to abortion in Western societies comes essentially from Christian groups. Scriptural Protestants tend to see abortion as a sin, but as a matter for the individual conscience. The Roman Catholic Church has a long tradition of condemnation of abortion. Between the time of Pope Innocent III (1161–1216) and Sixtus V (1521–1590), decretals were issued prohibiting abortion, with excommunication as the penalty. In 1869, Pius IX (1792–1878) reaffirmed Vatican opposition to all abortion, even on therapeutic grounds (for example, when the mother's life was gravely endangered). The 1930 encyclical *Casti Connubii* condemned direct abortion, even when medical opinion believed that both mother and baby would die without it. The Second Vatican Council (1965) condemned it once again.

The social issues

Outside Catholicism, from the mid-twentieth century there has been increased moral and social acceptance of abortion in the West. It is widely justified, by the public and by ethicists, to protect the life or health of the mother; to remedy injuries due to incest or rape; and to prevent defective babies. Feminists have supported it to promote a woman's right to control her own reproductive capacity and her body. But difficulties remain.

One major problem is the question of precisely when human life truly begins. It is a judgment that must be made as much on philosophical and human as on biological grounds. It is difficult to decide whether, or how far, or from what point, a fetus has all the rights and values of every other human being, or whether it should be viewed principally as a part of the mother.

Roy Porter

babies delivered at an earlier stage of gestation (some as young as 23 weeks). In 1988, there were 183,978 abortions performed in England and Wales, an increase of 5.5% on 1987 figures. In the UK, 20% of conceptions in 1988 were terminated by abortion, mostly in the 16-24 age group.

In April 1990, after 15 unsuccessful attempts to alter the 1967 act, Parliament approved a measure to lower the time limit on abortions to 24 weeks.

abracadabra magic word first recorded in a Latin poem of the 2nd century AD by the Gnostic poet Serenus Sammonicus. When the letters were written in the form of an inverted pyramid, so that the word could be read both across the top and up the right-hand side, it was used as a health amulet, to ward off illnesses.

Abraham c. 2300 BC. In the Old Testament, founder of the Jewish nation. In his early life he was called Abram. God promised him heirs and land for his people in Canaan (Israel), renamed him Abraham ('father of many nations'), and tested his faith by a command (later retracted) to sacrifice his son Isaac.

Abraham was born in Ur, in Sumeria, the son of Terah. With his father, wife Sarah, and nephew Lot, he migrated to Haran, N Mesopotamia, then to Canaan where he received God's promise of land. After visiting Egypt he separated from Lot at Bethel and settled in Hebron (now in Israel). He was still childless at the age of 76, subsequently had a son (Ishmael) with his wife's maidservant Hagar, and then, at the age of 100, a son Isaac with his wife Sarah. God's promise to Abraham that his descendants would be a nation and Canaan their land was fulfilled when the descendants of Abraham's grandson, Jacob, were led out of Egypt by Moses. Abraham was buried in Machpelah Cave, Hebron.

abraxas charm found engraved on ancient stones. The Greek letters of the word, when interpreted as numbers, total 365. The word was used by Egyptian Gnostics to describe the supreme being.

absolute music music that refers to nothing apart from itself, as opposed to programme music which is descriptive.

absolution in Christianity: the authority of the Church to pronounce God's forgiveness to a penitent sinner. The Church acts as Christ's representative, and in so far as the Church is filled with the Spirit of God, pronounces the judgement of God.

absolutism or *absolute monarchy* system of government in which the ruler or rulers have unlimited power. The principle of an absolute monarch, given a right to rule by God (see ◊divine right of kings), was extensively used in Europe during the 17th and 18th centuries. Absolute monarchy is contrasted with limited or constitutional monarchy, in which the sovereign's powers are defined or limited.

abstinence the practice of refraining from bodily or sensual pleasures in order to attain a higher spiritual state or a more thorough concentration on the sacred. It is integral to the practice of ◊asceticism (training in self-denial for religious benefit), common in Buddhism, Hinduism, and some forms of Christianity.

abstract art nonrepresentational art. Ornamental art without figurative representation occurs in most cultures. The modern abstract movement in sculpture and painting emerged in Europe and North America between 1910 and 1920. Two approaches produce different abstract styles: images that have been 'abstracted' from nature to the point where they no longer reflect a conventional reality, and nonobjective, or 'pure', art forms, without any reference to reality.

Abstract art began in the avant-garde movements of the late 19th century – Impressionism, Neo-Impressionism, and Post-Impressionism. These styles of painting reduced the importance of the original subject matter and began to emphasize the creative process of painting itself. In the first decade of the 20th century, some painters in Europe began to abandon the established Western conventions of imitating nature and of storytelling and developed a new artistic form and expression. Kandinsky is generally regarded as the first abstract artist. From 1910–14 he worked on two series, *Improvisations* and *Compositions*, in which he moved gradually towards total abstraction. His highly coloured canvases influenced many younger European artists. In France around 1907, the Cubists Picasso and Braque also developed a semi-abstract style; their pictures, some partly collage, were composed mainly of fragmented natural images. By 1912 Delaunay had pushed Cubism to complete abstraction. Many variations of abstract art developed in Europe and Russia, as shown in the work of Mondrian, Malevich, the Futurists, the Vorticists, and the Dadaists. Sculptors were inspired by the new freedom in form and content, and Brancusi's versions of *The Kiss* 1907–12 are among the earliest semi-abstract sculptures. Cubist-inspired sculptors such as Duchamp-Villon (1876–1918) and Lipchitz moved further towards abstraction, as did the Dadaist Hans Arp. Two exhibitions of European art, one in New York 1913 (the Armory Show), the other in San Francisco 1917, opened the way for abstraction in US art. Many painters, including the young Georgia O'Keeffe, experimented with new styles. Morgan Russell (1886–1953) and Stanton Macdonald-Wright (1890–1973) invented their own abstract style, Synchronism, a rival to Orphism, a similar style developed in France by Delaunay – both emphasized colour over form. Abstract art has dominated Western art from 1920 and has continued to produce many variations. In the 1940s it gained renewed vigour in the works of the Abstract Expressionists. In the 1960s Minimal art provoked outraged reactions from critics and the general public alike.

Abstract Expressionism US movement in abstract art that emphasized the act of painting, the expression inherent in the colour and texture of the paint itself, and the interaction of artist, paint, and canvas. Abstract Expressionism emerged in New York in the early 1940s. Arshile Gorky, Franz Kline, Jackson Pollock, and Mark Rothko are associated with the movement.

Abstract Expressionism may have been inspired by Hans Hofmann and Gorky, who were both working in the USA in the 1940s. Hofmann, who emigrated from Germany in the 1930s, had started to use dribbles and blobs of paint to create expressive abstract patterns, while Gorky, a Turkish Armenian refugee, was developing his highly coloured abstracts using wild organic forms. Abstract Expressionism was not a distinct school but rather a convergence of artistic personalities, each in revolt against the prevailing conventions in US art. The styles of the movement's exponents varied widely: Pollock's huge dripped and splashed work, Willem de Kooning's grotesque figures, Kline's strong calligraphic style, and Robert Motherwell's and Rothko's large, calm canvases. The movement made a strong impression on European painting in the late 1950s.

abstraction in philosophy, the process by which ◊universals and concepts are formed in our minds or by which we acquire general words. Many modern philosophers, following Ludwig ◊Wittgenstein, hold that no concepts are acquired by abstraction, because the ◊meaning of a word is its public use, not a private idea.

◊Aristotle held that circularity does not exist apart from circular things, and that we acquire the abstraction of circularity by induction – that is, by generalizing from coins, hoops, and wheels. English philosopher John ◊Locke thought that the meaning of a general word, such as 'triangle', was an abstract idea in the mind.

Absurd, Theatre of the avant-garde drama originating with a group of dramatists in the 1950s, including Beckett, Ionesco, Genet, and Pinter. Their work expressed the belief that in a godless universe human existence has no meaning or purpose and therefore all communication breaks down. Logical construction and argument gives way to irrational and illogical speech and to its ultimate conclusion, silence, as in Beckett's play *Breath* 1970.

I have too much respect for the idea of God to make it responsible for such an absurd world.

absurdity
Georges Duhamel, 1884–1966,
French novelist.
Le désert de Bièvres

Abu Bakr or *Abu-Bekr* 573–634. 'Father of the virgin', name used by Abd-el-Ka'aba from about 618 when the prophet ◊Muhammad married his daughter Ayesha. He was a close adviser to Muhammad in the period 622–32. On the prophet's death, he became the first caliph, adding Mesopotamia to the Muslim world and instigating expansion into Iraq and Syria.

He was one of the first to accept Islam, and after Muhammad's death he supervised the collection of Muhammad's prophetic revelations to form the Qur'an.

Abu Hanifah Al-Nu'man c. 700–780. Sunni religious leader and jurist. He was the founder of the Hanafi School, the earliest school of Islamic law, which dominates Turkey and India. He was born in Kufa, Iraq, and died in Baghdad.

Academy originally, the school of philosophy founded by ◊Plato in the gardens of Academe, NW of Athens; it was closed by the Byzantine emperor Justinian I, with the other pagan schools, in AD 529. The first academy (in the present-day sense of a recognized society established for the promotion of one or more of the arts and sciences) was the Museum of Alexandria, founded by Ptolemy Soter in the 3rd century BC.

accessibility the ease with which a place may be reached. An area with high accessibility will generally have a well-developed transport network and be centrally located or at least at a route centre. Many economic activities, such as retailing, commerce, and industry, require high accessibility for their customers and raw materials.

Accessibility can be measured by an *accessibility index* or matrix. In this method, a topological (simplified) map of the transport network is produced and a table constructed to show the number of links necessary to get from one destination to another. The place with the fewest links has the lowest ◊Shimbel index (highest accessibility). This method ignores all other factors, such as population density, distance, quality of link, and traffic flow. Another measure is the ◊beta index.

accounting the principles and practice of systematically recording, presenting, and interpreting financial accounts; financial record keeping and management of businesses and other organizations, from balance sheets to policy decisions, for tax or operating purposes. Forms of inflation accounting, such as CCA (current cost accounting) and CCP (current purchasing power) are aimed at providing valid financial comparisons over a period in which money values change.

The accountant's role was formerly one of recording economic events for the purposes of stewardship. However, the increasing complexity of business organizations has led accountants into the areas of providing information for decision makers and even to prediction and analysis, both formerly the function of economists.

Achilles Greek hero of Homer's *Iliad*. He was the son of Peleus, king of the Myrmidons in Thessaly, and of the sea nymph Thetis, who rendered him invulnerable, except for the heel by which she held him, by dipping him in the river Styx. Achilles killed Hector at the climax of the *Iliad*, and according to subsequent Greek legends was himself killed by Paris, who shot a poisoned arrow into Achilles' heel.

acquired character feature of the body that develops during the lifetime of an individual, usually as a result of repeated use or disuse, such as the enlarged muscles of a weightlifter.

French naturalist Jean Baptiste ◊Lamarck's theory of evolution assumed that acquired characters were passed from parent to offspring. Modern evolutionary theory does not recognize the inheritance of acquired characters because there is no reliable scientific evidence that it occurs, and because no mechanism is known whereby bodily changes can influence the genetic material. See also ◊central dogma.

action painting or *gesture painting* in abstract art, a form of Abstract Expressionism that emphasized the importance of the physical act of painting. Jackson Pollock, the leading exponent, threw, dripped, and dribbled paint on to canvases fastened to the floor. Another principal exponent was de Kooning.

The term 'action painting' was coined by the US art critic Harold Rosenberg 1952.

activism the attempt to precipitate political change through direct action rather than simply by theory and debate. It is a central belief of revolutionary and radical parties.

act of Congress in the USA, a bill or resolution passed by both houses of Congress, the Senate and the House of Representatives, which becomes law with the signature of the president. If vetoed by the president, it may still become law if it returns to Congress again and is passed by a majority of two-thirds in each house.

Acton John Emerich Edward Dalberg-, 1st Baron Acton 1834–1902. British historian and Liberal politician. Elected to Parliament 1859, he was a friend and adviser of Prime Minister Gladstone.

Power tends to corrupt and absolute power corrupts absolutely.

John Emerich Edward Dalberg-Acton,
1st Baron Acton
Letter to Mandell Creighton April 1887

Appointed professor of modern history at Cambridge in 1895, he planned and edited the *Cambridge Modern History* but did not live to complete more than the first two volumes.

acupuncture system of inserting long, thin metal needles into the body at predetermined points to relieve pain, as an anaesthetic in surgery, and to assist healing. The needles are rotated manually or electrically. The method, developed in ancient China and increasingly popular in the West, is thought to work by somehow stimulating the brain's own painkillers, the endorphins.

Grant that the old Adam in this Child may be so buried, that the new man may be raised up in him.

Adam
Common Prayer
Baptism Invocation of Blessing on the Child

Adam in the Old Testament, the first human. Formed by God from dust and given the breath of life, Adam was placed in the Garden of Eden, where ◊Eve was created from his rib and given to him as a companion. Because she tempted him, he tasted the forbidden fruit of the Tree of Knowledge of Good and Evil, for which trespass they were expelled from the Garden.

Adams John Couch 1819–1892. English astronomer who mathematically deduced the existence of the planet Neptune 1845 from the effects of its gravitational pull on the motion of Uranus, although it was not found until 1846 by J G ◊Galle. Adams also studied the Moon's motion, the Leonid meteors, and terrestrial magnetism.

Addams Jane 1860–1935. US sociologist and campaigner for women's rights. In 1889 she founded and led the social settlement of Hull House, Chicago, one of the earliest community centres. She was vice president of the National American Women Suffrage Alliance 1911–14, and in 1915 led the Women's Peace Party and the first Women's Peace Congress. She shared the Nobel Peace Prize 1931.

Her publications include *Newer Ideals of Peace* 1907 and *Twenty Years at Hull House* 1910.

added value or *value added* the sales revenue from selling a firm's products less the cost of the materials or purchases used in those products. An increasingly used indicator of relative efficiency within and between firms, although in the latter case open to distortion where mark-up varies between standard and premium-priced segments of a market.

Adi Granth or *Guru Granth Sahib* the holy book of Sikhism.

Adler Alfred 1870–1937. Austrian psychologist, founder of the School of Individual Psychology. In 1902 ◊Freud invited Adler and a few other psychologists to join him in forming a discussion circle, which later became the Vienna Psychoanalytic Society, but Adler's views began to diverge from those of Freud. He found the sexual theory of the neuroses and of mental life unacceptable, preferring instead to think of neurosis in terms of inferiority feelings and social maladjustments. He left the society in 1911 and founded his own Society for Free Analytic Research, which was later renamed the School of Individual Psychology.

Individual Psychology sees the individual as a unity, free, responsible, and goal-directed, and in the normal state knowing that happiness can only be achieved in the social group, working with and for others. Neurotics have to be convinced that the normal state is desirable and their feelings of inferiority, often expressed by a compensatory striving for superiority, replaced by a growing social interest.

Adler's books include *Study of Organ Inferiority and its Psychical Compensation* 1907, *The Neurotic Constitution* 1912, *The Practice and Theory of Individual Psychology* 1920, and *Understanding Human Nature* 1927.

Whenever a child lies you will always find a severe parent. A lie would have no sense unless the truth were felt to be dangerous.

Alfred Adler
New York Times 1949

Adonis in Greek mythology, a beautiful youth loved by the goddess ◊Aphrodite. He was killed while boar-hunting but was allowed to return from the underworld for six months every year to rejoin her. The anemone sprang from his blood.

Worshipped as a god of vegetation, he was known as ◊Tammuz in Sumerian legend. He seems also to have been identified with ◊Osiris, the Egyptian god of the underworld.

Adorno Theodor Wiesengrund 1903–1969. German philosopher, social theorist, musicologist, and critic of culture. His early writings show the influence of the Marxist thinking of Georg ◊Lukács and Ernst Bloch, as well as considerable interest in ◊Freud. Adorno was the main contributor to *The Authoritarian Personality* 1950, an important psychoanalytical and social research project stemming partly from Erich ◊Fromm's ideas, in which the well-known F-scale (F standing for fascism) was constructed.

Adorno was a leading member of the Institut für Sozialforschung (Institute for Social Research) at Frankfurt, which he joined in 1930. When the Nazis came to power, the

Institute moved with its director, Max ◊Horkheimer, to the USA and Adorno eventually followed, acquiring US citizenship. In the 1940s he collaborated with Horkheimer on *Dialectic of Enlightenment* 1947 (translated into English 1972), arguing that rationality had still not freed human beings from their mythic past and that domination of the natural world had led to the control of the social world. 'Progress' had turned out to be barbarism, and science the instrument of dehumanization. He returned to Germany 1949 and in 1951 published *Minima Moralia: Reflections from a Damaged Life*, a series of aphorisms in the style of ◊Nietzsche, many of which are concerned with the problems of exile. In *Negative Dialects* 1966 he is critical of all philosophers because they believed in some non-existent absolute or ultimate entity that would explain everything else. This was dangerous, he argued, because it led to totalitarian and oppressive thinking that turned the individual into an object to be manipulated. Adorno also wrote extensively on the aesthetics and sociology of music and art, including *Die Philosophie der neuen Musik* 1947 (published in translation as *The Philosophy of Modern Music* 1973).

Bibl. Jay, Martin *Adorno* (London, 1984)

Advaita Vedanta Hindu philosophy expounded by ◊Shankara, based on the Sanskrit scripture *Vedanta Sutra*, written by the mystic ◊Vyasa. It teaches that this world is *maya* (illusion), and that the Truth is one and indivisible. It opposes the philosophy of *dvaita*, 'dualism'.

Advent in the Christian calendar, the preparatory season for Christmas, including the four Sundays preceding it, beginning with the Sunday that falls nearest (before or after) St Andrew's Day (30 Nov).

Adventist person who believes that Jesus will return to make a second appearance on Earth. Expectation of the Second Coming of Christ is found in New Testament writings generally. Adventist views are held by the ◊Seventh-Day Adventists, Christadelphians, ◊Jehovah's Witnesses, and the Four Square Gospel Alliance.

advertising any of various methods used by a company to increase the sales of its products or to promote a brand name.

Advertising can be seen by economists as either beneficial (since it conveys information about a product and so brings the market closer to a state of ◊perfect competition) or as a hindrance to perfect competition, since it attempts to make illusory distinctions (such as greater sex appeal) between essentially similar products.

The UK's national advertising budget was £6 billion in 1988 (newspapers 40%; television 33%; magazines 20%; posters and radio taking the rest). The UK government spent over £120 million in 1988 on advertising.

More than £25 million a year is spent on advertising beer on television and in the press.

Aeneas in classical legend, a Trojan prince who became the ancestral hero of the Romans. According to ◊Homer, he was the son of Anchises and the goddess ◊Aphrodite. During the Trojan War he owed his life to the frequent intervention of the gods. The legend on which Virgil's epic poem the *Aeneid* is based describes his escape from Troy and his eventual settlement in Latium, on the Italian peninsula.

Aesir principal gods of Norse mythology – Odin, Thor, Balder, Loki, Freya, and Tyr – whose dwelling place was Asgard.

Aesop by tradition, a writer of Greek fables. According to the historian ◊Herodotus, he lived in the mid-6th century BC and was a slave of a Samian. The fables, which are ascribed to him, were collected at a later date and are anecdotal stories using animal characters to illustrate moral or satirical points.

aestheticism in the arts, the doctrine that holds art is an end in itself and does not need to have any moral, religious, political or educational purpose. The writer Theophile Gautier popularized the doctrine 'l'art pour l'art' ('art for art's sake') 1832, and it was taken up in mid-19th-century France by the Symbolist poets and painters. It flourished in the English ◊Aesthetic Movement of the late 19th century. An emphasis on form rather than content in art remained influential in the West well into the 20th century.

The idea developed from the 18th-century philosopher Immanuel Kant's view that art can only be judged by its own criteria and not by anything external to it.

Aesthetic Movement English artistic movement of the late 19th century, dedicated to the doctrine of 'art for art's sake' – that is, art as a self-sufficient entity concerned solely with beauty and not with any moral or social purpose. Associated with the movement were the artists Aubrey Beardsley and James McNeill Whistler and the writers Walter Pater and Oscar Wilde.

The idea of art for art's sake was current in Europe throughout the 19th century, but the English movement in the last two decades tended to advocate extremes of sensibility that attracted much ridicule. John ◊Ruskin and William ◊Morris were staunch critics of the Aesthetic Movement.

aesthetics branch of philosophy that deals with the nature of beauty, especially in art. It emerged as a distinct branch of enquiry in the mid-18th century.

The subject of aesthetics was introduced by Plato and enlarged upon by Aristotle, but the term was first used by the German philosopher Baumgarten (1714–1762). Other philosophers interested in this area were Immanuel ◊Kant, David ◊Hume, Benedetto ◊Croce, John ◊Dewey, and George ◊Santayana.

affirmative action government policy of positive discrimination that favours members of minority ethnic groups and women in such areas as employment and education, designed to counter the effects of long-term discrimination against them. In Europe, Sweden, Belgium, the Netherlands, and Italy actively promote affirmative action through legal and financial incentives. A Community Charter of the Fundamental Social Rights of Workers (The Social Chapter), adopted Dec 1989 by all EC members except the UK, assures the right of men and women to equal treatment.

In the UK the Sex Discrimination Act, 1975, and the Race Relations Act, 1976, are intended to eliminate discrimination on grounds of sex, race or colour and the Equal Opportunities Commission and the Commission for Racial Equality oversee their enforcement. The Criminal Justice Act, 1991, also places a duty on administrators of justice to avoid discrimination on grounds of race or sex. In general positive discrimination in favour of minority groups has not had wide political or popular support.

In the USA, the Equal Opportunities Act 1972 set up a commission to enforce the policy in organizations receiving public funds, so many private institutions and employers adopted voluntary affirmative action programmes at the same time. In the 1980s the policy was sometimes not rigorously enforced.

affluent society society in which most people have money left over after satisfying their basic needs such as food and shelter. They are then able to decide how to spend their excess ('disposable') income, and become 'consumers'. The term was popularized by the US economist John Kenneth ◊Galbraith.

Galbraith used the term to describe the Western industrialized nations, particularly the USA, in his book *The Affluent Society* 1958, in which he advocated using more of the nation's wealth for public spending and less for private consumption.

In the affluent society no useful distinction can be made between luxuries and necessaries.

affluent society
John Kenneth Galbraith, 1908–, Canadian-born US economist; he became a US citizen 1937.
The Affluent Society

African nationalism political movement for the unification of Africa. African nationalism has its roots among the educated elite (mainly 'returned' Americans of African descent and freed slaves or their descendants) in W Africa in the 19th century. Christian mission-educated, many challenged overseas mission control and founded independent churches. These were often involved in anticolonial rebellions, for example, in Natal 1906 and Nyasaland 1915. The Kitwala (Watchtower Movement) and Kimbanguist churches provided strong support for the nationalist cause in the 1950s. Early African political organizations included the Aborigines Rights Protection Society in the Gold Coast 1897, the African National Congress in South Africa 1912, and the National Congress of West Africa 1920. ◊Pan-Africanism.

There is always something new out of Africa.

Africa
Pliny, 23–79, Roman naturalist and writer.
Historia Naturalis II. 8

After World War I nationalists fostered moves for self-determination. The ◊Fourteen Points encouraged such demands in Tunisia, and delegates to London 1919 from the Native National Congress in South Africa stressed the contribution to the war effort by the South African Native Labour Corps. Most nationalist groups functioned within the territorial boundaries of single colonies, for example, the Tanganyika African Association and the Rhodesian Bantu Voters Association. One or two groups, including the National Congress of British West Africa, had wider pan-African visions. The first pan-African Congress was held in London 1900 and others followed after 1919.

Pan-African sentiment in Africa and the Americas was intensified with the Italian invasion of Ethiopia in 1935. By 1939 African nationalist groups existed in nearly every territory of the continent. Africa's direct involvement in World War II, the weakening of the principal colonial powers, increasing anticolonialism from America (the Atlantic Charter 1941 encouraged self-government), and Soviet criticism of imperialism inspired African nationalists.

Since 1958 pan-Africanism has become partially absorbed into wider Third World movements. In May 1963 it was decided to establish the Organization of African Unity (OAU).

afterlife belief that life does not end with death but continues in some form or in some place. Belief in an afterlife of some kind is a hallmark of all religions. Notions of what happens range from reincarnation into another body (Buddhists, Hindus, and Sikhs usually teach this) to being raised on the Last Day when God will end the world and judge everyone according to how they have lived (Christianity, Islam, and Judaism usually teach a form of this).

Agamemnon in Greek legend, a Greek hero, son of Atreus, king of Mycenae, and brother of Menelaus. He married Clytemnestra, and their children included Electra, Iphigenia, and Orestes. He sacrificed Iphigenia in order to secure favourable winds for the Greek expedition against Troy, and after a ten years' siege sacked the city, receiving Priam's daughter Cassandra as a prize. On his return home, he and Cassandra were murdered by Clytemnestra and her lover, Aegisthus. His children Orestes and Electra later killed the guilty couple.

Agassiz Jean Louis Rodolphe 1807–1873. Swiss-born US palaeontologist and geologist, one of the foremost scientists of the 19th century. He established his name through his work on the classification of the fossil fishes. Unlike Darwin, he did not believe that individual species themselves changed, but that new species were created from time to time.

Agassiz was the first to realize that an ice age had taken place in the northern hemisphere, when, in 1840, he observed ice scratches on rocks in Edinburgh. He is now criticized for holding racist views concerning the position of blacks in American society.

ageism discrimination against older people in employment, pensions, housing, and health care.

To combat it the American Association of Retired Persons (AARP) has 30 million members, and in 1988 a similar organization was founded in the UK. In the USA the association has been responsible for legislation forbidding employers to discriminate; for example, making it illegal to fail to employ, to dismiss, or to reduce working conditions or wages of people aged 40–69.

aggregate demand the total demand for goods and services in the economy. When aggregate demand or spending falls over a period of one to two years, the economy tends to go into recession, whilst a rise in aggregate demand tends to lead to booms in the economy.

The most persistent sound which reverberates through man's history is the beating of war drums.

aggression
Arthur Koestler, 1905–1983, Hungarian writer on culture and parapsychology.
Janus prologue

---

aggression in biology, behaviour used to intimidate or injure another organism (of the same or of a different species), usually for the purposes of gaining territory, a mate, or food. Aggression often involves an escalating series of threats aimed at intimidating an opponent without having to engage in potentially dangerous physical contact. Aggressive signals include roaring by red deer, snarling by dogs, the fluffing up of feathers by birds, and the raising of fins by some species of fish.

All they that take the sword shall perish with the sword.

aggression
Bible, the sacred book of the Jewish and Christian religions.
Matthew 26:52

---

aggression in politics, an unprovoked attack often involving an escalating series of threats aimed at intimidating an opponent. Examples of aggression in this century include the actions of Nazi Germany under Adolf Hitler in the 1930s, leading to World War II, and the invasion of Kuwait by Iraq in 1990.

agitprop Soviet government bureau established Sept 1920 in charge of Communist agitation and propaganda. The idea was developed by left-wing groups in the West for the use of theatre and the other arts to convey political messages.

Agni in Hindu mythology, the god of fire, the guardian of homes, and the protector of humans against the powers of darkness.

agnosticism belief that the existence of God cannot be proven; that in the nature of things the individual cannot know anything of what lies behind or beyond the world of natural phenomena. The term was coined 1869 by T H ◊Huxley.

Whereas an atheist (see ◊atheism) denies the existence of God or gods, an agnostic asserts that God or a First Cause is one of those concepts – others include the Absolute, infinity, eternity, and immortality – that lie beyond the reach of human intelligence, and therefore can be neither confirmed nor denied.

ahimsa ('noninjury') in Hinduism, Buddhism, and Jainism, the doctrine of respect for all life (including the lowest forms and even the elements themselves) and consequently nonviolence. It arises in part from the concept of karma, which holds that a person's actions (and thus any injury caused to any form of life) are carried forward from one life to the next, determining each stage of reincarnation.

Ahmadiyya Islamic religious movement founded by Mirza Ghulam Ahmad (1839–1908). His followers reject the doctrine that Muhammad was the last of the prophets and accept Ahmad's claim to be the Mahdi and Promised Messiah. In 1974 the Ahmadis were denounced as non-Muslims by other Muslims.

Ahriman or **Angra Mainyu** ('evil spirit') in ◊Zoroastrianism, the supreme evil spirit, lord of the darkness and death, waging war with his counterpart Ahura Mazda (Ormuzd) until a time when human beings choose to lead good lives and Ahriman is finally destroyed.

Ahura Mazda ('Wise Lord') or **Ormuzd** in ◊Zoroastrianism, the spirit of supreme good. As god of life and light he will finally prevail over his enemy, Ahriman.

aid, development money given or lent on concessional terms to developing countries or spent on maintaining agencies for this purpose. In the late 1980s official aid from governments of richer nations amounted to $45–60 billion annually whereas voluntary organizations in the West received about $2.4 billion a year for the Third World. The ◊World Bank is the largest dispenser of aid. In 1990 it transferred $467 billion to developing countries. All industrialized United Nations (UN) member countries devote a proportion of their gross national product to aid, ranging from 0.20% of GNP (Ireland) to 1.10% (Norway) (1988 figures). Each country spends more than half this contribution on direct bilateral assistance to countries with which they have historical or military links or hope to encourage trade. The rest goes to international organizations such as UN and World Bank agencies, which distribute aid multilaterally.

The UK development-aid budget in 1990 was 0.31% of GNP, with India and Kenya among the principal beneficiaries. The European Development Fund (an arm of the European Community) and the International Development Association (an arm of the World Bank) receive approximately 5% and 8% respectively of the UK development-aid budget.

In 1990, the US development-aid budget was 0.15% of GNP, with Israel and Egypt among the principal beneficiaries; Turkey, Pakistan, and the Philippines are also major beneficiaries. The United States Agency for International Development (USAID) is the State Department body responsible for bilateral aid. The USA is the largest contributor to, and thus the most powerful member of, the International Development Association.

In the UK, the Overseas Development Administration is the department of the Foreign Office that handles bilateral aid. The combined overseas development aid of all EC member countries is less than the sum ($20 billion) the EC spends every year on storing surplus food produced by European farmers.

aid, foreign financial and other assistance given by richer, usually industrialized, countries to low income, developing countries to promote economic ◊development (see ◊aid, development) or to provide relief from war damage or natural disasters.

AIDS (acronym for *acquired immune deficiency syndrome*) the gravest of the sexually transmitted diseases, or STDs. It is caused by the human immunodeficiency virus (HIV), now known to be a retrovirus, an organism first identified 1983. HIV is transmitted in body fluids, mainly blood and sexual secretions.

Sexual transmission of the AIDS virus endangers heterosexual men and women as well as high-risk groups, such as homosexual and bisexual men, prostitutes, intravenous drug-users sharing needles, and haemophiliacs and surgical patients treated with contaminated blood products. The virus itself is not selective, and infection is spreading to the population at large. The virus has a short life outside the body, which makes transmission of the infection by methods other than sexual contact, blood transfusion, and shared syringes extremely unlikely.

Infection with HIV is not synonymous with having AIDS; many people who have the virus in their blood are not ill, and only about half of those infected will develop AIDS within ten years. Some suffer AIDS-related illnesses but not the full-blown disease. However, there is no firm evidence to suggest that the proportion of those developing AIDS from being HIV-positive is less than 100%.

The effect of the virus in those who become ill is the devastation of the immune system, leaving the victim susceptible to (opportunistic) diseases that would not otherwise develop. In fact, diagnosis of AIDS is based on the appearance of rare tumours or opportunistic infections in unexpected candidates. Pneumocystis pneumonia, for instance, normally seen only in the malnourished or those whose immune systems have been deliberately suppressed, is common among AIDS victims and, for them, a leading cause of death.

The estimated incubation period is 9.8 years. Some AIDS victims die within a few months of the outbreak of symptoms, some survive for several years; roughly 50% are dead within three years. There is no cure for the disease, although the new drug zidovudine (AZT) was claimed to delay the onset of AIDS and diminish its effects. The search continues for an effective vaccine.

Aiken Howard 1900– . US mathematician and computer pioneer. In 1939, in conjunction with engineers from IBM, he started work on the design of an automatic calculator using standard business-machine components. In 1944 the team completed one of the first computers, the Automatic Sequence Controlled Calculator (known as the Mark 1), a programmable computer controlled by punched paper tape and using punched cards.

à Kempis Thomas see ◊Thomas à Kempis, religious writer.

Aladdin in the *Arabian Nights*, a poor boy who obtains a magic lamp: when the lamp is rubbed, a jinn (genie, or spirit) appears and fulfils its owner's wishes.

Alberti Leon Battista 1404–1472. Italian Renaissance architect, painter, philosopher, mathematician, and musician. He set out the principles of Classical architecture, as well as covering their modification for Renaissance practice, in *On Architecture* 1452.

His designs for the churches of San Sebastiano, begun 1460, and San Andrea 1470 (both in Mantua) – the only two extant buildings entirely of his design – are bold in their use of Classical architectural language. His treatises on painting (1436) and sculpture (c.1464) were the first to examine the theory as well as the technique of the subjects. He also wrote works on mathematics, ethics, religion, and grammar.

Albertus Magnus, St 1206–1280. German scholar of Christian theology, philosophy (especially ◊Aristotle), natural science, chemistry, and physics. He was known as 'doctor universalis' because of the breadth of his knowledge. Feast day 15 Nov.

He studied at Bologna and Padua, and entered the Dominican order 1223. He taught at Cologne and lectured from 1245 at Paris University. St Thomas ◊Aquinas was his pupil there, and followed him to Cologne 1248.

He became provincial of the Dominicans in Germany 1254, and was made bishop of Ratisbon 1260. Two years later he resigned and eventually retired to his convent at Cologne. He tried to reconcile Aristotelian thought with Christian teachings.

Albigenses heretical group of Christians (associated with the ◊Cathars) who flourished in S France near Albi and Toulouse during the 11th–13th centuries. They adopted the Manichean belief in the duality of good and evil and pictured Jesus as being a rebel against the cruelty of an omnipotent God.

The Albigensians showed a consistently anti-Catholic attitude with distinctive sacraments, especially the *consolamentum*, or baptism of the spirit. An inquisition was initiated against the Albigensians in 1184 by Pope Lucius III (although the ◊Inquisition as we know it was not established until 1233); it was, however, ineffective, and in 1208 a crusade (1208–29) was launched against them under the elder Simon de Montfort. Thousands were killed before the movement was crushed in 1244.

alchemy supposed technique of transmuting base metals, such as lead and mercury, into silver and gold by the philosopher's stone, a hypothetical substance, to which was also attributed the power to give eternal life.

This aspect of alchemy constituted much of the chemistry of the Middle Ages. More broadly, however, alchemy was a system of philosophy that dealt both with the mystery of life and the formation of inanimate substances. Alchemy was a complex and indefinite conglomeration of chemistry, astrology, occultism, and magic, blended with obscure and abstruse ideas derived from various religious systems and other sources. It was practised in Europe from ancient times to the Middle Ages but later fell into disrepute when ◊chemistry and ◊physics developed.

I always keep a supply of stimulant handy in case I see a snake – which / I also keep handy.

alcohol
W C Fields. Stage name of William Claude
Dukenfield Fields, 1879–1946,
US actor and screenwriter.
Time of Laughter C Ford

---

alcoholism chronic dependence on alcoholic liquor, thus a form of drug dependence. It is characterized as an illness when consumption of alcohol interferes with normal physical or emotional health.

Excessive consumption, especially frequent heavy drinking, may produce physical or psychological addiction, or both, and lead to nutritional and psychological disorders such as cirrhosis of the liver, heart disease, amnesia and dementia. Various types of alcoholism have been described for some of which there is evidence of genetic predisposition.

Wine is a mocker, strong drink is raging.

alcohol
Bible, the sacred book of the Jewish and
Christian religions.
Proverbs 20:1

In Britain, the cost of treating alcohol-related diseases in 1985 was estimated as at least £100 million. Alcohol consumption is measured in standard units. One unit is approximately equal to a single glass of wine or measure of spirits, or half a pint of normal-strength beer. The recommended maximum weekly intake is 21 units for men and 14 units for women.

aleatory term used to describe the use of random or chance elements in certain art forms.

Although Leonardo da Vinci recommended looking at blotches on walls as a means of initiating artistic ideas, aleatory practice has been mainly employed by 20th-century avant-garde artists. In ◊Dada, the artist Hans Arp made collages by dropping small pieces of paper onto a larger piece and fixing them where they landed. Similarly, his colleague Tristan Tzara created poetry by drawing sentences, extracted from newspapers, from out of a hat. In music, the major exponent has been John Cage who pioneered a method of composition in which the elements are assembled by using dice or a computer.

Alembert Jean le Rond d' 1717–1783. French mathematician and encyclopedist. He was associated with ◊Diderot as one of the leading ◊Encyclopédistes.

Alexander Samuel 1859–1938. Australian philosopher who originated the theory of emergent evolution: that the space-time matrix evolved matter; matter evolved life; life evolved mind; and finally God emerged from mind. His books include *Space, Time and Deity* 1920.

He was professor at Manchester University, England, 1893–1924.

Alexander technique method of correcting established bad habits of posture, breathing, and muscular tension which Australian therapist F M ◊Alexander maintained cause many ailments. Back troubles, migraine, asthma, hypertension, and some gastric and gynaecological disorders are among the conditions said to be alleviated by the technique, which is also effective in the prevention of disorders, particularly those of later life. The technique also acts as a general health promoter, promoting relaxation and enhancing vitality.

Alexandria, Library of library in Alexandria, Egypt, founded 330 BC by Ptolemy I and further expanded by Ptolemy II. It was the world's first state-funded scientific institution, and comprised a museum, teaching facilities, and a library that contained 700,000 scrolls, including much ancient Greek literature. It was burned down AD 640 at the time of the Arab conquest.

Alexandria, school of group of writers and scholars of Alexandria who made the city the chief centre of culture in the Western world from about 331 BC to AD 642. They include the poets Callimachus, Apollonius of Rhodes, and Theocritus; Euclid, pioneer of geometry;

Eratosthenes, the geographer; Hipparchus, who developed a system of trigonometry; the astronomer Ptolemy, who gave his name to the Ptolemaic system of astronomy that endured for over 1,000 years; and the Jewish philosopher Philo. The Gnostics and Neo-Platonists also flourished in Alexandria.

algebra system of arithmetic applying to any set of non-numerical symbols (usually letters), and the axioms and rules by which they are combined or operated upon; sometimes known as *generalized arithmetic*.

The basics of algebra were familiar in Babylon 2000 BC, and were practised by the Arabs in the Middle Ages. In the 9th century, the Arab mathematician Muhammad ibn-Mūsā al-◊Khwārizmī first used the words *hisäb al-jabr* ('calculus of reduction') as part of the title of a treatise. Algebra is used in many branches of mathematics, for example, matrix algebra and Boolean algebra (the latter method was first devised in the 19th century by the British mathematician George Boole and used in working out the logic for computers).

algorithm procedure or series of steps that can be used to solve a problem. In computer science, it describes the logical sequence of operations to be performed by a program. A ◊flow chart is a visual representation of an algorithm.

The word derives from the name of the 9th-century Arab mathematician Muhammad ibn-Mūsā al-◊Khwārizmī.

Ali c. 600–661. Cousin and son-in-law of the prophet Muhammad, one of the first to believe in Islam, and one of Muhammad's closest friends and supporters. Ali married Muhammad's daughter Fatima, with whom he had three sons: Hasan, Husayn, and Muhsin. In 656 Ali became the fourth Caliph or successor of the prophet. Shiah Muslims believe that Ali should have become ruler on the death of Muhammad, since he is his nominated ◊Wali.

alienation sense of isolation, powerlessness, and therefore frustration; a feeling of loss of control over one's life; a sense of estrangement from society or even from oneself. As a concept it was developed by the German philosophers ◊Hegel and ◊Marx; the latter used it as a description and criticism of the condition that developed among workers in capitalist society.

The term has also been used by non-Marxist writers and sociologists (in particular ◊Durkheim in his work *Suicide* 1897) to explain unrest in factories and to describe the sense of powerlessness felt by groups such as young people, black people, and women in Western industrial society.

Allah Islamic name for God.

A man's life of any worth is a continual allegory.

allegory
John Keats, 1795–1821,
English Romantic poet.
To George and Georgiana Keats, 1819

---

allegory in literature, the description or illustration of one thing in terms of another; a work of poetry or prose in the form of an extended ◊metaphor or parable that makes use of symbolic fictional characters.

An example of the use of symbolic fictional character in allegory is the romantic epic *The Faerie Queene* 1590–96 by Edmund Spenser in homage to Queen Elizabeth I. Allegory is often used for moral purposes, as in John Bunyan's *Pilgrim's Progress* 1678. Medieval allegory often used animals as characters; this tradition survives in such works as *Animal Farm* 1945 by George Orwell.

alliance agreement between two or more states to come to each other's assistance in the event of war. Formal alliances have played a large part in the diplomacy and warfare of states since antiquity. Alliances were criticized after World War I as having contributed to the outbreak of war but NATO has been a major part of the post-1945 structure of international relations (as was the Warsaw Pact until its dissolution 1991).

allocation of resources the way in which scarce resources are used in one way rather than another in the production and distribution of goods and services. When resources are allocated, there is an ◊opportunity cost involved (they cannot be used for other purposes). In a ◊market economy, it is mainly private firms that allocate resources in response to ◊market forces. ◊Economics is the study of how resources are allocated.

All Saints' Day or *All-Hallows* or *Hallowmas* festival on 1 Nov for all Christian saints and martyrs who have no special day of their own.

All Souls' Day festival in the Roman Catholic church, held on 2 Nov (following All Saints' Day) in the conviction that through prayer and self-denial the faithful can hasten the deliverance of souls expiating their sins in purgatory.

alma mater term applied to universities and schools, as though they are the foster mothers of their students. Also, the official school song. It was the title given by the Romans to Ceres, the goddess of agriculture.

alternative theatre general term for those kinds of theatre which, since the 1960s, have functioned outside the commercial mainstream, usually in an experimental style and in untraditional venues.

Althusser Louis 1918–1990. French philosopher and Marxist, born in Algeria, who argued that the idea that economic systems determine family and political systems is too simple. He attempted to show how the ruling class ideology of a particular era is a crucial form of class control.

Althusser divides each mode of production into four key elements – the economic, political, ideological, and theoretical – all of which interact. His structuralist analysis of capitalism sees individuals and groups as agents or bearers of the structures of social relations, rather than as independent influences on history. His works include *For Marx* 1965, *Lenin and Philosophy* 1969, *Essays in Self-Criticism* 1976, and his autobiography *The Future Lasts a Long Time* 1992.

He dismisses mainstream sociology as bourgeois and has influenced thinkers in fields as diverse as social anthropology, literature, and history.

In 1980, he murdered his wife and spent the next few years in mental hospitals.

altruism in biology, helping another individual of the same species to reproduce more effectively, as a direct result of which the altruist may leave fewer offspring itself. Female honey bees (workers) behave altruistically by rearing sisters in order to help their mother, the queen bee, reproduce, and forego any possibility of reproducing themselves.

Alvarez Luis Walter 1911–1988. US physicist who led the research team that discovered the Xi-zero atomic particle 1959. He had worked on the US atom bomb project for two years, at Chicago and Los Alamos, New Mexico, during World War II. He was awarded a Nobel prize 1968.

Alvarez was professor of physics at the University of California from 1945 and an associate director of the Lawrence Livermore Radiation Laboratory 1954–59. In 1980 he was responsible for the theory that dinosaurs disappeared because a meteorite crashed into Earth 70 million years ago, producing a dust cloud that blocked out the Sun for several years, and causing dinosaurs and plants to die.

Amar Das 1495–1574. Indian religious leader, third guru (teacher) of Sikhism 1552–74. He laid emphasis on equality and opposed the caste system. He initiated the custom of the *langar* (communal meal).

Amazon in Greek legend, a member of a group of female warriors living near the Black Sea, who cut off their right breasts to use the bow more easily. Their queen, Penthesilea, was killed by Achilles at the siege of Troy. The term Amazon has come to mean a large, strong woman.

The Amazons attacked ◊Theseus and besieged him at Athens, but were defeated, and Theseus took the Amazon Hippolyta captive; she later gave birth to Hippolytus.

ambiguity the possibility of more than one interpretation of a spoken or written expression; doubtful meaning. Ambiguity is much used in poetry.

Ambrose, St c. 340–397. One of the early Christian leaders and theologians known as the Fathers of the Church. Feast day 7 Dec.

Born at Trèves, in S Gaul, the son of a Roman prefect, Ambrose became governor of N Italy. In 374 he was chosen bishop of Milan, although he was not yet a member of the church. He was then baptized and consecrated. He wrote many hymns, and devised the regulation of church music known as the ***Ambrosian chant***, which is still used in Milan.

amen Hebrew word signifying affirmation ('so be it'), commonly used at the close of a Jewish or Christian prayer or hymn. As used by Jesus in the New Testament it was traditionally translated 'verily'.

Amerindian religions the religious beliefs of American Indians from Alaska to the tip of South America. They are numerous and often vastly different, and include ◊*Shamanism*, new forms of *Christianity*, and *Peyotism*.

There are certain trends which can offer forms of classification. Shamanism, which arrived over 8,000 years ago and slowly spread down from Alaska, is found in many cultures of the Americas. It incorporates a reverence for the natural world as a meeting place for the spiritual and material worlds. In recent centuries, the impact of Christianity has produced different responses: syncretistic forms such as Catholic Spiritists in Brazil who combine shamanism with Christianity, or rejection of Christianity itself but the adoption of many Christian notions, symbols, and beliefs. The use of stimulant drugs to enhance religious states is common in many Mid- and Central American cultures. Of these Peyotism, which emerged in the late 19th century, is the best known, combining pre-Christian elements such as music and chanting, with the Christian elements of healing, prayer, and the sacraments. Other communities have formed churches that are independent of the mainstream European Churches. Today there is a revival of interest in pre-Christian rituals, beliefs, and practices, especially in shamanism.

Ames Adelbert 1880–1955. US scientist who studied optics and the psychology of visual perception. He concluded that much of what a person sees depends on what he or she expects to see, based (consciously or unconsciously) on previous experience.

Amida Buddha the 'Buddha of immeasurable light'. Japanese name for *Amitābha*, the Buddha venerated in ◊Pure Land Buddhism. He presides over the Western Paradise (the Buddha-land of his own creation), and through his unlimited compassion and power to save, true believers can achieve enlightenment and be reborn.

Amish Christian group based on the ◊Mennonite Church, found today in the USA and Canada and characterized by its rejection of modern and urban ways of life. The Amish make no use of modern inventions and anyone marrying out of the community is cast out for ever. They hold to adult baptism and to a literal reading of the Bible. They are also one of the pacifist churches, alongside the Quakers and Mennonites.

When the Anabaptist movement of the 1520s and 1530s was suppressed, anabaptist communities fled into remote areas. The Amish were a splinter movement from one such group, the Mennonites, formed in the late 17th century. They were named after their leader Jakob Ammann (c. 1645–c. 1730), who set very strict standards and rejected the Mennonite Church as too secular. They were persecuted until the early 19th century. Many migrated to North America.

Ammon in Egyptian mythology, the king of the gods, the equivalent of Zeus (Roman Jupiter). The name is also spelled Amen/Amun, as in the name of the pharaoh Tutankh*amen*. In art, he is represented as a ram, as a man with a ram's head, or as a man crowned with feathers. He had temples at Siwa oasis, Libya, and at Thebes, Egypt; his oracle at Siwa was patronized by the classical Greeks.

Amnesty International human-rights organization established in the UK 1961 to campaign for the release of political prisoners worldwide; it is politically unaligned. Amnesty International has 700,000 members, and section offices in 43 countries. The organization was awarded the Nobel Peace Prize 1977.

Amos book of the Old Testament written c. 750 BC. One of the ◊prophets, Amos was a shepherd who foretold the destruction of Israel because of the people's abandonment of their faith.

Ampère André Marie 1775–1836. French physicist and mathematician who made many discoveries in electromagnetism and electrodynamics. He followed up the work of Hans ◊Oersted on the interaction between magnets and electric currents, developing a rule for determining the direction of the magnetic field associated with an electric current. The ampere is named after him.

Anabaptist member of any of various 16th-century radical Protestant groups. They believed in adult rather than child baptism, and sought to establish utopian communities. Anabaptist groups spread rapidly in N Europe, particularly in Germany, and were widely persecuted.

Notable Anabaptists included those in Moravia (the Hutterites) and Thomas Müntzer (1489–1525), a peasant leader who was executed for fomenting an uprising in Mühlhausen (now Mulhouse in E France). In Münster, Germany, Anabaptists controlled the city 1534–35. A number of Anabaptist groups, such as the Mennonites, Amish, and Hutterites, emigrated to North America, where they became known for their simple way of life and pacifism.

analects or *analecta* any collection of literary fragments taken from one or more sources. More specifically, the Analects are a selection of writings by the Chinese philosopher Confucius and his followers, the most important of the four books containing the teachings of ◊Confucianism.

Analogies decide nothing, that is true, but they can make one feel more at home.

analogies
Sigmund Freud, 1856–1939,
founder of psychoanalysis.
New Introductory Lectures on Psychoanalysis

analogy comparison of two different things, usually made to illustrate or explain complex or unfamiliar ideas. There is, for example, no similarity between a country's economy and a cake; yet a cake is frequently used as an analogy for the economy to illustrate that there are only a limited number of slices to share between the competing interests.

analogy in mathematics and in logic, a form of argument or process of reasoning from one case to another parallel case. Arguments from analogy generally have the following form: if some event or thing has the properties a and b, and if another event or thing has properties a, b and c, then the former thing or event has the property c, too. The *design argument* for the existence of God is an argument from analogy: it draws an analogy between the properties of order, design and purpose in a watch, a garden or some other artefact and the universe as a whole.

Arguments from analogy are not always sound and can mislead, and false analogies arise when the cases are insufficiently similar to support the reasoning. Things that are alike in some respects can be different in others – a whale lives in water and resembles a fish, but we cannot conclude from this that it is a fish. When arguments from analogy are compressed, they are called metaphors; and like other analogies, metaphors can mislead.

analysis branch of mathematics concerned with limiting processes on axiomatic number systems; ◊calculus of variations and infinitesimal calculus is now called analysis. In philosophy, examination of a concept or statement.

Conceptual analysis is explication of concepts – the search for the necessary and sufficient conditions that determine the meaning of a term. If we ask, for example, what a sister is, we want to know what all sisters have in common – which is, of course, being a female sibling. *Reductive (new-level) analysis* could involve analysing statements about sisters into statements of another kind, such as statements in a formal language about genetic relationships. *Logical (same-level) analysis* could involve analysing the different ways in which we speak about sisters ('Jane is the sister of Joan', 'All women are sisters') without making any claims about whether sisters actually exist or not and without being reductive in any way.

analytic in philosophy, a term derived from ◊Kant: the converse of ◊synthetic. In an analytic judgement, the judgement provides no new knowledge; for example: 'All bachelors are unmarried.'

Ananda 5th century BC. Favourite disciple of the Buddha. At his plea, a separate order was established for women. He played a major part in collecting the teachings of the Buddha after his death.

Anand Marg Indian religious sect, 'the pathway to bliss' that became popular in the West in the 1970s; their leader *Prahbat Ranjan Sarkar* (1923–90) was the subject of much controversy. Imprisoned for the alleged murder of defectors from the sect, he was released after acquittal in 1978.

anarchism political belief that society should have no government, laws, police, or other authority, but should be a free association of all its members. It does not mean 'without order'; most theories of anarchism imply an order of a very strict and symmetrical kind, but they maintain that such order can be achieved by cooperation. Anarchism must not be confused with nihilism (a purely negative and destructive activity directed against society); anarchism is essentially a pacifist movement.

We started off trying to set up a small anarchist community, but people wouldn't obey the rules.

anarchism
Alan Bennett, 1934 – , English dramatist.
Getting On I

Religious anarchism, claimed by many anarchists to be exemplified in the early organization of the Christian church, has found expression in the social philosophy of the Russian writer ◊Tolstoy and the Indian nationalist ◊Gandhi. The growth of political anarchism may be traced through the British Romantic writers William Godwin and Shelley to the 1848 revolutionaries P J ◊Proudhon in France and the Russian ◊Bakunin, who had a strong following in Europe.

Anarchism is a game at which the Police can beat you.

anarchism
George Bernard Shaw, 1856–1950,
Irish dramatist.
Misalliance

The theory of anarchism is expressed in the works of the Russian revolutionary ◊Kropotkin.

From the 1960s there were outbreaks of politically motivated violence popularly identified with anarchism; in the UK, the bombings and shootings carried out by the Angry Brigade 1968–71, and in the 1980s actions directed towards peace and animal-rights issues, and to demonstrate against large financial and business corporations.

anathema something that is shunned or cursed. The word is used in the Christian church in excommunication.

anatman in Buddhism, the central teaching that there is no soul, no self. It comes from the negative of atman, the Hindu notion of a soul which is eternal and which survives after death and enters another body. In Buddhist thought, such a notion is part of the delusion of self and of permanence which keeps us locked to the wheel of suffering. True release comes when one realises that there is no self, and thus all sense of being ceases.

Anaxogoras of Clazomenae c. 500–428 BC. Greek cosmologist and pre-Socratic philosopher. He speculated that everything consisted of 'seeds' which contained a little of every natural substance. Changes in things occurred by the exchange of portions of seeds. In the beginning, all natural substances were mixed together and Mind ('finest of all things and purest') started a rotation which formed the Earth by vortex action.

Anaxagoras studied under Anaximenes. He taught in Athens for 30 years (c. 480–450 BC), and his pupils included the politician Pericles, the playwright Euripides, and possibly the philosopher Socrates. He was prosecuted for impiety and banished, because he described the Sun as a white-hot lump of stone.

Anaximander c. 610–c. 546 BC. Greek astronomer and philosopher. He claimed that the Earth was a cylinder three times wider than it is deep, motionless at the centre of the universe, and he is credited with drawing the first geographical map. He said that the celestial bodies were fire seen through holes in the hollow rims of wheels encircling the Earth. According to Anaximander, the first animals came into being from moisture and the first humans grew inside fish, emerging once fully developed.

Anaximenes of Miletus c. 587–c. 527 BC. Greek cosmologist and pre-Socratic philosopher. He originated the important idea that one substance could account for the diversity of the world ($\Diamond$monism). This substance was air or mist. Rarefied, it became fire; condensed, water and earth.

Anaximenes was the teacher of Anaxagoras. He seems to have chosen air or mist as the basic substance because of its apparent connections with fire, rain, and breath in living creatures.

ancestor worship religious rituals and beliefs oriented towards deceased members of a family or group, as a symbolic expression of values or in the belief that the souls of the dead remain involved in this world and are capable of influencing current events.

Zulus used to invoke the spirits of their great warriors before engaging in battle; the Greeks deified their early heroes; and the ancient Romans held in reverential honour the $\Diamond$Manes, or departed spirits of their forebears. Ancestor worship is a part of $\Diamond$Confucianism, and recent ancestors are venerated in the Shinto religion of Japan.

ancien régime the old order; the feudal, absolute monarchy in France before the French Revolution 1789.

Anderson Carl David 1905–1991. US physicist who discovered the positive electron (positron) in 1932; he shared the Nobel Prize for Physics in 1936.

Carl Anderson was one of the pioneers in cosmic ray physics. He made two of the first discoveries in the field and launched what is now known as 'elementary particle physics'. The first discovery in 1932 was the positive electron or positron, a particle whose existence had been predicted by British theorist Paul Dirac. Anderson found that positrons were present in cosmic rays, energetic particles reaching Earth from outer space. For this discovery, Anderson shared the 1936 Nobel Prize for Physics with Victor Hess, the discoverer of cosmic rays. In 1937, Anderson discovered a new particle in cosmic rays, one with a mass between that of an electron and a proton. The new particle was first called a mesotron and then a meson muon. The discovery of the muon was a great step forward in physics; the muon was the first elementary particle to be discovered beyond the constituents of ordinary matter (proton, neutron, and electron). This could be said to be the birth of elementary particle physics.

Anderson Elizabeth Garrett 1836–1917. The first English woman to qualify in medicine. Refused entry into medical school, Anderson studied privately and was licensed by the Society of Apothecaries in London 1865. She was physician to the Marylebone Dispensary for Women and Children (later renamed the Elizabeth Garrett Anderson Hospital), a London hospital now staffed by women and serving women patients.

She helped found the London School of Medicine. She was the first woman member of the British Medical Association and the first woman mayor in Britain.

Andrewes Lancelot 1555–1626. Church of England bishop. He helped prepare the text of the Authorized Version of the Bible, and was known for the intellectual and literary quality of his sermons.

He was also bishop of Chichester (1605), Ely (1609), and Winchester (1618).

Andrews John 1813–1885. Irish chemist who conducted a series of experiments on the behaviour of carbon dioxide under varying temperature and pressure. In 1869 he introduced the idea of a critical temperature: 30.9°C in the case of carbon dioxide, beyond which no amount of pressure would liquefy the gas.

Andrew, St New Testament apostle. According to tradition, he went with John to Ephesus, preached in Scythia, and was martyred at Patras on an X-shaped cross (*St Andrew's cross*). He is the patron saint of Scotland. Feast day 30 Nov.

A native of Bethsaida, he was Simon Peter's brother. With Peter, James, and John, who worked with him as fishermen at Capernaum, he formed the inner circle of Jesus' 12 disciples.

androgyny (Greek *andro* 'male' *gyne* 'female') having both male and female sex organs or possessing characteristics and qualities of both sexes.

The use of androgynous figures in mythology and art is widespread: in Greek mythology, for example, the minor god Hermaphroditus became both male and female after the nymph Salacis was united with him in one body.

The concept of androgyny was further developed by the feminist movement. It emphasized that human personality is made up of both male and female characteristics, and if males developed their 'feminine' side and women their 'masculine' side differences could be lessened, and rigid stereotyping avoided.

Andromache in Greek legend, the loyal wife of Hector and mother of Astyanax. After the fall of Troy she was awarded to Neoptolemus, Achilles' son; she later married a Trojan seer called Helenus. Andromache is the heroine of Homer's *Iliad* and the subject of a play by Euripides.

Angad 1504–1552. Indian religious leader, second guru (teacher) of Sikhism 1539–52, succeeding Nanak. He popularized the alphabet known as *Gurmukhi*, in which the Sikh scriptures are written.

The nearer the Church the further from God.

Lancelot Andrewes
'Sermon on the Nativity' 1622

---

angel in Jewish, Christian, and Muslim belief, a supernatural being intermediate between God and humans. The Christian hierarchy has nine orders: *Seraphim, Cherubim, Thrones* (who contemplate God and reflect his glory), *Dominations, Virtues, Powers* (who regulate the stars and the universe), *Principalities, Archangels*, and *Angels* (who minister to humanity). In traditional Catholic belief every human being has a guardian angel. The existence of angels was reasserted by Pope John Paul II 1986. Muslims believe that the Qur'an was revealed to Muhammad by the angel Jibra'el (Gabriel).

Is man an ape or an angel? Now I am on the side of the angels.

angels
Benjamin Disraeli, Earl of Beaconsfield, 1804–1881, British Conservative politician and novelist.
Speech at meeting of Society for Increasing Endowments of Small Livings in the Diocese of Oxford 25 Nov 1864

Anglican Communion family of Christian churches including the Church of England, the US Episcopal Church, and those holding the same essential doctrines, that is the Lambeth Quadrilateral 1888, Holy Scripture as the basis of all doctrine, the Nicene and Apostles' Creeds, Holy Baptism and Holy Communion, and the historic episcopate.

In England the two archbishops head the provinces of Canterbury and York, which are subdivided into bishoprics. The Church Assembly 1919 was replaced 1970 by a General Synod with three houses (bishops, other clergy, and laity) to regulate church matters, subject to Parliament. A decennial

Lambeth Conference (so called because the first was held there 1867), attended by bishops from all parts of the Anglican Communion, is presided over by the archbishop of Canterbury; it is not legislative but its decisions are often put into practice. In 1988 it passed a resolution seen as paving the way for the consecration of women bishops (the first was elected in the USA Sept 1988).

---

*The angels keep their ancient places; /
Turn but a stone, and start a wing! / 'Tis
ye, 'tis your estrangèd faces, / That miss
the many-splendoured thing.*

angels
Francis Thompson, 1859–1907, English poet.
'The Kingdom of God'

Anglicanism see ◊Anglican Communion.

Anglo-Catholicism in the Anglican Church, the Catholic heritage of faith and liturgical practice which was stressed by the founders of the ◊Oxford Movement. The term was first used in 1838 to describe the movement, which began in the wake of pressure from the more Protestant wing of the Church of England. Since the Church of England voted in 1992 to ordain women as priests, some Anglo-Catholics have found it difficult to remain within the Church of England.

Angry Young Men journalistic term applied to a loose group of British writers who emerged in the 1950s after the creative hiatus that followed World War II. They expressed dissatisfaction with and revolted against the prevailing social mores, class distinction, and 'good taste'. It was typified by such works as John Osborne's *Look Back in Anger* 1956, Kingsley Amis's *Lucky Jim* 1954, Colin Wilson's *The Outsider* 1956, John Braine's *Room at the Top* 1957, and John Wain's *Hurry on Down* 1953. Also linked to the group was theatre critic Kenneth Tynan.

angst (German 'anxiety') emotional state of anxiety without a specific cause. In ◊Existentialism, the term refers to general human anxiety at having free will, that is, of being responsible for one's actions.

animal liberation loose international movement against the infliction of suffering on animals, whether for scientific, military, or commercial research, or in being raised for food. The movement was sparked by the book

Animal Liberation 1975 by Peter Singer and encompasses many different organizations.

---

*'Twould ring the bells of Heaven / The
wildest peal for years, / If Parson lost his
senses / And people came to theirs, / And
he and they together / Knelt down with
angry prayers / For tamed and shabby
tigers / And dancing dogs and bears, / And
wretched, blind, pit ponies, / And little
hunted hares.*

animal rights
Ralph Hodgson, 1871–1962, English poet.
'The Bells of Heaven'

---

animal sacrifice a practice common in early religions and still practised today in some parts of the world. Through the offering of an appropriate animal, cleansed and purified, the gods could be pacified or appeased and thus human life would be protected.

In the Hindu Vedic hymns sacrifice is a means of limiting and sanctifying the taking of life. In some cultures, sheep and goats or birds were the predominant animals of sacrifice – as in many cultures of the Near East in the pre-Christian era. In Hinduism, the horse was a major sacrificial animal in the earliest days of Vedic culture, while in ancient Greece, the ox or bull was most favoured. Sacrificed animals were sometimes used to help divination, as when the entrails of a sheep were examined by priests in ancient Greece to determine the likely fortunes of a war or action. At the festival of Eid ul Adha, Muslims sacrifice sheep to recall how God prevented Ibraham from sacrificing his son Isma'ail by providing a ram instead, thus showing that God forbade human sacrifice. (A parallel story appears in the Bible, but with Isaac as the intended victim).

---

*All animals, except man, know that the
principal business of life is to enjoy it – and
they do enjoy it as much as man and other
circumstances will allow.*

animals
Samuel Butler, 1835–1902, English writer.
The Way of All Flesh ch 19

---

animism the belief that everything, whether animate or inanimate, possesses a soul or spirit. It is a fundamental system of belief in certain

Animal Rights and Vivisection

Humans' relations with other living creatures have always been extremely varied and complicated, both in everyday life and conceptually. The Western Judaeo-Christian tradition regarded humans as essentially superior to the animal kingdom, because God had endowed them alone with immortal souls and therefore with the prospects of eternal salvation. Similar views were expressed philosophically by René Descartes (1596–1650), who maintained that humans alone had consciousness, whereas the 'brutes' were mere machines. Demurring from Descartes, Anglo-Saxon thinking contended that creatures had feelings, if not reason. It was nevertheless accepted that human life was of greater value than animal. Humans had the right to harness animals for power, to farm them and to eat them, to keep them as pets, and, some argued, to hunt them. Before 1800, only a tiny number of vegetarians dissented from this consensus.

The rise of vivisection

Increasingly from the eighteenth century, scientists extended their presumed 'right' to use animals by performing experiments upon them. After 1800, scientific vivisection became highly controversial. The matrix of anti-vivisection arguments and lobbies led to the rise of a counter tradition of 'animal rights' during the twentieth century.

Human use of animals for experimental purposes dates from pre-Christian times. Living animals were first used by the Alexandrian physicians Herophilus (c. 330–260 BC) and Erisistratus in the third century BC. Andreas Vesalius (1514–1564) created the modern science of anatomy by systematic dissection of and experimentation on living animals. William Harvey's (1578–1657) demonstration of the circulation of the blood (1628) relied on a combination of dissection and animal experimentation.

In the 1820s and 1830s extensive animal experiments by François Magendie (1783–1855) led to notable advances in neuro-physiology. The emergence of bacteriology and immunology in the 1880s hinged on experiments on living animals. Supporters of vivisection have argued (then and now) that such benefits provide great benefits for humans. The end justifies the means: animals suffer to prevent future human and animal suffering. Diabetes is often cited as an example of a disease tamed through a cure developed by the use of animal experimentation, and using a substance – insulin – taken from animal bodies.

Humanitarian dissension

Opposition to the experimental use of animals arose from the humanitarian and sentimental movements of the eighteenth century. The experiments of the Reverend Stephen Hales (1677–1761) and others inspired disapproving comments from literati such as Samuel Johnson (1709–1784). An organized antivivisection movement emerged in the nineteenth century, led by Frances Power Cobbe (1822–1904). A Royal Commission set up by the government of Benjamin Disraeli (1804–1881) in 1876 recommended regulation of the practice; the Cruelty to Animals Act of 1876 was passed. This act, still in force – although partially supplanted by the 1986 Scientific Procedures (Animals) Act – requires registration of laboratories, licensing of experimenters, certification for experiments, and meticulous record-keeping (its enforcement is limited). British antivivisectionists scorned this legislation, seeing it as a blank cheque for scientific cruelty.

The number of animal experiments has risen steadily. By 1980, over five million experiments were performed annually on vertebrates in Britain alone. Though nations like the USA and Germany have laws regulating animal experimentation, many countries – including France, Spain, Brazil, and Japan – still have no such legislation.

Antivivisectionists have attacked animal experiments on various grounds. Some contend that any scientific conclusions derived from animal experimentation are inherently misleading. Utilitarian arguments state that the benefits of experiments are outweighed by the pain inflicted, especially as many animals have been maimed and killed not for medical purposes but for cosmetic testing, military testing, psychological testing, and other non-medical purposes.

Freedom for animals?

Recently, the case has been argued for animal autonomy. Following the 'categorical imperative' of Immanuel Kant – a philosophical version of 'do unto others as you would be done by' – it is said that the end can never justify the means, because animals are ends in themselves, and should therefore be treated as autonomous, rights-bearing, moral agents. Such views have radical implications. Taken to their logical conclusion, they would entail universal vegetarianism, the closing of zoos, and the freeing of all pets and domesticated animals (for such relationships would be regarded as tantamount to slavery), and other far-reaching changes. The strong animal rights position would seem to require that all animals must be wild and that their 'rights' (to territory for instance) must be respected by humans.

Views along these lines might seem to have some appeal with respect to intelligent, sentient, higher primates (gorillas for instance); but it is not clear how far down the biological scale 'animal rights' philosophers, like Peter Singer and perhaps Mary Midgeley (1919–), would wish to go. Do fish have rights? Fleas? Bacteria? And what about plants? The attack on 'speciesism' (although lagging behind those on sexism and racism) is rapidly gaining ground in various practical ways, such as the opposition to wearing furs and the rise of vegetarianism. Its implications are difficult to calculate.

Roy Porter

religions, particularly those of some pre-industrial societies studied by anthropologists.

In philosophy, the term can be applied to the view that in all things consciousness, or something mindlike exists. In ◊developmental psychology, an animistic stage in the early thought and speech of the child has been described, notably by ◊Piaget.

ankh ancient Egyptian symbol (derived from the simplest form of sandal), meaning 'eternal life', as in Tut*ankh*amen. It consists of a T-shape surmounted by an oval.

Annales school or *total history* group of historians formed in France in 1929, and centred around the journal *Annales d'histoire économique et sociale* which pioneered new methods of historical enquiry. Its leading members included Fernand ◊Braudel, who coined the term total history, and Marc ◊Bloch. Their view was that to arrive at worthwhile conclusions on broad historical debates, all aspects of a society had to be considered. Thus they widened the scope of research away from political history to include social and economic factors as well.

The main criticism of this historical tradition comes from Marxists who complain that it has no overall theory of societal development.

anno Domini in the Christian chronological system, refers to dates since the birth of Jesus, denoted by the letters AD. There is no year 0, so AD 1 follows immediately after the year 1 BC (before Christ). The system became the standard reckoning in the Western world after being adopted by the English historian Bede in the 8th century. The abbreviations CE (Common Era) and BCE (before Common Era) are often used instead by scholars and writers as objective, rather than religious, terms.

The system is based on the calculations made 525 by Dionysius Exiguus, a Scythian monk, but the birth of Jesus should more correctly be placed about 4 BC.

Annunciation in the New Testament, the announcement to Mary by the archangel Gabriel that she was to be the mother of Christ; the feast of the Annunciation is 25 March (also known as Lady Day).

Anokhin Piotre Kuzmich 1897–1974. Russian-born psychologist who worked with V M Bechterev (1857–1927), and later with ◊Pavlov, in examining the physiological bases of animal behaviour.

He proposed that behaviour is a system of functions each relating to a definite goal and suggested that, even in simple ◊conditioning,

it is regulated by its consequences, and is essentially self-regulating rather than reflexively determined. His major ideas are collected in *Biology and Neurophysiology of the Conditioned Reflex and its Role in Adaptive Behaviour* 1974.

anomie in the social sciences, a state of 'normlessness' created by the breakdown of commonly agreed standards of behaviour and morality; the term often refers to situations where the social order appears to have collapsed. The concept was developed by the French sociologist Emile ◊Durkheim.

Durkheim used 'anomie' to describe societies in transition during industrialization. The term was adapted by the US sociologist Robert ◊Merton to explain deviance and crime in the USA as a result of the disparity between high goals and limited opportunities.

anorexia lack or loss of the desire to eat. The term is often used for *anorexia nervosa*, an eating disorder that may not actually involve loss of appetite. Anorexia nervosa is characterized by severe self-imposed restriction of food intake and weight loss that may lead, in women, to amenorrhoea. Other symptoms include an intense fear of gaining weight, distortion of body image, increased physical activity, and ◊depression.

Although the condition can occur with older women and, very rarely, with men, anorectics are usually adolescent girls or young women; their thin, waif-like appearance makes them easily recognizable. It can in some cases be fatal, usually due to suicide. ◊Bulimia nervosa may sometimes follow chronic anorexia nervosa.

The causes of anorexia nervosa are not really known; there is no firm evidence of genetic or biological factors, for example. Teenage pressures, particularly sexual ones such as the desire to attain an 'ideal' feminine figure, and family rivalries and hostilities may be contributive factors. The anorectic often sees her mother as domineering and thinks of herself as without an identity of her own. She desperately resists becoming a grown-up woman like her mother.

Anorexia nervosa is often associated with the symptoms of other mental disorders and ◊psychotherapy is an important part of the treatment for it.

Anselm, St c. 1033–1109. Medieval priest and philosopher. As abbot from 1078, he made the abbey of Bec in Normandy, France, a centre of scholarship in Europe. He was appointed archbishop of Canterbury by

William II of England 1093, but was later forced into exile. He holds an important place in the development of ◊Scholasticism.

As archbishop of Canterbury St Anselm was recalled from exile in 1100 by Henry I, with whom he bitterly disagreed on the investiture of the clergy; a final agreement gave the king the right of temporal investiture and the clergy that of spiritual investiture.

In his *Proslogion* he developed the ◊ontological argument, which infers God's existence from our capacity to conceive of a perfect Being. His *Cur deus homo?/Why did God Become Man?* treats the subject of the Atonement. Anselm was canonized 1494.

anthology collection of verse by various authors, particularly of shorter poems such as epigrams. The earliest known of these is the *Greek Anthology*, which includes a shorter collection by Meleager, known as the *Garland*.

Anthony Susan B(rownell) 1820–1906. US pioneering campaigner for women's rights who also worked for the antislavery and temperance movements. Her causes included equality of pay for women teachers, married women's property rights, and women's suffrage. In 1869, with Elizabeth Cady ◊Stanton, she founded the National Woman Suffrage Association.

The true Republic: men, their rights and nothing more; women, their rights and nothing less.

Susan B(rownell) Anthony
Motto of her newspaper *The Revolution*

She edited and published a radical women's newspaper, *The Revolution* 1868–70, and worked on the *History of Woman Suffrage* 1881–86. She organized the International Council of Women and founded the International Woman Suffrage Alliance in Berlin 1904. Her profile appears on the 1979 US dollar coin.

Anthony, St c. 251–356. Also known as Anthony of Thebes. He was the founder of Christian monasticism. At the age of 20, he renounced all his possessions and began a life of study and prayer, later seeking further solitude in a cave in the desert.

Anthony was born in Egypt. In 305 he founded the first cenobitic order, a community of Christians following a rule of life under a superior. Late in his life he went to Alexandria and preached against ◊Arianism. He lived to over 100, and a good deal is known about his life since a biography (by St Athanasius) has survived. Anthony's temptations in the desert were a popular subject in art; he is also often depicted with a pig and a bell.

anthropic principle in science, the idea that 'the universe is the way it is because if it were different we would not be here to observe it'. The principle arises from the observation that if the laws of science were even slightly different, it would have been impossible for intelligent life to evolve. For example, if the electric charge on the electron were only slightly different, stars would have been unable to burn hydrogen and produce the chemical elements that make up our bodies. Scientists are undecided whether the principle is an insight into the nature of the universe or a piece of circular reasoning.

An anthology is like all the plums and orange peel picked out of a cake.

anthologies
Sir Walter Alexander Raleigh,
1861–1922, English scholar.
Letter to Mrs Robert Bridges 15 Jan 1915

---

anthropology the study of humankind. Its development as a scientific discipline in the late 19th century coincided with the greatest moment of colonial expansion and it initially drew on the theory of ◊evolution, largely as a means of proving the inferiority of the so-called 'primitive' races. It gradually moved from being a theoretical subject to an empirical one which aimed to investigate the differences and diversity of the human species both past and present, physically, socially, and culturally.

Anthropology is a holistic science which is usually subdivided into four distinct disciplines: ◊archaeology, ◊linguistics, physical anthropology, and cultural/social anthropology. Physical anthropology is the study of the evolutionary history of man, largely through the analysis of early human fossil remains. Cultural anthropology (the preferred term in the USA) and social anthropology (the preferred term in the UK) both study the cultural and social organization of particular – usually pre-literate – societies, through the recording and analysis of data gathered during ◊fieldwork. The difference between the latter two is mainly one of emphasis. Finally, the term applied anthropology is used to describe the involvement of anthropologists, usually as advisers, in development programmes in the Third World – an involvement often criticized as being a form of neocolonialism.

anthropomorphism the attribution of human characteristics to animals, inanimate objects, or deities. It appears in the mythologies of many cultures and as a literary device in fables and allegories.

anthroposophy system of religious philosophy developed by the German mystic and educationist Rudolf ◊Steiner. Designed to develop the whole human being, anthroposophy stresses the importance of awakening latent spiritual perception by training the mind to rise above material things. Anthroposophists believe that an appreciation of art is one of the keys to spiritual development, and that music and colours have curative properties.

anti-art in the visual arts, work that is exhibited in a conventional context but makes fun of serious art or challenges the nature of art; it is characteristic of ◊Dada. Marcel Duchamp is credited with introducing the term c. 1914, and its spirit is summed up in his attempt to exhibit a urinal (*Fountain* 1917). The term is also used to describe other intentionally provocative art forms, for example, nonsense poetry.

Antichrist in Christian theology, the opponent of Christ. The appearance of the Antichrist is believed to signal the Second Coming, at which Christ will conquer his opponent. The concept may stem from the idea of conflict between Light and Darkness, which is present in Persian, Babylonian, and Jewish literature and which influenced early Christian thought.

The Antichrist may be a false messiah, or be connected with false teaching, or be identified with an individual, for example Nero at the time of the persecution of Christians, and the pope and Napoleon in later Christian history.

anticlericalism hostility to the influence of the clergy in affairs outside the sphere of the church. Identifiable from the 12th century onwards, it became increasingly common in France in the 16th century and especially after the French Revolution of 1789. More recently apparent in most western European states, anticlericalism takes many forms, for example, opposition to the clergy as reactionary and against the principles of liberalism and the enlightenment, also opposition to clerics as representatives of religion or as landowners, tax-gatherers, or state servants.

anticommunism fierce antagonism towards communism linked particularly with right-wing politician Joseph ◊McCarthy's activities in the USA during the 1950s.

Antigone in Greek legend, a daughter of Jocasta, by her son ◊Oedipus. She is the subject of a tragedy by ◊Sophocles.

anti-hero the protagonist of a novel or play who instead of displaying heroic or sympathetic characteristics is incompetent, foolish, and often immoral. Examples include Don Quixote in Cervantes' *Don Quixote* 1605 and Jimmy Porter in John Osborne's play *Look Back in Anger* 1957.

antimatter in physics, a form of matter in which most of the attributes (such as electrical charge, magnetic moment, and spin) of ◊elementary particles are reversed. Such particles (antiparticles) can be created in particle accelerators, such as those at CERN in Geneva, Switzerland, and at Fermilab in the USA.

antinomianism doctrine that Christians are freed by grace from the necessity of obeying any moral law, such as the Ten Commandments or church law. The term was first applied in the Reformation to Martin ◊Luther's collaborator Johann Agricola (1492–1566), who thought antinomianism followed from Luther's doctrine of justification by faith.

St ◊Paul has been called an antinomian because he said that Christ's teachings superseded the Mosaic law of Judaism. In the 16th and 17th centuries, the term was used of Anabaptists, Familists, Ranters, Independents, and other radical sects.

antinuclear movement organization or mass movement that opposes the proliferation of nuclear weapons and/or the use of nuclear energy.

As the nuclear arms race gathered momentum during the 1950s it began to be criticized by leading intellectual figures, notably Bertrand ◊Russell and Albert ◊Einstein. Russell was one of the founder members, in 1958, of the British Campaign for Nuclear Disarmament (CND) which every year held a mass march from London to Aldermaston, the site of the Atomic Weapons Research Establishment. Throughout the 1970s the increased use of nuclear energy as a major power source was opposed by the new environmental or ◊green movements. Membership of antinuclear movements grew during the 1980s as the Cold War appeared to intensify. Peaceful direct action included the setting up of a women's peace camp at the US air base at Greenham Common in Britain. (See ◊peace movement.)

anti-psychiatry school of thought derived from the ideas of Thomas Szasz (1920–), R D ◊Laing, and others, who have argued strenuously against the usefulness both of the concept of mental illness and of psychiatric treatment in general.

Szasz has argued, for example, that in most cases of incapacity due to psychological causes it is inappropriate to talk about illness. Not only can psychiatrists differ widely in their diagnoses, but it is also often difficult to determine whether or not someone is actually mentally ill. Furthermore, labelling someone as mentally ill can have unfortunate consequences due to the prejudice that persists in society. Adherents of anti-psychiatry see society as the cause of mental illness, application of the label 'mentally ill' as an attempt to cover up this fact, and treatment of the so-called mentally ill as a postponement of society's obligation to deal with the root of the problem.

Bibl. Szasz, TS *The Myth of Mental Illness* (New York, 1961)

antiracism and antisexism active opposition to ◊racism and ◊sexism; positive action or a set of policies, such as 'equal opportunity', can be designed to counteract racism and sexism, often on the part of an official body or an institution, such as a school, a business, or a government agency.

The growth of antiracist and antisexist policies in the UK in the 1980s, for example in education, reflected the belief that to ensure equality of opportunity, conscious efforts should be made to counteract the effects of unconscious racism and sexism as well as the effects of previous systematic ◊discrimination against members of minority ethnic groups and women.

anti-Semitism literally, prejudice against Semitic people (see ◊Semite), but in practice it has meant prejudice or discrimination against, and persecution of, the Jews as an ethnic group. Historically this was practised for almost 2,000 years by European Christians. Anti-Semitism was a tenet of Hitler's Germany, and in the Holocaust 1933–45 about 6 million Jews died in concentration camps and in local extermination ◊pogroms, such as the siege of the Warsaw ghetto. In eastern Europe, as well as in Islamic nations, anti-Semitism exists and is promulgated by neofascist groups. It is a form of ◊racism.

The destruction of Jerusalem AD 70 led many Jews to settle in Europe and throughout the Roman Empire. In the 4th century Christianity was adopted as the official religion of the Empire, which reinforced existing prejudice (dating back to pre-Christian times and referred to in the works of Seneca and Tacitus) against Jews who refused to convert. Anti-Semitism increased in the Middle Ages because of the Crusades and the Inquisition, and legislation forbade Jews to own land or be members of a craft guild; to earn a living they had to become moneylenders and traders (and were then resented when they prospered). Britain expelled many Jews 1290, but they were formally readmitted 1655 by Cromwell. From the 16th century Jews were forced by law in many cities to live in a separate area, or *ghetto*.

Late 18th- and early 19th-century liberal thought improved the position of Jews in European society. In the Austro-Hungarian Empire, for example, they were allowed to own land, and after the French Revolution the 'rights of man' were extended to French Jews 1790. The rise of 19th-century nationalism and unscientific theories of race instigated new resentments. Anti-Semitism became strong in Austria, France (see ◊Dreyfus), and Germany, and from 1881 pogroms in Poland and Russia caused refugees to flee to the USA (where freedom of religion was enshrined in the constitution), to the UK, and to other European countries as well as Palestine (see ◊Zionism).

In the 20th century, fascism and the Nazi Party's application of racial theories led to organized persecution and genocide. After World War II, the creation of Israel 1948 provoked Palestinian anti-Zionism, backed by the Arab world. Anti-Semitism is still fostered by extreme right-wing groups, such as the National Front in the UK and France and the Neo-Nazis in the USA and Germany.

Antisthenes c. 444 BC–c. 366 BC. Greek philosopher who is sometimes regarded as founder of the ◊Cynic school, but who also influenced ◊stoicism with his practical ethics. He believed that virtue could be taught. Virtue with physical exercise was the way to happiness.

Antisthenes was born in Athens. He studied under Gorgias the sophist and ◊Socrates, at whose death he was present. He disapproved of all speculation, and so was opposed to ◊Plato. Although not ascetic, he held that wealth and luxury were unimportant, as were established laws and conventions, birth, sex, and race. One of his pupils was ◊Diogenes the cynic.

antivivisection opposition to vivisection, that is, experiments on living animals, which is practised in the pharmaceutical and cosmetics industries on the grounds that it may result in discoveries of importance to medical science. Antivivisectionists argue that it is immoral to inflict pain on helpless creatures, and that it is unscientific because results achieved with animals may not be paralleled with human beings.

They also argue that it is unjust to make animals suffer in order that people may benefit, and that vivisection has not added to people's power over disease. Antivivisectionist groups, such as the Animal Liberation Front, sometimes take illegal action to draw attention to their cause.

Anu Mesopotamian sky god, commonly joined in a trinity with Enlil and Ea.

Anubis in Egyptian mythology, the jackal-headed god of the dead, son of ◊Osiris. Anubis presided over the funeral cult, including embalming, and led the dead to judgement.

It is the nature of human affairs to be fraught with anxiety.

> *anxiety*
> Anicius Manlius Severinus Boethius,
> 480 AD–524, Roman philosopher
> and Christian theologian.
> *The Consolation of Philosophy* II.iv

---

anxiety unpleasant, distressing emotion usually to be distinguished from fear. Fear is aroused by the perception of actual or threatened danger. Anxiety arises when the danger is unreal, imagined, or cannot be identified or clearly perceived and its outcome is unknown. It is a normal response in stressful situations, but is frequently experienced in, and is even a characteristic feature of, many mental disorders.

Anxiety is experienced as a feeling of suspense, helplessness, or alternating hope and despair together with excessive alertness and characteristic bodily changes such as tightness in the throat, disturbances in breathing and heartbeat, sweating, diarrhoea, and so on. In psychiatry, an anxiety state is a type of ◊neurosis in which anxiety resembling normal anxiety either seems to arise for no reason at all, or else is out of all proportion to what may have caused it. 'Phobic anxiety' refers to the irrational fear that characterizes ◊phobia.

Better to be despised for too anxious apprehensions, than ruined by too confident a security.

> *anxiety*
> Edmund Burke, 1729–1797, Anglo-Irish
> politician and political theorist.
> *Reflections on the Revolution in France*

◊Freud identified two important forms of anxiety: signal anxiety, which alerts the ◊ego to impending threats that might unbalance it, and primary anxiety, which occurs when its equilibrium is upset, as for example in ◊trauma or a nightmare. He also maintained that anxiety was a result of unsatisfied ◊libido and ◊repression, and that the most primitive from of anxiety originated in the individual's birth experience.

apartheid racial-segregation policy of the government of South Africa, which was legislated 1948, when the Afrikaner National Party gained power. Nonwhites (Bantu, coloured or mixed, or Indian) do not share full rights of citizenship with the 4.5 million whites (for example, the 23 million black people cannot vote in parliamentary elections), and many public facilities and institutions were until 1990 (and in some cases remain) restricted to the use of one race only; the establishment of Black National States is another manifestation of apartheid. In 1991 President de Klerk repealed the key elements of apartheid legislation.

The term 'apartheid' was coined in the late 1930s by the South African Bureau for Racial Affairs (SABRA), which called for a policy of 'separate development' of the races.

Internally, organizations opposed to apartheid were banned, for example the African National Congress and the United Democratic Front, and leading campaigners for its abolition have been, like Steve Biko, killed, or, like Archbishop Tutu, harassed. Anger at the policy has sparked off many uprisings, from Sharpeville 1960 and Soweto 1976 to the Crossroads squatter camps 1986.

Abroad, there are anti-apartheid movements in many countries. In 1961 South Africa was forced to withdraw from the Commonwealth because of apartheid; during the 1960s and 1970s there were calls for international ◊sanctions, especially boycotts of sporting and cultural links; and in the 1980s advocates of sanctions extended them into trade and finance.

The South African government's reaction to internal and international pressure was twofold: it abolished some of the more hated apartheid laws (the ban on interracial marriages was lifted 1985 and the pass laws, which restricted the movement of nonwhites, were repealed 1986); and it sought to replace the term 'apartheid' with 'plural democracy'. Under states of emergency 1985 and 1986 it used force to quell internal opposition, and from 1986 there was an official ban on the reporting of it in the media. In Oct 1989 President F W de Klerk permitted anti-apartheid demonstrations; the Separate Amenities Act was abolished 1990 and a new constitution promised. In 1990 Nelson Mandela, a leading figure in the African National Congress, was finally released. In 1991 the remaining major discriminating laws embodied in apartheid were repealed, including the Population Registration Act, which had made it obligatory for every citizen to be classified into one of nine racial groups.

The term has also been applied to similar movements and other forms of racial separation, for example social or educational, in other parts of the world.

aphasia a general term for the many types of disturbance in language that are due to brain damage, especially in the speech areas of the dominant hemisphere.

Symptom description and classification have never been straightforward. Classification systems are based on which part of the brain is thought to be affected or on which sensory or motor functions are impaired or language skills lost. The main types are: (a) Broca's aphasia – patient's speech and writing severely affected but with full understanding of spoken and written language; (b) ◊Wernicke's aphasia – speech and writing affected in expression (errors in grammar, wrong and non-existent words produced) and comprehension; (c) conduction aphasia – lesion in the arcuate fasciculus, the pathway connecting Wernicke's area with Broca's, resulting in speech that is semantically abnormal, and difficulty in repeating sentences and reading aloud; (d) aphasia due to lesions in the angular gyrus (a ridge on the side and toward the rear of the cortex) – difficulty in understanding spoken and written language and in naming objects; (e) global aphasia – language affected on a global scale, presumably due to lesions in both Broca's and Wernicke's area.

aphrodisiac any substance that arouses or increases sexual desire.

Sexual activity can be stimulated in humans and animals by drugs affecting the pituitary gland. Preparations commonly sold for the purpose can be dangerous (cantharidin) or useless (rhinoceros horn), and alcohol and cannabis, popularly thought to be effective because they lessen inhibition, may have the opposite effect.

Aphrodite in Greek mythology, the goddess of love (Roman Venus, Phoenician Astarte, Babylonian Ishtar); said to be either a daughter of Zeus (in Homer) or sprung from the foam of the sea (in Hesiod). She was the unfaithful wife of Hephaestus, the god of fire, and the mother of Eros.

Apis ancient Egyptian god with a human body and a bull's head, linked with Osiris (and later merged with him into the Ptolemaic god Serapis); his cult centres were Memphis and Heliopolis, where sacred bulls were mummified.

Apocrypha appendix to the Old Testament of the Bible, not included in the final Hebrew canon but recognized by Roman Catholics. There are also disputed New Testament texts known as Apocrypha.

He that toucheth pitch shall be defiled therewith.

Apocrypha
Ecclesiasticus 13:1

Apollinarius of Laodicea c. 310–c. 390. Bishop of Laodicea, whose views on the nature of Christ were condemned by the Council of Constantine 381, but who nonetheless laid the foundations for the later controversy over ◊Nestorianism. Rather than seeing the nature of Jesus as a human and divine soul somehow joined in the person of Christ, he saw Christ as having a divine mind only, and not a human one.

Apollo in Greek and Roman mythology, the god of sun, music, poetry, prophecy, agriculture, and pastoral life, and leader of the Muses. He was the twin child (with ◊Artemis) of Zeus and Leto. Ancient statues show Apollo as the embodiment of the Greek ideal of male beauty. His chief cult centres were his supposed birthplace on the island of Delos, in the Cyclades, and Delphi.

Apollonian term for the individuating, rationalizing, and conscious principle in human society used by the German philosopher

Friedrich ◊Nietzsche. In *The Birth of Tragedy from the Spirit of Music* 1872, his study of the origins of ancient Greek drama, Nietzsche contrasted the Apollonian principle to the Dionysiac, which he saw as collective, irrational, and lyrical.

Apollonius of Perga c. 260–c. 190 BC. Greek mathematician, called 'the Great Geometer'. In his work *Conic Sections* he showed that a plane intersecting a cone will generate an ellipse, a parabola, or a hyperbola, depending on the angle of intersection. In astronomy, he used a system of circles called epicycles and deferents to explain the motion of the planets; this system, as refined by Ptolemy, was used until the Renaissance.

Apollonius of Tyana early 1st century AD. Greek ascetic philosopher of the Neo-Pythagorean school. He travelled in Babylonia and India, where he acquired a wide knowledge of oriental religions and philosophies, and taught at Ephesus. He was said to have had miraculous powers but claimed only that he could see the future.

apologetics philosophical writings that attempt to refute attacks on the Christian faith. Apologists include ◊Justin Martyr, ◊Origen, St ◊Augustine, Thomas ◊Aquinas, Blaise ◊Pascal, and Joseph ◊Butler. The questions raised by scientific, historical, and archaeological discoveries have widened the field of apologetics.

apostasy public rejection of one's faith or taking up another faith. Julian the Apostate (332–63) was a Roman emperor who rejected the growth of Christianity in the Empire and tried to restore the older religions of Rome and Greece. Technically the term is used by the Roman Catholic Church to denote either someone who totally defects from the faith, or the abandonment of religious vows by a monk or nun.

a posteriori (Latin 'from the latter') in logic, an argument that deduces causes from their effects; inductive reasoning; the converse of ◊a priori.

apostle in the New Testament, any of the chosen 12 ◊disciples sent out by Jesus after his resurrection to preach the Gospel. In the earliest days of Christianity the term was extended to include some who had never known Jesus in the flesh, notably St Paul.

Apostles discussion group founded 1820 at Cambridge University, England; members have included the poet Tennyson, the philosophers G E ◊Moore and Bertrand ◊Russell, the writers Lytton Strachey and Leonard Woolf, the economist ◊Keynes, and the spies Guy Burgess and Anthony Blunt.

Apostles' Creed oldest of the three ancient ◊creeds of the Christian church; it probably dates from the 2nd century.

apostolic succession doctrine in the Christian church that certain spiritual powers were received by the first apostles directly from Jesus, and have been handed down in the ceremony of 'laying on of hands' from generation to generation of bishops.

apparatchik in a communist political system, an employee of the *apparat*, or state bureaucracy; that is, a full-time, senior party official.

appearance in philosophy, what is visible, or manifest to the senses, but is ultimately illusory. Hence, appearance is usually contrasted with reality, and so the term often occurs in ◊idealism and ◊scepticism.

appeasement historically, the conciliatory policy adopted by the British government, in particular under Neville Chamberlain, towards the Nazi and Fascist dictators in Europe in the 1930s in an effort to maintain peace. It was strongly opposed by Winston Churchill, but the Munich Agreement 1938 was almost universally hailed as its justification. Appeasement ended when Germany occupied Bohemia–Moravia March 1939.

Appleton Edward Victor 1892–1965. British physicist who worked at Cambridge under Ernest ◊Rutherford from 1920. He proved the existence of the Kennelly–Heaviside layer (now called the E layer) in the atmosphere, and the Appleton layer beyond it, and was involved in the initial work on the atom bomb. Nobel prize 1947.

appropriate technology simple or small-scale machinery and tools that, because they are cheap and easy to produce and maintain, may be of most use in the developing world; for example, hand ploughs and simple looms. This equipment may be used to supplement local crafts and traditional skills to encourage small-scale industrialization.

Many countries suffer from poor infrastructure and lack of capital but have the large supplies of labour needed for this level of technology. The use of appropriate technology was one of the recommendations of the Brandt Commission (1977–83), established to examine the problems of developing countries and identify corrective measures that would command international support.

April Fools' Day the first day of April, when it is customary in W Europe and the USA to expose people to ridicule by a practical joke, causing them to believe some falsehood or to go on a fruitless errand.

The victim is known in England as an April Fool; in Scotland as a gowk (cuckoo or fool); and in France as a *poisson d'avril* (April fish). There is a similar Indian custom on the last day of the Holi festival in late March.

a priori (Latin 'from what comes before') in logic, an argument that is known to be true, or false, without reference to experience; the converse of ◊a posteriori.

Aquinas St Thomas c. 1226–1274. Italian philosopher and theologian, the greatest figure of the school of ◊scholasticism. He was a Dominican monk, known as the 'Angelic Doctor'. In 1879 his works were declared the basis of Catholic theology. His *Summa contra Gentiles/Against the Errors of the Infidels* 1259–64 argues that reason and faith are compatible. He assimilated the philosophy of Aristotle into Christian doctrine.

He was born near Aquino in central Italy. He studied under Albert the Great ◊Albertus Magnus in both Paris and Cologne, and he taught in Paris 1256–72.

---

*Grace does not abolish nature,
but perfects it.*

St Thomas Aquinas
Medieval Thought: St Augustine to Ockham
G Leff

Working from fresh translations of ◊Aristotle into Latin by his fellow Dominican William of Moerbeke (1215–1286), Aquinas created a subtle philosophy, often described as Christian Aristotelianism. He also drew on the works of St ◊Augustine, ◊Avicenna, ◊Averroes, and the ◊neo-Platonists. In metaphysics, he contrasts a thing's ◊essence (that is, what makes it what it is) with its existence, though in God they coincide. He argued that the soul is immortal but cannot be permanently disembodied. Hence, he argues, immortality requires physical resurrection. He also developed five ways of demonstrating the existence of God. His theory of meaning relies on analogy: for instance, the term 'God's

wisdom' is to be understood by analogy with human wisdom. The philosophy of Aquinas is known as *Thomism*.

His unfinished *Summa Theologica*, begun 1265, deals with the nature of God, morality, and the work of Jesus.

arbitration submission of a dispute to a third, unbiased party for settlement. It may be personal litigation, a trade-union issue, or an international dispute.

The first permanent international court was established in The Hague in the Netherlands 1900, and the League of Nations set up an additional Permanent Court of International Justice 1921 to deal with frontier disputes and the like. The latter was replaced 1945 with the International Court of Justice under the United Nations. Another arbiter is the European Court of Justice, which rules on disputes arising out of the Rome treaties regulating the European Community. In the UK, the Advisory, Conciliation and Arbitration Service (ACAS) offers an arbitration service. In the United States Department of Labor there are sections concerned with employment standards and labour-management standards.

archaeology study of history (primarily but not exclusively the prehistoric and ancient periods), based on the examination of physical remains. Principal activities include preliminary field (or site) surveys, excavation (where necessary), and the classification, dating, and interpretation of finds. Since 1958 radiocarbon dating has been used to establish the age of archaeological strata and associated materials.

history Interest in the physical remains of the past began in the Renaissance among dealers in and collectors of ancient art. It was further stimulated by discoveries made in Africa, the Americas, and Asia by Europeans during the period of imperialist colonization in the 16th–19th centuries, such as the antiquities discovered during Napoleon's Egyptian campaign in the 1790s. Towards the end of the 19th century archaeology became an academic study, making increasing use of scientific techniques and systematic methodologies.

Related disciplines that have been useful in archaeological reconstruction include stratigraphy (the study of geological strata), dendrochronology (the establishment of chronological sequences through the study of tree rings), paleobotany (the study of ancient pollens, seeds, and grains), epigraphy (the study of inscriptions), and numismatics (the study of coins).

archetype typical or perfect specimen of its kind. In a more specialized sense, it also means one of the basic roles or situations, received from the ◊collective unconscious, in which people tend to cast themselves. The psychologist C G ◊Jung identified archetypes such as the Hero, the Terrible Mother (stepmother, witch), and the theme of death and rebirth. They are recurring motifs in myth, art, and literature.

The figure of the Wanderer condemned to roam the earth until released from a curse appears in the Greek legend of *Odysseus*, in the story of the Wandering Jew (told throughout Europe from the 16th century on), and in the hero of Wagner's opera *The Flying Dutchman*.

Eureka! I have found it!

Archimedes
Remark, quoted in Vitruvius Pollio
De Architectura IX

Archimedes c. 287–212 BC. Greek mathematician who made major discoveries in geometry, hydrostatics, and mechanics. He formulated a law of fluid displacement (Archimedes' principle), and is credited with the invention of the Archimedes screw, a cylindrical device for raising water.

He was born at Syracuse in Sicily. It is alleged that Archimedes' principle was discovered when he stepped into the public bath and saw the water overflow. He was so delighted that he rushed home naked, crying 'Eureka! Eureka!' ('I have found it! I have found it!') He used his discovery to prove that the goldsmith of the king of Syracuse had adulterated a gold crown with silver. Archimedes designed engines of war for the defence of Syracuse, and was killed when the Romans besieged the town.

Arendt Hannah 1906–1975. German-born US political philosopher. She studied with ◊Husserl and ◊Jaspers, but with the rise of the Nazis she moved to Paris and emigrated to the USA 1940. Her wide range of concerns includes modern totalitarianism, the nature of evil, and the erosion of public participation in the political process.

In *The Origins of Modern Totalitarianism*, 1951, she pointed out the similarities between Nazism and Soviet communism, and in her report on the trial of a leading Nazi war criminal, *Eichmann in Jerusalem* 1963, she coined the phrase 'the banality of evil' to describe how bureaucratic efficiency can facilitate the acceptance of the most terrible events.

Argos city in ancient Greece, at the head of the Gulf of Nauplia, which was once a cult centre of the goddess Hera. In the Homeric age the name 'Argives' was sometimes used instead of 'Greeks'. In the classical period Argos repeatedly, but unsuccessfully, contested supremacy in S Greece with Sparta.

argument from design or *teleological argument* or *physico-theological argument* line of reasoning, argued by English bishop William ◊Paley 1794, that the universe is so complex that it can only have been designed by a superhuman power, and that we can learn something of it (God) by examining the world. The argument from design became popular with Protestant theologians in the 18th century as a means of accommodating Newtonian science. It was attacked by Scottish philosopher David ◊Hume, among others.

Many versions of the argument exist, but all rely on the seeming pattern and order in the universe to take the view that it has a design or purpose (◊teleology). An alleged weakness in the argument is that it attempts a causal inference from the universe to God, when it only makes sense to speak of causal relations as holding between observable states of affairs.

The argument from design is one of four traditional arguments for the existence of God, the others being the ◊cosmological argument, the ◊moral argument, and the ◊ontological argument.

Argyris Chris 1923– . US psychologist, specializing in the personal development of individuals within organizations and the defence mechanisms managers employ to resist change. Argyris developed the 'Goal Congruence Theory' 1964 which stated that organizational design should ensure that the individual's needs for personal development are matched with the organization's needs for productivity.

Arianism system of Christian theology that denied the complete divinity of Jesus. It was founded about 310 by ◊Arius, and condemned as heretical at the Council of Nicaea 325.

Some 17th- and 18th-century theologians held Arian views akin to those of ◊Unitarianism (that God is a single being, and that there is no such thing as the Trinity). In 1979 the heresy again caused concern to the Vatican in the writings of such theologians as Edouard Schillebeeckx of the Netherlands.

Aristarchus of Samos c. 320–c. 250 BC. Greek astronomer. The first to argue that the Earth moves around the Sun, he was ridiculed for his beliefs. He was also the first astronomer to estimate the sizes of the Sun and Moon and their distances from the Earth.

His only surviving work is *Magnitudes and Distances of the Sun and Moon*, although ◊Archimedes quotes from another tract that no longer exists. Aristarchus produced methods for finding the relative distances of the Sun and Moon that were geometrically correct but rendered useless by inaccuracies in observation.

Aristippus c. 435–356 BC. Greek philosopher, founder of the ◊Cyrenaic or hedonist school. A pupil of Socrates, he developed the doctrine that pleasure is the highest good in life. He lived at the court of ◊Dionysius of Syracuse and then with Laïs, a courtesan, in Corinth.

A fully-equiped duke costs as much to keep up as two Dreadnoughts; and dukes are just as great a terror and they last longer.

aristocracy
David Lloyd George, 1863–1945,
Welsh Liberal politician,
prime minister of Britain 1916–22.
Speech at Newcastle 9 Oct 1909

aristocracy social elite or system of political power associated with landed wealth, as in western Europe; monetary wealth, as in Carthage and Venice; or religious superiority, as with the Brahmins in India. The Prussian (Junker) aristocracy based its legitimacy not only on landed wealth but also on service to the state. Aristocracies are also usually associated with monarchy but have frequently been in conflict with the sovereign over their respective rights and privileges. In Europe, their economic base was undermined during the 19th century by inflation and falling agricultural prices, leading to their demise as a political force after 1914.

Aristotle of Stagira 384–322 BC. Greek philosopher who advocated reason and mod-

eration. He began the systematic study of logic; his *Ethics* is a standard text; and he made major contributions to political theory, metaphysics, physics, astronomy, meteorology, biology, psychology, and literary criticism. Aristotle maintained that both sense experience and reason are necessary for knowledge.

When devoid of virtue, man is the most unscrupulous and savage of animals, and the worst in regard to sexual indulgence and gluttony.

Aristotle
Politics

He argued that humans are by nature social and moral, but that hierarchy and subordination are inevitable. His importance lies as much in his analytical methods as in his conclusions.

Aristotle was born in Stagira, a small town in Macedonia. He was the son of the physician to the king. In 367–347 BC he attended Plato's Academy in Athens, becoming tutor to Alexander the Great 342 BC. When Alexander succeeded to the throne of Macedonia in 335 BC, Aristotle opened his own school, the Lyceum, in Athens. It became known as the 'peripatetic school' because he walked up and down as he talked, and his works – including the *Politics*, the *Poetics*, the *Metaphysics*, the *Physics*, and *De Anima/On the Soul* – are a collection of his lecture notes. When Alexander died, Aristotle was forced to flee to Chalcis, where he died.

Aristotle was the first political theorist to try to classify constitutions, and to consider the role of law in states. In biology, he was the first to classify organisms into species and genera, and the first to notice the mammalian characteristics of whales and dolphins. In ethics, he held that the good life was the life of virtue and intellectual contemplation. The good person avoids both self-denial and self-indulgence, and aims for the mean – the moderate enjoyment of human appetites. He held that a

An aristocracy in a republic is like a chicken whose head has been cut off: it may run about in a lively way, but in fact it is dead.

aristocracy
Nancy Mitford, 1904–1973, English writer.
Noblesse Oblige

human being is a moral and physical unity: the soul is to the body as form is to matter, and similarly with reason and emotion.

Man by nature is a political animal.

Aristotle
Politics

Aristotle's influence has been immense. The neo-Platonists and the Roman philosopher ◊Boethius passed on his ideas to posterity. In the Middle Ages, Aristotle's philosophy became the foundation of Islamic philosophy, and later was incorporated into Christian theology, especially by Thomas ◊Aquinas. In the Italian Renaissance his conception of the good life was highly influential. Because medieval scholars had tended to accept his vast output without criticism, his reputation declined in tl.e 16th–18th centuries. Aristotle has been a major influence on late-19th- and 20th-century philosophy in the UK, the USA, and Germany.

This man (Aristotle) is ... an example which nature has devised to demonstrate supreme human perfection.

Averroës
Medieval Thought: St Augustine to Ockham
G Leff

---

arithmetic branch of mathematics concerned with the study of numbers and their properties. The fundamental operations of arithmetic are addition, subtraction, multiplication, and division. Raising to powers (for example, squaring or cubing a number), the extraction of roots (for example, square roots), percentages, fractions, and ratios are developed from these operations.

Forms of simple arithmetic existed in prehistoric times. In China, Egypt, Babylon, and early civilizations generally, arithmetic was used for commercial purposes, records of taxation, and astronomy. During the Dark Ages in Europe, knowledge of arithmetic was preserved in India and later among the Arabs. European mathematics revived with the development of trade and overseas exploration. Hindu-Arabic numerals replaced Roman numerals, allowing calculations to be made on paper, instead of by the abacus.

The essential feature of this number system was the introduction of zero, which allows us to have a *place–value* system. The decimal numeral system employs ten numerals (0,1,2,3,4,5,6,7,8,9) and is said to operate in 'base ten'. In a base-ten number, each position has a value ten times that of the position to its immediate right; for example, in the number 23 the numeral 3 represents three units (ones), and the number 2 represents two tens. The Babylonians, however, used a complex base-sixty system, residues of which are found today in the number of minutes in each hour and in angular measurement (6 x 60 degrees). The Mayas used a base-twenty system.

There have been many inventions and developments to make the manipulation of the arithmetic processes easier, such as the invention of ◊logarithms by Scottish mathematician John ◊Napier 1614 and of the slide rule in the period 1620–30. Since then, many forms of ready reckoners, mechanical and electronic calculators, and computers have been invented.

Modern computers fundamentally operate in base two, using only two numerals (0,1), known as a binary system. In binary, each position has a value twice as great as the position to its immediate right, so that for example binary 111 (111_2) is equal to 7 in the decimal system, and 1111 (1111_2) is equal to 15. Because the main operations of subtraction, multiplication, and division can be reduced mathematically to addition, digital computers carry out calculations by adding, usually in binary numbers in which the numerals 0 and 1 can be represented by off and on pulses of electric current.

Modular or modulo arithmetic, sometimes known as residue arithmetic, can take only a specific number of digits, whatever the value. For example, in modulo 4 (mod 4) the only values any number can take are 0, 1, 2, or 3. In this system, 7 is written as 3 mod 4, and 35 is also 3 mod 4. Notice 3 is the residue, or remainder, when 7 or 35 is divided by 4. This form of arithmetic is often illustrated on a circle. It deals with events recurring in regular cycles, and is used in describing the functioning of petrol engines, electrical generators, and so on. For example, in the mod 12, the answer to a question as to what time it will be in five hours if it is now ten o'clock can be expressed 10 + 5 = 3.

Arius c. 256–336. Egyptian priest whose ideas gave rise to ◊Arianism, a Christian belief which denied the complete divinity of Jesus.

He was born in Libya, and became a priest in Alexandria 311. In 318 he was excommunicated and fled to Palestine, but his theology spread to such an extent that the emperor ◊Constantine called a council at Nicaea 325 to resolve the question. Arius and his adherents were condemned and banished.

Arjan Indian religious leader, fifth guru (teacher) of Sikhism 1581–1606. He built the Golden Temple in Amritsar and compiled the *Adi Granth*, the first volume of Sikh scriptures. He died in Muslim custody.

Arjuna Indian prince, one of the two main characters in the Hindu epic ◊*Mahābhārata*.

Ark of the Covenant in the Old Testament, the chest that contained the Tablets of the Law as given to Moses. It is now the cupboard in a synagogue in which the ◊Torah scrolls are kept. The original ark was built under Moses' direction when the Israelites were wandering in the desert, and was carried on poles by the priests. King ◊David built the first Temple in Jerusalem to give a permanent home to the Ark, which was kept in the Holy of Holies.

Armageddon in the New Testament (Revelation 16), the site of the final battle between the nations that will end the world; it has been identified with Megiddo in Israel.

Armenian church form of Christianity adopted in Armenia in the 3rd century. The Catholicos, or exarch, is the supreme head, and Echmiadzin (near Yerevan) is his traditional seat.

About 295, Gregory the Illuminator (c. 257–332) was made exarch of the Armenian church, which has developed along national lines.

The Seven Sacraments (or Mysteries) are administered, and baptism is immediately followed by confirmation. Believers number about 2 million.

Arminius Jacobus. Latinized name of Jakob Harmensen 1560–1609. Dutch Protestant priest who founded Arminianism, a school of Christian theology opposed to ◊Calvin's doctrine of predestination. His views were developed by Simon Episcopius (1583–1643). Arminianism is the basis of Wesleyan ◊Methodism.

He was born in S Holland, ordained in Amsterdam 1588, and from 1603 was professor of theology at Leyden. He asserted that forgiveness and eternal life are bestowed on all who repent of their sins and sincerely believe in Jesus Christ. He was drawn into many

controversies, and his followers were expelled from the church and persecuted.

arms control attempts to limit the arms race between the superpowers by reaching agreements to restrict the production of certain weapons; see ◊disarmament.

Arnauld French family closely associated with ◊Jansenism, a Christian church movement that began in the 17th century. *Antoine Arnauld* (1560–1619) was a Parisian advocate, strongly critical of the Jesuits; along with the philosopher Pascal and others, he produced not only Jansenist pamphlets, but works on logic, grammar, and geometry. Many of his 20 children were associated with the abbey of Port Royal, a convent of Cistercian nuns near Versailles which became the centre of Jansenism. His youngest child, *Antoine* (1612-1694), the 'great Arnauld', was religious director there.

The men of culture are the true apostles of equality.

> **Matthew Arnold**
> *Culture and Anarchy*

Arnold Matthew 1822–1888. English poet and critic. His poems, characterized by their elegiac mood and pastoral themes, include *The Forsaken Merman* 1849, *Thyrsis* 1867 (commemorating his friend Arthur Hugh Clough), and *Dover Beach* 1867, which was widely regarded as one of the most eloquent expressions of the spiritual anxieties of Victorian England. Arnold's critical works include *Essays in Criticism* 1865 and 1888, and *Literature and Dogma* 1872. His most influential book was *Culture and Anarchy* 1869, in which he attacked the smugness and philistinism of the Victorian middle classes, and argued for a new culture based on the pursuit of artistic and intellectual values..

The son of Thomas Arnold, he was educated at public schools and Oxford University. After a short spell as an assistant master at Rugby, Arnold became a school inspector 1851–86. He published two unsuccessful volumes of anonymous poetry, but two further publications under his own name 1853 and 1855 led to his appointment as professor of poetry at Oxford. Arnold first used the word 'philistine' in its present sense in his attack on the cultural values of the middle classes.

Arnold of Brescia 1100–1155. Italian Augustinian monk, who attacked the holding of property by the Catholic church; he was hanged and burned, and his ashes thrown into the Tiber river.

Aron Raymond 1905–1983. French sociologist and political commentator who stressed the importance of the political element in social change. He saw industrial societies as characterized by pluralism and by a diversity of values and he was highly critical of ◊Marxism. He was professor of sociology at the Sorbonne, University of Paris, 1955–68 and wrote regularly for the newspaper *Le Figaro*.

Arrhenius Svante August 1859–1927. Swedish scientist, the founder of physical chemistry. Born near Uppsala, he became a professor at Stockholm in 1895, and made a special study of electrolysis. He wrote *Worlds in the Making* and *Destinies of the Stars*, and in 1903 received the Nobel Prize for Chemistry. In 1905 he predicted global warming as a result of carbon dioxide emission from burning fossil fuels.

Arrian lived 2nd century AD. Greek historian whose *Anabasis/Expedition* is the major literary source of information on the campaigns of Alexander the Great. A governor and commander under the Roman emperor Hadrian, his work was drawn with care from much earlier material.

Arrow Kenneth Joseph 1921– . US economist. He developed with Gerard ◊Debreu mathematical models of the conditions necessary for economic equilibrium, where demand and supply are equal. He also made a significant contribution to the development of the economics of social welfare, where he suggested that there were logical inconsistencies in attempting to analyse social welfare in terms of individual choices. He also carried out work on uncertainty and decision-making in economics, particularly on the effect of learning by doing on productivity. He was joint winner

of the Nobel Prize for Economics in 1972 with John ◊Hicks. His major works include *Social Choice and Individual Values* 1951 and *Essays in the Theory of Risk-bearing* 1971.

Bibl. Arrow, K J and Debreu, G 'Existence of an Equilibrium for a Competitive Economy' *Econometrica* (1954)

The history of art is the history of revivals.
art
Samuel Butler, 1835–1902, English writer.
Notebooks, 'Handel and Music'

---

art in the broadest sense, all the processes and products of human skill, imagination, and invention; the opposite of nature. In contemporary usage, definitions of art usually reflect aesthetic criteria, and the term may encompass literature, music, drama, painting, and sculpture. Popularly, the term is most commonly used to refer to the visual arts. In Western culture, aesthetic criteria introduced by the ancient Greeks still influence our perceptions and judgements of art.

Religion and art spring from the same root and are close kin. Economics and art are strangers.
art
Willa (Sibert) Cather, 1873–1947, US novelist and short-story writer.
Commonweal 17 Apr 1936

Two currents of thought run through our ideas about art. In one, derived from Aristotle, art is concerned with *mimesis* ('imitation'), the representation of appearances, and gives pleasure through the accuracy and skill with which it depicts the real world. The other view, derived from Plato, holds that the artist is inspired by the Muses (or by God, or by the inner impulses, or by the collective unconscious) to express that which is beyond appearances – inner feelings, eternal truths, or the essence of the age. In the Middle Ages the term 'art' was used, chiefly in the plural, to signify a branch of learning which was regarded as an instrument of knowledge. The seven *liberal arts* consisted of the *trivium*, that is grammar, logic, and rhetoric, and the *quadrivium*, that is arithmetic, music, geometry, and astronomy. In the visual arts of Western civilizations, painting and sculpture have been the

---

Do not imagine that Art is something which is designed to give gentle uplift and self-confidence. Art is not a brassière. *At least, not in the English sense. But do not forget that* brassière *is the French for life-jacket.*
art
Julian Barnes, 1946– , English writer.
Flaubert's Parrot

dominant forms for many centuries. This has not always been the case in other cultures. Islamic art, for example, is one of ornament, for under the Islamic religion artists were forbidden to usurp the divine right of creation by portraying living creatures. In some cultures masks, tattoos, pottery, and metalwork have been the main forms of visual art. Recent technology has made new art forms possible, such as photography and cinema, and today electronic media have led to entirely new ways of creating and presenting visual images.

Art is meant to disturb, science reassures.

art

Georges Braque, 1882–1963, French painter.
Pensées sur l'Art

Artaud Antonin 1896–1948. French theatre director, influenced by ◊Surrealism. Although his play, *Les Cenci/The Cenci* 1935, was a failure, his concept of the **Theatre of ◊Cruelty**, intended to release feelings usually repressed in the unconscious, has been an important influence on modern dramatists such as Jean Genet and on directors such as Peter Brook. Declared insane 1936, Artaud was confined in an asylum.

Artemis in Greek mythology, the goddess of chastity (Roman Diana), the young of all creatures, the Moon, and the hunt. She is the twin sister of ◊Apollo and was worshipped at cult centres throughout the Greek world, one of the largest of which was at ◊Ephesus. Her great temple there, reconstructed several times in antiquity, was one of the Seven Wonders of the World.

art for art's sake artistic theory; see ◊aestheticism.

artha in Hinduism, prosperity arising from economic development according to religious principles, one of the four aims of material life prescribed in Hindu scripture, *dharma-artha-kama-moksha* (religion-prosperity-sensual pleasure-liberation). The first three stages should eventually lead to the search for 'moksha', liberation from the cycle of birth and death.

art history the study of works of art. ◊Winckelmann laid the foundations for a systematic study of art history as early as the mid 18th century, but it did not become an academic discipline until 1844 when a chair was established at Berlin University. Two basic approaches had emerged by the end of the

19th century: the first considered art in relation to its cultural or social context (◊Burckhardt, ◊Taine); the second sought to analyse works of art in terms of such 'formal' properties as colour, line, and form (◊Wölfflin). A later approach, rejecting the formalism of Wölfflin, concentrated on ◊iconography, the study of the meaning of works of art (◊Panofsky).

Arthur 6th century AD. Legendary British king and hero in stories of ◊Camelot and the quest for the ◊Holy Grail. Arthur is said to have been born in Tintagel, Cornwall, and buried in Glastonbury, Somerset. He may have been a Romano-Celtic leader against pagan Saxon invaders.

The legends of Arthur and the knights of the Round Table were developed in the 12th century by Geoffrey of Monmouth, Chrétien de Troyes, and the Norman writer Wace. Later writers on the theme include the anonymous author of *Sir Gawayne and the Greene Knight* 1346, Thomas Malory, Tennyson, T H White, and Mark Twain.

arti or *arati* in Hinduism, a primary ritual for worship of the sacred image in a temple. A ghee (clarified butter) lamp, incense, flowers, and water are offered before the deity, using circular hand motions, to the accompaniment of bells and recitation of ◊mantras.

artificial intelligence (AI) branch of science concerned with creating computer programs that can perform actions comparable with those of an intelligent human. Current AI research covers such areas as planning (for robot behaviour), language understanding, pattern recognition, and knowledge representation.

Early AI programs, developed in the 1960s, attempted simulations of human intelligence or were aimed at general problem-solving techniques. It is now thought that intelligent behaviour depends as much on the knowledge a system possesses as on its reasoning power. Present emphasis is on ◊knowledge-based systems, such as ◊expert systems. Britain's largest AI laboratory is at the Turing Institute, University of Strathclyde, Glasgow. In May 1990 the first International Robot Olympics was held there, including table-tennis matches between robots of the UK and the USA.

Art Nouveau in the visual arts and architecture, decorative style of about 1890–1910, which makes marked use of sinuous lines reminiscent of unfolding tendrils, stylized flowers and foliage, and flame shapes. In England, it appears in the illustrations of Aubrey Beardsley; in Spain, in the architecture of

Antonio Gaudí; in France, in the architecture of Hector Guimard, the art glass of René Lalique, and the posters of Alphonse Mucha; in Belgium, in the houses and shops of Victor Horta; in the USA, in the lamps and metal work of Louis Comfort Tiffany; and in Scotland, in the interior and exterior designs of Charles Rennie Mackintosh. Art Nouveau took its name from a shop in Paris that opened 1895; it was also known as *Jugendstil* in Germany and *Stile Liberty* in Italy, after the fashionable London department store.

Arts and Crafts movement English social movement, largely antimachine in spirit, based in design and architecture and founded by William Morris in the latter half of the 19th century. It was supported by the architect A W Pugin and by John ◊Ruskin and stressed the importance of handcrafting. The ◊Art Nouveau style succeeded it.

Assassination – an accident of my trade.

assassination
Alfonso XIII of Spain, 1885–1941,
King of Spain.
Remark after an attempt on his life May 1906

Aryan Indo-European family of languages; also the hypothetical parent language of an ancient people who are believed to have lived between central Asia and E Europe and to have reached Persia and India in one direction and Europe in another sometime in the 2nd century BC, diversifying into the various Indo-European language speakers of later times. In Nazi Germany Hitler and other theorists erroneously propagated the idea of the Aryans as a white-skinned, blue-eyed, fair-haired master race.

Arya Samaj Hindu religious movement founded by Dayanand Saraswati (1824–1883) about 1875. He renounced idol worship and urged a return to the purer principles of the ◊Vedas (Hindu scriptures). For its time the movement was quite revolutionary in its social teachings, which included forbidding ◊caste practices, prohibiting child-marriage, and allowing widows to remarry.

Ascension Day or *Holy Thursday* in the Christian calendar, the feast day commemorating Jesus' ascension into heaven. It is the 40th day after Easter.

asceticism the renunciation of physical pleasure, for example, in eating, drinking, sexuality, and human company. Often for religious reasons, discomfort or pain may be sought.

Asgard in Scandinavian mythology, the place where the gods lived. It was reached by a bridge called Bifrost, the rainbow. One of its most sumptuous halls was ◊Valhalla.

ashram Indian community whose members lead a simple life of discipline and self-denial and devote themselves to social service. Noted ashrams are those founded by Mahatma Gandhi at Wardha and the poet Rabindranath Tagore at Santiniketan.

Ash Wednesday first day of Lent, the period in the Christian calendar leading up to Easter; in the Roman Catholic church the foreheads of the congregation are marked with a cross in ash, as a sign of penitence.

assassination murder, usually of a political, royal, or public person. The term derives from the order of the ◊Assassins, a Muslim sect that, in the 11th and 12th centuries, murdered officials to further its political ends.

Assassins, order of the militant offshoot of the Islamic Isma'ili sect 1089–1256, founded by Hassan Sabah (c. 1045–1124). Active in Syria and Persia, they assassinated high officials in every Muslim town to further their extremist political ends. Their headquarters from 1090 was the Alamut clifftop fortress in the Elburz Mountains, NW Iran.

Their leader, Hassan Sabah, became a missionary and rebel against the Seljuk Empire following his conversion to the sect. As grand master of the Assassins, he ran the order with strict asceticism. The assassins were members of a suicide squad: they remained at the scene of the crime to be martyred for their beliefs. Their enemies called them *hashishiyun* 'smokers of hashish'. Princes, viziers, and also Crusaders were among their victims. Hassan was a scholar and Alamut, built on a peak of 1,800 m/6,000 ft, held one of the largest libraries of the time.

asset in business accounting, a term that covers the land or property of a company or individual, payments due from bills, investments, and anything else owned that can be turned into cash. On a company's balance sheet, total assets must be equal to liabilities (money and services owed).

assisted area region that is receiving financial help from central government as part of a regional policy. Most policies concentrate on identifying and then assisting areas with lower-than-average incomes or higher unemployment rates, so that economic activity may be more equally distributed within the economy.

In the UK, areas with a high concentration of declining industries such as Clydeside and Tyneside are designated *development areas*, and new investment in these areas can qualify for government grants depending on its job-creating potential. Smaller areas around declining inner cities, docklands, or a major plant that has closed down are designated *enterprise zones*, where rent and rates are generally reduced and planning restrictions eased.

assize in medieval Europe, the passing of laws, either by the king with the consent of nobles, as in the Constitutions of ◊Clarendon 1164 by Henry II of England, or as a complete system, such as the *Assizes of Jerusalem*, a compilation of the law of the feudal kingdom of Jerusalem in the 13th century.

The term remained in use in the UK for the courts held by judges of the High Court in each county; they were abolished under the Courts Act 1971.

assurance form of long-term saving where individuals pay monthly premiums typically over 10 or 25 years and at the end receive a large lump sum. For example, a person may save £50 a month and at the end of 25 years receive a lump sum of £40,000. Assurance policies are offered by assurance companies which invest savers' monthly premiums typically in stocks, shares, and property.

Astarte alternative name for the Babylonian and Assyrian goddess ◊Ishtar.

Aston Francis William 1877–1945. English physicist who developed the mass spectrometer, which separates isotopes by projecting their ions (charged atoms) through a magnetic field. He received the Nobel Prize for Chemistry 1922.

astrological diagnosis casting of a horoscope to ascertain a person's susceptibility to specific kinds of disease. From statistical evidence that offspring tend to have the same planetary positions in their charts as a parent, astrologers infer that there is a significant correlation between genetic and planetary influences, and that medical horoscopes, by pinpointing pathological tendencies, can be a useful tool of preventative medicine.

astrology study of the relative position of the planets and stars in the belief that they influence or indicate events on Earth. The astrologer casts a ◊horoscope based on the time and place of the subject's birth. Astrology has no proven scientific basis, but has been widespread since ancient times. Western and Indian astrology is based on the 12 signs of the zodiac; Chinese astrology is based on a 60-year cycle and lunar calendar.

history A strongly held belief in ancient Babylon, astrology spread to the Mediterranean world, and was widely used by the Greeks and Romans. In Europe during the Middle Ages it had a powerful influence since kings and other public figures had their own astrologers; astrological beliefs are reflected in Elizabethan and Jacobean literature. In both Chinese and Hindu thought, the universe is seen as forming a pattern in which everything is linked. Human life should be lived in harmony with this pattern, and astrology is seen as one way of helping to do this.

popular prediction In the UK, the first edition of *Old Moore's Almanac*, which gives a forecast of the year ahead, appeared 1700, and there have been annual editions since. Astrological forecasts in newspapers and magazines are usually very simplistic.

astronomy science of the celestial bodies: the Sun, the Moon, and the planets; the stars and galaxies; and all other objects in the universe. It is concerned with their positions, motions, distances, and physical conditions; and with their origins and evolution. Astronomy thus divides into fields such as astrophysics, celestial mechanics, and cosmology.

Astronomy is perhaps the oldest recorded science; there are observational records from ancient Babylonia, China, Egypt, and Mexico. The first true astronomers, however, were the Greeks, who deduced the Earth to be a sphere, and attempted to measure its size. Ancient Greek astronomers included ◊Thales and ◊Pythagoras. ◊Eratosthenes of Cyrene measured the size of the Earth with considerable accuracy. Star catalogues were drawn up, the most celebrated being that of Hipparchus. The *Almagest*, by ◊Ptolemy of Alexandria, summarized Greek astronomy, and survived in its Arab translation. However, the Greeks still regarded the Earth as the centre of the universe, although this was doubted by some philosophers, notably ◊Aristarchus of Samos, who maintained that the Earth moves around the Sun.

Ptolemy, the last famous astronomer of the Greek school, died about AD 180, and little progress was made for some centuries. The Arabs revived the science, carrying out theoretical researches from the 8th and 9th centuries, and producing good star catalogues. Unfortunately, a general belief in the pseudo-science of astrology continued until the end of the Middle Ages (and has been revived from time to time).

The dawn of a new era came 1543, when a Polish canon, ◊Copernicus, published a work entitled *De Revolutionibus Orbium Coelestium/ About the Revolutions of the Heavenly Spheres*, in which he demonstrated that the Sun, not the Earth, is the centre of our planetary system. (Copernicus was wrong in many respects – for instance, he still believed that all celestial orbits must be perfectly circular.) Tycho ◊Brahe, a Dane, increased the accuracy of observations by means of improved instruments allied to his own personal skill, and his observations were used by the German mathematician Johannes ◊Kepler to prove the validity of the Copernican system. Considerable opposition existed, however, for removing the Earth from its central position in the universe; the Catholic Church was openly hostile to the idea, and, ironically, Brahe never accepted the idea that the Earth could move around the Sun. Yet before the end of the 17th century, the theoretical work of Isaac ◊Newton had established celestial mechanics.

The refracting telescope was invented about 1608, by Hans ◊Lippershey in Holland, and was first applied to astronomy by the Italian scientist ◊Galileo in the winter of 1609–10. Immediately, Galileo made a series of spectacular discoveries. He found the four largest satellites of Jupiter, which gave strong support to the Copernican theory; he saw the craters of the Moon, the phases of Venus, and the myriad faint stars of our Galaxy, the Milky Way. Galileo's most powerful telescope magnified only 30 times, but before long, larger telescopes were built, and official observatories were established.

Galileo's telescope was a refractor; that is to say, it collected its light by means of a glass lens or object glass. Difficulties with his design led Newton, in 1671, to construct a reflector, in which the light is collected by means of a curved mirror.

Theoretical researches continued, and astronomy made rapid progress in many directions. New planets were discovered – Uranus 1781 by William ◊Herschel, and Neptune 1846, following calculations by British astronomer John Couch ◊Adams and French astronomer Urbain Jean Joseph ◊Leverrier. Also significant was the first measurement of the distance of a star, when in 1838 the German astronomer Friedrich ◊Bessel measured the parallax of the star 61 Cygni, and calculated that it lies at a distance of about 6 light years (about half the correct value). Astronomical spectroscopy was developed,

first by Fraunhofer in Germany and then by people such as Pietro Angelo ◊Secchi and William Huggins, while Gustav ◊Kirchhoff successfully interpreted the spectra of the Sun and stars. By the 1860s good photographs of the Moon had been obtained, and by the end of the century photographic methods had started to play a leading role in research.

William Herschel, probably the greatest observer in the history of astronomy, investigated the shape of our Galaxy during the latter part of the 18th century, and concluded that its stars are arranged roughly in the form of a double-convex lens. Basically Herschel was correct, although he placed our Sun near the centre of the system; in fact, it is well out toward the edge, and lies 25,000 light years from the galactic nucleus. Herschel also studied the luminous 'clouds' or nebulae, and made the tentative suggestion that those nebulae capable of resolution into stars might be separate galaxies, far outside our own Galaxy. It was not until 1923 that US astronomer Edwin ◊Hubble, using the 2.5 m/100 in reflector at the Mount Wilson Observatory, was able to verify this suggestion. It is now known that the 'starry nebulae' are galaxies in their own right, and that they lie at immense distances. The most distant galaxy visible to the naked eye, the Great Spiral in Andromeda, is 2.2 million light years away; the most remote galaxy so far measured lies over 10 billion light years away. It was also found that galaxies tended to form groups, and that the groups were apparently receding from each other at speeds proportional to their distances.

This concept of an expanding and evolving universe at first rested largely on Hubble's law, relating the distance of objects to the amount their spectra shift towards red – the red shift. Subsequent evidence derived from objects studied in other parts of the electromagnetic spectrum, at radio and X-ray wavelengths, has provided confirmation. Radio astronomy established its place in probing the structure of the universe by demonstrating in 1954 that an optically visible distant galaxy was identical with a powerful radio source known as Cygnus A. Later analysis of the comparative number, strength, and distance of radio sources suggested that in the distant past these, including the ◊quasars discovered 1963, had been much more powerful and numerous than today. This fact suggested that the universe has been evolving from an origin, and is not of infinite age as expected under a ◊steady-state theory. The discovery 1965 of microwave background radiation suggested that residue survived the tremendous thermal power of the giant explosion, or ◊Big Bang, that brought the universe into existence.

Although the practical limit in size and efficiency of optical telescopes has apparently been reached, the siting of these and other types of telescope at new observatories in the previously neglected southern hemisphere has opened fresh areas of the sky to search. Australia has been in the forefront of these developments. The most remarkable recent extension of the powers of astronomy to explore the universe is in the use of rockets, satellites, space stations, and space probes. Even the range and accuracy of the conventional telescope may be greatly improved free from the Earth's atmosphere. The USA launched a large optical telescope, called the Hubble Space Telescope, permanently in space in April 1990. It is the most powerful optical telescope yet constructed, with a 2.4m/ 94.5 in mirror. It detects celestial phenomena seven times more distant (up to 14 billion light-years) than any land telescope. See also ◊black hole and ◊cosmology.

atavism (Latin *atavus* 'ancestor') in ◊genetics, the reappearance of a characteristic not apparent in the immediately preceding generations; in psychology, the manifestation of primitive forms of behaviour.

Ate in Greek mythology, the personification of infatuation, the failure to distinguish between good and bad courses of action.

Athanasian creed one of the three ancient ◊creeds of the Christian church. Mainly a definition of the ◊Trinity and ◊Incarnation, it was written many years after the death of Athanasius, but was attributed to him as the chief upholder of Trinitarian doctrine.

Athanasius, St 298–373. Bishop of Alexandria, supporter of the doctrines of the ◊Trinity and ◊Incarnation. He was a disciple of St Anthony the hermit, and an opponent of ◊Arianism in the great Arian controversy. Following the official condemnation of Arianism at the Council of Nicaea 325, Athanasius was appointed bishop of Alexandria 328. The Athanasian creed was not actually written by him, although it reflects his views.

Banished 335 by the emperor ◊Constantine because of his intransigence towards the defeated Arians, he was recalled in 346 but suffered three more banishments before his final reinstatement about 366.

atheism nonbelief in, or the positive denial of, the existence of a God or gods. A related concept is ◊agnosticism. Like theism, its opposite, atheism cannot be proved or disproved conclusively.

A little philosophy inclineth a man's mind to atheism; but depth in philosophy bringeth men's minds about to religion.

atheism
Francis Bacon, 1561–1626,
English philosopher, politician and essayist.
Essays, XVI 'Of Atheism'

Perhaps the strongest atheistic argument concerns the existence of ◊evil, which is hard to reconcile with the notion (in Christianity and other religions) that the world was created by an omnipotent, all-loving God: theologians have responded with a variety of theodicies, or justifications for the existence of evil.

The first openly atheistic book published in Britain was *Answer to Dr Priestley's Letters to a Philosophical Unbeliever* 1782 by Matthew Turner, a Liverpool doctor.

God never wrought miracle to convince atheism, because his ordinary works convince it.

atheism
Francis Bacon, 1561–1626, English
politician, philosopher, and essayist.
Essays, XVI 'Of Atheism'

Dogmatic atheism asserts that there is no God. *Sceptical atheism* maintains that the finite human mind is so constituted as to be incapable of discovering that there is or is not a God. *Critical atheism* holds that the evidence for theism is inadequate.

Athena in Greek mythology, the goddess of war, wisdom, and the arts and crafts (Roman Minerva), who was supposed to have sprung fully grown from the head of Zeus. In Homer's *Odyssey*, she is the protectress of ◊Odysseus and his son Telemachus. Her chief cult centre was Athens, where the Parthenon was dedicated to her.

atman in Hinduism, the individual soul or the eternal essential self.

atomic mass unit or *dalton unit* (symbol amu or u) unit of mass that is used to measure the relative mass of atoms and molecules. It is equal to one-twelfth of the mass of a carbon-12 atom, which is equivalent to the mass of a proton or 1.66×10^{-27} kg. The ◊relative atomic mass of an atom has no units; thus oxygen-16 has an atomic mass of 16 daltons, but a relative atomic mass of 16.

Neutrinos, they are very small. / They have no charge and have no mass / And do not interact at all.

atoms
John (Hoyer) Updike, 1932, US writer.
'Cosmic Gall'

Aton in ancient Egypt, the Sun's disc as an emblem of the single deity whose worship was promoted by ◊Ikhnaton in an attempt to replace the many gods traditionally worshipped.

atonement in Christian theology, the doctrine that Jesus suffered on the cross to bring about reconciliation and forgiveness between God and humanity.

Atonement is an action that enables a person separated from God by sin to be reconciled ('at one') with him. In ancient Judaism this was achieved through the sacrificial killing of animals.

Atonement, Day of Jewish holy day (*Yom Kippur*) held on the tenth day of Tishri (Sept–Oct), the first month of the Jewish year. It is a day of fasting, penitence, and cleansing from sin, ending the Ten Days of Penitence that follow *Rosh Hashanah*, the Jewish New Year.

audit official inspection of a company's accounts by a qualified accountant as required by law each year to ensure that the company balance sheet reflects the true state of its affairs.

augur member of a college of Roman priests who interpreted the will of the gods from signs or 'auspices' such as the flight of birds, the condition of entrails of sacrificed animals, and the direction of thunder and lightning. Their advice was sought before battle and on other important occasions. Consuls and other high officials had the right to consult the auspices themselves, and a campaign was said to be conducted 'under the auspices' of the general who had consulted the gods.

Augustan Age golden age of the Roman emperor Augustus, during which art and literature flourished. The name is also given to later periods which used Classical ideals, such as that of Queen Anne in England.

Augustine of Hippo, St 354–430. One of the early Christian leaders and writers known as the Fathers of the Church. He was converted to Christianity by Ambrose in Milan and became bishop of Hippo (modern Annaba, Algeria) 396. Among Augustine's many writings are his *Confessions*, a spiritual autobiography, and *De Civitate Dei/The City of God*, vindicating the Christian church and divine providence in 22 books.

Born in Thagaste, Numidia (now Algeria), of Roman descent, he studied rhetoric in Carthage, where he became the father of an illegitimate son, Adeodatus. He lectured in Tagaste and Carthage and for ten years was attached to the Manichaeist belief. In 383 he went to Rome, and on moving to Milan came under the influence of Ambrose. After prolonged study of ◊neo-Platonism he was baptized by Ambrose together with his son. Resigning his chair in rhetoric, he returned to Africa – his mother, St Monica, dying in Ostia on the journey – and settled in Thagaste. In 391, while visiting Hippo, Augustine was ordained priest, and in 396 he was appointed bishop of Hippo. He died there in 430, as the city was under siege by the Vandals.

Augustine's written output was vast, with 113 books and treatises, over 200 letters, and more than 500 sermons surviving. Many of Augustine's books resulted from his participation in three great theological controversies: he refuted ◊Manichaeism; attacked (and did much to eliminate) the exclusive N African ◊Donatists at the conference of Carthage 411; and devoted the last 20 years of his life to refute ◊Pelagius, maintaining the doctrine of original sin and the necessity of divine grace.

Augustine, St first archbishop of Canterbury, England. He was sent from Rome to convert England to Christianity by Pope Gregory I. He landed at Ebbsfleet in Kent 597, and soon after baptized Ethelbert, King of Kent, along with many of his subjects. He was consecrated bishop of the English at Arles in the same year, and appointed archbishop 601, establishing his see at Canterbury. Feast day 26 May.

Augustine was originally prior of the Benedictine monastery of St Andrew, Rome. In 603 he attempted unsuccessfully to unite the Roman and native Celtic churches at a conference on the Severn. He founded Christ Church, Canterbury, in 603, and the abbey of Saints Peter and Paul, now the site of Saint Augustine's Missionary College.

Augustinian member of a religious community that follows the Rule of St ◊Augustine of Hippo. It includes the Canons of

St Augustine, Augustinian Friars and Hermits, Premonstratensians, Gilbertines, and Trinitarians.

Aurobindo Ghose 1872–1950. Indian philosopher and founder of Aurobindo Ashram at Pondicherry, South India. He wrote extensively on Hindu theology and philosophy, proposing Integral Yoga to bring together body and soul, individual and community. Through his widespread influence on Hindu intelligentsia he strengthened the modern Hindu movement in the 1930s and 1940s. After his death his followers developed the city of Auroville at his ashram.

Austin J(ohn) L(angshaw) 1911–1960. British philosopher. Austin was a pioneer in the investigation of the way words are used in everyday speech. He is particularly remembered for his theory of speech acts. Speech acts are of three kinds – locutions (the uttering of meaningful sentences), illocutions (what one does in saying things, such as stating, promising, urging), and perlocutions (what one does by saying things, such as persuading, frightening, embarrassing). His lectures *Sense and Sensibilia* and *How to do Things with Words* were published posthumously in 1962.

Austin John 1790–1859. English jurist. His analysis of the chaotic state of the English legal system led him to define law as the enforceable command of a sovereign authority, thus distinguishing it from other kinds of rules and from morality. His work had a strong impact on jurisprudential thought, though many of his ideas were derived from his friend Jeremy ◊Bentham. He was professor of jurisprudence at the University of London 1826–35.

Australian Aboriginal religions beliefs associated with the creation legends recorded in the ◊Dreamtime stories.

autarchy national economic policy that aims at achieving self-sufficiency and eliminating the need for imports (by imposing tariffs, for example). Such a goal may be difficult, if not impossible, for a small country. Countries that take protectionist measures and try to prevent free trade are sometimes described as autarchical.

authoritarianism rule of a country by a dominant elite who repress opponents and the press to maintain their own wealth and power. They are frequently indifferent to activities not affecting their security, and rival power centres, such as trade unions and political parties, are often allowed to exist, although under tight control. An extreme form is ◊totalitarianism.

autocracy form of government in which one person holds absolute power. The autocrat has uncontrolled and undisputed authority. Russian government under the tsars was an autocracy extending from the mid-16th century to the early 20th century. The title *Autocratix* (a female autocrat) was assumed by Catherine II of Russia in the 18th century.

auto-da-fé (Portuguese 'act of faith') religious ceremony, including a procession, solemn mass, and sermon, which accompanied the sentencing of heretics by the Spanish ◊Inquisition before they were handed over to the secular authorities for punishment, usually burning.

automatic writing abnormal phenomenon, a type of ◊automatism, in which a person writes spontaneously, apparently without control over what is written. Automatic writing may sometimes arise as a symptom of mental disturbance.

The phenomenon has also occurred in connexion with that of mediumship, with ostensible communications from deceased persons taking the form of automatic scripts. Some individuals have attempted to develop a facility for automatic writing, often with the aim of gaining access to the unconscious mind. In psychology, there have been reports of its therapeutic use to stimulate memory in patients exhibiting varying degrees of mental dissociation.

automatism performance of actions without awareness or conscious intent. It is seen in sleepwalking and in some (relatively rare) psychotic states.

autonomy in politics, term used to describe political self-government of a state or, more commonly, a subdivision of a state. Autonomy may be based upon cultural or ethnic differences and often leads eventually to independence.

autosuggestion conscious or unconscious acceptance of an idea as true, without demanding rational proof, but with potential subsequent effect for good or ill. Pioneered by the French psychotherapist Emile ◊Coué (1857–1926) in healing, it is sometimes used in modern psychotherapy to conquer nervous habits and dependence on addictive substances such as tobacco and alcohol.

Avalokiteśvara in Mahāyāna Buddhism, one of the most important ◊bodhisattvas, seen as embodying compassion. Known as *Guanyin* in China and *Kannon* in Japan, he is one of the attendants of Amida Buddha.

Avalon in Celtic legend, the island of the blessed, or paradise; and in the legend of King ◊Arthur, the land of heroes, ruled over by ◊Morgan le Fay to which King Arthur is conveyed after his final battle with Mordred. It has been identified since the Middle Ages with Glastonbury in Somerset, SW England.

avant-garde in the arts, those artists or works that are in the forefront of new developments in their media. The term was introduced (as was 'reactionary') after the French Revolution, when it was used to describe any socialist political movement.

avatar in Hindu mythology, the descent of a deity to Earth in a visible form, for example the nine avatars of ◊Vishnu.

Ave Maria Christian prayer to the Virgin Mary, which takes its name from the archangel Gabriel's salutation to the Virgin Mary when announcing that she would be the mother of the Messiah (Luke 11:28).

Philosophy is the friend and milk-sister of the Law.

Averroës
The Decisive Treatise

Averroës (Arabic **Ibn Rushd**) 1126–1198. Arabian philosopher who argued for the eternity of matter and against the immortality of the individual soul. His philosophical writings, including commentaries on ◊Aristotle and on Plato's *Republic*, became known to the West through Latin translations. He influenced Christian and Jewish writers into the Renaissance, and reconciled Islamic and Greek thought in that philosophic truth comes through reason. St Thomas ◊Aquinas opposed this position.

Averroës was born in Córdoba, Spain, trained in medicine, and became physician to the caliph as well as judge of Seville and Córdoba. He was accused of heresy by the Islamic authorities and banished 1195. Later he was recalled, and died in Marrakesh. 'Averroism' was taught at Paris and elsewhere in the 13th century by the 'Averroists', who

No morality can be founded on authority, even if the authority were divine.

A(lfred) J(ules) Ayer
Essay on Humanism

defended a distinction between philosophical truth and revealed religion.

Avicenna (Arabic **Ibn Sina**) 979–1037. Arabian philosopher and physician. He was the most renowned philosopher of medieval Islam. His concept of God as the being in which essence and existence are identical gained wide currency, influencing ◊Maimonides and ◊Aquinas. His philosophical writings were influenced by al-Farabi, Aristotle, and the ◊neo-Platonists, and in turn influenced the scholastics of the 13th century. His *Canon Medicinae* was a standard work for many centuries.

A horse is simply a horse.

Avicenna
Medieval Thought: St Augustine to Ockham
G Leff

avidya in Hinduism and Buddhism, a lack of understanding of the true nature of reality. In Buddhism it also means a lack of understanding of the ◊Four Noble Truths. In its wider sense it denotes the root of all evil, for being unable to discern true reality means one is trapped in falsehood and thus in suffering and evil.

Avogadro Amedeo Conte di Quaregna 1776–1856. Italian physicist who proposed Avogadro's hypothesis on gases 1811. His work enabled scientists to calculate Avogadro's number, and still has relevance for today's atomic studies.

ayatollah honorific title awarded to Shi'ite Muslims in Iran by popular consent, as, for example, to Ayatollah Ruhollah ◊Khomeini.

If I had been someone not very clever, I would have done an easier job like publishing. That's the easiest job I can think of.

A(lfred) J(ules) Ayer
Remark

Ayer A(lfred) J(ules) 1910–1989. English philosopher. He wrote *Language, Truth and Logic* 1936, an exposition of the theory of 'logical positivism', presenting a criterion by which meaningful statements (essentially truths of logic, as well as statements derived from experience) could be distinguished from meaningless metaphysical utterances (for example, claims that there is a God or that the world external to our own minds is illusory).

He was Wykeham professor of logic at Oxford 1959–78. Later works included *Probability and Evidence* 1972 and *Philosophy in the Twentieth Century* 1982.

Ayurveda basically naturopathic system of medicine widely practised in India and based on principles derived from the ancient Hindu scriptures, the ◊Vedas. Hospital treatments and remedial prescriptions tend to be non-specific and to coordinate holistic therapies for body, mind, and spirit.

Azhar, El Muslim university and mosque in Cairo, Egypt. Founded 970 by Jawhar, commander in chief of the army of the Fatimid caliph, it is claimed to be the oldest university in the world. It became the centre of Islamic learning, with several subsidiary foundations, and is now primarily a school of Koranic teaching.

B

Baade Walter 1893–1960. German-born US astronomer who made observations that doubled the distance, scale, and age of the universe. Baade worked at Mount Wilson Observatory, USA, and discovered that stars are in two distinct populations according to their age, known as Population I (the younger) and Population II (the older). Later, he found that Cepheid variable stars of Population I are brighter than had been supposed, and that distances calculated from them were wrong. Baade's figures showed that the universe was twice as large as previously thought, and twice as old.

Baal divine title given to their chief male gods by the Phoenicians, or Canaanites. Their worship as fertility gods, often orgiastic and of a phallic character, was strongly denounced by the Hebrew prophets.

Baalbek city of ancient Syria, now in Lebanon, 60 km/36 mi NE of Beirut. It was originally a centre of Baal worship. The Greeks identified Baal with Helios, the Sun, and renamed Baalbek *Heliopolis*. Its ruins, including Roman temples, survive; the Temple of Bacchus, built in the 2nd century AD, is still almost intact.

Bab, the name assumed by Mirza Ali Mohammad 1819–1850. Persian religious leader, born in Shiraz, founder of ◊Babism, an offshoot of Islam. In 1844 he proclaimed that he was a gateway to the Hidden Imam, a new messenger of Allah who was to come. He gained a large following whose activities caused the Persian authorities to fear a rebellion, and who were therefore persecuted. The Bab was executed for heresy.

Babbage Charles 1792–1871. English mathematician who devised a precursor of the computer. He designed an analytical engine, a general-purpose mechanical computing device for performing different calculations according to a program input on punched cards (an idea borrowed from the Jacquard loom). This device was never built, but it embodied many of the principles on which present digital computers are based.

As a young man, Babbage assisted John ◊Herschel with his astronomical calculations. He became involved with calculating machines when he worked on his difference engine for the British Admiralty, which was partly built in 1822.

His most important book was *On the Economy of Machinery and Manufactures* 1832, an analysis of industrial production systems and their economics. Altogether he wrote about 100 books. In 1991, the British Science Museum completed Babbage's second difference engine (to demonstrate that it would have been possible to complete it with the materials then available), which evaluates polynomials up to the seventh power, with 30-figure accuracy.

Babel Hebrew name for the city of Babylon, chiefly associated with the *Tower of Babel* which, in the Genesis story in the Old Testament, was erected in the plain of Shinar by the descendants of Noah. It was a ziggurat, or staged temple, seven storeys high (100 m/ 300 ft) with a shrine of Marduk on the summit. It was built by Nabopolassar, father of Nebuchadnezzar, and was destroyed when Sennacherib sacked the city 689 BC.

Babi faith alternative name for ◊Baha'i faith.

Babism religious movement founded during the 1840s by Mirza Ali Mohammad ('the ◊Bab'). An offshoot of Islam, its main difference lies in the belief that Muhammad was not the last of the prophets. The movement split into two groups after the death of the Bab; Baha'ullah, the leader of one of these groups, founded the ◊Baha'i faith.

Babylonian captivity exile of Jewish deportees to Babylon after Nebuchadnezzar II's capture of Jerusalem in 586 BC. According to tradition, the captivity lasted 70 years, but Cyrus of Persia, who conquered Babylon, actually allowed them to go home in 536 BC. By analogy, the name has also been applied to the papal exile to Avignon, France, 1309–77.

Bacchus in Greek and Roman mythology, the god of fertility (see ◊Dionysus) and of wine; his rites (the *Bacchanalia*) were orgiastic.

Bachelard Gaston 1884–1962. French philosopher and scientist who argued for a creative interplay between reason and experience. He attacked both Cartesian and positivist positions, insisting that science was derived neither from first principles nor directly from experience.

He taught philosophy, first at Dijon and after 1940 at the University of Paris. His publications include *Le Rationalisme Appliqué/Applied Rationalism* 1949.

back to the land movement in late Victorian England that emphasized traditional values and rural living as a reaction against industrialism and urban society.

For some, this meant moving from city to country and becoming self-supporting; for example, by growing their own food. For others, their participation was limited to encouraging a rebirth of rural crafts and traditions, such as lacemaking, quilting, and folk music.

Movements loosely associated with back to the land include ◊vegetarianism, city idea, and conservation societies such as the National Trust that set out to preserve 'unspoilt' features of the countryside.

If a man will begin with certainties, he shall end in doubts; but if he will be content to begin with doubts, he shall end in certainties.

> **Francis Bacon**
> *The Advancement of Learning* bk I

Bacon Francis 1561–1626. English philosopher, essayist, and politician. His main philosophical achievement was in the philosophy of science. He criticized the Aristotelian and Platonic traditions of scientific method and advocated a new and thorough empiricism coupled with a more materialistic theory derived from Democritus. His political writings rely heavily on the scientifc opinions he thought his methods justified. He became Lord Chancellor 1618, and the same year confessed to bribe-taking, was fined £40,000 (which was later remitted by the king), and spent four days in the Tower of London.

His works include *Essays* 1597, *The Advancement of Learning* 1605, the *Novum Organum* 1620, and *The New Atlantis* 1626.

Bacon was ·born in London, studied law at Cambridge from 1573, was part of the embassy in France until 1579, and became a member of Parliament 1584. He was the nephew of Queen Elizabeth's adviser Lord Burghley, but turned against him when he failed to provide Bacon with patronage. He helped secure the execution of the Earl of Essex as a traitor 1601, after formerly being his follower. Bacon was accused of

ingratitude, but he defended himself in *Apology* 1604. The satirist Pope called Bacon 'the wisest, brightest, and meanest of mankind'. Knighted on the accession of James I 1603, he became Baron Verulam 1618 and Viscount St Albans 1621. His writing helped to inspire the founding of the Royal Society. The ***Baconian Theory***, originated by James Willmot in 1785, suggesting that the works of Shakespeare were written by Bacon, is not taken seriously by scholars.

Bacon Roger 1214–1292. English philosopher, scientist, and a teacher at Oxford University. He was interested in alchemy, the biological and physical sciences, and magic. Many discoveries have been credited to him, including the magnifying lens. He foresaw the extensive use of gunpowder and mechanical cars, boats, and planes.

In 1266, at the invitation of his friend Pope Clement IV, he began his *Opus Majus/Great Work*, a compendium of all branches of knowledge. In 1268 he sent this with his *Opus Minus/Lesser Work* and other writings to the pope. In 1277 Bacon was condemned and imprisoned by the church for 'certain novelties' (heresy) and not released until 1292.

Bacon was born in Somerset and educated at Oxford and Paris. He became a Franciscan monk and was in Paris until about 1251 lecturing on ◊Aristotle. He wrote in Latin and his works include *On Mirrors, Metaphysical* and *On the Multiplication of Species*. He followed the maxim 'Cease to be ruled by dogmas and authorities; look at the world!'

bad faith in the existentialist philosophy of Jean-Paul ◊Sartre, a type of moral self-deception, involving our behaving as a mere thing rather than choosing authentically. In bad faith, we evade responsibility and anxiety by not noticing possibilities of choice, or by behaving in a role others expect of us.

Sartre derives the concept from his metaphysical analysis of ◊being. Humans must strive to escape mere being-in-itself and to achieve their true being, being-for-itself.

Bagehot Walter 1826–1877. British writer and economist. His *The English Constitution* 1867, a classic analysis of the British political system, is still a standard work. *Physics and Politics* 1872, was one of the first books to apply the theory of evolution to politics. He was editor of the *Economist* magazine 1860–77.

Baha'i religion founded in the 19th century from a Muslim splinter group, ◊Babism, by the

Persian ◊Baha'ullah. His message in essence was that all great religious leaders are manifestations of the unknowable God and all scriptures are sacred. There is no priesthood: all Baha'is are expected to teach, and to work towards world unification. There are about 3.5 million Baha'is worldwide.

Great stress is laid on equality regardless of religion, race, or gender. Drugs and alcohol are forbidden, as is celibacy. Marriage is strongly encouraged; there is no arranged marriage, but parental approval must be given. Baha'is are expected to pray daily, but there is no set prayer. From 2–20 March, adults under 70 fast from sunrise to sunset. Administration is carried out by an elected body, the Universal House of Justice.

Baha'ullah title of Mirza Hosein Ali 1817–1892. Persian founder of the ◊Baha'i religion. Baha'ullah, 'God's Glory', proclaimed himself as the prophet the ◊Bab had foretold.

Bailly Jean Sylvain 1736–1793. French astronomer who wrote about the satellites of Jupiter and the history of astronomy. Early in the French Revolution, was president of the National Assembly and mayor of Paris, but resigned in 1791; he was guillotined during the Reign of Terror.

Bakunin Mikhail 1814–1876. Russian anarchist, active in Europe. In 1848 he was expelled from France as a revolutionary agitator. In Switzerland in the 1860s he became recognized as the leader of the anarchist movement. In 1869 he joined the First International (a coordinating socialist body) but, after stormy conflicts with Karl Marx, was expelled 1872.

Born of a noble family, Bakunin served in the Imperial Guard but, disgusted with tsarist methods in Poland, resigned his commission and travelled abroad. For his share in a brief revolt at Dresden 1849 he was sentenced to death. The sentence was commuted to imprisonment, and he was handed over to the tsar's government and sent to Siberia 1855. In 1861 he managed to escape to Switzerland. He had a large following, mainly in the Latin American countries. He wrote books and pamphlets, including *God and the State.*

balance of nature in ecology, the idea that there is an inherent equilibrium in most ◊ecosystems, with plants and animals interacting so as to produce a stable, continuing system of life on Earth. Organisms in the ecosystem are adapted to each other – for example, waste products produced by one species are used by another and resources used by some are replenished by others; the oxygen needed by animals is produced by plants while the waste product of animal respiration, carbon dioxide, is used by plants as a raw material in photosynthesis. The nitrogen cycle, the water cycle, and the control of animal populations by natural predators are other examples. The activities of human beings can, and frequently do, disrupt the balance of nature.

balance of payments in economics, an account of a country's debit and credit transactions with other countries. Items are divided into the *current account*, which includes both visible trade (imports and exports of goods) and invisible trade (services such as transport, tourism, interest, and dividends), and the *capital account*, which includes investment in and out of the country, international grants, and loans. Deficits or surpluses on these accounts are brought into balance by buying and selling reserves of foreign currencies.

A *balance of payments crisis* arises when a country's current account deteriorates because the cost of imports exceeds income from exports. In developing countries persistent trade deficits often result in heavy government borrowing overseas, which in turn leads to a debt crisis.

balance of power in politics, the theory that the best way of ensuring international order is to have power so distributed among states that no single state is able to achieve a dominant position. The term, which may also refer more simply to the actual distribution of power, is one of the most enduring concepts in international relations. Since the development of nuclear weapons, it has been asserted that the balance of power has been replaced by a *balance of terror*.

Balder in Norse mythology, the son of Odin and Freya and husband of Nanna, and the best, wisest, and most loved of all the gods. He was killed, at ◊Loki's instigation, by a twig of mistletoe shot by the blind god Hodur.

ballot the process of voting in an election. In political elections in democracies ballots are usually secret: voters indicate their choice of candidate on a voting slip that is placed in a sealed ballot box. *Ballot rigging* is a term used to describe elections that are fraudulent because of interference with the voting process or the counting of ◊votes.

Balmer Johann Jakob 1825–1898. Swiss physicist and mathematician who developed a formula in 1884 that gave the wavelengths of the light emitted by the hydrogen atom (the hydrogen spectrum). This simple formula played a central role in the development of spectral and atomic theory.

bank financial institution that uses funds deposited with it to lend money to companies or individuals, and also provides financial services to its customers.

In terms of assets, seven of the world's top ten banks were Japanese in 1988.

A ◊central bank (in the UK, the Bank of England) issues currency for the government and manages monetary policy and the exchange rate.

bankruptcy process by which the property of a person (in legal terms, an individual or corporation) unable to pay debts is taken away under a court order and divided fairly among the person's creditors, after preferential payments such as taxes and wages. Proceedings may be instituted either by the debtor (voluntary bankruptcy) or by any creditor for a substantial sum (involuntary bankruptcy). Until 'discharged', a bankrupt is severely restricted in financial activities.

Federal law distinguishes between complete bankruptcy and protection of the assets of a legal person for purposes of financial reorganization. This is commonly referred to as Chapter 11 bankruptcy, since it is provided for under Chapter 11 of the federal bankruptcy law, which allows businesses and individuals to continue to operate while reorganizing to pay debts.

When 'discharged' the person becomes free of most debts dating from the time of bankruptcy. The largest financial services bankruptcy, with liabilities of $3 billion, was filed by US securities firm Drexel Burnham Lambert in Feb 1990.

banshee in Gaelic folklore, a female spirit whose wailing outside a house foretells the death of one of its inhabitants.

baptism immersion in or sprinkling with water as a religious rite of initiation. It was practised long before the beginning of Christianity. In the Christian ceremony of infant baptism, sponsors or godparents make vows on behalf of the child, which are renewed by the child at confirmation. It is one of the seven sacraments. The *amrit* ceremony in Sikhism is sometimes referred to as baptism.

Baptism was universal in the Christian church from the first days, being administered to adults by immersion. The baptism of infants was not practised until the 2nd century, but became general in the 6th. Baptism by sprinkling (christening) when the child is named is now general among Western Christians, although some (notably the ◊Baptists) baptise adults by complete immersion. The Eastern Orthodox Church also practises immersion.

It is expedient that Baptism be administered in the vulgar tongue.

Publick Baptism of Infants
Introductory rubric

Baptist member of any of several Protestant and evangelical Christian groups that practise baptism by immersion only upon profession of faith. Baptists seek their authority in the Bible. They originated among English Dissenters who took refuge in the Netherlands in the early 17th century, and spread by emigration and, later, missionary activity. Of the world total of approximately 31 million, some 26.5 million are in the USA and 265,000 in the UK.

The Baptist Missionary Society, formed 1792, pioneered the 19th–century missionary movement which spread the Baptist creed through Europe and to British colonies. In 1905 the Baptist World Alliance was formed.

Barabbas in the New Testament, a condemned robber released by Pilate at Passover instead of Jesus to appease a mob.

Bardeen John 1908–1991. US physicist who won a Nobel prize 1956, with Walter Brattain and William Shockley, for the development of the transistor 1948. In 1972 he became the first double winner of a Nobel prize in the same subject (with Leon Cooper and John Schrieffer) for his work on superconductivity.

bar mitzvah in Judaism, initiation of a boy, which takes place at the age of 13, into the adult Jewish community; less common is the *bat* or *bas mitzvah* for girls aged 12. The child reads a passage from the Torah in the synagogue on the Sabbath, and is subsequently regarded as a full member of the congregation.

Barnabas, St in the New Testament, a 'fellow labourer' with St Paul; he went with St Mark on a missionary journey to Cyprus, his birthplace. Feast day 11 June.

Baroque in the visual arts and architecture, a style of the 17th and early 18th centuries characterized by extravagance in ornament, asymmetry of design, and great expressiveness; in music, a period lasting from about 1600 to 1750. The Baroque style dominated European art for most of the 17th century, exemplified in the work of artists such as Rubens and Bernini. In *architecture*, it often involved large-scale designs, for example Bernini's piazza in Rome and the palace of Versailles in France. In *music*, composers included Monteverdi, Vivaldi, J S Bach, and Handel.

In *painting*, Caravaggio, with his bold use of light and forceful compositions, was an early exponent, but the Carracci family was more typical of the early Baroque style, producing grandiose visions in ceiling paintings that deployed illusionistic displays of florid architectural decoration. In *sculpture*, the master of Baroque was Bernini, whose *Ecstasy of St Theresa* 1645–52 (Sta Maria della Vittoria, Rome) is a fine example of overt emotionalism. Most masterpieces of the new style emerged in churches and palaces in Rome, but the Baroque influence soon spread through Europe. The 19th-century Swiss art historian Burckhardt was the first to use the term 'baroque'.

Barth Karl 1886–1968. Swiss Protestant theologian. A socialist in his political views, he attacked the Nazis. His *Church Dogmatics* 1932–62 makes the resurrection of Jesus the focal point of Christianity.

Barthes Roland 1915–1980. French critic and theorist of ◊semiotics, the science of signs and symbols. One of the French 'new critics' and an exponent of ◊structuralism, he attacked traditional literary criticism in his first collection of essays *Writing Degree Zero* 1953. His main aim was to expose the bourgeois values and ideology he saw as implicit in the seemingly 'natural' and innocent language of French literature. For Barthes, a text was not a depiction of the world or the expression of an author's personality, but a system of signs in which meanings are generated solely by the interplay of these signs.

In *Mythologies* 1957 he used this structuralist approach to the study of signs in everyday life, looking at such things as toys, advertisements, and wrestling. This and similar studies had a profound influence on the study of popular culture.

S/Z 1970 and *The Pleasures of the Text* 1970 continue his ever more sophisticated analysis of literary texts. As he became aware of the difficulties inherent in structuralism, his work became more subjective and unorthodox. *Roland Barthes by Roland Barthes* 1975 is a highly imaginative autobiography, and *Camera Lucida* 1980 is both a reflection on photography and an elegy for his dead mother.

Bartlett Frederic Charles 1886–1969. English psychologist who put forward the view of sensory and memory processes as the expression of an underlying dynamic integration of an organism's past experience with its current situation and needs. The results of his extensive researches, centred on perception, recognition, and recall processes, are collected in his book *Remembering: A Study of Experimental and Social Psychology* 1932.

Bartlett studied at London and Cambridge universities and, with C S Myers (1873–1946) and W H R ◊Rivers (1864–1922), founded the Psychological Laboratory at Cambridge. He went on to become the first Professor of Experimental Psychology at Cambridge 1931. He also carried out influential work in applied and industrial psychology on problems associated with submarine detection, the design and control of aircraft, and the training of airforce personnel during both world wars.

Barzun Jacques Martin 1907– . French-born US historian and educator whose speciality was 19th-century European intellectual life. His book *The Modern Researcher* 1970 is recognized as a classic study of historical method. Among his many historical works is *Romanticism and the Modern Ego* 1943.

Barzun emigrated to the USA with his parents 1919. He was educated at Columbia University, earning a PhD in history 1932, and soon afterward joined the faculty there, becoming a member of the administration.

base rate in economics, the rate of interest to which most bank lending is linked, the actual rate depending on the status of the borrower. A prestigious company might command a rate only 1% above base rate, while an individual would be charged several points above.

basic economic problem in economics, the problem posed by the fact that human wants are infinite but resources are scarce. Resources therefore have to be allocated which then involves an ◊opportunity cost.

Basil, St c. 330–379. Cappadocian monk, known as 'the Great', founder of the Basilian monks. Elected bishop of Caesarea 370, Basil opposed the heresy of ◊Arianism. He wrote many theological works and composed the 'Liturgy of St Basil', in use in the Eastern Orthodox Church. Feast day 2 Jan.

Born in Caesarea, Anatolia, he studied in Constantinople and Athens, and visited the hermit saints of the Egyptian desert. He entered a monastery in Anatolia about 358, and developed a monastic rule based on community life, work, and prayer. These ideas form the basis of monasticism in the Greek Orthodox Church, and influenced the foundation of similar monasteries by St Benedict.

Teaching a Christian how he ought to live does not call so much for words as for daily example.

St Basil
Oration

Basov Nikolai Gennadievich 1912– . Soviet physicist who in 1953, with his compatriot Aleksandr Prokhorov, developed the microwave amplifier called a maser. They were both awarded the Nobel Prize for Physics 1964, which they shared with Charles Townes of the USA.

bastard feudalism late medieval development of ◊feudalism in which grants of land were replaced by money as rewards for service. Conditions of service were specified in a contract, or indenture, between lord and retainer. The system allowed large numbers of men to be raised quickly for wars or private feuds.

Bateson Gregory 1904–1980. British-born anthropologist and cyberneticist. His interests were wide-ranging – from the study of ritual in a New Guinea people to the exploration of communication methods in schizophrenics and dolphins – but all his work shows an interest in how systems operate and a willingness to break down the boundaries between intellectual disciplines. His publications include *Steps to an Ecology of Mind* 1973 and *Mind and Nature* 1978.

But the real travellers are only those who leave / For the sake of leaving.

Charles Pierre Baudelaire
'The Voyage'

Baudelaire Charles Pierre 1821–1867. French poet whose immensely influential work combined rhythmical and musical perfection with a morbid romanticism and eroticism, finding beauty in decadence and evil.

His first and best-known book of verse was *Les Fleurs du mal/Flowers of Evil* 1857. Its refinement and subtlety of feeling made it an important influence on modernist literature. He also wrote regularly as an art critic and his essay *The Painter of Modern Life*, which advocated the use of contemporary subject matter for painters, was an influence on Manet and ◊Impressionism.

Baudrillard Jean 1929– . French cultural theorist. Originally influenced by Marxism and structuralism in works such as *The System of Objects* 1968, Baudrillard evolved a critique of consumer society and of an information-world dominated by the reproduction of images, producing a state which he called 'hyper-reality'. His theories are expressed in a wide range of writings, including *In the Shadow of the Silent Majorities* 1978 and *Simulacra and Simulations* 1981.

Bauhaus German school of architecture and design founded 1919 at Weimar in Germany by the architect Walter ◊Gropius in an attempt to fuse all arts, design, architecture, and crafts into a unified whole. Moved to Dessau under political pressure 1925 (where it was housed in a building designed by Gropius), the school was closed by the Nazis 1933. Among the artists associated with the Bauhaus were the painters Klee and Kandinsky and the architect ◊Mies van der Rohe.

Its ideas were subsequently incorporated into teaching programmes in Europe and the USA, where many of its teachers and students emigrated. Gropius and Marcel Breuer worked together in the USA 1937–40 and the ◊International Style (of which Gropius' Bauhaus building 1925–26 is a hallmark) spread worldwide from there. In 1972 the *Bauhaus Archive* was installed in new premises in Berlin.

Bāul member of a Bengali mystical sect that emphasizes freedom from compulsion, from doctrine, and from social caste; they avoid all outward forms of religious worship. Not ascetic, they aim for harmony between physical and spiritual needs.

An oral tradition is passed down by gurus (teachers). The Bāuls make extensive use of music and poetry.

Bayes Thomas 1702–1761. English mathematician whose investigations into probability led to what is now known as Bayes' theorem.

Bayes' theorem in statistics, a theorem relating the ◊probability of particular events taking place to the probability that events conditional upon them have occurred.

For example, the probability of picking an ace at random out of a pack of cards is 4/52. If two cards are picked out, the probability of the second card being an ace is conditional on the first card: if the first card was an ace the probability will be 3/51; if not it will be 4/51. Bayes' theorem gives the probability that given that the second card is an ace, the first card is also.

Bayle Pierre 1647–1706. French critic and philosopher. In his *Dictionnaire historique et critique/Historical and Critical Dictionary* 1696, he wrote learned but highly sceptical articles attacking almost all of the contemporary religious, philosophical, moral scientific, and historical views. For example, he argued that Christianity was irrational, that Old Testament figures such as ◊David were immoral, and that all existing philosophies were inadequate. His scepticism greatly influenced the French Encyclopédistes and most Enlightenment thinkers.

Beadle George Wells 1903–1989. US biologist. Born in Wahoo, Nebraska, he was professor of biology at the California Institute of Technology 1946–61. In 1958 he shared a Nobel prize with Edward L Tatum for his work in biochemical genetics, forming the 'one-gene–one-enzyme' hypothesis (a single gene codes for a single kind of enzyme).

Beale Dorothea 1831–1906. British pioneer in women's education whose work helped to raise the standard of women's education and the status of women teachers.

She was headmistress of the Ladies' College at Cheltenham from 1858, and founder of St Hilda's Hall, Oxford, 1892.

Beard Charles Austin 1874–1948. US historian and a leader of the Progressive movement, active in promoting political and social reform. As a chief exponent of critical economic history, he published *An Economic Interpretation of the Constitution of the United States* 1913 and *The Economic Origins of Jeffersonian Democracy* 1915. With his wife, Mary, he wrote *A Basic History of the United States* 1944, long a standard textbook in the USA.

Born near Knightstown, Indiana, Beard earned a PhD from Columbia University 1904. He resigned from the Columbia faculty 1917 over issues of academic freedom. He helped found the New School for Social Research 1918.

Beat Generation or *Beat movement* sociological and literary phenomenon of the 1950s and early 1960s. Inspired by media responses to a loose grouping of writers, principally Jack Kerouac (who is credited with coining the term) and Allen Ginsberg, so-called beatniks responded to the conformist materialism of the period by adopting lifestyles derived from the tradition of Thoreau's social disobedience and Whitman's poetry of the open road. In addition to contemporary jazz music and the resurgence in Buddhist philosophy, they often used marijuana to affirm their anti-authoritarian liberty and licence to heighten experience.

Other prominent literary figures were novelist William Burroughs, poet and publisher Lawrence Ferlinghetti, poet Gregory Corso, and novelist John Clellon Holmes. The movement had no shared artistic credo beyond breaking the current literary orthodoxy, and its definition was largely historical. Most representative and influential were Kerouac's novel *On the Road* and Ginsberg's poem 'Howl', which used less conventionally structured forms to alternately celebrate the 'beatific' spirit of Beat and to indict the repressive 'beatness' of modern society.

beatification in the Catholic church, the first step toward ◊canonization. Persons who have been beatified can be prayed to, and the title 'Blessed' can be put before their names.

Beatitudes in the New Testament, the sayings of Jesus reported in Matthew 6: 1–12 and Luke 6: 20–38, depicting the spiritual qualities that characterize members of the Kingdom of God.

Beattie John Hugh Marshall 1915–1990. British anthropologist whose work on cross-cultural analysis influenced researchers in other fields, particularly philosophy. His book *Other Cultures: Aims, Methods and Achievements in Social Anthropology* 1964 has been translated into many languages. Beattie was appointed University Lecturer in Social Anthropology at Oxford 1953 and took up the Chair in Cultural Anthropology and Sociology of Africa in Leiden 1971.

Look thy last on all things lovely, / Every hour.

beauty
Walter de la Mare, 1873–1956, English poet.
Fare Well

---

beauty the property of, or combination of qualities in, objects giving rise to pleasure or delight. The branch of philosophy that deals with beauty is ◊aesthetics.

There are various philosophical theories about beauty. It may stand for a felt or intuited quality, or for a causal property evoking a special reaction in us, or even for the expression of nonpossessive love.

Beauvoir Simone de 1908–1986. French writer and feminist. A lifelong companion of the philosopher Jean-Paul ◊Sartre, she played a major role in French intellectual life from the 1940s to the 1980s. Her central themes were commitment, personal responsibility, and social and political freedom. *The Second Sex* 1949, one of the first major feminist texts, is an encyclopedic study of the role of women in society, drawing on literature, myth and history. She argues that the subservient position of women is the result of their systematic repression by a male-dominated society that denies their independence, identity and sexuality.

Women, she claims, must take responsibility for their own lives. The themes of choice and identity are explored in her novels, such as *She Came to Stay* 1943, and *Mandarins* 1954, generally regarded her best work of fiction. They also appear in what some regard will be her most enduring achievement, her extended autobiography. This gives a frank and vivid account not only of one woman's life from birth to old age, but also of intellectual life in the 20th century. The sequence includes *Memoirs of a Dutiful Daughter* 1954, *The Prime of Life* 1960, *The Force of Circumstance* 1963, and *All Said and Done* 1972. *Adieux* gives an intimate insight into her relationship with Sartre, and *Old Age* 1970 attacks society's indifference to the old.

Beccaria Cesare, Marese di Beccaria 1738–1794. Italian philanthropist, born in Milan. He opposed capital punishment and torture; advocated education as a crime preventative; influenced English philosopher Jeremy ◊Bentham; and coined the phrase 'the greatest happiness of the greatest number', the tenet of ◊utilitarianism.

Beckett Samuel 1906–1989. Irish novelist and dramatist who wrote in French and English. His *En attendant Godot* – first performed in Paris 1952, and then in his own translation as *Waiting for Godot* 1955 in London, and New York 1956 – is possibly the best-known example of Theatre of the ◊Absurd, in which life is taken to be meaningless. This genre is taken to further extremes in *Fin de Partie/Endgame* 1957 and *Happy Days* 1961. Nobel Prize for Literature 1969.

Originally a novelist and strongly influenced by James Joyce, Beckett also wrote successfully for radio in plays such as *All That Fall* 1957 and *Embers* 1959.

Becquerel Antoine Henri 1852–1908. French physicist who discovered penetrating radiation coming from uranium salts, the first indication of radioactivity, and shared a Nobel prize with Marie and Pierre ◊Curie 1903.

Bede c. 673–735. English theologian and historian, known as *the Venerable Bede*, active in Durham and Northumbria. He wrote many scientific, theological, and historical works. His *Historia Ecclesiastica Gentis Anglorum/ Ecclesiastical History of the English People* 731 is a seminal source for early English history.

Born at Monkwearmouth, Durham, he entered the local monastery at the age of seven, later transferring to Jarrow, where he became a priest in about 703. He devoted his life to writing and teaching; among his pupils was Egbert, archbishop of York.

Beelzebub in the New Testament, the leader of the devils, sometimes identified with Satan and sometimes with his chief assistant (see ◊devil). In the Old Testament Beelzebub was a fertility god worshipped by the ◊Philistines and other Semitic groups (Baal).

begging soliciting, usually for money and food. It is prohibited in many Western countries, and stringent measures were taken against begging in the former USSR. In the Middle East and Asia, almsgiving is often considered a religious obligation.

Legislation against begging is recorded in England from the 14th century and it is an offence to solicit alms on the public highway, to expose any sore or malformation to attract alms, to cause a child to beg, or to send begging letters containing false statements. In the 1980s begging reappeared in major UK cities and the 1824 Vagrancy Act was much used against young homeless people. By 1990 there were at least 60 convictions a week under the act and there were calls for its repeal.

behaviourism school of psychology originating in the USA, of which the leading exponent was John B ◊Watson. Behaviourists maintain that all human activity can ultimately be explained in terms of conditioned reactions or reflexes and habits formed in consequence. Leading behaviourists include Clark Hull (1884–1952), Edwin R ◊Guthrie, and B F ◊Skinner.

behaviour therapy the application of theories of behaviour or ◊learning theory, to the treatment of clinical conditions such as ◊phobias, ◊obsessions, and sexual and interpersonal problems. The symptoms of these disorders are regarded as unadaptive learned patterns of behaviour that the therapy can enable the patient to unlearn. For example, in treating a phobia the patient is taken gradually into the feared situation in about twenty sessions until the fear noticeably reduces.

This type of treatment is called desensitization. Among others are aversion (the behaviour to be unlearned being associated with an unpleasant stimulus such as a mild electric shock), operant ◊conditioning (behaviour shaped by reinforcing it with rewards or punishments), and special treatments like the bell and pad method for nocturnal enuresis (loud bell rings if patient urinates in bed).

being in philosophy, what is common to everything that there is. Being is a fundamental notion in ◊ontology and metaphysics generally, but particularly in idealism and existentialism.

Ancient Greek philosopher ◊Aristotle insisted that to say something exists adds nothing to its description. Being or existence is sometimes distinguished from subsistence, as by Austrian philosopher Alexius ◊Meinong. Idealist philosophers tend to believe that there are not only different kinds but also different degrees of being. The American W V O ◊Quine holds that 'to be is to be the value of a variable' in a system of formal logic – that is, that to be or exist is always to have a quality or feature. The ontological argument for the existence of God turns on whether being can be a predicate or property.

Belief is like love; it cannot be compelled.

belief

Arthur Schopenhauer, 1788–1860,
German philosopher.
Essays and Aphorisms

---

belief assent to the truth of propositions, statements, or facts. In philosophy, belief that something is the case is contrasted with ◊knowledge, because we only say we *believe* that something is the case when we are unjustified in claiming to *know* that it is.

Although they undoubtedly affect behaviour, beliefs cannot be analysed solely in terms of it, since I can believe that I am unselfish and yet still be very selfish. French philosopher René ◊Descartes held that the assent to the truth of a proposition is a matter of will, whereas the Scot David ◊Hume held that it is an emotional condition.

Bell Daniel 1919– . US sociologist who was editor of the report *Toward the Year 2000* 1968 which reflects his interest in contemporary history and social forecasting. In *The End of Ideology* 1960, he tried to show how the West, as a result of welfare state and mixed economy, had come to the 'end of the ideological age'.

Bell claimed the conflict between ideologies was to be seen mainly in developing countries or on the international stage. In *The Radical Right* 1963 he offered an explanation of ◊McCarthyism in terms of the extremities of minorities that had not adjusted to pluralistic society. *The Coming of Post-Industrial Society* underlined his view of the importance of scientific and technical knowledge in social and political life and predicted greater power for scientific elites.

He taught at Columbia University 1958–69, when he became professor of sociology at Harvard University. Prior to his appointment to the academic staff at Columbia, he had been a journalist on the magazine *Fortune*.

Bell John 1928–1990. British physicist who in 1964 devised a test to verify a point in ◊quantum theory: whether two particles that were once connected are always afterwards interconnected even if they become widely separated. As well as investigating fundamental problems in theoretical physics, Bell contributed to the design of particle accelerators.

One of the most profound thinkers in modern physics, Bell worked for 30 years at CERN, the European research laboratory near Geneva, Switzerland. He demonstrated how to measure the continued interconnection of particles that had once been closely connected, and put forward mathematical criteria that had to be obeyed if such a connection existed, as required by quantum theory. In the early 1980s, a French team tested Bell's criteria, and a connection between widely separated particles was detected.

Bellarmine Roberto Francesco Romolo 1542–1621. Italian Roman Catholic theologian and cardinal. He taught at the Jesuit College in Rome, and became archbishop of Capua 1602. His *Disputationes de controversersiis fidei christianae* 1581–93 was a major defence of Catholicism in the 16th century. He was canonized 1930.

Bell's theorem hypothesis of British physicist John Bell, that an unknown force, of which space, time, and motion are all aspects, continues to link separate parts of the universe that were once united, and that this force travels faster than the speed of light.

Belshazzar in the Old Testament, the last king of Babylon, son of Nebuchadnezzar.

During a feast (known as **Belshazzar's Feast**) he saw a message, interpreted by ◊Daniel as prophesying the fall of Babylon and death of Belshazzar.

Benedictine order religious order of monks and nuns in the Roman Catholic Church, founded by St ◊Benedict at Subiaco, Italy, in the 6th century. It had a strong influence on medieval learning and reached the height of its prosperity early in the 14th century.

St Augustine brought the order to England. A number of Oxford and Cambridge colleges have a Benedictine origin. At the Reformation there were nearly 300 Benedictine monasteries and nunneries in England, all of which were suppressed. The English novice house survived in France, and in the 19th century monks expelled from France moved to England and built abbeys at Downside, Ampleforth, and Woolhampton. The monks from Pierre-qui-vive, who went to England 1882, rebuilt Buckfast Abbey in Devon on the ruins of a Cistercian monastery.

benediction blessing recited at the end of a Christian service, particularly the Mass.

Benedict, St c. 480–c. 547. Founder of Christian monasticism in the West and of the ◊Benedictine order at the monastery of Monte Cassino, which he founded and where he wrote out his rule for monastic life. Feast day 11 July.

Born of wealthy parents at Nurcia in Umbria, he was sent to be educated in Rome, but fled from that city and spent three years in ascetic solitude. He founded 12 monasteries near Subiaco, and later migrated to Monte Cassino. He was visited shortly before his death by the Ostrogothic king Totila, whom he converted to the Christian faith.

benefice in the early Middle Ages, a donation of land or money to the Christian church as an act of devotion; from the 12th century, the term came to mean the income enjoyed by clergy.

Under the Carolingian dynasty, 'benefice' was used to mean a gift of land from a lord to a vassal, in which sense it is often indistinguishable from a fief.

Benjamin Walter 1892–1940. German Marxist critic and essayist. He wrote on literature, film, art and society, and is now regarded as one of the most important cultural critics of the 20th century. His works include *Einbahnstrasse/One-Way Street* 1928, a montage of aphorisms and essays, and *Illuminationen/Illuminations* 1961, a posthumous collection of some of his most important essays.

His works are a complex and unlikely blend of Marxism and Jewish mysticism. Rejecting more orthodox Marxist views, he was a staunch supporter of modernism, and wrote important essays on Kafka, Brecht, and Baudelaire, and on the relationship between technology, the arts, and society. See also ◊Marxist aesthetic theory.

Bentham Jeremy 1748–1832. English philosopher, legal and social reformer, and founder of ◊utilitarianism. The essence of his moral philosophy is found in the pronouncement of his *Principles of Morals and Legislation* (written 1780, published 1789): that the object of all legislation should be 'the greatest happiness for the greatest number'.

All punishment is mischief: all punishment in itself is evil.

Jeremy Bentham
Principles of Morals and Legislation

Bentham declared that the 'utility' of any law is to be measured by the extent to which it promotes the pleasure, good, and happiness of the people concerned. In 1776 he published *Fragments on Government*. He made suggestions for the reform of the poor law 1798, which formed the basis of the reforms enacted 1834, and in his *Catechism of Parliamentary Reform* 1817 he proposed annual elections, the secret ballot, and universal male suffrage. He was also a pioneer of prison reform.

In economics he was an apostle of *laissez-faire*, and in his *Defence of Usury* 1787 and *Manual of Political Economy* 1798 he contended that his principle of 'utility' was best served by allowing every man (sic) to pursue his own interests unhindered by restrictive legislation. He was made a citizen of the French Republic 1792.

Berdyaev Nikolai Alexandrovich 1874–1948. Russian philosopher who often challenged official Soviet viewpoints after the Revolution of 1917. Although appointed professor of philosophy in 1919 at Moscow University, he was exiled 1922 for defending Orthodox Christian religion. His books include *The Meaning of History* 1923 and *The Destiny of Man* 1935.

Berg Paul 1926– . US molecular biologist. In 1972, using gene-splicing techniques developed by others, Berg spliced and combined into a single hybrid DNA from an animal tumour virus (SV40) and DNA from a bacterial virus. Berg's work aroused fears in other workers and excited continuing controversy. For his work on recombinant DNA, he shared the 1980 Nobel Prize for Chemistry with Walter ◊Gilbert and Frederick ◊Sanger.

Berger John 1926– British left-wing art critic. In his best-known book, *Ways of Seeing* 1972, he valued art for social rather than aesthetic reasons. He also attacked museums for preserving what is by nature ephemeral.

Bergius Friedrich Karl Rudolph 1884–1949. German research chemist who invented processes for converting coal into oil and wood into sugar. He shared a Nobel prize 1931 with Carl Bosch for his part in inventing and developing high-pressure industrial methods.

Bergson Henri 1859–1941. French philosopher who believed that time, change, and development were the essence of reality. He thought that time was not a succession of distinct and separate instants but a continuous process in which one period merged imperceptibly into the next. Nobel Prize for Literature 1928.

Truth is the cry of all, but the game of few.

George Berkeley
Siris

Berkeley George 1685–1753. Irish philosopher and cleric. With ◊Locke and ◊Hume he is considered to be one of the British empiricists, but his philosophy is also described as subjective idealism – that is, the theory that nothing exists except in the mind. Berkeley argued that nothing exists apart from perception, and that the all-seeing mind of God makes possible the continued apparent existence of things. Everyday objects are collections of ideas or sensations, hence his dictum *esse est percipi* ('to exist is to be perceived'). He became bishop of Cloyne 1734.

Berlin Isaiah 1909– . Latvian-born British philosopher and historian of ideas. He emigrated to England with his family 1920, and was professor of social and political theory at Oxford 1957–67. In *The Hedgehog and the Fox* 1953 he wrote about Tolstoy's theory of irresistible historical forces; and in *Historical Inevitability* 1954 and *Four Essays on Liberty* 1969 he attacked all forms of historical determinism. His other works include *Karl Marx* 1939, and *Vico and Herder* 1976.

Liberty is liberty, not equality or fairness or justice or human happiness or a quiet conscience.

Isaiah Berlin
Two Concepts of Liberty

Bernadette, St 1844–1879. French saint, born in Lourdes in the French Pyrenees. In Feb 1858 she had a vision of the Virgin Mary in a grotto, and it became a centre of pilgrimage. Many sick people who were dipped in the water of a spring there were said to have been cured. Her feast day is 16 April.

Bernard Claude 1813–1878. French physiologist and founder of experimental medicine. Bernard first demonstrated that digestion is not restricted to the stomach, but takes place throughout the small intestine. He discovered the digestive input of the pancreas, several functions of the liver, and the vasomotor nerves which dilate and contract the blood vessels and thus regulate body temperature. This led him to the concept of the *milieu intérieur* ('internal environment') whose stability is essential to good health.

Bernard of Clairvaux, St 1090–1153. Christian founder in 1115 of Clairvaux monastery in Champagne, France. He reinvigorated the ◊Cistercian order, preached in support of the Second Crusade in 1146, and had the scholastic philosopher ◊Abelard condemned for heresy. Unlike Abelard, he had a deeply mystical approach to belief, and wrote many books on spirituality, the most influential being *On Loving God*. It is generally believed that his intense devotion to the Virgin Mary and the Infant Jesus prepared the way for a new strain of spirituality known as ◊*devotio moderna*. He is often depicted with a beehive. His feast day is 20 Aug.

Bernoulli Swiss family that produced many mathematicians and scientists in the 17th, 18th, and 19th centuries, in particular the brothers *Jakob* (1654–1705) and *Johann* (1667–1748).

Jakob and Johann were pioneers of Leibniz's calculus. Jakob used calculus to study the forms of many curves arising in practical situations, and studied mathematical probability (*Ars conjectandi* 1713); **Bernoulli numbers** are named after him. Johann developed exponential calculus and contributed to many areas of applied mathematics, including the problem of a particle moving in a gravitational field. His son, **Daniel** (1700–1782) worked on calculus and probability, and in physics proposed **Bernoulli's principle**, which states that the pressure of a moving fluid decreases the faster it flows (which explains the origin of lift on the aerofoil of an aircraft's wing). This and other work on hydrodynamics was published in *Hydrodynamica* 1738.

Bernstein Basil Bernard 1924– . British sociologist of education who has had considerable influence on teacher training and educational administration. Bernstein reported his research in several academic articles; many are published in *Class, Codes and Control. Vol 1: Theoretical Studies in the Sociology of Language* 1971. He observed that the language of working-class children, who were often socially disadvantaged, was considerably more restricted than that of middle-class children. This led him to study how social origins affect the ability to communicate with others.

He proposed a theory of 'restricted' and 'elaborated' codes, or forms of language, that characterize the language of working-class and middle-class children respectively. However, this does not imply that there is a direct or causal link between status and language ability, rather that it is the social relationships in which the child interacts and their communicative demands that shape linguistic potential. Bernstein taught day-release students at the City Day College, London, 1955–60 and then joined London University, where in 1963 he set up a sociological research unit.

Berrigan Daniel 1921– and Philip 1924– . US Roman Catholic priests. The brothers, opponents of the Vietnam War, broke into the draft-records offices at Catonsville, Maryland, to burn the files with napalm. They were sentenced in 1968 to three and six years' imprisonment respectively, but went underground. Subsequently Philip Berrigan was tried with others in 1972 for allegedly conspiring to kidnap President Nixon's adviser Henry Kissinger and blow up government offices in Washington DC; he was then sentenced to two years' imprisonment.

Bertholet Claude Louis 1748–1822. French chemist who carried out research into dyes and bleaches (introducing the use of chlorine as a bleach) and determined the composition of ammonia. Modern chemical nomenclature is based on a system worked out by Bertholet and Antoine ◊Lavoisier.

Berzelius Jöns Jakob 1779–1848. Swedish chemist who accurately determined more than 2,000 relative atomic and molecular masses. He devised (1813–14) the system of chemical symbols and formulae now in use and proposed oxygen as a reference standard for atomic masses. His discoveries include the elements cerium (1804), selenium (1817), and thorium (1828); he was the first to prepare silicon in its amorphous form and to isolate zirconium. The words *isomerism, allotropy,* and *protein* were coined by him.

Besant Annie 1847–1933. English socialist and feminist activist. Separated from her clerical husband in 1873 because of her freethinking views, she was associated with the radical atheist Charles Bradlaugh and the socialist ◊Fabian Society. She and Bradlaugh published a treatise advocating birth control and were prosecuted; as a result she lost custody of her daughter. In 1889 she became a disciple of Madame ◊Blavatsky. She thereafter preached theosophy and went to India. As a supporter of Indian independence, she founded the Central Hindu College 1898 and the Indian Home Rule League 1916, and became president of the Indian National Congress in 1917. Her *Theosophy and the New Psychology* was published 1904.

She was the sister-in-law of Walter Besant.

Bessel Friedrich Wilhelm 1784–1846. German astronomer and mathematician, the first person to find the approximate distance to a star by direct methods when he measured the parallax (annual displacement) of the star 61 Cygni in 1838. In mathematics, he introduced the series of functions now known as **Bessel functions**.

bestiary in medieval times, a book with stories and illustrations which depicted real and mythical animals or plants to illustrate a (usually Christian) moral. The stories were initially derived from the Greek *Physiologus*, a collection of 48 such stories, written in Alexandria around the 2nd century AD.

Translations of the *Physiologus* into vernacular languages (French, Italian, and English) date from the 13th century; illustrated versions are known from the 9th century. Much of later and contemporary folklore about animals derives from the bestiary, such as the myth of the phoenix burning itself to be born again.

beta index a mathematical measurement of the connectivity of a transport network. If the network is represented as a simplified topological map, made up of nodes (junctions or places) and edges (links), the beta index may be calculated by dividing the number of nodes by the number of edges. If the number of nodes is n and the number of edges is e, then the beta index β is given by the formula:

$$\beta = n/e$$

The higher the index number, the better connected the network is. If β is greater than 1, then a complete circuit exists.

Bethe Hans Albrecht 1906– . German-born US physicist who worked on the first atom bomb. He was awarded a Nobel prize 1967 for his discoveries concerning energy production in stars.

Bethe left Germany for England in 1933, and worked at Manchester and Bristol universities. In 1935 he moved to the USA where he became professor of theoretical physics at Cornell University; his research was interrupted by the war and by his appointment as head of the theoretical division of the Los Alamos atom bomb project. He has since become a leading peace campaigner, and opposed the US government's Strategic Defense Initiative (Star Wars) programme.

Bettelheim Bruno 1903–1990. Austrian-born US child psychologist. At the University of Chicago he founded a treatment centre for emotionally disturbed children based on the principle of a supportive home environment. Among his most influential books are *Love is Not Enough* 1950, *Truants from Life* 1954, and *Children of the Dream* 1962.

He was imprisoned in the Dachau and Buchenwald concentration camps 1933–35, about which he wrote *The Informed Heart*. He emigrated to the USA in 1939. His other books include *The Uses of Enchantment: The Meaning and Importance of Fairy Tales* 1976 and *A Good Enough Parent* 1987. He took his own life.

Beveridge Report, the popular name of *Social Insurance and Allied Services*, a report written by William Beveridge 1942 that formed the basis for the social reform legislation of the Labour Government of 1945–50.

Also known as the *Report on Social Security* it identified five 'giants': illness, ignorance, disease, squalor, and want. It proposed a scheme of social insurance from 'the cradle to the grave', and recommended a national health service, social insurance and assistance, family allowances, and full-employment policies.

Beza Théodore (properly *De Bèsze*) 1519–1605. French church reformer. He settled in Geneva, Switzerland, where he worked with the Protestant leader John Calvin and succeeded him as head of the reformed church there 1564. He wrote in defence of the burning of ◊Servetus (1554) and translated the New Testament into Latin.

Bhagavad-Gītā (Hindu 'the Song of the Blessed') religious and philosophical Sanskrit poem, dating from around 300 BC, forming an episode in the sixth book of the *Mahābhārata*, one of the two great Hindu epics. It is the supreme religious work of Hinduism.

bhakti (Sanskrit 'devotion') Hindu religious movement chiefly associated with the Vaishnava tradition of Vishnu worship. It emphasizes devotion to a personal God as the sole necessary means for achieving salvation. Its principal ancient text is *Bhagavad-Gītā*, but its popular writings are mostly in the form of devotional poems and songs.

The bhakti movement developed in South India around the Alvar poets (c. 6th–8th century AD), eventually finding expression in the writings of Ramanuja (died 1137). In North India it became in part a social protest movement, with such leading figures as ◊Kabir, Tulsi Das (probably 1543–1623), and Tukaram (17th century). In Bengal, ◊Caitanya led a popular bhakti movement which later gave rise to today's Hare Krishna movement. Nanak, influenced by Kabir, founded the Sikh religion.

Bhaktivedanta, Swami 1896–1977. Indian religious writer and teacher; founder of the International Society for Krishna Consciousness. He produced numerous scholarly translations and commentaries from Vedic devotional texts. By teaching devotion to Krishna as the universal religion, he did much to assist the spread of Hinduism in the West. He initiated over 5,000 disciples and established over 100 Hare Krishna communities outside India.

bhikku Buddhist monk who is totally dependent on alms and the monastic community (*sangha*) for support.

Bible the sacred book of the Jewish and Christian religions. The Hebrew Bible, recognized by both Jews and Christians, is called the ◊*Old Testament* by Christians. The ◊*New Testament* comprises books recognized by the Christian Church from the 4th century as canonical. The Roman Catholic Bible also includes the ◊*Apocrypha* (see ◊canon).

To every thing there is a season, and a time to every purpose under the heaven: / A time to be born, and a time to die.

Bible

Ecclesiastes 3:1

The first English translation of the entire Bible was by a priest, Miles Coverdale, 1535; the **Authorized Version** or **King James Bible** 1611, was long influential for the clarity and beauty of its language. A revision of the Authorized Version carried out 1959 by the British and Foreign Bible Society produced the widely used American translation, the Revised Standard Version. A conference of British churches 1946 recommended a completely new translation into English from the original Hebrew and Greek texts; work on this was carried out over the following two decades, resulting in the publication of the New English Bible (New Testament 1961, Old Testament and Apocrypha 1970). Another recent translation is the Jerusalem Bible, completed by Catholic scholars in 1966.

What is a man profited, if he shall gain the whole world, and lose his own soul.

Bible

Matthew 16:26

Missionary activity led to the translation of the Bible into the languages of people they were trying to convert, and by 1993 parts of the Bible had been translated into over 2,000 different languages, with 329 complete translations.

Bible society society founded for the promotion of translation and distribution of the Bible. The four largest branches are the British and Foreign Bible Society, founded in 1804, the

the Bible

The Books of the Old Testament			The Books of the New Testament		
name of book	chapters	date written	Habakkuk	3	c. 600 BC
			Zephaniah	3	3rd century BC
the Pentateuch or the Five Books of Moses			Haggai	2	c. 520 BC
Genesis	50	mid 8th–century BC	Zechariah	14	c. 520 BC
Exodus	40	950–586 BC	Malachi	4	c. 430 BC
Leviticus	27	mid 7th–century BC			
Numbers	36	850–650 BC			
Deuteronomy	34	mid-7th century BC	The Books of the New Testament		
			name of book	chapters	date written
Joshua	24	c. 550 BC	the Gospels		
Judges	21	c. 550 BC	Matthew	28	before AD 70
Ruth	4	end 3rd century BC	Mark	16	before AD 70
1 Samuel	31	c. 900 BC	Luke	24	AD 70–80
2 Samuel	24	c. 900 BC	John	21	AD 90–100
1 Kings	22	550–600 BC			
2 Kings	25	550–600 BC	The Acts	28	AD 70–80
1 Chronicles	29	c. 300 BC	Romans	16	AD 120
2 Chronicles	36	c. 300 BC	1 Corinthians	16	AD 57
Ezra	10	c. 450 BC	2 Corinthians	13	AD 57
Nehemiah	13	c. 450 BC	Galatians	6	AD 53
Esther	10	c. 200 BC	Ephesians	6	AD 140
Job	42	600–400 BC	Philippians	4	AD 63
Psalms	150	6th–2nd century BC	Colossians	4	AD 140
Proverbs	31	350–150 BC	1 Thessalonians	5	AD 50–54
Ecclesiastes	12	c. 200 BC	2 Thessalonians	3	AD 50–54
Song of Solomon	8	3rd century BC	1 Timothy	6	before AD 64
Isaiah	66	end 3rd century BC	2 Timothy	4	before AD 64
Jeremiah	52	604 BC	Titus	3	before AD 64
Lamentations	5	586–536 BC	Philemon	1	AD 60–62
Ezekiel	48	6th century BC	Hebrews	13	AD 80–90
Daniel	12	c. 166 BC	James	5	before AD 52
Hosea	14	c. 732 BC	1 Peter	5	before AD 64
Joel	3	c. 500 BC	2 Peter	3	before AD 64
Amos	9	775–750 BC	1 John	5	AD 90–100
Obadiah	1	6th–3rd century BC	2 John	1	AD 90–100
Jonah	4	600–200 BC	3 John	1	AD 90–100
Micah	7	end 3rd century BC	Jude	1	AD 75–80
Nahum	3	c. 626 BC	Revelation	22	AD 81–96

American Bible Society, the National Bible Society of Scotland, and the Netherlands Bible Society.

Biblical criticism study of the content and origin of the Bible. *Lower* or *textual criticism* is directed towards the recovery of the original text; *higher* or *documentary criticism* is concerned with questions of authorship, date, and literary sources; *historical criticism* seeks to ascertain the actual historical content of the Bible, aided by archaeological discoveries and the ancient history of neighbouring peoples.

bid-rent theory assumption that land value and rent decrease as distance from the central business district increases. Shops and offices have greater need for central, accessible locations than other users (such as those requiring land for residential purposes) and can pay higher prices. They therefore tend to be located within the expensive central area.

The bid-rent theory may also be true for farming, with the most intensive use being made of the relatively expensive land on the outskirts of towns. Other factors, including relief, communications, aspect, and land quality, may distort the relationship between price and location.

Big Bang in astronomy, the hypothetical 'explosive' event that marked the origin of the universe as we know it. At the time of the Big Bang, the entire universe was squeezed into a hot, superdense state. The Big Bang explosion threw this compacted material outwards, producing the expanding universe. The cause of the Big Bang is unknown; observations of the current rate of expansion of the universe suggest that it took place about 10 to 20 billion years ago. The Big Bang theory began modern ◊cosmology.

According to a modified version of the Big Bang, called the *inflationary theory*, the universe underwent a rapid period of expansion shortly after the Big Bang, which accounts for its current large size and uniform nature. The inflationary theory is supported by the most recent observations of the cosmic background radiation.

bilateralism in economics, a trade agreement between two countries or groups of countries in which they give each other preferential treatment. Usually the terms agreed result in balanced trade and are favoured by countries with limited foreign exchange reserves. Bilateralism is incompatible with free trade.

Bilateral agreements were common among the USSR and Eastern bloc countries, both between themselves and with the rest of the world. This was partly because their currencies were inconvertible and partly because bilateralism enabled them to make estimates of international trade in their economic plans.

bill of exchange form of commercial credit instrument, or IOU, used in international trade. In Britain, a bill of exchange is defined by the Bills of Exchange Act 1882 as an unconditional order in writing addressed by one person to another, signed by the person giving it, requiring the person to whom it is addressed to pay on demand or at a fixed or determinable future time a certain sum in money to or to the order of a specified person, or to the bearer. US practice is governed by the Uniform Negotiable Instruments Law, drafted on the same lines as the British, and accepted by all states by 1927.

Bill of Rights in the USA, the first ten amendments to the US ◊Constitution, incorporated 1791:

1 guarantees freedom of worship, of speech, of the press, of assembly, and to petition the government;
2 grants the right to keep and bear arms;
3 prohibits billeting of soldiers in private homes in peacetime;
4 forbids unreasonable search and seizure;
5 guarantees none be 'deprived of life, liberty or property without due process of law' or compelled in any criminal case to be a witness against himself or herself;
6 grants the right to speedy trial, to call witnesses, and to have defence counsel;
7 grants the right to trial by jury of one's peers;
8 prevents the infliction of excessive bail or fines, or 'cruel and unusual punishment';
9, 10 provide a safeguard to the states and people for all rights not specifically delegated to the central government.

Not originally part of the draft of the Constitution, the Bill of Rights was mooted during the period of ratification. Twelve amendments were proposed by Congress in 1789; the ten now called the Bill of Rights were ratified 1791.

Bill of Rights in Britain, an act of Parliament 1689 which established it as the primary governing body of the country. The Bill of Rights embodied the Declarations of Rights which contained the conditions on which William and Mary were offered the throne. It made provisions limiting royal prerogative with respect to legislation, executive power, money levies, courts, and the army and stipulated Parliament's consent to many government functions.

The act made illegal the suspension of laws by royal authority without Parliament's consent; the power to dispense with laws; the establishment of special courts of law; levying money by royal prerogative without Parliament's consent; and the maintenance of a standing army in peacetime without Parliament's consent. It also asserted a right to petition the sovereign, freedom of parliamentary elections, freedom of speech in parliamentary debates, and the necessity of frequent parliaments.

bimah in Judaism, raised platform in a synagogue from which the ◊Torah scroll is read.

bimetallism monetary system in which two metals, traditionally gold and silver, both circulate at a ratio fixed by the state, are coined by the mint on equal terms, and are legal tender to any amount. The system was in use in the 19th century.

Advocates of bimetallism have argued that the 'compensatory action of the double standard' makes for a currency more stable than one based only on gold, since the changes in the value of the two metals taken together may be expected to be less than the changes in one of them. One of the many arguments against the system is that the ratio of the prices of the metals is frozen regardless of the supply and demand.

Binet Alfred 1857–1911. French psychologist who founded the first psychology laboratory in France at the Sorbonne, Paris, 1889 and published, with Theodore Simon, the first ◊intelligence tests for children 1905.

The tests were standardized so that the last of a set of graded tests the child could successfully complete gave the level described as 'mental age'. If the test was passed by most children over 12, for instance, but failed by those younger, it was said to show a mental age of 12. The tests were fully revised 1911.

biochemistry science concerned with the chemistry of living organisms: the structure and reactions of proteins (such as enzymes), nucleic acids, carbohydrates, and lipids.

Its study has led to an increased understanding of life processes, such as those by which organisms synthesize essential chemicals from food materials, store and generate energy, and pass on their characteristics through their genetic material. A great deal of medical research is concerned with the ways in which these processes are disrupted. Biochemistry also has applications in agriculture and in the food industry (for instance, in the use of enzymes).

biodiversity (contraction of *biological diversity*) measure of the variety of the Earth's animal, plant, and microbial species; of genetic differences within species; and of the ecosystems that support those species. Its maintenance is important for ecological stability and as a resource for research into, for example, new drugs and crops. Research suggests that biodiversity is far greater than previously realized, especially among smaller organisms – for instance, it is thought that only 1–10% of the world's bacterial species have been identified. In the 20th century, however, the destruction of habitats is believed to have resulted in the most severe and rapid loss of diversity in the history of the planet.

The term came to public attention 1992 when an international convention for the preservation of biodiversity was signed by over 100 world leaders at the Earth Summit in Brazil. The convention called on industrialized countries to give financial and technological help to developing countries in order to allow them to protect and manage their natural resources, and profit from growing commercial demand for genes and chemicals from wild species. However, the convention was weakened when the USA refused to sign because of fears that it would undermine the patents and licenses of biotechnology companies.

bioeconomics theory put forward in 1979 by Chicago economist Gary Becker that the concepts of sociobiology apply also in economics. The competitiveness and self-interest built into human genes are said to make capitalism an effective economic system, whereas the selflessness and collectivism proclaimed as the socialist ideal are held to be contrary to human genetic make-up and to produce an ineffective system.

bioengineering the application of engineering to biology and medicine. Common applications include the design and use of artificial limbs, joints, and organs, including hip joints and heart valves.

biofeedback modification or control of a biological system by its results or effects. For example, a change in the position or trophic level of one species affects all levels above it.

Many biological systems are controlled by negative feedback. When enough of the hormone thyroxine has been released into the blood, the hormone adjusts its own level by 'switching off' the gland that produces it. In ecology, as the numbers in a species rise, the food supply available to each individual is reduced. This acts to reduce the population to a sustainable level.

biogenesis biological term coined 1870 by English scientist Thomas Henry Huxley to express the hypothesis that living matter always arises out of other similar forms of living matter. It superseded the opposite idea of spontaneous generation or abiogenesis (that is, that living things may arise out of nonliving matter).

There is properly no history; only biography.

biography

Ralph Waldo Emerson, 1803–1882, US philosopher, essayist, and poet.
Essays, 'History'

biography account of a person's life. When it is written by that person, it is an autobiography. Biography may consist simply of the factual details of a person's life told in chronological order, but has generally become a matter of interpretation as well as historical accuracy. Unofficial biographies (not sanctioned by the subject) have frequently led to legal disputes over both interpretation and facts.

Among ancient biographers are Xenophon, Plutarch, Tacitus, Suetonius, and the authors of the Gospels of the New Testament. Medieval biography was mostly devoted to religious edification and produced chronicles of saints and martyrs; among secular biographies are *Charlemagne* by Frankish monk Einhard (c. 770–840), *Alfred* by Welsh monk Asser (died c. 910), and *Petrarch* by Boccaccio.

Biography should be written by an acute enemy.

biography

Arthur James Balfour, 1st Earl of Balfour, 1848–1930.
Observer 30 Jan 1927

In England true biography begins with the early Tudor period and such works as *Sir Thomas More* 1626, written by his son-in-law William Roper (1498–1578). By the 18th century it became a literary form in its own right through Samuel Johnson's *Lives of the Most Eminent English Poets* 1779–81 and James Boswell's biography of Johnson 1791. Nineteenth-century biographers include Robert Southey, Elizabeth Gaskell, G H Lewes, J Morley, and Thomas Carlyle. The general ten-dency was to provide irrelevant detail and suppress the more personal facts. Lytton Strachey's *Eminent Victorians* opened the new era of frankness.

Twentieth-century biographers include Richard Ellmann (1918–1987), André Maurois (James Joyce and Oscar Wilde), Michael Holroyd (1935–) (Lytton Strachey and George Bernard Shaw), and Elizabeth Longford (Queen Victoria and Wellington).

The earliest **biographical dictionary** in the accepted sense was that of Pierre Bayle 1696, followed during the 19th century by the development of national biographies in Europe, and the foundation of the *English Dictionary of National Biography* 1882 and the *Dictionary of American Biography* 1928.

biology science of life. Strictly speaking, biology includes all the life sciences – for example, anatomy and physiology, cytology, zoology and botany, ecology, genetics, biochemistry and biophysics, animal behaviour, embryology, and plant breeding. During the 1990s an important focus of biological research will be the international ◊Human Genome Project, which will attempt to map the entire genetic code contained in the 23 pairs of human chromosomes.

biomass the total mass of living organisms present in a given area. It may be specified for a particular species (such as earthworm biomass) or for a general category (such as herbivore biomass). Estimates also exist for the entire global plant biomass. Measurements of biomass can be used to study interactions between organisms, the stability of those interactions, and variations in population numbers.

The burning of biomass (defined either as natural areas of the ecosystem or as forest, grasslands and fuelwoods) produces 3.5 million tonnes of carbon in the form of carbon dioxide each year, accounting for up to 40% of the world's annual carbon dioxide production.

biophysics application of physical laws to the properties of living organisms. Examples include using the principles of ◊mechanics to calculate the strength of bones and muscles, and ◊thermodynamics to study plant and animal energetics.

biorhythm rhythmic change, mediated by hormones, in the physical state and activity patterns of certain plants and animals that have seasonal activities. Examples include winter hibernation, spring flowering or breeding, and periodic migration. The hormonal changes themselves are often a response to changes in day length (photoperiodism); they signal the time of year to the animal or plant. Other biorhythms are innate and continue even if external stimuli such as day length are removed. These include a 24-hour or circadian rhythm, a 28-day or circalunar rhythm (corresponding to the phases of the Moon), and even a year-long rhythm in some organisms.

Such innate biorhythms are linked to an internal or biological clock, whose mechanism is still poorly understood. Often both types of rhythm operate; thus many birds have a circalunar rhythm that prepares them for the breeding season, and a photoperiodic response. There is also a nonscientific and unproven theory that human activity is governed by three biorhythms: the *intellectual* (33 days), the *emotional* (28 days), and the *physical* (23 days). Certain days in each cycle are regarded as 'critical', even more so if one such day coincides with that of another cycle.

Biot Jean 1774–1862. French physicist who studied the polarization of light. In 1804 he made a balloon ascent to a height of 5 km/ 3 mi, in an early investigation of the Earth's atmosphere.

biotechnology industrial use of living organisms to manufacture food, drugs, or other products. The brewing and baking industries have long relied on the yeast microorganism for fermentation purposes, while the dairy industry employs a range of bacteria and fungi to convert milk into cheeses and yoghurts. Enzymes, whether extracted from cells or produced artificially, are central to most biotechnological applications.

Recent advances include ◊genetic engineering, in which single-celled organisms with modified DNA are used to produce insulin and other drugs.

birth rate the number of live births per year per thousand of the population. Birth rate is a factor in ◊demographic transition. It is sometimes called *crude birth rate* because it takes in the whole population, including men and women who are too old to bear children.

The UK's birth rate has fallen from 28 at the beginning of the 20th century to 14 in 1990, owing to increased use of contraception, better living standards, and falling infant mortality. The birth rate remains high in developing countries – for example, in Malawi it stands at 56.3 (1985–90), in Burkina Faso at 47.1 (1985–90), in Honduras at 38 (1989), and in Bangladesh at 33 (1989).

Bismarck Otto Eduard Leopold, Prince von 1815–1898. German politician, prime minister of Prussia 1862–90 and chancellor of the German Empire 1871–90. He pursued an aggressively expansionist policy, waging wars against Denmark 1863–64, Austria 1866, and France 1870–71, which brought about the unification of Germany.

Bismarck was ambitious to establish Prussia's leadership within Germany and eliminate the influence of Austria. He secured Austria's support for his successful war against Denmark then, in 1866, went to war against Austria and its allies (the ◊Seven Weeks' War), his victory forcing Austria out of the German Bund and unifying the N German states into the North German Confederation under his own chancellorship 1867. He then defeated France, under Napoleon III, in the Franco-Prussian War 1870–81, proclaimed the German Empire 1871, and annexed Alsace-Lorraine. He tried to secure his work by the ◊Triple Alliance 1881 with Austria and Italy but ran into difficulties at home with the Roman Catholic Church and the socialist movement and was forced to resign by Wilhelm II 18 March 1890.

bivalence in logic, a principle or law that can be formulated as 'Every proposition is either true or false.'

If the principle of bivalence is true, then two-valued logic, in which true and false are in practice the two main truth-values of propositions, is the only possible logic. If the principle is false, then many-valued logics are possible, in which propositions can have values such as 'known to be false', 'known to be true', 'necessarily false', and 'necessarily true'.

'Every proposition is either true or false' is also one form of what is known as the law of the excluded middle.

Bjerknes Vilhelm Firman Koren 1862–1951. Norwegian scientist who developed the highly influential theory of polar fronts after working on Norwegian weather stations during World War I. This theory formed the basis of all modern weather forecasting and meteorological studies. He also developed hydrodynamic models of the oceans and the atmosphere and showed how weather prediction could be put on a statistical basis.

black English term first used 1625 to describe West Africans, now used to refer to Africans south of the Sahara and to people of African descent living outside Africa. In some countries such as the UK (but not in North America) the term is sometimes also used for people originally from the Indian subcontinent, for Australian Aborigines, and peoples of Melanesia.

The term 'black', at one time considered offensive by many people, was first adopted by militants in the USA in the mid-1960s to emphasize ethnic pride; they rejected the terms 'coloured' and 'Negro' as euphemistic. 'Black' has since become the preferred term in the USA and largely in the UK. Currently, US blacks often prefer the term 'Afro-American' or 'African-American'.

history Black Africans were first taken to the West Indies in large numbers as slaves by the Spanish in the early 16th century and to the North American mainland in the early 17th century. They were transported to South America by both the Spanish and Portuguese from the 16th century. African blacks were also taken to Europe to work as slaves and servants. Some of the indigenous coastal societies in W Africa were heavily involved in the slave trade and became wealthy on its proceeds. Sometimes, black sailors settled in European ports on the Atlantic seaboard, such as Liverpool and Bristol, England. Although blacks fought beside whites in the American Revolution, the US Constitution (ratified 1788) did not redress the slave trade, and slaves were given no ◊civil rights. Slavery was gradually abolished in the northern US states during the early 19th century, but as the South's economy had been based upon slavery, it was one of the issues concerning states' rights that led to the secession of the South, which provoked the American Civil War 1861–65. During the Civil War about 200,000 blacks fought in the Union (Northern) army, but in segregated units led by white officers.

The Emancipation Proclamation 1863 of President Abraham Lincoln officially freed the slaves (about 4 million), but it could not be enforced until the Union victory 1865 and the period after the war known as the Reconstruction. Freed slaves were often resented by poor whites as economic competitors, and vigilante groups in the South, such as the ◊Ku Klux Klan were formed to intimidate them. In addition, although freed slaves had full US citizenship under the 14th Amendment to the Constitution, and were thus entitled to vote, they were often disenfranchised in practice by state and local literacy tests and poll taxes.

A 'separate but equal' policy was established when the US Supreme Court ruled 1896 (*Plessy* v. *Ferguson*) that segregation was legal if equal facilities were provided for blacks and whites. The ruling was overturned 1954 (*Brown* v. *Board of Education*) with the Supreme Court decision outlawing segregation in state schools. This led to a historic confrontation in Little Rock, Arkansas, 1957 when Governor Orval Faubus attempted to prevent black students from entering Central High School, and President Eisenhower sent federal troops to enforce their right to attend.

Another landmark in the blacks' struggle for civil rights was the Montgomery bus boycott in Alabama 1955, which first brought Martin Luther ◊King Jr to national attention. In the early 1960s the civil-rights movement had gained impetus, largely under the leadership of King, who in 1957 had founded the Southern Christian Leadership Conference (SCLC), a coalition group advocating nonviolence. Moderate groups such as the National Association for the Advancement of Colored People (NAACP) had been active since early in the century; for the first time they were joined in large numbers by whites, in particular students, as in the historic march converging on Washington DC 1963 from all over the USA. At about this time, impatient with the lack of results gained through moderation, the militant ◊Black Power movements began to emerge, such as the Black Panther Party founded 1966, and black separatist groups such as the ◊Black Muslims gained support.

Increasing pressure led to the passage of federal legislation, the Civil Rights acts of 1964 and 1968, and the Voting Rights Act of 1965, under President Johnson; they guaranteed equal rights under the law and prohibited discrimination in public facilities, schools, employment, and voting. However, in the 1980s, despite some advances, legislation, and affirmative action (positive discrimination), blacks, who comprise some 12% of the US population, continued to suffer discrimination and inequality of opportunities in practice in such areas as education, employment, and housing. Despite these obstacles, many blacks have made substanital contributions in the arts, the sciences, and politics.

Black Davidson 1884–1934. Canadian anatomist. In 1927, when professor of anatomy at the Union Medical College, Peking (Beijing), he unearthed the remains of Peking man, an example of one of our human ancestors.

Black James 1924– . British physiologist, director of therapeutic research at Wellcome Laboratories (near London) from 1978. He was active in the development of beta-blockers (which reduce the rate of heartbeat) and anti-ulcer drugs. He shared the Nobel Prize for Medicine 1988 with US scientists Gertrude Elion (1918–) and George Hitchings (1905–).

Black Joseph 1728–1799. Scottish physicist and chemist who in 1754 discovered carbon dioxide (which he called 'fixed air'). By his investigations in 1761 of latent heat and specific heat, he laid the foundation for the work of his pupil James Watt.

Born in Bordeaux, France, Black qualified as a doctor in Edinburgh. In chemistry, he prepared the way for the scientists Henry Cavendish, Joseph ◊Priestley, and Antoine ◊Lavoisier.

black economy unofficial economy of a country, which includes undeclared earnings from a second job ('moonlighting'), and enjoyment of undervalued goods and services (such as company 'perks'), designed for tax evasion purposes. In industrialized countries, it has been estimated to equal about 10% of ◊gross domestic product.

Black Elk 1863–1950. Native American religious leader who tried to find ways of reconciling Native traditions with Christianity. His visions and ideas offered a new way of evaluating Native traditions within the new reality of white dominance. Though he continued his calling as a ◊shaman, he converted to christianity in 1886.

In our infinite ignorance we are all equal.

Karl Popper, Austrian Philosopher

Conjectures and Refutations

Blackett Patrick Maynard Stuart, Baron Blackett 1897–1974. British physicist. He was awarded a Nobel prize 1948 for work in cosmic radiation and his perfection of the Wilson cloud chamber.

black hole object in space whose gravity is so great that nothing can escape from it, not even light. Thought to form when massive stars shrink at the ends of their lives, a black hole sucks in more matter, including other stars, from the space around it. Matter that falls into a black hole is squeezed to infinite density at the centre of the hole. Black holes can be detected because gas falling towards them becomes so hot that it emits X-rays.

Satellites above the Earth's atmosphere have detected X-rays from a number of objects in our Galaxy that might be black holes. Massive black holes containing the mass of millions of stars are thought to lie at the centres of ◊quasars. Microscopic black holes may have been formed in the chaotic conditions of the ◊Big Bang. The English physicist Stephen ◊Hawking has shown that such tiny black holes could 'evaporate' and explode in a flash of energy.

How can the complexity of the universe and all its trivial details be determined by a simple set of equations?

Stephen Hawking, English physicist

Black Holes and Baby Universes

---

blacking in an industrial dispute, the refusal of workers to handle particular goods or equipment, or to work with particular people.

Blacking John 1928–1990. British anthropologist and ethnomusicologist who researched the relationship between music and body movement, and the patterns of social and musical organization. Blacking was from 1970 chair of social anthropology at Queen's University, Belfast, where he established a centre for ethnomusicology. His most widely read book is *How Musical is Man?* 1973.

black market illegal trade in rationed or otherwise scarce goods (for example, food, petrol, and clothing, during World War II and after).

Black Muslim member of a religious group founded 1929 in the USA and led, from 1934, by Elijah Muhammad (then Elijah Poole) (1897–1975) after he had a vision of ◊Allah. Its growth from 1946 as a black separatist organization was due to Malcolm X (1926–1965), the son of a Baptist minister who, in 1964, broke away and founded his own Organization for Afro-American Unity, preaching 'active self-defence'. Under the leadership of Louis Farrakhan, the movement underwent a recent revival.

black nationalism movement towards black separatism in the USA during the 1960s; see ◊Black Power.

Black Power movement towards black separatism in the USA during the 1960s, embodied in the ***Black Panther Party*** founded 1966 by Huey Newton and Bobby Seale. Its declared aim was the establishment of a separate black state in the USA established by a black plebiscite under the aegis of the United Nations. Following a National Black Political Convention 1972, a National Black Assembly was established to exercise pressure on the Democratic and Republican parties.

The Black Power concept arose when existing ◊civil rights organizations such as the National Association for Advancement of Colored People and the Southern Christian Leadership Conference were perceived to be ineffective in producing major change in the status of black people. Stokely Carmichael then advocated the exploitation of political and economic power and abandonment of nonviolence, with a move towards the type of separatism first developed by the ◊Black Muslims. Leaders such as Martin Luther King rejected this approach, but the Black Panther Party (so named because the panther, though not generally aggressive, will fight to the death under attack) adopted it fully and, for a time, achieved nationwide influence. Black Americans now generally prefer to be referred to as African-Americans in the same way that other Americans are called Italian-American, Greek-American and similar.

Black Stone in Islam, the sacred stone built into the east corner of the ◊Ka'aba which is a focal point of the *hajj*, or pilgrimage, to Mecca. There are a number of stories concerning its origin, one of which states that it was sent to Earth at the time of the first man, Adam; Muhammad declared that it was given to Abraham by the angel Jibra'el (Gabriel). It has been suggested that it is of meteoric origin.

black stump in Australia, an imaginary boundary between civilization and the outback, as in the phrase 'this side of the black stump'.

Blake William 1757–1827. English poet, artist, engraver, and visionary. His lyrics, as in *Songs of Innocence* 1789 and *Songs of Experience* 1794 express spiritual wisdom in radiant imagery and symbolism. Prophetic books like *The Marriage of Heaven and Hell* 1790, *America* 1793, and *Milton* 1804 yield their meaning to careful study. He created a new composite art form in engraving and hand-colouring his own works.

Blake was born in Soho, London, and apprenticed to an engraver 1771–78. He illustrated the Bible, works by Dante and Shakespeare, and his own poems. His figures are heavily muscled, with elongated proportions. In his later years he attracted a group of followers, including Samuel Palmer, who called themselves the Ancients. Henry Fuseli was another admirer. Blake's poem *Jerusalem* 1820 was set to music by Charles Parry (1848–1918).

blasphemy written or spoken insult directed against religious belief or sacred things with deliberate intent to outrage believers.

Blasphemy was originally defined as 'publishing any matter which contradicts the teaching of the Church of England'; since 1883 it has been redefined as a 'vilification' or attack on Christianity, likely to 'outrage the feelings of believers'. Blasphemy is still an offence in English common law, despite several recommendations (for example by the Law Commission 1985) that the law of blasphemy should be abolished or widened to apply to all religious faiths. In 1977 the magazine *Gay News* and its editor were successfully prosecuted for publishing a poem that suggested Jesus was a homosexual. In 1989 Salman Rushdie was accused by orthodox Muslims of blasphemy against the Islamic faith in his book *The Satanic Verses*, but the Court of Appeal held it was not blasphemous under English law. Demands have since been made to extend blasphemy laws to cover Islam, or abolish blasphemy laws entirely.

Blau Peter 1918– . US sociologist. In his studies of organizations, particularly bureaucracies, he has shown how a system of reciprocation and obligation can create social bonding and how less formal controls can increase involvement in decision making. His writings include *The Dynamics of Bureaucracy* 1952 and *On the Nature of Organizations* 1974.

Blavatsky Helena Petrovna (born Hahn) 1831–1891. Russian spiritualist and mystic, cofounder of the Theosophical Society (see ◊theosophy) 1875, which has its headquarters near Madras, India. In Tibet she underwent spiritual training and later became a Buddhist. Her books include *Isis Unveiled* 1877 and *The Secret Doctrine* 1888. She was declared a fraud by the London Society for Psychical Research 1885.

Bloch Felix 1905–1983. Swiss-US physicist who invented the analytical technique of nuclear magnetic resonance (NMR) spectroscopy 1946. For this work he shared the Nobel Prize for Physics 1952 with US physicist Edward Purcell (1912–).

Bloch Konrad 1912– . German-born US chemist whose research concerned cholesterol. Making use of the radioisotope carbon-14 (the radioactive form of carbon), Bloch was able to follow the complex steps by which the body chemically transforms acetic acid into cholesterol. For his work in this field Bloch shared the 1964 Nobel Prize for Medicine with Feodor Lynen (1911–1979).

Bloch Marc 1886–1944. French historian, leading member of the ◊Annales school. Professor of economic history at the Sorbonne from 1936, he undertook most of his research in medieval European history, exploring the relationship between freedom and servitude in his thesis *Kings and Serfs* 1920 and *Feudal Society* 1939–40. He held that economic structures and systems of belief were just as important to the study of history as legal norms and institutional practices, and pioneered the use of comparative history.

Forced out of teaching during World War II, he joined the Resistance 1943 but was captured and shot by the Germans 1944.

Bloomfield Leonard 1887–1949. American linguist, professor of linguistics at Chicago University 1927–40 and at Yale (from 1940). A major figure in the development of linguistics, he carried out extensive field research, notably on Tagalog (Filipino), spoken in the Philippines, and on the languages of North American Indians. His widely influential *Languages* 1933, regarded as a classic of linguistics, is a rigorous analysis of the theory and methodology of linguistic research.

Bloomfield's aim was to make linguistics a scientific discipline. This led him to adopt a behaviourist approach to research, concerned solely with what can be observed and measured – with form (phonology, syntax, and morphology) rather than meaning (semantics). He stressed that research should concentrate on the spoken rather than the written language, and argued that at any given time the sounds and forms of a language could be seen as a complete system, the history of their gradual evolution (the focus of 19th-century philosophy) being irrelevant. Bloomfield's ideas dominated American linguistics until the appearance of Noam ◊Chomsky's theories in the late 1950s.

Bloomsbury Group intellectual circle of writers and artists based in Bloomsbury, London, which flourished in the 1920s. It centred on the house of publisher Leonard Woolf (1880–1969) and his wife, novelist Virginia Woolf, and included the artists Duncan Grant and Vanessa Bell, the biographer Lytton Strachey, art critics Roger Fry and Clive Bell, and the economist Maynard ◊Keynes. Typically modernist, their innovatory artistic contributions represented an important section of the English avant-garde.

From their emphasis on close interpersonal relationships and their fastidious attitude towards contemporary culture arose many accusations of elitism.

They also held sceptical views on social and political conventions and religious practices.

Bloom's taxonomy term given to three educational objectives formulated by the US psychologist B S Bloom (1911–   ). The *cognitive* deals with knowledge and its application; the *affective* deals with emotions and values; the *psycho-motor* deals with physical and manipulative skills.

Bluebeard folktale character, popularized by the writer Charles ◊Perrault in France about 1697, and historically identified with Gilles de Rais. Bluebeard murdered six wives for disobeying his command not to enter a locked room, but was himself killed before he could murder the seventh.

To see a World in a Grain of Sand,
And a heaven in a Wild Flower,
Hold Infinity in the palm of your hand,
And Eternity in an hour.

William Blake
'Auguries of Innocence'

bluestocking learned woman; the term is often used disparagingly. It originated 1750 in England with the literary gatherings of Elizabeth Vesey (1715–1791), the wife of an Irish MP, in Bath, and Elizabeth Montagu, a writer and patron, in London. According to the novelist Fanny Burney, the term arose when the poet Benjamin Stillingfleet protested that he had nothing formal to wear. She told him to come in his 'blue stockings' – that is, ordinary clothes. The regulars at these gatherings became known as the Blue Stocking Circle.

Boas Franz 1858–1942. German-born US anthropologist. Joining the faculty of Clark University 1888, Boas became one of America's first academic anthropologists; he stressed the need to study 'four fields' – ethnology, linguistics, physical anthropology, and archaeology – before generalizations might be made about any one culture or comparisons about any number of cultures.

He began his career in geography but switched to ethnology when he joined a German scientific expedition to the Arctic 1883. In 1886 he travelled to the Pacific North-west to study the culture of the Kwakiutl Indian people, including their language. In 1896 he was appointed professor at Columbia University, where he trained the first generation of US anthropologists, such as Alfred Kroeber and Margaret Mead. From 1901 to 1905 he was also curator of the American Museum of Natural History in New York City. Boas spent much of his later career battling against unscientific theories of racial inequality.

Bode Johann Elert 1747–1826. German astronomer, director of the Berlin observatory. He published the first atlas of all stars visible to the naked eye, *Uranographia* 1801, and devised Bode's Law.

Bodhidharma 6th century AD. Indian Buddhist and teacher, founder of the Ch'an school (◊Zen is the Japanese derivation).

He was born near Madras, S India. About 520 he travelled to China where he met the emperor Wu and eventually settled at the Shao-lin monastery on the sacred Sung-shan mountain.

bodhisattva in Mahāyāna Buddhism, someone who seeks ◊enlightenment in order to help other living beings. A bodhisattva is free to enter ◊nirvana but voluntarily chooses to be reborn until all other beings have attained that state. Bodhisattvas are seen as intercessors to whom believers may pray for redemption.

Bodichon Barbara (born Leigh-Smith) 1827–1891. English feminist and campaigner for women's education and suffrage. She wrote *Women and Work* 1857, and was a founder of the magazine *The Englishwoman's Journal* 1858.

Born into a radical family that believed in female equality, she attended Bedford College, London. She was a founder of the college for women that became Girton College, Cambridge.

Bodin Jean 1530–1596. French political philosopher whose six-volume *De la République* 1576 is considered the first work on political economy.

An attorney in Paris, he published 1574 a tract explaining that prevalent high prices were due to the influx of precious metals from the New World. His theory of an ideal government emphasized obedience to a sovereign ruler.

body language nonverbal communication by largely unconscious signals of posture and movement. Sighing and laughing are also body language; though they rely principally on sound, they are often accompanied by gestures and are nonverbal.

Boehme Jakob 1575–1624. German mystic, who had many followers in Germany, Holland, and England. He claimed divine revelation of the unity of everything and nothing, and found in God's eternal nature a principle to reconcile good and evil. He was the author of the treatise *Aurora* 1612.

It is the nature of human affairs to be fraught with anxiety.
Anicius Manlius Severinus Boethius
The Consolation of Philosophy II.iv

Boethius Anicius Manlius Severinus AD 480–524. Roman philosopher who translated Aristotle's works on logic and wrote treatises on Christian theology, music, and mathematics. While imprisoned on suspicion of treason by the emperor Theodoric the Great, he wrote *De Consolatione Philosophiae/The Consolation of Philosophy*, a dialogue in prose, in which the lady, Philosophy, responds to Boethius' account of his misfortunes with Stoic, Platonic, and Christian advice. It was translated into European languages during the Middle Ages; English translations were written by Alfred the Great, Geoffrey Chaucer, and Queen Elizabeth I.

Bogomil member of a sect of Christian heretics who originated in 10th-century Bulgaria and spread throughout the Byzantine empire. Their name derives from Bogomilus, or Theophilus, probably a Greek Orthodox priest who taught in Bulgaria 927–950. Despite persecution, they were expunged by the Ottomans only after the fall of Constantinople 1453.

Bohr Aage 1922– . Danish physicist who produced a new model of the nucleus 1952, known as the collective model. For this work, he shared the 1975 Nobel Prize for Physics. He was the son of Niels Bohr.

Bohr Niels Henrik David 1885–1962. Danish physicist. His theoretic work produced a new model of atomic structure, now called the Bohr model, and helped establish the validity of ◊quantum theory.

After work with Ernest ◊Rutherford at Manchester, UK, he became professor at Copenhagen 1916, and founded there the Institute of Theoretical Physics of which he became director 1920. He was awarded the Nobel Prize for Physics 1922. Bohr fled from the Nazis in World War II and took part in work on the atomic bomb in the USA. In 1952, he helped to set up CERN, the

European nuclear research organization in Geneva.

Bolingbroke Henry St John, Viscount Bolingbroke 1678–1751. British Tory politician and philosopher. His political writings show the influence of ◊Machiavelli. The patriotic politician must oppose corruption not to further ambition, but to defend the constitution. Like Machiavelli's 'Prince', the patriotic king must be prepared to bring the government back to just principles. His scepticism about revealed religion (◊deism) in his posthumous works outraged Dr ◊Johnson.

His books, such as *Idea of a Patriot King* 1738, which argued for a leadership independent of party politics, and *The Dissertation upon Parties* 1735, laid the foundations for 19th-century Toryism. He was foreign secretary 1710–14 and a Jacobite conspirator.

Nations, like men, have their infancy.

Henry St John Bolingbroke, Viscount Bolingbroke
On the Study of History

Secretary of war 1704–08, he became foreign secretary in Robert Harley's ministry 1710, and in 1713 negotiated the Treaty of Utrecht. His plans to restore the 'Old Pretender' James Francis Edward Stuart were ruined by Queen Anne's death only five days after he had secured the dismissal of Harley 1714. He fled abroad, returning 1723, when he worked to overthrow Robert Walpole.

Bolívar Simón 1783–1830. South American nationalist, leader of revolutionary armies, known as **the Liberator**. He fought the Spanish colonial forces in several uprisings and eventually liberated his native Venezuela 1821, Colombia and Ecuador 1822, Peru 1824, and Bolivia (a new state named after him, formerly Upper Peru) 1825.

Born in Venezuela, he joined that country's revolution against Spain in 1810, and in the following year he declared Venezuela independent. His army was soon defeated by the Spanish, however, and he was forced to flee. Many battles and defeats followed, and it was not until 1819 that Bolívar won his first major victory, defeating the Spanish in Colombia and winning independence for that country. He went on to liberate Venezuela 1821 and (along with Antonio Sucre) Ecuador 1822. These three countries were united into the republic of Gran Colombia with Bolívar as its president. In 1824 Bolívar helped bring about the defeat of Spanish forces in Peru, and the area known as Upper Peru was renamed 'Bolivia' in Bolívar's honour. Within the next few years, Venezuela and Ecuador seceded from the union, and in 1830 Bolívar resigned as president. He died the same year, despised by many for his dictatorial ways but since revered as South America's greatest liberator.

Bollandist member of a group of Belgian Jesuits who edit and publish the *Acta Sanctorum*, the standard collection of saints' lives and other scholarly publications. They are named after John Bolland (1596–1665), who published the first two volumes 1643.

Bolshevik member of the majority of the Russian Social Democratic Party who split from the ◊Mensheviks 1903. The Bolsheviks, under ◊Lenin, advocated the destruction of capitalist political and economic institutions, and the setting-up of a socialist state with power in the hands of the workers. The Bolsheviks set the ◊Russian Revolution 1917 in motion. They changed their name to the Russian Communist Party 1918.

Boltzmann Ludwig 1844–1906. Austrian physicist who studied the kinetic theory of gases, which explains the properties of gases by reference to the motion of their constituent atoms and molecules.

He derived a formula, the *Boltzmann distribution*, which gives the number of atoms or molecules with a given energy at a specific temperature. The constant in the formula is called the *Boltzmann constant*.

Bon or *Bon po* the pre-Buddhist faith of many of the Tibetan peoples. Probably originally shamanistic in origin, it underwent a transformation in reaction to the arrival of Buddhism in Tibet in the 8th and 9th centuries. Bon pos are followers of this reformed Bon religion, which claims to have been founded in the distant past by Shenrab Mibo. Most of present-day Bon religious practice and sacred texts are clearly copied from Buddhism. Before the Chinese invasion of 1959 there were 350 specifically Bon monasteries.

Bonapartism political system of military dictatorship by an individual, ostensibly based on popular appeal, with frequent use of the ◊plebiscite. Derived from Napoleon's system of rule (1799–1815), the term has been applied to other regimes, for example that of Juan Perón in Argentina. In France, supporters of the Bonaparte family's claims to the French throne during the 19th century were known as

Bonapartists.

Bonaventura, St (John of Fidanza) 1221–1274. Italian Roman Catholic theologian. He entered the Franciscan order 1243, became professor of theology in Paris, and in 1256 general of his order. In 1273 he was created cardinal and bishop of Albano. Feast day 15 July.

Bondi Hermann 1919– . Viennese-born British cosmologist. In 1948 he joined with Fred ◊Hoyle and Thomas Gold (1920–) in developing the steady-state theory of cosmology, which suggested that matter is continuously created in the universe.

Bonhoeffer Dietrich 1906–1945. German Lutheran theologian and opponent of Nazism. Involved in a plot against Hitler, he was executed by the Nazis in Flossenburg concentration camp. His *Letters and Papers from Prison* 1953 became the textbook of modern radical theology, advocating the idea of a 'religionless' Christianity.

Boniface VIII Benedict Caetani c. 1228–1303. Pope from 1294. He clashed unsuccessfully with Philip IV of France over his taxation of the clergy, and also with Henry III of England.

Boniface exempted the clergy from taxation by the secular government in a bull (edict) 1296, but was forced to give way when the clergy were excluded from certain lay privileges. His bull of 1302 *Unam sanctam*, asserted the complete temporal and spiritual power of the papacy over secular rulers, but proved equally ineffective.

Bonner Yelena 1923– . Soviet human-rights campaigner. Disillusioned by the Soviet invasion of Czechoslovakia 1968, she resigned from the Communist Party after marrying her second husband, Andrei ◊Sakharov 1971, and became active in the dissident movement.

Buying books would be a good thing if one could also buy the time to read them in.

book

Arthur Schopenhauer, 1788–1860,
German philosopher.
Essays and Aphorisms

---

book portable written record. Substances used to make early books included leaves, bark, linen, silk, clay, leather, and papyrus. In about AD 100–150, the codex or paged book, as opposed to the roll or scroll, began to be adopted. Vellum (parchment of calfskin, lambskin, or kidskin) was generally used for book pages by the beginning of the 4th century, and its use lasted until the 15th. It was superseded by paper, which came to Europe from China (where it was made as early as AD 105, a mixture of bark and hemp fibres). Books only became widely available after the invention of the printing press in the 15th century. Printed text is also reproduced and stored in microform.

As good almost kill a man as kill a good book; who kills a man kills a reasonable creature, God's image; but he who destroys a good book, kills reason itself, kills the image of God, as it were in the eye.

book

John Milton, 1608–1674, English poet.
Areopagitica

Book of Hours see ◊Hours, Book of.

Book of the Dead ancient Egyptian book, known as the *Book of Coming Forth by Day*, buried with the dead as a guide to reaching the kingdom of Osiris, the god of the underworld. Similar practices were observed by Orphic communities (6th to 1st century BC) in S Italy and Crete, who deposited gold laminae, inscribed with directions about the next world, in the graves of their dead. An ancient Buddhist example is the Bardo Thödol from Tibet. In medieval times, Christians could obtain advice about dying from a book entitled *Ars Morendi/The Art of Dying*.

Don't believe what your eyes are telling you. All they show is limitation. Look with your understanding, find out what you already know, and you'll see the way to fly.

Richard Bach
Jonathan Livingstone Seagull

Boole George 1815–1864. English mathematician. In *The Mathematical Analysis of Logic* 1847 he established the basis of modern mathematical logic, by applying the methods of algebra to logic, logical operations 'and', 'or' and 'not' being represented by symbols. This *Boolean algebra* is also the basis of computer technology. His work greatly influenced ◊Frege and ◊Russell.

boom period in the ◊trade cycle when the economy is expanding and aggregate demand (total demand for goods and services) is rising quickly. It is characterized by falling or low unemployment but rising inflation.

Booth Charles 1840–1916. English sociologist,

author of the study *Life and Labour of the People in London* 1891–1903, and pioneer of an old-age pension scheme.

Booth William 1829–1912. British founder of the ◊Salvation Army 1878, and its first 'general'.

Born in Nottingham, the son of a builder, he experienced religious conversion at the age of 15. In 1865 he founded the Christian Mission in Whitechapel, E London, which became the Salvation Army 1878. *In Darkest England, and the Way Out* 1890 contained proposals for the physical and spiritual redemption of the many down-and-outs. His wife Catherine (1829–1890, born Mumford), whom he married 1855, became a public preacher about 1860, initiating the ministry of women. Their eldest son, **William Bramwell Booth** (1856–1929), became chief of staff of the Salvation Army 1880 and was general from 1912 until his deposition 1929. *Evangeline Booth* (1865–1950), seventh child of General William Booth, was a prominent Salvation Army officer, and 1934–39 was general. She became a US citizen.

Catherine Bramwell Booth (1884–1987), a granddaughter of William Booth, was a commissioner in the Salvation Army.

Bordet Jules 1870–1961. Belgian bacteriologist and immunologist who researched the role of blood serum in the human immune response. He was the first to isolate 1906 the whooping cough bacillus.

Born Max 1882–1970. German physicist who received a Nobel prize 1954 for fundamental work on the ◊quantum theory. He left Germany for the UK during the Nazi era.

Borromeo, St Carlo 1538–1584. Italian Roman Catholic saint and cardinal. He was instrumental in bringing the Council of Trent (1562–63) to a successful conclusion, and in drawing up the catechism that contained its findings. Feast day 4 Nov.

Born at Arona of a noble Italian family, Borromeo was created a cardinal and archbishop of Milan by his uncle Pope Pius IV 1560. He lived the life of an ascetic, and 1578 founded the community later called the Oblate Fathers of St Charles. He was canonized 1610.

Bosch Carl 1874–1940. German metallurgist and chemist. He developed Fritz ◊Haber's small-scale technique for the production of ammonia into an industrial high-pressure process that made use of water gas as a source of hydrogen. He shared the Nobel Prize for Chemistry 1931 with Friedrich Bergius.

Boscovich Ruggiero 1711–1787. Italian scientist. An early supporter of Newton, he developed a theory, popular in the 19th century, of the atom as a single point with surrounding fields of repulsive and attractive forces.

Bose Jagadis Chunder 1858–1937. Indian physicist and plant physiologist. Born near Dakha, he was professor of physical science at Calcutta 1885–1915, and studied the growth and minute movements of plants, and their reaction to electrical stimuli. He founded the Bose Research Institute, Calcutta.

Bose Satyendra Nath 1894–1974. Indian physicist who formulated the Bose–Einstein law of quantum mechanics with ◊Einstein which stated that more than one boson in a system (such as an atom) can possess the same energy state. A boson is an elementary particle whose spin can only take values that are whole numbers or zero. He was professor of physics at the University of Calcutta 1945–58.

Bothe Walther 1891–1957. German physicist who showed 1929 that the cosmic rays bombarding the Earth are composed not of photons but of more massive particles. Nobel Prize for Physics 1954.

Bourgeois Léon Victor Auguste 1851–1925. French politician. Entering politics as a Radical, he was prime minister in 1895, and later served in many cabinets. He was one of the pioneer advocates of the League of Nations. He was awarded the Nobel Peace Prize 1920.

How beastly the bourgeois is / Especially the male of the species.

bourgeoisie
D(avid) H(erbert) Lawrence, 1885–1930,
English writer.
'How Beastly the Bourgeois Is'

---

bourgeoisie (French) the middle classes. The French word originally meant 'the freemen of a borough'. It came to mean the whole class above the workers and peasants, and below the nobility. Bourgeoisie (and *bourgeois*) has also acquired a contemptuous sense, implying commonplace, philistine respectability. By socialists it is applied to the whole propertied class, as distinct from the proletariat.

The discreet charm of the bourgeoisie.

bourgeoisie
Buñuel, 1900–1983, Spanish film director.
Film title

Bowditch Nathaniel 1773–1838. US astronomer. He wrote *The New American Practical Navigator* 1802, having discovered many inaccuracies in the standard navigation guide of the day. His *Celestial Mechanics* 1829–39, was a translation of the first four volumes of French astronomer Pierre Laplace's *Traité de mécanique céleste* 1799–1825.

Born in Salem, Massachusetts, USA, Bowditch had little formal education but read widely as a merchant seaman during the years 1795–1803. In 1829 he became president of the American Academy of Arts and Sciences.

Bowlby John 1907–1990. English psychologist, honorary consultant to the Tavistock Clinic, London, and consultant in mental health for the World Health Organization (WHO) 1972–90. In his book *Child Care and the Growth of Love* 1953, an abridged version for the general reader of his report for the World Health Organization, *Maternal Care and Mental Health* 1951, he argued that a home environment for children is preferable to an institution, and stressed the bond between mother and child.

Boyle Charles, 4th Earl of Orrery 1676–1731. Irish soldier and diplomat. The *orrery*, a mechanical model of the solar system in which the planets move at the correct relative velocities, is named after him.

Boyle Robert 1627–1691. Irish physicist and chemist who published the seminal *The Sceptical Chymist* 1661. He formulated *Boyle's law* 1662.

He was the first chemist to collect a sample of gas, was one of the founders of the Royal Society, and endowed the Boyle Lectures for the defence of Christianity.

Boyle's law law stating that the volume of a given mass of gas at a constant temperature is inversely proportional to its pressure. For example, if the pressure of a gas doubles, its volume will be reduced by a half, and vice versa. The law was discovered in 1662 by Irish physicist and chemist Robert Boyle.

Bracton Henry de, died 1268. English judge, writer on English law, and chancellor of Exeter cathedral from 1264. The account of the laws and customs of the English attributed to Henry de Bracton, *De Legibus et consuetudinibus Anglie/The Laws and Customs of England*, the first of its kind, was not in fact written by him.

Bradley Francis Herbert 1846–1924. British philosopher who, influenced by ◊Hegel, argued for absolute idealism – the theory that there is only one ultimately real thing, the Absolute, which is spiritual in nature. In ethics, he attacked the ◊utilitarianism of J S ◊Mill.

His works include *Ethical Studies* 1876, *Principles of Logic* 1883, *Appearance and Reality* 1893, and *Truth and Reality* 1914.

Bradley James 1693–1762. English astronomer who in 1728 discovered the aberration of starlight. From the amount of aberration in star positions, he was able to calculate the speed of light. In 1748, he announced the discovery of nutation (variation in the Earth's axial tilt).

Bragg William Henry 1862–1942. British physicist. In 1915 he shared with his son *(William) Lawrence Bragg* (1890–1971) the Nobel Prize for Physics for their research work on X-rays and crystals.

Brahe Tycho 1546–1601. Danish astronomer who made accurate observations of the planets from which the German astronomer and mathematician Johann ◊Kepler proved that planets orbit the Sun in ellipses. His discovery and report of the 1572 supernova brought him recognition, and his observations of the comet of 1577 proved that it moved on an orbit among the planets, thus disproving the Greek view that comets were in the Earth's atmosphere.

Brahe was a colourful figure who wore a false nose after his own was cut off in a duel, and who took an interest in alchemy. In 1576 Frederick II of Denmark gave him the island of Hven, where he set up an observatory. Brahe was the greatest observer in the days before telescopes, making the most accurate measurements of the positions of stars and planets. He moved to Prague as imperial mathematician in 1599, where he was joined by Kepler, who inherited his observations when he died.

Brahma in Hinduism, the creator of the cosmos, who forms with ◊Vishnu and ◊Siva the Trimurti, or three aspects of the godhead, or absolute spirit.

In the Hindu creation myth, Brahma is born from the unfolding lotus flower that grows out of Vishnu's navel; after Brahma creates the world, Vishnu wakes and governs it for the duration of the cosmic cycle *kalpa*, the 'day of Brahma', which lasts for 4,200 million earthly years. Unlike Brahman, which is an impersonal principle and of neuter gender, Brahma is a personified god and of masculine gender.

brahmacari in Hinduism, a young man leading a life of disciplined religious study. In student life, the boy lives austerely in the ◊ashram (religious community) of his guru as a brahmacari, studying the Vedic literatures and begging for alms. In Hindu tradition the vow of brahmacari (celibacy) aids yogic practice and is sometimes maintained throughout life.

Brahman in Hinduism, the supreme being, an abstract, impersonal world-soul into whom the ◊atman, or individual soul, will eventually be absorbed when its cycle of rebirth is ended.

Brahmanism earliest stage in the development of ◊Hinduism. Its sacred scriptures are the ◊Vedas, with their accompanying literature of comment and explanation known as Brahmanas, Aranyakas, and ◊Upanishads.

Brahma Samaj Indian monotheistic religious movement, founded 1828 in Calcutta by ◊Ram Mohun Roy who attempted to recover the simple worship of the Vedas and purify and rationalize Hinduism. The movement had split into a number of sects by the end of the 19th century and is now almost defunct.

Braithwaite Richard Bevan 1900–1990. British philosopher, physicist, and mathematician. Though mainly a philosopher of science, he also tried to give an empiricist account of religious belief as belief in morally uplifting stories and to put moral choice on a rational basis by applying the mathematical theory of games to situations of moral conflict. He was professor of moral philosophy at Cambridge 1953–67.

Brandt Willy. Adopted name of Karl Herbert Frahm 1913–1992. German socialist politician, federal chancellor (premier) of West Germany 1969–74. He played a key role in the remoulding of the Social Democratic Party (SPD) as a moderate socialist force (leader 1964–87). As mayor of West Berlin 1957–66, Brandt became internationally known during the Berlin Wall crisis 1961. He chaired the ◊Brandt Commission on Third World problems 1977–83 and was a member of the European Parliament 1979–83. Nobel Peace Prize 1971.

Brandt, born in Lübeck, changed his name when he fled to Norway 1933 and became active in the anti-Nazi resistance. He returned 1945 and entered the Bundestag (federal parliament) 1949. In the 'grand coalition' 1966–69 he served as foreign minister and introduced *Ostpolitik*, a policy of reconciliation between East and West Europe, which was continued when he became federal chancellor 1969, and culminated in the 1972 signing of the Basic Treaty with East Germany.

Brandt Commission officially the Independent Commission on International Development Issues, established 1977 and chaired by the former West German chancellor Willy ◊Brandt. Consisting of 18 eminent persons acting independently of governments, the commission examined the problems of developing countries and sought to identify corrective measures that would command international support. It was disbanded 1983.

Its main report, published 1980 under the title *North–South: A Programme for Survival*, made detailed recommendations for accelerating the development of poorer countries (involving the transfer of resources to the latter from the rich countries).

Brattain Walter Houser 1902–1987. US physicist. In 1956 he was awarded a Nobel prize jointly with William ◊Shockley and John ◊Bardeen for their work on the development of the transistor, which replaced the comparatively costly and clumsy vacuum tube in electronics.

Braudel Fernand 1902–1985. French historian. While in a German prisoner-of-war camp during World War II he wrote *La Mediterranée et le monde mediterranéen à l'époque de Philippe II/The Mediterranean and the Mediterranean World in the Age of Philip II*, a work which revolutionized the writing of history by taking a global view of long-term trends.

Braudel taught in Algeria and Brazil before returning to France in 1938. He became a professor at the Collège de France (1949–72) and a leading member of the Annales school, editing the journal *Annales d'histoire économique et sociale*. During this period, he published extensively and championed the ideas of using the social sciences and problem-based research as a means of historical enquiry.

Food comes first, then morals.

Bertolt Brecht
Dreigroschenoper (Threepenny Opera)

Brecht Bertolt 1898–1956. German dramatist and poet, one of the most influential figures in 20th-century theatre. A committed Marxist, he sought to develop an 'epic theatre' which aimed to destroy the 'suspension of disbelief' usual in the theatre and so encourage audiences to develop an active and critical attitude to a play's subject. He adapted John Gay's *Beggar's Opera* as *Die Dreigroschenoper/*

The Threepenny Opera 1928, set to music by Kurt Weill. Later plays include *Mutter Courage/Mother Courage* 1941, set during the Thirty Years' War, and *Der kaukasische Kreidekreis/The Caucasian Chalk Circle* 1949.

As an anti-Nazi, he left Germany in 1933 for Scandinavia and the US. He became an Austrian citizen after World War II; in 1949 he established the Berliner Ensemble theatre group in East Germany. His other works include *Galileo* 1938, *Der gute Mensch von Setzuan/The Good Woman of Setzuan* 1943, and *Der aufhaltsame Aufstieg der Arturo Ui/The Preventable Rise of Arturo Ui* 1958.

Brenner Sidney 1927– . South African scientist, one of the pioneers of genetic engineering. Brenner discovered messenger RNA (a link between DNA and the ribosomes in which proteins are synthesized) 1960.

Brenner first studied medicine, moved into molecular biology at Oxford University and later settled at Cambridge. He worked for many years with Francis ◊Crick, doing much research on nematode worms.

Brentano Franz 1838–1916. German-Austrian philosopher and psychologist whose *Psychology from the Empirical Standpoint* 1874 developed the theory that mental phenomena can be identified as those which have ◊'intentionality' – that is, have an object within themselves. For example, fear is always fear of something and joy or sorrow are always about something.

Breton André 1896–1966. French author and poet, founder and theorist of ◊Surrealism. As one of the leaders of the ◊Dada art movement, he wrote (with Philippe Soupault) *Les Champs Magnetiques/Magnetic Fields* 1921, an experiment in automatic writing. He soon turned to Surrealism, publishing *Le Manifeste de surréalisme/Surrealist Manifesto* 1924. Influenced both by communism and Freud's theories, Breton believed that both on a personal and a political level surrealist techniques could shatter the inhibiting order and propriety of the conscious mind (bourgeois society) and release deep reserves of creative energy. Other works include *Najda* 1928, the story of his love affair with a medium.

Bretton Woods township in New Hampshire, USA, where the United Nations Monetary and Financial Conference was held in 1944 to discuss postwar international payments problems. The agreements reached on financial assistance and measures to stabilize exchange rates led to the creation of the International Bank for Reconstruction and Development in 1945 and the International Monetary Fund (IMF).

Breuer Josef 1842–1925. Viennese physician who conducted important research on the semi-circular canals in the ear and on the nervous control of breathing but is best known for his pioneering use of ◊hypnosis in treating ◊hysteria and his early collaboration with ◊Freud. One of the most famous case studies in the history of ◊psychoanalysis is that of Breuer's patient, Fräulein Anna O. (Her real name was Berthe Pappenheim. She later became famous as a social worker in Germany.) Breuer treated her bizarre hysterical symptoms by what she called their 'talking cue' or 'chimney sweeping', in which under hypnosis she would give her hallucinations and imaginings verbal expression. Breuer succeeded in getting her to recall traumatic incidents associated with her symptoms which she then 'talked away'. This method of employing ◊catharsis to diminish or reverse symptoms led to the beginnings of psychoanalysis. It is reported in Breuer's joint publication with Freud *Studien über Hysterie/Studies in Hysteria* 1895.

breviary in the Roman Catholic Church, the book of instructions for reciting the daily services. It is usually in four volumes, one for each season.

Brewster David 1781–1868. Scottish physicist who made discoveries about the diffraction and polarization of light, and invented the kaleidoscope.

Brezhnev Doctrine Soviet doctrine 1968 designed to justify the invasion of Czechoslovakia. It laid down for the USSR as a duty the direct maintenance of 'correct' socialism in countries within the Soviet sphere of influence. In 1979 it was extended, by the invasion of Afghanistan, to the direct establishment of 'correct' socialism in countries not already within its sphere. The doctrine was renounced by Mikhail ◊Gorbachev in 1989. Soviet troops were withdrawn from Afghanistan and the satellite states of E Europe were allowed to decide their own forms of government, with noncommunist and 'reform communist' governments being established from Sept 1989.

bridewealth or *brideprice* goods or property presented by a man's family to his prospective wife's as part of the marriage agreement. It was the usual practice among many societies in Africa, Asia, and the Pacific, and among many American Indian groups. In most

European and S Asian countries the alternative custom was ◊dowry.

Bridewealth is regarded as compensation to the woman's family for giving her away in marriage, and it usually means that the children she bears will belong to her husband's family group rather than her own. It may require a large amount of valuables such as livestock, shell items, or cash.

Bridgman Percy Williams 1882–1961. US physicist. His research into machinery producing high pressure led in 1955 to the creation of synthetic diamonds by General Electric. He was awarded the Nobel Prize for Physics 1946.

Born in Cambridge, Massachusetts, he was educated at Harvard, where he was Hollis Professor of Mathematics and Natural Philosophy 1926–50 and Higgins university professor 1950–54.

Broad Charles Dunbar 1887–1971. British philosopher, who appreciated the importance of science and psychology. His books include *Perception, Physics and Reality* 1914, and *Lectures on Psychic Research* 1962, discussing scientific evidence for survival after death.

Born in London, he was educated at Trinity College, Cambridge, and was Knightbridge professor of moral philosophy at the university 1933–53.

Broglie Louis de, 7th Duc de Broglie 1892–1987. French theoretical physicist. He established that all subatomic particles can be described either by particle equations or by wave equations, thus laying the foundations of wave mechanics. He was awarded the 1929 Nobel Prize for Physics.

Broglie Maurice de, 6th Duc de Broglie 1875–1960. French physicist. He worked on X-rays and gamma rays, and helped to establish the Einsteinian description of light in terms of photons. He was the brother of Louis de Broglie.

Brown Robert 1773–1858. Scottish botanist, best known today for his discovery 1827 of *Brownian movement*. As a botanist, his more lasting work was in the field of plant morphology. He was the first to establish the real basis for the distinction between gymnosperms (pines) and angiosperms (flowering plants).

Browne Robert 1550–1633. English Puritan leader, founder of the Brownists. He founded communities in Norwich, East Anglia, and in the Netherlands which developed into present-day ◊Congregationalism.

Browne, born in Stamford, Lincolnshire, preached in Norwich and then retired to Middelburg in the Netherlands, but returned after making his peace with the church and became master of Stamford Grammar School. In a work published in 1582 Browne advocated Congregationalist doctrine; he was imprisoned several times in 1581–82 for attacking Episcopalianism (church government by bishops). From 1591 he was a rector in Northamptonshire.

Browne Thomas 1605–1682. English author and physician. Born in London, he travelled widely in Europe before settling in Norwich 1637. His works display a richness of style as in *Religio Medici/The Religion of a Doctor* 1643, a justification of his profession; *Vulgar Errors* 1646, an examination of popular legend and superstition; *Urn Burial* and *The Garden of Cyrus* 1658; and *Christian Morals*, published posthumously in 1717.

Brüderhof Christian Protestant group with beliefs similar to the ◊Mennonites. They live in groups of families (single persons are assigned to a family), marry only within the Brüderhof (divorce is not allowed), and retain a 'modest' dress for women (cap or headscarf, and long skirts). In the USA they are known as Hutterites.

Originally established in Moravia, there are Brüderhof communities in the USA, and in Robertsbridge, E Sussex, UK; they support themselves by making children's toys.

Brunelleschi Filippo 1377–1446. Italian Renaissance architect. The first and one of the greatest of the Renaissance architects, he pioneered the scientific use of perspective. He was responsible for the construction of the dome of Florence Cathedral (completed 1438), a feat deemed impossible by many of his contemporaries. His use of simple geometries and a modified Classical language lend his buildings a feeling of tranquillity, to which many other early Renaissance architects aspired. His other works include the Ospedale degli Innocenti 1419 and the Pazzi Chapel 1429, both in Florence.

Bruno Giordano 1548–1600. Italian philosopher. He entered the Dominican order of monks 1563, but his sceptical attitude to Catholic doctrines forced him to flee Italy 1577. After visiting Geneva and Paris, he lived in England 1583–85, where he wrote some of his finest works. Drawing both on contemporary science (in particular the theories of Copernicus) and also on magic and esoteric wisdom, he developed a radical form of pantheism in which all things are aspects of a single, infinite reality animated by God as the 'world-soul'. He was arrested by the ◊Inquisition 1593 in Venice and burned at the stake for his adoption of Copernican astronomy and his heretical religious views. His views had a profound influence on Spinoza and Leibniz.

Brutalism architectural style of the 1950s and 1960s that evolved from the work of ◊Le Corbusier and Mies van der Rohe. Uncompromising in its approach, it stresses functionalism and honesty to materials; steel and concrete are favoured. The term was coined by Alison and Peter ◊Smithson who developed the style in the UK.

The Smithsons' design for Hunstanton School, Norfolk 1949–54, recalls the work of van der Rohe but is more brutally honest, exposing all of the services to view. The Park Hill Housing Estate, Sheffield 1961, by Jack Lynn and Ivor Smith makes use of the rough concrete (*béton brut*) characteristic of Le Corbusier's later work.

Buber Martin 1878–1965. Austrian-born Israeli philosopher, a Zionist and advocate of the reappraisal of ancient Jewish thought in contemporary terms. His book *I and Thou* 1923 posited a direct dialogue between the individual and God; it had great impact on Christian and Jewish theology. When forced by the Nazis to abandon a professorship in comparative religion at Frankfurt, he went to Jerusalem and taught social philosophy at the Hebrew University 1937–51.

Bucer Martin 1491–1551. German Protestant reformer, Regius professor of divinity at Cambridge University from 1549, who tried to reconcile the views of his fellow Protestants ◊Luther and ◊Zwingli with the significance of the eucharist.

Buchanan George 1506–1582. Scottish humanist. Forced to flee to France 1539 owing to some satirical verses on the Franciscans, he returned to Scotland about 1562 as tutor to Mary, Queen of Scots. He became principal of St Leonard's College, St Andrews 1566, and wrote *Rerum Scoticarum Historia/A History of Scotland* 1582, which was biased against Mary, Queen of Scots.

Buchner Eduard 1860–1917. German chemist who researched the process of fermentation. In 1897 he observed that fermentation could be produced mechanically, by cell-free extracts. Buchner argued that it was not the whole yeast cell that produced fermentation, but only the presence of the enzyme he named zymase. Nobel prize 1907.

Buddha 'enlightened one', title of Prince *Gautama Siddhārtha* c. 563–483 BC. Religious leader, founder of Buddhism, born at Lumbini in Nepal. At the age of 29 he left his wife and son and a life of luxury, to escape from the material burdens of existence. After six years of austerity he realized that ◊asceticism, like overindulgence, was futile, and chose the middle way of ◊meditation. He became enlightened under a bo, or bodhi tree near ◊Buddh Gaya. He began teaching at Varanasi, and founded the ◊Sangha, or order of monks. He spent the rest of his life travelling around N India, and died at Kusinagara in Uttar Pradesh.

Buddh Gaya village in Bihar, India, where Gautama became the ◊Buddha while sitting beneath a bo (*bodhi* 'wisdom') tree; a descendant of the original tree is preserved.

Buddhism one of the great world religions, which originated in India about 500 BC. It derives from the teaching of the ◊Buddha, who is regarded as one of a series of such enlightened beings; there are no gods. The Buddha's teaching consisted of the ◊Four Noble Truths: the fact of frustration or suffering; that suffering has a cause; that it can be ended; and that it can be ended by following the Noble Eightfold Path – right views, right intention, right speech, right action, right livelihood, right effort, right mindfulness, and right concentration – eventually arriving at nirvana, the extinction of all craving for things of the senses and release from the cycle of rebirth and ◊karma.

The main divisions in Buddhism are *Theravāda* (or Hīnayāna) in SE Asia and *Mahāyāna* in N Asia; *Lamaism* in Tibet and *Zen* in Japan are among the many Mahāyāna sects. There are over 300 million Buddhists worldwide.

scriptures The only complete canon of the Buddhist scriptures is that of the Sinhalese (Sri Lanka) Buddhists, in Pāli, but other schools have essentially the same canon in Sanskrit. The scriptures, known as ◊Tripitakas ('three baskets'), date from the 2nd to 6th centuries AD. There are three divisions: *vinaya* (discipline), listing rules of life; the sūtras (discourse), or *dharma* (doctrine), the exposition of Buddhism by the Buddha and his disciples; and *abhidharma* (further doctrine), later discussions on doctrine.

beliefs The self is not regarded as permanent, as it is subject to change and decay. It is attachment to the things that are essentially impermanent that causes delusion, suffering, greed, and aversion, the origin of karma, and they in turn create further karma and the sense of self is reinforced. Actions which incline towards selflessness are called 'skillful karma' and they are on the path leading to enlightenment. In the **Four Noble Truths** the Buddha acknowledged the existence and source of suffering, and showed the way of deliverance from it through the **Eightfold Path**. The aim of following the Eightfold Path is to break the chain of karma and achieve dissociation from the body by attaining *nirvana* ('extinguishing') the eradication of all desires, either in annihilation or by absorption of the self in the infinite. Supreme reverence is accorded to the historical Buddha (Śākyamuni, or, when referred to by his clan name, Gautama), who is seen as one in a long and ongoing line of Buddhas, the next one (Maitreya) being due c. AD 3000.

Theravāda Buddhism, the School of the Elders, also known as **Hīnayāna** or Lesser Vehicle, prevails in SE Asia (Sri Lanka, Thailand, and Myanmar), and emphasizes the mendicant, meditative life as the way to break the cycle of *samsāra*, or death and rebirth. Its three alternative goals are *arahat*: one who has gained insight into the true nature of things; *Paccekabuddha*, an enlightened one who lives alone and does not teach; and fully awakened *Buddha*. Its scriptures are written in Pāli, an Indo-Aryan language with its roots in N India. In India itself Buddhism had virtually died out by the 13th century, and was replaced by Hinduism. However, there are now about 5 million Buddhists in India and the number is growing.

Mahāyāna Buddhism, or Greater Vehicle arose at the beginning of the Christian era. This tradition emphasized the eternal, formless principle of the Buddha as the essence of all things. It exhorts the individual not merely to attain personal nirvana, but to become a trainee Buddha, or *bodhisattva*, and so save others; this meant the faithful could be brought to enlightenment by a bodhisattva without following the austerities of Theravāda, and the cults of various Buddhas and bodhisattvas arose. Mahāyāna Buddhism also emphasizes *shunyata*, or the experiential understanding of the emptiness of all things, even Buddhist doctrine.

Mahāyāna Buddhism prevails in N Asia (China, Korea, Japan, and Tibet). In the 6th century AD Mahāyāna spread to China with the teachings of the Indian monk Bodhidharma and formed Ch'an, which became established in Japan from the 12th century as **Zen Buddhism**. Zen emphasizes silent meditation with sudden interruptions from a master to encourage awakening of the mind. Japan also has the lay organization **Sōka Gakkai** (Value Creation Society), founded 1930, which equates absolute faith with immediate material benefit; by the 1980s it was followed by more than 7 million households.

Esoteric, Tantric, or **Diamond Buddhism** became popular in Tibet and Japan, and holds that enlightenment is already within the disciple and with the proper guidance (that is privately passed on by a master) can be realized.

budget estimate of income and expenditure for some future period, used in financial planning.

National budgets set out estimates of government income and expenditure and generally include projected changes in taxation and growth. Interim budgets are not uncommon, in particular, when dramatic changes in economic conditions occur. Governments will sometimes construct a budget deficit or surplus as part of macroeconomic policy.

Genius is only a great aptitude for patience.

Buffon
Attributed remark

Buffon George Louis Leclerc, Comte de 1707–1778. French naturalist and author of the 18th century's most significant work of natural history, the 44-volume *Histoire naturelle* (1749–67). In *The Epochs of Nature*, one of the volumes, he questioned biblical chronology for the first time, and raised the Earth's age from the traditional figure of 6,000 years to the seemingly colossal estimate of 75,000 years.

Bukharin Nikolai Ivanovich 1888–1938. Soviet politician and theorist. A moderate, he was the chief Bolshevik thinker after Lenin. Executed on Stalin's orders for treason 1938, he was posthumously rehabilitated 1988.

He wrote the major defence of war communism in his *Economics of the Transition Period* 1920. He drafted the Soviet constitution of 1936 but in 1938 was imprisoned and tried for treason in one of Stalin's 'show trials'. He pleaded guilty to treason, but defended his moderate policies and denied criminal charges. Nevertheless, he was executed, as were all other former members of Lenin's Politburo except ◊Trotsky, who was murdered, and ◊Stalin himself.

bulimia an eating disorder in which large amounts of food are consumed in a short time ('binge') usually followed by depression and self-criticism. The term is often used for **bulimia nervosa**, an emotional disorder in which eating is followed by deliberate vomiting and purging. This may be a chronic stage in ◊anorexia nervosa.

bull or **papal bull** document or edict issued by the pope; so called from the circular seals (medieval Latin *bulla*) attached to them. Some of the most celebrated bulls include Leo X's condemnation of Luther 1520 and Pius IX's proclamation of papal infallibility 1870.

Bull John. Imaginary figure personifying England.

A castle, called Doubting-Castle, the owner whereof was Giant Despair.

John Bunyan
The Pilgrim's Progress

Bunyan John 1628–1688. English author. A Baptist, he was imprisoned in Bedford 1660–72 for unlicensed preaching. During a second jail sentence 1675 he started to write *The Pilgrim's Progress*, the first part of which was published 1678. The fervour and imagination of this allegorical story of Christian's spiritual quest has ensured its continued popularity. Other works include *Grace Abounding* 1666, *The Life and Death of Mr Badman* 1680, and *The Holy War* 1682.

At 16, during the Civil War, he was conscripted into the Parliamentary army. Released 1646, he passed through a period of religious doubt before joining the ◊Baptists 1653. In 1660 he was committed to Bedford county jail for preaching, where he remained for 12 years, refusing all offers of release conditional on his not preaching again. During his confinement he wrote *Grace Abounding* describing his early spiritual struggles. Set free 1672, he was elected pastor of the Bedford congregation, but in 1675 he was again arrested and imprisoned for six months in the jail on Bedford Bridge, where he began *The Pilgrim's Progress*. The book was an instant success, and a second part followed 1684.

Burckhardt Jacob Christoph 1818–1897. Swiss art historian, professor of history at Basel University 1858–93, one of the founders of cultural history as a discipline. His *The Civilization of the Renaissance in Italy* 1860, intended as part of a study of world cultural history, profoundly influenced thought on the Renaissance.

bureaucracy organization whose structure and operations are governed to a high degree by written rules and a hierarchy of offices; in its broadest sense, all forms of administration, and in its narrowest, rule by officials.

The early civilizations of Mesopotamia, Egypt, China, and India were organized hierarchically, thus forming the bureaucratic tradition of government. The German sociologist Max ◊Weber saw the growth of bureaucracy in industrial societies as an inevitable reflection of the underlying shift from traditional authority to a rational and legal system of organization and control. In Weber's view, bureaucracy established a relation between legally enstated authorities and their subordinate officials. This relationship is characterized by defined rights and duties prescribed in written regulations.

Contemporary writers have highlighted the problems of bureaucracy, such as its inflexibility and rigid adherence to rules, so that today the term is often used as a criticism rather than its original neutral sense.

The greater the power, the more dangerous the abuse.

Edmund Burke
Speech on the Middlesex Election 1771

Burke Edmund 1729–1797. British Whig politician and political theorist, born in Dublin, Ireland. In Parliament from 1765, he opposed the government's attempts to coerce the American colonists, for example in *Thoughts on the Present Discontents* 1770, and supported the emancipation of Ireland, but denounced the French Revolution, for example in *Reflections on the Revolution in France* 1790.

Burke wrote *A Philosophical Inquiry into the Origin of our Ideas on the Sublime and Beautiful* 1756, on aesthetics. He was paymaster of the forces in Rockingham's government 1782 and in the Fox–North coalition 1783, and after the collapse of the latter spent the rest of his career in opposition. He attacked Warren Hastings's misgovernment in India and promoted his impeachment. Burke defended his inconsistency in supporting the American but not the French Revolution in his *Appeal from the New* to the Old Whigs 1791 and *Letter to a Noble Lord* 1796, and attacked the suggestion of peace with France in *Letters on a Regicide Peace* 1795–97. He retired 1794. He was a skilled orator and is regarded by British Conservatives as the greatest of their political theorists.

Better to be despised for too anxious apprehensions, than ruined by too confident a security.

Edmund Burke
Reflections on the Revolution in France

Burnell (Susan) Jocelyn (Bell) 1943–
British astronomer. In 1967 she discovered the first pulsar (rapidly flashing star) with Antony ◊Hewish and colleagues at Cambridge University, England.

Burnet Macfarlane 1899–1985. Australian physician, an authority on immunology and viral diseases. He was awarded the Order of Merit 1958 in recognition of his work on such diseases as influenza, poliomyelitis, and cholera, and shared the 1960 Nobel Prize for Medicine with Peter Medawar for his work on skin grafting.

Burnham James 1905–1987. US philosopher who argued in *The Managerial Revolution* 1941 that world control is passing from politicians and capitalists to the new class of business executives, the managers.

Burt Cyril Lodowic 1883–1971. English psychologist, a specialist in mental development and educational psychology. He was appointed psychologist to the London County Council 1913, the first such appointment in Britain. From 1931 to 1950 he was professor of psychology at University College, London. In *The Young Delinquent* 1925 he put forward the view that the causes of delinquency are largely environmental ones such as overcrowding, broken homes, and so on. He did important research on the measurement of educational abilities and on statistical methods of studying intelligence and personality, reported in *The Factors of Mind* 1940. His work influenced educational policy in the UK, particularly in the formulation of the 1944 Education Act. His investigations of the inheritance of intelligence, which relied on data obtained from twins separated at birth or in early infancy, were discredited after his death by evidence that he had falsified the data.

All poets are mad.

Robert Burton
Anatomy of Melancholy

Burton Robert 1577–1640. English philosopher who wrote an analysis of depression, *Anatomy of Melancholy* 1621, a compendium of information on the medical and religious opinions of the time, much used by later authors.

Born in Leicester, he was educated at Oxford, and remained there for the rest of his life as a fellow of Christ Church.

bushido chivalric code of honour of the Japanese military caste, the ◊samurai. Bushido means 'the way of the warrior'; the code stresses simple living, self-discipline, and bravery.

Buss Frances Mary 1827–1894. British pioneer in education for women. She first taught in a school run by her mother, and at 18 she founded her own school for girls in London, which became the North London Collegiate School in 1850. She founded the Camden School for Girls in 1871.

Her work helped to raise the status of women teachers and the academic standard of women's education in the UK. She is often associated with Dorothea ◊Beale, a fellow pioneer.

Butler Joseph 1692–1752. English priest and theologian who became dean of St Paul's in 1740 and bishop of Durham in 1750; his *Analogy of Religion* 1736 argued that it is no more rational to accept ◊deism (arguing for God as the first cause) than revealed religion (not arrived at by reasoning).

Butler Josephine (born Gray) 1828–1906. English social reformer. She promoted women's education and the Married Women's Property Act, and campaigned against the Contagious Diseases Acts of 1862–70, which made women in garrison towns suspected of prostitution liable to compulsory examination for venereal disease. Refusal to undergo examination meant imprisonment. As a result of her campaigns the acts were repealed in 1883.

Butskellism UK term for political policies tending towards the middle ground in an effort to gain popular support; the term was coined 1954 after R A Butler (moderate Conservative) and Hugh Gaitskell (moderate Labour politician).

Byron Augusta Ada 1815–1851. English mathematician, a pioneer in writing programs for Charles ◊Babbage's analytical engine. In 1983 a new, high-level computer language, ADA, was named after her. She was the daughter of the poet Lord Byron.

cabbala alternative spelling of ◊kabbala.

cabinet in politics, the group of ministers holding a country's highest executive offices who decide government policy. In Britain the cabinet system originated under the Stuarts. Under William and Mary it became customary for the sovereign to select ministers from the party with a parliamentary majority. The US cabinet, unlike the British, does not initiate legislation, and its members, appointed by the president, must not be members of Congress.

In the USA a cabinet system developed early and the term was used from 1793. Members are selected by the president and confirmed by the senate. They may neither be members of Congress nor speak there, being responsible to the president alone.

The first British 'cabinet councils' or subcommittees of the Privy Council undertook special tasks. When George I ceased to attend cabinet meetings, the office of prime minister, not officially recognized until 1905, came into existence to provide a chair (Robert Walpole was the first). Cabinet members are chosen by the prime minister; policy is collective and the meetings are secret, minutes being taken by the secretary of the cabinet, a high civil servant. Secrecy has been infringed in recent years by 'leaks', or unauthorized disclosures to the press.

caesarism political system similar to ◊Bonapartism, involving dictatorship by an individual supported by the army or a popular movement. The outward trappings of democracy are maintained but manipulated. The term originates with the system created by Julius Caesar that undermined the Roman Republic in the 1st century BC.

Cage John 1912–1992. US composer. A pupil of Arnold ◊Schoenberg, he maintained that all sounds should be available for musical purposes; for example, he used 24 radios, tuned to random stations, in *Imaginary Landscape No 4* 1951. He also worked to reduce the control of the composer over the music, introducing randomness (◊aleatory music) and inexactitude and allowing sounds to 'be themselves'. Cage's unconventional ideas have had a profound impact on 20th-century music. His work includes *4 Minutes and 33 Seconds* 1952, in which the pianist sits at the piano reading a score for that length of time but does not play.

Cain in the Old Testament, the first-born son of Adam and Eve. Motivated by jealousy, he murdered his brother Abel because the latter's sacrifice was more acceptable to God than his own.

Caitanya 1486–1534. Principal leader in Bengal of the ◊Bhakti movement which revitalised medieval Hinduism. He inspired a mass movement of devotion for Krishna, especially through *sankirtan*, public singing of the name of God accompanied by dancing and musical instruments. (The modern Hare Krishna movement is descended from Caitanya).

calculus branch of mathematics that permits the manipulation of continuously varying quantities, used in practical problems involving such matters as changing speeds, problems of flight, varying stresses in the framework of a bridge, and alternating current theory. *Integral calculus* deals with the method of summation or adding together the effects of continuously varying quantities. *Differential calculus* deals in a similar way with rates of change. Many of its applications arose from the study of the gradients of the tangents to curves.

There are several other branches of calculus, including calculus of errors and calculus of variation. Differential and integral calculus, each of which deals with small quantities which during manipulation are made smaller and smaller, compose the *infinitesimal calculus*. *Differential equations* relate to the derivatives of a set of variables and may include the variables. Many give the mathematical models for physical phenomena such as simple harmonic motion. Differential equations are solved generally through integrative means, depending on their degrees. If no known mathematical processes are available, integration can be performed graphically or by computers.

history Calculus originated with Archimedes in the 3rd century BC as a method for finding the areas of curved shapes and for drawing tangents to curves. These ideas were not developed until the 17th century, when the French philosopher René Descartes introduced coordinate geometry, showing how geometrical curves can be described and manipulated by means of algebraic expressions. Then the French mathematician Pierre de Fermat used these algebraic forms in the early stages of the development of differentiation. Later the German philosopher Gottfried Leibniz and the English scientist Isaac Newton advanced the study.

calendar division of the year into months, weeks, and days and the method of ordering the years. From year one, an assumed date of the birth of Jesus, dates are calculated backwards (BC 'before Christ' or BCE 'before common era') and forwards (AD, Latin *anno Domini* 'in the year of the Lord', or CE 'common era'). The **lunar month** (period between one new moon and the next) naturally averages 29.5 days, but the Western calendar uses for convenience a **calendar month** with a complete number of days, 30 or 31 (Feb has 28). For adjustments, since there are slightly fewer than six extra hours a year left over, they are added to Feb as a 29th day every fourth year (**leap year**), century years being excepted unless they are divisible by 400. For example, 1896 was a leap year; 1900 was not. 1996 is the next leap year.

The **month names** in most European languages were probably derived as follows: January from Janus, Roman god; February from *Februar*, Roman festival of purification; March from Mars, Roman god; April from Latin *aperire*, 'to open'; May from Maia, Roman goddess; June from Juno, Roman goddess; July from Julius Caesar, Roman general; August from Augustus, Roman emperor; September, October, November, December (originally the seventh–tenth months) from the Latin words meaning seventh, eighth, ninth, and tenth, respectively.

The **days of the week** are Monday named after the Moon; Tuesday from Tiu or Tyr, Anglo-Saxon and Norse god; Wednesday from Woden or Odin, Norse god; Thursday from Thor, Norse god; Friday from Freya, Norse goddess; Saturday from Saturn, Roman god; and Sunday named after the Sun.

All early calendars except the ancient Egyptian were lunar. The word calendar comes from the Latin *Kalendae* or *calendae*, the first day of each month on which, in ancient Rome, solemn proclamation was made of the appearance of the new moon.

The **Western** or **Gregorian calendar** derives from the **Julian calendar** instituted by Julius Caesar 46 BC. It was adjusted by Pope Gregory XIII 1582, who eliminated the accumulated error caused by a faulty calculation of the length of a year and avoided its recurrence by restricting century leap years to those divisible by 400. Other states only gradually changed from Old Style to New Style; Britain and its colonies adopted the Gregorian calendar 1752, when the error amounted to 11 days, and 3 Sept 1752 became 14 Sept (at the same time the beginning of the year was put back from 25 March to 1 Jan). Russia did not adopt it until the October Revolution of 1917, so that the event (then 25 Oct) is currently celebrated 7 Nov.

The **Jewish calendar** is a complex combination of lunar and solar cycles, varied by considerations of religious observance. A year may have 12 or 13 months, each of which normally alternates between 29 and 30 days; the New Year (Rosh Hashanah) falls between 5 Sept and 5 Oct. The calendar dates from the hypothetical creation of the world (taken as 7 Oct 3761 BC).

The **Chinese calendar** is lunar, with a cycle of 60 years. Both the traditional and, from 1911, the Western calendar are in use in China.

The **Muslim calendar**, also lunar, has 12 months of alternately 30 and 29 days, and a year of 354 days. This results in the calendar rotating around the seasons in a 30-year cycle. The era is counted as beginning on the day Muhammad fled from Mecca AD 622.

Calliope in Greek mythology, the Muse of epic poetry, and so the most important of all the ◊Muses.

Calvary in the New Testament, the site of Jesus' crucifixion at Jerusalem. Two chief locations are suggested: the site where the Church of the Sepulchre now stands, and the hill beyond the Damascus gate.

Calvin John (also known as **Cauvin** or **Chauvin**) 1509–1564. French-born Swiss Protestant church reformer and theologian. He was a leader of the Reformation in Geneva and set up a strict religious community there. His theological system is known as Calvinism, and his church government as ◊Presbyterianism. Calvin wrote (in Latin) *Institutes of the Christian Religion* 1536 and commentaries on the New Testament and much of the Old Testament.

Calvin, born in Noyon, Picardie, studied theology and then law, and about 1533 became prominent in Paris as an evangelical preacher. In 1534 he was obliged to leave

Paris and retired to Basel, where he studied Hebrew. In 1536 he accepted an invitation to go to Geneva, Switzerland, and assist in the Reformation, but was expelled 1538 because of public resentment against the numerous and too drastic changes he introduced. He returned to Geneva 1541 and, in the face of strong opposition, established a rigorous ◊theocracy (government on religious principles). In 1553 he had the Spanish theologian ◊Servetus burned for heresy. He supported the Huguenots in their struggle in France and the English Protestants persecuted by Queen Mary I.

Calvin Melvin 1911– . US chemist who, using radioactive carbon-14 as a tracer, determined the biochemical processes of photosynthesis, in which green plants use chlorophyll to convert carbon dioxide and water into sugar and oxygen. Nobel prize 1961.

Calvinism Christian doctrine as interpreted by John Calvin and adopted in Scotland, parts of Switzerland, and the Netherlands; by the ◊Puritans in England and New England, USA; and by the subsequent Congregational and Presbyterian churches in the USA. Its central doctrine is predestination, under which certain souls (the elect) are predestined by God through the sacrifice of Jesus to salvation, and the rest to damnation. Although Calvinism is rarely accepted today in its strictest interpretation, the 20th century has seen a Neo-Calvinist revival through the work of Karl ◊Barth.

Cambridge Platonists group of 17th-century English philosophers and Puritan theologians, centred on Cambridge University. In opposing the materialism of their contemporary Thomas Hobbes, they drew on Platonic and neo-Platonic ideas, stressing in particular the individual's innate spiritual and moral nature. Its leading members included the theologian Benjamin Whichcote (1609–83), Ralph Cudworth and Henry ◊More.

Camelot legendary seat of King ◊Arthur.

Camorra Italian secret society formed about 1820 by criminals in the dungeons of Naples and continued once they were freed. It dominated politics from 1848, was suppressed 1911, but many members eventually surfaced in the US ◊Mafia. The Camorra still operates in the Naples area.

Camp behaving in an exaggerated and even self-parodying way, particularly in female impersonation and among homosexuals. British entertainers Kenneth Williams (1926–1987) and Julian Clary and the Australian Barry Humphries have used camp behaviour to comic effect.

Campaign for Nuclear Disarmament (CND) non party-political British organization advocating the abolition of nuclear weapons worldwide. CND seeks unilateral British initiatives to help start the multilateral process and end the arms race. It was founded 1958.

The movement was launched by the philosopher Bertrand Russell and Canon John Collins and grew out of the demonstration held outside the government's Atomic Weapons Research Establishment at Aldermaston, Berkshire, at Easter 1956. CND held annual marches from Aldermaston to London 1959–63, after the initial march in 1958 which was routed from London to Aldermaston. From 1970 CND has also opposed nuclear power. Its membership peaked in the early 1980s, during the campaign against the presence of US Pershing and cruise nuclear missiles on British soil.

You know what charm is: a way of getting the answer yes without having asked any clear question.

Albert Camus
The Fall

Camus Albert 1913–1960. Algerian-born French writer. A journalist in France, he was active in the Resistance during World War II. His writings, such as *L'Etranger/The Outsider* 1942 and *Le Mythe de Sisyphe/The Myth of Sisyphus* 1943, owe much to ◊existentialism in their emphasis on the absurdity and arbitrariness of life. However his criticism of communism in *L'Homme Revolté/The Rebel* 1951 led to a protracted quarrel with ◊Sartre. He was awarded the Nobel Prize for Literature 1957.

Canaan ancient region between the Mediterranean and the Dead Sea, called in the Bible the 'Promised Land' of the Israelites. It was occupied as early as the 3rd millennium BC by the Canaanites, a Semitic-speaking people who were known to the Greeks of the 1st millennium BC as Phoenicians. The capital was Ebla (now Tell Mardikh, Syria).

The Canaanite Empire included Syria, Palestine, and part of Mesopotamia. It was conquered by the Israelites during the 13th to 10th centuries BC. Ebla was excavated 1976–77, revealing an archive of inscribed tablets dating from the 3rd millennium BC, which includes place names such as Gaza and Jerusalem (no excavations at the latter had suggested occupation at so early a date).

Candide satire by ◊Voltaire, published 1759. The hero experiences extremes of fortune in the company of Dr Pangloss, a personification of the popular belief of the time (partly based on a misunderstanding of ◊Leibniz) that 'all is for the best in the best of all possible worlds'. Voltaire exuberantly demonstrates that this idea is absurd and inhumane.

Candlemas in the Christian church, the Feast of the Purification of the Blessed Virgin Mary and the Presentation of the Infant Christ in the Temple, celebrated on 2 Feb; church candles are blessed on this day.

cannibalism or **anthropophagy** the practice of eating human flesh. The name is derived from the Caribs, a South American and West Indian people, alleged by the conquering Spaniards to eat their captives.

Cannon Annie Jump 1863–1941. US astronomer who, from 1896, worked at Harvard College Observatory and carried out revolutionary work on the classification of stars by examining their spectra. Her system, still used today, has spectra arranged according to temperature and runs from O through B, A, F, G, K, and M. O-type stars are the hottest, with surface temperatures of over 25,000 K.

canon in theology, the collection of writings that is accepted as authoritative in a given religion, such as the *Tripitaka* in Theravāda Buddhism. In the Christian church, it comprises the books of the ◊Bible.

The canon of the Old Testament was drawn up at the assembly of rabbis held at Jamnia in Palestine between AD 90 and 100; certain excluded books were included in the ◊Apocrypha. The earliest list of New Testament books is known as the Muratorian Canon (about 160–70). Bishop Athanasius promulgated a list (c. 365) which corresponds with that in modern Bibles.

canonical hours in the Catholic church, seven set periods of devotion: *matins* and *lauds*, *prime*, *terce*, *sext*, *nones*, *evensong* or *vespers*, and *compline*.

In the Anglican church, it is the period 8 a.m.–6 p.m. within which marriage can be legally performed in a parish church without a special licence.

canonization in the Catholic church, the admission of one of its members to the Calendar of ◊Saints. The evidence of the candidate's exceptional piety is contested before the Congregation for the Causes of Saints by the Promotor Fidei, popularly known as the *devil's advocate*. Papal ratification of a favourable verdict results in ◊beatification, and full sainthood (conferred in St Peter's basilica, the Vatican) follows after further proof.

Under a system laid down mainly in the 17th century, the process of investigation was seldom completed in under 50 years, although in the case of a martyr it took less time. Since 1969 the gathering of the proof of the candidate's virtues has been left to the bishop of the birthplace, and, miracles being difficult to substantiate, stress is placed on extraordinary 'favours' or 'graces' that can be proved or attested by serious investigation.

Many recent saints have come from the Third World where the expansion of the Catholic church is most rapid, for example the American Mohawk Indian Kateri Tekakwitha (died 1680), beatified 1980.

canon law rules and regulations of the Christian church, especially the Greek Orthodox, Roman Catholic, and Anglican churches. Its origin is sought in the declarations of Jesus and the apostles. In 1983 Pope John Paul II issued a new canon law code reducing offences carrying automatic excommunication, extending the grounds for annulment of marriage, removing the ban on marriage with non-Catholics, and banning trade union and political activity by priests.

The earliest compilations were in the East, and the canon law of the Eastern Orthodox Church is comparatively small. Through the centuries, a great mass of canon law was accumulated in the Western church which, in 1918, was condensed in the *Corpus juris canonici* under Benedict XV. Even so, this is supplemented by many papal decrees.

The canon law of the Church of England remained almost unchanged from 1603 until it was completely revised 1969, and is kept under constant review by the Canon Law Commission of the General Synod.

Canterbury historic cathedral city in Kent, England, on the river Stour, 100 km/62 mi SE of London; population (1984) 39,000. In 597 King Ethelbert welcomed ◊Augustine's mission to England here, and the city has since been the metropolis of the Anglican Communion and seat of the archbishop of Canterbury.

The Roman *Durovernum*, Canterbury was the Saxon capital of Kent. The present name derives from *Cantwarabyrig* (Old English 'fortress of the men of Kent').

Cantor Georg 1845–1918. German mathematician who followed his work on number theory and trigonometry by considering the foundations of mathematics. He defined real numbers and produced a treatment of irrational numbers using a series of transfinite numbers. Cantor's set theory has been used in the development of topology and real function theory.

capacity in economics, the maximum amount that can be produced when all the resources in an economy, industry, or firm are employed as fully as possible. Capacity constraints can be caused by lack of investment and skills shortages, and spare capacity can be caused by lack of demand.

capital in economics, the stock of goods used in the production of other goods. *Fixed capital* is durable, examples being factories, offices, plant, and machinery. *Circulating capital* is capital that is used up quickly, such as raw materials, components, and stocks of finished goods waiting for sale. *Private capital* is usually owned by individuals and private business organizations. *Social capital* is usually owned by the state and is the ◊infrastructure of the economy, such as roads, bridges, schools, and hospitals. Investment is the process of adding to the capital stock of a nation or business. *Financial capital* is accumulated or inherited wealth held in the form of assets, such as stocks and shares, property, and bank deposits.

capitalism economic system in which the principal means of production, distribution, and exchange are in private (individual or corporate) hands and competitively operated for profit. A ◊mixed economy combines the private enterprise of capitalism and a degree of state monopoly, as in nationalized industries and welfare services. Most capitalist economies are actually mixed economies, but some (such as the US and Japanese) have a greater share of the economy devoted to ◊free enterprise.

I think that Capitalism, wisely managed, can probably be made more efficient for attaining economic ends than any alternative system yet in sight, but that in itself it is in many ways extremely objectionable.

capitalism
John Maynard Keynes, 1st Baron Keynes, 1883–1946, English economist, whose *The General Theory of Employment, Interest, and Money* 1936 proposed the prevention of financial crises and unemployment by adjusting demand through government control of credit and currency.
End of Laissez-Faire pt 5

capital punishment punishment by death. Capital punishment is retained in 92 countries and territories (1990), including the USA (37 states), China, and Islamic countries. It was abolished in the UK 1965 for all crimes except treason. Methods of execution include electrocution, lethal gas, hanging, shooting, lethal injection, garrotting, and decapitation.

It is the unpleasant and unacceptable face of capitalism.

capitalism
Edward (Richard George) Heath, 1916, British politician and prime minister. On the Lonrho Scandal, *Hansard* 15 May 1973

Countries that have abolished the death penalty fall into three categories: those that have abolished it for all crimes (44 countries); those that retain it only for exceptional crimes such as war crimes (17 countries); and those that retain the death penalty for ordinary crimes but have not executed anyone since 1980 (25 countries and territories). The first country in Europe to abolish the death penalty was Portugal 1867. In the USA, the Supreme Court declared capital punishment unconstitutional 1972 (as a cruel and unusual punishment) but decided 1976 that this was not so in all circumstances. It was therefore reintroduced in some states, and in 1990 there were over 2,000 prisoners on death row (awaiting execution) in the USA. In Britain, the number of capital offences was reduced from over 200 at the end of the 18th century, until capital punishment was abolished 1866 for all crimes except murder, treason, piracy, and certain arson attacks. Its use was subject to the royal prerogative of mercy. The punishment was carried out by hanging (in public until 1866). Capital punishment for murder was abolished 1965 but still exists for treason. In 1990, Ireland abolished the death penalty for all offences. Many countries use capital punishment for crimes other than murder, including corruption and theft in the former Soviet Union and drug offences (Malaysia and elsewhere). In South Africa, over 1,500 death sentences were passed 1978–87. There were 1,500 executions in China 1983–89, and 64 in the USSR 1985–88, although the true figure may be higher in both cases. In 1989 the number of capital offences in the USSR was reduced to six. The International Covenant on Civil and Political Rights 1977 ruled out imposition of the death penalty on those under the age of 18. The covenant was signed by President Carter on behalf of the USA, but in 1989 the US Supreme Court decided that it could be imposed from the age of 16 for murder, and that the mentally retarded could also face the death penalty.

Capuchin member of the Franciscan order of monks in the Roman Catholic Church, instituted by the Italian monk Matteo di Bassi (died 1552), who wished to return to the literal observance of the rule of St ◊Francis of Assisi. The Capuchin rule was drawn up 1529 and the order recognized by the pope 1619. The name was derived from the French term for the brown habit and pointed hood (*capuche*) that they wore. The order has been involved in missionary activity.

cardinal in the Roman Catholic Church, the highest rank next to the pope. Cardinals act as an advisory body to the pope and elect him. Their red hat is the badge of office. The number of cardinals has varied; there were 151 in 1989.

Originally a cardinal was any priest in charge of a major parish, but in 1567 the term was confined to the members of the Sacred College, 120 of whom (below the age of 80) elect the pope and are themselves elected by him (since 1973). They advise on all matters of doctrine, canonizations, convocation of councils, liturgy, and temporal business.

cardinal number in mathematics, one of the series of numbers 0, 1, 2, 3, 4, ... Cardinal numbers relate to quantity, whereas ordinal numbers (first, second, third, fourth, ...) relate to order.

cargo cult Melanesian religious movement, dating from the 19th century. Adherents believe the arrival of cargo is through the agency of a messianic spirit figure, heralding a new paradise free of white dominance. The movement became active during and after World War II with the apparently miraculous dropping of supplies from aeroplanes.

Carmelite order mendicant order of friars in the Roman Catholic Church. The order was founded on Mount Carmel in Palestine by Berthold, a crusader from Calabria, about 1155, and spread to Europe in the 13th century. The Carmelites have devoted themselves largely to missionary work and mystical theology. They are known as **White Friars** because of the white overmantle they wear (over a brown habit).

The first Carmelites followed the example of Elijah, who according to the Old Testament is supposed to have lived on Mount Carmel. Following the rule which the patriarch of Jerusalem drew up for them about 1210, they lived as hermits in separate huts. About 1240, the Muslim conquests compelled them to move from Palestine and they spread to the west, mostly in France and England, where the order began to live communally. The most momentous reform movement was initiated by St ◊Teresa of Avila. In 1562 she founded a convent in Avila and, with the cooperation of St John of the Cross and others, she established a stricter order of barefoot friars and nuns (the **Discalced Carmelites**).

Carnap Rudolf 1891–1970. German philosopher, in the USA from 1935. He was a member of the Vienna Circle and an exponent of ◊logical positivism, the theory that the only meaningful propositions are those that can be verified empirically. He tried to show that metaphysics arose through our confusing talk about the world with talk about language. His books include *The Logical Syntax of Language* 1934 and *Meaning and Necessity* 1956. He was professor of philosophy at the University of California 1954–62.

What I tell you three times is true.

Lewis Carroll
The Hunting of the Snark Fit 1, 'The Landing'

Carpenter Edward 1844–1929. English socialist and writer. Inspired by the writings of ◊Thoreau, Walt Whitman, and William ◊Morris he abandoned the church in order to pursue his own form of socialism and to espouse such progressive causes as sexual reform, women's rights and vegetarianism. He lived openly as a homosexual and made a plea for sexual toleration in *Love's Coming of Age* 1896. His liberal idealism influenced later writers, including E M Forster and D H ◊Lawrence.

Carroll Lewis. Pen name of Charles Lutwidge Dodgson 1832–1898. English author of children's classics *Alice's Adventures in Wonderland* 1865 and its sequel *Through the Looking-Glass* 1872. Among later works was the mock-heroic 'nonsense' poem *The Hunting of the Snark* 1876. He was fascinated by the limits and paradoxes of language and thought, the exploration of which leads to the apparent nonsense of Alice's adventures. An Oxford don, he also published mathematical works.

Dodgson, born in Daresbury, Cheshire, was a mathematics lecturer at Oxford 1855–81.

There he first told the fantasy stories to Alice Liddell and her sisters, daughters of the dean of Christ Church. He was a prolific letter writer and inventor of games and puzzles, and was one of the pioneers of portrait photography.

carrying capacity in ecology, the maximum number of animals of a given species that a particular area can support. When the carrying capacity is exceeded, there is insufficient food (or other resources) for the members of the population. The population may then be reduced by emigration, reproductive failure, or death through starvation.

cartel agreement among national or international firms to fix prices for their products. A cartel may restrict supply (output) to raise prices in order to increase member profits. It therefore represents a form of ◊oligopoly. OPEC, for example, is an oil cartel.

National laws concerning cartels differ widely, and international agreement is difficult to achieve. Both the Treaty of Rome and the Stockholm Convention, governing respectively the ◊European Community (EC) and the ◊European Free Trade Association (EFTA), contain provisions for control. In Germany, cartels are the most common form of monopolistic organization. In the US, cartels are generally illegal. The Sherman Antitrust Act 1890 prohibited cartels, but legislation passed during the Great Depression permitted industries to enact 'codes of fair competition'. These were declared unconstitutional 1935, and public cartels in coal mining, oil production, and agriculture largely ended after World War II.

Carter Doctrine assertion 1980 by President Carter of a vital US interest in the Persian Gulf region (prompted by the Soviet invasion of Afghanistan and instability in Iran): any outside attempt at control would be met by military force if necessary.

Carthusian order Roman Catholic order of monks and, later, nuns, founded by St Bruno 1084 at Chartreuse, near Grenoble, France. Living chiefly in unbroken silence, they ate one vegetarian meal a day and supported themselves by their own labours; the rule is still one of severe austerity.

The first rule was drawn up by Guigo, the fifth prior. The order was introduced into England about 1178, when the first Charterhouse was founded at Witham in Somerset. They were suppressed at the Reformation, but there is a Charterhouse at Parkminster, Sussex, established 1833.

cartomancy practice of telling fortunes by cards, often ◊tarot cards.

Cassandra in Greek legend, the daughter of Priam, king of Troy. Her prophecies (for example, of the fall of Troy) were never believed, because she had rejected the love of the god Apollo. She was murdered with ◊Agamemnon by his wife Clytemnestra, having been awarded as a prize to the Greek hero on his sacking of Troy.

Cassirer Ernst 1874–1945. German philosopher, exponent of ◊neo-Kantianism. Immanuel ◊Kant had taught that human experience was conditioned by the categories or forms of thought to which all human experience was limited. Cassirer held that, in addition to Kant's list of categories, there are also forms of thought conditioning mythical, historical, and practical thinking. These forms of thought could be discovered by the study of language.

His main work is the three-volume *Die Philosophie der Symbolischen Formen/Philosophy of Symbolic Forms* 1923–29. Born in Breslau in Germany, he fled to the USA in 1932. He became a professor at Yale in 1941.

caste stratification of Hindu society into four main groups: **Brahmans** (priests), **Kshatriyas** (nobles and warriors), **Vaisyas** (traders and farmers), and **Sudras** (servants); plus a fifth group, **Harijan** (untouchables). No upward or downward mobility exists, as in classed societies. The system dates from ancient times, and there are more than 3,000 subdivisions.

In Hindu tradition, the four main castes are said to have originated from the head, arms, thighs, and feet respectively of Brahma, the creator; the members of the fifth were probably the aboriginal inhabitants of the country, known variously as Scheduled Castes, Depressed Classes, Untouchables, or Harijan (name coined by Gandhi, 'children of God'). This lowest caste handled animal products, garbage, and human wastes and so was considered to be polluting by touch, or even by sight, to others. Discrimination against them was made illegal 1947 when India became independent, but persists.

castration anxiety in psychoanalysis, the anxiety in men and boys arising from a usually imaginary threat to the genitals. It rarely refers to actual castration, but rather to the loss of the penis, or loss of the capacity for sexual pleasure, or a threat to masculinity.

Castro (Ruz) Fidel 1927– . Cuban communist politician, prime minister 1959–76, and president from 1976. He led two unsuccessful coups against the right-wing Batista regime and led the revolution that overthrew the dictator 1959. He raised the standard of living for most Cubans but dealt harshly with dissenters. Castro espoused Marxism-Leninism until, in 1974, he rejected Marx's formula 'from each according to his ability and to each according to his need' and decreed that each Cuban should 'receive according to his work'.

casuistry the application of an ethical theory to particular cases or types of case, especially in theology and dogmatics. Casuistry is contrasted with ◊situationism, which considers each moral situation as it arises and without reference to ethical theory or moral principles.

Most ethical theories can be shown to be inadequate, if sufficient effort is devoted to identifying increasingly subtle features in a particular moral situation. Hence, casuistry has fallen into disrepute.

catastrophe theory mathematical theory developed by René Thom in 1972, in which he showed that the growth of an organism proceeds by a series of gradual changes that are triggered by, and in turn trigger, large-scale changes or 'catastrophic' jumps. It also has applications in engineering – for example, the gradual strain on the structure of a bridge that can eventually result in a sudden collapse – and has been extended to economic and psychological events.

catastrophism theory that the geological features of the Earth were formed by a series of sudden, violent 'catastrophes' beyond the ordinary workings of nature. The theory was largely the work of Georges ◊Cuvier. It was later replaced by the concepts of ◊uniformitarianism and ◊evolution.

catchment area area from which water is collected by a river and its tributaries. In the social sciences the term may be used to denote the area from which people travel to obtain a particular service or product, such as the area from which a school draws its pupils.

catechism teaching by question and answer on the ◊Socratic method, but chiefly as a means of instructing children in the basics of the Christian creed. A person being instructed in this way in preparation for baptism or confirmation is called a *catechumen*.

A form of catechism was used for the catechumens in the early Christian church. Little books of catechism became numerous at the Reformation. Luther published simple catechisms for children and uneducated people,

---

The new catechism

Published in 1992 in most parts of the world, the English-language edition was not available until 1994 after the Vatican approved the acceptability of the 'inclusive', that is, non-sexist language with which the translation has been prepared. The *Catechism of the Catholic Church* is a book of some 700 pages containing the essential teaching of the Roman Catholic Church. It is the first 'universal' catechism since that produced in 1566 in the aftermath of the Protestant Reformation. This new catechism follows the Second Vatican Council 1961–64, but the initiative to produce it was only taken in 1985. The book is not in the traditional question and answer form, but contains commentaries on the Creed, the Ten Commandments, the Lord's Prayer, and other topics, the target readership being bishops and teachers of religion rather than the laity in general.

---

and a larger catechism for the use of teachers. The popular Roman Catholic catechism was that of Peter Canisius 1555; that with the widest circulation now is the 'Explanatory Catechism of Christian Doctrine'. Protestant catechisms include Calvin's Geneva Catechism 1537; that composed by ◊Cranmer and Ridley with additions by Overall 1549–1661, incorporated in the Book of Common Prayer; the Presbyterian Catechism 1647–48; and the Evangelical Free Church Catechism 1898.

categorical imperative technical term in the ethics of German philosopher Immanuel ◊Kant for his law of reason to which all moral rules must conform. The maxim 'Do not lie' conforms to the categorical imperative, and so is a moral rule, because a rational being can without inconsistency wish that everyone should obey it. Kant provides several formulations of the categorical imperative.

category in philosophy, a fundamental concept applied to being that cannot be reduced to anything more elementary. Aristotle listed ten categories: substance, quantity, quality, relation, place, time, position, state, action, and passion.

Cathar member of a religious group in medieval Europe usually numbered among the Christian heretics. Influenced by ◊Manichaeism, they started about the 10th century in the Balkans where they were called 'Bogomils', spread to SW Europe where they were often identified with the ◊Albigenses, and by the middle of the 14th century had been destroyed or driven underground by the Inquisition.

The Cathars believed that this world is under the domination of Satan, and men and women are the terrestrial embodiment of spirits who were inspired by him to revolt and were driven out of heaven. At death, the soul will be reincarnated (whether in human or animal form) unless it has been united through the Cathar faith with Christ.

For someone who has become a Cathar, death brings release, the Beatific Vision, and immortality in Christ's presence. Baptism with the spirit – the *consolamentum* – was the central rite, believed to remedy the disaster of the Fall. The spirit received was the Paraclete, the Comforter, and it was imparted by imposition of hands. The Believers, or *Credentes*, could approach God only through the Perfect (the ordained priesthood), who were implicitly obeyed in everything, and lived lives of the strictest self-denial and chastity.

catharsis emotional purging and purification brought about by the experience of pity and fear, as in tragic drama. Aristotle in his *Poetics* used the term to explain the audience's feelings of relief or pleasure in watching the suffering of characters in a tragedy.

cathedral Christian church containing the throne of a bishop or archbishop, which is usually situated on the south side of the choir. A cathedral is governed by a dean and chapter.

Formerly, cathedrals were distinguished as either monastic or secular, the clergy of the latter not being members of a regular monastic order. Some British cathedrals, such as Lincoln and York, are referred to as 'minsters', the term originating in the name given to the bishop and cathedral clergy who were often referred to as a *monasterium*. After the dissolution of the monasteries by Henry VIII, most of the monastic churches were refounded and are called Cathedrals of the New Foundation. Cathedrals of dioceses founded since 1836 include St Albans, Southwark, Truro, Birmingham, and Liverpool. There are cathedrals in most of the chief cities of Europe; UK cathedrals include Canterbury Cathedral (spanning the Norman to Perpendicular periods), Exeter Cathedral (13th-century Gothic), and Coventry Cathedral (rebuilt after World War II, consecrated 1962).

Catherine of Alexandria, St Christian martyr. According to legend she disputed with 50 scholars, refusing to give up her faith and marry Emperor Maxentius. Her emblem is a wheel, on which her persecutors tried to kill her (the wheel broke and she was beheaded). Feast day 25 Nov.

Catherine of Siena 1347–1380. Italian mystic, born in Siena. She persuaded Pope Gregory XI to return to Rome from Avignon 1376. In 1375 she is said to have received on her body the stigmata, the impression of Jesus' wounds. Her *Dialogue* is a classic mystical work. Feast day 29 April.

Catholic church whole body of the Christian church, though usually referring to the Roman Catholic Church (see ◊Roman Catholicism).

Caucasoid or **Caucasian** former racial classification used for any of the light-skinned peoples; so named because the German anthropologist J F Blumenbach (1752–1840) theorized that they originated in the Caucasus.

Cauchy Augustin Louis 1789–1857. French mathematician who employed rigorous methods of analysis. His prolific output included work on complex functions, determinants, and probability, and on the convergence of infinite series. In calculus, he refined the concepts of the limit and the definite integral.

In 1843 he published a defence of academic freedom of thought that was instrumental in the abolition of the oath of allegiance soon after the fall of Louis Philippe in 1848.

All is flux, nothing stays still.

causality
Heraclitus, c.544 BC–483 BC,
Greek philosopher.
quoted in *De Caelo* by Aristotle

---

causality in philosophy, a consideration of the connection between cause and effect, usually referred to as the 'causal relationship'. If an event is assumed to have a cause, two important questions arise: what is the relationship between cause and effect, and must it follow that every event is caused? The Scottish philosopher David ◊Hume considered these questions to be, in principle, unanswerable.

caveat emptor dictum that professes the buyer is responsible for checking the quality of nonwarrantied goods purchased.

Cavendish Henry 1731–1810. English physicist. He discovered hydrogen (which he called 'inflammable air') 1766, and determined the compositions of water and of nitric acid.

The ◊Cavendish experiment enabled him to discover the mass and density of the Earth.

A grandson of the 2nd duke of Devonshire, he devoted his life to scientific pursuits, living in rigorous seclusion in Clapham Common, London.

Cavendish experiment measurement of the gravitational attraction between lead and gold spheres, which enabled English physicist and chemist Henry Cavendish to calculate a mean value for the mass and density of Earth, using Newton's law of universal gravitation.

Cayley Arthur 1821–1895. British mathematician who developed matrix algebra, used by ◊Heisenberg in his elucidation of quantum mechanics.

CD-ROM (abbreviation for *compact-disc read-only memory*) computer storage device developed from the technology of the audio ◊compact disc. It consists of a plastic-coated metal disc, on which binary digital information is etched in the form of microscopic pits. This can then be read optically by passing a light beam over the disc. CD-ROMs typically hold about 550 ◊megabytes of data, and are used in distributing large amounts of text and graphics, such as encyclopedias, catalogues, and technical manuals.

Standard CD-ROMs cannot have information written onto them by computer, but must be manufactured from a master. Although recordable CDs, called CR-R discs, have been developed for use as computer discs, they are as yet too expensive for widespread use. A compact disc that can be overwritten repeatedly by a computer has also been developed; see ◊optical disc. The compact disc, with its enormous storage capacity, may eventually replace the magnetic disc as the most common form of backing store for computers.

Cecilia, St Christian patron saint of music, martyred in Rome in the 2nd or 3rd century, who is said to have sung hymns while undergoing torture. Feast day 22 Nov.

celestial mechanics the branch of astronomy that deals with the calculation of the orbits of celestial bodies, their gravitational attractions (such as those that produce the Earth's tides), and also the orbits of artificial satellites and space probes. It is based on the laws of motion and gravity laid down by Isaac ◊Newton.

celibacy way of life involving voluntary abstinence from sexual intercourse. In some religions, such as Christianity and Buddhism, celibacy is a requirement for certain religious roles, such as the priesthood or monastic life. Other religions, such as Judaism, strongly discourage celibacy.

censor in ancient Rome, either of two senior magistrates, high officials elected every five years to hold office for 18 months. Their responsibilities included public morality, a census of the citizens, and a revision of the senatorial list.

censor in Freudian psychology, the psychic function that prevents unacceptable unconscious impulses from reaching the conscious mind. This function leads to ◊repression of intolerable ideas, memories, or impulses.

This view of the censor as a mechanism of repression has received considerable criticism, notably from J P Sartre in *Being and Nothingness* 1975.

Censorship may be useful for the preservation of morality, but can never be so for its restoration.

censorship
Jean-Jacques Rousseau, 1712–1778, French philosopher and writer.
The Social Contract

---

censorship suppression by authority of material considered immoral, heretical, subversive, libellous, damaging to state security, or otherwise offensive. It is generally more stringent under totalitarian or strongly religious regimes and in wartime.

The British government uses the D-notice and the Official Secrets Act to protect itself. Laws relating to obscenity, libel, and blasphemy act as a form of censorship. The media exercise a degree of self-censorship. During the Gulf War 1991, access to the theatre of war was controlled by the US military: only certain reporters were allowed in and their movements were restricted. In the USA, despite First Amendment protection of free speech, attempts at censorship are made by government agencies or groups; the question is often tested in the courts, especially with respect to sexually explicit material. Recently, efforts have been made to suppress certain pieces of music and works of art, on such grounds as racial harassment and social depravity.

census official count of the population of a country, originally for military call-up and taxation, later for assessment of social trends as other information regarding age, sex, and occupation of each individual was included. They may become unnecessary as computerized databanks are developed.

The first US census was taken in 1790 and the first in Britain in 1801.

central bank the bank which has responsibility for issuing currency in a country. Often it is also responsible for foreign exchange dealings on behalf of the government, for supervising the banking system in the country, and for implementing monetary policy. The Bank of England is the central bank of the UK.

central dogma in genetics and evolution, the fundamental belief that genes can affect the nature of the physical body, but that changes in the body (for example, through use or accident) cannot be translated into changes in the genes.

central government in the UK, the part of the public sector controlled by government at Westminster, as opposed to local government which is controlled by local councillors in counties, boroughs, parishes, and so on.

Central Intelligence Agency (CIA) US intelligence organization established 1947. It has actively intervened overseas, generally to undermine left-wing regimes or to protect US financial interests; for example, in the Congo (now Zaire) and Nicaragua. From 1980 all covert activity by the CIA has by law to be reported to Congress, preferably beforehand, and must be authorized by the president. In 1990 the CIA's estimated budget was $10–12 billion. Robert James Woolsey became CIA director 1993.

Developed from the wartime Office of Strategic Services and set up by Congress, as part of the National Security Act, on the lines of the British Secret Service, the CIA was intended solely for use overseas in the Cold War. It was involved in, for example, the restoration of the Shah of Iran 1953, South Vietnam (during the Vietnam War), Chile (the coup against President Allende), and Cuba (the Bay of Pigs). On the domestic front, it was illegally involved in the Watergate political scandal and in the 1970s lost public confidence when US influence collapsed in Iran, Afghanistan, Nicaragua, Yemen, and elsewhere. A fire in the US embassy in Moscow 1991 led to the loss of much sensitive material and, in May, William Webster stepped down as director, following criticisms of the agency's intelligence gathering prior to the 1989 US invasion of Panama and the 1991 Gulf War. Robert Gates (deputy national security adviser 1989–91 and deputy director of the CIA 1986–89) became his successor. CIA headquarters is in Langley, Virginia. Past directors include William Casey, Richard Helms, and George Bush. The CIA director is also coordinator of all the US intelligence organizations. Domestic intelligence functions are performed by the Federal Bureau of Investigation.

centralization form of organization in a business where decision-making for the whole business is taken by individuals or groups of people at the centre of the business. This compares with 'decentralization', where decision-making is devolved throughout the whole business.

central planning system by which the state takes complete control over the running of the national economy. For example, in the Soviet Union from the 1920s, targets and strategies were all decided centrally, leaving little or no room for private initiative or enterprise.

Chadwick Edwin 1800–1890. English social reformer, author of the Poor Law Report 1834. He played a prominent part in the campaign which resulted in the Public Health Act 1848. He was commissioner of the first Board of Health 1848–54.

A self-educated protégé of Jeremy ◊Bentham and advocate of ◊utilitarianism, he used his influence to implement measures to eradicate cholera, improve sanitation in urban areas, and clear slums in British cities.

Chadwick James 1891–1974. British physicist. In 1932 he discovered the particle in the nucleus of an atom that became known as the neutron because it has no electric charge. He received the Nobel Prize for Physics 1935.

Chadwick studied at Cambridge under Ernest ◊Rutherford. He was Lyon Jones professor of physics at Liverpool 1935–48, and master of Gonville and Caius College, Cambridge 1948–59. In 1940 he was one of the British scientists reporting on the atom bomb.

chain of being in metaphysics, an ancient principle with many variations, originating in neo-Platonism. Essentially, the principle asserts the unity, continuity, and perfection of the universe. The principle assumes that the universe is a hierarchy of different grades of beings – the higher grades of beings possessing more reality or perfection than the lower ones. At the top of the hierarchy is the most perfect being of all – God – or, sometimes, the most perfect creature – Man. One version of the principle is that for the universe to be as perfect as possible, it must contain the greatest possible diversity in the greatest possible profusion compatible with the laws of nature. Another version is that nothing can remain a real but unactualized possibility throughout all time.

Bibl. Lovejoy, A O *The Great Chain of Being* (1936)

chain of command path down which orders and decisions are communicated, from the board of directors of a company at the top of the ◊hierarchy down to shop-floor workers at the bottom. The shorter the chain of command, the faster communication is likely to be. There is also less likely to be misinterpretation of communication. A short chain of command also tends to motivate workers because they are able to interact with those in positions of authority and see their decisions being implemented by workers below them.

Chalcedon, Council of ecumenical council of the early Christian church, convoked 451 by the Roman emperor Marcian, and held at Chalcedon (now Kadiköy, Turkey). The council, attended by over 500 bishops, resulted in the *Definition of Chalcedon*, an agreed doctrine for both the Eastern and Western churches.

The council was assembled to repudiate the ideas of ◊Eutyches on Jesus' divine nature subsuming the human; it also rejected the ◊Monophysite doctrine that Jesus had only one nature, and repudiated ◊Nestorianism. It reached a compromise definition of Jesus' nature which it was hoped would satisfy all factions: Jesus was one person in two natures, united 'unconfusedly, unchangeably, indivisibly, inseparably'.

chalice cup, usually of precious metal, used in celebrating the ◊Eucharist in the Christian church.

Chalmers Thomas 1780–1847. Scottish theologian. At the Disruption of the ◊Church of Scotland 1843, Chalmers withdrew from the church along with a large number of other priests, and became principal of the Free Church college, thus founding the ◊Free Church of Scotland.

As minister of Tron Church, Glasgow, from 1815, Chalmers became renowned for his eloquence and for his proposals for social reform. In 1823 he became professor of moral philosophy at St Andrews, and in 1828 of theology at Edinburgh.

chamber of commerce group of people in a locality, usually a town or city, who come together to form a chamber of commerce. They share ideas and concerns and act as a local ◊pressure group for business.

chance likelihood, or ◊probability, of an event taking place, expressed as a fraction or percentage. For example, the chance that a tossed coin will land heads up is 50%.

As a science, it originated when the Chevalier de Méré consulted ◊Pascal about how to reduce his gambling losses. In correspondence with another mathematician,

And a certain man drew a bow at a venture.

> *chance*
> Bible, the sacred book of the Jewish and
> Christian religions.
> 1 Kings 22:34

Pierre de ◊Fermat, Blaise Pascal worked out the foundations of the theory of chance. This underlies the science of statistics.

Chandrasekhar Subrahmanyan 1910– . Indian-born US astrophysicist who made pioneering studies of the structure and evolution of stars. The *Chandrasekhar limit* of 1.4 Suns is the maximum mass of a ◊white dwarf before it turns into a neutron star. Born in Lahore, he studied in Madras, India, and Cambridge, England, before emigrating to the USA. Nobel Prize for Physics 1983.

Chang Tao Ling lived 2nd century AD. Chinese Taoist and founder of salvationary or 'religious' ◊Taoism. He worked in Sichuan province as a healer. He combined Taoist teachings with shamanistic and healing or psychological rites to form the first popular mass movement in Taoism. He is worshipped as a Taoist deity and as the chief exorcist and demon-slayer of Taoist mythology.

Channing William Ellery 1780–1842. US minister and theologian. He became a leader of the Unitarian movement 1819, opposing the strict Calvinism of the New England Congregationalist churches. He was an instrumental figure in the establishment of the American Unitarian Association. In his later years, Channing devoted his energies to abolitionism in its campaign to end the institution of slavery.

Born in Newport, Rhode Island, Channing was educated at Harvard University. He was appointed minister of the Federal Street Congregationalist church in Boston 1803.

chantry in medieval Europe, a religious foundation in which, in return for an endowment of land, the souls of the donor and the donor's family and friends would be prayed for. A chantry Mass could be held at an existing altar, or in a specially constructed chantry chapel, in which the donor's body was usually buried.

Chantries became widespread in the later Middle Ages, reflecting the acceptance of the doctrine of ◊purgatory, together with the growth of individualistic piety (as in the ◊*devotio moderna*) and the decline in the popularity of monasteries, to which they were seen as an alternative. Their foundation required the consent of the local bishop and a licence from the king for the alienation of land. They were suppressed in Protestant countries during the Reformation, and abolished in England 1547.

chaos theory or *chaology* branch of mathematics which attempts to describe 'chaotic' systems – that is, systems whose behaviour is difficult to predict because there are so many variables or unknown factors (such as a weather system). Chaos theory, which attempts to predict the *probable* behaviour of such systems, based on a rapid calculation of the impact of as wide a range of elements as possible, emerged in the 1970s with the development of sophisticated computers. First developed for use in meteorology, it has also been used in such fields as economics.

The whole worl's in a state o' chassis!

chaos

Sean O'Casey. Adopted name of John Casey, 1884–1964, Irish dramatist.

Juno and the Paycock

---

chapel place of worship used by some Christian denominations; also, a part of a building used for Christian worship. A large church or cathedral may have several chapels.

chapter in the Christian church, the collective assembly of canons (priests) who together administer a cathedral.

Charcot Jean-Martin 1825–1893. French neurologist who studied hysteria, sclerosis, locomotor ataxia, and senile diseases. Among his pupils was Sigmund ◊Freud.

Charcot worked at a hospital in Paris, where he studied the way certain mental illnesses cause physical changes in the brain. He exhibited hysterical women at weekly public lectures, which became highly fashionable events.

charisma originally a theological term meaning the divine grace bestowed on a Christian in order to fulfil his or her mission. It was subsequently appropriated by Max ◊Weber to describe the special, indefinable power perceived in certain leaders by their followers.

charismatic movement late 20th-century movement within the Christian church that emphasizes the role of the Holy Spirit in the life of the individual believer and in the life of the church. See ◊Pentecostal movement.

charity originally a Christian term meaning a selfless, disinterested form of ◊love. This developed to include almsgiving or other actions performed by individuals to help the poor and needy. Today it refers to any independent agency (for example, Oxfam) that organizes such relief on a regular basis.

Charity shall cover the multitude of sins.

charity

Bible, the sacred book of the Jewish and Christian religions.

Peter 4:8

Charon in Greek mythology, the boatman who ferried the dead over the rivers Acheron and Styx to ◊Hades, the underworld. A coin placed on the tongue of the dead paid for their passage.

Chartism radical British democratic movement, mainly of the working classes, which flourished around 1838–48. It derived its name from the People's Charter, a six-point programme comprising universal male suffrage, equal electoral districts, secret ballot, annual parliaments, and abolition of the property qualification for, and payment of, members of Parliament. Greater prosperity, lack of organization, and rivalry in the leadership led to its demise.

chasuble the outer garment worn by the priest in the celebration of the Christian Mass. The colour of the chasuble depends on which feast is being celebrated.

The original writer is not he who refrains from imitating others, but he who can be imitated by none.

François Chateaubriand
Le Génie du Christianisme

Chateaubriand François René, vicomte de 1768–1848. French Romantic author. In exile from the French Revolution 1794–99, he wrote *Atala* 1801 (after his encounters with North American Indians) and the autobiographical *René* 1805, which formed part of *Le Génie du Christianisme/The Genius of Christianity* 1802 – a defense of the Christian faith in terms of its social, cultural and spiritual benefits to mankind.

chauvinism warlike, often unthinking patriotism, as exhibited by Nicholas Chauvin, one of Napoleon I's veterans and his fanatical admirer. In the mid-20th century the expression *male chauvinism* was coined to mean an assumed superiority of the male sex over the female.

chela in Hinduism, a follower or pupil of a guru (teacher).

chemistry science concerned with the composition of matter and of the changes that take place in it under certain conditions.

All matter can exist in three states: gas, liquid, or solid. It is composed of minute particles termed *molecules*, which are constantly moving, and may be further divided into *atoms*.

Molecules that contain atoms of one kind only are known as *elements*; those that contain atoms of different kinds are called *compounds*.

Chemical compounds are produced by a chemical action that alters the arrangement of the atoms in the reacting molecules. Heat, light, vibration, catalytic action, radiation, or pressure, as well as moisture (for ionization), may be necessary to produce a chemical change. Examination and possible breakdown of compounds to determine their components is *analysis*, and the building up of compounds from their components is *synthesis*. When substances are brought together without changing their molecular structures they are said to be *mixtures*.

Organic chemistry is the branch of chemistry that deals with carbon compounds. *Inorganic chemistry* deals with the description, properties, reactions, and preparation of all the elements and their compounds, with the exception of carbon compounds. *Physical chemistry* is concerned with the quantitative explanation of chemical phenomena and reactions, and the measurement of data required for such explanations. This branch studies in particular the movement of molecules and the effects of temperature and pressure, often with regard to gases and liquids.

Symbols are used to denote the elements. The symbol is usually the first letter or letters of the English or Latin name of the element – for example, C for carbon; Ca for calcium; Fe for iron (*ferrum*). These symbols represent one atom of the element; molecules containing more than one atom of an element are denoted by a subscript figure – for example, water is H_2O. In some substances a group of atoms acts as a single entity, and these are enclosed in parentheses in the symbol – for example $(NH_4)_2SO_4$ denotes ammonium sulphate.

The symbolic representation of a molecule is known as a *formula*. A figure placed before a formula represents the number of molecules of a substance taking part in, or being produced by, a chemical reaction – for example,

$2H_2O$ indicates two molecules of water. Chemical reactions are expressed by means of *equations* as in:

$$NaCl + H_2SO_4 \rightarrow NaHSO_4 + HCl$$

This equation states the fact that sodium chloride (NaCl) on being treated with sulphuric acid (H_2SO_4) is converted into sodium bisulphate (sodium hydrogensulphate, $NaHSO_4$) and hydrogen chloride (HCl).

Elements are divided into *metals*, which have lustre and conduct heat and electricity, and *nonmetals*, which usually lack these properties. The *periodic system*, developed by John Newlands in 1863 and established by Dmitri Mendeleyev in 1869, classified elements according to their relative atomic masses. Those elements that resemble each other in general properties were found to bear a relation to one another by weight, and these were placed in groups or families. Certain anomalies in this system were later removed by classifying the elements according to their atomic numbers. The latter is equivalent to the positive charge on the nucleus of the atom.

history Ancient civilizations were familiar with certain chemical processes – for example, extracting metals from their ores, and making alloys. The alchemists endeavoured to turn base (nonprecious) metals into gold, and chemistry evolved towards the end of the 17th century from the techniques and insights developed during alchemical experiments. Robert Boyle defined elements as the simplest substances into which matter could be resolved. The alchemical doctrine of the four elements (earth, air, fire, and water) gradually lost its hold, and the theory that all combustible bodies contain a substance called phlogiston (a weightless 'fire element' generated during combustion) was discredited in the 18th century by the experimental work of Joseph Black, Antoine Lavoisier, and Joseph Priestley (who discovered the presence of oxygen in air). Henry Cavendish discovered the composition of water, and John Dalton put forward the atomic theory, which ascribed a precise relative weight to the 'simple atom' characteristic of each element. Much research then took place leading to the development of ◊biochemistry, chemotherapy, and plastics.

cheque (US *check*) order written by the drawer to a commercial or central bank to pay a specific sum on demand.

Usually the cheque should bear the date on which it is payable, a definite sum of money to be paid, written in words and figures, to a named person or body, or to the bearer, and be signed by the drawer.

It is then payable on presentation at the bank on which it is drawn. If the cheque is 'crossed', as is usual British practice, it is not negotiable and can be paid only through a bank; in the USA a cheque is always negotiable.

cherub type of angel in Christian belief, usually depicted as a young child with wings. Cherubim form the second order of ◊angels.

Chicago School of Sociology the first university department of sociology, founded in Chicago 1892, under Albion Small. He was succeeded by Robert E Park, who with W I Thomas, Ernest Burgess, Louis Wirth, and R McKenzie created a centre for the social sciences in the 1920s and 1930s, studying urban life, including crime and deviance in Chicago, with its variety of urban communities, lifestyles, and ethnic subcultures.

A neo-Chicagoan school emerged in the 1940s under Erving ◊Goffman and Howard Becker.

Child Lydia Maria 1802–1880. US writer, social critic, and feminist, author of the popular women's guides *The Frugal Housewife* 1829 and *The Mother's Book* 1831. With her husband, David Child, she worked for the abolition of slavery, advocating educational support for black Americans. The Childs edited the weekly *National Anti-Slavery Standard* 1840–44.

Born in Medford, Massachusetts, USA, Child received little formal education but read widely and published several historical novels about life in colonial New England.

Child, Convention on the Rights of the United Nations document designed to make the wellbeing of children an international obligation. It was adopted 1989 and covers children from birth up to 18.

It laid down international standards for:
provision of a name, nationality, health care, education, rest, and play;
protection from commercial or sexual exploitation, physical or mental abuse, and engagement in warfare;
participation in decisions affecting a child's own future.

Children's Crusade ◊crusade by some 10,000 children from France, the Low Countries, and Germany, in 1212, to recapture Jerusalem for Christianity. Motivated by religious piety, many of them were sold into slavery or died of disease.

children's literature works specifically written for children. The earliest known illustrated children's book in English is *Goody Two Shoes* 1765, possibly written by Oliver Goldsmith. *Fairy tales* were originally part of a vast range of oral literature, credited only to the writer who first recorded them, such as Charles Perrault. During the 19th century several writers, including Hans Christian Andersen, wrote original stories in the fairy tale genre; others, such as the Grimm brothers, collected (and sometimes adapted) existing stories.

Early children's stories were written with a moral purpose; this was particularly true in the 19th century, apart from the unique case of Lewis Carroll's *Alice* books. The late 19th century was the great era of children's literature in the UK, with Lewis Carroll, Beatrix Potter, Charles Kingsley, and J M Barrie. It was also the golden age of illustrated children's books, with such artists as Kate Greenaway and Randolph Caldecott. In the USA, Louise May Alcott's *Little Women* 1868 and its sequels found a wide audience. Among the most popular 20th-century children's writers in English have been Kenneth Grahame (*The Wind in the Willows* 1908) and A A Milne (*Winnie the Pooh* 1926) in the UK; and, in the USA, Laura Ingalls Wilder (*Little House on the Prairie* 1935), E B White (*Stuart Little* 1945, *Charlotte's Web* 1952), and Dr Seuss (*Cat in the Hat* 1957). Canadian Lucy Maud Montgomery's series that began with *Anne of Green Gables* 1908 was widely popular.

Adventure stories have often appealed to children even when these were written for adults; examples include *Robinson Crusoe* by Daniel Defoe; the satirical *Gulliver's Travels* by Jonathan Swift, and *Tom Sawyer* 1876 and *Huckleberry Finn* 1884 by Mark Twain. Many recent children's writers have been influenced by J R R Tolkien whose *The Hobbit* 1937 and its sequel, the three-volume *Lord of the Rings* 1954–55, are set in the comprehensively imagined world of 'Middle-earth'. His friend C S Lewis produced the allegorical chronicles of Narnia, beginning with *The Lion, the Witch and the Wardrobe* 1950. Rosemary Sutcliff's *The Eagle of the Ninth* 1954, Philippa Pearce's *Tom's Midnight Garden* 1958, and Penelope Lively's *The Wild Hunt of Hagworthy* 1971 are other outstanding books by children's authors who have exploited a perennial fascination with time travel.

Writers for younger children combining stories and illustrations of equally high quality include Maurice Sendak (*Where the Wild Things Are* 1963) and Quentin Blake (*Mister Magnolia* 1980). Roald Dahl's *James and the Giant Peach* 1961 is the first of his popular children's books which summon up primitive emotions and have an imperious morality. More realistic stories for teenagers are written by US authors such as Judy Blume and S E Hinton.

chiliasm another word for millenarianism; see ◊millennium.

Chinese Revolution series of great political upheavals in China 1911–49 that eventually led to Communist Party rule and the establishment of the People's Republic of China. In 1912, a nationalist revolt overthrew the imperial Manchu dynasty. Led by Sun Yat-sen 1923–25 and by Chiang Kai-shek 1925–49, the nationalists, or Guomindang, were increasing challenged by the growing communist movement. The 10,000 km/6,000 mi **Long March** to the NW by the communists 1934–35 to escape from attacks by the Guomindang forces resulted in Mao Zedong's emergence as communist leader. During World War II 1939–45, the various Chinese political groups pooled military resources against the Japanese invaders. After World War II, the conflict reignited into open civil war 1946–49, until the Guomindang were defeated at Nanking and forced to flee to Taiwan. Communist rule was established in the People's Republic of China under the leadership of Mao.

chivalry code of gallantry and honour that medieval knights were pledged to observe. Its principal virtues were piety, honour, valour, courtesy, chastity, and loyalty. The word originally meant the knightly class of the feudal Middle Ages.

He was a verray parfit gentil knight.
chivalry
Geoffrey Chaucer, v. 1340–1400,
English writer.
Canterbury Tales, Prologue

Chivalry originated in feudal France and Spain, spreading rapidly to the rest of Europe and reaching its height in the 12th and 13th centuries. It was strengthened by the Crusades. The earliest orders of chivalry were the Knights Hospitallers and Knights Templars, founded to serve pilgrims to the Holy Land. Secular literature of the period takes knighthood and chivalry as its theme.

Chladni Ernst Florens Friedrich 1756–1827. German physicist, a pioneer in the field of acoustics. He developed an experimental technique whereby sand is vibrated on a metal plate, and settles into regular and symmetric patterns (**Chladni's figures**) indicating the nodes of the vibration's wave pattern.

choice in economics, decision about how resources are allocated. Each choice involves an ◊opportunity cost.

Chomsky Noam 1928– . US professor of linguistics. He proposed a theory of transformational generative grammar, which attracted widespread interest because of the claims it made about the relationship between language and the mind and the universality of an underlying language structure. He has been a leading critic of the imperialist tendencies of the US government.

Colourless green ideas sleep furiously.
Noam Chomsky
Example of a meaningless sentence,
in *Syntactic Structures*

Chomsky distinguished between knowledge and behaviour and maintained that the focus of scientific enquiry should be on knowledge. In order to define and describe linguistic knowledge, he posited a set of abstract principles of grammar that appear to be universal and may have a biological basis.

choreography art of creating and arranging ballet and dance for performance; originally, in the 18th century, the art of dance notation.

choropleth map map on which the average numerical value of some aspect of an area (for example, unemployment by county) is indicated by a scale of colours or isoline shadings. An increase in average value is normally shown by a darker or more intense colour or shading. Choropleth maps are visually impressive but may mislead by suggesting sudden changes between areas.

Christ the ◊Messiah as prophesied in the Hebrew Bible, or Old Testament.

christening Christian ceremony of ◊baptism of infants, including giving a name.

Christian follower of ◊Christianity, the religion derived from the teachings of Jesus. In the New Testament (Acts 11:26) it is stated that the first to be called Christians were the disciples in Antioch (now Antakya, Turkey).

Christian Democracy ideology of a number of parties active in Western Europe since World War II, especially in Italy, the former Federal Republic of Germany, and France. Christian Democrats are essentially moderate conservatives who believe in a mixed economy and in the provision of social welfare. They are opposed to both communism and fascism but are largely in favour of European integration.

Christianity world religion derived from the

Christianity: chronology

1st century	The Christian church is traditionally said to have originated at Pentecost, and separated from the parent Jewish religion by the declaration of saints Barnabas and Paul that the distinctive rites of Judaism were not necessary for entry into the Christian church.
3rd century	Christians were persecuted under the Roman emperors Severus, Decius, and Diocletian.
312	Emperor Constantine established Christianity as the religion of the Roman Empire.
4th century	A settled doctrine of Christian belief evolved, with deviating beliefs condemned as heresies. Questions of discipline threatened disruption within the Church; to settle these, Constantine called the Council of Arles 314, followed by the councils of Nicaea 325 and Constantinople 381.
5th century	Councils of Ephesus 431 and Chalcedon 451. Christianity was carried northwards by such figures as saints Columba and Augustine.
800	Holy Roman Emperor Charlemagne crowned by the pope. The church assisted the growth of the feudal system of which it formed the apex.
1054	The Eastern Orthodox Church split from the Roman Catholic Church.
11th–12th centuries	Secular and ecclesiastical jurisdiction were often in conflict; for example, Emperor Henry IV and Pope Gregory VII, Henry II of England and his archbishop Becket.
1096–1291	The church supported a series of wars in the Middle East, called the Crusades.
1233	The Inquisition was established to suppress heresy.
14th century	Increasing worldliness (against which the foundation of the Dominican and Franciscan monastic orders was a protest) and ecclesiastical abuses led to dissatisfaction and the appearance of the reformers Wycliffe and Huss.
early 16th century	The Renaissance brought a re-examination of Christianity in N Europe by the humanists Erasmus, More, and Colet.
1517	The German priest Martin Luther started the Reformation, an attempt to return to a pure form of Christianity, and became leader of the Protestant movement.
1519–64	In Switzerland the Reformation was carried out by Calvin and Zwingli.
1529	Henry VIII renounced papal supremacy and proclaimed himself head of the Church of England.
1545–63	The Counter-Reformation was initiated by the Catholic church at the Council of Trent.
1560	The Church of Scotland was established according to Calvin's Presbyterian system.
17th century	Jesuit missionaries established themselves in China and Japan. Puritans, Quakers, and other sects seeking religious freedom established themselves in North America.
18th century	During the Age of Reason, Christian dogmas were questioned, and intellectuals began to examine society in purely secular terms. In England and America, religious revivals occurred among the working classes in the form of Methodism and the Great Awakening. In England the Church of England suffered the loss of large numbers of Nonconformists.
19th century	The evolutionary theories of Darwin and the historical criticism of the Bible challenged the Book of Genesis. Missionaries converted people in Africa and Asia, suppressing indigenous faiths and cultures.
1948	The World Council of Churches was founded as part of the ecumenical movement to reunite various Protestant sects and, to some extent, the Protestant churches and the Catholic church.
1950s–80s	Protestant evangelicism grew rapidly in the USA, spread by television.
1969	A liberation theology of freeing the poor from oppression emerged in South America, and attracted papal disapproval.
1972	The United Reformed Church was formed by the union of the Presbyterian Church in England and the Congregational Church. In the USA, the 1960s–70s saw the growth of cults, some of them nominally Christian, which were a source of social concern.
1980s	The Roman Catholic Church played a major role in the liberalization of the Polish government; and in the USSR the Orthodox Church and certain sects were tolerated and even encouraged under President Gorbachev.
1989	Barbara Harris, first female bishop, ordained in the USA.
1992	The Church of England General Synod voted in favour of the ordination of women priests.

teaching of Jesus in the first third of the 1st century, with a present-day membership of about 1 billion. It is divided into groups or denominations that differ in some areas of belief and practice. Its main divisions are the Roman Catholic, Eastern Orthodox, and Protestant churches.

beliefs Christians believe in one God with three aspects: God the Father, God the Son (Jesus), and God the Holy Spirit, who is the power of God working in the world. God created everything that exists and showed his love for the world by coming to Earth as Jesus, and

suffering and dying in order to be reconciled with humanity. Christians believe that three days after his death by crucifixion Jesus was raised to life by God's power, appearing many times in bodily form to his followers, and that he is now alive in the world through the Holy Spirit. Christians speak of the sufferings they may have to endure because of their faith, and the reward of everlasting life in God's presence which is promised to those who have faith in Jesus Christ and who live according to his teaching.

Organized religion is making Christianity political, rather than making politics Christian.

Christianity

Laurens (Jan) Van der Post, 1906– , South African writer. *Observer* 9 Nov 1986

Christian Science or *the Church of Christ, Scientist* sect established in the USA by Mary Baker Eddy 1879. Christian Scientists believe that since God is good and is a spirit, matter and evil are not ultimately real. Consequently they refuse all medical treatment. The church has its own daily newspaper, the *Christian Science Monitor*.

Christian Science is regarded by its adherents as the restatement of primitive Christianity with its full gospel of salvation from all evil, including sickness and disease as well as sin. According to its adherents, Christian Science healing is brought about by the operation of truth in human conscience. There is no ordained priesthood, but there are public practitioners of Christian Science healing who are officially authorized. The headquarters of the First Church of Christ, Scientist, is in Boston, Massachusetts, with branches in most parts of the world. The textbook of Christian Science is Eddy's *Science and Health with Key to the Scriptures* 1875.

Christian Socialism in Britain, a 19th-century movement stressing the social principles of the Bible and opposed to the untrammelled workings of *laissez-faire* capitalism. Its founders were F D Maurice (1805–1872), Charles Kingsley, and the novelist Thomas Hughes.

In Europe, the establishment of Christian Socialist parties (the first was in Austria) was a direct response to the threat of socialism and therefore contained many conservative features.

Christians of St Thomas sect of Indian Christians on the Malabar Coast, named after the apostle who is supposed to have carried his mission to India. In fact the Christians of St Thomas were established in the 5th century by Nestorians from Persia. They now form part of the Assyrian church (see under ◊Nestorianism) and have their own patriarch.

Christmas Christian religious holiday, observed throughout the Western world on Dec 25 and traditionally marked by feasting and gift-giving. In the Christian church, it is the day on which the birth of Jesus is celebrated, although the actual birth date is unknown. Many of its customs have a non-Christian origin and were adapted from celebrations of the winter solstice.

Heap on more wood! – the wind is chill; But let it whistle as it will, We'll keep our Christmas merry still.

Christmas

Sir Walter Scott, 1771–1832, Scottish novelist and poet. *Marmion*

The choice of a date near the winter solstice owed much to the missionary desire to facilitate conversion of members of older religions, which traditionally held festivals at that time of year. Many Orthodox Christians use an older calendar, and celebrate Christmas on Jan 6.

Christopher, St patron saint of travellers. His feast day, 25 July, was dropped from the Roman Catholic liturgical calendar 1969.

Traditionally he was a martyr in Syria in the 3rd century, and legend describes his carrying the child Jesus over the stream; despite his great strength, he found the burden increasingly heavy, and was told that the child was Jesus Christ bearing the sins of all the world.

chromosome structure in a cell nucleus that carries the ◊genes. Each chromosome consists of one very long strand of DNA, coiled and folded to produce a compact body. The point on a chromosome where a particular gene occurs is known as its locus. Most higher organisms have two copies of each chromosome (they are diploid) but some have only one (they are haploid). There are 46 chromosomes in a normal human cell.

chronicles, medieval books modelled on the Old Testament Books of Chronicles. Until the later Middle Ages, they were usually written in Latin by clerics, who borrowed extensively from one another.

Two early examples were written by Gregory of Tours in the 6th century and by ◊Bede. In the later Middle Ages, vernacular chronicles appear, written by lay people, but by then the chronicle tradition was in decline, soon to be supplanted by Renaissance histories.

Chuang Tzu c. 370–300 BC. Chinese philosopher, the second most important writer in the Taoist tradition, following Lao Tzu. He was renowned for his wit, story telling, and discourses on the inadequacy of words to describe anything of meaning. Stories about him were collected into a book called the *Chuang Tzu*, which became one of the most influential books in the rise of philosophical Taoism.

church building designed as a Christian place of worship; also the Christian community generally, or a specific subdivision or denomination of it, for example the Roman Catholic Church or the Church of England. Churches were first built in the 3rd century, when persecution ceased under the Holy Roman emperor Constantine. The original church design was based on the Roman basilica, with a central nave, aisles either side, and an apse at one end. Many Western churches are built on an east–west axis with an altar at the east end, facing towards Jerusalem. The church as the whole body of Christians is taken to include both those who are alive (the church militant) and those who have died and are in heaven (the church triumphant).

Church Army religious organization within the Church of England founded 1882 by Wilson Carlile (1847–1942), an industrialist converted after the failure of his textile firm, who took orders 1880. Originally intended for evangelical and social work in the London slums, it developed along Salvation Army lines, and has done much work among ex-prisoners and for the soldiers of both world wars.

Church in Wales the Welsh Anglican Church, independent from the ◊Church of England.

The Welsh church became strongly Protestant in the 16th century, but in the 17th and 18th centuries declined as a result of being led by a succession of English-appointed bishops. Disestablished by an act of Parliament 1920, with its endowments appropriated, the Church in Wales today comprises six dioceses (with bishops elected by an electoral college of clergy and lay people) with an archbishop elected from among the six bishops.

Church of England established form of Christianity in England, a member of the Anglican Communion. It was dissociated from the Roman Catholic Church 1534. There were approximately 1,100,000 regular worshippers in 1988.

Two archbishops head the provinces of Canterbury and York, which are subdivided into bishoprics. The Church Assembly 1919 was replaced 1970 by a *General Synod* with three houses (bishops, other clergy, and laity) to regulate church matters, subject to Parliament and the royal assent. A *Lambeth Conference* (first held 1867), attended by bishops from all parts of the Anglican Communion, is held every ten years and presided over in London by the archbishop of Canterbury. It is not legislative but its decisions are often put into practice. The *Church Commissioners* for England 1948 manage the assets of the church (in 1989 valued at 2.64 billion) and endowment of livings. The

---

It is hard to tell where the MCC ends and the Church of England begins.

Church of England
J(ohn) B(oynton) Priestley, 1894–1984,
English novelist and playwright.
New Statesman 20 July 1962

---

main parties, all products of the 19th century, are: the *Evangelical* or *Low Church*, which maintains the church's Protestant character; the *Anglo-Catholic* or *High Church*, which stresses continuity with the pre-Reformation church and is marked by ritualistic practices, the use of confession, and maintenance of religious communities of both sexes; and the *Liberal* or *Modernist* movement, concerned with the reconciliation of the church with modern thought. There is also the *Pentecostal Charismatic* movement, emphasizing spontaneity and speaking in tongues.

Church of Scotland established form of Christianity in Scotland, first recognized by the state 1560. It is based on the Protestant doctrines of the reformer Calvin and governed on Presbyterian lines. The Church went through several periods of episcopacy in the 17th century, and those who adhered to episcopacy after 1690 formed the Episcopal Church of Scotland, an autonomous church in communion with the Church of England. In 1843, there was a split in the Church of Scotland (the Disruption), in which almost a third of its ministers and members left and formed the Free Church of Scotland. Its membership 1988 was about 850,000.

churinga or *tjuringa* in Australian Aboriginal culture, a sacred stone or wooden board, from 7 cm/2 in to 4 m/12 ft long, usually incised or painted with totemic designs.

They were made by men and kept hidden from women and uninitiated boys. Small ones were often attached to possum or human hair string and used as ◊bullroarers.

CIA abbreviation for the US ◊*Central Intelligence Agency*.

Cicero Marcus Tullius 106–43 BC. Roman orator, writer, and politician. His speeches and philosophical and rhetorical works are models of Latin prose, and his letters provide a picture of contemporary Roman life. As consul 63 BC he exposed the Roman politician Catiline's conspiracy in four major orations.

Born in Arpinium, Cicero became an advocate in Rome, spent three years in Greece studying oratory, and after the dictator Sulla's death distinguished himself in Rome with the prosecution of the corrupt Roman governor, Varres. When the First Triumvirate was formed 59 BC, Cicero was briefly exiled and devoted himself to literature. He sided with Pompey during the civil war (49–48) but was pardoned by Julius Caesar and returned to Rome. After Caesar's assassination 44 BC he supported Octavian (the future emperor Augustus) and violently attacked Antony in speeches known as the *Philippics*. On the reconciliation of Antony and Octavian he was executed by Antony's agents.

'Cinderella' traditional European fairy tale, of which about 700 versions exist, including one by Charles ◊Perrault. Cinderella is an ill-treated youngest daughter who is enabled by a fairy godmother to attend the royal ball. She captivates Prince Charming but must flee at midnight, losing a tiny glass slipper by which the prince later identifies her.

cinéma vérité school of documentary film-making that aims to capture truth on film by observing, recording, and presenting real events and situations as they occur without major directorial, editorial, or technical control. It first came into vogue around 1960 with the advent of lightweight cameras and sound equipment.

The American school of cinema vérité, called 'Direct Cinema', used the camera as a passive observer of events. Its main practitioners were Richard Leacock (1921–   ), D A Pennebaker (1930–   ), and Albert and David Maysles (1926–   , 1932–   ).

circular flow of income an economic model which describes how money and resources flow round the economy. In a simple circular flow model where there is no government and no foreign trade, money spent on consumer goods flows from households to companies, whilst money spent on wages, rents, interest, and profits flows from companies to house-

holds. Changes in the size of injections and ◊leakages from the circular flow will cause the level of national income to change.

Cistercian order Roman Catholic monastic order established at Cîteaux 1098 by St Robert de Champagne, abbot of Molesme, as a stricter form of the Benedictine order. Living mainly by agricultural labour, the Cistercians made many advances in farming methods in the Middle Ages. The ◊*Trappist*s, so called from the original house at La Trappe in Normandy (founded by Dominique de Rancé 1664), followed a particularly strict version of the rule.

A citizen of no mean city.

citizen
Bible, the sacred book of the Jewish and
Christian religions.
Acts 21:39

---

citizenship status as a member of a state. In most countries citizenship may be acquired either by birth or by naturalization. The status confers rights such as voting and the protection of the law and also imposes responsibilities such as military service, in some countries.

The UK has five different categories of citizenship, with varying rights. Under the British Nationality Act 1981, amended by the British Nationality (Falkland Islands) Act 1983 and the Hong Kong Act 1985, only a person designated as a *British citizen* has a right of abode in the UK; basically, anyone born in the UK to a parent who is a British citizen, or to a parent who is lawfully settled in the UK. Four other categories of citizenship are defined: *British dependent territories citizenship*, *British overseas citizenship*, *British subject*, and *Commonwealth citizen*. Rights of abode in the UK differ widely for each.

It sometimes happens that someone is a good citizen who has not the quality according to which someone is also a good man.

citizenship
St Thomas Aquinas, c.1226–1274, Italian
scholastic philosopher and theologian.
A History of Political Thought: The Middle Ages
W Ullmann

---

civil disobedience deliberate breaking of laws considered unjust, a form of nonviolent direct action; the term was coined by the US writer Henry Thoreau in an essay of that name

1849. It was advocated by Mahatma ◊Gandhi to prompt peaceful withdrawal of British power from India. Civil disobedience has since been employed by, for instance, the US civil-rights movement in the 1960s and the peace movement in the 1980s.

civilization highly developed human society with structured division of labour. The earliest civilizations evolved in the Old World from advanced neolithic farming societies in the Middle East (Sumer in 3500 BC; Egypt in 3000 BC), the Indus Valley (in 2500 BC), and China (in 2200 BC). In the New World, similar communities evolved civilizations in Mesoamerica (the Olmec in 1200 BC) and Peru (the Chavin in 800 BC).

Civilization advances by extending the number of important operations which we can perform without thinking about them.
civilization
Alfred North Whitehead, 1861–1947, English philosopher and mathematician.
Introduction to Mathematics

In anthropology, civilization is defined as an advanced sociopolitical stage of cultural evolution, whereby a centralized government (over a city, ceremonial centre, or larger region called a state) is supported by the taxation of surplus production, and rules the agricultural and, often, mercantile base. Non-food producers become specialists who govern, lead religious ritual, impose and collect taxes, record the past and present, plan and have executed monumental public works (irrigation systems, roads, bridges, buildings, tombs), and elaborate and formalize the style and traditions of the society. These institutions are based on the use of leisure time to develop writing, mathematics, the sciences, engineering, architecture, philosophy, and the arts. Archaeological remains of cities and ceremonial centres usually indicate the civilized state, with all the trappings of both style and content.

civil rights rights of the individual citizen. In many countries they are specified (as in the Bill of Rights of the US constitution) and guaranteed by law to ensure equal treatment for all citizens. In the USA, the struggle to obtain civil rights for former slaves and their descendants, both through legislation and in practice, has been a major theme since the Civil War.

civil-rights movement general term for efforts by American black people to improve their status in society after World War II. Following their significant contribution to the national effort in wartime, they began a sustained campaign for full civil rights which challenged racial discrimination. Despite favourable legislation such as the Civil Rights Act 1964 and the 1965 Voting Rights Act, growing discontent among urban blacks in northern states led to outbreaks of civil disorder such as the Watts riots in Los Angeles, Aug 1965. Another riot in the city 1992, following the acquittal of policemen charged with beating a black motorist, demonstrated continuing problems in American race relations. For full details see *history* under ◊black.

civil service body of administrative staff appointed to carry out the policy of a government. State administrations were developed in antiquity and have traditionally exercised great influence in imperial regimes. Members of the UK civil service may not take an active part in politics, and do not change with the government.

In Britain, civil servants were originally in the personal service of the sovereign. They were recruited by patronage, and many of them had only nominal duties. The great increase in public expenditure during the Napoleonic Wars led to a move in Parliament for reform of the civil service, but it was not until 1854 that two civil servants, Charles Trevelyan and Stafford Northcote, issued a report as a result of which recruitment by competitive examination, carried out under the Civil Service Commission 1855, came into force. Its recommendations only began to be effective when nomination to the competitive examination was abolished 1870. The two main divisions of the British civil service are the *Home* and *Diplomatic* services, the latter created 1965 by amalgamation of the Foreign, Commonwealth, and Trade Commission services. All employees are paid out of funds voted annually for the purpose by Parliament. Since 1968 the Civil Service Department has been controlled by the prime minister (as minister for the civil service), but everyday supervision is exercised by the Lord Privy Seal. In 1981 the secretary to the cabinet was also made head of the Home Civil Service. The present emphasis is on the professional specialist, and the *Civil Service College* (Sunningdale Park, Ascot, Berkshire) was established 1970 to develop training. Their permanence gives civil servants in the upper echelons an advantage over ministers, who are in office for a comparatively brief time, and in the 1970s and 1980s it was alleged that ministerial policies in conflict with civil-service views tended to be blocked from being put into practice. In 1988 it was decided to separate policy advice from executive functions in several departments.

civil society part of a society or culture outside the government and state-run institutions. For Karl ◊Marx and G W F ◊Hegel, civil society was that part of society where self-interest and materialism were rampant, although Adam ◊Smith believed that enlightened self-interest would promote the general good. Classical writers and earlier political theorists such as John ◊Locke used the term to describe the whole of a civilized society.

cladistics method of biological classification (taxonomy) that uses a formal step-by-step procedure for objectively assessing the extent to which organisms share particular characters, and for assigning them to taxonomic groups. Taxonomic groups (for example, species, genus, family) are termed *clades*.

Clancy of the Overflow an Australian folklore hero featuring in the bush ballads 'The Man from Snowy River' and 'Clancy of the Overflow' by A B Paterson.

Clare, St c. 1194–1253. Christian saint. Born in Assisi, Italy, at 18 she became a follower of St Francis, who founded for her the convent of San Damiano. Here she gathered the first members of the *Order of Poor Clares*. In 1958 she was proclaimed the patron saint of television by Pius XII, since in 1252 she saw from her convent sickbed the Christmas services being held in the Basilica of St Francis in Assisi. Feast day 12 Aug.

Any sufficiently advanced technology is indistinguishable from magic.

Arthur C(harles) Clarke
The Lost Worlds of 2001

Clarke Arthur C(harles) 1917– . English science-fiction and nonfiction writer, who originated the plan for a system of communications satellites in geostationary orbit 1945. His works include *Childhood's End* 1953 and *2001: A Space Odyssey* 1968 (which was made into a film by Stanley Kubrick), and *2010: Odyssey Two* 1982.

class in sociology, the main grouping of social stratification in industrial societies, based primarily on economic and occupational factors, but also referring to people's style of living or sense of group identity.

Within the social sciences, class has been used both as a descriptive category and as the basis of theories about industrial society. Theories of class may see such social divisions either as a source of social stability (see ◊Durkheim) or social conflict (see ◊Marx).

The most widely used descriptive classification in the UK divides the population into five main classes, with the main division between manual and nonmanual occupations. Such classifications have been widely criticized, however, on several grounds: they reflect a middle-class bias that brain is superior to brawn; they classify women according to their husband's occupation rather than their own; they ignore the upper class, the owners of land and industry.

class in biological classification, a group of related orders. For example, all mammals belong to the class Mammalia and all birds to the class Aves. Among plants, all class names end in 'idae' (such as Asteridae) and among fungi in 'mycetes'; there are no equivalent conventions among animals. Related classes are grouped together in a phylum.

classical economics school of economic thought that dominated 19th-century thinking. It originated with Adam ◊Smith's *The Wealth of Nations* 1776, which embodied many of the basic concepts and principles of the classical school. Smith's theories were further developed in the writings of John Stuart Mill and David Ricardo. Central to the theory were economic freedom, competition, and *laissez-faire* government. The idea that economic growth could best be promoted by free trade, unassisted by government, was in conflict with ◊mercantilism.

The belief that agriculture was the chief determinant of economic health was also rejected in favour of manufacturing development, and the importance of labour productivity was stressed. The theories put forward by the classical economists still influence economists today.

Classicism in art, music, and literature, a style that emphasizes the qualities traditionally considered characteristic of ancient Greek and Roman art, that is, reason, balance, objectivity, restraint, and strict adherence to form. The term Classicism (also ◊Neo-Classicism) is often used to characterize the culture of 18th-century Europe, and contrasted with 19th-century Romanticism.

classify in mathematics, to put into separate classes, or sets, which may be uniquely defined.

class interval in statistics, the range of each class of data, used when dealing with large amounts of data. To obtain an idea of the distribution, the data are broken down into convenient classes, which must be mutually exclusive and are usually equal. The class interval defines the range of each class; for example if the class interval is five and the data begin at zero, the classes are 0–4, 5–9, 10–14, and so on.

Clausewitz Karl von 1780–1831. Prussian officer and writer on war, born near Magdeburg. His uncompleted treatise *Vom Kriege/On War* 1833 exerted a powerful influence on military strategists well into the 20th century. Although he advocated the total destruction of an enemy's forces as one of the strategic targets of warfare, his most important idea was to see war as an extension of political policy and not as an end in itself.

Clausius Rudolf Julius Emanuel 1822–1888.

German physicist, one of the founders of the science of thermodynamics. In 1850 he enunciated its second law: heat cannot pass from a colder to a hotter body.

Clement of Alexandria c. AD 150–c. 215. Greek theologian and Father of the Church who applied Greek philosophical ideas to Christian doctrine, believing that Greek philosophy was a divine gift to humanity.

He saw Christ as the source of all human reason as well as the incarnation of the Word. He took an optimistic view of the ultimate fate of even the most wicked. His works include *The Exhortation to the Greeks* and *Miscellanies*. Probably born in Athens, he taught in Alexandria.

Clement of Rome, St lived late 1st century AD. One of the early Christian leaders and writers known as the Fathers of the Church. According to tradition he was the third or fourth bishop of Rome, and a disciple of St Peter. He wrote a letter addressed to the church at Corinth (First Epistle of Clement), and many other writings have been attributed to him.

Cleve Per Teodor 1840–1905. Swedish chemist and geologist who discovered the elements holmium and hulium 1879.

He also demonstrated that the substance didymium, previously supposed to be an element, was in fact two elements, now known as neodymium and praseodymium. Towards the end of his life he developed a method for identifying the age of glacial and post-glacial deposits from the diatom fossils found in them.

clinical ecology in medicine, ascertaining environmental factors involved in illnesses, particularly those manifesting nonspecific symptoms such as fatigue, depression, allergic reactions, and immune system malfunctions, and prescribing means of avoiding or minimizing these effects.

clinical psychology branch of ◊psychology dealing with the understanding and treatment of health problems, particularly mental disorders. The main problems dealt with include anxiety, phobias, depression, obsessions, sexual and marital problems, drug and alcohol dependence, childhood behavioural problems, psychoses (such as schizophrenia), mental handicap, and brain damage (such as dementia). Forensic psychology (concerned with criminal behaviour) and health psychology are other areas of work.

Assessment procedures assess intelligence and cognition (for example, in detecting the effects of brain damage) by using psychometric tests. *Behavioural approaches* are methods of treatment which apply learning theories to clinical problems. *Behaviour therapy* helps clients change unwanted behaviours (such as phobias, obsessions, sexual problems) and to develop new skills (such as improving social interactions). *Behaviour modification* relies on operant conditioning, making selective use of rewards (such as praise) to change behaviour. This is helpful for children, the mentally handicapped, and for patients in institutions, such as mental hospitals. *Cognitive therapy* is a new approach to treating emotional problems, such as anxiety and depression, by teaching clients how to deal with negative thoughts and attitudes. *Counselling*, developed by Rogers, is widely used to help clients solve their own problems. *Psychoanalysis*, as developed by Freud and Jung, is little used by clinical psychologists today. It emphasizes childhood conflicts as a source of adult problems.

cliometrics the use of statistics to measure and quantify all the salient elements of an economy. The data produced are sometimes used to construct counterfactual models where one element is removed and the consequences then measured. These methods, associated with the 'New Economic History', have been used to study the economic impact of railways in Britain, and more controversially, slavery in the USA.

clone group of cells or organisms arising by asexual reproduction from a single 'parent' individual. Clones therefore have exactly the same genetic make-up. The term has been adopted by computer technology, in which it describes a (nonexistent) device that mimics an actual one to enable certain software programs to run correctly.

closed shop any company or firm, public corporation, or other body that requires its employees to be members of the appropriate trade union. Usually demanded by unions, the closed shop may be preferred by employers as simplifying negotiation, but it was condemned by the European Court of Human Rights 1981.

In the USA the closed shop was made illegal by the Taft-Hartley Act 1947, passed by Congress over Truman's veto.

The practice became legally enforceable in the UK 1976, but was rendered largely inoperable by the Employment Acts 1980 and 1982. The European Community's social charter, for which the UK Labour Party announced its support 1989, calls for an end to the closed shop.

club association of persons formed for leisure, recreational, or political purposes.

Clubs based on political principles were common in the late 18th and early 19th centuries, for example the Jacobin Club in Paris in the 1790s and the English Carlton Club, founded in 1832 to oppose the Great Reform Bill. Sports and recreational clubs also originated in the 19th century, with the creation of working men's clubs in Britain and workers' recreation clubs elsewhere in Europe. Many of the London men's clubs developed from the taverns and coffee-houses of the 17th and 18th centuries. The oldest club is White's, evolved from a chocolate-house of the same name in 1693. Other historic London clubs include Boodles, 1762; Brooks's, 1764; the Portland (cards), 1816; the Athenaeum, 1824; the Garrick (dramatic and literary), 1831; the Reform (Liberal), 1836; the Savage (literary and art), 1857; the Press Club, 1882; the Royal Automobile, 1897. The Working Men's Club and Institute Union was founded in 1862, thus extending the range of social membership. Women's clubs include the Alexandra, 1883, and University Women's, 1887.

Cluniac order Christian religious order established 909 AD as a reform movement based on the ◊Benedictine order as part of the monastic foundation at Cluny, France. Its reforms extended to other monasteries in Germany, Italy, Spain, and England. Legally it came to an end in 1790, though its influence persisted. It stressed biblical scholarship and elaborate church ceremony.

Clytemnestra in Greek legend, the wife of ◊Agamemnon. With the help of her lover Aegisthus, she murdered her husband and his paramour Cassandra on his return from the Trojan War, and was in turn killed by her son Orestes.

From a very early age, I had imbibed the opinion, that it was every man's duty to do all that lay in his power to leave his country as good as he had found it.

William Cobbett
Political Register 22 Dec 1832

Cobbett William 1763–1835. British Radical politician and journalist, who published the weekly *Political Register* 1802–35. He spent much time in North America. His crusading essays on the conditions of the rural poor were collected as *Rural Rides* 1830.

Born in Surrey, the self-taught son of a farmer, Cobbett enlisted in the army 1784 and served in Canada. He subsequently lived in the USA as a teacher of English, and became a vigorous pamphleteer, at this time supporting the Tories. In 1800 he returned to England. With increasing knowledge of the sufferings of the farm labourers, he became a Radical and leader of the working-class movement. He was imprisoned 1809–11 for criticizing the flogging of British troops by German mercenaries. He visited the USA again 1817–19. He became a strong advocate of parliamentary reform, and represented Oldham in the Reformed Parliament after 1832.

Cockaigne, Land of in medieval English folklore, a mythical country of leisure and idleness, where fine food and drink were plentiful and to be had for the asking.

codex (plural *codices*) book from before the invention of printing: in ancient times these were wax-coated wooden tablets; later, folded sheets of parchment were attached to the boards, then bound together. The name 'codex' was used for all large works, collections of history, philosophy, and poetry, and during the Roman Empire designated collections of laws. During the 2nd century AD codices began to replace the earlier rolls. They were widely used from about 1200 onwards by the medieval Christian church to keep records.

Various codices record Mexican Indian civilizations just after the time of the Spanish Conquest about 1520. The *Codex Juris Canonici/Code of Canon Law* is the body of laws governing the Roman Catholic Church since 1918.

coeducation education of both boys and girls in one institution. In most countries coeducation has become favored over single-sex education, although there is some evidence to suggest that girls perform better in a single-sex institution, particularly in maths and science.

However, the new National Curriculum in the UK will make it impossible for girls to drop science and technology at an early stage. There has been a marked switch away from single-sex education and in favour of coeducation over the last 20 years in the UK. In the USA, 90% of schools and colleges are coeducational. In 1954, the USSR returned to its earlier coeducational system, which was partly abolished in 1944. In Islamic countries, coeducation is discouraged beyond the infant stage on religious principles.

coevolution evolution of those structures and behaviours within a species that can best be understood in relation to another species. For example, insects and flowering plants have evolved together: insects have produced mouthparts suitable for collecting pollen or drinking nectar, and plants have developed chemicals and flowers that will attract insects to them.

Coevolution occurs because both groups of organisms, over millions of years, benefit from a continuing association, and will evolve structures and behaviours that maintain this association.

cognition in psychology, a general term covering the functions involved in processing information – for example, perception (seeing, hearing, and so on), attention, memory, and reasoning.

cognitive dissonance state of psychological tension occurring when a choice has to be made between two equally attractive or equally unpleasant alternatives. The dissonance is greater the closer the alternatives are in attractiveness or unpleasantness.

Dissonance usually remains after the decision has been made and this motivates efforts to achieve a state of equilibrium, or consonance. The concept, first described by US psychologist Leon Festinger (1919–   ), has been one of the most influential in ◊social psychology and has led to much experimental research. Studies have focused on conditions that enhance or minimize dissonance and on how it can be resolved, for example, changes in the cognition or awareness of the decision situation, changes in attitude following compliance to a request to perform (typically, a role-playing task not nor-

mally voluntarily undertaken), and the effect of incentives on attitude changes following such tasks.

Bibl. Eiser, J Richard *Social Psychology: Attitudes, Cognition and Social Behaviour* (1986) ch. 4

cognitive psychology study of cognitive processes in humans and animals, covering their role in learning, memory, reasoning, and language development. Cognitive psychologists use a number of experimental techniques, including laboratory-based research with normal and brain-damaged subjects, as well as computer and mathematical models to test and validate theories.

The study of cognition was largely eschewed by psychologists for the early part of the 20th century following the demise of ◊introspection as a method of investigation and the rise of ◊behaviourism. However, several influential theorists, such as Edward Chase Tolman (1886–1959), continued to argue that in order to fully comprehend the determinants of behaviour cognitive processes must be studied and understood, and in 1957 Noam ◊Chomsky's examination of behaviourist approaches to language acquisition appeared. With the rise of telecommunications technology and digital computing, theorists, such as Donald Broadbent, developed information-processing models of the brain, later elaborated, for example, by Ulrich Neisser (1928–   ). More recently, the limitations of these approaches, for example, in elaborating the role of ◊emotion and motivation in cognitive processes, have become the focus of attention.

cognitive therapy also known as cognitive behaviour therapy methods of treating emotional disorders, such as ◊depression and ◊anxiety states, developed by the psychiatrist Aaron T Beck and others in the USA. Less concerned with the ◊unconscious and its manifestations, cognitive therapy focuses on the patient's conscious mental processes in the belief that problems may be due to faulty learning, wrong information, mistaken influences and so on. It encourages the patient to challenge the distorted and unhelpful thinking that is characteristic of depression, for example. The treatment may also include ◊behaviour therapy.

Coke Edward 1552–1634. Lord Chief Justice of England 1613–17. He was a defender of common law against royal prerogative; against Charles I he drew up the Petition of Right 1628, which defines and protects Parliament's liberties.

For a man's house is his castle.

Edward Coke
Institutes, 'Commentary upon Littleton',
Third Institute, ch 73

Coke was called to the Bar in 1578, and in 1592 became speaker of the House of Commons and solicitor-general. As attorney-general from 1594 he conducted the prosecution of Elizabeth I's former favourites Essex and Raleigh, and of the Gunpowder Plot conspirators. In 1606 he became Chief Justice of the Common Pleas, and began his struggle, as champion of the common law, against James I's attempts to exalt the royal prerogative. An attempt to silence him by promoting him to the dignity of Lord Chief Justice proved unsuccessful, and from 1620 he led the parliamentary opposition and the attack on Charles I's adviser Buckingham. Coke's *Institutes* are a legal classic, and he ranks as the supreme common lawyer.

Coke Thomas William 1754–1842. English pioneer and promoter of the improvements associated with the Agricultural Revolution. His innovations included regular manuring of the soil, the cultivation of fodder crops in association with corn, and the drilling of wheat and turnips.

He also developed a fine flock of Southdown sheep at Holkham, Norfolk, which were superior to the native Norfolks, and encouraged his farm tenants to do likewise. These ideas attracted attention at the annual sheep shearings, an early form of agricultural show, which Coke held on his home farm from 1776. By the end of the century these had become major events, with many visitors coming to see and discuss new stock, crops, and equipment.

Cold War ideological, political, and economic tensions 1945–90 between the USSR and Eastern Europe on the one hand and the USA and Western Europe on the other. The Cold War was exacerbated by propaganda, covert activity by intelligence agencies, and economic sanctions; it intensified at times of conflict anywhere in the world. Arms-reduction agreements between the USA and USSR in the late 1980s, and a diminution of Soviet influence in Eastern Europe, symbolized by the opening of the Berlin Wall 1989, led to a reassessment of positions, and the 'war' officially ended 1990.

Colenso John William 1814–1883. Bishop of Natal, South Africa, from 1853. He was the first to write down the Zulu language. He championed the Zulu way of life (including polygamy) in relation to Christianity, and applied Christian morality to race relations in South Africa.

Cold War: chronology

1947	The term 'Cold War' was first used by Bernard Baruch in a speech referring to the Truman Doctrine in April.
1950–53	The Korean War.
1956	The USSR intervened in Hungary to put down a revolution.
1962	The Cuban missile crisis.
1964–75	The USA participated in the Vietnam War.
1968	The USSR intervened in Czechoslovakia.
1972	SALT I accord on arms limitation signed by USA and USSR, beginning a thaw, or détente, in East–West relations.
1979	The USSR invaded Afghanistan.
1980–81	US support for the Solidarity movement in Poland. US president Reagan called the USSR an 'evil empire'.
1982	US covert and military intervention in Central America increased to aid right-wing groups.
1983	US president Reagan proposed to militarize space (Star Wars).
1986	Soviet leader Gorbachev made a proposal for nuclear disarmament that was turned down by Reagan.
1988	Soviet and US leaders reached accord on medium-range nuclear missiles.
1989	Widespread moves towards the abandonment of communism took place in Eastern European countries, including the opening of the Berlin Wall.
1990	Formal end of the Cold War declared in Nov. Treaty signed between NATO and Warsaw Pact countries on reduction of conventional forces in Europe. US president Bush announced the start of a 'new world order'.

Cole, Old King legendary British king, supposed to be the father of St Helena, who married the Roman emperor Constantius, father of Constantine; he is also supposed to have founded Colchester. The historical Cole was possibly a north British chieftain named Coel, of the 5th century, who successfully defended his land against the Picts and Scots. The nursery rhyme is recorded only from 1709.

Coleridge Samuel Taylor 1772–1834. English poet, one of the founders of the Romantic movement. A friend of Southey and Wordsworth, he collaborated with the latter on *Lyrical Ballads* 1798. His poems include 'The Rime of the Ancient Mariner', 'Christabel', and 'Kubla Khan'; critical works include *Biographia Literaria*.

Prose = words in their best order; poetry = the best words in the best order.

Samuel Taylor Coleridge
Table Talk 12 July 1827

While at Cambridge University, Coleridge was driven by debt to enlist in the Dragoons, and then in 1795, as part of an abortive plan to found a communist colony in the USA with Robert Southey, married Sarah Fricker, from whom he afterwards separated. He became addicted to opium and from 1816 lived in Highgate, London, under medical care. As a philosopher, he argued inferentially that even in registering sense-perceptions the mind was performing acts of creative imagination, rather than being a passive arena in which ideas interact mechanistically. A brilliant talker and lecturer, he was expected to produce some great work of philosophy or criticism. His *Biographia Literaria* 1817, much of it based on German ideas, is full of insight but its formlessness and the limited extent of his poetic output indicates a partial failure of promise.

Colet John c. 1467–1519. English humanist, influenced by the Italian reformer ◊Savonarola and the Dutch scholar ◊Erasmus. He reacted against the scholastic tradition in his interpretation of the Bible, and founded modern biblical exegesis. In 1505 he became dean of St Paul's Cathedral, London.

collective bargaining process whereby management, representing an employer, and a trade union, representing employees, agree to negotiate jointly terms and conditions of employment. Agreements can be company-based or industry-wide.

collective responsibility doctrine found in governments modelled on the British system of cabinet government. It is based on convention, or usage, rather than law, and requires that once a decision has been taken by the cabinet, all members of the government are bound by it and must support it or resign their posts.

collective unconscious in psychology, the shared pool of memories, ideas, modes of thought etc. that according to C G ◊Jung comes from the life experience of one's ancestors, indeed from the entire human race. It coexists with the personal ◊unconscious, which contains the material of individual experience, and may be regarded as an immense depository of ancient wisdom.

Primal experiences are represented in the collective unconscious by archetypes, symbolic pictures, or personifications that appear in ◊dreams and are the common element in myths, fairy tales, the literature of the world's religions, etc. Examples include the serpent, the sphinx, the Great Mother, the anima (representing the nature of woman), and the mandala (representing balanced wholeness, human or divine).

collectivism in politics, a position in which the collective (such as the state) has priority over its individual members. It is the opposite of ◊individualism, which is itself a variant of anarchy.

Collectivism, in a pure form impossible to attain, would transfer all social and economic activities to the state, which would assume total responsibility for them. In practice, it is possible to view collectivism as a matter of degree and argue that the political system of one state was more or less collectivist than that of another, for example in the provision of state-controlled housing.

collectivization policy pursued by the Soviet leader Stalin in the USSR after 1928 to reorganize agriculture by taking land into state ownership or creating collective farms. Much of this was achieved during the first two ◊five-year plans but only with much coercion and loss of life among the peasantry.

Collingwood Robin George 1889–1943. British philosopher, historian, and archaeologist who came to view philosophy as part of history, because any philosophical theory could be properly understood only within its own historical context and not from the point of view of the present. His aesthetic theory, outlined in *Principles of Art* 1938, bases art on expression and imagination.

Perfect freedom is reserved for the man who lives by his own work, and in that work does what he wants to do.

Robin George Collingwood
Speculum Mentis

He was professor of philosophy at Oxford, and also an authority on the history and archaeology of Roman Britain.

colonialism another name for ◊*imperialism*.

colour symbolism in the iconography of many faiths, certain colours signify certain deities, passions, or ideas. In ◊Taoism, white symbolises death, while in most Christian countries, white symbolises purity and is used for weddings. Blue is the colour associated with the Virgin Mary in Catholic symbolism, while in Hinduism it is the sacred colour associated with ◊Krishna. In many Christian traditions, the different festivals and seasons of the Church calendar are signalled by different colours used for the altar covering or priest's stole.

colour vision the ability of the eye to recognize different frequencies in the visible spectrum as colours, but it is also much more than just this. Colour vision is one of the ways in which the brain can acquire knowledge of the unchanging characteristics of objects. Colours are constructs of the brain, rather than physical features of objects or their surface. They remain more or less stable, and objects remain recognizable, in spite of the continuously changing illumination in which they are seen, a phenomenon known as *colour constancy*.

In 1802 Thomas ◊Young proposed that the enormous variety of colours in the visual spectrum could be accounted for by only three types of particle, or cell, in the retina, each corresponding to one of three colours – red, blue, or yellow. His idea was taken up and modified in the mid-19th century by ◊Helmholtz who argued that each type of light-sensitive cell, though sensitive to wavelengths over much of the spectrum, is especially sensitive to one of three types of wavelength – red, green, or blue. The Young–Helmholtz trichromatic, or three-colour, theory has inspired much research and has been particularly useful in explaining inherited colour defects (colour blindness), and the fact that a mixture of three coloured lights can match any other coloured light. However, it cannot explain the phenomenon of colour constancy and says little about what happens behind the retina.

◊Newton demonstrated in the 17th century that ordinary white light is a mixture of lights of different wavelengths, with long wavelengths appearing red, middle wavelengths green, short wavelengths blue, and so on. This led him to assume mistakenly, though not unreasonably, that an object's colour derives from the wavelengths it reflects. According to this theory, a red object, for example, would appear red because it mainly reflected long-wavelength, or red, light. But this common assumption is mistaken. A red object will still appear red when it is actually reflecting predominantly middle-wavelength or short-wavelength light. In a remarkable series of experiments, Edwin ◊Land showed that the brain registers the varying intensities of light, or lightnesses, in each of the long-, middle- and short-wavelength bands from all of the coloured surfaces in a scene, compares them simultaneously to produce three lightness records, and then compares these lightness records to construct colours. Land called his theory the retinex theory. It is receiving striking confirmation from physiological studies of single cells in the visual cortex, most notably by Semir Zeki, and from studies of patients who have become colour blind as a result of injury to the brain.

Bibl. Zeki, Semir *A Vision of the Brain* (Oxford, 1993) ch. 1–5, 23–27

Columba, St 521–597. Irish Christian abbot, missionary to Scotland. He was born in County Donegal of royal descent, and founded monasteries and churches in Ireland. In 563 he sailed with 12 companions to Iona, and built a monastery there that was to play a leading part in the conversion of Britain. Feast day 9 June.

From his base on Iona St Columba made missionary journeys to the mainland. Legend has it that he drove a monster from the river Ness, and he crowned Aidan, an Irish king of Argyll.

Columban, St 543–615. Irish Christian abbot. He was born in Leinster, studied at Bangor, and about 585 went to the Vosges, France, with 12 other monks and founded the monastery of Luxeuil. Later, he preached in Switzerland, then went to Italy, where he built the abbey of Bobbio in the Apennines. Feast day 23 Nov.

Mirth is always good, and cannot be excessive.

comedy
Benedict or Baruch Spinoza, 1632–1677,
Dutch philosopher of Portugese–Jewish
descent.
Ethics IV. xlii

---

comedy drama that aims to make its audience laugh, usually with a happy or amusing ending, as opposed to ◊tragedy. The comic tradition has enjoyed many changes since its Greek roots; the earliest comedy developed in ancient Greece, in the topical and fantastic satires of Aristophanes. Great comic dramatists include Shakespeare, Molière, Carlo Goldoni, Pierre de Marivaux, George Bernard Shaw, and Oscar Wilde. Genres of comedy include pantomime, satire, farce, black comedy, and *commedia dell'arte*.

All I need to make a comedy is a park, a policeman and a pretty girl.

comedy
Charlie (Charles Spencer) Chaplin,
1889–1977, English film actor and director.
My Autobiography

The comic tradition was established by the Greek dramatists Aristophanes and Menander, and the Roman writers Terence and Plautus. In medieval times, the Vices and Devil of the Morality plays developed into the stock comic characters of the Renaissance *Comedy of Humours* with such notable villains as Ben Jonson's Mosca in *Volpone*. The timeless comedies of Shakespeare and Molière were followed in England during the 17th century by the witty *comedy of manners* of Restoration writers such as George Etherege, William Wycherley, and William Congreve. Their often coarse but always vital comedies were toned down in the later Restoration dramas of Richard Sheridan and Oliver Goldsmith. Sentimental comedy dominated most of the 19th century, though little is remembered in the late 20th century, which prefers the realistic tradition of Shaw and the elegant social comedies of Wilde. The polished comedies of Nöel Coward and Terence Rattigan from the 1920s to 1940s were eclipsed during the late 1950s and the 1960s by a trend towards satire and cynicism as seen in the works of Joe Orton and Peter Nichols, alongside absurdist comedies by Samuel Beckett, Jean Genet, and Tom Stoppard. From the 1970s the 'black comedies' of Alan Ayckbourn have dominated the English stage, with the political satires of Dario Fo affecting the radical theatre.

Comenius see Jan Amos ◊Komensky, Moravian educationist.

Comintern acronym from *Communist* *◊International*.

command economy or *planned economy* type of economy where resources are allocated by the state through a system of planning. For example, in the former Soviet Union state planners decided what was to be produced. They passed orders down to factories, allocating raw materials, workers, and other factors of production to them. Factories were then told how much they should produce with these resources and where they should be sent. If there was a shortage of goods in the shops, then goods would be rationed through queueing. The ◊market mechanism plays little role in a command economy. However, historical experience this century suggests that planned economies have not produced as high growth as ◊free market or ◊mixed economies. For this reason, the command economies of Eastern Europe and the former Soviet Union are currently being transformed into mixed economies.

commensalism in biology, a relationship between two species whereby one (the commensal) benefits from the association, whereas the other neither benefits nor suffers. For example, certain species of millipede and silverfish inhabit the nests of army ants and live by scavenging on the refuse of their hosts, but without affecting the ants.

commodity something produced for sale. Commodities may be consumer goods, such as radios, or producer goods, such as copper bars. *Commodity markets* deal in raw or semi-raw materials that are amenable to grad-ing and that can be stored for considerable periods without deterioration.

Commodity markets developed to their present form in the 19th century, when industrial growth facilitated trading in large, standardized quantities of raw materials. Most markets encompass trading in *commodity futures* – that is, trading for delivery several months ahead. Major commodity markets exist in Chicago, Tokyo, London, and elsewhere. Though specialized markets exist, such as that for silkworm cocoons in Tokyo, most trade relates to cereals and metals. *Softs* is a term used for most materials other than metals.

Common Agricultural Policy (CAP) system of financial support for farmers in European Community (EC) countries. The most important way in which EC farmers are supported is through guaranteeing them minimum prices for part of what they produce.

CAP became extremely expensive in the 1970s and 1980s and led to overproduction of those agricultural products which were subsidized. In many years, far more was produced than could be sold and it had to be stored, creating 'mountains' and 'lakes' of produce. A large number of 'reforms' of CAP have been implemented in an attempt to solve these problems. However, CAP is likely to remain expensive for the EC taxpayer in the 1990s.

common difference the difference between any number and the next in an arithmetic sequence. For example, in the set 1, 4, 7, 10, ... , the common difference is 3.

common land unenclosed wasteland, forest, and pasture used in common by the community at large. Poor people have throughout history gathered fruit, nuts, wood, reeds, roots, game, and so on from common land; in dry regions of India, for example, the landless derive 20% of their annual income in this way, together with much of their food and fuel. Codes of conduct evolved to ensure that common resources were not depleted. But in the 20th century, in the Third World as elsewhere, much common land has been privatized or appropriated by the state, and what remains is overburdened by those dependent on it.

In the UK, ◊enclosure of common land by powerful landowners began in the 14th century, becoming widespread in the 15th and 16th centuries. It caused poverty, homelessness, and rural depopulation and led to revolts 1536, 1569, and 1608. Under the Commons Registration Act 1965, all remaining common land (such as village greens) had to be registered by a certain date; otherwise the rights of common were lost.

common law that part of the English law not embodied in legislation. It consists of rules of law based on common custom and usage and on judicial decisions. English common law became the basis of law in the USA and many other English-speaking countries.

Common law developed after the Norman Conquest 1066 as the law common to the whole of England, rather than local law. As the court system became established (under Henry II), and judges' decisions became recorded in law reports, the doctrine of *precedent* developed. This means that, in deciding a particular case, the court must have regard to the principles of law laid down in earlier reported cases on the same, or similar points, although the law may be extended or varied if the facts of the particular case are sufficiently different. Hence, common law (sometimes called 'case law' or 'judge-made law') keeps the law in harmony with the needs of the community where no legislation is applicable or where the legislation requires interpretation.

Common Market popular name for the *European Economic Community*; see ◊European Community (EC).

Commonsense is the most widely distributed commodity in the world, for everyone thinks himself so well endowed with it.

common sense
René Descartes, 1596–1650, French philosopher.
Discourse on Method

---

common sense in philosophy, the doctrine that we perceive the external world directly, that what we perceive is what there is and how things are. Common-sense realism has been held by Scottish mathematician Thomas ◊Reid and English philosopher G E ◊Moore. Although a useful antidote to complex metaphysical theories, common sense can mislead – for instance, common sense tells us that the world is flat.

Commons, House of the lower but more powerful of the two parts of the British and Canadian ◊parliaments.

In the UK, the House of Commons consists of 650 elected members of parliament each of whom represents a constituency. Its functions are to debate and legislate, and to scrutinize the activities of government.

commonwealth body politic founded on law for the common 'weal' or good. Political philosophers of the 17th century, such as Thomas Hobbes and John Locke, used the term to mean an organized political community. In Britain it was specifically applied to the regime (*the Commonwealth*) of Oliver Cromwell 1649–60.

commune group of people or families living together, sharing resources and responsibilities.

Communes developed from early 17th-century religious communities such as the Rosicrucians and Muggletonians, to more radical groups such as the ◊Diggers and the ◊Quakers. Many groups moved to America to found communes, such as the Philadelphia Society (1680s) and the ◊Shakers, which by 1800 had ten groups in North America. The Industrial Revolution saw a new wave of utopian communities associated with the ideas of Robert ◊Owen and Francois Charles ◊Fourier. Communes had a revival during the 1960s, when many small groups were founded. In 1970 it was estimated there were 2,000 communes in the USA, and 100 in England. The term also refers to a communal division or settlement in a communist country. In China, a policy of ◊Mao Zedong involved the grouping of villages within districts (averaging 30,000 people) and thus, cooperatives were amalgamated into larger units, the communes. In 1958 (the ◊Great Leap Forward) saw the establishment of peoples' communes (workers' combines) with shared living quarters and shared meals. Communes organized workers' brigades and were responsible for their own nurseries, schools, clinics, and other facilities. The term can also refer to the 11th-century to 12th-century association of burghers in north and central Italy. The communes of many cities asserted their independence from the overlordship of either the Holy Roman emperor or the pope, only to fall under the domination of oligarchies or despots during the 13th and 14th centuries.

communications in mass media, a term often used to describe features and developments in the fields of telegraphy, the telephone, radio, cinema, television, communications satellites, microcomputers, and newspapers.

The earliest practicable *telegraphic* instrument, invented by William Cooke and Charles Wheatstone, was patented in 1837. Telegraph links were established between Britain and France in 1850 and the first transatlantic cable was laid in 1858. The *telephone* was invented in 1876 by Alexander Graham Bell. In 1879 telephone exchanges were opened in London, Liverpool, and Manchester. In 1891 the first telephone cable was laid between England and France. Guglielmo Marconi, an Italian pioneer of telegraphy, succeeded in transmitting a *wireless* signal across the Atlantic Ocean from Cornwall to Newfoundland in 1896. The first *photographic* negative was produced by William Fox Talbot in 1839, and in the 1880s the 'box' camera was invented by US entrepreneur George Eastman. In *cinema* the first 'moving pictures' were shown in public in Paris in 1895. The first successful feature film with sound was *The Jazz Singer* 1927. The first working *television* system was demonstrated in London in 1926 by John Logie Baird. The first public television service in the world was started by the British Broadcasting Corporation (BBC) at Alexandra Palace in London 1936. The first *communications satellite* Telstar, was launched in July 1962 to carry TV signals across the Atlantic Ocean. Other satellites followed, and are used by individual countries for internal communications, or for business or military use. In the early 19th century Charles Babbage pioneered a very primitive form of *computer*. By the early 20th century, simple automatic calculating machines were coming into use. The first electronic computers were made in the USA after World War II. The first daily *newspaper* in the world, the *Daily Courant* appeared in 1702. In the later 19th and early 20th centuries, major technical changes in printing helped to reduce costs of newspaper production. In the late 1980s the production of newspapers was revolutionized with the introduction of more advanced technology and new printing methods.

Communion, Holy in the Christian church, another name for the ◊Eucharist.

Whether you like it or not, history is on our side. We will bury you.

communism
Nikita Sergeyevich Khrushchev, 1894–1971, Soviet politician, secretary general of the Communist Party 1953–64, premier 1958–64.
Speech to Western diplomats at reception in Moscow 18 Nov 1956

---

communism revolutionary socialism based on the theories of the political philosophers Karl ◊Marx and Friedrich ◊Engels, emphasizing common ownership of the means of production and a planned economy. The principle held is that each should work according to their capacity and receive according to their needs. Politically, it seeks the overthrow of capitalism through a proletarian revolution. The first communist state was the USSR after the revolution of 1917. Revolutionary socialist

parties and groups united to form communist parties in other countries (in the UK 1920). After World War II, communism was enforced in those countries that came under Soviet occupation. China emerged after 1961

Communism is Soviet power plus the electrification of the whole country.

communism
Vladimir Ilyich. Adopted name of Vladimir Ilyich Ulyanov Lenin, 1870–1924, Russian communist revolutionary leader.
Report to 8th Congress of the Communist Party 1920

---

as a rival to the USSR in world communist leadership, and other countries attempted to adapt communism to their own needs. The late 1980s saw a movement for more individual freedoms in many communist countries, culminating in the abolition or overthrow of communist rule in Eastern European countries and Mongolia, and further state repression in China. The failed hard-line coup in the USSR against President Gorbachev 1991 resulted in the effective abandonment of communism there. Communism, as the ideology of a nation state, now survives in only a handful of countries, notably China, Cuba, North Korea, Laos and Vietnam, and even in these countries it cannot be certain that the communist regimes will survive into the next century. In China, for example, it is doubtful whether economic liberalism, which is being increasingly practised, can live with political monism, and the retention of the communist ideology in Cuba is very much dependent on the survival of its charismatic leader.

Marx and Engels in the *Communist Manifesto* 1848 put forward the theory that human society, having passed through successive stages of slavery, feudalism, and capitalism, must advance to communism. This combines with a belief in economic determinism to form the central communist concept of *dialectical materialism*. Marx believed that capitalism had become a barrier to progress and needed to be replaced by a *dictatorship of the proletariat* (working class), which would build a socialist society. The Social Democratic parties formed in Europe in the second half of the 19th century professed to be Marxist, but gradually began to aim at reforms of capitalist society rather than at the radical social change envisaged by Marx. The Russian Social Democratic Labour Party, led by Lenin, remained Marxist, and after the Nov 1917 revolution changed its name to Communist Party to emphasize its difference from Social Democratic parties elsewhere. The communal basis of feudalism was still strong in Russia, and ◊Lenin and ◊Stalin were able to impose the communist system. China's communist revolution was completed 1949 under Mao Zedong.

Both China and the USSR took strong measures to maintain or establish their own types of 'orthodox' communism in countries on their borders (the USSR in Hungary and Czechoslovakia, and China in North Korea and Vietnam). In more remote areas (the USSR in the Arab world and Cuba, and China in Albania) and (both of them) in the newly emergent African countries, these orthodoxies were installed as the fount of doctrine and the source of technological aid.

In 1956 the Soviet premier Nikita Khrushchev denounced **Stalinism**, and there were uprisings in Hungary and Poland. During the late 1960s and the 1970s it was debated whether the state requires to be maintained as 'the dictatorship of the proletariat' once revolution on the economic front has been achieved, or whether it may then become the state of the entire people: Engels, Lenin, Khrushchev, and Liu Shaoqi held the latter view; Stalin and Mao the former. Many communist parties in capitalist countries, for example, Japan and the **Eurocommunism** of France, Italy, and the major part of the British Communist Party, have since the 1960s or later rejected Soviet dominance. In the 1980s there was an expansion of political and economic freedom in Eastern Europe: the USSR remained a single-party state, but with a relaxation of strict party orthodoxy and a policy of *perestroika* ('restructuring'), while the other Warsaw Pact countries moved towards an end to communist rule and its replacement by free elections within more democratic political systems.

In the Third World, Libya has attempted to combine revolutionary socialism with Islam; the extreme communist Khmer Rouge devastated Cambodia (then called Kampuchea) 1975–78; Latin America suffers from the US fear of communism in what it regards as its back yard, with the democratically elected Marxist regime in Chile violently overthrown 1973, and the socialist government of Nicaragua (until it fell 1990) involved in a prolonged civil war against US-backed guerrillas (Contras).

In 1991, the British Communist Party, with 6,300 card holders, changed its name to the Democratic Left. The red and black logo was replaced by a red (traditional), purple (women's suffrage), and green (environment) one.

community in the social sciences, the sense of identity, purpose, and companionship that comes from belonging to a particular place, organization, or social group. The concept dominated sociological thinking in the first half of the 20th century, and inspired the academic discipline of *community studies*.

community in ecology, an assemblage of plants, animals, and other organisms living within a circumscribed area. Communities are usually named by reference to a dominant feature such as characteristic plant species (for example, beech-wood community), or a prominent physical feature (for example, a freshwater-pond community).

community architecture movement enabling people to work directly with architects in the design and building of their own homes and neighbourhoods. Projects include housing at Byker, Newcastle, UK, by Ralph Erskine, and the work of the Lewisham Self-Build Housing Association, London 1977–80, pioneered by Walter Segal; the revitalization of the town of Bologna, Italy; and the University of Louvain, Belgium, by Lucien Kroll (1927–).

company in economics, a number of people grouped together as a business enterprise. Types of company include public limited companies, partnerships, joint ventures, sole proprietorships, and branches of foreign companies. Most companies are private and, unlike public companies, cannot offer their shares to the general public.

For most companies in Britain the liability of the members is limited to the amount of their subscription, under an act of 1855 promoted by Judge Lord Bramwell. This brought British law into line with European practice, which had already been largely adopted in the USA. This *limitation of liability* is essential when large capital sums must be raised by the contributions of many individuals. The affairs of companies are managed by directors, a public company having at least two, and their accounts must be audited. The development of multinational corporations, enterprises that operate in a number of countries, has been the cause of much controversy in recent years because of the conflict of interest that can occur. In developing countries, for example, the presence of multinationals may cause distortions in the marketplace.

comparative advantage law of international trade first elaborated by English economist David ◊Ricardo showing that trade becomes worthwhile if the cost of production of particular items differs between one country and another.

For example, if France can produce cheese at a cost of 100 units and milk at a cost of 300 units whilst Spain can produce cheese at 200 units and milk at 400 units, then France has an absolute advantage in the production of both cheese and milk because it can produce both more cheaply in absolute cost terms. However, it will still be advantageous for France to trade with Spain because in France milk is more expensive relative to cheese (milk costs three times more to produce than cheese) than in Spain (where milk costs only twice as much). So France would specialize in the production of cheese and Spain in the production of milk and they would trade.

comparative method in sociology, a term referring to the comparison of different societies or social groups as a means of elucidating their differences and/or similarities. It was originally used by philologists to analyse the common characteristics of different languages in order to trace their common origins.

comparative psychology branch of ◊psychology concerned with differences in the behaviour of various animal species; also the study of animal psychology in general. The most important area of research has been that of learning, covering topics such as ◊conditioning, ◊behaviourism, and the effects of reward and punishment on performance.

The effects of various drugs on psychological processes and behaviour has been an important area of study, as has maternal behaviour and interactions between mothers and offspring, particularly in mammals, together with the insights gained in our understanding of infant development. A number of experimental techniques are used including research under laboratory conditions and field studies where the behaviour of animals is observed under natural conditions.

comparative religion term first used in the late 19th century to mark the development of a critical examination of all religious phenomena with the dispassion of scientific analysis. It marked the beginnings of serious study in Western universities of non-Christian traditions and beliefs. The term has now fallen out of favour because such objectivity is impossible and because the concept of comparison implies that there is a degree of competition between the faiths.

competence and performance in linguistics, the potential and actual utterances of a speaker. As formulated by the linguist Noam ◊Chomsky, a person's linguistic competence is the set of internalized rules in his or her brain that makes it possible to understand and produce language – rules that stipulate, for example, the order words take to form a sentence. A person's performance consists of the actual phrases and sentences he or she produces on the basis of these inner rules.

competition rivalry in the marketplace between different business organizations. Firms can compete in many different ways including price, quality of products, availability, and delivery dates, and through advertising. In a market where ◊perfect competition is operating, it is assumed that all companies produce identical products and compete only on price. In markets characterized by an ◊oligopoly and other forms of ◊imperfect competition, goods are branded and there is much more emphasis on nonprice competition such as advertising. In a ◊monopoly, where there is only one producer, there is no competition. Governments attempt to increase competition through competition policy.

complex in psychology, a group of ideas and feelings that have become repressed because they are distasteful to the person in whose mind they arose, but which are still active in the depths of the person's unconscious mind, continuing to affect his or her life and actions even though he or she is no longer fully aware of their existence. Typical examples include the ◊Oedipus complex and the ◊inferiority complex.

complex number in mathematics, a number written in the form $a + ib$, where a and b are real numbers and i is the square root of -1 (that is, $i^2 = -1$); i used to be known as the 'imaginary' part of the complex number. Some equations in algebra, such as those of the form $x^2 + 5 = 0$, cannot be solved without recourse to complex numbers, because the real numbers do not include square roots of negative numbers.

The sum of two or more complex numbers is obtained by adding separately their real and imaginary parts, for example:

$$(a + bi) + (c + di) = (a + c) + (b + d)i$$

Complex numbers can be represented graphically on an Argand diagram, which uses rectangular Cartesian coordinates in which the x-axis represents the real part of the number and the y-axis the imaginary part. Thus the number $z = a + bi$ is plotted as the point (a, b). Complex numbers have applications in various areas of science, such as the theory of alternating currents in electricity.

componential analysis in linguistics, the analysis of the elements of a word's meaning.

The word *boy*, for example, might be said to have three basic meaning elements (or semantic properties): 'human', 'young,' and 'male'; and so might the word *murder*: 'kill', 'intentional', and 'illegal'.

composite function in mathematics, a function made up of two or more other functions carried out in sequence, usually denoted by ◊ or o, as in the relation (f ◊ g) x = f [g(x)].

Usually, composition is not commutative: (f ◊ g) is not necessarily the same as (g ◊ f).

comprehensive school in the UK, a secondary school which admits pupils of all abilities, and therefore without any academic selection procedure.

Most secondary education in the USA and the USSR has always been comprehensive, but most W European countries, including France and the UK, have switched from a selective to a comprehensive system within the last 20 years. In England, the 1960s and 1970s saw a slow but major reform of secondary education, in which most state-funded local authorities replaced selective grammar schools (taking only the most academic 20% of children) and secondary modern schools (for the remainder), with comprehensive schools capable of providing suitable courses for children of all abilities. By 1987, only 3% of secondary pupils were still in grammar schools. Scotland and Wales have switched completely to comprehensive education, while Northern Ireland retains a largely selective system.

Compton Arthur Holly 1892–1962. US physicist known for his work on X-rays. Working at Chicago 1923 he found that X-rays scattered by such light elements as carbon increased their wavelengths. Compton concluded from this unexpected result that the X-rays were displaying both wavelike and particlelike properties, since named the *Compton effect*. He shared a Nobel prize 1927 with Scottish physicist Charles Wilson (1869–1959).

computer programmable electronic device that processes data and performs calculations and other symbol-manipulation tasks. There are three types: the digital computer, which manipulates information coded as binary numbers; the analogue computer, which works with continuously varying quantities; and the hybrid computer, which has characteristics of both analogue and digital computers.

There are four classifications of digital computer, corresponding roughly to their size and intended use: microcomputers (including portable computers) are the smallest and most common, used in small businesses, at home, and in schools; minicomputers are found in medium-sized businesses and university departments (although the distinction between minicomputers and microcomputers is disappearing); mainframes, which can often service several hundred users simultaneously, are found in large organizations such as national companies; and supercomputers, mostly used for highly complex scientific tasks, such as analysing the results of weather forecasting.

computer simulation representation of a real-life situation in a computer program. For example, the program might simulate the flow of customers arriving at a bank. The user can alter variables, such as the number of cashiers on duty, and see the effect.

More complex simulations can model the behaviour of chemical reactions or even nuclear explosions. Computers also control the actions of machines – for example, a flight simulator models the behaviour of real aircraft and allows training to take place in safety. Computer simulations are very useful when it is too dangerous, time consuming, or simply impossible to carry out a real experiment or test.

Men are not allowed to think freely about chemistry and biology, why should they be allowed to think freely about political philosophy?

Auguste Comte
Positive Philosophy

Comte Auguste 1798–1857. French philosopher regarded as the founder of sociology, a term he coined 1830. He sought to establish sociology as an intellectual discipline, using a scientific approach (◊positivism) as the basis of a new science of social order and social development.

Comte, born in Montpellier, was expelled from the Paris Ecole Polytechnique for leading a student revolt 1816. In 1818 he became secretary to the socialist Saint-Simon and was much influenced by him. He began lecturing on the 'Positive Philosophy' 1826, but almost immediately succumbed to a nervous disorder and once tried to commit suicide in the river Seine. On his recovery he resumed his lectures and mathematical teaching. In his six-volume *Cours de philosophie positive* 1830–42 he argued that human thought and social development evolve through three stages: the theological, the metaphysical, and the positive or scientific. Although he originally sought to proclaim society's evolution to a new golden age of science, industry, and rational morality, his radical ideas were increasingly tempered by the political and social upheavals of his time. His

Computing: chronology

1614	John Napier invented logarithms.
1615	William Oughtred invented the slide rule.
1623	Wilhelm Schickard (1592–1635) invented the mechanical calculating machine.
1645	Blaise Pascal produced a calculator.
1672–74	Gottfried Leibniz built his first calculator, the Stepped Reckoner.
1801	Joseph-Marie Jacquard developed an automatic loom controlled by punch cards.
1820	The first mass-produced calculator, the Arithometer, was developed by Charles Thomas de Colmar (1785–1870).
1822	Charles Babbage completed his first model for the difference engine.
1830s	Babbage created the first design for the analytical engine.
1890	Herman Hollerith developed the punched-card ruler for the US census.
1936	Alan Turing published the mathematical theory of computing.
1938	Konrad Zuse constructed the first binary calculator, using Boolean algebra.
1939	US mathematician and physicist J V Atanasoff (1903–) became the first to use electronic means for mechanizing arithmetical operations.
1943	The Colossus electronic code-breaker was developed at Bletchley Park, England. The Harvard University Mark I or Automatic Sequence Controlled Calculator (partly financed by IBM) became the first program-controlled calculator.
1946	ENIAC (acronym for electronic numerator, integrator, analyser, and computer), the first general purpose, fully electronic digital computer, was completed at the University of Pennsylvania, USA.
1948	Manchester University (England) Mark I, the first stored-program computer, was completed. William Shockley of Bell Laboratories invented the transistor.
1951	Launch of Ferranti Mark I, the first commercially produced computer. Whirlwind, the first real- time computer, was built for the US air-defence system. Grace Murray Hopper of Remington Rand invented the compiler computer program.
1952	EDVAC (acronym for electronic discrete variable computer) was completed at the Institute for Advanced Study, Princeton, USA (by John Von Neumann and others).
1953	Magnetic core memory was developed.
1958	The first integrated circuit was constructed.
1963	The first minicomputer was built by Digital Equipment (DEC). The first electronic calculator was built by Bell Punch Company.
1964	Launch of IBM System/360, the first compatible family of computers. John Kemeny and Thomas Kurtz of Dartmouth College invented BASIC (Beginner's All-purpose Symbolic Instruction Code), a computer language similar to FORTRAN.
1965	The first supercomputer, the Control Data CD6600, was developed.
1971	The first microprocessor, the Intel 4004, was announced.
1974	CLIP–4, the first computer with a parallel architecture, was developed by John Backus at IBM.
1975	Altair 8800, the first personal computer (PC), or microcomputer, was launched.
1981	The Xerox Star system, the first WIMP system (acronym for windows, icons, menus, and pointing devices), was developed. IBM launched the IBM PC.
1984	Apple launched the Macintosh computer.
1985	The Inmos T414 transputer, the first 'off-the-shelf' microprocessor for building parallel computers, was announced.
1988	The first optical microprocessor, which uses light instead of electricity, was developed.
1989	Wafer-scale silicon memory chips, able to store 200 million characters, were launched.
1990	Microsoft released Windows 3, a popular windowing environment for PCs.
1992	Philips launched the CD-I (Compact-Disc Interactive) player, based on CD audio technology, to provide interactive multimedia programs for the home user.
1993	Intel launched the Pentium chip containing 3.1 million transistors and capable of 100 MIPs (millions of instructions per second). The Personal Digital Assistant (PDA), which recognizes user's handwriting, went on sale.

influence, however, continued in Europe and the USA until the early 20th century.

concentric-ring theory hypothetical pattern of land use within an urban area, where different activities occur at different distances from the urban centre. The result is a sequence of rings. The theory was first suggested by the US sociologist E W Burgess in 1925. He said that towns expand outwards evenly from an original core so that each zone grows by gradual colonization into the next outer ring.

In addition, the cost of land may decrease with increased distance from the city centre as demand for it falls (see ◊bid-rent theory). This means that commercial activity that can afford high land values will be concentrated in the city centre.

concept idea; in philosophy, the term 'concept' has superseded the more ambiguous '◊idea'. To have a concept of dog is to be able to distinguish dogs from other things, or to be able to think or reason about dogs in some way.

Conceptual realists hold that concepts are objectively existing ◊universals, like real ◊essences. Conceptualists hold that universals are mind-dependent concepts (this is the outlook of ◊nominalism).

Conceptual art (or *Concept art, Conceptualism*) style of art, originating in the 1960s in the USA, which aims to express ideas rather than create visual images. Its materials include, among others, photographs, written information, diagrams, sound, and video tapes. Continuing the tradition of

◊Dada and ◊anti-art, Conceptual art aims to raise questions about the nature of art by flouting artistic conventions. As well as its theorist Sol LeWitt (1928–), its practitioners include Joseph Kosuth (1945–), Allan Krapow, and Bruce Nauman (1941–).

Conceptual art overlaps with Performance art where it uses the human body as a medium for expression; some artists, such as Joseph Beuys, are practitioners of both.

Conchobar in Celtic mythology, king of Ulster whose intended bride, Deirdre, eloped with Noísi. She died of sorrow when Conchobar killed her husband and his brothers.

conciliar movement in the history of the Christian church, a 15th-century attempt to urge the supremacy of church councils over the popes, with regard to the ◊Great Schism and the reformation of the church. Councils were held in Pisa 1409, Constance 1414–18, Pavia–Siena 1423–24, Basle 1431–49, and Ferrara–Florence–Rome 1438–47.

After ending the Schism 1417 with the removal of John XXIII (1410–15), Gregory XII (1406–15), and Benedict XIII (1394–1423), and the election of Martin V (1417–31), the movement fell into disunity over questions of reform, allowing Eugenius IV (1431–47) to use the Ferrara–Florence–Rome council to reunite the church and reassert papal supremacy.

conclave secret meeting, in particular the gathering of cardinals in Rome to elect a new pope. They are locked away in the Vatican Palace until they have reached a decision. The result of each ballot is announced by a smoke signal – black for an undecided vote and white when the choice is made.

Wooden cells are erected near the Sistine Chapel, one for each cardinal, accompanied by his secretary and a servant, and all are sworn to secrecy. This section of the palace is then locked and no communication with the outside world is allowed until a new pope is elected.

concordat agreement regulating relations between the papacy and a secular government, for example, that for France between Pius VII and the emperor Napoleon, which lasted 1801–1905; Mussolini's concordat, which lasted 1929–78 and safeguarded the position of the church in Italy; and one of 1984 in Italy in which Roman Catholicism ceased to be the Italian state religion.

Condillac Étienne Bonnot de 1715–1780. French philosopher. He mainly followed the English philosopher John ◊Locke. However, his *Traité des sensations* 1754 claims that all mental activity stems from the transformation of sensations and that memory is an after-effect of sensation, while attention is the occupation of consciousness by one sensation to the exclusion of others. He was one of the French ◊Encyclopédistes. Born in Grenoble of noble parentage, he entered the church and was appointed tutor to Louis XV's grandson, the duke of Parma.

conditioning in psychology, two major principles of behaviour modification.

In *classical conditioning*, described by Ivan Pavlov, a new stimulus can evoke an automatic response by being repeatedly associated with a stimulus that naturally provokes a response. For example, the sound of a bell repeatedly associated with food will eventually trigger salivation, even if sounded without food being presented. In *operant conditioning*, described by US psychologists Edward Lee Thorndike (1874–1949) and Burrhus Frederic Skinner, the frequency of a voluntary response can be increased by following it with a reinforcer or reward.

Condorcet Marie Jean Antoine Nicolas Caritat, Marquis de Condorcet 1743–1794. French philosopher, mathematician, and politician, associated with the ◊*Encyclopédistes*. Though a keen supporter of the French Revolution, he opposed the execution of Louis XVI, and was imprisoned and poisoned himself. While in prison, he wrote *Esquisse d'un tableau historique des progrès de l'esprit humain/Historical Survey of the Progress of Human Understanding* 1795, in which he traced human development from barbarity to the brink of perfection. He wrote in support of pacifism, sexual equality, and social services. As a mathematician he made important contributions to the theory of probability.

conductive education specialized method of training physically disabled children suffering from conditions such as cerebral palsy. The method was pioneered at the Peto Institute in Budapest, Hungary, and has been taken up elsewhere.

confession in law, a criminal's admission of guilt. Since false confessions may be elicited by intimidation or ill-treatment of the accused, the validity of confession in a court of law varies from one legal system to another. For example, in England and Wales a confession, without confirmatory evidence, is sufficient to convict; in Scotland it is not. In the USA a confession that is shown to be coerced does not void a conviction as long as it is supported by independent evidence.

In England and Wales the jury should be told that the weight to be attached to confession depends on all the circumstances in which the confession was made. Special rules apply if the accused is mentally handicapped. The court also has discretionary power to exclude a confession, for example, where the police have broken the rules regarding the questioning or treatment of suspects. Confessions obtained by coercion have in the past led to wrongful imprisonment of, for example, the Birmingham Six.

confession in religion, the confession of sins practised in Roman Catholic, Orthodox, and most Far Eastern Christian churches, and since the early 19th century revived in Anglican and Lutheran churches. The Lateran Council of 1215 made auricular confession (self-accusation by the penitent to a priest, who in Catholic doctrine is divinely invested with authority to give absolution) obligatory once a year.

Both John the Baptist's converts and the early Christian church practised public confession. The Roman Catholic penitent in recent times has always confessed alone to the priest in a confessional box, but from 1977 such individual confession might be preceded by group discussion, or the confession itself might be made openly by members of the group.

confidence vote in politics, a test of support for the government in the legislature. In political systems modelled on that of the UK, the survival of a government depends on assembly support. The opposition may move a vote of 'no confidence'; if the vote is carried, it requires the government, by convention, to resign.

The last prime minister to be defeated in the House of Commons and forced to resign was Labour prime minister James Callaghan 1979. He lost the subsequent general election to Margaret Thatcher.

confirmation rite practised by a number of Christian denominations, including Roman Catholic, Anglican, and Orthodox, in which a previously baptized person is admitted to full membership of the church. In Reform Judaism there is often a confirmation service several years after the bar or bat mitzvah (initiation into the congregation).

Christian confirmation is believed to give the participant the gift of the Holy Spirit. In the Anglican church it consists in the laying on of hands by a bishop, while in the Roman Catholic and Orthodox churches the participant is anointed with oil. Except in the Orthodox churches, where infant confirmation is usual, the rite takes place around early adolescence. Until recently a child preparing for confirmation was required to learn by heart a series of questions and answers known as a ◊catechism.

Confucianism body of beliefs and practices based on the Chinese classics and supported by the authority of the philosopher Confucius. The origin of things is seen in the union of *yin* and *yang*, the passive and active principles. Human relationships follow the patriarchal pattern. For more than 2,000 years Chinese political government, social organization, and individual conduct was shaped by Confucian principles. In 1912, Confucian philosophy, as a basis for government, was dropped by the state.

The writings on which Confucianism is based include the ideas of a group of traditional books edited by Confucius, as well as his own works, such as the *Analects*, and those of some of his pupils. The ◊*I Ching* is included among the Confucianist texts.

doctrine Until 1912 the emperor of China was regarded as the father of his people, appointed by heaven to rule. The Superior Man was the ideal human and filial piety was the chief virtue. Accompanying a high morality was a kind of ancestor worship.

practices Under the emperor, sacrifices were offered to heaven and earth, the heavenly bodies, the imperial ancestors, various nature gods, and Confucius himself. These were abolished at the Revolution in 1912, but ancestor worship (better expressed as reverence and remembrance) remained a regular practice in the home. Under communism Confucianism continued. The defence minister Lin Biao was associated with the religion, and although the communist leader ◊Mao Zedong undertook an anti-Confucius campaign 1974–76, this was not pursued by the succeeding regime.

Confucius (Latinized form of *K'ung Fu-tzu*, 'Kong the master') 551 BC–479 BC. Chinese sage whose name is given to ◊Confucianism. He placed emphasis on moral order and the observance of the established patriarchal family and social relationships of authority, obedience, and mutual respect. *The Analects of Confucius*, a compilation of his teachings, was published after his death.

Congregationalism form of church government adopted by those Protestant Christians known as Congregationalists, who let each congregation manage its own affairs. The first Congregationalists were the Brownists, named after Robert Browne, who defined the congregational principle 1580.

In the 17th century they were known as Independents, for example, the Puritan leader Cromwell and many of his Ironsides, and in 1662 hundreds of their ministers were driven from their churches and established separate congregations. The Congregational Church in England and Wales and the Presbyterian Church in England merged in 1972 to form the United Reformed Church. The latter, like its counterpart the Congregational Union of Scotland, has no control over individual churches but is simply consultative. Similar unions have been carried out in Canada (United Church of Canada, 1925) and USA (United Church of Christ, 1957).

Congress national legislature of the USA, consisting of the House of Representatives (435 members, apportioned to the states of the Union on the basis of population, and elected for two-year terms) and the Senate (100 senators, two for each state, elected for six years, one-third elected every two years). Both representatives and senators are elected by direct popular vote. Congress meets in Washington DC, in the Capitol Building. An ◊act of Congress is a bill passed by both houses.

The Congress of the United States met for the first time on 4 March 1789. It was preceded by the Congress of the Confederation representing the several states under the Articles of Confederation from 1781 to 1789.

In 19th-century history, the term 'congress' refers to a formal meeting or assembly, usually for peace, where delegates assembled to discuss or settle a matter of international concern, such as the Congress of Vienna 1815, which divided up Napoleon's empire after the Napoleonic Wars; and the Congress of Paris 1856, which settled some of the problems resulting from the Crimean War.

Congress Party Indian political party, founded 1885 as the Indian National Congress. It led the movement to end British rule and was the governing party from independence 1947 until 1977, when Indira Gandhi lost the leadership she had held since 1966. Heading a splinter group, known as *Congress I*, she achieved an overwhelming victory in the elections of 1980, and reduced the main Congress Party to a minority.

The *Indian National Congress*, founded by the British colonialist Allan Hume (1829–1912), was a moderate body until World War I. Then, under the leadership of Mahatma Gandhi, it began a campaign of nonviolent noncooperation with the British colonizers. It was declared illegal 1932–34, but was recognized as the paramount power in India at the granting of independence in 1947. Dominated in the early years of Indian independence by Prime Minister Nehru, the party won the elections of 1952, 1957, and 1962. Under the leadership of Indira Gandhi from 1966, it went on to win the elections of 1967 and 1971, but was defeated for the first time in 1977.

connoisseur a person sufficiently equipped with knowledge and ◊taste to make critical judgements about art.

The term derives from the Italian *conoscitore* and in turn from the Latin *cognoscere* meaning to get to know. In 18th-century England connoisseurship was an attribute of a gentleman of refinement and ◊sensibility.

conscience inner sense of what is morally right and wrong. Austrian psychoanalyst Sigmund ◊Freud held that conscience is the ◊superego.

English theologian Joseph ◊Butler, the leading conscience theorist in ethics, saw the voice of conscience as 'the candle of the Lord'. He argued that conscience is the part of human nature that guides us towards the moral integration of the self. Critics of conscience theories argue that conscience is an unreliable guide.

conscientious objector person refusing compulsory service, usually military, on moral, religious, or political grounds.

The term originally denoted parents who objected to compulsory vaccination of their children.

Conscience is thoroughly well-bred and soon leaves off talking to those who do not wish to hear it.

conscience
Samuel Butler, 1835–1902, English writer.
Further Extracts from Notebooks

---

consciousness (Latin *conscire* 'to be aware') the state of being aware of oneself and one's surroundings, without hindrance from sleep, illness, drugs, or hypnotism. This awareness is not purely of external events or phenomena, but also of one's own feelings, beliefs, and mental events. Such introspective self-awareness, as opposed to merely responding to external stimuli, is generally taken to be a prerequisite for consciousness. This, however, sidesteps the question of animal consciousness, which is largely believed to be very different or even non-existent.

The inability of those in power to still the voices of their own consciences is the great force leading to change.

conscience
Kenneth (David) Kaunda, 1924, Zambian politician, president 1964–91.
Observer July 1965

Consciousness is poorly understood but it is often linked to our capacity for language. According to ◊Freud consciousness differs from unconsciousness in that it recognizes distinctions of space and time and is consistent. The unconscious frequently switches the meaning of symbols or events, as in dreams, and regularly accepts contradictions. Psychologists and neurologists have attempted to establish what processes are involved in consciousness, but with limited success, although recent studies in cognition and perception have greatly advanced our understanding of the workings of the mind.

One hotly contended issue is the ascription of conscious thought processes to animals. Many people wish to exclude animals from the category of conscious beings, but would admit that higher-order animals do exhibit a degree of self-awareness in addition to their responses to the outside world. However, there is generally considered to be a definite difference between the kind of self-examination and contemplation stemming from our consciousness of ourselves, and the level of self-awareness generally admitted to exist in, for example, a chimp. The difference is often felt to lie in our additional capacity to reason and discuss, although whether this is an inherent part of our consciousness or a faculty additional to it is unclear.

conscription legislation for all able-bodied male citizens (and female in some countries, such as Israel) to serve with the armed forces. It originated in France 1792, and in the 19th and 20th centuries became the established practice in almost all European states. Modern conscription systems often permit alternative national service for conscientious objectors.

In Britain conscription was introduced for single men between 18 and 41 in March 1916 and for married men two months later, but was abolished after World War I. It was introduced for the first time in peace April 1939, when all men aged 20 became liable to six months' military training. The National Service Act, passed Sept 1939, made all men between 18 and 41 liable to military service, and in 1941 women also became liable to be called up for the women's services as an alternative to industrial service. Men reaching the age of 18 continued to be called up until 1960.

consecration practice of investing buildings, objects, or people with special religious significance. It aims to establish in the visible world a concrete means of communion with the divine. The consecrated person or object is often considered to be transformed or empowered and is marked off from the everyday world. For example, a church building is consecrated for worship, usually by a bishop; clergy are consecrated in order to be able to act as God's representatives in the world.

consent, age of age at which consent may legally be given to sexual intercourse by a girl or boy.

In the UK it is 16 (21 for male homosexual intercourse). The Criminal Law Amendment Act 1885 raised the age of consent from 13 to 16, and that of abduction from 16 to 18, after a campaign by William Thomas Stead (1849–1912), editor of the *Pall Mall Gazette*, exposed the white slave trade from England to Paris and Brussels. Stead's purchase of a girl to demonstrate the existence of the trade led to his prosecution, conviction, and imprisonment for three months.

Rage and frenzy will pull down more in half an hour, than prudence, deliberation, and foresight can build up in a hundred years.

conservatism
Edmund Burke, 1729–1797, Anglo-Irish politician and political theorist.
Reflections on the Revolution in France

conservation in the life sciences, action taken to protect and preserve the natural world, usually from pollution, overexploitation, and other harmful features of human activity. The late 1980s saw a great increase in public concern for the environment, with membership of conservation groups, such as Friends of the Earth, rising sharply. Globally the most important issues include the depletion of atmospheric ozone by the action of chlorofluorocarbons (CFCs), the build-up of carbon dioxide in the atmosphere (thought to contribute to an intensification of the ◊greenhouse effect), and the destruction of the tropical rainforests (see ◊deforestation).

In the UK the conservation debate has centred on water quality, road-building schemes, the safety of nuclear power, and animal rights.

conservatism approach to government favouring the maintenance of existing institu-

The Race to Prevent Mass Extinction

About a million different living species have been identified so far. Recent studies in tropical forests – where biodiversity is greatest – suggest the true figure is nearer 30 million. Most are animals, and most of those are insects. Because the tropical forests are threatened, at least half the animal species could become extinct within the next century. There have been at least five 'mass extinctions' in our planet's history; the last removed the dinosaurs 65 million years ago. The present wave of extinction is on a similar scale, but hundreds of times faster.

There is conflict within the conservation movement over what is to be done about this. Some believe that *habitats* (the places where animals and plants live) should be conserved; others prefer to concentrate upon individual *species*. Both approaches have strengths and weaknesses, and they must operate in harmony.

Habitat protection

Habitat protection has obvious advantages. Many species benefit if land is preserved. Animals need somewhere to live; unless the habitat is preserved it may not be worth saving the individual animal. Habitat protection *seems* cheap; for example, tropical forest can often be purchased for only a few dollars per hectare. Only by habitat protection can we save more than a handful of the world's animals.

But there are difficulties. Even when a protected area is designated a 'national park', its animals may not be safe. All five remaining species of rhinoceros are heavily protected in the wild, but are threatened by poaching. Early in 1991 Zimbabwe had 1,500 black rhinos – the world's largest population. Patrols of game wardens shoot poachers on sight. Yet by late 1992, 1,000 of the 1,500 had been poached. In many national parks worldwide, the habitat is threatened by the local farmers' need to graze their cattle.

Computer models and field studies show that wild populations need several hundred individuals to be viable. Smaller populations will eventually go extinct in the wild, because of accidents to key breeding individuals, or epidemics. The big predators need vast areas. One tiger may command hundreds of square kilometres; a viable population needs an area as big as Wales or Holland. Only one of the world's five remaining subspecies of tiger – a population of Bengals in India – occupies an area large enough to be viable. All the rest (Indo-Chinese, Sumatran, Chinese and Siberian) seem bound to die out. Three other subspecies have gone extinct in the past 100 years – the latest, the Javan, in the 1970s.

Mosaic

Ecologists now emphasize the concept of *mosaic*. All animals need different things from their habitat, and a failure of supply of any one is disastrous. Giant pandas feed mainly on bamboo, but give birth in old hollow trees – of which there is a shortage. Birds commonly roost in one place, but feed in special areas far away. Nature reserves must either contain all essentials for an animal's life, or else allow access to such areas elsewhere. For many animals in a reserve, these conditions are not fulfilled. Hence year by year, after reserves are created, species go extinct: a process called *species relaxation*. The remaining fauna and flora may be a poor shadow of the original.

Interest is increasing in *captive breeding*, carried out mainly by the world's 800 zoos. Their task is formidable; each captive species should include several hundred individuals. Zoos maintain such numbers through *cooperative breeding*, organized regionally and coordinated by the Captive Breeding Specialist Group or the World Conservation Union, based in Minneapolis, Minnesota. Each programme is underpinned by a studbook, showing which individuals are related to which.

Genetic diversity

Breeding for conservation is different from breeding for livestock improvement. Livestock breeders breed *uniform* creatures by selecting animals conforming to some prescribed ideal. Conservation breeders maintain *maximum genetic diversity* by encouraging every individual to breed, including those reluctant to breed in captivity; by equalizing family size, so one generation's genes are all represented in the next; and by swapping individuals between zoos to prevent inbreeding.

Cooperative breeding programmes are rapidly diversifying; by the year 2000 there should be several hundred. They can only make a small impression on the 15 million endangered species, but they can contribute greatly to particular groups of animals, especially the land vertebrates – mammals, birds, reptiles, and amphibians. These include most of the world's largest animals, with the greatest impact on their habitats. There are 24,000 species of land vertebrate, of which 2,000 probably require captive breeding to survive. Zoos could save all 2,000, which would be a great contribution.

Captive breeding is not intended to establish 'museum' populations, but to provide a temporary 'lifeboat'. Things are hard for wild animals, but over the next few decades, despite the growing human population, it should be possible to establish more and safer national parks. The Arabian oryx, California condor, black-footed ferret, red wolf, and Mauritius kestrel are among the creatures so far saved from extinction by captive breeding and returned to the wild. In the future, we can expect to see many more.

Colin Tudge

tions and identified with a number of Western political parties, such as the British Conservative, US Republican, German Christian Democratic, and Australian Liberal parties. It tends to be explicitly nondoctrinaire and pragmatic but generally emphasizes free-enterprise capitalism, minimal government intervention in the economy, rigid law and order, and the importance of national traditions. Conservative philosophers include Edmund ◊Burke and Roger ◊Scruton.

Conservative Party UK political party, one of the two historic British parties; the name replaced *Tory* in general use from 1830 onwards. Traditionally the party of landed interests, it broadened its political base under Benjamin Disraeli's leadership in the 19th century. The present Conservative Party's free-market capitalism is supported by the world of finance and the management of industry.

Opposed to the *laissez-faire* of the Liberal manufacturers, the Conservative Party supported, to some extent, the struggle of the working class against the harsh conditions arising from the Industrial Revolution. The split of 1846 over Robert Peel's Corn Law policy led to 20 years out of office, or in office without power, until Disraeli 'educated' his party into accepting parliamentary and social change, extended the franchise to the artisan (winning considerable working-class support), launched imperial expansion, and established an alliance with industry and finance. The Irish Home Rule issue of 1886 drove Radical Imperialists and old-fashioned Whigs into alliance with the Conservatives, so that the party had nearly 20 years of office, but fear that Joseph Chamberlain's protectionism would mean higher prices led to a Liberal landslide in 1906. The Conservative Party fought a rearguard action against the sweeping reforms that followed and only the outbreak of World War I averted a major crisis. During 1915–45, except briefly in 1924 and 1929–31, the Conservatives were continually in office, whether alone or as part of a coalition, largely thanks to the breakup of the traditional two-party system by the rise of Labour. Labour swept to power after World War II, but the Conservative Party formulated a new policy in their Industrial Charter of 1947, visualizing an economic and social system in which employers and employed, private enterprise and the state, work to mutual advantage. Antagonism to further nationalization and postwar austerity returned the Conservatives to power in 1951 with a small majority, and prosperity kept them in office throughout the 1950s and early 1960s. Narrowly defeated in 1964 under Alec Douglas-Home, the Conservative

Party from 1965 elected its leaders, beginning with Edward Heath, who became prime minister 1970. The imposition of wage controls led to confrontation with the unions; when Heath sought a mandate Feb 1974, this resulted in a narrow defeat, repeated in a further election in Oct 1974. Margaret Thatcher replaced Heath, and under her leadership the Conservative Party returned to power in May 1979. Its economic policies increased the spending power of the majority, but also the gap between rich and poor; nationalized industries were sold off (see ◊privatization); military spending and close alliance with the USA were favoured, and the funding of local government was overhauled with the introduction of the ◊poll tax. Margaret Thatcher was re-elected in 1983 and 1987, but resigned in Nov 1990. The Conservative government continued in office under John Major, re-elected in 1992, repudiating some of the extreme policies of Thatcherism.

conspicuous consumption selection and purchase of goods for their social rather than their inherent value. These might include items with an obviously expensive brand-name tag. The term was coined by US economist Thorstein Veblen.

Constantine the Great c. AD 280–337. First Christian emperor of Rome and founder of Constantinople. He defeated Maxentius, joint emperor of Rome AD 312, and in 313 formally recognized Christianity. As sole emperor of the west of the empire, he defeated Licinius, emperor of the east, to become ruler of the Roman world 324. He presided over the church's first council at Nicaea 325. Constantine moved his capital to Byzantium on the Bosporus 330, renaming it Constantinople (now Istanbul).

Constantine was born at Naissus (Nis, Yugoslavia), the son of Constantius. He was already well known as a soldier when his father died in York in 306 and he was acclaimed by the troops there as joint emperor in his father's place. A few years later Maxentius, the joint emperor in Rome (whose sister had married Constantine), challenged his authority and mobilized his armies to invade Gaul. Constantine won a crushing victory outside Rome in 312. During this campaign he was said to have seen a vision of the cross of Jesus superimposed upon the sun, accompanied by the words: 'In this sign, conquer'. By the Edict of Milan 313 he formally recognized Christianity as one of the religions legally permitted within the Roman Empire and in 314 he summoned the bishops of the Western world to the Council of Arles. However, there has never been agreement on whether Constantine adopted Christianity for reasons of faith or as an act of imperial absolutism to further his power. Constantine increased the autocratic power of the emperor, issued legislation to tie the farmers and workers to their crafts in a sort of caste system, and enlisted the support of the Christian church. He summoned, and presided over, the first general council of the church in Nicaea 325. In 337 he set out to defend the Euphrates frontier against the Persians, but he died before reaching it, at Nicomedia in Asia Minor.

constitution body of fundamental laws of a state, laying down the system of government and defining the relations of the legislature, executive, and judiciary to each other and to the citizens. Since the French Revolution almost all countries (the UK is an exception) have adopted written constitutions; that of the USA (1787) is the oldest.

The constitution of the UK does not exist as a single document but as an accumulation of customs and precedents, together with laws defining certain of its aspects. Among the latter are Magna Carta 1215, the Petition of Right 1628, and the Habeas Corpus Act 1679, limiting the royal powers of taxation and of imprisonment; the Bill of Rights 1689 and the Act of Settlement 1701, establishing the supremacy of ◊Parliament and the independence of the judiciary; and the Parliament Acts 1911 and 1949, limiting the powers of the Lords. The Triennial Act 1694, the Septennial Act 1716, and the Parliament Act 1911 limited the duration of Parliament, while the Reform Acts of 1832, 1867, 1884, 1918, and 1928 extended the electorate. The proliferation of legislation during the 1970s, often carried on the basis of a small majority in the Commons and by governments elected by an overall minority of votes, led to demands such as those by the organization Charter 88 for the introduction of a written constitution as a safeguard for the liberty of the individual.

Constructivism revolutionary movement in Russian art and architecture, founded in Moscow 1917 by Vladimir Tatlin, which drew its inspiration and materials from modern industry and technology. Initially confined to sculpture, its ideas were later adopted and expanded upon in architecture. Associated with the movement was the artist and architect El Lissitzky, the artists Naum Gabo and Antoine Pevsner, and the architects Vladimir Melnikov and Alexander (1883–1959), Leonid (1880–1933), and Viktor (1882–1950) Vesnin. By 1932 official Soviet disap-

proval had brought the movement effectively to a close, but its ideas had already spread to Europe, influencing the ◊Bauhaus and de ◊Stijl schools of architecture and design. Today, Deconstructionism and much ◊High Tech architecture reflect its influence.

Inspired by Cubism and Futurism, Constructivist artists sought to produce abstract forms from industrial materials. Tatlin's early abstract pieces, made of wood, metal, and clear plastic, were hung on walls or suspended from ceilings. In architecture, the movement produced technologically advanced, machine-like buildings, as in the Vesnin brothers' design for the Pravda building, Leningrad (now St Petersburg) 1923. However, it was Tatlin's unrealized design for a monument to the Third International (his sole venture into engineering) which produced Constructivism's most potent architectural image: a huge, tilting, spiral, with revolving glass chambers – a cube, a cylinder, and a pyramid – suspended within its central core.

consumer price index yearly index of the cost of goods and services to the consumer needed for an average standard of living.

The US Department of Labor reforms its consumer price index (CPI), the most widely used measure of inflation, periodically, establishing a base year at 100. Prices 20% higher than those in the base year would thus be expressed as 120. The index is calculated on the spending habits of salaried employees, wage earners, and retired and unemployed persons in 85 metropolitan areas. The income of almost half the US population is related to the CPI through collective bargaining agreements, alimony, rent, and Social Security payments, all of which are linked to changes in the cost of living. The items making up the 'market basket' of typical consumer purchases are also revised periodically, reflecting changes in consumer spending habits.

consumer protection laws and measures designed to ensure fair trading for buyers. Responsibility for checking goods and services for quality, safety, and suitability has in the past few years moved increasingly away from the consumer to the producer.

In earlier days it was assumed that consumers could safeguard themselves by common sense, testing before purchase, and confronting the seller personally if they were dissatisfied. Today the technical complexities of products, the remoteness of outlets from the original producer, and pressures from advertising require protection for the consumer. In the USA, both federal and state governments make special provisions for consumer protection. In 1962

President Kennedy set out the four basic rights of the consumer: to safety, to be informed, to choose, and to be heard. There are many private consumer associations, and among the most vociferous of crusaders for greater protection has been Ralph Nader.

In Britain, an early organization for consumer protection was the British Standards Institution, set up in 1901, which certifies with a 'kitemark' goods reaching certain standards. Statutory protection is now given by acts such as the Trade Descriptions Act 1968 (making false descriptions of goods and services illegal), the Fair Trading Act 1973, the Unfair Contract Terms Act 1977, and the Consumer Safety Acts 1978 and 1987. In 1974 the government Department of Prices and Consumer Protection was set up.

Conspicuous consumption of valuable goods is a means of reputability to the gentleman of leisure.

consumption
Thorstein (Bunde) Veblen, 1857–1929, US
social critic.
Theory of the Leisure Class

---

consumption in economics, the purchase of goods and services for final use, as opposed to spending by firms on capital goods, known as capital formation.

In the official UK statistics, two types of consumption are measured: consumers' expenditure (spending by household) and government consumption.

In a consumer society there are inevitably two kinds of slaves: the prisoners of addiction and the prisoners of envy.

consumers
Ivan Illich, 1926, US radical philosopher and
activist, born in Austria.
Tools for Conviviality ch 3

---

containment US policy (adopted from 1947) that was designed to prevent the spread of communism.

continental drift in geology, the theory that, about 250–200 million years ago, the Earth consisted of a single large continent (Pangaea), which subsequently broke apart to form the continents known today. The theory was proposed 1912 by German meteorologist Alfred Wegener, but such vast continental movements could not be satisfactorily explained until the study of plate tectonics in the 1960s.

The term 'continental drift' is not strictly correct, since land masses do not drift through the oceans. The continents form part of a plate, and the amount of crust created at divergent plate margins must equal the amount of crust destroyed at subduction zones.

convent religious house for ◊nuns.

conventionalism the view that ◊a priori truths, logical axioms, or scientific laws have no absolute validity but are disguised conventions representing one of a number of possible alternatives. The French philosopher and mathematician Jules Henri Poincaré introduced this position into philosophy of science.

convergent evolution in biology, the independent evolution of similar structures in species (or other taxonomic groups) that are not closely related, as a result of living in a similar way. Thus, birds and bats have wings, not because they are descended from a common winged ancestor, but because their respective ancestors independently evolved flight.

convocation in the Church of England, the synods (councils) of the clergy of the provinces of Canterbury and York. The General Synod, established 1970, took over the functions and authority of the Convocation of Canterbury and York.

Cooper Leon 1930– . US physicist who in 1955 began work on the puzzling phenomenon of superconductivity. He proposed that at low temperatures electrons would be bound in pairs (since known as *Cooper pairs*) and in this state electrical resistance to their flow through solids would disappear. He shared the 1972 Nobel Prize for Physics with John ◊Bardeen and John Schrieffer (1931–).

cooperative movement banding together of groups of people for mutual assistance in trade, manufacture, the supply of credit, housing, or other services. The original principles of cooperative movement were laid down 1844 by the Rochdale Pioneers, under the influence of Robert ◊Owen, and by Francois Charles ◊Fourier in France.

Producers' cooperative societies, formed on a basis of co-partnership among the employees, exist on a large scale in France, Italy, Spain, and the ex-Soviet republics. (In 1988, Soviet economic cooperatives were given legal and financial independence and the right to appear in foreign markets and to set up joint ventures with foreign companies.) Agricultural cooperative societies have been formed in many countries for the collective purchase of seeds, fertilizers, and other commodities, while societies for cooperative marketing of agricultural produce are prominent in the USA, Ireland, Denmark, E Europe, and the ex-Soviet republics. Agricultural credit societies are strong in rural economies of Europe and Asia, including parts of India. The USA also has a cooperative farm credit system. In the UK the 1970s and 1980s saw a growth in the number of workers' cooperatives, set up in factories otherwise threatened by closure due to economic depression.

Cooperative Party political party founded in Britain 1917 by the cooperative movement to maintain its principles in parliamentary and local government. A written constitution was adopted 1938. The party had strong links with the Labour Party; from 1946 Cooperative Party candidates stood in elections as Cooperative and Labour Candidates and, after the 1959 general election, agreement was reached to limit the party's candidates to 30.

cope semicircular cape, without sleeves, worn by priests of the Western Christian church in processions and on some other formal occasions, but not when officiating at Mass.

Copernicus Nicolaus 1473–1543. Polish astronomer who believed that the Sun, not the Earth, is at the centre of the Solar System, thus defying the Christian church doctrine of the time. For 30 years he worked on the hypothesis that the rotation and the orbital motion of the Earth were responsible for the apparent movement of the heavenly bodies. His great work *De Revolutionibus Orbium Coelestium/About the Revolutions of the Heavenly Spheres* was not published until the year of his death.

Born at Torun on the Vistula, then under the Polish king, Copernicus studied at Kraków and in Italy, and lectured on astronomy in Rome. On his return to Pomerania 1505 he became physician to his uncle, the bishop of Ermland, and was made canon at Frauenburg, although he did not take holy orders. Living there until his death, he interspersed astronomical work with the duties of various civil offices.

Copt descendant of those Egyptians who adopted Christianity in the 1st century and refused to convert to Islam after the Arab conquest. They now form a small minority (about 5%) of Egypt's population. *Coptic* is a member of the Hamito-Semitic language family. It is descended from the language of the ancient Egyptians and is the ritual language of the Coptic Christian church. It is written in the Greek alphabet with some additional characters derived from demotic script.

The head of the Coptic church is the Patriarch of Alexandria, since 1971 Shenouda III (1923–), 117th pope of Alexandria. Imprisoned by President Sadat 1981, he is opposed by Muslim fundamentalists. Before the Arab conquest a majority of Christian Egyptians had adopted Monophysite views (that Christ had 'one nature' rather than being both human and divine). When this was condemned by the Council of Chalcedon 451, they became schismatic and were persecuted by the orthodox party, to which they were opposed on nationalistic as well as religious grounds. They readily accepted Arab rule, but were later subjected to persecution. They are mainly town-dwellers, distinguishable in dress and customs from their Muslim compatriots. They rarely marry outside their own religion.

copyright law applying to literary, musical, and artistic works (including plays, recordings, films, photographs, radio and television broadcasts, and, in the USA and the UK, computer programs), which prevents the reproduction of the work, in whole or in part, without the author's consent.

Copyright applies to a work, not an idea. For example, the basic plots of two novels might be identical, but copyright would be infringed only if it was clear that one author had copied from another. A translation is protected in its own right. The copyright holder may assign the copyright to another or license others to reproduce or adapt the work. In 1991, the US Supreme Court ruled that copyright does not exist in the information in a telephone directory since 'copyright rewards originality, not effort'.

In the UK and (since 1989) the USA, copyright lasts for a holder's lifetime plus 50 years, or (in the USA), a flat 75 years for a company copyright. Copyright is internationally enforceable under the Berne Convention 1886 (ratified by the UK, among others) and the Universal Copyright Convention 1952 (more widely ratified, including the USA, the former USSR, and the UK). Both conventions have been revised, most recently in Paris 1971. Under the Universal Copyright Convention, works must be marked with the copyright symbol accompanied by the name of the copyright owner and the year of its first publication. The Berne Convention gives a longer minimum period of protection of copyright. Under the UK Copyright, Designs, and Patents Act 1988, artists gained control of copyright over work commissioned by others; for example, additional payment must be made by the publisher commissioning the artwork if it is to be reused later. Artists were also enabled to object to the mutilation or distortion of their work. Photographers obtained the same 50-year copyright granted to other artists and the copyright itself was ruled to belong to whoever might have paid for the film used, as previously. Remedies for breach of copyright (piracy) include damages, account of profit, or an injunction. Computer software is specifically covered in the USA under the Copyright Act 1976 and the Computer Software Act 1980, and in the UK the Copyright (Computer Software) Amendment Act 1985 extended copyright to computer programs.

core curriculum term used to describe those subjects that are considered essential for a child's education and which must be studied by all.

Cori Carl 1896–1984 and Gerty 1896–1957. Husband-and-wife team of US biochemists, both born in Prague, who, together with Argentine physiologist Bernardo Houssay (1887–1971), received a Nobel prize 1947 for their discovery of how glycogen (animal starch) – a derivative of glucose – is broken down and resynthesized in the body, for use as a store and source of energy.

Cornforth John Warcup 1917– . Australian chemist. Using radioisotopes as markers, he found out how cholesterol is manufactured in the living cell and how enzymes synthesize chemicals that are mirror images of each other (optical isomers). He shared a Nobel prize 1975 with Swiss chemist Vladimir Prelog (1906–).

coronation ceremony of investing a sovereign with the emblems of royalty, as a symbol of inauguration in office. Since the coronation of Harold 1066, English sovereigns have been crowned in Westminster Abbey, London.

The kings of Scotland were traditionally crowned in Scone; French kings in Reims. The British coronation ceremony combines the Hebrew rite of anointing with customs of Germanic origin, for example, the actual crowning and the presentation of the monarch to his or her subjects to receive homage. It comprises the presentation to the people; the administration of the oath; the presentation of the Bible; the anointing of the sovereign with holy oil on hands, breast, and head; the presentation of the spurs and the sword of state, the emblems of knighthood; the presentation of the armils (a kind of bracelet), the robe royal, the orb, the ring, the sceptre with the cross, and the rod with the dove; the coronation with St Edward's crown; the benediction; the enthroning; and the homage of the princes of the blood and the peerage. The *consort* (the spouse of a sovereign) is anointed on the head, presented with a ring, crowned, and presented with the sceptre and the ivory rod.

corporal punishment physical punishment of wrongdoers – for example, by whipping. It is still used as a punishment for criminals in many countries, especially under Islamic law. Corporal punishment of children by parents is illegal in some countries, including Sweden, Finland, Denmark, and Norway.

It was abolished as a punishment for criminals in Britain 1967 but only became illegal for punishing schoolchildren in state schools 1986.

corporatism belief that the state in capitalist democracies should intervene to a large extent in the economy to ensure social harmony. In Austria, for example, corporatism results in political decisions often being taken after discussions between chambers of commerce, trade unions, and the government.

corporative state state in which the members are organized and represented not on a local basis as citizens, but as producers working in a particular trade, industry, or profession. Originating with the syndicalist workers' movement, the idea was superficially adopted by the fascists during the 1920s and 1930s. Catholic social theory, as expounded in some papal encyclicals, also favours the corporative state as a means of eliminating class conflict.

The concept arose in the political theories of the syndicalist movement of the early 20th century, which proposed that all industries should be taken over and run by the trade unions, a federation of whom should replace the state. Similar views were put forward in Britain by the guild socialists about 1906–25. Certain features of syndicalist theory were adopted and given a right-wing tendency by the fascist regime in Italy, under which employers' and workers' organizations were represented in the National Council of Corporations, but this was completely dominated by the Fascist Party and had no real powers. Corporative institutions were set up by the Franco and Salazar regimes in Spain and Portugal, under the influence of fascist and Catholic theories. In Spain representatives of the national syndicates were included in the Cortes (parliament), and in Portugal a corporative chamber existed alongside the National Assembly.

Corpus Christi feast celebrated in the Roman Catholic and Orthodox churches, and to some extent in the Anglican church, on the Thursday after Trinity Sunday. It was instituted in the 13th century through the devotion of St Juliana, prioress of Mount Cornillon, near Liège, Belgium, in honour of the ◊Real Presence of Christ in the Eucharist.

correlation the degree of relationship between two sets of information. If one set of data increases at the same time as the other, the relationship is said to be positive or direct. If one set of data increases as the other decreases, the relationship is negative or inverse. Correlation can be shown by plotting a best-fit line on a scatter diagram.

In statistics, such relations are measured by the calculation of coefficients of correlation. These generally measure correlation on a scale with 1 indicating perfect positive correlation, 0 no correlation at all, and –1 perfect inverse correlation. Correlation coefficients for assumed linear relations include the Pearson product moment correlation coefficient (known simply as the correlation coefficient), Kendall's tau correlation coefficient, or Spearman's rho correlation coefficient, which is used in nonparametric statistics (where the data are measured on ordinal rather than interval scales). A high correlation does not always indicate dependence between two variables; it may be that there is a third (unstated) variable upon which both depend.

corresponding society in British history, one of the first independent organizations for the working classes, advocating annual parliaments and universal male suffrage. The London Corresponding Society was founded 1792 by politicians Thomas Hardy (1752– 1832) and John Horne Tooke (1736–1812). It later established branches in Scotland and the provinces. Many of its activities had to be held in secret and government fears about the spread of revolutionary doctrines led to its banning 1799.

corroboree Australian Aboriginal ceremonial dance. Some corroborees record events in everyday life and are non-sacred, public entertainments; others have a religious significance and are of great ritual importance, relating to initiation, death, fertility, disease, war, and so on. The dancers' movements are prescribed by tribal custom and their bodies and faces are usually painted in clay in traditional designs. The dance is accompanied by song and music is provided by clapping sticks and the didjeridu. All these elements, as well as the dance itself, form the corroboree.

cosmogony study of the origin and evolution of cosmic objects, especially the Solar System.

cosmological argument any line of reasoning for the existence of God that proceeds from the inexplicable existence of the universe to an allegedly self-explanatory being, God. The cosmological argument originates in ancient Greece with Aristotle, but takes various forms. One version is that everything requires a cause, so God must exist as the first or sustaining cause of the universe.

In the Middle Ages, Thomas ◊Aquinas argued that the universe could have not existed, so there must be a being that could not but exist – that is, exists necessarily – on which it depends. Gottfried ◊Leibniz in the early 18th century also used the cosmological argument.

Like the ◊ontological argument, most versions of the cosmological argument rely on existence being a property or predicate, which Immanuel ◊Kant claimed was impossible. Another weakness is that the argument attempts a causal inference from the universe to God, when it only makes sense to speak of causal relations as holding between observable states of affairs.

The other two traditional arguments for the existence of God are the ◊argument from design and the ◊moral argument.

cosmological principle in astronomy, a hypothesis that any observer anywhere in the ◊universe has the same view that we have; that is, that the universe is not expanding from any centre but all galaxies are moving away from one another.

cosmology study of the structure of the universe. Modern cosmology began in the 1920s with the discovery that the universe is expanding, which suggested that it began in an explosion, the ◊Big Bang. An alternative – now discarded – view, the steady-state theory, claimed that the universe has no origin, but is expanding because new matter is being continually created.

cost-benefit analysis process whereby a project is assessed for its social and welfare benefits in addition to considering the financial return on investment. For example, this might take into account the environmental impact of an industrial plant or convenience for users of a new railway. A major difficulty is finding a way to quantify net social costs and benefits.

cost of living cost of goods and services needed for an average standard of living.

In Britain the cost-of-living index was introduced 1914 and based on the expenditure of a working-class family of a man, woman, and three children; the standard is 100. Known from 1947 as the Retail Price Index (RPI), it is revised to allow for inflation. Supplementary to the RPI are the Consumer's Expenditure Deflator (formerly Consumer Price Index) and the Tax and Price Index (TPI), introduced 1979. Comprehensive indexation has been advocated as a means of controlling inflation by linking all forms of income (such as wages and investment), contractual debts, and tax scales to the RPI. Index-linked savings schemes were introduced in the UK 1975. In the USA a consumer price index, based on the expenditure of families in the iron, steel, and related industries, was introduced 1890. The present index is based on the expenditure of the urban wage-earner and clerical-worker families in 46 large, medium, and small cities, the standard being 100. Increases in social security benefits are linked to it, as are many wage settlements.

Cotton John 1585–1652. English-born American religious leader. In England, his extreme Puritan views led to charges of heterodoxy being filed against him 1633. In the same year, he immigrated to the Massachusetts Bay Colony, where he was named teacher of Boston's First Congre-gational Church. A powerful force in the colony, he published widely circulated sermons and theological works.

Born in Derby, England, and educated at Cambridge University, Cotton was named vicar in Boston, Lincolnshire 1612 before the persecution of Puritans under Charles I forced him to leave the country.

Every day, in every way, I am getting better and better.

Emil Coué
Slogan that Coué advised
his patients to repeat.
De la suggestion et de ses applications (On Suggestion and its Applications)

Coué Emile 1857–1926. French psychological healer, the pioneer of ◊autosuggestion. He coined the slogan 'Every day, and in every way, I am becoming better and better.' Couéism reached the height of its popularity in the 1920s.

Council of Europe body constituted 1949 in Strasbourg, France (still its headquarters), to secure 'a greater measure of unity between the European countries'. The widest association of European states, it has a *Committee* of foreign ministers, a *Parliamentary Assembly* (with members from national parliaments), and a *European Commission* investigating violations of human rights.

The first session of the *Consultative Assembly* opened Aug 1949, the members then being the UK, France, Italy, Belgium, the Netherlands, Sweden, Denmark, Norway, the Republic of Ireland, Luxembourg, Greece, and Turkey; Iceland, Germany, Austria, Cyprus,

Switzerland, Malta, Portugal, Spain, Liechtenstein, Finland, and San Marino subsequently. With the collapse of communism in E Europe, the Council acquired a new role in assisting the establishment of Western-style democratic and accountable political systems in the region, and several countries applied for membership. Hungary joined 1990, Czechoslovakia and Poland 1991; Romania and Yugoslavia applied for membership 1991 and Albania for observer status.

counselling approach to treating problems, usually psychological ones, in which clients are encouraged to solve their own problems with support from a counsellor. There is some overlap with ◊psychotherapy although counselling is less concerned with severe psychological disorders.

Counter-Reformation movement initiated by the Catholic church at the Council of Trent 1545–63 to counter the spread of the ◊Reformation. Extending into the 17th century, its dominant forces included the rise of the Jesuits as an educating and missionary group and the deployment of the ◊Inquisition in Europe and the Americas.

counterurbanization movement of people and employment away from urban areas to smaller towns and villages in rural locations. Push factors within urban regions may be responsible – for example, congestion, high land prices, and population pressure – together with pull factors such as the perceived environmental quality of the countryside and improvements in transport systems.

countervailing power in economics, the belief that too much power held by one group or company can be balanced or neutralized by another, creating a compatible relationship, such as trade unions in the case of strong management in a large company, or an opposition party facing an authoritarian government.

coup d'état or *coup* forcible takeover of the government of a country by elements from within that country, generally carried out by violent or illegal means. It differs from a revolution in typically being carried out by a small group (for example, of army officers or opposition politicians) to install its leader as head of government, rather than being a mass uprising by the people.

Early examples include the coup of 1799, in which ◊Napoleon overthrew the Revolutionary Directory and declared himself first consul of France, and the coup of 1851 in which Louis Napoleon (then president) dissolved the French national assembly and a year later declared himself emperor. Coups of more recent times include the overthrow of the socialist government of Chile 1973 by a right-wing junta, the military seizure of power in Surinam Dec 1990, and the short-lived removal of Mikhail ◊Gorbachev from power in the USSR by hardline communists 19–22 Aug 1991.

Course in Miracles religious book by Helen Schucman, a research psychologist at Colombia University's School of Physicians and Surgeons in New York, USA. She claimed the book's content was revealed to her by a voice which she identified as that of Jesus. The book, first published in the early 1980s, stresses the need to listen to the voice of inner love from which comes forgiveness and healing. The book has been immensely successful and is popular with many within conventional religions.

courtly love medieval European code of amorous conduct between noblemen and noblewomen.

Originating in 11th-century Provence, it was popularized by troubadours under the patronage of Eleanor of Aquitaine, and codified by André le Chapelain. Essentially, it was concerned with the (usually) unconsummated love between a young bachelor knight and his lord's lady. The affair between Lancelot and Guinevere is a classic example. This theme was usually treated in an idealized form, but the relationship did reflect the social realities of noble households, in which the lady of the household might be the only noblewoman among several young unmarried knights. It inspired a great deal of medieval and 16th-century art and literature, including the 14th-century *Romance of the Rose* and Chaucer's *Troilus and Criseyde*, and was closely related to concepts of ◊chivalry.

couvade custom in some societies of a man behaving as if he were about to give birth when his child is being born, which may include feeling or appearing to feel real pain. It has been observed since antiquity in many cultures and may have begun either as a magic ritual or as a way of asserting paternity.

covenant solemn agreement between two parties. In Judaism, it describes especially the relationship between God and the Jewish people, based on God's promise to Abraham and his descendants in the book of Genesis: 'I will be your God and you will be my people.' Jewish life and practice are based on the covenant relationship with God: God gives his laws, recorded in the ◊Torah, and Jews have a special duty to keep those laws as their side of the covenant. The term also refers to other oaths such as that taken by the ◊Covenanters.

Covenanter in Scottish history, one of the Presbyterian Christians who swore to uphold their forms of worship in a National Covenant, signed 28 Feb 1638, when Charles I attempted to introduce a liturgy on the English model into Scotland.

A general assembly abolished episcopacy, and the Covenanters signed with the English Parliament the Solemn League and Covenant 1643, promising military aid in return for the establishment of Presbyterianism in England. A Scottish army entered England and fought at Marston Moor 1644. At the Restoration Charles II revived episcopacy in Scotland, evicting resisting ministers, so that revolts followed 1666, 1679, and 1685. However, Presbyterianism was again restored 1688.

Coverdale Miles 1488–1569. English Protestant priest whose translation of the Bible 1535 was the first to be printed in English. His translation of the psalms is that retained in the Book of Common Prayer.

Coverdale, born in Yorkshire, became a Catholic priest, but turned to Protestantism and 1528 went to the continent to avoid persecution. In 1539 he edited the Great Bible which was ordered to be placed in churches. After some years in Germany, he returned to England 1548, and in 1551 was made bishop of Exeter. During the reign of Mary I he left the country.

craft union union which represents skilled manual or 'craft' workers, traditionally trained through apprenticeship schemes. Craft unions were the first to be formed in the UK in the 19th century. An example of a craft union today is the Manufacturing, Science, and Finance Union (MSF).

Cranmer Thomas 1489–1556. English cleric, archbishop of Canterbury from 1533. A Protestant convert, he helped to shape the doctrines of the Church of England under Edward VI. He was responsible for the issue of the Prayer Books of 1549 and 1552, and supported the succession of Lady Jane Grey 1553.

Condemned for heresy under the Catholic Mary Tudor, he at first recanted, but when his life was not spared, resumed his position and was burned at the stake, first holding to the fire the hand which had signed his recantation. Cranmer suggested 1529 that the question of Henry VIII's marriage to Catherine of Aragon should be referred to the universities of Europe rather than to the pope, and in 1533 he declared it null and void.

creationism theory concerned with the origins of matter and life, claiming, as does the Bible in Genesis, that the world and humanity were created by a supernatural Creator, not more than 6,000 years ago. It was developed in response to Darwin's theory of ◊evolution; it is not recognized by most scientists as having a factual basis.

After a trial 1981–82 a US judge ruled unconstitutional an attempt in Arkansas schools to enforce equal treatment of creationism and evolutionary theory.

In the beginning God created the heaven and the earth.

creationism
Bible, the sacred book of the Jewish and Christian religions.
Genesis 1:1

creation myth legend of the origin of the world. All cultures have ancient stories of the creation of the Earth or its inhabitants. Often these involve the violent death of a primordial being from whose body everything then arises; the giant Ymir in Scandinavian mythology is an example. Marriage between heaven and earth is another common explanation, as in Greek mythology (Uranus and Gaia).

God made everything out of the void, but the void shows through.

creation
Paul Valéry, 1871–1945,
French poet and writer.
Mauvaises pensées et autres

creative accounting organizing and presenting company accounts in a way that, although desirable for the company concerned, relies on a liberal and unorthodox interpretation of general accountancy procedures.

Creative accounting has been much used by UK local authorities in recent years in an effort to avoid restrictions on expenditure imposed by central government.

credit in economics, means by which goods or services are obtained without immediate payment, usually by agreeing to pay interest. The three main forms are *consumer credit* (usually extended to individuals by retailers), *bank credit* (such as overdrafts or personal loans), and *trade credit* (common in the commercial world both within countries and internationally).

Consumer credit is increasingly used to pay for goods. In the USA 1989 it amounted to $711.8 billion, with about 18.5% of disposable income expended on hire-purchase and credit-card payments.

creed in general, any system of belief; in the Christian church the verbal confessions of faith expressing the accepted doctrines of the church. The different forms are the ◊Apostles' Creed, the ◊Nicene Creed, and the ◊Athanasian Creed. The only creed recognized by the Orthodox Church is the Nicene Creed.

The oldest is the **Apostles' Creed**, which, though not the work of the apostles, was probably first formulated in the 2nd century. The full version of the Apostles' Creed, as now used, first appeared about 750. The use of creeds as a mode of combating heresy was established by the appearance of the **Nicene Creed**, introduced by the Council of Nicaea 325 when ◊Arianism was widespread, and giving the orthodox doctrine of the Trinity. The Nicene Creed used today is substantially the same as the version adopted at the church council in Constantinople 381, with a ◊filioque clause added during the 5th and 8th centuries in the Western church. The **Athanasian Creed** is thought to be later in origin than the time of Athanasius (died 373), although it represents his views in a detailed exposition of the doctrines of the Trinity and the incarnation. Some authorities suppose it to have been composed in the 8th or 9th century but others place it as early as the 4th or 5th century.

cremation disposal of the dead by burning. The custom was universal among ancient Indo-European peoples, for example, the Greeks, Romans, and Teutons. It was discontinued among Christians until the late 19th century because of their belief in the bodily resurrection of the dead. Overcrowded urban cemeteries gave rise to its revival in the West. It has remained the usual method of disposal in the East.

Cremation was revived in Italy about 1870, and shortly afterwards introduced into the UK; the first crematorium was opened 1885 in Woking, Surrey. In the UK an application for cremation must be accompanied by two medical certificates. Cremation is usually carried out in gas-fired furnaces. Ashes are scattered in gardens of remembrance or elsewhere, or deposited in urns at the crematorium or in private graves.

crescent curved shape of the Moon when it appears less than half-illuminated. It also refers to any object or symbol resembling the crescent Moon. Often associated with Islam, it was first used by the Turks on their standards after the capture of Constantinople 1453, and appears on the flags of many Muslim countries. The **Red Crescent** is the Muslim equivalent of the Red Cross.

Crick Francis 1916– . British molecular biologist. From 1949 he researched the molecular structure of DNA, and the means whereby characteristics are transmitted from one generation to another. For this work he was awarded a Nobel prize (with Maurice ◊Wilkins and James ◊Watson) 1962.

crime behaviour or action that is punishable by criminal law. A crime is a public, as opposed to a moral, wrong; it is an offence committed against (and hence punishable by) the state or the community at large. Many crimes are immoral, but not all actions considered immoral are illegal.

The laws of each country specify which actions or omissions are criminal. These include serious moral wrongs, such as murder; wrongs that endanger state security, such as treason; wrongs that endanger disrupt an orderly society, such as evading taxes; and wrongs against the community, such as littering. Crime is socially determined and so what constitutes a crime may vary geographically and over time. Thus, an action may be considered a crime in one society but not in another, for example, drinking alcohol is not generally prohibited in the West, but is a criminal offence in many Islamic countries. Certain categories of crime though, such as violent crime and theft, are recognized almost universally.

Crime is dealt with in most societies by the judicial system, comprising the police, the courts, etc. These may impose penalties ranging from a fine to imprisonment to, in some instances, death, depending upon the severity of the offence and the penalty laid down by the country where the offence was committed.

The Italian physician Cesare Lombroso (1836–1909) is generally accredited with being the founder of criminology, the scientific study of criminal behaviour. He associated criminality with physical characteristics. Later criminologists have tended to draw more upon sociology and psychology than biology to formulate theories of crime.

critical mass in nuclear physics, the minimum mass of fissile material that can undergo a continuous chain reaction. Below this mass, too many neutrons escape from the surface for a chain reaction to carry on; above the critical mass, the reaction may accelerate into a nuclear explosion.

critical path analysis procedure used in the management of complex projects to minimize the amount of time taken. The analysis shows which subprojects can run in parallel with each other, and which have to be completed before other subprojects can follow on. By identifying the time required for each separate subproject and the relationship between the subprojects, it is possible to produce a planning schedule showing when each subproject should be started and finished in order to complete the whole project most efficiently. Complex projects may involve hundreds of subprojects, and computer applications packages for critical path analysis are widely used to help reduce the time and effort involved in their analysis.

Croce Benedetto 1866–1952. Italian philosopher, historian, and literary critic; an opponent of fascism. In his *Filosofia dello spirito/Philosophy of the Spirit* 1902–17, he argued that spirit is the sole reality. Like ◊Hegel, he held that ideas do not represent reality but *are* reality; but unlike Hegel, he rejected every kind of transcendence. For Croce, spirit is the world, and the history of the spirit is the history of human experience. Spirit contains four varieties of experience: aesthetics, logic, economics, and ethics.

A few honest men are better than numbers.
Oliver Cromwell
Letter to W. Spring, Sept 1643

Cromwell Oliver 1599–1658. English general and politician, Puritan leader of the Parliamentary side in the Civil War. He raised cavalry forces (later called *Ironsides*) which aided the victories at Edgehill 1642 and Marston Moor 1644, and organized the New Model Army, which he led (with General Fairfax) to victory at Naseby 1645. He declared Britain a republic ('the Commonwealth') 1649, following the execution of Charles I. As Lord Protector (ruler) from 1653, Cromwell established religious toleration and raised Britain's prestige in Europe on the basis of an alliance with France against Spain.

Cromwell was born at Huntingdon, NW of Cambridge, son of a small landowner. He entered Parliament 1629 and became active in events leading to the Civil War. Failing to secure a constitutional settlement with Charles I 1646–48, he defeated the 1648 Scottish invasion at Preston. A special commission, of which

Cromwell was a member, tried the king and condemned him to death, and a republic, known as 'the Common-wealth', was set up. The ◊Levellers demanded radical reforms, but he executed their leaders in 1649. He used terror to crush Irish clan resistance 1649–50, and defeated the Scots (who had acknowledged Charles II) at Dunbar 1650 and Worcester 1651. In 1653, having forcibly expelled the corrupt 'Rump' Parliament, he summoned a convention ('Barebone's Parliament'), soon dissolved as too radical, and under a constitution (Instrument of Govern-ment) drawn up by the army leaders, became Protector (king in all but name). The parliament of 1654–55 was dissolved as uncooperative, and after a period of military dictatorship, his last parliament offered him the crown; he refused because he feared the army's republicanism.

Cronus or *Kronos* in Greek mythology, ruler of the world and one of the ◊Titans. He was the father of Zeus, who overthrew him.

Crookes William 1832–1919. English scientist whose many chemical and physical discoveries included the metallic element thallium 1861, the radiometer 1875, and the Crookes high-vacuum tube used in X-ray techniques.

cross symbol of the Christian religion, in widespread use since the 3rd century. It is a symbol of the crucifixion of Jesus and the central significance of his suffering, death, and resurrection. The Latin cross is the most commonly used; other types are the Greek cross, St Anthony's cross, and St Andrew's cross. Symbolic crosses were used by pre-Christian cultures, for example the ancient Egyptian ◊ankh (St Anthony's cross with a loop at the top), symbol of life, and the swastika, used by Hindus, Buddhists, Celts, and N American Indians before it was adopted by the Nazis.

crowding out in economics, a situation in which an increase in government expenditure results in a fall in private-sector investment, either because it causes inflation or a rise in interest rates (as a result of increased government borrowing) or because it reduces the efficiency of production as a result of government intervention. Crowding out has been used in recent years as a justification of ◊supply-side economics such as the privatization of state-owned industries and services.

Crowley Aleister (Edward Alexander) 1875–1947. British occultist known as 'The Great Beast'. Along with the Irish poet W B Yeats he was a member of the Order of the Golden Dawn, a group of theosophists interested in the magic and ritual of the ◊Kabbala. However in 1909 he left to found his own order, the Argetitum Astrum. He was vehemently anti-Christian, allegedly practising black magic and advocating drug-taking and sexual magic as the means to deeper levels of consciousness. His beliefs are set out in *Magick in Theory and Practice* 1929. His other works include the novel *Diary of Drug Fiend* 1923 and he designed a tarot pack that bears his name. There was a revival of interest in his ideas in the 1960s.

crucifixion death by fastening to a cross, a form of capital punishment used by the ancient Romans, Persians, and Carthaginians, and abolished by the Roman emperor Constantine. Specifically, *the Crucifixion* refers to the execution by the Romans of ◊Jesus in this manner.

Cruelty, Theatre of theory advanced by Antonin ◊Artaud in his book *Le Théâtre et son double* 1938 and adopted by a number of writers and directors. It aims to substitute gesture and sound for spoken dialogue, and to shock the audience into awareness through the release of feelings usually repressed by conventional behaviour.

In the UK Artaud's ideas particularly influenced the producer and director Peter Brook.

crusade European war against non-Christians and heretics, sanctioned by the pope; in particular, the Crusades, a series of wars 1096–1291 undertaken by European rulers to recover Palestine from the Muslims. Motivated by religious zeal, the desire for land, and the trading ambitions of the major Italian cities, the Crusades were varied in their aims and effects.

1st Crusade 1095–99 led by Baldwin of Boulogne, Godfrey of Bouillon, and Peter the Hermit. Motivated by occupation of Anatolia and Jerusalem by the Seljuk Turks. The crusade succeeded in recapturing Jerusalem and establishing a series of Latin kingdoms on the Syrian coast. *2nd Crusade 1147–49* led by Louis VII of France and Emperor Conrad III; a complete failure. *3rd Crusade 1189–92* led by Philip II Augustus of France and Richard I of England. Failed to recapture Jerusalem, which had been seized by Saladin 1187. *4th Crusade 1202–04* led by William of Montferrata, and Baldwin of Hainault. Directed against Egypt but diverted by the Venetians to sack and divide Constantinople. *Children's Crusade 1212* thousands of children crossed Europe on their way to Palestine but many were sold into slavery in Marseille, or died of disease and hunger. *5th Crusade 1218–21* led by King Andrew of Hungary, Cardinal Pelagius, King John of Jerusalem, and King Hugh of Cyprus. Captured and then lost Damietta, Egypt. *6th Crusade 1228–29* led by the Holy Roman emperor Frederick II. Jerusalem recovered by negotiation with the sultan of Egypt, but the city was finally lost 1244. *7th and 8th Crusades 1249–54, 1270–72* both led by Louis IX of France. Acre, the last Christian fortress in Syria, was lost 1291.

Cubism revolutionary movement in early 20th-century painting, pioneering abstract forms. Its founders, Georges Braque and Pablo ◊Picasso, were admirers of Paul Cézanne and were inspired by his attempt to create a highly structured visual language. In *analytical Cubism* (1907–12) three-dimensional objects were split into facets and analysed before being 'reassembled' as complex two-dimensional images. In *synthetic Cubism* (after 1912) the images became simpler, the colours brighter, and collage was introduced. The movement attracted such artists as Juan Gris, Fernand Léger, and Robert Delaunay. Its message was that a work of art exists in its own right rather than as a representation of the real world.

Cuchulain Celtic hero, the chief figure in a cycle of Irish legends. He is associated with his uncle Conchobar, king of Ulster; his most famous exploits are described in *Taín Bó Cuailnge/The Cattle Raid of Cuchulain*.

Cudworth Ralph 1617–1688. English philosopher and leading member of the ◊Cambridge Platonists. He opposed the materialism of Thomas ◊Hobbes, and he tried to combine the science of his day with the Platonic tradition in metaphysics and theology. Holding that mechanical and atomic principles do not suffice to explain nature, he posited the existence of a Plastic Nature, or Platonic world-soul, to relate the material and spiritual orders.

His works include *The True Intellectual System of the Universe* 1678 and the posthumously published *A Treatise Concerning Eternal and Immutable Morality* 1731. Born in Aller in Somerset, he spent most of his life at Cambridge University, where he became Master of Clare Hall and then Master of Christ's College. He was professor of Hebrew 1645–88.

Culdee member of an ancient order of Christian monks that existed in Ireland and Scotland from before the 9th century to about

the 12th century AD, when the Celtic church, to which they belonged, was forced to conform to Roman usages. Some survived until the 14th century, and in Armagh, N Ireland, they remained until the dissolution of the monasteries in 1541.

cultural anthropology or *social anthropology* subdiscipline of anthropology that analyses human culture and society, the nonbiological and behavioural aspects of humanity. Two principal branches are ethnography (the study at first hand of living cultures) and ethnology (the comparison of cultures using ethnographic evidence).

Cultural Revolution Chinese mass movement 1966–69 begun by Communist Party chair ◊Mao Zedong, directed against the upper middle class – bureaucrats, artists, and academics – who were killed, imprisoned, humiliated, or 'resettled'. Intended to 'purify' Chinese communism, it was also an attempt by Mao to renew his political and ideological pre-eminence inside China. Half a million people are estimated to have been killed.

The 'revolution' was characterized by the violent activities of the semimilitary Red Guards, most of them students. Many established and learned people were humbled and eventually sent to work on the land, and from 1966 to 1970 universities were closed. Although the revolution was brought to an end in 1969, the resulting bureaucratic and economic chaos had many long-term effects. The ultra-leftist ◊Gang of Four, led by Mao's wife Jiang Qing and defence minister Lin Biao, played prominent roles in the Cultural Revolution. The chief political victims were Liu Shaoqi and ◊Deng Xiaoping, who were depicted as 'bourgeois reactionaries'. After Mao's death, the Cultural Revolution was criticized officially and the verdicts on hundreds of thousands of people who were wrongly arrested and persecuted were reversed.

culture in sociology and anthropology, the way of life of a particular society or group of people, including patterns of thought, beliefs, behaviour, customs, traditions, rituals, dress, and language, as well as art, music, and literature.

The concept of culture is difficult to define in a precise fashion, since it is employed by several intellectual disciplines in distinct and different ways. The primary use of the term is in the social sciences, where it refers to the whole way of life – both material and spiritual – of a particular society. The word culture is also commonly used to refer to the arts and intellectual activity in general: thus, a cultured (or cultivated) person is taken to mean someone who seeks to improve themselves by the contemplation of such things. This is sometimes called high culture, by way of contrast to ◊mass culture, or popular culture, which is more recreational and less concerned with intellectual improvement. The new academic discipline of Cultural Studies makes no qualitative distinction between the two, and analyses a cultural phenomenon such as the pop singer Madonna in much the same way as it would a novel by ◊Tolstoy.

The origins of the word are in the Latin word *cultura* meaning the cultivation of the soil, a meaning which still prevails in words such as agriculture and viticulture. From this root it was employed metaphorically to the intellect, so that the expression 'the culture of the mind', common in the 17th century, suggested both development and improvement. Culture was taken to be the process of achieving this. In the late 18th and early 19th centuries its meaning shifted from the process to the achievement: culture now meant 'a general state of intellectual and moral development in a society as a whole', and was more or less synonymous with the word civilization. Civilization (from the Latin *civis*, 'citizen') generally has a clearer history as a concept, and is often employed as the opposite of barbarism to mean a society that has reached a high level of cultural and political refinement.

In the late 19th century, the word culture entered the language of the new social sciences, famously in the work of E B Tylor who in *Primitive Culture* defined it as 'that complex whole which includes, knowledge, belief, art, morals, laws, customs, and any other capabilities and habits acquired by man as a member of society.' Initially ethnologists and anthropologists looked at non-Western cultures, partially with a view to proving their inferiority, despite the parallel rediscovery and appreciation of folklore and traditional customs within their own countries. Since then a more neutral use of the term has prevailed. Both Britain and the USA are multi-cultural, and this is widely regarded as enriching the fabric of their societies. That cultural differences can be emphasized in order to divide a society can be witnessed in such conflicts as the bloody civil war in former Yugoslavia.

The term culture is also used by microbiologists to refer to micro-organisms or tissue cells grown artificially for research, and by archaeologists to mean the surviving objects or artifacts that provide evidence of a social grouping.

Cupid in Roman mythology, the god of love, identified with the Greek ◊Eros.

curate in the Christian church, literally, a priest who has the cure of souls in a parish, and the term is so used in mainland Europe. In the Church of England, a curate is an unbeneficed cleric who acts as assistant to a parish priest, more exactly an 'assistant curate'.

Curie Marie (born Sklodovska) 1867–1934. Polish scientist. In 1898 she reported the possible existence of a new, powerfully radioactive element in pitchblende ores. Her husband, Pierre (1859–1906) abandoned his own researches to assist her, and in the same year they announced the existence of polonium and radium. They isolated the pure elements 1902. Both scientists refused to take out a patent on their discovery and were jointly awarded the Davy Medal 1903 and the Nobel Prize for Physics 1903, with Antoine ◊Becquerel. Marie Curie wrote a *Treatise on Radioactivity* 1910, and was awarded the Nobel Prize for Chemistry 1911.

Born in Warsaw, Marie Curie studied in Paris from 1891. Her decision to investigate the nature of uranium rays was influenced by the publication of Antoine ◊Becquerel's experiments. She took no precautions against radioactivity and died a victim of radiation poisoning. Her notebooks, even today, are too contaminated to handle. In 1904 Pierre was appointed to a chair in physics at the Sorbonne, and on his death in a street accident was succeeded by his wife.

currency the type of money in use in a country; for example, the US dollar, the Australian dollar, the UK pound sterling, the German Deutschmark, and the Japanese yen.

curriculum in education, the range of subjects offered within an institution or course.

Until 1988, the only part of the school curriculum prescribed by law in the UK was religious education. Growing concern about the low proportion of 14- and 16-year-olds opting to study maths, science, and technology, with a markedly low take-up rate among girls, led to the central government in the Education Reform Act 1988 introducing a compulsory national curriculum, which applies to all children of school age (5–16) in state schools. There are three core subjects in the curriculum: English, maths, and science, and seven foundation subjects: technology, history, geography, music, art, physical education, and a foreign language. The move towards central control of the curriculum has been criticized as it removes decision-making from the local authorities and schools, and tightens control over teachers.

Cuthbert, St died 687. Christian saint. A shepherd in Northumbria, England, he entered the monastery of Melrose, Scotland, after receiving a vision. He travelled widely as a missionary and because of his alleged miracles was known as the 'wonderworker of Britain'.

He became prior of Lindisfarne 664, and retired 676 to Farne Island. In 684 he became bishop of Hexham and later of Lindisfarne. Feast day 20 March.

Cuvier Georges, Baron Cuvier 1769–1832. French comparative anatomist. In 1799 he showed that some species have become extinct by reconstructing extinct giant animals that he believed were destroyed in a series of giant deluges. These ideas are expressed in *Recherches sur les ossiments fossiles de quadrupèdes* 1812 and *Discours sur les révolutions de la surface du globe* 1825.

In 1798 Cuvier produced *Tableau élémentaire de l'histoire naturelle des animaux*, in which his scheme of classification is outlined. He was professor of natural history in the Collège de France from 1799 and at the Jardin des Plantes from 1802; at the Restoration in 1815 he was elected chancellor of the University of Paris. Cuvier was the first to relate the structure of fossil animals to that of their living relatives. His great work *Le Règne animal/The Animal Kingdom* 1817 is a systematic survey.

cybernetics science concerned with how systems organize, regulate, and reproduce themselves, and also how they evolve and learn. In the laboratory, inanimate objects are created that behave like living systems. Applications range from the creation of electronic artificial limbs to the running of the fully automated factory where decision-making machines operate up to managerial level.

Cybernetics was founded and named in 1947 by US mathematician Norbert ◊Wiener.

Originally, it was the study of control systems using feedback to produce automatic processes.

cyclic patterns patterns in which simple ideas are repeated to form more complex designs. Some ◊functions show cyclic patterns, for example mapping round a circle.

Cynic school of Greek philosophy (Cynicism), founded in Athens about 400 BC by Antisthenes, a disciple of ◊Socrates, who advocated a stern and simple morality and a complete disregard of pleasure and comfort.

His followers, led by ◊Diogenes, not only showed a contemptuous disregard for pleasure, but despised all human affection as a source of weakness. Their 'snarling contempt' for ordinary people earned them the name of Cynic (Greek 'doglike').

Cyprian, St c. 210–258. Christian martyr, one of the earliest Christian writers, and bishop of Carthage about 249. He wrote a treatise on the unity of the church. Feast day 16 Sept.

Cyrenaic member of a school of Greek hedonistic philosophy (see ◊hedonism) founded about 400 BC by Aristippus of Cyrene. He regarded pleasure as the only absolutely worthwhile thing in life but taught that self-control and intelligence were necessary to choose the best pleasures.

Cyril and Methodius, Sts two brothers, both Christian saints: Cyril 826–869 and Methodius 815–885. Born in Thessalonica, they were sent as missionaries to what is today Moravia. They invented a Slavonic alphabet, and translated the Bible and the liturgy from Greek to Slavonic. The language (known as *Old Church Slavonic*) remained in use in churches and for literature among Bulgars, Serbs, and Russians up to the 17th century. The *cyrillic alphabet* is named after Cyril and may also have been invented by him. Feast day 14 Feb.

Dada or *Dadaism* artistic and literary movement founded 1915 in Zürich, Switzerland, by the Romanian poet Tristan Tzara (1896–1963) and others in a spirit of rebellion and disillusionment during World War I. Other Dadaist groups were soon formed by the artists Marcel Duchamp and Man Ray in New York, Francis Picabia in Barcelona, and Kurt Schwitters in Germany. The Dadaists produced deliberately anti-aesthetic images, often using photomontages with worded messages to express their political views, and directly scorned established art, as in Duchamp's *Mona Lisa* 1919, where a moustache and beard were added to Leonardo's classic portrait.

With the German writers Hugo Ball and Richard Huelsenbeck, Tzara founded the Cabaret Voltaire in Zürich 1916, where works by Hans Arp, the pioneer Surrealist Max Ernst, and others were exhibited. In New York in the same period the artist Man Ray met Duchamp and Picabia and began to apply Dadaist ideas to photography. The first international Dada exhibition was in Paris 1922. Dada had a considerable impact on early 20th-century art, questioning established artistic conventions and values. In the 1920s it evolved into Surrealism.

Daedalus in Greek legend, an Athenian artisan supposed to have constructed for King Minos of Crete the labyrinth in which the ◊Minotaur was imprisoned. When Minos became displeased with him, Daedalus fled from Crete with his son ◊Icarus using wings made by them from feathers fastened with wax.

Dahrendorf Ralf (Gustav) 1929– . German sociologist, director of the London School of Economics 1974–84. His works include *Life Chances* 1980, which sees the aim of society as the improvement of the range of opportunities open to the individual.

Daimon in Greek mythology and thought, a supernatural power, sometimes associated with the individual fates of human beings. The word 'demon' is derived from it.

Dalai Lama (Tibetan 'ocean-like guru') in Tibetan ◊Buddhism, the title of the second hierarch of the ◊Gelugpa monastic order. Also political ruler of Tibet from the 17th century until 1959.

The current Dalai Lama was born Tenzin Gyatso in 1935; he was chosen to be the 14th Dalai Lama in 1937 and enthroned at Lhasa in 1940. He has lived in exile since the Chinese seized full control of Tibet in 1959. He was awarded the Nobel Prize for Peace 1989.

In the 15th century, when the office was founded, the Dalai Lama was purely a religious title. The fifth Dalai Lama (1617–1682) united Tibet politically and assumed temporal as well as spiritual powers, though spiritually the Dalai Lama is still only second in rank in the Gelugpa school. The Dalai Lama is believed to be the reincarnation of Avalokitesvara and each successive Dalai Lama is a reincarnation of his predecessor.

Dalen Nils 1869–1937. Swedish industrial engineer who invented the light-controlled valve. This allowed lighthouses to operate automatically and won him the 1912 Nobel Prize for Physics.

Dalton John 1766–1844. English chemist who proposed the theory of atoms, which he considered to be the smallest parts of matter. He produced the first list of relative atomic masses in *Absorption of Gases* 1805 and put forward the law of partial pressures of gases (Dalton's law).

From experiments with gases he noted that the proportions of two components combining to form another gas were always constant.

From this he suggested that if substances combine in simple numerical ratios then the macroscopic weight proportions represent the relative atomic masses of those substances. He also propounded the law of partial pressures, stating that for a mixture of gases the total pressure is the sum of the pressures that would be developed by each individual gas if it were the only one present.

Dam (Henrik) Carl (Peter) 1895–1976. Danish biochemist who discovered vitamin K. For his success in this field he shared the 1943 Nobel Prize for Medicine with US biochemist Edward Doisy (1893–1986).

In 1928 Dam began a series of experiments to see if chickens could live on a cholesterol-free diet. The birds, it turned out, were able to metabolize their own supply. Yet they continued to die from spontaneous haemorrhages. Dam concluded that their diet lacked an unknown essential ingredient to control coagulation, which he eventually found in abundance in green leaves. Dam named the new compound vitamin K.

damnation in Christian and Muslim belief, a state of eternal punishment which will be undergone by those who are not worthy of salvation; sometimes equated with ◊hell.

The primrose way to the everlasting bonfire.

damnation
William Shakespeare, 1564–1616, English
dramatist and poet.
Macbeth II. iii

---

dance rhythmic movement of the body, usually performed in time to music. Its primary purpose may be religious, magical, martial, social, or artistic – the last two being characteristic of nontraditional societies. The pre-Christian era had a strong tradition of ritual dance, and ancient Greek dance still exerts an influence on dance movement today. Although Western folk and social dances have a long history, the Eastern dance tradition long predates the Western. The European classical tradition dates from the 15th century in Italy, the first printed dance text from 16th-century France, and the first dance school in Paris from the 17th century. The 18th century saw the development of European classical ballet as we know it today, and the 19th century saw the rise of Romantic ballet. In the 20th century modern dance firmly established itself as a separate dance idiom, not based on classical ballet, and many divergent styles and ideas have grown from a willingness to explore a variety of techniques and amalgamate different traditions.

history European dance is relatively young in comparison to that of the rest of the world. The first Indian book on dancing, the *Natya Sastra*, existed a thousand years before its European counterpart. The *bugaku* dances of Japan, with orchestra accompaniment, date from the 7th century and are still performed at court. When the Peking (Beijing) Opera dancers first astonished Western audiences during the 1950s, they were representatives of a tradition stretching back to 740, the year in which Emperor Ming Huang established the Pear Garden Academy. The first comparable

European institution, *L'Académie Royale de Danse*, was founded by Louis XIV 1661. In the European tradition social dances have always tended to rise upward through the social scale; for example, the medieval court dances derived from peasant country dances. One form of dance tends to typify a whole period, thus the galliard represents the 16th century, the minuet the 18th, the waltz the 19th, and the quickstep represents ballroom dancing in the first half of the 20th century. The nine dances of the modern world championships in ballroom dancing are the standard four (waltz, foxtrot, tango, and quickstep), the Latin-American styles (samba, rumba, cha-cha-cha, and paso doble), and the Viennese waltz. A British development since the 1930s, which has spread to some extent abroad, is 'formation' dancing in which each team (usually eight couples) performs a series of ballroom steps in strict coordination. Popular dance crazes have included the Charleston in the 1920s, jitterbug in the 1930s and 1940s, jive in the 1950s, the twist in the 1960s, disco and jazz dancing in the 1970s, and break dancing in the 1980s. In general, since the 1960s popular dance in the West has moved away from any prescribed sequence of movements and physical contact between participants, the dancers performing as individuals with no distinction between the male and the female role. Dances requiring skilled athletic performance, such as the hustle and the New Yorker, have been developed. In classical dance, the second half of the 20th century has seen a great cross-fertilization from dances of other cultures. Troupes visited the West, not only from the USSR and Eastern Europe, but from such places as Indonesia, Japan, South Korea, Nigeria, and Senegal. In the 1970s jazz dance, pioneered in the USA by Matt Mattox, became popular; it includes elements of ballet, modern, tap, Indian Classical, Latin American, and Afro-American dance. Freestyle dance is loosely based on ballet with elements of jazz, ethnic, and modern dance.

dance of death (German *Totentanz*, French *danse macabre*) popular theme in painting of the late medieval period, depicting an allegorical representation of death (usually a skeleton) leading the famous and the not-so-famous to the grave. One of the best-known representations is a series of woodcuts (1523–26) by Hans Holbein the Younger.

Daniel 6th century BC. Jewish folk hero and prophet at the court of Nebuchadnezzar; also the name of a book of the Old Testament, probably compiled in the 2nd century BC. It includes stories about Daniel and his companions Shadrach, Meshach, and Abednego, set during the Babylonian captivity of the Jews.

One of the best-known stories is that of Daniel in the den of lions, where he was thrown for refusing to compromise his beliefs, and was preserved by divine intervention. The book also contains a prophetic section dealing with the rise and fall of a number of empires.

In the middle of the road of our life.

Dante Alighieri
Divine Comedy Inferno I

Dante Alighieri 1265–1321. Italian poet. His masterpiece *La divina commedia/The Divine Comedy* 1307–21 is an epic account in three parts of his journey through Hell, Purgatory, and Paradise, during which he is guided part of the way by the poet Virgil; on a metaphorical level the journey is also one of Dante's own spiritual development. Other works include the philosophical prose treatise *Convivio/The Banquet* 1306–08, the first major work of its kind to be written in Italian rather than Latin; *Monarchia/On World Government* 1310–13, expounding his political theories; *De vulgari eloquentia/Concerning the Vulgar Tongue* 1304–06, an original Latin work on Italian, its dialects, and kindred languages; and *Canzoniere/Lyrics*, containing his scattered lyrics.

Dante was born in Florence, where in 1274 he first met and fell in love with Beatrice Portinari (described in *La vita nuova/New Life* 1283–92). His love for her survived her marriage to another and her death 1290 at the age of 24. He married Gemma Donati 1291.

In 1289 Dante fought in the battle of Campaldino, won by Florence against Arezzo, and from 1295 took an active part in Florentine politics. In 1300 he was one of the six Priors of the Republic, favouring the moderate 'White' Guelph party rather than the extreme papal 'Black' Ghibelline faction; when the Ghibellines seized power 1302, he was convicted in his absence of misapplication of public money, and sentenced first to a fine and then to death. He escaped from Florence and spent the remainder of his life in exile, in central and N Italy.

dark matter hypothetical matter that, according to current theories of ◊cosmology, makes up 90–99% of the mass of the universe but so far remains undetected.

Astronomers are unsure if it consists of unknown atomic particles (cold dark matter) or fast-moving neutrinos (hot dark matter) or a combination of both.

Dart Raymond 1893–1988. Australian-born South African paleontologist and anthropologist who in 1924 discovered the first fossil remains of the Australopithecenes, early hominids, near Taungs in Botswana. He named them *Australopithecus africanus*, and spent many years trying to prove to sceptics that they were early humans, since their cranial and dental characteristics were not apelike in any way. In the 1950s and 1960s, the ◊Leakey family found more fossils of this type and of related types in the Olduvai Gorge of E Africa, establishing that Australopithecines were hominids, walked erect, made tools, and lived as early as 5.5 million years ago. After further discoveries in the 1980s, they are today classified as *Homo sapiens australopithecus*, and Dart's assertions have been validated.

Darwin Charles Robert 1809–1882. English scientist who developed the modern theory of ◊evolution and proposed, with Alfred Russel Wallace, the principle of ◊natural selection. After research in South America and the Galápagos Islands as naturalist on HMS *Beagle* 1831–36, Darwin published *On the Origin of Species by Means of Natural Selection or the Preservation of Favoured Races in the Struggle for Life* 1859. This explained the evolutionary process through the principles of natural and sexual selection. It aroused bitter controversy because it disagreed with the literal interpretation of the Book of Genesis in the Bible.

Darwin also made important discoveries in many other areas, including the fertilization mechanisms of plants, the classification of barnacles, and the formation of coral reefs. Born at Shrewsbury, the grandson of Erasmus ◊Darwin, he studied medicine at Edinburgh and theology at Cambridge. By 1844 he had enlarged his sketch of ideas to an essay of his conclusions, but then left his theory for eight years while he studied barnacles. In 1858 he was forced into action by the receipt of a memoir from A R ◊Wallace, embodying the same theory. *On the Origin of Species* refuted earlier evolutionary theories, such as those of ◊Lamarck. Darwin himself played little part in the debates, but his *Descent of Man* 1871 added fuel to the theological discussion in which T H ◊Huxley and Haeckel took leading parts. Darwin then devoted himself chiefly to botanical studies until his death. Darwinism alone is not enough to explain the evolution of sterile worker bees, or altruism. ◊Neo-Darwinism, the current theory of evolution, is a synthesis of Darwin and genetics based on the work of ◊Mendel.

Darwin Erasmus 1731–1802. British poet, physician, and naturalist; he was the grandfather of Charles Darwin. He wrote *The Botanic Garden* 1792, which included a versification of the Linnaean system entitled 'The Loves of the Plants', and *Zoonomia* 1794–96, which anticipated aspects of evolutionary theory, but tended to ◊Lamarck's interpretation.

Darwinism, social in US history, an influential but contentious social theory, based on the work of Charles ◊Darwin and Herbert ◊Spencer, which claimed to offer a scientific justification for late 19th-century *laissez-faire* capitalism (the principle of unrestricted freedom in commerce).

Popularized by academics and by entrepreneurs such as Andrew Carnegie, social Darwinism was used to legitimize competitive individualism and a market economy unregulated by government; it argued that only the strong and resourceful businesses and individuals would thrive in a free environment.

Dasam Granth collection of the writings of the tenth Sikh guru (teacher), Gobind Singh, and of poems by a number of other writers. It is written in a script called Gurmukhi, the written form of Punjabi popularized by Guru Angad. It contains a retelling of the Krishna legends, devotional verse, and amusing anecdotes.

database in computing, a structured collection of data, which may be manipulated to select and sort desired items of information. For example, an accounting system might be built around a database containing details of customers and suppliers. In larger computers, the database makes data available to the various programs that need it, without the need for those programs to be aware of how the data are stored. The term is also sometimes used for simple record-keeping systems, such as mailing lists, in which there are facilities for searching, sorting, and producing records.

There are three main types (or 'models'): hierarchical, network, and relational, of which relational is the most widely used. A *free-text database* is one that holds the unstructured text of articles or books in a form that permits rapid searching.

A collection of databases is known as a *databank*. A database-management system (DBMS) program ensures that the integrity of the data is maintained by controlling the degree of access of the applications programs using the data. Databases are normally used by large organizations with mainframes or minicomputers.

A telephone directory stored as a database might allow all the people whose names start with the letter B to be selected by one program, and all those living in Chicago by another.

data protection safeguarding of information about individuals stored on computers, to protect privacy. The Council of Europe adopted, in 1981, a Data Protection Convention, which led in the UK to the Data Protection Act 1984. This requires computer databases containing personal information to be registered, and users to process only accurate information and to retain the information only for a necessary period and for specified purposes. Subject to certain exemptions, individuals have a right of access to their personal data and to have any errors corrected.

David c. 1060–970 BC. Second king of Israel. According to the Old Testament he played the harp for King Saul to banish Saul's melancholy; he later slew the Philistine giant Goliath with a sling and stone. After Saul's death David was anointed king at Hebron, took Jerusalem, and made it his capital.

David was celebrated as a secular poet and probably wrote some of the psalms attributed to him. He was the youngest son of Jesse of Bethlehem. While still a shepherd boy he was anointed by Samuel, a judge who ruled Israel before Saul. Saul's son Jonathan became David's friend, but Saul, jealous of David's prowess, schemed to murder him. David married Michal, Saul's daughter, but after further attempts on his life went into exile until Saul and Jonathan fell in battle with the Philistines at Gilboa.

Once David was king, Absalom, his favourite son, led a rebellion but was defeated and killed.

David sent Uriah (a soldier in his army) to his death in the front line of battle in order that he might marry his widow, Bathsheba. Their son Solomon became the third king.

In both Jewish and Christian belief, the messiah would be a descendant of David; Christians hold this prophecy to have been fulfilled by Jesus.

David, St or *Dewi* 5th–6th century. Patron saint of Wales, Christian abbot and bishop. According to legend he was the son of a prince of Dyfed and uncle of King Arthur; he was responsible for the adoption of the leek as the national emblem of Wales, but his own emblem is a dove. Feast day 1 March.

Tradition has it that David made a pilgrimage to Jerusalem, where he was consecrated bishop.

He founded 12 monasteries in Wales, including one at Menevia (now St Davids), which he made his bishop's seat; he presided over a synod at Brefi and condemned the ideas of the British theologian Pelagius.

Davis William Morris 1850–1934. Leading US physical geographer of the early 20th century. An influential analyst of landforms, in the 1890s he developed the organizing concept of the regular cycle of erosion, a theory that dominated geomorphology and physical geography for half a century.

Davisson Clinton Joseph 1881–1958. US physicist. With Lester Germer (1896–1971), he discovered that electrons can undergo diffraction, so proving Louis de ◊Broglie's theory that electrons, and therefore all matter, can show wavelike structure. George ◊Thomson carried through the same research independently, and in 1937 the two men shared the Nobel Prize for Physics.

Davy Humphry 1778–1829. English chemist. He discovered, by electrolysis, the metallic elements sodium and potassium in 1807, and calcium, boron, magnesium, strontium, and barium in 1808. In addition, he established that chlorine is an element and proposed that hydrogen is present in all acids. He invented the 'safety lamp' for use in mines where methane was present, enabling miners to work in previously unsafe conditions.

In 1802 he became professor at the Royal Institution, London. He was elected president of the Royal Society in 1820.

Dawkins Richard 1941– . British zoologist whose book *The Selfish Gene* 1976 popularized the theories of sociobiology (social behaviour in humans and animals in the context of evolution). A second book, *The Blind Watchmaker* 1986, explains the modern theory of evolution.

Dayananda Sarasvati 1824–1883. Hindu religious reformer who in 1875 founded the ◊Arya Samaj, a society named after the Aryans, who were believed to have originated the Vedic hymns. By returning to the original hymns of the Vedas, he tried to simplify and purify Hinduism.

deacon in the Roman Catholic and Anglican churches, an ordained minister who ranks immediately below a priest. In the Protestant churches, a deacon who is in training to become a minister or is a lay assistant.

Dead Sea Scrolls collection of ancient scrolls (rolls of writing) and fragments of scrolls found 1947–56 in caves on the W side of the Jordan, 12 km/7 mi S of Jericho and 2 km/l mi from the N end of the Dead Sea, at ◊Qumran. They include copies of Old Testament books a thousand years older than those previously known to be extant. The documents date mainly from about 150 BC–AD 68, when the monastic community that owned them, the Essenes, was destroyed by the Romans because of its support for a revolt against their rule.

The total of 800 manuscripts, containing all the books of the Old Testament except Esther, were publicly available for the first time 1986. Before this, only half the scrolls were published and only 15 scholars had access to them.

death permanent ending of all the functions that keep an organism alive. Death used to be pronounced when a person's breathing and heartbeat stopped. The advent of mechanical aids has made this point sometimes difficult to determine, and in controversial cases a person is now pronounced dead when the brain ceases to control the vital functions even if breath and heartbeat are maintained.

For removal of vital organs in transplant surgery, the World Health Organization in 1968 set out that the donor should exhibit no brain–body connection, muscular activity, blood pressure, or ability to breathe unaided by machine.

In religious belief death may be seen as the prelude to rebirth (as in Hinduism and Buddhism); under Islam and Christianity, there is the concept of a day of judgement and consignment to heaven or hell; Judaism concentrates not on an afterlife but on survival through descendants who honour tradition.

de Bono Edward 1933– . Maltese-born British medical doctor and psychologist whose concept of lateral thinking was first expounded in *The Use of Lateral Thinking* 1967. Lateral thinking is an approach to problem solving. It is not based on logical analytical reasoning, (which for de Bono is the process which follows lateral thinking), but on creative thinking. Its techniques are designed to free the mind from pre-conceptions and generate new approaches to a problem. De Bono's ideas have been widely adopted in business and management studies. His many books include *The Five Day Course in Thinking* 1969, *The Dog Exercising Machine* 1970, and *Po: Beyond Yes and No* 1972.

Deborah in the Old Testament, a prophet and judge (leader). She helped lead an Israelite army against the Canaanite general Sisera, who was killed trying to flee; her song of triumph at his death is regarded as an excellent example of early Hebrew poetry.

Debray Régis 1941– . French Marxist theorist. He was associated with Che ◊Guevara in the revolutionary movement in Latin America in the 1960s. In 1967 he was sentenced to 30 years' imprisonment in Bolivia but was released after three years. His writings on Latin American politics include *Strategy for Revolution* 1970. He became a specialist adviser to President Mitterrand of France on Latin American affairs.

Debreu Gerard 1921– . French-born US economist who developed mathematical economic models with Kenneth ◊Arrow), analysing the conditions for economic equilibrium where demand and supply are equal. He further developed such models in his major work, *Theory of Value* 1959, which integrates the theory of location of firms, the theory of capital, and the theory of behaviour under uncertainty into general economic equilibrium theory. He was awarded the Nobel Prize for Economics in 1983 for his work on general equilibrium theory.

Bibl. Arrow, K J and Debreu, G 'Existence of an Equilibrium for a Competitive Economy' *Econometrica* (1954)

debt something that is owed by a person, organization, or country, usually money, goods, or services. Debt usually occurs as a result of borrowing ◊credit. *Debt servicing* is the payment of interest on a debt. The *national debt* of a country is the total money owed by the national government to private individuals, banks, and so on; *international debt*, the money owed by one country to another, began on a large scale with the investment in foreign countries by newly industrialized countries in the late 19th to early 20th centuries. International debt became a global problem as a result of the oil crisis of the 1970s.

As a result of the ◊Bretton Woods Conference 1944, the World Bank (officially called the International Bank for Reconstruction and Development) was established 1945 as an agency of the United Nations to finance international development, by providing loans where private capital was not forthcoming. Loans were made largely at prevailing market rates ('hard loans') and therefore generally to the developed countries, who could afford them.

In 1960 the International Development Association (IDA) was set up as an offshoot of the World Bank to provide interest-free ('soft') loans over a long period to finance the economies of developing countries and assist their long-term development. The cash surpluses of Middle Eastern oil-producing countries were channelled by Western banks to Third World countries. However, a slump in the world economy and increases in interest rates resulted in the debtor countries paying an ever-increasing share of their national output in debt servicing (paying off the interest on a debt, rather than paying off the debt itself). As a result, many loans had to be **rescheduled** (renegotiated so that repayments were made over a longer term).

In 1980–81 Poland ceased making repayments on international debts. Today, the countries most at risk include Mexico and Brazil, both of which have a **debt-servicing ratio** (proportion of export earnings which is required to pay off the debt) of more than 50%. In May 1987 the world's largest bank, Citibank of New York, announced that it was writing off $3 billion of international loans, mainly due to Brazil's repeated rescheduling of debt repayments. The dangers of the current scale of international debt (the so-called **debt crisis**) is that the debtor country can only continue to repay its existing debts by means of further loans; for the Western countries, there is the possibility of a confidence crisis causing panic withdrawals of deposits and consequent collapse of the banking system.

major debtor nations: total external debt and debt service figures

country	total long-term debt as % of GNP		total long-term debt service as % of GNP	
	1970	1987	1970	1987
Argentina	23.8	65.5	5.1	5.8
Brazil	12.2	33.7	1.6	3.0
Mexico	16.2	69.6	3.5	8.2
Morocco	18.6	117.9	1.7	8.2
Nigeria	4.3	111.3	0.7	3.9
Philippines	21.8	69.4	4.3	6.9

debt-for-nature swap agreement under which a proportion of a country's debts are written off in exchange for a commitment by the debtor country to undertake projects for environmental protection. Debt-for-nature swaps were set up by environment groups in the 1980s in an attempt to reduce the debt problem of poor countries, while simultaneously promoting conservation.

To date, most debt-for-nature swaps have concentrated on setting aside areas of land, especially tropical rainforest, for protection and have involved private conservation foundations. The first swap took place 1987, when a US conservation group bought $650,000 of Bolivia's national debt from a bank for $100,000, and persuaded the Bolivian government to set aside a large area of rainforest as a nature reserve in exchange for never having to pay back the money owed. Other countries participating in debt-for-nature swaps are the Philippines, Costa Rica, Ecuador, and Poland. However, the debtor country is expected to ensure that the area of land remains adequately protected, and in practice this does not always happen. The practice has also produced complaints of neocolonialism.

Debye Peter 1884–1966. Dutch physicist. A pioneer of X-ray powder crystallography, he also worked on polar molecules, dipole moments, and molecular structure. In 1940, he went to the USA where he was professor of chemistry at Cornell University 1940–52. He was awarded the 1936 Nobel Prize for Chemistry.

decadence in literary and artistic criticism, the decline that follows a time of great cultural achievement. It is typified by world-weariness, self-consciousness, and the search for new stimulation through artistic refinement and degenerate behaviour. The term is used especially in connection with the *fin-de-siècle* styles of the late 19th century (symbolism, the Aesthetic Movement, and Art Nouveau). It has been applied to such artists and writers as Rimbaud, Oscar Wilde, and Aubrey Beardsley.

Decalogue ten commandments which, according to the Old Testament, were delivered by God to ◊Moses on Mount Sinai, stated in the books Exodus 20:1–17 and Deuteronomy 5:6–21. The Decalogue is recognized as the basis of morality by Jews and Christians.

decentralization the dispersion of a population away from a central point. A common form is ◊counterurbanization (in developed countries, the movement of industries and people away from cities). Examples in the UK include the move of the Department of Social Security to Newcastle and DVLA to Swansea.

decentralization form of organization in a business where decision-making for the business is taken by individuals or groups throughout the organization rather than at the centre. Decision-making is therefore 'devolved' throughout the business.

decision theory system of mathematical techniques for analysing decision-making problems, for example, over unpredictable factors. The system aims to minimize error. It includes game theory, risk analysis, and utility theory.

Declaration of Independence historic US document stating the theory of government on which the USA was founded, based on the right 'to life, liberty, and the pursuit of happiness'. The statement was issued by the Continental Congress 4 July 1776, renouncing all allegiance to the British crown and ending the political connection with Britain.

decolonization gradual achievement of independence by former colonies of the European imperial powers which began after World War I. The process of decolonization accelerated after World War II and the movement affected every continent: India and Pakistan gained independence from Britain 1947; Algeria gained independence from France 1962.

Deconstruction in literary theory, a radical form of ◊Structuralism, pioneered by the French philosopher Jacques ◊Derrida (1930–), which views text as a 'decentred' play of structures, lacking any ultimately determinable meaning. Through analysis of the internal structure of a text, particularly its contradictions, Deconstructionists demonstrate the existence of subtext meanings – often not those that the author intended – and hence illustrate the impossibility of attributing fixed meaning to a work. Roland ◊Barthes laid the foundations of Deconstruction in his book *Mythologies* 1957 in which he studied the inherent instability between sign and referent in a range of cultural phenomena, including not only literary works but also such things as advertising, cookery, wrestling, and so on.

Deconstructionism in architecture, a style that fragments forms and space by taking the usual building elements of floors, walls and ceilings and sliding them apart to create a sense of disorientation and movement. Its proponents include Zaha Hadid in the UK, Frank Gehry and Peter Eisenman in the USA, and Coop Himmelbau in Austria. Essentially Modernist, it draws inspiration from the optimism of the Soviet avant-garde of the 1920s.

decorum term derived from classical criticism meaning the proper or appropriate combination of elements within a work of art. Its later advocates believed that there was a 'correct' style for each genre: grandiloquent for tragedy, low for comedy, and so on, and that these styles should never be mixed.

decretum collection of papal decrees. The best known is that collected by Gratian (died 1159) about 1140, comprising some 4,000 items. The decretum was used as an authoritative source of canon law (the rules and regulations of the church).

Dedekind Richard 1831–1916. German mathematician, who made contributions to number theory. In 1872 he introduced the *Dedekind cut* (which divides a line of infinite length representing all real numbers) to categorize irrational numbers as fractions and thus increase their usefulness.

deduction in philosophy, a form of argument in which the conclusion necessarily follows from the premises. It would be inconsistent ◊logic to accept the premises but deny the conclusion.

Dee John 1527–1608. English alchemist, astrologer, and mathematician. He wrote on a wide range of subjects, including mathematics (such as his preface to the first English translation of Euclid), logic, geography, navigation, and astrology. His works were a typically Renaissance combination of scholarship, science, superstition and magic. He claimed to have transmuted metals into gold, although he died in poverty. He long enjoyed the favour of Elizabeth I, and was employed as a secret diplomatic agent.

Defender of the Faith one of the titles of the English sovereign, conferred on Henry VIII 1521 by Pope Leo X in recognition of the king's treatise against the Protestant Martin ◊Luther. It appears on coins in the abbreviated form *F.D.* (Latin *Fidei Defensor*).

deflation in economics, a reduction in the level of economic activity, usually caused by an increase in interest rates and reduction in the money supply, increased taxation, or a decline in government expenditure.

Deflation may be chosen as an economic policy to improve the balance of payments, by reducing demand and therefore cutting imports, and lowering inflation to stimulate exports. It can reduce wage increases but may also increase unemployment.

De Forest Lee 1873–1961. US physicist and inventor who perfected the triode valve and contributed to the development of radio, radar, and television.

Ambrose Fleming invented the diode valve 1904. De Forest saw that if a third electrode were added, the triode valve would serve as an amplifier and radio communications would become a practical possibility. He patented his discovery 1906.

de Gaulle Charles André Joseph Marie 1890–1970. French general and first president of the Fifth Republic 1958–69. He organized the Free French troops fighting the Nazis 1940–44, was head of the provisional French government 1944–46, and leader of his own Gaullist party. In 1958 the national assembly asked him to form a government during France's economic recovery and to solve the crisis in Algeria. He became president at the end of 1958, having changed the constitution to provide for a presidential system, and served until 1969.

Degenerate Art (German Entartete Kunst) art condemned by the Nazi regime, the name taken from a travelling exhibition mounted by the Nazi Party 1937 to show modern art as 'sick' and 'decadent' – a view that fitted with Nazi racial theories. The exhibition was paralleled by the official Great German Art Exhibition to display officially approved artists. However, five times as many people (more than 3 million) saw the former as the latter. Artists condemned included Beckmann, Nolde, Kandinsky, Matisse, Barlach, and Picasso.

deification the path whereby an individual can become a god. The deep distinction between mortal humans and immortal gods could be bridged through deification. Some Christians use the word in a more specific sense to refer to human participation in divine life through Christ, who is understood to be both God and human.

Deification was common in the ancient world, for example in Egypt and Rome, for rulers to become gods after their death. In the ancient mystery religions, such as the cults of Mithras and Dionysus, it meant union with the deity, achieved by undergoing initiation rituals.

deindustrialization decline in the share of manufacturing industries in a country's economy. Typically, industrial plants are closed down and not replaced, and service industries increase.

Deirdre in Celtic legend, the beautiful intended bride of ◊Conchobar. She eloped with Noísi, and died of sorrow when Conchobar killed him and his brothers.

deism belief in a supreme being; but the term usually refers to a movement of religious thought in the 17th and 18th centuries, characterized by the belief in a rational 'religion of nature' as opposed to the orthodox beliefs of Christianity. Deists believed that God is the source of natural law but does not intervene directly in the affairs of the world, and that the only religious duty of humanity is to be virtuous.

The father of English deism was Lord Herbert of Cherbury (1583–1648), and the chief exponents were John Toland (1670–1722), Anthony Collins (1676–1729), Matthew Tindal (1657–1733), Thomas Woolston (1670–1733), and Thomas Chubb (1679–1747). In France, the writer ◊Voltaire was the most prominent advocate of deism. In the USA, many of the country's founding fathers, including Benjamin ◊Franklin and Thomas ◊Jefferson, were essentially deists. Later, deism came to mean a belief in a personal deity who is distinct from the world and not very intimately interested in its concerns. See also ◊theism.

Delbruck Max 1906–1981. German-born US biologist who pioneered techniques in molecular biology, studying genetic changes occurring when viruses invade bacteria. He was awarded the Nobel Prize for Medicine 1969 which he shared with Salvador ◊Luria (1912–1951) and Alfred Hershey (1908–   ).

Delilah in the Old Testament, the Philistine mistress of ◊Samson. Following instructions from the lords of the Philistines she sought to find the source of Samson's great strength. When Samson eventually revealed that his physical power lay in the length of his hair, she had his head shaved while he slept and then delivered him into the hands of the Philistines.

Delors Jacques 1925–   . French socialist politician, finance minister 1981–84. As president of the European Commission from 1984 he has overseen significant budgetary reform and the move towards a free European Community market in 1992, with increased powers residing in Brussels.

Delphi city of ancient Greece, situated in a rocky valley north of the gulf of Corinth, on the southern slopes of Mount Parnassus, site of a famous ◊oracle in the temple of Apollo. The site was supposed to be the centre of the Earth and was marked by a conical stone, the *omphalos*. The oracle was interpreted by priests from the inspired utterances of the Pythian priestess until it was closed down by the Roman emperor Theodosius I AD 390.

A European Cultural Centre was built nearby 1966–67.

delusion in psychiatry, a false belief that is unshakeably held. Delusions are a prominent feature of schizophrenia and paranoia, but may also occur in severe depression and manic depression.

demand in economics, the quantity of a product that customers are able and willing to buy at any given price. It is a want backed by the ability to pay.

demand curve in economics, a curve on a graph which shows the relationship between the quantity demanded for a good and its price. It is downward-sloping, showing that as the price of the good goes down, the quantity demanded goes up. The demand curve will shift if there is a change in a variable which affects demand other than the price of the good.

demand-pull inflation rise in prices (inflation) caused by excess aggregate demand (total demand for goods and services) in the economy. For example, when the economy is in ◊boom, aggregate demand tends to be rising quickly, but inflation also rises quickly.

Demeter in Greek mythology, the goddess of agriculture (Roman Ceres), daughter of Kronos and Rhea, and mother of Persephone by Zeus. Demeter and Persephone were worshipped in a sanctuary at Eleusis, where one of the foremost ◊mystery religions of Greece was celebrated. She was later identified with the Egyptian goddess Isis.

demiurge the supernatural maker of the world who is subordinate to the Supreme Being or God. The term comes from the ancient Greek philosopher Plato's myth in the Timaeus about the divine creation of the universe. Plato's demiurge copies the ◊Forms onto the receptacle of space-time or womb of becoming.

We might have a two-party system, but one of the two parties would be in office and the other in prison.

democracy
Nikolai Ivanovich Bukharin, 1888–1938,
Soviet politician and theorist.
Attributed remark

democracy government by the people, usually through elected representatives. In the modern world, democracy has developed from the American and French revolutions.

Democracy is arguably the most misused word in contemporary society. It claims, or at the very least implies, rule by the people and yet it has been, and in some cases still is, used to describe quite despotic regimes. The real test of whether or not a political system can properly be called democratic is clear evidence that whatever government is in power it can be peacefully removed by a majority decision of the people, through a fair and open electoral system. There are few nation states today which do not claim to be democracies, but not all would qualify on the basis of this criterion.

The ballot is stronger than the bullet.

democracy

Abraham Lincoln, 1809–1865, 16th president
of the USA 1861–65, a Republican.
Speech 19 May 1856

Representative parliamentary government existed in Iceland from the 10th century and in England from the 13th century, but the British working classes were excluded almost entirely from the ◊vote until 1867, and women were admitted and property qualifications abolished only in 1918.

In *direct democracy* the whole people meets for the making of laws or the direction of executive officers, for example in Athens in the 5th century BC (and allegedly in modern Libya). Direct democracy today is represented mainly by the use of the ◊referendum, as in the UK, France, Switzerland, and certain states of the USA.

Democracy is the theory that the common people know what they want, and deserve to get it good and hard.

democracy

H(enry) L(ouis) Mencken, 1880–1956, US essayist and critic, known as 'the sage of Baltimore'.
Little Book in C major

It is often argued that the Western concept of democracy differs from that of the communist countries in that freedom of expression in those states is suppressed and political and economic power rests with the communist party. That is certainly so, but although the demise of communism in so many parts of the world has created more democratic institutions there are still many noncommunist countries where they do not exist.

Democratic Party one of the two main political parties of the USA. It tends to be the party of the working person, as opposed to the Republicans, the party of big business, but the divisions between the two are not clear cut. Its stronghold since the Civil War has traditionally been industrial urban centres and the Southern states, but conservative Southern Democrats were largely supportive of Republican positions and helped elect President Reagan.

Originally called Democratic Republicans, the party was founded by Thomas Jefferson 1792 to defend the rights of the individual states against the centralizing policy of the Federalists. The Democratic Party in the United States has never been a homogeneous unit and now comprises at least five significant factions. They are the southern conservative rump, the Conservative Democratic Forum (now much reduced); the northern liberals, moderate on defence and interventionists on economic and social issues; the radical liberals of the Midwest agricultural states; the Trumanite 'Defense Democrats', liberal on economic and social matters but hawks on defence; and the non-Congressional fringe, led by Jesse Jackson and seeking a 'rainbow' coalition of blacks, Hispanics, feminists, students, peace campaigners, and southern liberals.

The Democratic Party held power almost continuously 1800–60, and later returned with the presidencies of Grover Cleveland, Woodrow Wilson, Franklin D Roosevelt, Harry Truman, John F Kennedy, Lyndon B Johnson, Jimmy Carter, and, in 1992, Bill Clinton. From the 1930s the Democratic Party pursued a number of major policies which captured the hearts and minds of the American people, as well as making a significant contribution to their lives. They included Roosevelt's 'New Deal' and the 'Great Society' programme conceived by John Kennedy and implemented by Lyndon Johnson. The 'New Deal' aimed at pulling the country out of the 1930s depression and putting it back to work while the 'Great Society' programme, encompassing the Economic Opportunity Act, the Civil Rights Act, 1964, the Medicare and Voting Rights Act, 1965, and the Housing, Higher Education and Equal Opportunities Acts, sought to make America a better place for the ordinary, often disadvantaged, citizen. Roosevelt had the charisma and drive to see his policies through but Kennedy tragically did not live long enough to fulfill his ambitions. However, his successor, Johnson, although lacking his personal stature, had the invaluable ability, based on years of Congressional service, to deliver what his predecessor had promised.

Democritus c. 460–361 BC. Greek philosopher and speculative scientist who made a significant contribution to metaphysics with his atomic theory of the universe: all things originate from a vortex of atoms and differ according to the shape and arrangement of their atoms.

His concepts come to us through Aristotle's work in this area. His discussion of the constant motion of atoms to explain the origins of the universe was the most scientific theory proposed in his time.

demographic transition any change in birth and death rates; over time, these generally shift from a situation where both are high to a situation where both are low. This may be caused by a variety of social factors (among them education and the changing role of women) and economic factors (such as higher standard of living and improved diet). The **demographic transition model** suggests that it happens in four stages:
1) high birth rate, fluctuating but high death rate;
2) birth rate stays high, death rate starts to fall, giving maximum population growth;
3) birth rate starts to fall, death rate continues falling;
4) birth rate is low, death rate is low.

In some industrialized countries death rate exceeds birth rate, leading to a declining population. The history of many European countries follows the demographic transition model, but in poorer countries the pattern is far less clear. A population pyramid illustrates demographic composition, and the ◊Malthus theory gives a worst-case scenario of demographic change.

demography study of the size, structure, dispersement, and development of human populations to establish reliable statistics on such factors as birth and death rates, marriages and divorces, life expectancy, and migration.

Demography is significant in the social sciences as the basis for industry and for government planning in such areas as education, housing, welfare, transport, and taxation.

demonstration public show of support for, or opposition to, a particular political or social issue, typically by a group of people holding a rally, displaying placards, and making speeches. They usually seek some change in official policy by drawing attention to their cause with a media-worthy event.

Demonstrations can be static or take the form of elementary street theatre or processions. A specialized type of demonstration is the **picket**, in which striking or dismissed workers try to dissuade others from using or working in the premises of the employer.

In the UK, official response to demonstrations was first codified by the Public Order Act 1936. This was provoked by the Cable Street riot of that year, when an anti-Jewish march through East London by Oswald Mosley and 2,500 of his Blackshirts gave rise to violent clashes. Later demonstrations include the nonstop anti-apartheid presence in front of South Africa House in London April 1986–Feb 1990; the women's peace camp at Greenham Common; the picketing of the News International complex in Wapping, East London, by print workers 1986; and the anti-poll tax demonstrations in Trafalgar Square, London, March 1990.

The Public Order Act 1986 gave police extensive new powers to restrict demonstrations and pickets. It requires those organizing a demonstration to give seven days' notice to the police and gives the police the power to say where demonstrators should stand, how long they can stay, and in what numbers, if they believe the protest could cause 'serious disruption to the life of the community'. Police power to ban processions that they believe might result in serious public disorder has been used with increasing frequency in recent years (11 banning orders 1970–80 and 75 orders 1981–85).

Deng Xiaoping or **Teng Hsiao-ping** 1904– . Chinese political leader. A member of the Chinese Communist Party (CCP) from the 1920s, he took part in the Long March 1934–36. He was in the Politburo from 1955 until ousted in the Cultural Revolution 1966–69. Reinstated in the 1970s, he gradually took power and introduced a radical economic modernization programme. He retired from the Politburo 1987 and from his last official position (as chair of State Military Commission) March 1990, but remained influential behind the scenes.

Deng, born in Sichuan province into a middle-class landlord family, joined the CCP as a student in Paris, where he adopted the name Xiaoping ('Little Peace') 1925, and studied in Moscow 1926. After the Long March, he served as a political commissar to the People's Liberation Army during the civil war of 1937–49. He entered the CCP Politburo 1955 and headed the secretariat during the early 1960s, working closely with President Liu Shaoqi. During the Cultural Revolution Deng was dismissed as a 'capitalist roader' and sent to work in a tractor factory in Nanchang for 're-education'.

Deng was rehabilitated by his patron Zhou Enlai 1973 and served as acting prime minister after Zhou's heart attack 1974. On Zhou's death Jan 1976 he was forced into hiding but returned to office as vice premier July 1977. By Dec 1978, although nominally a CCP vice chair, state vice premier, and Chief of Staff to the PLA, Deng was the controlling force in China. His policy of 'socialism with Chinese characteristics', misinterpreted in the West as a drift to capitalism, had success in rural areas. He helped to oust Hua Guofeng in favour of his protégés Hu Yaobang (later in turn ousted) and Zhao Ziyang.

When Deng officially retired from his party and army posts, he claimed to have renounced political involvement. His reputation, both at home and in the West, was tarnished by his sanctioning of the army's massacre of more than 2,000 pro-democracy demonstrators in Tiananmen Square, Beijing, in June 1989.

Denis, St 3rd century AD. First bishop of Paris and one of the patron saints of France who was martyred by the Romans. Feast day 9 Oct.

St Denis is often confused with Dionysius the Areopagite, as well as with the dionysus mentioned in the New Testament. According to legend, he was sent as a missionary to Gaul in 250, and was beheaded several years later at what is today Montmartre in Paris, during the reign of Emperor Valerian. He is often represented as carrying his head in his hands.

deontology ethical theory that the rightness of an action consists in its conformity to duty, regardless of the consequences that may result from it. Deontological ethics is thus opposed to any form of utilitarianism or pragmatism.

depreciation in economics, the decline of a currency's value in relation to other currencies. Depreciation also describes the fall in value of an asset (such as factory machinery) resulting from age, wear and tear, or other circumstances. It is an important factor in assessing company profits and tax liabilities.

depression in economics, a period of low output and investment, with high unemployment. Specifically, the term describes two periods of crisis in world economy: 1873–96 and 1929–mid-1930s.

The term is most often used to refer to the world economic crisis precipitated by the Wall Street crash of 29 Oct 1929 when millions of dollars were wiped off US share values in a matter of hours. This forced the closure of many US banks involved in stock speculation and led to the recall of US overseas investments. This loss of US credit had serious repercussions on the European economy, especially that of Germany, and led to a steep fall in the levels of international trade as countries attempted to protect their domestic economies. Although most European countries experienced a slow recovery during the mid-1930s, the main impetus for renewed economic growth was provided by rearmament programmes later in the decade.

The Depression of 1873–96 centred on falling growth rates in the British economy but also affected industrial activity in Germany and the USA. The crisis in the British economy is now thought to have lasted longer than these dates suggest.

It's a recession when your neighbour loses his job; it's a depression when you lose yours.

depression
Harry S Truman, 1884–1972, 33rd president of the USA 1945–53.
Observer 13 Apr 1958

depression emotional state characterized by sadness, unhappy thoughts, apathy, and dejection. It is a normal response to major losses such as bereavement or unemployment. After childbirth, postnatal depression is quite common.

Depression is also a clinical syndrome or mental illness. Two main types have been described, though whether they are distinct or merely severe and milder forms of the same disorder has been a matter of some controversy. Endogenous depression is usually the more severe form and there is evidence of genetic predisposition to it. Neurotic, or reactive, depression is more usually a reaction to psychological stress. Both forms require treatment. ◊Electroconvulsive therapy (ECT) may be appropriate for endogenous depression, while anti-depressant drugs and psychotherapy, particularly ◊cognitive therapy, are more effective for neurotic depression.

In a real dark night of the soul it is always three o'clock in the morning, day after day.

depression
F Scott Fitzgerald, 1896–1940, US writer.
'Handle with Care'

In ◊manic depression, periods of depression may alternate with periods of mania.

Depression is the most common reason for people in the UK consulting a general practitioner.

deregulation US term for freeing markets from protection, with the aim of improving competitiveness. It often results in greater monopoly control.

An example is the deregulation of the US airline industry 1978, after which 14 new companies began flying. (By 1991 only one was left.) In Britain, the major changes in the City of London 1986 (the Big Bang) included deregulation.

Derrida Jacques 1930– . French philosopher who introduced the ◊deconstruction theory into literary criticism. His approach involves looking at how a text is put together in order to reveal its hidden meanings and the assumptions of the author. Derrida's main publications are *De la Grammatologie/Of Grammatology* 1967 and *La Voix et le phénomène/ Speech and Writing* 1967.

Derrida was born in Algeria. He taught in Paris at the Sorbonne 1960–64 and subsequently at the Ecole Normale Supérieure. His analysis of language draws on German philosophers Friedrich ◊Nietzsche, Edmund ◊Husserl, and Martin ◊Heidegger, and Swiss linguist Ferdinand de ◊Saussure. Although obscurely presented, his conclusions have some similarity to those of Anglo-American linguistic philosophers.

dervish in Iran and Turkey, a religious mendicant; throughout the rest of Islam a member of an Islamic religious brotherhood, not necessarily mendicant in character. The Arabic equivalent is **fakir**. There are various orders of dervishes, each with its rule and special ritual. The 'whirling dervishes' claim close communion with the deity through ecstatic dancing; the 'howling dervishes' gash themselves with knives to demonstrate the miraculous feats possible to those who trust in Allah.

Descartes René 1596–1650. French philosopher and mathematician. He believed that commonly accepted knowledge was doubtful because of the subjective nature of the senses, and attempted to rebuild human knowledge using as his foundation *cogito ergo sum* ('I think, therefore I am'). He also believed that the entire material universe could be explained in terms of mathematical physics, and founded coordinate geometry as a way of defining and manipulating geometrical shapes by means of algebraic expressions. Cartesian coordinates, the means by which points are represented in this system, are named after him. Descartes also established the science of optics, and helped to shape contemporary theories of astronomy and animal behaviour.

Commonsense is the most widely distributed commodity in the world, for everyone thinks himself so well endowed with it.

René Descartes
Discourse on Method

Born near Tours, Descartes served in the army of Prince Maurice of Orange, and in 1619, while travelling through Europe, decided to apply the methods of mathematics to metaphysics and science. He settled in the Netherlands 1628, where he was more likely

to be free from interference by the ecclesiastical authorities. In 1649 he visited the court of Queen Christina of Sweden, and shortly thereafter he died in Stockholm.

His works include *Discourse on Method* 1637, *Meditations on the First Philosophy* 1641, and *Principles of Philosophy* 1644, and numerous books on physiology, optics, and geometry.

design the conceptual and practical working out of the appearance of an artefact, with special reference to its effective functioning and to its aesthetic quality.

The term derives from the Italian word *disegno* which in Renaissance art theory meant the essential idea of a work of art and the expression of that idea through drawing.

Always design a thing by considering it in its larger context - a chair in a room, a room in a house, a house in an environment, an environment in a city plan.

design
Eero Saarinen, 1910–1961,
Finnish-born US architect.
Time July 1956

despotism arbitrary and oppressive rule of a despot or autocrat, whose decisions are not controlled by law or political institutions; another term for tyranny.

détente (French) reduction of political tension and the easing of strained relations between nations, for example, the ending of the Cold War 1989–90, although it was first used in the 1970s to describe the easing East–West relations, trade agreements, and cultural exchanges.

determinism thesis that every event whatsoever is an instance of some scientific law of nature; or that every event has at least one cause; or that nature is uniform. The thesis cannot be proved or disproved. Hence, it is often regarded as a methodological principle or rule of thumb, rather than a true or false statement. In philosophy, determinism is also the theory that we do not have ◊free will, because our choices and actions are caused.

It lies not in our power to love, or hate, / For will in us is over-rul'd by fate.

determinism
Christopher Marlowe, 1564–1593, English
poet and dramatist.
Hero and Leander I

Hard determinists hold that responsibility for our actions is an illusion. Soft determinists, or compatibilists, hold that causation is not a constraint or compulsion, and to act freely is not to act unpredictably. Indeterminists, or libertarians, hold that the self is outside of, but can intervene in, the causal chain.

deterrence underlying conception of the nuclear arms race: the belief that a potential aggressor will be discouraged from launching a 'first strike' nuclear attack by the knowledge that the adversary is capable of inflicting 'unacceptable damage' in a retaliatory strike. This doctrine is widely known as that of *mutual assured destruction (MAD)*. Three essential characteristics of deterrence are: the 'capability to act', 'credibility', and the 'will to act'.

There is a homely old adage which runs: 'Speak softly and carry a big stick; you will go far.'

deterrence
Theodore Roosevelt, 1858–1919, 26th president of the USA 1901–09, a Republican. Speech at Chicago 3 Apr 1903

---

de Tocqueville Alexis. French politician; see ◊Tocqueville, Alexis de.

Deuteronomy book of the Old Testament; fifth book of the ◊Torah. It contains various laws, including the laws for ◊kosher and the ten commandments, and gives an account of the death of Moses.

devaluation in economics, the lowering of the official value of a currency against other currencies, so that exports become cheaper and imports more expensive. Used when a country is badly in deficit in its balance of trade, it results in the goods the country produces being cheaper abroad, so that the economy is stimulated by increased foreign demand.

The increased cost of imported food, raw materials, and manufactured goods as a consequence of devaluation may, however, stimulate an acceleration in inflation, especially when commodities are rising in price because of increased world demand. *Revaluation* is the opposite process.

Devaluation of important currencies upsets the balance of the world's money markets and encourages speculation. Significant devaluations include that of the German mark in the 1920s and Britain's devaluation of sterling in the 1960s. To promote greater stability, many countries have allowed the value of their currencies to 'float', that is, to fluctuate in value.

developed world or *First World* or *the North* the countries that have a money economy and a highly developed industrial sector. They generally also have a high degree of urbanization, a complex communications network, high ◊GDP (over US $2,000) per person, low birth and death rates, high energy consumption, and a large proportion of the workforce employed in manufacturing or service industries (secondary to quaternary industrial sectors). The developed world includes the USA, Canada, Europe, Japan, Australia, and New Zealand.

developing world or *Third World* or *the South* countries with a largely subsistence economy where the output per person and the average income are both low. These countries typically have low life expectancy, high birth and death rates, poor communications, low literacy levels, high national debt, and low energy consumption per person. The developing world includes much of Africa and parts of Asia and South America. Terms like 'developing world' and 'less developed countries' are often criticized for implying that a highly industrialized economy (as in the ◊developed world) is a desirable goal.

development in the social sciences, the acquisition by a society of industrial techniques and technology; hence the common classification of the 'developed' nations of the First and Second Worlds and the poorer, 'developing' or 'underdeveloped' nations of the Third World. The assumption that development in the sense of industrialization is inherently good has been increasingly questioned since the 1960s.

Many universities today have academic departments of *development studies* that address the theoretical questions involved in proposing practical solutions to the problems of development in the Third World.

development aid see ◊aid, development.

developmental psychology branch of ◊psychology concerned with the study of changes that occur throughout the life-span, mainly in thought processes and behaviour but also in physical and neurological structure.

Research in this area may focus on changes that occur, for example, in all children regardless of culture and experience, on individual differences in development, or on the effects of specific social, cultural, or other contextual variables. Most of the work has been on child development, however, and the terms 'developmental psychology' and 'child psychology' have often been used interchangeably.

On a theoretical level, the study of development considers issues such as the relative importance of environment and biology in determining behaviour, whether development is continuous or a series of steps or phases, and to what extent specific personality traits contribute to an individual's behaviour over time. Although now regarded as an important area of psychological research, child development has only recently become the subject of systematic study, notably in the work of ◊Piaget, ◊Bowlby, and ◊Klein.

deviance abnormal behaviour; that is, behaviour that deviates from the norms or the laws of a society or group, and so invokes social sanctions, controls, or stigma.

Deviance is a relative concept: what is considered deviant in some societies may be normal in others; in a particular society the same act (killing someone, for example) may be either normal or deviant depending on the circumstances (in wartime or for money, for example). Some sociologists, such as Howard Becker, argue that the reaction of others, rather than the act itself, is what determines whether an act is deviant, and that deviance is merely behaviour other people so label.

The term may refer to minor abnormalities (such as nail-biting) as well as to criminal acts.

devil in Jewish, Christian, and Muslim theology, the supreme spirit of evil (*Beelzebub, Lucifer, Iblis*), or an evil spirit generally.

The devil, or Satan, is mentioned only in the more recently written books of the Old Testament, but the later Jewish doctrine is that found in the New Testament. The concept of the devil passed into the early Christian church from Judaism, and theology until at least the time of St Anselm represented the Atonement as primarily the deliverance, through Christ's death, of mankind from the

---

An apology for the Devil: It must be remembered that we have only heard one side of the case. God has written all the books.

devil

Samuel Butler, 1835–1902, English writer.
Notebooks ch 14

---

bondage of the devil. Jesus recognized as a reality the kingdom of evil, of which Satan or Beelzebub was the prince. In the Middle Ages the devil in popular superstition assumed the attributes of the horned fertility gods of paganism, and was regarded as the god of witches. The belief in a personal devil was strong during the Reformation, and the movement's

leader Luther regarded himself as the object of a personal Satanic persecution. With the development of liberal Protestantism in the 19th century came a strong tendency to deny the existence of a positive spirit of evil, and to explain the devil as merely a personification. However, the traditional conception was never abandoned by the Roman Catholic Church, and theologians, such as C S ◊Lewis, have maintained the existence of a power of evil.

Now the serpent was more subtil than any beast of the field.

devil

Bible, the sacred book of the Jewish and Christian religions.
Genesis 3:1

In Muslim theology, Iblis is one of the *jinn* (beings created by Allah from fire) who refused to prostrate himself before Adam, and who tempted Adam and his wife Hawwa (Eve) to disobey Allah, an act which led to their expulsion from Paradise. He continues to try to lead people astray, but at the Last Judgement he and his hosts will be consigned to hell.

devolution delegation of authority and duties; in the later 20th century, the movement to decentralize governmental power, as in the UK where a bill for the creation of Scottish and Welsh assemblies was introduced 1976 (rejected by referendums in Scotland and Wales 1979).

The word was first widely used in this sense in connection with Ireland, with the Irish Nationalist Party leader John Redmond claiming 1898 that the Liberals wished to diminish Home Rule into 'some scheme of devolution or federalism'.

devotio moderna movement of revived religious spirituality which emerged in the Netherlands at the end of the 14th century and spread into the rest of W Europe. Its emphasis was on individual, rather than communal, devotion, including the private reading of religious works.

The movement's followers were drawn from the laity, including women, and clergy. Lay followers formed themselves into associations known as Brethren of the Common Life. Among the followers of *devotio moderna* was Thomas ◊à Kempis, author of *De Imitatio Christi/Imitation of Christ*.

De Vries Hugo 1848–1935. Dutch botanist who conducted important research on osmosis in plant cells and was a pioneer in the study of plant evolution. His work led to the rediscovery of ◊Mendel's laws and the discovery of spontaneously occurring mutations.

For one man who thanks God that he is not as other men there are a few thousand to offer thanks that they are as other men, sufficiently as others to escape attention.

John Dewey
Human Nature and Conflict

Dewey John 1859–1952. US philosopher who believed that the exigencies of a democratic and industrial society demanded new educational techniques. He expounded his ideas in numerous writings, including *School and Society* 1899, and founded a progressive school in Chicago. A pragmatist thinker, influenced by William James, Dewey maintained that there is only the reality of experience and made 'inquiry' the essence of logic.

Dhammapada one of the most important Buddhist books, it forms a part of the Pali Canon of earliest texts. It consists of 423 verses, divided into 26 chapters, and deals primarily with practical aspects of Buddhist morality and wisdom and is popular with lay as well as monastic Buddhists, especially in those Southeast Asian countries where ◊Theravāda Buddhism is popular.

dharma in Hinduism, the consciousness of forming part of an ordered universe, and hence the moral duty of accepting the duties associated with one's station in life. In Buddhism, dharma is anything that increases generosity and wisdom, and so leads towards enlightenment.

For Hindus, correct performance of dharma has a favourable effect on their ◊karma (fate); this may enable them to be reborn to a higher caste or on a higher plane of existence, thus coming closer to the final goal of liberation from the cycle of reincarnation.

dialectic Greek term, originally associated with the philosopher Socrates' method of argument through dialogue and conversation. *Hegelian dialectic*, named after the German philosopher ◊Hegel, refers to an interpretive method in which the contradiction between a thesis and its antithesis is resolved through synthesis.

dialectical materialism political, philosophical, and economic theory of the 19th-century German thinkers Karl Marx and Friedrich Engels, also known as ◊Marxism.

Diamond Sūtra this forms part of the Perfection of Wisdom sutras (Prajnaparamita), first written down some time between the 2nd and 5th centuries AD. The Diamond Sutra (Vajracchedika – meaning thunderbolt sutra but popularly known as the Diamond Sutra) consists of 300 lines, the responses by the Buddha to questions put to him by Subhuti, one of his closest disciples. The text addresses such issues as the true nature of the Buddha, the meaning of his teachings, and the reality of the listener him or herself. The text has been very influential, especially in Chinese Buddhism, because of its discourse nature.

Diana in Roman mythology, the goddess of chastity, hunting, and the Moon, daughter of Jupiter and twin of Apollo. Her Greek equivalent is the goddess ◊Artemis.

dianetics form of psychotherapy developed by the US science-fiction writer L Ron Hubbard (1911–1986), which formed the basis for ◊Scientology. Hubbard believed that all mental illness and certain forms of physical illness are caused by 'engrams', or incompletely assimilated traumatic experiences, both pre- and postnatal. These engrams can be confronted during therapy with an auditor and thus exorcised. An individual free from engrams would be a 'Clear' and perfectly healthy.

Hubbard later expanded this theory: behind each mind is a nonphysical and immortal being, the Thetan, which has forgotten its true nature and is therefore trapped in a cycle of reincarnation, accumulating engrams with each lifetime. If these engrams are cleared, the individual will become an Operating Thetan, with quasi-miraculous powers.

During the 1970s and 80s the Church of Scientology was accused of having taken on a cultlike character and of financial duplicity.

diarchy the division of responsibility between two kinds of authority. Such an arrangement was implemented in India by the Montagu-Chelmsford report 1918 which recommended steps towards greater responsibilities for government.

Diaspora (Greek *'dispersion'*) dispersal of the Jews, initially from Palestine after the Babylonian conquest 586 BC, and then following the Roman sack of Jerusalem AD 70 and their crushing of the Jewish revolt of 135. The term has come to refer to all the Jews living outside Israel. It is sometimes applied to the enforced dispersal of other peoples, for example of the Armenians by the Turks between 1909 and 1915 and of Black Africans as a result of the slave trade.

dictatorship term or office of an absolute ruler, overriding the constitution. (In ancient Rome a dictator was a magistrate invested with emergency powers for six months.) Although dictatorships were common in Latin America during the 19th century, the only European example during this period was the rule of Napoleon III. The crises following World War I produced many dictatorships, including the regimes of Atatürk and Pi\\sudski (nationalist); Mussolini, Hitler, Primo de Rivera, Franco, and Salazar (all right-wing); and Stalin (Communist). More recent dictatorships have included those of General Pinochet in Chile and Nicolae Ceausescu in Romania.

dictatorship of the proletariat Marxist term for a revolutionary dictatorship established during the transition from capitalism to ◊communism after a socialist revolution.

Lexicographer. A writer of dictionaries, a harmless drudge.
                                    dictionaries
Samuel Johnson, known as 'Dr Johnson',
1709–1784, English lexicographer,
author, and critic.
Dictionary of the English Language

---

dictionary book that contains a selection of the words of a language, with their pronunciations and meanings, usually arranged in alphabetical order. The term *dictionary* is also applied to any usually alphabetic work of reference containing specialized information about a particular subject, art, or science; for example, a dictionary of music. Bilingual dictionaries provide translations of one language into another.

The first dictionaries of English (*glossa collectae*), in the 17th century, served to explain difficult words, generally of Latin or Greek origin, in everyday English. Samuel Johnson's *A Dictionary of the English Language* 1755 was one of the first dictionaries of standard English, and the first to give extensive coverage to phrasal verbs. Noah Webster's *An American Dictionary of the English Language* 1828 quickly became a standard reference work throughout North America. The many-volume *Oxford English Dictionary*, begun 1884 and subject to continuous revision (and now computerization), provides a detailed historical record of each word and, therefore, of the English language.

Diderot Denis 1713–1784. French philosopher. He is closely associated with the Enlightenment, the European intellectual movement for social and scientific progress, and was editor of the enormously influential *Encyclopédie* 1751–80.

An expanded and politicized version of the English encyclopedia '1728 of Ephraim Chambers (c. 1680–1740), this work exerted an enormous influence on contemporary social thinking with its materialism and anti-clericalism. Its compilers were known as ◊Encyclopédistes.

Diderot's materialism, most articulately expressed in *D'Alembert's Dream*, published after Diderot's death, sees the natural world as nothing more than matter and motion.

His account of the origin and development of life is purely mechanical.

Diels Otto 1876–1954. German chemist. In 1950 he and his former assistant, Kurt Alder (1902–1958), were jointly awarded the Nobel Prize for Chemistry for their research into the synthesis of organic chemical compounds.

diet the range of foods eaten by an animal. The basic components of a diet are a group of chemicals: proteins, carbohydrates, fats, vitamins, minerals, and water. Different animals require these substances in different proportions, but the necessity of finding and processing an appropriate diet is a very basic drive in animal evolution. For instance, all guts are adapted for digesting and absorbing food, but different guts have adapted to cope with particular diets.

The diet an animal needs may vary over its lifespan, according to whether it is growing, reproducing, highly active, or approaching death. For instance, an animal may need increased carbohydrate for additional energy, or increased minerals during periods of growth.

diffusionist approach explanatory concept that sees ideas, objects, or cultural traits as spreading from one culture or society to another, rather than independently invented.

Digambara ('sky-clad') member of a sect of Jain monks (see ◊Jainism) who practise complete nudity.

Diggers or *true ◊Levellers* English 17th-century radical sect that attempted to dig common land. The Diggers became prominent April 1649 when, headed by Gerrard Winstanley (c. 1609–1660), they set up communal colonies near Cobham, Surrey, and elsewhere. These colonies were attacked by mobs and, being pacifists, the Diggers made no resistance. The support they attracted alarmed the government and they were dispersed 1650. Their ideas influenced the early ◊Quakers.

Dilthey Wilhelm 1833–1911. German philosopher, a major figure in the interpretive tradition of ◊hermeneutics. He argued that the 'human sciences' (*Geisteswissenschaften*) could not employ the same methods as the natural sciences but must use the procedure of 'understanding' (*Verstehen*) to grasp the inner life of an alien culture or past historical period. Thus Dilthey extended the significance of hermeneutics far beyond the interpretation of texts to the whole of human history and culture.

diminishing returns, law of in economics, the principle that additional application of one factor of production, such as an extra machine or employee, at first results in rapidly increasing output but eventually yields declining returns, unless other factors are modified to sustain the increase.

Dinka religion the Dinka are a pastoral people of S Sudan, though recent warfare has driven them into other parts of Sudan, Somalia, and Kenya. They have been much studied by anthropologists because of their religion. It is dominated by Nhialic ('Sky') who is God, and speaks through a number of spirits who take possession of a person in order to speak through them. The sacrificing of oxen forms a central component of the faith, carried out by leaders known as the Spear-Masters. These powerful figures guide the destiny of the people.

Sell me to him. He needs a master.

Diogenes
(on being put up for sale at a slave auction)
Aspects of Antiquity M I Finley

Diogenes c. 412–323 BC. Ascetic Greek philosopher of the ◊Cynic school. He believed in freedom and self-sufficiency for the individual, and that the virtuous life was the simple life; he did not believe in social mores. His writings do not survive.

He was born at Sinope, captured by pirates, and sold as a slave to a Corinthian named Xeniades, who appointed Diogenes tutor to his two sons. He spent the rest of his life in Corinth. He is said to have carried a lamp during the daytime, looking for one honest man. The story of his having lived in a barrel arose when Seneca said that was where a man so crabbed ought to have lived.

Dionysia festivals of the god ◊Dionysus (Bacchus) celebrated in ancient Greece, especially in Athens. They included the lesser Dionysia in Dec, chiefly rural festivals, and the greater Dionysia, at the end of March, when new plays were performed.

Everyone is dragged on by their favourite pleasure

Virgil
Eclogue i.1

Dionysius the Areopagite c. 500 AD. Christian mystical theologian also known as Pseudo-Dionysius because falsely identified with the Dionysius converted by Paul in Acts 17:34. In the early 6th century letters written under his name appeared and were used to support the ◊Monophysite position. The authenticity of these letters is disputed, though they were widely influential in both the Western and Eastern churches.

Dionysus in Greek mythology, the god of wine (son of Semele and Zeus), and also of orgiastic excess, who was attended by women called maenads, who were believed to be capable of tearing animals to pieces with their bare hands when under his influence. He was identified with the Roman ◊Bacchus, whose rites were less savage.

diplomacy process by which states attempt to settle their differences through peaceful means such as negotiation or ◊arbitration.

Dirac Paul Adrien Maurice 1902–1984. British physicist who worked out a version of quantum mechanics consistent with special ◊relativity. The existence of the positron (positive electron) was one of its predictions. He shared the Nobel Prize for Physics 1933 with Austrian physicist Erwin Schrödinger (1887–1961).

Disarmament: chronology

1930s League of Nations attempt to achieve disarmament failed.
1968 US president Johnson's proposals for Strategic Arms Limitation Talks (SALT) were delayed by the Soviet invasion of Czechoslovakia.
1972–77 SALT I was in effect.
1979–85 SALT II, signed by the Soviet and US leaders Brezhnev and Carter, was never ratified by the US Senate, but both countries abided by it.
1986 US president Reagan revoked this pledge, against the advice of his European NATO partners.
1987 Reagan and the Soviet leader Gorbachev agreed to reduce their nuclear arsenals by 4% by scrapping intermediate-range nuclear weapons.
1990 Treaty signed between the USA and the USSR limiting both NATO and the Warsaw Pact to much reduced conventional weapons systems in Europe.
Jan 1991 President Bush announced decision to halve US military presence in Europe.
30–31 July 1991 Bush and Soviet president Gorbachev signed Strategic Arms Reduction Treaty (START) which limited both sides to no more than 6,000 nuclear warheads.
Sept–Oct 1991 Bush announced the unilateral reduction of about 2,400 US nuclear weapons, asking the Soviet Union to respond in kind. Gorbachev offered a package of unilateral cuts and proposals that surpassed the broad arms-control initiative presented by Bush.
Jan 1992 Bush and Russia's president, Boris Yeltsin, promised additional (60-80%) cuts in land- and sea-based long-range nuclear missiles. In addition, Bush promised an accelerated withdrawal of US troops from Europe and the halting of future production of the advanced B-2 bomber. Yeltsin announced that Russian long-range missiles would no longer be targeted on US cities.
June 1992 Yeltsin consented to the abandonment of strategic parity (equal balance of arms) and announced, with Bush, bilateral cuts in long-term nuclear weapons that far surpassed the terms of the 1991 START treaty. By 2003, it was promised, US warheads would be cut from 9,986 to 3,500, and Russian warheads from 10,237 to 3,000.
Jan 1993 START II treaty signed by Bush and Yeltsin in Moscow, committing both countries to reduce long-range nuclear weapons by two-thirds by the year 2003 and to do away with land-based, multiple warheads.

Dirichlet Peter Gustav Lejeune 1805–1859. German mathematician. His most important work was on the convergence of the Fourier series, which led him to the modern notion of a generalized function as represented in the form $f(x)$. He also made major contributions to number theory, producing *Dirichlet's theorem*: in every arithmetical sequence a, $a + d$, $a + 2d$, and so on, where a and d are relatively prime (that is, have no common divisors other than 1), there is an infinite number of prime numbers.

Dis in Roman mythology, the god of the underworld, also known as Orcus; he is equivalent to the Greek god Pluto, ruler of ◊Hades. Dis is also a synonym for the underworld itself.

disarmament reduction of a country's weapons of war. Most disarmament talks since World War II have been concerned with nuclear-arms verification and reduction, but biological, chemical, and conventional weapons have also come under discussion at the United Nations and in other forums. Attempts to limit the arms race (initially between the USA and the USSR and since 1992 between the USA and Russia) have included the Strategic Arms Limitation Talks (SALT) of the 1970s and the Strategic Arms Reduction Talks (START) of the 1980s–90s.

In the UK the Campaign for Nuclear Disarmament lobbies on this issue.

disassociation of sensibility divorce between intellect and emotion. T S ◊Eliot coined this phrase in 1921 in an essay on the metaphysical poets of the 17th century. He suggested that Donne, Marvell, and their contemporaries 'feel their thought as immediately as the odour of a rose' whereas later poets disengage intellect from emotion.

disciple follower, especially of a religious leader. The word is used in the Bible for the early followers of Jesus. The 12 disciples closest to him are known as the ◊apostles.

discrimination distinction made (social, economic, political, legal) between individuals or groups such that one has the power to treat the other unfavourably. *Negative discrimination*, often based on ◊stereotype, includes anti-Semitism, apartheid, caste, racism, sexism, and slavery. *Positive discrimination*, or 'affirmative action', is sometimes practised in an attempt to counteract the effects of previous long-term discrimination. Minorities and, in some cases, majorities have been targets for discrimination.

Discrimination may be on grounds of difference of colour, nationality, religion, politics, culture, class, sex, age, or a combination of such factors. Legislation has been to some degree effective in forbidding *racial discrimination*, against which there is a United Nations convention (1969).

National legislation in the UK includes the Race Relations Acts 1965 and 1976 and the Sex Discrimination Act of 1975.

disinvestment withdrawal of investments in a country for political reasons. The term is also used in economics to describe non-replacement of stock as it wears out.

It is generally applied to the ostensive removal of funds from South Africa in recent years by such multinational companies as General Motors and to the withdrawal of private investment funds (by universities, pension funds, and other organizations) from portfolios doing business in South Africa. Disinvestment may be motivated by fear of loss of business in the home market caused by adverse publicity or by fear of loss of foreign resources if the local government changes.

displacement in psychoanalysis, the transference of an emotion from the original idea with which it is associated to other ideas. It is usually thought to be indicative of ◊repression in that the emotional content of an unacceptable idea may be expressed without the idea itself becoming conscious.

Freud's original discussion of displacement focused on its occurrence in dreams, where strong emotions are often expressed in material which the subject usually finds of indifferent interest. As a defense mechanism, it is also associated with a number of afflictions including ◊phobias and ◊schizophrenia.

His Christianity was muscular.

**Benjamin Disraeli, Earl of
Beaconsfield**
Endymion

Disraeli Benjamin, Earl of Beaconsfield 1804–1881. British Conservative politician and novelist. Elected to Parliament 1837, he was chancellor of the Exchequer under Lord Derby 1852, 1858–59, and 1866–68, and prime minister 1868 and 1874–80. His imperialist policies brought India directly under the crown, and he was personally responsible for purchasing control of the Suez Canal. The central Conservative Party organization is his creation. His popular, political novels reflect an interest in social reform and include *Coningsby* 1844 and *Sybil* 1845.

Disruption, the split in the Church of Scotland 1843 when its Evangelical wing formed the Free Church of Scotland, hoping to recreate the spirit of John Knox and early Protestantism.

Dissenter former name for a Protestant refusing to conform to the established Christian church. For example, Baptists, Presbyterians, and Independents (now known as Congregationalists) were Dissenters.

dissident in one-party states, a person intellectually dissenting from the official line. Dissidents have been sent into exile, prison, labour camps, and mental institutions, or deprived of their jobs. In the USSR the number of imprisoned dissidents declined from more than 600 in 1986 to fewer than 100 in 1990, of whom the majority were ethnic nationalists. In China the number of prisoners of conscience increased after the 1989 Tiananmen Square massacre, and in South Africa, despite the release of Nelson ◊Mandela in 1990, numerous political dissidents remained in jail.

In the former USSR before the introduction of ◊glasnost, dissidents comprised communists who advocated a more democratic and humanitarian approach; religious proselytizers; Jews wishing to emigrate; and those who supported ethnic or national separatist movements within the USSR (among them Armenians, Lithuanians, Ukrainians, and Tatars). Their views were expressed through *samizdat* (clandestinely distributed writings) and sometimes published abroad. In the late 1980s Mikhail ◊Gorbachev lifted censorship, accepted a degree of political pluralism, and extended tolerance to religious believers. Almost 100,000 Jews were allowed to emigrate 1985–90. Some formerly persecuted dissidents, most prominently the physicist Andrei ◊Sakharov, emerged as supporters, albeit impatient, of the new reform programme.

Distributism campaign for land reform publicized by English writer G K Chesterton in his group the Distributist League, the journal of which he published from 1925. The movement called for a revival of smallholdings and a turn away from industrialization. Supporters included many Conservatives and traditional clergy.

diversification in business, a corporate strategy of entering distinctly new products or markets as opposed to simply adding to an existing product range. A company may diversify in order to spread its risks or because its original area of operation is becoming less profitable.

divination art of ascertaining future events or eliciting other hidden knowledge by supernatural or nonrational means. Divination played a large part in the ancient civilizations of the Egyptians, Greeks (see ◊oracle), Romans, and Chinese (see ◊*I Ching*), and is still practised throughout the world.

Divination generally involves the intuitive interpretation of the mechanical operations of chance or natural law. Forms of divination have included omens drawn from the behaviour of birds and animals; examination of the entrails of sacrificed animals; random opening of such books as the Bible; fortune-telling by cards (see ◊tarot cards) and palmistry; ◊dowsing; oracular trance-speaking; ◊automatic writing; necromancy, or the supposed raising of the spirits of the dead; and dreams, often specially induced.

Divine Light Mission religious movement founded in India in 1960, which gained a prominent following in the USA in the 1970s. It proclaims Guru Maharaj Ji (1957–   ) as the present age's successor to the gods or religious leaders Krishna, Buddha, Jesus, and Muhammad. He is believed to be able to provide his followers with the knowledge required to attain salvation.

Divine Principle sacred writings of the ◊Unification Church. The book, which offers a reinterpretation of the Bible, is also influenced by concepts from Buddhism, Islam, and Taoism.

divine right of kings Christian political doctrine that hereditary monarchy is the system approved by God, hereditary right cannot be forfeited, monarchs are accountable to God alone for their actions, and rebellion against the lawful sovereign is therefore blasphemous.

The doctrine had its origins in the anointing of Pepin in 751 by the pope after Pepin had usurped the throne of the Franks. It was at its peak in 16th- and 17th-century Europe as a weapon against the claims of the papacy – the court of Louis XIV of France pushed this to the limit – and was in 17th-century England maintained by the supporters of the Stuarts in opposition to the democratic theories of the Puritans and Whigs.

division of labour system of work where a task is split into several parts and done by different workers. For example, on a car assembly line, one worker will fit doors, another will make the engine block, and another will work in the paint shop. The division of labour is an example of ◊specialization.

divorce legal dissolution of a lawful marriage. It is distinct from an annulment, which is a legal declaration that the marriage was invalid. The ease with which a divorce can be obtained in different countries varies considerably and is also affected by different religious practices.

In the USA divorce laws differ from state to state. The grounds include adultery (in all states), cruelty, desertion, alcoholism, drug addiction, insanity, and declaration of irreconcilable differences or mutual incompatibility. Quick divorces in states with more liberal laws have been restricted by the imposition of minimum residence periods and by the right to challenge the divorce if one party has not been notified of the proceedings. Couples are increasingly negotiating prenuptial agreements that make an advance settlement of division of property and assets, including maintenance provisions. In some states, so-called no-fault divorce laws make divorces readily available to couples with no economic quarrels and with agreeable obligations to children.

The Roman Catholic Church does not permit divorce among its members, and under Pope John Paul II conditions for annulment have been tightened. Among Muslims a wife cannot divorce her husband, but he may divorce her by repeating the formula 'I divorce you' three times (called *talaq*). In Shi'ite law this must be pronounced either once or three times in the presence of two witnesses; in Sunni law it can be either oral or in writing. No reason need be given, nor does the wife have to be notified (although some Muslim countries, for example Pakistan, have introduced such a requirement). Property settlements by careful parents make this a right infrequently exercised.

Laws introduced in the USSR in the 1960s made divorce easy and cheap. Maintenance for a wife after divorce decreased in importance, but she was likely to benefit by a more equitable division of property.

In England, divorce could only be secured by the passing of a private act of Parliament until 1857, when the Matrimonial Causes Act set up the Divorce Court and provided limited grounds for divorce. The grounds for divorce were gradually liberalized by further acts of Parliament, culminating in the Divorce Reform Act 1969, under which the sole ground for divorce is the irretrievable breakdown of the marriage. This must be demonstrated by showing that the parties have lived apart for at least two years (or five years if one party does not consent to the divorce), or proving adultery, desertion, or unreasonable behaviour by one party. The court places great emphasis on provision for the custody and maintenance of any children. It may also order other financial arrangements, including the transfer of property.

Although not worded exactly the same, the grounds for divorce in Scotland are the same as in England and Wales. In England and Wales the Law Commission recommended

1990 that marital breakdown be provable after one year from the time that the parties lodge a sworn statement in court of their belief that the marriage has irretrievably broken down.

Diwali Hindu festival in Oct/Nov celebrating Lakshmi, goddess of light and wealth, as well as the New Year and the story of the *Rāmāyana*. It is marked by the lighting of lamps and candles (inviting the goddess into the house), feasting, and the exchange of gifts. For Sikhs, Diwali celebrates Guru Hargobind's release from prison.

Dix Dorothea Lynde 1802–1887. US educator and medical reformer. From 1841 she devoted herself to a campaign for the rights of the mentally ill, helping to improve conditions and treatment in public institutions for the insane in the USA, Canada, and Japan. During the American Civil War 1861–65, she served as superintendent of nurses.

Born in Hampden, Maine, and raised in Boston, Dix began her career as a teacher at a girls' school in Worcester, Massachusetts, and opened her own school in Boston 1821. Forced by ill health to retire in 1835, she travelled in Europe and published several books.

DNA (*deoxyribonucleic acid*) complex giant molecule that contains, in chemically coded form, all the information needed to build, control, and maintain a living organism. DNA is a ladderlike double-stranded nucleic acid that forms the basis of genetic inheritance in all organisms, except for a few viruses that have only ◊RNA. In organisms other than bacteria it is organized into ◊chromosomes and contained in the cell nucleus.

DNA is made up of two chains of nucleotide sub-units, with each nucleotide containing either a purine (adenine or guanine) or pyrimidine (cytosine or thymine) base. The bases link up with each other (adenine linking with thymine, and cytosine with guanine) to form base pairs that connect the two strands of the DNA molecule like the rungs of a twisted ladder. The specific way in which the pairs form means that the base sequence is preserved from generation to generation.

Hereditary information is stored as a specific sequence of bases. A set of three bases – known as a *codon* – acts as a blueprint for the manufacture of a particular amino acid, the sub-unit of a protein molecule. Geneticists identify the codons by the initial letters of the constituent bases – for example, the base sequence of codon CAG is cytosine–adenine–guanine. The meaning of each of the codons in the ◊genetic code has been worked out by molecular geneticists. There are four different bases, which means that there must be 4 x 4 x 4 = 64 different codons. Proteins are usually made up of only 20 different amino acids, so many amino acids have more than one codon (for example, GGT, GGC, GGA, and GGG all code for the same amino acid, glycine.)

The information encoded by the codons is transcribed (see ◊transcription) by messenger RNA and is then translated into amino acids in the ribosomes and cytoplasm. The sequence of codons determines the precise order in which amino acids are linked up during manufacture and, therefore, the kind of protein that is to be produced. Because proteins are the chief structural molecules of living matter and, as enzymes, regulate all aspects of metabolism, it may be seen that the genetic code is effectively responsible for building and controlling the whole organism.

The sequence of bases along the length of DNA can be determined by cutting the molecule into small portions, using restriction enzymes. This technique can also be used for transferring specific sequences of DNA from one organism to another.

Dobzhansky Theodosius 1900–1975. US geneticist of Ukrainian origin. A pioneer of modern genetics and evolutionary theory, he showed that genetic variability between individuals of the same species is very high and that this diversity is vital to the process of evolution. His book *Genetics and the Origin of Species* was published in 1937.

doctrine the official teaching of a particular religion. For example, in Christianity, the doctrine of the ◊Trinity does not appear in the Bible, but was developed in thought and debate, defined by church councils, and expressed in the creeds. Different branches of a faith may have slightly different doctrines, for example different Christian groups hold different doctrines about the ◊Eucharist.

documentary a film (sometimes a play) that relates actual events either by employing documents such as newspapers or archive material or by setting up cameras to record events as they happen.

Dōgen 1200–1253. Japanese Buddhist monk, founder of the Sōtō school of Zen, and the most important Zen master in Japanese history. He did not reject study, but stressed the importance of *zazen*, seated meditation, for its own sake. His teachings are outlined in the *Shōbogenzó*, the greatest work of Japanese religious literature.

dogma the authoritative truths accepted by members of a particular faith. In the Roman Catholic Church the dogmas are transmitted through scripture, or papal or church traditions. The teachings are believed to be handed down from the apostles and interpreted by the church fathers and canons. The Orthodox Church does not accept papal authority, while the Reformed Churches insist on scripture alone as the source of authority.

Doisy Edward 1893–1986. US biochemist. In 1939 he succeeded in synthesizing vitamin K, a compound earlier discovered by Carl ◊Dam, with whom he shared the 1943 Nobel Prize for Medicine.

Domagk Gerhard 1895–1964. German pathologist, discoverer of antibacterial sulphonamide drugs. He found in 1932 that a coal-tar dye called Prontosil red contains chemicals with powerful antibacterial properties. Sulphanilamide became the first of the sulphonamide drugs, used before antibiotics were discovered to treat a wide range of conditions, including pneumonia and septic wounds. Domagk was awarded the 1939 Nobel Prize for Physiology and Medicine.

Dome of the Rock building in Jerusalem dating from the 7th century AD that enshrines the rock from which, in Muslim tradition, Muhammad ascended to heaven on his ◊Night Journey. It stands on the site of the Jewish Temple and is visited by pilgrims.

dominant ideology belief or political dogma which characterizes the major institutions and social practices of a nation-state or of an ethnic group.

Ideologies provide the justification for a wide range of activities, extending from religious ritual to politics, economics, and relations with other nation-states. A dominant ideology will tend to combat or suppress the alternative codes of belief in a society, in contrast to pluralism which will tolerate them. Most dominant ideologies, such as medieval ◊feudalism, protestant ◊capitalism, or communism, have been strongly associated with ◊patriarchy.

Dominican order Roman Catholic order of friars founded 1215 by St Dominic. The Dominicans are also known as Friars Preachers, Black Friars, or Jacobins. The order is worldwide and there is also an order of contemplative nuns; the habit is black and white.

The first house was established in Toulouse, France, in 1215; in 1216 the order received papal recognition, and the rule was drawn up in 1220–21. They soon spread all over Europe, the first house in England being established in Oxford, UK, in 1221. The English Dominicans were suppressed in 1559, but were restored to a corporate existence in 1622. Dominicans have included Thomas Aquinas, Girolamo ◊Savonarola, and Bartolome de las Casas. In 1983 there were 7,200 friars and 4,775 nuns.

Dominic, St 1170–1221. Founder of the Roman Catholic Dominican order of preaching friars. Feast day 7 Aug.

Born in Old Castile, Dominic was sent by Pope Innocent III in 1205 to preach to the heretic Albigensians in Provence. In 1208 the Pope instigated the Albigensian crusade to suppress the heretics by force, and this was supported by Dominic. In 1215 the Dominican order was given premises at Toulouse; during the following years Dominic established friaries at Bologna and elsewhere in Italy, and by the time of his death the order was established all over W Europe.

domino theory idea popularized by US president Eisenhower in 1954 that if one country came under communist rule, adjacent countries were likely to fall to communism as well.

Used in the USA and Australia to justify intervention in SE Asia, the domino theory has also been invoked in reference to US involvement in Central America.

Donatist member of a puritanical Christian movement in 4th- and 5th-century N Africa, named after Donatus of Casae Nigrae, a 3rd-century bishop, later known as Donatus of Carthage.

The Donatists became for a time the major Christian movement in N Africa; following the tradition of ◊Montanism, their faith stressed the social revolutionary aspects of Christianity, the separation of church from state, and a belief in martyrdom and suffering. Their influence was ended by Bishop ◊Augustine of Hippo; they were formally condemned 412.

doppelgänger (German 'double-goer') apparition of a living person, a person's double, or a guardian spirit. The German composer and writer E T A Hoffman wrote a short story called *Die Doppelgänger* in 1821. English novelist Charles Williams used the idea to great effect in his novel *Descent into Hell* 1937.

Doppler Christian Johann 1803–1853. Austrian physicist. He became professor of experimental physics at Vienna. He described the ***Doppler effect***.

Doppler effect change in the observed frequency (or wavelength) of waves due to relative motion between the wave source and the observer. The Doppler effect is responsible for the perceived change in pitch of a siren as it approaches and then recedes, and for the red shift of light from distant stars. It is named after the Austrian physicist Christian Doppler (1803–1853).

Douglas Major (Clifford Hugh) 1879–1952. English social reformer, founder of the economic theory of *social credit*, which held that interest should be abolished, and credit should become a state monopoly. During a depression, the state should provide purchasing power by subsidizing manufacture and paying dividends to individuals; as long as there was spare capacity in the economy, this credit would not cause inflation.

Doukhobor member of a Christian group of Russian origin, now mainly found in Canada, also known as 'Christians of the Universal Brotherhood'.

They were long persecuted, mainly for refusing military service – the writer Tolstoy organized a relief fund for them – but in 1898 were permitted to emigrate and settled in Canada, where they number about 13,000, mainly in British Columbia and Saskatchewan. An extremist group, 'the Sons of Freedom', staged demonstrations and guerrilla acts in the 1960s, leading to the imprisonment of about 100 of them.

Some of the Doukhobor teachings resemble those of the Society of ◊Friends.

dove person who takes a moderate, sometimes pacifist, view on political issues. The term originated in the US during the Vietnam War. Its counterpart is a ◊hawk. In more general usage today, a dove is equated with liberal policies, and a hawk with conservative ones.

dove universal symbol of ◊peace and, to a lesser extent, of purity. In the biblical story of the Flood, Noah sends out a dove from the Ark, which returns bearing an olive branch – a symbol of reconciliation. In Judaism the dove represents the children of Israel, the beloved of God; in Christianity, it stands for God in the form of the Holy Spirit, the third person of the ◊Trinity.

The dove was one of the sacred animals associated with the Greek goddess ◊Aphrodite. In the Near East it is associated with fertility.

dowry property or money given by the bride's family to the groom or his family as part of the marriage agreement; the opposite of ◊bridewealth. In 1961 dowries were made illegal in India; however, in 1992 the Indian government reported more than 15,000 murders or suicides between 1988 and 1991 that were a direct result of insufficient dowries.

dowsing ascertaining the presence of water or minerals beneath the ground with a forked twig or pendulum. Unconscious muscular action by the dowser is thought to move the twig, usually held with one fork in each hand, possibly in response to a local change in the pattern of electrical forces. The ability has been known since at least the 16th century and, though not widely recognized by science, it has been used commercially and in archaeology.

Draco 7th century BC. Athenian politician, the first to codify the laws of the Athenian city-state. These were notorious for their severity; hence *draconian*, meaning particularly harsh.

dragon mythical reptilian beast, often portrayed as winged and breathing fire. An occasional feature of classical legend, dragons later held a central place as opponents of gods and heroes in Vedic, Teutonic (◊Siegfried), Anglo-Saxon, and Christian (St George) mythologies, possibly accounting for their heraldic role on medieval banners and weaponry.

In Christian art the dragon is linked with the devil; in traditional Chinese belief it is a symbol of divinity and royalty, associated with storms and rain.

drama, religious dramatic performance employed to tell a religious story either within a liturgical context (for example, Christian Nativity and Easter plays) or as part of a festival celebration (for example, Ancient Greek plays staged in honour of ◊Dionysus).

The connection between ritual and drama is very close and many religions, with the notable exception of Islam, have a theatrical element. The early Christians originally banned plays because of their ◊pagan connotations but by the Middle Ages religious plays were commonly performed both inside and outside churches. In Hindu religion, dramatic re-enactions of the lives of ◊Krishna and ◊Rama, using dance and music, have long been part of religious practice. The most famous tradition is the Kathakali, a form of dance drama, of S India.

Your old men shall dream dreams, your young men shall see visions.

dreams
Bible, the sacred book of the Jewish and
Christian religions.
Joel 2:28

dream an imagery experience during sleep in which memories, thoughts, and emotions present themselves dramatically and convincingly although when recalled they often seem bizarre. The characteristic and striking imagery of dreams is of hallucinatory quality. The function of dreams is still unclear. ◊Freud, for example, believed they protected the sleeper from disturbance, sometimes physical (e.g., a noise or bodily discomfort), but more often unacceptable thoughts and impulses invading consciousness from the ◊unconscious. He called these thoughts and impulses the latent content. They take the form of a wish and, because in their crude state they would disturb and wake up the sleeper, they have to be distorted and disguised by the dream-work in order to pass the ◊censor. The sleeper is thus presented with the innocuous 'manifest' content. Dream interpretation is therefore the 'royal road to...the unconscious'.

The eye of man hath not heard, the ear of man hath not seen, man's hand is not able to taste, his tongue to conceive, nor his heart to report, what my dream was.

dream
William Shakespeare, 1564–1616, English
dramatist and poet.
A Midsummer Night's Dream IV. i

For ◊Jung, dreams are as important as waking life. They can be instructive, creative, and even prophetic. The archetypes of the ◊collective unconscious appearing in dreams can assist in personal development.

The experimental study of dreams received considerable impetus from the discovery by the US psychologists, Nathaniel Kleitman and Eugene Aserinksy, of rapid-eye-movement (REM) sleep in the early 1950s. REM sleep occurs at roughly 70–90 minute intervals during sleep and dreams are usually reported if the sleeper is woken up at these times. Some dreaming is also reported in non-REM sleep, but most of it is properly called thinking or mentation.

Recently, a controversial view has been proposed by US psychologists, Allan Hobson and Robert McCarley. According to their 'activation-synthesis' hypothesis, the cortex is bombarded by neural impulses from the more primitive parts of the brain that initiate REM sleep. The brain, or mind, processes or interprets these chaotic impulses in terms of information stored in memory and the result, a synthesis, is the dream.

Bibl. Hobson, J Allan *The Dreaming Brain* (London, 1990)

We are such stuff / As dreams are made on, and our little life / Is rounded with a sleep.

dreams
William Shakespeare, 1564–1616, English
dramatist and poet.
The Tempest IV. i

Dreamtime or **Dreaming** mythical past of the Australian Aborigines, the basis of their religious beliefs and creation stories. In the Dreamtime spiritual beings shaped the land, the first people were brought into being and set in their proper territories, and laws and rituals were established. Belief in a creative spirit in the form of a huge snake, the Rainbow Serpent, occurs over much of Aboriginal Australia, usually associated with waterholes, rain, and thunder. A common feature of religions across the continent is the Aborigines' bond with the land.

The Dreamtime stories describe how giants and animals sprang from the earth, sea, and sky and crisscrossed the empty continent of Australia before returning into the earth. The places where they travelled or sank back into the land became mountain ranges, rocks, and sites full of sacred meaning. Rituals, which must be re-enacted at certain times of the year in order to maintain the life of the land, are connected with each site. Each Aborigine has a Dreamtime ancestor associated with a particular animal that the person must not kill or injure.

Drucker Peter 1909– . Austrian-born management guru, arguably the most influential theorist in the field and certainly the most widely read, with over 24 books to his name. He is particularly well known for setting out the theory of 'Management By Objectives' (MBO), now a field of management theory in its own right, in his classic *The Practices of Management* 1954. He was also responsible for the idea of privatization, although he referred to it as 'reprivatization'.

Drucker's five basic objectives for management – setting objectives, organization, motivation and communication, laying down performance targets, and personnel development – are still applicable today. His theory of MBO came from his experience with General Electric, where each manager was assigned a profit centre and set targets of 7% return on sales and 20% on investment to achieve. The targets were stringently applied and those who failed were sacked. Drucker reasoned that a business is ultimately judged by its bottom line of profit or loss, no matter what its other peripheral advantages or contributions to the community. Therefore, corporate goals should be divided into a list of objectives and targets to be attained and each assigned to units and individuals. MBO thus ensures that each individual in a ◊chain of command performs efficiently or, as in the case of General Electric, leaves the chain. Drucker's contribution to management theory and practice is phenomenal; he has few, if any, rivals of equal influence in the field.

Druidism religion of the Celtic peoples of the pre-Christian British Isles and Gaul. The word is derived from Greek *drus* 'oak'. The Druids regarded this tree as sacred; one of their chief rites was the cutting of mistletoe from it with a golden sickle. They taught the immortality of the soul and a reincarnation doctrine, and were expert in astronomy. The Druids are thought to have offered human sacrifices.

Druidism was stamped out in Gaul after the Roman conquest. In Britain their stronghold was Anglesey, Wales, until they were driven out by the Roman governor Agricola. They existed in Scotland and Ireland until the coming of the Christian missionaries. What are often termed Druidic monuments – cromlechs and stone circles – are of New Stone Age (Neolithic) origin, though they may later have been used for religious purposes by the Druids. A possible example of a human sacrifice by Druids is Lindow Man, whose body was found in a bog in Cheshire 1984.

Druse or *Druze* religious group in the Middle East of around 300,000 people. It began as a branch of ◊Shi'ite Islam, based on a belief in the divinity of the sixth Fatimid caliph, al-Hakim (996–1021), and that he will return at the end of time. Their particular doctrines are kept secret, even from the majority of members.

The Druse group was founded in Egypt in the 11th century, and then fled to Palestine to avoid persecution; today they occupy areas of Syria, Lebanon, and Israel.

dualism in philosophy, the belief that reality is essentially dual in nature. The French philosopher René ◊Descartes, for example, refers to thinking and material substance. These entities interact but are fundamentally separate and distinct.

Dualism is contrasted with ◊monism, the theory that reality is made up of only one substance.

Du Bois W(illiam) E(dward) B(urghardt) 1868–1963. US educator and social critic. Du Bois was one of the early leaders of the National Association for the Advancement of Colored People (NAACP) and the editor of its journal *Crisis* 1909–32. As a staunch advocate of black American rights, he came into conflict with Booker T ◊Washington opposing the latter's policy of compromise on the issue of slavery.

Born in Great Barrington, Massachusetts, Du Bois earned a PhD from Harvard 1895 and was appointed to the faculty of Atlanta University. In 1962 he established his home in Accra, Ghana.

Dubos René Jules 1901–1981. French-US microbiologist who studied soil microorganisms and became interested in their antibacterial properties.

The antibacterials he discovered had limited therapeutic use since they were toxic. However, he opened up a new field of research that eventually led to the discovery of such major drugs as penicillin and streptomycin.

Duguit Léon 1859–1928. French jurist. He attacked abstract notions of sovereignty and the state, believing that the law exists to promote social solidarity, that is, the interaction and interdependence of groups of people. When it fails to do so it should be rejected. He was professor of constitution law at the University of Bordeaux.

dukka Buddhist term for all suffering, evil, and disease. It is used to describe that which arises from the desire to hold onto pleasant experiences, feelings of comfort, or people we like, all of which are inevitably impermanent. From this clinging to the perishable arises suffering – dukka.

dumping in international trade, the selling of goods by one country to another at below marginal cost or at a price below that in its own country. Countries dump in order to get rid of surplus produce or to improve their competitive position in the recipient country. The practice is widely condemned by protectionists (opponents of free trade) because of the unfair competition it represents.

Dunant Jean Henri 1828–1910. Swiss philanthropist; the originator of the international relief agency, the Red Cross. At the Battle of Solferino 1859 he helped tend the wounded, and in *Un Souvenir de Solferino* 1862 he proposed the establishment of an international body for the aid of the wounded – an idea that was realized in the Geneva Convention 1864. He shared the 1901 Nobel Peace Prize.

Duns Scotus John c. 1265–c. 1308. Scottish monk, a leading figure in the theological and philosophical system of medieval ◊scholasticism. The church rejected his ideas, and the word *dunce* is derived from Dunses, a term of ridicule applied to his followers. In the medieval controversy over universals he advocated ◊nominalism, maintaining that classes of things have no independent reality. He belonged to the Franciscan order, and was known as Doctor Subtilis.

On many points he turned against the orthodoxy of Thomas ◊Aquinas; for example, he rejected the idea of a necessary world, favouring a concept of God as absolute freedom capable of spontaneous activity.

Durga Hindu goddess; one of the many names for the 'great goddess' ◊*Mahādevī*.

Durkheim Emile 1858–1917. French sociologist, one of the founders of modern sociology, who also influenced social anthropology. He worked to establish sociology as a respectable and scientific discipline, capable of diagnosing social ills and recommending possible cures.

He was the first lecturer in social science at Bordeaux University 1887–1902, professor of education at the Sorbonne in Paris from 1902, and the first professor of sociology there 1913. He examined the bases of social order and the effects of industrialization on traditional social and moral order.

His four key works are *De la division du travail social*/*The Division of Labour in Society* 1893, comparing social order in small-scale societies with that in industrial ones; *Les Régles de la méthode*/*The Rules of Sociological Method* 1895, outlining his own brand of functionalism and proclaiming ◊positivism as the way forward for sociology as a science; *Suicide* 1897, showing social causes of this apparently individual act; and *Les Formes élémentaires de la vie religieuse*/*The Elementary Forms of Religious Life* 1912, a study of the beliefs of Australian Aborigines, showing the place of religion in social solidarity.

Dutch Reformed Church the major Protestant church in the Netherlands. In theology it follows ◊Calvinism and in government it resembles ◊Presbyterianism. It was first organized during the revolt of the low countries against Spanish rule in the 16th century. The Reformed Church spread wherever the Dutch colonized or emigrated, with major centres in Indonesia, the West Indies, Sri Lanka, and South Africa, where the church gave theological support to apartheid in the 1930s and was expelled from the world community of Dutch Reformed Churches. Since the mid-1980s it has taken steps to distance itself from apartheid and to seek integration between the black and white churches that had been set up.

Render therefore unto Caesar the things which are Caesar's.

> *duty*
> Bible, the sacred book of the Jewish and
> Christian religions.
> Matthew 22:21

---

duty moral obligation experienced as a felt commandment of the moral law. The stoics in ancient Greece and Immanuel Kant in Germany (who coined the concept of the ◊categorical imperative) are the moral philosophers who have placed greatest emphasis on duty. Moral conflicts occur where a number of duties make apparently irreconcilable demands on us.

When a stupid man is doing something he is ashamed of, he always declares that it is his duty.

> *duty*
> George Bernard Shaw, 1856–1950,
> Irish dramatist.
> *Caesar and Cleopatra*

Duty is strongly emphasized in ◊Confucianism (especially duty to the state and to ancestors) and in Japanese culture, where it is divided into obligations (*on*) that can and therefore must be repaid, and continuous obligations, such as those to parents and country.

Duve Christian de 1917– . Belgian scientist, who shared the 1974 Nobel Prize for Medicine for his work on the structural and functional organization of the biological cell.

Dworkin Ronald 1931– . American jurist. A leading exponent of liberalism who has consistently challenged the positivist notion of law – that a legal system is the sum of its rules – by stressing the importance of moral principles or rights in assessing particular cases. His publications include *Taking Rights Seriously* 1977 and *Life's Dominion* 1993, a discussion of euthanasia and abortion in which he argues against the belief in fetal rights and in favour of the right to terminate a pregnancy when necessary.

He is professor of Jurisprudence at Oxford University and professor of Law at New York University.

dybbuk in Jewish folklore, the soul of a dead sinner which has entered the body of a living person.

dyslexia malfunction in the brain's synthesis and interpretation of sensory information, popularly known as 'word blindness'. Dyslexia is developed into developmental and acquired types. It results in poor ability in reading and writing, though the person may otherwise excel, for example, in mathematics. A similar disability with figures is called *dyscalculia*.

dystopia imaginary society whose evil qualities are meant to serve as a moral or political warning. The term was coined in the 19th century by the English philosopher John Stuart ◊Mill, and is the opposite of a Utopia. George Orwell's *1984* 194 9 and Aldous Huxley's *Brave New World* 1932 are examples of novels about dystopias. Dystopias are common in science fiction.

Ea or **Enki** A god (or sometimes goddess) who appears in the traditions of several ancient Middle Eastern religions such as the Hittites and the Babylonians. Ea was the Babylonian god of water and of wisdom. He was associated with the Babylonian creation story and in particular in the *Epic of ◊Gilgamesh,* with the creation of order out of the chaos of the primal waters. Ea was reputed to be the creator of humanity in some traditions.

earth science scientific study of the planet Earth as a whole, a synthesis of several traditional subjects such as ◊geology, meteorology, oceanography, geophysics, geochemistry, and ◊palaeontology.

The mining and extraction of minerals and gems, the prediction of weather and earthquakes, the pollution of the atmosphere, and the forces that shape the physical world all fall within its scope of study. The emergence of the discipline reflects scientists' concern that an understanding of the global aspects of the Earth's structure and its past will hold the key to how humans affect its future, ensuring that its resources are used in a sustainable way.

Most glorious Lord of life, that on this day / Didst make thy triumph over death and sin: / And, having harrow'd hell, didst bring / Captivity thence captive, us to win.

> **Easter**
> Edmund Spenser, c. 1552, English poet.
> *Amoretti* sonnet 68

Easter spring feast of the Christian church, commemorating the Resurrection of Jesus. The traditional greeting for Christians at Easter and for 40 days afterwards is 'Christ is risen!', to which the reply is 'He is risen indeed, Alleluya!' It is a moveable feast, falling on the first Sunday following the full moon after the vernal equinox (21 March), that is, between 22 March and 25 April.

The English name derives from Eostre, Anglo-Saxon goddess of spring, who was honoured in April.

Easter eggs, dyed and decorated or made of confectionery, symbolizing new life, are given as presents. Other foods traditionally eaten at Easter are those containing sugar, eggs, and butter – the foods that have not been eaten during ◊Lent. In some Orthodox churches the Easter service begins before midnight on Easter Saturday and continues until the early morning of Easter Sunday. Baskets of festive food are blessed in church and taken home for breakfast.

Ebbinghaus Hermann 1850–1909. German experimental psychologist. Influenced by ◊Fechner's *Elements of Psychophysics*, he applied quantitative principles to the study of higher mental processes, in particular to human memory.

Ebbinghaus invented nonsensical syllables, consonant-vowel-consonant letter groups that he believed (wrongly) had no meaning and would therefore all be equally difficult to memorize. Using himself as subject, he used this material to investigate learning and forgetting, publishing the results in his *Memory* 1885. It was the first research to attempt, experimentally, to isolate the principle factors that generate learning curves.

Psychology has a long past, but only a short history.

> **Hermann Ebbinghaus**
> *Summary of Psychology*

Although of great influence, Ebbinghaus's methods were later extensively criticised, notably by Frederic Charles ◊Bartlett.

Eccles John Carew 1903– . Australian physiologist who shared (with Alan ◊Hodgkin and Andrew ◊Huxley) the 1963 Nobel Prize for Medicine for work on conduction in the central nervous system. In some of his later works, he argued that the mind has an existence independent of the brain.

ecclesiastical law church law. In England, the Church of England has special ecclesiastical courts to administer church law. Each diocese has a consistory court with a right of appeal to the Court of Arches (in the archbishop of

Canterbury's jurisdiction) or the Chancery Court of York (in the archbishop of York's jurisdiction). They deal with the constitution of the Church of England, church property, the clergy, services, doctrine, and practice. These courts have no influence on churches of other denominations, which are governed by the usual laws of contract and trust.

Echo in Greek mythology, a nymph who pined away until only her voice remained, after being rejected by Narcissus.

Eckhart Johannes, called Meister Eckhart c. 1260–1327. German theologian and leader of a popular mystical movement. In 1326 he was accused of heresy, and in 1329 a number of his doctrines were condemned by the pope as heretical. His theology stressed the absolute transcendence of God, and the internal spiritual development through which union with the divine could be attained.

eclecticism in artistic theory, the use of motifs and elements from various styles, periods, and geographical areas. This selection and recombination of features from different sources is a characteristic of Victorian architecture, for example, J F Bentley's design for Westminster Cathedral, London 1895–1903, in Byzantine style.

ecology study of the relationship among organisms and the environments in which they live, including all living and nonliving components. The term was coined by the biologist Ernst Haeckel 1866.

Ecology may be concerned with individual organisms (for example, behavioural ecology, feeding strategies), with populations (for example, population dynamics), or with entire communities (for example, competition between species for access to resources in an ecosystem, or predator–prey relationships). Applied ecology is concerned with the management and conservation of habitats and the consequences and control of pollution.

econometrics application of mathematical and statistical analysis to the study of economic relationships, including testing economic theories and making quantitative predictions.

economic community organization of autonomous countries formed to promote trade.

economic growth rate of growth of output of all goods and services in an economy, usually measured as the percentage increase in gross domestic product or gross national product from one year to the next. It is regarded as an indicator of the rate of increase or decrease (if economic growth is negative) in the standard of living.

economic problem the problem that is faced because wants are infinite but resources are scarce. Therefore resources have to be allocated between competing uses. Economics is the study of how the economic problem is resolved.

Great Economists		
lived	*name*	*chief work published*
1723–1790	Adam Smith	The Wealth of Nations 1776
1766–1834	Thomas Malthus	Essay on the Principle of Population 1798
1772–1823	David Ricado	Principles of Political Economy 1817
1818–1883	Karl Marx	Das Kapital/Capital 1867–95
1834–1910	Léon Walras	Elements d'économie politique pure 1874–77
1842–1924	Alfred Marshall	Principles of Economics 1890
1883–1946	John Maynard Keynes	The General Theory of Employment, Interest and Money 1936
1883–1950	Joseph Schumpeter	Capitalism, Socialism and Democracy 1942
1908–	John Kenneth Galbraith	The Affluent Society 1958
1912–	Milton Friedman	Inflation: Causes and Consequences 1953

economics social science devoted to studying the production, distribution, and consumption of wealth. It consists of the disciplines of ◊*microeconomics*, the study of individual producers, consumers, or markets, and ◊*macroeconomics*, the study of whole economies or systems (in particular, areas such as taxation and public spending).

Economics is the study of how, in a given society, choices are made in the allocation of resources to produce goods and services for consumption, and the mechanisms and principles that govern this process. Economics seeks to apply scientific method to construct theories about the processes involved and to test them against what actually happens. Its two central concerns are the efficient allocation of available resources and the problem of reconciling finite resources with a virtually infinite desire for goods and services. Economics analyses the ingredients of economic efficiency in the production process, and the implications for practical policies, and examines conflicting demands for resources and the consequences of whatever choices are made, whether by individuals, enterprises, or governments.

Microeconomics and macroeconomics frequently overlap. They include the sub-discipline of *econometrics*, which analyses economic relationships using mathematical and statistical techniques. Increasingly sophisticated econometric methods are today being used for such topics as economic forecasting. Pioneers in this field include ◊Frisch and ◊Kantorovich.

Man does not live by GNP alone.

economics
Paul Samuelson, 1915, US economist and journalist.
Economics 1948

Economics aims to be either *positive*, presenting objective and scientific explanations of how an economy works, or *normative*, offering prescriptions and recommendations on what should be done to cure perceived ills. However, almost inevitably, value judgements are involved in all economists' formulations.

One of the pioneering works of ◊classical economics was Adam ◊Smith's *The Wealth of Nations* 1776. Alfred ◊Marshall was a founder of ◊neoclassical economics. John Maynard ◊Keynes criticized neoclassical economics for its analysis of output and employment in the whole economy. Milton ◊Friedman reasserted neoclassical principles of macroeconomics. Other major thinkers include David ◊Ricardo, Thomas ◊Malthus, J S ◊Mill, Karl ◊Marx, and Vilfredo ◊Pareto.

economies of scale internal economies of scale exist when there is a fall in the average cost of production as the scale of output rises in the long run. For example, there would sometimes be economies of scale present if a car manufacturer could manufacture cars at £5,000 per car if it produced 100,000 cars per year, but at £4,000 per car if it produced 200,000 cars per year. Economies of scale include technical economies, financial economies, managerial economies, and risk-bearing economies.

ecosystem in ◊ecology, an integrated unit consisting of the ◊community of living organisms and the physical environment in a particular area. The relationships among species in an ecosystem are usually complex and finely balanced, and removal of any one species may be disastrous. The removal of a major predator, for example, can result in the destruction of the ecosystem through overgrazing by herbivores.

Energy and nutrients pass through organisms in an ecosystem in a particular sequence (see ◊food chain): energy is captured through photosynthesis, and nutrients are taken up from the soil or water by plants; both are passed to herbivores that eat the plants and then to carnivores that feed on herbivores. These nutrients are returned to the soil through the decomposition of excrement and dead organisms, thus completing a cycle that is crucial to the stability and survival of the ecosystem.

ecstasy a state of exaltation where the self is transcended. It covers a range of phenomena from ◊mysticism to spirit possession and ◊shamanism. In Hinduism the achievement of ecstasy, *bhava*, is a sign of spiritual advancement on the yogic path.

ecumenical council meeting of church leaders worldwide to determine Christian doctrine; their results are binding on all church members. Seven such councils are accepted as ecumenical by both Eastern and Western churches, while the Roman Catholic Church accepts a further 14 as ecumenical.

ecumenical movement movement for reunification of the various branches of the Christian church. It began in the 19th century with the extension of missionary work to Africa and Asia, where the divisions created in Europe were incomprehensible; the movement gathered momentum from the need for unity in the face of growing secularism in Christian countries and of the challenge posed by such faiths as Islam. The *World Council of Churches* was founded 1948.

ecumenical patriarch head of the Eastern Orthodox Church, the patriarch of Istanbul (Constantinople). The Bishop of Constantinople was recognized as having equal rights with the Bishop of Rome 451, and first termed 'patriarch' in the 6th century. The office survives today but with only limited authority, mainly confined to the Greek and Turkish Orthodox churches.

Eddington Arthur Stanley 1882–1944. British astrophysicist, who studied the motions, equilibrium, luminosity, and atomic structure of the stars, and became a leading exponent of Einstein's relativity theory. In 1919 his observation of stars during an eclipse confirmed Einstein's prediction that light is bent when passing near the Sun. His book *The Nature of the Physical World* 1928 is a popularization of science. In *The Expanding Universe* 1933 he expressed the theory that in the spherical universe the outer galaxies or spiral nebulae are receding from one another.

Eddy Mary Baker 1821–1910. US founder of the Christian Science movement.

She was born in New Hampshire and brought up as a Congregationalist. Her pamphlet *Science of Man* 1869 was followed by *Science and Health with Key to the Scriptures* 1875, which systematically set forth the basis of Christian Science. She founded the Christian Science Association 1876. In 1879 the Church of Christ, Scientist, was established, and although living in retirement after 1892 she continued to direct the activities of the movement until her death.

Her faith in divine healing was confirmed by her recovery from injuries caused by a fall, and Christian Science follows this belief.

Edelman Gerald Maurice 1929– . US biochemist who worked out the sequence of 1330 amino acids that makes up human immunoglobulin, a task completed 1969. For this work he shared the Nobel Prize for Medicine 1972 with Rodney ◊Porter.

Eden, Garden of in the Old Testament book of Genesis and in the Qur'an, the 'garden' in which Adam and Eve lived after their creation, and from which they were expelled for disobedience.

Its location has often been identified with the Fertile Crescent in Mesopotamia (now in Iraq), and two of its rivers with the Euphrates and the Tigris.

Edom in the Old Testament, a mountainous area of S Palestine, which stretched from the Dead Sea to the Gulf of Aqaba. Its people were enemies of the Israelites.

Real education must ultimately be limited to one who insists on knowing, the rest is mere sheep-herding.

                            education
Ezra Pound, 1885–1972, US poet (who lived in London from 1909) and cultural critic.
                ABC of Reading ch 8

---

education process, beginning at birth, of developing intellectual capacity, manual skill, and social awareness, especially by instruction. In its more restricted sense, the term refers to the process of imparting literacy, numeracy, and a generally accepted body of knowledge.

history of education The earliest known European educational systems were those of ancient Greece. In Sparta the process was devoted mainly to the development of military skills; in Athens, to politics, philosophy, and public speaking, but both were accorded only to the privileged few.

In ancient China, formalized education received impetus from the imperial decree of 165 BC, which established open competitive examinations for the recruitment of members of the civil service, based mainly on a detailed study of literature.

The bodies of those that made such a noise and tumult when alive, when dead, lie as quietly among the graves of their neighbours as any others.

                        Jonathan Edwards
                        Procrastination

The Romans adopted the Greek system of education and spread it through Western Europe. Following the disintegration of the Roman Empire, widespread education vanished from Europe, although Christian monasteries preserved both learning and Latin. In the Middle Ages, Charlemagne's monastic schools taught the 'seven liberal arts': grammar, logic, rhetoric, arithmetic, geometry, music, and astronomy. These schools produced the theological philosophers of the Scholastic Movement, which in the 11th–13th centuries led to the foundation of the universities of Paris (the Sorbonne), Bologna, Padua, ◊Oxford University, and ◊Cambridge University. The capture of Constantinople, capital of the Eastern Roman Empire, by the Turks 1453 sent the Christian scholars there into exile across Europe, and revived European interest in learning.

Compulsory attendance at primary schools was first established in the mid-18th century in Prussia, and has since spread almost worldwide. Compulsory schooling in industrialized countries is typically from around age 6 to around age 15; public education expenditure is typically around 5% of GNP (Spain 3.2%, Japan 4.4%, Denmark 7.7%).

educational psychology the work of psychologists primarily in schools, including the assessment of children with achievement problems and advising on problem behaviour in the classroom.

The Major Educational Thinkers

author	work	central ideas or emphasis
Comenius	Didactica Magna 1628–32	education for all, regradless of class or sex, with knowledge made systematic and related to everyday life
	The Visible World in Pictures 1658	the first picture book for children
Rousseau	Emile 1762	a return to nature, with tolerance and example allowing a child's innate goodness and potential to develop unhindered
Pestalozzi	How Gertrude Teaches her Children 1801	the fostering of inner potential through pupil activity and object as well as through books
Froebel	Education of Man 1826	kindergarten system developed, based on self-motivated play, stimulating surrounding and encouragement rather than compulsion
Steiner	The Philosophy of Spiritual Activity 1894	development of the whole personality through art, drama and eurhythmics
Thorndike	Educational Psychology 1903	systematic use of intelligence tests
Montessori	The Montessori Method 1912	the importance of a stimulating environment and learning games, with an emphasis on movement and sense perception; children being allowed to develop at their own pace
Piaget	The Language and Thought of Children 1923	education based on meeting the specific needs of four invariable stages of intellectual development
Skinner	The Technology of Teaching 1969	programmed learning and 'teaching machines', based on behaviourist psychology
Illich	Deschooling Society 1971	schools to be replaced by education in and by the community

education, conductive training for the physically disabled; see ◊conductive education.

Edwards Jonathan 1703–1758. US theologian who took a Calvinist view of predestination (some are born to be saved, others to be damned) and initiated a religious revival, the 'Great Awakening'. His *The Freedom of the Will* 1754, defending ◊determinism, received renewed attention in the 20th century.

efficiency in a machine, the useful work output (work done by the machine) divided by the work input (work put into the machine), usually expressed as a percentage. In formula terms:

$$\text{efficiency} = \frac{\text{useful work output}}{\text{work input}} \times 100\%$$

or, because power is the rate at which work is done:

$$\text{efficiency} = \frac{\text{power input}}{\text{power output}} \times 100\%$$

Losses of energy caused by friction mean that efficiency is always less than 100%, although it can approach this for electrical machines with no moving parts (such as a transformer).

Because work output may be defined as the product of the machine's load and the distance moved by that load, and work input as the product of the effort and the distance moved by the effort, efficiency may be also be expressed as:

$$\text{efficiency} = \frac{\text{load} \times \text{distance load is moved}}{\text{effort} \times \text{distance effort moved}} \times 100\%$$

or, because the mechanical advantage (MA) of a machine is the ratio of the load to the effort, and its velocity ratio (VR) is the distance moved by the effort divided by the distance moved by the load, as:

$$\text{efficiency} = \frac{\text{mechanical advantage}}{\text{velocity ratio}} \times 100\%$$

efficiency in economics, production at lowest cost. Efficiency also relates to how resources are allocated. Resources are said to be allocated efficiently if business organizations are producing the best quality goods for the lowest price.

efficient cause in Aristotle's philosophy, one of the four causes of things. The efficient cause of a man, according to Aristotle, is his father. The other three causes of a man are flesh (material cause), the ◊form of man (formal cause), and the end, or purpose, of human life (final cause).

Only two of Aristotle's causes answer to English usage: the efficient and the final causes. The Greek word translated as 'cause' means something more like 'responsible factor' or 'necessary condition'.

egalitarianism belief that all citizens in a state should have equal rights and privileges. Interpretations of this can vary, from the notion of equality of opportunity to equality in material welfare and political decision-making. Some states clearly reject any thought of egalitarianism; most accept the concept of equal opportunities but recognize that people's abilities vary widely. Even those states which claim to be socialist find it necessary to have hierarchical structures in the political, social, and economic spheres. Egalitarianism was one of the principles of the French Revolution.

ego in psychology, a general term for the processes concerned with the self and a person's conception of himself or herself, encompassing values and attitudes. In Freudian psychology, the term refers specifically to the element of the human mind that represents the conscious processes concerned with reality, in conflict with the ◊id (the instinctual element) and the ◊superego (the ethically aware element). Initially, Freud used the term as a synonym for self-preservation.

egoism in ethics, the doctrine that we seek only our enlightened self-interest and that all our desires are self-referential. Notable ethical theorists who have held versions of egoism are ◊Aristotle, Thomas ◊Hobbes, and Benedict ◊Spinoza.

Egyptian religion in the civilization of ancient Egypt, totemic animals, believed to be the ancestors of the clan, were worshipped. Totems later developed into gods, represented as having animal heads. One of the main cults was that of ◊Osiris, the god of the underworld. Immortality, conferred by the magical rite of mummification, was originally the sole prerogative of the king, but was extended under the New Kingdom to all who could afford it; they were buried with the ◊Book of the Dead.

The hawk was sacred to *Ra* and *Horus*, the ibis to *Thoth*, the jackal to *Anubis*. The story of Osiris, who was murdered, mourned by his sister and wife Isis, and then rose again, was enacted in a fertility ritual. It was the wish of all who died to join Osiris in the Land of the West. Survival in the afterlife was largely dependant on the preservation of the body which required detailed methods of embalming and mummification. It was believed that the body and tomb contents were brought to life during a ceremony known as the 'Opening of the Mouth'. Those who could afford it were also buried with texts containing hymns and useful spells.

Ehrenfels Christian von 1859–1933. Austrian philosopher and psychologist who, in 1890, introduced the notion of ◊gestalt to explain observations of wholeness and object-constancy in perception.

For example, a circle which is still seen as a circle even after its size or colour has changed. A whole that retains its specific character when changes occur that affect all its parts he termed a *Gestalt* and its special property a *Gestalt quality*. His ideas were important in the early history of Gestalt psychology.

Eid ul-Adha Muslim festival which takes place during the ◊hajj, or pilgrimage to Mecca, and commemorates Abraham's willingness to sacrifice his son ◊Ishmael at the command of Allah.

Eid ul-Fitr Muslim festival celebrating the end of ◊Ramadan, the month of fasting.

Eigen Manfred 1927– . German chemist who worked on extremely rapid chemical reactions (those taking less than 1 millisecond). From 1954 he developed a technique by which very short bursts of energy could be applied to solutions, disrupting their equilibrium and enabling him to investigate momentary reactions such as the formation and dissociation of water.

For this work he shared the Nobel Prize in Chemistry 1967 with English chemists George Porter and Ronald Norrish (1897–1978).

Eightfold Path the fourth of the ◊Four Noble Truths of Buddhism, it outlines a path of discipline and correct behaviour which leads towards freedom from rebirth. The eight elements of the Path are: right understanding; right aspirations; right speech; right bodily action; right livelihood; right endeavour; right mindfulness; right concentration. The Eightfold Path is also known as the Middle Way, since it describes a course that lies between asceticism and sensual pleasure.

Einstein Albert 1879–1955. German-born US physicist who formulated the theories of ◊relativity, and worked on radiation physics and thermodynamics. In 1905 he published the special theory of relativity, and in 1915 issued his general theory of relativity. He received the Nobel Prize for Physics 1921. His latest conception of the basic laws governing the universe was outlined in his ◊unified field theory, made public 1953.

God is subtle but he is not malicious.

Albert Einstein
Remark made at Princeton University in 1921, later carved above the fireplace of the Common Room of Fine Hall (the Mathematical Institute)

Born at Ulm, in Württemberg, West Germany, he lived with his parents in Munich and then in Italy. After teaching at the polytechnic school at Zürich, he became a Swiss citizen and was appointed an inspector of patents in Berne. In his spare time, he took his PhD at Zürich. In 1909 he became a lecturer in theoretical physics at the university. After holding a similar post at Prague 1911, he returned to teach at Zürich 1912, and in 1913 took up a specially created post as director of the Kaiser Wilhelm Institute for Physics, Berlin. After being deprived of his position at Berlin by the Nazis, he emigrated to the USA 1933, and became professor of mathematics and a permanent member of the Institute for Advanced Study at Princeton, New Jersey. During World War II he worked for the US Navy Ordnance Bureau.

Eisai 1141–1215. Japanese Buddhist monk who introduced Zen and tea from China to Japan and founded the ◊Rinzai school.

Eisenstein Sergei Mikhailovich 1898–1948. Soviet film director who pioneered film theory and introduced the use of montage (the juxtaposition of shots to create a particular effect) as a means of propaganda, as in *The Battleship Potemkin* 1925.

The Soviet dictator Stalin banned the second (and last) part of Eisenstein's projected three-film epic *Ivan the Terrible* 1944–46. His other films include *Strike* 1925, *October* 1928, *Que Viva Mexico!* 1931–32, and *Alexander Nevsky* 1938.

elasticity in economics, the measure of response of one variable to changes in another. If the price of butter is reduced by 10% and the demand increases by 20%, the elasticity measure is 2. Such measures are used to test the effects of changes in prices and incomes on supply and demand. Inelasticity may exist in the demand for necessities such as water, the demand for which will remain the same even if the price changes considerably.

El Dorado fabled city of gold believed by the 16th-century Spanish and other Europeans to exist somewhere in the area of the Orinoco and Amazon rivers.

Eleatic school the pre-Socratic philosophers Parmenides and his follower Zeno, who lived in Elea (a Greek colony in S Italy) in the early 5th century BC. They taught that reality is single and unchanging, and that sense experience is illusory.

Melissus of Samos further developed Eleaticism. ◊Xenophanes of Colophon is often linked to the Eleatics.

election process of appointing a person to public office or a political party to government by voting. Elections were occasionally held in ancient Greek democracies; Roman tribunes were regularly elected.

The right to vote is almost the only universal right in the world today. Among all the sovereign contemporary states only five, Brunei, Oman, Qatar, Saudi Arabia, and the United Arab Emirates, do not have, and never have had, any political institutions which can, even in the loosest sense, be described as popularly representative. This does not necessarily mean that all countries in which citizens have the right to vote for a government have a free choice, and therefore enjoy democratic rule. Although elections are important, their form and methods are even more so.

The accursed power which stands on Privilege / (And goes with Women, and Champagne, and Bridge) / Broke – and Democracy resumed her reign: / (Which goes with Bridge, and Women and Champagne).

elections
(Joseph) Hilaire Pierre Belloc, 1870–1953.
'On a Great Election'

Since the near demise of communism throughout the world during the past decade there has been a clear movement away from one-party politics, where voting opportunities are strictly limited, to multi-party systems, where the choice is wide. The change has been evident in virtually all continents, including Europe, Africa, Asia, and Latin America.

The qualifications for voting have also been liberalized during the present century. New Zealand was the first country to give women the vote, in 1893, and, among economically advanced states, Switzerland was the last, in 1971. The minimum age for voting has also been reduced over the years. The age of 18 has now been almost universally adopted but some countries have adopted even lower figures. The age qualification in Iran for presidential elections is 15.

In England, elections have been used as a parliamentary process since the 13th century. The secret ballot was adopted 1872 and full equal voting rights won for women 1928. All registered members of the public aged 18 and over may vote in local, parliamentary, and European Parliament elections. The British House of Commons is elected for a maximum of five years; the prime minister can call a general election at any time.

electoral college in the US government, the indirect system of voting for the president and vice president. The people of each state officially vote not for the presidential candidate, but for a list of electors nominated by each party. The whole electoral-college vote of the state then goes to the winning party (and candidate). A majority is required for election.

The USA has as many electors as it has senators and representatives in Congress, so that the electoral college numbers 538 (535 state electors and 3 from the District of Columbia), and a majority of 270 electoral votes is needed to win. The system can lead to a presidential candidate being elected with a minority of the total vote over the whole country (as happened when Benjamin Harrison was elected over Grover Cleveland 1888). It has been proposed, for example by President Carter in 1977, to substitute a direct popular vote. A constitutional amendment to this effect failed in 1979, partly because minority groups argued that this would deprive them of their politically influential block vote in key states.

Electra in Greek legend, daughter of ◊Agamemnon and ◊Clytemnestra, and sister of ◊Orestes and Iphigenia. Her hatred of her mother for murdering her father and her desire for revenge, fulfilled by the return of her brother Orestes, made her the subject of tragedies by the Greek dramatists Aeschylus, Sophocles, and Euripides. In Euripides' tragedy she joins with Orestes in killing Clytemnestra.

electroconvulsive therapy (ECT) or *electroshock therapy* treatment for ◊depression, ◊manic depression, and some cases of ◊schizophrenia, given under anaesthesia and with a muscle relaxant. An electric current is passed through the brain to induce convulsions. The treatment can cause distress and loss of concentration and memory, and there is therefore much controversy about its use and effectiveness. However, it has saved probably thousands of depressives from suicide.

electromagnetic force one of the four fundamental ◊forces of nature, the other three being gravity, the strong nuclear force, and the weak nuclear force. The ◊elementary particle that is the carrier for the electromagnetic (em) force is the photon.

elementary particle in physics, a subatomic particle that is not made up of smaller particles, and so can be considered one of the fundamental units of matter. There are three groups of elementary particles: quarks, leptons, and gauge bosons.

Quarks, of which there are 12 types (up, down, charm, strange, top, and bottom, plus the antiparticles of each), combine in groups of three to produce heavy particles called baryons, and in groups of two to produce intermediate-mass particles called mesons. They and their composite particles are influenced by the strong nuclear force. *Leptons* are light particles. Again, there are 12 types: the electron, muon, tau; their neutrinos, the electron neutrino, muon neutrino, and tau neutrino; and the antiparticles of each. These particles are influenced by the weak nuclear force. *Gauge bosons* carry forces between other particles. There are four types: the gluons, photon, weakons, and graviton. The gluon carries the strong nuclear force, the photon the electromagnetic force, the weakons the weak nuclear force, and the graviton the force of gravity (see fundamental ◊forces).

elements, the four These are earth, air, fire, and water which the philosopher ◊Empedocles of Sicily believed made up the fundamental components of all matter, and which were destroyed and renewed through the action of love and discord.

This belief was shared by ◊Aristotle who also claimed that the elements were mutable and contained specific qualities: cold and dry for earth, hot and wet for air, hot and dry for fire, and cold and wet for water. The transformation of the elements formed the basis of medieval alchemy, and the belief that base metals could be turned into gold. The theory of the elements prevailed until the 17th century when Robert ◊Boyle redefined an a element as a substance 'simple or unmixed, not made of other bodies' and proposed the existence of a greater number than four. The symbolic significance of the elements still retains a hold on the modern imagination and reference to them can be found in the writings of ◊Jung and Rudolf ◊Steiner.

Eleusinian Mysteries ceremonies in honour of the Greek deities ◊Demeter, ◊Persephone, and ◊Dionysus, celebrated in the precincts of the temple of Demeter at Eleusis, in the territory of Athens. Demeter was the Greek goddess of grain.

Eliade Mircea 1907– . Hungarian-born philosopher and anthropologist of religion. He is a leading figure in the Phenomenology of Religion school, bringing anthropological insights and data to bear on the phenomena of religion. His influence has been extensive and his studies on previously marginalized religious groups, such as the shamans, have led to a major re-evaluation of many aspects of religious practice and history. His most significant books include *From Primitives to Zen: A Thematic Sourcebook of the History of Religion* and *Patterns in Comparative Religion*.

Elijah c. mid-9th century BC. In the Old Testament, a Hebrew prophet during the reigns of the Israelite kings Ahab and Ahaziah. He came from Gilead. He defeated the prophets of ◊Baal, and was said to have been carried up to heaven in a fiery chariot in a whirlwind. In Jewish belief, Elijah will return to Earth to herald the coming of the Messiah.

Eliot Charles William 1834–1926. US educator credited with establishing the standards of modern American higher education. He was appointed professor at the Massachusetts Institute of Technology (MIT) 1865 and was named president of Harvard University 1869. Under Eliot's administration, the college and its graduate and professional schools were reorganized and the curriculum and admission requirements standardized. He retired 1909.

Born in Boston and educated at Harvard, Eliot specialized in mathematics and chemistry and later took up the cause of educational reform.

Eliot T(homas) S(tearns) 1888–1965. US poet, playwright, and critic who lived in London from 1915. His first volume of poetry, *Prufrock and Other Observations* 1917, introduced new verse forms and rhythms; further collections include *The Waste Land* 1922, *The Hollow Men* 1925, and *Old Possum's Book of Practical Cats* 1939. His plays include *Murder in the Cathedral* 1935 and *The Cocktail Party* 1949. His critical works include *The Sacred Wood* 1920. He was awarded the Nobel Prize for Literature 1948.

Eliot was born in St Louis, Missouri, and was educated at Harvard, the Sorbonne, and Oxford. He settled in London 1915 and became a British subject 1927. He was for a time a bank clerk, later lecturing and entering publishing at Faber & Faber. As editor of the highly influential literary magazine *The Criterion* 1922–39, he was responsible for the critical re-evaluation of Metaphysical Poetry and Jacobean Drama, and wrote perceptively about ◊Dante, ◊Baudelaire, and Laforgue.

Prufrock and Other Observations expressed the disillusionment of the generation affected by World War I and caused a sensation with its experimental form and rhythms. His reputation was established by the desolate modernity of *The Waste Land*. *The Hollow Men* continued on the same note, but *Ash Wednesday* 1930 revealed the change in religious attitude that led him to join the Church of England in 1927. Among his other works are *Four Quartets* 1943, a religious sequence in which he seeks the eternal reality, and the poetic dramas *Murder in the Cathedral* (about Thomas à Becket); *The Cocktail Party*; *The Confidential Clerk* 1953; and *The Elder Statesman* 1958. His collection *Old Possum's Book of Practical Cats* was used for the popular British composer Andrew Lloyd Webber's musical *Cats* 1981. His critical works, which include *The Sacred Wood: Essays on Poetry* 1920, *The Idea of a Christian Society* 1940, and *Notes Toward a Definition of Culture* 1948, are conservative in tone, emphasizing the traditional values of ritual and community. He coined two important literary critical terms: ◊disassociation of sensibility and ◊objective correlative.

I grow old ... I grow old ... / I shall wear the bottoms of my trousers rolled.

T(homas) S(tearns) Eliot
'Love Song of J. Alfred Prufrock'

---

elite a small group with power in a society, having privileges and status above others. An elite may be cultural, educational, religious, political (also called 'the establishment' or 'the governing circles'), or social. Sociological interest has centred on how such minorities get, use, and hold on to power, and on what distinguishes elites from the rest of society.

Elizabeth in the New Testament, mother of John the Baptist. She was a cousin of Jesus' mother Mary, who came to see her shortly after the Annunciation; on this visit (called the Visitation), Mary sang the hymn of praise later to be known as the 'Magnificat'.

Ellis (Henry) Havelock 1859–1939. English psychologist and writer of many works on the psychology of sex, including *Studies in the Psychology of Sex* (seven volumes) 1898–1928. He was also a literary critic and essayist.

Elton Charles 1900–1991. British ecologist, a pioneer of the study of animal and plant forms in their natural environments, and of animal behaviour as part of the complex pattern of life. He defined the concept of ◊food chains and was an early conservationist, instrumental in establishing (1949) the Nature Conservancy Council of which he was a member 1949–56, and much concerned with the impact of introduced species on natural systems.

His books include *Animal Ecology and Evolution* 1930 and *The Pattern of Animal Communities* 1966.

Ely Richard Theodore 1854–1943. US economist and an early advocate of government economic intervention, central planning, and the organization of the labour force. He was appointed professor of political economy at Johns Hopkins University 1881 and in 1885 founded the American Economic Association. In 1892 he became chair of the department of economics at the University of Wisconsin before joined the faculty of Northwestern University 1925.

Born in Ripley, New York, USA, Ely was educated at Columbia University and received his PhD from the University of Heidelberg 1879. He retired from teaching 1933.

Elysium in Greek mythology, originally another name for the Islands of the Blessed, to which favoured heroes were sent by the gods to enjoy a life after death. Later a region in ◊Hades.

emancipation being liberated (originally applied to slaves); in contemporary use, being set free from servitude or subjection of any kind. The changing role of women in social, economic, and particularly in political terms in the 19th and 20th centuries is sometimes referred to as the 'emancipation of women' (see ◊women's movement).

In the UK, the 1829 Catholic Emancipation Act freed Roman Catholics from the civil disabilities imposed on them by English law. In 1861 the emancipation of Russian serfs was proclaimed. In 1862 President Abraham Lincoln issued an edict freeing all slaves, known as the Emancipation Proclamation; the Thirteenth Amendment of the Constitution declared the abolition of slavery throughout the USA.

Emancipation Proclamation in US history, President Lincoln's Civil War announcement, 22 Sept 1862, stating that from the beginning of 1863 all black slaves in states still engaged in rebellion against the federal government would be emancipated. Slaves in border states still remaining loyal to the Union were excluded.

embargo the legal prohibition by a government of trade with another country, forbidding foreign ships to leave or enter its ports.

Trade embargoes may be imposed on a country seen to be violating international laws.

The US Embargo Act 1807 was passed to prevent France and the UK taking measures to stop US ships carrying war weapons to European belligerents. It proved to be a counterproductive move, as did an embargo by Middle Eastern oil producers on oil shipments to W Europe in 1974.

The shot heard round the world.

Ralph Waldo Emerson
'Concord Hymn'

Emerson Ralph Waldo 1803–1882. US philosopher, essayist, and poet. He settled in Concord, Massachusetts, which he made a centre of ◊transcendentalism, and wrote *Nature* 1836, which states the movement's main principles emphasizing the value of self-reliance and the Godlike nature of human souls. His two volumes of *Essays* (1841, 1844) made his reputation: 'Self-Reliance' and 'Compensation' are among the best known.

Born in Boston, Massachusetts, and educated at Harvard, Emerson became a Unitarian minister. In 1832 he resigned and travelled to Europe, meeting the British writers Carlyle, Coleridge, and Wordsworth. On his return to Massachusetts in 1833 he settled in Concord. He made a second visit to England 1847 and incorporated his impressions in *English Traits* 1856. Much of his verse was published in the literary magazine *The Dial*. His poems include 'The Rhodora', 'Threnody', and 'Brahma'. His later works include *Representative Men* 1850 and *The Conduct of Life* 1870.

Emmert's law the perceived size of an afterimage is proportional to the distance of the surface on which it is projected. It is named after Emil Emmert (1844–1911) who observed it 1881. Emmert's law has been found to apply also to eidetic imagery (mental imagery that remains for some time after the stimulus has been removed).

In normal vision, size and distance are related: the further away an object is the smaller is its image on the retina, but it is perceived as distant rather than smaller due to a compensatory mechanism known as size constancy scaling. In the case of an afterimage, the size of the retinal image remains the same, but the same compensatory mechanism functions, making the afterimage appear larger when seen over a greater distance.

Bibl. Gregory, R L *Eye and Brain: the Psychology of Seeing* (London, 1966) ch. 9

emotion in philosophy, mental state of feeling, rather than thinking or knowing. In Western culture, ◊Romanticism has encouraged the view that reason and emotion are engaged in a perpetual battle, whereas ◊Classicism treats them as complementary aspects of being human and recommends rational reflection on which emotion is the most appropriate to feel in any particular circumstance.

Scottish 18th-century philosopher David Hume argues that reason is 'the slave of the passions', or emotions. US philosopher William James argued in the 1890s that emotional feeling arises from the behaviour associated with the emotion. We feel sorry because we cry, and angry because we strike, not vice versa.

Thanks to the human heart by which we live, / Thanks to its tenderness, its joys, and fears, / To me the meanest flower that blows can give / Thoughts that do often lie too deep for tears.

emotion
William Wordsworth, 1770–1850, English
Romantic poet.
Ode. Intimations of Immortality

emotion in psychology, a powerful feeling; a complex state of body and mind involving, in its bodily aspect, changes in the viscera and in facial expression and posture, and in its mental aspect, heightened perception, excitement and, sometimes, disturbance of thought and judgement. The urge to action is felt and impulsive behaviour may result.

As a subject area of both biology and psychology, emotion has aroused much controversy. Charles ◊Darwin, in his book *The Expression of Emotions in Man and Animals* 1872, argued that there are specific, fundamental emotions which are first aroused and then expressed in overt behaviour. William ◊James believed the opposite, namely that emotions actually are the feeling, or sensing, of the bodily changes as they occur when some exciting event or fact is perceived; the Danish physiologist, Carl Georg Lange (1834–1900), came independently to much the same conclusion. Their theoretical position, which became known as the ◊James–Lange theory, received considerable criticism at the start of the 20th century, notably from Walter Bradford Cannon (1871–1945) and P Bard who found physiological evidence for specific activity in

She … joined the vast armies of the benighted, who follow neither the heart nor the brain, and march to their destiny by catchwords.

emotion
E(dward) M(organ) Forster, 1879–1970,
English novelist.
A Room with a View

the nervous system, corresponding to emotional experience, that preceded the changes in the viscera and bodily behaviour. More recently it has been proposed, by Stanley Schachter and others, that the visceral changes are more or less the same for all emotions but that the quality of the feelings described – fear, joy, elation, and so on – depend on the individual's cognitive and perceptual evaluation of whatever is new, disruptive, or inconsistent in the environment.

Bibl. Frijda, Nico H *The Emotions* (1986)

emotivism a philosophical position in the theory of ethics. Emotivists deny that moral judgements can be true or false, maintaining that they merely express an attitude or an emotional response.

The concept came to prominence during the 1930s, largely under the influence of *Language, Truth and Logic* 1936 by A J ◊Ayer.

empathy the ability to project one's personality into (and so fully understand) the matter being contemplated.

Empedocles c. 490–430 BC. Greek philosopher and scientist. He lived at Acragas (Agrigentum) in Sicily, and proposed that the universe is composed of four elements – fire, air, earth, and water – which through the action of love and discord are eternally constructed, destroyed, and constructed anew. According to tradition, he committed suicide by throwing himself into the crater of Mount Etna.

empiricism in philosophy, the belief that all knowledge is ultimately derived from sense experience. It is suspicious of metaphysical schemes based on ◊a priori propositions, which are claimed to be true irrespective of experience. It is frequently contrasted with ◊rationalism.

Empiricism developed in the 17th and early 18th centuries through the work of John ◊Locke, George ◊Berkeley, and David ◊Hume, traditionally known as the British empiricist school.

emptiness in Buddhism, a central concept which may be interpreted in a variety of ways. Emptiness needs to be found for a proper state of meditation to be achieved: when a person is empty of all emotion, thought, and feelings, they are receptive to the ultimate emptiness or void of all phenomena. This insight, that nothing actually has reality of itself, lies at the heart of Buddhist philosophy in the Mahāyāna tradition. The Pali word for this Buddhist teaching is *sunnata*. It has a variety of meanings within the different traditions of Buddhism.

Empyrean in medieval and Renaissance thought, the name given to the outermost celestial sphere of pure fire, the highest heaven, and the home of God and the angels.

encyclical letter addressed by the pope to Roman Catholic bishops for the benefit of the people. The first was issued by Benedict XIV in 1740, but encyclicals became common only in the 19th century. They may be doctrinal (condemning errors), exhortative (recommending devotional activities), or commemorative.

Recent encyclicals include *Pacem in terris* (Pope John XXIII, 1963), *Sacerdotalis celibatus* (on the celibacy of the clergy, Pope Paul VI, 1967), and *Humanae vitae* (Pope Paul VI, 1967, on methods of contraception). Encyclicals are written in Latin and translated.

encyclopedia or *encyclopaedia* work of reference covering either all fields of knowledge or one specific subject. Although most encyclopedias are alphabetical, with cross-references, some are organized thematically with indexes, to keep related subjects together.

The earliest extant encyclopedia is the *Historia Naturalis/Natural History* AD 23–79 of ◊Pliny the Elder. The first alphabetical encyclopedia in English was the *Lexicon Technicum/ Technical Lexicon* 1704, compiled by John Harris. In 1728 Ephraim Chambers published his *Cyclopaedia*, which coordinated scattered articles by a system of cross-references and was translated into French 1743–45. This translation formed the basis of the *Encyclopédie* edited by Diderot and d'Alembert, published 1751–72. By this time the system of engaging a body of expert compilers and editors was established, and in 1768–71 the *Encyclopaedia Britannica* first appeared.

Other major encyclopedias include the Chinese encyclopedia printed 1726, the German *Conversations-Lexikon/Conversation Lexicon* of Brockhaus, and the French *Grand Dictionnaire Universel du XIXème Siècle/Great Universal Dictionary of the 19th Century* of Pierre Larousse 1866–76.

Encyclopédistes a group of 18th-century French intellectuals, who contributed to the *Encyclopédie* 1751–72. ◊Diderot and d'◊Alembert were the co-editors of the *Encyclopédie* until d'Alembert withdrew in 1757. The group of contributors also included ◊Voltaire, ◊Rousseau, and Holbach.

Endymion in Greek mythology, a beautiful young man loved by Selene, the Moon goddess. He was granted eternal sleep in order to remain forever young. Keats's poem *Endymion* 1818 is an allegory of searching for perfection.

Engels Friedrich 1820–1895. German social and political philosopher, a friend of, and collaborator with, Karl ◊Marx on *The Communist Manifesto* 1848 and other key works. His later interpretations of Marxism, and his own philosophical and historical studies such as *Origins of the Family, Private Property, and the State* 1884 (which linked patriarchy with the development of private property), developed such concepts as historical materialism. His use of positivism and Darwinian ideas gave Marxism a scientific and deterministic flavour which was to influence Soviet thinking.

In 1842 Engels's father sent him to work in the cotton factory owned by his family in Manchester, England, where he became involved with ◊Chartism. In 1844 his lifelong friendship with Karl Marx began, and together they worked out the materialist interpretation of history and in 1847–48 wrote the *Communist Manifesto*. Returning to Germany during the 1848–49 revolution, Engels worked with Marx on the *Neue Rheinische Zeitung/New Rhineland Newspaper* and fought on the barricades in Baden. After the defeat of the revolution he returned to Manchester, and for the rest of his life largely supported the Marx family.

Engels's first book was *The Condition of the Working Classes in England* 1845. He summed up the lessons of 1848 in *The Peasants' War in Germany* 1850 and *Revolution and Counter-Revolution in Germany* 1851. After Marx's death Engels was largely responsible for the wider dissemination of his ideas; he edited the second and third volumes of Marx's *Das Kapital* 1885 and 1894. Although Engels himself regarded his ideas as identical with those of Marx, discrepancies between their works are the basis of many Marxist debates.

Enkidu in the *Epic of* ◊*Gilgamesh*, the wild man created by the goddess Aruru who becomes a companion to Gilgamesh. After Gilgamesh has provoked the anger of the goddess Ishtar, Enkidu sickens and dies.

enlightenment in Buddhism, the term used to translate the Sanskrit *bodhi*, awakening: perceiving the reality of the world, or the unreality of the self, and becoming liberated from suffering (Sanskrit *duhkha*). It is the gateway to nirvana.

Enlightenment European intellectual movement that reached its high point in the 18th century. Enlightenment thinkers were believers in social progress and in the liberating possibilities of rational and scientific knowledge. They were often critical of existing society and were hostile to religion, which they saw as keeping the human mind chained down by superstition.

The American and French revolutions were justified by Enlightenment principles of human natural rights. Leading representatives of the Enlightenment were ◊Voltaire, ◊Lessing, and ◊Diderot.

Enlil in Sumerian mythology, the god of storms and the air, and head of the Heavenly court. His greatest weapon was the flood, and according to a stone pillar in Ur, the town's destruction in a storm was his work.

enosis movement, developed from 1930, for the union of Cyprus with Greece. The campaign (led by EOKA and supported by Archbishop Makarios) intensified from the 1950s. In 1960 independence from Britain, without union, was granted, and increased demands for union led to its proclamation 1974. As a result, Turkey invaded Cyprus, ostensibly to protect the Turkish community, and the island was effectively partitioned.

entropy in ◊thermodynamics, a parameter representing the state of disorder of a system at the atomic, ionic, or molecular level; the greater the disorder, the higher the entropy. Thus the fast-moving disordered molecules of water vapour have higher entropy than those of more ordered liquid water, which in turn have more entropy than the molecules in solid crystalline ice.

In a closed system undergoing change, entropy is a measure of the amount of energy unavailable for useful work. At absolute zero (−273°C/−459.67°F/0K), when all molecular motion ceases and order is assumed to be complete, entropy is zero.

environment in ecology, the sum of conditions affecting a particular organism, including physical surroundings, climate, and influences of other living organisms.

In common usage, 'the environment' often means the total global environment, without reference to any particular organism. In genetics, it is the external influences that affect an organism's development, and thus its phenotype.

Nothing was made by God for man to spoil or destroy.

environment
John Locke, 1632–1704, English philosopher.
The Second Treatise on Government IV. 31

environmental archaeology subfield of archaeology aimed at identifying processes, factors, and conditions of past biological and physical environmental systems and how they relate to cultural systems. It is a field where archaeologists and natural scientists combine to reconstruct the human uses of plants and animals and how societies adapted to changing environmental conditions.

enzyme biological catalyst produced in cells, and capable of speeding up the chemical reactions necessary for life by converting one molecule (substrate) into another. Enzymes are not themselves destroyed by this process. They are large, complex proteins, and are highly specific, each chemical reaction requiring its own particular enzyme. The enzyme fits into a 'slot' (active site) in the substrate molecule, forming an enzyme–substrate complex that lasts until the substrate is altered or split, after which the enzyme can fall away. The substrate may therefore be compared to a lock, and the enzyme to the key required to open it.

The activity and efficiency of enzymes are influenced by various factors, including temperature and pH conditions. Temperatures above 60°C/140°F damage (denature) the intricate structure of enzymes, causing reactions to cease. Each enzyme operates best within a specific pH range, and is denatured by excessive acidity or alkalinity.

Digestive enzymes include amylases (which digest starch), lipases (which digest fats), and proteases (which digest protein). Other enzymes play a part in the conversion of food energy into ATP; the manufacture of all the molecular components of the body; the replication of ◊DNA when a cell divides; the production of hormones; and the control of movement of substances into and out of cells.

Enzymes have many medical and industrial uses, from washing powders to drug production, and as research tools in molecular biology. They can be extracted from bacteria and moulds, and ◊genetic engineering now makes

The Enlightenment

The image of light has always been associated with wisdom and truth; darkness is traditionally linked with evil. The light (or white) versus dark (or black) dichotomy has innumerable cultural resonances. Until the seventeenth century, 'illumination' was mainly connected with mystical transports. From then, light and enlightenment have assumed secular connotations. Eighteenth-century critics liked to think of themselves as bringing light to a world long darkened by superstition, despotism, and ecclesiastical censorship. As a term, 'the Enlightenment' is now mainly used to characterize such currents of thought.

What is Enlightenment?
Was ist Aufklärung? (What is Enlightenment?) asked the German philosopher, Immanuel Kant (1724–1804), in 1784; and ever since, historians have tried to determine what the Enlightenment really was. In reality, the stream of ideas so denoted was diverse and varied. It spanned more than a century, from its early heroes like John Locke (1632–1704), Pierre Bayle (1647–1706) and Isaac Newton (1642–1727), through to such later thinkers as Marie Jean Condorcet (1743–1794), Erasmus Darwin (1731–1802), Johann Herder (1744–1803), Thomas Paine (1737–1809), and Thomas Jefferson (1743–1826), who lived to see the French Revolution, which was one of the bitter fruits of the Enlightenment. The movement grew ever more radical, culminating in democratic political programmes like that enunciated in Paine's *Rights of Man*.

A pan-European phenomenon
The Enlightenment was also geographically diverse. It is popularly seen as a French movement, involving Charles Louis Montesquieu (1689–1755), Voltaire (1694–1778), Denis Diderot (1713–1784), Jean le Rond d'Alembert (1717–1783), Claude Helvtius (1715–1771), Etienne Condillac (1715–1780), and the French-speaking Genevan Jean-Jacques Rousseau (1712–1778). But all Europe enjoyed ferments of ideas, albeit rather distinctive in nature. The French Enlightenment was preoccupied with the critique of despotism, feudalism, and the Roman Catholic Church. In Britain, intellectuals set greater store upon discovering the key to the operation of a free, constitutionally governed capitalist society. In most German states, in Spain and Portugal, and in Scandinavia, thinkers were concerned to educate absolutist rulers, to improve administration, modernize obsolete economies, and foster expertise. The Enlightenment was less a political party than a climate of criticism, a new conception of the social role of the intelligentsia.

The principles of Enlightenment
Certain principles were held in common. All men of the Enlightenment – women played second fiddle – believed in personal autonomy. All had to take responsibility for their own thinking and destiny. Truth could not be blindly accepted on authority. The progress of knowledge was the key to improvement, for, in the maxim of Francis Bacon (1561–1626), 'knowledge is power'. Experience was the key to valid knowledge, censorship was inadmissible, and intellectual freedom imperative. Hence, *philosophes* applauded the Scientific Revolution as the peak of intellectual emancipation. The science of Galileo (1564–1642), Newton, and others, emphasizing observation and experiment, provided models for intellectual progress.

Science – the keystone
Science revealed the uniformity of nature, governed by the laws of physics. The Enlightenment gloried in this vision of nature as harmonious, orderly, intelligible. It also challenged Christian pessimism about original sin. A few *philosophes* were atheists; for example, the Baron d'Holbach (1723–1789) and perhaps Diderot and the later Voltaire. Many, as for instance Locke in his *The Reasonableness of Christianity* (1695), wanted a rational faith, stripped of miracles and absurdities. Others, the Deists, rejected the Christian God, but affirmed a Divine Mechanic, who would underwrite universal order and justice. All applauded toleration and execrated bigotry.

The Enlightenment believed people could improve themselves by improving nature, offering a programme of progress through science, technology, and industry. Applied knowledge such as economics, jurisprudence, and public administration was crucial to Enlightenment strategies. For the *philosophes* wished to create new social sciences based on the natural sciences. This involved viewing people scientifically, as a product of their environment, endowed with uniform emotions and intellectual processes. If people were indeed machine-like, amenable to cause–effect analysis, they could (it followed) be reprogrammed to improve their social behaviour and achieve happiness. Education was important to *philosophes*. Jeremy Bentham (1748–1832), with his utilitarian philosophy ('the greatest happiness of the greatest number'), believed populations could be guided by government and the law to maximize pleasure.

Bringing back the glorious past
The Enlightenment looked back to antiquity for models of moral conduct. Politically, the *philosophes* were divided. Some, like Rousseau, admired small city states where all could be citizens. Pragmatists, like Voltaire, assumed the future lay with enlightened absolutists. Americans, like Benjamin Franklin (1706–1790), were fortunate enough to have a New World in which to construct a new republican order, based upon the sanctity of life, property, and the pursuit of happiness. The translation of Enlightenment principles into reality through the 'liberty, equality and fraternity' of the French Revolution proved equivocal. Nevertheless, the Enlightenment had profound consequences. The rise of the intelligentsia, belief in basic freedoms, and the conviction that people must be free to forge their own destinies – these are the legacies of the Enlightenment.

Roy Porter

it possible to tailor an enzyme for a specific purpose.

Eötvös Roland von, Baron 1848–1919. Hungarian physicist known for his work on gravity. His discovery that gravitational mass and inertial mass are the same greatly influenced the work of Einstein. He also developed a double-armed torsion balance, a device for measuring variations in gravity.

epic narrative poem or cycle of poems dealing with some great deed – often the founding of a nation or the forging of national unity – and often using religious or cosmological themes. The two major epic poems in the Western tradition are *The Iliad* and *The Odyssey*, attributed to Homer, and which were probably intended to be chanted in sections at feasts.

Greek and later criticism, which considered the Homeric epic the highest form of poetry, produced the genre of *secondary epic* – such as the *Aeneid* of Virgil, Tasso's *Jerusalem Delivered*, and Milton's *Paradise Lost* – which attempted to emulate Homer, often for a patron or a political cause. The term is also applied to narrative poems of other traditions: the Anglo-Saxon *Beowulf* and the Finnish *Kalevala*; in India the *Rāmāyana* and *Mahābhārata*; and the Babylonian *Epic of Gilgamesh*. All of these evolved in different societies to suit similar social needs and used similar literary techniques.

Epictetus c. AD 55–135. Greek Stoic philosopher who encouraged people to refrain from self-interest and to promote the common good of humanity. He believed that people were in the hands of an all-wise providence and that they should endeavour to do their duty in the position to which they were called.

Born at Hierapolis in Phrygia, he lived for many years in Rome as a slave but eventually secured his freedom. He was banished by the emperor Domitian from Rome in AD 89.

Epicureanism System of moral philosophy named after the Greek philosopher ◊Epicurus. He argued that pleasure is the basis of the ethical life, and that the most satisfying form of pleasure is achieved by avoiding pain, mental or physical. This is done by limiting desire as far as possible, and by choosing pleasures of the mind over those of the body.

Epicurus 341–270 BC. Greek philosopher, founder of Epicureanism, who taught at Athens from 306 BC. His view that all things are made up of atoms was influential in both Greek and Roman thinking (◊Lucretius). This atomism provided him with his theory of

knowledge, which stresses the role of sense perception, and his ethics, in which the most desired condition is a serene detachment based on the avoidance of anxiety and physical pain.

Epiphany festival of the Christian church, held 6 Jan, celebrating the coming of the Magi (the three Wise Men) to Bethlehem with gifts for the infant Jesus, and symbolizing the manifestation of Jesus to the world. It is the 12th day after Christmas, and marks the end of the Christmas festivities.

In many countries the night before Epiphany, called *Twelfth Night*, is marked by the giving of gifts. In the Orthodox church, the festival celebrated on this day is known as the *theophany* and commemorates the baptism of Jesus. Some Orthodox churches use an older calendar and celebrate Epiphany on 18 Jan.

episcopacy in the Christian church, a system of government in which administrative and spiritual power over a district (diocese) is held by a bishop.

The Roman Catholic, Orthodox, Anglican, and Episcopal churches (USA) are episcopalian; episcopacy also exists in some branches of the Lutheran Church, for example, in Scandinavia.

Episcopalianism US term for the Anglican Communion.

epistemology branch of philosophy that examines the nature of knowledge and attempts to determine the limits of human understanding. Central issues include how knowledge is derived and how it is to be validated and tested.

equality in political theory, the condition of being equal or the same in given respects, as advocated in liberalism, socialism, and feminism. Moral and political philosophers often discuss the complex relationships between the concepts of justice, fairness, freedom, rights, and equality.

The concept of equality is highly abstract, and it requires a great deal of background before it can be applied rigorously. Absolute equality is rarely advocated. Instead, debates about equality concern to what extent individuals or groups ought to have equality of opportunity, of respect, of rights, of treatment, of equality before the law, and so on.

equal opportunities the right to be employed or considered for employment without discrimination on the grounds of race, gender, or physical or mental handicap.

In 1946 a Royal Commission in the UK favoured equal pay for women in Britain. The Equal Pay Act of 1970 guaranteed (in theory) equal pay for equal work. The Sex Discrimination Act 1975 made it illegal to discriminate between men and women in a number of areas (though there were some exceptions). In 1975 the Equal Opportunities Commission was founded, with the power to oversee the operation of both the Equal Pay Act and the Sex Discrimination Act. The Commission was able to examine allegations of discrimination and to take legal action if necessary.

equation in mathematics, expression that represents the equality of two expressions involving constants and/or variables, and thus usually includes an equals sign (=). For example, the equation $A = r^2$ equates the area A of a circle of radius r to the product πr^2. The algebraic equation $y = mx + c$ is the general one in coordinate geometry for a straight line.

If a mathematical equation is true for all variables in a given domain, it is sometimes called an identity and denoted by ≡. Thus $(x + y)^2 \equiv x^2 + 2xy + y^2$ for all $x, y \in R$.

An *indeterminate equation* is an equation for which there is an infinite set of solutions – for example, $2x = y$. A *diophantine equation* is an indeterminate equation in which the solution and terms must be whole numbers (after Diophantus of Alexandria, c. AD 250).

equity system of law supplementing the ordinary rules of law where the application of these would operate harshly in a particular case; sometimes it is regarded as an attempt to achieve 'natural justice'. So understood, equity appears as an element in most legal systems, and in a number of legal codes judges are instructed to apply both the rules of strict law and the principles of equity in reaching their decisions.

In England equity originated in decisions of the Court of Chancery, on matters that were referred to it because there was no adequate remedy available in the Common Law courts. Gradually it developed into a distinct system of law, and until the 19th century, the two systems of common law and equity existed side by side, and were applied in separate law courts. The Judicature Acts 1873–75 established a single High Court of Justice, in which judges could apply both common law and equity to all their decisions. Equitable principles still exist side by side with principles of common law in many branches of the law.

Erasmus Desiderius c. 1466–1536. Dutch scholar and leading humanist of the Renais-

sance era, who taught and studied all over Europe and was a prolific writer. His pioneer translation of the Greek New Testament 1516 exposed the Vulgate as a second-hand document. Although opposed to dogmatism and abuse of church power, he remained impartial during Martin ◊Luther's conflict with the pope.

Erasmus was born in Rotterdam, and as a youth he was a monk in an Augustinian monastery near Gouda. After becoming a priest, he went to study in Paris 1495. He paid the first of a number of visits to England 1499, where he met the physician Thomas Linacre, the politician Thomas More, and the Bible interpreter John Colet, and for a time was professor of divinity and Greek at Cambridge University. He edited the writings of St Jerome, and published *Colloquia* (dialogues on contemporary subjects) 1519. In 1521 he went to Basel, Switzerland, where he edited the writings of the early Christian leaders.

Erasmus Prize prize awarded annually since 1958 to outstanding contributors to international understanding, usually in social or cultural fields. Previous winners include Martin ◊Buber, Herbert ◊Read, Robert ◊Schuman, and Jan ◊Tinbergen.

Erastianism belief that the church should be subordinated to the state. The name is derived from Thomas Erastus (1534–83), a German-Swiss theologian and opponent of Calvinism, who maintained in his writings that the church should not have the power of excluding people as a punishment for sin.

Eratosthenes c. 276–194 BC. Greek geographer and mathematician whose map of the ancient world was the first to contain lines of latitude and longitude, and who calculated the Earth's circumference with an error of about 10%. His mathematical achievements include a method for duplicating the cube, and for finding prime numbers (Eratosthenes' sieve).

Erigena Johannes Scotus 815–877. Medieval philosopher. He was probably Irish and, according to tradition, travelled in Greece and Italy. The French king Charles II (the Bald) invited him to France (before 847), where he became head of the court school. He is said to have visited Oxford, to have taught at Malmesbury, and to have been stabbed to death by his pupils. In his philosophy, he defied church orthodoxy in his writings on cosmology and predestination, and tried to combine Christianity with ◊neo-Platonism.

Erl-King in Germanic folklore, the king of the elves. He inhabited the Black Forest and lured children to their deaths. The Romantic writer J W Goethe's poem 'Erlkönig' was set to music by Franz Schubert 1816.

ERM abbreviation for ◊*Exchange Rate Mechanism*.

Eros in Greek mythology, boy-god of love, traditionally armed with bow and arrows. He was the son of ◊Aphrodite, and fell in love with ◊Psyche. He is identified with the Roman Cupid.

Esaki Leo 1925– . Japanese physicist who in 1957 noticed that electrons could sometimes 'tunnel' through the barrier formed at the junctions of certain semiconductors. The effect is now widely used in the electronics industry. For this early discovery Esaki shared the 1973 Nobel Prize for Physics with British physicist Brian Josephson and Norwegian-born US physicist Ivar Giaever (1929–).

Esau in the Old Testament, the son of Isaac and Rebekah, and the hirsute elder twin brother of Jacob. Jacob tricked the blind Isaac into giving him the blessing intended for Esau by putting on goatskins for Isaac to feel. Earlier Esau had sold his birthright to Jacob for a 'mess of red pottage'. Esau was the ancestor of the Edomites.

eschatology doctrines of the end of time. *Christian eschatology* concerns the end of this Earth and of time; the ◊Antichrist; the return of Jesus Christ to overthrow the Antichrist; and the culmination of history with the destruction of this world. In more general terms, it refers to the moral significance of the belief that time and history are working towards an ultimate end.

Islamic eschatology depicts the Earth devastated by fire and flood in the shape of Gog and Magog, followed by the reign of the ◊Mahdi. After this the Antichrist will reign, only to be overthrown by Jesus, who will bring everyone to judgement by God.

esotericism belief in an interior path where an individual gains insight and salvation from special knowledge (see ◊Gnosticism). The journey on this path requires an active imagination and in some cases the perceived presence of intermediary figures such as angels.

Esotericism was an element of the ◊mystery religions of the ancient world, and was introduced to Christianity in the early Middle Ages. There has been a revival of interest in esotericism in the second half of the 20th century with the development of the modern spiritual movements of ◊anthroposophy and ◊theosophy, which combine elements of Christianity, Buddhism, and Hinduism.

essence all that makes a thing what it is and is indispensable to the thing. Philosophers have often distinguished nominal essences from real essences. A *nominal essence* is a group of terms used to define a ◊concept: thus, the nominal essence of the concept of a horse could be 'anything that neighs and has a mane and four legs'. A *real essence* is either a group of ◊universals objectively given in nature (this is also called a ◊form) or (as in the work of John Locke) the underlying structure of an object; for example, its atomic structure.

Essene member of an ancient Jewish religious group located in the area near the Dead Sea c. 200 BC–AD 200, whose members lived a life of denial and asceticism, as they believed that the day of judgement was imminent.

The ◊Dead Sea Scrolls, discovered in 1947, are believed by some scholars to be the library of the community. John the Baptist may have been a member of the Essenes.

Establishment, the a perceived elite of the professional and governing classes (judges, civil servants, politicians, and so on) who collectively symbolize authority and the status quo.

And I saw a new heaven and a new earth: for the first heaven and the first earth were passed away; and there was no more sea.

eschatology
Revelation 21:1

---

estate in European history, an order of society that enjoyed a specified share in government. In medieval theory, there were usually three estates – the *nobility*, the *clergy*, and the *commons* – with the functions of, respectively, defending society from foreign aggression and internal disorder, attending to its spiritual needs, and working to produce the base with which to support the other two orders.

When parliaments and representative assemblies developed from the 13th century, their organization reflected this theory, with separate houses for the nobility, the commons (usually burghers and gentry), and the clergy.

Esther in the Old Testament, the wife of the Persian king Ahasuerus (Xerxes I), who prevented the extermination of her people by the king's vizier Haman. Their deliverance is celebrated in the Jewish festival of Purim. Her story is told in the Old Testament Book of Esther.

ether or **aether** in the history of science, a hypothetical medium permeating all of space. The concept originated with the Greeks, and has been revived on several occasions to explain the properties and propagation of light. It was supposed that light and other electromagnetic radiation – even in outer space – needed a medium, the ether, in which to travel. The idea was abandoned with the acceptance of ◊relativity.

Ethical Culture Movement movement during the late 19th and early 20th centuries designed to further the moral or ethical factor as the real substance and fundamental part of religion.

It originated in the New York Society for Ethical Culture founded by Felix Adler in 1876. Mainly Jewish at first, it soon attracted adherents of Christian and skeptical backgrounds. It had spread to England (where the first Ethical Society was founded 1888 by Dr Stanton Colt), Germany, and other countries by the turn of the century. In 1952 the International Humanist and Ethical Union was formed, with headquarters in Utrecht, the Netherlands.

ethics or **moral philosophy** branch of philosophy concerned with the systematic study of human values. It involves the study of theories of conduct and goodness, and of the meanings of moral terms. Ethics is closely linked to other disciplines, like anthropology, ethology, political theory, psychology, and sociology.

When devoid of virtue, man is the most unscrupulous and savage of animals, and the worst in regard to sexual indulgence and gluttony.

ethics
Aristotle, 384 BC–322 BC, Greek philosopher.
Politics

In ancient India and China, sages like Buddha and Lao Zi made recommendations about how people should live, as Jesus and Muhammad did in later centuries. However, ethics as a systematic study first appears with the Greek philosopher Socrates in the 5th century BC. Plato thought that objective standards (◊form) of justice and goodness existed beyond the everyday world. In his *Nicomachean Ethics*, Aristotle argued that virtue is natural and so leads to happiness, and that moral virtues are acquired by practice, like skills. The Cyrenaics and Epicureans were hedonists who believed in the wise pursuit of pleasure. The Stoics advocated control of the passions and indifference to pleasure and pain.

In the 17th century, the Dutch philosopher Spinoza and the English Thomas Hobbes both believed that morals were deducible from prudence, but Spinoza's moral theory is set in a pantheistic metaphysics. In the 18th century, Joseph Butler argued that virtue is natural and that benevolence and self-interest tend to coincide. The Scot David Hume, who influenced Jeremy Bentham, argued that moral judgements are based on feelings about pleasant and unpleasant consequences. For the German Immanuel Kant, morality could not have a purpose outside of itself, so the good person acts only from duty, not feeling or self-interest, and in accordance with the categorical imperative (the obligation to obey absolute moral law). Utilitarianism, devised by Bentham and refined by J S Mill in the 19th century, has been immensely influential, especially in social policy.

In the 20th century, British philosopher G E Moore argued in his influential *Principia Ethica* 1903 that the concept of goodness was simple and indefinable. The French Jean-Paul Sartre's existentialist emphasis on choice and responsibility has been influential, too. Stephen Toulmin (1922–) and others applied the techniques of linguistic analysis to ethics. But, like existentialism, linguistic analysis did not say what morality was about. The English novelist and philosopher Iris Murdoch has explored the relationship between goodness and beauty, while Mary Midgley has tried to update Aristotle's view of human nature by reference to studies of animal behaviour.

Increasingly, moral philosophers analyse major ethical problems, such as war, animal rights, abortion, euthanasia, and embryo research. ◊Medical ethics has recently emerged as a specialized branch of ethics.

ethnic cleansing the forced expulsion of one ethnic group by another; in particular the Serbian 'cleansing' of Muslim areas of Bosnia during the civil war of 1992– .

To further their aim of creating a Greater Serbia, Bosnian Serb forces compelled thousands of non-Serbs, Croats, and Muslims, to leave their homes which were then resettled by Serb families from other areas of former

Yugoslavia. Wholesale slaughter and other human rights atrocities were also allegedly used to implement this policy. As the war continued, evidence emerged that all sides of the conflict were involved to a greater or lesser degree.

Similar tactics were used by the Nazis in World War II, and the Khmer Rouge in Cambodia during the 1970s.

ethnicity people's own sense of cultural identity; a social term that overlaps with such concepts as race, nation, class, and religion.

Social scientists use the term *ethnic group* to refer to groups or societies that feel a common sense of identity, often based on a traditional shared culture, language, religion, and customs. It may or may not include common territory, skin colour, or common descent. The USA, for example, is often described as a *multi-ethnic society* because many members would describe themselves as members of an ethnic group (Jewish, black, or Irish, for example) as well as their national one (American).

ethnography study of living cultures, using anthropological techniques like participant observation (where the anthropologist lives in the society being studied) and a reliance on informants. Ethnography has provided many data of use to archaeologists as analogies.

ethnology study of contemporary peoples, concentrating on their geography and culture, as distinct from their social systems. Ethnologists make a comparative analysis of data from different cultures to understand how cultures work and why they change, with a view to deriving general principles about human society.

ethnomethodology the study of social order and routines used by people in their daily lives, to explain how everyday reality is created and perceived. Ethnomethodologists tend to use small-scale studies and experiments to examine the details of social life and structure (such as conversations) that people normally take for granted, rather than construct large-scale theories about society.

ethology comparative study of animal behaviour in its natural setting. Ethology is concerned with the causal mechanisms (both the stimuli that elicit behaviour and the physiological mechanisms controlling it), as well as the development of behaviour, its function, and its evolutionary history.

Ethology was pioneered during the 1930s by the Austrians Konrad Lorenz and Karl von Frisch who, with the Dutch zoologist Nikolaas Tinbergen, received the Nobel prize in 1973. Ethologists believe that the significance of an animal's behaviour can be understood only in its natural context, and emphasize the importance of field studies and an evolutionary perspective. A recent development within ethology is ◊sociobiology, the study of the evolutionary function of ◊social behaviour.

etymology study of the origin and history of words within and across languages. It has two major aspects: the study of the ◊phonetic and written forms of words, and of the ◊semantics or meanings of those words.

Etymological research has been particularly successful in tracing the development of words and word elements within the Indo-European language family. Since languages are always changing and usage differs among cultures, it is important to trace words to their original sources. Standard dictionaries of a language such as English typically contain etymological information within square brackets at the end of each entry.

Eucharist chief Christian sacrament, in which bread is eaten and wine drunk in memory of the death of Jesus. Other names for it are the *Lord's Supper, Holy Communion*, and (among Roman Catholics, who believe that the bread and wine are transubstantiated, that is, converted to the body and blood of Christ) the *Mass*. The doctrine of transubstantiation was rejected by Protestant churches during the Reformation.

The word comes from the Greek for 'thanksgiving', and refers to the statement in the Gospel narrative that Jesus gave thanks over the bread and the cup.

In Britain, members of the Church of England are required to participate in the Eucharist at least three times a year, with Easter as one. The service is not part of the worship of Quakers or the Salvation Army.

Euclid c. 330–c. 260 BC. Greek mathematician, who lived in Alexandria and wrote the *Stoicheia/Elements* in 13 books, of which nine deal with plane and solid geometry and four with number theory. His great achievement lay in the systematic arrangement of previous discoveries, based on axioms, definitions, and theorems.

Euclid's geometry texts remained in common usage for over 2,000 years.

Eudoxus of Cnidus c. 390–c. 340 BC. Greek mathematician and astronomer. He devised the first system to account for the motions of celestial bodies, believing them to be carried around the Earth on sets of spheres. Probably Eudoxus regarded these spheres as a mathematical device for ease of computation rather than as physically real, but the idea of celestial spheres was taken up by ◊Aristotle and became entrenched in astronomical thought until the time of Tycho ◊Brahe. Eudoxus also described the constellations in a work called *Phaenomena*, providing the basis of the constellation system still in use today.

eugenics study of ways in which the physical and mental quality of a people can be controlled and improved by selective breeding, and the belief that this should be done. The idea was abused by the Nazi Party in Germany during the 1930s to justify the attempted extermination of entire groups of people. Eugenics can be used to try to control the spread of inherited genetic abnormalities by counselling prospective parents.

The term was coined by Francis ◊Galton in 1883, and the concept was originally developed in the late 19th century with a view to improving human intelligence and behaviour.

In 1986 Singapore became the first democratic country to adopt an openly eugenic policy by guaranteeing pay increases to female university graduates when they give birth to a child, while offering grants towards house purchases for nongraduate married women on condition that they are sterilized after the first or second child.

Euler Leonhard 1707–1783. Swiss mathematician. He developed the theory of differential equations and the calculus of variations, and worked in astronomy and optics. He was a pupil of Johann ◊Bernoulli.

Euler became professor of physics at the University of St Petersburg in 1730. In 1741 he was invited to Berlin by Frederick the Great, where he spent 25 years before returning to Russia.

Eumenides in Greek mythology, appeasing name for the ◊Furies.

Eurocommunism policy followed by communist parties in Western Europe to seek power within the framework of national political initiative rather than by revolutionary means. In addition, Eurocommunism enabled these parties to free themselves from total reliance on the USSR.

European Community (EC) political and economic alliance consisting of the European

Coal and Steel Community (1952), ◊European Economic Community (EEC, popularly called the Common Market, 1957), and the European Atomic Energy Commission (Euratom, 1957). The original six members – Belgium, France, West Germany, Italy, Luxembourg, and the Netherlands – were joined by the UK, Denmark, and the Republic of Ireland 1973, Greece 1981, and Spain and Portugal 1986. Association agreements – providing for free trade within ten years and the possibility of full EC membership – were signed with Czechoslovakia, Hungary, and Poland 1991, subject to ratification, and with Romania 1992. The aims of the EC include the expansion of trade, reduction of competition, the abolition of restrictive trading practices, the encouragement of free movement of capital and labour within the community, and the establishment of a closer union among European people. The ◊Maastricht Treaty 1991 provides the framework for closer economic and political union but there have been delays over its ratification.

We are part of the community of Europe, and we must do our duty as such.

Europe

W E Gladstone, 1809–1898, Liberal politician and prime minister. Speech in Carnarvon, 1888

The EC has the following institutions: the *Commission* of 17 members pledged to independence of national interests, who initiate Community action (two members each from France, Germany, Italy, Spain, and the UK; and one each from Belgium, Denmark, Greece, Ireland, Luxembourg, Netherlands, and Portugal); the *Council of Ministers*, which makes decisions on the Commission's proposals; the ◊*European Parliament*, directly elected from 1979; the *Economic and Social Committee*, a consultative body; the *Committee of Permanent Representatives* (COMEPER), consisting of civil servants temporarily seconded by member states to work for the Commission; and the ◊*European Court of Justice*, to safeguard interpretation of the Rome Treaties (1957) that established the Community.

In 1992 there were more than 340 million people in the EC countries. A single market with free movement of goods and capital was established Jan 1993. A European Charter of Social Rights was approved at the Maastricht summit Dec 1991 by all members except the UK. The same meeting secured agreement on a treaty framework for European union, including political and monetary union, with a timetable for implementation, and for a new system of police and military EC cooperation. In May 1992 the bill to ratify the treaty was given a second reading. In June the Danish people voted narrowly against ratification in a national referendum, throwing the future of the treaty into doubt, but compromises agreed between all 12 nations at an Edinburgh summit Dec 1992 appeared to guarantee its survival.

Almost 60% of the EC's budget in 1990 was spent on supporting farmers (about 4 million people); of this, £4 billion a year went to dairy farmers, because the dairy quotas, which were introduced 1984, were 14% greater than EC consumption. The EC sheep policy cost over £1.7 billion in 1990, and 30 million tonnes of excess grain were exported annually at a subsidized price. Altogether it cost member countries' taxpayers almost £9 billion in 1989–90 to maintain the international competitiveness of the EC's overpriced produce under the ◊*Common Agricultural Policy*.

In 1963 and 1967 Britain's application for membership was blocked, largely by France under General de Gaulle.

European Court of Human Rights court that hears cases referred from the European Commission of Human Rights, if the commission has failed to negotiate a friendly settlement in a case where individuals' rights have been violated by a member state. The court sits in Strasbourg and comprises one judge for every state that is a party to the 1950 convention. Court rulings have forced the Republic of Ireland to drop its constitutional ban on homosexuality, and Germany to cease to exclude political left- and right-wingers from the civil service.

By 1991, 191 cases had been brought against the UK and violations of the convention found in two-thirds of these. They included illegal telephone tapping, interference with the post, unfair curbs on the press, and unjust restrictions on prisoners' access to lawyers.

European Court of Justice the court of the European Community (EC), which is responsible for interpreting Community law and ruling on breaches by member states and others

of such law. It sits in Luxembourg with judges from the member states.

European Economic Community (EEC) popularly called the *Common Market* organization established 1957 with the aim of creating a single European market for the products of member states by the abolition of tariffs and other restrictions on trade.

European Free Trade Association (EFTA) organization established 1960 consisting of Austria, Finland, Iceland, Norway, Sweden, Switzerland, and (from 1991) Liechtenstein, previously a nonvoting associate member. There are no import duties between members.

Of the original members, Britain and Denmark left (1972) to join the ◊European Community, as did Portugal (1985). In 1973 the EC signed agreements with EFTA members, setting up a free-trade area of over 300 million consumers. Trade between the two groups amounted to over half of total EFTA trade. A further pact signed Oct 1991 between the EC and EFTA provided for a European Economic Area (EEA) to be set up, allowing EFTA greater access to the EC market by ending many of the restrictions. The area would span 19 nations and 380 million people.

European Monetary System (EMS) attempt by the ◊European Community to bring financial cooperation and monetary stability to Europe. It was established 1979 in the wake of the 1974 oil crisis, which brought growing economic disruption to European economies because of floating exchange rates. Central to the EMS is the ◊*Exchange Rate Mechanism* (ERM), a voluntary system of semi-fixed exchange rates based on the European Currency Unit (ECU).

European Parliament the parliament of the ◊European Community, which meets in Strasbourg to comment on the legislative proposals of the Commission of the European Communities. Members are elected for a five-year term. The European Parliament has 518 seats, apportioned on the basis of population, of which the UK, France, Germany, and Italy have 81 each, Spain 60, the Netherlands 25, Belgium, Greece, and Portugal 24 each, Denmark 16, the Republic of Ireland 15, and Luxembourg 6.

Originally merely consultative, the European Parliament became directly elected 1979, and assumed increased powers. Though still not a true legislative body, it can dismiss

Euthanasia

Death has always been the great mystery, handed out by the gods or by fate. Humans have tried to tame death in two main ways. On the one hand, attempts have been made to prolong life or create earthly immortality. Alchemy centred on the quest for the elixir of life. The thirteenth-century monk, Roger Bacon (1214–1292), claimed that Christian medicine would surpass pagan science by conquering ageing. The Venetian architect, Luigi Cornaro (1475–1566), wrote a popular book to demonstrate how the pursuit of temperance would extend the lifespan up to 120 years. Francis Bacon and the philosophers of the Enlightenment expressed the hope that the advancement of science would produce the indefinite prolongation of life. Benjamin Franklin (1706–1790) boldly declared senescence to be not a natural process but a 'disease' to be cured, predicting that longevity might reach a thousand years or more. Marie Jean Condorcet (1743–1794), Erasmus Darwin (1731–1802), and William Godwin (1756–1836) speculated about virtually immortal life.

On the other hand, some have aimed at taming death by controlling its manner. Within traditional Christian culture, a good death (as prescribed by the *ars moriendi*, the art of dying well), was a Christian death: expiring in a state of grace, denouncing Satan, praying to the Lord, repenting one's sins, and (for Catholics) taking the sacraments. From the eighteenth century, the ideal death became more secular; and at this point the concept of euthanasia became relevant. In its original meaning, 'euthanasia' did not specifically mean the positive termination of life to end suffering (mercy killing) but referred to any means of bringing about an easy death.

Dying gracefully

Preferences were increasingly expressed in the Enlightenment, not for the dramatic Christian deathbed (with its emotional calling on God and denouncing Satan), but for a quiet and peaceful death. Dying, it was argued, should be like sleep. A serene death would demonstrate an untroubled conscience and crown a life well lived. This tallied with later Romantic notions of death's beauty, particularly among those who died young.

In the new conception of euthanasia popular in the nineteenth century, the doctor's task was to ensure a gentle death, by careful management and judicious application of opiates to dull pain and induce decease. According to the wishes of family or patient, the family doctor doubtless often became the agent of informal (and illegal) euthanasia.

Controversial issues

Thus there was a move toward an informal (and often unspoken) acceptance of euthanasia, whose existence social niceties compelled people to deny. This situation has continued, but has been rendered more complex and problematic in recent times. First, Adolf Hitler's (1899–1945) 'final solution' – of genocide for the Jews and mass extermination of the mentally ill, Romanies, and other victimized groups – twisted the concept of euthanasia for diabolical ends. Nazi genocide has created suspicion that any general legalization of euthanasia might be the thin end of the wedge, which in due course would lead to public euthanasia procedures for 'problem' or expensive people like the very old, poor, and senile.

Second, death now increasingly occurs in public institutions, notably hospitals. This may render the conduct of humane euthanasia more difficult, as physicians and nursing staff involved in such informal practices may be justifiably afraid that they thereby risk exposure and legal prosecution, particularly by Christian pressure groups, such as Life, who on transcendental grounds oppose mercy killing. Medical staff who put patients out of their dying agonies are from time to time subject to prosecutions, mainly brought by religious fundamentalists.

Dilemmas raised by medical advance

Yet the conditions of modern death have led to growing support for euthanasia, subject to proper safeguards. Thanks to high-tech life-support systems, it is now relatively easy to keep 'heart-dead' and even 'brain-dead' patients artificially alive. There is a growing feeling of repugnance at the 'cruelty' of the meaningless prolongation of the life of those who no longer have the possibility of consciousness, or who can feel only pain, incapacity, and the wish to be spared further agony. Hence, pressure has come about for the establishment of acceptable procedures for mercy killing, in circumstances in which it is clearly desired by the dying. One such device is the 'living will', a kind of assisted suicide.

Euthanasia under such circumstances can be reconciled with the professional ethics of the physician. It can be argued that, while it is the doctor's duty to save life, that duty does not run so far as to protract life by artificial means in any circumstances whatsoever. It may not be a duty of the doctor to provide resuscitation for a patient almost certain not to survive the effort.

The advance of modern medicine has thus created deep and novel dilemmas. Should a brain-dead patient be kept alive? Should a patient near death from excruciating cancer be resuscitated? Is it permissible to withhold medication from deeply malformed newborns? No categorical answers are available. Voluntary euthanasia is obviously open to abuse. But the more that medicine is able to manage life, the more it must find responsible ways of managing death.

Roy Porter

the whole Commission and reject the Community budget in its entirety. Full sittings are in Strasbourg; most committees meet in Brussels, and the seat of the secretariat is in Luxembourg. After the 1989 elections the Left held 260 seats (Socialist 180, Communist 41, Green 39); the Centre 203 (Christian Democrats 123, Liberals 44); Independents 16; Gaullists (with Fianna Fáil and SNP) 20; and the Right 55 (Conservatives 34, Right 21). Egon Klepsch (Germany) became president 1992.

Eurydice in Greek mythology, the wife of ◊Orpheus. She was a dryad, or forest nymph, and died from a snake bite. Orpheus attempted unsuccessfully to fetch her back from the realm of the dead.

eusociality form of social life found in insects such as honey bees and termites, in which the colony is made up of special castes (for example, workers, drones, and reproductives) whose membership is biologically determined. The worker castes do not usually reproduce. Only one mammal, the naked mole rat, has a social organization of this type. See also ◊social behaviour.

Euterpe in Greek mythology, one of the ◊Muses, of lyric poetry.

euthanasia in medicine, mercy killing of someone with a severe and incurable condition or illness. The Netherlands legalized voluntary euthanasia 1983, but is the only country to have done so.

Eutyches c. 384–456. Christian theologian. An archimandrite (monastic head) in Constantinople, he held that Jesus had only one nature, the human nature being subsumed in the divine (a belief which became known as ◊Monophysitism). He was exiled after his ideas were condemned as heretical by the Council of ◊Chalcedon 451.

evangelicalism the beliefs of some Protestant Christian movements that stress biblical authority, faith, and the personal commitment of the 'born again' experience.

Evangelical Movement in Britain, a 19th-century group that stressed basic Protestant beliefs and the message of the four Gospels. The movement was associated with Rev Charles Simeon (1783–1836). It aimed to raise moral enthusiasm and ethical standards among Church of England clergy.

Linked to the movement was the religious education provided by the ◊Bible Society and William ◊Wilberforce's campaign against the slave trade; it also attempted to improve the living conditions of the poor, and Evangelicals carried out missionary work in India.

evangelist person travelling to spread the Christian gospel, in particular the authors of the four Gospels in the New Testament: Matthew, Mark, Luke, and John.

Matthew, Mark, Luke, and John,
The Bed be blest that I lie on.

evangelist
anonymous

Evans-Pritchard Edward Evan 1902–1973. British anthropologist. His studies, in the 1920s and 1930s, of the Azande and the Nuer peoples of the southern Sudan were notable for attempting to understand both how a tribal society was organized and the way in which its people thought.

He was renowned for the elegance and clarity of his prose style in such works as *Witchcraft, Oracles and Magic among the Azande* 1937, and he regarded social anthropology as more of an art, like history, than a science. In 1946 he succeeded Alfred ◊Radcliffe-Brown as professor of social anthropology at the University of Oxford, a position he held until 1970.

Eve in the Old Testament, the first woman, wife of ◊Adam. She was tempted by Satan (in the form of a snake) to eat the fruit of the Tree of Knowledge of Good and Evil, and then tempted Adam to eat of the fruit as well, thus bringing about their expulsion from the Garden of Eden.

There are two versions of the creation myth in the Bible: in one of them, Eve was created simultaneously with Adam; in the other, she was created from his rib. In the Hebrew writings known as the Midrash, ◊Lilith was the first woman (and her children were the wives available to Eve's sons Cain and Abel).

Him there they found
Squat like a toad, close at the ear of Eve.

Eve
John Milton, 1608–1674, English poet.
Paradise Lost 1.799

Moral Evil and Human Nature

Evil is often divided into moral and natural evil. Moral evil originates in human action, while natural evil originates independently of human action, in, say, disease and natural disasters. Although some philosophers have argued that evil is unreal and illusory, most of us find such theories unconvincing. Assuming then that evil is not illusory, what is the nature of moral evil? Traditionally, there have been two answers to this question. One is that moral evil is nothing positive but entirely negative – an absence or privation of goodness. The other is that it is something positive and vital. In much Greek and Christian thought, moral evil is a negation, an absence or lack of moral goodness. Socrates (c. 469–339 BC) held that evil resulted from a type of ignorance or confusion: if the evil-doer understood the nature of his action, he would not do it, because wickedness hurts those who commit it. Evil actions arise from a disorder or lack in the self, from the denial of the unity of human needs and motivations. For Socrates, virtue, or moral goodness, is the health or harmony of the soul.

Original sin

In the Christian tradition, moral evil results from original sin, which St Paul seems to regard as a weakness leading to sin, rather than a sin in itself. St Augustine (354–430) and St Thomas Aquinas (c. 1226–1274) held that moral evil was a privation of the divine goodness: moral evil occurs in the absence of God, when human beings exclude the divine love from their lives. However, the modern theologian, John Hick, has argued, in his *Evil and the God of Love* (1968), the privation theory is inadequate as a description of experience.

For Hick, Goebbels or Milton's Satan represent 'a very positive and terrible moral evil'. Evil cannot be a privation, because 'hatred is not merely a lack of love'.

Absence of good

In her *Wickedness: a philosophical enquiry* (1985), the philosopher, Mary Midgley (1919–), argues that moral evil is a privation or absence, but that it is no less frightening for being so. Like darkness (which is an absence of light) and cold (which is an absence of heat), evil destroys but it cannot replace. Midgley also argues that evil arises in human beings from partial disintegration of the self – from the self-violation of our moral integrity. Morally evil actions and thoughts – such as occur when the negative emotions of hatred and resentment are indulged – are destructive of the wholeness of our nature. Having lost sight of its wholeness, a fractured self tends to concentrate on its fragments obsessively. Since obsession atrophies those faculties not involved in it, it leads to thoughtlessness and self-deception, from which spring further evil thoughts and actions.

A positive force

In contrast to the privation theory, both Manichaeism and neo-Platonism hold that evil is a positive, vital force. In Manichaeism, evil is a force in the universe at war with goodness. In the neo-Platonism of Plotinus (c. 205–270), evil has dominion over the material world. Both Manichaeism and neo-Platonism had considerable influence on early Christianity, and both doctrines still indirectly influence much Christian feeling. In Manichaeism and neo-Platonism, women were seen as doubly sinister – as tempting men to involvement in matter through sexual activity, and as drawing more souls into the material trap through childbirth. Arguably, the influence of Manichaeism and neo-Platonism on Christianity can be seen today in the opposition to the ordination of women.

Satan glorified – the Romantic view

In the nineteenth century, Romanticism revived the view that evil is something positive and even magnificent. Percy Bysshe Shelley (1792–1822) and William Blake (1757–1827) both admired and sympathized with the character of Satan in Milton's *Paradise Lost*. Arguably, their Romantic interpretation of Milton's Satan as a heroic rebel in revolt against a moral tyrant is mistaken: for the source of Satan's grandeur is not his vast pride and egotism, but rather the virtues, like courage, that he still retains. As Mary Midgley puts it, Milton's Satan's vices are parasitical on his virtues.

Back to Socrates – the disintegrating self

Of course, faced with the monstrously evil crimes committed by serial killers and mass murderers, it is very easy to assume that evil is a positive force – that is, something demonic and vital in its destructiveness. How else, we tend to think, could a nurse, Beverley Allitt, murder four sick children while they were under her care in hospital?

Socrates' answer would be that Beverley Allitt was probably capable of enormous self-deception and obsessiveness, to the point at which her moral feelings for her victims simply vanished. Moreover, perhaps medical technology and the administrative complexities of modern nursing provided scope for her to deceive herself about what she was doing. But whatever the explanation for her evil actions, Beverley Allitt does not seem to be vital, inspiring, magnificent, or heroic in any way. In the Socratic view, morally evil people, with their endless obsessions and self-deceptions, their indulged hatreds and resentments, are disintegrating selves, self-absorbed and self-destructive, banal and barren. If they are admirable in any respect, it is because they possess some vestige of virtue, some redeeming quality 'To be greatly and effectively wicked', as C S Lewis (1898–1963) observed, 'a man needs some virtue.'

P M Rowntree

evil what is bad for, or harmful to, human beings or animals. Evil is traditionally divided into moral and natural evil. *Moral evil* originates in human action, whereas *natural evil* originates independently of human action – for instance, earthquakes, or epidemics. The *problem of evil* is the difficulty of explaining the existence of evil if the world was created by a perfect and omnipotent God.

Evil can also be seen as illusory or real; and, when real, evil can be either a positive thing (the position of ◊Manichaeism) or a negative thing – the absence of goodness, just as darkness is the absence of light (the position of St ◊Augustine of Hippo).

evolution slow process of change from one form to another, as in the evolution of the universe from its formation in the ◊Big Bang to its present state, or in the evolution of life on Earth. Some Christians and Muslims deny the theory of evolution as conflicting with the belief that God created all things (see ◊creationism).

The idea of continuous evolution can be traced as far back as ◊Lucretius in the 1st century BC, but it did not gain wide acceptance until the 19th century following the work of Scottish geologist Charles ◊Lyell, French naturalist Jean Baptiste ◊Lamarck, English naturalist Charles ◊Darwin, and English biologist Thomas Henry ◊Huxley. Darwin assigned the major role in evolutionary change to ◊natural selection acting on randomly occurring variations (now known to be produced by spontaneous changes or mutations in the genetic material of organisms). Natural selection occurs because those individuals better adapted to their particular environments reproduce more effectively, thus contributing their characteristics (in the form of genes) to future generations. The current theory of evolution, called ◊Neo-Darwinism, combines Darwin's theory with Austrian biologist Gregor ◊Mendel's theories on genetics. Although neither the general concept of evolution nor the importance of natural selection is doubted by biologists, there remains dispute over other possible processes involved in evolutionary change. Besides natural selection and sexual selection, chance may play a large part in deciding which genes become characteristic of a population, a phenomenon called 'genetic drift'. It is now also clear that evolutionary change does not always occur at a constant rate, but that the process can have long periods of relative stability interspersed with periods of rapid change. This has led to new theories, such as the punctuated equilibrium model.

evolutionary stable strategy (ESS) in ◊sociobiology, an assemblage of behavioural or physical characters (collectively termed a 'strategy') of a population that is resistant to replacement by any forms bearing new traits, because the new traits will not be capable of successful reproduction.

ESS analysis is based on ◊game theory and can be applied both to genetically determined physical characters (such as horn length), and to learned behavioural responses (for example, whether to fight or retreat from an opponent). An ESS may be conditional on the context, as in the rule 'fight if the opponent is smaller, but retreat if the opponent is larger'.

ex cathedra (Latin 'from the throne') term describing a statement by the pope, taken to be indisputably true, and which must be accepted by Catholics.

Exchange Rate Mechanism (ERM) voluntary system for controlling exchange rates within the European Community's ◊European Monetary System. The member currencies of the ERM are fixed against each other within a narrow band of fluctuation based on a central European Currency Unit (ECU) rate, but floating against nonmember countries. If a currency deviates significantly from the central ECU rate, the European Monetary Cooperation Fund and the central banks concerned intervene to stabilize the currency.

The UK joined the ERM Oct 1990 but, unable to maintain the level of the pound, was forced to withdraw Sept 1992.

excommunication exclusion of an offender from the rights and privileges of the Roman Catholic Church; King John, Henry VIII, and Elizabeth I were all excommunicated.

existence in philosophy, what is common to everything that there is. Like ◊being, existence is a fundamental notion in metaphysics generally. Existence can be contrasted with being, as in some types of existentialism; or it can be contrasted with ◊essence, as in the work of Thomas Aquinas.

In medieval and rationalist metaphysics, existence is perfection. The ◊ontological argument – God is perfect; existence is a perfection; therefore, God exists necessarily – turns on whether existence can be a predicate or property, which German philosopher Immanuel Kant denied.

Life exists in the universe only because the carbon atom possesses certain exceptional properties.

existence
James Hopwood Jeans, 1877–1946, English mathematician and scientist.
Mysterious Universe

Out of Africa and the Eve Hypothesis

Most palaeoanthropologists recognize the existence of two human species during the last million years – *Homo erectus*, now extinct, and *H. sapiens*, the species which includes recent or 'modern' humans. In general, they believe that *H. erectus* was the ancestor of *H. sapiens*. How did the transition occur?

The multiregional model

There are two opposing views. The multiregional model says that *H. erectus* gave rise to *H. sapiens* across its whole range, which, about 700,000 years ago, included Africa, China, Java (Indonesia), and, probably, Europe. *H. erectus*, following an African origin about 1.7 million years ago, dispersed around the Old World, developing the regional variation that lies at the roots of modern 'racial' variation. Particular features in a given region persisted in the local descendant populations of today.

For example, Chinese *H. erectus* specimens had the same flat faces, with prominent cheekbones, as modern Oriental populations. Javanese *H. erectus* had robustly built cheekbones and faces that jutted out from the braincase, characteristics found in modern Australian Aborigines. No definite representatives of *H. erectus* have yet been discovered in Europe. Here, the fossil record does not extend back as far as those of Africa and eastern Asia, although a possible *H. erectus* jawbone more than a million years old was recently excavated in Georgia. Nevertheless, the multiregional model claims that European *H. erectus* did exist, and evolved into a primitive form of *H. sapiens*. Evolution in turn produced the Neanderthals: the ancestors of modern Europeans. Features of continuity in this European lineage include prominent noses and midfaces.

The multiregional model was first described in detail by Franz Weidenreich, a German palaeoanthropologist. It was developed further by the American Carleton Coon, who tended to regard the regional lineages as genetically separate. Most recently, the model has become associated with such researchers as Milford Wolpoff (USA) and Alan Thorne (Australia), who have re-emphasized the importance of gene flow between the regional lines. In fact, they regard the continuity in time and space between the various forms of *H. erectus* and their regional descendants to be so complete that they should be regarded as representing only one species – *H. sapiens*.

The Garden of Eden ...

The opposing view is that *H. sapiens* had a restricted origin in time and space. This is an old idea. Early in the twentieth century, workers such as Marcellin Boule (France) and Arthur Keith (UK) believed that the lineage of *H. sapiens* was very ancient, having developed in parallel with that of *H. erectus* and the Neanderthals. However, much of the fossil evidence used to support their ideas has been re-evaluated, and few workers now accept the idea of a very ancient and separate origin for modern *H. sapiens*.

Modern proponents of this approach focus on a recent and restricted origin for modern *H. sapiens*. This was dubbed the 'Garden of Eden' or 'Noah's Ark' model by the US anthropologist William Howells in 1976 because of the idea that all modern human variation had a localized origin from one centre. Howells did not specify the centre of origin, but research since 1976 points to Africa as especially important in modern human origins.

The consequent 'Out of Africa' model claims that *H. erectus* evolved into modern *H. sapiens* in Africa about 100,000–150,000 years ago. Part of the African stock of early modern humans spread from the continent into adjoining regions and eventually reached Australia, Europe, and the Americas (probably by 45,000, 40,000, and 15,000 years ago respectively). Regional ('racial') variation only developed during and after the dispersal, so that there is no continuity of regional features between *H. erectus* and present counterparts in the same regions.

Like the multiregional model, this view accepts that *H. erectus* evolved into new forms of human in inhabited regions outside Africa, but argues that these non-African lineages became extinct without evolving into modern humans. Some, such as the Neanderthals, were displaced and then replaced by the spread of modern humans into their regions.

... and an African Eve?

In 1987, research on the genetic material called mitochondrial DNA (mtDNA) in living humans led to the reconstruction of a hypothetical female ancestor for all present-day humanity. This 'Eve' was believed to have lived in Africa about 200,000 years ago. Recent re-examination of the 'Eve' research has cast doubt on this hypothesis, but further support for an 'Out of Africa' model has come from genetic studies of nuclear DNA, which also point to a relatively recent African origin for present-day *H. sapiens*.

Studies of fossil material of the last 50,000 years also seem to indicate that many 'racial' features in the human skeleton have developed only over the last 30,000 years, in line with the 'Out of Africa' model, and at odds with the million-year timespan one would expect from the multiregional model.

Chris Stringer

existence of God, arguments for in Western thought, there are four traditional lines of reasoning to support belief in the existence of God: the ◊argument from design, the ◊cosmological argument, the ◊moral argument, and the ◊ontological argument.

existentialism an anti-rationalist philosophical tendency and attitude to life concerned with the ◊being or existence of the free individual in an absurd or meaningless universe. Existentialists argue that philosophy must begin from the concrete situation of the individual in such a world, and that humans are responsible for and the sole judge of their actions as they affect others. All self-aware individuals can grasp or intuit their own existence and freedom, and individuals must not allow their choices to be constrained by anything – not even reason or morality. This freedom to choose leads to the notion of not-being or ◊nothingness, which can provoke angst or dread. Existentialism has many variants. The origin of existentialism is usually traced back to the Danish philosopher ◊Kierkegaard who emphasized the importance of pure choice in ethics and Christian belief; other existentialists include Martin ◊Heidegger in Germany and Jean-Paul ◊Sartre in France.

exobiology study of life forms that may possibly exist elsewhere in the universe, and of the effects of extraterrestrial environments on Earth organisms.

Exodus second book of the Old Testament, which relates the departure of the Israelites from slavery in Egypt, under the leadership of ◊Moses, for the Promised Land of Canaan. The journey included the miraculous parting of the Red Sea, with the Pharaoh's pursuing forces being drowned as the waters returned.

The Exodus is also recorded in the ◊Haggadah, which is read at the ◊seder (during the Jewish festival of Passover) to commemorate the deliverance. During the 40 years of wandering in the wilderness, Moses brought the ◊Ten Commandments down from Mount Sinai.

exorcism rite used in a number of religions for the expulsion of so-called evil spirits. In Christianity it is employed, for example, in the Roman Catholic and Pentecostal churches.

ex parte (Latin 'on the part of one side only') in law, term indicating that an order has been made after hearing only the party that made the application; for example, an ex parte injunction. It may also be used in law reports to indicate whom the application is on behalf of.

experiment in science, a practical test designed with the intention that its results will be relevant to a particular theory or set of theories. Although some experiments may be used merely for gathering more information about a topic that is already well understood, others may be of crucial importance in confirming a new theory or in undermining long-held beliefs.

The manner in which experiments are performed, and the relation between the design of an experiment and its value, are therefore of central importance. In general an experiment is of most value when the factors that might affect the results (variables) are carefully controlled; for this reason most experiments take place in a well-managed environment such as a laboratory or clinic.

experimental archaeology the controlled replication of ancient technologies and behaviour in order to provide hypotheses that can be tested by actual archaeological data. Experiments can range in size from the reproduction of ancient tools in order to learn about their processes of manufacture and use, and their effectiveness, to the construction of whole villages and ancient subsistence practices in long-term experiments.

experimental psychology branch of ◊psychology which applies scientific methods to the study of mental processes and behaviour.

This covers a wide range of fields of study including: *human and animal learning* in which learning theories describe how new behaviours are acquired and modified; *cognition*, the study of a number of functions, such as perception, attention, memory, and language; *physiological psychology*, which relates the study of cognition to different regions of the nervous system. ◊*Artificial intelligence* refers to the computer simulation of cognitive processes, such as language and problem-solving.

expert system computer program for giving advice (such as diagnosing an illness or interpreting the law) that incorporates knowledge derived from human expertise. It is a kind of ◊knowledge-based system containing rules that can be applied to find the solution to a problem. It is a form of ◊artificial intelligence.

explanation in science, an attempt to make clear the cause of any natural event, by reference to physical laws and to observations.

The extent to which any explanation can be said to be true is one of the chief concerns of philosophy, partly because observations may be wrongly interpreted, partly because explanations should help us predict how nature will behave. Although it may be reasonable to expect that a physical law will hold in the future, that expectation is problematic in that it relies on ◊induction, a much-criticized feature of human thought; in fact no explanation, however 'scientific', can be held to be true for all time, and thus the difference between a scientific and a common-sense explanation remains the subject of intense philosophical debate.

Expressionism style of painting, sculpture, and literature that expresses inner emotions; in particular, a movement in early 20th-century art in northern and central Europe. Expressionists tended to distort or exaggerate natural appearance in order to create a reflection of an inner world; the Norwegian painter Edvard Munch's *Skriket/The Scream* 1893 (National Gallery, Oslo) is perhaps the most celebrated example. Expressionist writers include August Strindberg and Frank Wedekind.

Other leading Expressionist artists were James Ensor, Oskar Kokoschka, and Chaïm Soutine. The *die Brücke* and *der Blaue Reiter* groups were associated with this movement, and the Expressionist trend in German art emerged even more strongly after World War I in the work of Max Beckmann and Georg Grosz.

extinction in biology, the complete disappearance of a species. In the past, extinctions are believed to have occurred because species were unable to adapt quickly enough to a naturally changing environment. Today, most extinctions are due to human activity. Some species, such as the dodo of Mauritius, the moas of New Zealand, and the passenger pigeon of North America, were exterminated by hunting. Others became extinct when their habitat was destroyed.

Mass extinctions are episodes during which whole groups of species have become extinct, the best known being that of the dinosaurs, other large reptiles, and various marine invertebrates about 65 million years ago. Another mass extinction occurred about 10,000 years ago when many giant species of mammal died out. This is known as the 'Pleistocene overkill' because their disappearance was probably hastened by the hunting activities of prehistoric humans. The greatest mass extinction occurred about 250 million years ago marking the Permian-Triassic boundary, when up to 96% of all living species became extinct. It was proposed 1982 that mass extinctions occur periodically, at approximately 26-million-year intervals.

The current mass extinction is largely due to human destruction of habitats, as in the tropical forests and coral reefs; it is far more serious and damaging than mass extinctions of the past because of the speed at which it occurs. Man-made climatic changes and pollution also make it less likely that the biosphere can recover and evolve new species to suit a changed environment. The rate of extinction is difficult to estimate, since most losses occur in the rich environment of the tropical rainforest, where the total number of existent species is not known. Conservative estimates put the rate of loss due to deforestation alone at 4,000 to 6,000 species a year. Overall, the rate could be as high as one species an hour, with the loss of one species putting those dependent on it at risk. Australia has the worst record for extinction: 18 mammals have disappeared since Europeans settled there, and 40 more are threatened.

The last mouse-eared bat (*Myotis myotis*) in the UK died 1990. This is the first mammal to have become extinct in the UK for 250 years, since the last wolf was exterminated.

extradition surrender, by one state or country to another, of a person accused of a criminal offence in the state or country to which that person is extradited.

When two nations are involved, extradition is usually governed by a treaty between the two countries concerned. A country usually will not allow extradition for political offences or an offence that it does not treat as a crime, even though it is a crime in the requesting country.

extrasensory perception (ESP) form of perception beyond and distinct from the known sensory processes. The main forms of ESP are clairvoyance (intuitive perception or vision of events and situations without using the senses); precognition (the ability to foresee events); and telepathy or thought transference (communication between people without using any known visible, tangible, or audible medium). Verification by scientific study has yet to be achieved.

extroversion or *extraversion* personality dimension described by ◊Jung and later by ◊Eysenck. The typical extrovert is sociable, impulsive, and carefree. The opposite of extroversion is ◊introversion.

Eysenck Hans Jurgen 1916– . German-born British psychologist, emeritus professor of psychology at London University and formerly director of the psychology department at the Institute of Psychiatry (Maudsley and Bethlem Royal Hospitals). Eysenck has contributed enormously to the study of ◊personality and to personality testing. He developed the Maudsley Personality Inventory to measure neuroticism, or emotional lability, and ◊extroversion; in a revised form this test is known as the Eysenck Personality Inventory, or EPI, and is widely used. He has also made important studies of emotionality and ◊conditioning, ◊behaviour therapy, and social attitudes. His contributions to the study of intelligence have at times been controversial, particularly his support of the view that ◊intelligence is largely heritable and that there *may* be a genetic basis for racial differences in ◊IQ. Much of the controversy is concerned with the methods of assessing intelligence and whether or not they are free of cultural bias. That intelligence has a physical basis and is heritable is shown, he argues, by objective physiological methods, such as measures of changes in EEG (brain wave) patterns evoked by a sudden stimulus. He is the most cited author in British psychology and his many publications include *The Dimensions of Personality* 1947, *The Scientific Study of Personality 1952, Behaviour Therapy and the Neuroses* 1960, *Crime and Personality* 1964, *The Decline and Fall of the Freudian Empire* 1985, and several books for the general reader.

Ezekiel lived c. 600 BC. In the Old Testament, a Hebrew prophet. Carried into captivity in Babylon by ◊Nebuchadnezzar 597, he preached that Jerusalem's fall was due to the sins of Israel. The book of Ezekiel begins with a description of a vision of supernatural beings.

Ezra in the Old Testament, a Hebrew scribe who was allowed by Artaxerxes, king of Persia (probably Artaxerxes I, 464–423 BC), to lead his people back to Jerusalem from Babylon 458 BC. He re-established the Mosaic law (laid down by Moses) and forbade intermarriage.

Fabian Society UK socialist organization for research, discussion, and publication, founded in London 1884. Its name is derived from the Roman commander Fabius Maximus, and refers to the evolutionary methods by which it hopes to attain socialism by a succession of gradual reforms. Early members included the playwright George Bernard Shaw and Beatrice and Sidney Webb. The society helped to found the Labour Representation Committee in 1900, which became the Labour Party in 1906.

fairy tale magical story, usually a folk tale in origin. Typically in European fairy tales, a poor, brave, and resourceful hero or heroine goes through testing adventures to eventual good fortune.

The Germanic tales collected by the ◊Grimm brothers have been retold in many variants. The form may also be adapted for more individual moral and literary purposes, as was done by Danish writer Hans Christian Andersen.

All I have written seems to me like so much straw ... compared with what has been revealed to me.

faith
St Thomas Aquinas, c.1226–1274, Italian
scholastic philosopher and theologian.
Aquinas F C Copleston

---

faith in religion, trust and belief in God's provision; the 'assurance of things hoped for, the conviction of things not seen' (St Paul). It can also mean a particular religion or set of beliefs.

The idea of faithfulness, in the sense of commitment or steadfastness, can be applied to both human beings and God. Faith includes moral or liturgical obedience, although in Christianity the Protestant reformers made a sharp distinction between faith (belief in Jesus Christ as the only way to salvation) and works (practical actions), which they taught did not bring salvation. In Hinduism, faith is defined as dependence on God in devotion. In Buddhism, faith is one of the five cardinal virtues, and is an essential part of the search for enlightenment.

Insofar as reason is hidden, let us be content with authority.

faith
Peter Abelard, 1079–1142, French
scholastic philosopher.
Medieval Thought: St Augustine to Ockham
G Leff

---

fakir originally a Muslim mendicant of some religious order, but in India a general term for an ascetic.

Falasha member of a small community of black Jews in Ethiopia. They suffered discrimination there, and, after being accorded Jewish status by Israel 1975, began a gradual process of resettlement in Israel. In the early 1980s only about 30,000 Falashim remained in Ethiopia. In 1991, 14,000 were airlifted out by Israel to escape famine in Ethiopia.

fallacy type of mistake in reasoning or inference. In Aristotelian logic (◊syllogism) and in modern formal logic, there are rules for detecting and preventing fallacies, and ensuring that an inference is valid.

Fallacies in everyday reasoning can be less easy to detect. Begging the question is a fallacy that occurs when one of the premises of an argument could not be known to be true unless the conclusion were first assumed to be true. Other fallacies include fallacies of ambiguity; of arguing against a person, rather than against what the person says; and of arguing that something is true simply because there is no evidence against it.

Fall of Man, the myth that explains the existence of evil as the result of some primeval wrongdoing by humanity. It occurs independently in many cultures. The biblical version, recorded in the Old Testament (Genesis 3), provided the inspiration for the epic poem *Paradise Lost* 1667 by John ◊Milton.

The Fall of Man (as narrated in the Bible) occurred in the Garden of Eden when the

Serpent tempted Eve to eat the fruit of the Tree of Knowledge. Disobeying God's will, she ate the fruit and gave some to Adam. This caused their expulsion from the Garden and, in Milton's words, 'brought death into the world and all our woe'.

Fallopius Gabriel. Latinized name of Gabriello Fallopio 1523–1562. Italian anatomist who discovered the Fallopian tubes, which he described as 'trumpets of the uterus', and named the vagina. As well as the reproductive system, he studied the anatomy of the brain and eyes, and gave the first accurate description of the inner ear.

Fallopius studied at Padua under Andreas ◊Vesalius, and later taught there and at Ferrara and Pisa.

falsificationism in philosophy of science, the belief that a scientific theory must be under constant scrutiny and that its merit lies only in how well it stands up to rigorous testing. It was first expounded by philosopher Karl ◊Popper in his *Logic of Scientific Discovery* 1934.

Such thinking also implies that a theory can only be held to be scientific if it makes predictions that are clearly testable. Critics of this belief acknowledge the strict logic of this process, but doubt whether the whole of scientific method can be subsumed into so narrow a programme. Philosophers and historians such as Thomas ◊Kuhn and Paul ◊Feyerabend have attempted to use the history of science to show that scientific progress has resulted from a more complicated methodology than Popper suggests.

All happy families resemble each other, but each unhappy family is unhappy in its own way.

families
Leo Nikolaievich Tolstoy, 1828–1910,
Russian novelist.
Anna Karenina

---

family in biological classification, a group of related genera. Family names are not printed in italic (unlike genus and species names), and by convention they all have the ending -idae (animals) or -aceae (plants and fungi). For example, the genera of hummingbirds are grouped in the hummingbird family, Trochilidae. Related families are grouped together in an order.

family planning spacing or preventing the birth of children. Access to family-planning

services is a significant factor in women's health as well as in limiting population growth. If all those women who wished to avoid further childbirth were able to do so, the number of births would be reduced by 27% in Africa, 33% in Asia, and 35% in Latin America; and the number of women who die during pregnancy or childbirth would be reduced by about 50%.

Children sweeten labours; but they make misfortunes more bitter.

family
Francis Bacon, 1561–1626, English
philosopher, politician and essayist.
Essays, VII 'Of Parents and Children'

The average number of pregnancies per woman is two in the industrialized countries, where 71% use family planning, as compared to six or seven pregnancies per woman in the Third World. According to a World Bank estimate, doubling the annual $2 billion spent on family planning would avert the deaths of 5.6 million infants and 250,000 mothers each year.

English philosopher Jeremy Bentham put forward the idea of birth control 1797, but it was Francis Place, a Radical, who attempted to popularize it in the 19th century, in a treatise entitled *Illustrations and Proofs of the Principle of Population* 1822. A US publication by Charles Knowlton *The Fruits of Philosophy: or The Private Companion of Young Married People* 1832 was reprinted in England in 1834. When a Bristol publisher was prosecuted for selling it 1876, two prominent freethinkers and radicals, Annie Besant and Charles Bradlaugh had the book published in London in order to provoke a test case in court. A successful outcome, and the resulting publicity, helped to spread information on birth control.

In the UK, family planning and birth control became acceptable partly through the efforts of Marie Stopes who opened a clinic in London in 1921. Other clinics subsequently opened in England were amalgamated to become the Family Planning Association 1930. Attitudes changed gradually from opposition to support: for example, in the 1930s the Family Planning Association in the UK ran clinics in hospitals and health centres; Sweden supported municipal clinics; while the USA set up some state public-health programmes incorporating birth control. In 1912 two articles by Margaret Sanger 'What every Woman should know' and 'What every girl should know' appeared in a New York socialist newspaper *The Call*, advocating birth control as one means of female emancipation. In 1916 she opened a clinic in Brooklyn, and helped to found the American Birth Control League. Internationally, in 1965, the United Nations Population Commission recommended the provision of technical assistance on birth control to member nations; while the World Health Organization instigated a programme of research.

Fanon Frantz 1925–1961. French political writer. His experiences in Algeria during the war for liberation in the 1950s led to the writing of *Les Damnés de la terre/The Wretched of the Earth* 1964, which calls for violent revolution by the peasants of the Third World.

Faraday Michael 1791–1867. English chemist and physicist. In 1821 he began experimenting with electromagnetism, and ten years later discovered the induction of electric currents and made the first dynamo. He subsequently found that a magnetic field will rotate the plane of polarization of light. Faraday also investigated electrolysis.

In 1812 he began researches into electricity, and made his first electrical cell. He became a laboratory assistant to Humphry Davy at the Royal Institution 1813, and in 1833 succeeded him as professor of chemistry. He delivered highly popular lectures at the Royal Institution, and published many treatises on scientific subjects. Deeply religious, he was a member of the Sandemanians (a small Congregationalist sect).

fasces in ancient Rome, bundles of rods carried in procession by the lictors (minor officials) in front of the chief magistrates, as a symbol of the latter's power over the lives and liberties of the people. An axe was included in the bundle. The fasces were revived in the 20th century as the symbol of ◊fascism.

fascism political ideology that denies all rights to individuals in their relations with the state; specifically, the totalitarian nationalist movement founded in Italy 1919 by Mussolini and followed by Hitler's Germany 1933.

Fascism was essentially a product of the economic and political crisis of the years after

---

The stars in their courses fought against Sisera.

fate
Bible, the sacred book of the Jewish and
Christian religions.
Judges 5:20

World War I. Units called *fasci di combattimento* (combat groups), from the Latin ◊fasces, were originally established to oppose communism. The fascist party, the *Partitio Nazionale Fascista*, controlled Italy 1922–43. Fascism protected the existing social order by forcible suppression of the working-class movement and by providing scapegoats for popular anger such as outsiders who lived within the state: Jews, foreigners, or blacks; it also prepared the citizenry for the economic and psychological mobilization of war.

The term 'fascist' is also applied to similar organizations in other countries, such as the Spanish Falange and the British Union of Fascists under Oswald Mosley. Neofascist groups still exist in many W European countries, in the USA (the ◊Ku Klux Klan and several small armed vigilante groups), France, Germany, Russia (Pamyat), and elsewhere.

fasting the practice of voluntarily going without food. It can be undertaken as a religious observance, a sign of mourning, a political protest (hunger strike), or for slimming purposes.

Fasting or abstinence from certain types of food or beverages occurs in most religious traditions. It is seen as an act of self-discipline that increases spiritual awareness by lessening dependence on the material world. In the Roman Catholic Church, fasting is seen as a penitential rite, a means to express repentance for sin. The most commonly observed Christian fasting is in Lent, from Ash Wednesday to Easter Sunday and recalls the 40 days Christ spent in the wilderness. Roman Catholics and Orthodox usually fast before taking communion and monastic communities observe regular weekly fasts. Devout Muslims go without food or water between sunrise and sunset during the month of Ramadan.

fatalism the view that the future is fixed, irrespective of our attempts to affect it. Seldom held as a philosophical doctrine, fatalism has been influential as an attitude towards life (as in ◊stoicism) and as a literary theme (for example, in the ◊Oedipus legend).

fata morgana a mirage, often seen in the Strait of Messina and traditionally attributed to the sorcery of ◊Morgan le Fay. She was believed to reside in Calabria, a region of S Italy.

fate a principle of what is ordained for human beings, which may also constrain gods in some mythologies. The related idea of ◊fatalism entails submission to fate, as this is perceived either to affect individuals or wider social groups. Fate may also be rendered as the 'destiny' of individuals or nations.

In classical mythology, the three ◊Fates wove and cut a thread of life for all mortals, and so fate is often associated with the timing and circumstances of an individual's death. In Christian thought, divine providence may play a similar role, balanced by the idea of free will. In Islam *kismet* entails submission to Allah, whereas in Hindu belief *karma*, as the sum of an individual's actions, determines an improved or worsened fate in the next life.

Fates in Greek mythology, the three female figures who determined the destiny of human lives. They were envisaged as spinners: Clotho spun the thread of life, Lachesis twisted the thread, and Atropos cut it off. They are analogous to the Roman Parcae and Norse Norns.

Father of the Church any of certain teachers and writers of the early Christian church, eminent for their learning and orthodoxy, experience, and sanctity of life. They lived between the end of the 1st and the end of the 7th century, a period divided by the Council of Nicaea 325 into the Ante-Nicene and Post-Nicene Fathers.

The Ante-Nicene Fathers include the Apostolic Fathers: Clement of Rome, Ignatius of Antioch, Polycarp of Smyrna, Barnabas, Justin Martyr, Clement of Alexandria, Origen, Tertullian, and Cyprian. Among the Post-Nicene Fathers are Cyril of Alexandria, Athanasius, John Chrysostom, Eusebius of Caesarea, Basil the Great, Ambrose of Milan, Augustine, Pope Leo I, Boethius, Jerome, Gregory of Tours, Pope Gregory the Great, and Bede.

fatwa in Islamic law, an authoritative legal opinion on a point of doctrine. In 1989 a fatwa calling for the death of English novelist Salman Rushdie was made by the Ayatollah ◊Khomeini of Iran, following publication of Rushdie's controversial and allegedly blasphemous book *The Satanic Verses*.

Faust legendary magician who sold his soul to the Devil. The historical Georg Faust appears to have been a wandering scholar and conjurer in Germany at the start of the 16th century. Goethe, Heine, Thomas Mann, and Paul Valéry all used the legend, and it inspired musical works by Schumann, Berlioz, Gounod, Boito, and Busoni.

Earlier figures such as Simon Magus (1st century AD, Middle Eastern practitioner of magic arts) contributed to the Faust legend. In 1587 the first of a series of Faust books appeared. Marlowe's tragedy, *Dr Faustus*, was acted in 1594. In the 18th century the story was a subject for pantomime in England and puppet plays in Germany, and was developed by ◊Goethe into his masterpiece.

Fauvism style of painting characterized by a bold use of vivid colours inspired by the work of van Gogh, Cézanne, and Gaugin. A short-lived but influential art movement, Fauvism originated in Paris 1905 with the founding of the Salon d'Automne by Henri Matisse and others, when the critic Louis Vauxcelles, on seeing a piece of conventional sculpture, said it was like 'Donatello amid wild beasts' (*'Donatello chez les fauves'*). Rouault, Dufy, Marquet, Derain, and Signac were early Fauves.

Fawcett Millicent Garrett 1847–1929. English suffragette, younger sister of Elizabeth Garrett ◊Anderson. A nonmilitant, she rejected the violent acts of some of her contemporaries in the suffrage movement. She joined the first Women's Suffrage Committee 1867 and became president of the Women's Unionist Association 1889.

Fayol Henri 1841–1925. A pioneer of management thought, generally regarded as the first to question the nature of management and put forward a theory designed to be applicable in all managerial contexts.

Fayol attempted to postulate his theory in such a way that the business procedures he had studied and developed as managing director of a mining and metallurgical combine in France could be applied to any organization, regardless of size or nature. He stipulated that managerial activity should involve five major elements: forecasting and planning; organizing; commanding; coordinating; and controlling. His ideas remained influential for much of this century.

February Revolution the first of the two political uprisings of the ◊Russian revolution in 1917 that led to the overthrow of the tsar and the end of the Romanov dynasty.

The immediate cause of the revolution was the inability of the tsardom to manage World War I. On 8 March (dating by the Western calendar, not adopted at that time in Russia) strikes and bread riots broke out in Petrograd (formerly St Petersburg), where the troops later mutinied and joined the rioters. A provisional government under Prince Lvov was appointed by the Duma (assembly) and Tsar Nicholas II abdicated on 15 March (27 Feb Julian calendar).

The Petrograd Soviet of Workers, Peasants and Soldiers (formed originally during the Russian revolution of 1905) was revived by the

Bolsheviks and opposed the provisional government, especially when ◊Lenin returned from Switzerland in April. On 16–18 July the Bolsheviks made an unsuccessful attempt to seize power and Lenin was forced into hiding in Finland. The provisional government tried to continue the war, but was weakened by serious misunderstandings between the prime minister, Kerensky, and the commander in chief, General Kornilov, who tried unsuccessfully to gain power in Sept 1917. Shortly afterwards the Bolsheviks seized power in the ◊October Revolution.

Febvre Lucien 1878–1956. French historian who in 1929 founded, with his colleague Marc ◊Bloch, the highly influential journal *Annales d'histoire économique et sociale*. His pupil Fernand ◊Braudel became the leading exponent of the *'Annales'* school of which Febvre and Bloch were the pioneers. This new kind of history emphasized economic and social change, studying human affairs and the impersonal forces that really influenced people rather than narrating the deeds of the famous or dealing with only dramatic events.

Drawing on research in social psychology and human geography, and influenced by the anthropologist and philosopher, Lucien ◊Lévy-Bruhl, Febvre developed the idea of 'collective mentalities' that went beyond individual thinkers, their beliefs and values and that differed from age to age. For example, in his classic *Le Problème de l'incroyance au XVIe siècle: La Religion de Rableais* 1942 (translated as *The Problem of Unbelief in the Sixteenth Century: The Religion ·of Rableais* 1982) he argues that Rableais and his contemporaries could not have been atheists because the mentality required for disbelief did not exist at the time. For much of his career he was a professor at Strasburg University and then president of the VIth section of the *Ecole Practique des Hautes Etudes* in Paris, now the *Ecole des Hautes Etudes en Sciences Sociales*. In this latter post he was succeeded by Braudel.

Fechner Gustav 1801–1887. German psychologist. He became professor of physics at Leipzig 1834, but in 1839 turned to the study of psychophysics (the relationship between physiology and psychology). He devised *Fechner's law*, a method for the exact measurement of sensation.

federalism system of government in which two or more separate states unite under a common central government while retaining a considerable degree of local autonomy. A federation should be distinguished from a *confederation*, a looser union of states for mutual assistance.

Switzerland, the USA, Canada, Australia, and Malaysia are all examples of federal government, and many supporters of the European Community see it as the forerunner of a federal Europe.

Federalist in US history, one who advocated the ratification of the US Constitution 1787–88 in place of the Articles of Confederation. The Federalists became in effect the ruling political party during the presidencies of George Washington and John Adams 1789–1801, legislating to strengthen the authority of the newly created federal government.

Federalist Papers, the in US politics, a series of 85 letters published in the newly independent USA in 1788, attempting to define the relation of the states to the nation, and making the case for a federal government. The papers were signed 'Publius', the joint pseudonym of three leading political figures: Alexander Hamilton, John Jay, and James Madison.

feedback in communication, when the person or group receiving information or a message reacts to it. This may, for example, take the form of a critical response (negative feedback), or it may be an affirmative response (positive feedback).

Feldenkrais method system for improving physical coordination and movement, devised by Moshe Feldenkrais. It aims to eliminate muscle strain and tension through a greater awareness of the body's mechanism, especially posture and breathing. It is used by many professional singers and dancers.

felicific calculus or *hedonic calculus* in ethics, a technique for establishing the rightness and wrongness of an action. Using the calculus, one can attempt to work out the likely consequences of an action in terms of the pain or pleasure of those affected by the action. The calculus is attributed to English utilitarian philosopher Jeremy Bentham.

fellah (plural *fellahin*) in Arab countries, a peasant farmer or farm labourer. In Egypt, approximately 60% of the fellah population live in rural areas, often in villages of 1,000–5,000 inhabitants.

One is not born a woman, one becomes one.

feminism; women's movement
Simone de Beauvoir, 1908–1986, French
socialist, feminist and writer.
The Second Sex

feminism an active belief in equal rights and opportunities for women; see ◊women's movement.

feminist criticism set of literary theories concerned with women as readers and writers of literary texts and as characters within them. Issues addressed include whether a specifically female writing exists, the way male authors perpetuate patriarchal attitudes through their writing, and the rehabilitation of neglected female authors.

feminist theology the critique of theology from an avowedly feminist perspective. Originating in the work of US scholars such as Mary Daly (1928–   ) in the 1970s, feminist theology has quickly become a major new branch of theology and has called into question many key concepts and terms within Christian and Jewish theology.

Feminist theologians are split between those who believe established religions such as Christianity or Judaism are fundamentally anti-women, and those who believe that such faiths can be purged of anti-feminist attitudes.

Fénelon Francois de Salingnac de la Mothe 1651–1715. Archbishop of Cambrai in France, member of the Quietist movement, and author of a book on mysticism which was subsequently banned.

Fénelon began his career working to convert the French Protestants back to Rome. He then moved on to be tutor to Louis XIV's grandson for whom he wrote *Télémaque* – one of the first educational novels. Through his acquaintance with the mystic Madame Guyon (1648–1717) in 1688 he became involved with ◊quietism which stressed the uselessness of human activity in the spiritual search. Appointed archbishop 1695, in 1697 he published his highly influential book on mysticism *Explication des maximes des saints sur la vie intérieure* which attracted much condemnation and was eventually banned by the Roman Catholic Church. Following this Fénelon submitted to the pope.

Fergus mac Roigh in Celtic legend, a king of Ulster, a great warrior. He was the tutor of ◊Cuchulain.

Fermat Pierre de 1601–1665. French mathematician, who with Blaise Pascal founded the theory of ◊probability and the modern theory of numbers and who made contributions to analytical geometry.

Fermat's last theorem states that equations of the form $x^n + y^n = z^n$ where x, y, z, and n are all integers have no solutions if $n > 2$. Fermat scribbled the theorem in the margin of a mathematics textbook and noted that he could have shown it to be true had he enough space in which to write the proof. Three hundred years later, the theorem remains unproven (and therefore, strictly speaking, constitutes a conjecture rather than a theorem).

Fermat's Principle in physics, the principle that a ray of light, or other radiation, moves between two points along the path that takes the minimum time. The principle is named after the French mathematician Pierre de Fermat who used it to deduce the laws of reflection and refraction.

Whatever Nature has in store for mankind, unpleasant as it may be, man must accept, for ignorance is never better than knowledge.

Enrico Fermi
Atoms in the Family

Fermi Enrico 1901–1954. Italian-born US physicist who proved the existence of new radioactive elements produced by bombardment with neutrons, and discovered nuclear reactions produced by low-energy neutrons. His theoretical work included study of the weak nuclear force, one of the fundamental forces of nature, and (with Paul Dirac) of the quantum statistics of fermion particles. He was awarded a Nobel prize 1938.

Born in Rome, he was professor of theoretical physics there 1926–38. Upon receiving the Nobel prize he and his family emmigrated to the US. He was professor at Columbia University, New York 1939–42 and from 1946 at the University of Chicago, where he had built the first US nuclear reactor 1942. This was the basis for studies leading to the atomic bomb and nuclear energy.

In 1954, the US Atomic Energy Commission made a special award to Fermi in recognition of his outstanding work in nuclear physics; these annual awards subsequently were known as Fermi awards.

fetishism in psychiatry, a sexual deviation or disorder, involving the transfer of erotic interest to an object, such as an item of clothing, associated with the loved one. The presence of this fetish is necessary for sexual gratification. The fetish may also be a part of the body not normally considered erogenous, such as the feet.

Fetishism is usually found only in men. According to ◊Freud, a young boy on seeing the female genitals, usually his mother's, for the first time takes the fact that there is no penis as evidence of the supposed threat of castration. The fetishist deals with his ◊castration anxiety by refusing to accept the fact of the 'missing penis' and substitutes the fetish for it.

In anthropology fetishism is the worship of inanimate objects, charms, or talismans, for example, imbued with supposed mysterious or supernatural qualities.

feudalism main form of social organization in medieval Europe. A system based primarily on land, it involved a hierarchy of authority, rights, and power that extended from the monarch downwards. An intricate network of duties and obligations linked royalty, nobility, lesser gentry, free tenants, villeins, and serfs. Feudalism was reinforced by a complex legal system and supported by the Christian church. With the growth of commerce and industry from the 13th century, feudalism gradually gave way to the class system as the dominant form of social ranking.

In return for military service the monarch allowed powerful vassals to hold land, and often also to administer justice and levy taxes. They in turn 'sublet' such rights. At the bottom of the system were the serfs, who worked on their lord's manor lands in return for being allowed to cultivate some for themselves, and so underpinned the system. They could not be sold as if they were slaves, but they could not leave the estate to live or work elsewhere without permission. The system declined from the 13th century, partly because of the growth of a money economy, with commerce, trade, and industry, and partly because of the many peasants' revolts 1350–1550. Serfdom ended in England in the 16th century, but lasted in France until 1789 and in the rest of Western Europe until the early 19th century. In Russia it continued until 1861.

Feuerbach Ludwig (Andreas) 1804–1872. German philosopher who argued that religion is the elevation of human qualities into an object of worship. His main work is *Das Wesen des Christentums/The Essence of Christianity* 1841. He influenced political theorist Karl Marx.

Feuerbach was born in Landshut, Bavaria. He studied philosophy under G W F Hegel in Berlin, but abandoned Hegel's idealism for a form of materialism. He also studied theology and science. *Das Wesen des Christentums/The Essence of Christianity* was translated into English by novelist George Eliot 1854.

Variety of opinion is necessary for objective knowledge.

Paul K Feyerabend
Against Method

Feyerabend Paul K 1924–1994. US philosopher of science, who rejected the attempt by certain philosophers (for instance ◊Popper) to find a methodology applicable to all scientific research. His works include *Against Method* 1975.

Although his work relies on historical evidence, Feyerabend argued that successive theories that apparently concern the same subject (for instance the motion of the planets) cannot in principle be subjected to any comparison that would aim at finding the truer explanation. According to this notion of incommensurability, there is no neutral or objective standpoint and therefore no rational way in which one theory can be chosen over another. Instead, scientific progress is claimed to be the result of a range of sociological factors working to promote politically convenient notions of how nature operates.

Feynman Richard P(hillips) 1918–1988. US physicist whose work laid the foundations of quantum electrodynamics. As a member of the committee investigating the *Challenger* space-shuttle disaster 1986, he demonstrated the lethal faults in rubber seals on the shuttle's booster rocket. For his work on the theory of radiation he shared the Nobel Prize for Physics 1965 with Julian Schwinger and Sin-Itiro Tomonaga (1906–1979).

One does not, by knowing all the physical laws as we know them today, immediately obtain an understanding of anything much.

Richard P(hillips) Feynman
The Character of Physical Law

Feynman was professor of physics at Caltech (California Institute of Technology) from 1950 until his death. In the course of his work he developed his remarkably simple and elegant system of Feynman diagrams to represent interactions between particles. He also contributed to many aspects of particle physics including the nature of the weak nuclear force and quark theory. Towards the end of his life he became widely known for his revealing autobiographies *Surely You're Joking, Mr Feynman!* 1985 and *What Do You Care What Other People Think?* 1988.

Fibonacci Leonardo, also known as *Leonardo of Pisa* c. 1175–c. 1250. Italian mathematician. He published *Liber abaci* in Pisa 1202, which was instrumental in the introduction of Arabic notation into Europe. From 1960, interest increased in *Fibonacci numbers*, in their simplest form a sequence in which each number is the sum of its two predecessors (1, 1, 2, 3, 5, 8, 13, ...). They have unusual characteristics with possible applications in botany, psychology, and astronomy (for example, a more exact correspondence than is given by ◊Bode's law to the distances between the planets and the Sun).

Man is what he eats.

Ludwig Feuerbach
Advertisement to Moleschott

Fichte Johann Gottlieb 1762–1814. German philosopher who developed a comprehensive form of subjective idealism, expounded in *The Science of Knowledge* 1794. He was an admirer of Immanuel ◊Kant.

In 1792, Fichte published *Critique of Religious Revelation*, a critical study of Kant's doctrine of the 'thing-in-itself'. For Fichte, the absolute ego posits both the external world (the non-ego) and finite self. Morality consists in the striving of this finite self to rejoin the absolute. In 1799 he was accused of atheism, and was forced to resign his post as professor of philosophy at Jena. He moved to Berlin, where he devoted himself to public affairs and delivered lectures, including *Reden an die deutsche Nation/Addresses to the German People* 1807–08, which influenced contemporary liberal nationalism.

Ficino Marsilio 1433–1499. Italian philosopher who created an influential synthesis of Platonism and medieval theology. He assigned to the human soul the central place in the hierarchy of the universe, and he believed that the soul ascended towards God through contemplation. His doctrine of platonic love became one of the most popular concepts of later Renaissance literature.

Ficino founded a Platonic Academy in Florence 1462. He was ordained a priest 1473 and retired 1494. He translated both Plato and Plotinus, the founder of ◊neo-Platonism, into Latin. His main work is *Theologica Platonica de immortalitate animae/Platonic Theology Concerning the Immortality of the Soul* 1482.

Fidei Defensor Latin for the title of 'Defender of the Faith' (still retained by British sovereigns) conferred by Pope Leo X on Henry VIII of England 1521 to reward his writing of a treatise against the Protestant Martin ◊Luther.

field studies study of ecology, geography, geology, history, archaeology, and allied subjects, in the natural environment as opposed to the laboratory.

The Council for the Promotion of Field Studies was established in Britain 1943, in order to promote a wider knowledge and understanding of the natural environment among the public; Flatford Mill, Suffolk, was the first of its research centres to be opened.

fieldwork in anthropology, the gathering and analysis of first-hand information through direct observation of a society or social group.

It was developed by William ◊Rivers and Bronislaw ◊Malinowski as a more scientific method of research, but its capacity for comprehensiveness and objectivity has been questioned.

fifth column group within a country secretly aiding an enemy attacking from without. The term originated 1936 during the Spanish Civil War, when General Mola boasted that Franco supporters were attacking Madrid with four columns and that they had a 'fifth column' inside the city.

figurative language grammatical usage that departs from everyday factual, plain, or literal language and is considered poetic, imaginative, or ornamental. The traditional forms, especially in literature, are the various figures of speech.

The sentence 'Justice is blind' is doubly figurative because it suggests that justice is a person (◊personification) rather than an abstract idea, and uses *blind* analogically to suggest that it is unbiased (◊metaphor).

filioque (Latin 'and the Son') a disputed term in the Christian ◊creeds from the 8th century, referring to the issue of whether the Holy Spirit proceeds from God only, or from God the Father and Son. Added by the Council of Frankfurt 794, the term was incorporated as Catholic doctrine in the 10th century.

final solution (to the Jewish question; German *Endlosung der Judenfrage*) euphemism used by the Nazis to describe the extermination of Jews (and other racial groups and opponents of the regime) before and during World War II. See ◊Holocaust.

fine arts (or *beaux arts*) art that exists primarily to create beauty, as opposed to the decorative or applied arts, which exist primarily for day-to-day use. They include painting, sculpture, some graphic art, and, despite its function, architecture. Music and poetry are sometimes called fine arts.

Finlandization political term for the tendency of a small state to shape its foreign policy so as to accommodate a much more powerful neighbour, taken from the example of Finland's foreign policy with respect to the USSR.

Finn Mac Cumhaill legendary Irish hero, identified with a general who organized an Irish regular army in the 3rd century. James Macpherson (1736–96) featured him (as Fingal) and his followers in the verse of his popular epics 1762–63, which were supposedly written by a 3rd-century bard, Ossian. Although challenged by the critic Dr Johnson, the poems were influential in the Romantic movement.

fire symbol of purity, purification, or divinity in many religions and cultures, in which sacrifice is or has been a central ritual. In Christianity, however, the fires of hell are traditionally opposed to the light of God and heaven.

In classical antiquity, fire was the attribute of Hestia, goddess of hearth and home, and in Rome the Vestal Virgins guarded the sacred flame of Vesta in her shrine in the Forum. In classical mythology, fire was stolen from the gods and given to humans by Prometheus. In Indian Vedic ritual, Agni was honoured as the sacrificial fire that mediated between gods and humans, and which was the responsibility of the Brahams. In Zoroastrianism, fire is the son of the supreme god Ahura Mazda. A remnant of symbolic purification still persists in the bonfires lit at Halloween to chase away evil spirits.

Firestone Shulamith 1945– . Canadian feminist writer and editor, whose book *The Dialectic of Sex: the Case for Feminist Revolution* 1970, which analysed the limited future of feminism under Marxist and Freudian theories, exerted considerable influence on feminist thought.

She was one of the early organizers of the women's liberation movement in the USA. Her other works include *Notes from the Second Year* 1970.

First Cause in philosophy, an argument for the existence of God as creator or cause of the world. The First Cause argument – a version of the ◊cosmological argument – turns on the idea that everything requires a cause or reason. God must exist to be the First Cause, because it is assumed either that an infinite regress of causes is impossible or that the existence of the universe itself needs explanation. For ◊Aristotle, matter has always existed, so the First Cause, or Prime Mover as he calls God, is not the First Cause in time but the cause of the universe's continuing existence – a sustaining cause, or reason for its existence. For Thomas ◊Aquinas, the First Cause is both a sustaining cause of the world and the First Cause in all the causal series that make up the world.

First World another name for ◊developed world.

Firth John Rupert 1890–1960. British linguist who, influenced by his friend and colleague, Bronislaw ◊Malinowski, made semantics central to his approach to linguistics and developed the latter's theory of the 'context of the situation'. Whatever anyone said or uttered must be understood in the entire context of the utterance, even including such non-linguistic factors as the status and personal history of the speakers, the social character of the situation, etc. In 1944 he was appointed to the professorship of general linguistics at London University, the first in Britain. His most important academic articles are set out in *Papers in Linguistics 1934–51* 1957 and *Selected Papers of J R Firth* 1968.

Firth described typical contexts of situation and 'typical repetitive events in the social process'. For example, the occurrence of ready-made, socially prescribed utterances such as 'How do you do?' He also studied phonological features of speech such as stress, intonation, and nasalization, which, he emphasized, varied considerably in different languages. He wrote two reasonably popular books, *Speech* 1930 and *The Tongues of Men* 1937.

Fischer Emil Hermann 1852–1919. German chemist who produced synthetic sugars and from these various enzymes. His descriptions of the chemistry of the carbohydrates and peptides laid the foundations for the science of ◊biochemistry. Nobel prize 1902.

Fischer Hans 1881–1945. German chemist awarded a Nobel prize 1930 for his discovery of haemoglobin in blood.

Fisher Irving 1867–1947. US economist who developed the ◊quantity theory of money from the quantity equation, which he formulated as $MV = PT$, M being the quantity of money in circulation (the money supply), V the velocity of circulation of money around the economy, P the average price level, and T the number of transactions (equivalent to output). This equation is sometimes known as the *Fisher equation*. The quantity theory assumes that V and T are relatively constant, and therefore suggests that an increase in the money supply causes inflation.

Fisher Ronald Aylmer 1890–1962. English statistician and geneticist. He modernized Charles Darwin's theory of evolution, thus securing the key biological concept of genetic change by ◊natural selection. Fisher developed several new statistical techniques and, applying his methods to genetics, published *The Genetical Theory of Natural Selection* 1930.

This classic work established that the discoveries of the geneticist Gregor Mendel could be shown to support Darwin's theory of evolution.

fission in physics, the splitting of a heavy atomic nucleus into two or more major fragments. It is accompanied by the emission of two or three neutrons and the release of large amounts of energy.

Fission occurs spontaneously in nuclei of uranium-235, the main fuel used in nuclear reactors. However, the process can also be induced by bombarding nuclei with neutrons because a nucleus that has absorbed a neutron becomes unstable and soon splits. The neutrons released spontaneously by the fission of uranium nuclei may therefore be used in turn to induce further fissions, setting up a chain reaction that must be controlled if it is not to result in a nuclear explosion.

Fitzgerald George 1851–1901. Irish physicist known for his work on electromagnetics. In 1895 he explained the anomalous results of the ◊Michelson–Morley experiment 1887 by supposing that bodies moving through the ether contracted as their velocity increased, an effect since known as the *Fitzgerald–Lorentz contraction*.

five pillars of Islam the five duties required of every Muslim: affirming that Allah is the one God and Muhammad is his prophet; daily *prayer* or ◊*salat*; giving *alms* or *zakat*; *fasting* during the month of Ramadan; and, if not prevented by ill health or poverty, the ◊hajj, or *pilgrimage* to Mecca, once in a lifetime.

five-year plan long-term strategic plan for the development of a country's economy. Five-year plans were from 1928 the basis of economic planning in the USSR, aimed particularly at developing heavy and light industry in a primarily agricultural country. They have since been adopted by many other countries.

flagellant religious person who uses a whip on him- or herself as a means of penance. Flagellation was practised in many religions from ancient times; notable outbreaks of this type of extremist devotion occurred in Christian Europe in the 11th–16th centuries.

flamen one of 15 sacrificial priests in ancient Rome. The office was held for life, but was terminated by the death of the flamen's wife (who assisted him at ceremonies) or by some misdemeanour.

Flamsteed John 1646–1719. English astronomer, who began systematic observations of the positions of the stars, Moon, and planets at the Royal Observatory he founded at Greenwich, London, 1676. His observations were published 1725.

Fleming Alexander 1881–1955. Scottish bacteriologist who discovered the first antibiotic drug, penicillin, in 1928. In 1922 he had discovered lysozyme, an antibacterial enzyme present in saliva, nasal secretions, and tears. While studying this, he found an unusual mould growing on a neglected culture dish, which he isolated and grew into a pure culture; this led to his discovery of penicillin. It came into use in 1941. In 1945 he won the Nobel Prize for Physiology and Medicine with Howard W Florey and Ernst B Chain, whose research had brought widespread realization of the value of penicillin.

Flood, the in the Old Testament, the Qur'an, and the *Epic of Gilgamesh* (an ancient Sumerian legend), a deluge lasting 40 days and nights, a disaster alleged to have obliterated all humanity except a chosen few (in the Old Testament and the Qur'an, the survivors were the family of ◊Noah and the pairs of animals sheltered on his ark).

The story may represent legends of a major local flood; for example, excavations at Ur in Iraq revealed 2.5 m/8 ft of water-laid clay dating before 4000 BC, over an area of about 645 km/400 mi by 160 km/100 mi.

flow chart diagram, often used in computing, to show the possible paths that data can take through a system or program.

A *system flow chart*, or *data flow chart*, is used to describe the flow of data through a complete data-processing system. Different graphic symbols represent the clerical operations involved and the different input, storage, and output equipment required. Although the flow chart may indicate the specific programs used, no details are given of how the programs process the data.

A *program flow chart* is used to describe the flow of data through a particular computer program, showing the exact sequence of operations performed by that program in order to process the data. Different graphic symbols are used to represent data input and output, decisions, branches, and subroutines.

Fludd Robert 1574–1637. English physician and mystical philosopher, influenced by ◊Paracelsus and ◊neo-Platonism. He defended the ◊Rosicrucians and the authenticity of the writings of Hermes Trismegistus.

He divided the world into the divine archetypes (the 'macrocosm'), and Man (the 'microcosm') who is a miniature representation of the universe. The macrocosm and microcosm are related by mystical correspondences. He published numerous works, including his *Apologia* 1616 and *The History of the Macrocosm and the Microcosm* 1617.

folklore the oral traditions and culture of a people, expressed in legends, riddles, songs, tales, and proverbs. The term was coined 1846 by W J Thoms (1803–85), but the founder of the systematic study of the subject was Jacob ◊Grimm.

The approach to folklore has varied greatly: the German scholar Max Müller (1823–1900) interpreted it as evidence of nature myths; James ◊Frazer was the exponent of the comparative study of early and popular folklore as mutually explanatory; Laurence Gomme (1853–1916) adopted a historical analysis; and Bronislaw ◊Malinowski and Alfred ◊Radcliffe-Brown examined the material as an integral element of a given living culture. Folklore overlaps with cultural anthropology but their roots and theoretical concerns are not the same.

folk religion popular religion which may be divergent from the official teachings and doctrines of the majority faith. Folk religions often combine the ancient indigenous beliefs of a region with a sophisticated religion of more recent date.

In China folk religion is the mixture of Taoist, Confucian, and Buddhist elements which constitute everyday religion in the villages, as distinct from the religious life of the Taoist and Buddhist monasteries. In southern Europe, it is the mixture of beliefs which focus around conventional Catholic notions such as the saints or the Mass. In northern Europe, it is the kind of popular religion which brings people to church for baptisms, marriages, and funerals, even if they do not attend at any other time.

food chain in ecology, a sequence showing the feeding relationships between organisms in a particular ◊ecosystem. Each organism depends on the next lowest member of the chain for its food.

Energy in the form of food is shown to be transferred from autotrophs, or producers, which are principally plants and photosynthetic microorganisms to a series of heterotrophs, or consumers. The heterotrophs comprise the herbivores, which feed on the producers; carnivores, which feed on the herbivores; and decomposers, which break down the dead bodies and waste products of all four groups (including their own), ready for recycling.

In reality, however, organisms have varied diets, relying on different kinds of foods, so that the food chain is an over-simplification. The more complex *food web* shows a greater variety of relationships, but again emphasises that energy passes from plants to herbivores to carnivores.

Environmental groups have used the concept of the food chain to show how poisons and other forms of pollution can pass from one animal to another, eventually resulting in the death of rare animals such as the golden eagle *Aquila chrysaetos*.

Force is not a remedy.

force
John Bright, 1811–1889, British Liberal politician.
Speech in Birmingham 1880

---

force majeure (French 'superior force') in politics, the use of force rather than the seeking of a political or diplomatic solution to a problem. By this principle, a government could end a strike by sending in troops, instead of attempting to conciliate the strikers.

Who overcomes / By force, hath overcome but half his foe.

force
John Milton, 1608–1674, English poet.
Paradise Lost bk 1

---

forces, fundamental in physics, the four fundamental interactions believed to be at work in the physical universe. There are two long-range forces: ◊*gravity*, which keeps the planets in orbit around the Sun, and acts between all particles that have mass; and the ◊*electromagnetic force*, which stops solids from falling apart, and acts between all particles with electric charge. There are two very short-range forces which operate only inside the atomic nucleus: the ◊*weak nuclear force*, responsible for the reactions that fuel the Sun and for the emission of beta particles from certain nuclei; and the ◊*strong nuclear force*, which binds together the protons and neutrons in the nuclei of atoms. The relative strengths of the four forces are: strong, 1; electromagnetic, 10^{-2}; weak, 10^{-6}; gravitational, 10^{-40}.

By 1971, US physicists Steven Weinberg and Sheldon Glashow, Pakistani physicist Abdus Salam, and others had developed a theory that suggested that the weak and electromagnetic forces were aspects of a single force called the **electroweak force**; experimental support came from observation at CERN in the 1980s. Physicists are now working on theories to unify all four forces.

Fordism mass production characterized by a high degree of job specialization, as typified by Ford motor company's early use of assembly lines. *Post-Fordism* management theory and practice emphasizes flexibility and autonomy of decision-making for nonmanagerial staff. It is concerned more with facilitating and coordinating tasks than with control. Mass-production techniques were influenced by US management consultant F W Taylor's book *Scientific Management*, which emphasized work study, work specialization, and managerial control.

forensic science the use of scientific techniques to solve criminal cases. A multidisciplinary field embracing chemistry, physics, botany, zoology, and medicine, forensic science includes the identification of human bodies or traces. Traditional methods such as fingerprinting are still used, assisted by computers; in addition, blood analysis, forensic dentistry, voice and speech spectograms, and ◊genetic fingerprinting are increasingly applied. Chemicals, such as poisons and drugs, are analysed by chromatography. Ballistics (the study of projectiles, such as bullets), another traditional forensic field, makes use of tools such as the comparison microscope and the electron microscope.

The first forensic laboratory was supposedly founded in Lyons, France in 1910 by Edmond Locard, although it is claimed that Locard's teacher, Alphonse Bertillon, had established one earlier, and that the laboratory in Lyons was founded by Jean Lacassagne. The science developed as a systematic discipline in the 1930s. In 1932 the US Federal Bureau of Investigation established a forensic science laboratory in Washington DC, and in the UK the first such laboratory was founded in London in 1935.

form in Greek and medieval European philosophy, that which makes a thing what it is. For ◊Plato, a Form was an immaterial, independent object, which could not be perceived by the senses and was known only by reason; thus, a horse was a thing participating in the Form of horseness. For ◊Aristotle, forms existed only in combination with matter: a horse was a lump of matter having the form of a horse – that is, the essential properties (see ◊essence) and powers of a horse. However, Aristotle, like the medieval philosophers after him, does not make it clear whether there is a different form for each individual, or only for each type or species.

In Platonic philosophy Form is generally capitalized and is synonymous with his use of ◊idea.

form in logic, the form of a proposition is the kind or species to which it belongs, such as the universal ('All x are y') or the negative ('No x are y'). Logical form is contrasted with the content, or what the proposition individually is about.

formalism in art, literature, and music, an emphasis on form and formal structures at the expense of content. Formalism also refers more narrowly to a Russian school of literary theory in the 1920s, which defined literature by its formal, aesthetic qualities, and did not recognize its social content.

Formalism fell into disrepute as an aesthetic self-indulgence and was the focus of the cultural purges of 1948 under Stalin. It was superseded by ◊Socialist Realism.

Fortin Jean 1750–1831. French physicist and instrument-maker who invented a mercury barometer that bears his name.

It measures atmospheric pressure by means of a column of mercury, formed by filling a tube, closed at one end, with mercury and upending it in a reservoir of the metal. At the upper end of the tube this leaves a gap (known as a Torricellian vacuum), which changes size with variations in atmospheric pressure, expressed as the height of the column of mercury in millimetres. On this scale, normal atmospheric pressure is 760 mm of mercury.

Foucault Jean Bernard Léon 1819–1868. French physicist who used a pendulum to demonstrate the rotation of the Earth on its axis, and invented the gyroscope.

He investigated heat and light, discovered eddy currents induced in a copper disc moving in a magnetic field, invented a polarizer, and made improvements in the electric arc.

Man is neither the oldest nor the most constant problem that has been posed for human knowledge.

Michel Foucault
The Order of Things

Foucault Michel 1926–1984. French philosopher who rejected phenomenology and existentialism. He was concerned with how forms of knowledge and forms of human subjectivity are constructed by specific institutions and practices. In particular, he was concerned to subvert conventional assumptions about social deviants – the insane, the sick, and the criminal – who, he believed are oppressed by the approved knowledge of the period in which they live.

Foucault was deeply influenced by ◊Nietzsche, and developed an analysis of the operation of power in society using Nietzschean concepts. His publications include *Histoire de la folie/Madness and Civilization* 1961 and *Les Mots et les Choses/The Order of Things* 1970.

found object French *object trouvé* in the visual arts, an object that has no intrinsic aesthetic value, such as a piece of wood or rusty machinery, but which is 'found' by an artist and displayed as a work of art or ◊anti-art. Its use was popular among the Surrealists.

Four Freedoms, the four kinds of liberty essential to human dignity as defined in an address to the US Congress by President F D ◊Roosevelt 6 Jan 1941: freedom of speech and expression, freedom of worship, freedom from want, freedom from fear.

Fourier François Charles Marie 1772–1837. French socialist. In *Le Nouveau monde industriel/The New Industrial World* 1829–30, he advocated that society should be organized in self-sufficient cooperative units of about 1,500 people, and marriage should be abandoned.

Fourier Jean Baptiste Joseph 1768–1830. French applied mathematician whose formulation of heat flow 1807 contains the proposal that, with certain constraints, any mathematical function can be represented by trigonometrical series. This principle forms the basis of *Fourier analysis*, used today in many different fields of physics. His idea, not immediately well received, gained currency and is embodied in his *Théorie analytique de la chaleur/The Analytical Theory of Heat* 1822.

Four Noble Truths in Buddhism, a summary of the basic concepts: life is suffering (Sanskrit *duhkha*); suffering has its roots in desire (*tanha*, clinging or grasping); the cessation of desire is the end of suffering, *nirvana*; and this can be reached by the Noble Eightfold Path of *dharma* (truth).

Fourteen Points the terms proposed by President Wilson of the USA in his address to Congress 8 Jan 1918, as a basis for the settlement of World War I. The creation of the League of Nations was one of the points.

Fowler William 1911– . US astrophysicist. In 1983 he and Subrahmanyan ◊Chandrasekhar were awarded the Nobel Prize for Physics for their work on the life cycle of stars and the origin of chemical elements.

I told them I lived in the virtue of that life and power that took away the occasion of all wars.

George Fox
on being offered a captaincy in the army

Fox George 1624–1691. English founder of the Society of ◊Friends. After developing his belief in a mystical 'inner light', he became a travelling preacher 1647, and in 1650 was imprisoned for blasphemy at Derby, where the name Quakers was first applied derogatorily to him and his followers, supposedly because he enjoined Judge Bennet to 'quake at the word of the Lord'.

He suffered further imprisonments, made a missionary journey to America in 1671–72, and wrote many evangelical and meditative works, including a *Journal*, published 1694.

Fox Margaret 1833–1893. Canadian-born US spiritual medium. With her sister, Katherine, she became famous for her psychic ability. The girls gave public demonstrations of their powers, sparking widespread public interest in spiritualism as a modern religious movement. In 1888 Margaret publicly confessed that her 'psychic powers' were a hoax.

Brought up in New York State, USA, the sisters moved to New York City 1850 and claimed to be able to communicate with 'departed spirits' from an early age.

Foxe John 1516–1587. English Protestant propagandist. He became a canon of Salisbury

1563. His *Book of Martyrs* 1563 luridly described persecutions under Queen Mary, reinforcing popular hatred of Roman Catholicism.

Fracastoro Girolamo c. 1478–1553. Italian physician known for his two medical books. He was born and worked mainly in Verona. His first book, *Syphilis sive morbus gallicus/Syphilis or the French disease* 1530, was written in verse. It was one of the earliest texts on syphilis, a disease Fracastoro named. In his second work, *De contagione/On contagion* 1546, he wrote, far ahead of his time, about 'seeds of contagion'.

fractal an irregular shape or surface produced by a procedure of repeated subdivision. Generated on a computer screen, fractals are used in creating models for geographical or biological processes (for example, the creation of a coastline by erosion or accretion, or the growth of plants).

Sets of curves with such discordant properties were developed in Germany by Georg Cantor (1845–1918) and Karl Weierstrass (1815–1897). The name was coined by the French mathematician Benoit Mandelbrod. Fractals are also used for computer art.

fraction in mathematics, a number that indicates one or more equal parts of a whole. Usually, the number of equal parts into which the unit is divided (denominator) is written below a horizontal line, and the number of parts comprising the fraction (numerator) is written above; thus $2/3$ or $3/4$. Such fractions are called *vulgar* or *simple* fractions. The denominator can never be zero.

A *proper fraction* is one in which the numerator is less than the denominator. An *improper fraction* has a numerator that is larger than the denominator, for example $3/2$. It can therefore be expressed as a mixed number, for example, $1\frac{1}{2}$. A combination such as $5/0$ is not regarded as a fraction (an object cannot be divided into zero equal parts), and mathematically any number divided by 0 is equal to infinity. A *decimal fraction* has as its denominator a power of 10, and these are omitted by use of the decimal point and notation, for example 0.04, which is $4/100$. The digits to the right of the decimal point indicate the numerators of vulgar fractions whose denominators are 10, 100, 1,000, and so on. Most fractions can be expressed exactly as decimal fractions ($1/3 = 0.333...$). Fractions are also known as the *rational numbers*, that is numbers formed by a ratio. *Integers* may be expressed as fractions with a denominator of 1.

franchise in business, the right given by one company to another to manufacture, distribute, or provide its products.

Examples of franchise operations in the UK include Benetton and the Body Shop. Many US companies use franchises to distribute their products. It is usual for US motor companies to give restricted franchise dealerships covering specified models, with the manufacturer fixing the quota and other stringent conditions of sale.

franchise in politics, the eligibility, right, or privilege to vote at public elections, especially for the members of a legislative body, or parliament. In the UK adult citizens are eligible to vote from the age of 18, with the exclusion of peers, the insane, and criminals.

In the UK it was 1918 before all men had the right to vote, and 1928 before women were enfranchised; in New Zealand women were granted the right as early as 1893.

Franciscan order Catholic order of friars, *Friars Minor* or *Grey Friars*, founded 1209 by ◊Francis of Assisi. Subdivisions were the strict Observants; the Conventuals, who were allowed to own property corporately; and the ◊Capuchins, founded 1529.

The Franciscan order included such scholars as the English scientist Roger Bacon. A female order, the *Poor Clares*, was founded by St ◊Clare 1215, and lay people who adopt a Franciscan regime without abandoning the world form a third order, *Tertiaries*.

Francis of Assisi, St 1182–1226. Italian founder of the Roman Catholic Franciscan order of friars 1209 and, with St Clare, of the Poor Clares 1212. In 1224 he is said to have undergone a mystical experience during which he received the stigmata (five wounds of Jesus). Many stories are told of his ability to charm wild animals, and he is the patron saint of ecology. His feast day is 4 Oct.

The son of a wealthy merchant, Francis changed his life after two dreams he had during an illness following spells of military service when he was in his early twenties. He resolved to follow literally the behests of the New Testament and live a life of poverty and service while preaching a simple form of the Christian gospel. In 1219 he went to Egypt to convert the sultan, and lived for a month in his camp. Returning to Italy, he resigned his leadership of the friars.

Francis of Sales, St 1567–1622. French bishop and theologian. He became bishop of Geneva 1602, and in 1610 founded the order of the Visitation, an order of nuns. He is the patron saint of journalists and other writers. His feast day is 24 Jan.

Francis of Sales was born in Savoy. His writings include *Introduction à la vie dévote/ Introduction to a Devout Life* 1609, written to reconcile the Christian life with living in the real world.

Franck James 1882–1964. US physicist. He was awarded a Nobel prize 1925 for his experiments of 1914 on the energy transferred by colliding electrons to mercury atoms, showing that the transfer was governed by the rules of ◊quantum theory.

Born and educated in Germany, he emigrated to the USA after publicly protesting against Hitler's racial policies. Franck participated in the wartime atomic-bomb project at Los Alamos but organized the 'Franck petition' 1945, which argued that the bomb should not be used against Japanese cities. After World War II he turned his research to photosynthesis.

Frank Ilya 1908– . Russian physicist known for his work on radiation. In 1934 Cherenkov had noted a peculiar blue radiation sometimes emitted as electrons passed through water. It was left to Frank and his colleague at Moscow University, Igor Tamm (1895–1971), to realize that this form of radiation was produced by charged particles travelling faster through the medium than the speed of light in the same medium. Frank shared the 1958 Nobel Prize for Physics with Cherenkov and Tamm.

Frankfurt School the members of the *Institute of Social Research*, set up at Frankfurt University, Germany, 1923 as the first Marxist research centre. With the rise of Hitler, many of its members went to the USA and set up the institute at Columbia University, New York. In 1969 the institute was dissolved.

In the 1930s, under its second director Max Horkheimer (1895–1973), a group that included Erich Fromm, Herbert Marcuse, and T W Adorno (1903–1969) attempted to update Marxism and create a coherent and viable social theory. Drawing on a variety of disciplines as well as the writings of Marx and Freud, they produced works such as *Authority and the Family* 1936 and developed a Marxist perspective known as *critical theory*. After World War II the institute returned to Frankfurt, although Marcuse and some others remained in the USA. The German and US branches diverged in the 1950s, and the institute was dissolved after Adorno's death, although Jurgen Habermas (1929-) and

others have since attempted to revive its theory and research programme.

Franklin Benjamin 1706–1790. US printer, publisher, author, scientist, and statesman. He proved that lightning is a form of electricity, distinguished between positive and negative electricity, and invented the lightning conductor. He was the first US ambassador to France 1776–85, and negotiated peace with Britain 1783. As a delegate to the Continental Congress from Pennsylvania 1785–88, he helped to draft the ◊Declaration of Independence and the US ◊Constitution.

But in this world nothing can be said to be certain, except death and taxes.

Benjamin Franklin
Letter to Jean Baptiste Le Roy 13 Nov 1789

Born in Boston, Franklin moved to Philadelphia as a young man and combined a successful printing business with scientific experiment and inventions; he authored and published the popular *Poor Richard's Almanac* 1733–58. A member of the Pennsylvania Assembly 1751–64, he was sent to Britain to lobby Parliament about tax grievances and achieved the repeal of the Stamp Act; on his return to the USA he was prominent in the deliberations leading up to independence. As ambassador in Paris he enlisted French help for the American Revolution.

Franklin Rosalind 1920–1958. English biophysicist whose research on X-ray diffraction of ◊DNA crystals helped Francis Crick and James D Watson to deduce the chemical structure of DNA.

Fraunhofer Joseph von 1787–1826. German physicist who did important work in optics. The dark lines in the solar spectrum (*Fraunhofer lines*), which reveal the chemical composition of the Sun's atmosphere, were accurately mapped by him.

Frazer James George 1854–1941. Scottish anthropologist, author of *The Golden Bough* 1890, a pioneer study of the origins of religion and sociology on a comparative basis. It exerted considerable influence on writers such as T S Eliot and D H Lawrence, but by the standards of modern anthropology, many of its methods and findings are unsound.

free association in psychoanalysis, therapeutic technique developed by ◊Freud in which the patient is encouraged to repeat whatever comes to mind without reservation. Freud claimed that, in the patient's unforced statements, unconscious wishes were unwittingly revealed, allowing analysis to proceed where the resistance or ◊repression usually manifest in personal disclosure would otherwise interfere.

The process of free association, which is still widely used in psychoanalysis today, is generally facilitated by the non-emotive prompting of the analyst.

Free Church the Protestant denominations in England and Wales that are not part of the Church of England; for example, the Methodist Church, Baptist Union, and United Reformed Church (Congregational and Presbyterian). These churches joined for common action in the Free Church Federal Council 1940.

Free Church of Scotland the body of Scottish Presbyterians who seceded from the Established Church of Scotland in the Disruption of 1843. In 1900 all but a small section (that retains the old name, and is known as the *Wee Frees*), combined with the United Presbyterian Church to form the United Free Church, which reunited with the Church of Scotland 1929.

freedom in political philosophy, the condition of personal liberty requiring either the absence of restraint (negative freedom) or self-mastery and self-realization (positive freedom), or both. Philosophers such as John ◊Locke, J S ◊Mill and Thomas ◊Hobbes hold the negative view of freedom. Philosophers such as Jean-Jacques ◊Rousseau, Georg ◊Hegel and the British neo-Hegelians – F H Bradley (1846–1924), T H Green (1836–1882) – hold a positive view of freedom.

The negative view of freedom tends to be held by those philosphers who think that the state is no more than the sum of the individuals composing it (◊mechanism). The positive view of freedom tends to be held by those philosophers who regard the state as an end to which its citizens are the means (◊organicism).

freedom of speech/the press the right to say or to print whatever one likes, unencumbered by any restrictions or controls from state institutions. The degree to which such freedom exists is usually taken to be a good indicator of how open and democratic a particular society is. Thus in totalitarian states the voicing of any dissenting opinion is repressed, whereas in liberal democracies the dissemination of accurate information and open and free discussion are regarded as integral to the political process.

Restrictions on press freedom date back to the beginning of printing in the late 15th century. In England, printing presses were licensed in order to control them, a practice that continued until 1695 when Parliament refused to renew the Printing Act. In the USA, the First Amendment to the constitution guarantees freedom of speech. In fact, very few countries permit complete freedom; restrictions preventing libel, slander, obscenity, and threats to national security are the norm in most countries. Furthermore, critics of the Western press would argue that although it is relatively free of government control, its opinions will always, in some ways, reflect the political sympathies of its proprietor.

free enterprise or *free market* economic system where private capital is used in business with profits going to private companies and individuals. The term has much the same meaning as ◊capitalism.

Freemasonry the beliefs and practices of a group of linked national organizations open to men over the age of 21, united by a common code of morals and certain traditional 'secrets'. Modern Freemasonry began in 18th-century Europe. Freemasons do much charitable work, but have been criticized in recent years for their secrecy, their male exclusivity, and their alleged use of influence within and between organizations (for example, the police or local government) to further each other's interests. There are approximately 6 million members.

beliefs Freemasons believe in God, whom they call the 'Great Architect of the Universe'.

history Freemasonry is descended from a medieval guild of itinerant masons, which existed in the 14th century and by the 16th was admitting men unconnected with the building trade. The term 'freemason' may have meant a full member of the guild or one working in free-stone, that is, a mason of the highest class. There were some 25 lodges in 17th-century Scotland, of which 16 were in centres of masonic skills such as stonemasonry.

The present order of *Free and Accepted Masons* originated with the formation in London of the first Grand Lodge, or governing body, in 1717, and during the 18th century spread from Britain to the USA, continental Europe, and elsewhere. In France and other European countries, freemasonry assumed a political and anticlerical character; it has been condemned by the papacy, and in some countries was suppressed by the state.

free thought post-Reformation movement opposed to Christian dogma.

It was represented in Britain in the 17th and 18th century by ◊deism; in the 19th century by the radical thinker Richard Carlile (1790–1843), a pioneer of the free press, and the Liberal politicians Charles Bradlaugh and Lord Morley (1838–1923); and in the 20th century by the philosopher Bertrand Russell.

The tradition is upheld in the UK by the National Secular Society 1866, the *Free Thinker* 1881, the Rationalist Press Association 1899, and the British Humanist Association 1963.

free trade economic system where governments do not interfere in the movement of goods between countries; there are thus no taxes on imports. In the modern economy, free trade tends to hold within economic groups such as the European Community (EC), but not generally, despite such treaties as ◊GATT 1948 and subsequent agreements to reduce tariffs. The opposite of free trade is ◊protectionism.

The case for free trade, first put forward in the 17th century, received its classic statement in Adam Smith's *Wealth of Nations* 1776. The movement towards free trade began with Pitt's commercial treaty with France 1786, and triumphed with the repeal of the Corn Laws 1846. According to traditional economic theory, free trade allows nations to specialize in those commodities which can be produced most efficiently. In Britain, superiority to all rivals as a manufacturing country in the Victorian age made free trade an advantage, but when that superiority was lost the demand for protection was raised, notably by Joseph Chamberlain. The Ottawa Agreements 1932 marked the end of free trade until in 1948 GATT came into operation. A series of resultant international tariff reductions was agreed in the Kennedy Round Conference 1964–67, and the Tokyo Round 1974–79 gave substantial incentives to developing countries.

In the 1980s recession prompted by increased world oil prices and unemployment swung the pendulum back towards protectionism, which discourages foreign imports by heavy duties, thus protecting home products. Within the European Community, a date of 1992 was agreed for the abolition of all protectionist tariffs.

free will the doctrine that human beings are free to control their own actions, and that these actions are not fixed in advance by God or fate. Some Jewish and Christian theologians assert that God gave humanity free will to choose between good and evil; others that God has decided in advance the outcome of all human choices (◊predestination), as in Calvinism.

Frege Friedrich Ludwig Gottlob 1848–1925. German philosopher, the founder of modern mathematical logic. He invented ◊quantification (specification as to quantity) in logic, and he introduced symbols for concepts like 'or' and 'if ... then', which are now in standard use in mathematics. His attempts to derive mathematics from logic influenced ◊Russell and ◊Whitehead, and his theory that a word has ◊meaning only in the context of a sentence greatly influenced ◊Wittgenstein.

His works include *Die Grundlagen der Arithmetik/The Foundations of Arithmetic* 1884 and *Berggriftsschrift/Conceptual Notation* 1879.

The *Grundgesetze der Arithmetik/Basic Laws of Arithmetic* was published 1903. His work, neglected for a time, has attracted renewed attention in recent years in Britain, as philosophical logic has replaced epistemology as the foundation for philosophy.

French Revolution the period 1789–99 that saw the end of the French monarchy.

Although the revolution began as an attempt to create a constitutional monarchy, by late 1792 demands for long-overdue reforms resulted in the proclamation of the First Republic. The violence of the revolution, attacks by other nations, and bitter factional struggles, riots, and counterrevolutionary uprisings consumed the republic. This helped bring the extremists to power, and the bloody Reign of Terror followed. French armies then succeeded in holding off their foreign enemies and one of the generals, ◊Napoleon, seized power 1799.

On 5 May 1789, after the monarchy had attempted to increase taxation and control of affairs, the ◊States General (three 'estates' of nobles, clergy, and commons) met at Versailles to try to establish some constitutional controls. Divisions within the States General led to the formation of a National Assembly by the third (commons) estate 17 June. Repressive measures by Louis XVI led to the storming of the Bastille by the Paris mob 14 July 1789.

On 20 June 1791 the royal family attempted to escape from the control of the Assembly, but Louis XVI was brought back a prisoner from Varennes and forced to accept a new constitution. War with Austria after 20 April 1792 threatened to undermine the revolution, but on 10 Aug the mob stormed the royal palace, and on 21 Sept the First French Republic was proclaimed.

On 21 Jan 1793 Louis XVI was executed.

The moderate ◊Girondins were overthrown 2 June by the ◊Jacobins, and control of the country was passed to the infamous Committee of Public Safety, and ◊Robespierre. The mass executions of the Reign of Terror (see ◊Terror, Reign of) began 5 Sept, and the excesses led to the overthrow of the Committee and Robespierre 27 July 1794. The Directory was established to hold a middle course between royalism and Jacobinism. It ruled until Napoleon seized power 1799 as dictator.

Fresnel Augustin 1788–1827. French physicist who refined the theory of polarized light. Fresnel realized in 1821 that light waves do not vibrate like sound waves longitudinally, in the direction of their motion, but transversely, at right angles to the direction of the propagated wave.

Freud Anna 1895–1982. Austrian-born founder of child psychoanalysis in the UK. Her work was influenced by the theories of her father, Sigmund Freud. She held that understanding of the stages of psychological development was essential to the treatment of children, and that this knowledge could only be obtained through observation of the child.

Anna Freud and her father left Nazi-controlled Vienna in 1938 and settled in London. There she began working in a Hampstead nursery. In 1947 she founded the Hampstead Child Therapy Course and Clinic, which specialized in the treatment of children and the training of child therapists.

Freud Sigmund 1865–1939. Austrian physician who pioneered the study of the unconscious mind. He developed the methods of ◊free association and dream interpretation that are basic techniques of ◊psychoanalysis, and formulated a psychodynamic approach to mental development based on internal conflict and ◊repression, utilizing the concepts of the ◊id, ◊ego, and ◊superego. His books include *The Interpretation of Dreams* 1900, *Totem and Taboo* 1913, and *Civilization and its Discontents* 1930.

Anatomy is destiny.

Sigmund Freud
Collected Writings

Freud studied medicine at the University of Vienna's medical faculty and later worked there on the medicinal properties of cocaine, just missing becoming the first to discover its local anaesthetic effects. He spent six months

in Paris, 1885–86, studying ◊hypnosis and the treatment of ◊hysteria under the French physiologist ◊Charcot, who believed that only hysterics could be hypnotized. He was later influenced by the rival view that everyone was susceptible to hypnosis held by two less-famous French physicians, Ambroise Auguste Liebeault and Hippolyte Bernheim, whom he visited in 1889, and particularly by Bernheim's demonstration that a person who had been hypnotized could with prompting actually recall everything that had happened during trance, though claiming to remember nothing at first. He was also influenced by the work on hysteria of the Viennese physician Josef ◊Breuer, with whom he collaborated. From 1886 to 1938 he had a private practice in Vienna, and his theories and writings drew largely on case studies of his own patients, who were mainly upper-middle class, middle-aged women. In the early 1900s a group of psychoanalysts gathered around Freud. Some of them later broke away and formed their own schools, notably Alfred ◊Adler in 1911 and C G ◊Jung in 1913. Following the Nazi occupation of Austria in 1938, Freud left for London, where he died fifteen and a half months later in 1939.

To us he is no more a person / Now but a whole climate of opinion.

Freud
W(ystan) H(ugh) Auden, 1907–1973,
English-born US poet.
'In Memory of Sigmund Freud'

The word 'psychoanalysis' was, like much of its terminology, coined by Freud, and many terms have passed into popular usage, not without distortion. The way that unconscious forces influence people's thoughts and actions was Freud's discovery, and his theory of the repression of infantile sexuality as the root of neuroses in the adult (as in the ◊Oedipus complex) was controversial. Later he also stressed the significance of aggressive drives. His work has changed the way people think about human nature and ◊sexuality. His theories have brought about a more open approach to sexual matters; antisocial behaviour is now understood to result in many cases from unconscious forces, and these new concepts have led to wider expression of the human condition in art and literature. Nevertheless, Freud's theories have caused disagreement among psychologists and psychiatrists, and his methods of psychoanalysis may not be applicable in every case.

Freya in Scandinavian mythology, the goddess of married love and the hearth, wife of Odin and mother of Thor. Friday is named after her.

Friedan Betty 1921– . US liberal feminist. Her book *The Feminine Mystique* 1963 started the contemporary ◊women's movement, both in the US and the UK. She was a founder of the National Organization for Women (NOW) 1966 (and its president 1966–70), the National Women's Political Caucus 1971, and the First Women's Bank 1973. Friedan also helped to organize the Women's Strike for Equality 1970 and called the First International Feminist Congress 1973. *The Fountain of Age* was published 1993.

Friedman Milton 1912– . US economist. A pioneer of ◊monetarism, he argued that inflation is 'always and everywhere a monetary phenomenon'. The implication for economic policy is that if the rate of growth of the ◊money supply should be limited to the rate of growth of output in the economy (through monetary policy such as changes in interest rates, it should be impossible for increases in costs, such as wages or imports, to be translated into a rise in prices in the economy as a whole. Friedman suggested that governments may lack the political will to control spending because of the effect of such policies on unemployment.

His advocacy of the use of monetary policy, and his rejection of ◊Keynesian economics stemmed from his belief in the self-regulating nature of ◊market forces, and the idea that there is a 'natural rate of unemployment'. He argued that this was determined by 'structural and institutional forces in the labour market', such as unemployment benefits and trade unions, and could not be reduced in the long term by increases in government spending.

He advocated the introduction of a negative income tax to replace social security benefits to be paid automatically when incomes fell below a certain level. He argued that this would increase incentives to take paid employment and reduce bureaucratic intervention.

Friedman's Permanent Income Hypothesis made a significant contribution to the theory of consumption. This hypothesis suggested that consumer spending depended on expectations of long-run, or permanent income, and did not fluctuate significantly with fluctuations in current income.

Friedman was professor of economics at Chicago University from 1948 to 1979. He was awarded the Nobel prize for Economics in 1976. His major published works include *A Theory of the Consumption Function* 1957, *Capitalism and Freedom* 1962, *A Monetary History of the United States 1867–1960* 1963, *A Theoretical Framework for Monetary Analysis* 1971, and *Free to Choose* 1980.

The friends thou hast, and their adoption tried, / Grapple them to thy soul with hoops of steel.

friendship
Wiliam Shakespeare, 1564–1616,
English dramatist and poet
Hamlet i. iii

---

friendship mutual benevolence that is independent of sexual or family love. Ancient Greek philosopher Aristotle distinguishes three levels of friendship: the useful (friendship as a common enterprise), the pleasant (friendship as entertaining companionship), and the good or virtuous (friendship as mutual esteem).

Friends, Society of or *Quakers* Christian Protestant group founded by George ◊Fox in England in the 17th century. They were persecuted for their nonviolent activism, and many emigrated to form communities elsewhere, for example in Pennsylvania and New England, USA. They now form a worldwide movement of about 200,000. Their worship stresses meditation and the freedom of all to take an active part in the service (called a meeting, held in a meeting house). They have no priests or ministers.

The name 'Quakers' may originate in Fox's injunction to 'quake at the word of the Lord'. Originally marked out by their sober dress and use of 'thee' and 'thou' to all as a sign of equality, they incurred penalties by their pacifism and refusal to take oaths or pay tithes. In the 19th century many Friends were prominent in social reform, for example, Elizabeth ◊Fry.

Quakers have exerted a profound influence on American life through their pacifism and belief in social equality, education, and prison reform.

Frisch Karl von 1886–1982. Austrian zoologist, founder with Konrad ◊Lorenz of ◊ethology, the study of animal behaviour. He specialized in bees, discovering how they communicate the location of sources of nectar by movements called 'dances'. He was awarded the Nobel Prize for Medicine 1973 together with Lorenz and Nikolaas ◊Tinbergen.

Frisch Otto 1904–1979. Austrian physicist who coined the term 'nuclear fission'. A refugee from Nazi Germany, he worked from 1943 on the atom bomb at Los Alamos, New Mexico, and later at Cambridge, England. He was the nephew of Lise ◊Meitner.

Frisch Ragnar 1895–1973. Norwegian economist, pioneer of ◊econometrics (the application of mathematical and statistical methods in economics). He shared the first Nobel Prize for Economics in 1969 with Jan ◊Tinbergen.

Froebel Friedrich August Wilhelm 1782–1852. German educationist who emphasized a holistic approach to education, aiming '...to make the pupil conscious of the esssential nature of things and of himself.' His system, described in *Education of Man* 1826, involved the use of instructive play, and built on the child's own interests and observations. In 1836 he founded the first kindergarten (German 'garden for children') in Blankenburg, Germany. He worked with and was influenced by ◊Pestalozzi.

Fröhlich Herbert 1905–1991. German-born English theoretical physicist who helped lay the foundations for modern theoretical physics in Britain. His main research interest was in solid-state physics, but he also became familiar with quantum field theory – the application of quantum theory to particle interactions. In particular, he proposed a theory to explain superconductivity using the methods of quantum field theory. He also made important advances in the understanding of low-temperature superconductivity and biological systems,

Fröhlich was one of many German scientists who left Germany at the time of World War II.

Fromm Erich 1900–1980. German psychoanalyst who moved to the USA 1933 to escape the Nazis. Influenced by ◊Marx and ◊existentialism as much as by ◊psychoanalysis, he believed that, though part of the natural world, human beings nonetheless experience a separation from nature and from other human beings which gives them the freedom to decide on the course their lives should take. Human life acquires its meaning from this freedom but ◊anxiety also appears. These views are expressed in his *Escape from Freedom* 1941 and *The Sane Society* 1955.

Fromm also wrote about the authoritarian personality (a term applied to a servile obedient person who wants to accept authority), particularly to explain the success of Nazism.

He urged people to give up the materialistic way of life for one based on meaningful love in *The Art of Loving* 1956 and *To Have or To Be* 1976, which became source books for alternative lifestyles.

Fry Elizabeth (born Gurney) 1780–1845. English Quaker philanthropist. She formed an association for the improvement of conditions for female prisoners 1817, and worked with her brother, *Joseph Gurney* (1788–1847), on an 1819 report on prison reform.

fugue in psychology, an abnormal state in which a person under emotional stress suddenly leaves home, apparently forgetting everything about his/her normal life, and assumes a new identity. The state is usually temporary and is probably due to ◊repression.

full employment in economics, a state in which the only unemployment is frictional (referring to people who are temporarily out of work while moving jobs), and when everyone wishing to work is able to find employment.

Full employment is unusual, although a few countries, including Sweden, Switzerland, and Japan, traditionally maintain low levels of unemployment. Communist countries usually claim full employment.

Fuller (Richard) Buckminster 1895–1983. US architect, engineer, and Futurist social philosopher who embarked on an unorthodox career in an attempt to maximize energy resources through improved technology. In 1947 he invented the lightweight geodesic dome, a hemispherical space-frame of triangular components linked by rods, independent of buttress or vault and capable of covering large-span areas. Within 30 years over 50,000 had been built.

Now there is one outstandingly important fact regarding Spaceship Earth, and that is that no instruction book came with it.

(Richard) Buckminster Fuller
Operating Manual for Spaceship Earth

He also invented a Dymaxion (a combination of the words 'dynamics' and 'maximum') house 1928 and car 1933 that were inexpensive and utilized his concept of using the least amount of energy output to gain maximum interior space and efficiency, respectively. Among his books are *Ideas and Integrities* 1963, *Utopia or Oblivion* 1969, and *Critical Path* 1981.

function in mathematics, a function f is a nonempty set of ordered pairs $(x, f(x))$ of which no two can have the same first element. Hence, if

$$f(x) = x^2$$

two ordered pairs are (−2,4) and (2,4). The set of all first elements in a function's ordered pairs is called the **domain**; the set of all second elements is the **range**. In the algebraic expression $y = 4x^3 + 2$, the dependent variable y is a function of the independent variable x, generally written as $f(x)$.

Functions are used in all branches of mathematics, physics, and science generally; for example, the formula

$$t = 2\pi \sqrt{\left(\frac{l}{g} \right)}$$

shows that for a simple pendulum the time of swing t is a function of its length l and of no other variable quantity (π and g, the acceleration due to gravity, are constants).

functionalism in the social sciences, the view of society as a system made up of a number of interrelated parts, all interacting on the basis of a common value system or consensus about basic values and common goals. Every social custom and institution is seen as having a function in ensuring that society works efficiently; deviance and crime are seen as forms of social sickness.

Functionalists often describe society as an organism with a life of its own, above and beyond the sum of its members. The French sociologists Comte and ◊Durkheim and the American ◊Parsons assumed functionalist approaches for their studies.

Functionalism in architecture and design, the principle of excluding everything that serves no practical purpose. Central to 20th-century ◊Modernism, the Functionalist ethic developed as a reaction against the 19th-century practice of imitating and combining earlier styles. Its finest achievements are in the realms of industrial architecture and office furnishings.

Leading exponents of Functionalism were the German ◊Bauhaus school, the Dutch group de ◊Stijl, and the Scandinavians, especially the Swedish and Finnish designers. Prominent architects in the field were Le Corbusier and Walter ◊Gropius.

fundamentalism in religion, an emphasis on basic principles or articles of faith. *Christian fundamentalism* emerged from a conference in Niagara 1895 which issued a statement of five fundamental beliefs (as a reaction to theological modernism and the historical criticism of the Bible) and insisted on belief in the literal truth of everything in the Bible. *Islamic fundamentalism* insists on strict observance of Muslim Shari'a law.

Christian fundamentalists (in the sense used by most 20th-century fundamentalist churches) believe in the literal truth of the Bible, the divinity of Christ, the Virgin Birth, the Atonement, and the resurrection of Christ as essential parts of their faith. Liberal theologians, while remaining Christian, have questioned all of these points.

funerary practice ritual or act surrounding the disposal of a dead body, by burial, cremation, or other means (such as exposure). Solemn acts such as the preparation of the body, song (laments), offering of gifts, the funeral procession, provision of a memorial, and mourning are subject to codes of procedure in most cultures.

There is evidence for ritualized burial as early as the Neanderthals, and further evidence from the upper Palaeolithic for the burial of skulls alone. By the third millennium BC graves began to be used for successive burials, and the monumental pyramids were constructed as tombs in Egypt. The Egyptian ◊*Book of the Dead* (c. 1600 BC) preserves magic formulas to be used in approaching the underworld. Cremation was practised by Indo-European groups (Greeks and Teutons), but because of Christian concern for the resurrection it was suppressed in Europe until the modern era; in Egypt, as in some other cultures, bodies were preserved by a process of embalming. Pyramids, beehive tombs in Mycenean Greece, neolithic barrows and bronze age tumuli, mausoleums, caves, catacombs, and ship burials (for example, Sutton Hoo) testify to the variety of burial, while decorated vases (from sub-Mycenean Greece) and plain urns have been used to contain the ashes of the cremated dead. In India, bodies may be set afloat into the sacred river Ganges; some native tribes of America practised ritual exposure.

Elaborate gifts placed with the dead, of valued or useful objects, are widely attested for many cultures, as is the decoration placed on sarcophagi, or the erection of memorial images; in ancient China, a terracotta army of 10,000 warriors guarded the tomb complex of the emperor Shi Huangdi (259–210 BC). In European societies, ceremonies at the Cenotaph or the tomb of the unknown soldier commemorate the loss of unidentified combatants in the two world wars of the 20th century. Death is almost universally understood as a rite of passage from one world to another, which must be fully supported by the performance of accepted rituals and confirmed by a period of mourning for the bereaved.

Funk Casimir 1884–1967. US biochemist, born in Poland, who pioneered research into vitamins.

Funk proposed that certain diseases are caused by dietary deficiencies. In 1912 he demonstrated that rice extracts cure beriberi in pigeons. As the extract contains an amine, he mistakenly concluded that he had discovered a class of 'vital amines', a phrase soon reduced to 'vitamins'.

Furies in Greek mythology, the Erinyes, appeasingly called the Eumenides ('kindly ones'). They were the daughters of Earth or of Night, represented as winged maidens with serpents twisted in their hair. They punished such crimes as filial disobedience, murder, inhospitality, and oath-breaking, but were also associated with fertility.

fusion in physics, the fusing of the nuclei of light elements, such as hydrogen, into those of a heavier element, such as helium. The resultant loss in their combined mass is converted into energy. Stars and thermonuclear weapons work on the principle of nuclear fusion.

Very high temperatures and pressures are thought to be required in order for fusion to take place. Under these conditions the atomic nuclei can approach each other at high speeds and overcome the mutual repulsion of their positive charges. At very close range another force, the ◊strong nuclear force, comes into play, fusing the particles together to form a larger nucleus. As fusion is accompanied by the release of large amounts of energy, the process might one day be harnessed to form the basis of commercial energy production. So far no successful fusion reactor – one able to produce the required conditions and contain the reaction – has been built. However, an important step along the road to fusion power was taken in November 1991. In an experiment that lasted 2 seconds, a 1.7 megawatt pulse of power was produced by the Joint European Torus (JET) at Culham, Oxfordshire, UK. This was the first time that a substantial amount of fusion power had been produced in a controlled experiment, as opposed to a bomb.

Futurism literary and artistic movement 1909–14, originating in Paris. The Italian poet Marinetti published the *Futurist Manifesto* 1909 urging Italian artists to join him in Futurism. In their works the Futurists eulogized the modern world and the 'beauty of speed and energy'. Combining the shifting geometric planes of Cubism with vibrant colours, they aimed to capture the dynamism of a speeding car or train by the simultaneous repetition of forms. As a movement Futurism died out during World War I, but the Futurists' exultation in war and violence was seen as an early manifestation of ◊fascism.

Gino Severini painted a topsy-turvy landscape as if seen from the window of a moving train, in *Suburban Train Arriving in Paris* 1915 (Tate Gallery, London), and Giacomo Balla represented the abstract idea of speed by the moving object in such pictures as *Abstract Speed-wake of a Speeding Car* 1919 (Tate Gallery, London). Umberto Boccioni, a sculptor, froze his figures as if they were several frames of a film moving at once.

The work of many Futurist painters, such as Carlo Carrá and Luigi Russolo (1885–1947), is characterized by forms fragmented by penetrating shafts of light. These, together with their use of colour, infuse a feeling of dynamic motion into their work. ◊Vorticism was a similar movement in Britain 1912–15, glorifying modern technology, energy, and violence.

fuzzy logic in mathematics and computing, a form of knowledge representation suitable for notions (such as 'hot' or 'loud') that cannot be defined precisely but which depend on their context. For example, a jug of water may be described as too hot or too cold, depending on whether it is to be used to wash one's face or to make tea. The central idea of fuzzy logic is *probability of set membership*. For instance, referring to someone 5 ft 9 in tall, the statement 'this person is tall' (or 'this person is a member of the set of tall people') might be about 70% true if that person is a man, and about 85% true if that person is a woman. Fuzzy logic enables computerized devices to reason more like humans, responding effectively to complex messages from their control panels and sensors.

The term 'fuzzy logic' was coined in 1965 by Iranian computer scientist Lofti Zadeh of the University of California at Berkeley, although the core concepts go back to the work of Polish mathematician Jan Lukasiewicz in the 1920s. It has been largely ignored in Europe and the USA, but was taken up by Japanese manufacturers in the mid-1980s and has since been applied to hundreds of electronic goods and industrial machines. For example, a vacuum cleaner launched in 1992 by Matsushita uses fuzzy logic to adjust its sucking power in response to messages from its sensors about the type of dirt on the floor, its distribution, and its depth.

G7 or *Group of Seven* the seven wealthiest nations in the world: the USA, Japan, Germany, France, the UK, Italy, and Canada. Since 1975 their heads of government have met once a year to discuss economic and, increasingly, political matters.

Till now man has been up against Nature, from now on he will be up against his own nature.

Dennis Gabor
Inventing the Future

Gabor Dennis 1900–1979. Hungarian-born British physicist. In 1947 he invented the holographic method of three-dimensional photography. He was awarded a Nobel prize 1971.

Gabriel in the New Testament, the archangel who foretold the birth of John the Baptist to Zacharias and of Jesus to the Virgin Mary. He is also mentioned in the Old Testament in the book of Daniel. In Muslim belief, Gabriel revealed the Koran to Muhammad and escorted him on his ◊Night Journey.

Gadamer Hans-Georg 1900– . German ◊hermeneutic philosopher. In *Truth and Method* 1960, he argued that 'understanding' is fundamental to human existence, and that all understanding takes place within a tradition. The relation between text and interpreter can be viewed as a dialogue, in which the interpreter must remain open to the truth of the text.

Gaia or *Ge* in Greek mythology, the goddess of the Earth. She sprang from primordial Chaos and herself produced Uranus, by whom she was the mother of the Cyclopes and ◊Titans.

Gaia hypothesis theory that the Earth's living and nonliving systems form an inseparable whole that is regulated and kept adapted for life by living organisms themselves. The planet therefore functions as a single organism, or a giant cell. Since life and environment are so closely linked, there is a need for humans to understand and maintain the physical environment and living things around them. The Gaia hypothesis was elaborated by British scientist James (Ephraim) Lovelock (1919-) in the 1970s.

Galahad in Arthurian legend, one of the knights of the Round Table. Galahad succeeded in the quest for the ◊Holy Grail because of his virtue. He was the son of ◊Lancelot of the Lake.

Galbraith John Kenneth 1908– . Canadian-born US economist; he became a US citizen 1937. Galbraith criticized the ◊neoclassical view that the economy was characterized by competitive market forces approximating to a state of ◊perfect competition. He suggested that large industrial corporations were constrained by the 'countervailing power' of other firms, trade unions, consumer groups and governments.

He argued that the motivation of large corporations depended on the influence of the 'technostructure' or departmental management, and that such corporations were motivated more by the desire for security and expansion, than the desire to maximize profits. Advertising is seen as a particularly important means of achieving market power and secure expansion.

As a result of this desire for expansion, Galbraith suggested that the 'Affluent Society' develops an economic imbalance devoting too many resources to the production of consumer goods, and not enough to public services and ◊infrastructure.

This commitment to the development of the public sector was in sympathy with ◊Keynesian economics. Galbraith was critical of the view put forward by the advocates of ◊monetarism that state spending was unable to reduce unemployment.

Galbraith became professor of economics at Harvard University in 1949. He was US Ambassador to India 1961 to 1963, and served as economic advisor to John F Kennedy. He taught economics at Harvard until 1975. His major published works include *American Capitalism* 1952, *The Affluent Society*

1958, *The New Industrial State* 1967, and *Economics and the Public Purpose* 1973.

Galen c. 130–c. 200. Greek physician whose ideas dominated Western medicine for almost 1,500 years. Central to his thinking were the theories of ◊humours and the threefold circulation of the blood. He remained the highest medical authority until Andreas Vesalius and William Harvey exposed the fundamental errors of his system.

Galen was born in Pergamum in Asia Minor. He attended the Roman emperor Marcus Aurelius. Although he made relatively few discoveries and relied heavily on the teachings of ◊Hippocrates, he wrote a large number of books, over 100 of which are known.

Galileo properly Galileo Galilei 1564–1642. Italian mathematician, astronomer, and physicist. He developed the astronomical telescope and was the first to see sunspots, the four main satellites of Jupiter, mountains and craters on the Moon, and the appearance of Venus going through 'phases', thus proving it was orbiting the Sun. In mechanics, Galileo discovered that freely falling bodies, heavy or light, had the same, constant acceleration (although the story of his dropping cannonballs from the Leaning Tower of Pisa is questionable) and that a body moving on a perfectly smooth horizontal surface would neither speed up nor slow down. He discovered in 1583 that each oscillation of a pendulum takes the same amount of time despite the difference in amplitude. He invented a hydrostatic balance, and discovered that the path of a projectile is a parabola.

Galileo was born in Pisa, and in 1589 became professor of mathematics at the university there; in 1592 he became a professor at Padua, and in 1610 was appointed chief mathematician to the Grand Duke of Tuscany. Galileo's observations and arguments were an unwelcome refutation of the ideas of ◊Aristotle taught at the (church-run) universities, largely because they made plausible for the first time the heliocentric (Sun-centred) theory of ◊Copernicus. Galileo's persuasive *Dialogues on the Two Chief Systems of the World* 1632 was banned by the church authorities in Rome; he was made to recant by the ◊Inquisition and put under house arrest for his last years.

Gall Franz Joseph 1758–1828. Austrian anatomist, instigator of the discredited theory of ◊phrenology.

Galle Johann Gottfried 1812–1910. German astronomer who located the planet Neptune in

1846, close to the position predicted by French mathematician Urbain Leverrier.

Gallo Robert Charles 1937– . US scientist credited with identifying the virus responsible for ◊AIDS. Gallo discovered the virus, now known as human immunodeficiency virus (HIV), in 1984; the French scientist Luc Montagnier (1932–) of the Pasteur Institute, Paris, discovered the virus, independently, in 1983. The sample in which Gallo discovered the virus was supplied by Montagnier, and it has been alleged that this may have been contaminated by specimens of the virus isolated by Montagnier a few months earlier.

Galois Evariste 1811–1832. French mathematician who originated the theory of groups. His attempts to gain recognition for his work were largely thwarted by the French mathematical establishment, critical of his lack of formal qualifications. Galois was killed in a duel before he was 21. The night before, he had hurriedly written out his unpublished discoveries on group theory, the importance of which would come to be appreciated more and more as the 19th century progressed.

Galton Francis 1822–1911. English scientist who studied the inheritance of physical and mental attributes in humans, with the aim of improving the human species. He discovered that no two sets of human fingerprints are the same, and is considered the founder of ◊eugenics.

Galvani Luigi 1737–1798. Italian physiologist who discovered galvanic, or voltaic, electricity in 1762, when investigating the contractions produced in the muscles of dead frogs by contact with pairs of different metals. His work led quickly to Alessandro Volta's invention of the electrical cell, and later to an understanding of how nerves control muscles.

game theory branch of mathematics that deals with strategic problems (such as those that arise in business, commerce, and warfare) by assuming that the people involved invariably try to win – that is, they are assumed to employ strategies that should give the greatest gain and the smallest loss. The theory was developed by Oscar Morgenstern (1902–1977) and John Von ◊Neumann during World War II.

Gamow George 1904–1968. Russian-born US cosmologist, nuclear physicist, and popularizer of science. His work in astrophysics included a study of the structure and evolution of stars and the creation of the elements. He also explained how the collision of nuclei in the solar interior could produce the nuclear reactions that power the Sun.

Gamow was also an early supporter of the ◊Big Bang theory of the origin of the universe. He predicted that the electromagnetic radiation left over from the universe's formation, should, after having cooled down during the subsequent expansion of the universe, manifest itself as a microwave background radiation with a temperature of 10K (–263°C/–442°F). In 1965 the cosmic background radiation was discovered, which had a temperature of 3K (–270°C/–454°F), or 3°C above absolute zero.

Gandhi Mohandas Karamchand, called *Mahatma* ('Great Soul') 1869–1948. Indian nationalist leader. A pacifist, he led the struggle for Indian independence from the UK by advocating nonviolent noncooperation (*satyagraha*, defence of and by truth) from 1915. He was imprisoned several times by the British authorities and was influential in the nationalist ◊Congress Party and in the independence negotiations 1947. He was assassinated by a Hindu nationalist in the violence that followed the partition of British India into India and Pakistan.

Gandhi was born in Porbandar and studied law in London, later practising as a barrister. He settled in South Africa where until 1914 he led the Indian community in opposition to racial discrimination. Returning to India, he emerged as leader of the Indian National Congress. He organized hunger strikes and events of civil disobedience, and campaigned for social reform, including religious tolerance and an end to discrimination against the so-called untouchable ◊caste.

Ganesh Hindu god, son of Siva and Parvati; he is represented as elephant-headed and is worshipped as a remover of obstacles.

Gang of Four in Chinese history, the chief members of the radical faction that played a key role in directing the ◊Cultural Revolution and tried to seize power after the death of the communist leader Mao Zedong 1976. It included his widow, ◊Jiang Qing; the other members were three young Shanghai politicians: Zhang Chunqiao, Wang Hongwen, and Yao Wenyuan. The coup failed and the Gang of Four were arrested. Publicly tried in 1980, they were found guilty of treason.

gangsterism organized crime, particularly in the USA as a result of the 18th Amendment (Prohibition) in 1919.

Bootlegging activities (importing or making illegal liquor) and 'speakeasies' (where alcohol could be illegally purchased) gave rise to rivalry that resulted in hired gangs of criminals (gangsters) and gun battles. One of the most notorious gangsters was Al Capone.

I've been accused of every death except the casualty list of the World War.

> **gangsters**
> Al(phonse) 'Scarface' Capone, 1898–1947,
> US gangster.
> Newspaper interview

---

garden city in the UK, a town built in a rural area and designed to combine town and country advantages, with its own industries, controlled developments, private and public gardens, and cultural centre. The idea was proposed by Ebenezer ◊Howard, who in 1899 founded the Garden City Association, which established the first garden city: Letchworth in Hertfordshire.

God Almighty first planted a garden; and, indeed, it is the purest of human pleasures.

> **garden**
> Francis Bacon, 1561–1626,
> English politician, philosopher, and essayist.
> *Essays*, 'Of Gardens'

Garvey Marcus (Moziah) 1887–1940. Jamaican political thinker and activist, an early advocate of black nationalism. He founded the UNIA (Universal Negro Improvement Association) in 1914, and moved to the USA in 1916, where he established branches in New York and other northern cities. Aiming to achieve human rights and dignity for black people through black pride and economic self-sufficiency, he was considered one of the first militant black nationalists. He led a Back to Africa movement for black Americans to establish a black-governed country in Africa. The Jamaican religion of ◊Rastafarianism is based largely on his ideas.

Gassendi Pierre 1592–1655. French physicist and philosopher who played a crucial role in the revival of atomism (the theory that the world is made of small, indivisible particles), and the rejection of Aristotelianism so characteristic of the period. He was a propagandist and critic of other views rather than an original thinker.

gaullism political philosophy deriving from the views of French political and military leader, Charles de Gaulle but not necessarily confined to Gaullist parties, or even to France. Its basic tenets are the creation and preservation of a strongly centralized state and an unwillingness to enter into international obligations at the expense of national interests.

Gauquelin Michel 1928–1991. French neo-astrologist. Gauquelin trained as a psychologist and statistician, but became widely known for neo-astrology, or the scientific measurement of the correlations between the exact position of certain planets at birth and individual fame. His work attracted strong criticism as well as much interest. His book *Neo-Astrology: a Copernican Revolution* was published posthumously 1991.

Gauquelin studied the relationship between planet and personality, discovering the 'Mars effect' that sports personalities were more likely to be born with Mars in the crucial positions, actors with Jupiter, and scientists and doctors with Saturn. Gauquelin studied thousands of eminent people to obtain his data, using thousands of non-eminent people as a control group.

Gauss Karl Friedrich 1777–1855. German mathematician who worked on the theory of numbers, non-Euclidean geometry, and the mathematical development of electric and magnetic theory. A method of neutralizing a magnetic field, used to protect ships from magnetic mines, is called 'degaussing'.

Gautama family name of the historical ◊Buddha.

Gawain in Arthurian legend, one of the knights of the Round Table who participated in the quest for the ◊Holy Grail. He is the hero of the 14th-century epic poem *Sir Gawayne and the Greene Knight*.

Gay-Lussac Joseph Louis 1778–1850. French physicist and chemist who investigated the physical properties of gases, and discovered new methods of producing sulphuric and oxalic acids. In 1802 he discovered the approximate rule for the expansion of gases now known as Charles's law.

gay politics political activity by homosexuals in pursuit of equal rights and an end to discrimination.

A gay political movement emerged in the late 1960s in New York with the founding of the Gay Liberation Front (GLF). It aimed to counter negative and critical attitudes to homosexuality and encouraged pride and solidarity among homosexuals. The appearance of the AIDS virus in the early 1980s has produced a new wave of hostility towards homosexuals but has also put them in the forefront of formulating an effective response to the epidemic and raising the public's awareness of its dangers.

Ge in Greek mythology, an alternative name for ◊Gaia, goddess of the Earth.

Geber Latinized form of *Jabir* ibn Hayyan c. 721–c. 776. Arabian alchemist. His influence lasted for more than 600 years, and in the late 1300s his name was adopted by a Spanish alchemist whose writings spread the knowledge and practice of alchemy throughout Europe.

The Spanish alchemist Geber probably discovered nitric and sulphuric acids, and he propounded a theory that all metals are composed of various mixtures of mercury and sulphur.

Gehenna another name for ◊hell; in the Old Testament, a valley S of Jerusalem where children were sacrificed to the Phoenician god Moloch and fires burned constantly.

Geiger Hans 1882–1945. German physicist who produced the Geiger counter. After studying in Germany, he spent the period 1907–12 in Manchester, England, working with Ernest Rutherford on radioactivity. In 1908 they designed an instrument to detect and count alpha particles, positively charged ionizing particles produced by radioactive decay.

In 1928 Geiger and Walther Müller produced a more sensitive version of the counter, which could detect all kinds of ionizing radiation.

Geisteswissenschaften the human and social sciences as opposed to the natural sciences (*Naturwissenschaften*). The term is a German translation of the phrase 'moral sciences' found in J S Mill's work *Logic*.

Gell-Mann Murray 1929– . US physicist. In 1964 he formulated the theory of the ◊quark as one of the fundamental constituents of matter. In 1969 he was awarded a Nobel prize for his work on elementary particles and their interaction.

He was R A Millikan professor of theoretical physics at the California Institute of Technology from 1967.

Gelugpa Tibetan Buddhist tradition founded by Tsongkhapa Lozang Dragpa (1357–1419). The ◊Dalai Lama is always a member of this tradition, though the actual head of the tradition is always the head abbot of the Ganden monastery, founded by Tsongkhapa.

The tradition follows a strict reading of the Vinaya (monastic rules laid down in the ◊Tripitaka, Buddhist scriptures). Gelugpa monks follow a celibate monastic way of life and undertake extensive philosophical scholarship. Tsongkhapa also taught that there was a graded path to enlightenment which the tradition is able to teach.

Gemara in Judaism, part of the ◊Talmud, the compilation of ancient Jewish law.

Gemeinschaft* and *Gesellschaft German terms (roughly, 'community' and 'association') coined by Ferdinand ◊Tönnies 1887 to contrast social relationships in traditional rural societies with those in modern industrial societies. He saw *Gemeinschaft* (traditional) as intimate and positive, and *Gesellschaft* (modern) as impersonal and negative.

In small-scale societies where everyone knows everyone else, the social order is seen as stable and the culture as homogeneous. In large urban areas life is faster and more competitive, and relationships are seen as more superficial, transitory, and anonymous.

gender differences differences between the sexes that are not anatomical or biological but are due to the influences of culture and society.

There are few, if any, differences in behaviour between baby boys and girls in the first weeks of life (which is not to say all babies behave in exactly the same way), but in nearly all societies, and classes of society the way a baby is regarded and handled by its parents and others varies according to its anatomical sex. Thus, gender roles are assigned from an early age and, through contact with peers and society at large, most children soon become aware of gender stereotypes, which are important in the development of ◊sexuality, especially during adolescence. In adult life, gender differences manifest themselves in the extent to which the attitudes and behaviour of men and women diverge, in public and private life, in their choice of occupation, their ambitions, and their aspirations. Male and female roles can also vary markedly from one society, or period in history, to another, pointing to the determining influence of culture on gender roles. It has been plausibly argued, however, that gender differences are purely arbitrary, that societies with different child-rearing practices have different attitudes toward men and women and their roles, and that in an ideal world gender differences could be abolished and many of the inequities of present-day society eliminated.

Bibl. Nicholson, John *A Question of Sex* (1979)

gene unit of inherited material, encoded by a strand of ◊DNA, and transcribed by ◊RNA. In higher organisms, genes are located on the chromosomes. The term 'gene', coined 1909 by the Danish geneticist Wilhelm Johannsen (1857–1927), refers to the inherited factor that consistently affects a particular character in an individual – for example, the gene for eye colour. Also termed a Mendelian gene, after Austrian biologist Gregor ◊Mendel, it occurs at a particular point or locus on a particular chromosome and may have several variants or alleles, each specifying a particular form of that character – for example, the alleles for blue or brown eyes. Some alleles show dominance. These mask the effect of other alleles known as recessive.

In the 1940s, it was established that a gene could be identified with a particular length of DNA, which coded for a complete protein molecule, leading to the 'one-gene-one-enzyme' principle. Later it was realized that proteins can be made up of several polypeptide chains, each with a separate gene, so this principle was modified to 'one-gene-one-polypeptide'. However, the fundamental idea remains the same, that genes produce their visible effects simply by coding for proteins; they control the structure of those proteins via the genetic code, as well as the amounts produced and the timing of production. In modern genetics, the gene is identified either with the cistron (a set of codons that determines a complete polypeptide) or with the unit of selection (a Mendelian gene that determines a particular character in the organism on which ◊natural selection can act). Genes undergo mutation and recombination to produce the variation on which natural selection operates.

gene bank collection of seeds or other forms of genetic material, such as tubers, spores, bacterial or yeast cultures, live animals and plants, frozen sperm and eggs, or frozen embryos. These are stored for possible future use in agriculture, plant and animal breeding, or in medicine, ◊genetic engineering, or the restocking of wild habitats where species have become extinct. Gene banks will be increasingly used as the rate of extinction increases, depleting the Earth's genetic variety (◊biodiversity).

General Agreement on Tarfiffs and Trade (GATT) organization within the United

Nations founded 1948 with the aim of encouraging free trade between nations through low tariffs, abolitions of quotas, and curbs on subsidies.

The latest rounds of talks, begun in Uruguary in 1986, intended to cut restrictions on trade of manufactured goods, agriculture, textiles, and services. The Uruguay round was scheduled to end in 1990, but reached a deadlock in Dec 1990 after negotiators failed to agree on a plan to reduce farm subsidies. However, in Nov 1992, the EC negotiator agreed to a scaled-down reduction in agricultural subsidies, but without the support of the French government. Farmers in France and other EC countries demonstrated against these cuts.

general strike refusal to work by employees in several key industries, with the intention of paralysing the economic life of a country. In British history, the General Strike was a nationwide strike called by the Trade Union Congress on 3 May 1926 in support of the miners' union. Elsewhere, the general strike was used as a political weapon by anarchists and others (see ◊syndicalism), especially in Spain and Italy.

The immediate cause of the 1926 General Strike was the report of a royal commission on the coal mining industry (*Samuel Report* 1926) which, among other things, recommended a cut in wages. The mine-owners wanted longer hours as well as lower wages. The miners' union under the leadership of A J Cook resisted with the slogan 'not a penny off the pay, not a minute on the day'. A coal strike started in early May 1926 and the miners asked the TUC to bring all major industries out on strike in support of the action; eventually it included more than 2 million workers. The Conservative government under Stanley Baldwin used troops, volunteers, and special constables to maintain food supplies and essential services, and had a monopoly on the information services, including BBC radio. After nine days the TUC ended the general strike, leaving the miners – who felt betrayed by the TUC – to remain on strike, unsuccessfully, until Nov 1926. The Trades Disputes Act of 1927 made general strikes illegal.

And the Lord God planted a garden eastward in Eden.

Genesis
Genesis 2:7

Genesis first book of the Old Testament, which includes the stories of the creation of the world, Adam and Eve, the Flood, and the history of the Jewish patriarchs Abraham, Isaac, Jacob, and Joseph (who brought his people to Egypt).

gene therapy medical technique for curing or alleviating inherited diseases or defects. In 1990 a genetically engineered gene was used for the first time to treat a patient.

genetic code the way in which instructions for building proteins, the basic structural molecules of living matter, are 'written' in the genetic material ◊DNA. This relationship between the sequence of bases (the subunits in a DNA molecule) and the sequence of amino acids (the subunits of a protein molecule) is the basis of heredity. The code employs codons of three bases each; it is the same in almost all organisms, except for a few minor differences recently discovered in some protozoa.

genetic engineering deliberate manipulation of genetic material by biochemical techniques. It is often achieved by the introduction of new ◊DNA, usually by means of a virus or plasmid. This can be for pure research or to breed functionally specific plants, animals, or bacteria. These organisms with a foreign gene added are said to be transgenic (see ◊transgenic organism).

In genetic engineering, the splicing and reconciliation of genes is used to increase knowledge of cell function and reproduction, but it can also achieve practical ends. For example, plants grown for food could be given the ability to fix nitrogen, found in some bacteria, and so reduce the need for expensive fertilizers, or simple bacteria may be modified to produce rare drugs. Developments in genetic engineering have led to the production of human insulin, human growth hormone, and a number of other bone-marrow stimulating hormones. New strains of animals have also been produced; a new strain of mouse was patented in the USA 1989 (the application was rejected in the European patent office). A vaccine against a sheep parasite (a larval tapeworm) has been developed by genetic engineering; most existing vaccines protect against bacteria and viruses. There is a risk that when transplanting genes between different types of bacteria (*Escherichia coli*, which lives in the human intestine, is often used) new and harmful strains might be produced. For this reason strict safety precautions are observed, and the altered bacteria are disabled in some way so they are unable to exist outside the laboratory.

genetic fingerprinting technique used for determining the pattern of certain parts of the genetic material ◊DNA that is unique to each individual. Like skin fingerprinting, it can accurately distinguish humans from one another, with the exception of identical siblings from multiple births. It can be applied to as little material as a single cell.

Genetic fingerprinting involves isolating DNA from cells, then comparing and contrasting the sequences of component chemicals between individuals. The DNA pattern can be ascertained from a sample of skin, hair, or semen. Although differences are minimal (only 0.1% between unrelated people), certain regions of DNA, known as **hypervariable regions**, are unique to individuals.

Genetic fingerprinting was discovered by Alec Jeffreys (1950–   ), and is now allowed as a means of legal identification. It is used in paternity testing, forensic medicine, and inbreeding studies.

The results of DNA tests have been accepted as evidence in many thousands of US court cases, although several courts have challenged the validity of conventional genetic fingerprinting. A new method that makes it possible to express the individuals' information in digital code will now be much more accurate than before.

genetics study of inheritance and of the units of inheritance (◊genes). The founder of genetics was Austrian biologist Gregor ◊Mendel, whose experiments with plants, such as peas, showed that inheritance takes place by means of discrete 'particles', which later came to be called genes.

Before Mendel, it had been assumed that the characteristics of the two parents were blended during inheritance, but Mendel showed that the genes remain intact, although their combinations change. Since Mendel, genetics has advanced greatly, first through breeding experiments and light-microscope observations (classical genetics), later by means of biochemical and electron-microscope studies (molecular genetics). An advance was the elucidation of the structure of ◊DNA by US biologist James Dewey Watson and British molecular biologist Francis Crick, and the subsequent cracking

of the ◊genetic code. These discoveries opened up the possibility of deliberately manipulating genes, or ◊genetic engineering.

Geneva Convention international agreement 1864 regulating the treatment of those wounded in war, and later extended to cover the types of weapons allowed, the treatment of prisoners and the sick, and the protection of civilians in wartime. The rules were revised at conventions held 1906, 1929, and 1949, and by the 1977 Additional Protocols.

The function of genius is to furnish cretins with ideas twenty years later.

genius
Louis Aragon, 1897–1982, French poet and novelist.
Traité du Style, 'Le Porte-Plume'

---

genius extraordinary intellectual, inventive, or creative gifts, or a person possessing them. The productions of genius may be astonishingly original and their apparently spontaneous appearance baffling and inexplicable, but there is no doubt that lengthy periods of intensive work and single-minded devotion to the task are involved.

Whether geniuses form a class of supremely gifted individuals is a much debated question. High ◊IQ, for example, is no predictor of genius.

genome the total information carried by the genetic code of a particular organism.

Genius does what it must, and Talent does what it can.

genius
Owen Meredith, 1831–1891, English statesman and poet.
'Last Words of a Sensitive Second-Rate Poet'

---

gentile any person who is not Jewish (the term 'non-Jew' is usually preferred now). In the Hebrew Bible the gentiles are included in the future promised for Israel, which is seen as leading all nations to God, but the word was sometimes used to indicate 'heathen', and the ◊Talmud contains warnings and restrictions about dealings with gentiles.

Jewish teaching has varied about the extent to which the Law should be applied to non-Jews. One of the main fears of modern Jews is that the distinctive Jewish identity, preserved for centuries, will be lost or diluted by marriage with gentiles, and it is therefore strongly discouraged. In the early years of Christianity there was much debate about the status of gentiles, since all the first Christians were Jews. St ◊Paul was influential in establishing the principle that salvation through Jesus Christ was open to Jews and non-Jews alike, and is thus known as 'the apostle to the gentiles'.

geochronology the branch of geology that deals with the dating of the Earth by studying its rocks and contained fossils. The geologic time chart is a result of these studies, dividing Earth time into eons, eras, periods, and epochs determined on the basis of absolute and relative dating methods. Absolute dating methods involve the measurement of radioactive decay over time in certain chemical elements found in rocks, whereas relative dating methods establish the sequence of deposition of various rock layers by identifying and comparing their contained fossils.

geography the study of the Earth's surface; its topography, climate, and physical conditions, and how these factors affect people and society. It is usually divided into *physical geography*, dealing with landforms and climates, and *human geography*, dealing with the distribution and activities of peoples on Earth.

geology science of the Earth, its origin, composition, structure, and history. It is divided into several branches: *mineralogy* (the minerals of Earth), *petrology* (rocks), *stratigraphy* (the deposition of successive beds of sedimentary rocks), *palaeontology* (fossils), and *tectonics* (the deformation and movement of the Earth's crust).

Geology is regarded as part of earth science, a more widely embracing subject that brings in meteorology, oceanography, geophysics, and geochemistry.

geometry branch of mathematics concerned with the properties of space, usually in terms of plane (two-dimensional) and solid (three-dimensional) figures. The subject is usually divided into *pure geometry*, which embraces roughly the plane and solid geometry dealt with in Euclid's *Elements*, and *analytical* or *coordinate geometry*, in which problems are solved using algebraic methods. A third, quite distinct, type includes the non-Euclidean geometries.

Geometry probably originated in ancient Egypt, in land measurements necessitated by the periodic inundations of the river Nile, and was soon extended into surveying and navigation. Early geometers were the Greek mathematicians Thales, Pythagoras, and Euclid. Analytical methods were introduced and developed by the French philosopher René Descartes in the 17th century. From the 19th century, various non-Euclidean geometries were devised by the Germans Karl Gauss and Georg Riemann, the Russian Nikolai Lobachevsky, and others. These proved significant in the development of the theory of relativity and in the formulation of atomic theory.

geomorphology branch of geology that deals with the nature and origin of surface landforms such as mountains, valleys, plains, and plateaus.

George Henry 1839–1897. US economist, born in Philadelphia. His *Progress and Poverty* 1879 suggested a 'single tax' on land, to replace all other taxes on earnings and savings. He hoped such a land tax would abolish poverty, by ending speculation on land values. George's ideas have never been implemented thoroughly, although they have influenced taxation policy in many countries.

George, St patron saint of England. The story of St George rescuing a woman by slaying a dragon, evidently derived from the ◊Perseus legend, first appears in the 6th century. The cult of St George was introduced into W Europe by the Crusaders. His feast day is 23 April.

He is said to have been martyred at Lydda in Palestine 303, probably under the Roman emperor Diocletian, but the other elements of his legend are of doubtful historical accuracy. His association with England probably began when his story became popular amongst medieval crusaders.

Germain Sophie 1776–1831. French mathematician, born in Paris. Although she was not allowed to study at the newly opened Ecole Polytechnique, she corresponded with the mathematicians ◊Lagrange and ◊Gauss. She is remembered for work she carried out in studying ◊Fermat's last theorem.

gerrymander in politics, the rearranging of constituency boundaries to give an unfair advantage to the ruling party. It is now used more generally to describe various kinds of political trickery.

The term derives from US politician Elbridge Gerry (1744–1814), who, while governor of Massachusetts 1812, reorganized an electoral district (shaped like a salamander) in favour of his party.

Gerson Jean 1363–1429. French theologian. He was leader of the concilliar movement, which argued for the supremacy of church councils over popes, and denounced ◊Huss at the Council of Constance 1415. His theological works greatly influenced 15th-century thought.

Gesell Arnold Lucius 1880–1961. US psychologist and educator, a pioneer of developmental psychology. He founded the Yale Clinic of Child Development which he directed 1911–48. Among the first to study the stages of normal development, he worked as a consultant to The Gesell Institute of Child Development, New Haven, Connecticut, which was founded 1950 to promote his educational ideas.

Born in Alma, Wisconsin, USA, Gesell received his PhD from Clark University 1906. Appointed to the Yale University faculty, he received a medical degree from Yale 1915 and became a professor of child hygiene, publishing both scholarly and popular works on the psychology of the child.

gestalt concept of a unified whole that is greater than, or different from, the sum of its parts; that is, a complete structure whose nature is not explained simply by analysing its constituent elements. A chair, for example, will generally be recognized as a chair despite great variations between individual chairs in such attributes as size, shape, and colour. The term was first used in psychology by the Austrian philosopher and psychologist Christian von ◊Ehrenfels in 1890. It has been adopted from German because there is no exact equivalent in English.

Gestalt psychology regards all mental phenomena as being arranged in organized, structured wholes as opposed to being composed of simple sensations. For example, learning is seen as a reorganizing of a whole situation (often involving insight), as opposed to the behaviourists' view that it consists of associations between stimuli and responses. Gestalt psychologists' experiments show that the brain is not a passive receiver of information, but that it structures all its input in order to make sense of it, a belief that is now generally accepted; however, other principles of Gestalt psychology have received considerable criticism. Max ◊Wertheimer, Wolfgang Köhler, and Kurt Koffka (1886–1941) were co-founders of Gestalt psychology.

Gestalt psychology provided the impetus for *Gestalt therapy*, a form of interpretative psychotherapy developed by Fritz and Laura Perls that adopts a holistic approach, emphasizing the development of both mind and body awareness and the development of personal responsibility.

Geulincx Arnold 1625–1669. Belgian philosopher who formed the theory of occasionalism, according to which God synchronizes body and mind, like two clocks that act together but have no influence on each other. Occasionalism was his solution to the ◊mind–body problem.

Geulincx was professor at Louvain 1646–58. To avoid persecution, he often used the pseudonym of Philaretus. His main works are *Quaestiones Quodlibeticae/Miscellaneous Questions* 1653 and *Metaphysica Vera/True Metaphysics* 1691.

ghat in Hinduism, broad steps leading down to one of the sacred rivers. Some of these, known as 'burning ghats', are used for cremation.

Ghazzali, al- 1058–1111. Muslim philosopher and Sufi (Muslim mystic). He was responsible for easing the conflict between the Sufi and the Ulema, a body of Muslim religious and legal scholars.

Initially, he believed that God's existence could be proved by reason, but later he became a wandering Sufi, seeking God through mystical experience; his book *Revival of the Religious Sciences* was written on his travels.

ghetto any deprived area occupied by a minority group, whether voluntarily or not. Originally a ghetto was the area of a town where Jews were compelled to live, decreed by a law enforced by papal bull 1555. The term came into use 1516 when the Jews of Venice were expelled to an island within the city which contained an iron foundry. Ghettos were abolished, except in E Europe, in the 19th century, but the concept and practice were revived by the Germans and Italians 1940–45.

ghost the spectre of a person who has died and who is believed to haunt places at certain times. Ghosts are often described as being indifferent to human presence, though a few are vengeful. Many faiths have special ceremonies – exorcisms – which are designed to get rid of ghosts.

Taoism celebrates a special festival every year for ghosts, seeing them as the unsettled spirits of those without descendants to pray for them and thus release them into the next world. In Western tradition, ghosts usually haunt places associated with a tragic moment in their lives.

Gibbs Josiah Willard 1839–1903. US theoretical physicist and chemist who developed a mathematical approach to thermodynamics. His book *Vector Analysis* 1881 established vector methods in physics.

Gibson James Jerome 1904–1979. US psychologist known for his influential and highly original work on visual perception. An outspoken critic of ◊Helmholtz's notion that perception involves unconscious inferences from sense data and learning-based associations, he proposed that perceptual information is gained directly from the environment, without the need for intermediate processing.

Educated at Princeton, Gibson went on to teach at Smith College, Massachusetts 1928–49, where he was influenced by Kurt Koffka (1886–1941), and at Cornell University 1949–72. In his experimental work he dispensed with the use of two-dimensional, static images and instead explored the perception of motion in freely moving subjects under natural conditions, publishing his results in *The Perception of the Visual World* 1950. He went on to develop what he called an ecological theory of perception in *Senses Considered as Perceptual Systems* 1966.

Gideon in the Old Testament, one of the Judges of Israel, who led a small band of Israelite warriors which succeeded in routing an invading Midianite army of overwhelming number in a surprise night attack.

Gilbert Walter 1932– . US molecular biologist who studied genetic control, seeking the mechanisms that switch genes on and off. By 1966 he had established the existence of the *lac* repressor, the molecule that suppresses lactose production. Further work on the sequencing of ◊DNA nucleotides won him a share of the 1980 Nobel Prize for Chemistry, with Frederick Sanger and Paul Berg.

Gilbert William 1544–1603. English scientist and physician to Elizabeth I and (briefly) James I. He studied magnetism and static electricity, deducing that the Earth's magnetic field behaves as if a bar magnet joined the North and South poles. His book on magnets, published 1600, is the first printed scientific book based wholly on experimentation and observation.

He erroneously thought that the planets were held in their orbits by magnetic forces.

Gilgamesh hero of Sumerian, Hittite, Akkadian, and Assyrian legend, and lord of the Sumerian city of Uruk. The 12 verse books of the *Epic of Gilgamesh* were recorded in a standard version on 12 cuneiform tablets by the Assyrian king Ashurbanipal's scholars in the 7th century BC, and the epic itself is older than Homer's *Iliad* by at least 1,500 years.

The *Epic*'s incident of the Flood is similar to the Old Testament account, since Abraham had been a citizen of the nearby city of Ur in Sumer.

There is no female mind. The brain is not an organ of sex. As well speak of a female liver.

Charlotte Perkins Gilman
Women and Economics

Gilman Charlotte Perkins 1860–1935. US feminist socialist poet, novelist, and historian, author of *Women and Economics* 1898, proposing the ending of the division between 'men's work' and 'women's work' by abolishing housework.

From 1909 to 1916 she wrote and published a magazine *The Forerunner* in which her feminist Utopian novel *Herland* 1915 was serialized.

Gilson Etienne Henry 1884–1978. French philosopher. He was famous for his historical studies of medieval philosophy, through which he became deeply influenced by Thomas ◊Aquinas, and for his contributions to the philosophy of ◊neo-Thomism. His works include *L'Esprit de la philosophie médiéval/The Spirit of Medieval Philosophy* 1932. Born in Paris, he taught at the Sorbonne from 1921 and later at the Collège de France. From 1945 he spent much time at the University of Toronto, Canada.

Girondin member of the right-wing republican party in the French Revolution, so called because a number of their leaders came from the Gironde region. They were driven from power by the ◊Jacobins 1793.

Glanville Ranalf died 1190. English justiciar from 1180 and legal writer. His *Treatise on the Laws and Customs of England* 1188 was written to instruct practising lawyers and judges and is now a historical source on medieval common law.

Glashow Sheldon Lee 1932– . US particle physicist. In 1964 he proposed the existence of a fourth 'charmed' ◊quark, and later argued that quarks must be coloured. Insights gained from these theoretical studies enabled Glashow to consider ways in which the ◊weak nuclear force and the ◊electromagnetic force (two of the fundamental forces of nature) could be unified as a single force now called the ◊electroweak force. For this work he shared the Nobel Prize for Physics 1979 with Abdus Salam and Steven Weinberg.

glasnost former Soviet leader Mikhail ◊Gorbachev's policy of liberalizing various aspects of Soviet life, such as introducing greater freedom of expression and information and opening up relations with Western countries. *Glasnost* was introduced and adopted by the Soviet government 1986.

Glasnost has involved the lifting of bans on books, plays, and films, the release of political ◊dissidents, the tolerance of religious worship, a reappraisal of Soviet history (destalinization), the encouragement of investigative journalism to uncover political corruption, and the sanctioning of greater candour in the reporting of social problems and disasters (such as the explosion at the Chernobyl nuclear plant). Under legislation introduced 1990, censorship of mass media was abolished; however, publication of state secrets, calls for the overthrow of the state by force, incitement of national or religious hatred, and state interference in people's private lives were prohibited. Journalists' rights to access were enshrined, and the right of reply instituted. Citizens gained the right to receive information from abroad.

Glastonbury market town in Somerset, England, on the river Brue; population (1981) 6,800. There is light industry and tourism. Nearby are two excavated lake villages thought to have been occupied for about 150 years before the Romans came to Britain. *Glastonbury Tor*, a hill with a ruined church tower, rises to 159 m/522 ft.

The first church on the site was traditionally founded in the 1st century by Joseph of Arimathea. Legend has it that he brought the Holy Grail to Glastonbury. The ruins of the Benedictine abbey built in the 10th and 11th centuries by Dunstan and his followers were excavated 1963 and the site of the grave of King Arthur and Queen Guinevere was thought to have been identified. One of Europe's largest pop festivals is held outside Glastonbury most years in June.

Glauber Johann 1604–1668. German chemist who discovered the salt known variously as 'Glauber's salt' and '*sal mirabile*'. He made his living selling patent medicines.

The salt, sodium sulphate decahydrate ($Na_2SO_4.10H_2O$), is produced by the action of sulphuric acid on common salt. It is now used as a laxative but was used by Glauber to treat almost any complaint.

global warming projected imminent climate change attributed to the ◊greenhouse effect.

glossolalia the gift of speaking in tongues, usually claimed to be unknown by the speaker and interpreted by someone else. It is referred to in the New Testament, Acts 2:4, and is believed to be a gift of the Holy Spirit. It is a distinct feature of many revivals, especially the ◊Pentecostal movement and the ◊charismatic movement in this century.

gnome in fairy tales, a small, mischievous spirit of the earth. The males are bearded, wear tunics and hoods, and often guard an underground treasure.

The *garden gnome*, an ornamental representation of these spirits, was first brought from Germany to England in 1850 by Charles Isham for his mansion Lamport Hall, Northamptonshire.

Gnosticism esoteric cult of divine knowledge (a synthesis of Christianity, Greek philosophy, Hinduism, Buddhism, and the mystery cults of the Mediterranean), which flourished during the 2nd and 3rd centuries and was a rival to, and influence on, early Christianity. The medieval French ◊Cathar heresy and the modern ◊Mandaeans (in S Iraq) descend from Gnosticism.

Gnostic 4th-century codices discovered in Egypt in the 1940s include the *Gospel of St Thomas* (unconnected with the disciple) and the *Gospel of Mary*, probably originating about AD 135. Gnosticism envisaged the world as a series of emanations from the highest of several gods. The lowest emanation was an evil god (the demiurge) who created the material world as a prison for the divine sparks that dwell in human bodies. The Gnostics

---

If God did not exist, it would be necessary to invent him.

God
Voltaire. Pen name of
François-Marie Arouet.
Épîtres

identified this evil creator with the God of the Old Testament, and saw the Adam and Eve story and the ministry of Jesus as attempts to liberate humanity from his dominion, by imparting divine secret wisdom.

Gobind Singh 1666–1708. Indian religious leader, the tenth and last guru (teacher) of ◊Sikhism, 1675–1708, and founder of the Sikh brotherhood known as the ◊Khalsa. On his death, the Sikh holy book, the *Guru Granth Sahib*, replaced the line of human gurus as the teacher and guide of the Sikh community.

During a period of Sikh persecution Gobind Singh asked those who were willing to die for their faith to join him, the first five willing to risk their lives were named the *pani pyares* 'the faithful ones' by him and proclaimed the first members of the Khalsa. He also introduced the names Singh (lion) for male Sikhs, and Kaur (princess) for female Sikhs.

I am Alpha and Omega, the beginning and the ending, saith the Lord.

God

Bible, the sacred book of the Jewish and Christian religions.
Revelation 1:7

God the concept of a supreme being, a unique creative entity, basic to several monotheistic religions (for example Judaism, Christianity, Islam); in many polytheistic cultures (for example Norse, Roman, Greek), the term 'god' refers to a supernatural being who personifies the force behind an aspect of life (for example Neptune, Roman god of the sea).

Since the 17th century, advances in science and the belief that the only valid statements were those verifiable by the senses have had a complex influence on the belief in God. (See also ◊monotheism, ◊polytheism, ◊deism, ◊theism, and ◊pantheism.)

goddess worship veneration of a female deity. It is a tradition known to have existed since prehistoric times, and continues today. It has frequently been connected with the worshipper's desire for their own fertility as well as that of their crops and livestock. The ancient Greeks, Romans, and Egyptians worshipped several female deities, including goddesses symbolizing fertility, wisdom, hunting, and the safety of the nation and its people. In many tribal religions and cultures, goddess worship forms a part within an over-all cosmology which often depicts the Earth as the mother goddess and the sky as the father god.

Both Hinduism and Buddhism have long traditions of goddess worship. In Hinduism, every deity is accompanied by a female counterpart, or goddess, such as Parvati–Shiva, Lakshmi–Vishnu, Sita–Rama and Radha–Krishna. Many temples are dedicated first to the goddess, who represents the merciful, loving side of the deity. In Buddhism, Tara or Guanyin are both often seen as goddesses of compassion. Such deities are usually considered officially as secondary deities, though popular devotion seems to accord them a higher significance.

In recent years considerable attention has been paid to earlier forms of goddess worship. Some scholars claim that prior to the rise of the main faiths, all worship was of the goddess; others see a time when both the male and female were venerated equally. All such scholars argue that the rise of patriarchy in religion has made the worship of the goddess either frightening to the men in control or has led to a debased form of goddess worship, as for instance in the cult of the Virgin Mary. There has been a rise in worship of the goddess in recent years and notions of the goddess are being raised in Christianity as a counterbalance to the patriarchy of traditional Christian theology and terminology.

Gödel Kurt 1906–1978. Austrian-born US mathematician and philosopher. He proved that a mathematical system always contains statements that can be neither proved nor disproved within the system; in other words, as a science, mathematics can never be totally consistent and totally complete. He worked on relativity, constructing a mathematical model of the universe that made travel back through time theoretically possible.

Godwin William 1756–1836. English philosopher, novelist, and father of Mary Shelley. His *Enquiry concerning Political Justice* 1793 advocated an anarchic society based on a faith in people's essential rationality. At first a Nonconformist minister, he later became an atheist. His first wife was Mary ◊Wollstonecraft.

Goeppert-Mayer Maria 1906–1972. German-born US physicist who studied the structure of the atomic nucleus. She shared the 1963 Nobel Prize for Physics with Eugene ◊Wigner and Hans Jensen (1907–1973).

Her explanation of the stability of particular atoms 1948 envisaged atomic nuclei as shell-like layers of protons and neutrons, with the most stable atoms having completely filled the outermost shells.

He who seizes the right moment, / Is the right man.

Johann Wolfgang von Goethe
Faust

Goethe Johann Wolfgang von 1749–1832. German poet, novelist, statesman, scholar and dramatist. Generally considered the founder of modern German literature, he was leader of the Romantic ◊*Sturm und Drang* movement. His works include the autobiographical *Die Leiden des Jungen Werthers/The Sorrows of the Young Werther* 1774 and the poetic play *Faust* 1808, his masterpiece. A visit to Italy 1786–88 inspired the classical dramas *Iphigenie auf Tauris/Iphigenia in Tauris* 1787 and *Torquato Tasso* 1790.

Among his many interests were geology, the occult, physics, philosophy, biology, comparative anatomy, and optics. His many works – in poetry, drama, fiction and science – made him known throughout Europe. Between 1775 and 1785 he served as prime minister at the court of Weimar.

His scientific research was characterized by a combination of keen observation and poetic intuition. He discovered the intermaxillary bone in the human jaw (thus anticipating Darwin's link between man and apes); and argued that the skull was a modification of the spine, and that all the parts of a plant are modifications of the leaf. In physics, he argued against Newton's theory of light.

Goffman Erving 1922–1982. Canadian social scientist. He studied the ways people try to create, present, and defend a self-image within the social structures surrounding, controlling, and defining human interaction. He also analysed human interaction and the ways people behave, for example, in public places. His works include *The Presentation of Self in Everyday Life* 1956, *Gender Advertisements* 1979, and *Forms of Talk* 1981.

Golden Age in classical mythology, the earliest period of human life, when human beings lived without labour and sorrow. This was followed by silver and bronze ages, the age of heroes, and the iron age of labour and strife.

The Greek poet ◊Hesiod describes the deteriorating conditions of humanity, starting during the reign of the god Cronus, in his poem *Works and Days*. In Roman belief, the reign of Saturn was the equivalent period. The term has since been applied to great periods of literature in national cultures: the late Republican and Augustan ages in Rome, and the 17th century in France and Spain.

Golden Calf in the Old Testament, image made by ◊Aaron in response to the request of the Israelites for a god when they despaired of Moses' return from Mount Sinai.

golden section visually satisfying ratio, first constructed by the Greek mathematician ◊Euclid and used in art and architecture. It is found by dividing a line AB at a point O such that the rectangle produced by the whole line and one of the segments is equal to the square drawn on the other segment. The ratio of the two segments is about 8:13 or 1:1.26, and a rectangle whose sides are in this ratio is called a *golden rectangle*. In van Gogh's picture *Mother and Child*, for example, the Madonna's face fits perfectly into a golden rectangle.

gold standard system under which a country's currency is exchangeable for a fixed weight of gold on demand at the central bank. It was almost universally applied 1870–1914, but by 1937 no single country was on the full gold standard. Britain abandoned the gold standard 1931; the USA abandoned it 1971. Holdings of gold are still retained because it is an internationally recognized commodity, which cannot be legislated upon or manipulated by interested countries.

golem in Jewish thought, anything that has a potential which has not yet been achieved. Adam is sometimes described as golem when he had been created from the Earth but God had not yet put breath in him. In late medieval and particularly post-17th century Jewish stories, certain holy rabbis were credited with the ability to make clay people who came alive as mechanical servants when certain letters forming one of the names of God were placed in their mouths or on their foreheads.

Gombrich Ernst 1909– . Austrian-born British art historian. His work on art history and theory is noted for its depth of analysis and the connections it makes with other fields, such as psychology. His best-known work is *The Story of Art* 1950, written for a popular audience.

He came to Britain in 1936 to work at the University of London Warburg Institute, where he was Director 1959–76.

good in philosophy, that property or characterization of a thing giving rise to commendation. *Intrinsic goods* are those things that we value in themselves, for their own sakes or as ends. Examples might be moral virtue, health, friendship, music or humour. *Extrinsic goods* are those that owe their goodness to things outside of themselves – for example, surgery is good in so far as it promotes health, or a cloud might be good in so far as it contributes to the overall beauty of a sunset. *Nonmoral good* can originate in human action (for example, taking exercise) or it can originate independently of human action (for example, good weather). *Moral good or goodness* (◊morality) originates in human action. ◊Ethics is, in part, the systematic study of theories about morality and goodness.

Many philosophers have identified a highest good. Others, such as Thomas ◊Hobbes, have denied that there is any such thing. Plato held that our highest good was experience of the ◊form of the Good – which is goodness itself and the transcendent source of goodness. ◊Aristotle held that it was an integrated life of virtuous behaviour and of intellectual contemplation. St ◊Augustine of Hippo and St Thomas ◊Aquinas, both Christian philosophers, held that the highest good is beatitude or a state of blessedness. Immanuel ◊Kant held that it was a community of rational people obeying the universal moral law given by reason (◊categorical imperative). Jeremy ◊Bentham held that it was a society in which there was the greatest happiness of the greatest number.

Good Friday in the Christian church, the Friday before Easter, which is observed with fasting and prayer in memory of the Crucifixion (the death of Jesus on the cross). In some places (notably Jerusalem) processions are held re-enacting Jesus's journey to the place of crucifixion.

Goodman Nelson 1906– . US philosopher who tried to dispel the confusions of everyday language by the use of formal logic. His alleged 'new riddle of induction' (◊Goodman's paradox) posits the lack of justification for the way in which we prefer one of the many conceivable characteristics of a set of things we have observed to other less obvious ones when we generalize about the set as a whole. In aesthetics, he attacked the idea that art represents reality by resembling it.

Born in Somerville, Mass., he initially worked as an art dealer after graduating. He taught at Harvard for most of his career, before becoming a professor at the University of Pennsylvania. His most important work is *The Structure of Appearance* 1951.

Goodman's paradox riddle of ◊induction (reasoning from the particular to the general) formulated by US philosopher Nelson Goodman (1906–). He invents a property 'grue', which applies to any green thing examined before a given time and also to any blue thing at any time, and uses it to show that in inductive reasoning some events do, and some do not, establish regularities from which we can make predictions, and that what determines our habits of classification is how deeply a property is entrenched in our thinking.

A prediction that all emeralds examined before the given time will be green, and a prediction that they will be 'grue', are both equally likely to be true. However, if, after the given time, we examine an emerald and it is 'grue', it must be blue and not green. Moreover, if the confirmation of predictions is defined in terms of past success, anything can be made to confirm anything else by inventing strange properties like 'grue'. Some philosophers have criticized the device of a time-linked property as artificial.

Gorbachev Mikhail Sergeyevich 1931– . Soviet president, in power 1985–91. He was a member of the Politburo from 1980. As general secretary of the Communist Party (CPSU) 1985–91, and president of the Supreme Soviet 1988–91, he introduced liberal reforms at home (*perestroika* and ◊*glasnost*), proposed the introduction of multiparty democracy, and attempted to halt the arms race abroad.

In the 1988 presidential election by members of the Soviet parliament, he was the sole candidate. He became head of state 1989. Gorbachev radically changed the style of Soviet leadership, encountering opposition to the pace of change in both conservative and radical camps, but he failed both to realize the depth of hostility this aroused against him in the CPSU and to distance himself from the party. In March 1990 he was elected to a five-year term as executive president with greater powers. He was awarded the Nobel Peace Prize 1990 but his international reputation suffered in the light of harsh state repression of nationalist demonstrations in the Baltic states.

At home his plans for economic reform failed to avert a food crisis in the winter of 1990–91 and his desire to preserve a single, centrally controlled USSR met with resistance from Soviet republics seeking more independence. Early in 1991, Gorbachev shifted to the right in order to placate the conservative wing of the party and appointed some of the hard-liners to positions of power. In late spring, he produced a plan for a new union treaty to sat-isfy the demands of reformers. This plan alarmed the hardliners, who, in late summer, temporarily removed him from office. He was saved from this attempted coup mainly by the efforts of Boris ◊Yeltsin and the ineptness of the plotters. Soon after his reinstatement, Gorbachev was obliged to relinquish his leader-ship of the party, renounce communism as a state doctrine, suspend all activities of the Communist Party (including its most powerful organs the Politburo and the Secretariat), and surrender many of his central powers to the states. During the following months he pressed for an agreement on his proposed union treaty in the hope of preventing a disintegration of the Soviet Union, but was unable to maintain con-trol and on 25 Dec 1991 resigned as president, effectively yielding power to Boris Yeltsin.

Gorgon in Greek mythology, any of three sis-ters, Stheno, Euryale, and Medusa, who had wings, claws, enormous teeth, and snakes for hair. Medusa, the only one who was mortal, was killed by ◊Perseus, but even in death her head was still so frightful that it turned the onlooker to stone.

Gospel in the New Testament generally, the message of Christian salvation; in particular the four written accounts of the life of Jesus by Matthew, Mark, Luke, and John. Although the first three give approximately the same account or synopsis (thus giving rise to the name 'Synoptic Gospels'), their differences from John have raised problems for theologians.

The so-called fifth Gospel, or *Gospel of St Thomas* (not connected with the disciple Thomas), is a 2nd-century collection of 114 sayings of Jesus. It was found in a Coptic translation contained in a group of 13 papyrus codices, discovered in Upper Egypt 1945, which may have formed the library of a Gnostic community (see ◊Gnosticism).

Gothic Revival the resurgence of interest in Gothic architecture, as displayed in the late 18th and 19th centuries, notably in Britain and the USA. Gothic Revival buildings include Barry and Pugin's Houses of Parliament, London 1836–65, and St Pancras Station, London 1865–71, by George Gilbert Scott; the Town Hall, Vienna 1872–83, by Friedrich von Schmidt (1825–1891); and Princeton University, USA.

The growth of Romanticism led some writ-ers, artists, and antiquaries to embrace a fasci-nation with Gothic forms that emphasized the

supposedly bizarre and grotesque aspects of the Middle Ages. During the Victorian period, however, a far better understanding of Gothic forms was achieved, and this resulted in some impressive Neo-Gothic architecture, as well as some desecration of genuine Gothic churches in the name of 'restoration'.

Science is all those things which are confirmed to such a degree that it would be unreasonable to withhold one's provisional consent.

Stephen Jay Gould
Lecture on Evolution

Gould Stephen Jay 1941– . US palaeontolo-gist and author. In 1972 he proposed the the-ory of punctuated equilibrium, suggesting that the evolution of species did not occur at a steady rate but could suddenly accelerate, with rapid change occurring over a few hundred thousand years. His books include *Ever Since Darwin* 1977, *The Panda's Thumb* 1980, *The Flamingo's Smile* 1985, and *Wonderful Life* 1990.

government any system whereby political authority is exercised. Modern systems of government distinguish between liberal democracies, totalitarian (one-party) states, and autocracies (authoritarian, relying on force rather than ideology). The Greek philosopher Aristotle was the first to attempt a systematic classification of governments. His main distinctions were between govern-ment by one person, by few, and by many (monarchy, oligarchy, and democracy), although the characteristics of each may vary between states and each may degenerate into tyranny (rule by an oppressive elite in the case of oligarchy or by the mob in the case of democracy).

Royalty is a government in which the attention of the nation is concentrated on one person doing interesting actions. A Republic is a government in which that attention is divided between many, who are all doing uninteresting actions.

government
Walter Bagehot, 1826–1877, British writer and economist.
The English Constitution

The French philosopher Montesquieu distinguished between constitutional governments – whether monarchies or republics – which operated under various legal and other constraints, and despotism, which was not constrained in this way. Many of the words used (dictatorship, tyranny, totalitarian, democratic) have acquired negative or positive connotations that make it difficult to use them objectively. The term *liberal democracy* was coined to distinguish Western types of democracy from the many other political systems that claimed to be democratic. Its principal characteristics are the existence of more than one political party, open processes of government and political debate, and a separation of powers. *Totalitarian* has been applied to both fascist and communist states and denotes a system where all power is centralized in the state, which in turn is controlled by a single party that derives its legitimacy from an exclusive ideology. *Autocracy* describes a form of government that has emerged in a number of Third World countries, where state power is in the hands either of an individual or of the army; normally ideology is not a central factor, individual freedoms tend to be suppressed where they may constitute a challenge to the authority of the ruling group, and there is a reliance upon force. Other useful distinctions are between *federal* governments (where powers are dispersed among various regions which in certain respects are self-governing) and *unitary* governments (where powers are concentrated in a central authority); and between *presidential* (where the head of state is also the directly elected head of government, not part of the legislature) and *parliamentary* systems (where the government is drawn from an elected legislature that can dismiss it).

No government ought to be without censors, and where the press is free, no one ever will.

government
Thomas Jefferson, 1743–1826, 3rd president of the USA.
Letter to George Washington 9 Sept 1792

grace in both Christianity and Sikhism, free or unmerited gift or privilege bestowed by God, whose favour, or revealing of himself, cannot be earned or attained by human efforts. In Christian thinking, grace also stands for God's presence in human history. In the Orthodox Church it refers to human participation in the divine life, while the Western church understands it more in terms of the power to heal humanity from its defects.

Grace does not abolish nature, but perfects it.

grace
St Thomas Aquinas, c.1226–1274, Italian scholastic philosopher and theologian.
Medieval Thought: St Augustine to Ockham
Gordon Leff

Graces in Greek mythology, three goddesses (Aglaia, Euphrosyne, Thalia), daughters of Zeus and Hera, personifications of pleasure, charm, and beauty; the inspirers of the arts and the sciences.

Graham Billy (William Franklin) 1918– . US Protestant evangelist, known for the dramatic staging and charismatic eloquence of his preaching. Graham has preached to millions during worldwide crusades and on television, bringing many thousands to a 'decision for Christ' (conversion to, or renewal of, Christian faith).

Graham Thomas 1805–1869. Scottish chemist who laid the foundations of physical chemistry (the branch of chemistry concerned with changes in energy during a chemical transformation) by his work on the diffusion of gases and liquids. *Graham's Law* 1829 states that the diffusion rate of a gas is inversely proportional to the square root of its density.

His work on colloids (which have larger particles than true solutions) was equally fundamental; he discovered the principle of dialysis, that colloids can be separated from solutions containing smaller molecules by the differing rates at which they pass through a semipermeable membrane (a process he termed 'osmosis'). The human kidney uses the principle of dialysis to extract nitrogenous waste.

grammar school in the UK, a secondary school catering for children of high academic ability, about 20% of the total, usually measured by the Eleven Plus examination. Most grammar schools have now been replaced by ◊comprehensive schools. By 1991 the proportion of English children in grammar schools was less than 3%.

In the USA, the term is sometimes used for a primary school (also called elementary school).

Gramsci Antonio 1891–1937. Italian Marxist who attempted to unify social theory and political practice. He helped to found the Italian Communist Party 1921 and was elected to parliament 1924, but was imprisoned by the Fascist leader Mussolini from 1926; his *Quaderni di carcere/Prison Notebooks* were published posthumously 1947.

Gramsci believed that politics and ideology were independent of the economic base, that no ruling class could dominate by economic factors alone, and that the working class could achieve liberation by political and intellectual struggle. His concept of **hegemony** argued that real class control in capitalist societies is ideological and cultural rather than physical, and that only the working class 'educated' by radical intellectuals could see through and overthrow such bourgeois propaganda.

His humane and gradualist approach to Marxism, specifically his emphasis on the need to overthrow bourgeois ideology, influenced European Marxists in their attempt to distance themselves from orthodox determinist Soviet communism.

Grandes Ecoles, les in France, selective higher education colleges which function alongside and independently of universities. Examples include the Ecole Polytechnique, the Ecole Normale Superieure, and the Ecole National d'Administration.

grand unified theory (GUT) in physics, a sought-for theory that would combine the theory of the strong nuclear force (called ◊quantum chromodynamics) with the theory of the weak nuclear and electromagnetic forces. The search for the grand unified theory is part of a larger programme seeking a ◊unified field theory, which would combine all the forces of nature (including gravity) within one framework.

granthi in Sikhism, the man or woman who reads from the holy book, the *Guru Granth Sahib*, during the service.

graphology the study of the writing system of a language. This study would include the number and formation of the letters, the spelling patterns, accents, and punctuation.

The range of writing systems varies so much that English speakers would not be able even to copy most of them; we would miss the fine distinctions in the formation of the letters. We probably would not be able to recognize many

of them as languages. However, with our alphabetical system we can represent most languages from the same family. *'Wo' d'Uelzecth durech d'wisen ze't/durch d'Fielsen d'Sauer brecht.'* This is Luxembourgian. We recognize the letters, but the use of apostrophes and capital letters seems to differ from English. A graphologist would study how this language works, and the rules that govern its writing.

gravity force of attraction that arises between objects by virtue of their masses. On Earth, gravity is the force of attraction between any object in the Earth's gravitational field and the Earth itself. It is regarded as one of the four fundamental ◊forces of nature, the other three being the ◊electromagnetic force, the ◊strong nuclear force, and the ◊weak nuclear force. The gravitational force is the weakest of the four forces, but it acts over great distances. The particle that is postulated as the carrier of the gravitational force is the graviton.

According to Newton's law of gravitation, all objects fall to Earth with the same acceleration, regardless of mass. For an object of mass m_1 at a distance r from the centre of the Earth (mass m_2), the gravitational force of attraction F equals Gm_1m_2/r^2, where G is the gravitational constant. However, according to Newton's second law of motion, F also equals m_1g, where g is the acceleration due to gravity; therefore $g = Gm_2/r^2$ and is independent of the mass of the object; at the Earth's surface it equals 9.806 metres per second per second.

Einstein's general theory of relativity treats gravitation not as a force but as a curvature of space and time around a body. Relativity predicts the bending of light and the red shift of light in a gravitational field; both have been observed. Another prediction of relativity is *gravitational waves*, which should be produced when massive bodies are violently disturbed. These waves are so weak that they have not yet been detected with certainty, although observations of a pulsar (which emits energy at regular intervals) in orbit around another star have shown that the stars are spiralling together at the rate that would be expected if they were losing energy in the form of gravitational waves.

Gray Asa 1810–1888. US botanist and taxonomist who became America's leading expert in the field. His major publications include *Elements of Botany* 1836 and the definitive *Flora of North America* 1838, 1843. He based his revision of the Linnaean system of plant classification on fruit form rather than gross morphology.

Born in Saquoit, New York, USA, Gray graduated from medical school but chose botany rather than medicine as his career. A friend and supporter of Charles ◊Darwin, he was one of the founders of the American National Academy of Sciences.

Great Awakening religious revival in the American colonies from the late 1730s to the 1760s, sparked off by George Whitefield (1714–1770), an itinerant English Methodist preacher whose evangelical fervour and eloquence made many converts. A second 'great awakening' occurred in the first half of the 19th century, establishing the evangelist tradition in US Protestantism.

Great Leap Forward change in the economic policy of the People's Republic of China introduced by ◊Mao Zedong under the second five-year plan of 1958–62. The aim was to achieve rapid and simultaneous agricultural and industrial growth through the creation of large new agro-industrial communes. The inefficient and poorly planned allocation of state resources led to the collapse of the strategy by 1960 and the launch of a 'reactionary programme', involving the use of rural markets and private subsidiary plots. More than 20 million people died in the Great Leap famines of 1959–61.

Great Schism in European history, the period 1378–1417 in which rival popes had seats in Rome and in Avignon; it was ended by the election of Martin V during the Council of Constance 1414–17.

Greek Orthodox Church see ◊Orthodox Church.

Greek religion the religion of Ancient Greece from the 8th to the 3rd centuries BC, with a pantheon of gods including ◊Zeus, his consort ◊Hera, ◊Athena the goddess of wisdom, ◊Hermes the god of war, and many others, who lived on Mount Olympus.

From the 8th century BC, a discernible form of Greek religion emerges from what was formerly a collection of local or tribal deities. Greek religion was based upon a network of mysteries (see ◊mystery religion) and sacred sites without a full-time professional priesthood. The mysteries were often associated with women, and appear to represent a very old strand in Greek religion. The oracles such as that at Delphi and the healing centres associated with the god of medicine, Aesculapius, formed major centres for Greek worship, as did the civic gods of each town who were

honoured through plays and performances. Under the influence of Plato, Greek religion of the last three centuries BC veered away from the pantheon of gods towards a more abstract notion of God as mind and as ultimate meaning, and a rejection of the notion, found in Homer, that human beings were the playthings of the gods of Mount Olympus.

Green Thomas Hill 1836–1882. English philosopher. He attempted to show the limitations of Herbert ◊Spencer and John Stuart ◊Mill, and advocated the study of the German philosophers Kant and Hegel. His chief works are *Prolegomena to Ethics* 1883 and *Principles of Political Obligation* 1895. He was professor of moral philosophy at Oxford from 1878.

greenhouse effect phenomenon of the Earth's atmosphere by which solar radiation, trapped by the Earth and re-emitted from the surface, is prevented from escaping by various gases in the air. The result is a rise in the Earth's temperature. The main greenhouse gases are carbon dioxide, methane, and chlorofluorocarbons (CFCs). Fossil-fuel consumption and forest fires are the main causes of carbon-dioxide build-up; methane is a byproduct of agriculture (rice, cattle, sheep). Water vapour is another greenhouse gas.

The United Nations Environment Programme estimates that by 2025 average world temperatures will have risen by 1.5°C with a consequent rise of 20 cm in sea level. Low-lying areas and entire countries would be threatened by flooding and crops would be affected by the change in climate. However, predictions about global warming and its possible climatic effects are tentative and often conflict with each other.

Dubbed the 'greenhouse effect' by Swedish scientist Svante Arrhenius, it was first predicted 1827 by French mathematician Joseph Fourier (1768–1830).

Green Man or *Jack-in-the-Green* in English folklore, figure dressed and covered in foliage, associated with festivities celebrating the arrival of spring. His face is represented in a variety of English church carvings, in wood or stone, often with a protruding tongue. Similar figures also occur in French and German folklore, the earliest related carvings being at Trier, France, on the river Mosel (about 200 AD).

green movement collective term for the individuals and organizations involved in efforts to protect the environment. The movement encompasses political parties such as the ◊Green Party and organizations like Friends of the Earth and Greenpeace.

Despite a rapid growth of public support, and membership of environmental organizations running into many millions worldwide, political green groups have failed to win significant levels of the vote in democratic societies.

Green Party political party aiming to 'preserve the planet and its people', based on the premise that incessant economic growth is unsustainable. The leaderless party structure reflects a general commitment to decentralization. Green parties sprang up in W Europe in the 1970s and in E Europe from 1988. Parties in different countries are linked to one another but unaffiliated with any pressure group. The party had a number of parliamentary seats in 1993: Austria 10, Belgium 36, Estonia 1, Finland 11, Georgia 11, Germany 8, Greece 1, Republic of Ireland 1, Italy 20, Luxembourg 4, the Netherlands 6, Portugal 2, Slovenia 7, and Switzerland 14; and 29 members in the European Parliament (Belgium 3, Denmark 1, France 9, Germany 8, Italy 5, the Netherlands 2, Portugal 1).

The British Green Party was founded 1973 as the Ecology Party (initially solely environmental). In the 1989 European elections, the British Green Party polled over 2 million votes but received no seats in Parliament, because Britain was the only country in Europe not to have some form of proportional representation. Internal disagreements from 1990 have reduced its effectiveness and popular appeal.

green revolution in agriculture, a popular term for the change in methods of arable farming in Third World countries. The intent is to provide more and better food for their populations, albeit with a heavy reliance on chemicals and machinery. It was instigated in the 1940s and 1950s, but abandoned by some countries in the 1980s. Much of the food produced is exported as cash crops, so that local diet does not always improve.

Measures include the increased use of tractors and other machines, artificial fertilizers and pesticides, as well as the breeding of new strains of crop plants (mainly rice, wheat, and corn) and farm animals. Much of the work is coordinated by the Food and Agriculture Organization of the United Nations.

The green revolution was initially successful in SE Asia; India doubled its wheat yield in 15 years, and the rice yield in the Philippines rose by 75%. However, yields have levelled off in many areas and some countries, which cannot afford the dams, fertilizers, and machinery required, have adopted intermediate technologies.

High-yield varieties of cereal plants require 70–90 kg/154–198 lb of nitrogen per hectare, more than is available to small farmers in poor countries. The rich farmers therefore enjoy bigger harvests, and the gap between rich and poor in the Third World has grown.

Human beings have an inalienable right to invent themselves; when that right is pre-empted it is called brain-washing.

Germaine Greer
The Times 1 Feb 1986

Greer Germaine 1939– . Australian-born feminist writer who achieved fame with the publication of *The Female Eunuch* 1970, a polemical study of how ◊patriarchy – through the nuclear family and capitalism – subordinates women by forcing them to conform to feminine stereotypes that effectively 'castrate' them.

It was immensely popular, and Greer became identified as a leading figure of the ◊women's movement. However, even at the time, the book was criticized by other feminists for placing too much emphasis on sexual liberation as the way forward. Since then she has published *The Obstacle Race* 1979, a study of women and painting; *Sex and Destiny: The Politics of Human Fertility* 1984, a critique of the politics of fertility and contraception which seemed to reverse her earlier position; and *The Change* 1991, a positive view of the menopause.

Gregory I St, *the Great* c. 540–604. Pope from 590 who asserted Rome's supremacy and exercised almost imperial powers. In 596 he sent St ◊Augustine to England. He introduced the choral *Gregorian chant* into the liturgy. Feast day 12 March.

Gregory VII or *Hildebrand* c. 1023–1085. Chief minister to several popes before his election to the papacy 1073. In 1077 he forced the Holy Roman emperor Henry IV to wait in the snow at Canossa for four days, dressed as a penitent, before receiving pardon. He was driven from Rome and died in exile. His feast day is 25 May.

He claimed power to depose kings, denied lay rights to make clerical appointments, and attempted to suppress simony (the buying and selling of church preferments) and to enforce clerical celibacy, making enemies of both rulers and the church.

Gresham Thomas c. 1519–1579. English merchant financier who founded and paid for the

Royal Exchange and propounded *Gresham's Law*: 'bad money tends to drive out good money from circulation'.

Grignard François Auguste-Victor 1871–1935. French chemist. In 1900 he discovered a series of organic compounds, the *Grignard reagents*, that found applications as some of the most versatile reagents in organic synthesis. Members of the class contain a hydrocarbon radical, magnesium, and a halogen such as chlorine. He shared the 1912 Nobel Prize for Chemistry.

Grimm brothers Jakob Ludwig Karl (1785–1863) and Wilhelm (1786–1859), philologists and collectors of German fairy tales such as Hansel and Gretel and Rumpelstiltskin. Joint compilers of an exhaustive dictionary of German, they saw the study of language and the collecting of folk tales as strands in a single enterprise.

Encouraged by a spirit of Romantic nationalism the brothers collected stories from friends, relatives, and villagers. *Kinder und Hausmärchen/ Nursery and Household Tales* were published as successive volumes 1812, 1815, and 1822. Jakob was professor of philology at Göttingen and formulator of Grimm's law. His *Deutsche Grammatick/German Grammar* 1819 was the first historical treatment of the Germanic languages.

Gropius Walter Adolf 1883–1969. German architect who lived in the USA from 1937. He was an early exponent of the ◊International Style defined by glass curtain walls, cubic blocks, and unsupported corners, for example, the model factory and office building at the 1914 Cologne Werkbund exhibition, designed with Adolph Meyer. A founder-director of the ◊Bauhaus school in Weimar 1919–28, he advocated teamwork in design and artistic standards in industrial production. He was responsible for the new Bauhaus premises at Dessau 1925–26, a hallmark of the International Style.

From 1937 he was professor of architecture at Harvard. His other works include the Fagus Works (a shoe factory in Prussia) 1911 and the Harvard Graduate Centre 1949–50.

gross domestic product (GDP) value of the output of all goods and services produced within a nation's borders, normally given as a total for the year. It thus includes the production of foreign-owned firms within the country, but excludes the income from domestically owned firms located abroad. See also ◊gross national product.

Since output is derived from expenditure on goods and services by firms, consumers, and government net of imports, and income (in the form of wages, salaries, interest, rent, and profits) is derived from the production of goods and services, GDP can be measured either by the sum of total output or expenditure or incomes. However, in practice there is usually a slight discrepancy between the three because of the highly complex calculations involved. GDP fluctuates in relation to the ◊trade cycle and ◊standard of living.

In the UK, the percentage increase in GDP from one year to the next is the standard measure of ◊economic growth.

Grosseteste Robert c. 1169–1253. English scholar and bishop. His prolific writings include scientific works, as well as translations of Aristotle, and commentaries on the Bible. He was a forerunner of the empirical school, being one of the earliest to suggest testing ancient Greek theories by practical experiment.

He was bishop of Lincoln from 1235 to his death, attempting to reform morals and clerical discipline, and engaging in controversy with Innocent IV over the pope's finances.

gross national product (GNP) the most commonly used measurement of the wealth of a country. GNP is defined as the total value of all goods and services produced by firms owned by the country concerned. It is measured as the ◊gross domestic product plus income from abroad, minus income earned during the same period by foreign investors within the country; see also ◊national income.

Grotius Hugo 1583–1645. Dutch jurist and politician. He held that the rules governing human and international relations were founded on human nature which is rational and social. These rules constitute a natural law binding on citizens, rulers, and God.

Born in Delft, he was educated at the University of London. He became a lawyer, and later received political appointments. In 1618 he was arrested as a republican and sentenced to imprisonment for life. His wife contrived his escape 1620, and he settled in France, where he composed the *De Jure Belli et Pacis/On the Law of War and Peace* 1625, the foundation of international law. He was Swedish ambassador in Paris 1634–45.

Not to know something is a great part of wisdom.

Hugo Grotius
Docta Ignorantia

group psychology area of ◊social psychology dealing with topics such as the formation and cohesion of groups, competition and conflict among group members and between groups, the influence of the group on the individual and vice-versa, communication within the group and between groups, and many other aspects of social interaction.

group psychotherapy or *group therapy* form of ◊psychotherapy carried out with groups of patients, of both sexes, who come together regularly with the therapist as group leader. They are encouraged to talk freely about themselves, their problems, and their feelings towards each other and the therapist.

There are many kinds of group psychotherapy; some are based on ◊psychoanalysis, others involve or are derived from psychodrama.

A group usually consists of six to eight patients who meet for treatment once or twice a week. A closed group keeps its membership for the duration of the treatment, about two years, whereas membership of an open group changes when patients leave or are discharged and new patients join the group.

growth see ◊economic growth.

Guanyin in Chinese Buddhism, the goddess of mercy. In Japan she is *Kwannon* or Kannon, an attendant of the Amida Buddha (Amitābha). Her origins were in India as the male bodhisattva Avalokiteśvara.

guardian spirit belief that people or places have guardian spirits who protect them. The belief is found worldwide and has a long history. Such spirits may be thought to dwell in rocks, rivers, or trees, while others are associated with crops or buildings. Many faiths teach that each person has a guardian spirit or angel who watches over them. In Islam there are believed to be two such angels, one on either shoulder. In many branches of Christianity it is believed that at birth everyone is given a guardian angel who is there to be turned to in times of stress or temptation. The Christian concept of patron saints – St Christopher, for example, is believed to protect travellers – may have developed from a belief in guardian spirits.

guerrilla irregular soldier fighting in a small unofficial unit, typically against an established or occupying power, and engaging in sabotage, ambush, and the like, rather than pitched battles against an opposing army. Guerrilla

tactics have been used both by resistance armies in wartime (for example, the Vietnam War) and in peacetime by national liberation groups and militant political extremists (for example the PLO; Tamil Tigers).

Government and co-operation are in all things the law of life; anarchy and competition the laws of death.

John Ruskin, 1819–1900,
English author and art critic.
Unto this Last

The term was first applied to the Spanish and Portuguese resistance to French occupation during the Peninsular War (1808–14). Guerrilla techniques were widely used in World War II – for example, in Greece and the Balkans. Political activists who resort to violence, particularly **urban guerrillas**, tend to be called 'freedom fighters' by those who support their cause, 'terrorists' by those who oppose it. Efforts by governments to put a stop to their activities have had only sporadic success. The Council of Europe has set up the European Convention on the Suppression of Terrorism, to which many governments are signatories. In the UK the Prevention of Terrorism Act 1984 is aimed particularly at the Irish Republican Army (IRA). The Institute for the Study of Terrorism was founded in London 1986.

What difference does it make to the dead, the orphans and the homeless, whether the mad destruction is wrought under the name of totalitarianism or the holy name of liberty or democracy?

Mohandas Gandhi
1869–1948, Indian Leader.
Non-violence in Peace and War
vol 1, ch 142

Guevara 'Che' Ernesto 1928–1967. Latin American revolutionary. He was born in Argentina and trained there as a doctor, but left his homeland 1953 because of his opposition to the right-wing president Perón. In effecting the Cuban revolution of 1959, he was second only to Castro and Castro's brother Raúl. In 1965 he went to the Congo to fight against white mercenaries, and then to Bolivia, where he was killed in an unsuccessful attempt to lead a peasant rising. He was an orthodox Marxist and renowned for his guerrilla techniques.

guild or *gild* medieval association, particularly of artisans or merchants, formed for mutual aid and protection and the pursuit of a common purpose, religious or economic. Guilds became politically powerful in Europe but after the 16th century their position was undermined by the growth of ◊capitalism.

Guilds fulfilling charitable or religious functions (for example, the maintenance of schools, roads, or bridges, the assistance of members in misfortune, or the provision of masses for the souls of dead members) flourished in western Europe from the 9th century but were suppressed in Protestant countries at the Reformation.

The earliest form of economic guild, the *guild merchant*, arose during the 11th and 12th centuries; this was an organization of the traders of a town, who had been granted a practical monopoly of its trade by charter. As the merchants often strove to exclude craftworkers from the guild, and to monopolize control of local government, the *craft guilds* came into existence in the 12th and 13th centuries. These, which included journeymen (day workers) and apprentices as well as employers, regulated prices, wages, working conditions, and apprenticeships, prevented unfair practices, and maintained high standards of craft; they also fulfilled many social, religious, and charitable functions. By the 14th century they had taken control of local government, ousting the guild merchant.

guild socialism early 20th-century movement in Britain whose aim was to organize and control the industrial life of the country through self-governing democratic guilds of workers. Inspired by Catholicism, it was antimaterialistic and attempted to arrest what it saw as a spiritual decline in modern civilization. The National Guilds League was founded 1915, and at the movement's height there were over 20 guilds, but the League was dissolved 1925.

Guillaume Charles 1861–1938. Swiss physicist who studied measurement and alloy development. He discovered a nickel–steel alloy, invar, which showed negligible expansion with rising temperatures. He was awarded the Nobel Prize for Physics 1920.

As the son of a clockmaker, Guillaume came early in life to appreciate the value of precision in measurement. He spent most of his life at the International Bureau of Weights and Measures in Sèvres, France, which established the standards for the metre, litre, and kilogram.

Guinevere Welsh *Gwenhwyfar* in British legend, the wife of King ◊Arthur. Her adulterous love affair with the knight ◊Lancelot of the Lake led ultimately to Arthur's death.

gulag Russian term for the system of prisons and labour camps used to silence dissidents and opponents of the Soviet regime.

In the Stalin era (1920s–1930s), thousands of prisoners died from the harsh conditions of these remote camps.

Gunter Edmund 1581–1626. English mathematician who became professor of astronomy at Gresham College, London 1619. He is reputed to have invented a number of surveying instruments as well as the trigonometrical terms 'cosine' and 'cotangent'.

Gurdjieff George Ivanovitch 1877–1949. Russian occultist and mystic who influenced the modern human-potential movement. His famous text is *Meetings with Remarkable Men* (English translation 1963). The mystic ◊Ouspensky was a disciple who expanded his ideas.

After years of wandering in central Asia, in 1912 Gurdjieff founded in Moscow the Institute for the Harmonious Development of Man, based on a system of raising consciousness (involving learning, group movement, manual labour, dance, and a minimum of sleep) known as the Fourth Way. After the 1917 Revolution he established similar schools in parts of Europe.

gurdwara Sikh place of worship and meeting. As well as a room housing the *Guru Granth Sahib*, the holy book, the gurdwara contains a kitchen and eating area for the *langar*, or communal meal.

guru (Hindi *gurū*) Hindu or Sikh leader, or religious teacher.

Guru Granth Sahib the holy book of ◊Sikhism, a collection of nearly 6,000 hymns by the first five and the ninth Sikh gurus, but also including the writings of some Hindus and Muslims. It is regarded as a living guru and treated with the respect that this implies.

Guru ◊Gobind Singh instructed Sikhs to look upon it as their guide, a symbolic representation of all the gurus. The original copy of the *Guru Granth Sahib* is kept in the Golden Temple in Amritsar which was built especially to house it. When the *Guru Granth Sahib* is moved, it must be accompanied by five

◊Khalsa Sikhs who correspond to the attendants who would accompany an honoured
person. The *Guru Granth Sahib* is taken into a
separate room at night; it must always be
approached with respect, and with clean
hands. The *Guru Granth Sahib* teaches that
there is one God and that all people are equal.
It accepts the concepts of ◊reincarnation and
the laws of ◊karma. It prohibits the use of
intoxicants and rejects both idol worship and
formal priesthood. It promotes the idea of
sewa, or service to others – Sikhs should give
their money or, more importantly, their time
and effort, to those in need.

Gutenberg Johann c. 1400–1468. German
printer, the inventor of printing from movable
metal type, based on the Chinese wood-block-
type method (although Laurens Janszoon
Coster has a rival claim).

Gutenberg began work on the process in
the 1440s and in 1450 set up a printing business in Mainz with Johann Fust (c.
1400–1466) as a backer. By 1455 he had produced the first printed Bible (known as the
Gutenberg Bible). Fust seized the press for
nonpayment of the loan, but Gutenberg is
believed to have gone on to print the Mazarin
and Bamberg bibles.

Guthrie Edwin R(ay) 1886–1959. US psychologist who attempted to develop a ◊learning theory in which the role of reinforcement (reward
or punishment) in a stimulus-response (S-R)
connection is secondary. Contiguity between
the stimulus and the response was the crucial
factor. Reinforcement merely brought the
learning trial or incident to an end, preventing
further responses that might become bonded to
the stimulus.

The teachings were at first transmitted orally, but this led to a large number of Hadith whose origin was in doubt; later, scholars such as Muhammad al-Bukhari (810–870) collected together those believed to be authentic, and these collections form the Hadith accepted by Muslims today.

Haeckel Ernst Heinrich 1834–1919. German scientist and philosopher. His theory of 'recapitulation', expressed as 'ontogeny repeats phylogeny' (or that embryonic stages represent past stages in the organism's evolution), has been superseded, but it stimulated research in embryology.

Born at Potsdam, he came professor of zoology at Jena 1865. He coined the term 'ecology', and is the author of bestselling general scientific works such as *The Riddles of the Universe*.

Haggadah (Hebrew 'telling') in Judaism, the part of the Talmudic literature not concerned with religious law (the Halakah), but devoted to folklore and legends of heroes. Also, the book (often richly illustrated) giving the order of service for the ◊seder meal at ◊Passover, including songs, prayers, and an account of the ◊Exodus of the Israelites from Egypt.

hagiography the writing of the lives of saints. These are usually expressed in glowing terms and as such hagiography tends to mean somewhat biased and over-ornate writings, frequently leaving much to be desired as historical records of the saints.

Hahn Kurt 1886–1974. German educationist. He was the founder of Salem School in Germany. After his expulsion by Hitler, he founded Gordonstoun School in Scotland and was its headmaster 1934–53. He cofounded the Atlantic College project 1960, and was associated with the Outward Bound Trust and the Duke of Edinburgh Award scheme.

Hahn Otto 1879–1968. German physical chemist who discovered nuclear fission. In 1938 with Fritz Strassmann (1902–1980), he discovered that uranium nuclei split when bombarded with neutrons, which led to the development of the atom bomb. He was awarded the Nobel Prize for Chemistry 1944.

He worked with Ernest Rutherford and William Ramsay, and became director of the Kaiser Wilhelm Institute for Chemistry 1928.

Haile Selassie Ras (Prince) Tafari ('the Lion of Judah') 1892–1975. Emperor of Ethiopia 1930–74. He pleaded unsuccessfully to the League of Nations against Italian conquest of his country 1935–36, and lived

Habermas Jürgen 1929– . German social theorist, a member of the ◊Frankfurt school. His central concern is how a meaningful engagement in politics and society is possible in a society dominated by science and the technology and bureaucracy based on it. In *Theory and Practice* 1963 and *Knowledge and Human Interest* 1968 he argues that reason, which had long been a weapon of intellectual and political freedom, has been appropriated by science. Far from being a disinterested pursuit of knowledge, it is an instrument for achieving a range of unquestioned social and political ends. In his *Theory of Communicative Action* 1981 he describes how a 'communicative rationality' can be developed, reclaiming lost ground and allowing rational political commitment.

hacking unauthorized access to a computer, either for fun or for malicious or fraudulent purposes. Hackers generally use microcomputers and telephone lines to obtain access. In computing, the term is used in a wider sense to mean using software for enjoyment or self-education, not necessarily involving unauthorized access. See also computer ◊virus.

Hades in Greek mythology, the underworld where spirits went after death, usually depicted as a cavern or pit underneath the Earth, the entrance of which was guarded by the three-headed dog Cerberus. It was presided over by the god Pluto or Hades (Roman Dis). Pluto was the brother of Zeus and married ◊Persephone, daughter of Demeter and Zeus.

Hadith collection of the teachings of ◊Muhammad and stories about his life, regarded by Muslims as a guide to living second only to the ◊Qur'an.

in the UK until his restoration 1941. He was deposed by a military coup 1974 and died in captivity the following year. Followers of the Rastafarian religion (see ◊Rastafarianism) believe that he was the Messiah, the incarnation of God (Jah).

hajj pilgrimage to ◊Mecca that should be undertaken by every Muslim at least once in a lifetime, unless he or she is prevented by financial or health difficulties. A Muslim who has been on hajj may take the additional name Hajji. Many of the pilgrims on hajj also visit Medina, where the prophet ◊Muhammad is buried.

halal conforming to the rules laid down by Islam. The term can be applied to all aspects of life, but usually refers to food permissible under Muslim dietary laws, including meat from animals that have been slaughtered in the correct ritual fashion.

Haldane J(ohn) B(urdon) S(anderson) 1892–1964. English scientist and writer. A physiologist and geneticist, Haldane was better known as a popular science writer of such books as *The Causes of Evolution* 1933 and *New Paths in Genetics* 1941.

Hale George Ellery 1868–1938. US astronomer who made pioneer studies of the Sun and founded three major observatories. In 1889 he invented the spectroheliograph, a device for photographing the Sun at particular wavelengths. In 1917 he established on Mount Wilson, California, a 2.5-m/100-in reflector, the world's largest telescope until superseded 1948 by the 5-m/200-in reflector on Mount Palomar, which Hale had planned just before he died.

In 1897 he founded the Yerkes Observatory in Wisconsin, with the largest refractor, 102 cm/40 in, ever built at that time.

Halicarnassus ancient city in Asia Minor (now Bodrum in Turkey), where the tomb of Mausolus, built about 350 BC by widowed Queen Artemisia, was one of the Seven Wonders of the World. The Greek historian Herodotus was born there.

Halley Edmond 1656–1742. English atronomer who not only identified 1705 the comet that was later to be known by his name, but also compiled a star catalogue, detected the proper motion of stars using historical records, and began a line of research that – after his death – resulted in a reasonably accurate calculation of the astronomical unit.

Halley calculated that the cometary sightings reported in 1456, 1531, 1607 and, most recently, in 1682, all represented reappearances of the same comet. He reasoned that the comet would follow a parabolic path and announced 1705 that it would reappear 1758. When it did, public acclaim for the astronomer was such that his name was irrevocably attached to it.

Halley was also a pioneer geophysicist and meteorologist and worked in many other fields including mathematics. He became the second Astronomer Royal 1720. He was a friend of Isaac ◊Newton, whose *Principia* he financed.

Hallowe'en evening of 31 Oct, immediately preceding the Christian feast of Hallowmas or All Saints' Day. Customs associated with Hallowe'en in the USA and the UK include children wearing masks or costumes, and 'trick or treating' – going from house to house collecting sweets, fruit, or money.

Hallowe'en is associated with the ancient Celtic festival of **Samhain**, which marked the end of the year and the beginning of winter. It was believed that on the evening of Samhain supernatural creatures were abroad and the souls of the dead were allowed to revisit their former homes.

Hamilton William D 1936– . New Zealand biologist. By developing the concept of inclusive fitness, he was able to solve the theoretical problem of explaining ◊altruism in animal behaviour in terms of ◊neo-Darwinism.

Hamilton William Rowan 1805–1865. Irish mathematician whose formulation of Isaac Newton's dynamics proved adaptable to ◊quantum theory, and whose 'quarternion' theory was a forerunner of the branch of mathematics known as vector analysis.

Handsome Lake 1735–1815. Native American religious leader who preached a combination of Christianity and Native traditions.

Born into the Seneca tribe, he became a typical victim of the arrival of white settlers. He collapsed from drink and depression in 1800, and was thought to be dead. During the funeral procession, he awoke and believed he had been resurrected to be a preacher. For the next 15 years he received messages from God which stressed a combination of the best in Christianity – as put forward by the Shakers in particular, and the best in Native traditions.

'Hansel and Gretel' folk tale of a brother and sister abandoned by their destitute parents and taken in by a witch who lives in a gingerbread cottage. She plans to fatten Hansel up for eating, but is tricked by Gretel, and the children return home with the witch's treasure. The story was collected by the brothers ◊Grimm and made into a children's opera by Engelbert Humperdinck, first performed 1893.

Hanukkah or *Hanukah* or *Chanukkah* in Judaism, an eight-day festival of lights that takes place at the beginning of Dec. It celebrates the recapture and rededication of the ◊Temple in Jerusalem by Judas Maccabaeus 164 BC.

During Hanukkah, candles are lit each night and placed in an eight-branched candlestick, or menorah: this commemorates the ◊Temple lamp that stayed miraculously lit for eight days on one day's supply of oil until a new supply could be made.

Hanuman in the Sanskrit epic ◊*Rāmāyana*, the Hindu monkey god and king of Hindustan (N India). He helped Rama (an incarnation of the god Vishnu) to retrieve his wife Sita, abducted by Ravana of Lanka (now Sri Lanka).

hara-kiri ritual suicide of the Japanese samurai (military caste) since the 12th century. Today it is illegal. It was carried out to avoid dishonor or to demonstrate sincerity, either voluntarily or on the order of a feudal lord. The correct Japanese term is *seppuku* and, traditionally, the ritual involved cutting open one's stomach with a dagger before one's head was struck off by another samurai's sword.

Hardy Sir Alister Clavering 1896–1985. English zoologist and researcher into religious experience. He conducted a number of research projects into religious experience, concluding that religious experiences were common and of certain types.

Clavering was professor of Zoology and Comparative Anatomy at Oxford 1946–65 and master of the Unitarian college, Manchester College, Oxford 1958–65. As a scientist and as a religious man (he was a Unitarian), he was interested to see if scientific methods could be applied to religious phenomena. Although he held back from claiming that his results proved that religious experience was genuine and therefore that God existed, his work has been cited as evidence for the existence of God by some and of the inappropriateness of scientific methodology in religion by others. His work is continued by the Alister Hardy Research centre in Oxford which is committed to scientific study of the nature and function of religious experience in the human species.

Hardy–Weinberg equilibrium in population ◊genetics, the theoretical relative frequency of different alleles within a given population of a species, when the stable endpoint of evolution in an undisturbed environment is reached.

Hare Krishna popular name for a member of the ◊International Society for Krishna Consciousness, derived from their chant.

Hargobind 1595–1644. Indian religious leader, sixth guru (teacher) of Sikhism 1606–44. He encouraged Sikhs to develop military skills in response to growing persecution. At the festival of ◊Diwali, Sikhs celebrate his release from prison.

Harijan member of the Indian ◊caste of untouchables. The compassionate term was introduced by Mahatma Gandhi during the independence movement.

Har Krishen 1656–1664. Indian religious leader, eighth guru (teacher) of ◊Sikhism 1661–64, who died at the age of eight.

Harlem Renaissance movement in US literature in the 1920s that used Afro-American life and black culture as its subject matter; it was an early manifestation of black pride in the USA. The centre of the movement was the Harlem section of New York City.

Harlem was the place where aspects of Afro-American culture, including jazz, flourished from the early 20th century, and attracted a new white audience. The magazine *Crisis*, edited by W E B DuBois (1868–1963), was a forum for the new black consciousness; writers associated with the movement include Langston Hughes (1902–1967), Zora Neale Hurston (1901–1960), James Weldon Johnson (1871–1938), and Countee Cullen (1903–1946).

Harpy (plural *Harpies*) in early Greek mythology, a wind spirit; in later legend the Harpies have horrific women's faces and the bodies of vultures.

Har Rai 1630–1661. Indian religious leader, seventh guru (teacher) of ◊Sikhism 1644–61.

Harris Louis 1921– . US pollster. He joined the Roper polling organization 1947 and became a partner in that firm 1954. Developing his own research techniques, he founded Louis Harris and Associates 1956. Hired by the 1960 Kennedy presidential campaign, Harris gained a national reputation and later served as a consultant to the CBS television network and as a political columnist.

Harrisson Tom 1911–1976. British anthropologist who set up ◊Mass Observation with Charles Madge 1937, the earliest of the organizations for the analysis of public opinions and attitudes.

Hart H(erbert) L(ionel) A(dolphus) 1907–1993. British jurist and philosopher. In his major work, *The Concept of Law* 1961, he argued that rules of obligation are felt to be necessary for society to function and that they are maintained through social pressure. A legal system is a union of primary rules (those which govern behaviour) and secondary rules (those which identify and modify primary rules). He was professor of jurisprudence at Oxford University 1952–68.

Harvard University oldest educational institution in the USA, founded 1636 at New Towne (later Cambridge), Massachusetts, and named after John Harvard (1607–1638), who bequeathed half his estate and his library to it. Women were first admitted 1969; the women's college of the university is *Radcliffe College*.

Hasan 625–670. Eldest grandson of the prophet Muhammad. He was the son of Ali bin Abu Talib and Muhammad's daughter Fatima. He was caliph for six months in 611 AD before resigning. It is through Hasan and his brother Husayn that the descendants of the prophet trace their lineage.

Hasid or *Hassid, Chasid* (plural *Hasidim, Hassidim, Chasidim*) member of a group of Orthodox Jews, originating in 18th-century Poland under the leadership of Israel Ba'al Shem Tov (c. 1700–1760). Hasidic teachings encourage prayer, piety, and 'serving the Lord with joy'. Many of their ideas are based on the ◊kabbala.

Hasidism spread against strong opposition throughout E Europe during the 18th and 19th centuries, led by charismatic leaders, the *zaddikim*.

The group emphasized ecstatic prayer, while denouncing the intellectual approach of talmudic academies. Hasidic men dress in the black suits and broad-brimmed hats of 18th-century European society, a tradition which they conservatively maintain. A resistance to modernization had led some Hasids to oppose Zionism, though others are active supporters of Israel.

hatha yoga system of exercises for the body and mind originally based on the teachings of ◊Patanjali. True hatha yoga includes his eight steps: *yama*, self-restraint; *niyama*, spiritual discipline; *asana*, sitting posture; *pranayama*, breath control; *pratyahara*, withdrawal of the senses; *dharana*, contemplation; *dhyana*, meditation; and *samadhi*, total absorption in God. In its modern popular form, particular emphasis is placed upon posture and breathing techniques to produce a state of physical and mental well-being.

hawk person who believes in the use of military action rather than mediation as a means of solving a political dispute. The term first entered the political language of the USA during the 1960s, when it was applied metaphorically to those advocating continuation and escalation of the Vietnam War. Those with moderate, or even pacifist, views were known as ◊doves. In general usage today, a hawk is associated with conservative policies.

Hawking Stephen 1942– . English physicist who has researched ◊black holes and gravitational field theory. His books include *A Brief History of Time* 1988, in which he argues that our universe is only one small part of a 'superuniverse' that has existed forever and that comprises an infinite number of universes like our own.

Professor of gravitational physics at Cambridge from 1977, he discovered that the strong gravitational field around a black hole can radiate particles of matter. Commenting on Einstein's remark, 'God does not play dice with the universe,' Hawking said: 'God not only plays dice, he throws them where they can't be seen.'

Confined to a wheelchair because of a muscular disease, he performs complex mathematical calculations entirely in his head.

Hawthorne effect an immediate improvement in industrial performance as a result of a change in conditions. Research at a Chicago electrical company showed that workers would initially interpret change as an indication of managerial concern and so increase productivity.

Hayek Friedrich August von 1899–1992. Austrian economist. Born in Vienna, he taught at the London School of Economics 1931–50. His *The Road to Serfdom* 1944 was a critical study of socialist trends in Britain. He won the 1974 Nobel Prize for Economics with Gunnar Myrdal.

Headstart US nursery-education project launched in the 1960s that aimed to boost the educational performance of children from deprived backgrounds. Early follow-up studies suggested that the results were not long-lasting, but later research indicated that the benefits of early education could be measured in terms of improved educational performance and job prospects in adult life.

health care implementation of the proper regimen to ensure long-lasting good health. Life expectancy is determined by overall efficiency of the body's vital organs and the rate at which these organs deteriorate. Fundamental health-care concerns are:

smoking This is strongly linked to heart disease, stroke, bronchitis, lung cancer, and other serious diseases.

exercise Regular physical exercise improves fitness, slows down the gradual decline in efficiency of the heart and lungs, and so helps to prolong life.

diet A healthy diet contains plenty of vegetable fibre, complex carbohydrates, vitamins, minerals, and enzymes, and polyunsaturated fats (which keep the level of blood cholesterol low), not saturated (animal) fats (which contribute to cholesterol storage in blood vessels).

weight Obesity (defined as generally being 20% or more above the desirable weight for age, sex, build, and height) is associated with many potentially dangerous conditions, such as coronary heart disease, diabetes, and stroke, as well as muscular and joint problems, and breathing difficulties.

alcohol Recommended maximum intake is no more than 21 units of alcohol a week for men, no more than 14 for women. (Half a pint of beer, one glass of wine, or a single measure of spirits is equivalent to one unit.) Doctors recommend at least two alcohol-free days a week. Excessive alcohol intake causes liver damage and may lead to dependence.

health education teaching and counselling on healthy living, including hygiene, nutrition, sex education, and advice on alcohol and drug abuse, smoking, and other threats to health. Health education in most secondary schools is also included within a course of personal and social education, or integrated into subjects such as biology, home economics, or physical education.

School governors were given specific responsibility for the content of sex education lessons in the 1986 Education Act.

health psychology development within ◊clinical psychology that applies psychological principles to promote physical well-being. For example, people with high blood pressure can learn methods such as relaxation, meditation, and lifestyle changes.

I have desired to go / Where springs not fail, / To fields where flies no sharp and sided hail / And a few lilies blow. / And I have asked to be / Where no storms come, / Where the green swell is in the havens dumb, / And out of the swing of the sea.

heaven
Gerard Manley Hopkins, 1844–1889,
English poet and Jesuit priest.
'Heaven-Haven'

---

heaven in Christianity and some other religions, the abode of God and the destination of the virtuous after death. In Islam, heaven is seen as a paradise of material delights, though such delights are generally accepted as being allegorical.

In traditional Christian teaching, the human body is reunited with the soul in heaven following the Last Judgement. Theolo-gians now usually describe it as a place or state in which the soul experiences the full reality of God.

Heaviside Oliver 1850–1925. British physicist. In 1902 he predicted the existence of an ionized layer of air in the upper atmosphere, which was known as the Kennelly – Heaviside layer but is now called the E layer of the ionosphere. Deflection from it makes possible the transmission of radio signals around the world, which would otherwise be lost in outer space.

His theoretical work had implications for radio transmission. His studies of electricity published in *Electrical Papers* 1892 had considerable impact on long-distance telephony.

Hebrew member of the Semitic people who lived in Palestine at the time of the Old Testament and who traced their ancestry to ◊Abraham of Ur, a city of Sumer.

Hebrew Bible the sacred writings of Judaism (some dating from as early as 1200 BC), called by Christians the ◊Old Testament. It includes the Torah (the first five books, ascribed to Moses), historical and prophetic books, and psalms, originally written in Hebrew and later translated into Greek (◊Septuagint) and other languages.

hedonism ethical theory that pleasure or happiness is, or should be, the main goal in life.

Hedonist sects in ancient Greece were the ◊Cyrenaics, who held that the pleasure of the moment is the only human good, and the ◊Epicureans, who advocated the pursuit of pleasure under the direction of reason. Modern hedonistic philosophies, such as those of the British philosophers Jeremy ◊Bentham and J S ◊Mill, regard the happiness of society, rather than that of the individual, as the aim.

The English have undertaken the weighty responsibility of being the missionaries of civilisation to the world … .

Georg Wilhelm Friedrich Hegel
The Philosophy of History

Hegel Georg Wilhelm Friedrich 1770–1831. German philosopher who conceived of mind and nature as two abstractions of one indivisible whole, Spirit. His system, which is a type of ◊idealism, traces the emergence of Spirit in the logical study of concepts and the process of world history.

For Hegel, concepts unfold, and in unfolding they generate the reality that is described by them. To understand reality is to understand our concepts, and vice-versa. The development of a concept involves three stages, which he calls dialectic. The dialectic moves from the thesis or indeterminate concept (for example, a thing in space) to the antithesis or determinate concept (for example, an animal) and then to the synthesis (for example, a cat) which is the resolution of what Hegel thinks is the contradiction between the indeterminate and determinate concepts. As logic, Hegel's dialectic is valueless. As an account of how intellectual and social development occurs, it is shrewd.

To Hegel, Spirit has purposes and ends of its own, which finite spirits serve. It lives only through human beings, but is not identical with the human spirit. In his social and political philosophy, he uses his dialectic to comprehend what he sees as the rationality of what already exists, and so to justify the Prussian State and Lutheran Christianity of his day as the supreme social synthesis. Leftist followers, including Karl Marx, tried to use Hegel's dialectic to show the inevitability of radical change and to attack both the religion and social order of their times.

Of all the great philosophers, Hegel is the most difficult to understand. Even so, his influence has been immense – ◊Marx and ◊Feuerbach in Germany; in Britain, the neo-

Hegelians such as F H ◊Bradley and J M E ◊McTaggart; in the USA, Josiah ◊ Royce; in Italy, ◊Croce; and in France, ◊Sartre. His works include *The Phenomenology of Spirit* 1807, *Encyclopedia of the Philosophical Sciences* 1817, and *Philosophy of Right* 1821.

He was professor of philosophy at Heidelberg 1817–18 and at Berlin 1818–31.

Hegel filled the universe with copulating contradictions.

Hegel
Bertrand Russell, 1872–1970, English philosopher and mathematical logician.
History of Western Philosophy ch. XXII

---

hegemony political dominance of one power over others in a group in which all are supposedly equal. The term was first used for the dominance of Athens over the other Greek city states, later applied to Prussia within Germany, and, in more recent times, to the USA and the USSR with regard to the rest of the world.

Hegira the flight of the prophet Muhammad; see ◊Hijrah.

Heidegger Martin 1889–1976. German philosopher, often classed as an existentialist (◊Existentialism). He believed that Western philosophy had 'forgotten' the fundamental question of the 'meaning of Being', and his work concerns the investigation of what he thought were the different types of ◊being appropriate to people and to things in general.

His works include *Sein und Zeit/Being and Time* 1927. Born in Baden, he taught mainly at the University of Freiburg. His sympathy with the Nazis damaged his reputation.

An expert is someone who knows some of the worst mistakes that can be made in his subject and how to avoid them.

Werner Carl Heisenberg
The Part and the Whole

Heisenberg Werner Carl 1901–1976. German physicist who developed ◊quantum theory and formulated the ◊uncertainty principle, which concerns matter, radiation, and their reactions, and places absolute limits on the achievable accuracy of measurement. He was awarded a Nobel prize 1932.

Helena, St c. 248–328. Roman empress, mother of Constantine the Great, and a convert to Christianity. According to legend, she discovered the true cross of Jesus in Jerusalem. Her feast day is 18 Aug.

Helicon mountain in central Greece, on which was situated a spring and a sanctuary sacred to the ◊Muses.

Heliopolis ancient Egyptian centre (the biblical *On*) of the worship of the sun god Ra, NE of Cairo and near the village of Matariah. Heliopolis was also the Greek name for ◊Baalbek.

The safest road to Hell is the gradual one.

hell

C(live) S(taples) Lewis, 1898–1963, literary critic and Christian apologist.
The Screwtape Letters

---

hell in various religions, a place of posthumous punishment. In Hinduism, Buddhism, and Jainism, hell is a transitory stage in the progress of the soul, but in Christianity and Islam it is eternal (◊purgatory is transitory). Judaism does not postulate such punishment.

In the Bible, the word 'hell' is used to translate Hebrew and Greek words all meaning 'the place of departed spirits, the abode of the dead'. In medieval Christian theology, hell is the place where unrepentant sinners suffer the torments of the damned, but the 20th-century tendency has been to regard hell as a state of damnation (that is, everlasting banishment from the sight of God) rather than a place.

Helmholtz Hermann Ludwig Ferdinand von 1821–1894. German physiologist, physicist, and inventor of the ophthalmoscope for examining the inside of the eye. He was the first to explain how the cochlea of the inner ear works, and the first to measure the speed of nerve impulses. In physics he formulated the law of conservation of energy, and worked in thermodynamics.

Helvetius Claude Adrien 1715–1771. French philosopher. In *De l'Esprit* 1758 he argued, following David ◊Hume, that self-interest, however disguised, is the mainspring of all human action and that since conceptions of good and evil vary according to period and locality there is no absolute good or evil. He also believed that intellectual differences are only a matter of education.

Helvetius's principle of artificial identity of interests (those manipulated by governments) influenced the utilitarian philosopher Jeremy ◊Bentham. *De l'Esprit* was denounced and burned by the public hangman.

henotheism belief that there are a number of gods, but that one particular god has a special relationship with a particular family, clan, or tribe. This means that for that group there is no other god, but allows for the existence of other gods. Some Biblical scholars see hints of this pre-monotheistic attitude in the Hebrew Bible – for example in Psalms 83:1.

Henotikon declaration published by Roman emperor Zeno 482, aimed at reconciling warring theological factions within the early Christian church. It refuted the Council of Chalcedon 451, and reaffirmed the heretical idea that Jesus was one person, not two. The declaration, not accepted by Rome, led to a complete split between Rome and Constantinople 484–519.

Henry Joseph 1797–1878. US physicist, inventor of the electromagnetic motor 1829 and of a telegraphic apparatus. He also discovered the principle of electromagnetic induction, roughly at the same time as Michael ◊Faraday, and the phenomenon of self-induction. A unit of inductance (henry) is named after him.

Another damned, thick, square book! Always scribble, scribble, scribble! Eh! Mr. Gibbon?

William Henry
Best's Literary Memorials

Henry William 1774–1836. British chemist. In 1803 he formulated **Henry's law**, which states that when a gas is dissolved in a liquid at a given temperature, the mass that dissolves is in direct proportion to the pressure of the gas.

Heracles in Greek mythology, a hero (Roman Hercules), son of Zeus and Alcmene, famed for strength. While serving Eurystheus, King of Argos, he performed 12 labours, including the cleansing of the Augean stables. Driven mad by the goddess Hera, he murdered his first wife Megara and their children, and was himself poisoned by mistake by his second wife wife Deianira.

Heraclitus c. 544–483 BC. Greek philosopher who believed that the cosmos is in a ceaseless state of flux and motion, fire being the fundamental material that accounts for all change and motion in the world. Nothing in the world ever stays the same, hence the dictum, 'one cannot step in the same river twice'.

All is flux, nothing is stationary.

Heraclitus
Quoted in Aristotle *De Caelo*

Herapath John 1790–1868. English mathematician. His work on the behaviour of gases, though seriously flawed, was acknowledged by the physicist James ◊Joule in his own more successful investigations.

herbalism prescription and use of plants and their derivatives for medication. Herbal products are favoured by alternative practitioners as 'natural medicine', as opposed to modern synthesized medicines and drugs, which are regarded with suspicion because of the dangers of side-effects and dependence.

Many are of proven efficacy both in preventing and curing illness. Medical herbalists claim to be able to prescribe for virtually any condition, except those so advanced that surgery is the only option.

Herbert Edward, 1st Baron Herbert of Cherbury 1583–1648. English philosopher, brother of the poet George Herbert. His virtual rejection of revelation and his advocacy of rational religion founded English ◊deism. His *De veritate* was published in 1624.

Hercules Roman form of ◊Heracles.

Herder Johann Gottfried von 1744–1803. German poet, critic, and philosopher. Herder's critical writings indicated his intuitive rather than reasoning trend of thought. He collected folk songs of all nations 1778, and in the *Ideen zur Philosophie der Geschichte der Menschheit/Outlines of a Philosophy of the History of Man* 1784–91 he outlined the stages of human cultural development.

Born in East Prussia, Herder studied at Königsberg where he was influenced by Kant, became pastor at Riga, and in 1776 was called to Weimar as court preacher. He gave considerable impetus to the *Sturm und Drang* (storm and stress) Romantic movement in German literature.

heresy (Greek *hairesis* 'parties' of believers) doctrine opposed to orthodox belief, especially in religion. Those holding ideas considered heretical by the Christian church have included Gnostics, Arians, Pelagians, Montanists, Albigenses, Waldenses, Lollards, and Anabaptists.

It is the customary fate of new truths to begin as heresies and to end as superstitions.

heresy
Thomas Henry Huxley, 1825–1895, English scientist and humanist
Science and Culture, 'The Coming of Age of the Origin of Species'

hermaphrodite organism that has both male and female sex organs. Hermaphroditism is the norm in species such as earthworms and snails, and is common in flowering plants. Cross-fertilization is the rule among hermaphrodites, with the parents functioning as male and female simultaneously, or as one or the other sex at different stages in their development.

Pseudo-hermaphrodites have the internal sex organs of one sex, but the external appearance of the other. The true sex of the latter becomes apparent at adolescence when the normal hormone activity appropriate to the internal organs begins to function.

hermeneutics philosophical tradition concerned with the nature of understanding and interpretation of human behaviour and social traditions. From its origins in problems of biblical interpretation, hermeneutics has expanded to cover many fields of enquiry, including aesthetics, literary theory, and science. ◊Dilthey, ◊Heidegger, and ◊Gadamer are influential contributors to this tradition.

Hermes in Greek mythology, a god, son of Zeus and Maia; messenger of the gods. He wore winged sandals, a wide-brimmed hat, and carried a staff around which serpents coiled. Identified with the Roman Mercury and ancient Egyptian Thoth, he protected thieves, travellers, and merchants.

Hermetism beliefs based on a collection of mystical texts of the 2nd–3rd centuries AD, supposed to have been the work of Hermes Trismegistus – the Thrice Great Hermes,

How can what an Englishman believes be heresy? It is a contradiction in terms.

heresy
George Bernard Shaw, 1856–1950, Irish dramatist.
St. Joan iv

another name for the ancient Egyptian god ◊Thoth. The texts drew upon Jewish, Egyptian, and Roman myths and beliefs, to present a mystical way of life.

The texts had a big impact on Renaissance Europe where they were believed to have been written by an Egyptian philosopher contemporary with Moses. The Jewish elements led to people believing that the texts had foretold the coming of Jesus and this enabled much of the mysticism and magic within the texts to be used by Christian writers. This strongly influenced the growth of Christian mysticism and fuelled a fascination with Egypt as a land of esoteric knowledge.

hermit religious ascetic living in seclusion, often practising extremes of mortification (such as the Stylites, early Christians who lived on top of pillars).

The Christian monastic movement developed as a way of organizing into communities the ascetic hermits living in the deserts of ancient Egypt and the Middle East.

Herodotus c. 484–424 BC. Greek historian. After four years in Athens, he travelled widely in Egypt, Asia, and the Black Sea region of eastern Europe, before settling at Thurii in S Italy 443 BC. He wrote a nine-book history of the Greek–Persian struggle that culminated in the defeat of the Persian invasion attempts 490 and 480 BC. Herodotus was the first historian to apply critical evaluation to his material, while also recording divergent opinions.

heroism outstanding bravery or courage on the part of an individual, often in exceptional circumstances. Heroism is frequently displayed in a military context and official honours such as the British Victoria Cross or the French Croix de Valeur may be awarded in recognition of this. However, most states also now recognize civilian heroism; for example, in Britain, the George Cross is awarded to civilians displaying exceptional courage or resource. The award is often made to police officers or firefighters who frequently face dangerous situations in the course of their duty.

The term comes from Greek mythology, where the child resulting from the union between a human and a god or goddess was known as a hero. As much early Greek literature focused on the doings of gods and heroes the term then came to mean the main protagonist in a book or play. These heroes frequently displayed superhuman characteristics and exceptional feats of bravery, strength, and military endeavour, so the term then came to mean anyone displaying exceptional resource.

Hero of Alexandria Greek mathematician and engineer, probably of the 1st century AD, who invented an automatic fountain and a kind of stationary steam-engine, described in his book *Pneumatica*.

hero-worship idolizing someone as if they were endowed with superhuman attributes. The term is used when a person is the focus of unusual adulation by another and does not necessarily imply that they display heroic attributes.

Herschel Caroline Lucretia 1750–1848. German-born English astronomer, sister of William ◊Herschel, and from 1772 his assistant in England. She discovered eight comets and was awarded the Royal Astronomical Society's gold medal for her work on her brother's catalogue of star clusters and nebulae.

Herschel John Frederick William 1792–1871. English scientist and astronomer, son of William ◊Herschel. He discovered thousands of close double stars, clusters, and nebulae, reported 1847. A friend of the photography pioneer Fox Talbot, Herschel coined the terms 'photography', 'negative', and 'positive', discovered sodium thiosulphite as a fixer of silver halides, and invented the cyanotype process; his inventions also include astronomical instruments.

During the early days of photography he gave lectures on the subject and exhibited his own images.

Herschel William 1738–1822. German-born English astronomer. He was a skilled telescope maker, and pioneered the study of binary stars and nebulae. He discovered the planet Uranus 1781 and infrared solar rays 1801. He catalogued over 800 double stars, and found over 2,500 nebulae, catalogued by his sister Caroline ◊Herschel; this work was continued by his son John ◊Herschel. By studying the distribution of stars, William established the basic form of our Galaxy, the Milky Way.

Born in Hanover, Germany, he went to England 1757 and became a professional musician and composer while instructing himself in mathematics and astronomy, and constructing his own reflecting telescopes. While searching for double stars, he found Uranus, and later several of its satellites. This brought him instant fame and, in 1782, the post of private astronomer to George III. He discovered the motion of binary stars around one another, and recorded it in his *Motion of the Solar System in Space* 1783. In 1789 he built, at Slough, a 1.2 m/4 ft telescope of 12 m/40 ft focal length (the largest in the world at the time), but he made most use of a more satisfactory 46 cm/18 in instrument.

Hertz Heinrich 1857–1894. German physicist who studied electromagnetic waves, showing that their behaviour resembles that of light and heat waves.

He confirmed ◊Maxwell's theory of electromagnetic waves. The unit of frequency, the *hertz*, is named after him.

Herzl Theodor 1860–1904. Austrian founder of the *Zionist* movement. He was born in Budapest and became a successful playwright and journalist, mainly in Vienna. The ◊Dreyfus case convinced him that the only solution to the problem of anti-Semitism was the resettlement of the Jews in a state of their own. His book *Jewish State* 1896 launched political ◊Zionism, and he became the first president of the World Zionist Organization 1897.

Hesiod Greek poet, supposed to have lived a little later than Homer, and according to his own account born in Boeotia. He is the author of *Works and Days*, a moralizing and didactic poem of rural life, and the *Theogony*, an account of the origin of the world and of the gods. Both poems include the myth of ◊Pandora.

Hess Victor 1883–1964. Austrian physicist who emigrated to the USA shortly after sharing a Nobel prize in 1936 for the discovery of cosmic radiation.

heterosexuality sexual preference for, or attraction mainly to, persons of the opposite sex. Long regarded as the only acceptable expression of ◊sexuality, this has been challenged by both feminists and the gay rights movement as oppressive.

heuristics in computing, a process by which a program attempts to improve its performance by learning from its own experience.

Hevesy Georg von 1885–1966. Swedish chemist, discoverer of the element hafnium. He was the first to use a radioactive isotope (radioactive form of an element) to follow the steps of a biological process, for which he won the Nobel Prize for Chemistry 1943.

Hewish Antony 1924– . British radio astronomer who was awarded, with Martin ◊Ryle, the Nobel Prize for Physics 1974 for his work on pulsars, rapidly rotating neutron stars that emit pulses of energy.

Heyerdahl Thor 1914– . Norwegian ethnologist. He sailed on the ancient-Peruvian-style raft ◊Kon-Tiki from Peru to the Tuamotu Archipelago along the Humboldt Current 1947, and in 1969–70 used ancient-Egyptian-style papyrus reed boats to cross the Atlantic. His experimental approach to historical reconstruction is not regarded as having made any important scientific contribution.

His expeditions were intended to establish that ancient civilizations could have travelled the oceans in similar fashion, but his theories are largely discounted by anthropologists, who rely on linguistic, sociological, and archaeological information. His voyages are described in *Kon-Tiki*, translated into English 1950, and *The Ra Expeditions*, translated 1971. He also crossed the Persian Gulf 1977, written about in *The Tigris Expedition*, translated 1981.

Hicks John Richard 1904– . British economist who developed a theoretical framework for Keynesian analysis (known as IS–LM analysis) with an expenditure sector incorporating investment and savings (IS, investment–savings) and a monetary sector incorporating the demand for and supply of money (LM, liquidity–money). The extent to which an increase in the money supply affects expenditure depends on the sensitivity of expenditure to changes in interest rates. He was joint winner of the Nobel Prize for Economics in 1972 with Kenneth ◊Arrow.

He also developed, in his work *Theory of Wages* 1963, a model of industrial disputes which relates the length of strikes to the expected net costs of the strike to unions and management.

Bibl. 'Mr Keynes and the Classics, a suggested interpretation' *Econometrica* (April 1937)

The Peter Principle: In a Hierarchy Every Employee Tends to Rise to His Level of Incompetence.

> *hierarchy*
> Laurence J Peter, 1910–1990, Canadian
> writer and teacher.
> *The Peter Principle*

---

hierarchy structure consisting of different levels of authority in a business organization, one above the other. At the top of the hierarchy of a company, for example, is the chairperson and at the bottom is the shop-floor worker. Each worker in the hierarchy should have a job description that clearly sets out his or her duties and position within it.

hieroglyphic Egyptian writing system of the mid-4th millennium BC–3rd century AD, which combines picture signs with those indicating letters. The direction of writing is normally from right to left, the signs facing the beginning of the line. It was deciphered 1822 by the French Egyptologist J F Champollion (1790–1832) with the aid of the *Rosetta Stone*, which has the same inscription carved in hieroglyphic, demotic, and Greek.

High Church group in the ◊Church of England that emphasizes aspects of Christianity usually associated with Catholicism, such as ceremony and hierarchy. The term was first used in 1703 to describe those who opposed Dissenters, and later for groups such as the 19th-century ◊Oxford Movement.

higher education in most countries, education beyond the age of 18 leading to a university or college degree or similar qualification.

High Tech (abbreviation for *high technology*) in architecture, an approach to design, originating in the UK in the 1970s, which concentrates on technical innovation of a high order and celebrates structure and services as a means of creating exciting forms and spaces. The Hong Kong and Shanghai Bank, Hong Kong 1986, designed by Norman Forster, is a masterpiece of High Tech architecture.

Other outstanding examples are the Lloyds Building in the City of London, 1986, by Richard Rogers, which dramatically exhibits the service requirements of a large building, and Nicholas Grimshaw's Financial Times printing works, London 1988.

Hijab in Islam, the Arabic term for the seclusion of women enjoined by the Qur'an. It also refers to the modest, covering dress worn by Muslim women when outside their homes and at any time when they are in the presence of men not closely related to them.

Hijrah or *Hegira* the journey from Mecca to Medina of the prophet Muhammad, which took place AD 622 as a result of the persecution of the prophet and his followers. The Muslim calendar dates from this event, and the day of the Hijrah is celebrated as the Muslim New Year.

Hilbert David 1862–1943. German mathematician who founded the formalist school with the publication of *Grundlagen der Geometrie/ Foundations of Geometry* 1899, which was based on his idea of postulates. He attempted to put mathematics on a logical foundation through defining it in terms of a number of basic principles, which ◊Gödel later showed to be impossible; nonetheless, his attempt greatly influenced 20th-century mathematicians.

Hildegard of Bingen 1098–1179. German scientific writer, abbess of the Benedictine convent of St Disibode, near the Rhine, from 1136. She wrote a mystical treatise, *Liber Scivias* 1141, and an encyclopedia of natural history, *Liber Simplicis Medicinae* 1150–60, giving both Latin and German names for the species described, as well as their medicinal uses; it is the earliest surviving scientific book by a woman.

Hillel 1st century BC Hebrew scholar, lawyer, and teacher; member of the Pharisaic movement (see ◊Pharisee). His work was accepted by later rabbinic Judaism and is noted for its tolerance.

Hinduism religion originating in N India about 4,000 years ago, which is superficially and in some of its forms polytheistic, but has a concept of the supreme spirit, ◊Brahman, above the many divine manifestations. These include the triad of chief gods (the Trimurti): ◊Brahma, ◊Vishnu, and ◊Shiva (creator, preserver, and destroyer). Central to Hinduism are the beliefs in reincarnation and ◊karma; the oldest scriptures are the *Vedas*. Temple worship is almost universally observed and there are many festivals. There are over 805 million Hindus worldwide. Women are not regarded as the equals of men but should be treated with kindness and respect. Muslim influence in N India led to the veiling of women and the restriction of their movements from about the end of the 12th century.

roots Hindu beliefs originated in the Indus Valley civilization about 4,500 years ago. Much of the tradition that is now associated with Hinduism stems from the ritual and religion of the Aryans who invaded N India about 3,000 years ago.

scriptures The Veda collection of hymns, compiled by the Aryans, was followed by the philosophical Upanishads, centring on the doctrine of Brahman, and the epics *Rāmāyana* and *Mahābhārata* (which includes the *Bhagavad- Gītā*), all from before the Christian era.

beliefs Hindu belief and ritual can vary greatly even between villages. Some deities achieve widespread popularity such as Krishna, Hanuman, Lakshmi, and Durga; others, more localized and specialized, are referred to particularly in times of sickness or need. Some deities manifest themselves in different incarnations or avatars such as Rama and Krishna, both avatars of the god Vishnu.

Underlying this multifaceted worship is the creative strength of Brahman, the Supreme Being. Hindus believe that all living things are part of Brahman: they are sparks of atman or divine life that transmute from one body to another, sometimes descending into the form of a plant or an insect, sometimes the body of a human. This is all according to its karma or past actions which are the cause of its sufferings or joy as it rises and falls in samsara (the endless cycle of birth and death). Humans have the opportunity, through knowledge and devotion, to break the karmic chain and achieve final liberation or moksha. The atman is then free to return to Brahman. The creative force of the universe is recognized in the god Brahma. Once he has brought the cosmos into being it is sustained by Vishnu and then annihilated by the god Siva, only to be created once more by Brahma. Vishnu and Siva are, respectively, the forces of light and darkness, preservation and destruction, with Brahma as the balancing force that enables the existence and interaction of life. The cosmos is seen as both real and an illusion (maya), since its reality is not lasting; the cosmos is itself personified as the goddess Maya.

practice Hinduism has a complex of rites and ceremonies performed within the framework of the *jati* or caste system under the supervision of the Brahman priests and teachers. In India, caste is traditionally derived from the four classes of early Hindu society: brahmans (priests), kshatriyas (nobles and warriors), vaisyas (traders and cultivators), and sudras (servants). A fifth class, the untouchables, regarded as polluting in its origins, remained (and still largely remains) on the edge of Hindu society. The Indian Constituent Assembly 1947 made discrimination against the Scheduled Castes or Depressed Classes illegal, but strong prejudice continues.

Western influence The International Society for Krishna Consciousness (ISKON), the Western organization of the Hare Krishna movement, was introduced to the West by Swami Prabhupada (1896–1977). Members are expected to lead ascetic lives. It is based on devotion to Krishna which includes study of the *Bhagavad-Gītā*, temple and home ritual, and the chanting of the name Hare (saviour) Krishna. Members are expected to avoid meat, eggs, alcohol, tea, coffee, drugs, and gambling. Sexual relationships should be for procreation within the bonds of marriage.

Hinshelwood Cyril Norman 1897–1967. English chemist. He shared the 1956 Nobel Prize for Chemistry with Nikolai Semenov for his work on chemical chain reactions. He also studied the chemistry of bacterial growth.

Hipparchus c. 190–c. 120 BC. Greek astronomer who invented trigonometry, calculated the lengths of the solar year and the lunar month, discovered the precession of the equinoxes, made a catalogue of 800 fixed stars, and advanced Eratosthenes' method of determining the situation of places on the Earth's surface by lines of latitude and longitude.

Turn on, tune in and drop out.
hippies
Timothy Leary, 1920– , US psychologist who popularized LSD.
The Politics of Ecstasy

---

hippie member of a youth movement of the late 1960s, also known as *flower power*, which originated in San Francisco, California, and was characterized by nonviolent anarchy, concern for the environment, and rejection of Western materialism. The hippies formed a politically outspoken, antiwar, artistically prolific counterculture in North America and Europe. Their colourful psychedelic style, inspired by drugs such as LSD, emerged in fabric design, graphic art, and music by bands such as Love (1965–71), the Grateful Dead, Jefferson Airplane (1965–74), and Pink Floyd.

Hippocrates c. 460–c. 370 BC. Greek physician, often called the father of medicine. Important Hippocratic ideas include cleanliness (for patients and physicians), moderation in eating and drinking, letting nature take its course, and living where the air is good. He believed that health was the result of the '◊humours' of the body being in balance; imbalance caused disease. These ideas were later adopted by ◊Galen.

He was born and practised on the island of Kos and died at Larissa. He is known to have discovered aspirin in willow bark. The *Corpus Hippocraticum*, a group of some 70 works, is attributed to him but was probably not written by him, although the works outline his approach to medicine. They include *Aphorisms* and the *Hippocratic Oath*, which embodies the essence of medical ethics.

historical materialism the application of the principles of ◊dialectical materialism to history and sociology. This decrees that the social, political, and cultural superstructure of a society is determined by its economic base and that developments are therefore governed by laws with no room for the influence of individuals. In this theory, change occurs through the meeting of opposing forces (thesis and antithesis) which leads to the production of a higher force (synthesis).

historicism term referring to two contrasting views on the nature of historical and social research. The first claims that historians must interpret each age in terms of its values, assumptions, and concerns, and that a modern perspective uncritically distorts historical phenomena. The second argues for the need to understand historical change in terms of broad, all-embracing laws of historical growth and development. ◊Popper used the term in this second sense (in the *Poverty of Historicism* 1957) to attack the theories of Hegel and Marx, both of whom saw the course of history as working towards a goal.

If Cleopatra's nose had been shorter, the whole face of the earth would have changed.

                                 history
Blaise Pascal, 1623–1662, French
philosopher and mathematician.
Pensés II.162

history record of the events of human societies. The earliest surviving historical records are the inscriptions denoting the achievements of Egyptian and Babylonian kings. As a literary form in the Western world, historical writing or **historiography** began with the Greek Herodotus in the 5th century BC, who was first to pass beyond the limits of a purely national outlook. Contemporary historians make extensive use of statistics, population figures, and primary records to justify historical arguments.

There is always something rather absurd about the past.

                                 history
Max Beerbohm, 1872–1956,
British caricaturist and author.
1880

A generation later, Thucydides brought to history a strong sense of the political and military ambitions of his native Athens. His close account of the Peloponnesian War was continued by ◊Xenophon. Later Greek history and Roman history tended towards rhetoric;

Sallust tried to recreate the style of Thucydides, but Livy wrote an Augustan history of his city and its conquests, while Tacitus expressed his cynicism about the imperial dynasty. Medieval history was dominated by a religious philosophy sustained by the

History, n. An account, mostly false, of events, mostly unimportant, which are brought about by rulers, mostly knaves, and soldiers, mostly fools.

                                 history
Ambrose (Gwinett) Bierce, 1842–c. 1914,
US author.
Cynic's Word Book

Christian church. English chroniclers of this period are Bede, William of Malmesbury, and Matthew Paris. France produced great chroniclers of contemporary events in Froissart and Comines. The Renaissance revived historical writing and the study of history both by restoring classical models and by creating the science of textual criticism. A product of the new secular spirit was Machiavelli's *History of Florence* 1520–23. This critical approach continued into the 17th century but the 18th century ◊Enlightenment disposed of the attempt to explain history in theological terms, and an interpretive masterpiece was produced by Edward Gibbon, *The Decline and Fall of the Roman Empire* 1776–88. An attempt to formulate a **historical method** and a philosophy of history, that of the Italian Giovanni Vico, remained almost unknown until the 19th century. Romanticism left its mark on 19th-century historical writing in the tendency to exalt the contribution of the individual 'hero', and in the introduction of a more colourful and dramatic style and treatment, variously illustrated in the works of the French historian Jules Michelet (1798–1874), and the British writers Carlyle and Macaulay. During the 20th century the study of history has been revolutionized, partly through the contributions of other disciplines, such as the sciences and anthropology. The deciphering of the Egyptian and Babylonian inscriptions was of great importance. Researchers and archaeologists have traced developments in prehistory, and have revealed forgotten civilizations such as that of Crete. Anthropological studies of primitive society and religion, which began with James Frazer's *Golden Bough* 1890, have attempted to analyse the bases of later forms of social organization and belief. The changes brought about by the Industrial Revolution and the accompanying perception of economics as a science forced historians to turn their attention to economic questions. Marx's attempt to find in economic development the most significant, although not the only, determining factor in social change, has influenced many historians. History from the point of view of ordinary people is now recognized as an important element in historical study. Associated with this is the collection of spoken records known as *oral history*. A comparative study of civilizations is offered in A J Toynbee's *Study of History* 1934–54, and on a smaller scale by J M Roberts's *History of the World* 1992. Contemporary historians make a distinction between historical evidence or records, historical writing, and historical method or approaches to the study of history. The study of historical method is also known as *historiography*.

history of ideas discipline that studies the history and development of ideas and theories in terms of their origins and influences. The historian of ideas seeks to understand their significance in their original contexts.

Hitler Adolf 1889–1945. German Nazi dictator, born in Austria. He was *Führer* (leader) of the Nazi Party from 1921 and author of *Mein Kampf/My Struggle* 1925–27. As chancellor of Germany from 1933 and head of state from 1934, he created a dictatorship by playing party and state institutions against each other and continually creating new offices and appointments. His position was not seriously challenged until the 'Bomb Plot' 20 July 1944 to assassinate him. In foreign affairs, he reoccupied the Rhineland and formed an alliance with the Italian Fascist Mussolini 1936, annexed Austria 1938, and occupied the Sudetenland under the Munich Agreement. The rest of Czechoslovakia was annexed March 1939. The Hitler–Stalin pact was followed in Sept by the invasion of Poland and the declaration of war by Britain and France. He committed suicide as Berlin fell.

Born at Braunau-am-Inn, the son of a customs official, he spent his early years in poverty in Vienna and Munich. After serving as a volunteer in the German army during World War I, he was employed as a spy by the military authorities in Munich and in 1919 joined, in this capacity, the German Workers' Party. By 1921 he had assumed its leadership, renamed it the National Socialist German Workers' Party (Nazi Party for short), and provided it with a programme that mixed nationalism with ◊anti-Semitism. Having led an unsuccessful uprising in Munich 1923, he

was sentenced to nine months' imprisonment during which he wrote his political testament, *Mein Kampf*. The party did not achieve national importance until the elections of 1930; by 1932, although Field Marshal Hindenburg defeated Hitler in the presidential elections, it formed the largest group in the Reichstag (parliament). As the result of an intrigue directed by Chancellor Franz von Papen, Hitler became chancellor in a Nazi–Nationalist coalition 30 Jan 1933. The opposition was rapidly suppressed, the Nationalists removed from the government, and the Nazis declared the only legal party. In 1934 Hitler succeeded Hindenburg as head of state. Meanwhile, the drive to war began; Germany left the League of Nations, conscription was reintroduced, and in 1936 the Rhineland was reoccupied. Hitler and Mussolini, who were already both involved in Spain, formed an alliance (the Axis) 1936, joined by Japan 1940. Hitler conducted the war in a ruthless but idiosyncratic way, took and ruled most of the neighbouring countries with repressive occupation forces, and had millions of Slavs, Jews, Romanies, homosexuals, and political enemies killed in concentration camps and massacres. He narrowly escaped death 1944 from a bomb explosion at a staff meeting, prepared by high-ranking officers. On 29 April 1945, when Berlin was largely in Soviet hands, he married his mistress Eva Braun in his bunker under the chancellery building and on the following day committed suicide with her.

No arts; no letters; no society; and which is worst of all, continual fear and danger of violent death; and the life of man, solitary, poor, nasty, brutish, and short.

Thomas Hobbes
Leviathan pt 1, ch 13

Hobbes Thomas 1588–1679. English philosopher and the first thinker since Aristotle to attempt to develop a comprehensive theory of nature. He analysed everything, including human behaviour, in terms of matter and motion. He is now best remembered for his political philosophy, in which he defended absolute sovereignty as the only way to ensure security and prevent life from being 'solitary, poor, nasty, brutish and short', as he alleged it was in the state of nature. He based this absolute sovereignty on a ◊social contract among individuals, but the sovereign has duties only to God. In *Leviathan* 1651, he advocates absolutist government as the only means of ensuring order and security; he saw this as deriving from the social contract.

He was tutor to the exiled Prince Charles (later Charles II).

Hobson John Atkinson 1858–1940. British economist and publicist who was a staunch opponent of the Boer War 1899–1902. He condemned it as a conflict orchestrated by and fought for the preservation of finance capitalism at the expense of the British working class.

In his *Imperialism: A Study* 1902, he argued that imperial expansion was driven by a search for new markets and opportunities for investment overseas. Resultant under-consumption of finance capital in the domestic arena stifled the development of social welfare policies which would benefit the impoverished classes.

Hodgkin Alan Lloyd 1914– . British physiologist engaged in research with Andrew Huxley on the mechanism of conduction in peripheral nerves 1946–60. In 1963 they shared the Nobel Prize for Physiology and Medicine with John Eccles.

Hodgkin Dorothy Crowfoot 1910–1994. English biochemist who analysed the structure of penicillin, insulin, and vitamin B_{12}. Hodgkin was the first to use a computer to analyse the molecular structure of complex chemicals, and this enabled her to produce three-dimensional models. She was awarded the Nobel Prize for Chemistry 1964.

Hofmann August Wilhelm von 1818–1892. German chemist who studied the extraction and exploitation of coal tar derivatives. Hofmann taught chemistry in London from 1845 until his return to Berlin in 1865.

In 1881 he devised a process for the production of pure primary amines from amides.

Hofmeister Wilhelm 1824–1877. German botanist. He studied plant development and determined how a plant embryo, lying within a seed, is itself formed out of a single fertilized egg (ovule).

Hofmeister also discovered that mosses and ferns display an alternation of generations, in which the plant has two forms, spore-forming and gamete-forming.

Hofstadter Robert 1915–1990. US highenergy physicist who revealed the structure of the atomic nucleus. He demonstrated that the nucleus is composed of a high-energy core and a surrounding area of decreasing density. He shared the 1961 Nobel Prize for Physics with Rudolf Mössbauer.

Hofstadter helped to construct a new highenergy accelerator at Stanford University, California, with which he showed that the proton and the neutron have complex structures and cannot be considered elementary particles.

Hohfield Wesley N(ewcomb) 1879–1918. American jurist. In his posthumously published *Fundamental Legal Conceptions as Applied to Judicial Reasoning* 1919 he criticized the imprecision of much legal terminology and formulated a system of jural relationships:

Jural Right	Privilege	Power	Immunity	*correlatives*
Duty	No- Right	Liability	Disability	
Jural Right	Privilege	Power	Immunity	*opposites*
No-Right	Duty	Disability	Liability	

If all the year were playing holidays, / To sport would be as tedious as to work; / But when they seldom come, they wish'd for come.

holiday
William Shakespeare, 1564–1616,
English dramatist and poet.
1 Henry IV I. ii

holiday period of allowed absence from work. The word derives from medieval *holy days*, which were saints' days when no work was done.

Holidays became a legal requirement in Britain under the Bank Holidays Acts 1871 and 1875. Under the Holidays with Pay Act 1938, paid holidays (initially one week per year) were made compulsory in many occupations; 11 million people were entitled to a holiday in 1939. By 1955, 96% of manual labourers had two weeks' holiday.

holiness in religion, the separation of a person or thing from the common or profane to a divine use; when used of God, those qualities that set him apart from humanity and the world. The concept is particularly found in Christianity and Judaism.

People or things dedicated to God's service may be holy in different senses: *invoking reverence*, for example the 'holy of holies' in the ◊Temple in Jerusalem; *relating to God*, for example the Holy Trinity; *pure and chaste*, as in the injunction to live a holy life.

holism in philosophy, the concept that the whole is greater than the sum of its parts.

holistic medicine umbrella term for an approach that virtually all alternative therapies profess, which considers the overall health and lifestyle profile of a patient, and treats specific ailments not primarily as conditions to be alleviated but rather as symptoms of more fundamental disease.

The first formal link between conventional and alternative holistic medicine was established in 1989 between the Hammersmith Hospital (London) and the Bristol Cancer Health Centre. Conventional therapy and holistic treatment (including a vegan diet, counselling, and complete relaxation) were combined.

Hollerith Herman 1860–1929. US inventor of a mechanical tabulating machine, the first device for data processing. Hollerith's tabulator was widely publicized after being successfully used in the 1890 census. The firm he established, the Tabulating Machine Company, was later one of the founding companies of IBM.

After attending the Columbia University School of Mines, Hollerith worked on the 1880 US census and witnessed the huge task of processing so much information. In 1882 he became an instructor at the Massachusetts Institute of Technology, where he developed his machine for counting and collating census data.

Holmes Oliver Wendell Jr 1841–1935. American jurist. He was an associate justice of the US Supreme Court, 1902–32, where he became known as the 'Great Dissenter' because of his liberal attitudes and his frequent opposition to the often conservative judgements of his colleagues. His approach to the Law was practical rather than based on abstract principles, and he frequently championed the rights of workers against exploitative contracts and oppressive labour laws. His book *The Common Law* 1881 is still regarded as a classic.

Holocaust, the the annihilation of an estimated 6 million Jews by the Hitler regime 1933–45 in the numerous extermination and concentration camps, most notably Auschwitz, Sobibor, Treblinka, and Maidanek in Poland, and Belsen, Buchenwald, and Dachau in Germany. An additional 10 million people died during imprisonment or were exterminated; among them were Ukrainian, Polish, and Russian civilians and prisoners of war, gypsies, socialists, homosexuals, and others (labelled 'defectives'). Victims were variously starved, tortured, experimented on, and worked to death. Millions were executed in gas chambers, shot, or hanged. It was euphemistically termed the ◊final solution (of the Jewish question).

Holy Communion another name for the ◊Eucharist, a Christian sacrament.

Holy Grail in medieval Christian legend, the dish or cup used by Jesus at the Last Supper, supposed to have supernatural powers. Together with the spear with which he was wounded at the Crucifixion, it was an object of quest by King Arthur's knights in certain stories incorporated in the Arthurian legend.

According to one story, the blood of Jesus was collected in the Holy Grail by ◊Joseph of Arimathaea at the Crucifixion, and he brought it to Britain where he allegedly built the first church, at Glastonbury. At least three churches in Europe possess vessels claimed to be the Holy Grail.

Holy Land Christian term for Israel, because of its association with Jesus and the Old Testament.

Holy Office tribunal of the Roman Catholic Church that deals with ecclesiastical discipline; see ◊Inquisition.

holy orders Christian priesthood, as conferred by the laying on of hands by a bishop. It is held by the Roman Catholic, Orthodox, and Anglican churches to have originated in Jesus' choosing of the apostles.

The Anglican church has three orders (bishop, priest, and deacon); the Roman Catholic Church includes also subdeacon, acolyte, exorcist, reader, and door-keepers, and, outside the priesthood, ◊tertiary.

Holy Spirit third person of the Christian ◊Trinity, also known as the Holy Ghost or the Paraclete, usually depicted as a white dove.

Holy Week in the Christian church, the last week of ◊Lent, when Christians commemorate the events that led up to the crucifixion of Jesus. Holy Week begins on Palm Sunday and includes Maundy Thursday (which commemorates the Last Supper) and ◊Good Friday.

homeopathy or *homoeopathy* system of medicine based on the principle that symptoms of disease are part of the body's self-healing processes, and on the practice of administering extremely diluted doses of natural substances found to produce in a healthy person the symptoms manifest in the illness being treated. Developed by German physician Samuel Hahnemann (1755–1843), the system is widely practised today as an alternative to allopathic medicine, and many controlled tests and achieved cures testify its efficacy.

Homer according to ancient tradition, the author of the Greek narrative epics, the *Iliad* and the *Odyssey* (both derived from oral tradition). Little is known about the man, but modern research suggests that both poems should be assigned to the 8th century BC, with the *Odyssey* the later of the two. The predominant dialect in the poems indicates that Homer may have come from an Ionian Greek settlement, such as Smyrna or Chios, as was traditionally believed.

The epics, dealing with military values, social hierarchy, and the emotions and objectives of an heroic class of warriors, supported or opposed by the gods, had an immediate and profound effect on Greek society and culture and were a major influence on the Roman poet Virgil in the composition of his *Aeneid*. In the Renaissance a revival of the study of Greek brought translations from Alexander Pope and George Chapman. Modern writers influenced by Homer include James Joyce and Nikos Kazantzakis.

homosexuality sexual preference for, or attraction to, persons of one's own sex; in women it is referred to as ◊lesbianism. Both sexes use the term 'gay'. Men and women who are attracted to both sexes are referred to as bisexual. The extent to which homosexual behaviour is caused by biological or psychological factors is an area of disagreement among experts.

Although some ancient civilizations (notably ancient Greece and Confucian China) accepted homosexuality, other societies have punished homosexual acts. In 12th-century Europe sodomy was punishable by burning and since then homosexuals have suffered varying degrees of prejudice and prosecution. In the latter half of the 20th century discrimination against homosexuals has decreased as a result of pressure from 'gay rights' campaigners. However, laws against homosexuality differ from country to country. In the USA, for example, many states prohibit homosexual acts while in the EC countries (except the Isle of Man) homosexuality between consenting adults is legal. Male homosexuals fear further discrimination as a result of the discovery of the ◊AIDS virus.

In 1991 the Isle of Man rejected the decriminalization of male homosexual acts and is the only EC country to treat homosexuality as criminal. In Denmark 11 couples of gay men were legally married (termed 'registered partnership') under Danish law in Oct 1989. They have all the legal rights of married couples except for adoption.

Hōnen 1133–1212. Japanese Buddhist monk who founded the ◊Pure Land school of Buddhism.

honour dignity, social rank, or privilege. Originating in the *cursus honorum* at Rome, a standard 'course of honours' through public office to the consulate, the concept of honour held a dual sense of dignity and rank in aristocratic societies.

The louder he talked of his honour, the faster we counted our spoons.

honour
Ralph Waldo Emerson, 1803–1882,
US philosopher, essayist, and poet.
Conduct of Life, 'Worship'

The formal attributes of honour persisted in such phrases as 'word of honour' and 'man of honour' until the modern era, with duelling classed as an 'affair of honour'. Military and civil distinction is reflected in the US Medal of Honor and the French Légion d'honneur, founded by Napoleon I; an Honours List of awards for public service or achievement still exists in the UK. Honour was also used of a woman's reputation, notably for chastity or fidelity.

Content thyself to be obscurely good. / When vice prevails, and impious men bear sway, / The post of honour is a private station.

honour
Joseph Addison, 1672–1719, English writer.
Cato IV. iv

Hook Sidney 1902–1989. US philosopher, noted for his interpretations of John ◊Dewey and Karl ◊Marx. He held that our ideas are not true or false propositions but guides to action and experiment, and that Marx held that knowledge was primarily an activity, too. Accordingly, he saw philosophy as an empirical discipline, similar to the social sciences. He attacked Martin ◊Heidegger's notion of being. Born in New York, he taught at New York University 1927–69. His works include *From Hegel to Marx* 1936 and *The Quest for Being* 1961.

Hooke Robert 1635–1703. English scientist and inventor, originator of ◊*Hooke's law*, and considered the foremost mechanic of his time. His inventions included a telegraph system, the spirit level, marine barometer, and sea gauge. He coined the term 'cell' in biology.

Hooke was born at Freshwater on the Isle of Wight, the son of a priest. He studied elasticity, furthered the sciences of mechanics and microscopy, and helped improve such scientific instruments as watches, microscopes, telescopes, and barometers. He was elected to the Royal Society 1663, and became its curator for the rest of his life. He was professor of geometry at Gresham College, London, and designed several buildings, including the College of Physicians, London.

Hooker Joseph Dalton 1817–1911. English botanist who travelled to the Antarctic and made many botanical discoveries. His works include *Flora Antarctica* 1844–47, *Genera Plantarum* 1862–83, and *Flora of British India* 1875–97.

In 1865 he succeeded his father, William Jackson Hooker (1785–1865), as director of the Royal Botanic Gardens, Kew, England.

Hooke's law law stating that the deformation of a body is proportional to the magnitude of the deforming force, provided that the body's elastic limit (see ◊elasticity) is not exceeded. If the elastic limit is not reached, the body will return to its original size once the force is removed. It was discovered by Robert Hooke 1676.

For example, if a spring is stretched by 2 cm by a weight of 1 N, it will be stretched by 4 cm by a weight of 2 N, and so on; however, once the load exceeds the elastic limit for the spring, Hooke's law will no longer be obeyed and each successive increase in weight will result in a greater extension until finally the spring breaks.

Hooper John c. 1495–1555. English Protestant reformer and martyr. He adopted the views of ◊Zwingli and was appointed bishop of Gloucester 1550. He was burned to death for heresy.

Hopi religion the Hopi are the chief religious exponents of traditional Native American religion. They see themselves charged with maintaining the balance between the upper and lower worlds. Through an elaborate cycle of festivals and rituals, the Hopi keep these worlds in harmony, thus ensuring the continuity of life on earth. The name Hopi means 'peaceful people' and they seem to have been long revered by other Native Americans for their priestly role.

Hopkins Frederick Gowland 1861–1947. English biochemist whose research into diets revealed the existence of trace substances, now known as vitamins. Hopkins shared the 1929 Nobel Prize for Physiology and Medicine with Christiaan Eijkman, who had arrived at similar conclusions.

While studying diets, Hopkins noticed that, of two seemingly identical diets, only one was able to support life. He concluded that one must contain trace substances, or accessory food factors, lacking in the other. Among these were certain amino acids which the body cannot produce itself. The other factors were later named vitamins.

Horkheimer Max 1895–1973. German social theorist and director of the Institut für Sozialforschung (Institute for Social Research) at Frankfurt from 1930.

When the Nazis came to power, he moved with the Institute to Columbia University, New York and later to California. He returned to Frankfurt 1949 and became rector of the university there 1951. In his seminal papers of the 1930s which have been collected under the title *Kritische Theorie* 1968 (translated as *Critical Theory: Selected Essays* 1972), he argues that only a radical transformation in social theory and practice will cure modern civilization of its sickness. The analysis of society is partly a function of social life – its concepts, as well as what it studies, are products of social and economic processes – but it is also autonomous. 'Critical theory' has to discover and describe the social origins of knowledge in order to emancipate human beings. He rejected ◊empiricism and ◊positivism and believed technology posed a threat to culture and civilization because the physical sciences upon which it is based ignored human values.

He collaborated with, among others, Theodor W ◊Adorno, on *Dialectic of Enlightenment* 1947, and also with Herbert ◊Marcuse.

horoscope in Western astrology, a chart of the position of the Sun, Moon, and planets relative to the zodiac at the moment of birth, used to assess a person's character and forecast future influences.

In casting a horoscope, the astrologer draws a circular diagram divided into 12 sections, or houses, showing the 12 signs of the zodiac around the perimeter and the Sun, Moon, and planets as they were at the subject's time and place of birth. These heavenly bodies are supposed to represent different character traits and influences, and by observing their positions and interrelations the astrologer may gain insight into the subject's personality and foretell the main outlines of his or her career.

Horus in ancient Egyptian mythology, the hawkheaded sun god, son of Isis and Osiris, of whom the pharaohs were declared to be the incarnation.

hospital facility for the care of the sick, injured, and incapacitated.

In ancient times, temples of deities such as Aesculapius offered facilities for treatment and by the 4th century, the Christian church had founded hospitals for lepers, cripples, the blind, the sick, and the poor. The oldest surviving hospital in Europe is the 7th-century Hôtel Dieu, Paris; in Britain, the most ancient are St Bartholomew's 1123 and St Thomas's 1200; and in the Americas the Hospital of Jesus of Nazareth, Mexico, 1524. Medical knowledge advanced during the Renaissance, and hospitals became increasingly secularized after the Reformation. In the 19th century, further progress was made in hospital design, administration, and staffing (Florence Night-ingale played a significant role in this). In the 20th century there has been an increasing trend towards specialization and the inclusion of maternity wards. Modern hospitals have abandoned the single-room Nightingale design for wards in favour of four- or six-bedded rooms, where patients have more privacy.

Hounsfield Godrey (Newbold) 1919– . British engineer, a pioneer of tomography, the application of computer techniques to X-raying the human body. He shared the Nobel Prize for Physiology and Medicine 1979 with the US physicist Allan Cormack (1924–   ).

Hours, Book of in medieval Europe, a collection of liturgical prayers for the use of the faithful.

Books of Hours appeared in England in the 13th century, and contained short prayers and illustrations, with each prayer suitable for a different hour of the day, in honour of the Virgin Mary. The enormous demand for Books of Hours was a stimulus for the development of Gothic illumination. A notable example is the *Très Riches Heures du Duc de Berry*, illustrated in the early 15th century by the Limbourg brothers.

Howard Ebenezer 1850–1928. English town planner and pioneer of the ideal of the ◊garden city, through his book *Tomorrow: A Peaceful Path to Real Reform* 1898 (republished as *Garden Cities of Tomorrow* 1902).

Influenced by Walt Whitman, ◊Emerson, and above all by Edward Bellamy's utopian novel *Looking Backward*, Howard aimed to halt the unregulated growth of industrial cities and to replace them with model 'garden cities'. In these, every house was to have its own plot of land, land usage was to be arranged zonally with civic amenities at the centre and factories on the edge of the city,

and the whole city was to be surrounded by a 'green belt'.

Howard John 1726–1790. English philanthropist whose work to improve prison conditions is continued today by the *Howard League for Penal Reform*.

On his appointment as high sheriff for Bedfordshire 1773, he undertook a tour of English prisons which led to two acts of Parliament 1774, making jailers salaried officers and setting standards of cleanliness. After touring Europe 1775 he published his *State of the Prisons in England and Wales, with an account of some Foreign Prisons* 1777. He died of typhus fever while visiting Russian military hospitals at Kherson in the Crimea.

Howe Samuel Gridley 1801–1876. US educational reformer. A close associate of Horace Mann and Dorothea ◊Dix, he campaigned for expanded public education and better mental health facilities. He served as chairman of the Massachusetts Board of State Charities 1865–74.

Born in Boston, Howe was educated at Brown University and received an MD degree from Harvard 1824. A Philhellene, he spent seven years in Greece during its War of Independence 1821–29. As director of a school for the blind in Boston 1831, he developed innovative educational techniques that were widely emulated.

Space isn't remote at all. It's only an hour's drive away if your car could go straight upwards.

Fred(erick) Hoyle
Observer Sept 1979

Hoyle Fred(erick) 1915–   . English astronomer and writer. In 1948 he joined with Hermann ◊Bondi and Thomas Gold (1920–   ) in developing the steady-state theory. In 1957, with Geoffrey and Margaret Burbidge (1925– and 1919–   ) and William Fowler, he showed that chemical elements heavier than hydrogen and helium are built up by nuclear reactions inside stars. He has suggested that life originates in the gas clouds of space and is delivered to the Earth by passing comets. His science-fiction novels include *The Black Cloud* 1957.

His work on the evolution of stars was published in *Frontiers of Astronomy* 1955. He lectured in mathematics at Cambridge University 1945–58, when he became professor of astronomy. He was director of the Cambridge Institute of Theoretical Astronomy from 1967. He held numerous research and visiting posts at institutions in England and America, including Manchester University from 1972, and at University College, Cardiff from 1975.

Hsun Tzu 300–230 BC. Sceptical rationalist Chinese philosopher who argued that human nature is essentially evil and needs to be constrained into moral behaviour by laws and punishments.

Hubbard L(afayette) Ron(ald) 1911–1986. US science-fiction writer of the 1930s and 40s, founder in 1954 of ◊Scientology.

Despite his later claims to be a war hero, he was in fact relieved of his command in the Navy for incompetence.

Hubble Edwin Powell 1889–1953. US astronomer who discovered the existence of other galaxies outside our own, and classified them according to their shape. His theory that the universe is expanding is now generally accepted.

At Mount Wilson observatory in 1923 he discovered Cepheid variable stars in the Andromeda galaxy, proving it to lie far beyond our own Galaxy. In 1925 he introduced the classification of galaxies as spirals, barred spirals, and ellipticals. In 1929 he announced ◊*Hubble's law*, which states that the galaxies are moving apart at a rate that increases with their distance.

Hubble's law the law that relates a galaxy's distance from us to its speed of recession as the universe expands, announced in 1929 by Edwin Hubble. He found that galaxies are moving apart at speeds that increase in direct proportion to their distance apart. The rate of expansion is known as *Hubble's constant*.

Whom the gods wish to destroy they first call promising.

hubris
Cyril Connolly, 1903–1974, English critic and author.
Enemies of Promise ch 13

---

hubris in Greek thought, an act of transgression, often violent. In ancient Greek tragedy, hubris was believed to offend the gods, and to lead to retribution.

Huggins William 1824–1910. British astronomer. He built a private observatory at Tulse Hill, London, in 1856, where he embarked on research in spectrum analysis that marked the beginning of astrophysics.

Hughes Charles Evans 1862–1948. US jurist and public official, appointed to the US Supreme Court by President Taft 1910. He resigned 1916 to accept the Republican nomination for president, losing narrowly to the incumbent Wilson. He served as secretary of state 1921–25 under President Harding. As Supreme Court chief justice 1930–41 in the Hoover administration, he presided over the constitutional tests of ◊New Deal legislation.

Born in Glens Falls, New York, Hughes received his law degree from Columbia University 1884. After joining the Columbia law faculty 1891–93, he directed a state investigation of public utilities 1905 and served two terms as New York governor 1906–10. He retired from the from the US Supreme Court 1941.

Huguenot French Protestant in the 16th century; the term referred mainly to Calvinists. Severely persecuted under Francis I and Henry II, the Huguenots survived both an attempt to exterminate them (the *Massacre of St Bartholomew* 24 Aug 1572) and the religious wars of the next 30 years. In 1598 Henry IV (himself formerly a Huguenot) granted them toleration under the *Edict of Nantes*. Louis XIV revoked the edict 1685, attempting their forcible conversion, and 400,000 emigrated.

Some of the nobles adopted Protestantism for political reasons, causing the civil wars 1592–98. The Huguenots lost military power after the revolt at La Rochelle 1627–29, but were still tolerated by the chief ministers Richelieu and Mazarin. Provoked by Louis XIV they left, taking their industrial skills with them; 40,000 settled in Britain, where their descendants include the actor David Garrick and the textile manufacturer Samuel Courtauld. Many settled in North America, founding new towns. Only in 1802 was the Huguenot church again legalized in France.

Huitzilopochtli a central deity in Aztec religion. The Aztecs sacrificed thousands of human lives to him each year, especially at the great festival of Panquetzalitzili (the raising of the banners) which celebrated his supremacy as a god of war and courage.

He was the guardian deity of the city of Tenochtitlan. A fierce warrior god, reputed to have slain 400 of his own siblings, he was often depicted as a giant eagle.

Huizinga Johan 1872–1945. Dutch historian and in his time a leading intellectual and popular writer. He is probably best known for his

The Waning of the Middle Ages 1919, an account of cultural decline in 14th- and 15th-century Burgundy.

Huizinga preferred broad themes and his writings ranged widely from classical Indian drama and Oriental cultural history to Western history from the 12th century to the present day. His eclecticism is brilliantly displayed in *Homo Ludens* 1938, a classic study of culture as play. His *Dutch Civilization in the Seventeenth Century* 1933 is an important contribution to Dutch history, as is his biography of Erasmus (*Erasmus* 1924) whose heir many consider him to be.

Huizinga was educated at Groningen University and studied briefly at Leipzig University. He taught Indian literature at the University of Amsterdam before being appointed professor of history at Groningen in 1905. From 1915 he was professor of general history at London University and became rector of Leyden University 1933.

Hulme T(homas) E(rnest) 1881–1917. British philosopher, critic, and poet, killed on active service in World War I. His *Speculations* 1924 influenced T S ◊Eliot and his few poems inspired ◊Imagism.

humanism belief in the high potential of human nature rather than in religious or transcendental values. Humanism culminated as a cultural and literary force in 16th-century Renaissance Europe in line with the period's enthusiasm for classical literature and art, growing individualism, and the ideal of the all-round male who should be statesman and poet, scholar and warrior. Sir Philip Sidney is a great exemplar of Renaissance humanism.

Renaissance humanism originated in the literary studies undertaken in Italian universities in the 13th and 14th centuries. It gained momentum with the scholarly study of literary texts and the concomitant rediscovery of the great body of ancient Greek literature for the West.

Human Genome Project research scheme, begun 1988, to map the complete nucleotide (see nucleic acid) sequence of human ◊DNA. There are approximately 80,000 different ◊genes in the human genome, and one gene may contain more than 2 million nucleotides. The knowledge gained is expected to help prevent or treat many crippling and lethal diseases, but there are potential ethical problems associated with knowledge of an individual's genetic make-up, and fears that it will lead to ◊genetic engineering.

The Human Genome Organization (HUGO) coordinating the project expects to spend $1 billion over the first five years, making this the largest research project ever undertaken in the life sciences. Work is being carried out in more than 20 centres around the world. By the beginning of 1991, some 2,000 genes had been mapped. Concern that, for example, knowledge of an individual's genes may make that person an unacceptable insurance risk has led to planned legislation on genome privacy in the USA, and 3% of HUGO's funds have been set aside for researching and reporting on the ethical implications of the project. Each strand of DNA carries a sequence of chemical building blocks, the nucleotides. There are only four different types, but the number of possible combinations is immense. The different combinations of nucleotides produce different proteins in the cell, and thus determine the structure of the body and its individual variations. To establish the nucleotide sequence, DNA strands are broken into fragments, which are duplicated (by being introduced into cells of yeast or the bacterium *Escherichia coli*) and distributed to the research centres. Genes account for only a small amount of the DNA sequence. Over 90% of DNA appears not to have any function, although it is perfectly replicated each time the cell divides, and handed on to the next generation. Many higher organisms have large amounts of redundant DNA and it may be that this is an advantage, in that there is a pool of DNA available to form new genes if an old one is lost by mutation.

human rights civil and political rights of the individual in relation to the state.

Human Rights, Universal Declaration of charter of civil and political rights drawn up by the United Nations 1948. They include the right to life, liberty, education, and equality before the law; to freedom of movement, religion, association, and information; and to a nationality. Under the European Convention of Human Rights 1950, the Council of Europe established the *European Commission of Human Rights* (headquarters in Strasbourg, France), which investigates complaints by states or individuals, and its findings are examined by the ◊*European Court of Human Rights* (established 1959), whose compulsory jurisdiction has been recognized by a number of states, including the UK.

Human Rights Day is 10 Dec, commemorating the adoption of the Universal Declaration of Human Rights by the UN General Assembly. The declaration is not legally binding, and the frequent contraventions are monitored by organizations such as ◊Amnesty International. Human rights were also an issue at the Helsinki Conference.

In 1988 the European Court condemned as unlawful the UK procedure of holding those suspected of terrorism for up to seven days with no judicial control.

human sacrifice the ritual slaughter of human beings in the belief that through the offering of such sacrifices to a deity, powers and forces will be given to those making the sacrifice, or that the anger of the deity will be assuaged or placated. Human sacrifice is mentioned in the Hebrew Bible as being practiced in the area of Palestine. Hinduism records such practices at a similar time, and in a few extreme cases, such as the worship of the goddess ◊Kali, such practices continued in India until the 19th century. The Aztecs practiced human sacrifice on a considerable scale.

human species, origins of evolution of humans from ancestral ◊primates. The African apes (gorilla and chimpanzee) are shown by anatomical and molecular comparisons to be the closest living relatives of humans. Humans are distinguished from apes by the size of their brain and jaw, their bipedalism, and their elaborate culture. Molecular studies put the date of the split between the human and African ape lines at 5–10 million years ago.

There are only fragmentary remains of ape and **hominid** (of the human group) fossils from this period; the oldest known hominids, found in Ethiopia and Tanzania, date from 3.5 to 4 million years ago. These creatures are known as *Australopithecus afarensis*, and they walked upright. They were either direct ancestors or an offshoot of the line that led to modern humans. They may have been the ancestors of *Homo habilis* (considered by some to be a species of *Australopithecus*), who appeared about a million years later, had slightly larger bodies and brains, and were probably the first to use stone tools. *Australopithecus robustus* and *A. africanus* also lived in Africa at the same time, but these are not generally considered to be our ancestors.

Over 1.5 million years ago, *Homo erectus*, believed by some to be descended from *H. habilis*, appeared in Africa. The *erectus* people had much larger brains, and were probably the first to use fire and the first to move out of Africa. Their remains are found as far afield as China, western Asia, Spain, and S Britain. Modern humans, *H. sapiens sapiens*, and the Neanderthals, *H. sapiens neanderthalensis*, are probably descended from *H. erectus*.

Neanderthals were large-brained and heavily built, probably adapted to the cold conditions of the ice ages. They lived in Europe and the Middle East, and died out about 40,000 years ago, leaving *H. sapiens sapiens* as the only remaining species of the hominid group.

There are currently two major views of human evolution: the *'Out of Africa' model*, according to which, *H. sapiens* emerged from *H. erectus* in Africa and then spread throughout the world; and the *multiregional model*, according to which, selection pressures led to the emergence of similar advanced types of *H. sapiens* from *H. erectus* in different parts of the world at around the same time.

Analysis of DNA in recent human populations suggests that *H. sapiens* originated about 200,000 years ago in Africa from a single female ancestor, 'Eve'. The oldest known fossils of *H. sapiens* also come from Africa, dating from 150,000–100,000 years ago. Separation of human populations would have occurred later, with separation of Asian, European, and Australian populations taking place between 100,000 and 50,000 years ago.

Creationists believe that the origin of the human species is as written in the book of Genesis in the Old Testament of the Bible.

Avarice, the spur of industry.

David Hume
'Of Civil Liberty'

Hume David 1711–1776. Scottish philosopher whose *A Treatise of Human Nature* 1739–40 is a central text of British ◊empiricism. He examined meticulously our modes of thinking and concluded that our thinking is more habitual than rational. Consequently, he not only held that speculative metaphysics was impossible, but also arrived at generally sceptical positions about reason, causation, necessity, identity, and the self.

The Christian religion not only was at first attended with miracles, but even at this day cannot be believed by any reasonable person without one.

David Hume
Essays, 'On Miracles'

Hume became secretary to the British embassy in Paris 1763. His *History of Great Britain* 1754–62 was popular within his lifetime but *A Treatise of Human Nature* was indifferently received. However, the German philosopher Immanuel Kant claimed that Hume's scepticism woke him from his 'dogmatic slumbers'. Among Hume's other publications is the *Enquiry concerning the Principles of Morals* 1751.

Blessed are the meek: for they shall inherit the earth.

humility

Bible, the sacred book of the Jewish and Christian religions.
Matthew 5:5

---

humility in Christianity, Islam, and Judaism, an attitude which recognizes human imperfection and human dependence on God. It is also enjoined in relation to other people: to consider others before self and to be predisposed to serve others.

humours, theory of theory attributed to ◊Hippocrates and prevalent in classical and medieval times that the human body was composed of four kinds of fluid: phlegm, blood, choler or yellow bile, and melancholy or black bile. Physical and mental states (temperaments) and disorders were explained by different proportions of humours in individuals.

An excess of phlegm produced a 'phlegmatic', or calm, temperament; of blood a 'sanguine', or passionate, one; of yellow bile a 'choleric', or irascible, temperament; and of black bile a 'melancholy', or depressive, one. ◊Galen connected the theory to that of the four ◊elements: the phlegmatic was associated with water, the sanguine with air, the choleric with fire, and the melancholic with earth. An imbalance of the humours could supposedly be treated by diet.

Husayn 627–680. Second grandson of the prophet Muhammad. He was the son of Ali bin Abu Talib and Muhammad's daughter Fatima. He was murdered at Karbala (modern Iraq), and his death is commemorated every year by Shia Muslims. It is through Husayn and his brother Hasan that Muhammad's descendants trace their lineage.

Huss John (Czech *Jan*) c. 1373–1415. Bohemian Christian church reformer, rector of Prague University from 1402, who was excommunicated for attacks on ecclesiastical abuses. He was summoned before the Council of Constance 1414, defended the English

reformer John Wycliffe, rejected the pope's authority, and was burned at the stake. His followers were called Hussites.

Husserl Edmund (Gustav Albrecht) 1859–1938. German philosopher, regarded as the founder of ◊phenomenology, the study of mental states as consciously experienced. His early phenomenology resembles linguistic philosophy because he examined the meaning and our understanding of words. His main works are *Logical Investigations* 1900, *Phenomenological Philosophy* 1913, and *The Crisis of the European Sciences* 1936.

He hoped phenomenology would become the science of all sciences. He influenced Martin ◊Heidegger and affected sociology through the work of Alfred Schütz (1899–1959).

Hussite follower of John ◊Huss. Opposed to both German and papal influence in Bohemia, the Hussites waged successful war against the Holy Roman Empire from 1419, but Roman Catholicism was finally re-established 1620.

Hutchinson Anne Marbury 1591–1643. American colonial religious leader. In 1634, she and her family followed John ◊Cotton to Massachusetts Bay Colony 1634. Preaching a unique theology which emphasized the role of faith, she gained a wide following. The colony's leaders, including Cotton, felt threatened by Hutchinson and in 1637 she was banished and excommunicated. Settling in Long Island, she and her family were killed by American Indians.

Born in England, Hutchinson was noted for her intellect and forceful personality.

Hutterian Brethren Christian group; see ◊Mennonite.

Hutton James 1726–1797. Scottish geologist, known as the 'founder of geology', who formulated the concept of ◊uniformitarianism. In 1785 he developed a theory of the igneous origin of many rocks.

His *Theory of the Earth* 1788 proposed that the Earth was indefinitely old. Uniformitarianism suggests that past events could be explained in terms of processes that work today. For example, the kind of river current that produces a certain settling pattern in a bed of sand today must have been operating many millions of years ago, if that same pattern is visible in ancient sandstones.

Huxley Andrew 1917– . English physiologist, awarded the Nobel Prize for Physiology or Medicine 1963 with Alan Hodgkin and John Eccles, for work on nerve impulses, discovering

Illness: Health, Disease and the Humours

The term 'disease' comes from 'dis-ease', and this provides a clue to some of its complexities. In medical parlance, 'disease' is an objective malady, typically caused by some pathogen (such as bacteria or a virus); but it is also the state of being sick (dis-eased), which may be a subjective condition. It is possible to have a disease without being or feeling ill; or to feel sick while having no disease. In an extreme case, this is called hypochondria.

A cursed visitation?

In ancient civilizations, disease was routinely interpreted as the consequence of sin, crime or moral fault, as precipitated by evil spirits, or as the work of black magic. Disease was thus personalized and given a moral or religious meaning; hence health was to be recovered by some act of propitiation or counter-magic such as prayer, sacrifice, or the performance of ritual. In most tribal societies, disease is thus a public matter, put to rights, by the witch-doctor or medicine man, through public ceremonial. Beliefs of this kind continued to play a major role throughout the Middle Ages and into the sixteenth and seventeenth centuries, with disease being associated with the work of Satan and with demonic possession. Plagues and pestilences were believed to be visitations from God, to punish or try sinful people. Protestants long continued to see disease as the finger of Providence.

The Greek analysis

It was Greek civilization that first, by contrast, viewed disease in a more naturalistic light, seeing it not as an evil assault from outside but as an internal breakdown. Above all, Hippocrates (c. 460–370 BC), often called the father of Greek medicine, developed the notion that health and disease hinged upon the quality and balance of the 'humours' within the body.

Four basic qualities characterized the four elements (air, water, fire, and earth) which had their analogues in the four humours of the body: blood, phlegm, choler (yellow bile), and black bile. Hot and dry corresponded to fire and yellow bile, hot and moist to air and blood, cold and dry to earth and black bile, cold and moist to water and phlegm. The humours related to the broader order of things, including the four seasons, so that humanity in health and disease was explicable in terms of natural philosophy. The humours were products of digested food and of metabolism, and a person's functions were regulated from the anatomical centres of the liver, heart, and brain, which were the seats of the natural soul (appetites), the vital soul (the passions), and the rational soul (wisdom, judgment, will).

A person was in good health if the body, its parts and humours, had the proper temperament. Otherwise disease, an imbalance of the main constitutional fluids, would strike. Disease could be fought by restoring the balance of the humours – thus anaemia would be countered by eating plenty of red meat and drinking red wine to make more blood. It was thought apoplexy (over-heating of the blood) could be countered by blood-letting.

Greek medicine emphasized the natural origin of even supposedly 'sacred' diseases like epilepsy. It also valued the cultivation of good health through temperance in eating, drinking, and the regulation of sleep, exercise, sex, and the passions.

Other theories

Greek theories had great currency within medicine until the last couple of centuries, and still carry popular appeal. Plagues and epidemics were harder to explain. As well as the idea of divine intervention, 'miasmatism' grew popular: epidemics, it was believed, derived from miasmas, or bad gases and smells given off from the soil, from rotting animal and vegetable matter, and from filth. The public health movements of the nineteenth century were founded on the idea of combating such miasmas, which supposedly caused typhus, typhoid, and cholera.

Another theory was 'contagionism', the notion that disease spread through the transmission of a certain unknown entity from person to person. This seemed fairly plausible in the case of diseases like syphilis. The poisonous agent of such contagion long, however, remained a mystery, until the work of Louis Pasteur (1822–1895) and Robert Koch (1843–1910) in the 1870s conclusively demonstrated the presence of injurious bacteria and similar living micro-organisms. Late nineteenth-century tropical medicine also began to grasp the parasitic (insect-borne) nature of diseases like malaria.

The scientific era

The discovery of the specificity of infectious disease was a tremendous breakthrough, putting medicine on a scientific basis and leading in the twentieth century to specific biological cures, such as antibiotics. Chronic disorders, mental diseases, degenerative disorders, and what are often called psychosomatic conditions have remained more difficult both to characterize and especially to cure.

Critics today widely argue that much modern Western medicine puts the cart before the horse by channeling more resources into curative than into preventive medicine. Scientific medicine's emphasis upon the body as a machine, to be understood primarily in terms of basic science (chemistry, physiology, anatomy) is also challenged by alternative medicine, with its more holistic concept of the unity of mind and body and its insistence that health and disease are located no less in the mind than in the body.

Roy Porter

how ionic mechanisms are used in nerves to transmit impulses.

Logical consequences are the scarecrows of fools and the beacons of wise men.

Thomas Henry Huxley
Science and Culture, 'On the Hypothesis that Animals are Automatic'

Huxley Thomas Henry 1825–1895. English scientist and humanist. Following the publication of Charles Darwin's *On the Origin of Species* 1859, he became known as 'Darwin's bulldog', and for many years was a prominent champion of evolution. In 1869, he coined the word 'agnostic' to express his own religious attitude. His grandsons include Aldous, Andrew, and Julian Huxley.

He wrote *Man's Place in Nature* 1863, textbooks on physiology, and innumerable scientific papers. His later books, such as *Lay Sermons* 1870, *Science and Culture* 1881, and *Evolution and Ethics* 1893 were expositions of scientific humanism.

Huygens Christiaan 1629–1695. Dutch mathematical physicist and astronomer who proposed the wave theory of light. He developed the pendulum clock, discovered polarization, and observed Saturn's rings.

hymn song in praise of a deity. Examples include Ikhnaton's hymn to the Aton in ancient Egypt, the ancient Greek Orphic hymns, Old Testament psalms, extracts from the New Testament (such as the 'Ave Maria'), and hymns by the British writers John Bunyan ('Who would true valour see') and Charles Wesley ('Hark the herald angels sing'). Gospel music and carols are forms of Christian hymn singing.

Other Christian hymn writers include Reginald Heber (1783–1826) ('From Greenland's icy mountains'), Henry Francis Lyte (1793–1847) ('Abide with me'), John S B Monsell (1811–1875) ('Fight the good fight'), and Sabine Baring-Gould (1834–1924) ('Onward Christian soldiers'). William Blake's poem 'Jerusalem' was set to music by Hubert Parry.

Hypatia c. 370–c. 415. Greek philosopher, born in Alexandria. She studied neo-Platonism in Athens, and succeeded her father Theon as professor of philosophy at Alexandria. She was murdered, it is thought by Christian fanatics.

hyperinflation rapid and uncontrolled ◊inflation, or increases in prices, usually associated with political and/or social instability (as in Germany in the 1920s).

hypnosis artificially induced temporary state of relaxation or altered attention characterized by heightened suggestibility. There is evidence that, with susceptible persons, the sense of pain may be diminished, memory of past events enhanced, and illusions or hallucinations experienced. Post-hypnotic amnesia (forgetting what happened during hypnosis) and post-hypnotic suggestion (performing an action after hypnosis that had been suggested during it) have also been demonstrated.

Hypnosis has a number of uses in medicine. Hypnotically induced sleep, for example, may assist the healing process, and hypnotic suggestion may help in dealing with the symptoms of emotional and psychosomatic disorders. Franz Anton Mesmer (1743–1815), the Viennese physician, is said to be the discoverer of hypnosis but he called it 'animal magnetism', believing it to be a physical force or fluid. The term 'hypnosis' was invented by James Braid (1795–1860), the British physician and surgeon who was the first to regard it as a psychological phenomenon. The Scottish surgeon, James Esdaile (1805–1859), working in India, performed hundreds of operations in which he used hypnosis to induce analgesia (insensitivity to pain) or general anaesthesia (total insensitivity).

Hypnosis has also been used by charlatans and entertainers until laws such as the Hypnosis Act 1952 in the UK controlled its exploitation.

Gibson, H B *Hypnosis: Its Nature and Therapeutic Uses* (London, 1977)

hypnotherapy use of hypnotic trance and post-hypnotic suggestions to relieve stress-related conditions such as insomnia and hypertension, or to break health-inimical habits or addictions.

The hypnotic trance was discovered by Austrian physician Friedrich Anton Mesmer and first used clinically in the 1840s by Scottish physician James Braid (1795–1860), who coined the term 'hypnosis'. Though it is an effective method of modifying behaviour, its effects are of short duration unless it is used as an adjunct to ◊psychotherapy.

hypothesis proposition assumed for the sake of argument. To hypothesize is to suggest an idea and then examine its plausibility in relation to the facts and the consequences if it were proven to be true.

'Now take, for instance, the theory that the prime minister is dead and being impersonated in his public appearances. He has certainly said some odd things lately and ...'.

hysteria in psychology and psychiatry, a term used to describe several different symptoms and to refer to at least one well-known disorder. This is conversion hysteria, one of the neuroses, the symptoms of which include paralysis, tics, tremors, changes in pain sensitivity, blindness, deafness, ◊anorexia, ◊bulimia, amnesia, ◊fugues, and somnambulism. The term is also applied to a personality disorder unconnected with the neurosis often referred to as hysterical personality, but now called histrionic personality. The characteristic features of this disorder include attention-seeking, over-dramatizing situations, labile emotions, suggestibility, and sexual provoca-tiveness but anxiety and frigidity in sexual situations.

Following Jean-Martin ◊Charcot, ◊Freud initially considered the often bizarre symptoms of conversion hysteria to symbolize repressed and forgotten sexual traumas and thus to discharge the anxiety aroused by repressed sexual conflict. At first he thought these traumas were actual seductions or childhood sexual abuse (the 'seduction' theory) but revised this view later when he realized that they were imagined events, or phantasies, arising from childhood sexual desires and auto-erotic activities, and that the patients' memories were fictitious. This is known as the 'phantasy' theory.

I

Iblis the Muslim name for the ◊devil.

Ibn 'Arabi Abu Bakr Muhammad bin Ali Muhyi al-Din 1165–1240. Andalusian-born mystic and teacher who settled and died in Damascus. To Ibn 'Arabi love was more important than knowledge, a theory which is totally rejected by traditional Muslim lawyers. A prolific writer, he combined inner devotion with an analytical mind, concluding the unity of faiths despite their apparent divergency. He wrote an estimated 400 books and treatises, among which is his famous *al-Futuhat al-Makiyya/The Makkan Inspirations*.

Ibn Hanbal Ahmad 780–855. Founder of the last of the four main schools of Sunni Islamic Law. He was particularly renowned for his knowledge of the ◊Hadith of the prophet Muhammad (traditions concerning his life and sayings).

He was born in Baghdad and instructed by Imam ◊Shafi'i. His main work, the *Musnad/ The Reliable* contained 30,000 hadith. Included amongst his pupils were Ismail al-Bukhari and Muslim Ibn Daud. Modern ◊Wahabis adhere to his teachings.

Ibn Sina Arabic name of ◊Avicenna, scholar, and translator.

Icarus in Greek legend, the son of ◊Daedalus, who with his father escaped from the labyrinth in Crete by making wings of feathers fastened with wax. Icarus plunged to his death when he flew too near the Sun and the wax melted.

I Ching or **Book of Changes** ancient Chinese book of divination based on 64 hexagrams, or patterns of six lines. The lines may be 'broken' or 'whole' (yin or yang) and are generated by tossing yarrow stalks or coins. The enquirer formulates a question before throwing, and the book gives interpretations of the meaning of the hexagrams.

The *I Ching* is thought to have originated in the 2nd millennium BC, with commentaries added by Confucius and later philosophers. It is proto-Taoist in that it is not used for determining the future but for making the enquirer aware of inherent possibilities and unconscious tendencies.

icon in the Orthodox Church, a representation of Jesus, Mary, an angel, or a saint, in painting, low relief, or mosaic. The painted icons were traditionally done on wood. After the 17th century in Russia, a *riza*, or gold and silver covering which leaves only the face and hands visible (and may be adorned with jewels presented by the faithful in thanksgiving), was often added as protection.

Icons were regarded as holy objects, based on the doctrine that God became visible through Christ. Icon painting originated in the Byzantine Empire, but many examples were destroyed by the ◊iconoclasts in the 8th and 9th centuries. The Byzantine style of painting predominated in the Mediterranean region and in Russia until the 12th century, when Russian, Greek, and other schools developed. Andrei Rublev (c. 1365–1430) was a renowned Russian icon painter.

iconoclast literally, a person who attacks religious images, originally in obedience to the injunction of the Second Commandment not to worship 'graven images'. Under the influence of Islam and Judaism, an iconoclastic movement calling for the destruction of religious images developed in the Byzantine Empire, and was endorsed by the Emperor Leo III in 726. Fierce persecution of those who made and venerated icons followed, until iconoclasm was declared a heresy in the 9th century.

The same name was applied to those opposing the use of images at the Reformation, when there was much destruction in churches. Figuratively, the term is used for a person who attacks established ideals or principles.

iconography in art history, significance attached to symbols that can help to identify subject matter (for example, a saint holding keys usually represents St Peter) and place a work of art in its historical context. The pioneer of this approach was Erwin ◊Panofsky.

iconology a more detailed form of ◊iconography that analyses the meaning of pictorial motifs and symbols within the context of their original significance. It is an approach to art history pioneered by Erwin ◊Panofsky.

iconostasis screen separating the altar from the body of the church in Orthodox churches. It is usually covered with large icons of Christ, Mary the Mother of God, John the Baptist, and the saint of the church, with a row of smaller icons at the top showing the main feasts of the church year.

id in Freudian psychology, the mass of motivational or instinctual elements of the human mind, whose activity is largely governed by the arousal of specific need states, which Freud termed *triebe* or instinctual drives. The id is regarded as the ◊unconscious element of the human psyche, and is said to be in conflict with the ◊ego and the ◊superego.

One of the greatest pains to human nature is the pain of a new idea.

idea

Walter Bagehot, 1826–1877, British writer and economist.
Physics and Politics

---

idea in philosophy, a term that has had a variety of technical usages; modern philosophers prefer more specific terms like 'sense datum', 'image', and '◊concept'. An ◊innate idea is a concept not derived from experience.

Plato's Ideas (also called ◊Forms) were immaterial objects outside the mind, universals or essences existing objectively in nature. In later Greek and in medieval philosophy, ideas tended to be in the mind of God. Since the 17th century, 'idea' has nearly always been used for something in or having reference to the mind. For Immanuel Kant, an idea was a representation of something that cannot be experienced. For G W F Hegel, the term meant something like the overall pattern or purpose in the universe.

I am an idealist. I don't know where I'm going but I'm on the way.

idealism

Carl August Sandburg, 1878–1967, US poet.
Incidentals

---

idealism in philosophy, the theory that states that the external world is fundamentally immaterial and a dimension of the mind. Objects in the world exist but, according to this theory, they lack substance.

identity in philosophy, the sameness of a person, which may continue in spite of changes in bodily appearance, personality, intellectual abilities, memory, and so on. In psychology, identity refers to one's conception of oneself and sense of continuous being, particularly as an individual distiguishable from, but interacting, with others.

ideology set of ideas, beliefs, and opinions about the nature of people and society, providing a framework for a theory about how people should live, as well as how society is or should be organized. A nation's ideology is usually reflected in the political system it creates.

idiot savant (French 'knowledgeable idiot') person who has a specific musical, mathematical, or mnemonic skill which has developed at the expense of general intelligence. An idiot savant is educationally slow but may be able to calculate the day of the week for any date, or memorize a large quantity of text. Most idiots savants are male.

idolatry in Christianity, Islam, and Judaism, the turning away from God to other objects of religious devotion. In the Hebrew Bible it is specifically forbidden in the the second of the ◊Ten Commandments. Islam forbids the use of any pictures or other images of living beings, because of the danger of transferring admiration and wonder from God to the image or the artist. Christianity has interpreted the command variously at different times and places. Some groups, notably in certain Protestant churches, avoid all images, while others, such as the Roman Catholic and Orthodox, encourage the use of pictures and statues as pointers, or ◊icons, to God. The word idol is highly prejudicial to Hindus who practice *arcana* – the worship of an image of the deity – as an important element in their path of devotion.

Ignatius Loyola, St 1491–1556. Spanish noble who founded the ◊Jesuit order 1540, also called the Society of Jesus.

His deep interest in the religious life began in 1521, when reading the life of Jesus while recuperating from a war wound. He visited the Holy Land in 1523, studied in Spain and Paris, where he took vows with St Francis Xavier, and was ordained 1537. He then moved to Rome and with the approval of Pope Paul III began the Society of Jesus, sending missionaries to Brazil, India, and Japan, and founding Jesuit schools. Feast day 31 July.

Ignatius of Antioch, St lived 1st–2nd century AD. Christian martyr. Traditionally a disciple of St John, he was bishop of Antioch, and was thrown to the wild beasts in Rome. He wrote seven epistles, important documents of the early Christian church. Feast day 1 Feb.

Ikhnaton or *Akhenaton* King of Egypt of the 18th dynasty (c. 1379–1362 BC), who may have ruled jointly for a time with his father Amenhotep III. He developed the cult of the Sun, ◊Aton, rather than the rival cult of Ammon, and removed his capital to Akhetaton. Some historians believe that his attention to religious reforms rather than imperial defence led to the loss of most of Egypt's possessions in Asia.

Ikhnaton's favourite wife was Nefertiti, and two of their six daughters were married to his successors Smenkhare and Tutankaton (later known as Tutankhamen).

In a consumer society there are inevitably two kinds of slaves: the prisoners of addiction and the prisoners of envy.

Ivan Illich
Tools for Conviviality ch 3

Illich Ivan 1926– . US radical philosopher and activist, born in Austria. His works, which include *Deschooling Society* 1971, *Towards a History of Need* 1978, and *Gender* 1983, are a critique of contemporary economic development, especially in the Third World.

Illich was born in Vienna and has lived in the USA and Latin America. He believes that modern technology and bureaucratic institutions are destroying peasant skills and self-sufficiency and creating a new form of dependency: on experts, professionals, and material goods. True liberation, he believes, can only be achieved by abolishing the institutions on which authority rests, such as schools and hospitals.

illusion generally, a delusion, deception, or false perception. Illusion is, like ◊appearance, usually contrasted with reality. The concept is often used in the philosophy of perception and in epistemology. It is only by trusting some experiences that we can identify others as illusory, so the occurrence of illusions does not mean that everything is illusory.

Imagism movement in Anglo-American poetry that flourished 1912–14 and affected much US and British poetry and critical thinking thereafter. A central figure was Ezra Pound, who asserted the principles of free verse, complex imagery, and poetic impersonality.

Pound encouraged Hilda Doolittle to sign her verse H D Imagiste and in 1914 edited the *Des Imagistes* anthology. Poets subsequently influenced by this movement include T S Eliot, William Carlos Williams, Wallace Stevens, and Marianne Moore. Imagism established modernism in English-language verse.

imam (Arabic 'leader') in a mosque, the leader of congregational prayer, but generally any notable Islamic leader.

IMF abbreviation for ◊*International Monetary Fund*.

Immaculate Conception in the Roman Catholic Church, the belief that the Virgin Mary was, by a special act of grace, preserved free from ◊original sin from the moment she was conceived. This article of the Catholic faith was for centuries the subject of heated controversy, opposed by St Thomas Aquinas and other theologians, but generally accepted from about the 16th century. It became a dogma in 1854 under Pope Pius IX.

immortality in religious belief, a state of perpetual life attributed to divine beings, mythical or angelic. A belief in immortality is common to many religions, though each has its own conception of perpetual life.

Every parting is a foretaste of death, and every reunion a foretaste of the resurrection.

immortality
Arthur Schopenhauer, 1788–1860,
German philosopher.
Essays and Aphorisms

In some mythologies, for example Greek and Chinese, heroes or sages can become divine and therefore immortal. The ancient Egyptians believed in physical resurrection and took great care in the preservation of the dead body and the provision of food and material goods for the dead person. In Christian and Muslim thinking immortality also refers to the belief that human beings will enter a new form of eternal existence after physical death. Hinduism teaches that the soul, atman, has no beginning and no end; it is indestructible and transmigrates into another body after death.

imperfect competition competition amongst firms that supply branded products. Firms therefore compete not just on price, as in ◊perfect competition, but on the type of good they supply. In an ◊oligopoly, the market is dominated by a few firms offering strongly branded products and new firms find it difficult to establish themselves in the industry, whereas in monopolistic competition there are many small firms, branding is weaker, and entry to the industry is easier.

An empire founded by war has to maintain itself by war.

imperialism

Charles Montesquieu, 1689–1755, French philosophical historian. *Considérations sur les causes de la grandeur des Romains et de leur décadence* ch 8

---

imperialism policy of extending the power and rule of a government beyond its own boundaries. A country may attempt to dominate others by direct rule or by less obvious means such as control of markets for goods or raw materials. The latter is often called ◊neocolonialism.

In the 19th century imperialism was synonymous with the establishment of colonies, and at this time imperialism was overt and often flamboyant. Britain, for example, revelled in its expansionist policies, initially in the pursuit of trade, and its colonies and dominions all bore evidence of rule by the 'mother country'. Places, such as Victoria in Australia and Canada, the Victoria Falls in Rhodesia, Victoria Lake in Tanganyika, and Victoria Peak in Hong Kong, are examples of this boastful display of empire. As the British Empire was progressively dismembered after World War II, traditional imperialism was continued by the Soviet Union, but in other areas of the world it became less obvious, and more subtle. As the superpower of the

---

The conquest of the earth, which mostly means the taking it away from those who have a different complexion or slightly flatter noses than ourselves, is not a pretty thing when you look into it.

imperialism

Joseph Conrad. Pen name of Joseph Jozef Konrad Korzeniowski, 1857–1924, English novelist, born in the Ukraine of Polish parents. *Heart of Darkness* ch 1

West, the United States, while espousing democratic, egalitarian virtues, secured and protected its interests by economic pressure,

and sometimes military intervention, in many parts of the world, and particularly in its own 'backyard'. Japan, on the other hand carried out a much more discreet form of economic imperialism, becoming a superpower to rival the United States without having recourse to military might. Today many so-called Third World countries, heavily dependent on the leading industrial nations, are subject to this new brand of imperialism, or neocolonialism, significant proportions of their national product being allocated purely to the payment of interest on accumulated international debts.

imply to lead logically to. For example, if $2x = 10$, then $x = 5$. The second statement follows from the first.

Impressionism movement in painting that originated in France in the 1860s and dominated European and North American painting in the late 19th century. The Impressionists wanted to depict real life, to paint straight from nature, and to capture the changing effects of light. The term was first used abusively to describe Monet's painting *Impression, Sunrise* 1872 (Musée Marmottan, Paris); other Impressionists were Renoir and Sisley, and the style was adopted for periods by Cézanne, Manet, Degas, and others.

The starting point of Impressionism was the 'Salon des Refusés', an exhibition in 1873 of work rejected by the official Salon. This was followed by the Impressionists' own exhibitions 1874–86, where their work aroused fierce opposition. Their styles were diverse, but all experimented with effects of light and movement created with distinct brushstrokes and fragments of colour juxtaposed on the canvas rather than mixed on the palette. By the 1880s, the movement's central impulse had dispersed, and a number of new styles emerged, later described as Post-Impressionism.

imprinting in ◊ethology, the process whereby a young animal learns to recognize both specific individuals (for example, its mother) and its own species.

Imprinting is characteristically an automatic response to specific stimuli at a time when the animal is especially sensitive to those stimuli (the **sensitive period**). Thus, goslings learn to recognize their mother by following the first moving object they see after hatching; as a result, they can easily become imprinted on other species, or even inanimate objects, if these happen to move near them at this time. In chicks, imprinting occurs only between 10 and 20 hours after hatching. In mammals, the mother's attachment to her infant may be a form of imprinting made possible by a sensitive period; this period may be as short as the first hour after giving birth.

incarnation assumption of living form (plant, animal, human) by a deity, for example the gods of Greece and Rome, Hinduism, and Christianity (Jesus as the second person of the Trinity).

incentive in economics, a measure which persuades economic agents to adopt a particular course of action. For example, it can be argued that lower income-tax rates provide an incentive for people to work harder. Higher indirect taxes on alcohol provide a disincentive for people to drink. An *incentive scheme*, where an employer will offer a bonus to staff who achieve a certain target, is a way of motivating workers.

incest sexual intercourse between persons thought to be too closely related to marry; the exact relationships that fall under the incest taboo vary widely from society to society. A biological explanation for the incest taboo is based on the necessity to avoid inbreeding.

Within groups in which ritual homosexuality is practised, for example in New Guinea, an incest taboo applies also to these relations, suggesting that the taboo is as much social as biological in origin.

incomes policy government-initiated exercise to curb ◊inflation by restraining rises in incomes, on either a voluntary or a compulsory basis; often linked with action to control prices, in which case it becomes a prices and incomes policy.

In Britain incomes policies have been applied at different times since the 1950s, with limited success. An alternative to incomes policy, employed by the post-1979 Conservative government in Britain, is monetary policy, which attempts to manage the economy by controlling the quantity of money in circulation (◊money supply).

income tax direct tax levied on personal income, mainly wages and salaries, but which may include the value of receipts other than in cash. It is one of the main instruments for achieving a government's income redistribution objectives. In contrast, *indirect taxes* are duties payable whenever a specific product is purchased; examples include VAT and customs duties.

Most countries impose income taxes on company (corporation) profits and on individuals (personal), although the rates and systems differ widely from country to country. In the case of companies in particular, income tax returns are prepared by an accountant, who will take advantage of the various exemptions, deductions, and allowances available. Personal income taxes are usually progressive so that the poorest members of society pay little or no tax, while the rich make much larger contributions. In the 1980s many countries have undergone tax reforms that have led to simplification and reductions in income-tax rates. This has had the effect of stimulating economic activity by increasing consumer spending and in some cases has discouraged tax evasion. In the UK the rates of tax and allowances are set out yearly in the annual Finance Act, which implements the recommendations agreed to by the House of Commons in the budget presented by the chancellor of the Exchequer. William Pitt introduced an income tax 1799–1801 to finance the wars with revolutionary France; it was reimposed 1803–16 for the same purpose, and was so unpopular that all records of it were destroyed when it was abolished. Peel reintroduced the tax in 1842 and it has been levied ever since, forming an important part of government finance. At its lowest, 1874–76, it was 0.83%; at its highest, 1941–46, the standard rate was 50%. In the UK, employees' tax is deducted under the PAYE system.

incubus in the popular belief of the Middle Ages, male demon who had sexual intercourse with women in their sleep. Supposedly the women then gave birth to witches and demons. *Succubus* is the female equivalent.

index in economics, an indicator of a general movement in wages and prices over a specified period.

For example, the retail price index (RPI) records changes in the ◊cost of living. The *Financial Times* Industrial Ordinary Share Index (FT) indicates the general movement of the London Stock Exchange market in the UK; the US equivalent is the Dow Jones Index.

Index Librorum Prohibitorum the list of books formerly officially forbidden to members of the Roman Catholic Church. The process of condemning books and bringing the Index up to date was carried out by a congregation of cardinals, consultors, and examiners from the 16th century until its abolition 1966.

individualism in politics, a view in which the individual takes precedence over the collective: the opposite of ◊collectivism. The term *possessive individualism* has been applied to the writings of John ◊Locke and Jeremy ◊Bentham,

Personal Happiness and the Cult of the Individual

The idea of happiness has a complex history. Few have denied the desirability of happiness, though many have tried to distinguish 'true' happiness from happiness 'as commonly understood', and religions and philosophies have often prized happiness (as in Aristotle's *eudaimonia*, or total well-being) while demeaning some inferior alternative called (mere) 'pleasure'. While moralists have had certain reservations, psychologists have been more wholehearted about hedonism and in certain fields (e.g. medicine) pleasure has found ready approval as the opposite of pain.

Historically, philosophies that make the goal of happiness or pleasure their central theme have tended to be worldly and individualistic, even where, as does Benthamite utilitarianism, they seek to achieve the 'greatest happiness of the greatest number'.

Happiness – a moral end

For the Greeks, happiness tends to be equated with faring well or doing well. Socrates (469–399 BC) refined this notion, stressing the importance not of external prosperity but of goodness and justice. Plato's (c. 428–347 BC) writings tend to portray the achievement of happiness as a moral end, distinct from the indulgence of appetite. Stoicism had similar reservations about pleasure, and the Epicureans, despite the popular associations of their name, stressed the avoidance of pain rather than the gratification of the passions.

Within Judaeo-Christianity, happiness became associated with blessedness, walking in the ways of God, and with heavenly salvation. Bodily pleasure was typically shunned as sinful, and various puritanical movements stressed commandments of prohibition ('Thou Shalt Not'), asceticism, self-denial, and the mortification of the flesh. The Christian idea of blessedness became connected with the love of God.

A function of freedom

With the gradual secularization of values, especially associated with the eighteenth-century Enlightenment, the concept of happiness became increasingly linked to science, individualism, liberalism and freedom, and the hope of progress. Happiness was represented as a right, to be fulfilled alongside such other rights as liberty (of person and speech) and the security of property. Utopian thinking, from Thomas More's (1478–1535) *Utopia* (1516), began to conceptualize the elements of happy societies. With the rise of the notion of progress, old myths of the 'Golden Age' – a lost time of bliss – gave way to the notion that happiness lay in an attainable future state.

Philosophical ideas

In the later seventeenth century, the concept of happiness became increasingly important in moral philosophy. For Thomas Hobbes (1588–1679), happiness was viewed as the satisfaction of appetite. Francis Hutcheson (1694–1746) and Adam Smith (1723–1790) stressed that

happiness was based on sympathy and benevolence; Smith, meanwhile, developed an economic theory which argued that the selfish behaviour of individuals in a free market would maximize economic progress and benefits for all – a version of Bernard Mandeville's 'private vices, public benefits' paradox. John Locke's (1632–1704) psychological hedonism stimulated the accent on pleasure in the writings of French *philosophes* like Claude Helvtius (1715–1771) and Etienne Condillac (1715–1780), who viewed pleasure and pain as the sole motives of action.

The pleasure principle

The philosophy of pleasure was most systematically advocated by Jeremy Bentham (1748–1832), whose utilitarianism embraced the notion that 'the greatest happiness of the greatest number' was the only meaningful, scientific, consistent criterion of good and evil. Bentham upheld a psychological hedonism in which pleasure is the goal of all purposive behaviour. He attempted to work out a 'felicific calculus' in which the value of a given unit of pleasure (or pain) could be calculated by judging it for qualities like intensity, duration, certainty or uncertainty, propinquity or remoteness, fecundity, purity, and the extent or number of persons affected. Bentham believed that such a 'felicific calculus' would be practically useful in assessing rational scales of punishment (too little pain would not deter; too much would unnecessarily detract from utility). Bentham's pleasure–pain theory was frankly hedonistic, secular, and individualistic. Even broadly sympathetic critics, like John Stuart Mill (1806–1873), berated it for failing to make allowance for different qualities of happiness – 'higher' and 'lower' pleasures. Crude utilitarianism thus made no allowance for self-perfection. Moreover, psychologically speaking, Mill believed that the conscious pursuit of pleasure was necessarily self-defeating.

During the last two centuries, psychological hedonism has become the bedrock of many theories of human (and animal) behaviour, including behaviourist psychology. Within evolutionary biology, the pursuit of sensory happiness in the guise of survival, and the survival of the fittest, forms a key mechanism. For Sigmund Freud (1856–1939), pleasure was a basic instinct, initially taking the form of sexual gratification or libido. Since full pursuit of the 'pleasure principle' appears incompatible with civilized order, the drive for pleasure is either thwarted (causing neurosis) or sublimated into art, religion, work, and other creative or productive activity.

Thus Freud – and by extension modern values – in many respects reversed the priorities of earlier theologians and philosophers. They saw happiness, based on higher values, as the experience of truth, and hedonism as a kind of illusion, or at least less valuable. Freud, by contrast, saw the drive for sensory and sexual gratification as the ultimate truth about the human animal.

Roy Porter

describing society as comprising individuals interacting through market relations.

Comrades! We must abolish the cult of the individual decisively, once and for all.

individualism

Nikita Sergeyevich Khrushchev, 1894–1971,
Soviet politician, premier 1958–64.
Speech to the secret session of 20th Congress
of the Communist Party 25 Feb 1956

Indra Hindu god of the sky, shown as a four-armed man on a white elephant, carrying a thunderbolt. The intoxicating drink ◊soma is associated with him.

induction in philosophy, the process of observing particular instances of things in order to derive general statements and laws of nature. It is the opposite of ◊deduction, which moves from general statements and principles to the particular.

Induction was criticized by the Scottish philosopher David ◊Hume because it relied upon belief rather than valid reasoning. In the philosophy of science, the 'problem of induction' is a crucial area of debate: however much evidence there is for a proposition, there is the possibility of a future counter-instance that will invalidate the explanation. Therefore, it is argued, no scientific statement can be said to be true.

indulgence in the Roman Catholic Church, the total or partial remission of temporal punishment for sins which remain to be expiated after penitence and confession have secured exemption from eternal punishment. The doctrine of indulgence began as the commutation of church penances in exchange for suitable works of charity or money gifts to the church, and became a great source of church revenue. This trade in indulgences roused Luther in 1517 to initiate the Reformation. The Council of Trent 1563 recommended moderate retention of indulgences, and they continue, notably in 'Holy Years'.

industrial democracy means whereby employees may have a share in the decisions taken by the firm in which they work, and, therefore, a share of responsibility for its success or failure.

In 1975 the UK government led by Harold Wilson appointed a Commission of Inquiry on Industrial Democracy, chaired by Sir Alan Bullock. The Bullock Report 1977 produced an explicit model for adoption by company boards but its suggestions were never taken seriously by British management.

Although there are a small number of firms in Britain that operate some form of industrial democracy, it is in mainland European countries, particularly Sweden and Germany, that the most successful examples are to be found.

industrialization policy usually associated with modernization of developing countries where the process normally starts with the manufacture of simple goods that can replace imports. It is essential for economic development and largely responsible for the growth of cities.

Industrial Revolution the sudden acceleration of technical and economic development that began in Britain in the second half of the 18th century. The traditional agrarian economy was replaced by one dominated by machinery and manufacturing, made possible through technical advances such as the steam engine. This transferred the balance of political power from the landowner to the industrial capitalist and created an urban working class. From 1830 to the early 20th century, the Industrial Revolution spread throughout Europe and the USA and to Japan and the various colonial empires.

The great initial invention was the steam engine, originally developed for draining mines but rapidly put to use in factories and on the railways.

infallibility inability to err in matters of ◊doctrine. In Christianity different beliefs are found. Some believe that only God is infallible, others believe that God, in the person of the Holy Spirit, so guides the church or its leaders that in certain circumstances infallibility is conferred. One tradition is that the church as a whole is infallible, so that doctrines are true if accepted by the whole church. The first ◊Vatican Council formulated the doctrine that the pope is infallible when speaking on matters of doctrine *ex cathedra* ('from the throne', an official, formal pronouncement in his office as pope). It is not meant to imply that the pope's every utterance is infallible. This doctrine has been the subject of much discussion both within the Roman Catholic Church and with other churches.

inference deduction or conclusion drawn from what has been implied rather than directly stated; a reading between the lines.

If you heard a member of Parliament saying that the prime minister was always making mistakes, you might infer that he was a member of the opposition. This would be a reasonable inference, but it could be wrong.

An important aspect of the National Curriculum in English is the ability to infer meaning, to understand what is hinted (the subtext) as well as what is directly stated. 'It is a truth universally acknowledged, that a single man in possession of a good fortune must be in want of a wife.' Jane Austen means that a rich, unmarried man is seen as a potential husband: everybody wants him to marry their daughter. That is not what she says, but what she implies. It is easier to pick up such inferences in context, as you get to know your author. Reading implications, taking inferences, is an important skill in the study of English.

A common error is to confuse *infer* and *imply*. *Imply* means 'to hint at'; *infer* means 'to draw conclusions from'.

No one can make you feel inferior without your consent.

inferiority complex
(Anna) Eleanor Roosevelt, 1884–1962, US social worker, lecturer, and First Lady.
Catholic Digest

---

inferiority complex in psychology, as described by Alfred ◊Adler, a ◊complex, or cluster of repressed fears, arising from the inferiority of an organ or part of the body and leading to feelings of general inferiority. Adler believed everyone suffered from inferiority feelings and the desire or determination to relieve them determined one's lifestyle. Failure to deal with them could lead to neurotic symptoms. The term is also used in a popular sense to describe general feelings of inferiority and the overcompensation that often ensues.

infinite series in mathematics, a series of numbers consisting of a denumerably infinite sequence of terms. The sequence n, n^2, n^3, ... gives the series $n + n^2 + n^3 + ...$. For example, $1 + 2 + 3 + ...$ is a divergent infinite arithmetic series, and $8 + 4 + 2 + 1 + \frac{1}{2} + ...$ is a convergent infinite geometric series that has a sum to infinity of 16.

infinity mathematical quantity that is larger than any fixed assignable quantity; symbol ∞. By convention, the result of dividing any number by zero is regarded as infinity.

inflation in economics, a rise in the general level of prices. The many causes include *cost-push inflation* that occurred 1974 as a result

of the world price increase in oil, thus increasing production costs. *Demand-pull inflation* results when overall demand exceeds supply. Suppressed inflation occurs in controlled economies and is reflected in rationing, shortages, and black market prices. Deflation, a fall in the general level of prices, is the reverse of inflation.

information technology collective term for the various technologies involved in processing and transmitting information. They include computing, telecommunications, and microelectronics.

infrastructure relatively permanent facilities that service an industrial economy. Infrastructure usually includes roads, railways, other communication networks, energy and water supply, and education and training facilities. Some definitions also include sociocultural installations such as health-care and leisure facilities.

Inge William 1860–1954. English philosopher and dean of St Paul's in London 1911–1934. As a Christian Platonist and an expert on ◊Plotinus, he believed that self-disciplined prayer admitted the individual to an eternal world of light and peace. As a social commentator, he inclined to rather pessimistic and politically conservative views, and he became known as 'the gloomy Dean'.

Born in Crayke, North Yorkshire, he taught at Eton and at Oxford University before joining the church. His works include *Christian Mysticism* 1899, *Christian Ethics and Modern Problems* 1930, and *The End of an Age* 1948.

initiative device whereby constitutional voters may play a direct part in making laws. A proposed law is drawn up and signed by petitioners, and submitted to the legislature. A ◊*referendum* may be taken on a law that has been passed by the legislature but that will not become operative unless the voters assent to it. Switzerland was the first country to make use of the device.

innate idea in philosophy, a ◊concept prior to, and not derived from, experience. The term is traditional and was revived in the 20th century by certain linguists, notably the American Noam ◊Chomsky, who holds that we have an innate tendency to learn and to use certain grammatical structures.

Innocent III 1161–1216. Pope from 1198 who asserted papal power over secular princes, in particular over the succession of Holy Roman Emperors. He also made King John of England his vassal, compelling him to accept

Stephen Langton as archbishop of Canterbury. He promoted the fourth Crusade and crusades against the non-Christian Livonians and Letts, and the Albigensian heretics of S France.

Greediness closed Paradise; it beheaded John the Baptist.

Innocent III
De Contemptu Mundi

Innocents' Day or **Childermas** Christian festival, celebrated 28 Dec in memory of the **Massacre of the Innocents**, the children of Bethlehem who were allegedly slaughtered by King Herod after the birth of Jesus.

Inquisition tribunal of the Roman Catholic Church established 1233 to suppress heresy (dissenting views), originally by excommunication. Sentence was pronounced during a religious ceremony, the ◊auto-da-fé. The Inquisition operated in France, Italy, Spain, and the Holy Roman Empire, and was especially active following the ◊Reformation; it was later extended to the Americas. Its trials were conducted in secret, under torture, and penalties ranged from fines, through flogging and imprisonment, to death by burning.

During the course of the Spanish Inquisition, until its abolition 1834, some 60,000 cases were tried. The Roman Inquisition was established 1542 to combat the growth of Protestantism. The Inquisition or Holy Office (renamed Sacred Congregation for the Doctrine of the Faith 1965) still deals with ecclesiastical discipline.

insanity in a medical or legal context, any mental disorder in which the patient cannot be held responsible for their actions. The term is no longer used to refer to ◊psychosis.

insider trading or *insider dealing* illegal use of privileged information in dealing on a stock exchange, for example when a company takeover bid is imminent. Insider trading is in theory detected by the Securities and Exchange Commission (SEC) in the USA, and by the Securities and Investment Board (SIB) in the UK. Neither agency, however, has any legal powers other than public disclosure and they do not bring prosecutions themselves.

In the UK, insider trading was made illegal by the Company Securities (Insider Dealing) Act 1985, and in 1989 it was ruled that the perpetrator was equally guilty whether the information was solicited or unsolicited.

I dare not alter these things, they come to me from above.

inspiration
Alfred Austin, 1835–1913, British poet.
Rejecting the accusation of writing
ungrammatical verse

---

inspiration spiritual influence which allows a person to think, speak, or act in a way that transcends ordinary human abilities. It can refer to a wide variety of religious experiences, including the presence of a 'spiritus' or breath responsible for the inspiration. Religious scriptures are often believed to be inspired, although this may be understood in a variety of ways. Muslims believe that the ◊Qur'an was directly revealed, word for word, by God through the prophethood of ◊Muhammad. Christians disagree about the inspiration of the Bible: some believe it is the directly inspired word of God, while others give more importance to the human abilities of the writers, while still stressing God's influence on them.

Work brings inspiration, if inspiration is not discernible at the beginning.

inspiration
Igor Stravinsky, 1882–1971, Russian-born
composer.
Chronicles of My Life

---

instinct in ◊ethology, behaviour found in all equivalent members of a given species (for example, all the males, or all the females with young) that is presumed to be genetically determined.

'Be a good animal, true to your instincts,' was his motto.

instinct
D(avid) H(erbert) Lawrence, 1885–1930,
English writer whose work expresses his belief
in emotion and the sexual impulse as creative
and true to human nature.
White Peacock

Examples include a male robin's tendency to attack other male robins intruding on its territory and the tendency of many female mammals to care for their offspring. Instincts differ from reflexes in that they involve very much more complex actions, and learning often plays an important part in their development.

Institute for Advanced Study department of Princeton University in New Jersey, USA, established 1933 to encourage gifted scientists to further their research uninterrupted by teaching duties or an imposed research scheme. Its first professor was Albert Einstein.

insurance contract guaranteeing compensation to the payer of a premium against loss by fire, death, accident, and so on, which is known as *assurance* in the case of a fixed sum and *insurance* where the payment is proportionate to the loss.

intellect aspect of the mind concerned with cognitive processes, such as remembering, imagining, conceptualising, reasoning, understanding, and judging. The term is also used to refer to these rational, or higher, thought processes.

Intelligence is quickness to apprehend as distinct from ability, which is capacity to act wisely on the thing apprehended.
intelligence
Alfred North Whitehead, 1861–1947, English philosopher and mathematician.
Dialogues 15 Dec 1939

intelligence in psychology, a general concept that summarizes the abilities of an individual in reasoning and problem solving, particularly in novel situations. These consist of a wide range of verbal and nonverbal skills and therefore some psychologists dispute a unitary concept of intelligence. See ◊intelligence test.

intelligence services in military and political affairs, services which obtain 'intelligence' (information), often secretly or illegally, about other countries or residents thought to be subversive of the state. *Counter-intelligence* is information obtained on the activities of hostile agents. Much intelligence is gained by technical means, such as satellites and the electronic interception of data.

The British intelligence services consist of MI5, the security service, which is responsible directly to the prime minister for internal security, MI6, the secret intelligence service, which operates mainly under Foreign Office control, and the Government Communications Head-

quarters (GCHQ) which carries out electronic surveillance for the other two branches. Although it is well known that GCHQ is based at Cheltenham, in Gloucestershire, information about the other two operations has been deliberately withheld until quite recently. It has now been revealed that the director-general of MI5 is Stella Rimington and the chief of MI6 is Sir Colin McColl. Indeed, MI5 published a booklet 1993 giving information about itself, which is available to the general public. MI5 has been based in Gower Street, in London's Bloomsbury district, but will soon move to Thames House, on Millbank. MI6 will shortly move from Century House, Waterloo, to Vauxhall Cross, at Vauxhall Bridge. In future the accounts of all three branches of the services will be audited by the National Audit Office, serving the controller and auditor general, and the House of Commons. It is expected that legislation will be passed during the 1993–94 parliamentary session to give powers to a House of Commons select committee to scrutinize the work of the services.

intelligence test test that attempts to measure innate intellectual ability, rather than acquired ability.

It is now generally believed that a child's ability in an intelligence test can be affected by his or her environment, cultural background, and teaching. There is scepticism about the accuracy of intelligence tests, but they are still widely used as a diagnostic tool when children display learning difficulties. 'Sight and sound' intelligence tests, developed by Christopher Brand in 1981, avoid cultural bias and the pitfalls of improvement by practice. Subjects are shown a series of lines being flashed on a screen at increasing speed, and are asked to identify in each case the shorter of a pair; and when two notes are relayed over headphones, they are asked to identify which is the higher. There is a close correlation between these results and other intelligence test scores.

Workers in this field have included Francis ◊Galton, Alfred Binet (1857–1911), Cyril ◊Burt, and Hans ◊Eysenck. Binet devised the first intelligence test in 1905. The concept of intelligence quotient (IQ) was adopted by US psychologist Lewis Terman in 1915. The IQ is calculated according to the formula: IQ = MA/CA × 100, in which MA is 'mental age' (the age at which an average child is able to perform given tasks) and CA is 'chronological age', hence an average person has an IQ of 100. Intelligence tests were first used on a large scale in World War I in 1917 for 2 million drafted men in the USA. They were widely used in UK education as part of the Eleven Plus selection procedures, on the assumption that inborn intelligence was unalterable. Most psychologists now accept a much broader definition of intelligence, including spatial, creative, and problem-solving abilities which are often highly sought after in adult life but not measured by conventional intelligence tests.

intelligentsia in 19th-century Russia, a section of the middle class including lawyers, doctors, teachers, engineers, and some military men, who advocated the adoption of Western ideas as a cure for the country's backwardness. They also supported political and social reform but were baulked by an autocratic tsarist regime. This group eventually provided much of the leadership for the revolutionary movements of the early 20th century.

The intelligence are to the intelligentsia what a gentleman is to a gent.

Inteligensia
Stanley Baldwin, 1st Earl Baldwin of
Bewdley, 1867–147. English politician.
Stanley Baldwin

---

intentionality in philosophy, the property of consciousness whereby it is directed towards an object, even when this object does not exist in reality (such as 'the golden mountain'). Intentionality is a key concept in the German phenomenologist Edmund ◊Husserl's philosophy.

interdict ecclesiastical punishment that excludes an individual, community, or realm from participation in spiritual activities except for communion. It was usually employed against heretics or realms whose ruler was an excommunicant.

intermediate technology application of mechanics, electrical engineering, and other technologies, based on inventions and designs developed in scientifically sophisticated cultures, but utilizing materials, assembly, and maintenance methods found in technologically less advanced regions (known as the Third World).

Intermediate technologies aim to allow developing countries to benefit from new techniques and inventions of the 'First World', without the burdens of costly maintenance and supply of fuels and spare parts that in the Third World would represent an enormous and probably uneconomic overhead. See also ◊appropriate technology.

International, the coordinating body established by labour and socialist organizations, including:
First International or *International Working Men's Association* 1864–72, formed in London under Karl ◊Marx.
Second International 1889–1940, founded in Paris.
Third (Socialist) International or *Comintern* 1919–43, formed in Moscow by the Soviet leader Lenin, advocating from 1933 a popular front (communist, socialist, liberal) against the German dictator Hitler.
Fourth International or *Trotskyist International* 1936, somewhat indeterminate, anti-Stalinist.
Revived Socialist International 1951, formed in Frankfurt, Germany, a largely anti-communist association of social democrats.

International Brigade international volunteer force on the Republican side in the Spanish Civil War 1936–39.

Internationale international revolutionary socialist anthem; composed 1870 and first sung 1888. The words by Eugène Pottier (1816–1887) were written shortly after Napoleon III's surrender to Prussia; the music is by Pierre Degeyter. It was the Soviet national anthem 1917–44.

international law body of rules generally accepted as governing the relations between countries, pioneered by Hugo ◊Grotius, especially in matters of human rights, territory, and war.

Neither the League of Nations nor the United Nations proved able to enforce international law, successes being achieved only when the law coincided with the aims of a predominant major power – for example, in the Korean War. The scope of the law is now extended to space – for example, the 1967 treaty that (among other things) banned nuclear weapons from space.

International Monetary Fund (IMF) specialized agency of the United Nations, with its headquarters in Washington, DC, established under the 1944 Bretton Woods agreement and operational since 1947. It seeks to promote international monetary cooperation and the growth of world trade, and to smooth multilateral payment arrangements among member states.

IMF stand-by loans are available to members in balance-of-payments difficulties (the amount being governed by the member's quota), usually on the basis of acceptance of instruction on stipulated corrective measures.

International Society for Krishna Consciousness (ISKCON) or *Gaudiya Vaisnavism* Hindu sect based on the demonstration of intense love for ◊Krishna (an incarnation of the god Vishnu), especially by chanting the mantra 'Hare Krishna'. Members wear distinctive yellow robes, and men often have their heads partly shaven. Their holy books are the Hindu scriptures and particularly the *Bhagavad-Gītā,* which they study daily.

The sect was introduced to the West by Swami Prabhupada (1896–1977). Members believe that by chanting the mantra and meditating on it they may achieve enlightenment and so remove themselves from the cycle of ◊reincarnation. They are expected to live ascetic lives, avoiding meat, eggs, alcohol, tea, coffee, and other drugs, and gambling; sexual relationships should only take place within marriage and solely for procreation.

The sect has about 5,000 members in the UK. Their centre of worship in Britain is Bhakti-Vedanta Manor in Letchmore Heath, Hertfordshire.

International Style or *International Modern* architectural style, an early and influential phase of the ◊Modern Movement, originating in Western Europe in the 1920s, but finding its fullest expression in the 1930s, notably in the USA. Although sometimes used to refer to the Modern Movement as a whole, it here describes an architectural output, centred around the 1920s and 1930s, with distinct stylistic qualities: a dominance of geometric, especially rectilinear, forms; emphasis on asymmetrical composition; large expanses of glazing; and white rendered walls. Important buildings in what could be termed the 'classic' period of the style are ◊Gropius' Bauhaus building, Dessau, Germany 1925–26, ◊Le Corbusier's Villa Savoye, Poissy, France 1927–31, Aalto's Viipuri Library, Finland (now in Russia) 1927–35, and Mies van der Rohe's Barcelona Pavilion 1929.

Philip Johnson and Alfred Barr coined the term 'International Style' 1932 to describe the work of ◊Le Corbusier, ◊Gropius, and ◊Mies van der Rohe (among others) during the preceding decade.

intertextuality theory in literary criticism that draws attention to the interdependence of literary texts.

As part of a movement stemming from the work of the French philosopher Jacques ◊Derrida which has been popularly known as 'deconstruction', the principles of intertextuality are as thoroughly demonstrated in the critical writings of its advocates as in the literary works they discuss. Behind assertions of intertextuality lies the more general theory that authors cannot achieve a 'closure' of their writings as self-contained artefacts in the manner assumed by much traditional literary criticism.

introspection observing or examining the contents of one's own mind or consciousness. For example, 'looking' at and describing a 'picture' or image in the 'mind's eye', or trying to examine what is happening when one performs mental arithmetic.

Its use as an approach to the study of the mind has a history dating back, at least, to Socrates, it was first proposed as an experimental method by Wilhelm ◊Wundt and employed routinely in his laboratory, established 1879, in accord with his view that psychology is 'the science of inward and immediate experience'. The method was further developed by Wundt's pupil Edward Bradford Titchener (1867–1927) and by members of the Wurtzberg School around the turn of the century. Wundt eventually became dissatisfied with this method of enquiry and, following severe criticism as to the reliability of introspective data, the method fell into disuse. So grave were the problems with its methodology that, following the advent of ◊behaviourism, the systematic study of mental processes was largely eschewed by psychologists for half a century, only returning as a course of serious study in the 1960s.

introversion preoccupation with the self, generally coupled with a lack of sociability. In psychology, introversion is usually regarded as one extreme on a continuum of personality traits, with ◊extroversion at the other extreme.

The term was first used by ◊Jung 1924 in his description of ◊schizophenia where he noted that 'interest does not move towards the object but recedes towards the subject'. It is also used within ◊psychoanalysis to refer to the turning of the instinctual drives towards objects of fantasy rather than the pursuit of real objects. Another term for this sense is fantasy cathexis.

intuition rapid, unconscious thought process. In philosophy, intuition is that knowledge of a concept which does not derive directly from the senses. Thus, we may be said to have an intuitive idea of God, beauty, or justice. The concept of intuition is similar to Bertrand ◊Russell's theory of knowledge by acquaintance. In both cases, it is contrasted with empirical knowledge (see ◊empiricism).

intuitionism in mathematics, the theory that propositions can be built up only from intuitive concepts that we all recognize easily, such as unity or plurality. The concept of ◊infinity, of which we have no intuitive experience, is thus not allowed.

investment in general usage, the purchase of any asset with the potential to give future financial benefit to the buyer, such as a house, stocks and shares, deposits in a building society, a grand master painting, or even private education.

In economics, the term is used far more strictly. It is spending solely on ◊capital goods and services. This capital is then used in the production of goods and services for consumption at a later date. Fixed investment, or fixed capital formation, includes buildings, machinery, and equipment but excludes stocks of material used in production. Economists also recognize that spending on education and training is a form of investment which increases the human capital of the economy.

Iona island in the Inner Hebrides; area 850 hectares/2,100 acres. A centre of early Christianity, it is the site of a monastery founded 563 by St ◊Columba. It later became a burial ground for Irish, Scottish, and Norwegian kings. It has a 13th-century abbey.

IQ (abbreviation for *intelligence quotient*) the ratio between a subject's 'mental' and chronological ages, multiplied by 100. A score of 100 ± 10 in an ◊intelligence test is considered average.

Irish nationalism political movement objecting to British rule of Ireland (which had no elected government of its own but sent members to the British Parliament in Westminster) and campaigning for Home Rule.

In the Easter Rising 1916 an armed rebellion that aimed to secure Irish independence from British rule was crushed by the British army. In 1919 fighting broke out in Ireland between the British army and the Irish Republican Army (IRA), a guerrilla unit formed by the political group Sinn Fein. In the 1921 treaty partitioning Ireland, southern Ireland became independent (Irish Free State 1922) with the province of Northern Ireland voting to remain part of Britain.

Iron Curtain in Europe after World War II, the symbolic boundary of the ◊Cold War between capitalist West and communist East. The term was popularized by the UK prime minister Winston Churchill from 1945.

An English traveller to Bolshevik Russia, Mrs Snowden, used the term with reference to the Soviet border in 1920. The Nazi minister Goebbels used it a few months before Churchill in 1945 to describe the divide between Soviet dominated and other nations that would follow German capitulation.

irony literary technique that achieves the effect of 'saying one thing and meaning another' through the use of humour or mild sarcasm. It can be traced through all periods of literature, from classical Greek and Roman epics and dramas to the good-humoured and subtle irony of Chaucer to the 20th-century writer's method for dealing with nihilism and despair, as in Samuel Beckett's *Waiting for Godot*.

The Greek philosopher Plato used irony in his dialogues, in which Socrates elicits truth through a pretence of naivety. Sophocles' use of dramatic irony also has a high seriousness, as in *Oedipus Rex*, where Oedipus prays for the discovery and punishment of the city's polluter, little knowing that it is himself. Later, 18th-century scepticism provided a natural environment for irony, with Jonathan ◊Swift using the device as a powerful weapon in *Gulliver's Travels* and elsewhere.

Iroquois religion the name Iroquois is a blanket term used to cover the five Native American peoples known individually as the Mohawk, Seneca, Onondaga, Cayuga, and Oneida, all of whom are linked linguistically. They believe in twin forces, good and evil created by the birth of two twins, Ioskeha (good) and Tawiscara (bad). Humanity was created by Ioskeha but Tawiscara created great suffering and troubles. Eventually Ioskeha created the medicine men who are able to bring healing and try to restore the balance of good on the Earth.

irrationalism feature of many philosophies rather than a philosophical movement. Irrationalists deny that the world can be comprehended by conceptual thought, and often see the human mind as determined by unconscious forces.

irredentist person who wishes to reclaim the lost territories of a state. The term derives from an Italian political party founded about 1878 intending to incorporate Italian-speaking areas into the newly formed state.

Isaac in the Old Testament, Hebrew patriarch, son of ◊Abraham and Sarah, and father of Esau and Jacob.

Isaiah 8th century BC. In the Old Testament, the first major Hebrew prophet. The son of Amos, he was probably of high rank, and lived largely in Jerusalem. The book of Isaiah in the Old Testament was traditionally thought to be written by him. It is now thought that large parts of it were the work of at least two other writers.

Ishmael in the Old Testament, son of ◊Abraham and his wife Sarah's Egyptian maid Hagar; traditional ancestor of ◊Muhammad and the Arab people. He and his mother were driven away by Sarah's jealousy. Muslims believe that it was Ishmael, not Isaac, whom God commanded Abraham to sacrifice, and that Ishmael helped Abraham build the ◊Ka'aba in Mecca.

Ishtar Mesopotamian goddess of love and war, worshipped by the Babylonians and Assyrians, and personified as the legendary queen Semiramis.

Isis the principal goddess of ancient Egypt. She was the daughter of Geb and Nut (Earth and Sky), and as the sister-wife of Osiris searched for his body after his death at the hands of his brother, Set. Her son Horus then defeated and captured Set but cut off his mother's head because she would not allow Set to be killed. She was later identified with Hathor. The cult of Isis ultimately spread to Greece and Rome.

Islam religion founded in the Arabian peninsula in the early 7th century AD. It emphasizes the oneness of God, his omnipotence, benificence, and inscrutability. The sacred book is the **Qur'an** of the prophet ◊Muhammad, the Prophet or Messenger of Allah. There are two main Muslim sects: ◊**Sunni** and ◊**Shi'ite**. Other schools include ◊**Sufism**, a mystical movement originating in the 8th century.

beliefs The fundamental beliefs of Islam are contained in the Adhan: 'I bear witness that there is no God but Allah and Muhammad is the Prophet of Allah.' Other beliefs include Creation, Fall of Adam, angels and ◊jinns, heaven and hell, Day of Judgment, God's predestination of good and evil, and the succession of scriptures revealed to the prophets, including Moses and Jesus, but of which the perfect, final form is the **Qur'an** or **Koran**, divided into 114 **suras** or chapters, said to have been divinely revealed to Muhammad; the original is said to be preserved beside the throne of Allah in heaven.

Islamic law Islam embodies a secular law (the **Shari'a** or 'Highway'), which is clarified

---

Islam: chronology

571	Birth of the prophet Muhammad.
610	First revelation to Muhammad in the cave at Mount Hira.
622	Muhammad and other Muslims moved to Medina – the Hijrah. Start of Islamic calendar.
624	Battle of Badr, when a small Muslim army defeated the forces of Mecca outside Medina.
630	Conquest of Mecca by Muslims.
632	Death of Muhammad.
7th century	Military campaigns spread Islam into Arabia, the Middle East, Egypt, other parts of North Africa, and Persia.
661	Martyrdom of Ali.
680	Martyrdom of Husayn.
711–21	Attacks on Constantinople; conquest of Spain and S France.
700–900	Development of systematic theology and schools of Islamic law.
900–1100	Development of Sufism.
11th–13th centuries	Christian crusades against Muslim rule in the Middle East.
12th century	Islamic culture and scholarship flourished in Spain.
13th century	Mongol invasions destroyed much Islamic culture in Central Asia. Rise of Ottoman Empire.
1453	Fall of Constantinople to the Ottoman Empire.
1492	Expulsion of Muslims from Spain.
16th century	Art and architecture flourished in the Ottoman Empire.
18th–19th century	Decline in areas controlled by Muslim governments, hastened by the rise of colonial expansion by Christian Europe, especially in India and Indonesia.
1778	Wahhabi reform and renewal movement declared jihad on the Ottomans.
1922	Mustafa Kemal abolished Turkish Sultanate.
1924	King Abd al-Aziz conquered Mecca and Medina – formation of Saudi Arabia.
1928	Hasan al-Banna founded the Muslim Brotherhood.
1947	Creation of Pakistan.
1948	Creation of the state of Israel resulted in Palestinian refugees.
1960s	'Black Muslim' movement (later 'Nation of Islam') founded by Elijah Muhammad in the United States.
1979	Islamic revolution in Iran.
1979	A group led by theological students at the University of Medina proclaimed one of their group as Mahdi and held the holy places of Mecca against the army for two weeks.
1980–89	Iran–Iraq war.
1988	Publication of Salman Rushdie's *The Satanic Verses*, resulting in the Ayatollah Khomeini issuing a fatwa against him the following year.

Islamic calendar 1414–1415 (June 1993–1995)

The beginning of the month in the Islamic calendar depends on the visibility of the new moon; therefore dates may differ from those stated here

Hijrah month	1414 AH	1415AH
1 Muharram	20 June 1993	9 June 1994
1 Safar	20 July 1994	9 July 1994
1 Rabi'a I	18 Aug 1993	7 Aug 1994
1 Rabi'a II	17 Sept 1993	6 Sept 1994
1 Jumada I	16 Oct 1993	5 Oct 1994
1 Jamada II	15 Nov 1993	4 Nov 1994
1 Rajab	14 Dec 1993	4 Dec 1994
1 Sha'ban	13 Jan 1994	2 Jan 1995
1 Ramadan	11 Feb 1994	31 Jan 1995
1 Shawwal	13 March 1994	2 March 1995
1 Dhul-Qi'da	11 April 1994	31 March 1995
1 Dhul-Hijja	11 May 1994	30 April 1995
important days	1414AH	1415AH
Hirah New Year	20 June 1993	9 June 1994
Ashura'	29 Aug 1993	18 June 1994
Birthday of the prophet Muhammad	29 Aug 1993	18 Aug 1994
Lailat-ul-Isra'wai Mi'raj	8 Jan 1994	29 Dec 1994
Lailat-ul-Bara'h	26 Jan 1994	15 Jan 1995
Ramadan	11 Feb 1994	31 Jan 1995
Lailat-ul-Qadr	8 March 1994	25 Feb 1995
Eid-ul-Fitr	13 March 1994	2 March 1995
Arafat	19 May 1994	2 March 1995
Eid-ul-Adha	20 May 1994	9 May 1995

AH – *anno Hegirae*, the Muslim era

for Shi'ites by reference to their own version of the *sunna*, 'practice' of the Prophet as transmitted by his companions and embodied in the Hadith; the Sunni sect also takes into account *ijma'*, the endorsement by universal consent of practices and beliefs among the faithful. For the Sufi, the *Shari'a* is the starting point on the 'Sufi Path' to self-enlightenment. A *mufti* is a legal expert who guides the courts in their interpretation. (In Turkey until the establishment of the republic 1924 the mufti had supreme spiritual authority.)

organization There is no organized church or priesthood, although Muhammad's descendants (the Hashim family) and popularly recognized holy men, mullahs, and ayatollahs are accorded respect.

observances The Shari'a includes the observances known as the 'Five Pillars of the Faith' which are binding to all adult male believers. The observances include: *shahada* or profession of the faith; *salat* or worship five times a day facing the holy city of ◊Mecca (the call to prayer is given by a muezzin, usually from the minaret or tower of a mosque); *zakat* or obligatory almsgiving; *saum* or fasting sunrise to sunset through Ramadan (ninth month of the year, which varies with the calendar); and the ◊*hajj* or pilgrimage to Mecca at least once in a lifetime.

history Islam began as a militant and missionary religion, and between 711 and 1492 spread east into India, west over N Africa, then north across Gibraltar into the Iberian peninsula. During the Middle Ages, Islamic scholars preserved ancient Greco-Roman learning, while the Dark Ages prevailed in Christian Europe. Islam was seen as an enemy of Christianity by European countries during the Crusades, and Christian states united against a Muslim nation as late as the Battle of Lepanto 1571. Driven from Europe, Islam remained established in N Africa and the Middle East. Islam is a major force in the Arab world and is a focus for nationalism among the peoples of the Central Asian Republics. It is also a significant factor in Pakistan, Indonesia, Malaysia, and parts of Africa.

Islam is the second largest religion in the UK. In 1987 the manifesto *The Muslim Voice* demanded rights in the UK for Muslim views on education (such as single-sex teaching) and on the avoidance of dancing, mixed bathing, and sex education.

And do not say, regarding anything, 'I am going to do that tomorrow', but only, 'if God will'.

Islam
Qur'an, sacred book of Islam.
18:23–24

Islamic Conference Organization (ICO) association of 44 states in the Middle East, Africa, and Asia, established 1971 to promote Islamic solidarity between member countries, and to consolidate economic, social, cultural, and scientific cooperation. Headquarters in Niger.

The ICO also aims to 'support international peace and security; to coordinate efforts to safeguard the holy places; to support Palestinians in their efforts to liberate their lands; and to strengthen the struggle of all Muslim people to safeguard their dignity and independence.' Mozambique and Nigeria have observer status.

Islamic fundamentalism the fundamental basis of Islam is the ◊Qur'an; the 20th-century movement often referred to by non-Muslims as Islamic fundamentalism, rejects the influence of the West and seeks a return to a pure, undiluted form of Islam, based upon a literal understanding of the Qur'an.

Different schools place different emphases on the meaning of the Qur'an and, with the impact of Western thought as a result of colonialism, a wide range of interpretations of Islam have arisen.

isolationism in politics, concentration on internal rather than foreign affairs; a foreign policy having no interest in international affairs that do not affect the country's own interests.

In the USA, isolationism is usually associated with the Republican Party, especially politicians of the Midwest (for example, the Neutrality Acts 1935–39). Intervention by the USA in both world wars was initially resisted. In the 1960s some Republicans demanded the removal of the United Nations from American soil.

Israel ancient kingdom of N Palestine, formed after the death of Solomon by Jewish peoples seceding from the rule of his son Rehoboam and electing Jeroboam in his place. It is named after the descendants of Jacob, whose name was changed to Israel. His 12 sons are the ancestors of the Jewish tribes.

Jews believe the land of Israel was given to them for ever by God when he brought them out of Egypt under ◊Moses' guidance. The name is therefore sometimes used to describe the Jews themselves, as in the People of Israel, or Israelites when referring to Biblical times. See also ◊Zionism.

Ithaca (Greek *Itháki*) Greek island in the Ionian Sea, area 93 sq km/36 sq mi. Important in pre-classical Greece, Ithaca was (in Homer's poem) the birthplace of Odysseus, though this is sometimes identified with the island of Leukas (some archaeologists have equated ancient Ithaca with Leukas rather than modern Ithaca).

Ivy League eight long-established colleges and universities in the US with prestigious academic and social reputations: Brown, Columbia, Cornell, Dartmouth, Harvard, Pennsylvania, Princeton, and Yale. The members of the Ivy League compete in intercollegiate athletics.

Jacob in the Old Testament, Hebrew patriarch, son of Isaac and Rebecca, who obtained the rights of seniority from his twin brother Esau by trickery. He married his cousins Leah and Rachel, serving their father Laban seven years for each, and at the time of famine in Canaan joined his son Joseph in Egypt. His 12 sons were the traditional ancestors of the 12 tribes of Israel.

Jacob François 1920– . French biochemist who, with Jacques Monod, pioneered research into molecular genetics and showed how the production of proteins from ◊DNA is controlled. He shared the Nobel Prize for Medicine in 1965.

Jacobin member of an extremist republican club of the French Revolution founded at Versailles 1789, which later used a former Jacobin (Dominican) friary as its headquarters in Paris. Helped by Danton's speeches, they proclaimed the French republic, had the king executed, and overthrew the moderate ◊Girondins 1792–93. Through the Committee of Public Safety, they began the Reign of Terror, led by ◊Robespierre. After his execution 1794, the club was abandoned and the name 'Jacobin' passed into general use for any left-wing extremist.

Jade Emperor in Chinese religion, the supreme god, Yu Huang, of pantheistic Taoism, who watches over human actions and is the ruler of life and death.

Jahilliyah the time that predates the emergence of Islam in the 7th century. The legacy of that pagan period is called jahili to indicate its lack of knowledge about Islam.

Jahweh another spelling of ◊Jehovah, the Lord (meaning God) in the Hebrew Bible, used by some writers instead of *Adonai* (Lord) or *Hashem* (the Name) – all names used to avoid the representation of God in any form.

Jainism ancient Indian religion, sometimes regarded as an offshoot of Hinduism. Jains emphasize the importance of not injuring living beings, and their code of ethics is based on sympathy and compassion for all forms of life. They also believe in ◊karma but not in any deity. It is a monastic, ascetic religion. There are two main sects: the Digambaras and the Swetambaras. Jainism practises the most extreme form of nonviolence (*ahimsā*) of all Indian sects, and influenced the philosophy of Mahatma Gandhi. Jains number approximately 6 million; there are Jain communities throughout the world but the majority live in India.

Jainism's sacred books record the teachings of Mahavira (c. 540–468 BC), the last in a line of 24 great masters called Tirthankaras (or *jainas*). Mahavira was born in Vessali (now Bihar), E India. He became an ascetic at the age of 30, achieved enlightenment at 42, and preached for 30 years.

During the 3rd century BC two divisions arose regarding the extent of austerities. The Digambaras ('sky-clad') believe that enlightenment can only occur when all possessions have been given up, including clothes, and that it can only be achieved when a soul is born into a human male body. Monks of this sect go naked on the final stages of their spiritual path. The Swetambaras ('white-clad') believe that both human sexes can achieve enlightenment and that nakedness is not a prerequisite.

Jakobson, Roman Osipovic 1896–1982. Russian-born American linguist, member of the ◊Prague school.

Jakobson was educated at the Lazarev institute of Oriental Languages and Moscow University, where he was influenced by the writings of ◊Saussure, ◊Gestalt psychology and Russian ◊formalism. In 1920 he left Moscow for Prague where he co-founded the Prague Linguistic Circle, the 'cradle of the structuralist movement in modern linguistics', and with the Russian linguist, Nikolai Trubetzkoy, produced a structural theory of phonology (the study of language sounds). He taught at the T G Masaryk University at Brno from 1933 to 1939. Forced to leave Czechoslovakia by the Nazis, he taught in Scandinavia before emigrating to the USA. He held professorships at Columbia, Harvard and MIT, and was president of the Linguistic Society of America in 1956. His publications include *Language, Aphasia and Phonological Universals* 1941, in which he shows that there is an order (possibly universal) in which speech structures are acquired and that the first to appear in children are the last to go in aphasics. In *Fundamentals of Language* 1956, which he wrote with Morris Halle, he suggests that there is a limited universal set of distinctive features underlying the sound patterns in all languages. His later work incorporates ideas from ◊cybernetics and the mathematical theory of communication, but throughout the emphasis is on language as it operates.

Man, biologically considered, and whatever else he may be into the bargain, is simply the most formidable of all the beasts of prey, and, indeed, the only one that preys systematically on its own species.

William James
Atlantic Monthly Dec 1904

James William 1842–1910. US psychologist and philosopher. As a psychologist, James was among the first to take an approach emphasizing the ends or purpose of behaviour and to advocate a scientific, experimental psychology.

Although on his own admission unsuited to experimental work himself, he established one of the first psychological laboratories at Harvard University in 1875. In his classic, two-volume *Principles of Psychology* 1890, which secured his reputation as one of the most influential psychologists in the history of the field, he introduced the notion of the 'stream of consciousness' (thought or consciousness or subjective life regarded as a conscious flow rather than as separate bits) and propounded the theory of ◊emotions now associated with his name, the ◊James–Lange theory. James' main philosophical ideas are set out in *Pragmatism, a New Name for Some Old Ways of Thinking* 1907, an attempt to give an account of truth in terms of its satisfactory outcomes that owes much to C S ◊Peirce's ideas on ◊pragmatism, and *Essays in Radical Empiricism* 1912 in which he proposed that ultimate reality consists of 'pure experience', defining this as 'the immediate flux of life

---

An idea, to be suggestive, must come to the individual with the force of a revelation.

William James
Varieties of Religious Experience

---

which furnishes the material to our later reflection'. James wrote extensively on abnormal psychology and had much to contribute to the study of the ◊paranormal. The relevance of such ideas to the understanding of religious experience is the main theme in his still widely read *The Variety of Religious Experience: A Study in Human Nature* 1902.

For much of his working life James taught at Harvard University, where he had studied medicine, but travelled to Europe several times to visit academic institutions in Britain, France, and Germany. He was the brother of the novelist, Henry James.

James–Lange theory in psychology, the theory that ◊emotions are actually the feeling, or sensing, of the bodily changes as they occur when some exciting event or fact is perceived. For example, if we encounter a dangerous animal bodily changes occur – we tremble, the heart beats faster, and so on – and we are afraid, fear being the perception of the trembling, rapid heart beat, etc. rather than the emotional reaction to a terrifying situation.

It is named after the US psychologist, William ◊James, and the Danish physician, Carl Georg Lange (1834–1900), who arrived at this view independently in the 1880s.

Janmastami in the Hindu calendar, the birthday of ◊Krishna. One of the major Hindu festivals, it falls in the Hindu month of Julan (around August) and is a time of fasting followed by feasting, often accompanied by dance-dramas depicting the life of Krishna.

Jansen Cornelius 1585–1638. Dutch Roman Catholic theologian, founder of ◊*Jansenism* with his book *Augustinus* 1640. He held that the performance of God's commandments is impossible for human beings without special grace from God. Since the operation of God's grace is irresistible, the destiny of all humans is therefore pre-determined.

He became professor at Louvain, Belgium, 1630, and bishop of Ypres, Belgium, 1636.

Jansenism Christian teaching of Cornelius ◊Jansen. Jansenists emphasized the predestinatory aspect of St Augustine of Hippo's teaching, that people are saved by God's grace not by their own will-power, because all spiritual initiatives are God's.

The ◊Jesuits disagreed with this because they believed their spiritual exercises trained the will to turn toward God. The philosopher ◊Pascal and the theologian Antoine ◊Arnauld who had links with the abbey of ◊Port Royal were supporters of Jansenism. Jansenists were declared heretics 1653 and excommunicated 1719.

Jansky Karl Guthe 1905–1950. US radio engineer who discovered that the Milky Way galaxy emanates radio waves; he did not follow up his discovery, but it marked the birth of radioastronomy.

Jansky was born in Norman, Oklahoma. In 1928 he joined the Bell Telephone Laboratories, New Jersey, where he investigated causes of static that created interference on radio-telephone calls.

Janus in Roman mythology, the god of doorways and passageways, patron of the beginning of the day, month, and year, after whom January is named; he is represented as having two faces, one looking forwards and one back. In Roman ritual, the doors of Janus in the Forum were closed when peace was established.

Japanese religions Japan is dominated by two main religions: Shintoism and various forms of Japanese Buddhism. Many Japanese, while saying they are not religious, will practice elements of both religions at appropriate times during the year and during central moments of their life.

Shintoism is the aboriginal religion of Japan and pre-dates Buddhism by at least 1,000 years. The title means 'way of the gods'. These gods, known as *kami*, are essentially seen as being present in the forces of nature and thus Shintoism is very much tied up with worship of nature. It can be said that Shintoism sees the whole of the land and water of Japan as sacred; Mount Fuji is one of the most sacred elements of the Japanese landscape. The status of the Emperor is accorded by virtue of his being a direct descendant of the Shinto sun goddess. *Japanese Buddhism* was initiated by contacts with Buddhism in Korea and especially in China. It soon developed into three main schools, the Shingon, Tendai, and Zen. Within the Tendai, the emphasis on the Buddha nature inherent within each person led to Amida Buddhism with its belief in the salvationary powers of ◊Amida Buddha.

Japji Sikh morning hymn which consists of verses from the beginning of the holy book *Guru Granth Sahib*.

Jaspers Karl 1883–1969. German philosopher, often described as an existentialist. His voluminous writings are filled with highly subjective paraphrases of the great philosophers, followed by appeals to the reader to be concerned with his or her own existence. He believed that apes are degenerate humans. His works include *General Psychopathology* 1913

and *Philosophy* 1932. He studied medicine and psychology, and in 1921 became professor of philosophy at Heidelberg.

Jataka collections of Buddhist legends compiled at various dates in several countries; the oldest and most complete has 547 stories. They were collected before AD 400.

They give an account of previous incarnations of the Buddha, and the verse sections of the text form part of the Buddhist canon. The Jataka stories were one of the sources of inspiration for the fables of Aesop.

J-curve in economics, a graphic illustration of the likely effect of a currency devaluation on the balance of payments. Initially, there will be a deterioration as import prices increase and export prices decline, followed by a decline in import volume and upsurge of export volume.

Life exists in the universe only because the carbon atom possesses certain exceptional properties.

James Hopwood Jeans
Mysterious Universe

Jeans James Hopwood 1877–1946. British mathematician and scientist. In physics he worked on the kinetic theory of gases, and on forms of energy radiation; in astronomy, his work focused on giant and dwarf stars, the nature of spiral nebulae, and the origin of the cosmos. He did much to popularize astronomy.

A little rebellion now and then is a good thing.

Thomas Jefferson
Letter to James Madison 30 Jan 1787

Jefferson Thomas 1743–1826. 3rd president of the USA 1801–09, founder of the Democratic Republican Party. He published *A Summary View of the Rights of America* 1774 and as a member of the Continental Congresses of 1775–76 was largely responsible for the drafting of the ◊Declaration of Independence. He was governor of Virginia 1779–81, ambassador to Paris 1785–89, secretary of state 1789–93, and vice president 1797–1801.

Jefferson was born in Virginia into a wealthy family. His interests included music, painting, architecture, and the natural sciences; he was very much a product of the 18th-century

Enlightenment. His political philosophy of 'agrarian democracy' placed responsibility for upholding a virtuous American republic mainly upon a citizenry of independent yeoman farmers. Ironically, his two terms as president saw the adoption of some of the ideas of his political opponents, the ◊Federalists.

Jeffreys Alec John 1950– . British geneticist who discovered the DNA probes necessary for accurate ◊genetic fingerprinting so that a murderer or rapist could be identified by, for example, traces of blood, tissue, or semen.

Jehovah also *Jahweh* in the Old Testament the name of God, revealed to Moses; in Hebrew texts of the Old Testament the name was represented by the letters YHVH (without the vowels 'a o a') as it was regarded as too sacred to be pronounced.

The terms *Adonai* ('Lord') and *Hashem* ('the Name') were also used in order to avoid directly naming God.

Jehovah's Witness member of a religious organization originating in the USA 1872 under Charles Taze Russell (1852–1916). Jehovah's Witnesses attach great importance to Christ's second coming, which Russell predicted would occur 1914, and which Witnesses still believe is imminent. All Witnesses are expected to take part in house-to-house preaching; there are no clergy.

Witnesses believe that after the second coming the ensuing Armageddon and Last Judgment, which entail the destruction of all except the faithful, are to give way to the Theocratic Kingdom. Earth will continue to exist as the home of humanity, apart from 144,000 chosen believers who will reign with Christ in heaven. Witnesses believe that they should not become involved in the affairs of this world, and their tenets, involving rejection of obligations such as military service, have often brought them into conflict with authority. Because of a biblical injunction against eating blood, they will not give or receive blood transfusions. Adults are baptized by total immersion.

The Watch Tower Bible and Tract Society and the Watch Tower Students' Association form part of the movement, which is believed to have about 6 million members worldwide in the 1990s.

When Russell died 1916, he was succeeded by Joseph Rutherford (died 1942).

Jeremiah 7th–6th century BC. Old Testament Hebrew prophet, whose ministry continued 626–586 BC. He was imprisoned during Nebuchadnezzar's siege of Jerusalem on suspicion of intending to desert to the enemy. On the city's fall, he retired to Egypt.

Jerome, St c. 340–420. One of the early Christian leaders and scholars known as the Fathers of the Church. His Latin versions of the Old and New Testaments form the basis of the Roman Catholic Vulgate. He is usually depicted with a lion. Feast day 30 Sept.

Jespersen Jens Otto Harry 1860–1943. Danish linguist, author of the classic seven-volume *Modern English Grammar* 1909–49. At the beginning of his career he was concerned with ◊phonetics and comparative ◊philology. Later his enormous contribution to the study of English occupied much of his time, but he also worked on general linguistic theory and on syntax (which deals with the rules governing the way words are put together in sentences).

He wrote, for example, on traditional 'notional' grammar, which assumes that there are universal categories of grammar that apply to all languages, such as the parts of speech – nouns, verbs and so on, and tense and mood. His other works include *Language* 1922 and *The Philosophy of Grammar* 1924. He was professor of English at Copenhagen University 1893–1925.

Jesuit member of the largest and most influential Roman Catholic religious order (also known as the *Society of Jesus*) founded by ◊Ignatius Loyola 1534, with the aims of protecting Catholicism against the Reformation and carrying out missionary work. During the 16th and 17th centuries Jesuits were missionaries in Japan, China, Paraguay, and among the North American Indians. The order had (1991) about 29,000 members (15,000 priests plus students and lay members), and their schools and universities are renowned.

history The Society of Jesus received papal approval 1540. Its main objects were defined as educational work, the suppression of heresy, and missionary work among non-believers (its members were not confined to monasteries). Loyola infused into the order a spirit of military discipline, with long and arduous training. Their political influence resulted in their expulsion during 1759–68 from Portugal, France, and Spain, and suppression by Pope Clement XIV 1773. The order was revived by Pius VII 1814, but has since been expelled from many of the countries of Europe and the Americas, and John Paul II criticized the Jesuits 1981 for supporting revolution in South America.

Their head (general) is known as the 'Black Pope' from the colour of his cassock; in 1983 Pieter-Hans Kolvenbach was elected general.

Jesus c. 4 BC–AD 29 or 30. Hebrew preacher on whose life and teachings Christianity is founded. According to the accounts of his life in the four Gospels, he was born in Bethlehem, Palestine, son of God and the Virgin Mary, and brought up by Mary and her husband Joseph as a carpenter in Nazareth. After adult baptism, he gathered 12 disciples, but his preaching antagonized the Roman authorities and he was executed by crucifixion. Three days later there came reports of his resurrection and, later, his ascension to heaven.

Jesus' teaching centres on two commandments: that his followers love others as they love themselves, and that they worship and love God. His followers were, moreover, to live life with purity of heart, sensitivity to others, and without pride or anxiety.

Simple though Jesus' teaching may seem, it soon became complicated by the various ways in which Christians interpreted it. Although many individual Christians and Christian institutions have departed from the high standards of his teachings, his life and thought remain a continuing influence on the world.

Through his legal father Joseph, Jesus belonged to the tribe of Judah and the family of David, the second king of Israel, a heritage needed by the Messiah for whom the Hebrew people were waiting. In AD 26/27 his cousin John the Baptist proclaimed the coming of the promised Messiah and baptized Jesus, who then made two missionary journeys through the district of Galilee. His teaching, summarized in the Sermon on the Mount, aroused both religious opposition from the ◊Pharisees and secular opposition from the party supporting the Roman governor, Herod Antipas. When Jesus returned to Jerusalem (probably in AD 29), a week before the Passover festival, he was greeted by the people as the Messiah, and the Hebrew authorities (aided by the apostle Judas) had him arrested and condemned to death, after a hurried trial by the Sanhedrin (supreme Jewish court). The Roman procurator, Pontius Pilate, confirmed the sentence, stressing the threat posed to imperial authority by Jesus' teaching. Christians believe that he was God in human form, who died willingly to reconcile God and humanity, and was raised from death by the power of God. They worship him as the second person of the ◊Trinity.

Jevons William Stanley 1835–1882. British economist who introduced the concept of *marginal utility*: the increase in total utility (satisfaction or pleasure of consumption) relative to a unit increase of the goods consumed.

Jew follower of ◊Judaism, the Jewish religion. The term is also used to refer to those who claim descent from the ancient Hebrews, a Semitic people of the Middle East. Today, some may recognize their ethnic heritage but not practise the religious or cultural traditions. The term came into use in medieval Europe, based on the Latin name for Judeans, the people of Judah. Prejudice against Jews is termed ◊anti-Semitism.

Jezebel in the Old Testament, daughter of the king of Sidon. She married King Ahab of Israel, and was brought into conflict with the prophet Elijah by her introduction of the worship of Baal.

Jiang Qing or *Chiang Ching* 1914–1991. Chinese communist politician, third wife of the party leader Mao Zedong. In 1960 she became minister for culture, and played a key role in the 1966–69 Cultural Revolution as the leading member of the Shanghai-based Gang of Four, who attempted to seize power 1976. Jiang was imprisoned 1981.

Jiang was a Shanghai actress when in 1937 she met Mao Zedong at the communist headquarters in Yan'an; she became his wife 1939. She emerged as a radical, egalitarian Maoist. Her influence waned during the early 1970s and her relationship with Mao became embittered. On Mao's death Sept 1976, the ◊Gang of Four, with Jiang as a leading figure, sought to seize power by organizing military coups in Shanghai and Beijing. They were arrested for treason by Mao's successor Hua Guofeng and tried 1980–81. The Gang were blamed for the excesses of the Cultural Revolution, but Jiang asserted during her trial that she had only followed Mao's orders as an obedient wife. This was rejected, and Jiang received a death sentence Jan 1981, which was subsequently commuted to life imprisonment.

jihad in Islam, the effort to uphold the faith and live in accordance with Islam. It is sometimes used to mean a holy war undertaken by Muslims against nonbelievers. In the *Mecca Declaration* 1981, the Islamic powers pledged a jihad against Israel, though not necessarily military attack.

Jim Crow the systematic practice of segregating black Americans, which was common in the South until the 1960s. *Jim Crow laws* are laws designed to deny civil rights to blacks or to enforce the policy of segregation, which existed until Supreme Court decisions and civil-rights legislation of the 1950s and 1960s (Civil Rights Act 1964, Voting Rights Act 1965) denied their legality. See also ◊black.

Jim Crow was originally a derogatory term white Americans used for a black person.

jingoism blinkered, warmongering patriotism. The term originated in 1878, when the British prime minister Disraeli developed a pro-Turkish policy, which nearly involved the UK in war with Russia. His supporters' war song included the line 'We don't want to fight, but by jingo if we do ... '.

jinn in Muslim mythology, class of spirits able to assume human or animal shape.

Joachim of Fiore c. 1132–1202. Italian mystic, born in Calabria. In his mystical writings he interpreted history as a sequence of three ages, that of the Father, Son, and Holy Spirit, the last of which, the age of perfect spirituality, was to begin in 1260. His messianic views were taken up enthusiastically by many followers.

Joan mythical Englishwoman supposed to have become pope in 855, as John VIII, and to have given birth to a child during a papal procession. The myth was exposed in the 17th century.

Joan of Arc, St 1412–1431. French military leader. In 1429 at Chinon, NW France, she persuaded Charles VII that she had a divine mission to expel the occupying English from N France and secure his coronation. She raised the siege of Orléans, defeated the English at Patay, north of Orléans, and Charles was crowned in Reims. However, she failed to take Paris and was captured May 1430 by the Burgundians, who sold her to the English. She was found guilty of witchcraft and heresy by a tribunal of French ecclesiastics who supported the English. She was burned to death at the stake in Rouen 30 May 1431. In 1920 she was canonized.

Job c. 5th century BC. In the Old Testament, Hebrew leader who in the **Book of Job** questioned God's infliction of suffering on the righteous while enduring great sufferings himself.

Although Job comes to no final conclusion, his book is one of the first attempts to explain the problem of human suffering in a world believed to be created and governed by a God who is all-powerful and all-good.

John XXIII Angelo Giuseppe Roncalli 1881–1963. Pope from 1958. He improved relations with the USSR in line with his encyclical *Pacem in Terris/Peace on Earth* 1963, established Roman Catholic hierarchies in newly emergent states, and summoned the Second Vatican Council, which reformed church liturgy and backed the ecumenical movement.

John Chrysostom, St 345–407. Christian scholar, hermit, preacher, and Eastern Orthodox bishop of Constantinople 398–404. He was born in Antioch (now Antakya, Turkey). He was given the name 'Chrysostom' ('golden mouth') because of his eloquence. Feast day 13 Sept.

John of Damascus, St c. 676–c. 754. Orthodox theologian and hymn writer, a defender of icon worship against the ◊iconoclasts (image-breakers). Contained in his *The Fountain of Knowledge* is *An Accurate Exposition of the Orthodox Faith*, an important chronicle of theology from the 4th to 7th centuries. He was born in Damascus, Syria. Feast day 4 Dec.

John of the Cross, St 1542–1591. Spanish Roman Catholic Carmelite friar from 1564, who was imprisoned several times for attempting to impose the reforms laid down by St Teresa. His verse describes spiritual ecstasy. Feast day 24 Nov.

He was persecuted and sent to the monastery of Ubeda until his death. He was beatified 1674 and canonized 1726.

John Paul II Karol Wojtyla 1920– . Pope from 1978, the first non-Italian to be elected pope since 1522. He was born near Kraków, Poland. He has upheld the tradition of papal infallibility, condemned artificial contraception, women priests, married priests, and modern dress for monks and nuns – views that have aroused criticism from liberalizing elements in the church.

In 1939, at the beginning of World War II, Wojtyla was conscripted for forced labour by the Germans, working in quarries and a chemical factory, but from 1942 studied for the priesthood illegally in Kraków. After the war he taught ethics and theology at the universities of Lublin and Kraków, becoming archbishop of Kraków 1964. In 1967 he was made a cardinal. He was shot and wounded by a Turk in an attempt on his life 1981. Although he has warned against the involvement of priests in political activity, he opposed the Gulf War 1991 and has condemned arms manufacturers as sinful. Through his extensive travels, he has had more contact with Catholics worldwide than any previous pope.

John, St 1st century AD. New Testament apostle. Traditionally, he wrote the fourth Gospel and the Johannine Epistles (when he was bishop of Ephesus), and the Book of Revelation (while exiled to the Greek island of Patmos). His emblem is an eagle; his feast day 27 Dec.

St John is identified with the unnamed 'disciple whom Jesus loved'. Son of Zebedee, born in Judaea, he and his brother James were Galilean fishermen. Jesus entrusted his mother to John at the Crucifixion, where John is often shown dressed in red, with curly hair. Another of his symbols is a chalice with a little snake in it.

If you call a dog Hervey, I shall love him.

Samuel Johnson, known as
'Dr Johnson'
Boswell *Life of Johnson* vol i

Johnson Samuel, known as 'Dr Johnson', 1709–1784. English lexicographer, author, and critic, also a brilliant conversationalist and the dominant figure in 18th-century London literary society. His *Dictionary*, published 1755, remained authoritative for over a century, and is still remarkable for the vigour of its definitions. In 1764 he founded the Literary Club, whose members included the painter Joshua Reynolds, the political philosopher Edmund Burke, the dramatist Oliver Goldsmith, the actor David Garrick, and James ◊Boswell, Johnson's biographer.

Born in Lichfield, Staffordshire, Johnson became first an usher and then a literary hack. In 1735 he married Elizabeth Porter and opened a private school. When this proved unsuccessful he went to London with his pupil David Garrick, becoming a regular contributor to the *Gentleman's Magazine* and publishing the poem *London* 1738. Other works include the satire imitating Juvenal, *Vanity of Human Wishes* 1749, the philosophical romance *Rasselas* 1759, an edition of Shakespeare 1765, and the classic *Lives of the Most Eminent English Poets* 1779–81. His first meeting with Boswell was 1763. A visit with Boswell to Scotland and the Hebrides 1773 was recorded in *Journey to the Western Isles of Scotland* 1775. He was buried in Westminster Abbey and his house, in Gough Square, London, is preserved as a museum; his wit and humanity are documented in Boswell's classic biography *Life of Samuel Johnson* 1791.

John the Baptist, St c. 12 BC–c. AD 27. In the New Testament, an itinerant preacher. After preparation in the wilderness, he proclaimed the coming of the Messiah and baptized Jesus in the river Jordan. He was later executed by Herod Antipas at the request of Salome, who demanded that his head be brought to her on a platter.

John was the son of Zacharias and Elizabeth (a cousin of Jesus' mother). He and Jesus are often shown together as children.

As an adult, he is depicted with a shaggy beard and robes.

Joliot-Curie Irène (born Curie) 1897–1956 and Frédéric (born Joliot) 1900–1958. French physicists who made the discovery of artificial radioactivity, for which they were jointly awarded the 1935 Nobel Prize for Chemistry.

Irène was the daughter of Marie and Pierre ◊Curie and began work at her mother's Radium Institute in 1921. In 1926 she married Frédéric, a pupil of her mother's, and they began a long and fruitful collaboration. In 1934 they found that certain elements exposed to radiation themselves become radioactive.

Jonah 7th century BC. Hebrew prophet whose name is given to a book in the Old Testament. According to this, he fled by ship to evade his mission to prophesy the destruction of Nineveh. The crew threw him overboard in a storm, as a bringer of ill fortune, and he spent three days and nights in the belly of a whale before coming to land.

Joseph in the New Testament, the husband of the Virgin Mary, a descendant of King David of the Tribe of Judah, and a carpenter by trade. Although Jesus was not the son of Joseph, Joseph was his legal father. According to Roman Catholic tradition, he had a family by a previous wife, and was an elderly man when he married Mary.

Joseph in the Old Testament, the 11th and favourite son of ◊Jacob, sold into Egypt by his jealous half-brothers. After he had risen to power there, they and his father joined him to escape from famine in Canaan.

Joseph Père. Religious name of Francis Le Clerc du Tremblay 1577–1638. French Catholic Capuchin monk. He was the influential secretary and agent to Louis XIII's chief minister Cardinal Richelieu, and nicknamed *L'Eminence Grise* ('the Grey Eminence') in reference to his grey habit.

Joseph of Arimathaea, St 1st century AD. In the New Testament, a wealthy Hebrew, member of the Sanhedrin (supreme court), and secret supporter of Jesus. On the evening of the Crucifixion he asked the Roman procurator Pilate for Jesus' body and buried it in his own tomb. Feast day 17 March.

According to tradition he brought the Holy Grail to England about AD 63 and built the first Christian church in Britain, at Glastonbury.

Josephson Brian 1940– . British physicist, a leading authority on superconductivity. In 1973 he shared a Nobel prize for his theoretical predictions of the properties of a supercurrent through a tunnel barrier (the Josephson effect), which led to the development of the Josephson junction.

Joshua 13th century BC. In the Old Testament, successor of Moses, who led the Jews in their return to and conquest of the land of Canaan. The city of Jericho was the first to fall – according to the Book of Joshua, the walls crumbled to the blast of his trumpets.

Joule James Prescott 1818–1889. English physicist whose work on the relations between electrical, mechanical, and chemical effects led to the discovery of the first law of thermodynamics.

Joule was born in Salford, Lancashire, into a wealthy brewery-owning family. He was educated mainly by private tutors, including the scientist John ◊Dalton, and dedicated his life to precise scientific research. Until neighbours protested, he kept a steam engine in his house in Manchester. He determined the mechanical equivalent of heat (*Joule's equivalent*), and the SI unit of energy, the joule, is named after him.

Jowett Benjamin 1817–1893. English scholar. He promoted university reform, including the abolition of the theological test for degrees, and translated Plato, Aristotle, and Thucydides.

Jowett was ordained in 1842. He became Regius professor of Greek at Oxford University 1855, and Master of Balliol College 1870.

Judah or *Judaea* or *Judea* district of S Palestine. After the death of King Solomon 937 BC, Judah adhered to his son Rehoboam and the Davidic line, whereas the rest of Israel elected Jeroboam as ruler of the northern kingdom. In New Testament times, Judah was the Roman province of Judaea, and in current Israeli usage it refers to the southern area of the West Bank.

Judah Ha-Nasi 'the Prince' c. AD 135– c. 220. Jewish scholar who with a number of colleagues edited the collection of writings known as the ◊Mishna, which formed the basis of the ◊Talmud, in the 2nd century AD.

Judaism the religion of the ancient Hebrews and their descendants the Jews, based, according to the Old Testament, on a covenant between God and Abraham about 2000 BC, and the renewal of the covenant with Moses about 1200 BC. It rests on the concept of one

---

Jewish calendar 5754 and 5755 (Sept 1993–Sept 1995)

Jewish month	AM 5754	AM 5755
1 Tishri	16 Sept 1993	6–7 Sept 1994
1 Mercheshvan	16 Oct 1993	5–6 Oct 1994
1 Kislev	15 Nov 1993	4 Nov 1994
1 Tebet	15 Dec 1993	3–4 Dec 1994
1 Shebat	13 Jan 1994	2 Jan 1995
1 Adar*	12 Feb 1994	1 Feb/3 March 1995
1 Nisan	13 March 1994	1 April 1995
1 Lyar	12 April 1994	1 May 1995
1 Sivan	11 May 1994	30 May 1995
1 Tammuz	10 June 1994	10 June 1995
1 Av	9 July 1994	28 July 1995
1 Elul	8 Aug 1994	27 Aug 1995

Jewish fasts and festivals

date in Jewish calendar	fast/festival	date in 1994
1–2 Rishri	Rosh HashAnah (New Year)	6–7 Sept
3 Tishri	Fast of Gedaliah*	8 Sept
10 Tishri	Yom Kippur (Day of Atonement)	15 Sept
15–21 Tishri	Succot (Feast of Tabernacles)	20–26 Sept
22 Tishri	Shemini Ayzeret	27 Sept
23 Tishri	Sinchat Torah	28 Sept
25 Kislev	Hanukkah (Dedication of the Temple) begins	28Nov–5 Dec
10 Tebet	Fast of Tevet	13 Dec
13 Adar	Fast of Esther†	24 Feb
14 Adar	Purim	25 Feb
15 Adar	Shushan Purim	26 Feb
14 Nisan	Taanit Behorim (Fast of the Firstborn)	24 March
15–22 Nisan	Pesach (Passover)	27 March–3 April
27 Nisan	Yon Ha-Shoah (Holocaust Day)	8 April
4 Lyar	Yon Ha'Zikharon (Remembrance Day)	13 April
5 Lyar	Yom Ha'Atzmaut (Independence Day)	14 April
18 Lyar	33rd Day of Counting the Omer	29 April
28 Lyar	Yom Yerushalayim (Jerusalem Day)	9 May
6–7 Sivan	Shavuot (Festival of Weeks)	16–17 May
17 Tammuz	Fast of 17 Tammuz**	26 June
9 Av	Fast of 9 Av**	17 July

* Ve-Adar in leap years
** If these dates fall on the Sabbath the fast is kept on the following day.
† This fast is observed on 11 Adar (for 11Ve-Adar in leap years) if 13 Adar falls on a Sabbath.
AM anno mundi, in the year of the world

---

eternal invisible God, whose will is revealed in the Torah and who has a special relationship with the Jewish people. The Torah comprises the first five books of the Bible (the Pentateuch), which contains the history, laws, and guide to life for correct behaviour. Besides those living in Israel, there are large Jewish populations today in the USA, the former USSR (mostly Russia, Ukraine, Belarus, and Moldova), the UK and Commonwealth nations, and in Jewish communities throughout the world. There are approximately 18 million Jews, with about 9 million in the Americas, 5 million in Europe, and 4 million in Asia, Africa, and the Pacific.

scriptures The Talmud combines the Mishna, rabbinical commentary on the law handed down orally from AD 70 and put in writing about 200, and the Gemara, legal discussions in the schools of Palestine and Babylon from the 3rd and 4th centuries. The Haggadah is a part of the Talmud dealing with stories of heroes. The Midrash is a collection of commentaries on the scriptures written AD 400–1200, mainly in Palestine. Along with the

Judaism: chronology

c. 2000 BC	Led by Abraham, the ancient Hebrews emigrated from Mesopotamia to Canaan.
18th century–1580 BC	Some settled on the borders of Egypt and were put to forced labour.
13th century BC	They were rescued by Moses, who aimed at their establishment in Palestine. Moses received the Ten Commandments from God and brought them to the people. The main invasion of Canaan was led by Joshua about 1274.
12th–11th centuries BC	During the period of Judges, ascendancy was established over the Canaanites.
c. 1000 BC	Complete conquest of Palestine and the union of all Judea was achieved under David, and Jerusalem became the capital.
10th century BC	Solomon succeeded David and enjoyed a reputation for great wealth and wisdom; but his lack of a constructive policy led, after his death, to the secession of the north of Judea (Israel) under Jeroboam, with only the tribe of Judah remaining under the house of David as the southern kingdom of Judah.
9th–8th centuries BC	Assyria became the dominant power in the Middle East. Israel purchased safety by tribute, but the basis of the society was corrupt, and prophets such as Amos, Isaiah, and Micah predicted destruction. At the hands of Tiglathpileser and his successor Shalmaneser IV, the northern kingdom (Israel) was made into Assyrian provinces after the fall of Samaria 721, although the southern kingdom of Judah was spared as an ally.
586–458 BC	Nebuchadnezzar took Jerusalem and carried off the major part of the population to Babylon. Judaism was retained during exile, and was reconstituted by Ezra on the return to Jerusalem.
520 BC	The Temple, originally built by Solomon, was restored.
c. 444 BC	Ezra promulgated the legal code that was to govern the future of the Jewish people.
4th–3rd centuries BC	After the conquest of the Persian Empire by Alexander the Great, the Syrian Seleucid rulers and the Egyptian Ptolemaic dynasty struggled for Palestine, which came under the government of Egypt, although with a large measure of freedom.
2nd century BC	With the advance of Syrian power, Antiochus IV attempted intervention in the internal quarrels of the Hebrews, even desecrating the Temple, and a revolt broke out 165 led by the Maccabee family.
63 BC	Judaea's near-independence ended when internal dissension caused the Roman general Pompey to intervene, and Roman suzerainty was established.
1st century AD	A revolt led to the destruction of the Temple 66-70 by the Roman emperor Titus. Judean national sentiment was encouraged by the work of Rabbi Johanan ben Zakkai (c. 20–90), and following him the president of the Sanhedrin (supreme court) was recognized as the patriarch of Palestinian Jewry.
2nd–3rd centuries	Greatest of the Sanhedrin presidents was Rabbi Judah (c. 135–220), who codified the traditional law in the Mishna. The Palestinian Talmud (c. 375) added the Gemara to the Mishna.
4th–5th centuries	The intellectual leadership of Judaism passed to the descendants of the 6th-century exiles in Babylonia, who compiled the Babylonian Talmud.
8th–13th centuries	Judaism enjoyed a golden era, producing the philosopher Saadiah, the poet Jehudah Ha-levi (c. 1075–1141), the codifier Moses Maimonides, and others.
14th–17th centuries	Where Christianity became the dominant or state religion, the Jews were increasingly segregated from mainstream life and trade by the Inquisition, anti-Semitic legislation, or by expulsion. The Protestant and Islamic states, and their colonies, allowed for refuge. Persecution led to messianic hopes strengthened by the 16th century revival of Kabbalism, culminating in the messianic movement of Shabbatai Sevi in the 17th century.
18th–19th centuries	Outbreaks of persecution increased with the rise of European nationalism. Reform Judaism, a rejection of religious orthodoxy and an attempt to interpret it for modern times, began in Germany 1810 and soon was established in England and the USA. In the late 19th century, large numbers of Jews fleeing persecution (pogrom) in Russia and E Europe emigrated to the USA, leading to the development of large Orthodox, Conservative, and Reform communities there. Many became Americanized and lost interest in religion.
20th century	Zionism (founded 1896) is a movement dedicated to achieving a secure homeland where the Jewish people would be free from persecution; this led to the establishment of the state of Israel 1948. Liberal Judaism (more radical than Reform) developed in the USA. In 1911 the first synagogue in the UK was founded. The Nazi regime 1933–45 exterminated 6 million European Jews. Hundreds of thousands of survivors went to Palestine to form the nucleus of the new state of Israel, to the USA, and to other countries. Although most Israeli and American Jews were not affiliated with synagogues after the 1950s, they continued to affirm their Jewish heritage. Both Orthodox and Hasidic Judaism, however, flourished in their new homes and grew rapidly in the 1970s and 1980s.

Torah they are regarded as authoritative sources of Jewish ritual, worship, and practice.

observances The synagogue (in US non-Orthodox usage temple) is the local building for congregational worship (originally simply the place where the Torah was read and expounded); its characteristic feature is the Ark, the enclosure where the Torah scrolls are kept. Rabbis are ordained teachers schooled in the Jewish law and ritual who act as spiritual leaders and pastors of their communities; some devote themselves to study. Religious practices include: circumcision, daily services in Hebrew, observance of the Sabbath (sunset on Friday to sunset Saturday) as a day of rest, and, among Orthodox Jews, strict dietary laws (see ◊kosher). High holy days include *Rosh Hashanah* marking the Jewish New Year (first new moon after the autumn equinox) and, a week later, the religious fast *Yom Kippur* (Day of Atonement). Other holidays are celebrated throughout the year to commemorate various events of Biblical history.

divisions In the late Middle Ages, when Europe and W Asia were divided into Christian and Islamic countries, the Jewish people also found itself divided into two main groups. Jews in central and eastern Europe, namely in Germany and Poland, were called *Ashkenazi*. *Sephardic* Jews can trace their tradition back to the Mediterranean countries, particularly Spain and Portugal under Muslim rule. When they were expelled in 1492 they settled in North Africa, the Levant, the Far East, and northern Europe. The two traditions differ in a number of ritual and cultural ways but their theology and basic Jewish practice is the same. The Hasidic Jews of eastern Europe and some North African and Oriental countries also differ from other groups in their rites but they, too, maintain the concept of divine authority. In the 19th and early 20th centuries there was a move by some Jewish groups away from traditional or orthodox observances. This trend gave rise to a number of groups within Judaism. *Orthodox Jews*, who form the majority, assert the supreme authority of the Torah, adhere to all the traditions of Judaism, including the strict dietary laws (see ◊kosher) and the segregation of women in the synagogue. *Reform Judaism* rejects the idea that Jews are the chosen people, has a liberal interpretation of the dietary laws, and takes a critical attitude towards the Torah. *Conservative Judaism* is a compromise between Orthodox and Reform in its acceptance of the traditional law, making some allowances for modern conditions, although its services and ceremonies are closer to Orthodox than to Reform.

Liberal Judaism, or *Recontructionism*, goes further than Reform in attempting to adapt Judaism to the needs of the modern world and to interpret the Torah in the light of current scholarship. In all the groups except Orthodox, women are not segregated in the synagogue, and there are female rabbis in both Reform and Liberal Judaism. In the 20th century many people who call themselves Jews prefer to identify Judaism with a historical and cultural tradition rather than with strict religious observance, and a contemporary debate (complicated by the history of non-Jewish attitudes towards Jews) centres on the question of how to define a Jew. As in other religions, fundamentalist movements have emerged, for example, Gush Emunim.

Judas Iscariot 1st century AD. In the New Testament, the disciple who betrayed Jesus. Judas was the treasurer of the group. At the last Passover supper, he arranged, for 30 pieces of silver, to point out Jesus to the chief priests so that they could arrest him. Afterwards Judas was overcome with remorse and committed suicide.

Jude, St 1st century AD. Supposed half-brother of Jesus and writer of the Epistle of Jude in the New Testament; patron saint of lost causes. Feast day 28 Oct.

Judges book of the Old Testament, describing the history of the Israelites from the death of Joshua to the reign of Saul, under the command of several leaders known as Judges (who deliver the people from repeated oppression).

judiciary in constitutional terms, the system of courts and body of judges in a country. The independence of the judiciary from other branches of the central authority is generally considered to be an essential feature of a democratic political system. This independence is often written into a nation's constitution and protected from abuse by politicians.

Juggernaut or *Jagannath* a name for ◊Vishnu, the Hindu god, meaning 'Lord of the World'. His temple is in Puri, Orissa, India. A statue of the god, dating from about 318, is annually carried in procession on a large vehicle (hence the word 'juggernaut'). Devotees formerly threw themselves beneath its wheels.

Julius II 1443–1513. Pope 1503–13. A politician who wanted to make the Papal States the leading power in Italy, he formed international alliances first against Venice and then against France. He began the building of St Peter's Church in Rome 1506 and was the patron of the artists Michelangelo and Raphael.

Junayd (al-)bin Muhammad al-Baghdadi Eminent Muslim Sufi mystic who advocated the integration of mysticism into ordinary life.

His family was originally from Nahawand (S Iran) although he lived and taught in Baghdad. He disapproved of ecstatic mysticism, and of seeking union with God, advocating instead a settled, sober way of life and a constant awareness of God. His distinctive Sufi personality stems from the ability to combine his knowledge of Islamic law learnt from Imam Shafi with his Sufi commitment developed with his Sufi Master al-Saqati.

Jung Carl Gustav 1875–1961. Swiss psychiatrist who collaborated with Sigmund ◊Freud 1907–13. Their disagreement turned on the importance of sexuality in causing psychological problems, Jung seeing it as only one among several primary human drives. Jung then founded his own school of Analytical Psychology.

Jung developed an analytical conception of personality viewed from a philosophical, religious, and mystical perspective and based on the interaction between conscious, personal unconscious, and ◊collective unconscious systems. He studied religion and dream symbolism, and introduced the terms 'introversion' and 'extroversion'. He saw the mind as a self-regulating system, and he stressed the importance of the individual's search for meaning in life. The central theme of his work is the idea – taken from Plato's *Republic* – that mental health is characterized by the unity of the personality, while poor mental health is manifested by disunity of the personality. His books include *Modern Man in Search of a Soul* 1933.

Juno in Roman mythology, the principal goddess, identified with the Greek ◊Hera. The wife of Jupiter and queen of heaven, she was concerned with all aspects of women's lives.

junta the military rulers of a country after an army takeover. Notable recent examples of juntas are Argentina, with Juan Peron and his successors; Chile, with Augusto Pinochet; Paraguay, with Afredo Stroessner; Peru, with Manuel Odria; and Uruguay, with Juan Bordaberry. Juntas rarely remain collective councils: most of them result in domination by one leading member.

Jupiter or *Jove* in Roman mythology, the chief god, identified with the Greek ◊Zeus. He was god of the sky, associated with lightning and thunderbolts; protector in battle; and bestower of victory. The son of Saturn, he married his sister Juno, and reigned on Mount Olympus as lord of heaven. His most famous temple was on the Capitoline Hill in Rome.

jurisprudence the science of law in the abstract – that is, not the study of any particular laws or legal system, but of the principles upon which legal systems are founded.

Justice is truth in action.

justice

Benjamin Disraeli, Earl of Beaconsfield, 1804–1881, British Conservative politician and novelist.

Speech in House of Commons 11 Feb 1851

---

justice a goal of political activity and a subject of political enquiry since the Greek philosopher Plato. The term has been variously defined as fairness, equity, rightness, the equal distribution of resources, and positive discrimination in favour of underprivileged groups. It is most directly applied to the legal systems of states, and to decisions made by the recognized authorities within them.

It is not merely of some importance, but is of fundamental importance that justice should not only be done, but should manifestly and undoubtedly be seen to be done.

justice

Gordon Hewart, 1870–1943, English lawyer and politician.

Rex v Sussex Justices 9 Nov 1923

Justin, St c. 100–c. 163. One of the early Christian leaders and writers known as the Fathers of the Church. Born in Palestine of a Greek family, he was converted to Christianity and wrote two *Apologies* in its defence. He spent the rest of his life as an itinerant missionary, and was martyred in Rome. Feast day 1 June.

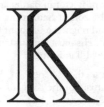

Ka in ancient Egyptian religion, the energy or life-force of the dead which dwelt beside the mummy in the tomb and would perish unless provided with sustenance by the family of the deceased.

Ka'aba (Arabic 'chamber') in Mecca, Saudi Arabia, the oblong building in the quadrangle of the Great Mosque, into the NE corner of which is built the Black Stone declared by the prophet Muhammad to have been given to Abraham by the angel Jibra'el (Gabriel), and revered by Muslims. All Muslims face towards the Ka'aba when they pray, and it is the focus of the ◊hajj (pilgrimage).

kabbala or *cabbala* (Hebrew 'tradition') ancient esoteric Jewish mystical tradition of philosophy containing strong elements of pantheism yet akin to neo-Platonism. Kabbalistic writing reached its peak between the 13th and 16th centuries. It is largely rejected by current Judaic thought as medieval superstition, but is basic to the ◊Hasid group.

Among its earliest documents are the *Sefir Jezirah/The Book of Creation*, attributed to Rabbi Akiba (died 120). The *Zohar/Book of Light* was written in Aramaic in about the 13th century.

Kabir Indian religious poet and teacher. His exact dates are disputed, but it seems certain that he was alive in the later part of the 15th century. He rejected the external practices of Islam and Hinduism to teach a simple, direct faith in the one God, attracting many followers from among both Hindus and Muslims.

He was born a Muslim in Varanasi and lived as an illiterate weaver. The first Sikh guru, ◊Nanak, was influenced by Kabir's message. Kabir's present-day Hindu followers number about 4 million.

kaddish Jewish prayer in praise of God, normally regarded as a prayer to be said by the bereaved on behalf of a deceased parent, although there is no mention of death or mourning in it. It is of ancient date and is in Aramaic apart from the last sentence, which is in Hebrew.

A male mourner is traditionally required to chant the kaddish at three services each day except the Sabbath for a period of eleven months. The words of the the Christian doxology are derived from the kaddish prayer.

Kafkaesque term used to evoke the nightmarish atmosphere which exists in the fiction of the Czech novelist Franz Kafka (1883–1924). In his novels *Der Prozess/The Trial* 1925 and *Der Schloss/The Castle* 1926 (written in German) the protagonist experiences a mounting sense of powerlessness and anxiety in the face of a menacing and omniscient bureaucracy.

kalam Islamic scholastic theology. Kalam was founded by al-Ashari (873–935), whose Ashariyya school was the dominant school of scholastic theology.

Kalam has always been of secondary importance to shariah (law), and currently the Ashrai kalam is seen by traditional Muslim scholars as a departure from Islamic theology, which is textually based. Moses is described as *kalim Allah* 'the speaker to God', because he spoke directly to him.

Kaldor Nicholas 1908–1986. British economist, born in Hungary, special adviser 1964–68 and 1974–76 to the UK government. He was a firm believer in long-term capital gains tax, selective employment tax, and a fierce critic of monetarism. He advised several Third World governments on economic and tax reform.

Kalecki Michal 1899–1970. Polish-born economist who settled in England in the 1930s. In the late 1940s, he moved to the US to work in the United Nations secretariat. In 1955 he resigned in protest against McCarthyism and returned to Poland. Independently of John Maynard ◊Keynes, he analysed the failure of ◊market forces to bring about full employment in his book, *Essays on Business Cycle Theory* 1933, and in an article in *The Political Quarterly* 1943. He also analysed the effects of uncertainty on economic activity in *Studies in Economic Dynamics* 1943.

Kali in Hindu mythology, the goddess of destruction and death. She is the wife of ◊Siva.

Kali-Yuga in Hinduism, the last of the four *yugas* (ages) that make up one cycle of creation. The Kali-Yuga, in which Hindus believe we are now living, is characterized by wickedness and disaster, and leads up to the destruction of this world in preparation for a new creation and a new cycle of yugas.

Kalki in Hinduism, the last avatar (manifestation) of ◊Vishnu, who will appear at the end of the Kali-Yuga, or final age of the world, to destroy it in readiness for a new creation.

kama one of the four aims of material life prescribed in Hindu scripture. These aims are *dharma-artha-kama-moksha* (religion-prosperity-sensual pleasure-liberation). From religion followed prosperity, which in turn brought kama. When satiated one would then seek moksha – release from the cycle of birth and death.

Kamerlingh-Onnes Heike 1853–1926. Dutch physicist who worked mainly in the field of low-temperature physics. In 1911, he discovered the phenomenon of superconductivity (enhanced electrical conductivity at very low temperatures), for which he was awarded the 1913 Nobel Prize for Physics.

Kandinsky Wassily 1866–1944. Russian painter, a pioneer of abstract art. Born in Moscow, he travelled widely, settling in Munich 1896. Between 1910–14 he produced the series *Improvisations* and *Compositions*, the first known examples of purely abstract work in 20th-century art. He was an originator of the *Blaue Reiter* movement 1911–12. From 1921 he taught at the ◊Bauhaus school of design. He moved to Paris 1933, becoming a French citizen 1939.

Kandinsky originally experimented with Post-Impressionist styles and Fauvism. His highly coloured works had few imitators, but his theories on composition, published in *Concerning the Spiritual in Art* 1912, were taken up by the abstractionists.

Two things fill the mind with ever-increasing wonder and awe ... the starry heavens above me and the moral law within me.

Immanuel Kant
Critique of Practical Reason conclusion

Kant Immanuel 1724–1804. German philosopher who developed a highly influential synthesis, known as 'critical' philosophy, of British ◊empiricism, with its stress on experience and experiment, and continental European ◊rationalism, with its stress on mathematical reasoning. In ethics, Kant argued that right action cannot be based on feelings or inclinations but conforms to a law given by reason, the *categorical imperative*.

Kant's whole life was spent in Königsberg (in what was then East Prussia), where he became professor of logic and metaphysics 1770.

Kant asked what it is possible for the human mind to know. He concluded that the categories or conceptual apparatus of the human understanding give experience its form and limits. Since the knower and what is known are mutually dependent in his critical philosophy, Kant believed that he had countered the arguments of both sceptics and speculative metaphysicians. Kant's influnece has been immense, particularly in Germany. His works include *Kritik der reinen Vernunft/Critique of Pure Reason* 1781, *Kritik der praktischen Vernunft/Critique of Practical Reason* 1788, and *Kritik der Urteilskraft/Critique of Judgement* 1790.

Kantorovich Leonid 1912–1986. Soviet mathematical economist whose theory that decentralization of decisions in a planned economy could only be made with a rational price system earned him a share (with Tjalling C Koopmans) of the 1975 Nobel Prize for Economics.

Kapitza Peter 1894–1984. Soviet physicist who in 1978 shared a Nobel prize for his work on magnetism and low-temperature physics. He was assistant director of magnetic research at the Cavendish Laboratory, Cambridge, England, 1924–32, before returning to the USSR to work at the Russian Academy of Science.

Karaite member of an 8th-century Jewish group which denied the authority of rabbinic tradition, recognizing only the authority of the scriptures.

karma (Sanskrit 'action') in Hinduism, the sum of a human being's actions, carried forward from one life to the next, resulting in an improved or worsened fate. Buddhism has a similar belief, except that no permanent personality is envisaged, the karma relating only to the physical and mental elements carried on from birth to birth, until the power holding them together disperses in the attainment of nirvana.

Karytikeya or *Skanda* Hindu god of war. He is the chief military commander of the *devas* (heavenly beings), and is the son of Shiva and Parvati and brother of Ganesh. His mount is a peacock. In South India he is popular as

Subrahmanya and Muruga and many temples are dedicated to him.

Katz Bernard 1911– . British biophysicist. He shared the 1970 Nobel Prize for Medicine with Ulf von Euler (1905–1983) and Julius Axelrod for work on the biochemistry of the transmission and control of signals in the nervous system, vital in the search for remedies for nervous and mental disorders.

Kautsky Karl 1854–1938. German socialist theoretician who opposed the reformist ideas of Edouard Bernstein from within the Social Democratic Party. In spite of his Marxist ideas he remained in the party when its left wing broke away to form the German Communist Party (KPD).

Keble John 1792–1866. Anglican priest and religious poet. His sermon on the decline of religious faith in Britain, preached 1833, heralded the start of the ◊Oxford Movement, a Catholic revival in the Church of England. Keble College, Oxford, was founded 1870 in his memory.

Keble was professor of poetry at Oxford 1831–41. He wrote four of the *Tracts for the Times* (theological treatises in support of the Oxford Movement), and from 1835 was vicar of Hursley in Hampshire.

Kekulé von Stradonitz Friedrich August 1829–1896. German chemist whose theory 1858 of molecular structure revolutionized organic chemistry. He proposed two resonant forms of the benzene ring.

Kelly Petra 1947–1992. German politician and activist. She was a vigorous campaigner against nuclear power and other environmental issues and founded the German Green Party 1972. She was a member of parliament 1983–90, but then fell out with her party over her assertive and domineering style of leadership. She died at the hands of her lover, the former general Gert Bastian.

Born in Germany, Kelly was brought up in the USA and was influenced by the civil rights movement there. She worked briefly in the office of Robert Kennedy and, returning to Germany, she joined the EEC as a civil servant 1972. Her goal, to see the ecological movement as a global organization, became increasingly frustrated by the provincialism of the German Green Party.

Kelsen Hans 1881–1973. Austrian-American jurist and philosopher. In analysing the structure of law he argued that a legal system was a hierarchy of norms. Each norm, or legal proposition, was validated by a previous norm leading back to a fundamental postulate or *Grundnorm*, for example, the will of the Queen in Parliament. Thus the law and the state were essentially the same. This he called the pure theory of law; pure because it was free from any ethical, ideological, or sociological considerations.

Kempe Margery c. 1373–c. 1439. English Christian mystic. She converted to religious life after a period of mental derangement, and travelled widely as a pilgrim. Her *Boke of Margery Kempe* about 1420 describes her life and experiences, both religious and worldly. It has been called the first autobiography in English.

Thus, the glory of the world passes away!
Thomas à Kempis
Imitatio Christi

Kempis Thomas à. Medieval German monk and religious writer; see ◊Thomas à Kempis.

Kendall Edward 1886–1972. US biochemist. In 1914 he isolated the hormone thyroxine, the active compound of the thyroid gland. He went on to work on secretions from the adrenal gland, among which he discovered a compound E, which was in fact the steroid cortisone. For this Kendall shared the 1950 Nobel Prize for Medicine with Philip Hench (1896–1965) and Tadeus Reichstein.

Kendrew John 1917– . British biochemist. Kendrew began, in 1946, the ambitious task of determining the three-dimensional structure of the major muscle protein myoglobin. This was completed in 1959 and won for Kendrew a share of the 1962 Nobel Prize for Chemistry with Max Perutz.

And so, my fellow Americans: ask not what your country can do for you – ask what you can do for your country.
John F(itzgerald) 'Jack' Kennedy
Inaugural address 20 Jan 1962

Kennedy John F(itzgerald) 'Jack' 1917–1963. 35th president of the USA 1961–63, a Democrat; the first Roman Catholic and the youngest person to be elected president. In foreign policy he carried through the unsuccessful Bay of Pigs invasion of Cuba, and in 1963 secured the withdrawal of Soviet missiles from the island. His programme for reforms at home, called the **New Frontier**, was posthumously executed by Lyndon Johnson. Kennedy was assassinated while on a visit to Dallas, Texas, on 22 Nov 1963 by Lee Harvey Oswald (1939–1963), who was within a few days shot dead by Jack Ruby (1911–1967).

Son of successful financier Joseph Kennedy, John was born in Brookline, Massachusetts, educated at Harvard, and served in the navy in the Pacific during World War II. In 1946 he was elected to the House of Representatives and in 1952 to the Senate from Massachusetts. In 1953 he married socialite Jacqueline Lee Bouvier (1929–   ). In 1960 he defeated Richard Nixon for the presidency, partly as a result of televised debates, and brought academics and intellectuals to Washington as advisers. The US involvement in the Vietnam War began during Kennedy's administration.

A number of conspiracy theories have been spun around the Kennedy assassination, which was investigated by a special commission headed by Chief Justice Earl Warren. The commission determined that Oswald acted alone, although this is extremely unlikely. A later congressional committee re-examined the evidence and determined that Kennedy 'was probably assassinated as a result of a conspiracy'. Oswald was an ex-marine who had gone to live in the USSR 1959 and returned when he could not become a Soviet citizen. Ruby was a Dallas nightclub owner, associated with the underworld and the police.

Kepler Johannes 1571–1630. German mathematician and astronomer. He formulated what are now called **Kepler's laws** of planetary motion: (1) the orbit of each planet is an ellipse with the Sun at one of the foci; (2) the radius vector of each planet sweeps out equal areas in equal times; (3) the squares of the periods of the planets are proportional to the cubes of their mean distances from the Sun.

Born in Württemberg, Kepler became assistant to Tycho ◊Brahe 1600, and succeeded him 1601 as imperial mathematician to the emperor Rudolph II. Kepler observed in 1604 a supernova, the first visible since the one discovered by Brahe 1572. His analysis of Brahe's observations of the planets, observations published by Kepler in his *Rudolphine Tables* 1627, led to the discovery of his three laws, the first two of which he published in *Astronomia Nova* 1609 and the third in *Harmonices Mundi* 1619. Kepler lived in turbulent times and was faced with many taxing domestic problems, not least of which was the unsuccessful prosecution in Wittenberg 1618 of his mother for witchcraft.

Keynes John Maynard, 1st Baron Keynes 1883–1946. English economist whose *The General Theory of Employment, Interest and Money* 1936 argued that a lack of demand for goods and rising unemployment could be countered by increased government expenditure to stimulate the economy. Keynes's theories made a major contribution to the study of ◊macroeconomics.

The important thing for Government is not to do things which individuals are doing already, and to do them a little better or a little worse; but to do those things which at present are not done at all.

John Maynard Keynes, 1st Baron Keynes
End of Laissez-Faire pt 4

Keynes led the British delegation at the Bretton Woods Conference 1944, which set up the International Monetary Fund.

His theories were widely accepted in the aftermath of World War II, and he was one of the most influential economists of the 20th century. His ideas are today often contrasted with those of ◊monetarism.

Keynes was Fellow of King's College, Cambridge. He worked at the Treasury during World War I, and took part in the peace conference as chief Treasury representative, but resigned in protest against the financial terms of the treaty. He justified his action in *The Economic Consequences of the Peace* 1919. His later economic works aroused much controversy.

Keynesian economics the economic theory of English economist John Maynard ◊ Keynes, which argues that a fall in national income, lack of demand for goods, and rising unemployment should be countered by increased government expenditure to stimulate the economy. It is opposed by monetarists (see ◊monetarism).

Khomeini Ayatollah Ruhollah 1900–1989. Iranian Shi'ite Muslim leader, born in Khomein, central Iran. Exiled for opposition to the Shah from 1964, he returned when the Shah left the country 1979, and established a fundamentalist Islamic republic. His rule was marked by a protracted war with Iraq, and suppression of opposition within Iran, executing thousands of opponents.

Khorana Har Gobind 1922– . Indian-born US biochemist who in 1976 led the team that first synthesized a biologically active gene. In 1968 he shared the Nobel Prize for Medicine for research on the interpretation of the genetic code and its function in protein synthesis.

Khwārizmī, al- Muhammad ibn-Mūsā c. 780–c. 850. Persian mathematician from Khwarizm (now Khiva, Uzbekistan), who lived and worked in Baghdad. He wrote a book on algebra, from part of whose title (*al-jabr*) comes the word 'algebra', and a book in which he introduced to the West the Hindu–Arabic decimal number system.

The word 'algorithm' is a corruption of his name.

He also compiled astronomical tables and was responsible for introducing the concept of zero into Arab mathematics.

kibbutz Israeli communal collective settlement with collective ownership of all property and earnings, collective organization of work and decision-making, and communal housing for children. A modified version, the *Moshav Shitufi*, is similar to the collective farms that were typical of the former USSR. Other Israeli cooperative rural settlements include the *Moshav Ovdim*, which has equal opportunity, and the similar but less strict *Moshav* settlement.

Kierkegaard Søren (Aabye) 1813–1855. Danish philosopher and theologian. He is often considered to be the founder of ◊existentialism because of his stress on pure choice and the absurdity of the Christian faith. Disagreeing with the German dialectical philosopher ◊Hegel, he argued that no system of thought could explain the unique experience of the individual. He defended Christianity, suggesting that God cannot be known through reason, but only through a 'leap of faith'. He became hostile to the established church, however, and his beliefs caused much controversy. He was a prolific author, but his chief works are *Either-Or* 1843, *Concept of Dread* 1844, and *Postscript* 1846, which summed up much of his earlier writings.

I want to be the white man's brother, not his brother-in-law.

Martin Luther King Jr
New York Journal-American 10 Sept 1962

King Martin Luther Jr 1929–1968. US civil-rights campaigner, black leader, and Baptist minister. He first came to national attention as leader of the Montgomery, Alabama, bus boycott 1955, and was one of the organizers of the massive (200,000 people) march on Washington DC 1963 to demand racial equality. An advocate of nonviolence, he was awarded the Nobel Peace Prize 1964. He was assassinated in Memphis, Tennessee, supposedly by James Earl Ray (1928–).

Born in Atlanta, Georgia, son of a Baptist minister, King founded the Southern Christian Leadership Conference 1957. A brilliant and moving speaker, he was the symbol of, and leading figure in, the campaign for integration and equal rights in the late 1950s and early 1960s. In the mid-1960s his moderate approach was criticized by black militants. He was the target of intensive investigation by the federal authorities, chiefly the FBI under J Edgar Hoover. His personal life was scrutinized and criticized by those opposed to his policies. King's birthday (15 Jan) is observed on the third Monday in Jan as a public holiday in the USA.

Injustice anywhere is a threat to justice everywhere.

Martin Luther King Jr
Letter from Birmingham jail, Alabama
16 Apr 1963

James Earl Ray was convicted of the murder, but there is little evidence to suggest that he committed the crime. Various conspiracy theories concerning the FBI, the CIA, and the Mafia have been suggested.

kin selection in biology, the idea that ◊altruism shown to genetic relatives can be worthwhile, because those relatives share some genes with the individual that is behaving altruistically and may continue to reproduce.

Alarm-calling in response to predators is an example of a behaviour that may have evolved through kin selection: relatives that are warned of danger can escape and continue to breed, even if the alarm caller is caught.

Kinsey Alfred 1894–1956. US researcher whose studies of male and female sexual behaviour 1948–53, based on questionnaires, were the first serious published research on this topic.

The Institute for Sex Research at Indiana University, founded 1947, continues the objective study of human sexual behaviour.

Many misconceptions, social class differences, and wide variations in practice and expectations have been discovered as a result of Kinsey's work.

kinship in anthropology, human relationship based on blood or marriage, and sanctified by law and custom. Kinship forms the basis for most human societies and for such social groupings as the family, clan, or tribe.

The social significance of kinship varies from society to society. Most human societies have evolved strict social rules, customs, and taboos regarding kinship and sexual behaviour (such as the prohibition of incest), marriage, and inheritance.

Kirchhoff Gustav Robert 1824–1887. German physicist who with Bunsen used the spectroscope to show that all elements, heated to incandescence, have their individual spectra.

kitsch in the arts, anything claiming to have an aesthetic purpose but which is tawdry and tasteless. It usually applies to cheap sentimental works produced for the mass market, such as those found in souvenir shops and chain stores, but it is also used for any art that is considered in bad taste.

In the 1960s ◊Pop art began to explore the potential of kitsch, and since the 1970s pop culture and various strands of ◊Post-Modernism have drawn heavily on it. The US artist Jeff Koons employs kitsch extensively.

Klaproth Martin Heinrich 1743–1817. German chemist who first identified the elements uranium, zirconium, cerium, and titanium.

At 16 he was apprenticed to an apothecary; he began research in 1780. The first professor of chemistry at the University of Berlin, he is sometimes called 'the father of analytical chemistry'.

Klein Melanie 1882–1960. British psychoanalyst, born in Vienna. She was a pioneer of child analysis. She analysed children as young as two, believing that by observing them at play their behaviour and emotional states could be interpreted and their vivid phantasy life revealed.

The latter, she found, involves phantasies of a sexual and aggressive nature, including manifestations of the ◊Oedipus complex, that orthodox Freudians would not recognize as occurring so early in childhood. She was influenced by ◊Freud's writings and the ideas, particularly on ◊object relations, of one of his followers, the Berlin analyst Karl Abraham with whom she had analysis.

kleptomania behavioural disorder characterized by an overpowering desire to possess articles for which one has no need. In kleptomania, as opposed to ordinary theft, there is no obvious need or use for what is stolen and sometimes the sufferer has no memory of the theft.

knowledge often defined as justified true ◊belief, although philosophers dispute what would count as justification here, and some philosophers have argued that knowledge does not involve but replaces belief. The philosophy of knowledge is ◊epistemology.

I am sufficiently proud of my knowing something to be modest about my not knowing all.

        knowledge
Vladimir Nabokov, 1899–1977,
Russian-born US writer.
Lolita

For Plato, knowledge is of the ◊Forms or universals, whereas belief is of changing, material things. For English philosopher John Locke, knowledge is 'the perception of the agreement or disagreement of two ideas'. French mathematician René Descartes thought his '*Cogito, ergo sum*/I think, therefore I am' was an item of certain knowledge.

English philosopher Gilbert Ryle contrasts knowing *how* and knowing *that*: moral knowledge is knowing how to behave, whereas factual knowledge is knowing that something is the case.

knowledge-based system (KBS) computer program that uses an encoding of human knowledge to help solve problems. It was discovered during research into ◊artificial intelligence that adding ◊heuristics (rules of thumb) enabled programs to tackle problems that were otherwise difficult to solve by the usual techniques of computer science.

Chess-playing programs have been strengthened by including knowledge of what makes a good position, or of overall strategies, rather than relying solely on the computer's ability to calculate variations.

Knox John c. 1505–1572. Scottish Protestant reformer, founder of the Church of Scotland. He spent several years in exile for his beliefs, including a period in Geneva where he met John ◊Calvin. He returned to Scotland 1559 to promote Presbyterianism. His books include *First Blast of the Trumpet Against the Monstrous Regiment of Women* 1558.

Originally a Roman Catholic priest, Knox is thought to have been converted by the reformer George Wishart. When Wishart was burned for heresy, Knox went into hiding, but later preached the reformed doctrines.

The First Blast of the Trumpet Against the Monstrous Regiment of Women.

John Knox
Pamphlet title

Captured by French troops in Scotland 1547, he was imprisoned in France, sentenced to the galleys, and released only by the intercession of the British government 1549. In England he assisted in compiling the Prayer Book, as a royal chaplain from 1551. On Mary's accession 1553 he fled the country and in 1557 was, in his absence, condemned to be burned. In 1559 he returned to Scotland. He was tried for treason but acquitted 1563. He wrote a *History of the Reformation in Scotland* 1586.

Knox Ronald Arbuthnott 1888–1957. British Roman Catholic scholar, whose translation of the Bible (1945–49) was officially approved by the Roman Catholic Church.

Son of an Anglican bishop, he became chaplain to the University of Oxford following his ordination 1912, but resigned 1917 on his conversion, and was Catholic chaplain 1926–39.

kōan in Zen Buddhism, a superficially nonsensical question or riddle used by a Zen master to help a pupil achieve satori (◊enlightenment). It is used in the Rinzai school of Zen.

A *kōan* supposedly cannot be understood through the processes of logic; its solution requires attainment of a higher level of insight. An often repeated example is 'What is the sound of one hand clapping?'

Koestler Arthur 1905–1983. Hungarian author. Imprisoned by the Nazis in France 1940, he escaped to England. His novel *Darkness at Noon* 1940, regarded as his masterpiece, is a fictional account of the Stalinist purges, and draws on his experiences as a prisoner under sentence of death during the Spanish Civil War.

Born in Budapest, and educated as an engineer in Vienna, he became a journalist in Palestine and the USSR. He joined the Communist party in Berlin 1931, but left it

1938 (he recounts his disillusionment with communism in *The God That Failed* 1950). His account of being held by the Nazis is contained in *Scum of the Earth* 1941.

Koestler's other novels include *Thieves in the Night* 1946, *The Lotus and the Robot* 1960, and *The Call Girls* 1972. His nonfiction includes *The Yogi and the Commissar* 1945, *The Sleepwalkers* 1959, *The Act of Creation* 1964, *The Ghost in the Machine* 1967, *The Roots of Coincidence* 1972, *The Heel of Achilles* 1974, and *The Thirteenth Tribe* 1976.

Autobiographical works include *Arrow in the Blue* 1952 and *The Invisible Writing* 1954. He was a member of the Voluntary Euthanasia Society, and committed suicide with his wife, after suffering for a long time from Parkinson's disease.

The most persistent sound which reverberates through man's history is the beating of war drums.

Arthur Koestler
Janus prologue

Köhler Wolfgang 1887–1967. Estonian-born German psychologist, co-founder with Max ◊Wertheimer and Kurt Koffka (1886–1941) of the ◊Gestalt school of psychology. Based on his study of the behaviour of apes in a colony on Tenerife, he developed the controversial hypothesis that problem-solving is dependent on a process of insight – a concept central to gestalt theory – rather than on trial-and-error learning, as was more commonly believed. He published his experiments and observations from this period in *The Mentality of Apes* 1925.

Köhler was appointed to the chair of psychology at Berlin 1921, largely on the basis of work done in the field of physics – which he believed to be vital to the future of psychology – but emigrated to the USA 1934. Other important works inspired by gestalt principles include *Gestalt Psychology* 1929, *The Place of Value in the World of Facts* 1938, and *Dynamics in Psychology* 1940.

Kollontai Alexandra 1872–1952. Russian revolutionary, politician, and writer. In 1905 she published *On the Question of the Class Struggle*, and, as commissar for public welfare, was the only female member of the first Bolshevik government. She campaigned for domestic reforms such as acceptance of free love, simplification of divorce laws, and collective child care.

In 1896, while on a tour of a large textile factory with her husband, she saw the appalling conditions endured by factory workers in Russia. Thereafter she devoted herself to improving conditions for working women. She was harassed by the police for her views and went into exile in Germany 1914. On her return to the USSR 1917 she joined the Bolsheviks. She was sent abroad by Stalin, first as trade minister, then as ambassador to Sweden 1943.

Kollontai took part in the armistice negotiations ending the Soviet-Finnish War 1944. She toured the USA to argue against its involvement in World War I and organized the first all-Russian Congress of Working and Peasant Women 1918. In 1923 she published *The Love of Worker Bees*.

Komensky Jan Amos (known as *Comenius*) 1592–1670. Moravian pastor and educationist who believed that a universal Christian brotherhood could be achieved through the improvement of education. He thought that understanding and not coercion was the key to learning and that teaching should build on the sense experiences of the child. His major work *Didactica Magna/The Great Didactic* 1657 had a lasting influence throughout Europe.

Kon-Tiki legendary creator god of Peru and sun king who ruled the country later occupied by the Incas and was supposed to have migrated out into the Pacific. The name was used by explorer Thor ◊Heyerdahl for his raft (made of nine balsawood logs), which he sailed from Peru to the Tuamotu Islands, near Tahiti, on the Humboldt current 1947, in an attempt to show that ancient inhabitants of South America might have reached Polynesia. He sailed from 28 April to 7 Aug 1947, with five companions, over about 8,000 km/ 5,000 mi. The Tuamotu Archipelago was in fact settled by Austronesian seafarers, and Heyerdahl's theory is largely discounted by anthropologists.

Koran (alternatively transliterated as ◊*Qur'an*) sacred book of ◊Islam. Written in the purest Arabic, it contains 114 *suras* (chapters), and is stated to have been divinely revealed to the prophet ◊Muhammad about 616.

Kornberg Arthur 1918– . US biochemist. In 1956, Kornberg discovered the enzyme DNA-polymerase, which enabled molecules of ◊DNA to be synthesized for the first time. For this work Kornberg shared the 1959 Nobel Prize for Medicine with Severo ◊Ochoa.

Korsch Karl 1886–1961. German Marxist philosopher who argued in *Marxism and Philosophy* 1923 against the ◊dialectical materialism of ◊Engels. Always critical of the Soviet variety of Marxism, Korsch also criticized, in *Karl Marx* 1938, the early, or 'Hegelian', Marx of ◊Adorno and ◊Marcuse. He believed that the well-being of theory and practice depended on the continued reinterpretation of Marxism. His 'ultra-leftism' led to his expulsion from the Communist Party in 1926.

He studied at the University of Jena and taught philosophy there until the Nazis came to power, when he emigrated to the USA. He returned to Europe 1950 and lectured in Germany and Switzerland.

kosher conforming to religious law with regard to the preparation and consumption of food; in Judaism, conforming to the Mosaic law of the Book of Deuteronomy. For example, only animals that chew the cud and have cloven hooves (cows and sheep, but not pigs) may be eaten. There are rules governing their humane slaughter and their preparation (such as complete draining of blood) which also apply to fowl. Only fish with scales and fins may be eaten; shellfish may not. Milk products may not be cooked or eaten with meat or poultry, or until four hours after eating them. Utensils for meat must be kept separate from those for milk as well.

There have been various explanations for the origins of these laws, particularly hygiene: pork and shellfish spoil quickly in a hot climate. Many Reform Jews no longer feel obliged to observe these laws.

Kovalevsky Sonja Vasilevna 1850–1891. Russian mathematician who received a doctorate from Göttingen University 1874 for her dissertation on partial differential equations. She was professor of mathematics at the University of Stockholm from 1884. In 1886 she won the Prix Bordin of the French Academy of Sciences for a paper on the rotation of a rigid body about a point, a problem the 18th-century mathematicians Euler and Lagrange had both failed to solve.

Krafft-Ebing Baron Richard von 1840–1902. German pioneer psychiatrist and neurologist. He published *Psychopathia Sexualis* 1886.

Educated in Germany, Krafft-Ebing became professor of psychiatry at Strasbourg 1872. His special study was the little understood relationship between minor paralysis in the insane and syphilis, a sexually transmitted disease. In 1897 he performed an experiment which conclusively showed that his paralysed patients must previously have been infected with syphilis, the first clear example of personality change induced by a specified brain disease. He also carried out a far-reaching study of sexual behaviour.

Krebs Hans 1900–1981. German-born British biochemist who discovered the citric acid cycle, also known as the *Krebs cycle*, the final pathway by which food molecules are converted into energy in living tissues. For this work he shared with Fritz Lipmann the 1953 Nobel Prize for Medicine.

Krishna incarnation of the Hindu god ◊Vishnu. The devotion of the ◊bhakti movement is usually directed towards Krishna; an example of this is the ◊International Society for Krishna Consciousness. Many stories are told of Krishna's mischievous youth, and he is the charioteer of Arjuna in the *Bhagavad-Gītā.*

Krishna Consciousness Movement popular name for the ◊International Society for Krishna Consciousness.

Kristeva Julia 1941– . Bulgarian-born psychoanalyst and literary theorist. Drawing upon Freudian psychoanalysis and structuralist linguistics, she has analysed the relationship between language, society, and the self. In *Semeiotiké* 1969 she argues that the self is not a stable, autonomous entity, but the product of language.

Consequently, those elements which are repressed in the well-ordered language of bourgeois society (the 'dominant social discourse') become the repressed elements (the unconscious) of the self. She examines the political and cultural implications of this position in *The Revolution in Poetic Language* 1974, in which she claims that poetry is essentially an expression of the irrational, of those repressed elements that form the unconscious. Poetry (and such disruptors as laughter and pleasure) challenges the order, rationality, and repressive control of the dominant social discourse, and so shows that revolution is possible at both the personal and political level. *Polylogue* 1977 and *Love Stories* 1983 express her growing interest in the relationship between language, the body, and the limits of personal identity, with her analyses of sexuality and the 'feminine' becoming an important part of feminist debates. Among her more accessible books are *About Chinese Women* 1974, a feminist study of the Cultural Revolution, and *Les Samourais* 1991, a novel containing a thinly disguised portrait of several figures who have recently dominated French intellectual life.

Kroeber Alfred Louis 1876–1960. US anthropologist. His extensive research into and analysis of the culture of California, Plains, Mexican, and South American Indians dramatically broadened the scope of anthropological studies. His textbook *Anthropology* 1923, 1948 remains a classic and influential work.

Born in Hoboken, New Jersey, USA, Kroeber was the first student of Franz ◊Boas to receive a PhD from Columbia University 1901. After establishing a department of anthropology at the University of California at Berkeley, he led archaeological expeditions to New Mexico beginning 1915.

Kronos or *Cronus* in Greek mythology, the ruler of the world and one of the ◊Titans. He was the father of Zeus, who overthrew him.

Kropotkin Peter Alexeivich, Prince Kropotkin 1842–1921. Russian anarchist. Imprisoned for revolutionary activities 1874, he escaped to the UK 1876 and later moved to Switzerland. Expelled from Switzerland 1881, he went to France, where he was imprisoned 1883–86. He lived in Britain until 1917, when he returned to Moscow. Among his works are *Memoirs of a Revolutionist* 1899, *Mutual Aid* 1902, and *Modern Science and Anarchism* 1903.

Kropotkin was a noted geologist and geographer. In 1879 he launched an anarchist journal, *Le Révolté.* Unsympathetic to the Bolsheviks, he retired from politics after the Russian Revolution.

Kuanyin transliteration of ◊Guanyin, goddess of mercy in Chinese Buddhism.

Kuhn Richard 1900–1967. Austrian chemist. Working at Heidelberg University in the 1930s, Kuhn succeeded in determining the structures of vitamins A, B_2, and B_6. He was awarded the 1938 Nobel Prize for Chemistry, but was unable to receive it until after World War II.

Kuhn Thomas S 1922– . US historian and philosopher of science, who showed that social and cultural conditions affect the directions of science. *The Structure of Scientific Revolutions* 1962 argued that even scientific knowledge is relative, dependent on the ◊*paradigm* (theoretical framework) that dominates a scientific field at the time.

Such paradigms (for example, Darwinism and Newtonian theory) are so dominant that they are uncritically accepted as true, until a 'scientific revolution' creates a new orthodoxy. Kuhn's ideas have also influenced ideas in the social sciences.

Kuiper Gerard Peter 1905–1973. Dutch-born US astronomer who made extensive studies of the Solar System. His discoveries included the atmosphere of the planet Mars and that of Titan, the largest moon of the planet Saturn.

Kuiper was adviser to many NASA exploratory missions, and pioneered the use of telescopes on high-flying aircraft. The Kuiper Airborne Observatory, one such telescope, is named after him.

Ku Klux Klan US secret society dedicated to white supremacy, founded 1866 in the southern states of the USA to oppose Reconstruction after the American Civil War and to deny political rights to the black population. Members wore hooded white robes to hide their identity, and burned crosses at their night-time meetings. Today the Klan has evolved into a paramilitary extremist group that has forged loose ties with other white supremacist groups.

Its violence led the government to pass the restrictive Ku Klux Klan Acts of 1871. The society re-emerged 1915 in Atlanta, Georgia, and increased in strength during the 1920s as a racist, anti-Semitic, anti-Catholic, and anti-Communist organization. It was publicized in the 1960s for terrorizing civil-rights activists and organizing racist demonstrations.

Kulpe Oswald 1862–1915. German psychologist and philosopher. In philosophy, he was attacked by the followers of Immanuel Kant for believing that metaphysics was possible.

His psychology is similar to the ◊phenomenology of Edmund Husserl.

Kulpe was a disciple of German physiologist Wilhelm ◊Wundt, and was professor at Würzburg 1894–1909, Bonn 1909–12, and Munich 1912–23. His psychological research concerned perception, judgement, and thought, and his works include *Grundriss der Psychologie/Outline of Psychology* 1893.

kundalini in Hindu thought, a flow of life energy existing within everyone. It is believed to lie coiled at the base of the spine, and by the practice of kundalini yoga can be raised from the first *chakra* (centre of spiritual power) step by step to the seventh *chakra* at the top of the skull, burning away obstacles on the spiritual path.

Küng Hans 1928– . Swiss Roman Catholic theologian who was barred from teaching by the Vatican 1979 'in the name of the Church' because he had cast doubt on papal infallibility, and on whether Christ was the son of God.

Kuznets Simon 1901–1985. Russian-born economist who emigrated to the USA 1922. He developed theories of national income and economic growth, used to forecast the future, in *Economic Growth of Nations* 1971. He won the Nobel Prize for Economics 1971.

Kwannon or *Kannon* in Japanese Buddhism, a female form (known to the West as 'goddess of mercy') of the bodhisattva ◊Avalokiteśvara. Kwannon is sometimes depicted with many arms extending compassion.

labelling in sociology, defining or describing a person in terms of his or her behaviour; for example, describing someone who has broken a law as a criminal. Labelling theory deals with human interaction, behaviour, and control, particularly in the field of deviance.

Labelling has been seen as a form of social control in that labels affect both a person's self-image and other people's expectations and reactions. Crucial factors include who labels a person (for example, only a court can convict a criminal), and whether the label persists.

labour one of the factors of production, used to produce goods and provide services. Wages are the reward for labour. The quantity of labour in a modern economy is determined by the size of the population and the extent to which young and old people and women are prepared to take paid work.

For example, the labour force in the UK has gone down over the past 30 years because more and more young people are staying longer in education and because workers are tending to retire earlier. However, this has been more than offset by an increase in the total population of working age and by a growth in the number of women taking paid jobs rather than staying at home. The quality of the labour force is determined by education and training. The more highly trained and educated the labour force is, the more productive it will be.

Labour Party UK political party based on socialist principles, originally formed to represent workers. It was founded in 1900 and first held office in 1924. The first majority Labour government 1945–51 introduced ◊nationalization and the National Health Service, and expanded social security. Labour was again in power 1964–70 and 1974–79. The party

leader is elected by Labour members of Parliament.

The Labour Party, the Trades Union Congress, and the cooperative movement together form the National Council of Labour, whose aims are to coordinate political activities and take joint action on specific issues. Although the Scottish socialist Keir Hardie and John Burns, a workers' leader, entered Parliament independently as Labour members in 1892, it was not until 1900 that a conference representing the trade unions, the Independent Labour Party (ILP), and the ◊Fabian Society founded the Labour Party, known until 1906, when 29 seats were gained, as the Labour Representation Committee. All but a pacifist minority of the Labour Party supported World War I, and in 1918 a socialist programme was first adopted, with local branches of the party set up to which individual members were admitted. By 1922 the Labour Party was recognized as the official opposition, and in 1924 formed a minority government (with Liberal support) for a few months under the party's first secretary Ramsay MacDonald. A second minority government in 1929 followed a conservative policy, and in 1931 MacDonald and other leaders, faced with a financial crisis, left the party to support the national government. The ILP seceded in 1932. In 1936–39 there was internal dissension on foreign policy; the leadership's support of nonintervention in Spain was strongly criticized and Stafford Cripps, Aneurin Bevan, and others were expelled for advocating an alliance of all left-wing parties against the government of Neville Chamberlain. The Labour Party supported Winston Churchill's wartime coalition, but then withdrew and took office for the first time as a majority government under Clement Attlee, party leader from 1935, after the 1945 elections. The welfare state was developed by nationalization of essential services and industries, a system of national insurance was established in 1946, and the National Health Service was founded in 1948. Defeated in 1951, Labour was split by disagreements on further nationalization, and unilateral or multilateral disarmament, but achieved unity under Hugh Gaitskell's leadership 1955–63. Under Harold Wilson the party returned to power 1964–70 and, with a very slender majority, 1974–79. James Callaghan, who had succeeded Wilson in 1976, was forced to a general election in 1979 and lost. Michael Foot was elected to the leadership in 1980; Neil Kinnock succeeded him in 1983 after Labour had lost another general election. The party adopted a policy of unilateral nuclear disarmament in 1986 and expelled the left-wing faction Militant Tendency, but rifts remained. Labour lost the 1987 general election, a major reason being its non-nuclear policy. In spite of the Conservative government's declining popularity, Labour was defeated in the 1992 general election, following which Neil Kinnock stepped down as party leader; John Smith succeeded him July 1992.

labour theory of value in classical economics, the theory that the price (value) of a product directly reflects the amount of labour it involves. According to the theory, if the price of a product falls, either the share of labour in that product has declined or that expended in the production of other goods has risen. ◊Marx adopted and developed the theory but it was not supported by all classical economists. The British economist, Thomas ◊Malthus, was a dissenter.

Labyrinth in Greek legend, the maze designed by the Athenian artisan Daedalus at Knossos in Crete for King Minos, as a home for the Minotaur – a monster, half man and half bull. After killing the Minotaur, ◊Theseus, the prince of Athens, was guided out of the Labyrinth by a thread given to him by the king's daughter, Ariadne.

Lacan Jacques 1901–1981. French psychoanalyst and theorist. His attempt to reinterpret Sigmund ◊Freud in terms of the structural linguistics of Ferdinand de ◊Saussure has influenced studies in literature, social ideology, aesthetics, and philosophy, but has had little effect on the practice of psychoanalysis. His main work is *Ecrits/Writings* 1966.

Lacan rejects the notion of a stable, coherent, autonomous self and argues that the self is formed in a complex network (the 'symbolic order') of language and social customs. It follows that the self is inherently unstable and 'neurotic'. In Lacan's theories, Freud's Oedipal stage is replaced by the child's entry in to language and society, the secure sense of narcissistic self-sufficiency giving way to a realization of difference, alienation, and loss.

Lady Day Christian festival (25 March) of the Annunciation of the Virgin Mary; until 1752 it was the beginning of the legal year in England, and it is still a quarter day (date for the payment of quarterly rates or dues).

Lagrange Joseph Louis 1736–1813. French mathematician. His *Mécanique analytique* 1788 applied mathematical analysis, using principles established by Newton, to such

problems as the movements of planets when affected by each other's gravitational force. He presided over the commission that introduced the metric system in 1793.

Lailat ul-Barah Muslim festival, the *Night of Forgiveness*, which takes place two weeks before the beginning of the fast of Ramadan (the ninth month of the Islamic year) and is a time for asking and granting forgiveness.

Lailat ul-Isra Wal Mi'raj Muslim festival that celebrates the prophet Muhammad's ◊Night Journey.

Lailat ul-Qadr Muslim festival, the *Night of Power*, which celebrates the giving of the Qu'ran to Muhammad. It falls at the end of Ramadan.

We are effectively destroying ourselves by violence masquerading as love.

R(onald) D(avid) Laing

Politics of Experience

Laing R(onald) D(avid) 1927–1989. Scottish psychiatrist and psychotherapist whose writings, influenced by ◊existentialism, inspired the ◊anti-psychiatry movement. He observed interactions between people in an attempt to understand and describe their experience and thinking.

In *The Divided Self* 1959 he criticized the psychiatrist's role as one that, with its objective scientific outlook, depersonalized the patient. By investigating the personal interactions within the families of diagnosed schizophrenics, he found that the seemingly bizarre behaviour normally regarded as indicating the illness began to make sense. He also wrote on interpersonal perception and on power and decision-making.

laissez faire theory that the state should not intervene in economic affairs, except to break up a monopoly. The phrase originated with the Physiocrats, 18th-century French economists whose maxim was *laissez faire et laissez passer* (literally, 'let go and let pass' – that is, leave the individual alone and let commodities circulate freely). The degree to which intervention should take place is still one of the chief problems of economics. The Scottish economist Adam ◊Smith justified the theory in *The Wealth of Nations*.

Before the 17th century, control by guilds, local authorities, or the state, of wages, prices, employment, and the training of workmen, was taken for granted. As capitalist enterprises developed in the 16th and 17th centuries, entrepreneurs shook off the control of the guilds and local authorities. By the 18th century this process was complete. The reaction against *laissez faire* began in the mid-19th century and found expression in the factory acts and elsewhere. This reaction was inspired partly by humanitarian protests against the social conditions created by the ◊Industrial Revolution and partly by the wish to counter popular unrest of the 1830s and 1840s by removing some of its causes.

The 20th century has seen an increasing degree of state intervention to promote social benefits, which after World War II in Europe was extended into the field of nationalization of leading industries and services. However, from the 1970s, *laissez-faire* policies were again pursued in the UK and the USA. European Community efforts to incorporate social benefits in monetary-union legislation have been rejected by the UK government.

Lakshmi Hindu goddess of wealth and beauty, consort of Vishnu; her festival is ◊Diwali.

Lamaism religion of Tibet and Mongolia, a form of Mahāyāna Buddhism. Buddhism was introduced into Tibet in AD 640, but the real founder of Lamaism was the Indian missionary Padma Sambhava who began his activity about 750. The head of the church is the ◊Dalai Lama, who is considered an incarnation of the Bodhisattva Avalokiteśvara. On the death of the Dalai Lama great care is taken in finding the infant in whom he has been reincarnated.

In the 15th century Tsongkhapa founded the sect of Gelu-Pa (virtuous), which has remained the most powerful organization in the country. The Dalai Lama, residing at the palace of Potala in Lhasa, exercised both spiritual and temporal authority as head of the Tibetan state until 1959, aided by the ◊Panchen Lama.

Before Chinese Communist rule, it was estimated that one in four of Tibet's male population was a Lamaist monk, but now their numbers are greatly reduced. Prayer-wheels and prayer-flags, on which were inscribed prayers, were formerly a common sight in the Tibetan countryside; when these were turned by hand or moved by the wind, great spiritual benefit was supposed to accrue.

Lamarck Jean Baptiste de 1744–1829. French naturalist whose theory of evolution, known as *◊Lamarckism*, prepared the way for Darwin's theory. His works include *Philosophie Zoologique/ Zoological Philosophy* 1809 and *Histoire naturelle des animaux sans vertèbres/Natural History of Invertebrate Animals* 1815–22.

Lamarckism theory of evolution, now discredited, advocated during the early 19th century by French naturalist Jean Baptiste Lamarck. It differed from the Darwinian theory of evolution.

The theory was based on the idea that ◊acquired character was inherited: he argued that particular use of an organ or limb strengthens it, and that this development may be 'preserved by reproduction'. For example, he suggested that giraffes have long necks because they are continually stretching them to reach high leaves; according to the theory, giraffes that have lengthened their necks by stretching will pass this characteristic on to their offspring.

Lamb Willis 1913– . US physicist who revised the quantum theory of Paul ◊Dirac. The hydrogen atom was thought to exist in either of two distinct states carrying equal energies. More sophisticated measurements by Lamb in 1947 demonstrated that the two energy levels were not equal. This discrepancy, since known as the *Lamb shift* won him the 1955 Nobel Prize for Physics.

Lambeth Conference meeting of bishops of the Anglican Communion every ten years, presided over by the archbishop of Canterbury; its decisions on doctrinal matters are not binding.

Lammas medieval festival of harvest, celebrated 1 Aug. At one time it was an English quarter day (date for payment of quarterly rates or dues), and is still a quarter day in Scotland.

Lancelot of the Lake in British legend, one of King ◊Arthur's knights, the lover of Queen Guinevere. Originally a folk hero, he first appeared in the Arthurian cycle of tales in the 12th century.

Landau Lev Davidovich 1908–1968. Russian theoretical physicist. He was awarded the 1962 Nobel Prize for Physics for his work on liquid helium.

land reform theory that ownership of land should be shared among the workers, the peasants, and the agricultural workers.

Landsteiner Karl 1868–1943. Austrian-born immunologist who discovered the ABO blood group system 1900–02, and aided in the discovery of the Rhesus blood factors 1940. He also discovered the polio virus. He was awarded a Nobel prize in 1930.

Landsteiner worked at the Vienna Pathology Laboratory, and the Rockefeller Institute for Medical Research, New York, where he was involved in the discovery of the MN blood groups in 1927. In 1936 he wrote *The Specificity of Serological Reactions*, which helped establish the science of immunology. He also developed a test for syphilis.

Lanfranc c. 1010–1089. Italian archbishop of Canterbury from 1070; he rebuilt the cathedral, replaced English clergy by Normans, enforced clerical celibacy, and separated the ecclesiastical from the secular courts.

His skill in theological controversy did much to secure the church's adoption of the doctrine of transubstantiation. He came over to England with William the Conqueror, whose adviser he was.

Lanfranc was born in Pavia, Italy; he entered the monastery of Bec, Normandy, in 1042, where he opened a school; St Anselm, later his successor, was his pupil there.

Langevin Paul 1872–1946. French physicist who contributed to the studies of magnetism and X-ray emissions. During World War I he invented an apparatus for locating enemy submarines. The nuclear institute at Grenoble is named after him.

Langley Samuel Pierpoint 1834–1906. US astronomer, scientist, and inventor of the bolometer. His steam-driven aeroplane flew for 90 seconds in 1896 – the first flight by an engine-equipped aircraft.

He was professor of physics and astronomy at the Western University of Pennsylvania 1866–87, and studied the infrared portions of the solar system.

Langmuir Irving 1881–1957. US scientist who invented the mercury vapour pump for producing a high vacuum, and the atomic hydrogen welding process; he was also a pioneer of the thermionic valve. In 1932 he was awarded a Nobel prize for his work on surface chemistry.

language human communication through speech, writing, or both. Different nationalities or ethnic groups typically have different languages or variations on particular languages; for example, Armenians speaking the Armenian language and the British and Americans speaking distinctive varieties of the English language. One language may have various dialects, which may be seen by those who

use them as languages in their own right. The term is also used for systems of communication with language-like qualities, such as *animal language* (the way animals communicate), *body language* (gestures and expressions used to communicate ideas), *sign language* (gestures for the deaf or for use as a lingua franca, as among American Indians), and *computer languages* (such as BASIC and COBOL).

The limits of my language mean the limits of my world.

language
Ludwig Wittgenstein, 1889–1951, Austrian philosopher.
Tractatus Logico-Philosophicus

Natural human language has a neurological basis centred on the left hemisphere of the brain and is expressed through two distinct media in most present-day societies: mouth and ear (the medium of sound, or *phonic medium*), and hand and eye (the medium of writing, or *graphic medium*). Language appears to develop in all children under normal circumstances, either as a unilingual or multilingual skill, crucially between the ages of one and five, and as a necessary interplay of innate and environmental factors. Any child can learn any language, under the appropriate conditions. When forms of language are as distinct as Dutch and Arabic, it is obvious that they are different languages. When, however, they are mutually intelligible, as are Dutch and Flemish, a categorical distinction is harder to make. Rather than say that Dutch and Flemish are dialects of a common Netherlandic language, as some scholars put it, Dutch and Flemish speakers may, for traditional reasons that include ethnic pride and political distinctness, prefer to talk about two distinct languages. To strengthen the differences among similar languages, groups may emphasize those differences (for example, the historical distancing of Portuguese from Castilian Spanish) or adopt different scripts (Urdu is written in Arabic script, its relative Hindi in Devanagari script). From outside, Italian appears to be a single language; inside Italy, it is a standard variety resting on a base of many very distinct dialects. The terms 'language' and 'dialect' are not therefore easily defined and distinguished. English is today the most widespread world language, but it has so many varieties (often mutually unintelligible) that scholars now talk about 'Englishes' and even 'the English languages' – all, however, are united for international purposes by Standard English. When scholars decide that languages are cognate (that is, have a common origin), they group them into a **language family**. Membership of a family is established through a range of correspondences, such as *f* and *p* in certain English and Latin words (as in *father/pater* and *fish/piscis*). By such means, English and Latin are shown to have long ago shared a common 'ancestor'. Some languages, such as French, Spanish, and Italian, fall easily into family groups, while others, such as Japanese, are not easy to classify, and others still, such as Basque, appear to have no linguistic kin anywhere (and are known as **isolates**). The families into which the languages of the world are grouped include the Indo-European (the largest, with subfamilies or branches from N India to Ireland), the Hamito-Semitic or Afro-Asiatic (with a Hamitic branch in N Africa and a Semitic branch in W Asia and Africa, and containing Arabic, Hebrew, and Berber), the Finno-Ugric (including Finnish and Hungarian), the Sino-Tibetan (including Chinese and Tibetan), the Malayo-Polynesian

---

If a lion could talk, we could not understand him.

language
Ludwig Wittgenstein, 1889–1951, Austrian philosopher.
Philosophical Investigations

---

or Austronesian (including Malay and Maori), and the Uto-Aztecan (one of many American Indian families, including Ute and Aztec or Nahuatl). Linguists estimate that there may be 4,000–5,000 distinct languages in the world. The number is uncertain because: (1) it is not always easy to establish whether a speech form is a distinct language or a dialect of another language; (2) some parts of the world remain incompletely explored (such as New Guinea); and (3) the rate of **language death** is often unknown (for example, in Amazonia, where many undescribed American Indian languages have died out). It is also difficult to estimate the precise number of speakers of many languages, especially where communities mix elements from several languages elsewhere used separately (as in parts of India). The Indo-European language family is considered to have some 2 billion speakers worldwide, Sino-Tibetan about 1,040 million, Hamito-Semitic some 230

Main Language Groups	
language	number of speakers (millions)
Mandarin	907
English	456
Hindi	383
Spanish	362
Russian	293
Arabic	208
Bengali	189
Portuguese	177
Malay-Indonesian	148
Japanese	126
French	123
German	119
Urdu	96
Punjabi (Punjab, Pakistan, India)	89
Korean (Korea, China, Japan)	73
Telugu (Andhra Pradesh, SE India)	71
Marathi (Maharashtra, India)	67
Tamil (Tamil Nadu, India, Sri Lanka)	67
Cantonese (China, Hong Kong)	65
Wu (Shanghai region, China)	64
Italian	63
Javanese (Java, Indonesia)	61
Vietnamese	61
Turkish	57
Min (SE China, Taiwan, Malaysia)	50
Thai	49
Swahili	46
Ukrainian	46
Polish	44
Kannada (S India)	43
Tagalog (Philippines)	43
Gujarati (WC India, S Pakistan)	39
Hausa (N Nigeria, Niger, Cameroon)	36
Malayalam (Kerala, India)	35
Persian (Iran, Afghanistan)	34
Hakka (SE China)	33
Burmese (Myanmar)	31
Oriya (C and E India)	31
Romanian	26
Sundanese (Sunda Strait, Indonesia)	25
Assamese (India, Bangladesh)	23
Dutch-Flemish (Netherlands, Belgium)	21
Pashtu (Pakistan, Afghanistan, Iran)	21
Serbo-Croatian	20
Yoruba (SW Nigeria, Zou, Benin)	19
Amharic (Ethiopia)	18
Igbo (Lower Niger, Nigeria)	17
Sindhi (SE Pakistan, W India)	17
Azerbaijani	15
Zhuang (S China)	15
Hungarian	14
Nepali (Nepal, NE India, Bhutan)	14
Cebuano (Bohol Sea, Philippines)	13
Fula (Cameroon, Nigeria)	13
Sinhalese (Sri Lanka)	13
Uzbek	13
Czech	12
Malagasy (Madagascar)	12
Greek	11
Afrikaans (Southern Africa)	10
Byelorussian	10
Kurdish (SW of Caspian Sea)	10
Madurese (Madura, Indonesia)	10
Oromo (W Ethiopia, N Kenya)	10

million, and Malayo-Polynesian some 200 million. Chinese (which may or may not be a single language) is spoken by around 1 billion people, English by some 350 million native speakers and at least the same number of non-natives, Spanish by 250 million, Hindi 200 million, Arabic 150 million, Russian 150 million, Portuguese 135 million, Japanese 120 million, German 100 million, French 70 million, Italian 60 million, Korean 60 million, Tamil 55 million, and Vietnamese 50 million.

language, philosophy of offshoot of logic concerned with the analysis of such notions as truth, facts, meaning, concept, and sentence. It is different from *linguistic philosophy*, which is not a subject but an approach to philosophy involving ordinary language. The philosophy of language is connected to ◊epistemology, ◊metaphysics, and the philosophy of mind.

langue and parole linguistic term introduced by Ferdinand de ◊Saussure to distinguish between language as a unified system shared by its speakers (*langue*) and as the particular utterance of an individual (*parole*). An approximate English translation would be 'language and speech'.

Lankavatara Sutra one of the most important and influential Buddhist texts. It was written around 300 AD and is found in the canon of the Yogacara school, which emerged in the 5th century. This school emphasized the need for calm meditation prior to the development of wisdom and understanding. The Yogacara school profoundly influenced the development of later Mahāyāna traditions in Tibet and China where the Lankavatara Sutra was most popular.

Lao Zi or *Lao Tzu* c. 604–531 BC. (Chinese 'the old master') Chinese philosopher, commonly regarded as the founder of ◊Taoism, with its emphasis on the Tao, the inevitable and harmonious way of the universe. Nothing certain is known of his life, and he is variously said to have lived in the 6th or the 4th century BC. The *Tao Tê Ching*, the Taoist scripture, is attributed to him but apparently dates from the 3rd century BC.

Laplace Pierre Simon, Marquis de Laplace 1749–1827. French astronomer and mathematician. In 1796, he theorized that the solar system originated from a cloud of gas (the nebular hypothesis). He studied the motion of the Moon and planets, and published a five-volume survey of celestial mechanics, *Traité de méchanique céleste* 1799–1825. Among his

mathematical achievements was the development of probability theory.

lares **and** *penates* in Roman mythology, spirits of the farm and of the store cupboard, often identified with the family ancestors, whose shrine was the centre of worship in Roman homes.

Las Casas Bartolomé de 1474–1566. Spanish missionary, historian, and colonial reformer, known as *the Apostle of the Indies*. He was one of the first Europeans to call for the abolition of Indian slavery in Latin America. He took part in the conquest of Cuba in 1513, but subsequently worked for American Indian freedom in the Spanish colonies. *Apologetica historia de las Indias* (first published 1875–76) is his account of Indian traditions and his witnessing of Spanish oppression of the Indians.

Las Casas sailed to Hispaniola in the West Indies in 1502 and was ordained priest there in 1512. From Cuba he returned to Spain in 1515 to plead for the Indian cause, winning the support of the Holy Roman emperor Charles V. In what is now Venezuela he unsuccessfully attempted to found a settlement of free Indians. In 1530, shortly before the conquest of Peru, he persuaded the Spanish government to forbid slavery there. In 1542 he became bishop of Chiapas in S Mexico. He returned finally to Spain in 1547.

Laski Harold 1893–1950. British political theorist. Professor of political science at the London School of Economics from 1926, he taught a modified Marxism and published *A Grammar of Politics* 1925 and *The American Presidency* 1940. He was chairman of the Labour Party 1945–46.

Latimer Hugh 1490–1555. English Christian church reformer and bishop. After his conversion to Protestantism in 1524 he was imprisoned several times but was protected by Cardinal Wolsey and Henry VIII. After the accession of the Catholic Mary, he was burned for heresy.

Latimer was appointed bishop of Worcester in 1535, but resigned in 1539. Under Edward VI his sermons denouncing social injustice won him great influence, but he was arrested in 1553, once Mary was on the throne, and two years later he was burned at the stake in Oxford.

Latitudinarian in the Church of England from the 17th century, a member of a group of priests, which included J R Tillotson (1630–1694, archbishop of Canterbury) and

Edward Stillingfleet (1635–1699, bishop of Worcester), who were willing to accept modifications of forms of church government and worship to accommodate Dissenters (Protestants who refused to conform to the established church).

Latter-day Saint member of the Christian group commonly known as the ◊Mormons.

Laud William 1573–1645. English priest; archbishop of Canterbury from 1633. Laud's High Church policy, support for Charles I's unparliamentary rule, censorship of the press, and persecution of the Puritans all aroused bitter opposition, while his strict enforcement of the statutes against enclosures and of laws regulating wages and prices alienated the propertied classes. His attempt to impose the use of the Prayer Book on the Scots precipitated the English Civil War. Impeached by Parliament 1640, he was imprisoned in the Tower of London, summarily condemned to death, and beheaded.

Laue Max Theodor Felix von 1879–1960. German physicist who was a pioneer in measuring the wavelength of X-rays by their diffraction through the closely spaced atoms in a crystal. His work led to the powerful technique (X-ray diffraction) now used to elucidate the structure of complex biological materials such as ◊DNA. He was awarded a Nobel prize in 1914.

Lavoisier Antoine Laurent 1743–1794. French chemist. He proved that combustion needed only a part of the air, which he called oxygen, thereby destroying the theory of phlogiston (an imaginary 'fire element' released during combustion). With Pierre de Laplace, the astronomer and mathematician, he showed that water was a compound of oxygen and hydrogen. In this way he established the basic rules of chemical combination.

law body of rules and principles under which justice is administered or order enforced in a state or nation. In western Europe there are two main systems: Roman law and English law. US law is a modified form of English law.

 Roman law, first codified in 450 BC and finalized under Justinian AD 528–534,

---

Law is a bottomless pit.

law
John Arbuthnot, 1667–1735, Scottish writer and physician.
The History of John Bull

---

advanced to a system of international law (*jus gentium*), applied in disputes between Romans and foreigners or provincials, or between provincials of different states. Church influence led to the adoption of Roman law throughout western continental Europe, and it was spread to eastern Europe and parts of Asia by the French *Code Napoléon* in the 19th century. Scotland and Québec (because of their French links) and South Africa (because of its link with Holland) also have it as the basis of their legal systems.

They [the poor] have to labour in the face of the majestic equality of the law, which forbids the rich as well as the poor to sleep under bridges, to beg in the streets, and to steal bread.

law
Anatole France. Pen name of Jacques Anatole Thibault, 1844–1924, French writer.
The Red Lily ch 7

 English law derives from Anglo-Saxon customs, which were too entrenched to be broken by the Norman Conquest and still form the basis of the ◊common law, which by 1250 had been systematized by the royal judges. Unique to English law is the doctrine of *stare decisis* (Latin 'to stand by things decided'), which requires that courts abide by former precedents (or decisions) when the same points arise again in litigation. These two concepts are the basis for US law.

The system of ◊*equity* developed in the Court of Chancery, where the Lord Chancellor considered petitions, and the ordinary rules were mitigated where their application would operate harshly in some cases. In the 19th century there was major reform of the law (for example, the abolition of many capital offences, in which juries would not in any case convict) and of the complex system of courts. The 1989 Green Paper proposed (1) omitting the Bar's monopoly of higher courts, removing demarcation between barristers and solicitors; (2) cases to be taken on a 'no-win, no-fee' basis (as already happens in Scotland).

Law William 1686–1761. English cleric. His work *A Serious Call to a Devout and Holy Life* 1728, with its emphasis on self-denial and humility, influenced John Wesley, the founder of ◊Methodism. His Jacobite opinions caused him to lose his fellowship at Emmanuel College, Cambridge, in 1714.

law of nature scientific generalization that both explains and predicts physical phenomena; laws of nature are generally assumed to be descriptive of, and applicable to, the world. The three laws of ◊thermodynamics are examples.

However, the first of Isaac ◊Newton's laws of motion discusses the behaviour of a moving body not acted on by a net force, and this neither applies to the world nor describes it, because there are no such bodies. Hence, some philosophers of science have argued that the laws of nature are rules governing scientists' expectations and so are prescriptive rather than descriptive. Others have argued that laws are idealized descriptions to which the world approximates, as triangles on a blackboard approximate to Euclidean triangles.

I like to write when I feel spiteful; it's like having a good sneeze.

D(avid) H(erbert) Lawrence
Letter to Lady Cynthia Asquith 1913

Lawrence D(avid) H(erbert) 1885–1930. English writer whose work expresses his belief in emotion and the sexual impulse as creative and true to human nature. The son of a Nottinghamshire miner, Lawrence studied at University College, Nottingham, and became a teacher. His writing first received attention after the publication of the semi-autobiographical *Sons and Lovers* 1913, which includes a portrayal of his mother (died 1911). Other novels include *The Rainbow* 1915, *Women in Love* 1921, and *Lady Chatterley's Lover* 1928. Lawrence also wrote short stories (for example 'The Woman Who Rode Away') and poetry.

In 1914 he married Frieda von Richthofen, ex-wife of his university professor, with whom he had run away in 1912. Frieda was the model for Ursula Brangwen in *The Rainbow*, which was suppressed for obscenity, and its sequel, *Women in Love*. Lawrence's travels in search of health (he suffered from tuberculosis, from which he eventually died near Nice) prompted books such as *Mornings in Mexico* 1927. *Lady Chatterley's Lover* was banned as obscene in the UK until 1960.

Lawrence Ernest O(rlando) 1901–1958. US physicist. His invention of the cyclotron particle accelerator pioneered the production of artificial radioisotopes.

He was professor of physics at the University of California, Berkeley, from 1930 and director from 1936 of the Radiation Laboratory, which he built into a major research centre for nuclear physics. He was awarded a Nobel prize in 1939.

Lawrence, St Christian martyr. Probably born in Spain, he became a deacon of Rome under Pope Sixtus II. According to tradition, when summoned to deliver the treasures of the church, he displayed the beggars in his charge, for which he was broiled on a gridiron. Feast day 10 Aug.

lay reader in the Church of England, an unordained member of the church who is permitted under licence from the bishop of the diocese to conduct some public services.

Lazarus in the New Testament, the brother of Martha, a friend of Jesus, raised by him from the dead. Lazarus is also the name of a beggar in a parable told by Jesus (Luke 16).

The final test of a leader is that he leaves behind him in other men the conviction and the will to carry on.

leadership
Walter Lippmann, 1889–1974, US liberal political commentator.
New York Herald Tribune 14 Apr 1945

---

leadership role taken which involves organizing others and taking decisions. A leader in a work organization may be an *autocratic leader*, someone who perhaps listens to advice but ultimately makes decisions on his or her own, or he or she may be a *democratic leader*, allowing others to participate in the decision-making process.

League of Nations international organization formed after World War I to solve international disputes by arbitration. Established in Geneva, Switzerland, 1920, the league included representatives from states throughout the world, but was severely weakened by the US decision not to become a member, and had no power to enforce its decisions. It was dissolved 1946. Its subsidiaries included the *International Labour Organization* and the *Permanent Court of International Justice* in The Hague, Netherlands, both now under the auspices of the ◊United Nations.

The League of Nations was suggested in US president Woodrow Wilson's 'Fourteen Points' in 1917 as part of the peace settlement for World War I. The league covenant was drawn up by the Paris peace conference in

1919 and incorporated into the Versailles and other peace treaties. The member states undertook to preserve the territorial integrity of all, and to submit international disputes to the league. There were a number of important subsidiary organizations:

International Labour Organization (ILO) formed in 1920, based in Geneva and concerned primarily with working conditions and social welfare. *High Commission for Refugees* (Nansen Office) created to assist refugees, primarily from the USSR and Eastern Europe. Built on the work of the Norwegian explorer Fridtjof Nansen as first high commissioner, the High Commission declined in importance after his death and the entry of the USSR to the league. It formed the basis for post-1945 refugee work by the United Nations.

Permanent Court of Justice created in The Hague in 1921 and based on ideas for some form of international court put forward at the Hague congress 1907; now known as the International Court of Justice (see ◊United Nations). The league enjoyed some success in the humanitarian field (international action against epidemics, drug traffic, and the slave trade), in organizing population exchanges after the Paris peace conferences had established new national boundaries, and in deferring arguments over disputed territories and former German colonies by mandating a league member to act as a caretaker of administration for a specified period of time, or until a permanent solution could be found. Mandates were created for Palestine (Britain), SW Africa (South Africa), and the free city of Danzig (Gdańsk).

In the political and diplomatic field, the league was permanently hampered by internal rivalries and the necessity for unanimity in the decision-making process. No action was taken against Japan's aggression in Manchuria in 1931; attempts to impose sanctions against Italy for the invasion of Ethiopia 1935–36 collapsed; no actions were taken when Germany annexed Austria and Czechoslovakia, nor when Poland was invaded. Japan in 1932 and Germany in 1933 simply withdrew from the league, and the expulsion of the USSR in 1939 had no effect on the Russo-Finnish war. Long before the outbreak of World War II, diplomacy had abandoned international security and reverted to a system of direct negotiation and individual alliances.

leakage in economics, money which leaves the ◊circular flow of income. The three main leakages are usually said to be savings, taxes, and imports.

Leakey Richard 1944– . British archaeologist. In 1972 he discovered at Lake Turkana, Kenya, an apelike skull, estimated to be about 2.9 million years old; it had some human characteristics and a brain capacity of 800 cu cm. In 1984 his team found an almost complete skeleton of *Homo erectus* some 1.6 million years old. He is the son of Louis and Mary Leakey.

learning curve graphical representation of the improvement in performance of a person executing a new task.

learning theory a theory, or body of theories, about how behaviour in animals and human beings is acquired or modified by experience.

Many learning theories have been proposed, the main ones being: (a) *S-R theories*, which regard learning as the establishment of an association between stimuli (S) and responses (R) that is strengthened if followed by a 'satisfying state of affairs' (◊Thorndike's Law of Effect) or by reinforcement that involves drive reduction, for example, food reducing hunger (C L Hull's systematic theory of behaviour); (b) the theory of *classical* ◊*conditioning*, originally described by ◊Pavlov; (c) the theory of *operant* ◊*conditioning* developed by B F ◊Skinner; and (d) *cognitive learning theories*, such as E C Tolman's 'purposive behaviourism'.

Several more recent theories have attempted to explain learning in specific areas, such as paired-associate word learning, learning of social skills, and so on, rather than learning in general.

leaven element inducing fermentation. The term is applied to the yeast added to dough in bread making; it is used figuratively to describe any pervasive influence, usually in a good sense, although in the Old Testament it symbolized corruption, and unleavened bread was used in sacrifice. During the Jewish festival of Passover, all leaven is removed from the house.

Leavis F(rank) R(aymond) 1895–1978. English literary critic. With his wife Q D Leavis (1906–81) he co-founded and edited the review *Scrutiny* 1932–53. He championed the work of D H Lawrence and James Joyce and in 1962 attacked C P Snow's theory of 'The Two Cultures' (the natural alienation of the arts and sciences in intellectual life). His other works include *New Bearings in English Poetry* 1932 and *The Great Tradition* 1948. He was a lecturer at Cambridge University.

Leavitt Henrietta Swan 1868–1921. US astronomer who in 1912 discovered the *period–luminosity law* that links the brightness of a Cepheid variable star to its period of variation. This law allows astronomers to use Cepheid variables as 'standard candles' for measuring distances in space.

Lebedev Peter Nikolaievich 1866–1912. Russian physicist. He proved by experiment that light exerts a minute pressure upon a physical body, thereby confirming James Maxwell's theoretic prediction.

Lebensphilosophie (German) philosophy of life.

Lebensraum theory developed by Hitler for the expansion of Germany into E Europe, and in the 1930s used by the Nazis to justify their annexation of neighbouring states on the grounds that Germany was overpopulated.

Lebenswelt term used by Edmund ◊Husserl in his later philosophy to distinguish the lived world of ordinary individuals from the world of science. The main task of ◊phenomenology is the understanding of the *Lebenswelt*.

Leblanc Nicolas 1742–1806. French chemist who in 1790 developed a process for making soda ash (sodium carbonate, Na_2CO_3) from common salt (sodium chloride, $NaCl$).

In the *Leblanc process*, salt was first converted into sodium sulphate by the action of sulphuric acid, which was then roasted with chalk or limestone (calcium carbonate) and coal to produce a mixture of sodium carbonate and sulphide. The carbonate was leached out with water and the solution crystallized. Leblanc devised this method of producing soda ash (for use in making glass, paper, soap, and various other chemicals) to win a prize offered in 1775 by the French Academy of Sciences, but the Revolutionary government granted him only a patent (1791), which they seized along with his factory three years later. A broken man, Leblanc committed suicide.

Leclanché Georges 1839–1882. French engineer. In 1866 he invented a primary electrical cell, the *Leclanché cell*, which is still the basis of most dry batteries. A Leclanché cell consists of a carbon rod (the anode) inserted into a mixture of powdered carbon and manganese dioxide contained in a porous pot, which sits in a glass jar containing an electrolyte (conducting medium) of ammonium chloride solution, into which a zinc cathode is inserted. The cell produces a continuous current, the carbon mixture acting as a depolarizer; that is, it prevents hydrogen bubbles from forming on the anode and increasing resistance. In a dry battery, the electrolyte is made in the form of a paste with starch.

Le Corbusier assumed name of Charles-Edouard Jeanneret 1887–1965. Swiss-born French architect, an early and influential exponent of the Modern Movement and one of the most innovative of 20th-century architects. His distinct brand of Functionalism first appears in his town-planning proposals of the early 1920s, which advocate 'vertical garden cities' (multistorey villas, zoning of living and working areas, and traffic separation) as solutions to urban growth and chaos. From the 1940s several of his designs for multi-storey villas were realised, notably Unités d'Habitations, Marseilles 1947–52 (now demolished), using his modulor system of standard-sized units mathematically calculated according to the proportions of the human figure (see ◊Fibonacci, ◊golden section).

Le Corbusier was originally a painter and engraver, but turned his attention to the problems of contemporary industrial society. His books *Vers une architecture/Towards a New Architecture* 1923 and *Le Modulor* 1948 have had worldwide significance for town planning and building design.

Leda in Greek legend, the wife of Tyndareus and mother of ◊Clytemnestra. Zeus, who came to her as a swan, was the father of her other children: Helen of Troy and the twins Castor and Pollux.

Lederberg Joshua 1925– . US geneticist who showed that bacteria can reproduce sexually, combining genetic material so that offspring possess characteristics of both parent organisms.

Lederberg is considered a pioneer of ◊genetic engineering, a science that relies on the possibility of artificially shuffling genes from cell to cell. He realized that bacteriophages, viruses which invade bacteria, can transfer genes from one bacterium to another, a discovery that led to the deliberate insertion by scientists of foreign genes into bacterial cells. In 1958 he shared the Nobel Prize for Medicine with George ◊Beadle and Edward Tatum.

Lee Tsung-Dao 1926– . Chinese physicist whose research centred on the physics of ◊weak nuclear forces. In 1956 Lee proposed that weak nuclear forces between elementary particles might disobey certain key assumptions, for instance, the conservation of parity. He shared the 1957 Nobel Prize for Physics with his colleague Yang Chen Ning (1922–).

Leeuwenhoek Anton van 1632–1723. Dutch pioneer of microscopic research. He ground his own lenses, some of which magnified up to 200 times. With these he was able to see individual red blood cells, sperm, and bacteria, achievements not repeated for more than a century.

left wing in politics, the socialist parties. The term originated in the French National Assembly of 1789, where the nobles sat in the place of honour to the right of the president, and the commons sat to the left. This arrangement has become customary in European parliaments, where the progressives sit on the left and the conservatives on the right. It is also usual to speak of the right, left, and centre, when referring to the different elements composing a single party.

legislative process procedures by which the laws of a country are enacted.

In the UK, legislation can be initiated in either the House of Commons or the House of Lords, but usually in the former. It is introduced as a bill, which is given a formal first reading, when no debate occurs. At the second reading the principles behind the bill are debated and at the next stage it is considered in detail by a standing committee or by the whole House. This is followed by the report stage, when the results of committee deliberations are reported and further amendments can be accepted. Finally, the bill is given a third reading. Once it has completed this process in one of the two Houses it must follow a similar course in the other House. It is then submitted for formal royal assent and the bill then becomes an act.

The exception to the process of passing through both Houses applies to financial bills, or the financial parts of all bills; these are exempt from consideration by the Lords.

legislature law-making body or bodies in a political system. Some legislatures are unicameral (having one chamber), and some bicameral (with two).

In most democratic countries with bicameral legislatures the 'lower', or popular, chamber is the more powerful but there are exceptions, the most notable being in the USA, where the upper chamber, the ◊Senate, is constitutionally more powerful than the lower, the House of Representatives. Most lower or single chambers are popularly elected and upper chambers are filled by appointees or a mixture of appointed and elected members. In the USA, both chambers are elected, whereas in the UK, the lower chamber, the House of Commons, is elected and the upper chamber, the House of Lords, is filled by hereditary members or appointees.

Leibniz or *Leibnitz* Gottfried Wilhelm 1646–1716. German mathematician and philosopher. Independently of, but concurrently with, the British scientist Isaac Newton he developed the branch of mathematics known as ◊calculus. In his metaphysical works, such as *The Monadology* 1714, he argued that everything consisted of innumerable units, *monads*, the individual properties of which determined each thing's past, present, and future. Monads, although independent of each other, interacted predictably; this meant that Christian faith and scientific reason need not be in conflict and that 'this is the best of all possible worlds'. His optimism is satirized in Voltaire's *Candide*.

leisure class term applied by Thorstein ◊Veblen in *The Theory of the Leisure Class* 1899 to those people (aristocrats, bourgeoisie, nouveaux riches) who regarded work, particularly manual labour, as beneath them. Status was maintained not by the accumulation of wealth but by ◊conspicuous consumption.

Lemaître Georges Edouard 1894–1966. Belgian cosmologist who in 1927 proposed the ◊Big Bang theory of the origin of the universe. He predicted that the entire universe was expanding, which the US astronomer Edwin ◊Hubble confirmed. Lemaître suggested that the expansion had been started by an initial explosion, the Big Bang, a theory that is now generally accepted.

Lenard Philipp Eduard Anton 1862–1947. German physicist who investigated the photoelectric effect (light causes metals to emit electrons) and cathode rays (the stream of electrodes emitted from the cathode in a vacuum tube). He was awarded a Nobel prize in 1905.

In later life he became obsessed with the idea of producing a purely 'Aryan' physics free from the influence of ◊Einstein and other Jewish physicists.

Lenin Vladimir Ilyich. Adopted name of Vladimir Ilyich Ulyanov 1870–1924. Russian revolutionary, first leader of the USSR, and communist theoretician. Active in the 1905 Revolution, Lenin had to leave Russia when it failed, settling in Switzerland in 1914. He returned to Russia after the February revolution of 1917 (see ◊Russian Revolution). He led the Bolshevik revolution in Nov 1917 and became leader of a Soviet government, concluded peace with Germany, and organized a successful resistance to White Russian (pro-tsarist) uprisings and foreign intervention 1918–20. His modification of traditional Marxist doctrine to fit conditions prevailing in Russia became known as *Marxism–Leninism*, the basis of communist ideology.

Lenin was born on 22 April, 1870 in Simbirsk (now renamed Ulyanovsk), on the river Volga, and became a lawyer in St Petersburg. His brother was executed in 1887 for attempting to assassinate Tsar Alexander III. A Marxist from 1889, Lenin was sent to Siberia for spreading revolutionary propaganda 1895–1900. He then edited the political paper *Iskra* ('The Spark') from abroad, and visited London several times. In *What Is to be Done?* 1902 he advocated that a professional core of Social Democratic Party activists should spearhead the revolution in Russia, a suggestion accepted by the majority (*bolsheviki*) at the London party congress 1903. From Switzerland he attacked socialist support for World War I as aiding an 'imperialist' struggle, and wrote *Imperialism* 1917.

Communism is Soviet power plus the electrification of the whole country.

Vladimir Ilyich Lenin. Adopted name of Vladimir Ilyich Ulyanov
Report to 8th Congress of the Communist Party 1920

After the renewed outbreak of revolution in Feb/March 1917, he returned to Russia in April and called for the transfer of power to the soviets (workers' councils). From the overthrow of the provisional government in Nov 1917 until his death, Lenin effectively controlled the Soviet Union, although an assassination attempt in 1918 injured his health. He founded the Third (Communist) ◊International in 1919. With communism proving inadequate to put the country on its feet, he introduced the private-enterprise ◊New Economic Policy 1921. His embalmed body is in a mausoleum in Red Square, Moscow. In 1898 he married **Nadezhda Konstantinova Krupskaya** (1869–1939), who shared his work and wrote *Memories of Lenin*.

Leninism modification of ◊Marxism by ◊Lenin which argues that in a revolutionary situation the industrial proletariat is unable to develop a truly revolutionary consciousness without strong leadership.

The responsibility for this is taken on by the Communist Party which acts as the 'vanguard of the proletariat' in leading it to revolution, before then assuming political control in a ◊dictatorship of the proletariat. Only when the proletariat achieves a full socialist awareness will the power of the party, and ultimately the state itself, wither away.

Lent in the Christian church, the 40-day period of fasting that precedes Easter, beginning on Ash Wednesday, but omitting Sundays. It is a time of reflection and repentance, and commemorates the forty days that Jesus spent fasting in the desert before beginning the public ministry.

Leo XIII Gioacchino Pecci 1810–1903. Pope from 1878. After a successful career as a papal diplomat, he established good relations between the papacy and European powers, the USA, and Japan. He remained intransigent in negotiations with the Italian government over the status of Rome, insisting that he keep control over part of it.

He was the first pope to emphasize the duty of the church in matters of social justice. His encyclical *Rerum novarum* 1891 pointed out the moral duties of employers towards workers.

Leonardo da Vinci 1452–1519. Italian painter, sculptor, architect, engineer, and scientist. One of the greatest figures of the Italian Renaissance, he was active in Florence, Milan, and, from 1516, France. As state engineer and court painter to the duke of Milan, he painted the *Last Supper* mural about 1495 (Sta Maria delle Grazie, Milan), and on his return to Florence painted the *Mona Lisa* (Louvre, Paris) about 1503–06. His notebooks and drawings show an immensely inventive and enquiring mind, studying aspects of the natural world from anatomy to aerodynamics.

Leonardo was born at Vinci in Tuscany and studied under Verrocchio in Florence in the 1470s. His earliest dated work is a sketch of the Tuscan countryside 1473 (Uffizi, Florence); other early works include drawings, portraits, and religious scenes, such as the unfinished *Adoration of the Magi* (Uffizi). About 1482 he went to the court of Lodovico Sforza in Milan. In 1500 he returned to Florence (where he was architect and engineer to Cesare Borgia in 1502), and then to Milan in 1506. He went to France in 1516 and died at Château de Cloux, near Amboise, on the Loire. Apart from portraits, religious themes, and historical paintings, Leonardo's greatest legacies were his notebooks and drawings. He influenced many of his contemporary artists, including Michelangelo, Raphael, Giorgione, and Bramante. He also revolutionized painting style. Instead of a white background, he used a dark one to allow the overlying colour a more three-dimensional existence. He invented 'aerial perspective' whereby the misty atmosphere changes the colours of the landscape as it dissolves into the distance, and also *sfumato*, the blurring of outlines through the use of subtle gradations of tone – both give his pictures their characteristic air of mysteriousness. His principle of grouping figures within an imaginary pyramid, linked by their gestures and facial expressions, became a High Renaissance compositional rule. His two versions of the Madonna and child with St Anne, *Madonna of the Rocks* (Louvre, Paris, and National Gallery, London) exemplify all these ideas. Other chief works include the *Mona Lisa* (wife of Zanoki del Gioconda, hence also known as *La Gioconda*) and the *Battle of Anghiari* 1504–05, formerly in the Palazzo Vecchio, Florence.

Le Play Frédéric 1806–1882. French mining engineer and social scientist. His comprehensive reports for the mining industry, which covered the social conditions of workers as well as manufacturing and management methods, provided the basis for empirical sociology.

He believed that the family was the basic social unit and that its condition of well-being and stability was the best way of judging the state of society in general.

leprechaun (Old Irish 'small body') in Irish folklore, a fairy in the shape of an old man, sometimes conceived as a cobbler, with a hidden store of gold.

Le Roy Ladurie Emmanuel Bernard 1929– . French historian, a pupil of Fernand ◊Braudel and, like him, a leading member of the '*Annales*' school. The importance he attaches to customs, rituals, and symbols is seen in *Le Carneval de Romans/The Carnival in Romans* 1979, a study of a riot in a small French town in 1580.

His doctoral thesis *Les Paysans de Languedoc* 1966 (abridged and translated as *The Peasants of Languedoc* 1974) dealt with economic and social changes in a region of southern France from the 15th to 18th centuries and especially with 'the activities, the struggles, and the thoughts of the people themselves'. *Montaillou village occitan 1294–1324* 1975 (abridged and translated as *Montaillou: Cathars and Catholics in a French Village* 1978) was a bestseller in both France and Britain. His belief that ecological and demographic factors determined the conditions of life in rural Europe is supported at length in *Le Territoire de l'historien* 1973 (selections from Vol. 1 translated 1979 as *The Territory of the Historian*; selections from Vol. 2 translated 1981 as *The Mind and Method of the Historian*).

lesbianism ◊homosexuality (sexual attraction to one's own sex) between women, so called from the Greek island of Lesbos (now Lesvos), the home of Sappho the poet and her followers to whom the behaviour was attributed.

less developed country (LDC) any country late in developing an industrial base, and dependent on cash crops and unprocessed minerals. The Group of 77 was established in 1964 to pressure industrialized countries into giving greater aid to less developed countries.

The terms 'less developed' and 'developing' imply that industrial development is desirable or inevitable; many people prefer to use 'Third World'.

A man who does not lose his reason over certain things has none to lose.

Gotthold Ephraim Lessing
Emilia Galotti

Lessing Gotthold Ephraim 1729–1781. German dramatist and critic. His plays include *Miss Sara Sampson* 1755, *Minna von Barnhelm* 1767, *Emilia Galotti* 1772, and the verse play *Nathan der Weise* 1779. His works of criticism *Laokoon* 1766 and *Hamburgische Dramaturgie* 1767–68 influenced German literature. He also produced many theological and philosophical writings.

Laokoon analysed the functions of poetry and the plastic arts; *Hamburgische Dramaturgie* reinterpreted Aristotle and attacked the restrictive form of French classical drama in favour of the freer approach of Shakespeare.

Lethe in Greek mythology, a river of the underworld whose waters, when drunk, brought forgetfulness of the past.

Levellers democratic party in the English Civil War. The Levellers found wide support among Cromwell's New Model Army and the yeoman farmers, artisans, and small traders, and proved a powerful political force 1647–49. Their programme included the establishment of a republic, government by a parliament of one house elected by male suffrage, religious toleration, and sweeping social reforms.

Cromwell's refusal to implement this programme led to mutinies by Levellers in the army, which, when suppressed by Cromwell in 1649, ended the movement. They were led by John Lilburne.

Leverrier Urbain Jean Joseph 1811–1877. French astronomer who predicted the existence and position of the planet Neptune, discovered in 1846.

leviathan in the Old Testament, a sea monster, later associated in Christian literature with Satan. The term was also used to describe the monstrous qualities of wealth or power invested in one person, as in the political treatise *Leviathan* by the English philosopher Thomas ◊Hobbes.

Lévi-Strauss Claude 1908–1990. French anthropologist who, influenced by the linguistics of ◊Saussure and ◊Jakobson, helped to formulate the principles of ◊structuralism – a methodology which instead of focusing on the significance of individual elements within a cultural system stressed their interdependence and relatedness.

In his analyses of kinship, myth, and symbolism he argued that, though the superficial appearance of these factors might vary between societies, their underlying structures were universal and could best be understood in terms of binary oppositions: left and right, male and female, nature and culture, the raw and the cooked, etc. His works include *Tristes Tropiques* 1955 – an intellectual autobiography – and the four-volume *Mythologiques/ Mythologies* 1964–71.

The spirit of reform has been too much concerned with private 'rights', and not enough concerned with the public order that makes them possible.

liberalism
Roger Scruton, 1944–   , English philosopher and social critic.
The Meaning of Conservatism

---

levitation counteraction of gravitational forces on a body. As claimed by medieval mystics, spiritualist mediums, and practitioners of transcendental meditation, it is unproven. In the laboratory it can be produced scientifically; for example, electrostatic force and acoustical waves have been used to suspend water drops for microscopic study. It is also used in technology, for example, in magnetic levitation as in maglev trains.

Levite in the Old Testament, a member of one of the 12 tribes of Israel, descended from Levi, a son of ◊Jacob. The Levites performed the lesser services of the Temple; the high priesthood was confined to the descendants of Aaron, the brother of Moses.

Lévy-Bruhl Lucien 1857–1939. French anthropologist and philosopher. For most of his career he was mainly concerned with analysing the differences between modern and primitive mentalities. In *How Natives Think* 1910, he argued that primitive thought operated through its own system of rules. This he described as 'pre-logical' because it ignored logic and accepted contradiction. He significantly revised his views toward the end of his life.

Libby Willard Frank 1908–1980. US chemist whose development in 1947 of radiocarbon dating as a means of determining the age of organic or fossilized material won him a Nobel prize in 1960.

liberal arts or *the arts* collective term for the visual arts, music, and literature together with certain subjects of study, such as philosophy, history, languages, and sociology. The concept dates back to the classical idea of the pursuits worthy of a free man (which were seen as intellectual rather than manual).

As usual the Liberals offer a mixture of sound and original ideas. Unfortunately none of the sound ideas is original and none of the original ideas is sound.

liberalism
(Maurice) Harold Macmillan, 1st Earl of Stockton, 1894–1986, British Conservative politician, prime minister 1957–63; foreign secretary 1955 and chancellor of the Exchequer 1955–57.
Speech to London Conservatives 7 Mar 1962

---

liberalism political and social theory that favours representative government, freedom of the press, speech, and worship, the abolition of class privileges, the use of state resources to protect the welfare of the individual, and international ◊free trade. It is historically associated with the Liberal Party in the UK and the Democratic Party in the USA.

Liberalism developed during the 17th–19th centuries as the distinctive theory of the industrial and commercial classes in their struggle against the power of the monarchy, the church, and the feudal landowners. Economically it was associated with ◊*laissez faire*, or nonintervention. In the late 19th and early 20th centuries its ideas were modified by the acceptance of universal suffrage and a certain amount of state intervention in economic affairs, in order to ensure a minimum standard of living and to remove extremes of poverty and wealth. The classical statement of liberal principles is found in *On Liberty* and other works of the British philosopher J S ◊Mill.

Liberal Party British political party, the successor to the ◊Whig Party, with an ideology of liberalism. In the 19th century, it represented the interests of commerce and industry. Its outstanding leaders were Palmerston, Gladstone, and Lloyd George. From 1914 it declined, and the rise of the Labour Party pushed the Liberals into the middle ground. The Liberals joined forces with the Social Democratic Party (SDP) as the Alliance for the 1983 and 1987 elections. In 1988, a majority of the SDP voted to merge with the Liberals to form the Social and Liberal Democrats.

The term 'Liberal', used officially from about 1840 and unofficially from about 1815, marked a shift of support for the party from aristocrats to include also progressive industrialists, backed by supporters of the utilitarian reformer ◊Bentham, Nonconformists (especially in Welsh and Scottish constituencies), and the middle classes. During the Liberals' first period of power 1830–41, they promoted parliamentary and municipal government reform and the abolition of slavery, but their *laissez-faire* theories led to the harsh Poor Law of 1834. Except for two short periods the Liberals were in power 1846–66, but the only major change was the general adoption of free trade. Liberal pressure forced Peel to repeal the Corn Laws 1846, thereby splitting the Tory party. Extended franchise in 1867 and Gladstone's emergence as leader began a new phase, dominated by the Manchester school with a programme of 'peace, retrenchment, and reform'. Gladstone's 1868–74 government introduced many important reforms, including elementary education and vote by ballot. The party's left, mainly composed of working-class Radicals and led by Charles Bradlaugh (a lawyer's clerk) and Joseph Chamberlain (a wealthy manufacturer), repudiated *laissez faire* and inclined towards republicanism, but in 1886 the Liberals were split over the policy of Home Rule for Ireland, and many became Liberal Unionists or joined the Conservatives. Except for 1892–95, the Liberals remained out of power until 1906, when, reinforced by Labour and Irish support, they returned with a huge majority. Old-age pensions, National Insurance, limitation of the powers of the Lords, and the Irish Home Rule Bill followed. Lloyd George's alliance with the Conservatives 1916–22 divided the Liberal Party between him and his predecessor Asquith, and although reunited in 1923 the Liberals continued to lose votes. They briefly joined the National Government 1931–32. After World War II they were reduced to a handful of members of Parliament. A revival began under the leadership 1956–67 of Jo Grimond and continued under Jeremy Thorpe, who resigned after a period of controversy within the party in 1976. After a caretaker return by Grimond, David Steel became the first party leader in British politics to be elected by party members who were not MPs. In 1977–78 Steel entered into an agreement to support Labour in any vote of confidence in return for consultation on measures undertaken. He resigned in 1988 and was replaced by Paddy Ashdown.

liberation theology Christian theory of Jesus' primary importance as the 'Liberator', identifying with the poor and devoted to freeing them from oppression (Matthew 19:21, 25:35, 40). Initiated by the Peruvian priest Gustavo Gutierrez in *The Theology of Liberation* 1969, and enthusiastically (and sometimes violently) adopted in Latin America, it embodies a Marxist interpretation of the class struggle, especially by Third World nations. It has been criticized by some Roman Catholic authorities including Pope John Paul II.

One of its leaders is Leonardo Boff (1939–), a Brazilian Franciscan priest.

Liberator, the title given to Simón ◊Bolívar, South American revolutionary leader; also a title given to Daniel O'Connell, Irish political leader; and to Bernardo O'Higgins, Chilean revolutionary.

libertarianism political theory that upholds the rights of the individual above all other considerations and seeks to minimize the power of the state to the safeguarding of those rights.

At its most extreme it sees the state as having no legitimate power to interfere with people's lives, since permission for such interference has not been granted by the individual concerned. Individuals should be free to do whatever they like so long as it does not affect the rights of others. Recent advocates have included the philosopher Robert ◊Nozick.

liberty in its medieval sense, a franchise, or collection of privileges, granted to an individual or community by the king, and the area over which this franchise extended.

liberty, equality, fraternity (*liberté, egalité, fraternité*) motto of the French republic from 1793.

It was changed 1940–44 under the Vichy government to 'work, family, fatherland'.

libido in Freudian psychology, the energy of the sex instinct, which is found even in a newborn child. The libido develops through a number of phases, described by ◊Freud in his theory of infantile ◊sexuality.

The source of libido is the ◊id. Freud extended his usage of the term as his ideas on instinct developed but never used it, as ◊Jung and several other psychologists did, outside the sexual context.

Liddell Hart Basil 1895–1970. British military strategist. He was an exponent of mechanized warfare, and his ideas were adopted in Germany in 1935 in creating the 1st Panzer Division, combining motorized infantry and tanks. From 1937 he advised the UK War Office on army reorganization.

Liebig Justus, Baron von 1803–1873. German chemist, a major contributor to agricultural chemistry. He introduced the theory of radicals and discovered chloroform and chloral.

Lieh Tzu collection of Chinese sayings, stories, and teachings ascribed to Lieh Tzu who, if he existed, lived in China around the 4th century BC. The book reflects early ◊Taoist philosophical notions of the 4th–3rd centuries BC. The text stresses the Tao as the supreme origin of all existence and takes a hostile stance to ◊Confucianism. Lieh Tzu is the third major figure in philosophical Taoism, after ◊Lao Zi and ◊Chuang Tzu.

There is an ambush everywhere from the army of accidents; therefore the rider of life runs with loosened reins.

life
Hâfiz, 1326–1390, Persian lyric poet.
Diwan

---

life ability to grow, reproduce, and respond to such stimuli as light, heat, and sound. It is thought that life on Earth began about 4 billion years ago. The earliest fossil evidence of life is threadlike chains of cells discovered in 1980 in deposits in NW Australia that have been dated as 3.5 billion years old.

It seems probable that the original atmosphere of Earth consisted of carbon dioxide, nitrogen, and water, and that complex organic molecules, such as amino acids, were created when the atmosphere was bombarded by ultraviolet radiation or by lightning. Attempts to replicate these conditions in the laboratory have successfully shown that amino acids, purine and pyrimidine bases (base pairs in ◊DNA), and other vital molecules can be created in this way. It has also been suggested that life could have reached Earth from elsewhere in the universe in the form of complex organic molecules present in meteors or comets, but others argue that this is not really an alternative explanation because these primitive life forms must then have been created elsewhere by much the same process. Normally life is created by living organisms (a process called ◊biogenesis).

Everything that lives, / Lives not alone, nor for itself.

life
William Blake, 1757–1827, English poet, artist, engraver, and visionary.
Book of Thel 2

---

life sciences scientific study of the living world as a whole, a new synthesis of several traditional scientific disciplines including ◊biology, zoology, and botany, and newer, more specialized areas of study such as ◊biophysics and ◊sociobiology.

This approach has led to many new ideas and discoveries as well as to an emphasis on ◊ecology, the study of living organisms in their natural environments.

Lighthill James 1924– . British mathematician who specialized in the application of mathematics to high-speed aerodynamics and jet propulsion.

Lilith in the Old Testament, an Assyrian female demon of the night. According to Jewish tradition in the ◊Talmud, she was the wife of Adam before Eve's creation.

limbo in Christian theology, a region for the souls of those who were not admitted to the vision of God in heaven (believed to be the destiny of those who are saved). *Limbus infantum* was a place where unbaptized infants enjoyed inferior blessedness, and *limbus patrum* was where the prophets of the Old Testament dwelt. The word was first used in this sense in the 13th century by St Thomas Aquinas.

limits to growth the belief, based on computer calculations, that the steadily rising population growth combined with the rapid depletion of the Earth's natural resources will lead to environmental catastrophe by the beginning of the 21st century.

This prediction was first propounded in the 1970s by the Club of Rome, a group of European intellectuals and businessmen. As a solution they advocated zero population growth, the reduction of output, and an emphasis on food production and recycling.

No man is good enough to govern another man without that other's consent.

Abraham Lincoln
Speech 1854

Lincoln Abraham 1809–1865. 16th president of the USA 1861–65, a Republican. In the American Civil War, his chief concern was the preservation of the Union from which the Confederate (Southern) slave states had seceded on his election. In 1863 he announced the freedom of the slaves with the Emancipation Proclamation. He was re-elected in 1864 with victory for the North in sight, but was assassinated at the end of the war.

Lincoln was born in a log cabin in Kentucky. Self-educated, he practised law from 1837 in Springfield, Illinois. He was a member of the state legislature 1832–42, and was known as Honest Abe. He joined the new Republican Party in 1856, and was elected president in 1860 on a minority vote. His refusal to concede to Confederate demands for the evacuation of the federal garrison at Fort Sumter, Charleston, South Carolina, precipitated the first hostilities of the Civil War. In the Gettysburg Address 1863, he declared the aims of preserving a 'nation conceived in liberty, and dedicated to the proposition that all men are created equal'. Re-elected with a large majority in 1864 on a National Union ticket, he advocated a reconciliatory policy towards the South 'with malice towards none, with charity for all'. Five days after General Lee's surrender, Lincoln was shot in a theatre audience by an actor and Confederate sympathizer, John Wilkes Booth.

lingam in Hinduism, the phallic emblem of the god ◊Siva, the *yoni* being the female equivalent.

linguistics scientific study of language. Linguistics has many branches, such as origins (historical linguistics), the changing way language is pronounced (phonetics), derivation of words through various languages (etymology), development of meanings (semantics), and the arrangement and modifications of words to convey a message (grammar). Applied linguistics is the use of linguistics to aid understanding in other areas of language-based study, such as dictionary compilation and foreign language teaching.

Linnaeus Carolus 1707–1778. Swedish naturalist and physician. His botanical work *Systema naturae* 1735 contained his system for classifying plants into groups depending on shared characteristics (such as the number of stamens in flowers), providing a much-needed framework for identification. He also devised the concise and precise system for naming plants and animals, using one Latin (or Latinized) word to represent the genus and a second to distinguish the species.

For example, in the Latin name of the daisy, *Bellis perennis*, *Bellis* is the name of the genus to which the plant belongs, and *perennis* distinguishes the species from others of the same genus. By tradition the generic name always begins with a capital letter. The author who first described a particular species is often indicated after the name, for example, *Bellis perennis* Linnaeus, showing that the author was Linnaeus.

Nature does not make jumps.

Carolus Linnaeus
Philosophia Botanica

Lipmann Fritz 1899–1986. US biochemist. He investigated the means by which the cell acquires energy and highlighted the crucial role played by the energy-rich phosphate molecule, adenosine triphosphate (ATP). For this and further work on metabolism, Lipmann shared the 1953 Nobel Prize for Medicine with Hans Krebs.

liquidation in economics, the winding up of a company by converting all its assets into money to pay off its liabilities.

An estimated 22,440 UK businesses went into liquidation in 1991, with a further 6,466 businesses failing in the first three months of 1992.

liquidity in economics, the state of possessing sufficient money and/or assets to be able to pay off all liabilities. *Liquid assets* are those such as shares that may be converted quickly into cash, as opposed to property.

litany in the Christian church, a form of prayer or supplication led by a priest with set responses by the congregation. It was introduced in the 4th century.

literacy ability to read and write. The level at which functional literacy is set rises as society becomes more complex, and it becomes increasingly difficult for an illiterate person to find work and cope with the other demands of everyday life.

Nearly 1 billion adults in the world, most of them women, are unable to read or write. Africa has the world's highest illiteracy rate: 54% of the adult population. Asia has 666 million illiterates, 75% of the world total. Surveys in the USA, the UK, and France in the 1980s found far greater levels of functional illiteracy than official figures suggest, as well as revealing a lack of basic general knowledge, but no standard of measurement has been agreed. For example, in a 1988 survey, one in six Britons could not find their country on a map, and in the USA 12% of 12-year-olds in 1991 could not find their country on a map; 25 million US adults could not decipher a road sign.

literary criticism establishment of principles governing literary composition, and the assessment and interpretation of literary works. Contemporary criticism offers analyses of literary works from structuralist, semiological, feminist, Marxist, and psychoanalytical perspectives, whereas earlier criticism tended to deal with moral or political ideas, or with a literary work as a formal object independent of its creator.

The earliest systematic literary criticism was the *Poetics* of Aristotle; a later Greek critic was the author of the treatise *On the Sublime*, usually attributed to Longinus. Horace and Quintilian were influential Latin critics. The Italian Renaissance introduced humanist criticism, and the revival of classical scholarship exalted the authority of Aristotle and Horace. Like literature itself, European criticism then applied Neo-Classical, Romantic, and modern approaches.

literati term applied, sometimes disparagingly, to the learned and well-read. It was originally used by Robert ◊Burton to describe the literate class in China.

Little Red Book book of aphorisms and quotations from the speeches and writings by ◊Mao Zedong, in which he adapted Marxist theory to Chinese conditions. Published 1966, the book was printed in huge numbers and read widely at the start of the ◊Cultural Revolution.

liturgy in the Christian church, any service for public worship; the term was originally limited to the celebration of the ◊Eucharist.

loa spirit in ◊voodoo. Loas may be male or female, and include Maman Brigitte, the loa of death and cemeteries, and Aida-Wedo, the rainbow snake. Believers may be under the protection of one particular loa.

Lobachevsky Nikolai Ivanovich 1792–1856. Russian mathematician who concurrently with, but independently of, Karl ◊Gauss and the Hungarian János Bolyai (1802–1860), founded non-Euclidean geometry. Lobachevsky published the first account of the subject in 1829, but his work went unrecognized until Georg ◊Riemann's system was published.

lobby individual or pressure group that sets out to influence government action. The lobby is prevalent in the USA, where the term originated in the 1830s from the practice of those wishing to influence state policy waiting for elected representatives in the lobby of the Capitol.

Under the UK lobby system, certain parliamentary journalists are given unofficial access to confidential news.

local government that part of government dealing mainly with matters concerning the inhabitants of a particular area or town, usually financed at least in part by local taxes. In the USA and UK, local government has comparatively large powers and responsibilities.

Historically, in European countries such as France, Germany, and the USSR, local government tended to be more centrally controlled than in Britain, although German cities have a tradition of independent action, as exemplified in Berlin, and France from 1969 moved towards regional decentralization. In the USA the system shows evidence of the early type of settlement (for example in New England the town is the unit of local government, in the South the county, and in the N central states the combined county and township). A complication is the tendency to delegate power to special authorities in such fields as education. In Australia, although an integrated system similar to the British was planned, the scattered nature of settlement, apart from the major towns, has prevented implementation of any uniform tiered arrangement.

England and Wales are divided into counties (Scotland into regions) and these are subdivided into districts.

Locke John 1632–1704. English philosopher. His *Essay Concerning Human Understanding* 1690 maintained that experience was the only source of knowledge (empiricism), and that 'we can have knowledge no farther than we have ideas' prompted by such experience. For Locke, the physical universe is a mechanical system of material bodies, composed of corpuscules or 'invisible particles'. *Two Treatises on Government* 1690 helped to form contemporary ideas of liberal democracy.

Locke studied at Oxford, practised medicine, and in 1667 became secretary to the Earl of Shaftesbury. He consequently fell under suspicion as a Whig and in 1683 fled to Holland, where he lived until the 1688 revolution brought William of Orange to the English throne. In later life he published many works on philosophy, politics, theology, and economics; these include *Letters on Toleration* 1689–92 and *Some Thoughts concerning Education* 1693. His *Two Treatises on Government* supplied the classical statement of Whig theory and enjoyed great influence in America and France. It supposed that governments derive their authority from popular consent (regarded as a 'contract'), so that a government may be rightly overthrown if it infringes such fundamental rights of the people as religious freedom. He believed that at birth the mind was a blank, and that all ideas came from sense impressions.

It is one thing to show a man that he is in error, and another to put him in possession of the truth.

John Locke
Essay Concerning Human Understanding

---

logarithm or **log** the exponent or index of a number to a specified base – usually 10. For example, the logarithm to the base 10 of 1,000 is 3 because $10^3 = 1,000$; the logarithm of 2 is 0.3010 because $2 = 10^{0.3010}$. Before the advent of cheap electronic calculators, multiplication and division could be simplified by being replaced with the addition and subtraction of logarithms.

For any two numbers x and y (where $x = b^a$ and $y = b^c$) $x \times y = b^a \times b^c = b^{a + c}$; hence we would add the logarithms of x and y, and look up this answer in antilogarithm tables. Tables of logarithms and antilogarithms are available that show conversions of numbers into logarithms, and vice versa. For example, to multiply 6,560 by 980, one looks up their logarithms (3.8169 and 2.9912), adds them together (6.8081), then looks up the antilogarithm of this to get the answer (6,428,800). *Natural* or *Napierian logarithms* are to the base e, an irrational number equal to approximately 2.7183.

The principle of logarithms is also the basis of the slide rule. With the general availability of the electronic pocket calculator, the need for logarithms has been reduced. The first log tables (to base e) were published by the Scottish mathematician John Napier in 1614. Base-ten logs were introduced by the Englishman Henry Briggs (1561–1631) and Dutch mathematician Adriaen Vlacq (1600–1667).

logic branch of philosophy that studies valid reasoning and argument. It is also the way in which one thing may be said to follow from, or be a consequence of, another (deductive logic). Logic is generally divided into the traditional formal logic of ◊Aristotle and the symbolic logic derived from Friedrich ◊Frege and Bertrand ◊Russell.

Aristotle's *Organon* is the founding work on logic, and Aristotelian methods, as revived in the medieval church by the French scholar Peter Abelard in the 12th century, were used in the synthesis of ideas aimed at in ◊scholasticism. As befitted the spirit of the Renaissance, the English philosopher Francis Bacon considered many of the general principles used as premises by the scholastics to be groundless; he envisaged that in natural philosophy principles worthy of investigation would emerge by 'inductive' logic, which works backward from the accumulated facts to the principle that accounts for them.

In 1965, the concept of ◊fuzzy logic was proposed to enable computer-controlled devices to deal with vague concepts.

logical atomism philosophical theory that seeks to analyse thought and discourse in terms of indivisible components, or atomic propositions, like 'Jane is clever', 'Tom loves Jane'. Atomic propositions are true if they correspond directly to atomic facts. One of many difficulties with the theory is how negative propositions (such as 'Jane does not love Tom') can correspond to atomic facts. The theory is associated with the 20th-century philosophers Bertrand Russell and, in his early period, Ludwig Wittgenstein.

logical positivism doctrine that the only meaningful propositions are those that can be verified empirically. Metaphysics, religion, and aesthetics are therefore meaningless. However, the doctrine itself cannot be verified empirically and so is self-refuting. Logical positivists have expended much effort in trying to solve this problem.

Logical positivism was characteristic of the ◊Vienna Circle in the 1920s and 1930s, and was influenced by Friedrich Frege, Bertrand Russell, and Ludwig Wittgenstein.

logos a term in Greek, Hebrew, and Christian philosophy and theology. It was used by Greek philosophers as the embodiment of 'reason' in the universe. Under Greek influence the Jews came to conceive of 'wisdom' as an aspect of

God's activity. The Jewish philosopher ◊Philo Judaeus (1st century AD) attempted to reconcile Platonic, Stoic, and Hebrew philosophy by identifying the logos with the Jewish idea of 'wisdom'. Several of the New Testament writers took over Philo's conception of the logos, which they identified with Christ and hence with the second person of the Trinity.

Lohengrin in late 13th-century Germanic legend, a hero, son of ◊Parsifal. Lohengrin married Princess Elsa, who broke his condition that she never ask his origin, and he returned to the temple of the ◊Holy Grail. Wagner based his German opera *Lohengrin* 1847 on the story.

Lokayata Indian school of materialistic philosophy and literature based on the idea that there are no gods and experience is the only true source of knowledge. The Lokayata school opposed the ◊caste system and strongly objected to the worship of deities and to professional religious groups.

In the ◊Vedas (early Hindu scriptures) there are signs of a sceptical viewpoint which dismisses the divine and belief in life after death and insists upon the material world as ultimate reality. By the time of the Buddha these views began to take a more defined shape with its own school of philosophy and literature.

Loki in Norse mythology, one of the ◊Aesir (the principal gods), but the cause of dissension among the gods, and the slayer of ◊Balder. His children are the Midgard serpent Jörmungander, which girdles the Earth, the wolf Fenris, and Hela, goddess of death.

Lollard follower of the English religious reformer John ◊Wycliffe in the 14th century. The Lollards condemned the doctrine of the transubstantiation of the bread and wine of the Eucharist, advocated the diversion of ecclesiastical property to charitable uses, and denounced war and capital punishment. They were active from about 1377; after the passing of the statute *De heretico comburendo* ('The Necessity of Burning Heretics') 1401 many Lollards were burned, and in 1414 they raised an unsuccessful revolt in London, known as Oldcastle's rebellion.

The movement began at Oxford University, where Wycliffe taught, but thereafter included nonacademics, merchants, lesser clergy, and a few members of Richard II's court. Repression began in Henry IV's reign. The 1414 revolt was known as Oldcastle's rebellion, and the Lollards subsequently went underground; much of their policy was advocated by the early Protestants.

The name is derived from the Dutch *lollaert* (mumbler), applied to earlier European groups accused of combining pious pretensions with heretical belief. Lollardy lingered on in London and East Anglia, and in the 16th century became absorbed into the Protestant movement.

Lombroso Cesare 1836–1909. Italian criminologist. His major work is *L'uomo delinquente/The Delinquent Man* 1889. He held the now discredited idea that there was a physically distinguishable 'criminal type'.

loneliness feeling of sadness that results from being solitary and isolated. Loneliness can occur at various stages in life and in different situations. An adolescent in an ◊identity crisis, for example, may be afraid of forming close relationships and be lonely as a result. In the elderly, isolation resulting from degenerative disease, particularly that affecting sight, hearing, or mobility, or due to social factors, such as loss of a spouse or close friends, often leads to loneliness and ◊depression.

Lord's Prayer in the New Testament, the prayer taught by Jesus to his disciples. It is sometimes called 'Our Father' or 'Paternoster' from the opening words in English and Latin respectively.

Lord's Supper in the Christian church, another name for the ◊Eucharist.

Lorelei in Germanic folklore, a river nymph of the Rhine who lures sailors onto the rock where she sits combing her hair. She features in several poems, including 'Die Lorelei' by the German Romantic writer Heine. The *Lurlei* rock S of Koblenz is 130 m/430 ft high.

Lorentz Hendrik Antoon 1853–1928. Dutch physicist, winner (with his pupil Pieter ◊Zeeman) of a Nobel prize in 1902 for his work on the Zeeman effect.

Lorentz spent most of his career trying to develop and improve James ◊Maxwell's electromagnetic theory. He also attempted to account for the anomalies of the ◊Michelson–Morley experiment by proposing, independently of George Fitzgerald, that moving bodies contracted in their direction of motion. He took the matter further with his method of transforming space and time coordinates, later known as Lorentz transformations, which prepared the way for Albert Einstein's theory of ◊relativity.

Lorenz Konrad 1903–1989. Austrian ethologist. Director of the Max Planck Institute for the Physiology of Behaviour in Bavaria

1955–73, he wrote the studies of ethology (animal behaviour) *King Solomon's Ring* 1952 and *On Aggression* 1966. In 1973 he shared the Nobel Prize for Medicine with Nikolaas Tinbergen and Karl von Frisch.

It is a good morning exercise for a research scientist to discard a pet hypothesis every day before breakfast. It keeps him young.

Konrad Lorenz
The So-Called Evil

Lorenz sympathized with Nazi views on eugenics, and in 1938 applied to join the Nazi party.

Lorenz Ludwig Valentine 1829–1891. Danish mathematician and physicist. He developed mathematical formulae to describe phenomena such as the relation between the refraction of light and the density of a pure transparent substance, and the relation between a metal's electrical and thermal conductivity and temperature.

loss the opposite of ◊profit, when ◊revenues are less than costs.

Lot in the Old Testament, Abraham's nephew, who escaped the destruction of Sodom. Lot's wife disobeyed the condition of not looking back at Sodom and was punished by being turned into a pillar of salt.

Lotus-Eaters in Homer's *Odyssey*, a mythical people living on the lotus plant, which induced travellers to forget their journey home.

Lotus Sūtra scripture of Mahāyāna Buddhism. It is Buddha Śākyamuni's final teaching, emphasizing that everyone can attain Buddhahood with the help of ◊bodhisattvas. The original is in Sanskrit (*Saddharmapundarīka Sū\tra*) and is thought to date from some time after 100 BC.

Twice or thrice had I loved thee, / Before I knew thy face or name. / So in a voice, so in a shapeless flame, / Angels affect us oft, and worshipped be.

love
John Donne, 1571–1631, English
metaphysical poet.
'Air and Angels'

---

love affectionate or passionate devotion to another being. The Greeks often distinguished fondness or ◊friendship (*philia*), erotic love (*eros*), and selfless love (*agape*).

Plato and Aristotle both hold that love is ultimately the desire of the imperfect for the perfect, whereas in Christianity love arises from the concern of the perfect (God) for the imperfect (human beings).

St Augustine defines virtue as *ordo amoris* ('the order of love'), which occurs when the love of God replaces the love of self. For St Thomas Aquinas, natural love concerns the passions and will, whereas supernatural love is natural love to which has been added habitual unselfishness.

Love, all alike, no season knows, nor clime, / Nor hours, days, months, which are the rags of time.

love
John Donne, 1571–1631, English
metaphysical poet.
'The Sun Rising'

Lovejoy Arthur Oncken 1873–1962. US philospher, noted for his analysis and application of the scope and methods of the study of the history of ideas. He advocated identifying the implicit ideas of a period in history, and then subjecting them to logical analysis. One of his techniques was what he called philosophical semantics – the investigation of recurrent terms and phrases in the literature of a period.

His works include his classic study *The Great Chain of Being* 1936 (◊chain of being), *Essays in the History of Ideas* 1948 and *Revolt against Dualism* 1930. He taught for some 40 years at the John Hopkins University.

Lovell Bernard 1913– . British radio astronomer, director (until 1981) of Jodrell Bank Experimental Station (now Nuffield Radio Astronomy Laboratories).

During World War II he worked at the Telecommunications Research Establishment (1939–45), and in 1951 became professor of radio astronomy at the University of Manchester. His books include *Radio Astronomy* 1951 and *The Exploration of Outer Space* 1961.

Lowell Percival 1855–1916. US astronomer who predicted the existence of a 'Planet X' beyond Neptune, and started the search that led to the discovery of Pluto in 1930. In 1894 he founded the Lowell Observatory at Flagstaff, Arizona, where he reported seeing

Love

Love is affectionate or passionate devotion to another being or to an inanimate thing. We can love ourselves, other people, pets, and God. We can love work, games, hobbies, and other activities. We can love traditions, institutions, countries, and nations. We can love York Minster, the *Mona Lisa*, landscapes, money, cream cakes, or cricket bats.

False or true?

Love can be false or true. False love gravitates toward what is false or evil: we can love a fantasy or a delusion (as in unrequited romantic love), or we can love wrongdoing. Yet, as the philosopher and novelist Iris Murdoch (1919–) has argued, even false, impure, self-absorbed, or fantasy love is refined by an object that is morally good. True love, however, gravitates toward what is morally good: as Plato (c. 428–347 BC) argues in *The Symposium*, love involves the desire of the imperfect for the perfect. Moreover, true love of all kinds involves not only affection but also unconditional devotion, loyalty, and constancy: 'Love is not love. Which alters when it alteration finds', as William Shakespeare (1564–1616) observed. In certain respects, true love can even survive and transcend the death of the one who is loved.

In all its forms, true love involves a desire and concern for the flourishing, or the good, of whatever or whomever is loved. When we love an inanimate object, an activity, or an institution, we cherish it with a passionate devotion. But the concern we feel when we love such things cannot be returned. By contrast, true love for another being (animal, person, or God) is or can be returned: it involves reciprocity.

Erotic love

Roughly speaking, the Greeks distinguished three types or aspects of love – erotic love (*eros*), fondness or friendship (*philia*), and selfless love (*agape*). Each of these types of love has its distinctive features. Erotic love (*eros*) is sexual love. True erotic love involves sensual desire and passionate adoration. While desire has a tendency to wither with time, true erotic love has a tendency to grow. Rooted in our animality, true erotic love extends far beyond it; and, over time, erotic love acquires many of the qualities of family affection and of friendship.

In erotic love, moreover, we find sexual ecstasy. The contemporary philosopher Richard Spilsbury has argued, in his *Providence Lost: a critique of Darwinism* (1974), that it is implausible to suggest that the remarkable harmony between the interests of the species and individual ecstasy came about solely through evolution. The sheer joy of love, sexual and non-sexual, is far greater than can be explained by reference to biological utility or Freudian psychology. The mystery of love is a genuine mystery – the mystery of how non-material values are related to the material processes of the world around us.

Family and friends

The Greeks tended to group both family affection and friendship under one term (*philia*). However, we tend to distinguish friendship from family affection, because we can choose our friends but not our relatives. Unlike the Greeks, we tend to see friendship as a mutual benevolence that is independent of sexual or family love.

Furthermore, we tend to think of family love in terms of its types – paternal, maternal, sibling (love between brothers and sisters), and filial (love of children for parents), as well as love for other relatives beyond the nuclear family. When we are infants, we tend to experience the love poured out on us first as maternal and later as paternal. The child's experience of its mother's passionate devotion lays the foundations not only of self-respect but also of moral feeling, of all sympathy for others. 'We begin', as Edmund Burke (1729–1797) said, 'our public affections in our families.'

Loving ourselves

If we love others truly, we can love ourselves truly. True love of one's self is not selfishness: rather, it is a proper concern for one's self. Both Plato and Aristotle argue, in effect, that an appropriate concern for one's self involves an appropriate concern for others – that concern for others is part of true happiness and well-being.

Loving our neighbour

Selfless love (*agape*) is the most spiritual love. In the New Testament, it is the love for one's neighbour, or charity, through which God's love reaches the world. Charity is not only an emotion but also a discipline. St Augustine (354–430) defined virtue itself as the order of love – which occurs when the love of God displaces the old loves of self and of worldly pleasures.

St Paul (c. AD 3–68), in a celebrated passage (I Corinthians 13: 4–7), sketches the nature of charity. It is the reverse of jealousy, boastfulness, arrogance or rudeness; it is patient and kind, not resentful or irritable; and it is sympathetic, encouraging, optimistic, and unselfish. In self-sacrificial love, we discover a greater sense of self. Or, as both St Augustine and Benedict Spinoza (1632–1677) would have it, one must lose oneself in order to find oneself, and in so doing one finds God.

In so far as it involves self-sacrifice and personal discipline, love transforms, purifies, and redeems. Since we cannot love others unless we love ourselves, loving makes us more whole, integrated, and fulfilled; and loving makes the boundaries of the self seem less rigid and more permeable. Perhaps Christ meant this when he indicated that we could have life 'more abundantly' by loving our neighbour (John 10: 10).

Love the healer

The redemptive, joyous, and life-enhancing character of love contrasts markedly with the character of indulged hatred and its derivatives (such as chronic anger and resentment). Hatred is by nature reflexive and turns in upon itself. Part of every hater hates himself for hating others. Consequently, hatred spawns self-hatred. Because it corrodes self-respect and fractures the integrity of the self, all hatred is ultimately self-destructive. In contrast, the practice of true love unifies the self, which is why modern psychotherapists often see personal maturity as a growth in the capacity to love.

P M Rowntree

'canals' (now known to be optical artefacts) on the surface of Mars.

Loyola founder of the Jesuits. See ◊Ignatius Loyola.

Lucas Robert 1937– . US economist, leader of the University of Chicago school of 'new classical' macroeconomics, which contends that wage and price adjustment is almost instantaneous and that the level of unemployment at any time must be the natural rate (it cannot be reduced by government action except in the short term and at the cost of increasing inflation).

Lucifer in Christian theology, another name for the ◊devil, the leader of the angels who rebelled against God. Lucifer is also another name for the morning star (the planet Venus).

Nothing can be created out of nothing.
(Titus Lucretius Carus) Lucretius
De Rerum Natura

Lucretius (Titus Lucretius Carus) c. 99–55 BC. Roman poet and philosopher of ◊Epicureanism whose *De Rerum Natura/On the Nature of The Universe* envisaged the whole universe as a combination of atoms, and had some concept of evolutionary theory.

According to Lucretius, animals were complex but initially quite fortuitous clusters of atoms, only certain combinations surviving to reproduce.

Luddite one of a group of people involved in machine-wrecking riots in N England 1811–16. The organizer of the Luddites was referred to as General Ludd, but may not have existed. Many Luddites were hanged or transported to penal colonies, such as Australia.

The movement, which began in Nottinghamshire and spread to Lancashire, Cheshire, Derbyshire, Leicestershire, and Yorkshire, was primarily a revolt against the unemployment caused by the introduction of machines in the ◊Industrial Revolution.

Lukács György Szegedy von 1885–1971. Hungarian philosopher and literary critic. Lukács was one of the leading, and most controversial, Marxist writers on aesthetics and the sociology of literature. When the Hungarian communist uprising was put down in 1919, he emigrated first to Germany and then, in 1930, to Russia, returning to Hungary in 1945. He was a member of the short-lived Hungarian revolutionary government of 1956 and was briefly imprisoned when it was ended with the arrival of Soviet tanks.

Influenced by Georg ◊Simmel and Max ◊Weber, he wrote two of his best books on literature, *Soul and Form* 1910 and *The Theory of the Novel* 1916, before he became a communist in 1918. In his important collection of essays on Marxism, *History and Class Consciousness* 1923, he discussed ◊reification, reintroducing ◊alienation as a central concept, and argued that bourgeois thought was 'false consciousness'. His views were considered unorthodox by Russian communist leaders and he had to make a humiliating public retraction of his 'errors' in Moscow in 1930. Lukács may have accepted that acting wickedly was an unfortunate but necessary communist duty, but he could not have approved of Stalin's policies and misdeeds, and consistently protested against demands that literature should support them. Rejected by official socialist literature, he was also an outsider to the dominant literary movements of the 'free world'. He repudiated the view held by both, according to him, that 'literature and art really can be manipulated according to the needs of the day.' He argued for ◊realism in literature and opposed ◊modernism, particularly the work of Joyce and Kafka.

Luke, St 1st century AD. Traditionally the compiler of the third Gospel and of the Acts of the Apostles in the New Testament. Luke is supposed to have been a Greek physician born in Antioch (Antakiyah, Turkey) and to have accompanied Paul after the ascension of Jesus. Feast day 18 Oct.

Lully Raymond c. 1232–1315. Spanish theologian and philosopher famous for his desire to convert Muslims which led to his being stoned to death in Algeria. He also invented a mechanistic method of learning and of solving all problems by application of key fundamental notions. His followers, known as Lullists, continued this methodology and spirituality, and were accused of mixing religious mysticism with alchemy.

Lumbini birthplace of ◊Buddha in the foothills of the Himalayas near the Nepalese-Indian frontier. A sacred garden and shrine were established here in 1970 by the Nepalese government.

Lumpenproletariat the poorest of the poor: beggars, tramps, and criminals (according to Karl Marx).

Lupercalia Roman festival celebrated 15 Feb. Goats were sacrificed at the Lupercal, the cave where Romulus and Remus, the twin founders of Rome, were supposedly suckled by a wolf (*lupus*). Youths then ran around the boundaries of the city carrying whips made from the hides of the sacrificed goats, blows from which were believed to cure sterility in women.

Luria Salvador Edward 1912–1991. Italian-born US physician who was a pioneer in molecular biology, internationally known for his research in the field of virology and ◊genetics. With fellow biologists Max Delbruck and Alfred Hershey, the three were cited for their 'discoveries concerning the replication mechanism and the genetic structure of viruses,' which 'set the solid foundation on which modern molecular biology rests.' Luria and Delbruek also received the Louisa Gross Horwitz Prize for their work on genetics of bacteria and bacteriophage, and Laurie won the Nobel Prize in Medicine 1969.

Luria was born in Turin, Italy, into a distinguished Northern Italian Jewish family. He went to Paris in 1938, where he became a research fellow at the Institut du Radium. In 1940 Luria emigrated to the US. From 1943 he taught at a number of universities and in 1959 became a professor at the Massachusetts Institute of Technology (MIT), where he taught until his death. After joining MIT he organized a new teaching and research programme in the field of microbiology and later founded the MIT Center for Cancer Research which he directed from 1972 to 1985. He urged his students to form a strong world view and for some time taught a course in world literature to graduate students at MIT and at Harvard Medical School to ensure their involvement in the arts. Luria was an ardent pacifist and was identified with efforts to keep science humanistic.

I can do no other.

Martin Luther
Speech at the Diet of Worms 18 Apr 1521

Luther Martin 1483–1546. German Christian church reformer, the instigator of the Protestant revolution; one of the major branches of Protestantism, Lutheranism, is named after him. While a priest at the University of Wittenberg, Luther wrote an attack on the sale of indulgences (remissions of punishment for sin). The Holy Roman emperor Charles V summoned him to the Diet (meeting of dignitaries of the Holy Roman Empire) of Worms in Germany, in 1521,

where he refused to retract his objections. Originally intending reform, his protest led to schism, with the emergence, following the Augsburg Confession 1530 (a statement of the Protestant faith), of a new Protestant church.

Luther was born in Eisleben, the son of a miner; he studied at the University of Erfurt, spent three years as a monk in the Augustinian convent there, and in 1507 was ordained priest. Shortly afterwards he attracted attention as a teacher and preacher at the University of Wittenberg; and in 1517, after returning from a visit to Rome, he attained nationwide celebrity for his denunciation of the Dominican monk Johann Tetzel (1455–1519), one of those sent out by the Pope to sell indulgences as a means of raising funds for the rebuilding of St Peter's Basilica in Rome.

On 31 Oct 1517, Luther nailed on the church door in Wittenberg a statement of 95 theses concerning indulgences, and the following year he was summoned to Rome to defend his action. His reply was to attack the papal system even more strongly, and in 1520 he publicly burned in Wittenberg the papal bull (edict) that had been launched against him. On his way home from the imperial Diet of Worms he was taken into 'protective custody' by the elector of Saxony in the castle of Wartburg. Later he became estranged from the Dutch theologian Erasmus, who had formerly supported him in his attacks on papal authority, and engaged in violent controversies with political and religious opponents. After the Augsburg Confession 1530, Luther gradually retired from the Protestant leadership.

Lutheranism form of Protestant Christianity derived from the life and teaching of Martin Luther; it is sometimes called Evangelical to distinguish it from the other main branch of European Protestantism, the Reformed. The most generally accepted statement of Lutheranism is that of the *Augsburg Confession* 1530 but Luther's Shorter Catechism also carries great weight. It is the largest Protestant body, including some 80 million persons, of whom 40 million are in Germany, 19 million in Scandinavia, 8.5 million in the USA and Canada, with most of the remainder in central Europe.

Lutheranism is the principal form of Protestantism in Germany, and is the state religion of Denmark, Norway, Sweden, Finland, and Iceland. The organization may be episcopal (Germany, Sweden) or synodal (the Netherlands and USA): the Lutheran World Federation has its headquarters in

Geneva. In the USA, Lutheranism is particularly strong in the Midwest, where several churches were originally founded by German and Scandinavian immigrants.

Lyceum ancient Athenian gymnasium and garden, with covered walks, where the philosopher Aristotle taught. It was SE of the city and named after the nearby temple of Apollo Lyceus.

Lycurgus Spartan lawgiver. He was believed to have been a member of the royal house of the ancient Greek city-state of Sparta, who, while acting as regent, gave the Spartans their constitution and system of education. Many modern scholars believe him to be purely mythical.

Lyell Charles 1797–1875. Scottish geologist. In his *Principles of Geology* 1830–33, he opposed the French anatomist Georges Cuvier's theory that the features of the Earth were formed by a series of catastrophes, and expounded the Scottish geologist James Hutton's view, known as ◊uniformitarianism, that past events were brought about by the same processes that occur today – a view that influenced Charles Darwin's theory of evolution.

Lyell trained and practised as a lawyer, but retired from the law 1827 and devoted himself full time to geology and writing. He implied that the Earth was much older than the 6,000 years of prevalent contemporary theory, and provided the first detailed description of the Tertiary period, dividing it into the Eocene, Miocene, and older and younger Pliocene periods. Although it was only in old age that he accepted that species had changed through evolution, he nevertheless provided Darwin with a geological framework within which evolutionary theories could be placed. Darwin simply applied Lyell's geological method – explaining the past through what is observable in the present – to biology.

lying deliberately making false statements with the intention to deceive or mislead. Lying may sometimes be justified, for example, for self-protection or to deceive the enemy in wartime.

The question of whether it is ever right to tell a lie has frequently been discussed by moral philosophers, especially with reference to difficult situations, such as whether a doctor should withold the truth from a patient with a fatal disease or whether one should protect a friend or client with a lie when telling the truth would be a betrayal of confidence. In pathological lying the mendacity has no moral justification. The pathological liar is typically an imposter or swindler, adopting a false persona with the aim, say, of obtaining money under false pretences.

Bibl. Bok, Sissela *Lying: Moral Choice in Public and Private Life* (Sussex, 1978)

It is always the best policy to speak the truth – unless, of course, you are an exceptionally good liar.

lying
Jerome K(lapka) Jerome, 1859–1927,
English journalist and writer.
The Idler Feb 1892

Lyotard, Jean François 1924– . French philosopher, one of the leading theorists of ◊Post-Modernism. His central concern is the role of knowledge in contemporary society. A member of Marxist groups in the 1950s and 60s, he became disillusioned with the ideology of revolution, and developed a radical scepticism towards all attempts to make sense of history and society. In *The Postmodern Condition* 1979 he argued that in an advanced post-industrial society in which capitalism had appropriated all values, technology, science and the mass media, it is necessary to abandon the desire for truth, for rational and coherent accounts ('grand narratives') of the world, whether these are scientific, religious, historical or political. (He defines Post-Modernism not as a stage succeeding Modernism, but as an attitude of 'incredulity' towards grand narratives). Such monolithic theories should, he argues, be rejected in favour of a plurality of 'small narratives', in which the emphasis is on the local and the personal. The world is not rational but 'fabulous' – it needs to be seen in terms of myths rather than all-embracing theories. Politically and culturally, this involves a shift to the individual. Grand narratives are authoritarian, defining the individual in terms of pre-existing theories; small narratives require an involvement in their ever-evolving creation. These views were further developed in *The Differend* 1983. *Just Gaming* which focuses on justice, shows his indebtedness, in his notion of small narratives, to ◊Wittgenstein's 'language games'. Lyotard's ideas have had a great impact on the development of recent artistic practice.

Lysenko Trofim Denisovich 1898–1976. Soviet biologist who believed in the inheritance of ◊acquired character (changes acquired in an individual's lifetime) and used his position under Joseph Stalin officially to exclude Gregor ◊Mendel's theory of inheritance. He was removed from office after the fall of Khrushchev in 1964.

proposal to go ahead with ratification in Nov was passed by only a small majority, prompting British prime minister John Major to delay ratification until after a second Danish national referendum. These results contrasted with a clear 'yes' vote in low-income countries such as Spain and Ireland, which stood to benefit substantially from the treaty. However, after agreement on a series of compromises at a summit in Edinburgh 11 Dec, ratification by all 12 nations was completed July 1993.

Maat Egyptian goddess of truth and justice. The souls of the dead were weighed against the feather of truth (her symbol) or against her statue. The Egyptians believed that all things were governed by Maat.

Mabinogion, the collection of medieval Welsh myths and folk tales put together in the mid-19th century and drawn from two manuscripts: *The White Book of Rhydderch* 1300–25 and *The Red Book of Hergest* 1375–1425.

The *Mabinogion* proper consists of four tales, three of which concern a hero named Pryderi. Other stories in the medieval source manuscripts touch on the legendary court of King ◊Arthur.

Maccabee or ***Hasmonaean*** member of an ancient Hebrew family founded by the priest Mattathias (died 166 BC) who, with his sons, led the struggle for independence against the Syrians in the 2nd century BC. Judas (died 161) reconquered Jerusalem 164 BC, and Simon (died 135) established its independence 142 BC. The revolt of the Maccabees lasted until the capture of Jerusalem by the Romans 63 BC. The story is told in four books of the ◊Apocrypha.

McCarthyism is Americanism with its sleeves rolled.

McCarthyism
Joseph McCarthy, 1908–1957,
US right-wing politician.
Speech in Wisconsin 1952

Maastricht Treaty treaty on European union, signed 10 Dec 1991 by leaders of ◊European Community (EC) nations at Maastricht in the Netherlands, at a meeting convened to agree on terms for political union. The treaty was formally endorsed by the ◊European Parliament April 1992 but its subsequent rejection by the Danish in a June referendum placed its future in jeopardy. The Treaty was eventually ratified by Denmark, after a second referendum May 1993, and by the United Kingdom July 1993. However, economic recession and financial instability in most major EC countries has placed doubts on the ability of the Community to achieve monetary union within the timescale prescribed by the Treaty.

A draft treaty on political union, proposed by Luxembourg premier Jacques Santer in June 1991, became the focus of EC discussions in the months leading up to the summit at Maastricht in Dec 1991, at which a revised treaty was signed. Issues covered by the treaty included a revision of the Community's desion-making process and the establishment of closer links on foreign and military policy. The British government demanded that any reference to federalism be removed from the treaty. Discussions on greater economic and monetary integration, a highly divisive issue, were also held.

Throughout 1992 the parliaments of EC nations voted on whether or not to go ahead and ratify the treaty, in some cases opting to put the question to the people in the form of a national referendum (Denmark, France, Spain, Ireland). A clear 'no' vote in a June Danish referendum, together with Britain and Italy's subsequent enforced withdrawal from the European ◊Exchange Rate Mechanism (ERM), caused repercussions throughout the Community. The French voted only narrowly in favour in Sept and a British government

McCarthyism political persecution or witch-hunt of the type associated with the US senator Joseph McCarthy.

At the height of US anxiety about the communist 'threat' during the 1950s, McCarthy accused many public officials and private citizens of being Communist Party members or sympathizers. Most of his evidence was fabricated, but the Congressional committees, where his claims were investigated, destroyed many careers and created an atmosphere of suspicion and paranoia, especially in liberal intellectual circles.

The dark flame of his male pride was a little suspicious of having its leg pulled.

machismo
Stella (Dorothea) Gibbons, 1902–1989,
English journalist.
Cold Comfort Farm ch 7

McClintock Barbara 1902–1992. US geneticist who discovered jumping ◊genes (genes that can change their position on a chromosome from generation to generation). This would explain how originally identical cells take on specialized functions as skin, muscle, bone, and nerve, and also how ◊evolution could give rise to the multiplicity of species. Nobel prize 1983.

McCulloch Warren Sturgis 1899–1969. US neurophysiologist. Although his initial work, conducted at Yale in the 1930s, concentrated on primate physiology, he is best-known for his development of cybernetic and computational models of the brain, undertaken initially at the University of Illinois and later, from 1952, at the Massachusetts Institute of Technology (MIT).

The work of his research group at MIT was published in several influential papers, including *What the frog's eye tells the frog's brain* 1959, which detailed the way in which information is transmitted from the retina to the brain to detect significant features or events in the frog's environment.

McGuffey William Holmes 1800–1873. US educator. He is best remembered for his series the *Eclectic Readers* which became standard reading textbooks throughout the USA in the 19th century. He was president of Cincinnati College 1836–39 and Ohio University 1839–45.

Born in Claysville, Pennsylvania, USA, and raised in Ohio, McGuffey attended Washington University and Jefferson College.

Mach Ernst 1838–1916. Austrian philosopher and physicist. He was an empiricist, believing that science is a record of facts perceived by the senses, and that acceptance of a scientific law depends solely on its standing the practical test of use; he opposed concepts such as Newton's 'absolute motion'. He researched airflow, and ◊Mach numbers are named after him.

Machiavelli Niccolò 1469–1527. Italian

politician and author whose name is synonymous with cunning and cynical statecraft. In his most celebrated political writings, *Il principe/The Prince* 1513 and *Discorsi/Discourses* 1531, he discussed ways in which rulers can advance the interests of their states (and themselves) through an often amoral and opportunistic manipulation of other people.

Machiavelli was born in Florence and was second chancellor to the republic 1498–1512. On the accession to power of the Medici family 1512, he was arrested and imprisoned on a charge of conspiracy, but in 1513 was released to exile in the country. *The Prince*, based on his observations of Cesare Borgia, is a guide for the future prince of a unified Italian state (which did not occur until the Risorgimento in the 19th century). In *L'Arte della guerra/The Art of War* 1520 Machiavelli outlined the provision of an army for the prince, and in *Historie fiorentine/History of Florence* he analysed the historical development of Florence until 1492. Among his later works are the comedies *Clizia* 1515 and *La Mandragola/The Mandrake* 1524.

machine politics organization of a local political party to ensure its own election by influencing the electorate, and then to retain power through control of key committees and offices. The idea of machine politics was epitomized in the USA in the late 19th century, where it was used to control individual cities, most notably Chicago and New York.

machismo in Latin American culture, the idea of a tough swaggering masculinity or virility. Since the resurgence of ◊feminism in the 1970s it has been applied to any man who projects an invulnerable and aggressive manner.

Mach number ratio of the speed of a body to the speed of sound in the undisturbed medium through which the body travels. Mach 1 is reached when a body (such as an aircraft) has a velocity greater than that of sound ('passes the sound barrier'), namely 331 m/1,087 ft per second at sea level. It is named after Austrian physicist Ernst ◊Mach.

McLuhan (Herbert) Marshall 1911–1980. Canadian theorist of communication, famed for his views on the effects of technology on modern society. He coined the phrase 'the medium is the message', meaning that the form rather than the content of information has become crucial. His works include *The Gutenberg Galaxy* 1962 (in which he coined the phrase 'the global village' for the worldwide electronic society then emerging), *Under-standing Media* 1964, and *The Medium Is the Massage* [sic] 1967.

McMillan Edwin Mattison 1907– . US physicist. In 1940 he discovered neptunium, the first transuranic element, by bombarding uranium with neutrons. He shared a Nobel prize with Glenn ◊Seaborg 1951 for their discovery of transuranic elements. In 1943 he developed a method of overcoming the limitations of the cyclotron, the first accelerator, for which he shared, 20 years later, an Atoms for Peace award with I Veksler, director of the Soviet Joint Institute for Nuclear Research, who had come to the same discovery independently. McMillan was a professor at the University of California 1946–73.

McPherson Aimee Semple 1890–1944. Canadian-born US religious leader. As a popular preacher, 'Sister Aimee' reached millions through radio broadcasts of her weekly sermons, in which she emphasized the power of faith. She established the Church of the Four-Square Gospel in Los Angeles 1918.

Born in Ingersoll, Ontario, USA, McPherson worked as a missionary to China before becoming an itinerant evangelist in the USA, gaining a large following through her revival tours. She committed suicide 1944.

macrobiotics dietary system of organically grown wholefoods. It originates in Zen Buddhism, and attempts to balance the principles of ◊yin and yang, thought to be present in foods in different proportions.

macroeconomics division of economics concerned with the study of whole (aggregate) economies or systems, including such aspects as government income and expenditure, the balance of payments, fiscal policy, investment, inflation, and unemployment. It seeks to understand the influence of all relevant economic factors on each other and thus to quantify and predict aggregate national income.

Modern macroeconomics takes much of its inspiration from the work of John Maynard ◊Keynes, who suggested that governments could manage the economy by adjusting demand through control of government expenditure, taxation, and by credit. **Keynesian macroeconomics** thus analyses aggregate supply and demand and holds that markets do not continuously 'clear' (quickly attain equilibrium between supply and demand) and may require intervention if objectives such as full employment are thought desirable. Keynesian macroeconomic formulations were generally accepted well into the postwar era and have been refined and extended by the **neo-Keynesian school**, which contends that in a recession the market will clear only very slowly and that full employment equilibrium may never return without significant demand management (by government). At the same time, however, **neo-classical economics** has experienced a recent resurgence, using tools from ◊microeconomics to challenge the central Keynesian assumption that resources may be underemployed and that full employment equilibrium requires state intervention. Another important school is **new classical economics**, which seeks to show the futility of Keynesian demand-management policies and stresses instead the importance of **supply-side economics**, believing that the principal factor influencing growth of national output is the efficient allocation and use of labour and capital. A related school is that of the **Chicago monetarists**, led by Milton ◊Friedman, who have revived the old idea that an increase in money supply leads inevitably to an increase in prices rather than in output; however, whereas the new classical school contends that wage and price adjustment are almost instantaneous and so the level of employment at any time must be the natural rate, the Chicago monetarists are more gradualist, believing that such adjustment may take some years.

McTaggart John McTaggart Ellis 1866–1925. English philosopher, who was a follower of ◊Hegel and argued for atheism, the immortality of the soul, and the unreality of time. McTaggart's ingenious arguments give his work lasting interest. His great work is *The Nature of Existence* 1927.

When a heroine goes mad she always goes into white satin.

madness
Richard Brinsley Sheridan, 1751–1816, Irish dramatist and politician.
The Critic

---

madness state of having a disordered mind; extreme folly or infatuation. Its synonym, ◊insanity, is no longer used to mean ◊psychosis but is used primarily in medical and legal contexts to refer to mental disorders in which patients cannot be held responsible for their actions.

Madonna Italian name for the Virgin ◊Mary, meaning 'my lady'.

maenad in Greek mythology, one of the women participants in the orgiastic rites of ◊Dionysus; maenads were also known as **Bacchae**.

Madness

Madness has always attracted attention as a dreadful affliction, defying medicine's powers, yet deeply fascinating, and associated, in the 'holy fool' or the *distrait* genius, with insight, creativity, and vision. Some have seen method in madness, or a higher reason exposing hypocrisy.

No consensus exists about the cause and cure of psychiatric disorder. Some even question its reality. The 'anti-psychiatrists' of the 1960s argued that mental illness was not a disease but a label pinned on deviants. Perhaps what is known as 'schizophrenia' is a rational way of coping with an irrational society.

Demonic possession

History reveals profound shifts in the theory of insanity. In ancient times, deranged behaviour was regarded as possession by demons. Greek heroes are driven to frenzy by the Furies. The idea of supernatural madness was reinforced by Christianity, spiritual disturbance being seen as a symptom of the war for the soul waged between God and Satan. Religious insanity could be holy, manifest in ecstasies and prophetic powers. But mostly it was evil, provoked by the Devil.

The idea of madness as demonic possession was challenged by the Scientific Revolution, which depicted the universe in regular and mechanical terms. Moreover, after the Thirty Years War and the English Civil War, opinion turned against the religious lunatic fringe. The ruling orders denied the 'revelations' of visionaries. Now the 'possessed' were judged simply crackbrained, and early Methodists diagnosed as victims of religious mania.

A bodily affliction

A new theory was advanced: lunacy as an organic disorder. Here doctors built upon Greek medicine, whose theory of humours presupposed regular, internal, physiological causes for disordered states. An excess of 'choler' (yellow bile), would cause mania, too much black bile or 'melancholy' would induce depression. Seventeenth-century physicians elaborated these ideas, but 'humoral' medicine itself came under fire from anatomists who, inspired by the new 'mechanical philosophy', saw the body as a machine, with psychiatric disorders attributable to the nerves.

Organic theorists saw themselves as humane: lunacy could no longer threaten the soul. Viewed as a bodily affliction, insanity was expected to yield to drugs and other physical treatments, such as blood-lettings, purges, shocks, and the like.

A psychological disorder

When these somatic initiatives failed, a new movement developed, arguing that madness was not, after all, an organic disorder but psychological, the product of bad habits or trauma; it required psychiatric treatments. Such views also had a history, for moralists and playwrights had long shown the inner conflicts of the passions, while John Locke (1632–1704) had explained madness as due to rampant imagination.

Around 1800, figures like Philippe Pinel (1745–1826) in France, Chiarugi in Italy, William (1732–1822) and Samuel (1784–1857) Tuke in England, and Reil in Germany were arguing that insanity could best be corrected by 'moral therapy', a psychotherapy stressing reason and humanity. The right place for this was the lunatic asylum – homely, secluded, tranquil.

Institutionalization

In earlier centuries madhouses were few, lunatics mostly being kept within the family or allowed to wander. Things changed after 1650, and irrational people were increasingly institutionalized. Especially after 1800, the numbers 'shut up' (in both senses) skyrocketed. In Britain, a mere 5,000 people were confined in asylums by 1800; this had leapt to 100,000 by 1900, and 150,000 by 1950. By then, approximately 500,000 people were certified insane in the USA.

The impetus for this massive sequestration came from well-meaning reformers. Progressive mental-health professionals argued that the insane should be managed via a comprehensive system of purpose-built, well-staffed institutions, where personal attention, occupational therapy, and a supportive environment would cure them.

It didn't work. The insane rarely recovered as predicted. Asylums slowly deteriorated, becoming the dustbins of the incurable. Pessimistic psychiatrists rationalized this by arguing that institutional care had brought to light thousands of hopeless degenerates previously hidden from view. But critics alleged that the madness in the asylums was largely due to institutionalization. Optimism faded, and fatalism infected mental health policy, until the 1950s, when the voices of the anti-psychiatrists chimed with civil rights movements.

The talking cure

In recent times, new hope has come from many quarters. Freud introduced the 'talking cure', the conviction that, through free associations of words and ideas, the causes of neuroses would surface. Freud was cautious and expected no miracle cures; few occurred. Yet his insights into unconscious processes have proved immensely fruitful, particularly in the fields of child and family therapy.

High-tech fixes

The twentieth century has also seen a succession of high-tech, quick-fix procedures. Insulin therapy had its hour, the theory being that the reduction of blood-sugar levels induced by insulin injections would produce convulsions and coma that would bring remission from serious syndromes. The 1930s saw the introduction of another 'panacea': electro-convulsive therapy (ECT). Slightly later, lobotomies and leucotomies were developed. Each produced certain improvements. But the trigger-happy attitudes of the promoters of 'desperate remedies', and the growing evidence of relapses and side-effects, undermined confidence.

For that reason, breakthroughs in psychopharmacology in the 1950s were rapturously received: psychiatry seemed to have found its penicillin. Neuroleptics like chlorpromazine and lithium (for manic-depressive conditions) had remarkable success in stabilizing behaviour, enabling patients to resume life in the outside world. Community care was much touted; but now its difficulties and drawbacks have become apparent.

Psychiatry remains a house divided against itself. For all the strides made in neurology, we still understand all too little about the true causes of mental illness.

Roy Porter

Mafia secret society reputed to control organized crime such as gambling, loansharking, drug traffic, prostitution, and protection; connected with the ◊Camorra of Naples. It originated in Sicily in the late Middle Ages and now operates chiefly there and in countries to which Italians have emigrated, such as the USA and Australia.

It began as a society that avenged wrongs against Sicilian peasants by means of terror and vendetta. In 19th-century Sicily the Mafia was employed by absentee landlords to manage their *latifundia* (landed estates), and through intimidation it soon became the unofficial ruling group. Despite the expropriation and division of the *latifundia* after World War II, the Mafia remains powerful in Sicily. The Italian government has waged periodic campaigns of suppression, notably 1927, when the Fascist leader Mussolini appointed Cesare Mori (1872–?) as prefect of Palermo. Mori's methods were, however, as suspect as those of the people he was arresting, and he was fired 1929. A further campaign was waged 1963–64.

The Mafia grew during Prohibition in the USA. Main centres are New York, Las Vegas, Miami, Atlantic City, and Chicago. Organization is in 'families', each with its own boss, or *capo*. A code of loyalty and secrecy, combined with intimidation of witnesses, makes it difficult to bring criminal charges against its members. However, Al Capone was sentenced for federal tax evasion and Lucky Luciano was deported. Recent cases of the US government versus the Mafia implicated Sicilian-based operators in the drug traffic that plagues much of the Western world (the 'pizza connection'). In 1992 John Gotti, reputedly head of the Gambino 'family' of the Mafia, was convicted.

The Mafia, also known in the USA as *La Cosa Nostra* ('our affair') or the Mob, features frequently in fiction; for example, in the *Godfather* films from 1972 based on a book by Mario Puzo.

Magendie François 1783–1855. French doctor. A pioneer of modern experimental physiology, Magendie helped to introduce into medicine the range of plant-derived compounds known as alkaloids as well as strychnine, morphine and codeine, and quinine. His numerous works include the *Elements of Physiology* 1816–17.

magi (singular *magus*) priests of the Zoroastrian religion of ancient Persia, noted for their knowledge of astrology. The term is used in the New Testament of the Latin Vulgate Bible where the Authorized Version gives 'wise men'. The magi who came to visit the infant Jesus with gifts of gold, frankincense, and myrrh (the *Adoration of the Magi*) were in later tradition described as 'the three kings' – Caspar, Melchior, and Balthazar.

magic art of controlling the forces of nature by supernatural means such as charms and ritual. The central ideas are that like produces like (*sympathetic magic*) and that influence carries by contagion or association; for example, by the former principle an enemy could be destroyed through an effigy, by the latter principle through personal items such as hair or nail clippings. See also ◊witchcraft.

It is now generally accepted that most early religious practices and much early art were rooted in beliefs in magical processes. There are similarities between magic and the use of symbolism in religious ritual. Under Christianity existing magical rites were either suppressed (although they survived in modified form in folk custom and superstition) or replaced by those of the church itself. Those still practising the ancient rites were persecuted as witches.

magic square in mathematics, a square array of different numbers in which the rows, columns, and diagonals add up to the same total. A simple example employing the numbers 1 to 9, with a total of 15, is:

6	7	2
1	5	9
8	3	4

Magna Carta in English history, the charter granted by King John 1215, traditionally seen as guaranteeing human rights against the excessive use of royal power. As a reply to the king's demands for excessive feudal dues and attacks on the privileges of the church, Archbishop Langton proposed to the barons the drawing-up of a binding document 1213. John was forced to accept this at Runnymede (now in Surrey) 15 June 1215.

Magna Carta begins by reaffirming the rights of the church. Certain clauses guard against infringements of feudal custom: for example, the king was prevented from making excessive demands for money from his barons without their consent. Others are designed to check extortions by officials or maladministration of justice: for example, no freeman to be arrested, imprisoned, or punished except by the judgement of his peers or the law of the land. The privileges of London and the cities were also guaranteed.

As feudalism declined Magna Carta lost its significance, and under the Tudors was almost forgotten. During the 17th century it was rediscovered and reinterpreted by the Parliamentary party as a democratic document. Four original copies exist, one each in Salisbury and Lincoln cathedrals and two in the British Library.

Magnificat in the New Testament, the song of praise sung by Mary, the mother of Jesus, on her visit to her cousin Elizabeth shortly after the Annunciation; it is used in the liturgy of some Christian churches.

Mahābhārata Sanskrit Hindu epic consisting of 18 books and 90,000 stanzas, probably composed in its present form about 300 BC. It forms with the *Rāmāyana* the two great epics of the Hindus. It contains the ◊*Bhagavad-Gītā*, or *Song of the Lord*, an episode in the sixth book.

The poem, set on the plain of the Upper Ganges, deals with the fortunes of the rival families of the Kauravas and the Pandavas and reveals the ethical values of ancient Indian society and individual responsibility in particular.

Mahādeva (Sanskrit 'great god') title given to the Hindu god ◊Siva.

Mahādevī (Sanskrit 'great goddess') title given to Sakti, the consort of the Hindu god Siva. She is worshipped in many forms, including her more active manifestations as Kali or Durga and her peaceful form as Parvati.

maharishi Hindu guru (teacher), or spiritual leader. The Maharishi Mahesh Yogi influenced the Beatles and other Westerners in the 1960s.

mahatma (Sanskrit 'great soul') title conferred on Mohandas ◊Gandhi by his followers as the first great national Indian leader.

Mahavira c. 599–527 BC. Indian sage, from whose teachings the Jain faith arose. At the age of 30 he turned from a life of comfort to asceticism which he practised for 12 years. At the end of this time he began to bring together a group of followers who were to be the bridge-builders who would pass on right knowledge and right conduct to others.

A contemporary of the ◊Buddha, Mahavira lived in N India and is believed by the Jains to be the 24th *tirthankara* or bridge-builder. The *tirthankaras* come to each era of time and preach the way to right knowledge and right conduct. After 30 years of building his community, he died in the town of Pava.

Mahāyāna one of the two major forms of ◊Buddhism, common in N Asia (China, Korea, Japan, and Tibet). Veneration of ◊bodhisattvas (those who achieve enlightenment but remain on the human plane in order to help other living beings) is a fundamental belief in Mahāyāna, as is the idea that everyone has within them the seeds of Buddhahood.

A synthesis of Mahāyāna doctrines is found in the Sūtra of the Golden Light, stressing that people should obey reason (prajñā), which enables them to tell right from wrong; an act of self-sacrifice is the highest triumph of reason. The Lotus Sūtra describes the historical Buddha as only one manifestation of the eternal Buddha, the ultimate law (dharma) of the cosmos and the omnipresent and compassionate saviour.

Mahdi in Islam, the title of a coming messiah who will establish a reign of justice on Earth. The title has been assumed by many Muslim leaders, notably the Sudanese sheik Muhammad Ahmed (1848–1885), who headed a revolt 1881 against Egypt and 1885 captured Khartoum.

His great-grandson *Sadiq el Mahdi* (1936–), leader of the Umma party in Sudan, was prime minister 1966–67. He was imprisoned 1969–74 for attempting to overthrow the military regime.

mahr the gift (dowry) of money or property from the bridegroom to the bride without which an Islamic marriage is not valid. Normally the amount of the mahr is a part of the marriage contract. It becomes payable when the bride demands it. Part of it may be 'deferred', payable in the event of widowhood or divorce.

Maimonides Moses (Moses Ben Maimon) 1135–1204. Spanish-born Jewish philosopher and physician. Known as one of the greatest Hebrew scholars, he attempted to reconcile faith and reason. His codification of Jewish law is known as the *Mishneh Torah/Torah Reviewed* 1180; he also formulated the *Thirteen Principles*, which summarize the basic beliefs of Judaism.

Maimonides was born in Córdoba, Spain; he left Spain 1160 to escape the persecution of the Jews and settled in Fez, and later in Cairo, where he was personal physician to Sultan Saladin. His philosophical classic *More nevukhim/The Guide to the Perplexed* 1176–91 helped to introduce Aristotelian thought into medieval philosophy. He also wrote ten books on medicine.

Maine de Biran Marie-François-Pierre 1766–1824. French thinker and politician who speculated that the self is an active power developed through experience. He developed a philosophy in which the will was the source of human freedom. He was councillor of state 1816.

Maine de Biran was a member and treasurer of the chamber of deputies (national assembly) 1814. His main works include *L'Influence d'habitude/The Influence of Habit* 1802 and *Essai sur les fondements de la psychologie/Essay on the Foundations of Psychology* 1812.

Maitreya the Buddha to come, 'the kindly one', a principal figure in all forms of ◊Buddhism; he is known as *Mi-lo-fo* in China and *Miroku* in Japan. Buddhists believe that a Buddha appears from time to time to maintain knowledge of the true path; Maitreya is the next future Buddha.

Makarenko Anton Semyonovitch 1888–1939. Russian educationist. In his work with homeless orphans and delinquents, after the Russian Revolution, he encouraged children to take responsibility not just for themselves but, more importantly, for the good of the community as a whole. His ideas have been criticized for being implicitly totalitarian.

Malcolm X adopted name of Malcolm Little 1926–1965. US black nationalist leader. While serving a prison sentence for burglary 1946–53, he joined the ◊Black Muslims sect. On his release he campaigned for black separatism, condoning violence in self-defence, but 1964 modified his views to found the Islamic, socialist Organization of Afro-American Unity, preaching racial solidarity. He was assassinated.

If someone puts his hand on you, send him to the cemetery.

Malcolm X. *Adopted name of*
Malcolm Little
Malcolm X Speaks

He was born in Omaha, Nebraska, but grew up in foster homes in Michigan, Massachusetts, and New York. Convicted of robbery 1946, he spent seven years in prison, becoming a follower of Black Muslim leader Elijah Muhammad and converting to Islam. In 1952 he officially changed his name to Malcolm X to signify his rootlessness in a racist society. Having become an influential national and international leader, Malcolm X publicly broke with the Black Muslims 1964. A year later he was assassinated by Black Muslim opponents while addressing a rally in Harlem, New York City. His *Autobiography of Malcolm X* was published 1964.

Malebranche Nicolas 1638–1715. French philosopher. His *De la Recherche de la vérité/Search after Truth* 1674–78 was inspired by René ◊Descartes; he maintained that exact ideas of external objects are obtainable only through God.

Malik Abu Abdallah Malik ibn Anas 716–795 AD. Founder of the Maliki school of Sunni Islamic law, which dominates in N Africa. His main work was *Muwatta/The Simplified*, a book about Islamic law which was intended to be a bridge between the complexity of scholars and the simplicity of ordinary people, giving a guide for Muslims to follow.

He was born in Medina; his first teacher was Sahl ibn Sa'd, a companion of the prophet Muhammad. He was a close acquaintance of the jurist Abu Hanifa. His main pupil was Al-Shafi'i.

Malinowski Bronislaw 1884–1942. Polish-born British anthropologist, one of the founders of the theory of ◊functionalism in the social sciences. In two expeditions to the Trobriand Islands, 1915–16 and 1917–18, his detailed studies of the islanders led him to see customs and practices in terms of their function in creating and maintaining social order.

His ◊fieldwork involved a revolutionary system of 'participant observation' whereby the researcher became completely involved in the life of the people studied. He wrote several influential monographs on the islanders, including *Argonauts of the Pacific*.

Malthus Thomas Robert 1766–1834. English economist and cleric. His *Essay on the Principle of Population* 1798 (revised 1803) argued for population control, since populations increase in geometric ratio and food supply only in arithmetic ratio, and influenced Charles ◊Darwin's thinking on natural selection as the driving force of evolution.

Malthus saw war, famine, and disease as necessary checks on population growth. Later editions of his work suggested that 'moral restraint' (delaying marriage, with sexual abstinence before it) could also keep numbers from increasing too quickly, a statement seized on by later birth-control pioneers (the 'neo-Malthusians').

Malthus theory projection of population growth made by Thomas Malthus. He based his theory on the ◊population explosion that was already becoming evident in the 18th century, and argued that the number of people would increase faster than the food supply. Population would eventually reach a resource limit (◊overpopulation). Any further increase would result in a population crash, caused by famine, disease, or war.

Malthus was not optimistic about the outcome and suggested that only 'moral restraint' (birth control) could prevent crisis. Recent famines in Ethiopia and other countries, where drought, civil war, and poverty have reduced agricultural output, might suggest that Malthus was correct. In the USA, the UK, and many other countries, the agricultural revolution boosted food production, and contraception led to a decline in ◊birth rate; and in some countries ◊population control policies have been introduced.

Better authentic mammon than a bogus god.

mammon
Louis MacNeice, 1907–1963, Irish-born British poet.
Autumn Journal

Mammon evil personification of wealth and greed; originally a Syrian god of riches, cited in the New Testament as opposed to the Christian god.

management process or technique of managing a business. Systems vary according to the type of organization, company, and objectives.

Since the early 1970s, there has been a growing demand for learned management skills, such as those taught in the Harvard Business School, USA, and at the London Business School. By contrast, in Japan, such skills are learned on the job; employees tend to spend their careers with the same company and towards the end of them will acquire management status.

In Europe, there has been a trend toward management by consensus, rather than by the individual.

Mandaean member of the only surviving Gnostic group of Christianity (see ◊Gnosticism). The Mandaeans live near the Euphrates, S Iraq, and their sacred book is the *Ginza*. The group claims descent from John the Baptist, but its incorporation of Christian, Hebrew, and indigenous Persian traditions keeps its origins in dispute.

mandala symmetrical design in Hindu and Buddhist art, representing the universe; used in some forms of meditation.

Mandela Nelson (Rolihlahla) 1918– . South African politician and lawyer, president of the African National Congress (ANC) from 1991. As organizer of the then banned ANC, he was imprisoned 1964. In prison he became a symbol of unity for the worldwide anti-apartheid movement. In Feb 1990 he was released, the ban on the ANC having been lifted, and he entered into negotiations with the government about a multiracial future for South Africa. In Sept 1992, Mandela and President de Klerk agreed to hasten the creation of an interim government under which reforms could take place. In Feb 1993 they agreed to the formation of a government of national unity after free, nonracial elections in late 1993 or early 1994.

He was married to the South African civil-rights activist Winnie Mandela 1955–92.

Mandela was born near Umbata, in what is today Transkei, the son of a local chief. In a trial of several ANC leaders, he was acquitted of treason 1961, but was once more arrested 1964 and given a life sentence on charges of sabotage and plotting to overthrow the government. In July 1991 he was elected, unopposed, to the presidency of the ANC. In 1993, jointly with F W de Klerk, he won the Nobel Peace Prize.

Mandelbrot Benoit B 1924– . Polish-born US scientist who coined the term *fractal geometry* to describe 'self-similar' shape, a motif that repeats indefinitely, each time smaller. The concept is associated with ◊chaos theory.

Manes in ancient Rome, the spirits of the dead, worshipped as divine and sometimes identified with the gods of the underworld (Dis and Proserpine).

manic depression or *manic depressive* ◊*psychosis* mental disorder that can take several forms. There may be recurring episodes of varying degrees of severity of ◊depression or of mania, for example, inappropriate elation, agitation, and rapid thought and speech. Chronic mania may sometimes continue for years without interruption. Some manic depressive patients have only manic attacks, others only depressive, and in others the alternating or circular form exists.

Manichaeism religion founded by the prophet Mani (Latinized as Manichaeus, c. 216–276). Despite persecution Manichaeism spread and flourished until about the 10th century. Based on the concept of dualism, it held that the material world is evil, an invasion of the spiritual realm of light by the powers of darkness; particles of divine light imprisoned in evil matter were to be rescued by messengers such as Jesus, and finally by Mani himself.

Mani proclaimed his creed in 241 at the Persian court. Returning from missions to China and India, he was put to death at the instigation of the Zoroastrian priesthood.

manifesto published prospectus of a political party, setting out the policies that the party will pursue if elected to govern. When elected to power a party will often claim that the contents of its manifesto constitute a mandate to introduce legislation to bring these policies into effect. The term has also been used for documents setting out the aims and aspirations of artistic movements, such as ◊Surrealism.

manna sweetish exudation obtained from many trees such as the ash and larch, and used in medicine. The manna of the Bible is thought to have been from the tamarisk tree, or a form of lichen. The Bible (Exodus 16) relates how God provided manna for the Israelites in the desert when there was no other food.

Mannerism in painting, sculpture, and architecture, a style characterized by a subtle but conscious breaking of the 'rules' of classical composition – for example, displaying the human body in an off-centre, distorted pose, and using harsh, non-blending colours. The term was coined by Giorgio ◊Vasari and used to describe the 16th-century reaction to the peak of Renaissance Classicism. Strictly speaking, it refers to a style developed by painters and architects working in Italy (primarily Rome and Florence) during the years 1520 to 1575, beginning with, and largely derived from, the later works of Michelangelo in painting and architecture. It includes the works of the painters Giovanni Rosso and Parmigianino and the architect Giulio Romano.

In both painting and architecture, Mannerist works have the effect of unsettling the viewer, who is expected to understand the norms that the painting or building is deliberately violating. The term has been extended to cover similar styles in other arts and in other countries, for example, the works of the Italian sculptor Giambologna and the Spanish painter El Greco.

Mannheim Karl 1893–1947. Hungarian sociologist who settled in the UK 1933. In *Ideology and Utopia* 1929 he argued that all knowledge, except in mathematics and physics, is ideological, a reflection of class interests and values;

that there is therefore no such thing as objective knowledge or absolute truth.

Mannheim distinguished between ruling class ideologies and those of utopian or revolutionary groups, arguing that knowledge is thus created by a continual power struggle between rival groups and ideas. Later works such as *Man and Society* 1940 analysed contemporary mass society in terms of its fragmentation and susceptibility to extremist ideas and totalitarian governments.

Manning Henry Edward 1808–1892. English Catholic priest, one of the leaders of the ◊Oxford Movement. In 1851 he was converted from the Church of England to Roman Catholicism, and in 1865 became archbishop of Westminster (head of the English Catholic Church). He was created a cardinal 1875.

Manning left the Colonial Office for the Church of England, becoming archdeacon of Chichester 1840. Following his conversion to Catholicism he founded in 1857 the congregation of the Oblates of St Charles Borromeo, dedicated to social reform and Catholic education. In 1875 he held an ardent dispute (*The Vatican Decrees*) with Gladstone on the question of papal infallibility.

mantra in Hindu or Buddhist belief, a word repeatedly intoned to assist concentration and develop spiritual power; for example, *om*, which represents the names of Brahma, Vishnu, and Siva. Followers of a guru may receive their own individual mantra.

Manu in Hindu mythology, the founder of the human race, who was saved by ◊Brahma from a deluge.

manufacturing base share of the total output in a country's economy contributed by the manufacturing sector. This sector has greater potential for productivity growth than the service sector, which is labour-intensive; in manufacturing, productivity can be increased by replacing workers with technically advanced capital equipment. It is also significant because of its contribution to exports.

In the UK there was an absolute decline in manufacturing output 1979–82. In 1980 output returned to its 1979 level, though still below its 1973 level. (Other Western countries and Japan enjoyed an average growth of manufacturing output 1973–86 of 2.3%.) The UK had its first-ever deficit in the balance of manufacturing trade 1983; the deficit has tended to widen since then. Yet the manufacturing sector accounted for about 60% of exports 1988. Free-market economists (adherents of ◊monetarism) argue that the decline in manufacturing reflects market conditions and that attempts by government to intervene would be inefficient. Others argue for an industrial strategy to promote an internationally more competitive manufacturing industry, including increased funding for relevant training and research and development.

Maoism form of communism based on the ideas and teachings of the Chinese communist leader ◊Mao Zedong. It involves an adaptation of ◊Marxism to suit conditions in China and apportions a much greater role to agriculture and the peasantry in the building of socialism, thus effectively bypassing the capitalist (industrial) stage envisaged by Marx.

Maori religion the religion of the original inhabitants of New Zealand, having the god Io at its peak, who acts through an array of gods, spirits and ancestors, for example Rangi the sky god and Papa-tua-Kuku the earth mother who gave birth to all creation, and the gods who look after creation. The religious functionaries are called *tohungas*; they keep the balance between the different realms of the gods, the ancestors, guardians, and ghosts as well as the monsters. The world of the dead is seen as the most dangerous because its overlaps with this world. It is filled with *mana* – a sort of dynamic holy power – which can spill over into this world causing great troubles, or conversely endowing great powers. The world of nature is imbued with great power and sanctity and it is essential for human wellbeing that the land is content and cared for. Many Maoris are now Christians who try to draw in elements of their traditional culture. In recent years there has been a return to more traditional Maori beliefs and practices in order to stress distinct Maori identity.

Letting a hundred flowers blossom and a hundred schools of thought contend is the policy for promoting progress in the arts and the sciences and a flourishing socialist culture in our land.

Mao Zedong or Mao Tse-tung
Speech in Peking 27 Feb 1957

Mao Zedong or *Mao Tse-tung* 1893–1976. Chinese political leader and Marxist theoretician. A founder of the Chinese Communist Party (CCP) 1921, Mao soon emerged as its leader. He organized the Long March 1934–35 and the war of liberation 1937–49, following which he established a People's

Republic and communist rule in China; he headed the CCP and government until his death. His influence diminished with the failure of his 1958–60 ◊Great Leap Forward, but he emerged dominant again during the 1966–69 ◊Cultural Revolution. Mao adapted communism to Chinese conditions, as set out in the ◊*Little Red Book*.

Mao, son of a peasant farmer in Hunan province, was once library assistant at Beijing University and a headmaster in Changsha. He became chief of CCP propaganda under the Guomindang (nationalist) leader Sun Yat-sen (Sun Zhong Shan) until dismissed by Sun's successor Chiang Kai-shek (Jiang Jie Shi). In 1931–34 Mao set up a communist republic in Jiangxi and, together with Zhu De, marshalled the Red Army in the Long March to Shaanxi to evade Guomindang suppressive tactics. In Yan'an 1936–47, he built up a people's republic and married his third wife ◊Jiang Qing 1939. CCP head from 1935, Mao set up an alliance with the nationalist forces 1936–45 aimed at repelling the Japanese invaders. Civil war with the Guomindang was renewed from 1946 to 1949, when the Mao defeated them at Nanjing and established the People's Republic and CCP rule under his leadership. During the civil war, he successfully employed mobile, rural-based guerrilla tactics. Mao served as party head until his death Sept 1976 and as state president until 1959. After the damages of the Cultural Revolution, the Great Helmsman, as he was called, worked with his prime minister Zhou Enlai to oversee reconstruction.

Mao's writings and thoughts dominated the functioning of the People's Republic 1949–76. He wrote some 2,300 publications, comprising 3 million words; 740 million copies of his *Quotations* have been printed. Adapting communism to Chinese conditions, he stressed the need for rural rather than urban-based revolutions in Asia, for reducing rural–urban differences, and for perpetual revolution to prevent the emergence of new elites. Mao helped precipitate the Sino-Soviet split 1960 and was a firm advocate of a nonaligned Third World strategy. Since 1978, the leadership of Deng Xiaoping has reinterpreted Maoism and criticized its policy excesses, but many of Mao's ideas remain valued.

Mara in Buddhism, a supernatural being who attempted to distract the Buddha from the meditations that led to his enlightenment. In Hinduism, a goddess of death.

Marcus Aurelius Antoninus AD 121–180. Roman emperor from 161 and Stoic philosopher. He wrote the philosophical *Meditations*.

Born in Rome, he was adopted by his uncle, the emperor Antoninus Pius, whom he succeeded in 161. He conceded an equal share in the rule to Lucius Verus (died 169).

Let thy every action, word and thought be that of one who is prepared at any moment to quit this life
Marcus Aurelius Antoninus
Meditations

Marcus Aurelius spent much of his reign warring against the Germanic tribes and died in Pannonia, where he had gone to drive back the invading Marcomanni.

Men exist for the sake of one another. Either teach them or bear with them.
Marcus Aurelius Antonius
Meditations

Marcuse Herbert 1898–1979. German political philosopher, in the USA from 1934; his theories combining Marxism and Freudianism influenced radical thought in the 1960s. His books include *One-Dimensional Man* 1964.

Marcuse preached the overthrow of the existing social order by using the system's very tolerance to ensure its defeat; he was not an advocate of violent revolution. A refugee from Hitler's Germany, he became professor at the University of California at San Diego 1965.

Mardi Gras (French 'fat Tuesday' from the custom of using up all the fat in the household before the beginning of ◊Lent) Shrove Tuesday. A festival was traditionally held on this day in Paris, and there are carnivals in many parts of the world, including New Orleans, Louisiana; Italy; and Brazil.

marginal cost pricing in economics, the setting of a price based on the additional cost to a firm of producing one more unit of output (the marginal cost), rather than the actual average cost per unit (total production costs divided by the total number of units produced). In this way, the price of an item is kept to a minimum, reflecting only the extra cost of labour and materials.

Marginal cost pricing may be used by a company during a period of poor sales with the additional sales generated allowing it to remain operational without a reduction of the labour force.

marginal efficiency of capital in economics, effectively the rate of return on investment in a given business project compared with the rate of return if the capital were invested at prevailing interest rates.

marginal utility in economics, the measure of additional satisfaction (utility) gained by a consumer who receives one additional unit of a product or service. The concept is used to explain why consumers buy more of a product when the price falls.

An individual's demand for a product is determined by the marginal utility (and the point at which he has sufficient quantity). The greater the supply of the item available to him, the smaller the marginal utility. In total utility, supply is the main price determinant. The total utility of diamonds is low because their use is mainly decorative, but because of their rarity, the price is high, and the marginal utility is high. On the other hand, the total utility of bread is high because it is essential, but its marginal utility may be very low because it is plentiful, making it much cheaper than diamonds.

Mariotte Edme 1620–1684. French physicist and priest known for his recognition in 1676 of ◊Boyle's law about the inverse relationship of volume and pressure in gases, formulated by Irish physicist Robert Boyle 1672. He had earlier, in 1660, discovered the eye's blind spot.

Maritain Jacques 1882–1973. French Catholic philosopher. Originally a disciple of Henri ◊Bergson, he later became the best-known exponent of neo-Thomism, applying the methods of St Thomas ◊Aquinas to contemporary philosophical problems. He distinguished three contemporary types of knowledge – scientific, metaphysical, and mystical. His works include *Introduction à la Philosophie/Introduction to Philosophy* 1920.

Mark in Celtic legend, king of Cornwall, uncle of ◊Tristan, and suitor and husband of Isolde.

market any situation where buyers and sellers are in contact with each other. This could be a street market or it could be a world market where buyers and sellers communicate via letters, faxes, telephones, and representatives.

In a perfect or *free market*, there are many buyers and sellers, so that no single buyer or seller is able to influence the price of the product; there is therefore ◊perfect competition in the market. In an *imperfect market* either a few buyers or sellers (or even just one) dominate the market.

market economy free market economy where most resources are allocated through markets rather than through state planning.

market forces in economics, the forces of demand (a want backed by the ability to pay) and supply (the willingness and ability to supply).

Some economists argue that resources are allocated most efficiently when producers are able to respond to consumer demand without intervention from 'distortions' such as governments and trade unions, and that profits and competition between firms and individuals provide sufficient incentives to produce efficiently (◊monetarism). Critics of this view suggest that market forces alone may not be efficient because they fail to consider ◊social costs and benefits, and may also fail to provide for the needs of the less well off, since private firms aiming to make a profit respond to the ability to pay.

marketing promoting goods and services to consumers. In the 20th century, marketing has played an increasingly larger role in determining company policy, influencing product development, pricing, methods of distribution, advertising, and promotion techniques.

Marketing skills are beginning to appear on the curriculum of some schools and colleges.

market research process of gaining information about customers in a market through field research or desk research. *Field research* involves collecting *primary data* by interviewing customers or completing questionnaires. *Desk research* involves collecting *secondary data* by looking at information and statistics collected by others and published, for example, by the government.

Markov Andrei 1856–1922. Russian mathematician, formulator of the ◊Markov chain, an example of a stochastic (random) process.

Markov chain in statistics, an ordered sequence of discrete states (random variables) $x_1, x_2, ..., x_i, ..., x_n$ such that the probability of x_i depends only on n and/or the state x_{i-1} which has preceded it. If independent of n, the chain is said to be homogeneous.

Mark, St 1st century AD. In the New Testament, Christian apostle and evangelist whose name is given to the second Gospel. It was probably written AD 65–70, and used by the authors of the first and third Gospels. Feast day 25 April.

His first name was John, and his mother, Mary, was one of the first Christians in Jerusalem. He was a cousin of Barnabas, and accompanied Barnabas and Paul on their first missionary journey. He was a fellow worker with Paul in Rome, and later became Peter's interpreter after Paul's death. According to tradition he was the founder of the Christian church in Alexandria, and St Jerome says that he died and was buried there. He is the patron saint of Venice, and his emblem is a winged lion.

Maronite member of a Christian group deriving from refugee Monothelites (Christian heretics) of the 7th century. They were subsequently united with the Roman Catholic Church and number about 400,000 in Lebanon and Syria, with an equal number scattered in southern Europe and the Americas.

Marr David Courtenay 1945–1980. English psychologist known for his development of computer-based models of the visual system. From 1975 he worked at the artificial intelligence laboratory of the Massachusetts Institute of Technology (MIT). Drawing on current findings in neurophysiology and the psychology of vision, he applied his models to a number of issues, notably the problem of how objects in the perceptual field are represented within the brain. His findings are summarized in *Vision* 1982, published posthumously.

Marr first became aware of the potential benefits of ◊computer simulation of brain function while a senior research fellow at Kings' College, Cambridge, and following his move to MIT, devoted the remaining years of his life to work in this field. He was a leukaemia sufferer.

Marrano term of abuse applied to Spanish or Portuguese Jews who, during the 14th and 15th centuries, converted to Christianity to escape death or persecution at the hands of the ◊Inquisition. Many continued to adhere secretly to Judaism and carry out Jewish rites. During the Spanish Inquisition thousands were burned at the stake as heretics.

marriage legally or culturally sanctioned union of one man and one woman (monogamy); one man and two or more women (polygamy); one woman and two or more men (polyandry). The basis of marriage varies considerably in different societies (romantic love in the West; arranged marriages in some other societies), but most marriage ceremonies, contracts, or customs involve a set of rights and duties, such as care and protection, and there is generally an expectation that children will be born of the union to continue the family line and maintain the family property.

In different cultures and communities there are various conventions and laws that limit the choice of a marriage partner. *Restrictive factors* include: age limits, below which no marriage is valid; degrees of consanguinity or other special relationships within which marriage is either forbidden or enjoined; economic factors such as ability to pay a dowry; rank, caste, or religious differences or expectations; medical requirements, such as the blood tests of some US states; the necessity of obtaining parental, family, or community consent; the negotiations of a marriage broker in some cultures, as in Japan or formerly among Jewish communities; colour – for example, marriage was illegal until 1985 between 'European' and 'non-European' people in South Africa, until 1967 between white and black people in some southern US states and between white and Asian people in some western US states.

I have never understood this liking for war. It panders to instincts already catered for within the scope of any respectable domestic establishment.
marriage
Alan Bennett, 1934– , English dramatist, screenwriter, and actor.
Forty Years On I

rights In Western cultures, social trends have led to increased legal equality for women within marriage: in England married women were not allowed to hold property in their own name until 1882; in California community property laws entail the equal division of all assets between the partners on divorce. Other legal changes have made ◊divorce easier, notably in the USA and increasingly in the UK, so that remarriage is more and more frequent for both sexes within the lifetime of the original partner.

law In most European countries and in the USA civil registration of marriage, as well as (or instead of) a religious ceremony, is obligatory. Common-law marriages (that is, cohabitation as man and wife without a legal ceremony) are recognized (for inheritance purposes) in, for example, Scotland and some states of the USA. As a step to international agreement on marriage law the United Nations in 1962 adopted a convention on consent to marriage, minimum age for marriage, and registration.

In England marriages can be effected according to the rites of the Church of England or those of other faiths, or in a superintendent registrar's office.

I married beneath me, all women do.
marriage
Nancy Astor, 1879–1964, American-born British politician.
Dictionary of National Biography 1961–1970

Marshall Alfred 1842–1924. English economist, professor of economics at Cambridge University 1885–1908. A pioneer of ◊neoclassical economics, Marshall derived the relationship between demand for a product and its price from the concept of marginal utility, the extra satisfaction gained by a consumer from an additional purchase. Marshall suggested that a consumer will stop increasing consumption of a product when the price he or she has to pay is greater than the marginal utility derived from it. Since marginal utility declines as more is consumed, the demand for a product falls as price rises. From this a graph of the ◊demand curve could be drawn, showing how quantity demanded varies with price. The term ◊elasticity was used by Marshall to denote the response of demand to changes in price. On the supply side, higher prices are needed to persuade firms to increase output. The market price is determined where the demand curve and ◊supply curve intersect. Marshall therefore stressed the importance of supply and demand for the determination of prices in markets.

Marshall also emphasised the importance of time in determining the responsiveness of supply to demand. He identified three distinct time periods: the market period, in which all supply is fixed; the short period, in which supply can only be increased within the current capacity, and the long period, in which capacity (i.e. land, buildings and machinery) can be increased. His major published works include *Principles of Economics* 1890 and *Industry and Trade* 1919.

Marshall Plan programme of US economic aid to Europe, set up at the end of World War II, totalling $13,000 billion 1948–52. Officially known as the European Recovery Programme, it was announced by Secretary of State George C Marshall in a speech at Harvard June 1947, but it was in fact the work of a State Department group led by Dean Acheson. The perceived danger of communist takeover in postwar Europe was the main reason for the aid effort.

Martineau Harriet 1802–1876. English journalist, economist, and novelist who wrote popular works on economics, children's stories, and articles in favour of the abolition of slavery.

Martin, St 316–400. Bishop of Tours, France, from about 371, and founder of the first monastery in Gaul. He is usually represented as tearing his cloak to share it with a beggar. His feast day is Martinmas, 11 Nov.

Born in Pannonia, SE Europe, a soldier by profession, Martin was converted to Christianity, left the army, and lived for ten years as a recluse. After being elected bishop of Tours, he worked for the extinction of idolatry and the extension of monasticism in France.

martyr one who voluntarily suffers death for refusing to renounce a religious faith. The first recorded Christian martyr was St Stephen, who was killed in Jerusalem shortly after the apostles began to preach.

Marx Karl (Heinrich) 1818–1883. German philosopher, economist, and social theorist whose account of change through conflict is known as historical, or dialectical, materialism (see ◊Marxism). His *Das Kapital/Capital* 1867–95 is the fundamental text of Marxist economics, and his systematic theses on class struggle, history, and the importance of economic factors in politics have exercised an enormous influence on later thinkers and political activists.

Marx was born in Trier, the son of a lawyer, and studied law and philosophy at Bonn and Berlin. During 1842–43, he edited the *Rheinische Zeitung/Rhineland Newspaper* until its suppression. In 1844 he began his life-long collaboration with Friedrich ◊Engels, with whom he developed the Marxist philosophy, first formulated in their joint works, *Die heilige Familie/The Holy Family* 1844 and *Die deutsche Ideologie/ German Ideology* 1846 (which contains the theory demonstrating the material basis of all human activity: 'Life is not determined by consciousness, but consciousness by life'), and Marx's *Misère de la philosophie/ Poverty of Philosophy* 1847. Both joined the Communist League, a German refugee organization, and in 1847–48 they prepared its programme, *The Communist Manifesto*. During the 1848 revolution Marx edited the *Neue Rheinische Zeitung/New Rhineland Newspaper*, until he was expelled from Prussia 1849.

He then settled in London, where he wrote *Die Klassenkämpfe in Frankreich/Class Struggles in France* 1849, *Die Achtzehnte Brumaire des*

> *Religion is the sigh of the oppressed creature, the sentiment of the heartless world, and the soul of soulless conditions. It is the opium of the people.*
>
> **Karl Marx**
> *Marx in his own Words* Ernst Fischer

Louis Bonaparte/The 18th Brumaire of Louis Bonaparte 1852, *Zur Kritik der politischen ökonomie/Critique of Political Economy* 1859, and his monumental work *Das Kapital/ Capital*. In 1864 the International Working Men's Association was formed, whose policy Marx, as a member of the general council, largely controlled. Although he showed extraordinary tact in holding together its diverse elements, it collapsed 1872 due to Marx's disputes with the anarchists, including the Russian ◊Bakunin. The second and third volumes of *Das Kapital* were edited from his notes by Engels and published posthumously. Marx's philosophical work owes much to the writings of ◊Hegel, though he rejected Hegel's idealism.

Marxism philosophical system, developed by the 19th-century German social theorists ◊Marx and ◊Engels, also known as *dialectical materialism*, under which matter gives rise to mind (materialism) and all is subject to change (from dialectic; see ◊Hegel). As applied to history, it supposes that the succession of feudalism, capitalism, socialism, and finally the classless society is inevitable. The stubborn resistance of any existing system to change necessitates its complete overthrow in the *class struggle* – in the case of capitalism, by the proletariat – rather than gradual modification.

Social and political institutions progressively change their nature as economic developments transform material conditions. The orthodox belief is that each successive form is 'higher' than the last; perfect socialism is seen as the ultimate rational system, and it is alleged that the state would then wither away. Marxism has proved one of the most powerful and debated theories in modern history, inspiring both dedicated exponents (Lenin, Trotsky, Stalin, Mao) and bitter opponents. It is the basis of ◊communism.

Marxism–Leninism term used by ◊Stalin and his supporters to define their own views as the orthodox position of ◊Marxism as a means of refuting criticism. It has subsequently been employed by other communist parties as a yardstick for ideological purity.

Marxist aesthetic theory the thought relating to the arts in Marxist countries. Early Marxists saw art as a means of communicating socialist ideals to the masses, covering subjects relevant to their everyday lives ('proletarian art'). In the Soviet Union, ◊Socialist Realism became dominant 1932, ousting Formalism, which emphasized form over content. Modernism, with its emphasis on abstraction and the individual artist's personal feelings, was dismissed as decadent by socialist critics such as Georg Lukacs.

The term also refers, albeit differently, to Marxist artists working in Western Europe. The ◊Frankfurt School championed Modernism and saw art as portraying reality only indirectly. Critics such as ◊Marcuse and Max Horkheimer (1895–1973) believed in the autonomy and creativity of art an antidote to repressive ideology. Walter ◊Benjamin was interested in the way that technological developments made art accessible to the masses, challenging the elitist nature of art. Other Western Marxist theorists include Lucien Goldmann (1913–1970) and Louis ◊Althusser.

Mary in the New Testament, the mother of Jesus through divine intervention (see ◊Annunciation), wife of ◊Joseph. The Roman Catholic Church maintains belief in her ◊Immaculate Conception and bodily assumption into heaven, and venerates her as a mediator. Feast day (the Assumption) 15 Aug.

Traditionally her parents were elderly and named Joachim and Anna. Mary (Hebrew *Miriam*) married Joseph and accompanied him to Bethlehem. Roman Catholic doctrine assumes that the brothers of Jesus were Joseph's sons by an earlier marriage, and that she remained a virgin. Pope Paul VI proclaimed her 'Mother of the Church' 1964.

Mary Magdalene, St 1st century AD. In the New Testament, the woman whom Jesus cured of possession by evil spirits, was present at the Crucifixion and burial, and was the first to meet the risen Jesus. She is often identified with the woman of St Luke's gospel who anointed Jesus' feet, and her symbol is a jar of ointment; feast day 22 July.

Maskelyne Nevil 1732–1811. English astronomer who accurately measured the distance from the Earth to the Sun by observing a transit of Venus across the Sun's face 1769. In 1774 he measured the mass of the Earth by noting the deflection of a plumb line near Mount Schiehallion in Scotland.

He was the fifth Astronomer Royal 1765–1811. He began publication 1766 of the *Nautical Almanac*, containing tables for navigators.

masochism desire to subject oneself to physical or mental pain, humiliation, or punishment, for erotic pleasure, to alleviate guilt, or out of destructive impulses turned inwards. The term is derived from Leopold von ◊Sacher-Masoch.

mass in physics, the quantity of matter in a body as measured by its inertia. Mass determines the acceleration produced in a body by a given force acting on it, the acceleration being inversely proportional to the mass of the body. The mass also determines the force exerted on a body by ◊gravity on Earth, although this attraction varies slightly from place to place. In the SI system, the base unit of mass is the kilogram.

At a given place, equal masses experience equal gravitational forces, which are known as the weights of the bodies. Masses may, therefore, be compared by comparing the weights of bodies at the same place. The standard unit of mass to which all other masses are compared is a platinum-iridium cylinder of 1 kg, which is kept at the International Bureau of Weights and Measures in Sèvres, France.

Mass in Christianity, the celebration of the ◊Eucharist.

mass culture culture associated with products that are mass-produced to meet popular demand. Traditionally mass or popular culture has been deemed inferior to high culture but since the 1960s there has been a partial relaxing of these distinctions. 'Lowbrow' products, such as pop music and cinema, have been taken more seriously and 'highbrow' activities, such as opera and reading of novels, have attempted to become more accessible and less elitist.

mass observation study of the details of people's daily lives through observation and interview. A society of the name was founded in London 1937 for the purpose, employing a panel of observers and a number of trained investigators, and publishing the results.

materialism philosophical theory that there is nothing in existence over and above matter and matter in motion. Such a theory excludes the possibility of deities. It also sees mind as an attribute of the physical, denying idealist theories that see mind as something independent of body; for example, Descartes' theory of 'thinking substance'.

Like most other philosophical ideas, materialism probably arose among the early Greek thinkers. The stoics and the Epicureans were materialists, and so were the ancient Buddhists. Among later materialists have been Hobbes, Diderot, d'Holbach, Büchner, and Haeckel; Hume, J S Mill, Huxley, and Spencer showed materialist tendencies.

God has been replaced, as he has all over the West, with respectability and air conditioning.

materialism

(Imamu) Amiri Baraka. Born LeRoi Jones, 1934– , US poet, dramatist and black activist.
Midstream

---

mathematics science of spatial and numerical relationships. The main divisions of *pure mathematics* include geometry, arithmetic, algebra, calculus, and trigonometry. Mechanics, statistics, numerical analysis, computing, the mathematical theories of astronomy, electricity, optics, thermodynamics, and atomic studies come under the heading of *applied mathematics*.

early history Prehistoric human beings probably learned to count at least up to ten on their fingers. The Chinese, Hindus, Babylonians, and Egyptians all devised methods of counting and measuring that were of practical importance in their everyday lives. The first theoretical mathematician is held to be Thales of Melitus (c. 580 BC) who is believed to have proposed the first theorems in plane geometry. His disciple ◊Pythagoras established geometry as a recognized science among the Greeks. The later school of Alexandrian geometers (4th and 3rd centuries BC) included ◊Euclid and ◊Archimedes. Our present decimal numerals are based on a Hindu–Arabic system that reached Europe about AD 100 from Arab mathematicians of the Middle East such as ◊Khwārizmī.

Europe Western mathematics began to develop from the 15th century. Geometry was revitalized by the invention of coordinate geometry by René Descartes 1637; Blaise Pascal and Pierre de Fermat developed probability theory, John Napier invented logarithms, and Isaac Newton and Gottfried Leibniz developed calculus. In Russia, Nikolai Lobachevsky rejected Euclid's parallelism and developed non-Euclidean geometry, a more developed form of which (by Georg Riemann) was later utilized by Einstein in his relativity theory.

the present Higher mathematics has a powerful tool in the high-speed electronic computer, which can create and manipulate mathematical 'models' of various systems in science, technology, and commerce. Modern additions to school syllabuses such as sets, group theory, matrices, and graph theory are sometimes referred to as 'new' or 'modern' mathematics.

Mather Cotton 1663–1728. American theologian and writer. He was a Puritan minister in Boston, and wrote over 400 works of history, science, annals, and theology, including *Magnalia Christi Americana/The Great Works of Christ in America* 1702, a vast compendium of early New England history and experience. Mather appears to have supported the Salem witch-hunts.

matriarchy form of social organization in which women head the family, and descent and relationship are reckoned through the female line.

Matriarchy, often associated with polyandry (one wife with several husbands), occurs in certain parts of India, in the South Pacific, Central Africa, and among some North American Indian peoples. In *matrilineal* societies, powerful positions are usually held by men but acceded to through female kin.

matrix in mathematics, a square ($n \times n$) or rectangular ($m \times n$) array of elements (numbers or algebraic variables). They are a means of condensing information about mathematical systems and can be used for, among other things, solving simultaneous linear equations and transformations.

Much early matrix theory was developed by the British mathematician Arthur ◊Cayley, although the term was coined by his contemporary James Sylvester (1814–1897).

matter in physics, anything that has mass and can be detected and measured. All matter is made up of atoms, which in turn are made up of ◊elementary particles; it exists ordinarily as a solid, liquid, or gas. The history of science and philosophy is largely taken up with accounts of theories of matter, ranging from the hard 'atoms' of Democritus to the 'waves' of modern quantum theory.

Matthew, St 1st century AD. Christian apostle and evangelist, the traditional author of the first Gospel. He is usually identified with Levi, who was a tax collector in the service of Herod

Mathematics: chronology

c. 2500 BC The people of Mesopotamia (now Iraq) developed a positional numbering (place-value) system, in which the value of a digit depends on its position in a number.

c. 2000 BC Mesopotamian mathematicians solved quadratic equations (algebraic equations in which the highest power of a variable is 2).

876 BC A symbol for zero was used for the first time, in India.

c. 550 BC Greek mathematician Pythagoras formulated a theorem relating the lengths of the sides of a right-angled triangle. The theorem was already known by earlier mathematicians in China, Mesopotamia, and Egypt.

c. 450 BC Hipparcos of Metapontum discovered that some numbers are irrational (cannot be expressed as the ratio of two integers).

300 BC Euclid laid out the laws of geometry in his book *Elements*, which was to remain a standard text for 2,000 years.

c. 230 BC Eratosthenes developed a method for finding all prime numbers.

c. 100 BC Chinese mathematicians began using negative numbers.

c. 190 BC Chinese mathematicians used powers of 10 to express magnitudes.

c. AD 210 Diophantus of Alexandria wrote the first book on algebra.

c. 600 A decimal number system was developed in India.

829 Persian mathematician Muhammad ibn-Mūsā al-Khwārizmī published a work on algebra that made use of the decimal number system.

1202 Italian mathematician Leonardo Fibonacci studied the sequence of numbers (1, 1, 2, 3, 5, 8, 13, 21, ...) in which each number is the sum of the two preceding ones.

1550 In Germany, Rheticus published trigonometrical tables that simplified calculations involving triangles.

1614 Scottish mathematician John Napier invented logarithms, which enable lengthy calculations involving multiplication and division to be carried out by addition and subtraction.

1623 Wilhelm Schickard invented the mechanical calculating machine.

1637 French mathematician and philosopher René Descartes introduced coordinate geometry.

1654 In France, Blaise Pascal and Pierre de Fermat developed probability theory.

1666 Isaac Newton developed differential calculus, a method of calculating rates of change.

1675 German mathematician Gottfried Wilhelm Leibniz introduced the modern notation for integral calculus, a method of calculating volumes.

1679 Leibniz introduced binary arithmetic, in which only two symbols are used to represent all numbers.

1684 Leibniz published the first account of differential calculus.

1718 Jakob Bernoulli in Switzerland published his work on the calculus of variations (the study of functions that are close to their minimum or maximum values).

1746 In France, Jean le Rond d'Alembert developed the theory of complex numbers.

1747 D'Alembert used partial differential equations in mathematical physics.

1798 Norwegian mathematician Caspar Wessel introduced the vector representation of complex numbers.

1799 Karl Friedrich Gauss of Germany proved the fundamental theorem of algebra: the number of solutions of an algebraic equation is the same as the exponent of the highest term.

1810 In France, Jean Baptiste Joseph Fourier published his method of representing functions by a series of trigonometric functions.

1812 French mathematician Pierre Simon Laplace published the first complete account of probability theory.

1822 In the UK, Charles Babbage began construction of the first mechanical computer, the difference machine, a device for calculating logarithms and trigonometric functions.

1827 Gauss introduced differential geometry, in which small features of curves are described by analytical methods.

1829 In Russia, Nikolai Ivanovich Lobachevsky developed hyperbolic geometry, in which a plane is regarded as part of a hyperbolic surface, shaped like a saddle. In France, Evariste Galois introduced the theory of groups (collections whose members obey certain simple rules of addition and multiplication).

1844 French mathematician Joseph Liouville found the first transcendental number, which cannot be expressed as an algebraic equation with rational coefficients. In Germany, Hermann Grassmann studied vectors with more than three dimensions.

1854 George Boole in the UK published his system of symbolic logic, now called Boolean algebra.

1858 English mathematician Arthur Cayley developed calculations using ordered tables called matrices.

1865 August Ferdinand Möbius in Germany described how a strip of paper can have only one side and one edge.

1892 German mathematician Georg Cantor showed that there are different kinds of infinity and studied transfinite numbers.

1895 Jules Henri Poincaré published the first paper on topology, often called 'the geometry of rubber sheets'.

1931 In the USA, Austrian-born mathematician Kurt Gödel proved that any formal system strong enough to include the laws of arithmetic is either incomplete or inconsistent.

1937 English mathematician Alan Turing published the mathematical theory of computing.

1944 John Von Neumann and Oscar Morgenstern developed game theory in the USA.

1945 The first general purpose, fully electronic digital computer, ENIAC (electronic numerator, integrator, analyser, and computer), was built at the University of Pennsylvania, USA.

1961 Meteorologist Edward Lorenz at the Massachusetts Institute of Technology, USA, discovered a mathematical system with chaotic behaviour, leading to a new branch of mathematics – chaos theory.

1962 Benit Mandelbrot in the USA invented fractal images, using a computer that repeats the same mathematical pattern over and over again.

1975 US mathematician Mitchell Feigenbaum discovered a new fundamental constant (approximately 4.669201609103), which plays an important role in chaos theory.

1980 Mathematicians worldwide completed the classification of all finite and simple groups, a task that took over a hundred mathematicians more than 35 years to complete and whose results took up more than 14,000 pages in mathematical journals.

1989 A team of US computer mathematicians at Amdahl Corporation, California, discovered the highest known prime number (it contains 65,087 digits).

1993 Andrew Wiles proved Fermat's last theorem, one of the most baffling challenges of mathematics.

Antipas, and was called by Jesus to be a disciple as he sat by the Lake of Galilee receiving customs dues. His emblem is a man with wings; feast day 21 Sept.

Mauchly John William 1907–1980. US physicist and engineer who, in 1946, constructed the first general-purpose computer, the ENIAC, in collaboration with John Eckert. Their company was bought by Remington Rand 1950, and they built the UNIVAC 1 computer 1951 for the US census.

The idea for ENIAC grew out of work carried out by the two during World War II on ways of automating the calculation of artillery firing tables for the US Army.

Maundy Thursday in the Christian church, the Thursday before Easter. The ceremony of washing the feet of pilgrims on that day was instituted in commemoration of Jesus' washing of the apostles' feet and observed from the 4th century to 1754.

In Britain it was performed by the English sovereigns until the time of William III, and *Maundy money* is still presented by the sovereign to poor people each year.

Maurice (John) Frederick Denison 1805–1872. Anglican cleric from 1834, cofounder with Charles Kingsley of the Christian Socialist movement. He was deprived of his professorships in English history, literature, and divinity at King's College, London, because his *Theological Essays* 1853 attacked the doctrine of eternal punishment; he became professor of moral philosophy at Cambridge 1866.

Mauss Marcel 1872–1950. French sociologist and anthropologist. His initial studies concentrated on religion, especially the nature and function of sacrifice. His best-known work is *The Gift* 1954 in which he argues that the exchange of gifts creates a system of reciprocity which is fundamental to the ordering of society.

Maxwell James Clerk 1831–1879. Scottish physicist. His main achievement was in the understanding of electromagnetic waves: *Maxwell's equations* bring together electricity, magnetism, and light in one set of relations. He contributed to every branch of physical science – studying gases, optics, and the sensation of colour. His theoretical work in magnetism prepared the way for wireless telegraphy and telephony.

Born in Edinburgh, he was professor of natural philosophy at Aberdeen 1856–60, and then of physics and astronomy at London. In 1871, he became professor of experimental physics at Cambridge. His principal works include *Perception of Colour, Colour Blindness* 1860, *Theory of Heat* 1871, *Electricity and Magnetism* 1873, and *Matter and Motion* 1876.

maya (Sanskrit 'illusion') in Hindu philosophy, mainly in the *Vedānta*, the cosmos which Isvara, the personal expression of Brahman, or the ◊atman, has called into being. This is real, yet also an illusion, since its reality is not everlasting.

Mayan religion religion of the Maya people of Central America. The religion of pre-conquest Central America has survived in different ways. In some rural areas, it has continued almost unchanged, while in other areas there are heavy influences from Catholicism, which in its turn is influenced by Mayan traditions. In pre-conquest times, the main deities were the Earth Lord, who protected the crops, the Father Sun, the Mother Moon, and the Morning Star who was the warriors' god. Today the Mother Moon is often linked to the Virgin Mary but the Earth Lord is to be found worshipped as before, though local saints also have a role in crop protection. The Mayans believe that each person has an animal spirit which inhabits a creature born at the same time. Should the animal be killed, the person also dies. Like most Central American traditional religions, it is shamanistic in basis.

May Day first day of May. In many countries it is a national holiday in honour of labour.

Traditionally the first day of summer, in parts of England it is still celebrated as a pre-Christian magical rite; for example, the dance around the maypole (an ancient fertility symbol).

Mayer Julius Robert von 1814–1878. German physicist who in 1842 anticipated James ◊Joule in deriving the mechanical equivalent of heat, and Hermann von ◊Helmholtz in the principle of conservation of energy.

Maynard Smith John 1920– . British biologist. He applied game theory to animal behaviour and developed the concept of the ◊evolutionary stable strategy (ESS) as a mathematical technique for studying the evolution of behaviour.

His books include *The Theory of Evolution* 1958 and *Evolution and the Theory of Games* 1982.

McGregor Douglas 1906–1964. US social psychologist, famous for his motivational theory of work and management based on the concept of 'Theory X' and 'Theory Y' set out in his *The Human Side of Enterprise* 1960.

These two theories describe two different ways that managers view their workforces. Theory X managers assume that humans are naturally lazy, dislike work, and shun responsibility and so have to be coerced through a system of rewards, threats, and punishment to perform their allotted task. Theory Y, however, assumes that people want to work and take on responsibility, and indeed have an innate psychological need to do so. Work and responsibility provide not only financial but also emotional security and self-esteem, thereby satisfying many other higher-order needs than allowed by Theory X. Obviously each has implications for managerial practice across a broad spectrum of organizations.

Mead George Herbert 1863–1931. US philosopher and social psychologist who helped to found the philosophy of ◊pragmatism.

He taught at the University of Chicago during its prominence as a centre of social scientific development in the early 20th century, and is regarded as the founder of ◊symbolic interactionism. His work on group interaction had a major influence on sociology, stimulating the development of role theory, ◊phenomenology, and ◊ethnomethodology.

Human beings do not carry civilization in their genes.

Margaret Mead
New York Times Magazine April 1964

Mead Margaret 1901–1978. US anthropologist who popularized cultural relativity and challenged the conventions of Western society with *Coming of Age in Samoa* 1928 and subsequent works. Her fieldwork has later been criticized. She was a popular speaker on civil liberties, ecological sanity, feminism, and population control.

Meade James Edward 1907– . British Keynesian economist. He shared a Nobel prize in 1977 for his work on trade and capital movements, and published a four-volume *Principles of Political Economy* 1965–76.

mean in mathematics, a measure of the average of a number of terms or quantities. The simple *arithmetic mean* is the average value of the quantities, that is, the sum of the quantities divided by their number. The *weighted mean* takes into account the frequency of the terms that are summed; it is calculated by multiplying each term by the number of times it occurs, summing the results and dividing

this total by the total number of occurrences. The *geometric mean* of n quantities is the nth root of their product. In statistics, it is a measure of central tendency of a set of data.

meaning what is meant by words or things. In the philosophy of language, there are various theories about the meaning of words and sentences; for example, that a meaningful proposition must be possible to check (◊verifiability). When things (or life itself) have meaning, it is because we understand them ('Clouds mean rain') or they have significance ('This ring means a lot to me').

Perhaps the most influential theory of meaning is German philosopher Ludwig ◊Wittgenstein's use theory, which states that the meaning of a word or expression is to be found in its use. For Wittgenstein, the meaning of a word or sentence is not subjective and private but public, because it requires social conventions for its use.

mean life in nuclear physics, the average lifetime of a nucleus of a radioactive isotope.

Mecca (Arabic *Makkah*) city in Saudi Arabia and, as birthplace of Muhammad, the holiest city of the Islamic world; population (1974) 367,000. In the centre of Mecca is the Great Mosque, in the courtyard of which is the ◊Ka'aba, the sacred shrine containing the black stone believed to have been given to Abraham by the angel Jibra'el (Gabriel).

It also contains the well Zam-Zam, associated by tradition with the biblical characters Hagar and Ishmael. Most pilgrims come via the port of Jiddah.

mechanics branch of physics dealing with the motions of bodies and the forces causing these motions, and also with the forces acting on bodies in equilibrium. It is usually divided into dynamics and statics.

Quantum mechanics is the system based on the ◊quantum theory that has superseded Newtonian mechanics in the interpretation of physical phenomena on the atomic scale.

mechanism in philosophy, a system of adapted parts working together, as in a machine. Mechanists hold that all natural phenomena admit of mechanical explanation, and that no reference to teleology (purpose or design) is necessary. In political philosophy, mechanists (like English thinkers Thomas Hobbes, John Locke, Jeremy Bentham, and J S Mill) see the state as more or less the sum of the individuals composing it, and not as an entity in its own right (which is ◊organicism).

mechanization the use of machines in place of manual labour or the use of animals. Until the 1700s there were few machines available to help people in the home, on the land, or in industry. There were no factories, only cottage industries, in which people carried out work, such as weaving, in their own homes for other people. The 1700s saw a long series of inventions, initially in the textile industry, that ushered in a machine age and brought about the ◊Industrial Revolution.

Among the first inventions in the textile industry were those made by John Kay (flying shuttle, 1773), James Hargreaves (spinning jenny, 1764), and Richard Arkwright (water frame, 1769). Arkwright pioneered the mechanized factory system by installing many of his spinning machines in one building and employing people to work them.

Medea in Greek legend, the sorceress daughter of the king of Colchis. When Jason reached Colchis, she fell in love with him, helped him acquire the Golden Fleece, and they fled together. When Jason later married Creusa, daughter of the king of Corinth, Medea killed his bride with the gift of a poisoned garment, and then killed her own two children by Jason.

mediation technical term in ◊Hegel's philosophy, and in Marxist philosophy influenced by Hegel, describing the way in which an entity is defined through its relations to other entities.

medical ethics moral guidelines for doctors. Traditionally these have been set out in the Hippocratic Oath (introduced by Greek physician ◊Hippocrates and including such injunctions as the command to preserve confidentiality, to help the sick to the best of one's ability, and to refuse fatal draughts), but in the late 20th century rapidly advancing technology has raised the question of how far medicine should intervene in natural processes.

Lack of resources also confronts doctors, particularly surgeons, with the question of which patients to select for treatment. The right to voluntary ◊euthanasia is another problem of medical ethics.

meditation act of spiritual contemplation, practised by members of many religions or as a secular exercise. It is a central practice in Buddhism, but there are established traditions of meditation in all the major religions. See also ◊transcendental meditation (TM).

medusa the free-swimming phase in the life cycle of a coelenterate, such as a jellyfish or coral. The other phase is the sedentary *polyp*.

megalithic religions the beliefs of those cultures which raised the megalithic monuments such as Stonehenge, the stone circles found across Ireland and Scotland, and the great sacred sites such as Avebury in England. Little is known about the religion of these people, though much is speculated about them. Probably the megalithic monuments were related to the movement of the Sun and acted as centres of calculation for the seasons of the year. There are approximately 50,000 megalithic monuments across Europe; they were clearly focal points for considerable numbers of communities and may have had a social as well as specifically religious function.

Meinecke Friedrich 1862–1954. German historian who endeavoured to combine intellectual and political history and produce a synthesis of cultural and political values. Meinecke worked in the Prussian State Archives for fourteen years before becoming a professional historian. His first important book was *Cosmopolitanism and the National State* 1908, an account of how the Enlightenment's ideals gave way to the nationalism of the Romantics.

His other major works include *Machiavellism* 1924, concerned with the ideas of statecraft and their development from the 15th century to the time of Frederick the Great, and *Historicism* 1936 which deals with the beginnings and development of historicism from ◊Vico onward. Meinecke's critical reaction and opposition to the Nazi state are explained in his book *The German Catastrophe* 1946.

Mein Kampf book dictated by Adolf ◊Hitler to Rudolf Hess 1923–24 during Hitler's jail sentence for his part in the abortive 1923 Munich beer-hall putsch. Part autobiography, part political philosophy, the book presents Hitler's ideas of German expansion, anticommunism, and anti-Semitism. It was published in two volumes, 1925 and 1927.

Meinong Alexius 1853–1920. Austrian philosopher who held that nonexistents – like the golden mountain, the round square, or dragons – have classifiable natures. He also distinguished many different types of existence, most notably subsistence, which he believed is the type of existence possessed by states of mind.

Meinong was professor of philosophy at Graz from 1889 until his death. His works include *über Annahmen/On Assumptions* 1902. His philosophical psychology influenced English philosophers Bertrand Russell and G E Moore.

Medical Ethics: The Crossroads Reached?

With advances in medical science, doctors often face agonizing moral decisions. Babies can now be kept alive with handicaps so severe that they would have died soon after birth a few years ago. What, for instance, should doctors do about a baby born with its brain outside its head? Many people would agree that it would be wrong to prolong the life of such a baby, but if a doctor lets the baby die, is this the same as killing it?

Similarly, some doctors have argued that nothing should be done to prolong the life of babies born with spina bifida, because such babies otherwise experience terrible suffering. (Adults with spina bifida often disagree, believing that their lives are worthwhile despite their suffering.) Yet the same doctors argue against infanticide for spina bifida babies, on the grounds that it would brutalize staff, traumatize parents, and reduce respect for human life.

Handicap and the quality of life

With less severe forms of handicap, the issue is even less clear. The quality of the lives of Down's syndrome children is usually not unbearably awful, and they can live enjoyable and serene lives. But what about a Down's Syndrome baby born with a life-threatening condition, such as a serious intestinal blockage? Some years ago, the parents of just such a child – baby Alexandra – wanted her to die, believing that nature had 'made its own arrangements to terminate a life which could not be fruitful'. The doctor would not operate without their consent. Eventually, the local social services department succeeded in persuading the courts to overturn the parents' decision.

A rather different judgement was given in the case of Dr Arthur, a senior consultant paediatrician in Derby. He was asked to examine a newly born Down's Syndrome baby, whose parents were very distressed. Dr Arthur noted: 'Parents do not wish it to survive. Nursing care only.' He prescribed a sedative to alleviate the baby's distress, as and when it arose. Three days later, the baby died of bronchopneumonia. Dr Arthur was charged with murder; but the prosecution's case fell apart when it emerged that a post-mortem examination had shown that the baby had potentially fatal heart, lung, and brain defects. Dr Arthur was then charged with attempted murder, but was acquitted. The judge observed that it was lawful to treat a baby with sedation and nursing care only, if certain criteria were met – that the child was rejected by its parents and was irreversibly disabled.

Dominant themes

There are, of course, many other issues in medical ethics, apart from whether severely handicapped babies should be allowed to die. Here, there is space to mention only the main themes.

1. *Respect for Life*: Since we generally accept that we may kill other people in war and in self-defence, is life absolutely sacred or not? Is it right to preserve life if the quality of that life is likely to be poor? Should doctors preserve life at all costs and by extraordinary means?

And if not, where should doctors draw the line? Is switching off a life-support machine the same as murder? In general, since we distinguish between an act and its omission, is there a difference between killing someone and letting someone die?

2. *Patient Autonomy*: This theme arises in a variety of medical contexts – such as medical confidentiality, voluntary euthanasia, or experimentation on humans. Since patients must give informed consent to an experimental procedure, how much information is the patient to be given, and how detailed should it be? The problem is particularly acute in the case of randomly controlled trials which require the patient's agreement to receiving at random alternative forms of treatment.

3. *Resource Allocation*: What are the ethical and rational principles of distribution for medical resources? Where expensive but life-saving treatments are available, how should they be rationed? When kidney dialysis machines were novel and scarce, some doctors treated patients on a 'first come, first served' basis, while others gave precedence to younger patients or those with dependents.

4. *Reproductive Technologies*: Should a doctor prescribe the Pill to a 12-year-old girl? Should post-coital 'contraceptives' – 'morning after' pills – be prescribed? Is abortion murder? If embryos resulting from in vitro fertilization are frozen in case the implanted embryo should miscarry, what is to be done with these embryos if both parents die, as happened in Australia in 1984? Should post-menopausal women have fertility treatment? Should surrogate mothers be permitted to rent their wombs to the highest bidder? If a surrogate mother changes her mind and decides to keep the baby, should she be entitled to do so? Should parents be able to choose the sex of their babies? If homosexuality has a genetic basis, should parents be able to abort a fetus carrying 'gay genes'? As genetic engineering and screening become available, what sort of people should there be? As we enter the 21st century, this is perhaps the most challenging ethical issue of all.

Moral philosophy in medical ethics

Medical ethics has been described, rather unfairly, as an adventure playground for moral philosophers. To anyone unfamiliar with philosophy, the fact that different philosophers come to different conclusions about the same problems in medical ethics is frustrating. But, then, philosophers can often do little more than clarify the questions to be answered or considered by busy doctors who frequently have to make difficult decisions under stress.

Moreover, in society at large, no single moral outlook currently prevails on matters of birth, of death, of suffering, and of sexuality: there is moral pluralism, and a lack of moral consensus. However, by clarifying the issues, philosophers can help to build a consensus in medical ethics. Perhaps, though, such consensus is unlikely to emerge without consensus on not only an overall philosophy of medicine that clarifies what medicine is for, but also an overall moral philosophy that clarifies what human life is for and what its ends are.

P M Rowntree

Meitner Lise 1878–1968. Austrian physicist who worked with Otto ◊Hahn and was the first to realize that they had inadvertently achieved the fission of uranium. Driven from Nazi Germany because of her Jewish origin, she later worked in Sweden, where she published the results of their work. She refused to work on the atom bomb.

melancholia depressive disposition attributed to the influence of one of the ◊humours in pre-scientific thought; melancholia was thought to be particularly characteristic of writers and thinkers.

The psychological states associated with it were assembled and analysed by Robert ◊Burton in his *Anatomy of Melancholy* 1621.

Melanchthon Philip. Assumed name of Philip Schwarzerd 1497–1560. German theologian who helped Luther prepare a German translation of the New Testament. In 1521 he issued the first systematic formulation of Protestant theology, reiterated in the *Confession of ◊Augsburg* 1530.

Melanchthon, a humanist, was professor of Greek at Wittenberg from 1518; he adopted the name 'Melanchthon' as the Greek form of his family name, meaning 'black earth'. There he came under ◊Luther's influence, and became an evangelical theologian. He also translated and wrote commentaries on the Bible.

I have been here before, / But when or how I cannot tell: / I know the grass beyond the door, / The sweet keen smell, / The sighing sound, the lights around the shore.

memory
Dante Gabriel Rossetti, 1828–1882, English poet and painter.
'Sudden Light'

---

memory ability to store and recall observations and sensations. Memory does not seem to be based in any particular part of the brain; it may depend on changes to the pathways followed by nerve impulses as they move through the brain. Memory can be improved by regular use, the connections between nerve cells (neurons) becoming 'well-worn paths' in the brain. Events stored in *short-term memory* are forgotten quickly, whereas those in *long-term memory* can last for many years, enabling recall of information and recognition of people and places over long periods of time. Research is just beginning to uncover the biochemical and electrical bases of the human memory.

Mencius Latinized name of Mengzi c. 372–289 BC. Chinese philosopher and moralist, in the tradition of orthodox ◊Confucianism. Mencius considered human nature innately good, although this goodness required cultivation, and based his conception of morality on this conviction.

Born in Shantung (Shandong) province, he was founder of a Confucian school. After 20 years' unsuccessful search for a ruler to put into practice his enlightened political programme, based on people's innate goodness, he retired. His teachings are preserved as the *Book of Mengzi*.

Mendel Gregor Johann 1822–1884. Austrian biologist, founder of ◊genetics. His experiments with successive generations of peas gave the basis for his theory of particulate inheritance rather than blending, involving dominant and recessive characters; see ◊Mendelism. His results, published 1865–69, remained unrecognized until the early 20th century.

Mendel was abbot of the Augustinian abbey at Brünn (now Brno, Czech Republic) from 1868.

Mendeleyev Dmitri Ivanovich 1834–1907. Russian chemist who framed the periodic law in chemistry 1869, which states that the chemical properties of the elements depend on their relative atomic masses. This law is the basis of the periodic table of elements, in which the elements are arranged by atomic number and organized by their related groups.

For this work, Mendeleyev and Lothar Meyer (who presented a similar but independent classification of the elements) received the Davy medal in 1882. From his table Mendeleyev predicted the properties of elements then unknown (gallium, scandium, and germanium).

Mendelism in genetics, the theory of inheritance originally outlined by Austrian biologist Gregor Mendel. He suggested that, in sexually reproducing species, all characteristics are inherited through indivisible 'factors' (now identified with ◊genes) contributed by each parent to its offspring.

mendicant order religious order dependent on alms. In the Roman Catholic Church there are four orders of mendicant friars: Franciscans, Dominicans, Carmelites, and Augustinians. Buddhism has similar orders.

Menninger Karl Augustus 1893–1990. US psychiatrist, instrumental in reforming public mental-health facilities. With his father, prominent psychiatrist Charles Menninger, he founded the Menninger Clinic in Topeka 1920 and with his brother William (1900–1966), also a psychiatrist, established the Menninger Foundation 1941.

Born in Topeka, Kansas, USA, and educated at the University of Kansas, Menninger received his MD degree from Harvard University 1917. Among his influential books are *The Human Mind* 1930, *Man Against Himself*, and *The Vital Balance* 1963.

Mennonite member of a Protestant Christian group, originating as part of the ◊Anabaptist movement in Zürich, Switzerland, 1523. Members refuse to hold civil office or do military service, and reject infant baptism. They were named Mennonites after Menno Simons (1496–1559), leader of a group in Holland. Persecution drove other groups to Russia and North America.

When the Mennonites came under persecution, some settled in Germantown, Pennsylvania. The *Hutterian Brethren* (named after Jacob Hutter who died in 1536) hold substantially the same beliefs, and Hutterian principles are the basis of the *◊Brüderhof*. Of the 600,000 Mennonites in the world, some 250,000 are in the USA.

menorah seven-branched candlestick symbolizing Judaism and the state of Israel. Also, the candelabrum (having eight branches and a *shammes*, or extra candle with which to light the others) used on ◊Hanukkah.

Mensa International organization founded in the UK 1945 with membership limited to those passing an '◊intelligence' test. It has been criticized by many who believe that intelligence is not satisfactorily measured by IQ (intelligence quotient) tests alone. In recent years, Mensa has started to fund special schools and activities for high-IQ children in the UK.

Menshevik member of the minority of the Russian Social Democratic Party, who split from the ◊Bolsheviks 1903. The Mensheviks believed in a large, loosely organized party and that, before socialist revolution could occur in Russia, capitalist society had to develop further. During the Russian Revolution they had limited power and set up a government in Georgia, but were suppressed 1922.

mental handicap arrested or incomplete development of mental capacities. It can be very mild, but in more severe cases is associated with social problems and difficulties in living independently. A person may be born with a mental handicap (for example, Down's syndrome) or may acquire it through brain damage.

Clinically, mental handicap is graded as profound, severe, moderate, or mild, roughly according to ◊IQ and the sufferer's ability to cope with everyday tasks. Among its many causes are genetic defect (phenylketonuria), chromosomal errors (Down's syndrome), infection before birth (rubella) or in infancy (meningitis), trauma (brain damage at birth or later), respiratory arrest at the time of birth, toxins (lead poisoning), physical deprivation (lack of, or defective, thyroid tissue as in cretinism), and psychological deprivation (lack of stimulation due to social isolation).

Bibl. Tredgold, R F Wolff, H H (eds) *UCH Handbook of Psychiatry* (London, 1975)

mental health well-being and soundness of mind, not only in terms of intellectual abilities, but also in terms of the capability to deal with everyday problems, and the capacity to get on well with other people and to form and sustain relationships.

In ◊psychoanalysis, much prominence is given to the importance of the relationship between a child and its mother and, since the publication of John ◊Bowlby's *Maternal Care and Mental Health* 1951, a considerable body of research by psychologists and ethologists has confirmed that a warm, intimate, and continuous relationship is essential to a child's intellectual and social development and mental health. Separation from, or loss of, the mother, or surrogate mother, can retard the development of language and intellectual skills as well as severely disrupt a child's emotional life. In puberty and adolescence, the important developmental factor is membership of a peer group. Through peer-group relationships the young person establishes his, or her, ◊identity. When a crisis arises the mentally healthy person is normally able to cope. However, a crisis in the life of a person whose emotional and social development has been inadequate will bring distress and can often result in instability and mental illness.

Bibl. Bowlby, John *Child Care and the Growth of Love* (Harmondsworth, 1965)

mental illness abnormal working of the mind. Since normal working cannot easily be defined, the borderline between mild mental illness and normality is a matter of opinion (not to be confused with normative behaviour; see ◊norm), and so is usually defined in terms of impairment in individual function. Mild forms are known as *neuroses*, affecting the emotions, whereas more severe forms, *psychoses*, distort conscious reasoning.

mental test any of various standardized methods of assessing or measuring mental abilities and personality traits. Where selected for their reliability and validity, mental tests are indispensible aids in assessing educational attainment, in the clinical assessment of mental disorders and their treatment, and in careers guidance and job selection.

Of the various types of mental test, ◊intelligence tests are among the most widely used, though their reliability and validity have frequently been called into question. In education, tests of attainment have been used for many years to assess language development, reading, elementary mathematics, and other school subjects. There are also tests of aptitude and special abilities, as well as the numerous tests employed by the occupational psychologist whose concern is with personnel selection, performance appraisal, and job analysis. In psychology, personality tests have contributed significantly to the scientific study of ◊personality, as well as having important applications in clinical and occupational psychology.

Bibl. Kline, P *Handbook of Psychological Testing* (London, 1992)

Mephistopheles or *Mephisto* another name for the ◊devil, or an agent of the devil, associated with the ◊Faust legend.

mercantilism economic theory, held in the 16th–18th centuries, that a nation's wealth (in the form of bullion or treasure) was the key to its prosperity. To this end, foreign trade should be regulated to create a surplus of exports over imports, and the state should intervene where necessary (for example, subsidizing exports and taxing imports). The bullion theory of wealth was demolished by Adam ◊Smith in Book IV of *The Wealth of Nations* 1776.

Mercator Gerardus 1512–1594. Latinized form of the name of the Flemish map-maker Gerhard Kremer. He devised the first modern atlas, showing *Mercator's projection* in which the parallels and meridians on maps are drawn uniformly at 90°. It is often used for navigational charts, because compass courses can be drawn as straight lines, but the true area of countries is increasingly distorted the further north or south they are from the equator.

meritocracy system (of, for example, education or government) in which selection is by performance (in education, by competitive examinations), which therefore favours intelligence and ability rather than social position or wealth.

The result is the creation of an elite group. The term was coined by Michael Young in his *The Rise of the Meritocracy* 1958.

Merleau-Ponty Maurice 1908–1961. French philosopher, one of the most significant contributors to ◊phenomenology after Edmund ◊Husserl. He attempted to move beyond the notion of a pure experiencing consciousness, arguing in *The Phenomenology of Perception* 1945 that perception is intertwined with bodily awareness and with language. In his posthumously published work *The Visible and the Invisible* 1964, he argued that our experience is inherently ambiguous and elusive and that the traditional concepts of philosophy are therefore inadequate to grasp it.

Merlin legendary magician and counsellor to King ◊Arthur. Welsh bardic literature has a cycle of poems attributed to him, and he may have been a real person. He is said to have been buried in a cave in the park of Dynevor Castle, Dyfed.

Merton Louis Thomas 1915–1968. US Trappist Christian monk who felt that contemporary society was suffering an inward crisis and stood in need of contemplative reflection. His poetic and spiritual writings include an autobiography, *The Seven Storey Mountain* 1946. His writings were directed to those living a monastic life, but his influence is much wider.

Merton Robert King 1910– . US sociologist, who undertook exemplary studies of several topics, including ◊deviance and ◊anomie, role theory, the sociology of knowledge, and historical sociology. His *Science, Technology and Society in Seventeenth Century England* 1938 had a considerable influence on historians of science.

He continued Max ◊Weber's work on the link between Protestantism and capitalism by considering the enormous amount of scientific inquiry carried out during the 17th century in terms of social and cultural change. In *Social Theory and Social Structure* 1951 Merton accepted that the task of sociology is to discover 'systematic regularity' in social phenomena, but was doubtful about grand, all-inclusive theories. Instead he preferred 'middle-range theories', a few careful theories explaining a limited number of phenomena.

Educated at Harvard University, where he was a pupil of Talcott ◊Parsons, Merton taught at Columbia University, New York, where, from 1941, he co-directed the Bureau of Applied Social Research with the Viennese-born naturalized US sociologist, Paul F Lazarsfeld.

Merton thesis theory, suggested by the American sociologist Robert K ◊Merton, that the development of science has been strongly influenced by cultural, social, and economic forces – an extension of Max ◊Weber's idea of a strong link between Protestantism and the rise of capitalism.

In *Science, Technology and Society in Seventeenth Century England* 1938, Merton argued that, in an age when scientific enquiry was not regarded as an end in itself, particular requirements in the fields of mining, navigation, and the military were prioritized, and their achievement given a high level of recognition. Such endeavours could be justified in terms of Puritan values: it was work that benefited the well-being of others as well as revealing the hand of God in the workings of ◊Nature. Merton's research, which included the analysis of much biographical data, is seen as having initiated the sociology of science.

mesmerism former term for ◊hypnosis, after Franz Anton Mesmer.

Messiah in Judaism and Christianity, the saviour or deliverer. Jews from the time of the Old Testament exile in Babylon have looked forward to the coming of the Messiah. Christians believe that the Messiah came in the person of ◊Jesus, and hence called him the Christ.

Messier Charles 1730–1817. French astronomer who discovered 15 comets and in 1781 published a list of 103 star clusters and nebulae. Objects on this list are given M (for Messier) numbers, which astronomers still use today, such as M1 (the Crab nebula) and M31 (the Andromeda galaxy).

metalanguage any language which describes, in technical terms, the properties of another language. Thus linguistics is a scientific language about language.

metamorphosis in mythology, a transformation from one shape to another, animate or inanimate, almost inevitably through the intervention of a god. The Roman poet Ovid composed his *Metamorphoses* on this theme.

In classical mythology, metamorphosis often occurs as a result of an erotic intrigue; as the god may change shape to approach a lover (Zeus becomes a swan, a bull, or a shower of gold), so the object of desire may also be transformed (Daphne becomes a laurel tree in order to escape from Apollo). In many cultures, the symbolic or totemic association of animals with gods may be represented in mythical narratives as a form of metamorphosis.

metaphor figure of speech using an analogy or close comparison between two things that are not normally treated as if they had anything in common. Metaphor is a common means of extending the uses and references of words.

If we call people cabbages or foxes, we are indicating that in our opinion they share certain qualities with those vegetables or animals: an inert quality in the case of cabbages, a cunning quality in the case of foxes, which may lead on to calling people 'foxy' and saying 'He really foxed them that time', meaning that he tricked them. If a scientist is doing research in the *field* of nuclear physics, the word 'field' results from comparison between scientists and farmers (who literally work in fields). Such usages are metaphorical.

Metaphysical Painting Italian *pittura metafisica* Italian painting style, conceived 1917 by Giorgio de Chirico and Carlo Carrá, which sought to convey a sense of mystery through the use of dreamlike imagery. Reacting against both Cubism and Futurism, it anticipated Surrealism in the techniques it employed, notably the incongruous juxtaposition of familiar objects. Though short-lived – it had disbanded by the early 1920s – its influence was considerable.

metaphysics branch of philosophy that deals with first principles, in particular 'being' (◊ontology) and 'knowing' (◊epistemology), and that is concerned with the ultimate nature of reality. It has been maintained that no certain knowledge of metaphysical questions is possible.

Epistemology, or the study of how we know, lies at the threshold of the subject. Metaphysics is concerned with the nature and origin of existence and of mind, the interaction between them, the meaning of time and space, causation, determinism and free will, personality and the self, arguments for belief in God, and human immortality. The foundations of metaphysics were laid by ◊Plato and ◊Aristotle. St Thomas ◊Aquinas, basing himself on Aristotle, produced a metaphysical structure that is accepted by the Catholic church. The subject has been advanced by Descartes, Spinoza, Leibniz, Berkeley, Hume, Locke, Kant, Hegel, Schopenhauer, and Marx; and in the 20th century by Bergson, Bradley, Croce, McTaggart, Whitehead, and Wittgenstein.

metempsychosis another name for ◊reincarnation.

Methodism evangelical Protestant Christian movement that was founded by John ◊Wesley 1739 within the Church of England, but became a separate body 1795. The Methodist Episcopal Church was founded in the USA 1784. There are over 50 million Methodists worldwide.

Methodist doctrines are contained in Wesley's sermons and *Notes on the New Testament*. A series of doctrinal divisions in the early 19th century were reconciled by a conference in London 1932 that brought Wesleyan methodists, primitive methodists, and United methodists into the Methodist Church. The church government is presbyterian in Britain and episcopal in the USA. Supreme authority is vested in the annual conference (50% ministers, 50% lay people); members are grouped under 'class leaders' and churches into 'circuits'.

Expansion in the 19th century in developing industrial areas enabled people to overcome economic depression or change by spiritual means. Its encouragement of thrift and simple living helped many to raise their economic status. Smaller Methodist groups such as the Primitive Methodists and the Methodist New Connexion provided leadership in early trade unionism in disproportion to their size. Mainstream Wesleyans at first were politically conservative but identified increasingly with Gladstonian liberalism in the second half of the 19th century.

Methodius, St c. 825–884. Greek Christian bishop, who with his brother ◊Cyril translated much of the Bible into Slavonic. Feast day 14 Feb.

Methuselah in the Old Testament, Hebrew patriarch who lived before the Flood; his lifespan of 969 years makes him a byword for longevity.

metropolitan in the Christian church generally, a bishop who has rule over other bishops (termed *suffragans*). In the Orthodox Church, a metropolitan has a rank between an archbishop and a ◊patriarch.

In the Church of England, the archbishops of York and Canterbury are both metropolitans.

Metternich Klemens (Wenzel Lothar). Prince von Metternich 1773–1859. Austrian politician, the leading figure in European diplomacy after the fall of Napoleon. As foreign minister 1809–48 (as well as chancellor from 1821), he tried to maintain the balance of power in Europe, supporting monarchy and repressing liberalism. At the Congress of Vienna 1815 he advocated coop-

eration by the great powers to suppress democratic movements. The revolution of 1848 forced him to flee to ther UK; he returned 1851 as a power behind the scenes.

Meyerhold Vsevolod 1874–1940. Russian actor and director. Before the revolution of 1917 he developed a strong interest in commedia dell'arte and stylized acting. He developed a system of actor-training known as bio-mechanics, which combined insights drawn from sport, the circus, and modern studies of time and motion. He produced the Russian poet Mayakovsky's futurist *Mystery-Bouffe* 1918 and 1921, and later his *The Bed Bug* 1929.

A member of the Moscow Art Theatre, he was briefly director of its Studio theatre under Stanislavsky 1905. He receive state support from 1920, but was arrested 1938 and shot under the Stalinist regime.

mezuza in Judaism, a small box containing a parchment scroll inscribed with a prayer, the Shema from Deuteronomy 6:4–9; 11:13–21, which is found on the doorpost of every home and every room in a Jewish house, except the bathroom.

Michael in the Old Testament, an archangel, referred to as the guardian angel of Israel. In the New Testament Book of Revelation he leads the hosts of heaven to battle against Satan. In paintings, he is depicted with a flaming sword and sometimes a pair of scales. Feast day 29 Sept (Michaelmas).

Michaelmas Day in Christian church tradition, the festival of St Michael and all angels, observed 29 Sept.

It is one of the English quarter days.

Michelangelo Buonarroti 1475–1564. Italian sculptor, painter, architect, and poet, active in his native Florence and in Rome. His giant talent dominated the High Renaissance. The marble *David* 1501–04 (Accademia, Florence) set a new standard in nude sculpture. His massive figure style was translated into fresco in the Sistine Chapel 1508–12 and 1536–41 (Vatican). Other works in Rome include the dome of St Peter's basilica. His influence, particularly on the development of ◊Mannerism, was profound.

Born near Florence, he was a student of Ghirlandaio and trained under the patronage of Lorenzo de' Medici. His patrons later included several popes and Medici princes. In 1496 he completed the *Pietà* (St Peter's, Rome), a technically brilliant marble sculpture that established his reputation. Also in Rome he began the great tomb of Pope Julius II: *The Slaves* about 1513 (Louvre, Paris) and *Moses* about 1515 (San Pietro in Vincoli, Rome) were sculpted for this unfinished project. His grandiose scheme for the ceiling of the Sistine Chapel tells the Old Testament story from Genesis to the Deluge, and on the altar wall he later added a vast and dramatic *Last Judgement* 1536–41. From 1516 to 1534 he was again in Florence, where his chief work was the design of the Medici sepulchral chapel in San Lorenzo. Returning to Rome he became chief architect of St Peter's in 1547. His friendship with Vittoria Colonna (1492–1547), a noblewoman,inspired many of his sonnets and madrigals. There are collections of his drawings in the Uffizi, Florence, and the Louvre, Paris.

Michels Robert 1876–1936. German social and political theorist. Originally a radical, he became a critic of socialism and Marxism, and in his last years supported Hitler and Mussolini. In *Political Parties* 1911 he propounded the **Iron Law of Oligarchy**, arguing that in any organization or society, even a democracy, there is a tendency towards rule by the few in the interests of the few, and that ideologies such as socialism and communism were merely propaganda to control the masses. He believed that the rise of totalitarian governments – both fascist and communist – in the 1930s confirmed his analysis and proved that the masses were incapable of asserting their own interests.

Michelson Albert Abraham 1852–1931. German-born US physicist. In conjunction with Edward Morley, he performed in 1887 the **Michelson–Morley experiment** to detect the motion of the Earth through the postulated ether (a medium believed to be necessary for the propagation of light).

The failure of the experiment indicated the nonexistence of the ether, and led ◊Einstein to his theory of ◊relativity. Michelson was the first American to be awarded a Nobel prize, in 1907.

He invented the **Michelson interferometer** and made precise measurement of the speed of light. From 1892 he was professor of physics at the University of Chicago.

Michotte Albert 1881–1965. Belgian experimental psychologist known for his investigations of perceptual causality. By means of ingenious and careful experimentation, he studied the dynamic organization of the perceptual world and was particularly concerned with the role of language in the analysis of perceptual phenomena. His book *La Perception de la Causalité/The Perception of Causality* 1946 has become a classic.

In his experiments, subjects looking through a slit saw what appeared to them as two small rectangular spots in motion. Alternatively, they looked at a screen on which small moving shapes were projected. When one object A was seen to bump into another B, A appeared to give B a push or set it in motion, which Michotte termed the launching effect. If object A on reaching object B was seen to move with it and at the same speed, A appeared to carry B, which he termed the entraining effect. Michotte observed these phenomena, and others, under various experimental conditions. His work is important not least because it is a scientific investigation of a topic that has mainly been the province of philosophers.

Bibl. Michotte, A *The Perception of Causality* (London, 1963)

microeconomics the division of economics concerned with the study of individual decision-making units within an economy: a consumer, firm, or industry. Unlike ◊macro-economics, it looks at how individual markets work and how individual producers and consumers make their choices and with what consequences. This is done by analysing how relevant prices of goods are determined and the quantities that will be bought and sold.

For simplicity, microeconomics begins by analysing a market in which there is **perfect competition**, a theoretical state that exists only when no individual producer or consumer can influence the market price. In the real world, there is always imperfect competition for various reasons (monopoly practices, barriers to trade, and so on), and microeconomics examines what effect these have on wages and prices.

Underlying these and other concerns of microeconomics is the concept of **optimality**, first advanced by Vilfredo ◊Pareto in the 19th century. Pareto's perception of the most efficient state of an economy, when there is no scope to reallocate resources without making someone worse off, has been of great influence.

middle class term applied to those members of society who earn their living by nonmanual labour. Their income is usually higher than that of the working class in recognition of greater skills. The subdivisions **upper-middle class** and **lower-middle class** refer respectively to the more skilled professions (doctors, lawyers, and so on) and white-collar workers (lower management, shopkeepers, and so on).

Karl ◊Marx used the term ◊bourgeoisie to refer to the capitalist class who do not live by the sale of their labour.

Middle Way the path to enlightenment, taught by Buddha, which avoids the extremes of indulgence and asceticism.

Midgley Mary 1919– . English moral philosopher, who has used studies of animal behaviour (◊ethology) to support a broadly Aristotelian ethics. She has also argued that our moral concern should extend to animals. Midgley taught at the University of Newcastle upon Tyne from 1963 until her retirement. Her publications include *Beast and Man: The Roots of Human Nature* 1978, *Animals and Why They Matter* 1983, and *Wickedness: a Philosophical Enquiry* 1984.

Midrash medieval Hebrew commentaries on the Bible, in the form of sermons, in which allegory and legendary illustration are used. They were compiled mainly in Palestine between AD 400 and 1200.

Mies van der Rohe Ludwig 1886–1969. German architect, a leading exponent of the ◊International Style, who practised in the USA from 1937. He succeeded Walter ◊Gropius as director of the ◊Bauhaus 1929–33. He designed the bronze-and-glass Seagram building in New York City 1956–59 and numerous apartment buildings.

He became professor at the Illinois Technical Institute 1938–58, for which he designed a new campus on characteristically functional lines from 1941. He also designed the National Gallery, Berlin 1963–68.

mihrab in Islamic architecture, niche in the wall of a mosque indicating the direction of Mecca to those taking part in prayers.

Milarepa 1040–1123. The greatest of all Tibetan Buddhist sages, seen as the founder of one of the four major schools of Tibetan Buddhism, the Kagyu school, whose central purpose is meditation.

Milarepa's life is told in a classic of Buddhist spirituality written down in the 15th century. After an early life of hardship and of powerful evil magic, Milarepa repented and went to study Buddhism under the master Marpa. From him he learnt the importance of solitary meditation, even walling himself up for years at a time. Milarepa is not just beloved by the Kagyu school which he founded; he stands as the paragon of the Tibetan mystic and hermit and is a popular figure of devotion.

Milinda (2nd century BC) Indian name for *Menander*, the Greek ruler of Bactria (E Afghanistan) whose discourses with the Buddhist monk Nagasena are recorded in the *Milindapanha/Questions of Milinda* an important ◊Theravada text, in which certain key Buddhist teachings are explored.

Mill James 1773–1836. Scottish philosopher and political theorist who contributed to the development of the theory of ◊utilitarianism, the theory of ethics in which the rightness of an action depends on how much it increases happiness. In political theory, he rejected natural rights as a basis for representative institutions, which he advocated on the purely utilitarian grounds that they lead to the greatest happiness of the greatest number. He is remembered for the rigorous education he gave his son John Stuart Mill.

Born near Montrose, Mill moved to London 1802. Associated for most of his working life with the East India Company, he wrote a vast *History of British India* 1817–18. He was one of the founders of University College, London, together with his friend and fellow utilitarian Jeremy Bentham.

Ask yourself whether you are happy, and you cease to be so.

John Stuart Mill
Autobiography ch 5

Mill John Stuart 1806–1873. English philosopher and economist who wrote *On Liberty* 1859, the classic philosophical defence of liberalism, and *Utilitarianism* 1863, a version of the 'greatest happiness for the greatest number' principle in ethics. His progressive views inspired *On the Subjection of Women* 1869.

He was born in London, the son of James Mill. In 1822 he entered the East India Company, where he remained until retiring in 1858. In 1826, as described in his *Autobiography* 1873, he passed through a mental crisis; he found his father's bleakly intellectual utilitarianism emotionally unsatisfying and abandoned it for a more human philosophy influenced by Coleridge. In *Utilitarianism*, he states that actions are right if

---

No great improvements in the lot of mankind are possible, until a great change takes place in the fundamental constitution of their modes of thought.

John Stuart Mill
Autobiography ch 7

---

they bring about happiness and wrong if they bring about the reverse of happiness. *On Liberty* moved away from the utilitarian notion that individual liberty was necessary for economic and governmental efficiency and advanced the classical defence of individual freedom as a value in itself and the mark of a mature society; this change can be traced in the later editions of *Principles of Political Economy* 1848. He sat in Parliament as a Radical 1865–68 and introduced a motion for women's suffrage. His philosophical and political writings include *A System of Logic* 1843 and *Considerations on Representative Government* 1861.

millennium period of 1,000 years. Some quasi-Christian groups, such as Jehovah's Witnesses, believe that Jesus will return to govern the Earth in person at the next millennium, the 6001st year after the creation (as located by Archbishop Usher at 4004 BC).

This belief, *millenarianism*, also called chiliasm (from the Greek for 1,000), was widespread in the early days of Christianity. As hopes were disappointed, belief in the imminence of the second coming tended to fade, but millenarian views have been expressed at periods of great religious excitement, such as the Reformation.

Miller Stanley 1930– . US chemist. In the early 1950s, under laboratory conditions, he tried to imitate the original conditions of the Earth's atmosphere (a mixture of methane, ammonia, and hydrogen), added an electrical discharge, and waited. After a few days he found that amino acids, the ingredients of protein, had been formed.

Miller William 1782–1849. US religious leader. Ordained as a Baptist minister 1833, Miller predicted that the Second Advent would occur 1844. Many of his followers sold their property in expectation of the end of the world. Although Miller's movement disbanded soon after, his teachings paved the way for later Adventist sects.

Born in Pittsfield, Massachusetts, and raised in New York, Miller later settled in Vermont. Convinced that the Second Coming of Jesus was imminent, he began to preach about the millennium.

Millett Kate 1934– . US radical feminist lecturer, writer, and sculptor whose book *Sexual Politics* 1970 was a landmark in feminist thinking. She was a founding member of the **National Organization of Women** (NOW). Later books include *Flying* 1974, *The Prostitution Papers* 1976, *Sita* 1977, and *The Loony Bin Trip* 1991, describing a period of manic depression and drug therapy.

Millikan Robert Andrews 1868–1953. US physicist, awarded a Nobel prize 1923 for his determination of the electric charge on an electron 1913.

His experiment, which took five years to perfect, involved observing oil droplets, charged by external radiation, falling under gravity between two horizontal metal plates connected to a high-voltage supply. By varying the voltage, he was able to make the electrostatic field between the plates balance the gravitational field so that some droplets became stationary and floated. If a droplet of weight W is held stationary between plates separated by a distance d and carrying a potential difference V, the charge, e, on the drop is equal to Wd/V.

Mills C Wright 1916–1962. US sociologist whose concern for humanity, ethical values, and individual freedom led him to criticize the US establishment.

Originally in the liberal tradition, Mills later adopted Weberian and even Marxist ideas. He aroused considerable popular interest in sociology with such works as *White Collar* 1951; *The Power Elite* 1956, depicting the USA as ruled by businessmen, military experts, and politicians; and *Listen, Yankee* 1960.

Milstein César 1927– . Argentine-born British molecular biologist who developed monoclonal antibodies, giving immunity against specific diseases. He shared the Nobel Prize for Medicine 1984.

Milstein, who settled in Britain 1961, was engaged on research into the immune system at the Laboratory of Molecular Biology in Cambridge. He and his colleagues devised a means of accessing the immune system for purposes of research, diagnosis, and treatment. They developed monoclonal antibodies (MABs), cloned cells that, when introduced into the body, can be targeted to seek out sites of disease. The full potential of this breakthrough is still being investigated. However, MABs, which can be duplicated in limitless quantities, are already in use to combat disease. Milstein shared the Nobel Prize for Medicine 1984 with two colleagues, Georges Köhler and Niels Jerne.

As good almost kill a man as kill a good book; who kills a man kills a reasonable creature, God's image; but he who destroys a good book, kills reason itself, kills the image of God, as it were in the eye.

John Milton
Areopagitica

Milton John 1608–1674. English poet whose epic *Paradise Lost* 1667 is one of the landmarks of English literature. Early poems including *Comus* (a masque performed 1634) and *Lycidas* (an elegy 1638) showed Milton's superlative lyric gift. Latin secretary to Oliver Cromwell during the Commonwealth period, he also wrote many pamphlets and prose works, including *Areopagitica* 1644, which opposed press censorship.

Born in London and educated at Christ's College, Cambridge, Milton was a scholarly poet, ambitious to match the classical epics, and with strong theological views. Of polemical temperament, he published prose works on republicanism and church government. His middle years were devoted to the Puritan cause and pamphleteering, including one on divorce (*The Doctrine and Discipline of Divorce* 1643, which was based on his own experience of marital unhappiness) and another (*Areopagitica*) advocating freedom of the press. From 1649 he was (Latin) secretary to the Council of State. His assistants (as his sight failed) included Andrew Marvell. He married Mary Powell 1643, and their three daughters were later his somewhat unwilling scribes. After Mary's death 1652, the year of his total blindness, he married twice more, his second wife Catherine Woodcock dying in childbirth, while Elizabeth Minshull survived him for over half a century. *Paradise Lost* 1667 and the less successful sequel *Paradise Regained* 1671 were written when he was blind and in some political danger (after the restoration of Charles II), as was *Samson Agonistes* 1671, a powerful if untheatrical play. He is buried in St Giles's, Cripplegate, London.

The mind is its own place, and in it self /
Can make a Heav'n of Hell, a Hell of
Heav'n.

mind
John Milton, 1608–1674, English poet.
Paradise Lost bk 1

---

mind in philosophy, the presumed mental or physical being or faculty that enables a person to think, will, and feel; the seat of the intelligence and of memory; sometimes only the cognitive or intellectual powers, as distinguished from the will and the emotions.

Mind may be seen as synonymous with the merely random chemical reactions within the brain, or as a function of the brain as a whole, or (more traditionally) as existing independently of the physical brain, through which it expresses

itself, or even as the only reality, matter being considered the creation of intelligence. The relation of mind to matter may be variously regarded. See ◊mind–body problem.

Like a long-legged fly upon the stream /
His mind moves upon silence.

mind
W(illiam) B(utler) Yeats, 1865–1939,
Irish poet.
'Long-Legged Fly'

---

mind–body problem a central problem in philosophy, concerning what mind is and how it relates to the body. Answers range from idealist views that only the mind is real to materialist views that the body alone is real or that mental phenomena are identical with certain physical ones.

The idealist and the materialist views are both *monist* views – that is, that body and mind are one substance (◊monism). Other monist views are Aristotelianism (that the mind is to the body as ◊form is to matter), neutral monism (English philospher Bertrand Russell's theory that physical and mental phenomena can be analysed in terms of a common underlying reality), and the double-aspect theory (that mind and matter as a whole are two aspects of a single substance). The double-aspect theory can refer either to individual minds and their corresponding bodies or to mind and matter as a whole; the latter view was advanced by Benedict Spinoza.

◊*Dualism* asserts the distinctness of mind and body, as in Cartesian dualism (that of French philosopher René ◊Descartes. Cartesian dualism is a type of interactionism – that is, the theory that mind and body are different substances but still interact. There are several other dualist theories. Epiphenomenalism is the theory that mind has distinctive and irreducible qualities but that it has no power over the body. Psycho-physical parallelism is the theory that every mental event has a physical counterpart, and vice-versa, but that mind and body do not interact. A version of psycho-physical parallelism is occasionalism, which is the theory put forward by Belgian philosopher Arnold ◊Geulincx that body and mind do not interact but are synchronized by God.

Minerva in Roman mythology, the goddess of intelligence, and of handicrafts and the arts, equivalent to the Greek ◊Athena. From the earliest days of ancient Rome, there was a

Mind-body Dualism and the Riddle of Human Consciousness

There is nothing self-evidently correct about dividing up human beings into one component called 'mind' and another called 'body' – or, more broadly, dividing up Nature into mind and matter. Dualistic thinking, however, has become embedded within our culture. Yet there have always been thinkers who have denied the polar-opposite categories of mind and body. Some have argued that 'mind' is a philosophical delusion, others have maintained that only the spiritual is real. Monists and holists have tried to transcend the habit of thinking in terms of diametrically opposite pairs. The history of philosophies of mind and body is an unresolved series of reflections about human nature.

Soul over body

In the Classical world, the healthy, well-formed body held a place of honour. Great store was set by athletic training. The visual arts gloried in the human frame, and art generally portrayed a complementarity between the body's geometry and the cosmos. Meanwhile, Greek philosophers fleshed out correspondences between microcosm (humans) and macrocosm (the universe).

Yet, though the body was prized by the Greeks, it was subordinated to the soul. Physical appetites aroused philosophical distrust; reason proclaimed the monarchy of mind. Sensory gratification, argued Plato (c. 428–347 BC), is at best passing, and finally a cheat; the soul's transports, by contrast, are transcendent. Though rarely advocating stringent asceticism, the Classical view was that the body should obey the mind. Against a backdrop of war, carnage, and sacrifice under the Roman Empire, philosophy increasingly questioned the Aristotelian notion of earthly corporeal fulfilment and idealized the mind. Stoics mocked the vanity of human wishes: be not passion's slave, they urged.

Christianity accentuated this growing contempt for the flesh. The flesh was regarded as filthy, its sight shameful, its lusts sinful. The golden rule was therefore 'Thou Shalt Not'. Temporal existence was seen as a vale of tears; pain, pestilences, and plagues as divine punishments. The essence of a human lay in the immortal soul. The Genesis story shows humanity punished for the sins of the flesh (sexuality). Thereafter Man is doomed to toil, while 'unto the woman', the Lord declared, 'in pain thou shalt bring forth children' (Genesis 3:16). For Judaeo-Christianity the flesh was corrupt and prey to Satan. Only the sacrifice of God's Son would suffice to bear away the sins of the world.

But this points to Christianity's singularity among world religions: the Godhead becomes *human*. The Christian faith has a heartfelt hope of *redeeming* the flesh. Over the centuries, the Roman Catholic Church espoused doctrines of immanence, fulfilling the text: 'And the Word was made flesh, and dwelt among us.' Catholicism attested the real presence in the Mass of the body and the blood of Christ (transubstantiation) and emphasized the healing properties of relics. Medieval piety humanized Christ and created the cult of the Virgin – in both ways rendering the notion of the divine more physical.

Such temporizing with base flesh was opposed by those seeking a spiritual faith, like Medieval Cathars and other heretics who saw the physical as diabolically infected. Broadly speaking, Christianity engaged with the body – God became flesh – but the flesh had to be mastered, through asceticism and monasticism. Protestantism proved no more indulgent: Martin Luther (1438–1546), Ulrich Zwingli (1484–1531) and John Calvin (1509–1564) upheld Original Sin, carnal turpitude, the servitude of the will, and the real presence of Satan and of Hellfire to come.

The philosophical approach

From around the seventeenth century, discussion about mind–/body relations increasingly took place in philosophical and scientific terms. René Descartes (1596–1650) in his *Discourse on Method* (1637) spelt out the most influential scientific metaphysics of mind and body. Descartes posited a sigle, indivisible, nonmaterial, intellectual faculty of consciousness, the thinking part: I *think*, therefore I am. Everything else about human life – emotions, desires, instincts, and physiological processes – was devolved upon the body and deemed merely mechanical, matter in motion. Descartes' drastic clarification of man into two fundamentally disparate continents, mind and body, promised rich dividends, for it seemingly elevated the soul onto an unassailable metaphysical pedestal, while everything else ('extension': res extensa) was material and hence a legitimate terrain for scientific investigation.

Science enters the fray

But certain Enlightenment *philosophes* began to draw upon science to deny dualism. Spirit or soul, some argued, was merely an invention of the priests, and consciousness should be treated as an offshoot of the body. A strong advocate of this view was the French doctor, Julien La Mettrie (1709–1751), who advanced a materialist vision of humans as predetermined machines, whose consciousness arose from, and was subservient to, their bodily needs, via their senses. Some nineteenth-century scientists took this reductionist attack further. Karl Marx (1818–1883) debunked dualistic idealism as the false consciousness symptomatic of the people's alienation: religion was the opium of the people. Nineteenth-century biology, medicine, and natural history undermined supernaturalism. Evolution postulated continuity of function from lower creatures to mighty humans.

Traditional mind–/body dualism became the target of other assaults, notably from neuroscientists. Phrenologists claimed that the brain was the organ of mind. Neurologists took up this line, exploring the physical basis of thought. Twentieth-century logical positivists and behaviourists denied the validity of speaking about people in terms of traditional 'mentalist' entities like intentions and goals: behaviour was to be explained by external conditioning and reinforcement.

Scientists have increasingly claimed that they possess, or shortly will, the solution to the old conundrum of mind and body, largely through extending the traditional domain of the physical, for instance by claiming that all mental activity can be mapped upon the brain. That project has a long pedigree. It has many supporters. To many, however, it cannot resolve the problem of the 'ghost in the machine', the riddle of human consciousness.

Roy Porter

temple to her on the Capitoline Hill, near the Temple of Jupiter.

Minimalism movement in abstract art (mostly sculpture) and music toward severely simplified composition. Minimal art developed in the USA in the 1950s in reaction to ◊Abstract Expressionism, shunning its emotive approach in favour of impersonality and elemental, usually geometric, shapes. It has found its fullest expression in sculpture, notably in the work of Carl Andre, who employs industrial materials in modular compositions. In music, from the 1960s, it has manifested itself in large-scale statements based on layers of imperceptibly shifting repetitive patterns; major Minimalist composers are Steve Reich and Philip Glass.

Minoan religion the Minoan civilization, centred on the Greek island of Crete, emerged during the 3rd millenium BC and reached its height around 1500 BC before being apparently wiped out by an earthquake around 1450 BC. Its focus was the worship of the goddess in many different forms, though that of the Snake goddess is most common. Minoan religion celebrated the fertility of the land, sea, and air and was linked to a cycle of agricultural and possibly even pre-agricultural festivals. The famous bull of Minoan civilization was believed to be the goddess' son, a symbol of her creative powers and strength.

Minotaur in Greek mythology, a monster, half man and half bull, offspring of Pasiphaë, wife of King Minos of Crete, and a bull. It lived in the Labyrinth at Knossos, and its victims were seven girls and seven youths, sent in annual tribute by Athens, until ◊Theseus killed it, with the aid of Ariadne, the daughter of Minos.

minster in the UK, a church formerly attached to a monastery: for example, York Minster. Originally the term meant a monastery, and in this sense it is often preserved in place names, such as Westminster.

miracle event that cannot be explained by the known laws of nature and is therefore attributed to divine intervention.

Mirandola Italian 15th-century philosopher. See ◊Pico della Mirandola.

Mishna or *Mishnah* collection of commentaries on written Hebrew law, consisting of discussions between rabbis, handed down orally from their inception in AD 70 until about 200, when, with the Gemara (the main body of rabbinical debate on interpretations of the Mishna) it was committed to writing to form the Talmud.

missal in the Roman Catholic Church, a service book containing the complete office of Mass for the entire year. A simplified missal in the vernacular was introduced 1969 (obligatory from 1971): the first major reform since 1570.

mission organized attempt to spread a religion. Throughout its history Christianity has been the most assertive of missionary religions; Islam has also played a missionary role. Missionary activity in the Third World has frequently been criticized for its disruptive effects on indigenous peoples and their traditional social, political, and cultural systems.

Mitchell Juliet 1940– . British psychoanalyst and writer. She came to public notice with an article in *New Left Review* 1966 entitled 'Women: The Longest Revolution,' one of the first attempts to combine socialism and feminism using Marxist theory to explain the reasons behind women's oppression. She published *Women's Estate* 1971 and *Psychoanalysis and Feminism* 1974.

Mithraism a ◊mystery religion based on the worship of the Persian god of light ◊Mithras. Spreading throughout Asia Minor, it was introduced into the Roman Empire about 68 BC. By about AD 250, it rivalled Christianity in strength.

A bath in the blood of a sacrificed bull formed part of the initiation ceremony of the Mithraic cult, which spread rapidly, gaining converts especially among soldiers. In 1954 remains of a Roman temple dedicated to Mithras were discovered in the City of London.

Mithras in Persian mythology, the god of light. Mithras represented the power of goodness, and promised his followers compensation for present evil after death. He was said to have captured and killed the sacred bull, from whose blood all life sprang.

mitre in the Christian church, the headdress worn by bishops, cardinals, and mitred abbots at solemn services. There are mitres of many different shapes, but in the Western church they usually take the form of a tall cleft cap. The mitre worn by the pope is called a tiara.

mixed economy type of economic structure that combines the private enterprise of capitalism with a degree of state monopoly. In mixed economies, governments seek to control the public services, the basic industries, and those industries that cannot raise sufficient capital investment from private sources. Thus a measure of economic planning can be combined with a measure of free enterprise. A notable example was US President F D Roosevelt's ◊New Deal in the 1930s.

mnemonics any technique used to aid or improve the memory. Mnemonic systems usually involve additional organization of the information to be learnt or recalled.

An early mnemonic device, The Method of Loci, first described by Cicero 55 BC, involves taking a strict sequence of locations with which one is familiar, such as one might find in walking through one's house. When one wishes to remember a series of items in a list, the mnemonic system is employed by associating an item with each location in sequence. In recall, the location is called to mind and the item associated with it retrieved. Other mnemonics may be structured using rhythm and rhyme, such as the mnemonic used to recall the number of days in each month of the year. Further examples include the acronym FACE, for the notes between the lines of the musical stave, or the sentence 'Every Good Boy Deserves Favours', for the notes on the lines.

mobility in economics, the degree of movement of the factors of production from one occupation to another (occupational mobility) or from one region to another (regional mobility). The labour mobility of unskilled workers is not very great in the UK, for example, because of the lack of knowledge about jobs between one part of the country and another and because it is so difficult to find affordable housing in some areas.

Möbius August Ferdinand 1790–1868. German mathematician, discoverer of the ◊Möbius strip and considered one of the founders of ◊topology.

Möbius strip structure made by giving a half twist to a flat strip of paper and joining the ends together. It has certain remarkable properties, arising from the fact that it has only one edge and one side. If cut down the centre of the strip, instead of two new strips of paper, only one long strip is produced. It was invented by the German mathematician August Möbius.

model simplified version of some aspect of the real world. Models are produced to show the relationships between two or more factors, such as land use and the distance from the centre of a town (see ◊concentric-ring theory).

Because models are idealized, they give only a general guide to what may happen.

Modernism in the arts, a general term used to describe the 20th century's conscious attempt to break with the artistic traditions of the 19th century; it is based on a concern with form and the exploration of technique as opposed to content and narrative. In the visual arts, direct representationalism gave way to abstraction (see ◊abstract art); in literature, writers experimented with alternatives to orthodox sequential storytelling, such as ◊stream of consciousness; in music, the traditional concept of key was challenged by atonality; and in architecture, Functionalism ousted decorativeness as a central objective.

Critics of Modernism have found in it an austerity that is seen as dehumanizing. ◊Post-Modernism developed as a reaction to Modernism, but has had to compete with new and divergent Modernist trends, for example ◊High Tech in architecture.

Mohammed alternative form of ◊Muhammad, founder of Islam.

Mohammedanism misnomer for ◊Islam (Muhammad is the prophet of Islam).

Mohs Friedrich 1773–1839. German mineralogist who 1812 devised *Mohs' scale* of minerals, classified in order of relative hardness.

Moissan Henri 1852–1907. French chemist. For his preparation of pure fluorine 1886, Moissan was awarded the 1906 Nobel Prize for Chemistry. He also attempted to create artificial diamonds by rapidly cooling carbon heated to high temperatures. His claims of success were treated with suspicion.

moksha in Hinduism, liberation from the cycle of reincarnation and from the illusion of ◊maya. In Buddhism, ◊enlightenment.

molecular biology study of the molecular basis of life, including the biochemistry of molecules such as ◊DNA, ◊RNA, and proteins, and the molecular structure and function of the various parts of living cells.

There are living systems; there is no 'living matter'.

Jacques Monod
Lecture Nov 1967

---

molecular clock use of rates of ◊mutation in genetic material to calculate the length of time elapsed since two related species diverged from each other during evolution. The method can be based on comparisons of the DNA or of widely occurring proteins, such as haemoglobin.

Since mutations are thought to occur at a constant rate, the length of time that must have elapsed in order to produce the difference between two species can be estimated. This information can be compared with the evidence obtained from palaeontology to reconstruct evolutionary events.

molecule group of two or more atoms bonded together. A molecule of an element consists of one or more like atoms; a molecule of a compound consists of two or more different atoms bonded together. Molecules vary in size and complexity from the hydrogen molecule (H_2) to the large macromolecules of proteins. They are held together by ionic bonds, in which the atoms gain or lose electrons to form ions, or by covalent bonds, where electrons from each atom are shared in a new molecular orbital.

According to the molecular or kinetic theory of matter, molecules are in a state of constant motion, the extent of which depends on their temperature, and exert forces on one another.

The shape of a molecule profoundly affects its chemical, physical, and biological properties. Optical isomers (molecules that are mirror images of each other) rotate plane polarized light in opposite directions; isomers of drug molecules may have have different biological effects; and enzyme reactions are crucially dependent on the shape of the enzyme and the substrate on which it acts.

The symbolic representation of a molecule is known as its formula. The presence of more than one atom is denoted by a subscript figure – for example, one molecule of the compound water, having two atoms of hydrogen and one atom of oxygen, is shown as H_2O.

The existence of molecules was inferable from Italian physicist Amedio ◊Avogadro's hypothesis 1811, but only became generally accepted 1860 when proposed by Italian chemist Stanislao Cannizzaro.

Molinos Miguel de 1640–1697. Spanish mystic and Roman Catholic priest. He settled in Rome and wrote several devotional works in Italian, including the *Guida spirituale/Spiritual Guide* 1675, which aroused the hostility of the Jesuits. In 1687 he was sentenced to life imprisonment. His doctrine is known as ◊quietism.

Moloch or *Molech* in the Old Testament, a Phoenician deity worshipped in Jerusalem in the 7th century BC, to whom live children were sacrificed by fire.

monad philosophical term deriving from the work of Gottfried Leibniz, suggesting a soul or metaphysical unit that has a self-contained life. The monads are independent of each other but coordinated by a 'pre-established harmony'.

Monarchianism form of belief in the Christian Trinity that emphasizes the undifferentiated unity of God. It was common in the early 3rd century.

monasticism devotion to religious life under vows of poverty, chastity, and obedience, known to Judaism (for example ◊Essenes), Buddhism, and other religions, before Christianity. In Islam, the Sufis formed monastic orders from the 12th century.

Mond Ludwig 1839–1909. German chemist who perfected a process for recovering sulphur during the manufacture of alkali.

Mond moved to England 1862 and became a British subject 1867. In 1873, he helped to found the firm of Brunner, Mond, and Company, which pioneered the British chemical industry. His son *Alfred Mond, 1st Baron Melchett* (1868–1930), was a founder of Imperial Chemical Industries (ICI).

monetarism economic policy, advocated by the economist Milton ◊Friedman and the Chicago school of economists, that proposes control of a country's money supply to keep it in step with the country's ability to produce goods, with the aim of curbing inflation. Cutting government spending is advocated, and the long-term aim is to return as much of the economy as possible to the private sector, allegedly in the interests of efficiency.

Central banks (in the USA, the Federal Reserve Bank) use the discount rate and other tools to restrict or expand the supply of money to the economy. Unemployment may result from some efforts to withdraw government 'safety nets', but monetarists claim it is less than eventually occurs if the methods of ◊Keynesian economics are adopted. Monetarist policies were widely adopted in the 1980s in response to the inflation problems caused by spiralling oil prices in 1979. See also ◊deregulation, ◊privatization.

Additionally, credit is restricted by high interest rates, and industry is not cushioned against internal market forces or overseas competition (with the aim of preventing 'overmanning', 'restrictive' union practices, and 'excessive' wage demands).

money any common medium of exchange acceptable in payment for goods or services or for the settlement of debts; legal tender.

Money is usually coinage (invented by the Chinese in the second millennium BC) and paper notes (used by the Chinese from about AD 800). Developments such as the cheque and credit card fulfil many of the traditional functions of money.

money supply quantity of money in circulation in an economy at any given time. It can include notes, coins, and clearing-bank and other deposits used for everyday payments. Changes in the quantity of lending are a major determinant of changes in the money supply. One of the main principles of ◊monetarism is that increases in the money supply in excess of the rate of economic growth are the chief cause of inflation.

In Britain there are several definitions of money supply. M0 was defined as notes and coins in circulation, together with the operational balance of clearing banks with the Bank of England. The M1 definition encompasses M0 plus current account deposits; M2, now rarely used, covers the M1 items plus deposit accounts; M3 covers M2 items plus all other deposits held by UK citizens and companies in the UK banking sector. In May 1987 the Bank of England introduced new terms including M4 (M3 plus building society deposits) and M5 (M4 plus Treasury bills and local authority deposits).

monism in philosophy, the theory that reality is made up of only one substance. This view is usually contrasted with ◊dualism, which divides reality into two substances, matter and mind. The Dutch philosopher Baruch Spinoza saw the one substance as God or Nature. Monism is also sometimes used as a description of a political system in which only one party is permitted to operate.

monk man belonging to a religious order under the vows of poverty, chastity, and obedience, and living under a particular rule; see ◊monasticism.

Monnet Jean 1888–1979. French economist. The originator of Winston Churchill's offer of union between the UK and France 1940, he devised and took charge of the French modernization programme under Charles de Gaulle 1945. In 1950 he produced the 'Shuman Plan' initiating the coordination of European coal and steel production in the European Coal and Steel Community (ECSC), which developed into the Common Market (EC).

Monod Jacques 1910–1976. French biochemist who shared the 1965 Nobel Prize for Medicine (with two colleagues) for research in genetics and microbiology.

monogamy practice of having only one husband or wife at a time in ◊marriage and the opposite of ◊polygamy, the practice of having more than one spouse. Monogamy occurs to some extent in all human societies and is usually prevalent – possibly because it is only the relatively rich who can afford to support more than one spouse.

Monophysite member of a group of Christian heretics of the 5th–7th centuries who taught that Jesus had one nature, in opposition to the orthodox doctrine (laid down at the Council of Chalcedon 451) that he had two natures, the human and the divine. Monophysitism developed as a reaction to ◊Nestorianism and led to the formal secession of the Coptic and Armenian churches from the rest of the Christian church. Monophysites survive today in Armenia, Syria, and Egypt.

monopoly in economics, the domination of a market for a particular product or service by a single company, which can therefore restrict competition and keep prices high. In practice, a company can be said to have a monopoly when it controls a significant proportion of the market (technically an ◊oligopoly).

In communist countries the state itself has the overall monopoly; in capitalist ones some services, such as transport or electricity supply, may be state monopolies.

In the UK, monopoly was originally a royal grant of the sole right to manufacture or sell a certain article. The Fair Trading Act 1973 defines a monopoly supplier as one having 'a quarter of the market', and the Monopolies and Mergers Commission controls any attempt to reach this position (in the USA 'antitrust laws' are similarly used). The Competition Act of 1980 covers both private monopolies and possible abuses in the public sector. A *monopsony* is a situation in which there is only one buyer; for example, most governments are the only legal purchasers of military equipment inside their countries.

monotheism belief or doctrine that there is only one God; the opposite of ◊polytheism which is the belief in the existence of more than one god. Monotheism involves belief in a personal deity, unlike the impersonal deity of ◊pantheism. Elements of monotheism exist in many religions but it is central to Judaism, Islam, and Christianity. Islam is the most uncompromising, whereas Christianity's doctrine of the holy trinity makes it the least monotheistic of the three. See also ◊religion.

Monothelite member of a group of Christian heretics of the 7th century who sought to reconcile the orthodox and ◊Monophysite theologies by maintaining that, while Christ possessed two natures, he had only one will. Monothelitism was condemned as a heresy by the Third Council of Constantinople 680.

Monroe Doctrine declaration by US president James Monroe 1823 that any further European colonial ambitions in the western hemisphere would be threats to US peace and security, made in response to proposed European intervention against newly independent former Spanish colonies in South America. In return the USA would not interfere in European affairs. The doctrine, subsequently broadened, has been a recurrent theme in US foreign policy, although it has no basis in US or international law.

At the time of the declaration, the USA was militarily incapable of enforcing its sweeping proclamations. The impetus for and the power behind the doctrine came from the British, whose commercial interests were at risk in the event of a Franco-Spanish reassertion of colonial influence. President Theodore Roosevelt drew on the doctrine to proclaim a US right to intervene in the internal affairs of Latin American states.

monstrance in the Roman Catholic Church, a vessel used from the 13th century to hold the Host (bread consecrated in the Eucharist) when exposed at benediction or in processions.

Montagu Ashley 1905– . British-born US anthropologist. As a critic of theories of racial determinism, he was a forceful defender of human rights and wrote such important works as *Man's Most Dangerous Myth: The Fallacy of Race* 1942. In 1950 he helped draft the definitive Unesco 'Statement on Race'.

Born in London, Montagu was educated at the University of London, Columbia University, and the University of Florence. He received his PhD from Columbia under Franz ◊Boas 1937. He became well known for popularizing social issues, such as 'psychosclerosis', the so-called hardening of the psyche, in *Growing Young* 1981.

Montaigne Michel Eyquem de 1533–1592. French writer, regarded as the creator of the essay form. In 1580 he published the first two volumes of his *Essais*; the third volume appeared in 1588. Montaigne deals with all aspects of life from an urbanely sceptical viewpoint. Through the translation by John Florio in 1603, he influenced Shakespeare and other English writers.

He was born at the Château de Montaigne near Bordeaux, studied law, and in 1554 became a counsellor of the Bordeaux *parlement*. Little is known of his earlier life, except that he regularly visited Paris and the court of Francis II. In 1571 he retired to his estates, relinquishing his magistracy. He toured Germany, Switzerland, and Italy 1580–81, returning upon his election as mayor of Bordeaux, a post he held until 1585.

If you press me to say why I loved him, I feel that it can only be expressed by replying 'Because it was him; because it was me'.

Michel Eyquem de Montaigne
Explaining his friendship with
Etienne de La Boëtie, *Essays* I, 28

Montanism movement within the early Christian church that strove to return to the purity of primitive Christianity. It originated in Phrygia in about 156 with the teaching of a prophet named Montanus, and spread to Anatolia, Rome, Carthage, and Gaul. The theologian ◊Tertullian was a Montanist.

Montesquieu Charles Louis de Secondat, baron de la Brède 1689–1755. French political philosopher and historian, author of the *Lettres persanes/Persian Letters* 1721. *De l'Esprit des lois/The Spirit of the Laws* 1748, a 31-volume philosophical disquisition on politics and sociology as well as legal matters, advocated the separation of powers within government, that is, separation of the legislative, executive, and judicial functions. He saw his model for such a state from the viewpoint of the Tory opposition to Robert Walpole and the Whigs. The doctrine of the separation of powers became the basis of liberal constitutions.

Born near Bordeaux, Montesquieu became adviser to the Bordeaux parliament 1714. After the success of *Lettres persanes*, he adopted a literary career, writing *Considérations sur les causes de la grandeur des Romains et de leur décadence/Considerations on the Greatness and Decadence of the Romans* 1734.

Montessori Maria 1870–1952. Italian educationist and the first woman to qualify as a doctor in Italy. She specialized in paediatric medicine and psychiatry. Working with mentally handicapped children, she developed the **Montessori method**, an educational system for all children based on an informal approach, incorporating instructive play, though emphasizing the value of work, and allowing children to develop at their own pace. For this children are given a wide variety of materials carefully graded to permit repetition, self-correction and self-education. She wrote *The Montessori Method* 1912 and *The Secret of Childhood* 1936.

Moody Dwight Lyman 1837–1899. US evangelist. During the American Civil War 1861–65, he provided medical and moral support to the troops. In the 1870s he became a popular evangelist and founded the Northfield Seminary (now School) for girls 1879 and the Mount Hermon School for boys 1881, both in Massachusetts.

Born in East Northfield, Massachusetts, USA, Moody moved to Boston as a young man and joined the Congregational Church 1856. Later settling in Chicago, he devoted himself to preaching among the poor. In 1889 he founded the Chicago (later Moody) Bible Institute.

Moon natural satellite of the Earth. The Moon is illuminated by the Sun, and goes through a cycle of phases of shadow, waxing from new to full, and waning back to new every 29.53 days. In many religions and in popular superstition, the lunar cycle was believed to affect many aspects of life, from birth and death, to the propitious times to harvest crops, slaughter livestock, do business and go to war. The Druids, for example, avoided fighting till after the full Moon. The full Moon is also associated with an increase in disturbance in the mentally ill.

Moonie popular name for a follower of the ◊Unification Church, a religious sect founded by Sun Myung Moon.

I ... use the word 'beautiful' to denote that of which the admiring contemplation is good in itself.

G(eorge) E(dward) Moore
Principia Ethica ch VI

Moore G(eorge) E(dward) 1873–1958. British philosopher who generally defended ◊commonsense views of the world and what is said about it in ordinary language. In ethics, he held that any attempt to identify goodness with another concept such as happiness was a fallacy – the 'naturalistic fallacy'.

Educated at Trinity College, Cambridge University, he was professor of philosophy at the university 1925–39, and edited the journal *Mind*, to which he contributed 1921–47. His books include *Principia Ethica* 1903, and *Some Main Problems of Philosophy* 1953.

moral argument one of four traditional lines of reasoning for the existence of God. It has several subtle forms. One is that without a just God to ensure that virtue is rewarded by happiness, morality would be impossible; and since morality is possible, God must exist.

The moral argument was originated by German philosopher Immanuel ◊Kant, who claimed to have demolished the ◊cosmological argument and the ◊ontological argument. The remaining traditional argument is the ◊argument from design.

To make our idea of morality centre on forbidden acts is to defile the imagination and to introduce into our judgments of our fellow-men a secret element of gusto.

morality
Robert Louis Stevenson, 1850–1894, Scottish novelist and poet.
Across the Plains, 'A Christmas Sermon'

morality in ethics, a morality can be defined as having three essential components: (1) a community of responsible agents, for morality concerns our behaviour towards others and their behaviour towards us; (2) a shared set of nonmaterial values, such as fairness, truth, and compassion, the pursuit of which constitutes one aim of community life (this distinguishes a morality from an economic system); (3) a way of life involving a code of behaviour (this distinguishes a morality from, say, a set of aesthetic values).

Although he accepted that morality requires a community of responsible agents, Immanuel Kant argued that the distinguishing feature of morality is that it involves judgements that conform to a law of reason (the ◊categorical imperative).

Moral Rearmament (MRA) international movement calling for 'moral and spiritual renewal', founded by the Christian evangelist F N D Buchman in the 1920s as the *Oxford Group*. It based its teachings on the 'Four Absolutes' (honesty, purity, unselfishness, love).

Later, as the MRA (1938), it became more involved in political and social issues, particularly during the Cold War period when its anticommunist orientation found a receptive climate.

Moravian member of the Christian Protestant *Moravian Brethren*. An episcopal church that grew out of the earlier Bohemian Brethren, it was established by the Lutheran Count Zinzendorf in Saxony 1722.

Persecution of the Bohemian Brethren began 1620, and they were held together mainly by the leadership of their bishop, Comenius. Driven out of Bohemia in 1722, they spread into Germany, England, and North America. In 1732 missionary work began.

There are about 63,000 Moravians in the USA, and small congregations in the UK and the rest of Europe.

More Henry 1614–1687. English philosopher, theologian and member of the ◊Cambridge Platonists. He denied ◊Descartes's division of mind and matter (Cartesian dualism), maintaining that mind or spirit had extension in space. Mind or spirit could penetrate material objects, and was the only cause of motion in things, and the only cause (as the soul) of actions by people.

His works include *Philosophical Poems* 1647 and *Divine Dialogues* 1660. Born at Grantham, he was educated at Cambridge. He took orders, but declined all preferment (including two deaneries and a bishopric), devoting himself instead to the study of Plato and his followers.

Morgan Lewis Henry 1818–1881. US anthropologist who pioneered the study of NE American Indian culture and was adopted by the Iroquois.

Morgan Thomas Hunt 1866–1945. US geneticist, awarded the 1933 Nobel Prize for Medicine for his pioneering studies in classical ◊genetics. He was the first to work on the fruit fly *Drosophila*, which has since become a major subject of genetic studies. He helped establish that the genes were located on the chromosomes, discovered sex chromosomes, and invented the techniques of genetic mapping.

Morgan le Fay in the romance and legend of the English king ◊Arthur, an enchantress and healer, ruler of ◊Avalon and sister of the king, whom she tended after his final battle. In some versions of the legend she is responsible for the suspicions held by the king of his wife Guinevere.

Morley Edward 1838–1923. US physicist who collaborated with Albert ◊Michelson on the *Michelson–Morley experiment* 1887. In 1895 he established precise and accurate measurements of the densities of oxygen and hydrogen.

Mormon or *Latter-day Saint* member of a Christian group, the Church of Jesus Christ of Latter-day Saints, founded at Fayette, New York, USA in 1830 by Joseph ◊Smith. According to Smith, Mormon was an ancient prophet in North America; his *Book of Mormon* is accepted by Mormons as part of the Christian scriptures. Smith said he found the book, inscribed on golden tablets, with the help of the angel Moroni in 1827, and that he translated it from 'reformed Egyptian' by using special spectacles. Originally persecuted, the Mormons migrated West under Brigham ◊Young's leadership and prospered. Today the worldwide membership of the Mormon church is about 6 million.

The *Book of Mormon* describes American Indians as descendants of ancient Hebrews who came to North America across the Pacific. Christ is said to have appeared to them after his ascension to establish his church in the New World. The Mormon church claims to be a reestablishment of this pure, original Christianity by divine intervention. The church grew rapidly, especially in the Midwest, but its controversial doctrines and rumours that Smith had taken several wives (as allowed in the Old Testament) provoked persecution, and Smith was killed in Illinois. Further settlements were rapidly established despite opposition, and in 1847 Brigham Young led a westward migration of most of the church's members to the Valley of the Great Salt Lake in what is now Utah. The Mormons under Young openly practised polygamy, but the church repudiated the practice in 1890, following Congressional pressure related to the proposed admission of Utah as a state. Mormons hold several doctrines not held by other Christians, including the belief that God has a physical body and that human beings may become gods, just as God was once a man. They advocate a strict sexual morality, large families, and respect for authority. They forbid the consumption of alcohol, coffee, tea, and tobacco.

Morpheus in Greek and Roman mythology, the god of dreams, son of Hypnos or Somnus, god of sleep.

morphing the metamorphosis of one shape or object into another by computer-generated animation. First used in film-making in 1990, it has transformed cinema special effects. Conventional animation is limited to two dimensions; morphing enables the creation of three-dimensional transformations.

To create such effects, the start and end of the transformation must be specified on screen using a wire-frame model that mathematically defines the object. To make the object three-dimensional, the wire can be extruded from a cross-section or turned as on a lathe to produce and evenly turned surface. This is then rendered, or filled in and shaded. Once the beginning and end objects have been created the computer can calculate the morphing process.

morphology in biology, the study of the physical structure and form of organisms, in particular their soft tissues.

morphology in the study of language, the analysis of the formation of words, the breaking-down of a language into morphemes.

Morrigan in Celtic mythology, a goddess of war and death who could take the shape of a crow.

Morris Henry 1889–1961. British educationalist. He inspired and oversaw the introduction of the 'village college' and community school education, which he saw as regenerating rural life. His ideas were also adopted in urban areas.

Morris emphasized the value of providing single-site centres of continuing education and leisure activity for both adults and children alike. He persuaded Walter ◊Gropius, together with Maxwell Fry, to design the Village College at Impington, near Cambridge, 1939. He was chief education officer for Cambridgeshire 1922–54.

Dreamer of dreams, born out of my due time, / Why should I strive to set the crooked straight?

William Morris
The Earthly Paradise 'An Apology'

Morris William 1834–1896. English designer, a founder of the ◊Arts and Crafts movement, socialist, and writer who shared the Pre-Raphaelite painters' fascination with medieval settings. In 1861 he co-founded a firm that designed and produced furniture, carpets, and a wide range of decorative wallpapers, many of which are still produced today. His Kelmscott Press, set up 1890 to print beautifully designed books, influenced printing and book design. The prose romances *A Dream of John Ball* 1888 and *News from Nowhere* 1891 reflect his socialist ideology. He also lectured on socialism.

Morris abandoned his first profession, architecture, to study painting, but had a considerable influence on such architects as William Lethaby and Philip ◊Webb. As a founder of the Arts and Crafts movement, Morris did much to raise British craft standards. His first book of verse was *The Defence of Guenevere* 1858.

William Morris was born in Walthamstow, London, and educated at Oxford, where he formed a lasting friendship with the Pre-Raphaelite artist Edward Burne-Jones and was influenced by the art critic John Ruskin and the painter and poet Dante Rossetti.

Morris published several volumes of verse romances, notably *The Life and Death of Jason* 1867 and *The Earthly Paradise* 1868–70; a visit to Iceland 1871 inspired *Sigurd the Volsung* 1876 and general interest in the ◊sagas. He joined the Social Democratic Federation 1883, but left it 1884 because he found it too moderate, and set up the Socialist League. To this period belong the critical and sociological studies *Signs of Change* 1888 and *Hopes and Fears for Art* 1892, and the narrative poem 'The Pilgrims of Hope' 1885.

Mosca Gaetano 1858–1941. Italian jurist, politician, and political scientist. Mosca was elected a deputy in the Italian parliament 1908 and became a life senator 1919. His most famous work *Elementi di scienza politica* 1896 (translated as *The Ruling Class* 1939) set out his theory of the political elite. In all societies, the majority is ruled by a minority in the upper stratum of society and, in the endless struggle for power, the membership of the elite political class is determined by natural selection.

Although his theory of the elite appears to justify fascism, Mosca spurned both Mussolini and Hitler. He was a professor at the University of Rome from 1923 and taught both there and at the universities of Palermo and Turin.

Moseley Henry Gwyn-Jeffreys 1887–1915. English physicist. From 1913 to 1914 he devised the series of atomic numbers (reflecting the charges of the nuclei of different elements) that led to the revision of the ◊Mendeleyev's periodic table of the elements.

A student of Ernest ◊Rutherford, Moseley devoted his career to research on the structure of the atom. He concluded that the atomic number is equal to the charge on the nucleus; therefore his periodic table was arranged by atomic number (instead of atomic mass, as presented by Mendeleyev). When the elements are so arranged, problems appearing in the Mendeleyev version are resolved.

Moses c. 13th century BC. Hebrew lawgiver and judge who led the Israelites out of Egypt to the promised land of Canaan. The Torah describes how on Mount Sinai he received from Jehovah the oral and written Law, including the ◊*Ten Commandments* engraved on tablets of stone. The first five books of the Old Testament – in Judaism, the Torah – are ascribed to him.

According to the Torah, the infant Moses was hidden among the bulrushes on the banks of the Nile when the pharaoh commanded that all newborn male Hebrew children should be destroyed. He was found by a daughter of Pharaoh, who reared him. Eventually he became the leader of the Israelites in their ◊*Exodus* from Egypt and their 40 years' wandering in the wilderness.

He died at the age of 120, after having been allowed a glimpse of the Promised Land from Mount Pisgah.

Moslem alternative spelling of *Muslim*, a follower of ◊Islam.

mosque in Islam, a place of worship. Chief features are: the dome; the minaret, a balconied turret from which the faithful are called to prayer; the mihrab, or prayer niche, in one of the interior walls, showing the direction of the holy city of Mecca; and an open court surrounded by porticoes.

The earliest mosques were based on the plan of Christian basilicas, although different influences contributed towards their architectural development. Mosques vary a great deal in style in various parts of the world.

Mott Nevill Francis 1905– . English physicist who researched the electronic properties of metals, semiconductors, and noncrystalline materials. He shared the Nobel Prize for Physics 1977 with US physicists Philip Anderson (1923–) and John Van Vleck (1899–1980).

Mo Tzu c. 470–391 BC. Chinese philosopher whose pragmatism and anti-Confucian teachings are summarized in a book also called *Mo Tzu*. His followers formed a group known as the Mohists. The core of Mo Tzu's teaching was frugality, universal love, and the rejection and condemnation of warfare.

Mo Tzu attacked what he saw as the empty formulas of the Confucians by stating that nothing should be undertaken unless it was of clear benefit to the people. He saw this as the necessary guiding principle that governments should follow. He held that if universal love was the norm, nations would not go to war with each other, people would not harm each other, and the wastefulness of dispute and warfare would thus be avoided, benefiting everyone.

Moundbuilder member of any of the various North American Indian peoples of the Midwest and the South who built earth mounds, from about 300 BC. The mounds were linear and pictographic in form for tombs, such as the Great Serpent Mound in Ohio, and truncated pyramids and cones for the platforms of chiefs' houses and temples. The Hopewell and Natchez were Moundbuilders.

The Moundbuilders carried out group labour projects under the rule of an elite. An important site is Monk's Mound in Mississippi. They were in decline by the time of the Spanish invasion, but traces of their culture live on in the folklore of the Choctaw and Cherokee Indians.

Mudra in Hindu religious dance, ritualized body gestures, especially of the hand and fingers.

mufti Muslim legal expert who guides the courts in their interpretation. In Turkey the *grand mufti* had supreme spiritual authority until the establishment of the republic in 1924.

Muhammad or *Mohammed, Mahomet* c. 570–632. The final prophet of Islam, born in Mecca on the Arabian peninsula. In about 616 he began to preach the worship of one God, who is believed to have revealed to him the words of the ◊Qur'an in a series of revelations that continued throughout his life. In 622 he and his followers escaped persecution in Mecca by moving to Medina. The flight, known as the Hijra or Hegira, marks the beginning of the Islamic era.

Muhammad was a shepherd and and trader, and married Khadija, a widow, in 595. He spent time in meditation, and received his first revelation in 610.

At first he doubted its divine origin, but later began to teach others, who recorded the words of his revelations and wrote them down. They were collected after his death to form the Qur'an. The move to Medina resulted in the first Islamic community, which for many years fought fierce battles against fierce opposition from Mecca and from neighbouring tribes. In 630 the Muslim army defeated that of Mecca and the city came under Muslim rule. By the time of Muhammad's death in 632 Islam had spread to the whole Arabian peninsula. After his death the leadership of the Muslims was disputed. Muslims believe that he was the final prophet, although they recognized other, earlier prophets, including Ibrahim (Abraham) and Isa (Jesus). Muhammad is not worshipped, but honoured by the words 'Peace be upon him', whenever Muslims mention his name.

muhrim the close relatives of the opposite sex, detailed by the ◊Qur'an, whom a Muslim may not marry. A Muslim may not mix freely with any member of the opposite sex outside these prohibited degrees.

Muller Hermann Joseph 1890–1967. US geneticist who discovered the effect of radiation on genes by his work on fruit flies. He was awarded the Nobel Prize for Medicine 1946.

Müller Johannes Peter 1801–1858. German comparative anatomist whose studies of nerves and sense organs opened a new chapter in physiology by demonstrating the physical nature of sensory perception. His name is associated with a number of discoveries, including the *Müllerian ducts* in the mammalian fetus and the lymph heart in frogs.

Mulliken Robert Sanderson 1896–1986. US chemist and physicist who received the 1966 Nobel Prize for Chemistry for his development of the molecular orbital theory.

multicultural education education aimed at preparing children to live in a multiracial society by giving them an understanding of the culture and history of different ethnic groups.

The initiative for multicultural teaching in the UK rose out of the Swann Report 1985 against racism and racial disadvantage in schools.

multilateralism trade among more than two countries without discrimination over origin or destination and regardless of whether a large trade gap is involved.

Unlike ◊bilateralism, multilateralism does not require the trade flow between countries to be of the same value.

multimedia computer system that combines audio and video components to create an interactive application that uses text, sound, and graphics (still, animated, and video sequences). For example, a multimedia database of musical instruments may allow a user not only to search and retrieve text about a particular instrument but also to see pictures of it and hear it play a piece of music.

Multimedia systems are still at an early stage of development. ◊CD-ROM is frequently used as a backing storage for such systems because of its high storage capacity.

In training applications based on multimedia, the student's responses to questions displayed using pictures, text, and sound are monitored by the computer and the student's route through the training material is adjusted accordingly.

multiplier in economics, the theoretical concept, formulated by John Maynard Keynes, of the effect on national income or employment by an adjustment in overall demand. For example, investment by a company in a new plant will stimulate new income and expenditure, which will in turn generate new investment, and so on, so that the actual increase in national income may be several times greater than the original investment.

Every generation revolts against its fathers and makes friends with its grandfathers.

Lewis Mumford
The Brown Decade

Mumford Lewis 1895–1990. US urban planner and social critic, concerned with the adverse effect of technology on contemporary society.

His books, including *Technics and Civilization* 1934 and *The Culture of Cities* 1938, discussed the rise of cities and proposed the creation of green belts around large conurbations. His view of the importance of an historical perspective in urban planning for the future is reflected in his major work *The City in History* 1961.

Murchison Roderick 1792–1871. Scottish geologist responsible for naming the Silurian period (in his book *The Silurian System* 1839).

He surveyed Russia 1840–45. In 1855 he became director-general of the UK Geological Survey.

Muses, The in Greek mythology, the nine daughters of Zeus and Mnemosyne (goddess of memory) and inspirers of the creative arts: Calliope represented epic poetry; Clio, history; Erato, love poetry; Euterpe, lyric poetry; Melpomene, tragedy; Polyhymnia, sacred song; Terpsichore, dance; Thalia, comedy; and Urania, astronomy.

museum a place or building for the storage and display of works of art, scientific specimens, or other objects of cultural importance.

In Ancient Greece the *mouseion* was a temple dedicated to the ◊Muses. By the Renaissance, the term museum was applied to the room where a scholar examined and studied his collection of classical antiquities. The notion of a national or state collection which could be viewed by the general public began as a result of the French Revolution and the opening of the Louvre Gallery in 1793. Before that, the British Museum had been established by an Act of Parliament in 1759, but access was limited to scholars. More recently, museums have sought to widen the uses of their collections by combining the aims of scholarship and conservation with a more entertaining approach for the ordinary visitor.

music art of combining sounds into a coherent perceptual experience, typically in accordance with fixed patterns and for an aesthetic purpose. Music is generally categorized as classical, jazz, pop music, country and western, and so on.

The notes I handle no better than many pianists. But the pauses between the notes – ah, that is where the art resides!

music
Artur Schnabel, 1882–1951,
Austrian pianist and composer.
Chicago Daily News 11 June 1958

The Greek word *mousikē* covered all the arts presided over by the Muses. The various civilizations of the ancient and modern world developed their own musical systems. Eastern music recognizes subtler distinctions of pitch than does Western music and also differs from Western music in that the absence, until recently, of written notation ruled out the composition of major developed works; it fostered melodic and rhythmic patterns, freely interpreted (as in the Indian *raga*) by virtuosos.

Muslim or *Moslem* a follower of ◊Islam.

Muslim Brotherhood the most prominent Sunni Islamic movement, founded 1928 by Hasan al-Banna (1906–1949). Its overall aim is the foundation of an Islamic state governed by Islamic law. The movement also operates under different names, such as the People of the Call (Ahl al-Da'wa) in Algeria, and Islamic Party (al Hizb al-Islami) in Tunisia.

It is active throughout the Arab world, and generally retains strong popular support, although banned in most countries (since 1980, membership has been punishable by death in Syria). The movement has gained political acceptance in Jordan, in 1989 winning 20 out of 80 seats in the House of Representatives, and joining the government in 1991.

mutation in biology, a change in the genes produced by a change in the ◊DNA that makes up the hereditary material of all living organisms. Mutations, the raw material of evolution, result from mistakes during replication (copying) of DNA molecules. Only a few improve the organism's performance and are therefore favoured by ◊natural selection. Mutation rates are increased by certain chemicals and by radiation.

Common mutations include the omission or insertion of a base (one of the chemical subunits of DNA); these are known as *point mutations*. Larger-scale mutations include removal of a whole segment of DNA or its inversion within the DNA strand. Not all mutations affect the organism, because there is a certain amount of redundancy in the genetic information. If a mutation is 'translated' from DNA into the protein that makes up the organism's structure, it may be in a nonfunctional part of the protein and thus have no detectable effect. This is known as a *neutral mutation*, and is of importance in ◊molecular clock studies because such mutations tend to accumulate gradually as time passes. Some mutations do affect genes that control protein production or functional parts of protein, and most of these are lethal to the organism.

Myers F(rederic) W(illiam) H(enry) 1843–1901. English classical scholar and psychic researcher, a founder 1882 and one of the first presidents, 1900, of the Society for Psychical Research and one of its most indefatigable investigators of the ◊paranormal.

He collaborated with Edmund Gurney (1847–1888) and Frank Podmore (1856–1910) on *Phantasms of the Living* 1886, the first thorough study of 'crisis' apparitions – cases in which an apparition is 'seen' by someone roughly twelve hours either side of another's death or encounter with danger. His *Human Personality and its Survival of Bodily Death* 1903, which was published posthumously, is a remarkable account of 19th century psychical research, dealing with, among other topics, sleep, ◊hypnotism, ◊genius, ◊automatism, and ◊telepathy, a term he coined.

Myrdal Gunnar 1898–1987. Swedish economist, author of many works on development economics. He shared a Nobel prize in 1974 with F A Hayek.

mystery religion any of various cults of the ancient world, open only to the initiated; for example, the cults of Demeter (see ◊Eleusinian Mysteries), Dionysus, Cybele, Isis, and ◊Mithras. Underlying some of them is a fertility

Western Music: chronology

AD 590 St Gregory the Great was elected pope. Under his rule, music attained new heights, initiating Gregorian chant.

1026 The Italian monk Guido d'Arezzo completed his treatise *Micrologus*. He founded modern notation and tonic sol-fa.

1207 Minnesingers (poet-musicians) Walther von der Vogelweide, Tannhauser, and Wolfram von Eschenbach competed in a song contest at Wartburg Castle, later celebrated in Wagner's opera *Die Meistersinger von Nürnberg*.

1240 The earliest known canon, *Sumer is Icumen In*, was composed around this year.

1280 *Carmina Burana*, a collection of students' songs, was compiled in Benediktbeurn, Bavaria; Carl Orff was later inspired by their subject matter.

1288 France's greatest troubadour, Adam de la Halle, died in Naples.

1320 *Ars nova*, a tract by Philippe de Vitry, gave its name to a new, more graceful era in music.

1364 Music's first large-scale masterpiece, the *Notre Dame Mass* of Guillaume de Machaut, was performed in Rheims to celebrate the coronation of Charles V of France.

1453 John Dunstable, England's first composer of significance, died in London.

1473 The earliest known printed music, the *Collectorium super Magnificat* by Johannes Gerson, was published in Esslingen, near Stuttgart.

1521 Josquin Desprez, the leading musician of his time, died in Condé-sur-Escaut, Burgundy.

1564 Production of violins began at the workshop of Andrea Amati in Cremona.

1575 Thomas Tallis and William Byrd jointly published their *Cantiones sacrae*, a collection of 34 motets.

1576 Hans Sachs, the most famous of the Meistersinger (mastersinger) poets and composers, died in Nuremberg.

1597 The first opera, *La Dafne* by Jacopo Peri, was staged privately at the Corsi Palazzo in Florence.

1610 Monteverdi's *Vespers* was published in Venice.

1637 The world's first opera house opened in Venice.

1644 Antonio Stradivarius was born. More than 600 of his violins, made in Cremona, survived into the 20th century.

1672 The violinist John Banister inaugurated the first season of public concerts in London.

1709 Bartolemmeo Cristofori unveiled the first fortepiano in Florence.

1721 Bach completed his six *Brandenburg Concertos* for Baroque orchestra.

1722 Jean-Philippe Rameau's book *Traité de l'harmonie* was published, founding modern harmonic theory.

1725 Vivaldi's orchestral suite *The Four Seasons* was published in Amsterdam.

1732 Covent Garden Theatre opened in London.

1742 Handel's *Messiah* received its world premiere in Dublin.

1757 Johann Stamitz died in Mannheim, where he had made important contributions to the development of the symphony and raised the status of the orchestra.

1761 Haydn took up liveried service as vice kapellmeister with the aristocratic Esterházy family, to whom he was connected until his death 1809.

1788 Mozart completed his last three symphonies, numbers 39–41, in six weeks.

1798 The *Allgemeine Musikalische Zeitung*, a journal of music criticism, was first published in Leipzig.

1805 Beethoven's *Eroica Symphony* vastly expanded the horizons of orchestral music.

1814 Maelzel invented the metronome.

1815 Schubert's output for this year included 2 symphonies, 2 masses, 20 waltzes, and 145 songs.

1821 Weber's *Der Freischütz/The Marksman* introduced heroic German Romanticism to opera.

1828 The limits of instrumental virtuosity were redefined by violinist Paganini's Vienna debut.

1830 Berlioz's dazzlingly avant-garde and programmatic *Symphonie fantastique* startled Paris concertgoers.

1831 Grand opera was inaugurated with *Robert le diable* by Giacomo Meyerbeer.

1851 Jenny Lind, a singer managed by P T Barnum, earned $176,675 from nine months' concerts in the USA.

1842 The Vienna Philharmonic Orchestra gave its first concerts.

1854 In Weimar, Liszt conducted the premieres of his first symphonic poems.

1855 Like most orchestras around this date, the New York Philharmonic for the first time sat down while playing (cellists were already seated).

1865 Wagner's opera *Tristan and Isolde* scaled new heights of expressiveness using unprecedented chromaticism. Schubert's *Unfinished Symphony* (1822) was premiered in Vienna.

1875 The first of a series of collaborations between Arthur Sullivan and the librettist W S Gilbert, *Trial by Jury*, was given its premiere.

1876 Wagner's *The Ring of the Nibelung* was produced in Bayreuth. Brahms' *First Symphony* was performed in Karlsruhe.

1877 Edison invented the cylindrical tin-foil phonograph.

1883 The Metropolitan Opera House opened in New York with a production of Gounod's *Faust*.

1885 Liszt composed *Bagatelle without Tonality* (his *Faust Symphony* of 1857 opened with a 12-note row).

1894 Debussy's *Prélude à l'après-midi d'un faune* anticipated 20th-century composition with its use of the whole-tone scale.

1895 Henry Wood conducted the first Promenade Concert at the Queen's Hall in London.

1899 Scott Joplin's *Maple Leaf Rag* was published in Sedalia, Missouri.

1902 Caruso recorded ten arias in a hotel room in Milan, the success of which established the popularity of the phonograph. By the time of his death 1921 he had earned $2 million from sales of his recordings.

1908 Saint-Saëns became the first leading composer to write a film score, for *L'Assassinat du duc de Guise*.

1911 Irving Berlin had his first big success as a songwriter with *Alexander's Ragtime Band*.

1912 Schoenberg's atonal *Pierrot Lunaire*, for reciter and chamber ensemble, foreshadowed many similar small-scale quasi-theatrical works.

1913 Stravinsky's ballet *The Rite of Spring* precipitated a riot at its premiere in Paris.

Western Music: chronology

1919	Schoenberg, who was experimenting with serial technique, set up the Society for Private Musical Performances in Vienna, which lasted until 1921.
1922	Alessandro Moreschi, last of the castrati, died in Rome.
1925	Louis Armstrong made his first records with the Hot Five. Duke Ellington's Washingtonians also started recording.
1927	Jerome Kern's *Showboat*, with libretto by Oscar Hammerstein II, laid the foundations of the US musical.
1932	The BBC Symphony Orchestra was founded in London under Sir Adrian Boult.
1937	Arturo Toscanini, one of the greatest conductors in the history of music, began his 17-year association with the NBC Symphony Orchestra.
1938	Prokofiev's score for Eisenstein's *Alexander Nevsky* raised film music to new levels. Big-band music became popular.
1939	Elisabeth Lutyens was one of the first English composers to use 12-note composition in her *Chamber Concerto No 1* for nine instruments.
1940	Walt Disney's *Fantasia* introduced classical music, conducted by Leopold Stokowski, to a worldwide audience of film-goers.
1941	The 'Proms' moved to the Royal Albert Hall.
1942	In Chicago, John Cage conducted the premiere of his *Imaginary Landscape No 3*, scored for marimbula, gongs, tin cans, buzzers, plucked coil, electric oscillator, and generator.
1945	Bebop jazz was initiated. The jazz greats Charlie Parker and Dizzy Gillespie first recorded together.
1954	Stockhausen's *Electronic Studies* for magnetic tape were broadcast in Cologne. Edgard Varèse's *Déserts*, the first work to combine instruments and prerecorded magnetic tape, was performed in Paris. Elvis Presley made his first rock-and-roll recordings.
1955	Pierre Boulez's *Le Marteau sans maître*, for contralto and chamber ensemble, was performed in Baden-Baden. Its formidable serial technique and exotic orchestration was acclaimed by the avant-garde. The Miles Davis Quintet with John Coltrane united two of the most important innovators in jazz.
1956	The first annual Warsaw Autumn festival of contemporary music was held. This became important for the promotion of Polish composers such as Lutoslawski and Penderecki.
1957	Leonard Bernstein's *West Side Story* was premiered in New York. A computer, programmed at the University of Illinois by Lejaren Hiller and Leonard Isaacson, composed the *Illiac Suite* for string quartet.
1963	Shostakovich's opera *Lady Macbeth of Mezensk*, earlier banned and condemned in the Soviet newspaper *Pravda* 1936, was produced in a revised version as *Katerina Ismailova*.
1965	Robert Moog invented a synthesizer that considerably widened the scope of electronic music. The film soundtrack of *The Sound of Music*, with music by Rodgers and lyrics by Hammerstein, was released, and stayed in the sales charts for the next two years. Bob Dylan used electric instrumentation on *Highway 61 Revisited*.
1967	The Beatles' album *Sgt Pepper's Lonely Hearts Club Band*, which took over 500 hours to record, was released. The first Velvet Underground album was released. Psychedelic rock spread from San Francisco, and hard rock developed in the UK and the USA.
1969	Peter Maxwell Davies' theatre piece *Eight Songs for a Mad King*, for vocalist and six instruments, was premiered under his direction in London by the Pierrot Players, later to become the Fires of London ensemble.
1972	Bob Marley's LP *Catch a Fire* began popularization of reggae beyond Jamaica.
1976	Philip Glass' opera *Einstein on the Beach*, using the repetitive techniques of minimalism, was given its first performance in Paris. Punk rock arrived with the Sex Pistols' *Anarchy in the UK*.
1977	The Institute for Research and Coordination of Acoustics and Music (IRCAM) was founded in Paris under the direction of Pierre Boulez, for visiting composers to make use of advanced electronic equipment.
1981	MTV (Music Television) started broadcasting nonstop pop videos on cable in the USA, growing into a worldwide network in the following decade.
1983	Messiaen's only opera, *Saint François d'Assise*, was given its first performance in Paris. Lutoslawski's *Third Symphony* was premiered to worldwide acclaim by the Chicago Symphony Orchestra under Georg Solti. Compact discs were launched in the West.
1986	Paul Simon's *Graceland* album drew on and popularized world music.
1990	Many record chain stores ceased to stock seven-inch singles, accelerating the decline of vinyl records' share of the market.
1991	US rap group NWA declared not obscene by a UK court. Various attempts, especially in the USA, to limit freedom of speech in popular music were generally unsuccessful.
1992	DCC (Digital Compact Cassettes) and MiniDisc (MD), two new audio formats, were launched by Philips and Sony, respectively.

ritual, in which a deity undergoes death and resurrection and the initiates feed on the flesh and blood to attain communion with the divine and ensure their own life beyond the grave. The influence of mystery religions on early Christianity was considerable.

mysticism religious belief or spiritual experience based on direct, intuitive communion with the divine. It does not always involve an orthodox deity, though it is found in all the major religions – for example, kabbalism in Judaism, Sufism in Islam, and the bhakti movement in Hinduism. The mystical experience is often rooted in asceticism and can involve visions, trances, and ecstasies; many religious traditions prescribe meditative and contemplative techniques for achieving mystical experience. Official churches fluctuate between acceptance of mysticism as a form of special grace, and suspicion of it as a dangerous deviation, verging on the heretical.

myth traditional tale of gods, goddesses, heroes, or heroines. Myths are not based on actual events (although there might be a historical element) but are imaginary, fabulous tales that often offer explanations of natural phenomena, such as the coming of spring or the creation of the world.

mythology study and interpretation of the stories symbolically underlying a given culture and of how they relate to similar stories told in other cultures. These stories describe gods and other supernatural beings, with whom humans may have relationships, and may be intended to explain the workings of the universe, nature, or human history.

Ancient mythologies, with the names of the chief god of each, include those of Egypt (Osiris), Greece (Zeus), Rome (Jupiter), India (Brahma), and the Teutonic peoples (Odin or Woden).

mythopoeia composition of stories or myths, usually in a narrative form such as epic poetry. The term may include the reshaping of traditional stories by a poet, and an acknowledgement of the art of storytelling.

Nagel Ernest 1901–1985. US philosopher who specialized in the philosophy of science and logic. He analysed the logical structure of scientific enquiries; and, in particular, he argued that the social sciences are capable of making useful general laws and explanations. He also held that the world contains no ultimate ingredients beyond matter.

His *The Structure of Science: Problems in the Logic of Scientific Explanation* 1961 is a modern classic in this field. He was born at Novemesto in Czechoslovakia, emigrated to the USA in 1911, and became a US citizen in 1919. He was professor of philosophy at Columbia University.

Namier Lewis Bernstein (Ludwik Bernsztajn vel Niemirowski) 1888–1960. Polish historian, who became a British citizen after coming to Britain 1906. His two major books, *The Structure of Politics at the Accession of George III* 1929 and *England in the Age of the American Revolution* 1930, challenged accepted interpretations of 18th-century British history in terms of Whig–Tory rivalry.

Their success led to his appointment as professor of history at Manchester University from 1931–53. He also made contributions to the study of 19th-century European history, in particular with *1848: The Revolution of the Intellectuals* 1946, and wrote many essays and reviews collected in *Avenues of History* 1952, *Personalities and Powers* 1955, and *Vanished Supremacies* 1958.

After coming to Britain, Namier studied at Balliol College, Oxford. During the First World War he worked in the Foreign Office, and thereafter in business, while working on his two major studies of 18th century British politics.

Nanak 1469–c. 1539. first guru of Sikhism, a religion based on the unity of God and the equality of all human beings. He was strongly opposed to caste divisions.

He was born in the Punjab, to a Hindu family in an area deeply divided between Muslims and Hindus. After training to be an accountant like his father, he found himself increasingly attracted to a life of prayer and meditation. He appears to have had a conversion experience which led to his saying, 'There is neither Hindu nor Muslim, so whose path shall I follow? I shall follow God's path. God is neither Hindu nor Muslim and the path which I follow is God's.' For many years he travelled around India and other countries teaching this message. At the age of 50 he founded a town in the Punjab called Kartapur, where many people came to live as his disciples. Guru Nanak insisted that everyone was equal, so all sat down at the same table to eat. On his deathbed, Guru Nakak announced his friend Lehna as his successor, and gave him the name Angad – 'part of me'.

Napier John 1550–1617. Scottish mathematician who invented ◊logarithms 1614 and 'Napier's bones', an early mechanical calculating device for multiplication and division.

Soldiers! From the summit of these pyramids, forty centuries look down upon you.

Napoleon
Exhortation to his troops before the Battle of the Pyramids 1798

Napoleon I Bonaparte 1769–1821. Emperor of the French 1804–14 and 1814–15. A general from 1796 in the Revolutionary Wars, in 1799 he overthrew the ruling Directory (see ◊French Revolution) and made himself dictator. From 1803 he conquered most of Europe (the *Napoleonic Wars*) and installed his brothers as puppet kings. After the Peninsular War and retreat from Moscow 1812, he was forced to abdicate 1814 and was banished to the island of Elba. In March 1815 he reassumed power but was defeated by British forces at the Battle of Waterloo and exiled to the island of St Helena. His internal administrative reforms and laws are still evident in France.

While retaining and extending the legal and educational reforms of the Jacobins, Napoleon replaced the democratic constitution established by the Revolution with a centralized despotism, and by his ◊concordat with Pius VII conciliated the Catholic church. The

Code Napoléon remains the basis of French law.

narcissism in psychology, an exaggeration of normal self-respect and self-involvement which may amount to mental disorder when it precludes relationships with other people. Named after legendary beautiful Greek youth, ◊Narcissus.

Narcissus in Greek legend, a beautiful youth who rejected the love of the nymph ◊Echo and was condemned to fall in love with his own reflection in a pool. He pined away and in the place where he died a flower sprang up that was named after him.

National Association for the Advancement of Colored People (NAACP) US civil-rights organization dedicated to ending inequality and segregation for African-Americans through nonviolent protest. Founded 1910, its first aim was to eradicate lynching. The NAACP campaigned to end segregation in state schools; it funded test cases that eventually led to the Supreme Court decision 1954 outlawing school segregation, although it was only through the ◊civil-rights movement of the 1960s that desegregation was achieved. In 1987 the NAACP had about 500,000 members, black and white.

The NAACP was founded by a group of white liberals, including William Walling, Oswald Villard, social worker Jane Addams, philosopher John Dewey, and novelist William Dean Howells. Most of the officials were white, but most of the members were drawn from the ranks of the black bourgeoisie. It merged with the Niagara Movement founded 1905 by W E B DuBois. During World War II its membership increased from 50,000 to 400,000. The organization has been criticized by militants and black separatists for its moderate stance and its commitment to integration. See also *history* under ◊black.

national debt debt incurred by the central government of a country to its own people and institutions and also to overseas creditors. A government can borrow from the public by means of selling interest-bearing bonds, for example, or from abroad. Traditionally, a major cause of national debt was the cost of war but in recent decades governments have borrowed heavily in order to finance development or nationalization, to support an ailing currency, or to avoid raising taxes.

Government budgets are often planned with a deficit that is funded by overseas borrowing. In the 1980s most governments adopted monetary policies designed to limit their borrowing requirements, both to reduce the cost of servicing the debt and because borrowing money tends to cause inflation.

On 31 March 1988 the UK national debt was £197,295 million, or £3,465 per head of population.

In Britain the national debt is managed by the Bank of England, under the control of the Treasury. The first issue of government stock in Britain was made in 1693, to raise a loan of £1 million. Historically, increases of the national debt have been caused by wartime expenditure; thus after the War of the Spanish Succession 1701–14 it reached £54 million. By 1900 it reached £610 million but World War I forced it up, by 1920, to £7,828 million and World War II, by 1945, to £21,870,221,651. Since then other factors have increased the national debt, including nationalization expenditure and overseas borrowing to support the pound. However, as a proportion of gross domestic product, the national debt has fallen since 1945 and stabilized at about 40–45%. In the 1970s it stood at over £35,000 million.

As a proportion of gross national product, net government debt in the UK has been falling steadily since 1975 when it stood at 58% and by 1988 it was only 45%. By contrast, in Italy, it continued to increase growing from 60% to 110% over the same period.

The US national debt was $2,436,453,269 in 1870 and $1,132,357,095 in 1905, but had risen to $24,299,321,467 by 1920 and it has since risen almost continuously, reaching $1,823,103 million in 1985.

national income the total income of a state in one year, including both the wages of individuals and the profits of companies. It is equal to the value of the output of all goods and services during the same period. National income is equal to gross national product (the value of a country's total output) minus an allowance for replacement of ageing capital stock.

Nations, like men, are teachable only in their youth; with age they become incorrigible.

nationalism
Jean-Jacques Rousseau, 1712–1778, French social philosopher.
The Social Contract

---

nationalism in politics, a movement that consciously aims to unify a nation, create a state, or liberate it from foreign or imperialistic rule.

Nationalist movements became a potent factor in European politics during the 19th century; since 1900 nationalism has become a strong force in Asia and Africa and in the late 1980s revived strongly in E Europe.

Stimulated by the French Revolution, movements arose in the 19th century in favour of national unification in Germany and Italy and national independence in Ireland, Italy, Belgium, Hungary, Bohemia, Poland, Finland, and the Balkan states. Revival of interest in the national language, history, traditions, and culture has accompanied and influenced most political movements. See also ◊African nationalism, ◊Irish nationalism.

Nationalism is an infantile sickness. It is the measles of the human race.

nationalism
Albert Einstein, 1879–1955, German-born US physicist.
Albert Einstein, the Human Side
H Dukas and B Hoffman

In political terms, nationalism can be pursued as an ideology which stresses the superiority of a nation and its inhabitants compared with other nations and peoples. Most countries enjoy, and wish to demonstrate, national pride but – carried to an extreme – nationalism can produce dangerous regimes and political systems (such as that in Nazi Germany in the 1930s).

In the second half of the 20th century a strongly national literary and political movement has developed in Scotland and Wales.

nationalization policy of bringing a country's essential services and industries under public ownership. It was pursued, for example, by the UK Labour government 1945–51. In recent years the trend towards nationalization has slowed and in many countries (the UK, France, and Japan) reversed (◊privatization). Assets in the hands of foreign governments or companies may also be nationalized; for example, Iran's oil industry, the Suez Canal, and US-owned fruit plantations in Guatemala, all in the 1950s.

In the UK, acts were passed nationalizing the Bank of England, coal, and most hospitals in 1946; transport and electricity in 1947; gas in 1948; and iron and steel in 1949. In 1953 the succeeding Conservative government provided for the return of road haulage to private enterprise and for decentralization of the railways. It also denationalized iron and steel in

1953, but these were renationalized by the next Labour government in 1967. In 1977 Callaghan's Labour government nationalized the aircraft and shipbuilding industries. With the advent of a Conservative government 1979, the process was reversed in the form of privatization.

National Socialism official name for ◊Nazism in Germany; see also ◊fascism.

Nation of Islam former name of the group more commonly known as the ◊Black Muslims. This US group was radically changed after the death of its founder Elijah Muhammad (1897–1975). The majority of followers now practise orthodox Islam although a minority retain the group's original name together with the group's original anti-white attitudes.

nativity Christian festival celebrating a birth: *Christmas* is celebrated 25 Dec from AD 336 in memory of the birth of Jesus in Bethlehem; *Nativity of the Virgin Mary* is celebrated 8 Sept by the Catholic and Eastern Orthodox churches; *Nativity of John the Baptist* is celebrated 24 June by the Catholic, Eastern Orthodox, and Anglican churches.

Naturalism in the arts, an approach that advocated the factual and realistic representation of the subject of a painting or novel with no stylization. Naturalism also refers specifically to a movement in literature and drama that originated in France in the late 19th century with the writings of Emile ◊Zola and the brothers Goncourt. Similar to ◊Realism in that it was concerned with everyday life, Naturalism also held that people's fates were determined by heredity, environment, and social forces beyond their control.

Zola, the chief theorist of the movement, demonstrates the characteristic accuracy of reportage in his Rougon-Macquart sequence of novels (1871–93), which shows the working of heredity and environment in one family. Other Naturalists writers include Guy de Maupassant and Alphonse Daudet in France, Gerhart Hauptmann in Germany, and Theodore Dreiser in America.

natural justice the concept that there is an inherent quality in law which compares favourably with arbitrary action by a government. It is largely associated with the idea of the rule of law. For natural justice to be present it is generally argued that no one should be a judge in his or her own case, and that each party in a dispute has an unalienable right to be heard and to prepare their case thoroughly (the rule of *audi alterem partem*).

natural law the idea that fundamental laws exist in nature which are common to all mankind. Natural law is distinct from positive law which is those laws imposed on man by man.

natural philosophy or ***philosophy of nature*** former name for ◊physics, used in the days before physics was separated from philosophy and became a discipline in its own right. The term began to fall out of use in the late 18th century.

natural selection the process whereby gene frequencies in a population change through certain individuals producing more descendants than others because they are better able to survive and reproduce in their environment. The accumulated effect of natural selection is to produce adaptations such as the insulating coat of a polar bear or the spadelike forelimbs of a mole. The process is slow, relying firstly on random variation in the genes of an organism being produced by ◊mutation and secondly on the genetic recombination of sexual reproduction. It was recognized by Charles Darwin and English naturalist Alfred Russel Wallace as the main process driving ◊evolution.

natural theology in Christianity, learning about God from creation, using reason alone. In Greek and Roman philosophy, discourse on the 'divine' nature of things, rather than their accidental or transient nature. Thomas ◊Aquinas was the first great proponent of Christian natural theology. It became a part of Roman Catholic dogma in 1870 at the first ◊Vatican Council.

Don't you find it a beautiful clean thought, a world empty of people, just uninterrupted grass, and a hare sitting up?

nature
D(avid) (H)erbert Lawrence, 1885–1930, English writer.
Women in Love

nature the living world, including plants, animals, fungi, and all microorganisms, and naturally formed features of the landscape, such as mountains and rivers.

Historically the word nature has had a multiplicity of meanings which can conveniently be reduced to two. Firstly, it refers to the essence or innate quality of a thing – that which makes it what it is. An example of this would be human nature – those universal characteristics which are common to all people. Secondly, it refers to the material world and to those phenomena that function independently of humans. This definition of nature is often contrasted with the artificial

The rainbow comes and goes, / And lovely is the rose, / The moon doth with delight / Look round her when the heavens are bare, / Waters on a starry night / Are beautiful and fair; / The sunshine is a glorious birth: / But yet I know, where'er I go, / That there hath passed away a glory from the earth.

nature
William Wordsworth, 1770–1850, English Romantic poet.
Ode. Intimations of Immortality

and the conventional, i.e., with human modifications of the natural order of things. Whether nature is superior or inferior to human uses and transformations of it has long been debated. Certainly many have believed that a time existed when humans and nature were part of one harmonious whole. Christians identify this period with Adam and Eve's life before the ◊Fall. For ◊Rousseau and the Romantics a pure state of nature could still be found in the behaviour of animals, children, and 'noble savages'. Such diverse figures as ◊Diogenes and ◊Thoreau have attempted to abandon the human world and return to a more natural state. Similar ideas can be found in the ecological movement, which has attacked the spoliation of nature by industry.

One impulse from a vernal wood / May teach you more of man, / Of moral evil and of good, / Than all the sages can.

nature
William Wordsworth, 1770–1850, English Romantic poet.
'The Tables Turned'

In earlier times the natural was also contrasted with the supernatural: the sub-lunary world – which followed ultimately predictable laws – with the super-lunary world – the world of the ideal and the spiritual. In the Middle Ages a further distinction was made between the passive, created world, *natura naturata*, and the active physical force which created it, *natura naturans*. Such a force was often personified: as Gods like ◊Persephone and ◊Gaia by the Ancient Greeks, and later as Mother Nature. The Romantics, exemplified by the poetry of Wordsworth, venerated this notion of nature as an active presence in the world.

nature-nurture controversy or *environ-ment-heredity controversy* long-standing dispute among philosophers and psychologists over the relative importance of environment, that is upbringing, experience, and learning ('nurture'), and heredity, that is genetic inheritance ('nature'), in determining the make-up of an organism, particularly with regard to human personality and intelligence.

One area of contention is the reason for differences between individuals, for example, in performing intelligence tests. The environmentalist position assumes that individuals do not differ significantly in their inherited mental abilities and that subsequent differences are due to learning, or to differences in early experiences. Opponents insist that certain differences in the capacities of individuals (and hence their behaviour) can be attributed to inherited differences in their genetic make-up.

Nazarite or *Nazirite* in the Old Testament, a Hebrew under a vow to God to observe certain rules, including not to cut his hair, drink wine, or have contact with dead bodies. Some took the vow for life, others for only a certain period. ◊Samson and ◊Samuel in the Old Testament were Nazarites from birth.

Nazism ideology based on racism, nationalism, and the supremacy of the state over the individual. The German Nazi party, the *Nationalsozialistische Deutsche Arbeiter-partei* (National Socialist German Workers' Party), was formed from the German Workers' Party (founded 1919) and led by Adolf ◊Hitler 1921-45.

During the 1930s, many similar parties were created throughout Europe and the USA, although only those of Austria, Hungary, and Sudetenland were of major importance. These parties collaborated with the German occupation of Europe 1939-45. After the Nazi atrocities of World War II (see ◊Holocaust), the party was banned in Germany, but today parties with Nazi or neo-Nazi ideologies exist in many countries.

Nazi-related movements were founded in the UK 1932 by Oswald Mosley and 1962 by Colin Jordan (National Socialist Movement),

and in 1967 the National Front was formed. In the USA the American Nazi Party was founded 1958 by George Lincoln Rockwell.

necessity in economics, good or service whose consumption is seen as essential in order to maintain a minimum standard of living in a society, for example food or shelter.

need human requirement. In business studies, needs are ranked in order of priority. According to US psychologist Abraham Maslow, basic or primary needs are the physical needs for food, shelter, clothing, and water. Social needs for love and respect from family, friends, and others in a group come next. Higher needs are the personal needs for status, recognition, responsibility, creativity, and achievement.

Thy necessity is yet greater than mine.

need

Philip Sidney, 1554-1586, English poet and soldier.
On giving his water-bottle to a critically wounded soldier at the Battle of Zutphen 1586

Needham Joseph 1900– . British biochemist and sinologist known for his work on the history of Chinese science. He worked first as a biochemist concentrating mainly on problems in embryology. In the 1930s he learned Chinese and began to collect material. The first volume of his *Science and Civilisation in China* was published in 1954 and by 1989 fifteen volumes had appeared.

negligence in law, doing some act that a 'prudent and reasonable' person would not do, or omitting to do some act that such a person would do. Negligence may arise in respect of a person's duty towards an individual or towards other people in general. Breach of the duty of care that results in reasonably foreseeable damage is a tort.

Contributory negligence is a defence sometimes raised where the defendant to an action for negligence claims that the plaintiff by his own negligence contributed to the cause of the action.

A person's duty towards an individual may cover parenthood, guardianship, trusteeship, or a contractual relationship; a person's duty towards other people may include the duties owed to the community, such as care upon the public highway, and the maintenance of structures in a safe condition.

négritude concept that reasserts black African cultural and aesthetic values against European colonialism; most simply, black intuition is opposed to European logic. It has been current since the 1930s, when it was used originally among French-speaking African writers and intellectuals to emphasize their pride in their own culture. Its adherents have included L S Senghor and the Martinique poet, playwright, and politician Aimé Césaire.

Neil A(lexander) S(utherland) 1883–1973. British educationist. In 1924, partially in reaction to his own repressive upbringing, he founded a school, Summerhill, where liberal and progressive ideas such as self-government by pupils and the voluntary attendance of lessons achieved remarkable results, especially with problem children.

Nemesis in Greek mythology, the goddess of retribution, who especially punished hubris (Greek *hybris*), violent acts carried through in defiance of the gods and human custom.

nemesis theory theory of animal extinction, suggesting that a sister star to the Sun caused the extinction of groups of animals such as dinosaurs. The theory holds that the movement of this as yet undiscovered star disrupts the ◊Oort cloud of comets every 26 million years, resulting in the Earth suffering an increased bombardment from comets at these times. The theory was proposed in 1984 to explain the newly discovered layer of iridium – an element found in comets and meteorites – in rocks dating from the end of dinosaur times. However, many palaeontologists deny any evidence for a 26-million-year cycle of extinctions.

neoclassical economics school of economic thought based on the work of 19th-century economists, such as Alfred ◊Marshall, using ◊marginal analysis to modify theories of ◊classical economics. Neoclassical economics placed greater emphasis on mathematical techniques and theories of the firm. Neoclassicists believed competition to be the regulator of economic activity that would establish equilibrium between demand and supply through the operation of ◊market forces. John Maynard ◊Keynes criticized neoclassical economics for its analysis of output and employment in the whole economy. Milton ◊Friedman reasserted neoclassical principles of macroeconomics.

Neo-Classicism movement in art and architecture in Europe and North America about 1750–1850, a revival of classical Greek and Roman art. It superseded the Rococo style and was partly inspired by the excavation of the Roman cities of Pompeii and Herculaneum. The architect Piranesi was an early Neo-Classicist; in sculpture Antonio Canova and in painting Jacques Louis David were exponents.

Other notable Neo-Classicists include (in sculpture) Thorwaldsen, Flaxman, and the American Horatio Greenough (1805–1852), (in painting) Ingres and Mengs, and (in architecture) Robert Adam. The movement drew very largely on the Greek cultural studies of the German art historian J J ◊Winckelmann.

neocolonialism disguised form of ◊imperialism, by which a country may grant independence to another country but continue to dominate it by control of markets for goods or raw materials.

This system was analysed in the Ghanaian leader Kwame Nkrumah's book *Neo-Colonialism, the Last Stage of Imperialism* 1965.

Neo-Confucianism vigorous intellectual response by Confucian scholars to the rise of both Buddhism and Taoism in China, beginning during the Sung dynasty (960–1126 AD). Its core cosmology and philosophy were set out by Chou Tun I (1017– 1073) who saw all reality (the twin forces of yin and yang, the five elements, and from these all life forms) as coming from an ultimate source which he termed Wu Chi (Original Non-Being).

This was further developed by two outstanding scholars. The most influential was Chu Hsi (1130–1200) who is associated with the School of Principle which sought to apply Chou Tun I's model to all phenomena in order to investigate their properties and purpose, seeking always to reduce them to the core elements of fundamental principle (li) and core energy (chi). Chu Hsi was the best exponent of this school and is particularly important for his prodigious output of writings, especially those on cosmology and the I Ching. The second scholar was Lu Chiu Yuan (1139–1193) who developed the School of Mind tradition. This turned inwards, seeking within the mind and the individual a microcosm of the universe within each person, which could be purified by meditation.

neoconservatism a version of conservatism that emerged in the USA in opposition to the liberal social and political attitudes of the 1960s. It advocates a traditional approach to morality and family life, extols the virtues of Western capitalism as a system that encourages individual initiative and freedom, and attacks the notion of the state as the promoter of equality and as a provider of welfare.

neo-Darwinism the modern theory of ◊evolution, built up since the 1930s by integrating the 19th-century English scientist Charles ◊Darwin's theory of evolution through natural selection with the theory of genetic inheritance founded on the work of the Austrian biologist Gregor ◊Mendel.

neo-Kantianism philosophical movement started about 1865 in Germany by Otto Liebmann (1840–1912), which lasted until the 1920s. Neo-Kantianism abandoned the wild speculations of the followers of G W F Hegel and advocated a return to the theories of Immanuel ◊Kant. The physicist Albert Einstein's philosophy of science is neo-Kantian.

neopaganism the rise of interest and practice of supposedly pagan ideas, festivals, and rituals since the mid-19th century. Often inspired by a dislike of both modern industrial society and traditional Christianity, neopaganism is both a romantic and anti-urban phenomenon. In most cases, the rituals which are performed have only tenuous links with any pagan past, as there is no provable line of descent in Europe. For example, the costumes and rituals of the Druids at Stonehenge on Midsummer's night were invented during the 19th century.

At its more serious level, neo-paganism does not try to reinvent the past, but sees itself as drawing inspiration for a new form of spirituality and response to nature from models perceived to have been followed by the ancient pagans. As such it represents a genuine spiritual search for new ways of expressing contemporary spirituality.

neo-Platonism school of philosophy that flourished in the late Roman Empire (3rd–6th centuries AD) and influenced Christian and metaphysical thought. The central figure was ◊Plotinus (205–270) who held that the ultimate goal of mystical union with the One or Good (which is the source of all being) could be achieved by intense moral and intellectual discipline.

The term neo-Platonism is a nineteenth century invention. Leading neo-Platonists after Plotinus include Porphyry (3rd century AD), Proclus (5th century AD) and Boethius (480–524). Many later philosophers, including Nicholas of Cusa (1401–1464), Marsilio Ficino (1433–1499), and the ◊Cambridge Platonists in the 17th century, were influenced by neo-Platonism. In the 20th century, William Inge (1860–1954), Dean of St Paul's, was a Christian neo-Platonist.

Nernst (Walther) Hermann 1864–1941. German physical chemist. His investigations, for which he won the 1920 Nobel Prize for Chemistry, were concerned with heat changes in chemical reactions. He proposed in 1906 the principle known as the **Nernst heat theorem** or the third law of thermodynamics: the law states that chemical changes at the temperature of ◊absolute zero involve no change of ◊entropy (disorder).

nervous breakdown popular term for a reaction to overwhelming psychological stress. It has no equivalent in medicine: patients said to be suffering from a nervous breakdown may in fact be going through an episode of depression, manic depression, anxiety, or even schizophrenia.

Nestorianism Christian doctrine held by the Syrian ecclesiastic Nestorius (died c. 457), patriarch of Constantinople 428–431. He asserted that Jesus had two natures, human and divine. He was banished for maintaining that Mary was the mother of the man Jesus only, and therefore should not be called the Mother of God. Today the Nestorian Church is found in small communities in Syria, Iraq, Iran, and India.

Nestorius and his followers fled from persecution in the Byzantine Empire after the Council of Ephesus 431 banned him and his teachings. They migrated to Persia and from here launched one of the most significant missionary movements of the churches. By the end of the 8th century they had spread from Persia to China and from Central Asia through Afghanistan to India, probably becoming the most numerous church in the world by the 9th century.

However, the Mongol invasions and the consolidation of Islam through these areas have now reduced this church to its present-day numbers of around 100,000.

neurasthenia obsolete term for nervous exhaustion, covering mild ◊depression and various symptoms of ◊neurosis. Formerly thought to be a bodily malfunction, it is now generally considered to be mental in origin. Dating from the mid-19th century, the term became widely used to describe the symptoms of soldiers returning from the front in World War I.

neurolinguistics the study of the neurological basis of language, particularly how the brain controls the processes of speech, through the analysis of speech disorders. Both clinical disorders, such as aphasia where the patient is physically and mentally capable of using language but experiences problems, and ordinary 'slips of the tongue', are analysed to understand how the basic speech system can go wrong.

neurology the branch of medicine concerned with the study and treatment of the brain, spinal cord, and peripheral nerves.

neuropsychology branch of neurology that overlaps with psychiatry and psychology and which is mainly concerned with the cerebral cortex, specifically those disorders of perception, memory, language, and behaviour that result from brain injury or disease.

A central concern of neuropsychology has been the question of how mental functions, such as perception, memory, and the initiation and control of actions, are related to the structure of the brain. Some researchers, for example Carl Broca and Carl ◊Wernicke, have favoured a holistic approach, believing that the whole brain is involved in any type of mental activity or action, while others, for example Huglings Jackson and Kurt Goldstein (1878–1965), have searched for evidence of the localization of specific functions in separate areas. The ultimate aim, however, has always been to understand the mechanisms of cognition and behaviour – in short, to discover how the brain works. Studies of the effects of specific brain injuries and the changes in cognition and behaviour associated with them as, for example, in ◊aphasia, together with carefully conducted experimental work with animals, have thrown light on certain aspects of cerebral functioning and also indicated ways of treating brain-damaged patients and helping them to understand their disease.

Bibl. Luria, A R *The Working Brain: An Introduction to Neuropsychology* (Harmondsworth, 1973)

If I were a medical man, I should prescribe a holiday to any patient who considered his work important.

neurosis

Bertrand Russell, 1872–1970, English philosopher and mathematical logician.
The Conquest of Happiness ch 5

---

neurosis in psychology, a general term referring to emotional disorders, such as anxiety, depression, and obsessions. The main disturbance tends to be one of mood; contact with reality is relatively unaffected, in contrast to the effects of ◊psychosis.

neuroticism personality dimension described by Hans Eysenck. People with high neuroticism are worriers, emotional, and moody.

neutrality the legal status of a country that decides not to choose sides in a war. Certain states, notably Switzerland and Austria, have opted for permanent neutrality. Neutrality always has a legal connotation. In peacetime, neutrality towards the big power alliances is called ***nonalignment***.

new age movement of the late 1980s characterized by an emphasis on the holistic view of body and mind, alternative (or complementary) medicines, personal growth therapies, and a loose mix of theosophy, ecology, oriental mysticism, and a belief in the dawning of an astrological age of peace and harmony.

Drawing on the hippie counterculture of the 1960s, new-age ideas include ◊monism and ◊pantheism, preferring intuition and direct experience to rationality and science. Critics of new-age thinking argue that it is so eclectic that it is incoherent. Nonetheless, new-age principles have inspired many business organizations to decentralize and produce less rigid management hierarchies. The rise of European ◊Green parties provided the new-age philosophy with a practical and political forum for its ideas.

New Criticism in literature, a US movement dominant in the 1930s and 1940s stressing the autonomy of the text without biographical and other external interpolation, but instead requiring close readings of its linguistic structure. The major figures of New Criticism include Allen Tate, John Crowe Ransom, R P Blackmur, W K Wimsatt, Cleanth Brooks, and Robert Pen Warren. The term was coined by J E Spingarn in 1910.

New Deal in US history, programme introduced by President F D Roosevelt 1933 to counter the Great ◊Depression, including employment on public works, farm loans at low rates, and social reforms such as old-age and unemployment insurance, prevention of child labour, protection of employees against unfair practices by employers, and loans to local authorities for slum clearance.

The ***Public Works Administration*** was given $3.3 billion to spend on roads, public buildings, and similar developments (the Tennessee Valley Authority was a separate project). The ***Agricultural Adjustment***

Administration raised agricultural prices by restriction of output. In 1935 Harry L Hopkins was put in charge of a new agency, the **Works Progress Administration** (WPA), which in addition to taking over the public works created something of a cultural revolution with its federal theatre, and writers' and arts projects. When the WPA was disbanded 1943 it had found employment for 8.5 million people.

Some of the provisions of the New Deal were declared unconstitutional by the Supreme Court 1935–36. The New Deal encouraged the growth of trade-union membership, brought previously unregulated areas of the US economy under federal control, and revitalized cultural life and community spirit. Although full employment did not come until World War II, the New Deal did bring political stability to the industrial-capitalist system.

New Economic Policy (NEP) economic policy of the USSR 1921–29 devised by the Soviet leader Lenin. Rather than requisitioning all agricultural produce above a stated subsistence allowance, the state requisitioned only a fixed proportion of the surplus; the rest could be traded freely by the peasant. The NEP thus reinstated a limited form of free-market trading, although the state retained complete control of major industries.

The NEP was introduced in March 1921 after a series of peasant revolts and the Kronstadt uprising. Aimed at re-establishing an alliance with the peasantry, it began as an agricultural measure to act as an incentive for peasants to produce more food. The policy was ended in 1928 by Stalin's first Five-Year Plan, which began the collectivization of agriculture.

Newlands John Alexander Reina 1838–1898. English chemist who worked as an industrial chemist; he prepared in 1863 the first periodic table of the elements arranged in order of relative atomic masses, and pointed out the 'Law of Octaves' whereby every eighth element has similar properties. He was ridiculed at the time, but five years later Russian chemist Dmitri Mendeleyev published a more developed form of the table, also based on atomic masses, which forms the basis of the one used today (arranged by atomic number).

New Left term covering a wide range of radical political theories and movements that emerged in the late 1950s, largely in reaction to the perceived failures of traditional left-wing organizations.

Inspired by the US Civil Rights movement, the New Left favoured political ◊activism as a way of challenging the hegemony of state institutions. It appealed to the young educated middle class more than to the politically dispossessed and was a major influence on the developing green movement as well as on ◊gay politics and the ◊women's movement.

May He support us all the day long, till the shades lengthen, and the evening comes, and the busy world is hushed, and the fever of life is over, and our work is done!

John Henry Newman
Sermon, 1834. 'Wisdom and Innocence'

Newman John Henry 1801–1890. English Roman Catholic theologian. While still an Anglican, he wrote a series of *Tracts for the Times*, which gave their name to the Tractarian Movement (subsequently called the ◊Oxford Movement) for the revival of Catholicism. He became a Catholic 1845 and was made a cardinal 1879. In 1864 his autobiography, *Apologia pro vita sua*, was published.

Newman, born in London, was ordained in the Church of England 1824, and in 1827 became vicar of St Mary's, Oxford. There he was influenced by the historian R H Froude and the Anglican priest Keble, and in 1833 published the first of the *Tracts for the Times*. They culminated in *Tract 90* 1841 which found the Thirty-Nine Articles of the Anglican church compatible with Roman Catholicism, and Newman was received into the Roman Catholic Church in 1845. He was rector of Dublin University 1854–58 and published his lectures on education as *The Idea of a University* 1873. His poem *The Dream of Gerontius* appeared in 1866, and *The Grammar of Assent*, an analysis of the nature of belief, in 1870. He wrote the hymn 'Lead, kindly light' 1833.

New Style the Gregorian ◊calendar introduced in 1582 and now used throughout most of the Christian world.

new technology collective term applied to technological advances made in such areas as telecommunications, nuclear energy, space satellites, and computers.

New Testament the second part of the ◊Bible, recognized by the Christian church from the 4th century as sacred doctrine. The New Testament includes the Gospels, which tell of the life and teachings of Jesus, the history of the early church, the teachings of St Paul, and mystical writings. It was written in Greek during the 1st and 2nd centuries AD, and the individual sections have been ascribed to various authors by Biblical scholars.

I do not know what I may appear to the world, but to myself I seem to have been only a boy playing on the sea-shore, and diverting myself in now and then finding a smoother pebble or a prettier shell than ordinary, whilst the great ocean of truth lay all undiscovered before me.

Isaac Newton
Isaac Newton L T More

Newton Isaac 1642–1727. English physicist and mathematician who laid the foundations of ◊physics as a modern discipline. He discovered the law of ◊gravity, created calculus, discovered that white light is composed of many colours, and developed the three standard laws of motion still in use today. During 1665–66, he discovered the binomial theorem, and differential and integral calculus, and also began to investigate the phenomenon of gravitation. In 1685, he expounded his universal law of gravitation. His *Philosophiae naturalis principia mathematica*, usually referred to as *Principia*, was published in 1687, with the aid of Edmond ◊Halley.

Born at Woolsthorpe, Lincolnshire, he was educated at Grantham grammar school and Trinity College, Cambridge, of which he became a Fellow in 1667. He was elected a Fellow of the Royal Society in 1672, and soon afterwards published his *New Theory about Light and Colours. De Motu corporum in gyrum/ On the motion of bodies in orbit* was written in 1684. Newton resisted James II's attacks on the liberties of the universities, and sat in the parliaments of 1689 and 1701/1702 as a Whig. Appointed warden of the Royal Mint in 1696, and master in 1699, he carried through a reform of the coinage. He was elected president of the Royal Society in 1703, and was knighted in 1705. Most of the last 30 years of his life were taken up by studies of theology and chronology, and experiments in alchemy. He was buried in Westminster Abbey.

Newtonian physics ◊physics based on the concepts of Isaac ◊Newton, before the formulation of ◊quantum theory or ◊relativity theory.

new town centrally planned urban area. In the UK, new towns were partly designed to accommodate the overspill from large cities and towns with provision for housing, employment, and other amenities after World War II, when the population was rapidly expanding and city centres had either decayed or been destroyed. In 1976 the policy, which had been criticized for disrupting family groupings and local communities, destroying small shops and specialist industries, and leading to the decay of city centres, was abandoned.

In order to stimulate employment in depressed areas, 14 new towns were planned between 1946 and 1950, with populations of 25,000–60,000, among them Cwmbran and Peterlee, and eight near London to relieve congestion there. Another 15, with populations up to 250,000, were established 1951–75, but by then a static population and cuts in government spending halted their creation.

New Wave (French *nouvelle vague*) French literary movement of the 1950s, a cross-fertilization of the novel, especially the ◊*nouveau roman* (Marguerite Duras, Alain Robbe-Grillet, Nathalie Sarraute), and film (directors Jean-Luc Godard, Alain Resnais, and François Truffaut).

Nibelungenlied *Song of the Nibelungs*, anonymous 12th-century German epic poem, derived from older sources. The composer Richard Wagner made use of the legends in his *Ring* cycle.

◊Siegfried, possessor of the Nibelung treasure, marries Kriemhild (sister of Gunther of Worms) and wins Brunhild as a bride for Gunther. However, Gunther's vassal Hagen murders Siegfried, and Kriemhild achieves revenge by marrying Etzel (Attila) of the Huns, at whose court both Hagen and Gunther are killed.

Nicaea, Council of Christian church council held in Nicaea (modern Iznik, Turkey) in 325, called by the Roman emperor Constantine. It condemned ◊Arianism as heretical and upheld the doctrine of the Trinity in the ◊Nicene Creed.

Nicene Creed one of the fundamental ◊creeds of Christianity, promulgated by the Council of ◊Nicaea 325.

niche in ecology, the 'place' occupied by a species in its habitat, including all chemical, physical, and biological components, such as what it eats, the time of day at which the species feeds, temperature, moisture, the parts of the habitat that it uses (for example, trees or open grassland), the way it reproduces, and how it behaves.

It is believed that no two species can occupy exactly the same niche, because they would be in direct competition for the same resources at every stage of their life cycle.

Nicholas of Cusa or *Nicolaus Cusanus* 1401–1464. German philosopher, involved in the transition from scholasticism to the philosophy of modern times. He argued that knowledge is learned ignorance (*docta ignorantia*) since God, the ultimate object of knowledge, is above the opposites by which human reason grasps the objects of nature. He also asserted that the universe is boundless and has no circumference, thus breaking with medieval cosmology.

Nicholas, St also known as *Santa Claus* 4th century AD. In the Christian church, patron saint of Russia, children, merchants, sailors, and pawnbrokers; bishop of Myra (in modern Turkey). His legendary gifts of dowries to poor girls led to the custom of giving gifts to children on the eve of his feast day, 6 Dec, still retained in some countries, such as the Netherlands; elsewhere the custom has been transferred to Christmas Day. His emblem is three balls.

God, give us the serenity to accept what cannot be changed; Give us the courage to change what should be changed; Give us the wisdom to distinguish one from the other.

Reinhold Niebuhr
Reinhold Niebuhr Richard Wightman Fox

Niebuhr Reinhold 1892–1971. US Protestant theologian, a Lutheran minister. His *Moral Man and Immoral Society* 1932 attacked depersonalized modern industrial society but denied the possibility of fulfilling religious and political utopian aspirations, a position that came to be known as Christian Realism. Niebuhr was a pacifist, activist, and socialist but advocated war to stop totalitarianism in the 1940s.

Morality is the herd instinct in the individual.

Friedrich Wilhelm Nietzsche
The Joyous Science

Nietzsche Friedrich Wilhelm 1844–1900. German philosopher who rejected the accepted absolute moral values and the 'slave morality' of Christianity. He argued that 'God is dead' and therefore people were free to create their own values. His ideal was the *übermensch*, or 'Superman', who would impose his will on the weak and worthless. Nietzsche claimed that knowledge is never objective but always serves some interest or unconscious purpose.

His insights into the relation between thought and language were a major influence on philosophy. Although claimed as a precursor by Nazism, many of his views are incompatible with totalitarian ideology. He is a profoundly ambivalent thinker whose philosophy can be appropriated for many purposes.

Born in Röcken, Saxony, he attended Bonn and Leipzig universities and was professor of Greek at Basel, Switzerland, 1869–80. He had abandoned theology for philology, and was influenced by the writings of Schopenhauer and the music of Wagner, of whom he became both friend and advocate. Both these attractions passed, however, and ill-health caused his resignation from the university. He spent his later years in northern Italy, in the Engadine, and in southern France. He published *Morgenröte/The Dawn* 1880–81, *Die fröhliche Wissenschaft/The Gay Science* 1881–82, *Also sprach Zarathustra/ Thus Spoke Zarathustra* 1883–85, *Jenseits von Gut und Böse/Between Good and Evil* 1885–86, *Zur Genealogie der Moral/Towards a Genealogy of Morals* 1887, and *Ecce Homo* 1888. He suffered a permanent breakdown in 1889 from overwork and loneliness.

Night Journey or *al-Miraj* (Arabic 'the ascent') in Islam, the journey of the prophet Muhammad, guided by the archangel Jibra'el (Gabriel), from Mecca to Jerusalem, where he met the earlier prophets, including Adam, Moses, and Jesus; he then ascended to paradise, where he experienced the majesty of Allah, and was also shown hell.

Nihilist member of a group of Russian revolutionaries in the reign of Alexander II 1855–81. The name, popularized by the writer Turgenev, means 'one who approves of nothing' (Latin *nihil*) belonging to the existing order. In 1878 the Nihilists launched a guerrilla campaign leading to the murder of the tsar 1881.

nikah Muslim marriage contract. In Islam ◊marriage is not a sacrament but a legal, binding contract between a man and a woman. The acceptance of the contract by the spouses involves a mutual commitment to live together according to the teachings of Islam. The contract involves a mutual exchange of rights and responsibilities.

Nike in Greek mythology, the goddess of victory, represented as 'winged', as in the statue from Samothrace in the Louvre, Paris. One of the most beautiful architectural monuments of Athens was the temple of Nike Apteros.

Nobel Prize: recent winners

Peace
1982   Alva Myrdal (Sweden) and Alfonso Garcia Robles (Mexico)
1983   Lech Walesa (Poland)
1984   Bishop Desmond Tutu (South Africa)
1985   International Physicians for the Prevention of Nuclear War
1986   Elie Wiesel (USA)
1987   President Oscar Arias Sanchez (Costa Rica)
1988   The United Nations peacekeeping forces
1989   The Dalai Lama (Tibet)
1990   President Mikhail Gorbachev (USSR)
1991   Aung San Suu Kyi (Myanmar)
1992   Rigoberta Menche (Guatemala)
1993   Nelson Mandela and Frederik Willem de Klerk (South Africa)

Literature
1982   Gabriel García Marquez (Colombia)
1983   William Golding (UK)
1984   Jaroslav Seifert (Czechoslovakia)
1985   Claude Simon (France)
1986   Wole Soyinka (Nigeria)
1987   Joseph Brodsky (USSR/USA)
1988   Naguib Mahfouz (Egypt)
1989   Camilo José Cela (Spain)
1990   Octavio Paz (Mexico)
1991   Nadine Gordimer (South Africa)
1992   Derek Walcott (St Lucia)
1993   Toni Morrison (American)

Economics
1982   George J Stigler (USA)
1983   Gérard Debreu (USA)
1984   Richard Stone (UK)
1985   Franco Modigliani (USA)
1986   James Buchanan (USA)
1987   Robert Solow (USA)
1988   Maurice Allais (France)
1989   Trygve Haavelmo (Norway)
1990   Harry M Markowitz (USA), Merton H Miller (USA), and William F Sharpe (USA)
1991   Ronald H Coase (USA)
1992   Gary S Becker (USA)
1993   Robert Fogel and Douglass North (USA)

Chemistry
1982   Aaron Klug (UK)
1983   Henry Taube (US)
1984   Bruce Merrifield (US)
1985   Herbert A Hauptman (US) and Jerome Karle (US)
1986   Dudley Herschbach (US), Yuan Lee (US), and John Polanyi (Canada)
1987   Donald Cram (US), Jean-Marie Lehn (France), and Charles Pedersen (US)
1988   Johann Deisenhofer (West Germany), Robert Huber (West Germany), and Hartmut Michel (West Germany)
1989   Sydney Altman (US) and Thomas Cech (US)
1990   Elias James Corey (US)
1991   Richard R Ernst (Switzerland)
1992   Rudolph A Marcus (US)
1993   Kary Mullis (USA) and Michael Smith (Canada)

Physics
1982   Kenneth G Wilson (US)
1983   Subrahmanyan Chandrasekhar (US) and William A Fowler (US)
1984   Carlo Rubbia (Italy) and Simon van der Meer (Netherlands)
1985   Klaus von Klitzing (West Germany)
1986   Ernst Ruska (West Germany), Gerd Binnig (West Germany), and Heinrich Rohrer (Switzerland)
1987   Georg Bednorz (West Germany) and Alex Müller (Switzerland)
1988   Leon Lederman, Melvin Schwartz, and Jack Steinberger (US)
1989   Norman Ramsey (US), Hans Dehmeit (US), and Wolfgang Paul (West Germany)
1990   Richard E Taylor (Canada), Jerome I Friedman (US), and Henry W Kendall (US)
1991   Pierre-Gilles de Gennes (France)
1992   Georges Charpak (France)
1993   Joseph Taylor (USA) and Russell Hulse (USA)

Physiology or Medicine
1982   Sune Bergström (Sweden), Bengt Samuelson (Sweden), and John Vane (UK)
1983   Barbara McClintock (US)
1984   Niels Jerne (Denmark), Georges Köhler (West Germany), and César Milstein (UK)
1985   Michael Brown (US) and Joseph L Goldstein (US)
1986   Stanley Cohen (US) and Rita Levi-Montalcini (Italy)
1987   Susumu Tonegawa (Japan)
1988   James Black (UK), Gertrude Elion (US), and George Hitchings (US)
1989   Michael Bishop (US) and Harold Varmus (US)
1990   Joseph Murray (US) and Donnall Thomas (US)
1991   Erwin Neher (Germany) and Bert Sakmann (Germany)
1992   Edmond Fisher (US) and Edwin Krebs (US)
1993   Phillip Sharp (USA) and Richard Roberts (UK)

nirvana in Buddhism, the attainment of perfect serenity by the eradication of all desires. To some Buddhists it means complete annihilation, to others it means the absorption of the self in the infinite.

Noah in the Old Testament, the son of Lamech and father of Shem, Ham, and Japheth, who, according to God's instructions, built a ship, the ark, so that he and his family and specimens of all existing animals might survive the ◊Flood. There is also a Babylonian version of the tale, the *Epic of Gilgamesh*.

Nobel Alfred Bernhard 1833–1896. Swedish chemist and engineer. He invented dynamite in 1867 and ballistite, a smokeless gunpowder, in 1889. He amassed a large fortune from the manufacture of explosives and the exploitation of the Baku oilfields in Azerbaijan, near the Caspian Sea. He left this fortune in trust for the endowment of five ◊Nobel prizes.

Nobel prize annual international prize, first awarded 1901 under the will of Alfred ◊Nobel, Swedish chemist, who invented dynamite. The interest on the Nobel endowment fund is divided annually among the persons who have made the greatest contributions in the fields of physics, chemistry, medicine, literature, and world peace.

The first four are awarded by academic committees based in Sweden, while the peace prize is awarded by a committee of the Norwegian parliament. A sixth prize, for economics, financed by the Swedish National Bank, was first awarded 1969. The prizes have a large cash award and are given to organizations - such as the United Nations peacekeeping forces, which received the Nobel Peace Prize in 1988 - as well as individuals.

Noble Savage, the ◊Enlightenment idea of the virtuous innocence of 'savage' peoples, often embodied in the American Indian, and celebrated by the writers J J Rousseau, Chateaubriand (in *Atala* 1801), and James Fenimore Cooper.

nominalism in philosophy, the theory that objects of general terms (red - dog) have nothing in common except the general term. Nominalists deny that the meaning of a general term is an independently accessible thing, concept or ◊universal. Nominalists also deny that any particular thing has an independently real ◊essence. Consequently, nominalism makes our classifications arbitrary. The opposite of nominalism is ◊realism, and the dispute between these two theories has continued since at least the 11th century. Leading nominalists include William of ◊Occam, Thomas ◊Hobbes, Nelson ◊Goodman, and W V O ◊Quine.

Nonconformist in religion, originally a member of the Puritan section of the Church of England clergy who, in the Elizabethan age, refused to conform to certain practices, for example the wearing of the surplice and kneeling to receive Holy Communion.

After 1662 the term was confined to those who left the church rather than conform to the Act of Uniformity requiring the use of the Prayer Book in all churches. It is now applied mainly to members of the Free churches.

non-objective art art that is not representational. The paintings of Piet Mondrian, for example, consist of very simple, brightly coloured, geometric forms. See ◊abstract art.

nonrenewable resource natural resource, such as coal or oil, that takes thousands or millions of years to form naturally and can therefore not be replaced once it is consumed. The main energy sources used by humans are nonrenewable; ◊renewable resources, such as solar, tidal, and geothermal power, have so far been less exploited.

nonviolence the principle or practice of abstaining from the use of violence. The Indian nationalist leader Mahatma Gandhi adopted a campaign of passive resistance 1907–14 in response to the attempts by the Transvaal government to discriminate against Indians in South Africa. Later, in India, Gandhi employed nonviolent methods, including the boycotting of British goods and hunger strikes. Martin Luther ◊King led a nonviolent civil-rights movement in the USA. He organized a boycott against segregated seating on the buses in Montgomery, Alabama. In June 1963 he led a peaceful demonstration in Washington and in March 1965 led a civil-rights march from Selma to Montgomery.

norm informal guideline about what is, or is not, considered normal social behaviour (as opposed to rules and laws, which are formal guidelines). Such shared values and expectations may be measured by statistical sampling and vary from one society to another and from one situation to another; they range from crucial taboos such as those against incest or cannibalism to trivial customs and traditions, such as the correct way to hold a fork. Norms play a key part in social control and social order.

North American Indian religions beliefs and myths of the North American Indians. Common features include a belief that everything in nature is alive and contains powerful forces that can be helpful or harmful to humans. The forces must be treated with respect, and so hunting and other activities require ritual and preparation. Certain people are believed to be in contact with the spirit world (◊shamans) and to have special powers, but each individual can also seek power and vision through ordeals and fasting.

Northrop John 1891–1987. US chemist. In the 1930s he crystallized a number of enzymes, including pepsin and trypsin, showing conclusively that they were proteins. He shared the 1946 Nobel Prize for Chemistry with Wendell ◊Stanley and James ◊Sumner.

North–South divide geographical division of the world that theoretically demarcates the rich from the poor. The South includes all of Asia except Japan, Australia, and New Zealand; all of Africa, the Middle East, Central and South America. The North includes Europe, the USA,

Canada, and all republics of the former Soviet Union. Newly industrialized countries such as South Korea and Taiwan could, however, be said to have more in common with the industrialized North than with ◊Third World countries.

The gulf between rich and poor is widening: in 1880 the average income of a European was twice that of an Indian or Chinese; by 1965 the ratio was 40:1; in 1991 it was 70:1. The richest 20% of the world's people had (1992) 150 times the income of the poorest 20%.

Nostradamus Latinized name of Michel de Notredame 1503–1566. French physician and astrologer of Jewish origin who was consulted by Catherine de Medici and Charles IX of France. His book of prophecies in verse, *Centuries* 1555, makes obscure and cryptic predictions about world events up until the year 3797.

Some interpreters have claimed that he successfully foretold the rise of Napoleon and Hitler and the political impact of the Kennedy brothers. His books were banned by the Catholic Church.

nothingness nonbeing. The concept is much used in ◊existentialism, as in the title of Jean-Paul Sartre's work *L'Etre et le néant/Being and Nothingness* 1943.

In logic, it is an error to assume that every subject of a grammatical sentence is the name of a thing. So when 'nothingness' is used as the subject of a grammatical sentence, it must not be assumed that 'nothingness' is itself a thing, or the name of anything.

Nothing can be created out of nothing.

nothing
(Titus Lucretius Carus) Lucretius, c. 99,
Roman poet and Epicurean philosopher.
De Rerum Natura

In Buddhism, nothingness is the essence of enlightenment. Some philosophers think that the problem of why something, rather than nothing, exists is the deepest metaphysical conundrum, whereas others consider it irrelevant.

nouveau roman (French 'new novel') experimental literary form produced in the 1950s by French novelists of the ◊New Wave, including Alain Robbe-Grillet and Nathalie Sarraute. In various ways, these writers seek to eliminate character, plot, and authorial subjectivity in order to present the world as a pure, solid 'thing in itself'.

Robbe-Grillet's *Le Voyeur* 1955 and Sarraute's *Le Planetarium* 1959 are critically successful examples. Michel Butor, Claude Ollier, and Marguerite Duras also contribute to this form, which is sometimes labelled the 'anti-novel' because of its subversion of traditional methods.

novel extended fictional prose narrative, often including some sense of the psychological development of the central characters and of their relationship with a broader world. The modern novel took its name and inspiration from the Italian *novella*, the short tale of varied character which became popular in the late 13th century. As the main form of narrative fiction in the 20th century, the novel is frequently classified according to genres and subgenres such as the historical novel, detective fiction, fantasy, and ◊science fiction.

The European novel is said to have originated in Greece in the 2nd century BC. Ancient Greek examples include the *Daphnis and Chloë* of Longus; almost the only surviving Latin work that could be called a novel is the *Golden Ass* of Apuleius (late 2nd century), based on a Greek model. There is a similar, but until the 19th century independent, tradition of prose narrative including psychological development in the Far East, notably in Japan, with for example *The Tale of Genji* by Murasaki Shikibu (978–c.1015). The works of the Italian writers Boccaccio and Matteo Bandello (1485–1561) were translated into English in such collections as William Painter's *Palace of Pleasure* 1566–67, and inspired the Elizabethan novelists, including John Lyly, Philip Sidney, Thomas Nash, and Thomas Lodge. In Spain, Cervantes's *Don Quixote* 1604 contributed to the development of the novel through its translation into other European languages, but the 17th century was dominated by the French romances of Gauthier de Costes de La Calprenède (1614–1663) and Madelaine de Scudéry (1607–1691), although William Congreve and Aphra Behn continued the English tradition.

In the 18th century the realistic novel was established in England by the work of Daniel Defoe, Samuel Richardson, Henry Fielding, Laurence Sterne, and Tobias Smollett. Horace Walpole, and later Mary Shelley, developed the Gothic novel; in the early 19th century Sir Walter Scott developed the historical novel, and Jane Austen wrote 'novels of manners'. Celebrated novelists of the Victorian age in Britain were Charles Dickens, William Thackeray, the Brontës, George Eliot, Anthony Trollope, and Robert Louis

Stevenson. Great European novelists of the 19th century were Victor Hugo, Honoré de Balzac, the two Dumas, George Sand, and Emile Zola in France; Goethe and Jean Paul in Germany; Gogol, Turgenev, Dostoievsky, and Tolstoy in Russia; and, in the USA, Fenimore

---

Of course I draw from life – but I always pulp my acquaintance before serving them up. You would never recognize a pig in a sausage.

novel
Frances Trollope, 1780–1863,
English novelist.
Remark

Cooper, Herman Melville, Nathaniel Hawthorne, and Mark Twain. In Britain the transition period from Victorian times to the 20th century includes George Meredith, Samuel Butler, Thomas Hardy, George Gissing, Henry James, Rudyard Kipling, Joseph Conrad, George Moore, H G Wells, Arnold Bennett, and John Galsworthy. Slightly later are W Somerset Maugham, E M Forster, James Joyce, D H Lawrence, Ivy Compton-Burnett, and Virginia Woolf – the last four being especially influential in the development of novel technique. Among those who began writing in the 1920s are J B Priestley, Richard Hughes, Aldous Huxley, Christopher Isherwood, Graham Greene, V S Pritchett, Evelyn Waugh, Elizabeth Bowen, Rose Macaulay, and Rosamund Lehmann. The 1930s produced Nigel Balchin, Joyce Cary, Lawrence Durrell, and George Orwell, and more recent British writers include Anthony Powell, John Fowles, Kingsley Amis, Anthony Burgess, Iris Murdoch, Angela Carter, Doris Lessing, Salman Rushdie, and Martin Amis. Twentieth-century European novelists include Lion Feuchtwanger, Thomas Mann, Franz Kafka, Ernst Wiechert, Stefan Zweig, Christa Wolff, Heinrich Böll, and Gunter Grass (Germany); André Gide, Marcel Proust, Jules Romains, François Mauriac, Michel Butor, Nathalie Sarraute, and Alain Robbe-Grillet (France); Gabriele d'Annunzio, Ignazio Silone, Alberto Moravia, Italo Calvino, Primo Levi, and Natalia Ginzburg (Italy); Maxim Gorky, Mikhail Sholokhov, Aleksei Tolstoi, Boris Pasternak, and Alexander Solzhenitsyn (Russia); Arturo Baréa, Pío Baroja, and Ramón Pérez de Ayala (Spain). In the Americas contemporary novelists include Mario Vargas Llosa and Gabriel García Márquez (Latin America); Morley

Callaghan, Robertson Davies, and Margaret Atwood (Canada); and Ernest Hemingway, William Faulkner, Bernard Malamud, Eudora Welty, Vladimir Nabokov, and Saul Bellow (USA).

Noyce Robert Norton 1927–1990. US scientist and inventor, with Jack Kilby, of the integrated circuit (chip), which revolutionized the computer and electronics industries in the 1970s and 1980s. In 1968 he and six colleagues founded Intel Corporation, which became one of the USA's leading semiconductor manufacturers.

Noyes John Humphrey 1811–1886. US religious and communal leader. He formulated the 'doctrine of free love' 1837 and in 1848 founded the Oneida Community in central New York which served as a forum for his social experiments. In 1879 Noyes was forced to move to Canada to avoid legal action against him. The former community, which made silverware and steel traps, became a joint stock company 1881.

Born in Brattleboro, Vermont, Noyes was educated at Dartmouth and the Andover Seminary. While at Yale Divinity School, he announced that he had achieved human perfection and was promptly expelled. An advocate of alternative forms of marriage, he founded a religious society in Putney, Vermont 1836.

Nozick Robert 1938– . US political philosopher, who argues that the state's existence can be justified only when it is limited to the narrow function of protection against force, theft, and fraud, and to the enforcement of contracts. Any more extensive activities by the state will inevitably violate individual rights (see ▷rights, natural). His main work is *Anarchy, State and Utopia* 1974.

nuclear family the basic family unit of mother, father, and children. This is the familial norm of industrial societies in contrast to less developed countries where the extended family (nuclear family plus assorted kin) is more common.

nuclear warfare war involving the use of nuclear weapons. The worldwide total of nuclear weapons in 1990 was about 50,000, and the number of countries possessing nuclear weapons stood officially at five – USA, USSR, UK, France, and China – although some other nations were thought either to have a usable stockpile of these weapons (Israel) or the ability to produce them quickly (Brazil, India, Pakistan, South Africa).

Nuclear-weapons research began in Britain 1940, but was transferred to the USA after it entered World War II. The research programme, known as the Manhattan Project, was directed by J Robert Oppenheimer.

atom bomb The original weapon relied on use of a chemical explosion to trigger a chain reaction. The first test explosion was at Alamogordo, New Mexico, 16 July 1945; the first use in war was by the USA against Japan 6 Aug 1945 over Hiroshima and three days later at Nagasaki.

hydrogen bomb A much more powerful weapon than the atom bomb, it relies on the release of thermonuclear energy by the condensation of hydrogen nuclei to helium nuclei (as happens in the Sun). The first detonation was at Eniwetok Atoll, Pacific Ocean, 1952 by the USA.

neutron bomb or enhanced radiation weapon (ERW) A very small hydrogen bomb that has relatively high radiation but relatively low blast, designed to kill (in up to six days) by a brief neutron radiation that leaves buildings and weaponry intact.

nuclear methods of attack now include aircraft bombs, missiles (long- or short-range, surface to surface, air to surface, and surface to air), depth charges, and high-powered land-mines ('atomic demolition munitions') to destroy bridges and roads.

The major subjects of disarmament negotiations are **intercontinental ballistic missiles** (ICBMs), which have from 1968 been equipped with clusters of warheads (which can be directed to individual targets) and are known as multiple independently targetable re-entry vehicles (MIRVs). The 1980's US-designed MX (Peacekeeper) carries up to ten warheads in each missile. In 1989, the UK agreed to purchase submarine-launched Trident missiles from the USA. Each warhead has eight independently targetable re-entry vehicles (each nuclear-armed) with a range of about 6,400 km/4,000 mi to eight separate targets within about 240 km/150 mi of the central aiming point. The Trident system was scheduled to enter service within the Royal Navy in the mid-1990s.

Nuclear methods of defence include:

antiballistic missile (ABM) Earth-based systems with two types of missile, one short-range with high acceleration, and one comparatively long-range for interception above the atmosphere;

Strategic Defense Initiative (announced by the USA 1983 to be operative from 2000; popularly known as the 'Star Wars' programme) 'directed energy weapons' firing laser beams would be mounted on space stations, and by burning holes in incoming missiles would either collapse them or detonate their fuel tanks.

The worldwide total of nuclear weapons in 1990 was about 50,000, and the number of countries possessing nuclear weapons stood officially at five – USA, USSR, UK, France and China – although some other nations were thought to have a usable stockpile of these weapons (Israel) or the ability to produce them quickly (Brazil, India, Pakistan, South Africa). Successive arms-reduction treaties between 1990 and 1993 have, however, resulted in agreements to reduce the worldwide figure to approximately 10,000 by 2003. In the 1991 Minsk Agreement – 'The Creation of the Commonwealth of Independent States' – Belarus, Ukraine, and Kazakhstan declared they would become non-nuclear.

The UK nuclear warhead programme costs £607 million a year.

nuclear winter possible long-term effect of a widespread nuclear war. In the wake of the destruction caused by nuclear blasts and the subsequent radiation, it has been suggested that atmospheric pollution by dust, smoke, soot, and ash could prevent the Sun's rays from penetrating for a period of time sufficient to eradicate most plant life on which other life depends, and create a new Ice Age.

Even after it had settled, ash would still reflect the Sun's rays and delay the planet's return to normal warmth. Insects, grasses, and sea life would have the best prospects of survival, as well as microorganisms. The cold would be intense, and a great increase in snow and ice worldwide would occur.

number theory in mathematics, the abstract study of the structure of number systems and the properties of positive integers (whole numbers). For example, the theories of factors and prime numbers fall within this area as do the work of mathematicians Giuseppe Peano (1858–1932), Pierre de Fermat, and Karl Gauss.

nun woman belonging to a religious order under the vows of poverty, chastity, and obedience, and living under a particular rule. Christian convents are ruled by a superior (often elected), who is subject to the authority of the bishop of the diocese or sometimes directly to the pope. See ◊monasticism.

It is possible that the institution of Christian communities for nuns preceded the establishment of monasteries. The majority of the male orders have their female counterparts.

Oakeshott Michael Joseph 1901–1990. English philosopher. In political theory, he advocated a sceptical and conservative attitude: the purpose of politics is not to provide wealth or well-being, but simply to keep the ship of state afloat. He was professor of political science at the London School of Economics 1950–69. His main publications are *Experience and its Modes* 1933, *Rationalism in Politics* 1962 and *On Civilization* 1969.

Nearly always a philosopher hides a secret ambition, foreign to philosophy, and often it is that of the preacher.

Michael Oakeshott
Experience and its Modes ch 1

---

obedience carrying out instructions or commands; submitting to authority. Obedience became an important topic in ◊social psychology in the 1960s and 1970s as a result of extensive research by US psychologist Stanley Milgram (1933–1984), which appeared to show that a high proportion of ordinary individuals would obey instructions that involved inflicting severe pain on others.

Obeying orders when disobedience results in punishment is understandable (even if not always morally justifiable), but Milgram claimed that many people would willingly obey orders, even if not threatened with punishment. The subjects in his experiments were required to act as 'teachers' for a 'learner' who, unknown to them, was a confederate of the experimenter. Using a simulated shock generator, they were told to administer electric shocks, of increasing strengths, every time the 'learner' made a mistake. In some experiments as many as 60% of the subjects, when the experimenter told them

to continue, administered shocks that they believed would seriously harm the 'learner'. Although distressed by their actions, the subjects felt the experimenter was responsible. Milgram's work has not been accepted uncritically, but it has generated much discussion and stimulated further research.

Bibl. Eiser, J Richard *Social Psychology: Attitudes, Cognition and Social Behaviour* (1986) ch 8

Oberon in folklore, king of the elves or fairies and, according to the 13th-century French romance *Huon of Bordeaux*, an illegitimate son of Julius Caesar. Shakespeare used the character in *A Midsummer Night's Dream*.

obi or *obeah* form of witchcraft practised in the West Indies. It combines elements of Christianity and African religions, such as snake worship.

objective correlative phrase suggested by T S ◊Eliot in a discussion of Shakespeare's *Hamlet*. Recognizing that the hero's emotion in the play was excessive and inexplicable, Eliot suggested that dramatists must find an exact, sensuous equivalent, or 'objective correlative', for any emotion they wish to express. He gave an example from *Macbeth* where Lady Macbeth's state of mind in the sleepwalking scene is communicated to the audience by a skilful building-up of images and actions.

object relations in psychoanalysis, the emotional relations between subject and object which, through a process of identification, are believed to constitute the developing ego. In this context, the word 'object' refers to any person or thing, or representational aspect of them, with which the subject forms an intense emotional relationship.

Object relations were first described by Karl Abraham in an influential paper, published 1924, in which he developed Freud's ideas on infantile sexuality and the development of the ◊libido. Object relations theory has become one of the central themes of post-Freudian psychoanalysis, particularly through the writings of Melanie ◊Klein, Ronald Fairbairn, and Donald ◊Winnicott, all deeply influenced by Abraham. They have each developed distinct, though complementary, approaches to analysis, evolving theories of personal development based on early parental attachments.

observation in science, the perception of a phenomenon – for example, examining the Moon through a telescope, watching mice to discover their mating habits, or seeing how a plant grows.

Traditionally, observation was seen as entirely separate from theory, free from preconceptions and therefore lending support to the idea of scientific objectivity. However, as the preceding examples show, observations are ordered according to a pre-existing theory; for instance, one cannot observe mating behaviour without having decided what mating behaviour might look like. In addition many observations actually affect the behaviour of the observed (for instance, of mating mice).

obsession persistently intruding thought, emotion, or impulse, often recognized by the sufferer as irrational, but nevertheless causing distress. It may be a brooding on destiny or death, or chronic doubts interfering with everyday life, such as fearing the gas is not turned off and repeatedly checking, or impulses leading to the continual repetition of actions, for example, repeatedly washing one's hands. In obsessive–compulsive ◊neurosis, these intrusions compel the patient to reluctantly perform rituals or ceremonies however absurd or distasteful they may seem.

Occam or *Ockham* William of c. 1300–1349. English philosopher and scholastic logician who revived the fundamentals of ◊nominalism. As a Franciscan monk he defended evangelical poverty against Pope John XXII, becoming known as the Invincible Doctor. He was imprisoned in Avignon, France, on charges of heresy 1328 but escaped to Munich, Germany, where he died. The principle of reducing assumptions to the absolute minimum is known as *Occam's razor*.

occult vague term describing a wide range of activities connected with the supernatural, from seances to black magic, from reading one's horoscopes in the newspaper to child abuse. The term has come to have a largely sinister connotation and association with Satanism and witchcraft. The occult sciences include the study and practice of such paranormal phenomena as telepathy and clairvoyance.

occupational psychology study of human behaviour at work. It includes dealing with problems in organizations, advising on management difficulties, and investigating the relationship between humans and machines (as in the design of aircraft controls). Another area is ◊psychometrics and the use of assessment to assist in selection of personnel.

occupational therapy form of therapy or treatment that requires patients to do something purposeful. Almost all psychiatric clinics

or units have an occupational therapy department, in which patients are encouraged to undertake tasks that enable them to express their feelings and thoughts. These typically involve group activity so that personal relationships can develop.

Tasks can range from agricultural or simple manufacturing work to craft activities such as basketwork or model-making. Art therapy, a form of occupational therapy in which patients express their feelings through painting, sculpture, pottery, and the like, has been particularly successful.

Ochoa Severo 1905–1993. Spanish-born US biochemist. He discovered an enzyme able to assemble units of the nucleic acid ◊RNA in 1955, while working at New York University. For his work towards the synthesis of ◊RNA, Ochoa shared the 1959 Nobel Prize for Medicine with Arthur ◊Kornberg.

Ockham William. English philosopher; see ◊Occam.

October Revolution second stage of the ◊Russian Revolution 1917, when, on 24 Oct (6 Nov in the Western calendar), the Bolshevik forces under Trotsky, and on orders from Lenin, seized the Winter Palace and arrested members of the Provisional Government. The following day the Second All-Russian Congress of Soviets handed over power to the Bolsheviks.

Odin chief god of Scandinavian mythology, the **Woden** or **Wotan** of the Germanic peoples. A sky god, he lives in Asgard, at the top of the world-tree, and from the Valkyries (the divine maidens) receives the souls of heroic slain warriors, feasting with them in his great hall, Valhalla. The wife of Odin is Freya and Thor is their son. Wednesday is named after Odin.

Odysseus chief character of Homer's *Odyssey*, king of the island of Ithaca; he is also mentioned in the *Iliad* as one of the leaders of the Greek forces at the siege of Troy. Odysseus was distinguished among Greek leaders for his cleverness and cunning. He appears in other later tragedies.

Oedipus in Greek legend, king of Thebes who unwittingly killed his father, Laius, and married his mother, Jocasta, in fulfilment of a prophecy. When he learned what he had done, he put out his eyes. His story was dramatized by the Greek tragedian Sophocles.

Left to die at birth because Laius had been warned by an oracle that his son would kill him, Oedipus was saved and brought up by the king of Corinth. Oedipus later killed Laius in a quarrel (without recognizing him). Because Oedipus saved Thebes from the Sphinx, he was granted the Theban kingdom and Jocasta (wife of Laius and his own mother) as his wife. After four children had been born, the truth was discovered. Jocasta hanged herself, Oedipus blinded himself, and as an exiled wanderer was guided by his daughter, Antigone, to a final resting-place at Colonus, near Athens.

Oedipus complex in psychology, term coined by Sigmund ◊Freud for the unconscious antagonism of a son to his father, whom he sees as a rival for his mother's affection. For a girl antagonistic to her mother, as a rival for her father's affection, the term is *Electra complex*.

Freud saw this as a universal part of childhood development, which in most children is resolved during late childhood. Contemporary theory places less importance on the Oedipus/Electra complex than did Freud and his followers.

Oersted Hans Christian 1777–1851. Danish physicist who founded the science of electromagnetism. In 1820 he discovered the magnetic field associated with an electric current.

Ohm Georg Simon 1787–1854. German physicist who studied electricity and discovered the fundamental law that bears his name. The SI unit of electrical resistance is named after him, and the unit of conductance (the reverse of resistance) was formerly called the mho, which is Ohm spelled backwards.

Ohm's law law that states that the current flowing in a metallic conductor maintained at constant temperature is directly proportional to the potential difference (voltage) between its ends. The law was discovered by German physicist Georg ◊Ohm 1827.

If a current of I amperes flows between two points in a conductor across which the potential difference is V volts, then V/I is a constant called the resistance R ohms between those two points. Hence:

$$V/I = R$$
or
$$V = IR$$

Not all conductors obey Ohm's law; those that do are called *ohmic conductors*.

Olbers Heinrich 1758–1840. German astronomer. A medical doctor, Olbers was a keen amateur astronomer and a founder member of the *Celestial Police*, a group of astronomers who attempted to locate a supposed 'missing planet' between Mars and Jupiter.

During his search he discovered two asteroids, Pallas 1802 and Vesta 1807. Also credited to Olbers are a number of comet discoveries, a new method of calculating cometary orbits, and the stating of ◊Olbers' paradox. In 1928 Olbers retired from medicine to devote himself to astronomy.

Olbers' paradox question put forward 1826 by Heinrich Olbers, who asked: If the universe is infinite in extent and filled with stars, why is the sky dark at night? The answer is that the stars do not live infinitely long, so there is not enough starlight to fill the universe. A wrong answer, frequently given, is that the expansion of the universe weakens the starlight.

Old Believers section of the Russian Orthodox Church which was excommunicated in 1667 for refusing to accept the liturgical reforms of the Moscow Patriarch Nikon, particularly the new way of crossing oneself during prayer. Much persecuted, they are still strong in many country areas of Russia where their initial following was based.

Old Catholic one of various breakaway groups from Roman Catholicism – including those in Holland (such as the *Church of Utrecht*, who separated from Rome 1724 after accusations of ◊Jansenism) and groups in Austria, Czechoslovakia, Germany, and Switzerland – who rejected the proclamation of ◊papal infallibility of 1870. Old Catholic clergy are not celibate.

The Old Catholic Church entered full communion with the Church of England 1931. Anglican and Old Catholic bishops have joined in the consecration of new bishops so that their consecration can be traced back to the time of an undivided church.

Oldenburg Henry 1615–1677. German official, residing in London from 1652, who founded and edited in 1665 the first-ever scientific periodical *Philosophical Transactions*. He was secretary to the Royal Society 1663–77 and through his extensive correspondence acted as a clearing house for the science of the day.

Old Man of the Sea in the *Arabian Nights*, a man who compels strangers to carry him until they drop, encountered by Sinbad the Sailor on his fifth voyage. Sinbad escapes by getting him drunk. In Greek mythology, the Old Man of the Sea describes ◊Proteus, an attendant of the sea god Poseidon.

Old Testament Christian term for the Hebrew ◊Bible, which is the first part of the Christian Bible. It contains many books (39 for Christians, or 24 for Jews, depending on how they are divided), which include the origins of the world, the history of the ancient Hebrews and their covenant with God, prophetical writings, and religious poetry. The first five books (The five books of Moses) are traditionally ascribed to Moses and known as the Pentateuch (by Christians) or the Torah (by Jews).

The language of the original text was Hebrew, dating from the 12th–2nd centuries BC. The earliest known manuscripts containing part of the text were found among the ◊Dead Sea Scrolls. The traditional text (translated first into Greek and then other languages) was compiled by rabbinical authorities around the 2nd century AD.

Olga, St wife of Igor, the Scandinavian prince of Kiev. Her baptism around 955 was a decisive step in the Christianization of Russia.

oligarchy rule of the few, in their own interests. It was first identified as a form of government by the Greek philosopher Aristotle. In modern times there have been a number of oligarchies, sometimes posing as democracies; the paramilitary rule of the Duvalier family in Haiti, 1957–86, is an example.

oligopoly in economics, a situation in which a few companies control the major part of a particular market and concert their actions to perpetuate such control. This may include an agreement to fix prices (a ◊cartel).

Olives, Mount of range of hills E of Jerusalem, associated with the Christian religion: a former chapel (now a mosque) marks the traditional site of Jesus' ascension to heaven, with the Garden of Gethsemane at its foot.

Om sacred word in Hinduism, used to begin prayers and placed at the beginning and end of books. More accurately written as 'aum', the three sounds are symbolic of the Hindu ◊Trimurti, or trinity of gods.

Omar Khayyám c. 1050–1123. Persian astronomer, mathematician, and poet. In the West, he is chiefly known as a poet through Edward Fitzgerald's version of *The Rubaiyat of Omar Khayyám* 1859.

Khayyám was born in Nishapur. He founded a school of astronomical research and assisted in reforming the calendar. The result of his observations was the *Jalālī* era, begun 1079. He wrote a study of algebra, which was known in Europe as well as in the East.

ombudsman official who acts on behalf of the private citizen in investigating complaints against the government. The post is of Scandinavian origin; it was introduced in Sweden 1809, Denmark 1954, and Norway 1962, and spread to other countries from the 1960s.

The first Commonwealth country to appoint an ombudsman was New Zealand 1962; the UK followed 1966 with a parliamentary commissioner; and Hawaii was the first US state to appoint an ombudsman, 1967. The UK Local Government Act 1974 set up a local ombudsman, or commissioner for local administration, to investigate maladministration by local councils, police, health or water authorities. In the 1980s, ombudsmen were appointed to private bodies such as banks 1986, insurance companies 1983, and building societies 1988.

omphalos in classical antiquity, a conical navel-stone, thought to mark the centre of the world, notably that in the temple of Apollo at ◊Delphi in Greece.

one-party state state in which there is a ban, constitutional or unofficial, on the number of political parties permitted to stand for election. In some cases there may be no legal alternative parties. For example, in the USSR up until the 1990s members of only one political party stood for election; in other instances a few token members of an opposition party may be tolerated, as in Mexico; or one party may be permanently in power with no elections.

Onsager Lars 1903–1976. Norwegian-born US physical chemist. He worked on the application of the laws of thermodynamics to systems not in equilibrium, and received the 1968 Nobel Prize for Chemistry.

ontological argument one of four traditional lines of reasoning to support the existence of God. Crudely, the argument is that God has all perfections; existence is a perfection, so God exists necessarily. The argument dates back to 11th-century scholar St ◊Anselm.

In various forms, the ontological argument has been used by René Descartes, Gottfried Leibniz, and Benedict Spinoza, and by several 20th-century philosophers. In the 18th century Immanuel Kant criticized the argument, saying that ◊being or existence is not a property or predicate.

The other three traditional arguments are the ◊argument from design, the ◊cosmological argument, and the ◊moral argument.

ontology that branch of philosophy concerned with the study of being. In the 20th century, ◊Heidegger distinguished between an 'ontological' enquiry (an enquiry into 'Being') and an 'ontic' enquiry (an enquiry into a specific kind of entity).

Oort Jan Hendrik 1900–1992. Dutch astronomer. In 1927, he calculated the mass and size of our Galaxy, the Milky Way, and the Sun's distance from its centre, from the observed movements of stars around the Galaxy's centre. In 1950 Oort proposed that comets exist in a vast swarm, now called the *Oort cloud*, at the edge of the solar system.

In 1944 Oort's student Hendrik van de Hulst (1918–   ) calculated that hydrogen in space would emit radio waves at 21 cm/8.3 in wavelength, and in the 1950s Oort's team mapped the spiral structure of the Milky Way from the radio waves given out by interstellar hydrogen.

open-door policy economic philosophy of equal access by all nations to another nation's markets.

The term was suggested by US secretary of state John Hay Sept 1899 to allow all nations free access to trade with China, and hence a rejection of a sphere-of-influence agreement for Chinese trade.

Open University institution established in the UK 1969 to enable mature students without qualifications to study to degree level without regular attendance. Open University teaching is based on a mixture of correspondence courses, TV and radio lectures and demonstrations, personal tuition organized on a regional basis, and summer schools.

Announced by Harold Wilson 1963 as a 'university of the air', it was largely created by Jennie Lee, minister for the arts, from 1965. There are now over 30 similar institutions in other countries, including Thailand and South Korea.

operating system (OS) in computing, a program that controls the basic operation of a computer. A typical OS controls the peripheral devices, organizes the filing system, provides a means of communicating with the operator, and runs other programs.

Some operating systems were written for specific computers, but some are accepted standards. These include CP/M (by Digital Research) and MS-DOS (by Microsoft) for microcomputers. Unix (developed at AT&T's Bell Laboratories) is the standard on workstations, minicomputers, and super computers; it is also used on desktop PCs and mainframes.

operations research business discipline that uses logical analysis to find solutions to managerial and administrative problems, such as the allocation of resources, inventory control, competition, and the identification of information needed for decision-making.

Typically, a problem is identified by researchers and a model constructed; then solution techniques are applied to the model to solve the problems. Key skills required include mathematics, economics, and engineering, and computers are increasingly being used.

Operations research was developed as a discipline in the UK during World War II in response to the need to improve the efficiency of military systems. Its use spread, and by the 1950s methods were being adapted to improve management of industrial systems in the USA.

opinion poll attempt to measure public opinion by taking a survey of the views of a representative sample of the electorate; the science of opinion sampling is called *psephology*. Most standard polls take random samples of around a thousand voters which gives results that should be accurate to within three percentage points, 95% of the time. The first accurately sampled opinion poll was carried out by George Gallup during the US presidential election 1936.

Opinion polls have encountered criticism on the grounds that their publication may influence the outcome of an election. Rather than simply predicting how people will vote, poll results may alter voters' intentions – for example, by establishing one party as likely to win and making the voters wish to join the winning side, or by making the lead of one party seem so great that its supporters feel they need not bother to vote.

Oppenheimer J(ulius) Robert 1904–1967. US physicist. As director of the Los Alamos Science Laboratory 1943–45, he was in charge of the development of the atom bomb (the Manhattan Project). When later he realized the dangers of radioactivity, he objected to the development of the hydrogen bomb, and was alleged to be a security risk 1953 by the US Atomic Energy Commission (AEC).

Oppenheimer was the son of a German immigrant. Before World War II he worked with the physicist Ernest Rutherford in Cambridge. He was rehabilitated by the AEC 1963 when it granted him the Fermi award for accomplishments in physics.

opportunity cost in economics, that which has been foregone in order to achieve an objective. A family may choose to buy a new television set and forgo their annual holiday; the holiday represents the opportunity cost.

In decision-making, economists prefer to look at the opportunity cost because it requires a rational approach (all alternatives are examined), while an accountant's view of cost is more concerned with the way in which money is spent and the profit or loss that results.

optics branch of physics that deals with the study of light and vision — for example, shadows and mirror images, lenses, microscopes, telescopes, and cameras. For all practical purposes light rays travel in straight lines, although Albert ◊Einstein demonstrated that they may be 'bent' by a gravitational field. On striking a surface they are reflected or refracted with some absorption of energy, and the study of this is known as geometrical optics.

Opus Dei Roman Catholic institution advocating holiness in everyday life. Founded in Madrid 1928 by Jose Maria Escriva de Balaguer (1902–1975), who was beatified 1992, it now has over 1,000 priests and 75,000 lay members in more than 80 countries. It has been the subject of controversy because of allegations about secret right-wing involvement in politics, finance, and education.

oracle Greek sacred site where answers (also called oracles) were given by priests of a diety to enquirers about personal affairs or state policy. These were often ambivalent. The earliest was probably at Dodona (in Epirus), where priests interpreted the sounds made by the sacred oaks of ◊Zeus, but the most celebrated was that of Apollo at ◊Delphi.

ordeal, trial by in tribal societies and in Europe in medieval times, a method of testing guilt of an accused person based on the belief in heaven's protection of the innocent. Examples of such ordeals are walking barefoot over heated iron, dipping the hand into boiling water, and swallowing consecrated bread (causing the guilty to choke).

In Europe the practice originated with the Franks in the 8th century, and survived until the 13th century. In another ordeal, the accused would be bound and thrown into cold water; if he or she sank, it would prove innocence, but remaining afloat showed guilt.

ordination religious ceremony by which a person is accepted into the priesthood or monastic life in various religions. Within the Christian church, ordination authorizes a person to administer the sacraments.

ordination of women Many Protestant denominations, such as the Methodists and Baptists, ordain women as ministers, as do many churches in the Anglican Communion. In 1988 the first female bishop was elected within the Anglican Communion (in Massachusetts, USA). The Anglican church in England and Australia voted in favour of the ordination of women priests Nov 1992. The Roman Catholic and Eastern Orthodox churches refuse to ordain women.

Orestes in Greek legend, the son of ◊Agamemnon and ◊Clytemnestra, who killed his mother on the instructions of Apollo because she and her lover Aegisthus had murdered his father, and was then hounded by the ◊Furies until he was purified, and acquitted of the crime of murder.

organicism in political philosophy, a theory about the nature of the state, making an analogy between the state and an organism. The theory owes much to the ancient Greek political philosophers, especially Aristotle.

Some organicists, notably the German G W F Hegel, seem to hold that the state is a superperson, and an end to which its citizens are the means. French Enlightenment philosopher Jean-Jacques Rousseau and British neo-Hegelian T H Green are also organicists.

orientalism the study of Islam and the Muslim world by Western, non-Muslim scholars. Historically there has been conflict between orientalists and Muslim scholars. Orientalists believe Muslim theologians do not display scientific standards of analysis, while Muslims believe orientalists are deficient in understanding and motivated by the nature of the colonial prejudice.

Origen c. 185–c. 254. Christian theologian. By drawing on Greek philosophy and on scripture, he produced allegorical interpretations of the Bible that disturbed the more orthodox. For example, he held that the Fall occurred when spiritual beings became bored with the adoration of God and turned their attention to inferior things. He also compiled a vast synopsis of versions of the Old Testament, called the *Hexpla*. Eusebius says that Origen castrated himself to ensure his celibacy, but as Origen disapproves of such actions in his Biblical commentaries it may be just malicious gossip.

Origen taught in Alexandria and Caesarea. He was imprisoned and tortured during the persecution of Decius 250.

original sin Christian doctrine that the ◊fall of man rendered humanity predisposed to sin and unable to achieve salvation except through divine grace and the redemptive power of Christ.

Ormuzd another name for *Ahura Mazda*, the good god of ◊Zoroastrianism.

Orpheus mythical Greek poet and musician. The son of Apollo and a muse, he married Eurydice, who died from the bite of a snake. Orpheus went down to Hades to bring her back and her return to life was granted on condition that he walk ahead of her without looking back. But he did look back and Eurydice was irretrievably lost. In his grief, he offended the ◊maenad women of Thrace, and was torn to pieces by them.

Orphism ancient Greek mystery cult, of which the Orphic hymns formed a part. Secret rites, accompanied by a harsh lifestyle, were aimed at securing immortality.

Remains of an Orphic temple were found 1980 at Hungerford, Berkshire, England.

Orphism French style of abstract painting, derived from ◊Cubism, in which colour harmonies take precedence over form. The term 'Orphic Cubism' (later Orphism) was first used by the poet Guillaume Apollinaire 1913 to describe the mystical, visionary qualities he perceived in the first ◊non-objective art works of Robert Delaunay. These sought to develop a visual equivalent to music through the interplay of light and colour on pure abstract form. Other noted Orphists were Frank Kupka and Fernard Leger.

Delaunay's innovative style greatly influenced his contemporaries, notably members of the *Blaue Reiter* group in Munich and the Synchronists in the USA.

The poet begins where the man ends. The man's lot is to live his human life, the poet's to invent what is nonexistent.

José Ortega y Gasset
The Dehumanization of Art

Ortega y Gasset José 1883–1955. Spanish philosopher and critic. He considered communism and fascism the cause of the downfall of Western civilization. His *Toward a Philosophy of History* 1941 contains philosophical reflections on the state and an interpretation of the meaning of human history.

Orthodox Church or *Eastern Orthodox Church* or *Greek Orthodox Church* federation of self-governing Christian churches mainly found in E and SE Europe, the former USSR, and parts of Asia. The centre of worship is the Eucharist. There is a married clergy, except for bishops; the Immaculate Conception is not accepted. The highest rank in the church is that of Ecumenical Patriarch, or Bishop of Istanbul. There are approximately 130 million adherents (1990).

The church's teaching is based on the Bible, and the ◊Nicene Creed (as modified by the Council of Constantinople 381) is the only confession of faith used. The celebration of the Eucharist has changed little since the 6th century. The ritual is elaborate, and accompanied by singing in which both men and women take part, but no instrumental music is used. Besides the seven sacraments, the prayer book contains many other services for daily life. During the marriage service, the bride and groom are crowned.

Its adherents include Greeks, Russians, Romanians, Serbians, Bulgarians, Georgians, and Albanians. In the last 200 years the Orthodox Church has spread into China, Korea, Japan, and the USA, as well as among the people of Siberia and central Asia. Some of the churches were founded by the apostles and their disciples; all conduct services in their own languages and follow their own customs and traditions, but are in full communion with one another. There are many monasteries, including several on Mount Athos in Greece, which has flourished since the 10th century. The senior church of Eastern Christendom is that of Constantinople (Istanbul).

To see what is in front of one's nose needs a constant struggle.

George Orwell. Pen name of Eric Arthur Blair
Tribune 22 Mar 1946

Orwell George. Pen name of Eric Arthur Blair 1903–1950. English author. His books include the satirical fable *Animal Farm* 1945, which included such slogans as 'All animals are equal, but some are more equal than others', and the prophetic *Nineteen Eighty-Four* 1949, portraying the catastrophic excesses of state control over the individual. Other works include *Down and Out in Paris and London* 1933. A deep sense of social conscience and antipathy towards political dictatorship characterize his work.

Born in India and educated in England, he served for five years in the Burmese police force, an experience reflected in the novel *Burmese Days* 1935. Life as a dishwasher and tramp were related in *Down and Out in Paris and London,* and service for the Republican cause in the Spanish Civil War in *Homage to Catalonia* 1938. He also wrote numerous essays.

All animals are equal but some animals are more equal than others.

George Orwell. Pen name of Eric Arthur Blair
Animal Farm ch 10

Osborn Henry Fairfield 1857–1935. US palaeontologist. He made his first fossil-hunting expedition to the West 1877. He was staff palaeontologist with the US Geological Survey 1900–24 and president of the American Museum of Natural History 1908–33.

Born in Fairfield, Connecticut, USA, Osborn was educated at Princeton University. Appointed to the Princeton faculty 1881, he was named professor of biology at Columbia 1891. In the same year, he also began to serve as curator of vertebrate palaeontology at the American Museum of Natural History.

Osiris ancient Egyptian god, the embodiment of goodness, who ruled the underworld after being killed by Set. The sister-wife of Osiris was Isis or Hathor, and their son ◊Horus captured his father's murderer. The pharaohs were thought to be his incarnation.

Under Ptolemy I's Greco-Egyptian empire Osiris was developed (as a means of uniting his Greek and Egyptian subjects) into **Serapis** (Osiris+Apis, the latter being the bull god of Memphis who carried the dead to the tomb), elements of the cults of Zeus and Hades being included; the greatest temple of Serapis was the Serapeum in Alexandria. The cult of Osiris, and that of Isis, later spread to Rome.

ostracism deliberate exclusion of an individual, or group, from society. It was an ancient Athenian political device to preserve public order. Votes on pieces of broken pot (Greek *ostrakon*) were used to exile unpopular politicians for ten years.

Ostwald Wilhelm 1853–1932. German chemist who devised the Ostwald process (the oxidation of ammonia over a platinum catalyst to give nitric acid). His work on catalysts laid the foundations of the petrochemical industry. He won the Nobel Prize for Chemistry 1909.

other, the in philosophy, a term often used when discussing the relationship between the subject (the knower) and the object (the known) or in analysing the nature of knowledge, of morality, or of being or existence. Our sense of the otherness of things or people arises from each individual's sense of 'I' or first-person perspective on the world.

Otto Rudolf 1869–1937. German Lutheran theologian who was professor of systematic theology at the University of Marburg 1919–37. In his major work, *The Idea of the Holy* 1917, he explores the sense of the numinous, which is common to all major religious experiences and beyond reason, knowledge, or any other term.

Oughtred William 1575–1660. English mathematician, credited as the inventor of the slide rule 1622. His major work *Clavis mathematicae/The Key to Mathematics* 1631 was a survey of the entire body of mathematical knowledge of his day. It introduced the '×' symbol for multiplication, as well as the abbreviations 'sin' for sine and 'cos' for cosine.

Ouspensky Peter 1878–1947. Russian mystic and journalist. Originally a scientist, he became an adherent of Gurdjieff but broke with him 1924. He expanded ◊Gurdjieff's ideas in terms of other dimensions of space and time. His works include *In Search of the Miraculous.*

out-of-the-body experience (OBE) experience in which the world is apparently perceived from somewhere outside the body. A person having such an experience may perceive his or her real physical body below, often from the perspective of a nonphysical body which in some cases appears attached to the physical body by a cord. The experience has most often been reported by those who have temporarily 'died' but have then been resuscitated after a period of unconsciousness.

The nonphysical body may 'travel' to locations nearby or even 'visit' places hundreds of miles away. The experience, reported by people of many different ages and cultures, is deeply impressive and has understandably given support to the widely held belief that one has a spirit or soul that leaves the body for another world at death. In some societies, sorcerers and shamans are believed to be able to send their souls to distant places to obtain information or to bring back the lost soul of a sick person. OBEs fall within the bounds of ◊parapsychology and many studies have been carried out on reported experiences, without conclusive results.

Bibl. Blackmore, Susan J *Beyond the Body: An Investigation of Out-of-the-Body Experiences* (London, 1982)

overhead in economics, fixed costs in a business that do not vary in the short term. These might include property rental, heating and lighting, insurance, and administration costs.

overpopulation too many people for the resources available in an area (such as food, land, and water). The consequences were first set out in the ◊Malthus theory.

Although there is often a link between overpopulation and population density, high densities will not always result in overpopulation. In many countries, resources are plentiful and the ◊infrastructure and technology are well developed. This means that a large number of people can be supported by a small area of land. In some developing countries, such as Bangladesh, Ethiopia, and Brazil, insufficient food, minerals, and energy, and inequitable income distribution result in poverty and often migration in search of better living conditions. Here even low population densities may amount to overpopulation. Overpopulation may also result from a decrease in resources or an increase in population or a combination of both.

Owen Richard 1804–1892. British anatomist and palaeontologist. He attacked the theory of ◊natural selection and in 1860 published an anonymous and damaging review of Charles ◊Darwin's work. He was Director of the Natural History Museum, London, 1856–1883 and was responsible for the first public exhibition of dinosaurs.

Owen Robert 1771–1858. British socialist, born in Wales. In 1800 he became manager of a mill at New Lanark, Scotland, where by improving working and housing conditions and providing schools he created a model community. His ideas stimulated the ◊cooperative movement (the pooling of resources for joint economic benefit).

From 1817 Owen proposed that 'villages of cooperation', self-supporting communities run on socialist lines, should be founded; these, he believed, would ultimately replace private ownership. His later attempt to run such a community in the USA failed.

Oxford Movement also known as *Tractarian Movement* or *Catholic Revival* movement that attempted to revive Catholic religion in the Church of England. Cardinal Newman dated the movement from ◊Keble's sermon in Oxford 1833. The Oxford Movement by the turn of the century had transformed the Anglican communion, and survives today as Anglo-Catholicism.

Oxford University oldest British university, established during the 12th century, the earliest existing college being founded 1249. After suffering from land confiscation during the Reformation, it was reorganized by Elizabeth I 1571. In 1985 there were 9,000 undergraduate and 3,000 postgraduate students.

Besides the colleges, notable academic buildings are the Bodleian Library (including the New Bodleian, opened 1946, with a capacity of 5 million books), the Divinity School, the Radcliffe Camera, and the Sheldonian Theatre. The university is governed by the Congregation of the University; Convocation, composed of masters and doctors, has a delaying power. Normal business is conducted by the Hebdomadal Council.

Pachomius, St 292–346. Egyptian Christian, the founder of the first Christian monastery, near Dendera on the river Nile.

Originally for Copts (Egyptian Christians), the monastic movement soon spread to include Greeks.

Sometime they'll give a war and nobody will come.

pacificism

Carl August Sandburg, 1878–1967, US poet.
The People

---

pacifism belief that violence, even in self-defence, is unjustifiable under any conditions and that arbitration is preferable to war as a means of solving disputes. In the East, pacifism has roots in Buddhism, and nonviolent action was used by Mahatma ◊Gandhi in the struggle for Indian independence.

Pacifist sentiment in Europe before and during World War I persuaded many to become conscientious objectors and refuse to fight, even when conscripted. They were imprisoned and in some cases executed.

As a result of the carnage in the war, pacifism became more acceptable in the 1920s and 1930s, and organizations like the Peace Pledge Union in Britain were initiated. During World War II, conscientious objectors who refused to bear arms were often placed in noncombatant units such as the British Pioneer Corps, or in medical units.

pagan usually, a member of one of the pre-Christian cultures of N Europe, primarily Celtic or Norse, linked to the stone circles (see ◊megalithic religions) and to an agricultural calendar of which the main festivals are the summer and winter solstices and Beltane, the spring festival.

The term was and often still is used as a dismissive phrase, signifying ignorance or 'primitive' religion. It can cover a range of activities, largely agricultural and closely associated with veneration of nature. In the 8th–12th centuries the Church set itself to eradicate the rural practices which were found to be continuing even after the population had officially converted to Christianity. This gave paganism a strong anti-Christian emphasis, which is one of its attractions for some people today.

pain sense that gives an awareness of harmful effects on or in the body. It may be triggered by stimuli such as trauma, inflammation, and heat. Pain is transmitted by specialized nerves and also has psychological components controlled by higher centres in the brain. Drugs that control pain are also known as analgesics.

A pain message to the brain travels along the sensory nerves as electrical impulses. When these reach the gap between one nerve and another, biochemistry governs whether this gap is bridged and may also either increase or decrease the attention the message receives or modify its intensity in either direction. The main type of pain transmitter is known simply as 'substance P', a neuropeptide concentrated in a certain area of the spinal cord. Substance P has been found in fish, and there is also evidence that the same substances that cause pain in humans (for example, bee venom) cause a similar reaction in insects and arachnids (for instance, spiders).

Since the sensation of pain is transmitted by separate nerves from that of fine touch, it is possible in diseases such as syringomyelia to have no sense of pain in a limb, yet maintain a normal sense of touch. Such a desensitized limb is at great risk of infection from unnoticed cuts and abrasions.

These are the times that try men's souls.

Thomas Paine
The American Crisis

Paine Thomas 1737–1809. English left-wing political writer, active in the American and French revolutions. His pamphlet *Common Sense* 1776 ignited passions in the American Revolution; others include *The Rights of Man* 1791 and *The Age of Reason* 1793. He advocated republicanism, deism, the abolition of slavery, and the emancipation of women.

Paine, born in Thetford, Norfolk, was a friend of US scientist and politician Benjamin Franklin and went to America 1774, where he published several republican pamphlets and fought for the colonists in the revolution. In 1787 he returned to Britain. *The Rights of Man* is an answer to the conservative theorist Burke's *Reflections on the Revolution in France*. In 1792, Paine was indicted for treason and escaped to France, to represent Calais in the National Convention. Narrowly escaping the guillotine, he regained his seat after the fall of Robespierre. Paine returned to the USA 1802 and died in New York.

My country is the world, and my religion is to do good.

Thomas Paine
The Rights of Man

palaeontology in geology, the study of ancient life that encompasses the structure of ancient organisms and their environment, evolution, and ecology, as revealed by their fossils. The practical aspects of palaeontology are based on using the presence of different fossils to date particular rock strata and to identify rocks that were laid down under particular conditions, for instance giving rise to the formation of oil.

The use of fossils to trace the age of rocks was pioneered in Germany by Johann Friedrich Blumenbach (1752–1830) at Göttingen, followed by ◊Cuvier and Alexandre Brongniart (1770–1847) in France 1811.

The term palaeontology was first used in 1834, during the period when the first dinosaur remains were discovered.

Paley William 1743–1805. English Christian theologian and philosopher. He put forward the ◊argument from design theory, which reasons that the complexity of the universe necessitates a superhuman creator and that the existence of this being (God) can be deduced from a 'design' seen in all living creatures. His views were widely held until challenged by Charles ◊Darwin. His major treatises include *The Principles of Moral and Political Philosophy* 1785, *A View of the Evidences of Christianity* 1794, and *Natural Theology* 1802.

Palladio Andrea 1518–1580. Italian Renaissance architect noted for his harmonious and balanced classical structures. He designed numerous palaces and country houses in and around Vicenza, Italy, making use of Roman classical forms, symmetry, and proportion. The Villa Malcontenta and the Villa Rotonda are examples of houses designed from 1540 for

patrician families of the Venetian Republic. He also designed churches in Venice and published his studies of classical form in several illustrated books.

His ideas were revived in England in the early 17th century by Inigo Jones and in the 18th century by Lord Burlington and later by architects in Italy, Holland, Germany, Russia, and the USA. Examples of 'Palladian' buildings include Washington's home at Mount Vernon, USA, the palace of Tsarskoe Selo in Russia, and Prior Park, England.

Palm Sunday in the Christian calendar, the Sunday before Easter and first day of Holy Week, commemorating Jesus' entry into Jerusalem, when the crowd strewed palm leaves in his path.

Pan in Greek mythology, the god of flocks and herds (Roman **Sylvanus**), shown as a man with the horns, ears, and hoofed legs of a goat, and playing a shepherd's panpipe (or syrinx).

Pan-Africanism An anti-colonial movement which believed in the innate unity of all black Africans and their descendants overseas, and which advocated a united Africa. It was founded 1900 at the first Pan-African Conference in London.

Support for the movement was fuelled by the Italian invasion of Ethiopia 1933. By the time of the sixth Pan-African Conference 1945, national independence dominated the agenda and the conference was attended by several future African leaders, including Kwame Nkrumah of Ghana and Jomo Kenyatta of Kenya. In 1963, the Organisation of African Unity (OAU) was founded to foster cooperation among the newly independent African nations and to continue to fight colonialism, especially in South Africa.

Panathenaea major festival of ancient Athens. Held annually in the summer, but with greater ceremony every fourth year, it included sacrifices, musical and poetical competitions, and athletic games. Parts of the procession, in which an embroidered robe was brought to the statue of the goddess Athene, were illustrated in the frieze of the Parthenon.

Panchen Lama 10th incarnation 1935–1989. Tibetan spiritual leader, second in importance to the ◊Dalai Lama. A protégé of the Chinese since childhood, the present Panchen Lama is not universally recognized. When the Dalai Lama left Tibet 1959, the Panchen Lama was deputed by the Chinese to take over, but was stripped of power 1964 for refusing to denounce the Dalai Lama. He did not appear again in public until 1978.

Pandora in Greek mythology, the first mortal woman. Zeus sent her to Earth with a box of evils (to counteract the blessings brought to mortals by ◊Prometheus' gift of fire); she opened the box, and the evils all flew out. Only hope was left inside as a consolation.

Pan-Germanism movement that developed during the 19th century to encourage unity between German- and Dutch-speaking peoples in Austria, the Netherlands, Flanders, Luxembourg, and Switzerland. Encouraged by the unification of Germany after 1871, the movement had an increasingly high profile in the period up to 1914.

Pan-Germanism also had an impact in Belgium (Flemish separatism) and in Poland during World War I. Despite the defeat of Germany in 1919, its ideas were revived under Hitler's plans to expand through Europe.

Is not a woman's life, is not her health, are not her limbs more valuable than panes of glass? There is no doubt of that, but most important of all, does not the breaking of glass produce more effect upon the Government?

Emmeline Pankhurst
Speech 16 Feb 1912

Pankhurst Emmeline (born Goulden) 1858–1928. English suffragette. Founder of the Women's Social and Political Union 1903, she launched the militant suffragette campaign 1905. In 1926 she joined the Conservative Party and was a prospective Parliamentary candidate.

She was supported by her daughters *Christabel Pankhurst* (1880–1958), political leader of the movement, and *Sylvia Pankhurst* (1882–1960). The latter was imprisoned nine times under the 'Cat and Mouse Act', and was a pacifist in World War I.

Panofsky Erwin 1892–1968. German art historian who lived and worked in the USA from 1931. He pioneered ◊iconography, the study of the meaning of works of art, in such works as *Studies in Iconology* 1939 and *Meaning in the Visual Arts* 1955, and in so doing profoundly influenced the development of ◊art history as a discipline.

pantheism doctrine that regards all of reality as divine, and God as present in all of nature and the universe. It is expressed in ◊Egyptian religion and ◊Brahmanism; stoicism and neo-

Platonism can be interpreted in pantheistic terms. Pantheistic philosophers include Bruno, Spinoza, Fichte, Schelling, and Hegel.

The Papacy is not other than the Ghost of the deceased Roman Empire, sitting crowned upon the grave thereof.

papacy
Thomas Hobbes, 1588–1679, English political philosopher.
Leviathan pt 4, ch 47

---

papacy the office of the ◊pope or bishop of Rome, as head of the Roman Catholic Church.

papal infallibility doctrine formulated by the Roman Catholic Vatican Council 1870, which stated that the pope, when speaking officially on certain doctrinal or moral matters, was protected from error by God, and therefore such rulings could not be challenged.

Paracelsus Adopted name of Theophrastus Bombastus von Hohenheim 1493–1541. Swiss physician, alchemist, and scientist. He developed the idea that minerals and chemicals might have medical uses (iatrochemistry). He introduced the use of laudanum (which he named) for pain-killing purposes. Considered by some to be something of a charlatan, his books were also criticized because of their mystical content. However, his rejection of the ancients and insistence on the value of experimentation make him a leading figure in early science.

He lectured in Basel on the need for observational experience rather than traditional lore in medicine: he made a public bonfire of the works of his predecessors Avicenna and Galen. He was the disseminator in Europe of the medieval Islamic alchemists' theory that matter is composed of only three elements: salt, sulphur, and mercury.

paradigm all those factors, both scientific and sociological, that influence the research of the scientist. The term, first used by the US historian of science T S ◊Kuhn, has subsequently spread to social studies and politics.

paradise in various religions, a place or state of happiness. Examples are the Garden of ◊Eden and the Messianic kingdom; the Islamic paradise of the Qur'an is a place of sensual pleasure.

paradox statement that seems contradictory but contains an element of truth. The truth is emphasized by the unexpected form of expression. The Bible is a rich source of paradox: 'Love your enemies'; 'The first shall be last and the last shall be first.'

In philosophy, paradoxes relying on purely logical or mathematical terms are called logical paradoxes or paradoxes of ◊set theory, for example, Russell's Paradox which asks whether the class of all classes that are not members of themselves is a member of itself. (If yes, no; and if no, yes.) Paradoxes depending on notions such as ◊meaning or designation are called semantic paradoxes; for example, the liar paradox – 'this statement is false' is false if true and true if false. In pragmatic paradoxes, there is a contradiction not in what is said but in what is done in saying it, for example, 'It is raining but I do not believe it'. The second part of the utterance frustrates the normal intentions of uttering the first. Other philosophical paradoxes apparently show that indispensable notions are inconsistent – for example, ◊Zeno's paradoxes apparently show that our notions of space, time, and motion are inconsistent.

paranoia in psychiatry, true paranoia is a rare disorder, or group of disorders, characterized by the gradual appearance of one or more delusions that, although persistent, are not really bizarre, for example, being constantly followed by the secret police, being loved by someone at a distance, believing oneself to be of great importance or in special relation to God. In chronic paranoia, the patient exhibits a rigid system of false beliefs and opinions, but there are no hallucinations and the patient is in other respects normal.

In disorders known as paranoid states there are again delusions of persecution or grandeur but they are not systematized. In paranoid ◊schizophrenia, the patient suffers from many delusions which are unsystematized and incoherent, is extremely suspicious, and experiences hallucinations and the feeling that external reality has altered.

paranormal phenomena that are not within the range of, or explicable by, established science.

Paranormal phenomena include ◊*extrasensory perception* (ESP) which takes in clairvoyance, precognition, and telepathy; *psychokinesis* (PK), the movement of objects from one position to another by human mental concentration; and *mediumship*, supposed contact with the spirits of the dead, usually via an intermediate 'guide' in the other world. Paranormal phenomena are usually attributed to the action of an unknown factor, ◊psi. ◊Parapsychology is the study of such phenomena.

Bibl. Edge, Hoyt L, Morris, Robert L, Palmer, John, and Rush, Joseph H *Foundations of Parapsychology: Exploring the Boundaries of Human Capability* (Boston and London, 1986)

parapsychology study of ◊paranormal phenomena, which are generally subdivided into two types: ◊extrasensory perception (ESP) or the paracognitive, and psychokinesis (PK) or the paraphysical, movement of an object, apparently without use of physical force or energy. The faculty allegedly responsible for such phenomena, and common to humans and other animals, is known as ◊*psi*.

There have been many reports of sporadic paranormal phenomena, the most remarkable being reports by one person, or occasionally more, of apparitions or hallucinatory experiences associated with another person's death. There have also been investigations of recurrent paranormal phenomena such as hauntings, poltergeist manifestations, and mental and physical mediumship. However, most research in parapsychology has been experimental.

In a typical ESP experiment, one or more percipients try to guess targets, such as randomly ordered drawings or symbols on cards, that are presented one at a time to one or more 'agents', or 'senders'.

In a PK experiment, the subject may try to cause or influence a physical event, such as the fall of a mechanically released die (making it come up six, for example) or a particular movement of a light appearing in a ring of lamps in a random event generator (apparatus in which lamps are lit at random by, for example, the emission of electrons from a radioactive source). Many ingeniously designed experiments have been carried out to demonstrate the existence of psi, but the data are disputable and the evidence, therefore, remains inconclusive.

The first Society for Psychical Research was established in London 1882 by scientists, philosophers, classical scholars, and spiritualists. Over a century later, despite continued scepticism within the scientific establishment as a whole, a chair of parapsychology was established 1984 at Edinburgh University, endowed by the Hungarian author Arthur Koestler.

Pareto Vilfredo 1848–1923. Italian economist and political philosopher. A vigorous opponent of socialism and liberalism, he justified inequality of income on the grounds of his empirical observation (*Pareto's law*) that income distribution remained constant whatever efforts were made to change it.

Pareto was born in Paris. He produced the first account of society as a self-regulating and interdependent system that operates independently of human attempts at voluntary control. A founder of welfare economics, he put forward a concept of 'optimality', which contends that optimum conditions exist in an economic system if no one can be made better off without at least one other person becoming worse off.

Give me fruitful error any time, full of seeds, bursting with its own corrections. You can keep your sterile truth for yourself.

Vilfredo Pareto
The Mind and Society

---

parity in economics, equality of price, rate of exchange, wages, and buying power. Parity ratios may be used in the setting of wages to establish similar status to different work groups. Parity in international exchange rates means that those on a par with each other share similar buying power. In the USA, agricultural output prices are regulated by a parity system.

Parkinson's Law A formula invented by the political analyst C. Northcote Parkinson, which states that 'work expands so as to fill the time available for its completion.'

parliament legislative body of a country. The world's oldest parliament is the Icelandic Althing which dates from about 930. The UK Parliament is usually dated from 1265. The legislature of the USA is called ◊Congress and comprises the House of Representatives and the Senate.

In the UK, Parliament is the supreme legislature, comprising the **House of Commons** and the **House of Lords**. The origins of Parliament are in the 13th century, but its powers were not established until the late 17th century. The powers of the Lords were curtailed 1911, and the duration of parliaments was fixed at five years, but any parliament may extend its own life, as happened during both world wars. The UK Parliament meets in the Palace of Westminster, London.

history Parliament originated under the Norman kings as the Great Council of royal tenants-in-chief, to which in the 13th century representatives of the shires were sometimes summoned. The Parliament summoned by Simon de Montfort 1265 (as head of government in the Barons' War) set a precedent by including representatives of the boroughs as well as the shires. Under Edward III the burgesses and knights of the shires began to meet separately from the barons, thus forming the House of Commons. By the 15th century Parliament had acquired the right to legislate, vote, and appropriate supplies, examine public accounts, and impeach royal ministers. The powers of Parliament were much diminished under the Yorkists and Tudors but under Elizabeth I a new spirit of independence appeared. The revolutions of 1640 and 1688 established parliamentary control over the executive and judiciary, and finally abolished all royal claim to tax or legislate without parliamentary consent. During these struggles the two great parties (Whig and Tory) emerged, and after 1688 it became customary for the sovereign to choose ministers from the party dominant in the Commons. The English Parliament was united with the Scottish 1707, and with the Irish 1801–1922. The ◊franchise was extended to the middle classes 1832, to the urban working classes 1867, to agricultural labourers 1884, and to women 1918 and 1928. The duration of parliaments was fixed at three years 1694, at seven 1716, and at five 1911. Payment of MPs was introduced 1911. A *public bill* that has been passed is an act of Parliament.

Parmenides c. 510–450 BC. Greek pre-Socratic philosopher, head of the Eleatic school (so called after Elea in S Italy). Against Heraclitus' doctrine of Becoming, Parmenides advanced the view that nonexistence was impossible, that everything was permanently in a state of being. Despite evidence of the senses to the contrary, motion and change are illusory – in fact, logically impossible – because their existence would imply a contradiction. Parmenides saw speculation and reason as more important than the evidence of the senses.

Parnassus mountain in central Greece, height 2,457 m/8,064 ft, revered by the ancient Greeks as the abode of Apollo and the Muses. The sacred site of Delphi lies on its southern flank.

Parsee or *Parsi* follower of the religion ◊Zoroastrianism. The Parsees fled from Persia after its conquest by the Arabs, and settled in India in the 8th century AD. About 100,000 Parsees now live mainly in Bombay State.

Parsifal in Germanic legend, one of the knights who sought the ◊Holy Grail; the father of ◊Lohengrin.

Parsons Talcott 1902–1979. US sociologist who attempted to integrate all the social sciences into a science of human action. A prolific writer and probably the most influential sociologist since World War II, Parsons converted to ◊functionalism under the influence of ◊Malinowski.

Like ◊Durkheim and ◊Weber, Parsons wanted to describe convincingly logical types of social relation applicable to all groups however small or large. His great achievement was to construct a system or general theory of social action to include all its aspects, drawing on several disciplines and reinterpreting previous theories. His first attempt at this systematization appeared in *The Structure of Social Action* 1937, followed by *Essays in Sociological Theory, Pure and Applied* 1942. In *The Social System* 1951, he argued that the crucial feature of societies, as with biological organisms, is homeostasis and that their parts can only be understood in terms of the whole.

Parsons began his career as a biologist and later became interested in economics and sociology. He studied in Heidelberg, where he read Max Weber, whose *The Protestant Ethic and the Spirit of Capitalism* 1904 he translated 1930. He taught at Harvard University from 1931 until his death and set up the Department of Social Relations there.

Parvati in Hindu mythology, the consort of Siva in one of her gentler manifestations, and the mother of Ganesh, the elephant-headed god; she is said to be the daughter of the Himalayas.

The eternal silence of these infinite spaces the terrifies me.

Blaise Pascal
Pensées

Pascal Blaise 1623–1662. French philosopher and mathematician. He contributed to the development of hydraulics, the ◊calculus, and the mathematical theory of ◊probability.

In mathematics, Pascal is known for his work on conic sections and, with Pierre de Fermat, on the probability theory. In physics, Pascal's chief work concerned fluid pressure and hydraulics. **Pascal's principle** states that the pressure everywhere in a fluid is the same, so that pressure applied at one point is transmitted equally to all parts of the container. This is the principle of the hydraulic press and jack.

Pascal's triangle is a triangular array of numbers in which each number is the sum of the pair of numbers above it. Plotted at equal distances along a horizontal axis, the numbers in the rows give the binomial probability distribution with equal probability of success and failure, such as when tossing fair coins.

Pascal's wager involves the application of probability theory to religious belief. If God and an afterlife exist, we could face infinite suffering in Hell. Therefore, it must be rational to act as though they do exits, however low the probability, because the sacrifice of pleasure is only finite.

The heart has its reasons which reason knows nothing of.

Blaise Pascal
Pensées

In 1654 Pascal went into the Jansenist monastery of Port Royal and defended a prominent Jansenist, Antoine Arnauld (1612–1694), against the Jesuits in his *Lettres Provinciales* 1656. His *Pensées* 1670 was part of an unfinished defence of the Christian religion.

Passover also called **Pesach** in Judaism, an eight-day spring festival which commemorates the exodus of the Israelites from Egypt and the passing over by the Angel of Death of the Jewish houses, so that only the Egyptian firstborn sons were killed, redressing Pharaoh's murdering of all Jewish male infants. Unleavened bread (matzah) is eaten as no yeast (leaven) is allowed in a Jewish home during the festival. On the first night of the festival the seder meal is eaten as the story of the Exodus is told.

Passy Frédéric 1822–1912. French economist who shared the first Nobel Peace Prize 1901 with Jean-Henri Dunant. He founded the International League for Permanent Peace 1867, and was co-founder, with the English politician William Cremer (1828–1908), of the Inter-Parliamentary Conferences on Peace and on Arbitration 1889.

Pasteur Louis 1822–1895. French chemist and microbiologist who discovered that fermentation is caused by microorganisms. He also developed a vaccine for rabies, which led to the foundation of the Institut Pasteur in Paris 1888.

Pasteur saved the French silkworm industry by identifying two microbial diseases that were decimating the worms. He discovered the pathogens responsible for anthrax and chicken cholera, and developed vaccines for these diseases. He inspired his pupil Joseph Lister's work in antiseptic surgery. **Pasteurization** to make dairy products free from the tuberculosis bacteria is based on his discoveries.

pastoral a work of art, literature, music or a musical play that depicts the countryside or rural life, often in an idyllic way. The Pastoral scenes were popular in classical Greece and Rome (for instance, Virgil's *Eclogues*), and again from the 15th to 18th centuries (for example, G F Handel's masque *Acis and Galatea* 1718). They were frequently peopled with shepherds and shepherdesses or with mythological figures, such as nymphs and satyrs.

Patanjali Indian author of the Yoga-sutras which propound the philosophy of yoga. According to Patanjali, yoga consists of eight steps: *yama* (self-restraint); *niyama* (spiritual discipline); *asana* (sitting posture); *pranayama* (breath control); *pratyahara* (withdrawal of the senses); *dharana* (contemplation); *dhyana* (meditation); and *samadhi* (total absorption in God).

Paternoster in the Roman Catholic Church, the Lord's Prayer. The opening words of the Latin version are *Pater noster*.

pathetic fallacy in the arts, the presentation of natural events and objects as controlled by human emotions, so that in some way they express human sorrow or joy. The phrase was invented by John Ruskin in *Modern Painters* 1843–60 to describe the ascription of human feelings to the outside world.

patriarch in the Old Testament, one of the ancestors of the human race, and especially those of the ancient Hebrews, from Adam to Abraham, Isaac, Jacob, and his sons (who became patriarchs of the Hebrew tribes). In the Orthodox Church, the term refers to the leader of a national church.

patriarchy a form of social organization in which a man heads and controls the family unit. This definition has been broadened by feminists to describe the dominant position of men and male values throughout society.

Patrick, St 389–c. 461. Patron saint of Ireland. Born in Britain, probably in S Wales, he was carried off by pirates to six years' slavery in Antrim, Ireland, before escaping either to Britain or Gaul – his poor Latin suggests the former – to train as a missionary. He is variously said to have landed again in Ireland 432 or 456, and his work was a vital factor in the spread of Christian influence there. His symbols are snakes and shamrocks; feast day 17 March.

Patrick is credited with founding the diocese of Armagh, of which he was bishop, though this was probably the work of a 'lost apostle' (Palladius or Secundinus). Of his writings only his *Confessio* and an *Epistola* survive.

patronage power to give a favoured appointment to an office or position in politics, business, or the church; or sponsorship of the arts. Patronage was for centuries bestowed mainly by individuals (in Europe often royal or noble) or by the church. In the 20th century, patrons have tended to be political parties, the state, and – in the arts – private industry and foundations.

In Britain, where it was nicknamed 'Old Corruption', patronage existed in the 16th century, but was most common from the Restoration of 1660 to the 19th century, when it was used to manage elections and ensure party support. Patronage was used not only for the preferment of friends, but also as a means of social justice, often favouring, for example, the families of those in adversity. Political patronage has largely been replaced by a system of ◊meritocracy (in which selection is by open competition rather than by personal recommendation).

Ecclesiastical patronage was the right of selecting a person to a living or benefice, termed an advowson.

Salaried patronage was the nomination to a salaried post: at court, in government, the Church of England, the civil service, the armed services, or to the East India Company. The Northcote–Trevelyan report on the civil service 1854 advised the replacement of patronage in the civil service by open competitive examination, although its recommendations were carried out only later in the century. Commissions in the British army were bought and sold openly until the practice was abolished in 1871. Church livings were bought and sold as late as 1874.

Patronage survives today in the political honours system (awards granted to party supporters) and the appointment of university professors, leaders of national corporations, and government bodies, which is often by invitation rather than by formal application. Selection on grounds other than solely the basis of ability lives on today with the practice of positive ◊discrimination.

Paul VI Giovanni Battista Montini 1897–1978. Pope from 1963. His encyclical *Humanae Vitae/Of Human Life* 1968 reaffirmed the church's traditional teaching on birth control, thus following the minority report of the commission originally appointed by Pope John rather than the majority view.

He was born near Brescia, Italy. He spent more than 25 years in the Secretariat of State

Patronage: Still Alive and Well?

Michelangelo had the Medici family, Josef Haydn (1732–1809) had the Prince of Esterhazy, Vincent Van Gogh (1853–1890) had his brother Theo. Artists, like everyone else, need to be paid for the work they produce. In the Middle Ages this was not as complicated an issue as it is today. The function of the artist was largely the same as that of any other craftsman or artisan. The artist was paid for what he produced, but he only produced what was wanted. A commission was a legally binding contract between the artist and his client. If an altarpiece was requested, the details of the contract might specify subject matter and the quality of the materials, as well as the size of the work and the date it was to be completed. The artist's imagination functioned within strictly limited parameters. Patronage was a different kind of financial arrangement but it did not, in fact, allow the artist any greater freedom. The protection of an aristocratic patron might guarantee temporary financial security and provide a stimulating intellectual atmosphere in which to work, but the artist was still an employee and never much more than a glorified servant. Michelangelo (1475–1564) was regarded as the greatest artist of his age, whose genius would reflect well on those who supported him, but Pope Julius II (1443–1513) could still command him to paint the ceiling of the Sistine Chapel even though he had no desire to do so.

The artist as visionary

The notion of a disinterested form of patronage, with the patron making no demands upon the artist but simply enjoying the proximity of genius and the fruits of that genius, really dates from the end of the eighteenth century. As the power and wealth of the aristocracy started to decline, a new conception of the artist emerged which was to provide him with greater autonomy but less security. In the Age of Romanticism the artist became a visionary whose work, arrived at through intense personal struggle, constituted a kind of autobiography of the psyche, rather than something that could be created to order. In effect he became a freelance, producing whatever he wanted to produce. If he failed to find a market or a patron (if he went 'unrecognized') and finished up starving in a garret, he could always reassure himself that his artistic integrity had been preserved. The history of art since the Romantic era is littered with examples of this clichéd scenario. On the one hand, there is an example like the Russian composer Pyotr Tchaikovsky (1848–1893), who was regularly supplied with money and encouragement from a patron, Baroness von Meck, whom he never met. On the other hand the English painter Benjamin Robert Haydon (1786–1846) who, persisting in a grandiose style and manner that nobody much cared for, desperately borrowed money from his friends until his death by suicide.

Patronage was therefore something of a hit and miss affair: fortunate for those who found it, a disaster for those who did not. Of course there was always the possibility of state intervention. Just like any private individual, the state could function simply as a client or, more systematically, as a source of patronage.

The French Salon of the nineteenth century was an annual exhibition controlled by the Academie des Beaux Arts, an official organization which also ran the state art schools. In order to gain public exposure and establish any sort of reputation, an artist needed to be selected for the Salon. But selection meant having to conform to the officially recognized style as laid down by the Academie. The vast number of rejections, and the high quality of many of them, eventually led the Emperor, Napoleon III (1852–1870), to set up a rejects salon (the Salon des Réfuses). However the exhibition was largely derided by both critics and public alike – Edouard Manet (1832–1883) and Paul Cézanne (1839–1906) coming in for particular abuse – and the experiment was never repeated.

The state supplies

Where state control of the arts is absolute – as in the Soviet Union from the time of Joseph Stalin (1879–1953) until its demise – the result will always be a uniform official style, from which it is impossible to deviate and still continue to work openly. Different problems occur in modern liberal democracies where the ideal, in theory, is for the state to be a disinterested benefactor and to offer incentives for individuals, and more recently for businesses, to do the same. In practice this still means that the agents of the state, like The Arts Council in Britain or the National Endowment for the Arts in the USA, have to make choices about who deserves funding and who does not. In Britain the Royal Opera House, the Royal Shakespeare Company, and the Royal National Theatre jointly receive more money than all the other subsidized theatres and their competitors in the commercial sector. But even prestigous national institutions are not secure: funding can be withdrawn or switched around at will. For all those who applauded the diverse and modern policy of the recent French Arts minister Jack Lang, there were those who claimed that such a policy was at the expense of France's national heritage and the upkeep of buildings like Chartres Cathedral. Artists may like to be paid, but they can rarely expect to have a regular income guaranteed. Not many people can, but few employments are so susceptible as the arts to the vagaries of both politics and taste. It is worth remembering that both Harmensz van Rembrandt (1606–1669) and Wolfgang Amadeus Mozart (1756–1791) died penniless.

Joe Staines

0

under Pius XI and Pius XII before becoming archbishop of Milan in 1954. In 1958 he was created a cardinal by Pope John, and in 1963 he succeeded him as pope, taking the name of Paul as a symbol of ecumenical unity.

Pauli Wolfgang 1900–1958. Austrian physicist who originated the *exclusion principle*: in a given system no two fermions (electrons, protons, neutrons, or other elementary particles of half-integral spin) can be characterized by the same set of ◊quantum numbers. He also predicted the existence of neutrinos. He was awarded a Nobel prize 1945 for his work on atomic structure.

Pauling Linus Carl 1901–1994. US chemist, author of fundamental work on the nature of the chemical bond and on the discovery of the helical structure of many proteins. He also investigated the properties and uses of vitamin C as related to human health. He won the Nobel Prize for Chemistry 1954. An outspoken opponent of nuclear testing, he also received the Nobel Peace Prize in 1962.

What would I have made of you, had I found you alive?

St Paul
(while weeping at Virgil's tomb)
Bluff Your Way In The Classics Ross Leckie

Paul, St c. AD 3–c. AD 68. Christian missionary and martyr; in the New Testament, apostle and author of 13 epistles. Originally opposed to Christianity, he took part in the stoning of St Stephen. He was converted by a vision on the road to Damascus. After his conversion he made great missionary journeys, for example to Philippi and Ephesus, becoming known as the Apostle of the Gentiles (non-Jews). His emblems are a sword and a book; feast day 29 June.

The Jewish form of his name is Saul. He was born in Tarsus (now in Turkey), son of well-to-do Pharisees, and had Roman citizenship. On his return to Jerusalem after his missionary journeys, he was arrested, appealed to Caesar, and (as a citizen) was sent to Rome for trial about 57 or 59. After two years in prison, he may have been released before his final arrest and execution under the emperor Nero.

St Paul's theology was rigorous on such questions as sin and atonement, and his views on the role of women were adopted by the Christian church generally.

Pavlov Ivan Petrovich 1849–1936. Russian physiologist noted particularly for his research on the physiology of digestion, for which he was awarded the Nobel Prize 1904. His work on classical ◊conditioning, published in *Conditioned Reflexes* 1927 and *Lectures on Conditioned Reflexes* 1928, had a great impact on behaviourism, though Pavlov himself thought behaviourism's claims to be scientifically ridiculous. He also carried out pioneering work on experimentally induced ◊neurosis in animals.

Pax in Roman mythology, the goddess of peace, equivalent to the Greek Irene.

The wolf also shall dwell with the lamb, and the leopard shall lie down with the kid.

peace
Bible, the sacred book of the Jewish and Christian religions.
Isaiah 11:7

peace a concept with two distinct meanings. On the one hand it can be defined negatively as the absence of war and hostility; on the other hand it suggests the idea of harmony and wholeness achieved through a proper relationship with God.

Attempts to achieve the cessation of war have taken varying and sometimes paradoxical forms. The 200-year Pax Romana of the Roman Empire was achieved through military strength, and military parity between states is often cited as a guarantee of peace. On the other hand, ◊pacifism – the belief that no violence can be justified – has been central to many faiths including ◊Jainism, ◊Buddhism, and the ◊Quakers. The Jain concept of ahimsa, respect for all living things, was an influence on Gandhi. For Muslims and Jews, peace is an ideal of social well-being as well as an aspect of the Godhead, and their respective word for it, *sala'am* and *shalom*, is the customary greeting between the faithful.

Peace to him that is far off, and to him that is near.

peace
Bible, the sacred book of the Jewish and Christian religions.
Isaiah 57:19

Peace Corps US organization of trained men and women, inspired by the British programme Voluntary Service Overseas (VSO) and established by President Kennedy 1961. The Peace Corps provides skilled volunteer workers for Third World countries, especially in the fields of teaching, agriculture, and health, for a period of two years.

Living among the country's inhabitants, workers are paid only a small allowance to cover their basic needs and maintain health. Over 130,000 Americans have been involved.

peace movement collective opposition to war. The Western peace movements of the late 20th century can trace their origins to the pacifists of the 19th century and conscientious objectors during World War I. The campaigns after World War II have tended to concentrate on nuclear weapons, but there are numerous organizations devoted to peace, some wholly pacifist, some merely opposed to escalation.

In the UK, the Peace Pledge Union may be the oldest organization in the peace movement, the Campaign for Nuclear Disarmament the largest, and the Greenham Common women the most publicized.

Peale Norman Vincent 1898– . US religious leader. Through his radio programme and book *The Art of Living* 1948, he became one of the best- known religious figures in the USA. His *The Power of Positive Thinking* 1952 became a national bestseller. Peale was elected president of the Reformed Church in America in 1969.

Born in Bowersville, Ohio, USA, Peale was educated at Ohio Wesleyan University and was ordained in the Methodist Episcopal Church in 1922. After serving congregations in Brooklyn 1924–27 and Syracuse 1927–32, he became pastor of the Marble Collegiate Church in New York City.

Pearson Karl 1857–1936. British statistician who followed Francis Galton in introducing statistics and probability into genetics and who developed the concept of ◊eugenics (improving the human race by selective breeding). He introduced the term standard deviation into statistics.

peer group in the social sciences, people who have a common identity based on such characteristics as similar social status, interests, age, or ethnic group. The concept has proved useful in analysing the power and influence of co-workers, school friends, and ethnic and religious groups in socialization and social behaviour.

Peirce Charles Sanders 1839–1914. US philosopher, phsyicist, and logician, founder of ◊pragmatism (which he later called pragmaticism), who argued that genuine conceptual distinctions must be correlated with some differences of practical effect. He wrote extensively on the logic of scientific enquiry, suggesting that truth could be conceived of as the object of an ultimate consensus.

He (William James) is so concrete, so living; I, a mere table of contents, so abstract, a very snarl of twine.

Charles Sanders Peirce
A Hundred Years of Philosophy J Passmore

Pelagianism the teachings of the Christian British theologian Pelagius (c. 360–c. 420). He taught the primacy of individual free will committed to perfectionist ideas. The Roman Catholic Church officially banned the teaching, which denied ◊original sin and granted salvation to unbaptized infants. Pelagianism is optimistic about human nature and opposed to ◊Manichaeism which encouraged moral pessimism.

Pelagius 360–420. British theologian. He taught that each person possesses free will (and hence the possibility of salvation), denying Augustine's doctrines of predestination and original sin. Cleared of heresy by a synod in Jerusalem 415, he was later condemned by the pope and the emperor.

penance Roman Catholic sacrament, involving confession of sins and receiving absolution, and works performed (or punishment self-inflicted) in atonement for sin. Penance is worked out nowadays in terms of good deeds rather than routine repetition of prayers.

penates the household gods of a Roman family; see ◊*lares and penates*.

Penrose Lionel Sharples 1898–1972. English physician and geneticist, known for his pioneering work on mental retardation and Down's syndrome. Early in his career, he advanced the study of ◊schizophrenia and developed a test for its diagnosis.

Penrose worked as research medical officer at the Royal Eastern Counties Institution, Colchester 1930–39, during which time he produced an influential survey of patients and their families (*A Clinical and Genetic Study of 1,280 Cases of Mental Defect* 1938) showing that there were very many different types and causes of mental defect and that normality and subnormality were on a continuum. His subsequent work concentrated on the causative factors of Down's syndrome. He was the first to demonstrate the significance of the mother's age.

He was director of psychiatric research for Ontario, Canada 1939–45. In 1945 he was appointed to the Galton professorship of eugenics at London University and elected a Fellow of the Royal Society 1953.

pensée insight or saying; a mainly literary term. A *pensée* need not be as pointed as an epigram nor as moralizing as a maxim. The *Pensées* 1670 of French thinker Blaise Pascal are his notes for an unwritten defence of Christianity.

Penston Michael 1943–1990. British astronomer at the Royal Greenwich Observatory 1965–90. From observations made with the Ultraviolet Explorer Satellite of hot gas circulating around the core of the galaxy NGC 4151, he and his colleagues concluded that a black hole (an object whose gravity is so great that nothing can escape from it) of immense mass lay at the galaxy's centre.

Pentateuch Greek (and Christian) name for the first five books of the Bible, ascribed to Moses, and called the ◊*Torah* by Jews.

Pentecost in Judaism, the festival of *Shavuot*, celebrated on the 50th day after ◊Passover in commemoration of the giving of the Ten Commandments to Moses on Mount Sinai, and the end of the grain harvest; in the Christian church, Pentecost is the day on which the apostles experienced inspiration of the Holy Spirit, commemorated on Whit Sunday.

Pentecostal movement Christian revivalist movement inspired by the baptism in the Holy Spirit with 'speaking in tongues' experienced by the apostles at the time of Pentecost. It represents a reaction against the rigid theology and formal worship of the traditional churches. Pentecostalists believe in the literal word of the Bible and in faith healing. It is an intensely missionary faith, and recruitment has been rapid since the 1960s: worldwide membership is estimated at more than 25 million, and it is the world's fastest growing sector of Christianity.

The Pentecostal movement dates from 4 April 1906 when members of the congregation of the Azusa Street Mission in Los Angeles experienced 'baptism in the Spirit'. From this phenomenon it is sometimes also known as the Tongues movement. Its appeal was to the poor and those alienated by the formalism and modernist theology of established denominations. It combined a highly emotional, informal approach to worship with an ethical emphasis on sobriety and hard work, and it became a way for poor and marginal groups to improve their economic and social status while retaining their religious faith. The services are informal, with gospel music and exclamations of 'Hallelujah'.

The movement spread, and took hold in revivalist areas of Wales and N England, but was less successful there than in Scandinavia, South America, and South Africa. In the USA, where the largest grouping is the Assemblies of God, members of the movement total more than 0.5 million. It has been spoken of as the 'third force' in Christendom, and a serious challenge to Roman Catholicism and traditional Protestantism.

perception an individual's assessment or personal ideas of the real world. People's perception of the world is necessarily based on incomplete or unreliable information. Perception affects the attitude of people to events.

Perey Marguérite (Catherine) 1909–1975. French nuclear chemist who discovered the radioactive element francium in 1939. Her career, which began as an assistant to Marie Curie 1929, culminated with her appointment as professor of nuclear chemistry at the University of Strasbourg 1949 and director of its Centre for Nuclear Research 1958.

perfect competition in economics, a market situation in which there are many potential and actual buyers and sellers, each being too small to be an individual influence on the price; the market is open to all and the products being traded are homogeneous. At the same time, the producers are seeking the maximum profit and consumers the best value for money.

There are many economic, social, and political barriers to perfect competition, not least because the underlying assumptions are unrealistic and in conflict. Nevertheless some elements are applicable in free trade.

peri in Persian myth, a beautiful, harmless being, ranking between angels and evil spirits. Peris were ruled by Eblis, the greatest of evil spirits.

permissive society society in which the prevailing ethic is one of tolerance, liberalism, and sexual freedom. The term is often used to describe the years in the West from the 1950s to the 1970s.

perpetual motion the idea that a machine can be designed and constructed in such a way that, once started, it will continue in motion indefinitely without requiring any further input of energy (motive power). Such a device contradicts the two laws of thermodynamics that state that (1) energy can neither be created nor destroyed (the law of conservation of energy) and (2) heat cannot by itself flow from a cooler to a hotter object. As a result, all practical (real) machines require a continuous supply of energy, and no heat engine is able to convert all the heat into useful work.

Perrault Charles 1628–1703. French author of the fairy tales *Contes de ma mère l'oye/Mother Goose's Fairy Tales* 1697, which include 'Sleeping Beauty', 'Little Red Riding Hood', 'Blue Beard', 'Puss in Boots', and 'Cinderella'.

Perrin Jean 1870–1942. French physicist who produced the crucial evidence that finally established the atomic nature of matter. Assuming the atomic hypothesis, Perrin demonstrated how the phenomenon of Brownian movement could be used to derive precise values for ◊Avogadro's number. He was awarded the 1926 Nobel Prize for Physics.

Persephone in Greek mythology, a goddess (Roman Proserpina), the daughter of Zeus and Demeter, and queen of the underworld. She was carried off to the underworld as the bride of Pluto, who later agreed that she should spend six months of the year above ground with her mother. The myth symbolizes the growth and decay of vegetation and the changing seasons.

personality individual's characteristic way of behaving across a wide range of situations. Two broad dimensions of personality are ◊extroversion and ◊neuroticism. A number of more specific personal traits have also been described, including ◊psychopathy (antisocial behaviour).

personality cult practice by which a leader is elevated to a pre-eminent status through a massive propaganda campaign. In the USSR, the cult of personality was developed by Joseph Stalin in the 1930s. More recently, both Mao Zedong in China and Kim-Il-Sung in North Korea have used similar techniques to reinforce their leadership and power.

Its promotion of the individual was in marked contrast to the primacy of the masses espoused in the 1920s. Stalin's image was portrayed everywhere; factories, streets, and a city were named after him. He was able to take

credit for the regime's successes without taking responsibility for the failures. In some respects, this system had echoed the semi-divine cult status of Russian tsars in the 19th century.

personification figure of speech (poetic or imaginative expression) in which animals, plants, objects, and ideas are treated as if they were human or alive ('Clouds chased each other across the face of the Moon'; 'Nature smiled on their work and gave it her blessing'; 'The future beckoned eagerly to them').

perspective the realistic representation of a three-dimensional object in two dimensions. In a perspective drawing, vertical lines are drawn parallel from the top of the page to the bottom. Horizontal lines, however, are represented by straight lines which meet at one of two perspective points. These perspective points lie to the right and left of the drawing at a distance which depends on the view being taken of the object.

Perutz Max 1914– . Austrian-born British biochemist who shared the 1962 Nobel Prize for Chemistry with John Kendrew for work on the structure of the haemoglobin molecule.

Perutz moved to Britain in 1936 to work with John Bernal (1901–1971) at Cambridge University. After internment in Canada as an alien during World War II he returned to Cambridge and completed his research in 1959.

Pesach Jewish name for the ◊Passover festival.

Pestalozzi Johann Heinrich 1746–1827. Swiss educationalist who advocated the French philosopher Jean-Jacques Rousseau's 'natural' principles (of natural development and the power of example), and described his own theories in *Wie Gertrude ihre Kinder lehrt/How Gertrude Teaches her Children* 1801. He stressed the importance of mother and home in a child's education.

International Children's Villages named after Pestalozzi have been established, for example at Sedlescombe, East Sussex, UK.

The Peter Principle: In a Hierarchy Every Employee Tends to Rise to His Level of Incompetence.

Laurence J Peter
The Peter Principle

Peter Laurence J 1910–1990. Canadian writer and teacher, author (with Raymond Hull) of *The Peter Principle* 1969, in which he outlined the theory that people tend to be promoted into positions for which they are incompetent.

Peter, St Christian martyr, the author of two epistles in the New Testament and leader of the apostles. He is regarded as the first bishop of Rome, whose mantle the pope inherits. His real name was Simon, but he was nicknamed Kephas ('Peter', from the Greek for 'rock') by Jesus, as being the rock upon which he would build his church. His emblem is two keys; feast day 29 June.

Originally a fisherman of Capernaum, on the Sea of Galilee, Peter may have been a follower of John the Baptist, and was the first to acknowledge Jesus as the Messiah. Tradition has it that he later settled in Rome; he was martyred during the reign of the emperor Nero, perhaps by crucifixion. Bones excavated from under the Basilica of St Peter's in the Vatican 1968 were accepted as those of St Peter by Pope Paul VI.

Peter's pence in the Roman Catholic Church, a voluntary annual contribution to papal administrative costs; during the 10th–16th centuries it was a compulsory levy of one penny per household.

Peter the Hermit 1050–1115. French priest whose eloquent preaching of the First ◊Crusade sent thousands of peasants marching against the Turks, who massacred them in Asia Minor. Peter escaped and accompanied the main body of crusaders to Jerusalem.

Petit Alexis 1791–1820. French physicist, co-discoverer of *Dulong and Petit's law*, which states that the specific heat capacity of an element is inversely proportional to its relative atomic mass.

phallus model of the male sexual organ, used as a fertility symbol in ancient Greece, Rome, Anatolia, India, and many other parts of the world. In Hinduism it is called the *lingam*, and is used as the chief symbolical representation of the deity Siva.

Pharisee member of a conservative Jewish group that arose in the 2nd century BC in protest against all movements favouring compromise with Hellenistic culture. The Pharisees were devout adherents of the law, both as found in the Torah and in the oral tradition known as the Mishna.

They were opposed by the Sadducees on several grounds: the Sadducees did not acknowledge the Mishna; the Pharisees opposed Greek and Roman rule of their country; and the Pharisees held a number of beliefs – such as the existence of hell, angels, and demons, the resurrection of the dead, and the future coming of the Messiah – not found in the Torah.

The Pharisees rejected political action, and in the 1st century AD the left wing of their followers, the *Zealots*, broke away to pursue a revolutionary nationalist policy. After the fall of Jerusalem, Pharisee ideas became the basis of orthodox Judaism as the people were dispersed throughout the W Roman empire.

phenomena in philosophy, a technical term used in Immanuel ◊Kant's philosophy, describing things as they appear to us, rather than as they are in themselves.

phenomenalism philosophical position that argues that statements about objects can be reduced to statements about what is perceived or perceivable. Thus English philosopher John Stuart Mill defined material objects as 'permanent possibilities of sensation'. Phenomenalism is closely connected with certain forms of ◊empiricism.

phenomenology the philosophical perspective, founded by the German philosopher Edmund ◊Husserl, that concentrates on phenomena as objects of perception (rather than as facts or occurrences that exist independently) in attempting to examine the ways people think about and interpret the world around them. It has been practised by the philosophers Martin ◊Heidegger, Jean-Paul ◊Sartre, and Maurice ◊Merleau-Ponty.

In contrast to positivism or 'scientific' philosophy, phenomenology sees reality as essentially relative and subjective.

philanthropy the love felt by an individual towards mankind. It is expressed through acts of generosity and ◊charity and seeks to promote the greater happiness and prosperity of humanity.

The term derives from the Greek but the notion of caring for more than oneself and one's immediate family is the basis for all civilizations. It can be found in the writings of ◊Confucius and ◊Mencius and it is a central tenet of Judaism where it is considered not just a virtue but an obligation. To do good works and to relieve suffering is to recognize one's fellow beings equally as children of God. Philanthropy, like charity and ◊aid, has sometimes been accused of perpetuating poverty and inequality by victimizing the recipients rather than encouraging self-help.

Philip Neri, St 1515–1595. Italian Roman Catholic priest who organized the Congregation of the Oratory. He built the oratory over the church of St Jerome, Rome, where prayer meetings were held and scenes from the Bible performed with music, originating the musical form oratorio. Feast day 26 May.

Phillips Wendell 1811–1884. US reformer. After attending the World Anti-Slavery Convention in London 1840, he became an outspoken proponent of the abolition of slavery. In addition to abolition he espoused a variety of other social causes, including feminism, prohibition, unionization, and improved treatment of American Indians.

Born in Boston and educated at Harvard University, Phillips was admitted to the bar 1834. Critical of the Mexican War 1846–48 and the conduct of the American Civil War 1861–65 by President Lincoln, Phillips was a reform candidate for governor of Massachusetts 1870.

Phillips curve graph showing the relationship between percentage changes in wages and unemployment, and indicating that wages rise faster during periods of low unemployment as employers compete for labour. The implication is that the dual objectives of low unemployment and low inflation are inconsistent. The concept has been widely questioned since the early 1960s because of the apparent instability of the wages/unemployment relationship. It was developed by the British economist A(lban) W(illiam) Phillips (1914–1975), who plotted graphically wage and unemployment changes between 1861 and 1957.

Philistine member of a seafaring people of non-Semitic origin who founded city-states on the Palestinian coast plain in the 12rth century bc, adopting a Semitic language and religion. They were at war with the Israelites in the 11th–10th centuries bc (hence the pejorative use of their name in Hebrew records for anyone uncivilized in intellectual and artistic terms). They were largely absorbed into the kingdom of Israel under King David, about 1000 BC.

Philo Judaeus lived 1st century AD. Jewish philosopher of Alexandria who in AD 40 undertook a mission to Caligula to protest against the emperor's claim to divine honours. In his writings Philo Judaeus attempts to reconcile Judaism with Platonic and stoic ideas.

philology in historical ◊linguistics, the study of the development of languages. It is also an obsolete term for the study of literature.

In this sense the scholars of Alexandria, who edited the Greek epics of Homer, were philologists. The Renaissance gave great impetus to this kind of study. Dutch scholars took the lead in the 17th century while Richard Bentley made significant contributions in England. *Comparative philology* arose at the beginning of the 19th century from the study of Sanskrit, under Franz Bopp's (1791–1867) leadership. It was originally mainly concerned with the Indo-European languages, while the Romantic movement greatly inspired the establishment of national philology throughout Europe and Asia.

philosophes the leading intellectuals of pre-revolutionary 18th-century France, including Condorcet, Diderot, Rousseau, and Voltaire. Their role in furthering the principles of the enlightenment and extolling the power of human reason made them question the structures of the *ancien régime*, and they were held responsible by some for influencing the revolutionaries of 1789.

Do not all charms fly / At the mere touch of cold philosophy?

philosophy
John Keats, 1795–1821, English Romantic poet.
Lamia pt 2

---

philosophy the systematic analysis and critical examination of fundamental problems, such as the nature of matter, mind, reality, language, identity, self, free will, perception, causation, science, mathematics, time, space, and moral judgements. Traditionally, philosophy has three branches: logic (study of valid inference), epistemology (theory of knowledge), and metaphysics (the nature of existence). Modern philosophy also includes aesthetics, ethics, political theory, the philosophy of science, and the philosophy of religion. Originally, philosophy included all intellectual endeavour, but over time branches of philosophy (such as physics) have become separate areas of study.

Anyone who has had a glimpse of the range and subtlety of the thought of Plato or of a Hegel will long ago have despaired of becoming a philosopher.

philosophy
Michael Oakeshott, 1901–1990, English philosopher and political theorist.
Experience and its Modes ch 1

In the ancient civilizations of India and China, various sages set out their views and reflections about life and ultimate reality; but philosophy as a systematic and rational endeavour originated in Greece in the 6th century BC with the Milesian school (Thales, Anaximander, Anaximenes). Both these and the later pre-Socratics (Pythagoras, Xenophon, Parmenides, Zeno of Elea, Empe-

The Great Philosophers

name	dates	nationality	representative work
Heraclitus	c. 544–483 BC	Greek	On Nature
Parmenides	c. 510–c. 450 BC	Greek	fragments
Socrates	469–399 BC	Greek	—
Plato	428–347 BC	Greek	Republic; Phaedo
Aristotle	384–322 BC	Greek	Nichomachaen Ethics; Metaphysics
Epicurus	341–270 BC	Greek	fragments
Lucretius	c. 99–55 BC	Roman	On the Nature of Things
Plotinus	AD 205–270	Greek	Enneads
Augustine	354–430	N African	Confessions; City of God
Aquinas	c. 1225–1274	Italian	Summa Theologica; Summa contra Gentiles
Duns Scotus	c. 1266–1308	Scottish	Opus Oxoniense
William of Occam	c. 1285–1349	English	Commentary of the Sentences
Nicholas of Cusa	1401–1464	German	De Docta Ignorantia
Giordano Bruno	1548–1600	Italian	De la Causa, Principio e Uno
Bacon	1561–1626	English	Novum Organum; The Advancement of Learning
Hobbes	1588–1679	English	Leviathan
Descartes	1596–1650	French	Discourse on Method; Meditations on the First Philosophy
Spinoza	1632–1677	Dutch	Ethics
Locke	1632–1704	English	Essay Concerning Human Understanding
Leibniz	1646–1716	German	The Monadology
Berkeley	1685–1753	Irish	A Treatise Concerning Principles of Human Knowledge
Hume	1711–1776	Scottish	A Treatise of Human Nature
Rousseau	1712–1778	French	The Social Contract
Kant	1724–1804	German	The Critique of Pure Reason
Fichte	1762–1814	German	The Science of Knowledge
Hegel	1770–1831	German	The Phenomenology of Spirit
Schelling	1775–1854	German	System of Transcendental Idealism
Schopenhauer	1788–1860	German	The World as Will and Idea
Mill	1806–1873	English	Utilitarianism
Kierkegaard	1813–1855	Danish	Concept of Dread
Pierce	1839–1914	US	How to Make our Ideas Clear
Nietzsche	1844–1900	German	Thus Spake Zarathustra
Husserl	1859–1938	German	Logical Investigations
Russell	1872–1970	English	Principia Mathematica
Wittgenstein	1889–1951	Austrian	Tractatus Logico–Philosophicus; Philosophical Investigations
Heidegger	1889–1976	German	Being and Time
Sartre	1905–1980	French	Being and Nothingness
Merleau-Ponty	1908–1961	French	The Phenomenology of Perception
Quine	1908–	US	Word and Object

docles, Anaxagoras, Heraclitus, Democritus) were lively theorists, and ideas like atomism, developed by Democritus, occur in later philosophies. In the 5th century BC, Socrates laid the foundation of ethics; Plato evolved his metaphysical theory of ◊Forms; and Aristotle invented syllogistic logic and developed his ethics, political theory, and metaphysics. Later schools include the Epicureans (Epicurus); stoics (Zeno of Citium); sceptics (Pyrrho); and the neo-Platonists, who infused a mystic element into the system of Plato (Philo, Plotinus).

The closure of the Athenian schools of philosophy by Justinian AD 529 marks the end of ancient philosophy, although the Roman philosopher Boethius passed on the outlines of Greek philosophy to the West. Greek thought also survived in the Arab philosophers Avicenna and Averroes, and in the Jewish philosophers Avencebrol (1021–1058) and Maimonides. In the early medieval period, Johannes Scotus Erigena formulated a neo-Platonic system. The 12th century saw the recovery of the texts of Aristotle, which stimulated the scholastic philosophers Anselm, Abelard, Albertus Magnus, Thomas Aquinas, Duns Scotus, and William of Occam.

Philosophy is the product of wonder.

Alfred North Whitehead
Nature and Life ch 1

In the 17th century, René Descartes, Gottfried Leibniz, and B Spinoza mark the beginning of modern philosophy with their rationalism and faith in mathematical proof. In the 17th and 18th centuries, the British empiricists (John Locke, George Berkeley,

THE HISTORY AND DEVELOPMENT OF WESTERN PHILOSOPHY

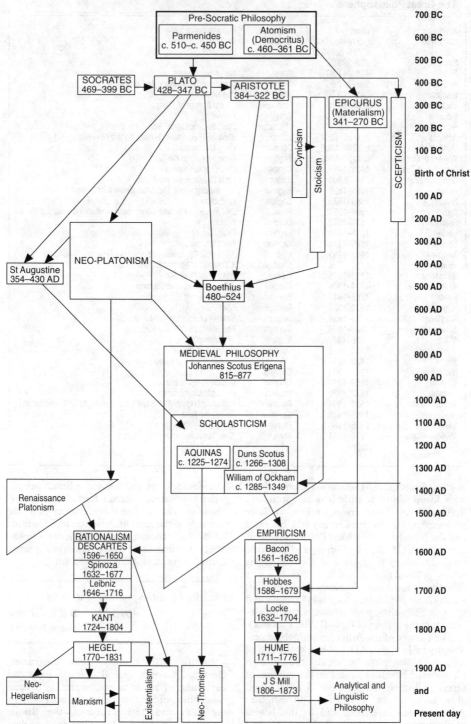

Key: Names in capitals indicate people or schools of particular importance. Arrows indicate influence. The tapering shapes of Renaissance Platonism and Medieval Philosophy indicate that these schools died out only slowly.

David Hume) turned to science and sense experience for guidance on what can be known and how. The German philosopher Immanuel Kant tried to define what we can know and to rebut both scepticism and speculative metaphysics in his critical philosophy.

In the early 19th century, classical German idealists (J G Fichte, F W J Schelling, G W F Hegel) rejected Kant's limitation on human knowledge. Notable also in the 19th century are the pessimistic atheism of Arthur Schopenhauer; the work of Friedrich Nietzsche and Søren Kierkegaard, which led to 20th-century existentialism; the pragmatism of William James and John Dewey; and neo-Hegelianism at the turn of the century (F H Bradley, T H Green, Josiah Royce). Among 20th-century movements are logical positivism (Rudolf Carnap, Karl Popper, Alfred Ayer); neo-Thomism, the revival of the medieval philosophy of Aquinas (Jacques Maritain); existentialism (Martin Heidegger, Jean-Paul Sartre, Karl Jaspers); phenomenology (Edmund Husserl, Maurice Merleau-Ponty); and analytical and linguistic philosophy (Bertrand Russell, G E Moore, Ludwig Wittgenstein, Gilbert Ryle, Willard Quine). Under the influence of Russell's work on formal logic and Wittgenstein's *Philosophical Investigations*, English-speaking philosophers have paid great attention to the nature and limits of language, particularly in relation to the language used to formulate philosophical problems.

phobia excessive irrational fear of an object or situation – for example, agoraphobia (fear of open spaces and crowded places), acrophobia (fear of heights), and claustrophobia (fear of enclosed places). ◊Behaviour therapy is one form of treatment.

phonetics identification, description, and classification of sounds used in articulate speech. These sounds are codified in the International Phonetic Alphabet (a highly modified version of the English/Roman alphabet).

A *phoneme* is the range of sound that can be substituted without change of meaning in the words of a particular language, for example – r and l form a single phoneme in Japanese but are two distinct phonemes in English. The study of phonemes is called phonemics, a branch of linguistics.

phrenology study of the shape and protuberances of the skull, based on the (now discredited) theory of the Viennese physician Dr Franz Josef Gall that such features revealed measurable psychological and intellectual traits.

phylogeny historical sequence of changes that occurs in a given species during the course of its ◊evolution. It was once erroneously associated with ontogeny (the process of development of a living organism).

physics branch of science concerned with the laws that govern the structure of the universe, and the forms of matter and energy and their interactions. For convenience, physics is often divided into branches such as nuclear physics, particle physics, solid- and liquid-state physics, electricity, electronics, magnetism, optics, acoustics, heat, and thermodynamics. Before this century, physics was known as *natural philosophy*.

Physics: recent chronology

1960	The Mössbauer effect of atom emissions was discovered by Rudolf Mössbauer; the first maser was developed by US physicist Theodore Maiman (1927–).
1963	Maiman developed the first laser.
1964	Murray Gell-Mann and George Zweig discovered the quark.
1971	The theory of superconductivity was announced, where electrical resistance in some metals vanishes above absolute zero.
1973	The discovery of pulsars was made by Antony Hewish.
1979	The discovery of the asymmetry of elementary particles was made by US physicists James W Cronin and Val L Fitch.
1982	The discovery of processes involved in the evolution of stars was made by Subrahmanyan Chandrasekhar and William Fowler.
1983	Evidence of the existence of weakons (W and Z particles) was confirmed at CERN, validating the link between the weak nuclear force and the electromagnetic force.
1986	The first high-temperature superconductor was discovered, able to conduct electricity without resistance at a temperature of 35K.
1989	Stanley Pons and Martin Fleischmann claimed to have achieved nuclear fusion at room temperature and pressure (cold fusion). CERN's Large Electron–Positron Collider (LEP), a particle accelerator with a circumference of 27 km/16.8 mi, came into operation.
1991	LEP experiments demonstrated the existence of three generations of elementary particles, each with two quarks and two leptons.
1992	Japanese researchers developed a material that becomes superconducting at −103°C/−153°F (about 45°C/80°F warmer than the previous record).
1993	Top quark discovered at Fermilab, the US particle-physics laboratory, near Chicago, USA

physiocrat member of a school of 18th-century French economists including François Quesnay (1694–1774) and Mirabeau who believed in the bounty of nature and the inherent goodness of man. They held that governments should intervene in society only where individuals' liberties were infringed. Otherwise there should be a *laissez-faire* system with free trade between states. Adam Smith was much influenced by their ideas.

physiological psychology a branch of ◊experimental psychology concerned with physiological and neurological processes as the basis of experience and behaviour. It overlaps considerably with fields such as ◊anatomy, physiology, ◊neurology, and ◊biochemistry.

Piaget Jean 1896–1980. Swiss biologist, philosopher and developmental psychologist – he thought of himself as a genetic epistemologist – whose painstaking observations of children have been enormously influential in early childhood research and on school curricula and teaching methods.

After taking his doctorate in zoology at the University of Neuchâtel, Piaget turned to psychology first in Zürich and then in Paris where he worked on reasoning tests for children in ◊Binet's laboratory. In 1921 he was appointed Director of Studies at the Institut J J Rousseau in Geneva. There he began his detailed experimental work on children's language and thinking, their ideas about movement, causality, force, space, time etc. and their understanding of dreams, life and morality. He published this research in several books, the first being *The Language and Thought of the Child* 1923. Most important were his studies of intellectual development in infancy, which, with his wife Valentine Chatenay, he carried out with his own children as subjects. They are reported in *The Origins of Intelligence in the Child* 1936, *The Child's Construction of Reality* 1936, and *Play, Dreams and Imitation in Childhood* 1946. He investigated abstract and tacit thinking by 'externalizing' it – getting the child to manipulate simple objects, toys etc. and talk while doing so. He examined the development of symbolic thinking and the child's understanding of logic, number, geometry, time, etc., which he regarded as passing through various stages characterized by special modes of thought. His later work was mainly theoretical and interdisciplinary and was an attempt to produce a biologically orientated theory of knowledge emphasizing activity, overt or internalized, and structure.

Piaget held professorships at Neuchâtel, the Sorbonne and Geneva and received many honorary degrees. In 1955 he founded the Centre for the Study of Genetic Epistemology in Geneva.

Picasso Pablo Ruiz Y 1881–1973. Spanish artist, active chiefly in France, one of the most inventive and prolific talents in 20th-century art. His Blue Period 1901–04 and Rose Period 1905–06 preceded the revolutionary *Les Demoiselles d'Avignon* 1907 (Metropolitan Museum of Art, New York), which paved the way for Cubism. In the early 1920s he was considered a leader of the Surrealist movement. In the 1930s his work included metal sculpture, book illustration, and the mural *Guernica* 1937 (Prado, Madrid), a comment on the bombing of civilians in the Spanish Civil War. He continued to paint into his eighties.

Picasso was born in Málaga, son of an art teacher, José Ruiz Blasco, and an Andalusian mother, Maria Picasso López; he stopped using the name Ruiz in 1898. He was a precocious artist by the age of 10, and at 16 was holding his first exhibition. In 1900 he made an initial visit to Paris, where he was to settle. From 1946 he lived mainly in the south of France where, in addition to painting, he experimented with ceramics, sculpture, sets for ballet (for example *Parade* 1917 for Diaghilev), book illustrations (such as Ovid's *Metamorphoses*), and portraits (Stravinsky, Valéry, and others).

Pico della Mirandola Count Giovanni 1463–1494. Italian mystic philosopher. Born at Mirandola, of which his father was prince, he studied Hebrew, Chaldean, and Arabic, showing particular interest in the Jewish and theosophical system, the ◊kabbala. His attempt to reconcile the religious base of Christianity, Islam, and the ancient world earned Pope Alexander VI's disapproval.

Pietism religious movement within Lutheranism in the 17th century which emphasized spiritual and devotional faith rather than theology and dogma. It was founded by Philipp Jakob Spener (1635–1705), a minister in Frankfurt, Germany, who emphasized devotional meetings for 'groups of the Elect' rather than biblical learning; he wrote the *Pia Desideria* 1675. The movement was for many years associated with the University of Halle (founded 1694), Germany.

Pigou Arthur Cecil 1877–1959. British economist whose notion of the 'real balance effect' (the 'Pigou effect') contended that employment was stimulated by a fall in prices, because the latter increased liquid wealth and thus demand for goods and services.

pilgrimage journey to sacred places inspired by religious devotion. For Hindus, the holy places include Varanasi and the purifying river Ganges; for Buddhists, the places connected with the crises of Buddha's career; for the ancient Greeks, the shrines at Delphi and Ephesus among others; for Jews, the sanctuary at Jerusalem; and for Muslims, Mecca.

Among Christians, pilgrimages were common by the 2nd century, and as a direct result of the growing frequency and numbers of pilgrimages there arose numerous hospices catering for pilgrims, the religious orders of knighthood, and the Crusades. The great centres of Christian pilgrimages have been, or still are, Jerusalem, Rome, the tomb of St James of Compostela in Spain, the shrine of Becket in Canterbury, England, and the holy places at La Salette and Lourdes in France.

The three major centres of pilgrimage in medieval England were Canterbury, Bury (the shrine of St Edmund), and Walsingham, Norfolk. Walsingham is still a site of pilgrimage each Easter.

Pincus Gregory Goodwin 1903–1967. US biologist who, together with Min Chueh Chang (1908–) and John Rock (1890–1984), developed the contraceptive pill in the 1950s.

As a result of studying the physiology of reproduction, Pincus conceived the idea of using synthetic hormones to mimic the condition of pregnancy in women. This effectively prevents impregnation.

Pirenne Henri 1862–1935. Belgian historian and prolific writer whose most remarkable achievement is his seven-volume *Histoire de Belgique* 1900–32. He also wrote numerous books and articles on the Middle Ages, among the best-known being *Belgian Democracy, Its Early History* 1910.

In *Mohammed and Charlemagne* 1939, he argued that the Middle Ages properly began with the rise of Islam, which disrupted Western European trade in the Mediterranean and thus led to a decline in European towns.

Pius IX 'Pio Nono' (Giovanni Maria Mastai-Ferretti) 1792–1878. Pope from 1846. He never accepted the incorporation of the Papal States and of Rome in the kingdom of Italy. He proclaimed the dogmas of the Immaculate Conception of the Virgin 1854 and papal infallibility 1870; his pontificate was the longest in history.

Originally a liberal, he became highly reactionary as papal territories were progressively lost. He refused to set foot outside the Vatican following the Italian occupation of Rome, regarding himself as a prisoner, and forbade Catholics to take any part in politics in Italy. He centred power in the Vatican, refusing compromise with modern spiritual ideas. His devotion inspired a cult following that continues to this day. The first stage in his canonization was begun 1985.

Pius XII (Eugenio Pacelli) 1876–1958. Pope from 1939. He was conservative in doctrine and politics, and condemned ◊Modernism. He proclaimed the dogma of the bodily assumption of the Virgin Mary 1950 and in 1951 restated the doctrine (strongly criticized by many) that the life of an infant must not be sacrificed to save a mother in labour. He was criticized for failing to speak out against atrocities committed by the Germans during World War II and has been accused of collusion with the Nazis.

pixel (acronym for *picture element*) single dot on a computer screen. All screen images are made up of a collection of pixels, with each pixel being either off (dark) or on (illuminated, possibly in colour). The number of pixels available determines the screen's resolution. Typical resolutions of microcomputer screens vary from 320 × 200 pixels to 640 × 480 pixels, but screens with over 1,000 × 1,000 pixels are now quite common for high-quality graphic (pictorial) displays.

The number of bits (binary digits) used to represent each pixel determines how many colours it can display: a two-bit pixel can have four colours; an eight-bit (one-byte) pixel can have 256 colours. The higher the resolution of a screen and the more colours it is capable of displaying, the more memory will be needed in order to store that screen's contents.

Plains Indian member of any of the North American Indian peoples of the Great Plains, which extend over 3,000 km/2,000 mi from Alberta to Texas. The various groups include Blackfoot, Cheyenne, Comanche, Pawnee, and the Dakota or Sioux.

Planck Max 1858–1947. German physicist who framed the quantum theory 1900. His research into the manner in which heated bodies radiate energy led him to report that energy is emitted only in indivisible amounts, called quanta, the magnitudes of which are proportional to the frequency of the radiation. His discovery ran counter to classical physics and is held to have marked the commencement of the modern science. Nobel Prize for Physics 1918.

planned economy see ◊command economy.

plastic arts the arts that are produced by modelling or moulding, chiefly sculpture and ceramics.

Plato c. 428–347 BC. Greek philosopher, pupil of Socrates, teacher of Aristotle, and founder of the Academy school of philosophy. He was the author of philosophical dialogues on such topics as metaphysics, ethics, and politics.

Central to his teachings is the theory of ◊Forms, which are located outside the everyday world – timeless, motionless, and absolutely real.

Plato's philosophy has influenced Christianity and European culture, directly as well as through Augustine, the Florentine Platonists during the Renaissance, and countless others.

Born of a noble family, he entered politics on the aristocratic side, and in philosophy became a follower of Socrates. He travelled widely after Socrates' death, and founded the educational establishment, the Academy, in order to train a new ruling class.

Of his work, some 30 dialogues survive, intended for performance either to his pupils or to the public. The principal figure in these ethical and philosophical debates is Socrates and the early ones employ the Socratic method, in which he asks questions and traps the students into contradicting themselves; for example, *Ion*, on poetry. Other dialogues include the *Symposium*, on love, *Phaedo*, on immortality, and *Apology* and *Crito*, on Socrates' trial and death. It is impossible to say whether Plato's Socrates is a faithful representative of the real man or an articulation of Plato's own thought. Plato's philosophy rejects scientific rationalism (establishing facts through experiment) in favour of arguments, because mind, not matter, is fundamental, and material objects are merely imperfect copies of abstract and eternal 'ideas'. His political philosophy is expounded in two treatises, *The Republic* and *The Laws*, both of which describe ideal states. Platonic love is inspired by a person's best qualities and seeks their development.

plebiscite referendum or direct vote by all the electors of a country or district on a specific question. Since the 18th century plebiscites have been employed on many occasions to decide to what country a particular area should belong; for example, in Upper Silesia and elsewhere after World War I, and in the Saar 1935.

Plethon George Gemisthos 1353–1452. Byzantine philosopher who taught for many years at Mistra in Asia Minor.

A Platonist, he maintained a resolutely anti-Christian stance and was the inspiration for many of the ideas of the 15th-century Florentine Platonic Academy.

Plotinus AD 205–AD 270. Egyptian originator of the philosophy now called ◊neo-Platonism. He held that the ultimate goal of mystical union with the One or Good (the source of all being) can be achieved by intense moral and intellectual discipline. From the One or Good, the various levels of reality emanate timelessly.

The first level is the Divine Intellect, in which the ◊Ideas are living intelligences and archetypes of the things of the world of sense. The next level is the Soul, the active principle forming and ordering the visible universe. People can choose to live on the level of the lower Soul (Nature) or the higher Soul (Intellect). Neo-Platonism has had a deep influence on Christian and metaphysical thought.

Born in Egypt, Plotinus studied from the age of 28 under Ammonius Saccas (died AD 243) in Alexandria. In AD 244 he went to Rome, where he founded a philosophy school. His treatises in Greek, the *Enneads*, were edited by his pupil Porphyry.

pluralism in political science, the view that decision-making in contemporary liberal democracies is the outcome of competition among several interest groups in a political system characterized by free elections, representative institutions, and open access to the organs of power. This concept is opposed by corporatism and other approaches that perceive power to be centralized in the state and its principal elites (the ◊Establishment).

pluralism in philosophy, the belief that reality consists of several different elements, not just two – matter and mind – as in ◊dualism.

Plymouth Brethren fundamentalist Christian Protestant group characterized by extreme simplicity of belief, founded in Dublin about 1827 by the Reverend John Nelson Darby (1800–1882). The Plymouth Brethren have no ordained priesthood, affirming the ministry of all believers, and maintain no church buildings. They hold prayer meetings and Bible study in members' houses.

An assembly of Brethren was held in Plymouth 1831 to celebrate the group's arrival in England, but by 1848 the movement had split into 'Open' and 'Closed' Brethren. The latter refuse communion with those not of their persuasion. A further subset of the Closed Brethren is the 'Exclusive' Brethren, who have strict rules regarding dress and conduct.

In the UK, the Plymouth Brethren are mainly found in the fishing villages of NE Scotland. There are some 65,000 in the USA, divided into eight separate groups. Worldwide membership is about 1.5 million, including members in the Caribbean, India, and Burma. Famous members include Dr Barnado.

pogrom unprovoked violent attack on an ethnic group, particularly Jews, carried out with official sanction. The Russian pogroms against Jews began 1881, after the assassination of Tsar Alexander II, and again in 1903–06; persecution of the Jews remained constant until the Russian Revolution. Later there were pogroms in E Europe, especially in Poland after 1918, and in Germany under Hitler (see ◊Holocaust).

Poincaré Jules Henri 1854–1912. French mathematician who developed the theory of differential equations and was a pioneer in ◊relativity theory. He suggested that Isaac Newton's laws for the behaviour of the universe could be the exception rather than the rule. However, the calculation was so complex and time-consuming that he never managed to realize its full implication.

He also published the first paper devoted entirely to ◊topology (the branch of geometry that deals with the unchanged properties of figures).

Poisson Siméon Denis 1781–1840. French applied mathematician. In probability theory he formulated the *Poisson distribution*, which is widely used in probability calculations. He published four treatises and several hundred papers on aspects of physics, including mechanics, heat, electricity and magnetism, elasticity, and astronomy.

Polanyi Michael 1891–1976. Hungarian chemist, social scientist, and philosopher. As a scientist, he worked on thermodynamics, X-ray crystallography and physical adsorption. As a philosopher and social scientist, he was concerned about the conflicts between personal freedom and central planning, and the impact of the conflict upon scientists. He also analysed the nature of knowledge, skills, and discovery.

His works include *Personal Knowledge* 1958, *Knowing and Being* 1969, and *Scientific Thought and Social Reality* 1974. Born in Budapest, he studied medicine there and later turned to chemistry. In 1933 he resigned from the Kaiser Wilhelm Institute in Berlin over the dismissal of Jewish scientists, and he moved to Manchester University, England, to be professor of physical chemistry. He became professor of social studies at Manchester in 1948.

police civil law-and-order force. In the UK it is responsible to the Home Office, with 56 autonomous police forces, generally organized on a county basis; mutual aid is given in circumstances such as mass picketing in the 1984–85 miners' strike, but there is no national police force or police riot unit (such as the French CRS riot squad). The predecessors of these forces were the ineffective medieval watch and London's Bow Street runners, introduced 1749 by Henry Fielding which formed a model for the London police force established by Robert Peel's government 1829 (hence 'peelers' or 'bobbies'); the system was introduced throughout the country from 1856.

Landmarks include: *Criminal Investigation Department* detective branch of the London Metropolitan Police (New Scotland Yard) 1878, recruited from the uniformed branch (such departments now exist in all UK forces); women police 1919; motorcycle patrols 1921; two-way radio cars 1927; personal radio on the beat 1965; and *Special Patrol Groups* (SPG) 1970, squads of experienced officers concentrating on a specific problem (New York has the similar Tactical Patrol Force). Unlike most other police forces, the British are armed only on special occasions, but arms issues grow more frequent. In 1985 London had one police officer for every 268 citizens.

Other police forces include the Garda Síochána in the Republic of Ireland, the Carabinieri in Italy, the Guardia Civil in Spain, the Royal Canadian Mounted Police ('Mounties') in Canada, the Police Nationale (under the Ministry of the Interior) for the cities and the Gendarmerie (part of the army) elsewhere in France.

In the UK, police expenditure increased by 55% in real terms in the period 1979 to 1990. In 1991, the force claimed to clear up 26% of all recorded crimes, although this is estimated to be only 7% of the total committed.

polis in ancient Greece, a city-state, the political and social centre of most larger Greek communities. Originally a citadel on a rock or hill, in classical times the polis consisted of a walled city with adjoining land, which could be extensive. Membership of a polis as a citizen, participation in its cults and festivals, and the protection of its laws formed the basis of classical Greek civilization, which was marked by intense inter-city rivalries and conflicts until the Hellenistic period.

political correctness (PC) shorthand term for a set of liberal attitudes about education and society, and the terminology associated with them. To be politically correct is to be sensitive to unconscious racism and sexism and to display environmental awareness. However, the real or alleged enforcement of PC speech codes ('people of colour' instead of

The Major Political Thinkers

name	book	central ideas
Plato	Republic 4th century BC	the ideal state, rationally constructed, would be based on justice and the 'good', and ruled by philosophers
Aristotle	Politics 4th century BC	people are 'political animals' who realize their true potential through political action, the ideal state being ruled by the aristocracy
Cicero	The Republic 1st century BC	the fundamental importance of individual rights based on 'natural law'
St Augustine	The City of God 5th century AD	though the state is a product of man's fallen nature, it may also become an expression of his desire for justice
Aquinas	Summa Theologica late 13th century	the state, essential to the realization of man's potential, is an expression of God's purpose
Dante	On World Government 1310–13	the need for a world state governed by an emperor
Machiavelli	Prince 1513	the concern of rulers should be the brutal realities of power
Hobbes	Leviathan 1651	natural rights must be willingly surrendered (the 'social contract') in support of absolute sovereignty
Locke	Two Treatises on Civil Government 1690	government must be based on the natural rights of man (classic expression of liberalism)
Montesquieu	Spirit of the Laws 1748	the need for a separation of power within government to prevent tyranny
Rousseau	Social Contract 1762	government must be subordinate to the rights of the people as expressed in the 'general will'
Burke	Reflections on the French Revolution 1790	the state is a living organism, needing gradual reform based on traditional values (classic expression of conservatism)
Paine	The Rights of Man 1791	revolution is legitimate if it establishes justice and equal rights for all
Hegel	The Philosophy of Rights 1821	the state is the highest expression of the historical/spiritual process, the individual being completely subordinate to the state
Saint-Simon	The Industrial System 1821	class conflict will be eliminated when a socialist state governed by technicians and scientists is established
Proudhon	What is Property? 1840	property and the state must be abolished if society is to be free and just (the classic expression of anarchism)
Marx and Engels	Communist Manifesto 1848	class conflict will lead to revolution and, with the collapse of capitalism, the creation of the perfect socialist state (the classic expression of communism)
J S Mill	On Liberty 1859	the highest form of government, democracy, must be based both on wide suffrage and on respect for minority rights
Bakunin	God and the State 1882	revolutionary violence is necessary to create the anarchist society of complete individual freedom

'coloured people', 'differently abled' instead of 'disabled', and so on) at more than 130 US universities by 1991 attracted derision and was criticized as a form of thought-policing.

political party association of like-minded people organized with the purpose of seeking and exercising political power. A party can be distinguished from an interest or ⊅pressure group which seeks to influence governments rather than aspire to office, although some pressure groups, such as the Green movement, have over time transformed themselves into political parties.

Although politics, as an activity, has been practised for thousands of years, political parties seem to have been largely a product of the 19th century, eventually epitomized by the major British parties, the Whigs and the Tories. Although the US constitution contains no reference to parties, the Republican and Democratic parties became essential elements of the political system, reflecting the country's history and social and economic structure. The one-party state, in which party and state institutions became enmeshed, was the distinguishing feature of the political system established in Russia by Lenin (and later Stalin) after World War I.

political science the study of politics and political life. Originally it concentrated on the state and how it was organized, but more recently it has come to include the analysis of all those institutions and groups which possess and exercise political power.

Political Power: Does it Inevitably Corrupt?

In 1887, the English historian Lord Acton wrote, in a letter to Bishop Mandell Creighton, a sentence set to become one of the world's most familiar quotations: 'Power tends to corrupt and absolute power corrupts absolutely.' The link between power and corruption had long been recognized. William Pitt, Earl of Chatham, said in a speech in the House of Lords in 1770, had said, 'Unlimited power is apt to corrupt the minds of those who possess it.' In the 4th century BC, the Greek philosopher, Plato, argued in *The Republic* that only politicians who would gain no personal advantage from the policies they pursued would be fit to govern. This is recognized also in the aphorism that those who want to hold power are most likely those least fit to do so.

Contemporary corruption

The present century has produced numerous examples of corrupt political leaders: the Duvaliers of Haiti; Ferdinand Marcos of the Philippines; Idi Amin of Uganda; Nicolae Ceausescu of Romania; Erich Honecker of East Germany; Jean-Bédel Bokassa of the Central African Republic; Josef Stalin of the former USSR. There are many more examples. The world's liberal democracies were thought to be relatively immune from corruption of the sort found in less developed politics, but revelations of widespread Mafia corruption in Italy, involving some of the country's most respected politicians, have brought the problem to light again right at the centre of European life.

Corruption is not an absolute condition. It can range from the acts of violence perpetrated by outright dictators to rules being bent and a blind eye turned to acts that a completely moral society would consider offensive. Political corruption can mean anything from buying votes or obtaining financial support by giving rewards only accessible by governments, to the elimination of people standing in the way of those in power.

In 1993 serious allegations of corruption, involving varying levels of government, surfaced in countries as diverse as Australia, Bolivia, Brazil, Bulgaria, France, Haiti, India, Italy, Japan, Malaysia, Paraguay, South Africa, Spain, and the USA. In Brazil, the allegations caused the president's resignation and a subsequent action for impeachment. In Italy, political leaders resigned and a major judicial inquiry was instigated as links were alleged between politicians, including former prime ministers, and the Italian Mafia. In Japan, the prime minister was discredited and removed from office.

The common factors

An analysis of worldwide political corruption reveals common factors. First, in many cases a person, regime, or party has been continuously in power for a long period. Second, and flowing from the first, power rather than public service has become the main purpose of political life. Third, with the retention of power the main objective, virtually any action is acceptable if it furthers this end. In other words, morality and probity take second place to the essential objective of maintaining power. Inevitably, this involves politicians granting favours to win votes ('pork barrel' politics), or granting favours to obtain money to finance their parties. It is an insidious process, with one favour demanding another and one shady deal leading to the next.

Public opinion

The most obvious effect of political corruption is a loss of public esteem for politicians and political life. The cynical view that 'politics is a dirty business' becomes a reality; people enter politics not from a sense of public service but in pursuit of personal power and advancement. The debate in the UK about the funding of political parties illustrates this very well. There is a growing sense that the Conservative Party has been in office too long for its own and the nation's good; that it has become so accustomed to being in power that it has forgotten why it was put there in the first place; that, because it wants to remain in power, almost anything is acceptable if power can be retained.

Solutions

So it would seem that Lord Acton was right, human nature being what it is. The evidence is there for all to see, right across the world. There are probably few politicians whose hands are absolutely clean. Is there an answer? There is certainly not a simple or instant one. In most countries it will be a long-haul process. The theory of multiparty politics, in which there is always an effective opposition ready to take over should the party in power falter, should be made more of a reality. Government should be opened up much more to public scrutiny and this should include the accountability of political parties for their funds. Most important of all, however, public esteem for politicians should be restored. This can only be done by the politicians themselves, demonstrating by deeds that they see themselves as elected to serve, rather than to profit.

Denis Derbyshire

Many major philosophers, including ◊Aristotle, ◊Hobbes, and ◊Rousseau, have been concerned with defining the political institutions which are necessary for a properly functioning civil society. Political science, however, differs from political philosophy or ◊political theory in being more descriptive rather than prescriptive, more concerned with how political institutions actually function than with how they ought to function.

political theory the philosophical questioning of the assumptions underlying political life, for example the grounds on which an individual is obliged to obey the state. It also attempts to formulate theories of how political institutions can be perfected by the empirical observation of existing institutions.

politics ruling by the consent of the governed; an activity whereby solutions to social and economic problems are solved and different aspirations are met by the process of discussion and compromise rather than by the application of decree or force.

The first requirement of a statesman is that he be dull. This is not always easy to achieve.

politicians
Dean (Gooderham) Acheson, 1893–1971,
US politician.
Observer 21 June 1970

A much misused term, it has been expounded by Bernard Crick in his classic *In Defence of Politics* 1962. Its popular description as 'the art of the possible' was probably first used by Otto von Bismarck of Prussia, in a recorded conversation in 1867. Both Bismarck and Crick were making the point that politics is essentially an activity and not a science, or set of rules. It is an activity based on diversity: diverse opinions about aims to be achieved and means to achieve them. Politicians accept this diversity as a fact of life and seek to resolve conflicting views by discussion and compromise, rather than diktat and violence.

Finality is not the language of politics.

politics
Benjamin Disraeli, Earl of Beaconsfield,
1804–1881, British Conservative politician
and novelist.
Speech in House of Commons 28 Feb 1859

Winston Churchill characteristically expounded the nature of politics when he said that 'Jaw jaw is better than war war.'

poll tax tax levied on every individual, without reference to income or property. Being simple to administer, it was among the earliest taxes (introduced in England 1377), but because of its indiscriminate nature (it is a regressive tax, in that it falls proportionately more heavily on poorer people) it has often been criticized.

In the USA, the tax was widely used as a means of disenfranchising poor blacks in southern states. It was made unconstitutional under the 24th Amendment 1964 for federal elections and 1966 for state races. In England, the poll tax of 1377 contributed to the Peasants' Revolt of 1381 and was abolished 1698. In April 1989, the *community charge*, a type of poll tax, was introduced in Scotland by the British government, and subsequently in England and Wales 1990, replacing the property-based local taxation (the rates). Its unpopularity led to the announcement 1991 of a replacement, a 'council tax', based both on property values and on the size of households, introduced 1993–94.

polluter-pays principle the idea that whoever causes pollution is responsible for the cost of repairing any damage. The principle is accepted in British law but has in practice often been ignored; for example, farmers causing the death of fish through slurry pollution have not been fined the full costs of restocking the river.

poltergeist unexplained phenomenon that invisibly moves objects or hurls them about, starts fires, or causes other mischief.

polyandry system whereby a woman has more than one husband at the same time. It is found in many parts of the world, for example, in Madagascar, Malaysia, and certain Pacific isles, and among certain Inuit and South American Indian groups. In Tibet and parts of India, polyandry takes the form of the marriage of one woman to several brothers, as a means of keeping intact a family's heritage and property.

Polycarp, St c. 69–c. 155. Christian martyr allegedly converted by St John the Evangelist. As bishop of Smyrna (modern Izmir, Turkey), he carried on a vigorous struggle against various heresies for over 40 years. He was burned alive at a public festival; feast day 26 Jan.

polygamy the practice of having more than one spouse at the same time. It is found among many peoples. Normally it has been confined to the wealthy and to chiefs and nobles who can support several women and their offspring, as among ancient Egyptians, Teutons, Irish, and Slavs. Islam limits the number of legal wives a man may have to four. Certain Christian sects – for example, the Anabaptists of Münster, Germany, and the Mormons – have practised polygamy because it was the norm in the Old Testament.

In pious times, ere priestcraft did begin, /
Before polygamy was made a sin.

polygamy
John Dryden, 1631–1700, English poet and dramatist.
Absalom and Achitophel pt 1

polytheism the worship of many gods, as opposed to ◊monotheism (belief in one god). Examples are the religions of ancient Egypt, Babylon, Greece, Rome, Mexico, and modern Hinduism.

Poncelet Jean-Victor 1788–1867. French mathematician and military engineer who advanced projective geometry. His book *Traité des propriétés projectives des figures*, started in 1814 and completed 1822, deals with the properties of plane figures that remain unchanged when projected.

poor law English system for poor relief, established by the Poor Relief Act 1601. Each parish was responsible for its own poor, paid for by a parish tax. The care of the poor was transferred to the Ministry of Health 1918, but the poor law remained in force until 1930.

Poor law was reformed in the 19th century. After the Royal Commission on the Poor Law 1834, 'outdoor' relief for able-bodied paupers was abolished and replaced by workhouses run by unions of parishes. Conditions in such workhouses were designed to act as a deterrent for all but the genuinely destitute, but the Andover workhouse scandal 1847 removed some of the greatest corruptions and evils of the system.

Pop art movement of British and American artists in the mid-1950s and 1960s, reacting against the elitism of abstract art. Pop art imagery was drawn from advertising, comic strips, film, and television. Early exponents in the UK were Richard Hamilton, Peter Blake (1932–), and Eduardo Paolozzio, and in the USA Jasper Johns, Jim Dine, Andy Warhol, Roy Lichtenstein, and Claes Oldenburg. In its eclecticism and its sense of irony and playfulness, Pop art helped to prepare the way for the Post-Modernism of the 1970s and 1980s.

Pop art was so named by the British critic Lawrence Alloway (1926–). Richard Hamilton described it in 1957 as 'popular, transient, expendable, low-cost, mass-produced, young, witty, sexy, gimmicky, glamorous, and big business'. The artists often used repeating images and quoted from others' work.

pope the bishop of Rome, head of the Roman Catholic Church, which claims he is the spiritual descendant of St Peter. Elected by the Sacred College of Cardinals, a pope dates his pontificate from his coronation with the tiara, or triple crown, at St Peter's Basilica, Rome. The pope had great political power in Europe from the early Middle Ages until the Reformation.

Popov Alexander 1859–1905. Russian physicist who devised the first aerial, in advance of Marconi (although he did not use it for radio communication). He also invented a detector for radio waves.

We may become the makers of our fate when we have ceased to pose as its prophets.

Karl Popper
The Open Society and its Enemies Introduction

Popper Karl (Raimund) 1902–1994. Austrian philosopher of science and history. Popper's main interest was the precise status of scientific claims. In *The Logic of Scientific Discovery* 1934 and *Conjectures and Refutations* 1963 he argued that what distinguishes science from metaphysics and 'pseudoscience' is that its claims are in principle falsifiable – they leave open the possibility that they might be wrong. If a claim cannot, even in principle, be shown to be false, it is not scientific. For Popper, ◊Freud's theories are pseudoscience, for despite their claim to scientific status there is no way they can be put to the test.

In two influential works, *The Open Society and its Enemies* 1945 and *The Poverty of Historicism* 1957 he analysed the nature of social and historical research. He attacked the ◊historicism of Plato, Hegel, and Marx, all of whom saw social and historical change in terms of all-embracing laws of human development. His argument is that history is profoundly influenced by the growth of knowledge; but as the growth of knowledge is unpredictable and always open to new developments, its influence on the course of history is unpredictable. Popper's other works include *Objective Knowledge* 1972 and *Unended Quest* 1976, his autobiography.

His major work on the philosophy of science is *The Logic of Scientific Discovery* 1935. Other works include *The Poverty of Historicism* 1957 (about the philosophy of social science), *Conjectures and Refutations* 1963, and *Objective Knowledge* 1972.

More people are killed out of righteous stupidity than out of wickedness.

Karl Popper
Conjectures and Refutations

Born and educated in Vienna, Popper became a naturalized British subject 1945 and was professor of logic and scientific method at the London School of Economics 1949–69. He opposed Wittgenstein's view that philosophical problems are merely pseudoproblems. Popper's view of scientific practice has been criticized by T S ◊Kuhn and other writers.

population control measures taken by some governments to limit the growth of their countries' populations by trying to reduce ◊birth rates. Propaganda, freely available contraception, and tax disincentives for large families are some of the measures that have been tried.

The population-control policies introduced by the Chinese government are the best known. In 1979 the government introduced a 'one-child policy' that encouraged ◊family planning and penalized couples who have more than one child. It has been only partially successful since it has been difficult to administer, especially in rural areas, and has in some cases led to the killing of girls in favour of sons as heirs.

population explosion the rapid and dramatic rise in world population that has occurred over the last few hundred years. Between 1959 and 1990, the world's population increased from 2.5 billion to over 5 billion people. It is estimated that it will be at least 6 billion by the end of the century. Most of this growth is now taking place in the ◊developing world, where rates of natural increase are much higher than in developed countries. Concern that this might lead to ◊overpopulation has led some countries to adopt ◊population control policies.

pornography obscene literature, pictures, photos, or films considered to be of no artistic merit and intended only to arouse sexual desire. Standards of what is obscene and whether a particular work has artistic value are subjective, hence there is often difficulty in determining whether a work violates the obscenity laws. Opponents of pornography claim that it is harmful and incites violence to women and children. Others oppose its censorship claiming that it is impossible to distinguish pornography from art.

Porter George 1920– . English chemist. From 1949 he and Ronald Norrish (1897–1978) developed the technique by which flashes of high energy are used to bring about and study extremely fast chemical reactions. He shared the 1967 Nobel Prize for Chemistry with Norrish and German chemist Manfred Eigen.

Porter was director of the Royal Institution 1966–85 and president of the Royal Society 1885–90. In the 1960s he became a familiar figure through his appearances on British television.

Porter Michael 1947– . US management theorist and expert on competitive strategy, and professor of Management at Harvard Business School. His first book *Competitive Strategy* 1980 set out his theory on strategies for competitive advantage and is regarded by many as the definitive work in the field. He later applied the same theory to countries in his *Competitive Advantage of Nations* 1990 to explain why some countries are richer than others.

Porter Rodney Robert 1917–1985. British biochemist. In 1962 Porter proposed a structure for human immunoglobulin in which the molecule was seen as consisting of four chains. Porter was awarded, with Gerald Edelman, the 1972 Nobel Prize for Medicine.

Port Royal former Cistercian convent, SW of Paris, founded in 1204. In 1626 its inmates were moved to Paris, and the buildings were taken over by a male community which became a centre of Jansenist teaching. During the second half of the 17th century the community was subject to periodic persecutions (◊Jansenism being unpopular with the French authorities) and finally in 1709 was dispersed; the following year the buildings were destroyed by order of Louis XIV.

Poseidon in Greek mythology, the chief god of the sea (Roman **Neptune**), brother of Zeus and Pluto. The brothers dethroned their father, Kronos, and divided his realm, Poseidon taking the sea; he was also worshipped as god of earthquakes. His sons were the merman sea god Triton and the Cyclops Polyphemus.

positivism theory that confines genuine knowledge within the bounds of science and observation. The theory is associated with the French philosopher Auguste Comte and ◊empiricism. *Logical positivism* developed in the 1920s. It rejected any metaphysical world beyond everyday science and common sense, and confined statements to those of formal logic or mathematics.

On the basis of positivism, Comte constructed his 'Religion of Humanity', in which the object of adoration was the Great Being, that is, the personification of humanity as a whole. Logical positivism influenced, and became more widely known through, the work of A J ◊Ayer and the ◊Vienna Circle.

possible world in philosophy, a consistent set of propositions describing a logically, if not physically, possible state of affairs. The term was invented by German philosopher ◊Leibniz who argued that God chose to make real one world from an infinite range of possible worlds. Since God could only choose the best, our world is 'the best of all possible worlds'.

In the 20th century, philosophers have used Leibniz's metaphysics as a set of logical doctrines and the concept of possible worlds is now used as a tool in modal logic (the formal logic of possibility and necessity). The concept can help to analyse the ontological argument of St ◊Anselm, which aims to prove the necessary existence of God. It can also be used to explain terms like *necessary truth* or *contingent truth*. A necessary truth, such as 2 + 2 = 4, is one that is true in all possible worlds, while a contingent truth, such as 'Italy is a republic', is one that is true only in some possible worlds.

Post-Impressionism movement in painting that followed ◊Impressionism in the 1880s and 1890s, incorporating various styles. The term was first used by the British critic Roger Fry in 1910 to describe the works of Paul Cézanne, Vincent van Gogh, and Paul Gauguin. Thought differing greatly in style and aims, these painters sought to go beyond Impressionism's concern with the ever-changing effects of light.

Post-Modernism late 20th-century movement in architecture and the arts that rejects the preoccupation of ◊Modernism with purity of form and technique. Post-Modern designers and architects use an amalgam of style elements from the past, such as the Classical and the Baroque, and apply them in a witty and parodic way that emphasizes surface rather than depth.

The implication is that in an age of mass media and multiculturalism, clarity and coherence of meaning are no longer possible. This collapse of progress and signification is seen by some cultural critics, for instance Jean ◊Baudrillard and Jean-Francois Lyotard, as symptomatic of society as a whole.

poststructuralism movement in 20th-century philosophy, cultural theory, and literary criticism which debates and contests the theoretical assumptions of ◊structuralism, rejecting the conclusion that there are fundamental structures in language and cultural systems which provide a key to meaning.

Following the work of the French philosopher Jacques ◊Derrida, poststructuralist critics point to the free play of meaning in the 'texts' constituted by sign systems, which are considered to be open to a multiplicity of interpretations. As a discipline of thought, poststructuralism draws heavily on traditional categories of rhetorical study, such as metaphor and metonymy.

poujadist member of an extreme right-wing political movement in France led by Pierre Poujade (1920–), which was prominent in French politics 1954–58. Known in France as the *Union de Défense des Commerçants et Artisans*, it won 52 seats in the national election of 1956. Its voting strength came mainly from the lower-middle-class and petit-bourgeois sections of society but the return of de Gaulle to power 1958, and the foundation of the Fifth Republic led to a rapid decline in the movement's fortunes.

Pound Roscoe 1870–1964. American jurist. He was the leading exponent of what became known as sociological jurisprudence: the idea that the law must be sufficiently flexible to take into account social realities in order to provide the maximum of people's wants with the minimum of friction and waste. He regarded this as a form of social engineering that required the balancing of competing interests, classified as individual, public, and social interests. His major published work is the 5-volume *Jurisprudence*.

Anyone who has ever struggled with poverty knows how extremely expensive it is to be poor.

poverty
James Baldwin, 1924–1987, US writer and civil-rights activist.
Nobody Knows My Name, Fifth Avenue, Uptown: a letter from Harlem'

---

poverty condition that exists when the basic needs of human beings (shelter, food, and clothing) are not being met. Many different definitions of poverty exist, since there is little agreement on the standard of living considered to be the minimum adequate level (known as the *poverty level*) by the majority of people.

Absolute poverty, where people lack the necessary food, clothing, or shelter to survive, can be distinguished from *relative poverty*. In ◊Third World countries, a significant proportion of the population may suffer from

Post-Modernism: the beginning of the end?

The Seagram Building (1954–58) in New York – a glass and steel tower designed by Mies Van der Rohe – is a classic of Modernism. The AT&T Building (1978–83) in New York – a glass and steel tower with a Chippendale-style pediment stuck on the top – is a classic of Post-Modernism. The first takes itself completely seriously, the second undercuts its own seriousness by the humorous addition of an incongruous detail.

Functionality confounded –Modernism goes wrong

For Modernist architects a house was 'a machine for living in', a building that serviced particular needs just as a factory or a museum does. The architect's task was not to give rein to his own artistic expression, but to find the form that best fitted the function. The Modernist despised 19th-century architecture with its profusion of styles and surfeit of decoration. The Austrian architect Adolf Loos, writing in 1892, even went so far as to associate an excess of ornamentation with criminal depravity. But although 19th-century styles were rejected, 19th-century values, like belief in progress and in the perfectibility of social institutions, were not. The Modernist project to destroy slums and to build the model cities of the future began in earnest after World War II. Twenty-five years later confidence in this project was rapidly waning. Tower blocks and high-density housing were starting to be seen as the problem rather than the solution. The dynamiting, in St Louis, Missouri, of the Pruitt-Igoe housing estate in 1972 – just 14 years after it went up – became a symbol of the destruction of the god that failed. What could possibly fill the vacuum?

Return of the decorative – with a sting in the tail

The answer, initially, was wit and a return to ornamentation. The Post-Modern architect/designer sought to replace the austere, functional aesthetic of Modernism with a dizzying mélange of hybrid styles. The classical language of columns and the orders was mixed in with modern materials and brilliant colours. Pastiche, parody and playful quotation from the past became the order of the day. James Stirling's Staatsgalerie Stuttgart (1980–84) combines classical references with polychromatic marble and high-tech detailing. Notions of good and bad taste became irrelevant. The architect Robert Venturi proposed Las Vegas as the archetypal modern city – an instant city of signs and symbols, with no depth or meaning beyond what is visible. In Post-Modern design, form no longer followed function; it positively undermined it. Nowhere was this more spectacularly apparent than in Jean-Paul Gaultier's costume designs for the pop star Madonna – the ultimate Post-Modern entertainer: manufactured, provocative, deliberately blurring public and private, fact and fantasy; and above all ironic.

Loss of faith – loss of reality?

So is Post-Modernism just another style? A witty reaction to the perceived brutality of late Modernism? Or is it part of a more wide-ranging cultural condition? According to the critic Jean-Francois Lyotard, the prevailing mood of our age is one of ˙incredulity towards meta-narratives'. In other words, there is no longer any faith in the great belief systems of the past, in history, progress, or truth. Our capacity to hold such beliefs has been eroded by the constant bombardment of images and information available to us through the new technology and the mass media. Marshall MacLuhan's 'global village' has come to pass, but instead of making us more enlightened it has befuddled us. We can no longer make sense of the world because there is no cohesive world to make sense of. Instead we occupy a state of what Jean Baudrillard has called 'hyperreality', an unreal world of dreams and fantasy, of 'simulacra' – the world of TV, of the shopping mall, of video games, of Disneyland. Politics has ended, people have been reduced to mindless consumers, and the dominant language is the language of packaging and advertising. According to Baudrillard, there is no point in trying to resist the hyperreal, we should simply enjoy it.

Such a view has been criticized, especially by the left, as being absurdly negative – apocalyptic even. However, as a cultural critique, albeit of an exaggerated kind, Post-Modernism functions best when it analyses the extremes of mass-consumerism and the media.

Or Apocalypse Now?

But this manic consumerism is essentially a phenomenon of the first World, and of the USA in particular. Even taking into account the pervasiveness of US cultural imperialism, the experience of many other parts of the world is completely different. The world of Islam, for instance, or China, occupies a very different reality from that posited by Baudrillard. Perhaps Post-Modernism could be usefully understood as a form of millenarianism – along with religous fundamentalism, the 'new world order', the 'end of history', and the 'Age of Aquarius' – just one of the many attempts to deal with the impending sense of rootlessness and anxiety which seems to be emerging as the millennium draws to a close.

Joe Staines

absolute poverty. In developed countries, a significant proportion of the population may suffer from relative poverty, which has been defined as the inability of a citizen to participate fully in economic terms in the society in which he or she lives. Examples of relative poverty in developed countries might include not being able to afford to heat the house adequately, to buy and run a car, or to go on holiday.

Come away; poverty's catching.

poverty
Aphra Behn, 1640–1689, English author and
adventuress.
The Rover, Part II III.i

---

poverty cycle set of factors or events by which poverty, once started, is likely to continue unless there is outside intervention. Once an area or a person has become poor, this tends to lead to other disadvantages, which may in turn result in further poverty. The situation is often found in inner-city areas and shanty towns. Applied to countries, the poverty cycle is often called the *development trap*. One way of breaking the cycle may be through ◊aid.

Powell Cecil Frank 1903–1969. English physicist. From the 1930s he and his team at Bristol University investigated the charged subatomic particles in cosmic radiation by using photographic emulsions carried in weather balloons. This led to his discovery of the pion (pi meson) 1946, a particle whose existence had been predicted by the Japanese physicist Hideki Yukawa 1935. Powell was awarded a Nobel prize in 1950.

pragmatism philosophical tradition that interprets truth in terms of the practical effects of what is believed and, in particular, the usefulness of these effects. The US philosopher Charles ◊Peirce is often accounted the founder of pragmatism; it was further advanced by William James.

Prague School group of linguists, including Roman ◊Jakobson and Nicolai Trubetzkoy, who were active in Prague in the late 1920s and early 1930s. Their theory of phonology analysed sounds into sets of oppositions.

prana the life force, or airs, within the body, divided by Hindu philosophy into ten classifications beginning with the breath, and including the air of digestion, of evacuation, of relaxation, of opening and closing the eyes and mouth, of contraction, of circulation, and of sustenance. The seat of the life airs is the heart. Prana is closely connected with ◊yoga: calm

breathing brings calmness of mind. The practice of *pranayama* (breath control) is the fourth of the eight limbs of yoga.

prasada in Hinduism, consecrated food, normally vegetarian, that is prepared for the deity either in the temple or in the home, and then distributed to the faithful as a blessing. The offering and receiving of prasada is an essential part of Hindu daily life.

The wish for prayer is itself a prayer.

prayer
Georges Bernanos, 1888–1948,
French author.
Diary of a Country Priest ch 2

---

prayer address to divine power, ranging from a magical formula to attain a desired end, to selfless communication in meditation. Within Christianity the Catholic and Orthodox churches sanction prayer to the Virgin Mary, angels, and saints as intercessors, whereas Protestantism limits prayer to God alone. Muslims pray only to God (see ◊salat), five times each day, using a set pattern of words and movements, followed by personal prayer. Times for prayer are signalled by a *muezzin* (caller). Hindu prayer may be addressed to any god, or to the supreme godhead. It often includes chanting the scriptures in Sanskrit, and the sacred sound 'om' or 'aum'. In Judaism there are traditional prayers related to many everyday tasks or situations, and congregational prayers are said at the synagogue every day. It is the duty of every adult male Jew to attend these if possible, and help form part of the *minyan*, or quorum of 10 which is necessary for congregational prayers. Sikhs repeat morning and evening prayers taken from the *Guru Granth Sahib*.

He prayeth well, who loveth well / Both man and bird and beast. / He prayeth best, who loveth best / All things both great and small.

prayer
Samuel Taylor Coleridge, 1772–1834,
English poet, one of the founders of the
Romantic movement.
The Ancient Mariner pt 7

---

predestination in Christian theology, the doctrine asserting that God has determined all events beforehand, including the ultimate salvation or damnation of the individual human soul. Today Christianity in general accepts that humanity has free will, though some forms, such as Calvinism, believe that salvation can only be attained by the gift of God. The concept of predestination is also found in Islam.

The theory of predestination caused the early-5th-century controversy between Augustine of Hippo, who claimed the absolute determination of choice by God, and Pelagius, who upheld the doctrine of free will. Martin Luther and John Calvin adopted the Augustinian view at the Reformation, although in differing degrees, but Jacobus Arminius adopted the Pelagian standpoint.

prehistory human cultures before the use of writing. A classification system (◊Three Age System) was devised 1816 by Danish archaeologist Christian Thomsen, based on the predominant materials used by early humans for tools and weapons: Stone Age, Bronze Age, Iron Age.

Stone Age Stone, mainly flint, was predominant. The Stone Age is divided into:

Old Stone Age (Palaeolithic) 3,500,000–5000 BC. Tools were chipped into shape by early humans, or hominids, from Africa, Asia, the Middle East, and Europe as well as later Neanderthal and Cro-Magnon people; the only domesticated animals were dogs. Some Asians crossed the Bering land-bridge to inhabit the Americas. Cave paintings were produced 20,000–8,000 years ago in many parts of the world; for example, Altamira, Spain; Lascaux, France; India; and Australia.

Middle Stone Age (Mesolithic) and *New Stone Age* (Neolithic). Stone and bone tools were ground and polished as well as chipped. In Neolithic times, agriculture and the domestication of goats, sheep, and cattle began. Stone Age cultures survived in the Americas, Asia, Africa, Oceania, and Australia until the 19th and 20th centuries.

Bronze Age Bronze tools and weapons began approximately 5000 BC in the Far East, and continued in the Middle East until about 1200 BC; in Europe this period lasted from about 2000 to 500 BC.

Iron Age Iron was hardened (alloyed) by the addition of carbon, so that it superseded bronze for tools and weapons; in the Old World generally from about 1000 BC.

Premonstratensian Roman Catholic monastic order founded 1120 by St Norbert (c. 1080-1134), a German bishop, at Prémontré, N France. Members were known as White Canons. The rule was a stricter version of that of the St Augustine Canons.

Presbyterianism system of Christian Protestant church government, expounded during the Reformation by John Calvin, which gives its name to the established Church of Scotland, and is also practised in England, Wales, Ireland, Switzerland, North America, and elsewhere. There is no compulsory form of worship and each congregation is governed by presbyters or elders (ordained or lay), who are of equal rank. Congregations are grouped in presbyteries, synods, and general assemblies.

president in government, the usual title of the head of state in a republic; the power of the office may range from the equivalent of a constitutional monarch to the actual head of the government.

pre-Socratic philosophy the ideas of the usually speculative ancient Greek cosmologists who mainly preceded Socrates (469–399 BC). The pre-Socratics range from ◊Thales (early 6th century BC) to ◊Democritus (later 5th century BC). The school is defined more by an outlook and a range of interests than by any chronological limit. Unlike Socrates and the ◊sophists, who were both primarily concerned with ethics and politics, the pre-Socratics were mainly concerned with the search for universal principles to explain the whole of nature, its origin and our destiny.

Other pre-Socratics are Pythagoras, Xenophanes of Colophon, Parmenides, Zeno of Elea, Anaximander, Empedocles, Heraclitus, Diogenes of Apollonia, and Protagoras of Abdera. Only short passages from the works of the pre-Socratic philosophers have survived.

press, freedom of absence of political ◊censorship in the press or other media, a concept regarded as basic to Western democracy. Access to and expression of views are, however, in practice restricted by the commercial interests of the owners and advertisers. In the UK the government imposed a ban 1988 on broadcast interviews with Provisional IRA members, which was upheld by the courts 1989.

pressure group or *interest group* or *lobby* association that puts pressure on governments or parties to ensure laws and treatment favourable to its own interest. Pressure groups have played an increasingly prominent role in contemporary Western democracies. In general they fall into two types: groups concerned with a single issue, such as nuclear disarmament, and groups attempting to promote their own interest, such as oil producers.

Prester John legendary Christian prince. During the 12th and 13th centuries, Prester John was believed to be the ruler of a powerful empire in Asia. From the 14th to the 16th century, he was generally believed to be the king of Abyssinia (now Ethiopia) in N E Africa.

price value put on a commodity at the point of exchange. In a free market it is determined by the market forces of demand and supply. In an imperfect market, firms face a trade-off between charging a higher price and losing sales, or charging a lower price and gaining sales.

Priestley Joseph 1733–1804. English chemist and Presbyterian minister. He identified the gas oxygen 1774. In 1791 his chapel and house were sacked by a mob because of his support for the French Revolution. He emigrated to the USA 1794.

Prigogine Ilya 1917– . Russian-born Belgian chemist who, as a highly original theoretician, has made major contributions to the field of thermodynamics for which work he was awarded the 1977 Nobel Prize for Physics. Earlier theories had considered systems at or about equilibrium. Prigogine began to study 'dissipative' or non-equilibrium structures frequently found in biological and chemical reactions.

primary data facts and figures that have been collected through direct investigation, for example, through observation, interviews, or questionnaires. Counting the number of customers entering a supermarket for one hour would be an example of primary data collection.

Primary data contrasts with secondary data which is data collected by another source. Primary data is often important in ◊market research.

primary education the education of children between the ages of 5 and 11 in the state school system in England and Wales, and up to 12 in Scotland. About 100 million children in the world have no access to primary education, and many children leave primary school unable to read or write.

prime minister or *premier* head of a parliamentary government, usually the leader of the largest party. In countries with an executive president, the prime minister is of lesser standing, whereas in those with dual executives, such as France, power is shared with the president.

The first prime minister in Britain is usually considered to have been Robert Walpole, but the office was not officially recognized until 1905. In some countries, such as Australia, a distinction is drawn between the prime minister of the whole country and the premier of an individual state.

prime number number that can be divided only by 1 or itself, that is, having no other factors. There is an infinite number of primes, the first ten of which are 2, 3, 5, 7, 11, 13, 17, 19, 23, and 29 (by definition, the number 1 is excluded from the set of prime numbers). The number 2 is the only even prime because all other even numbers have 2 as a factor.

Over the centuries mathematicians have sought general methods (algorithms) for calculating primes, from ◊Eratosthenes' sieve to programs on powerful computers.

In 1989 researchers at Amdahl Corporation, Sunnyvale, California, calculated the largest known prime number. It has 65,087 digits, and is more than a trillion trillion trillion times as large as the previous record holder. It took over a year of computation to locate the number and prove it was a prime.

Primitive Methodism Protestant Christian movement, an offshoot of Wesleyan ◊Methodism, that emerged in England 1811 when evangelical enthusiasts organized camp meetings at places such as Mow Cop 1807. Inspired by American example, open-air sermons were accompanied by prayers and hymn singing. In 1932 the Primitive Methodists became a constituent of a unified Methodist church.

Hugh Bourne (1772–1852) and William Clowes, who were both expelled from the Wesleyan Methodist circuit for participating in camp meetings, formed a missionary campaign that led to the development of Primitive Methodist circuits in central, eastern and northern England. They gained a strong following in working-class mining and agricultural communities, and concentrated on villages and towns rather than major urban centres. Primitive Methodism as a separate group was exported to the USA in 1829 and then to Canada, Australia, New Zealand, South Africa, and Nigeria.

Primitivism the influence on modern art (Kirchner, Modigliani, Picasso, Gauguin, and others) of the indigenous arts of Africa, Oceania, the Americas, and also of Western folk art.

prior, prioress in a Christian religious community, the deputy of an abbot or abbess, responsible for discipline. In certain Roman Catholic orders, the prior or prioress is the principal of a monastery or convent.

prism in mathematics, a solid figure whose cross section is constant in planes drawn perpendicular to its axis. A cube, for example, is a rectangular prism with all faces (bases and sides) the same shape and size. A cylinder is a prism with a circular cross section.

prism in optics, a triangular block of transparent material (plastic, glass, silica) commonly used to 'bend' a ray of light or split a beam into its spectral colours. Prisms are used as mirrors to define the optical path in binoculars, camera viewfinders, and periscopes. The dispersive property of prisms is used in the spectroscope.

privacy the right of the individual to be free from secret surveillance (by scientific devices or other means) and from the disclosure to unauthorized persons of personal data, as accumulated in computer data banks. Always an issue complicated by considerations of state security, public welfare (in the case of criminal activity), and other factors, it has been rendered more complex by present-day technology.

computer data All Western countries now have computerized-data protection. In the USA the Privacy Act 1974 requires that there should be no secret data banks and that agencies handling data must ensure their reliability and prevent misuse (information gained for one purpose must not be used for another). The public must be able to find out what is recorded and how it is used, and be able to correct it. Under the Freedom of Information Act 1967, citizens and organizations have the right to examine unclassified files.

In Britain under the Data Protection Act 1984 a register is kept of all businesses and organizations that store and process personal information, and they are subject to a code of practice set out in the act.

media In the UK, a bill to curb invasions of privacy by the media failed to reach the statute book in 1989. It would have enabled legal action against publication, or attempted publication, of private information without consent. In the USA the media have a working rule that private information is made public only concerning those who have entered public life, such as politicians, entertainers, and athletes.

private enterprise business unit where economic activities are in private hands and are carried on for private profit, as opposed to national, municipal, or cooperative ownership.

private sector part of the economy that is owned and controlled by private individuals and business organizations such as private and public limited companies. In a ◊free market economy, the private sector is responsible for allocating most of the resources within the economy. This contrasts with the ◊public sector where economic resources are owned and controlled by the state.

privatization policy or process of selling or transferring state-owned or public assets and services (notably nationalized industries) to private investors. Privatization of services involves the government contracting private firms to supply services previously supplied by public authorities.

Supporters of privatization argue that the public benefits from theoretically greater efficiency from firms already in the competitive market, and the release of resources for more appropriate use by government. Those against privatization believe that it transfers a country's assets from all the people to a controlling minority, that public utilities such as gas and water become private monopolies, and that a profit-making state-owned company raises revenue for the government.

In many cases the trend toward privatization has been prompted by dissatisfaction with the high level of subsidies being given to often inefficient state enterprise. The term 'privatization' is used even when the state retains a majority share of an enterprise.

The policy has been pursued by the post-1979 Conservative administration in the UK, and by recent governments in France, Japan (Nippon Telegraph and Telephone Corpor-ation 1985, Japan Railways 1987, Japan Air Lines 1987), Italy, New Zealand, and elsewhere.

By 1988 the practice had spread worldwide with communist countries such as China and Cuba selling off housing to private tenants.

probability likelihood, or chance, that an event will occur, often expressed as odds, or in mathematics, numerically as a fraction or decimal. In general, the probability that n particular events will happen out of a total of m possible events is n/m. A certainty has a probability of 1; an impossibility has a probability of 0. Empirical probability is defined as the number of successful events divided by the total possible number of events.

In tossing a coin, the chance that it will land 'heads' is the same as the chance that it will land 'tails', that is, 1 to 1 or even; mathematically, this probability is expressed as $^1/_2$ or 0.5. The odds against any chosen number coming up on the roll of a fair die are 5 to 1; the probability is $^1/_6$ or 0.1666... . If two dice are rolled there are 6 x 6 = 36 different possible combinations. The probability of a double (two numbers the same) is $^6/_{36}$ or $^1/_6$ since there are six doubles in the 36 events: (1,1), (2,2), (3,3), (4,4), (5,5), and (6,6).

Probability theory was developed by the French mathematicians Blaise Pascal and Pierre de Fermat in the 17th century, initially in response to a request to calculate the odds of being dealt various hands at cards. Today probability plays a major part in the mathematics of atomic theory and finds application in insurance and statistical studies.

probation in law, the placing of offenders under supervision of probation officers in the community, as an alternative to prison.

There are strict limits placed on travel, associations, and behaviour. Often an offender is required to visit a probation officer on a regular schedule. Failure to abide by the regulations can result in imprisonment.

Juveniles are no longer placed on probation, but under a 'supervision' order. The *probation service* assists the families of those imprisoned, gives the prisoner supervisory aftercare on release, and assists in preventive measures to avoid family breakdown.

process theology in Christianity, an attempt to absorb evolutionary ideas into theology and philosophy by seeing God as part of a wider evolutionary drive towards greater fulfilment and perfection in all aspects of existence. It began in the early 20th century under religious philosophers A N ◊Whitehead and Charles Hartshorne, and has been influential in the USA and UK in presenting a positivist attitude to modern science, though this has often led to an uncritical acceptance of all scientific developments.

productivity in economics, the output produced by a given quantity of labour, usually measured as output per person employed in the firm, industry, sector, or economy concerned. Productivity is determined by the quality and quantity of the fixed ◊capital used by labour, and the effort of the workers concerned.

The level of productivity is a major determinant of cost-efficiency: higher productivity tends to reduce average costs of production. Increases in productivity in a whole economy are a major determinant of economic growth. It is important to distinguish between the rate of growth of productivity and the level of productivity, since at lower levels of productivity, higher rates of productivity growth may be achieved.

profit amount by which total ◊revenue exceeds total cost. It is the reward for risk-taking for shareholders in a business organization. *Gross profit* is the difference between sales revenue and the direct cost of production. *Net profit* is total revenue minus total direct and indirect cost (for example, overheads, the cost of running the business). *Normal profit* is the profit needed to keep a firm from switching its resources into the production of other goods and services. *Abnormal profit* is profit earned over and above normal profit. *Pre-tax profit* is profit before corporation tax and any other taxes on profit have been paid; *post-tax profit is profit after tax.* Retained profit is profit not

distributed to shareholders but kept back to invest in the business.

profit-sharing system whereby an employer pays the workers a fixed share of the company's profits. It originated in France in the early 19th century and was widely practised for a time within the cooperative movement.

program set of instructions that controls the operation of a computer. There are two main kinds: applications programs, which carry out tasks for the benefit of the user – for example, word processing; and systems programs, which control the internal workings of the computer. A utility program is a systems program that carries out specific tasks for the user.

Programs can be written in any of a number of programming languages but are always translated into machine code before they can be executed by the computer.

programme music music that tells a story, depicts a scene or painting, or illustrates a literary or philosophical idea, such as Richard Strauss's *Don Juan.*

Progress ... is not an accident, but a necessity.... It is part of nature.

progress
Herbert Spencer, 1820–1903,
English philosopher.
Social Statics I. ch 2

---

progress forward movement or advance. Science progresses, providing more comprehensive theories about the world, and these theories can be tested. In the humanities, assessment of progress involves interpretation and is therefore harder, though not necessarily any less rational. Metaphysical philosophies of history as a form of purposive evolution (such as in the works of German thinkers G W F Hegel and Karl Marx) try to show that progress (variously defined) is inevitable, as it is in ◊teleology (the belief that all change serves a purpose).

progressive education teaching methods that take as their starting point children's own aptitudes and interests, and encourage them to follow their own investigations and lines of inquiry.

Prokhorov Aleksandr 1916– . Russian physicist whose fundamental work on microwaves in 1955 led to the construction of the first practical maser (the microwave equivalent of the laser) by Charles Townes, for which they shared the 1964 Nobel Prize for Physics.

Progress and the Idea of Perfectability

Graeco-Roman thinking espoused notions of individual growth and improvement, but on the whole, Classical thinking tended to look back to some lost Paradise or Golden Age, an era of pristine innocence, simple virtue, and pure wisdom, corrupted by the passage of time. The course of events was one of decay and decline, or at most a cyclical pattern of change, rather than betterment.

Prophecies of doom
With regard to temporal affairs, Christianity embraced a similar vision. After original sin and the expulsion from Paradise, life on Earth had been characterized by the reign of disease, decay, and death. According to the Old Testament, ancient patriarchs like Methuselah had lived for many centuries – proof that humans had been stronger and more righteous in the past. On the basis of biblical prophecies, it was widely believed by theologians from the Middle Ages through to the seventeenth century that the world was decaying (*mundus senescens*) and would soon come to an end, ushering in the millennium, the second coming of Christ. Christianity offered at best an oblique theory of progress – temporal sin and misery would be followed by eternal bliss. In general, the Christian vision was pessimistic; sinners could not pull themselves up by their own bootstraps; they needed to be redeemed.

The approach to perfection
The notion that temporal affairs were improving, that better times lay ahead, and within human grasp – the essence of the idea of progress – developed in the early modern period. The discovery of the New World, together with the advent of printing, gunpowder, and other technological breakthroughs, offered convincing proof that 'Moderns' were outstripping 'Ancients', at least in certain departments of life.

The writings of Francis Bacon (1561–1626) early in the seventeenth century offered an inspiring and comprehensive vision of future progress based upon science, technology, and industry. Many contemporaries, including René Descartes (1596–1650) and the founders of the Royal Society (1660), looked to the natural sciences as the proof and the best engine of progress. Leading thinkers of the Enlightenment attempted to fuse the Graeco-Roman image of the wise, ethical man with Bacon's modern scientific vision of social betterment ('knowledge is power') in a philosophy that underlined the human race's unlimited capacity for individual and social amelioration in the future. The word 'perfectibility' came into vogue to express more optimistic conceptions of mankind. Jean-Jacques Rousseau believed humans had a capacity for perfectibility, viewed as a potential for self-rule and moral progress, that set human beings apart from all other creatures; this was a significant advance as it denied the significance of original sin.

Humanity (emphasized many Enlightenment philosophers) was infinitely malleable; it could be improved by education, by environmental management, and by inner effort. The ability to change and learn was cumulative and had no limits. Certain thinkers, notably Marie Jean Condorcet (1743–1794) and William Godwin (1756–1836), even began to think in terms of the indefinite prolongation of individual life on earth.

Philosophy of history
Late Enlightenment and nineteenth-century thinkers began to systematize the idea of progress in terms of philosophies of history which specified a series of successive economic, political, or cultural epochs marking the advance of civilization as a whole. In his two discourses of 1750, Anne Robert Turgot (1727–1781) saw progress as the key to universal history, spelling out the theme with regard to the rise and fall of nations and empires, the development of the sciences and arts, religions, morals, and manners. Progress was uneven, Turgot admitted, yet overall 'manners become more gentle, the human mind becomes more enlightened, isolated nations draw nearer to each other, commerce and politics connect all parts of the world and the whole mass of the human race, alternative between calm and agitation, good and bad conditions, marches always, though slowly, towards greater perfection.' Such views were developed further by Condorcet, Claude St Simon (1760–1825), Auguste Comte (1798–1857), and (in dialectical form) by Georg Hegel (1770–1831) and Karl Marx (1818–1883). Hegel saw human history as the progress of Mind, or self-consciousness; offering an opposing materialist viewpoint, Marx claimed true progress lay in humanity's economic ability to free itself from natural necessity through labour. The Marxist concept of predetermined proletarian revolution became the world's most widely espoused theory of necessary progress in the late nineteenth and twentieth centuries.

Progress – a fantasy?
Since World War I, both individual and global notions of perfectibility and progress have been questioned in the West. As popular fears of science and technology increase, prophets of scientific and physical progress have been rejected as offering dystopias not utopias: for example, the message of Aldous Huxley's (1894–1963) *Brave New World*. Sigmund Freud's (1865–1939) theories of the workings of the unconscious mind suggest that traditional rational notions of progress amount to nothing but sublimation. Basic instincts (sex and death) are masked by a veneer of civilization, which itself may breed neurosis. An age of affluence has eroded earlier faith in material progress.

Roy Porter

Programming Languages

language	main uses	description
ALGOL (algorithmic language)	scientific applications	early algebraic language, little used today, but precursor of such languages as ADA and PASCAL
ADA	process and machine control (particularly military)	Developed by US Department of Defense. Named after English mathematician and supporter of Babbage, Ada Byron
assembler languages	jobs needing detailed control of the hardware, fast execution, and small program sizes	fast and efficient but require considerable effort and skill
BASIC (beginner's all-purpose symbolic instruction code)	mainly in education, business, and the home, and among non-professional programmers, such as engineers	easy to learn; early versions lacked the features of other languages
C	systems programming; general programming	fast and efficient; widely used as a general-purpose language; especially popular among professional programmers
C++	object-oriented applications	adds object-oriented features to C
COBOL (common business-oriented language)	business programming	strongly oriented towards data processing work; easy to learn but very verbose; widely used on mainframes
FORTH	control applications	reverse Polish notation language
FORTRAN (formula translation)	scientific and computational work	based on mathematical formulae; popular among engineers, scientists, and mathematicians
LISP (list processing)	artificial intelligence	symbolic language with a reputation for being hard to learn; popular in the academic and research communities
LOGO	teaching mathematical concepts	high-level language, popular with schools
Modula-2	systems and real-time programming; general programming	highly structured; intended to replace Pascal for 'real-world' applications
OBERON	general programming	small, compact language incorporating many of the features of PASCAL and Modula-2
PASCAL (*program appliqué à la sélection et la compilation automatique de la littérature*)	general-purpose language	highly structured; widely used for teaching programming in universities
PROLOG (programming in logic)	artificial intelligence	symbolic-logic programming system, originally intended for theorem solving but now used more generally in artificial intelligence
Smalltalk	object-oriented applications	the original language developed for object-oriented programming

proletariat in Marxist theory, those classes in society that possess no property, and therefore depend on the sale of their labour or expertise (as opposed to the capitalists or bourgeoisie, who own the means of production, and the petty bourgeoisie, or working small-property owners). They are usually divided into the industrial, agricultural, and intellectual proletariat.

The term is derived from Latin *proletarii*, 'the class possessing no property', whose contribution to the state was considered to be their offspring, *proles*.

Prometheus in Greek mythology, a ◊Titan who stole fire from heaven for the human race. In revenge, Zeus had him chained to a rock where an eagle came each day to feast on his liver, which grew back each night, until he was rescued by the hero ◊Heracles.

propaganda systematic spreading of information or disinformation, usually to promote a religious or political doctrine with the intention of instilling particular attitudes or responses. As a system of disseminating information it was thought to be a legitimate instrument of government but became notorious through the deliberate distortion of facts, or the plain publication of falsehoods, by totalitarian regimes, notably Nazi Germany.

The word is derived from the activities of a special sacred congregation of the Catholic

Church (*de propaganda fide*) which sought to spread the faith and recruit members.

In the USA in the 1980s, the term 'public diplomacy' was introduced. Government-sponsored reports and articles were presented to the media as independent sources, especially on the subject of Central America.

There are various forms of propaganda: black propaganda (a pack of lies), grey propaganda (half-truths and distortions), and white propaganda (the truth).

property the right to control the use of a thing (such as land, a building, a work of art, or a computer program). In English law, a distinction is made between **real property**, which involves a degree of geographical fixity, and **personal property**, which does not. Property is never absolute, since any society places limits on an individual's property (such as the right to transfer that property to another). Different societies have held widely varying interpretations of the nature of property and the extent of the rights of the owner of that property.

The debate about private and public property began with the Greeks. For Plato, an essential prerequisite for the guardians of his *Republic* was that they owned no property, while Aristotle saw private property as an equally necessary prerequisite for political participation. The story of Creation in the Bible was interpreted variously as a state of original communism destroyed by the Fall (by Thomas More in his *Utopia* 1516), and hence a justification of the monastic ideal, in which property is held in common, or as justifying the institution of private property, since Adam was granted dominion over all things in Eden. The philosopher John Locke argued that property rights to a thing are acquired by expending labour on it. Adam Smith saw property as a consequence of the transition of society from an initial state of hunting (in which property did not exist) to one of flock-rearing (which depended on property for its existence).

Karl Marx contrasted an Asiatic mode of production, a mythical age in which all property was held in common, with the situation under capitalism in which the only 'property' of the worker, labour, was appropriated by the capitalist. One of Marx's achievements was to reawaken the debate over property in terms that are still being used today.

prophet person thought to speak from divine inspiration or one who foretells the future. In the Bible, the chief prophets were Elijah, Amos, Hosea, and Isaiah. In Islam, ◊Muhammad is believed to be the last and greatest of a long line of prophets beginning with Adam and including Moses and Jesus.

In the Bible, one of the succession of saints and seers who preached and prophesied in the Hebrew kingdoms in Palestine from the 8th century BC until the suppression of Jewish independence in 586 BC, and possibly later. The prophetic books of the Old Testament constitute a division of the Hebrew Bible. Some Christians, especially adherents of the ◊Pentecostal movement and ◊charismatic movement, believe in modern-day prophets.

A prophet is not without honour, save in his own country and in his own house.
prophet
Bible, the sacred book of the Jewish and Christian religions.
Matthew 13:57

---

proportional representation (PR) electoral system in which distribution of party seats corresponds to their proportion of the total votes cast, and minority votes are not wasted (as opposed to a simple majority, or 'first past the post', system).

Forms include: **party list** (PLS) or additional member system (AMS). As recommended by the Hansard Society 1976 for introduction in the UK, three-quarters of the members would be elected in single-member constituencies on the traditional majority-vote system, and the remaining seats be allocated according to the overall number of votes cast for each party (a variant of this is used in Germany); **single transferable vote** (STV), in which candidates are numbered in order of preference by the voter, and any votes surplus to the minimum required for a candidate to win are transferred to second preferences, as are second-preference votes from the successive candidates at the bottom of the poll until the required number of elected candidates is achieved (this is in use in the Republic of Ireland).

In France 1985 it was proposed to introduce a system under which, after ruling out parties with less than a 5% poll in each *département*, the votes for the rest would be divided by the number of seats to obtain an electoral quotient (for example, if the quotient were 15,000 votes, party A with 30,000 votes would win two seats, and party B with 12,000 would win none); unallocated seats would be distributed in a second round when each party's poll would be divided by the number of seats it had already won, plus one (that is, party A would now be credited with only 10,000 votes; party B, having won no seat so far, would be credited with its original 12,000, and so gain a seat).

Man is the measure of all things.

Protagoras
Quoted in Plato *Theaetetus*

Protagoras of Abdera c. 485–c. 420 BC. Greek ◊sophist, or travelling lecturer who taught rhetorical and political skills for a fee. In his dictum that 'Man is the measure of all things', Protagoras was probably both denying that there is any objective truth (◊relativism) and also criticizing the theory of Parmenides and the ◊Eleatic school that reality is single and unchanging.

protectionism in economics, the imposition of heavy duties or import quotas by a government as a means of discouraging the import of foreign goods likely to compete with domestic products. Price controls, quota systems, and the reduction of surpluses are among the measures taken for agricultural products in the European Community. The opposite practice is ◊free trade.

Protestantism one of the main divisions of Christianity, which emerged from Roman Catholicism at the ◊Reformation. The chief denominations are the Anglican Communion (Episcopalian in the USA), Baptists, Lutherans, Methodists, Pentecostals, and Presbyterians, with a total membership of about 300 million.

Protestantism takes its name from the protest of Martin ◊Luther and his supporters at the Diet of Spires 1529 against the decision to reaffirm the edict of the Diet of Worms against the Reformation. The first conscious statement of Protestantism as a distinct movement was the Confession of Augsburg 1530. The chief characteristics of original Protestantism are the acceptance of the Bible as the only source of truth, the universal priesthood of all believers, and forgiveness of sins solely through faith in Jesus Christ. The Protestant church minimalizes the liturgical aspects of Christianity and emphasizes the preaching and hearing of the word of God before sacramental faith and practice. The many interpretations of doctrine and practice are reflected in the various denominations. The ecumenical movement of the 20th century has unsuccessfully attempted to reunite various Protestant denominations and, to some extent, the Protestant churches and the Catholic church. During the last 20 years there has been a worldwide upsurge in Christianity taking place largely outside the established church.

Proteus in Greek mythology, the warden of the sea beasts of the sea god Poseidon, who possessed the gift of prophecy and could transform himself into any form he chose to evade questioning.

Proudhon Pierre Joseph 1809–1865. French anarchist, born in Besançon. He sat in the Constituent Assembly of 1848, was imprisoned for three years, and had to go into exile in Brussels. He published *Qu'est-ce que la propriété/What is Property?* 1840 and *Philosophie de la misère/Philosophy of Poverty* 1846; the former contains the dictum 'property is theft'.

Proust Joseph Louis 1754–1826. French chemist. He was the first to state the principle of constant composition of compounds – that compounds consist of the same proportions of elements wherever found.

Prout William 1785–1850. British physician and chemist. In 1815 Prout published his hypothesis that the relative atomic mass of every atom is an exact and integral multiple of the hydrogen atom. The discovery of isotopes (atoms of the same element that have different masses) in the 20th century bore out his idea.

Proverbs book of the Old Testament traditionally ascribed to the Hebrew king ◊Solomon. The Proverbs form a series of maxims on moral and ethical matters.

psalm sacred poem or song of praise. The Book of Psalms in the Old Testament is divided into five books containing 150 psalms in all. They are traditionally ascribed to David, the second king of Israel.

psi in parapsychology, a hypothetical faculty common to humans and other animals said to be responsible for extrasensory perception (ESP) and other forms of paranormal phenomena.

Psyche late Greek personification of the soul as a winged girl or young woman. The goddess Aphrodite was so jealous of Psyche's beauty that she ordered her son Eros, the god of love, to make Psyche fall in love with the worst of men. Instead, he fell in love with her himself.

psychiatry branch of medicine dealing with the diagnosis and treatment of mental disorder, normally divided into the areas of *neurotic conditions* including anxiety, depression, and hysteria and *psychotic disorders* such as schizophrenia. Psychiatric treatment consists of analysis, drugs, or electroconvulsive therapy.

In practice there is considerable overlap between psychiatry and clinical ◊psychology, the fundamental difference being that psychiatrists are trained medical doctors (holding an MD degree) and may therefore prescribe drugs, whereas psychologists may hold a PhD but do not need a medical qualification to practise. See also ◊psychoanalysis.

Psychology: chronology

1846	E H Weber reported on his pioneering quantitative investigations on touch in *On Touch and Common Sensibility*.
1860	G T Fechner published his *Elements of Psychophysics*, in which he presented the first statistical treatment of psychological data.
1879	Wilhelm Wundt founded the first psychological laboratory in Leipzig.
1885	H Ebbinghaus published his experimental researches on memory.
1890	William James published the first comprehensive psychology text, *Principles of Psychology*.
1895	Joseph Breuer and Sigmund Freud published *Studies on Hysteria*, containing the first writings on psychoanalysis.
1896	The first clinical psychology clinic founded, by Lightner Witmer at the University of Pennsylvania, and first use of the term 'clinical psychology'.
1900	Freud's *The Interpretation of Dreams* published.
1905	Alfred Binet and Théodore Simon developed the first effective intelligence test.
1906	Ivan Pavlov first lectured in the West on conditioned reflexes.
1908	The first textbooks of social psychology, by William McDougall and E A Ross, appear.
1910	Max Wertheimer, Wolfgang Köhler, and Kurt Koffka founded the Gestalt School in Frankfurt.
1913	J B Watson's article *Psychology as a Behaviorist Views it* published and the behaviourist movement thus launched.
1923	Jean Piaget's *The Language and the Thought of the Child* published, the first of his many books on the development of thinking.
1927	C Spearman proposed in *The Abilities of Man*, that two kinds of factor comprise intelligence, a general factor ('g') and specific factors.
1929	H Berger published his findings on the electroencephalogram (EEG).
1938	B F Skinner published *The Behavior of Organisms*, detailing his studies of operant conditioning and his radical behaviourism.
1943	C L Hull published his influential book *Principles of Behavior: An Introduction to Behavior Theory*, the most rigorous account of conditioning and learning from the perspective of behaviourism.
1947	Hans Eysenck published *Dimensions of Personality*, a large-scale study of neuroticism and introversion–extraversion.
1948	Nobert Wiener coined the term 'cybernetics' and published *Cybernetics: Control and Communication in the Animal and Machine*.
1949	D O Hebb's classic *Organization of Behaviour* re-emphasized the role of central (brain) processes in the explanation of behaviour.
1950	Alan Turing's famous article *Computing Machinery and Intelligence* published, in which he proposes a test of whether a machine can be said to think.
1950	*The Authoritarian Personality* by Theodor W Adorno and others published.
1953	E Aserinksy and N Kleitman publish the first account of rapid-eye-movement (REM) sleep.
1957	L Festinger's *A Theory of Cognitive Dissonance* published.
1957	Noam Chomsky published *Syntactic Structures*, a seminal work in psycholinguistics, that revolutionized the study of language.
1958	A Newell and H A Simon, with J C Shaw, published their article on human problem-solving, the first account of the information-processing approach to human psychology.
1958	Donald E Broadbent published his influential book *Perception and Communication*, a detailed account of information-processing psychology.
1960	G A Miller, E Galanter, and K Pribam applied the idea of a hierarchically structured computer program to the whole of psychology in their *Plans and the Structure of Behaviour*.
1961	A Newell and H A Simon published their pioneering computational model of human problem-solving, the General Problem Solver.
1962	M S Gazzaniga, J E Bogen, and R W Sperry first reported on the 'split-brain' phenomenon in epileptic patients.
1963	Stanley Milgram published his first studies of obedience and the conditions under which individuals will inflict harm when instructed to.
1967	Konovski published *Integrative Activity of the Brain*, an influential melding of conditioning principles with sensation and motivation.
1967	Ulric Neisser's *Cognitive Psychology* marked renewed interest in the study of cognition after years in which behaviourism had dominated.
1968	R C Atkinson and R M Shiffin developed their theory of interacting memory systems in cognitive processing.
1970	T Shallice and E K Warrington provided the first of much evidence from brain-damaged patients that short-term memory is in parallel with long-term memory and is best viewed as a collection of separate processing modules.
1972	E Tulving distinguished episodic memory (for personal experience) and semantic memory (for general knowledge and facts about the world).
1983	J A Fodor published *The Modularity of Mind* arguing that the mind is a set of independent, computational input systems and central systems, or more general cognitive processes, corresponding to what the individual 'believes'.
1985	A new view of intelligence proposed by Robert J Sternberg in his *Beyond IQ: A Triarchic Theory of Intelligence*.
1986	J L McClelland and D E Rumelhart developed complex computational networks using parallel processing to simulate human learning and categorization.
1988	An important collection of articles by psychologists, neuropsychologists, and others published in *Consciousness in Contemporary Science*, edited by A J Marcel and E Bisiach.
1989	The mathematician, Roger Penrose, in his *The Emperor's New Mind*, argues that the computational account of the mind is incomplete, particularly concerning consciousness.
1992	The philosopher, John Searle, in *The Rediscovery of the Mind*, argues for the return of consciousness to its position as the central topic in psychology and cognitive science.

psychic person allegedly possessed of parapsychological, or paranormal, powers.

Property is theft.
Pierre Joseph Proudhon
What is Property?

---

psychoanalysis theory and treatment method for neuroses, developed by Sigmund ◊Freud. The main treatment method involves the free association of ideas, and their interpretation by patient and analyst. It is typically prolonged.

Psychoanalysis emphasizes that the impact of early childhood sexuality and experiences stored in the unconscious can lead to the development of adult emotional problems. Treatment involves recognizing these long-buried events in order to relieve actual pressure. Modern approaches, drawing from Freud's ideas, tend to be briefer and more problem-focused.

psychology systematic study of human and animal behaviour. The first psychology laboratory was founded 1879 by Wilhelm ◊Wundt at Leipzig, Germany. The subject includes diverse areas of study and application, among them the roles of instinct, heredity, environment, and culture; the processes of sensation, perception, learning, and memory; the bases of motivation and emotion; and the functioning of thought, intelligence, and language. Significant psychologists have included Gustav Fechner, founder of psychophysics; Wolfgang Köhler, one of the ◊gestalt or 'whole' psychologists; Sigmund Freud and his associates Carl Jung, Alfred Adler, and Hermann Rorschach (1884–1922); William James, Jean Piaget; Carl Rogers; Hans Eysenck; J B Watson; and B F Skinner.

Psychology has a long past, but only a short history.
psychology
Hermann Ebbinghaus, 1850–1909,
German psychologist.
Summary of Psychology

Experimental psychology emphasizes the application of rigorous and objective scientific methods to the study of a wide range of mental processes and behaviour, whereas *social psychology* concerns the study of individuals within their social environment; for example, within groups and organizations. This has led to the development of related fields such as *occupational psychology*, which studies human behaviour at work, and *educational psychology*.

Clinical psychology concerns the understanding and treatment of mental health disorders, such as anxiety, phobias, or depression; treatment may include behaviour therapy, cognitive therapy, counselling, psychoanalysis, or some combination of these.

Modern studies have been diverse, for example the psychological causes of obesity; the nature of religious experience; and the underachievement of women seen as resulting from social pressures. Other related subjects are the nature of sleep and dreams, and the possible extensions of the senses, which leads to the more contentious ground of ◊parapsychology.

psychometrics measurement of mental processes. This includes intelligence and aptitude testing to help in job selection and in the clinical assessment of cognitive deficiencies resulting from brain damage.

psychopathy or *psychopathic personality* personality disorder characterized by chronic antisocial behaviour (violating the rights of others, often violently) and an absence of feelings of guilt about the behaviour.

Because the term 'psychopathy' has been used loosely in the past to refer to any mental disorder, many psychiatrists and psychologists prefer the term 'antisocial personality disorder', though this also includes cases in which absence or a lesser degree of guilt is not a characteristic feature.

psychosis or *psychotic disorder* general term for a serious mental disorder where the individual commonly loses contact with reality and may experience hallucinations (seeing or hearing things that do not exist) or delusions (fixed false beliefs). For example, in a paranoid psychosis, an individual may believe that others are plotting against him or her. A major type of psychosis is ◊schizophrenia (which may be biochemically induced).

psychotherapy treatment approaches for psychological problems involving talking rather than surgery or drugs. Examples include ◊cognitive therapy and ◊psychoanalysis.

Ptah Egyptian god, the divine potter, a personification of the creative force. He was worshipped at Memphis, and was often portrayed as a mummified man. He was said to be the father of Imhotep, the physician and architect.

Ptolemy (Claudius Ptolemaeus) c. 100–AD 170. Egyptian astronomer and geographer who worked in Alexandria. His *Almagest* developed the theory that Earth is the centre of the universe, with the Sun, Moon, and stars revolving around it. In 1543 the Polish astronomer ◊Copernicus proposed an alternative to the *Ptolemaic system*. Ptolemy's *Geography* was a standard source of information until the 16th century.

public good good which possesses the characteristics of nonexcludability and nonrivalry. Nonexcludability means that once a good is provided it is impossible to prevent anyone benefiting from it. For example, once a street light is provided, it is impossible to prevent anyone walking under it from enjoying its benefits. Nonrivalry means that consumption of the good by one person does not reduce the amount available for consumption by other people. The fact that one person benefits from a street lamp does not prevent others from benefiting from it as well.

Because of these characteristics, the private sector is reluctant to provide public goods. Consumers are likely to want to be *free riders*, hoping that they can benefit from the good without having to pay for it. Public goods are therefore normally provided by government and paid for by everyone through the taxation system. Commonly given examples of public goods are defence, the judiciary, the police, and street lighting.

public sector part of the economy that is owned and controlled by the state, namely central government, local government, and government enterprises. In a ◊command economy, the public sector allocates most of the resources in the economy. The opposite of the public sector is the ◊private sector where resources are allocated by private individuals and business organizations.

Most goods and services provided by the public sector in any economy are allocated on the basis of need rather than through ability to pay. For example, in the National Health Service, patients are treated because of the seriousness of their medical complaint and not because of how much they can afford to pay in fees. However, some products produced by the public sector are sold, for example rail services or postal services. Most of this production has been privatized in the UK since 1979.

public spending expenditure by government, covering the military, health, education, infrastructure, development projects, and the cost of servicing overseas borrowing.

A principal source of revenue to cover public expenditure is taxation. Most countries present their plans for spending in their annual budgets.

pūjā worship, in Hinduism, Buddhism, and Jainism.

punctuated equilibrium model evolutionary theory developed by Niles Eldridge and US palaeontologist Stephen Jay Gould 1972 to explain discontinuities in the fossil record. It claims that periods of rapid change alternate with periods of relative stability (stasis), and that the appearance of new lineages is a separate process from the gradual evolution of adaptive changes within a species. The pattern of stasis and more rapid change is now widely accepted, but the second part of the theory remains unsubstantiated.

Purana one of a number of sacred Hindu writings dealing with ancient times and events, and dating from the 4th century AD onwards. The 18 main texts include the *Vishnu Purāna* and *Bhāgavat Purāna*, which encourage devotion to Vishnu, above all in his incarnation as Krishna.

purdah seclusion of women practised by some Islamic and Hindu peoples. It had begun to disappear with the adoption of Western culture, but the ◊fundamentalism of the 1980s revived it; for example, the wearing of the chador (an all-enveloping black mantle) in Iran. The Qur'an actually lays down only 'modesty' in dress.

Pure Land Buddhism dominant form of Buddhism in China and Japan. It emphasizes faith in and love of Buddha, in particular Amitābha (Amida in Japan, Amituofo in China), the ideal 'Buddha of boundless light', who has vowed that all believers who call on his name will be reborn in his Pure Land, or Western Paradise. This also applies to women, who had been debarred from attaining salvation through monastic life. There are over 20 million Pure Land Buddhists in Japan.

Amidism developed in China in the 3rd century, where the Pure Land school was, according to tradition, founded by the monk Hui Yuan (334–417); it spread in Japan from the 10th century.

The basic teachings are found in the *Sukhāvati vyūhua/Pure Land Sūtra*. The prayer *Namu Amida Butsu* or *Nembutsu* was in some sects repeated for several hours a day. The *True Pure Land* school (Jōdo Shinshū), founded by the Japanese monk Shinran (1173–1262), held that a single, sincere invocation was enough and rejected monastic discipline and the worship of all other Buddhas; this has become the largest school.

purgatory in Roman Catholic belief, a purificatory state or place where the souls of those who have died in a state of grace can expiate their venial sins, with a limited amount of suffering.

Purim Jewish festival celebrated in Feb or March (the 14th of Adar in the Jewish calendar), commemorating ◊Esther, who saved the Jews from destruction in 473 BC in Persia.

The festival includes a complete reading of the Book of Esther (the megilla) in the synagogue, during which the listeners respond with stamping, whistling, and hissing to the names of the evil characters.

Puritan from 1564, a member of the Church of England who wished to eliminate Roman Catholic survivals in church ritual, or substitute a presbyterian for an episcopal form of church government. The term also covers the separatists who withdrew from the church altogether. The Puritans were identified with the parliamentary opposition under James I and Charles I, and after the Restoration were driven from the church, and more usually known as ◊Dissenters or ◊Nonconformists.

The Puritan hated bear-baiting, not because it gave pain to the bear, but because it gave pleasure to the spectators.

Puritan

Thomas Babington Macaulay, Baron Macaulay, 1800–1859, English historian.
History of England

Pusey Edward Bouverie 1800–1882. English Church of England priest from 1828. In 1835 he joined J H ◊Newman in issuing the *Tracts for the Times*. After Newman's conversion to Catholicism, Pusey became leader of the High Church Party or Puseyites, striving until his death to keep them from conversion.

Pygmalion in Greek legend, a king of Cyprus who fell in love with an ivory statue he had carved. When Aphrodite brought it to life as a woman, Galatea, he married her.

Pyke Margaret 1893–1966. British birth-control campaigner. In the early 1930s she became secretary of the National Birth Control Association (later the Family Planning Association, FPA), and campaigned vigorously to get local councils to set up family-planning clinics. She became chair of the FPA in 1954.

Pyrrho of Elis c. 360–c. 270 BC. Greek philosopher, founder of the school of ◊scepticism. He extended doubt about sense experience to both logic and morals. He believed that peace of mind could be attained by renouncing all claims to knowledge; consequently, there could never be any reason for preferring one way of life to another. In practice, this meant conforming to whatever the local customs were.

Pythagoras c. 580–500 BC. Greek mathematician and philosopher who formulated Pythagoras' theorem.

Much of his work concerned numbers, to which he assigned mystical properties. For example, he classified numbers into triangular ones (1, 3, 6, 10,...), which can be represented as a triangular array, and square ones (1, 4, 9, 16,...), which form squares. He also observed that any two adjacent triangular numbers add to a square number (for example, $1 + 3 = 4$; $3 + 6 = 9$; $6 + 10 = 16$;...). Pythagoras was the founder of a politically influential religious brotherhood in Croton, S Italy (suppressed in the 5th century). Its tenets included the immortality and ◊transmigration of souls.

Pythagoras' theorem in geometry, a theorem stating that in a right-angled triangle, the area of the square on the hypotenuse (the longest side) is equal to the sum of the areas of the squares drawn on the other two sides. If the hypotenuse is h units long and the lengths of the other sides are a and b, then $h^2 = a^2 + b^2$.

The theorem provides a way of calculating the length of any side of a right-angled triangle if the lengths of the other two sides are known. It is also used to determine certain trigonometrical relationships such as $\sin^2 \theta + \cos^2 \theta = 1$.

qiblah direction in which Muslims face to pray: the direction of Mecca. In every mosque this is marked by a niche (mihrab) in the wall.

quadrivium in medieval education, the four advanced liberal arts (arithmetic, geometry, astronomy, and music) which were studied after mastery of the trivium (grammar, rhetoric, and logic).

Quaker popular name, originally derogatory, for a member of the Society of ◊Friends.

quantification in logic, specification of quantity or number. There are two main quantifiers: the universal quantifier (For all *x* ...) and the existential quantifier (For at least one/some *x* ...). Either of these quantifiers can be defined in terms of the other plus negation – just as 'some' can be defined as 'not all' in everyday speech. The quantifier shift ◊fallacy is that of arguing from 'Every nice girl loves a sailor' to 'At least one sailor is loved by every nice girl'. The latter implies, but is not implied by, the former.

quantity theory of money economic theory claiming that an increase in the amount of money in circulation causes a proportionate increase in prices.

The theory dates from the 17th century and was elaborated by the US economist Irving Fisher (1867–1947). Supported and developed by Milton Friedman, it forms the theoretical basis of ◊monetarism.

quantum chromodynamics (QCD) in physics, a theory describing the interactions of ◊quarks, the elementary particles that make up all ◊hadrons (subatomic particles such as protons and neutrons). In quantum chromodynamics, quarks are considered to interact by exchanging particles called gluons, which carry the ◊strong nuclear force, and whose role is to 'glue' quarks together. The mathematics involved in the theory is complex, and although a number of successful predictions have been made, as yet the theory does not compare in accuracy with quantum electrodynamics, upon which it is modelled. See ◊elementary particles and ◊forces, fundamental.

quantum mechanics branch of physics dealing with the interaction of ◊matter and radiation, the structure of the atom, the motion of atomic particles, and with related phenomena (see ◊elementary particle and ◊quantum theory).

quantum number in physics, one of a set of four numbers that uniquely characterize an electron and its state in an atom. The *principal quantum number* n defines the electron's main energy level. The *orbital quantum number* l relates to its angular momentum. The *magnetic quantum number* m describes the energies of electrons in a magnetic field. The *spin quantum number* m_s gives the spin direction of the electron.

The principal quantum number, defining the electron's energy level, corresponds to shells (energy levels) also known by their spectroscopic designations K, L, M, and so on. The orbital quantum number gives rise to a series of subshells designated s, p, d, f, and so on, of slightly different energy levels. The magnetic quantum number allows further subdivision of the subshells (making three subdivisions p_x, p_y, and p_z in the p subshell, for example, of the same energy level). No two electrons in an atom can have the same set of quantum numbers (the ◊Pauli exclusion principle).

quantum theory or *quantum mechanics* in physics, the theory that ◊energy does not have a continuous range of values, but is, instead, absorbed or radiated discontinuously, in multiples of definite, indivisible units called quanta. Just as earlier theory showed how light, generally seen as a wave motion, could also in some ways be seen as composed of discrete particles (photons), quantum theory shows how atomic particles such as electrons may also be seen as having wavelike properties. Quantum theory is the basis of particle physics, modern theoretical chemistry, and the solid-state physics that describes the behaviour of the silicon chips used in computers.

The theory began with the work of Max Planck 1900 on radiated energy, and was extended by Albert Einstein to electromagnetic radiation generally, including light. Danish physicist Niels Bohr used it to explain the spectrum of light emitted by excited hydrogen atoms. Later work by Erwin Schrödinger, Werner Heisenberg, Paul Dirac, and others elaborated the theory to what is called quantum mechanics (or wave mechanics).

quark in physics, the ◊elementary particle that is the fundamental constituent of all hadrons (baryons, such as neutrons and protons, and mesons). There are six types, or 'flavours': up, down, top, bottom, strange, and charm, each of which has three varieties, or 'colours': red, yellow, and blue (visual colour is not meant, although the analogy is useful in many ways). To each quark there is an antiparticle, called an antiquark. See ◊quantum chromodynamics.

quasar (from *quasi*-stell*ar* object or QSO) one of the most distant extragalactic objects known, discovered 1964–65. Quasars appear starlike, but each emits more energy than 100 giant galaxies. They are thought to be at the centre of galaxies, their brilliance emanating from the stars and gas falling towards an immense ◊black hole at their nucleus.

Quasar light shows a large red shift, indicating that they are very distant. Some quasars emit radio waves, which is how they were first identified 1963, but most are radio-quiet. The furthest are over 10 billion light years away.

Quesnay François 1694–1774. French economic philosopher who was head of the school of physiocrats – the first systematic school of political economy. He held that land was the main source of wealth, and advocated noninterference by government in economic matters.

Quesnay was consulting physician to Louis XV at Versailles, where he became interested in economics. His political economy is summed up in his *Tableau economique/ Economic Scene* 1758.

Quetelet Lambert Adolphe Jacques 1796–1874. Belgian statistician. He developed tests for the validity of statistical information, and gathered and analysed statistical data of many kinds. From his work on sociological data came the concept of the 'average person'.

quietism a religious attitude, displayed periodically in the history of Christianity, consisting of passive contemplation and meditation to achieve union with God. The founder of modern quietism was the Spanish priest ◊Molinos who published a *Guida Spirituale/Spiritual Guide* 1675.

Quine Willard Van Orman 1908– . US philosopher and logician who holds to a highly scientific view of the world. He is often described as a ◊nominalist because he believes that ◊universals do not have any real existence

outside of thought and language, and a ◊pragmatist because he holds that our minds group together properties in the ways that are most useful for us. Quine is famous for his slogan, 'to be is to be the value of a variable' in a system of formal logic. By this, he means that we commit ourselves to the existence of something only when we can say that it has a quality or feature, and that existence itself is not a quality or feature (◊being).

Quine's theory of the indeterminacy of translation states that assured translation between two languages (or even within one language) is impossible in principle, because the designation of any two words or phrases as synonymous is impossible to justify completely.

Quine's most famous work is *Word and Object* 1960. He was Professor of Philosophy at Harvard University until his retirement.

Qumran or *Khirbet Qumran* archaeological site in Jordan, excavated from 1951, in the foothills NW of the Dead Sea. Originally an Iron Age fort (6th century BC), it was occupied in the late 2nd century BC by a monastic community, the ◊Essenes, until the buildings were burned by Romans AD 68. The monastery library once contained the ◊Dead Sea Scrolls, which had been hidden in caves for safekeeping and were discovered 1947.

Qur'an (or *Koran*) the holy book of Islam. It is stated to have been divinely revealed through the angel Jibra'el (Gabriel) to the prophet Muhammad between about AD 610 and his death in 632, to address the rising problems and questions that the Muslims faced. The Qur'an is the prime source of all Islamic ethical and legal doctrines and is followed by the ◊Hadith or the traditions of Muhammad. The style and structure of the Qur'an is said to be the basic miracle given to Muhammad by God: that is, the text itself is divine, and Islamic law forbids touching Qur'an without ritual cleansing.

The Qur'an is divided into 114 *suras* (chapters), some very long, others consisting only of a few words. It includes many events also described in the Hebrew Bible but narrated from a different viewpoint. Other issues are also discussed by the Qur'an, giving injunctions relevant to situations that needed alteration or clarification.

Until very recently the Qur'an was memorized by every Muslim, and it is a prescription of Islam that every Muslim should learn at least twelve verses by heart. Once thought by Islamic scholars to be impossible to translate, it has today been translated into all major languages.

perform less well than they should because of a foreign or hostile environment.

The Swann Report 1986 found that this was the case in British schools and recommended methods of combating racial disadvantage, and local authorities are increasingly adopting anti-racist policies and attempting to give their curricula a multicultural dimension. (See ◊multicultural education.)

It comes as a great shock to see Gary Cooper killing off the Indians and, although you are rooting for Gary Cooper, that the Indians are you.

racism
James Baldwin, 1924–1987, US writer and civil-rights activist.
Speech at Cambridge University 17 Feb 1965

---

rabbi in Judaism, the chief religious leader of a synagogue or the spiritual leader (not a hereditary high priest) of a Jewish congregation; also, a scholar of Judaic law and ritual from the 1st century AD.

I go to seek a great perhaps.

Rabelais
Attributed remark on his deathbed

Rabelais François 1495–1553. French satirist, monk, and physician whose name has become synonymous with bawdy humour. He was educated in the Renaissance humanist tradition and was the author of satirical allegories, including *La Vie inestimable de Gargantua/The Inestimable Life of Gargantua* 1535 and *Faits et dits héroïques du grand Pantagruel/Heroic Deeds and Sayings of the Great Pantagruel* 1533, about two giants (father and son).

race in anthropology, term sometimes applied to a physically distinctive group of people, on the basis of their difference from other groups in skin colour, head shape, hair type, and physique. Formerly anthropologists divided the human race into three hypothetical racial groups: Caucasoid, Mongoloid, and Negroid. However, scientific studies have produced no proof of definite genetic racial divisions. Many anthropologists today, therefore, completely reject the concept of race, and social scientists tend to prefer the term ethnic group (see ◊ethnicity).

Rachel in the Old Testament, the favourite wife of ◊Jacob, and mother of ◊Joseph and Benjamin.

racial disadvantage in education, a situation in which children from ethnic minority groups

racism belief in, or set of implicit assumptions about, the superiority of one's own ◊race or ethnic group, often accompanied by prejudice against members of an ethnic group different from one's own. Racism may be used to justify ◊discrimination, verbal or physical abuse, or even genocide, as in Nazi Germany, or as practised by European settlers against American Indians in both North and South America.

Many social scientists believe that even where there is no overt discrimination, racism exists as an unconscious attitude in many individuals and societies, based on a ◊stereotype or preconceived idea about different ethnic groups, which is damaging to individuals (both perpetrators and victims) and to society as a whole. See also ◊ethnicity.

For the black man there is only one destiny. And it is white.

racism
Frantz Fanon, 1925–1961, French political writer.
Black Skin White Masks

Radcliffe-Brown Alfred 1881–1955. British anthropologist who, influenced by Emile ◊Durkheim, developed the theory of ◊structural functualism in which aspects of society were analysed in terms of their contribution to the overall social structure or system.

Radha in the Hindu epic ◊*Mahābhārata*, the wife of a cowherd who leaves her husband for love of Krishna (an incarnation of the god

Vishnu). Her devotion to Krishna is seen by the mystical ◊bhakti movement as the ideal of the love between humans and God.

Radhasoami the Supreme Being of the Radhasoami faith, founded 1861 by Shiv Dayal Singh (1818–878) near Agra, N India. The faith teaches a blend of ◊yoga and ◊bhakti derived, yet distinct, from Hindu tradition. Its principal centre is now the Radha Soami Satsang in Beas, in the Punjab, where the present leader is Charan Singh (1916–   ), a grandson of the original founder. There are over 2 million followers of the Radhasoami faith worldwide.

radical in politics, anyone with opinions more extreme than the main current of a country's major political party or parties. It is more often applied to those with left-wing opinions, although the radical right also exists.

Ragnarök (German *Götterdämmerung*) in Norse mythology, the ultimate cataclysmic battle between gods and forces of evil, from which a new order will come.

Rahner Karl 1904–1984. German Catholic theologian, he joined the ◊Jesuits 1922, studying first philosophy and then theology. His major work is a sixteen-volume series *Schriften zur Theologie*, published in English in 20 volumes as *Theological Investigations*, begun in 1954 when he was teaching at Innsbruck and finished in 1984 after he had retired from the post of professor at Munich (1964–67) and Munster (1967–71). In this series he attempts a systematic theological exploration linking the historical and the transcendent, especially by relating salvation history to the history of evolution and the world. He was considered too radical by many in the Catholic church but was one of the more influential advisers to the Second Vatican Council.

rainbow coalition or *rainbow alliance* in politics, from the mid-1980s, a loose, left-of-centre alliance of people from several different sections of society that are traditionally politically underrepresented, such as nonwhite ethnic groups. Its aims include promoting minority rights and equal opportunities.

'Rainbow' is a translation of French *Arc-en-Ciel*, a name applied in 1984 to an alliance of 20 Euro-MPs from various countries who supported Green environmental policies. The term was taken up by Jesse Jackson's US presidential campaign, which sought to represent an alliance of nonwhite political groupings.

Rainbow Serpent in Australian Aboriginal belief, a creative spirit being common to religions throughout much of the country. Sometimes male, sometimes female, it has the form of a giant python surrounded by rainbows and is associated with water and with fertility. In W Arnhem Land it is known as Ngaljod and is held responsible for monsoonal storms and floods. See ◊Dreamtime.

Rajneesh meditation meditation based on the teachings of the Indian Shree Rajneesh (born Chaadra Mohan Jain 1931–1990), established in the early 1970s. Until 1989 he called himself *Bhagwan* (Hindi 'God'). His followers, who number about half a million worldwide, regard themselves as Sannyas, or Hindu ascetics; they wear orange robes and carry a string of prayer beads. They are not expected to observe any specific prohibitions but to be guided by their instincts.

Rajneesh initially set up an ashram, or religious community, in Poona, NW India. He gained many followers, both Indian and Western, but his teachings also created considerable opposition, and in 1981 the Bhagwan moved his ashram to Oregon, USA, calling himself 'guru of the rich'. He was deported 1985 after pleading guilty to immigration fraud, and died 1990.

He taught that there is a basic energy in the world, bio-energy, and that individuals can release this by *dynamic meditation*, which involves breathing exercises and explosive physical activity. His followers are encouraged to live in large groups, so that children may grow up in contact with a variety of people.

Rama incarnation of ◊Vishnu, the supreme spirit of Hinduism. He is the hero of the epic poem the ◊*Rāmāyana*, and he is regarded as an example of morality and virtue.

Ramadan in the Muslim calendar, the ninth month of the year. Throughout Ramadan a strict fast is observed during the hours of daylight; Muslims are encouraged to read the whole Qur'an in commemoration of the Night of Power (which falls during the month) when, it is believed, Muhammad first received his revelations from the angel Jibra'el (Gabriel).

Ramakrishna 1834–1886. Hindu sage, teacher, and mystic (one dedicated to achieving oneness with or a direct experience of God or some force beyond the normal world). Ramakrishna claimed that mystical experience was the ultimate aim of religions, and that all religions which led to this goal were equally valid.

Ramakrishna's most important follower, Swami Vivekananda (1863–1902), set up the Ramakrishna Society 1887, which now has centres for education, welfare, and religious teaching throughout India and beyond.

Ramanuja 1017–1137. Indian teacher and philosopher of ◊Vaishnavism. He taught the path of self-surrender to a personal God and laid the foundation for the ◊bhakti movement in Hinduism. He looked upon individual souls as distinct from God and advocated devotion as superior to knowledge. He countered Sankara's advaita (non-dual) philosophy of pure monism with *vishishtadvaita*, 'non-duality in difference'.

Rāmāyana Sanskrit epic of c. 300 BC, in which ◊Rama (an incarnation of the god Vishnu) and his friend Hanuman (the monkey chieftain) strive to recover Rama's wife, Sita, abducted by the demon king Ravana.

Ram Das 1534–1581. Indian religious leader, fourth guru (teacher) of Sikhism 1574–81, who founded the Sikh holy city of Amritsar.

Ram Mohan Roy 1772–1833. Indian religious reformer. He campaigned to reform some of the old customs of traditional Hinduism such as suttee (the suicide of widows) and the privilege of the priests. He was influenced by Christianity and founded the ◊Brahma Samaj movement 1828 'to teach and practice the worship of the one, supreme, undivided eternal God'. He was in the forefront of the modern Hindu movement in India.

Ramsey Ian Thomas 1915–1972. English theologian who argued that the essential character of religious language is in its 'disclosures' which allow a deeper level of perception of religious truth. He offered a new slant on the problem of analogy – how the language of this world can be the vehicle of a religious dimension beyond this world.

Ramus Petrus, Latinized name of Pierre de la Ramée 1515–1572. French philosopher and logician who sought to improve the syllogistic logic of Greek philosopher ◊Aristotle with the rhetoric of Roman orator ◊Cicero. In the 17th century, Ramism was a serious rival to Aristotelian logic in Britain, New England, and Germany.

Aristotelian logic had also been criticized by Italian scholar Lorenzo ◊Valla. Francis I suppressed Ramus's works 1544, but Henry II lifted the ban 1547. From 1551, Ramus was professor of philosophy and eloquence at the Collège de France. Around 1561 he became a Protestant. He was murdered by hired assassins. His works include *Dialectique/Dialectic* 1555.

Rand Ayn. Adopted name of Alice Rosenbaum 1905–1982. Russian-born US novelist. Her novel *The Fountainhead* 1943 (made into a film 1949), describing an idealistic architect who destroys his project rather than see it altered, displays her persuasive blend of vehement anti-communism and fervent philosophy of individual enterprise.

random number one of a series of numbers having no detectable pattern. Random numbers are used in computer simulation and computer games. It 'is impossible for an ordinary computer to generate true random numbers, but various techniques are available for obtaining pseudo-random numbers – close enough to true randomness for most purposes.

Ranke Leopold von 1795–1886. German historian, pioneer of empirical research and the analysis of sources. His ideas were often regarded as the beginning of 'modern' history. His most famous work is *History of the Popes in the 16th and 17th centuries* 1834–36, but he published extensively on a wide range of topics including the development of the German peoples.

He was professor of history at Berlin University from 1825 until his death.

Ranters English religious sect, one of the many groups which arose during the English Civil War in the mid-17th century. Known for their ecstatic shoutings during services, they rejected much of mainstream Christianity, relying instead upon inner experience for vindication of their teachings. They were renowned for their licentiousness.

Raoult François 1830–1901. French chemist. In 1882, while working at the University of Grenoble, Raoult formulated one of the basic laws of chemistry. *Raoult's law* enables the relative molecular mass of a substance to be determined by noting how much of it is required to depress the freezing point of a solvent by a certain amount.

rapprochement improvement of relations between two formerly antagonistic states, such as the agreement between Britain and France in 1904 which ended decades of colonial rivalry.

Rastafarianism religion originating in the West Indies, based on the ideas of Marcus ◊Garvey, who called on black people to return to Africa and set up a black-governed country there. When Haile Selassie (*Ras Tafari*, 'Lion of Judah') was crowned emperor of Ethiopia 1930, this was seen as a fulfilment of prophecy and some Rastafarians acknowledged him as an incarnation of God (*Jah*), others as a prophet. The use of ganja (marijuana) is a sacrament. There are no churches. There were about one million Rastafarians by 1990.

Rastafarians identify themselves with the Chosen People, the Israelites, of the Bible. Ethiopia is seen as the promised land, while all countries outside Africa are **Babylon**, the place of exile. Many Rastafarians do not cut their hair, because of Biblical injunctions against this, but wear it instead in long dreadlocks, often covered in woollen hats in the Rastafarian colours of red, green, and gold. Food laws are very strict.

The term *I-tal* is used for food as close as possible to its natural state. Medicines should be made from natural herbs. Meetings are held regularly for prayer, discussion, and celebration, and at intervals there is a very large meeting, or Nyabingi. Rastafarians use a distinct language, in particular using the term 'I and I' for 'we' to stress unity.

rationalism in theology, the belief that human reason rather than divine revelation is the correct means of ascertaining truth and regulating behaviour. In philosophy, rationalism is the view that self-evident ◊a priori propositions are the sole basis of all knowledge, not the experience of the senses. It is usually contrasted with ◊empiricism, which argues that all knowledge must ultimately be derived from the senses.

The philosophers Descartes, Leibniz, and Spinoza, are known as the continental rationalists, and are usually contrasted with the British empiricists (Locke, Berkeley, and Hume).

Rawls John 1921– . US philosopher. In *A Theory of Justice* 1971, he revived the concept of the ◊social contract, arguing that if we did not know which position we were to occupy in society we would choose to live in a society in which there was equal liberty and the minimum of social and economic inequalities. His ideas have influenced left-of-centre parties throughout the world.

Ray John 1627–1705. English naturalist who devised a classification system accounting for nearly 18,000 plant species. It was the first system to divide flowering plants into monocotyledons and dicotyledons, with additional divisions made on the basis of leaf and flower characters and fruit types.

Rayleigh John W Strutt, 3rd Baron 1842–1919. British physicist who wrote the standard *Treatise on Sound*, experimented in optics and microscopy, and, with William Ramsay, discovered argon. Nobel prize 1904.

reactionary pejorative term applied to those people who are seen as resistant to change and progress.

Read Herbert 1893–1968. British art critic, poet, and academic, whose writings during the 1930s made modern art accessible to the public. His books include *The Meaning of Art* 1931 and the influential *Education Through Art* 1943.

He was one of the founders of the Institute of Contemporary Arts in London.

reader-response theory literary theory which sees the reader as an active participant in establishing the meaning of a text.

Reagan doctrine US foreign policy which, during the presidency of Ronald Reagan 1981–89, stressed the potential threat of the Soviet Union. It also provided economic and military support for anticommunist, authoritarian regimes (for example, El Salvador) while attempting to undermine and destabilize left-wing governments (for example, Nicaragua).

realism in philosophy, the theory that universals (properties such as 'redness') have an existence independent of the human mind (◊universal). Realists hold that the ◊essence of things is objectively given in nature, and that our classifications are not arbitrary. As such, realism is contrasted with ◊nominalism, the theory that universals are merely names or general terms.

More generally, realism is any philosophical theory that emphasizes the existence of some kind of things or objects, in contrast to theories that dispense with the things in question in favour of words, ideas or logical constructions. In particular, the term stands for the theory that there is a reality quite independent of the mind. In this sense, realism is opposed to ◊idealism, the theory that only minds and their contents exist.

Realism in the arts and literature, an unadorned, naturalistic approach to subject matter. Realism also refers more specifically to a movement in mid-19th-century European art and literature, a reaction against Romantic and Classical idealization and a rejection of conventional academic themes (such as mythology, history, and sublime landscapes) in favour of everyday life and carefully observed social settings. The movement was particularly important in France, where it had political overtones; the painters Gustave Courbet and Honoré

Daumier, two leading Realists, both used their art to expose social injustice.

Courbet's work was controversial both for its scale and subject matter; his *Burial at Ornans* 1850, a large-scale canvas depicting life-size, ordinary people attending a burial, is typical. Other Realists include the novelists Balzac, Flaubert, Stendhal, Eliot, Fontane, Dostoevsky, Gogol, and Tolstoy. Realism was superceded by ◊Impressionism in painting and ◊Naturalism in literature.

realpolitik belief that the pragmatic pursuit of self-interest and power, backed up by force when convenient, is the only realistic option for a great state. The term was coined 1859 to describe Bismarck's policies.

real presence in Christianity, the doctrine that Christ is really present in the properly consecrated ◊Eucharist. The Roman Catholic Church holds to a metaphysical theory about the real presence, ◊*transubstantiation*, which is the doctrine that only the appearance of the consecrated bread and wine remain and that its actual substance becomes Christ's body and blood. The Lutheran Churches hold to another metaphysical theory about it, *consubstantiation*, which is the doctrine that the substances of the bread and wine and of Christ's body and blood co-exist in union with one another. The Anglican Churches avoid metaphysical speculation about the real presence and regard it as a mystery.

reception theory literary theory which concentrates on the way a work is received by its contemporary readership and throughout its ensuing history.

Its leading exponent, Hans Robert Jauss, argues that the meaning of a text changes as its readership's horizon of expectation and knowledge changes.

recession in economics, a fall in business activity lasting more than a few months, causing stagnation in a country's output. A serious recession is called a *slump*.

recidivism the tendency of criminals to fall repeatedly into crime.

rector Anglican priest, formerly entitled to the whole of the ◊tithes levied in the parish, as opposed to a *vicar* (Latin 'deputy') who was only entitled to part.

recycling processing of industrial and household waste (such as paper, glass, and some metals and plastics) so that it can be reused.

This saves expenditure on scarce raw materials, slows down the depletion of ◊nonrenewable resources, and helps to reduce pollution and the problem of waste disposal.

The USA recycles only around 13% of its waste, compared to around 33% in Japan. However, all US states encourage or require local recycling programmes to be set up. It was estimated 1992 that 4,000 cities collected waste from 71 million people for recycling. Most of these programmes were set up in 1989–92. Around 33% of newspapers, 22% of office paper, 64% of aluminium cans, 3% of plastic containers, and 20% of all glass bottles and jars were recycled.

Most British recycling schemes are voluntary, and rely on people taking waste items to a central collection point. However, some local authorities, such as Leeds, now ask householders to separate waste before collection, making recycling possible on a much larger scale.

red informal term for a leftist, revolutionary, or communist, which originated in the 19th century in the form 'red republican', meaning a republican who favoured a social as well as a political revolution, generally by armed violence. Red is the colour adopted by socialist and communist parties.

Red Cross international relief agency founded by the Geneva Convention 1864 at the instigation of the Swiss doctor Henri ◊Dunant to assist the wounded and prisoners in war. Its symbol is a symmetrical red cross on a white ground. In addition to dealing with associated problems of war, such as refugees and the care of the disabled, the Red Cross is increasingly concerned with victims of natural disasters – floods, earthquakes, epidemics, and accidents.

Prompted by war horrors described by Dunant, the Geneva Convention laid down principles to ensure the safety of ambulances, hospitals, stores, and personnel distinguished by the Red Cross emblem. The Muslim equivalent is the *Red Crescent*.

The British Red Cross Society was founded 1870, and incorporated 1908. It works in close association with the St John Ambulance Association.

red tape derogatory term for bureaucratic methods, derived from the fastening for departmental bundles of documents in Britain.

referendum procedure whereby a decision on proposed legislation is referred to the electorate for settlement by direct vote of all the people. It is most frequently employed in Switzerland, the first country to use it, but has become increasingly widespread. In 1992 several European countries (Ireland, Denmark, France) held referenda on whether or not to ratify the ◊Maastricht Treaty on closer European economic and political union.

A referendum was held in the UK for the first time 1975 on the issue of membership of the European Community. Critics argue that referenda undermine parliamentary authority, but they do allow the elector to participate directly in decision-making. Similar devices are the *recall*, whereby voters are given the opportunity of demanding the dismissal from office of officials, and the ◊*initiative*.

Reformation religious and political movement in 16th-century Europe to reform the Roman Catholic Church, which led to the establishment of Protestant churches. Anticipated from the 12th century by the Waldenses, Lollards, and Hussites, it was set off by German priest Martin ◊Luther 1517, and became effective when the absolute monarchies gave it support by challenging the political power of the papacy and confiscating church wealth.

reformism improvement of the political and social order by gradual change and reform rather than by sudden revolutionary transformation.

refugee person fleeing from oppressive or dangerous conditions (such as political, religious, or military persecution) and seeking refuge in a foreign country. In 1991 there were an estimated 17 million refugees worldwide, whose resettlement and welfare were the responsibility of the United Nations High Commission for Refugees (UNHCR). An estimated average of 3,000 people a day become refugees.

The term was originally applied to the French Huguenots who came to England after toleration of Protestantism was withdrawn with the revocation of the Edict of Nantes in 1685. Major refugee movements in 20th-century Europe include: Jews from the ◊pogroms of Russia 1881–1914 and again after the Revolution; White Russians from the USSR after 1917; Jews from Germany and other Nazi-dominated countries 1933–45; the displaced people of World War II; and from 1991 victims of the the civil wars in Croatia and Bosnia-Herzegovina.

Many Chinese fled the mainland after the communist revolution of 1949, especially to Taiwan and Hong Kong; many Latin Americans fled from Cuba, Colombia, Brazil, Chile, Argentina, and Central America when new governments took power; and many boat people left Vietnam after the victory of the North over the South. Refugee movements created by natural disasters and famine have been widespread, most notably in Ethiopia and Sudan, where civil war has also contributed. Between 1985 and 1989 the number of refugees doubled worldwide, and the Gulf War 1991 created 1.5 million refugees, though many were later able to return to their homes.

In 1990 the largest single refugee groupings were: Afghans (about 6 million, temporarily settled in Iran and Pakistan); Ethiopians (1.3 million, mostly Eritreans who have moved to Sudan); Mozambicans (1.2 million, displaced mostly to Malawi); Iraqis (600,000, predominantly Kurds who have settled in Iran); Somalis (400,000); Sudanese (400,000); Sri Lankan Tamils (300,000, who have fled to India); and Cambodians (300,000, who live in refugee camps in Thailand). UNHCR's budget was $550 million in 1990.

A distinction is usually made by Western nations between 'political' refugees and so-called 'economic' refugees, who are said to be escaping from poverty rather than persecution, particularly when the refugees come from low-income countries. The latter group often become illegal immigrants. International law recognizes the right of the persecuted to seek asylum but does not oblige states to provide it. Only 0.17% of W Europe's population are refugees.

Internally displaced people, who have been forced to leave their homes but not crossed their country's borders, are not recognized as refugees; they are estimated to number over 30 million (1991).

Since 1920, international organizations have been set up to help refugees, including the Nansen Office for Russian refugees in the 1920s, and the United Nations High Commission for Refugees in 1945. In 1970 there were 2.5 million refugees worldwide, in 1985 10 million, in 1990 15 million.

regent person who carries out the duties of a sovereign during the sovereign's minority, incapacity, or lengthy absence from the country. In England since the time of Henry VIII, Parliament has always appointed a regent or council of regency when necessary.

Rehoboam king of Judah about 932–915 BC, son of Solomon. Under his rule the Jewish nation split into the two kingdoms of *Israel* and *Judah*. Ten of the tribes revolted against him and took Jeroboam as their ruler, leaving

Rehoboam only the tribes of Judah and Benjamin.

Reich Wilhelm 1897–1957. Austrian doctor, who emigrated to the USA 1939. He combined ◊Marxism and ◊psychoanalysis to advocate the positive effects of directed sexual energies and sexual freedom. His works include *Die Sexuelle Revolution/The Sexual Revolution* 1936–45 and *Die Funktion des Orgasmus/The Function of the Orgasm* 1948.

Reichian therapy general term for a group of body-therapies based on the theory propounded in the 1930s by Wilhelm Reich, that many functional and organic illnesses are attributable to constriction of the flow of vital energies in the body by tensions that become locked into the musculature. Bioenergetics and Rolfing are related approaches.

Reid Thomas 1710–1796. Scottish mathematician and philosopher. His *Enquiry into the Human Mind on the Principles of Common Sense* 1764 attempted to counter the sceptical conclusions of Hume. He believed that the existence of the material world and the human soul is self-evident 'by the consent of ages and nations, of the learned and unlearned'.

reification alleged social process whereby relations between human beings are transformed into impersonal relations between things. Georg Lukács, in *History and Class Consciousness* 1923, analyses this process as characteristic of capitalist society.

Later Marxists have developed this analysis, thus extending Marx's early critique of alienation in the *Paris Manuscripts* 1844.

reincarnation belief that after death the human soul or the spirit of an animal may live again in another human or animal. It is part of the teachings of many religions and philosophies, for example ancient Egyptian and Greek (the philosophies of Pythagoras and Plato), Buddhism, Hinduism, Jainism, certain Christian heresies (such as the Cathars), and theosophy. It is also referred to as *transmigration* or metempsychosis.

relativism philosophical position that denies the possibility of objective truth independent of some specific social or historical context or conceptual framework.

relativity in physics, the theory of the relative rather than absolute character of motion and mass, and the interdependence of matter, time, and space, as developed by German physicist Albert ◊Einstein in two phases:

special theory (1905) Starting with the premises that (1) the laws of nature are the same for all observers in unaccelerated motion, and (2) the speed of light is independent of the motion of its source, Einstein postulated that the time interval between two events was longer for an observer in whose frame of reference the events occur in different places than for the observer for whom they occur at the same place.

general theory of relativity (1915) The geometrical properties of space-time were to be conceived as modified locally by the presence of a body with mass. A planet's orbit around the Sun (as observed in three-dimensional space) arises from its natural trajectory in modified space-time; there is no need to invoke, as Isaac Newton did, a force of ◊gravity coming from the Sun and acting on the planet. Einstein's theory predicted slight differences in the orbits of the planets from Newton's theory, which were observable in the case of Mercury. The new theory also said light rays should bend when they pass by a massive object, owing to the object's effect on local space-time. The predicted bending of starlight was observed during the eclipse of the Sun 1919, when light from distant stars passing close to the Sun was not masked by sunlight.

Einstein showed that for consistency with premises (1) and (2), the principles of dynamics as established by Newton needed modification; the most celebrated new result was the equation $E = mc^2$, which expresses an equivalence between mass (m) and energy (E), c being the speed of light in a vacuum. Although since modified in detail, general relativity remains central to modern astrophysics and ◊cosmology; it predicts, for example, the possibility of ◊black holes. General relativity theory was inspired by the simple idea that it is impossible in a small region to distinguish between acceleration and gravitation effects (as in a lift one feels heavier when the lift accelerates upwards), but the mathematical development of the idea is formidable. Such is not the case for the special theory, which a nonexpert can follow up to $E = mc^2$ and beyond.

relic part of some divine or saintly person, or something closely associated with them. Christian examples include the arm of St Teresa of Avila, the blood of St Januarius, and the ◊True Cross. Buddhist relics include the funeral ashes of the historic Buddha, placed in a number of stupas or burial mounds.

In medieval times relics were fiercely fought for, and there were a vast number of fakes. The cult was condemned by Protestant reformers but upheld by the Roman Catholic Church at the Council of Trent in the mid-16th century. Parallel nonreligious examples of the phenomenon include the display of the preserved body of Lenin in Moscow, Russia.

> One religion is as true as another.
>
> religion
> Robert Burton, 1577–1640, English
> philosopher.
> Anatomy of Melancholy

religion code of belief or philosophy that often involves the worship of a ◊God or gods. Belief in a supernatural power is not essential (absent in, for example, Buddhism and Confucianism), but faithful adherence is usually considered to be rewarded, for example, by escape from human existence (Buddhism), by a future existence (Christianity, Islam), or by worldly benefit (Sōka Gakkai Buddhism). Among the chief religions are: *ancient and pantheist* religions of Babylonia, Assyria, Egypt, Greece, and Rome; *oriental* Hinduism, Buddhism, Jainism, Parseeism, Confucianism, Taoism, and Shinto; *'religions of a book'* Judaism, Christianity (the principal divisions are Roman Catholic, Eastern Orthodox, and Protestant), and Islam (the principal divisions are Sunni and Shi'ite); *combined derivation* such as Baha'ism, the Unification Church, and Mormonism.

> There is only one religion, though there are a hundred versions of it.
>
> religion
> George Bernard Shaw, 1856–1950,
> Irish dramatist.
> Arms and the Man preface

Comparative religion studies the various faiths impartially, but often with the hope of finding common ground, to solve the practical problems of competing claims of unique truth or inspiration. The earliest known attempt at a philosophy of religious beliefs is contained in fragments written by Xenophanes in Greece 6th century BC, and later Herodotus and Aristotle contributed to the study. In 17th-century China, Jesuit theologians conducted comparative studies. Towards the end of the 18th century English missionary schools in Calcutta compared the Bible with sacred Indian texts. The work of Charles Darwin in natural history and the growth of anthropology stimulated fresh investigation of religious beliefs; work by the Sanskrit scholar Max Müller (1823–1900), the Scottish anthropologist James Frazer, the German sociologist Max Weber, and the Romanian scholar Mircea Eliade has formed the basis for modern comparative religion.

> A shadow in a dream is Man.
>
> religion
> Pindar, c.552 BC–442 BC, Greek poet.
> Pythian VIII

remote sensing gathering and recording information from a distance. Space probes have sent back photographs and data about planets as distant as Neptune. In archaeology, surface survey techniques provide information without disturbing subsurface deposits.

Satellites such as *Landsat* have surveyed all the Earth's surface from orbit. Computer processing of data obtained by their scanning instruments, and the application of so-called false colours (generated by the computer), have made it possible to reveal surface features invisible in ordinary light. This has proved valuable in agriculture, forestry, and urban planning, and has led to the discovery of new deposits of minerals.

Renaissance period and intellectual movement in European cultural history that is traditionally seen as ending the Middle Ages and beginning modern times. The Renaissance started in Italy in the 14th century and flourished in W Europe until about the 17th century.

The aim of Renaissance education was to produce the 'complete human being' (*Renaissance man*), conversant in the humanities, mathematics and science (including their application in war), the arts and crafts, and athletics and sport; to enlarge the bounds of learning and geographical knowledge; to encourage the growth of scepticism and free thought, and the study and imitation of Greek and Latin literature and art. The revival of interest in classical Greek and Roman culture inspired artists such as Leonardo da Vinci, Michelangelo, and Dürer, architects such as Brunelleschi and Alberti, and writers such as Petrarch and Boccaccio. Scientists and explorers proliferated as well.

Science and Religion: Enemies or Partners?

In recent years the truce between science and religion has shown itself to be uneasy. Public perception of the status and role of science in society has shifted from approval, and a conviction that science has all the answers, to ambivalence. This leaves many scientists defensive about their particular contribution in society. Any suggestion that scientists might have something to learn from theology was roundly dismissed on 1 April 1993 by the editor of *Nature*, a leading scientific weekly magazine. He asserted that the creation of a lectureship in theology and the natural sciences, funded by a £1 million endowment from the English author Susan Howatch and named the Starbridge Lectureship after her best-selling series, was nonacademic and amounted to a university's giving in to pressure to accept finances from what he believed to be 'dubious' sources. His lead article attracted a flurry of correspondence from both scientists and theologians.

Natural partners
One position is that science and religion are partners rather than enemies. According to this view, it was the belief in a divine creator that allowed the first scientific investigations to take place. Both Christians and Muslims perceived the world as a product of divine creation. Scientists eagerly studied creation as a way of finding out the wisdom of God as revealed in it. The early scientists, including Johannes Kepler, Galileo Galilei, Robert Boyle, René Descartes, Francis Bacon, Blaise Pascal, John Ray, Isaac Newton, and Michael Faraday, were all concerned to relate their scientific studies to their faith. The areas of theology and natural science can coexist if theology is seen as bringing in layers of meaning that are missing from purely scientific accounts. Some Christians argue that science itself requires a leap of faith that is at least as strong as religious commitment, and some scientists would urge us to see our religious predisposition as having survival value, if religious belief leads to an overall increase in 'goodness'. In this view, our genetic make-up is not conditioned by selfish competition but by altruism.

Secular v sacred
An alternative view is that science and religion are incompatible. Science is a form of knowledge that can be proved, while religion cannot be proved and so is, by implication, not knowledge. The church resisted the teaching of the early scientists, such as Galileo, because he seemed to be able to do away with the necessary existence of God for the creation of the universe. Science responded to such attacks by becoming increasingly secular and working in detachment from the teaching of the Christian church or other religions. Established science tended to equate religious teachings with superstitious ornamentations of life of no intellectual value. Science began to explain religion as a way of responding psychologically to pressures in society. Belief in miracles and other supernatural events was seen as a function of a fantasy world created by the religious participants. The origin of humanity, crucially attributed to a creator god in religion, is explained by scientific principles according to the theory of evolution, where only those populations that best fit the environment survive. The weak and defenceless are weeded out in the process.

The power of the scientist
Scientists are popularly perceived as either innocent bystanders with regard to the way the technology for which they have provided the basis has been used, or scapegoats who can be blamed for contemporary problems such as the ecological crisis. The application of scientific ideas by other parties such as politicians, industrial entrepreneurs, and the military, has changed the face of our planet and broken up ancient, more stable social structures and religious patterns of living. Scientists injected the original ideas into our cultures, even if they were not involved in their implementation.

A living planet?
In the last 30 years there has been an increased interest in cross-disciplinary studies. One of the pioneers of work of this type is James Lovelock, who argues that the world as a whole behaves rather like a giant organism. The composition of the atmosphere is controlled by the sum total of life on the planet. He is most controversial when he mixes his scientific hypothesis with an ancient belief in the Earth goddess, Gaia. Such controversy stems from the unease of the scientific establishment about the academic worth of religious ideas, since such ideas are a matter of opinion and cannot be proved in any objective sense.

Ethics – the common ground
In establishing the policy for future scientific practice, questions of faith are also raised. What kind of guidelines can we draw up in deciding what the limits of medical research should be? Do we need to take a wider ethical approach when using advances in biological technology that were unimaginable in earlier centuries? Advances in genetics, and genetic engineering in particular, posit a future in which scientists may be able to produce certain characteristics or eliminate 'undesirable' ones in humans, as well as other animals – a future where even the role of creator is usurped by science. An appreciation by scientists of religious concerns is more likely to lead to a lasting contribution by science to society; and an understanding of science by the religious is more likely to prevent a retreat into fanaticism.

Celia Deane-Drummond

The beginning of the Italian Renaissance is usually dated in the 14th century with the writers Petrarch and Boccaccio. The invention of printing (mid-15th century) and geographical discoveries helped spread the new spirit. Exploration by Europeans opened Africa, Asia, and the New World to trade, colonization, and imperialism. Biblical criticism by the Dutch humanist Erasmus and others contributed to the Reformation, but the Counter-Reformation almost extinguished the movement in 16th-century Italy. In the visual arts Renaissance painting and sculpture later moved towards ◊Mannerism.

Figures of the Renaissance include the politician Machiavelli, the poets Ariosto and Tasso, the philosopher Bruno, the physicist Galileo, and the artists Michelangelo, Cellini, and Raphael in Italy; the writers Rabelais and Montaigne in France, Cervantes in Spain, and Camoëns in Portugal; the astronomer Copernicus in Poland; and the politicians More and Bacon, and the writers Sidney, Marlowe, and Shakespeare in England.

The term 'Renaissance' was first used to describe the period of time in the 18th century. Especially in Italy, where the ideals of the Renaissance were considered to have been fulfilled by the great masters, the period 1490–1520 is known as the **High Renaissance**, and painting of the period described as **High Renaissance Classicism**.

Renan (Joseph) Ernest 1823–1892. French theologian and historian. Professor of Hebrew at the Collège de France, his *La Vie de Jésus/The Life of Jesus*, published 1863, controversially denied the supernatural element of Christ's life and mission. It was the first work in a series on the history of the origins of Christianity.

renewable resource natural resource that is replaced by natural processes in a reasonable amount of time. Soil, water, forests, plants, and animals are all renewable resources as long as they are properly conserved.

renunciation in religion, giving something up, an element of almost every ethical system. At one extreme is hedonism, with individual pleasure as the goal, and only limited renunciation, at the other extreme is ◊asceticism. Buddhism is based on renunciation of personal desires, and Hinduism seeks eventually, after many lifetimes, the abandonment of ties to the physical world, and the spirit of true renunciation is the recognition that everything belongs to God. In Christianity the idea of renunciation was most pronounced in medieval asceticism.

repentance in religion, to turn back to God in remorse at one's past actions. In the Hebrew Bible it is sometimes used of God who 'repents of the evil' proposed. The call for repentance of humanity is a call to return to a relationship of dependence on God as his creatures, and is found in Christianity, Judaism, and Islam along with a God who is merciful and forgiving. The New Testament stresses the idea of turning around and conversion.

The Moving Finger writes; and, having writ / Moves on: nor all thy Piety nor Wit / Shall lure it back to cancel half a Line, / Nor all thy Tears wash out a Word of it.

repentance
Edward Fitzgerald, 1809–1883, English poet and translator.
Rubaiyat of Omar Khayyám

repression in psychoanalysis, a mental process that ejects and excludes from consciousness ideas, impulses, or memories that would otherwise threaten emotional stability.

In ◊Freud's early writings, repression is controlled by the ◊censor, a hypothetical mechanism or agency that allows ideas, memories, and so on from the ◊unconscious to emerge into consciousness only if distorted or disguised, as for example in ◊dreams.

republic country where the head of state is not a monarch, either hereditary or elected, but usually a president whose role may or may not include political functions.

Republican Party one of the USA's two main political parties, formed 1854. It is considered more conservative than the Democratic Party, favouring capital and big business and opposing state subvention and federal controls. In the late 20th century most presidents have come from the Republican Party, but in Congress Republicans have been outnumbered.

The party was founded by a coalition of ◊slavery opponents, who elected their first president, Abraham ◊Lincoln, in 1860. The early Republican Party supported protective tariffs and favoured genuine settlers (homesteaders) over land speculators. Towards the end of the century the Republican Party was identified with US imperialism and industrial expansion. With few intermissions, the Republican Party controlled Congress from the 1860s until defeated by the ◊New Deal Democrats 1932.

Conservative tendencies and an antagonism of the legislature to the executive came to the fore after Lincoln's assassination, when Andrew Johnson, his Democratic and Southern successor, was impeached (although not convicted), and General Grant was elected to the presidency 1868 and 1872. In the bitter period following the Civil War the party was divided into those who considered the South a beaten nation and those who wished to reintegrate the South into the country as a whole, but Grant carried through a liberal Reconstruction policy in the South.

The party became divided during Theodore Roosevelt's attempts at regulation and control of big business, and in forming the short-lived Progressive Party 1912, Roosevelt effectively removed the liberal influence from the Republican Party.

The Republican Party remained in eclipse until the election of Eisenhower 1952, more his personal triumph than that of the party, whose control of Congress was soon lost and not regained by the next Republican president, Nixon, 1968. Both Nixon and his successor, Ford, pursued active foreign policies; the latter was defeated by Carter in the presidential election 1976. However, the party enjoyed landslide presidential victories for Reagan and also carried the Senate 1980–86. Bush won the 1988 presidential election but faced a Democratic Senate and House of Representatives, and in 1992 lost the presidency to the Democrat Bill Clinton.

Rerum Novarum encyclical letter on the condition of the working classes written 1891 by Pope Leo XIII in response to the conditions arising from the Industrial Revolution. It condemned socialism as an infringement of the right of the individual to hold private property but advocated the idea of a just wage, and stated that the place of women was in the home. The principles of Catholic social teaching which it sets out have inspired debate and discussion ever since.

research the primary activity in science, a combination of theory and experimentation directed towards finding scientific explanations of phenomena. It is commonly classified into two types: *pure research*, involving theories with little apparent relevance to human concerns; and *applied research*, concerned with finding solutions to problems of social importance – for instance in medicine and engineering. The two types are linked in that theories developed from pure research may eventually be found to be of great value to society.

Scientific research is most often funded by government and industry, and so a nation's wealth and priorities are likely to have a strong influence on the kind of work undertaken.

In 1989 the European Community (EC) Council adopted a revised programme on research and technological development for the period 1990–94, requiring a total Community finance of 5,700 million ECUs, to be apportioned as follows: information and communications technology 2,221 million; industrial and materials technologies 888 million; life sciences and technologies 741 million; energy 814 million; human capacity and mobility 518 million; environment 518 million.

In the UK, government-funded research and development in 1989–90 was £4.8 billion, representing 3.8% of total central government expenditure. This amount was distributed between the Ministry of Defence (£2.2 billion), civil departments (£1 billion), and the science base (£1.6 billion), the latter comprising the combined total for the Research Councils, University Funding Council, and the Polytechnics and Colleges Funding Council.

resistance movement opposition movement in a country occupied by an enemy or colonial power, especially in the 20th century; for example, the French resistance to Nazism in World War II.

During World War II, resistance in E Europe took the form of ◊guerrilla warfare, for example in Yugoslavia, Greece, Poland, and by *partisan* bands behind the German lines in the USSR. In more industrialized countries, such as France (where the underground movement was called the *maquis*), Belgium, and Czechoslovakia, sabotage in factories and on the railways, propaganda, and the assassination of Germans and collaborators were the main priorities.

Most resistance movements in World War II were based on an alliance of all anti-fascist parties, but there was internal conflict between those elements intent only on defeat of the enemy, and those who aimed at establishing communist governments, as in Yugoslavia and Greece.

After World War II the same methods were used in Palestine, South America, and European colonial possessions in Africa and Asia to unsettle established regimes.

resurrection in Christian, Jewish, and Muslim belief, the rising from the dead that all souls will experience at the Last Judgement. The Resurrection also refers to Jesus rising from the dead on the third day after his crucifixion, a belief central to Christianity and celebrated at Easter.

Behold, I shew you a mystery; We shall not all sleep but we shall all be changed, / In a moment, in the twinkling of an eye, at the last trump.

       resurrection
Bible, the sacred book of the Jewish and Christian religions.
1 Corinthians 15:51

---

retail price index (RPI) indicator of variations in the ◊cost of living, superseded in the USA by the consumer price index.

retrovirus any of a family (*Retroviridae*) of viruses containing the genetic material ◊RNA rather than the more usual ◊DNA.

For the virus to express itself and multiply within the infected cell, its RNA must be converted to DNA. It does this by using a built-in enzyme known as reverse transcriptase (since the transfer of genetic information from DNA to RNA is known as transcription, and retroviruses do the reverse of this). Retroviruses include those causing ◊AIDS and some forms of leukemia.

Revelation last book of the New Testament, traditionally attributed to the author of the Gospel of St John but now generally held to be the work of another writer. It describes a vision of the end of the world, of the Last Judgement, and of a new heaven and earth ruled by God from Jerusalem.

revelation the unveiling of something hidden, so that it may be seen for what it is. In the Bible it means God showing himself active in human history and as creator, and can come through actions or the words of prophets. In Christian belief Jesus Christ is the ultimate revelation of God. In Islam God's most complete and final revelation was that given through Muhammad and recorded as the ◊Qur'an.

revenge an action, usually of a violent nature, meted out by, or on behalf of, the victim of a wrongdoing against the perpetrator by way of retribution or repayment.

The desire for revenge is deep-rooted and is encoded in many cultures both ancient and modern. It differs from punishment in that it is usually performed by the victim or his or her kin as direct compensation for the wrong committed and not by a separate agency, such as the state, as an official act of disapproval. Revenge is an action which restores the honour of the wronged party; in primitive societies this extended to the whole group and was therefore a social obligation. Not to take revenge was a sign of weakness which prolonged disgrace for the individual and the group. In modern societies revenge is seen as 'taking the law into your own hands' and is approved or disapproved of according to the effectiveness of the actual law. Many of the Greek tragedies, notably the *Oresteia* of Aeschylus, depict individuals trapped in an endless cycle of murder and revenge. In English literature Shakespeare's play *Hamlet* is the best-known example of a Revenge Tragedy, a genre that flourished 1580–1640.

Vengeance is mine; I will repay, saith the Lord.

       revenge
Bible, the sacred book of the Jewish and Christian religions.
Romans 12:19

---

revenue money received from the sale of a product. *Total revenue* can be calculated by multiplying the average price received by the total quantity sold. *Average revenue* is the average price received and is calculated by dividing total revenue by total quantity sold. *Marginal revenue* is the revenue gained from the sale of an additional unit of output.

revisionism political theory derived from Marxism that moderates one or more of the basic tenets of Marx, and is hence condemned by orthodox Marxists.

The first noted Marxist revisionist was Eduard Bernstein, who in Germany in the 1890s questioned the inevitability of a breakdown in capitalism. After World War II the term became widely used by established communist parties, both in E Europe and Asia, to condemn movements (whether more or less radical) that threatened the official party policy.

revolution any rapid, far-reaching, or violent change in the political, social, or economic structure of society. It is usually applied to political change: examples include the American Revolution, where colonists broke free from their colonial ties and established a sovereign, independent nation; the ◊French Revolution, where an absolute monarchy was overthrown by opposition from inside the country and a popular uprising; and the ◊Russian Revolution, where a repressive monarchy was overthrown by those seeking to institute widespread social and economic changes based on a socialist model.

Every revolutionary ends as an oppressor or a heretic.

revolutionary
Albert Camus, 1913–1960, Algerian-born French writer.
The Rebel

While political revolutions are often associated with violence, other types of change can have just as much impact on society. Most notable is the Industrial Revolution of the mid-18th century, which caused massive economic and social changes. In the 1970s and 1980s a high-tech revolution based on the silicon chip took place, facilitating the widespread use of computers.

Those who make peaceful revolution impossible will make violent revolution inevitable.

revolution
John F(itzgerald) 'Jack' Kennedy, 1917–1963, 35th president of the USA 1961–63, a Democrat; the first Roman Catholic and the youngest person to be elected president.
Speech at White House 13 Mar 1962

---

revolutions of 1848 series of revolts in various parts of Europe against monarchical rule. While some of the revolutionaries had republican ideas, many more were motivated by economic grievances. The revolution began in France with the overthrow of Louis Philippe and then spread to Italy, the Austrian Empire, and Germany, where the short-lived Frankfurt Parliament put forward ideas about political unity in Germany. None of the revolutions enjoyed any lasting success, and most were violently suppressed within a few months.

revolutions of 1989 popular uprisings in many countries of Eastern Europe against communist rule, prompted by internal reforms in the USSR that permitted dissent within its sphere of influence. By 1990 nearly all the Warsaw Pact countries had moved from one-party to pluralist political systems, in most cases peacefully but with growing hostility between various nationalist and ethnic groups.

Until the late 1980s, any discontent, however widespread, had been kept in check by the use or threat of military force controlled from Moscow. Mikhail Gorbachev's official encouragement of *perestroika* (radical restructuring) and ◊*glasnost* (greater political openness), largely for economic reasons, allowed popular discontent to boil over. Throughout the summer and autumn of 1989 the Eastern European states broke away from the communist bloc, as the Soviet republics were to do during the next two years. Bulgaria, Czechoslovakia, and Hungary achieved bloodless coups; Poland held free elections; East Germany took the first steps towards reunification with West Germany; Romania's revolution was short and bloody. Yugoslavia held multiparty elections 1990 but then broke up into civil war. Albania held elections 1991.

Revolutionary Wars

1791	Emperor Leopold II and Frederick William II of Prussia issued the *Declaration of Pillnitz* inviting the European powers to restore the French king Louis XVI to power.
1792	France declared war on Austria, which formed a coalition with Prussia, Sardinia, and (from 1793), Britain, Spain, and the Netherlands; victories for France at Valmy and Jemappes.
1793	French reverses until the reorganization by Lazare Carnot.
1795	Prussia, the Netherlands, and Spain made peace with France.
1796	Sardinia was forced to make peace by the Italian campaign of Napoleon I, then a commander.
1797	Austria was compelled to make peace with France under the Treaty of Campo-Formio.
1798	Napoleon's fleet, after its capture of Malta, was defeated by the British admiral Nelson in Egypt at the Battle of the Nile (Aboukir Bay), and Napoleon had to return to France without his army; William Pitt the Younger, Britain's prime minister, organized a new coalition with Russia, Austria, Naples, Portugal, and Turkey.
1798–99	The coalition mounted its major campaign in Italy (under the Russian field marshal Suvorov), but dissension led to the withdrawal of Russia.
1799	Napoleon, on his return from Egypt, reorganized the French army.
1800	Austrian army defeated by Napoleon at Marengo in NW Italy 14 June, and again 3 Dec (by General Moreau) at Hohenlinden near Munich; the coalition collapsed.
1801	Austria made peace under the Treaty of Lunéville; Sir Ralph Abercromby defeated the French army by land in Egypt at the Battle of Alexandria, but was himself killed.
1802	Treaty of Amiens truce between France and Britain, followed by the Napoleonic Wars.

Reynolds Osborne 1842–1912. British physicist and engineer who studied fluid flow and devised the ◊*Reynolds number*, which relates to turbulence in flowing fluids.

Reynolds number number used in fluid mechanics to determine whether fluid flow in a particular situation (through a pipe or around an aircraft body) will be turbulent or smooth. The Reynolds number is calculated using the flow velocity, viscosity of the fluid, and the dimensions of the flow channel. It is named after British engineer Osborne ◊Reynolds.

rhetoric traditionally, the art of public speaking and debate. Rhetorical skills are valued in such occupations as politics, teaching, law, religion, and broadcasting.

Accomplished rhetoricians need not be sincere in what they say; they should, however, be effective, or at least entertaining. Nowadays, 'rhetoric' is often a pejorative term (for example, 'Cut the rhetoric and tell us what you really think').

Rhine Joseph Banks 1895–1980. US parapsychologist who from 1927 onward conducted, at Duke University, North Carolina, many of the best known laboratory experiments in ◊parapsychology.

He was the first to make extensive use of Zener cards, named after K E Zener a psychologist colleague, each containing one of five symbols, in card-guessing experiments to investigate clairvoyance and ◊telepathy. His report of these experiments in *Extra-Sensory Perception* 1934 made ESP a common term. He also investigated psychokinesis in experiments in which subjects tried to influence the fall of dice. This work is described in *The Reach of The Mind* 1947.

Ricardo David 1772–1823. English economist, author of *Principles of Political Economy* 1817. Among his discoveries were the principle of ◊comparative advantage (that countries can benefit by specializing in goods they produce efficiently and trading internationally to buy others), and the law of diminishing returns (that continued increments of capital and labour applied to a given quantity of land will eventually show a declining rate of increase in output).

Richards I(vor) A(rmstrong) 1893–1979. English literary critic. He collaborated with C K Ogden and wrote *Principles of Literary Criticism* 1924. In 1939 he went to Harvard University, USA, where he taught detailed attention to the text and had a strong influence on contemporary US literary criticism.

Richardson Owen Willans 1879–1959. British physicist. He studied the emission of electricity from hot bodies, giving the name thermionics to the subject. At Cambridge University, he worked under J J ◊Thomson in the Cavendish Laboratory. Nobel prize 1928.

Richter Burton 1931– . US particle physicist. In the 1960s he designed the Stanford Positron–Electron Accelerating Ring (SPEAR), a machine designed to collide positrons and electrons at high energies. In 1974 Richter and his team used SPEAR to produce a new subatomic particle, the (psi) meson. This was the first example of a particle formed from a charmed quark, the quark whose existence had been postulated by Sheldon Glashow ten years earlier. Richter shared the 1976 Nobel Physics Prize with Samuel Ting, who had discovered the particle independently.

Richter Charles Francis 1900–1985. US seismologist, deviser of the Richter scale used to measure the strength of the waves from earthquakes.

Ricoeur Paul 1913– . French philosopher who under the influence of ◊existentialism and Sigmund ◊Freud reflected at length on the nature of language and interpretation, subjectivity and the will. His works include *Le voluntaire et l'involuntaire/Freedom and Nature: the Voluntary and the Involuntary* 1950, *L'homme faillible/Fallible Man* 1960, and *La symbolique du mal/ The Symbolism of Evil* 1960. Born in Valence, he taught at the Sorbonne and elsewhere.

Riemann Georg Friedrich Bernhard 1826–1866. German mathematician whose system of non-Euclidean geometry, thought at the time to be a mere mathematical curiosity, was used by Einstein to develop his general theory of ◊relativity.

Riesman David 1909– . US sociologist, author of *The Lonely Crowd: A Study of the Changing American Character* 1950. He made a distinction among 'inner-directed', 'tradition-directed', and 'other-directed' societies; the first using individual internal values, the second using established tradition, and the third, other people's expectations, to develop cohesiveness and conformity within a society.

rights an individual's automatic entitlement to certain freedoms and other benefits, usually, in liberal democracies such as the UK, in the context of the individual's relationship with the government of the country. The struggle to assert political and civil rights against arbitrary government has been a major theme of Western political history.

The true Republic: men, their rights and nothing more; women, their rights and nothing less.

rights
Susan B(rownell) Anthony, 1820–1906, US campaigner for women's rights.
Motto of her newspaper *Revolution*

---

rights, natural doctrine, deriving from medieval philosophy but articulated by John ◊Locke, that human beings as individuals have certain absolute moral claims or entitlements. Locke identified three natural rights: to life, liberty, and property. The first two are also included in the Universal Declaration of ◊Human Rights, and most states pay at least lip service to the concept of ◊rights.

The doctrine of natural rights has been criticized on the grounds that no rights are absolute and that natural rights are a myth.

Bibl. Nozick, Robert *Anarchy, State and Utopia* (1974)

right wing the more conservative or reactionary section of a political party or spectrum. It originated in the French national assembly 1789, where the nobles sat in the place of honour on the president's right, whereas the commons were on his left (hence ◊left wing).

Rig-Veda oldest of the ◊Vedas, the chief sacred writings of Hinduism. It consists of hymns to the Aryan gods, such as Indra, and to nature gods.

Rinzai (Chinese **Lin-ch'i**) school of Zen Buddhism introduced to Japan from China in the 12th century by the monk Eisai and others. It emphasizes rigorous monastic discipline and sudden enlightenment by meditation on a ◊*kōan* (paradoxical question).

risk capital or *venture capital* finance provided by venture capital companies, individuals, and merchant banks for medium- or long-term business ventures that are not their own and in which there is a strong element of risk.

In recent years, there has been a large growth in the number of UK companies specializing in providing venture capital.

rites in religion, specific rituals or actions central to acts of worship or to a person's life – such as rites of passage (for example baptisms and funerals) or the rite of consecration of the bread and wine in the Christian ◊Eucharist.

rites of passage term used to describe those rituals that accompany the most significant moments (birth, puberty, marriage, and so on) in an individual's life. The term was coined by the French ethnographer and folklorist Charles-Arnold Kurr van Gennep (1873–1957).

ritual in religious devotion or service, the practice of certain set formulas which either mark a particular event in a person's life – such as birth rituals or death rituals, or which form a patterned daily, weekly, or annual cycle, for example Sunday services in Christian churches, or the Saturday Sabbath for Jews.

ritual slaughter either the killing of animals for religious purposes, such as sacrifice in order to appease a god, or, as in Islam and Judaism, the killing of an animal for food according to strict religious rules.

In Judaism, *shechitah* (ritual slaughter), whilst not prescribed in the Hebrew Bible, has been practiced from very early on. Both Muslim and Jewish laws try to reduce the likely suffering for an animal and under the Jewish *shechitah*, only those qualified and without infirmity can conduct the slaughter. Following a prayer of blessing, the animal's windpipe is severed in one cut. Argument rages as to whether ritual slaughter is inherently more or less cruel to animals than the processes of stunning and then cutting laid down in, for example, EEC legislation. In Hinduism, dispensation is given for the slaughter of goats, accompanied by the ◊mantra, whispered in the animal's ear: 'I am killing you now, but in a future incarnation you will have the right to kill me.'

Rivers William 1864–1922. British anthropologist and psychologist. His systematic study of kinship relations and his emphasis on ◊fieldwork helped to establish anthropology as a more scientific discipline.

As a psychologist he argued that perception was culturally conditioned and he applied the theories of Sigmund ◊Freud in his treatment of World War I shell-shock victims.

RNA *ribonucleic acid* nucleic acid involved in the process of translating ◊DNA, the genetic material into proteins. It is usually single- stranded, unlike the double-stranded DNA, and consists of a large number of nucleotides strung together, each of which comprises the sugar ribose, a phosphate group, and one of four bases (uracil, cytosine, adenine, or guanine). RNA is copied from DNA by the assemblage of free nucleotides against an unwound portion (a single strand) of the DNA, with DNA serving as the template. In this process, uracil (instead of the thymine in DNA) is paired with adenine, and guanine with cytosine, forming base pairs that then separate. The RNA then travels to the ribosomes where it serves to assemble proteins from free amino acids. In a few viruses, such as ◊retroviruses, RNA is the only hereditary material.

RNA occurs in three major forms, each with a different function in the synthesis of protein molecules. *Messenger RNA* (mRNA) acts as the template for protein synthesis. Each codon (a set of three bases) on the RNA molecule is matched up with the corresponding amino acid, in accordance with the ◊genetic code. This process (translation) takes place in the ribosomes, which are made up of proteins and *ribosomal RNA* (rRNA). *Transfer RNA* (tRNA) is responsible for combining with specific amino acids, and then matching up a special 'anticodon' sequence of its own with a codon on the mRNA. This is how the genetic code is translated into proteins.

Robbins Lionel (Baron Robbins of Clare Market) 1898– . British economist, best known for his work on the nature of economic analysis. He defined economics as 'the science which studies human behaviour as a relationship between ends and scarce means which have alternative uses.' He stressed the role of scarcity and constraints in economic decision-making, and distinguished positive and normative economics. Positive economics is concerned with hypotheses about economic relationships which can be tested by empirical evidence. Normative economics involves value judgements such as 'unemployment should be reduced to 5%'. Robbins' view was that economists should not make value judgements and should concern themselves with positive economics.

He chaired the committee of inquiry to review the pattern of higher education which recommended the extension of degree courses to polytechnics (now mostly universities) in its report, now known as *The Robbins Report*, 1963.

Robespierre Maximilien François Marie Isidore de 1758–1794. French politician in the ◊French Revolution. As leader of the ◊Jacobins in the National Convention, he supported the execution of Louis XVI and the overthrow of the right-wing republican Girondins, and in July 1793 was elected to the Committee of Public Safety. A year later he was guillotined; many believe that he was a scapegoat for the Reign of Terror since he ordered only 72 executions personally.

Robespierre, a lawyer, was elected to the National Assembly of 1789–91. His defence of democratic principles made him popular in Paris, while his disinterestedness won him the nickname of 'the Incorruptible'. His zeal for social reform and his attacks on the excesses of the extremists made him enemies on both right and left; a conspiracy was formed against him, and in July 1794 he was overthrown and executed by those who actually perpetrated the Reign of Terror.

Robin Hood in English legend, an outlaw and champion of the poor against the rich, said to have lived in Sherwood Forest, Nottinghamshire, during the reign of Richard I (1189–99). He feuded with the sheriff of Nottingham, accompanied by Maid Marian and a band of followers known as his 'merry men'. He appears in ballads from the 13th century, but his first datable appearance is in Langland's *Piers Plowman* about 1377.

Robinson Joan (Violet) 1903–1983. British economist who introduced Marxism to Keynesian economic theory. She expanded her analysis in *Economics of Perfect Competition* 1933.

Robinson Robert 1886–1975. English chemist, Nobel prizewinner 1947 for his research in organic chemistry on the structure of many natural products, including flower pigments and alkaloids. He formulated the electronic theory now used in organic chemistry.

Rococo movement in the arts and architecture in 18th-century Europe, tending towards lightness, elegance, delicacy, and decorative charm. The term 'Rococo' is derived from the French *rocaille* (rock- or shell-work), a style of interior decoration based on S-curves and scroll-like forms. Watteau's paintings and Sèvres porcelain belong to the French Rococo vogue. In the 1730s the movement became widespread in Europe, notably in the churches and palaces of S Germany and Austria. Chippendale furniture is an English example of the French Rococo style.

Other Rococo features include the use of fantastic ornament and pretty, naturalistic details. The architectural and interior design of the Amalienburg pavilion at Nymphenburg near Munich, Germany, and the Hôtel de Soubise pavilion in Paris, are typical of the movement. The painters Boucher and Fragonard both painted typically decorative Rococo panels for Parisian *hôtels* (town houses).

Rogers Carl 1902–1987. US psychologist who developed the client-centred approach to counselling and psychotherapy. This stressed the importance of clients making their own decisions and developing their own potential (self-actualization).

He emphasized the value of genuine interest on the part of a therapist who is also accepting and empathetic. Rogers's views became widely employed.

O liberty! O liberty! what crimes are committed in thy name!

Jeanne Manon Roland de la Platière
Remark on seeing a statue of Liberty as she was taken to the scaffold

---

Roland de la Platière Jeanne Manon (born Philipon) 1754–1793. French intellectual politician whose salon from 1789 was a focus of democratic discussion. Her ideas were influential after her husband Jean Marie Roland de la Platière (1734–1793) became minister of the interior 1792. As a supporter of the ◊Girondin party, opposed to Robespierre and Danton, she was condemned to the guillotine 1793 without being allowed to speak in her own defence. While in prison she wrote *Mémoires*.

role in the social sciences, the part(s) a person plays in society, either in helping the social system to work or in fulfilling social responsibilities towards others. *Role play* refers to the way in which children learn adult roles by acting them out in play (mothers and fathers, cops and robbers). Everyone has a number of roles to play in a society: for example, a woman may be an employee, mother, and wife at the same time.

Sociologists distinguish between formal roles, such as those of a doctor or politician, and informal roles, such as those of mother or husband, which are based on personal relationships. Social roles involve mutual expectations: a doctor can fulfil that role only if the patients play their part; a father requires the support of his children. They also distinguish between ascribed roles (those we are born with) and achieved roles (those we attain).

Role conflict arises where two or more of a person's roles are seen as incompatible.

Roman Catholicism one of the main divisions of the Christian religion, separate from the Orthodox Church from 1054, and headed by the pope. For history and beliefs, see ◊Christianity. Membership is about 585 million worldwide, concentrated in S Europe, Latin America, and the Philippines.

The Protestant churches separated from the Catholic with the Reformation in the 16th century, to which the Counter-Reformation was the Catholic response. An attempt to update Catholic doctrines in the late 19th century was condemned by Pope Pius X in 1907, and more recent moves have been rejected by John Paul II.

doctrine The focus of liturgical life is the Mass or Eucharist, and attendance is obligatory on Sundays and Feasts of Obligation such as Christmas or Easter. The Roman Catholic differs from the other Christian churches in that it acknowledges the supreme jurisdiction of the pope, infallible when he speaks *ex cathedra* ('from the throne'); in the doctrine of the Immaculate Conception (which states that the Virgin Mary, the mother of Jesus, was conceived without the original sin with which all other human beings are born); and in according a special place to the Virgin Mary.

organization Since the Second Vatican Council 1962–66, major changes have taken place. They include the use of vernacular or everyday language instead of Latin in the liturgy, and increased freedom amongst the religious and lay orders. The pope has an episcopal synod of 200 bishops elected by local hierarchies to collaborate in the government of the church. The priesthood is celibate and there is a strong emphasis on the monastic orders.

Under John Paul II from 1978, power has been more centralized, and bishops and cardinals have been chosen from the more traditionally minded clerics and from the Third World.

Roman religion religious system that retained early elements of animism (with reverence for stones and trees) and totemism, and had a strong domestic base in the ◊lares and *penates*, the cult of Janus and Vesta. It also had a main pantheon of gods derivative from the Greek one, which included Jupiter and Juno, Mars and Venus, Minerva, Diana, Ceres, and many lesser deities.

The deification of dead emperors served a political purpose and also retained the idea of family – that is, that those who had served the national family in life continued to care, as did one's ancestors, after their death. By the time of the empire, the educated classes tended towards stoicism or scepticism, but the following of mystery cults, especially within the army (see ◊Mithras), proved a strong rival to early Christianity.

Romanticism: An Idea and its Legacy

William Blake (1757–1827), in his famous painting of Sir Isaac Newton (1795), depicts the great scientist seated, in classical profile, holding a pair of compasses with which he measures the world. The feeling behind the image is ambivalent, but for Blake – Romantic poet and visionary artist – Newton was essentially an enemy: the supreme rationalist who had succeeded in reducing the mysterious workings of the world to the logic of the machine. This attitude encapsulates one of the most important aspects of the Romantic Movement (a movement of many facets and contradictory impulses): its reaction against the optimistic programme of the Enlightenment, against the belief that all things would eventually be known and understood if and when they were subjected to the cold, objective light of reason.

For the Romantics such a belief was reductive and demeaning because it rejected the idea of the infinite and the transcendent and, by implication, anything beyond the material and the empirical. Against this they argued that man was not simply a cog in a machine but a being able, in Blake's memorable words, 'to see a world in a grain of sand, and heaven in a wild flower ...', in other words capable, through the faculty of the imagination of seeing the spiritual rerality behind the physical appearance of things. Maximilien François Marie Isidore de Robespierre (1758–1794), at the height of the French Revolution, had abolished traditional religion and replaced it with a cult of Reason. Now that the revolutionary experiment had ended, Romanticism began to reinstate the spiritual dimension in a number of ways: François René Chateaubriand (1768–1848) attempted to revitalize the Christian tradition; the poet William Wordsworth (1770–1850), among others, practised a form of pantheistic nature worship; William Blake followed his own highly personal and mystical vision

Individuality emphasized

What all the many manifestations of Romanticism had in common was an emphasis on individuality. Developing out of the 18th-century cult of sensibility, it stressed the validity of subjectivity and emotion. Art became, for the first time, a form of self-expression. The Romantic artist, even when he refused to acknowledge the term, saw himself as a superior being, the possessor of a unique vision, subject only to the limitations of his own imagination. Hence the tendency for subject matter to be frequently drawn from the world of the bizarre, the fantastic, or the exotic. The painter Francisco Goya (1746–1828) inscribed plate 43 of his series of etchings, 'Los Caprichos' 1799, with the words 'the sleep of reason produces monsters', and time and again Romanticism presents us with nightmare images of the uncontrollable and the extreme – from the opulent brutality of Eugéne Delacroix's (1798–1863) paintings to the supernatural horror of the Gothic novel. It was this pursuit of the morbid and irrational, specifically in the weird tales of E T A. Hoffmann, that led Johan Wolfgang von Goethe (1749–1832) to describe Romanticism as a 'sickness' and Classicism as 'health'.

However not all Romantic artists gave rein to the darker sides of their imaginations. Nature was as frequently depicted as an ideal of purity and serenity, as it was as a place of wildness and elemental power. To be in touch with nature was to be more yourself. Landscape painters increasingly studied directly from nature, even though their finished works continued to be produced in the studio. The English painter John Constable (1776–1837) attempted, and often succeeded, in synthesizing in his work an objective approach to natural phenomena with a sense of the personal and poetic. That a non mechanistic science could be reconcilable with the world of the imagination can be seen, not just in the work of Constable, but in the writings of Samuel Taylor Coleridge (1772–1834), Novalis (1772–1801) and Victor Hugo (1802–1885), where science is seen as opening a door onto the Infinite.

Inherent conservatism

Many cultural historian have stressed the conservative nature of Romanticism – despite the diversity of specific political opinion within it. The French Revolution, welcomed by many including Wordsworth, came to be seen as a nightmare of rationality that failed to take into account individual feeling and human nature. Napoleon (1769–1821) was initially admired as a man of destiny who would rescue the true aims of the Revolution and cast down the petty despots of Europe. Disillusionment came when he declared himself Emperor in 1804 – thus causing Ludwig van Beethoven (1770–1827) to delete the dedication to him of the Eroica Symphony – but he continued to maintain a hold on the Romantic imagination as a man of superhuman will and vision who had dared much but tragically failed. Such hero-worship can also be found in the cult of Lord Byron (1788–1824) – the melancholic Romantic hero par excellence – as well as in the biographical and historical writings of Thomas Carlyle (1795–1881). Carlyle also shared with many writers a nostalgia for the Middle Ages, as a simpler more authentic time whose spirit survived, and could be reproduced, in Gothic architecture. This search for a greater naturalness and authenticity is clearly a legacy of Jean-Jacques Rousseau (1712–78). It can been seen in the period's growing admiration for national traditions and folklore, for instance, the tales collected by the Brothers Grimm (Jakob Ludwig Karl, 1785–1863 and Wilhelm 1786–1859), which developed, particularly in German-speaking countries, into a wider sense of national identity as the unique spirit of a particular people. The combination of these ideas, most clearly articulated by the German philosopher Johann Gottfried von Herder (1744–1803), has been identified as the seed from which fascism grew.

Joe Staines

Romanticism in literature, music, and the visual arts, a style that emphasizes the imagination, emotions, and creativity of the individual artist. Romanticism also refers specifically to late-18th- and early-19th-century European culture, as contrasted with 18th-century ◊Classicism.

Inspired by the ideas of Jean Jacques ◊Rousseau and by contemporary social change and revolution (US, French), Romanticism emerged as a reaction to 18th-century values, asserting emotion and intuition over rationalism, the importance of the individual over social conformity, and the exploration of natural and psychic wildernesses over classical restraint. Major themes of Romantic art and literature include a love of atmospheric landscapes (see ◊sublime); nostalgia for the past, particularly the Gothic; a love of the primitive, including folk traditions; cult of the hero figure, often an artist or political revolutionary; romantic passion; mysticism; and a fascination with death.

In *literature*, Romanticism is represented by Novalis, Brentano, Eichendorff, and Tieck in Germany, who built on the work of the Sturm and Drang movement; Wordsworth, Coleridge, Shelley, Byron, and Walter Scott in Britain; and Victor Hugo, Lamartine, George Sand, and Dumas Père in France. The work of the US writers Poe, Melville, Longfellow, and Whitman reflects the influence of Romanticism.

In *art*, Caspar David Friedrich in German and J M W Turner in England are outstanding landscape painters of the Romantic tradition, while Henry Fuseli and William Blake represent a mystical and fantastic trend. The French painter Delacroix is often cited as the quintessential Romantic artist.

In *music*, the term is loosely applied to most 19th compositions but is associated particularly with programme music, such as the *Symphonie fantastique* by Berlioz; the song cycle, as developed by Schubert; and, most significantly, opera, culminating in the late Romanticism of Wagner and Verdi.

Rome, Treaties of two international agreements signed 25 March 1957 by Belgium, France, West Germany, Italy, Luxembourg, and the Netherlands, which established the European Economic Community (◊European Community) and the European Atomic Energy Commission (EURATOM).

The terms of the economic treaty, which came into effect 1 Jan 1958, provided for economic cooperation, reduction (and eventual removal) of customs barriers, and the free movement of capital, goods, and labour between the member countries, together with common agricultural and trading policies. Subsequent new members of the European Community have been obliged to accept these terms.

rood alternative name for the cross of Christ, often applied to the large crucifix placed on a beam or screen at the entrance to the chancel of a church.

Roosevelt Franklin D(elano) 1882–1945. 32nd president of the USA 1933–45, a Democrat. He served as governor of New York 1929–33. Becoming president during the Great Depression, he launched the ◊*New Deal* economic and social reform programme, which made him popular with the people. After the outbreak of World War II he introduced lend-lease for the supply of war materials and services to the Allies and drew up the Atlantic Charter of solidarity. Once the USA had entered the war 1941, he spent much time in meetings (including the Québec, Tehran, and ◊Yalta conferences with Allied leaders).

Born in Hyde Park, New York, of a wealthy family, Roosevelt was educated in Europe and at Harvard and Columbia universities, and became a lawyer. In 1910 he was elected to the New York state senate. He held the assistant secretaryship of the navy in Wilson's administrations 1913–21, and did much to increase the efficiency of the navy during World War I. He suffered from polio from 1921 but returned to politics, winning the governorship of New York State in 1929.

When he first became president 1933, Roosevelt inculcated a new spirit of hope by his skilful 'fireside chats' on the radio and his inaugural-address statement: 'The only thing we have to fear is fear itself.' Surrounding himself by a 'Brain Trust' of experts, he immediately launched his reform programme. Banks were reopened, federal credit was restored, the gold standard was abandoned, and the dollar devalued. During the first hundred days of his administration, major legislation to facilitate industrial and agricultural recovery was enacted. In 1935 he introduced the Utilities Act, directed against abuses in the large holding companies, and the Social Security Act, providing for disability and retirement insurance. The presidential election 1936 was won entirely on the record of the New Deal. During 1935–36 Roosevelt was involved in a conflict over the composition of the Supreme Court, following its nullification of major New Deal measures as unconstitutional. In 1938 he introduced measures for farm relief and the improvement of working conditions.

In his foreign policy, Roosevelt endeavoured to use his influence to restrain Axis aggression, and to establish 'good neighbour' relations with other countries in the Americas. Soon after the outbreak of war, he launched a vast rearmament programme, introduced conscription, and provided for the supply of armaments to the Allies on a 'cash-and-carry' basis. In spite of strong isolationist opposition, he broke a long-standing precedent in running for a third term; he was re-elected 1940. He announced that the USA would become the 'arsenal of democracy'. Roosevelt was eager for US entry into the war on behalf of the Allies. In addition to his revulsion for Hitler, he wanted to establish the USA as a world power, filling the vacuum he expected to be left by the breakup of the British Empire. He was restrained by isolationist forces in Congress, and some argued that he welcomed the Japanese attack on Pearl Harbor.

Public opinion, however, was in favour of staying out of the war, so Roosevelt and the military chiefs deliberately kept back the intelligence reports received from the British and others concerning the imminent Japanese attack on the US naval base at Pearl Harbor in Hawaii.

The deaths at Pearl Harbor 7 Dec 1941 incited public opinion, and the USA entered the war. From this point on, Roosevelt concerned himself solely with the conduct of the war. He participated in the Washington 1942 and Casablanca 1943 conferences to plan the Mediterranean assault, and the conferences in Québec, Cairo, and Tehran 1943, and Yalta 1945, at which the final preparations were made for the Allied victory. He was re-elected for a fourth term 1944, but died 1945.

Rorschach test in psychology, method of diagnosis involving the use of inkblot patterns that subjects are asked to interpret, to help indicate personality type, degree of intelligence, and emotional stability. It was invented by the Swiss psychiatrist Hermann Rorschach (1884–1922).

Rorty Richard McKay 1931– . US philosopher. Rorty's main concern has been to trace the personal and social implications of our changing perception of human identity, and his work draws inspiration from US philosopher John ◊Dewey and German social theorist Jürgen ◊Habermas.

In his *Contingency, Irony and Solidarity* 1989, Rorty argues that language, self, and community are determined by history and are not expressions of an essential human nature. When we accept that human identity is not fixed, he argues, we then need to reconcile two seemingly conflicting consequences: at the personal level, the possibility of autonomy and self-creation; and at the public level, the need to create a freer and less cruel society.

rosary string of beads used in a number of religions, including Buddhism, Christianity, and Islam. The term also refers to a form of prayer used by Catholics, consisting of 150 ◊Ave Marias and 15 ◊Paternosters and Glorias, or to a string of 165 beads for keeping count of these prayers; it is linked with the adoration of the Virgin Mary.

Roscellinus Johannes c. 1050–c. 1122. Philosopher regarded as the founder of ◊scholasticism because of his defence of ◊nominalism (the idea that classes of things are simply names and have no objective reality) against ◊Anselm.

Rosh Hashanah two-day holiday that marks the start of the Jewish New Year (first new moon after the autumn equinox), traditionally announced by blowing a ram's horn (a ◊shofar).

Rosicrucians group of early 17th-century philosophers who claimed occult powers and employed the terminology of ◊alchemy to expound their mystical doctrines (said to derive from ◊Paracelsus). The name comes from books published in 1614 and 1615, attributed to Christian Rosenkreutz ('rosy cross'), most probably a pen name but allegedly a writer living around 1460. Several societies have been founded in Britain and the USA that claim to be their successors, such as the Rosicrucian Fraternity (1614 in Germany, 1861 in the USA).

Rousseau was the first militant low-brow.

Jean-JacquesRousseau
Isaiah Berlin 1906– ,
philosopher and historian of ideas.
The Observer 9 November, 1952

Rousseau Jean-Jacques 1712–1778. French social philosopher and writer. In his *Du Contrat social/Social Contract* 1762, he argued that government is justified only if sovereignty stays with the people. Hence he rejected representative democracy in favour of direct democracy, modelled on the Greek *polis* and the Swiss *canton.* His ideas had a significant influence on the French Revolution and on ◊Romanticism. His characterization of the state as a person reappeared in Hegel's political theory (see ◊organicism). In the novel *Emile* 1762 he outlined a new theory of education.

Rousseau was born in Geneva, Switzerland. *Discourses on the Origins of Inequality* 1754 made his name: he denounced civilized society and postulated the paradox of the superiority of the '◊noble savage'. *Social Contract* stated that a government could be legitimately overthrown if it failed to express the general will of the people. *Emile* was written as an example of how to elicit the unspoiled nature and abilities of children, based on natural development and the power of example.

Rousseau's ideas were condemned by philosophers, the clergy, and the public, and he lived in exile in England for a year, being helped by Scottish philosopher David Hume until they fell out. He was a contributor to the *Encyclopédie* and also wrote operas. *Confessions*, published posthumously 1782, was a frank account of his occasionally immoral life and was a founding work of autobiography.

Rowbotham Sheila 1943– . British socialist, feminist, historian, lecturer, and writer. Her pamphlet *Women's Liberation and the New Politics* 1970 laid down fundamental approaches and demands of the emerging ◊women's movement.

Rowbotham taught in schools and then became involved with the Workers' Educational Association. An active socialist since the early 1960s, she has contributed to several left-wing journals. Her books include *Hidden from History*, *Women's Consciousness, Man's World* both 1973, *Beyond the Fragments* 1979, and *The Past is Before Us* 1989.

Royce Josiah 1855–1916. US idealist philosopher who in *The Conception of God* 1895 and *The Conception of Immortality* 1900 interpreted Christianity in philosophical terms. His philosophy saw God as cosmic purpose, which man embraces.

Rudra early Hindu storm god, most of whose attributes were later taken over by ◊Siva.

rule of law doctrine that no individual, however powerful, is above the law. The principle had a significant influence on attempts to restrain the arbitrary use of power by rulers and on the growth of legally enforceable human rights in many Western countries. It is often used as a justification for separating legislative from judicial power.

Rumford Benjamin Thompson, Count Rumford 1753–1814. American-born British physicist. In 1798, impressed by the seemingly inexhaustible amounts of heat generated in the boring of a cannon, he published his theory that heat is a mode of vibratory motion, not a substance.

Rumford spied for the British in the American Revolution, and was forced to flee from America to England 1776. He travelled in Europe, and was created a count of the Holy Roman Empire for services to the elector of Bavaria 1791. He founded the Royal Institute in London 1799.

Government and co-operation are in all things the laws of life; anarchy and competition the laws of death.

John Ruskin
Unto this Last

Ruskin John 1819–1900. English art critic and social critic. He published five volumes of *Modern Painters* 1843–60 and *The Seven Lamps of Architecture* 1849, in which he stated his philosophy of art. His writings hastened the appreciation of painters considered unorthodox at the time, such as J M W Turner and the Pre-Raphaelite Brotherhood. His later writings were concerned with social and economic problems.

Born in London, the only child of a prosperous wine-merchant, Ruskin was able to travel widely and was educated at Oxford. In 1848 he married Euphemia 'Effie' Chalmers Gray, but six years later the marriage was annulled.

In *The Stones of Venice* 1851–53, he drew moral lessons from architectural history. From 1860 he devoted himself to social and economic problems, in which he adopted an individual and radical outlook exalting the 'craftsman'. He became increasingly isolated in his views. To this period belong a series of lectures and pamphlets (*Unto this Last* 1860, *Sesame and Lilies* 1865 on the duties of men and women, *The Crown of Wild Olive* 1866).

Ruskin was Slade professor of art at Oxford 1869–79, and he made a number of social experiments, such as St George's Guild, for the establishment of an industry on socialist lines. His last years were spent at Brantwood, Cumbria.

Ruskin College was founded in Oxford 1899 by an American, Walter Vrooman, to provide education in the social sciences for working people. It is supported by trade unions and other organizations.

Three passions, simple but overwhelmingly strong, have governed my life: the longing for love, the search for knowledge, and unbearable pity for the suffering of mankind.

Bertrand Russell, 3rd Earl Russell
Autobiography prologue

Russell Bertrand (Arthur William), 3rd Earl Russell 1872–1970. English philosopher and mathematician who contributed to the development of modern mathematical logic and wrote about social issues. His works include *Principia Mathematica* 1910–13 (with A N ◊Whitehead), in which he attempted to show that mathematics could be reduced to a branch of logic; *The Problems of Philosophy* 1912; and *A History of Western Philosophy* 1946. He was an outspoken liberal pacifist.

The grandson of Prime Minister John Russell, he was educated at Trinity College, Cambridge, where he read mathematics and specialized in philosophy, later becoming a lecturer. Russell's pacifist attitude in World War I lost him the lectureship, and he was imprisoned for six months for an article he wrote in a pacifist journal. His *Introduction to Mathematical Philosophy* 1919 was written in prison. He and

A sense of duty is useful in work, but offensive in personal relations. People wish to be liked, not to be endured with patient resignation.

Bertrand Russell, 3rd Earl Russell
Conquest of Happiness ch 10

his wife ran a progressive school 1927–32. After visits to the USSR and China, he went to the USA 1938 and taught at many universities. In 1940, a US court disqualified him from teaching at City College of New York because of his liberal moral views. He later returned to England and was a fellow of Trinity College. He was a life-long pacifist except during World War II. From 1949 he advocated nuclear disarmament and until 1963 was on the Committee of 100, an offshoot of the Campaign for Nuclear Disarmament.

All science is either physics or stamp collecting.

Ernest Rutherford
Rutherford at Manchester J B Birks

Among his other works are *Principles of Mathematics* 1903, *Principles of Social Reconstruction* 1917, *Marriage and Morals* 1929, *An Enquiry into Meaning and Truth* 1940, *New Hopes for a Changing World* 1951, and *Autobiography* 1967–69.

Russell Charles Taze 1852–1916. US religious figure, founder of the ◊Jehovah's Witness sect 1872.

Russell Dora Winifred (born Black) 1894–1986. English feminist who married Bertrand ◊Russell 1921. The 'openness' of their marriage (she subsequently had children by another man) was a matter of controversy. She was a founding member of the National Council for Civil Liberties in 1934.

She was educated at Girton College, Cambridge, of which she became a Fellow. In 1927 the Russells founded the progressive Beacon Hill School in Hampshire. After World War II she actively supported the Campaign for Nuclear Disarmament.

Russian revolution two revolutions Feb–March and Oct–Nov 1917. Food shortages, war weariness, and a breakdown in government control created mass demonstrations in Petrograd, which led to the overthrow of Tsar Nicholas II and the Romanov dynasty. The resulting provisional government, led by Kerensky, proved incapable of solving the pressing economic and social problems of the state. The Bolsheviks, under ◊Lenin attracted widespread support for their policies which included ending the war and redistributing land to the peasantry. In October, Bolshevik workers and sailors seized government buildings and took over power. Lenin's success in maintaining control, ending the war with the Central Powers and defeating pro-Tsarist forces culminated in the establishment of the Union of Soviet Socialist Republics.

Ruth in the Old Testament, Moabite ancestor of David (king of Israel) by her second marriage to Boaz. When her first husband died, she preferred to stay with her mother-in-law, Naomi, rather than return to her own people.

Rutherford Ernest 1871–1937. New Zealand-born British physicist, a pioneer of modern atomic science. His main research was in the

---

Russian Revolution: chronology (Western calendar)

1894	Beginning of the reign of Tsar Nicholas II.
1898	Formation of the Social Democratic Party among industrial workers under the influence of Plekhanov and Lenin.
1901	Formation of the Socialist Revolutionary Party.
1903	Split in Social Democratic Party at the party's second congress (London Conference) into Bolsheviks and Mensheviks.
1905	Jan: 'Bloody Sunday', where repression of workers in St Petersburg led to widespread strikes and the '1905 Revolution'. Oct: strikes and the first 'soviet' (local revolutionary council) in St Petersburg. October constitution provided for new parliament (Duma). Dec: insurrection of workers in Moscow. Punitive repression by the 'Black Hundreds'.
1914	July: outbreak of war between Russia and the Central Powers.
1917	March: outbreak of riots in Petrograd (St Petersburg). Tsar Nicholas abdicated. Provisional government established under Prince Lvov. Power struggles between government and Petrograd soviet. April: Lenin arrived in Petrograd. He demanded the transfer of power to soviets; an end to the war; the seizure of land by the peasants; control of industry by the workers. July: Bolsheviks attempted to seize power in Petrograd. Trotsky arrested and Lenin in hiding. Kerensky became head of a provisional government. Sept: Kornilov coup failed owing to strike by workers. Kerensky's government weakened. Nov: Bolshevik Revolution. Military revolutionary committee and Red Guards seized government offices and the Winter Palace, arresting all the members of the provisional government. Second All-Russian Congress of Soviets created the Council of Peoples Commissars as new governmental authority. Led by Lenin, with Trotsky as commissar for war and Stalin as commissar for national minorities. Land Decree ordered immediate distribution of land to the peasants. Banks were nationalized and national debt repudiated. Elections to the Constituent Assembly gave large majority to the Socialist Revolutionary Party. Bolsheviks a minority.
1918	Jan: Constituent Assembly met in Petrograd but almost immediately broken up by Red Guards. March: Treaty of Brest-Litovsk marked the end of the war with the Central Powers but with massive losses of territory. July: murder of the tsar and his family.
1918–20	Civil War in Russia between Red Army led by Trotsky and White Russian forces. Red Army ultimately victorious.
1923	6 July: constitution of USSR adopted.

---

field of radio-activity, and he discovered alpha, beta, and gamma rays. He named the nucleus, and was the first to recognize the nuclear nature of the atom. Nobel prize 1908.

Ryle Gilbert 1900–1976. British philosopher. His *The Concept of Mind* 1949 set out to show that the distinction between an inner and an outer world in philosophy and psychology cannot be sustained. He ridiculed the mind–body dualism of ◊Descartes as the doctrine of 'the Ghost in the Machine'.

The dogma of the Ghost in the Machine.
Gilbert Ryle
The Concept of Mind ch 1

Ryle Martin 1918–1984. English radio-astronomer. At the Mullard Radio Astronomy Observatory, Cambridge, he developed the technique of sky-mapping using 'aperture synthesis', combining smaller dish aerials to give the characteristics of one large one. His work on the distribution of radio sources in the universe brought confirmation of the ◊Big Bang theory. He won, with Antony ◊Hewish, the Nobel Prize for Physics 1974.

Ryobu Shinto in Japan, a syncretistic version of ◊Shintoism which combined with elements of Buddhism. It is based upon the writings of Gyogi (670–749) and involves the joint celebration of each other's ceremonies by Buddhist and Shinto priests. It was popular in rural areas where the Buddhist priests had to accommodate themselves to Shinto deities and believers. It was banned during the Meiji period (1868–1912) because it was seen as a watering down of Shintoism.

S

Sabatier Paul 1854–1951. French chemist. He found in 1897 that if a mixture of ethylene and hydrogen was passed over a column of heated nickel, the ethylene changed into ethane. Further work revealed that nickel could be used to catalyse numerous chemical reactions. Sabatier shared the 1912 Nobel Prize for Chemistry with François Grignard.

Sabbatarianism belief held by some Protestant Christians in the strict observance of Sunday as the Sabbath, following the fourth commandment of the ◊Bible. It began in the 17th century.

Sabbatarianism has taken various forms, including an insistence on the Sabbath lasting a full 24 hours; prohibiting sports and games and the buying and selling of goods on the Sabbath; and ignoring public holidays when they fall on a Sunday.

Sabbath the seventh day of the week, commanded by God in the Old Testament as a sacred day of rest; in Judaism, from sunset Friday to sunset Saturday. Some Christians regard Sunday (the first day of the week, the day of the ◊Resurrection) as the Sabbath.

Sabeans religious group mentioned favourably in the ◊Qur'an alongside Jews and Christians as 'People of the Book'. They were thought to be the same as the ◊Mandaeans.

Sacher-Masoch Leopold von 1836–1895. Austrian novelist. His books dealt with the sexual pleasure of having pain inflicted on oneself, hence ◊masochism.

sacrament in Christian usage, observances forming the visible sign of inward grace. In the Roman Catholic Church there are seven sacraments: baptism, Holy Communion (Eucharist or Mass), confirmation, rite of reconciliation (confession and penance), holy orders, matrimony, and the anointing of the sick.

Only the first two are held to be essential by the Church of England.

sacred in ancient religion, that holy place belonging to the gods, in contrast to profane places where the gods are absent. More recently the term is used to mean anything holy or relating to God that is set apart from the profane world. The Sacred Heart of Jesus has become an object of devotion in the Roman Catholic Church, originating with the medieval mystics.

sacred cow any person, institution, or custom that is considered above criticism. The term comes from the Hindu belief that cows are sacred and must not be killed.

Sacred Thread ceremony Hindu initiation ceremony which marks the passage to maturity for boys of the upper three castes; it usually takes place between the ages of five and twelve. It is regarded as a second birth and the castes whose males are entitled to undergo the ceremony are called 'twice born'.

sacrifice in religion, the act of sanctifying or dedicating an object to a god, as a religious act of self-denial. Through it the giver seeks to enter into communion with a supernatural being. In some religions, and especially in earlier times, an animal or a human being may be killed as a sacrifice (see ◊human sacrifice). Many faiths today encourage believers to give up something they value as a sacrifice, or to give offerings of food.

The Hebrew Bible gives instructions for a number of different sacrifices in different circumstances, and also records Abraham's willingness to sacrifice his son Isaac when God asked it of him (at the last moment God provided a ram instead). A similar story is found in Islam, with Ishmael as the intended victim. For Christians, the supreme sacrifice (compared with the sacrificial lamb of the Old Testament) was that of Jesus Christ giving himself to be killed on the cross.

Sadducee (Hebrew 'righteous') member of the ancient Hebrew political party and religious group of ◊Judaism that formed in pre-Roman Palestine in the first century BC. They were the group of priestly aristocrats in Jerusalem until the final destruction of the Temple AD 70.

They opposed the ◊Pharisees and favoured Hellenization. They stood for the hereditary high priesthood, the Temple, and sacrifice. Sadducees denied the immortality of the soul and the existence of angels, and maintained the religious law in all its strictness. Many of their ideas and practices resurfaced in medieval Jewish groups after Pharisee ideas dominated the dispersed Jews of the western Roman empire.

Sade Donatien Alphonse François, Comte de, known as the *Marquis de Sade* 1740–1814. French author who was imprisoned for sexual offences and finally committed to an asylum. He wrote plays and novels dealing explicitly with a variety of sexual practices, including ◊sadism.

sadhu in Hinduism, a wandering holy man who devotes himself to the goal of moksha, or liberation from the cycle of reincarnation.

sadism tendency to derive pleasure (usually sexual) from inflicting physical or mental pain on others. The term is derived from the Marquis de ◊Sade.

sadomasochism a form of deviant sexual behaviour that combines ◊sadism and ◊masochism. The term was coined by sexologist Richard von Krafft-Ebing (1840–1902) 1907.

saga prose narrative written down in the 11th–13th centuries in Norway and Iceland. The sagas range from family chronicles, such as the *Landnamabok* of Ari (1067–1148), to legendary and anonymous works such as the *Njala* saga.

Other sagas include the *Heimskringla* of Snorri Sturluson celebrating Norwegian kings (1178–1241), the *Sturlunga* of Sturla Thordsson (1214–1284), and the legendary and anonymous *Laxdaela* and *Grettla* sagas. 'Family saga' is often used of a novel whose protagonists span two or more generations.

Sagan Carl 1934– . US physicist and astronomer, renowned for his popular science writings and broadcasts. His books include *Cosmic Connection: An Extraterrestrial Perspective* 1973; *Broca's Brain: Reflections on the Romance of Science* 1979; *Cosmos* 1980, based on his television series of that name; and the science-fiction novel *Contact* 1985.

Sagan became professor of astronomy and space science at Cornell University, New York, in 1970. His research concerned the chemistry and physics of planetary atmospheres, the origin of life on Earth, the probable climatic effects of nuclear war, and the possibility of life on other planets.

saint holy man or woman respected for their wisdom, spirituality, and dedication to their faith; in the New Testament and in some Christian groups, all Christians are called saints. Within the Roman Catholic Church a saint is officially recognized through ◊canonization by the pope. Many saints are associated with miracles and canonization usually occurs after a thorough investigation of the lives and miracles attributed to them. In the Orthodox Church saints are recognized by the patriarch and Holy Synod after recommendation by local churches. The term is also used in Buddhism for individuals who have led a virtuous and holy life, such as Kūkai (775–835), founder of the Japanese Buddhist Shingon group. For individual saints, see under forename, for example ◊Paul, St.

In 1970 Pope Paul VI revised the calendar of saints' days: excluded were Barbara, Catherine, Christopher, and Ursula (as probably nonexistent); optional veneration might be given to George, Januarius, Nicholas (Santa Claus), and Vitus; insertions for obligatory veneration include St Thomas More and the Uganda martyrs.

In the revised Calendar of Saints 1970, only 58 saints were regarded as of worldwide importance. In 1980 the Church of England added 20 saints from the Post-Reformation era, including Josephine Butler, Thomas More, King Charles I, John Bunyan, and William Wilberforce.

St John, Order of (full title *Knights Hospitallers of St John of Jerusalem*) oldest order of Christian chivalry, named from the hospital at Jerusalem founded about 1048 by merchants of Amalfi for pilgrims, whose travel routes the knights defended from the Muslims. Today there are about 8,000 knights (male and female), and the Grand Master is the world's highest ranking Roman Catholic lay person.

On being forced to leave Palestine, the knights went to Cyprus 1291, to Rhodes 1309, and to Malta (granted to them by Emperor Charles V) 1530. Expelled by Napoleon (on his way to Egypt) 1798, they established their headquarters in Rome (Palazzo di Malta).

Saint-Simon Claude Henri, Comte de 1760–1825. French socialist who fought in the American Revolution and was imprisoned during the French Revolution. He advocated an atheist society ruled by technicians and industrialists in *Du Système industrielle/The Industrial System* 1821.

Sakharov Andrei Dmitrievich 1921–1989. Soviet physicist, known both as the 'father of the Soviet H-bomb' and as an outspoken human-rights campaigner. In 1948 he joined

Patron Saints

saint	occupation	saint	occupation
Adam	gardeners	Honoratus	bakers
Albert the Great	scientists	Isidore	farmers
Alphonsus Liguori	theologians	Ivo	lawyers
Amand	brewers, hotelkeepers	James	labourers
Andrew	fishermen	Jean-Baptiste Vianney	priests
Angelico	artists	Jerome	librarians
Anne	miners	Joan of Arc	soldiers
Apollonia	dentists	John Baptist de la Salle	teachers
Augustine	theologians	John Bosco	labourers
Barbara	builders, miners	John of God	book trade, nurses, printers
Bernadino (Feltre)	bankers	Joseph	carpenters
Bernadino of Siena	advertisers	Joseph (Arimathea)	gravediggers, undertakers
Camillus de Lellis	nurses	Joseph (Cupertino)	astronauts
Catherine of Alexandria	librarians, philosophers	Julian the Hospitaler	hotelkeepers
Cecilla	musicians, poets, singers	Lawrence	cooks
Christopher	motorists, sailors	Leonard	prisoners
Cosmos and Damian	barbers, chemists, doctors, surgeons	Louis	sculptors
		Lucy	glassworkers, writers
Crispin	shoemakers	Luke	artists, butchers, doctors, glass-workers, sculptors surgeons
Crispinian	shoemakers		
David	poets		
Dismas	undertakers	Martha	cooks, housewives, servants, waiters
Dominic	astronomers		
Dorothy	florists	Martin of Tours	soldiers
Eligins	blacksmiths, jewellers metalworkers	Matthew	accountants, bookkeepers tax collectors
Eramus	sailors	Michael	grocers, policemen
Fiacre	gardeners, taxi drivers	Our Lady of Loreto	aviators
Florian	firemen	Peter	fishermen
Francis de Sales	authors, editors, journalists	Raymond Nonnatus	midwives
Francis of Assis	merchants	Sebastian	athletes, soldiers
Francis of Paola	sailors	Thérèse of Lisieux	florists
Gabriel	messengers, postal workers, radio workers, television workers	Thomas (Apostle)	architects, builders
		Thomas Aquinas	philosophers, scholars, students, theologians
Genesius	actors, secretaries	Thomas More	lawyers
George	soldiers	Vitus	actors, comedians, dancers
Gregory	singers	Wenceslaus	brewers
Gregory the Great	muscians, teachers	Zita	sevants
Homobonus	tailors		

Igor Tamm in developing the hydrogen bomb; he later protested against Soviet nuclear tests and was a founder of the Soviet Human Rights Committee, winning the Nobel Peace Prize 1975. In 1980 he was sent to internal exile in Gorky (now Nizhni-Novgorod) for criticizing Soviet action in Afghanistan. At the end of 1986 he was allowed to return to Moscow and resume his place in the Soviet Academy of Sciences.

He was elected to the Congress of the USSR People's Deputies (CUPD) 1989, where he emerged as leader of its radical reform grouping prior to his death later the same year.

Sakti or *Shakti* the female principle in ◊Hinduism.

Sākyamuni the historical ◊Buddha, called *Shaka* in Japan (because Gautama was of the Śakya clan).

Salam Abdus 1926– . Pakistani physicist. In 1967 he proposed a theory linking the electromagnetic and weak nuclear forces, also arrived at independently by Steven Weinberg. In 1979 he was the first person from his country to receive a Nobel prize, which he shared with Weinberg and Sheldon Glashow.

Abdus Salam became a scientist by accident, when he won a scholarship to Cambridge in 1945 from the Punjab Small Peasants' welfare fund; he had intended to join the Indian civil service. He subsequently worked on the structure of matter at the Cavendish Laboratory.

salat or *salah* the daily prayers that are one of the Five Pillars of ◊Islam.

Muslims are required to pray five times a day, the first prayer being before dawn and the last after dusk. Prayer must be preceded by ritual washing and may be said in any clean place, facing the direction of Mecca. The prayers, which are recited in Arabic, follow a fixed series of words and movements.

Salic law a law adopted in the Middle Ages by several European royal houses, excluding women from succession to the throne. The name derives mistakenly from the Salian or northern division of the Franks, who supposedly practised it.

In Sweden 1980 such a provision was abrogated to allow Princess Victoria to become crown princess.

Salk Jonas Edward 1914– . US physician and microbiologist. In 1954 he developed the original vaccine that led to virtual eradication of paralytic polio in industrialized countries. He was director of the Salk Institute for Biological Studies, University of California, San Diego, 1963–75.

salon meeting place provided by a wealthy host or hostess for writers, artists, and musicians. The term was first used in 17th-century Paris to describe the gatherings of artists and intellectuals in the houses of rich and cultured ladies. The tradition of the 'literary hostess' has continued in Europe and the USA.

saltation in biology, the idea that an abrupt genetic change can occur in an individual, which then gives rise to a new species. The idea has now been largely discredited, although the appearance of polyploid individuals can be considered an example.

All things excellent are as difficult as they are rare.

salvation
Benedict (Baruch) Spinoza, 1632–1677, Dutch philosopher of Portugese-Jewish descent.
The Ethics V. xlii scholium

---

salvation being saved. In Christianity individuals are thought of as being saved from eternal punishment through Christ's death on the cross, although this may be understood in different ways. In Buddhism, especially in Chinese and Japanese Buddhism, people can be saved from the endless cycle of reincarnation through ◊bodhisattvas or through ◊Amida Buddha. In Hinduism, especially in the bhakti tradition, devotion to a god can bring salvation from reincarnation, open to those who have realised their true nature as *brahman* (spirit).

I know that my redeemer liveth, and that he shall stand at the latter day upon the earth: / And though after my skin worms destroy this body, yet in my flesh shall I see God.

salvation
Bible, the sacred book of the Jewish and Christian religions.
Job 19:25

Salvation Army Christian evangelical, social-service, and social-reform organization, originating 1865 in London, England, with the work of William ◊Booth. Today a worldwide organization, it has four million members in over 70 countries. It has military titles for its officials, is renowned for its brass bands, and its weekly journal is the *War Cry*.

Originally called the Christian Revival Association, it was renamed the East London Christian Mission in 1870 and from 1878 has been known as the Salvation Army. Doctrine and ritual have never been primary concerns of the Salvation Army, which devotes itself to preaching redemption from a sinful life.

samadhi in Hinduism and Buddhism, a total absorption in meditation. For Buddhists it is one of the three main components (with *prajna*, wisdom, and *sila*, ethical living) in the Buddhist path to ◊nirvana. It refers to meditation and to clearing the mind of all thoughts. In such a state, the individual is receptive to enlightenment. In Hinduism it represents a trance-like state in which mental activity ceases.

Samaritan member or descendant of the colonists forced to settle in Samaria (now N Israel) by the Assyrians after their occupation of the ancient kingdom of Israel 722 BC. Samaritans adopted a form of Judaism, but adopted only the Pentateuch, the five books of Moses of the Old Testament, and regarded their temple on Mount Gerizim as the true sanctuary.

They remained a conservative, separate people and declined under Muslim rule, with only a few hundred, in a small community at Nablus, surviving today.

Samaritans voluntary organization aiding those tempted to suicide or despair, established in 1953 in the UK. Groups of lay people, often consulting with psychiatrists, psychotherapists, and doctors, offer friendship and counselling to those using their emergency telephone numbers, day or night.

The Samaritans were founded at St Stephen's Church, Walbrook, London, by the rector, Chad Varah (1911–ㅤ), and subsequently extended throughout Britain and overseas. They are inspired by the story of the 'good Samaritan' of the New Testament, who aided an injured traveller who had been attacked and robbed, instead of 'walking by on the other side of the road'.

Samkhya or *Sankhya* Hindu philosophy of discrimination between matter and spirit taught in the ◊Upanishads. One of the six orthodox doctrines of Hindu philosophy, Samkhya describes the universe as two forms, *prakriti* (nature) and *purusha* (the individual spirit). Matter is divided into 25 elements, beginning with earth, water, fire, air, and space. The 25th element is time. Samkhya seeks that which is beyond these 25 elements, namely pure spirit.

samsara in Hinduism and Buddhism, the cycle of repeated birth and death in the material world, which is held to be a place of suffering. The goal of yoga is release from samsara.

samskaras in Hindu tradition, the ceremonies that mark the passage of life. The 14 samskaras are conception, blessing the child during pregnancy, the birth ceremony, name-giving, first leaving of the house, receiving the first solid food, shaving the head, receiving initiation from a guru, receiving the sacred thread, second shaving of the head, lighting the sacred fire, marriage, death, and cremation.

Samson 11th century BC. In the Old Testament, a hero of Israel. He was renowned for exploits of strength against the Philistines, which ended when his lover Delilah cut off his hair, the source of his strength, as told in the Book of Judges.

Samuel 11th–10th centuries BC. In the Old Testament, the last of the judges who ruled the ancient Hebrews before their adoption of a monarchy, and the first of the prophets; the two books bearing his name cover the story of Samuel and the reigns of kings Saul and David.

Samuelson Paul 1915–ㅤ. US economist. He became professor at the Massachusetts Institute of Technology 1940 and was awarded a Nobel prize 1970 for his application of scientific analysis to economic theory. His books include *Economics* 1948, a classic textbook, and *Linear Programming and Economic Analysis* 1958.

Man does not live by GNP alone.

Paul Samuelson
Economics 1948

---

samurai member of the military caste in Japan from the mid-12th century until 1869, when the feudal system was abolished and all samurai pensioned off by the government. A samurai was an armed retainer of a *daimyō* (large landowner) with specific duties and privileges and a strict code of honour. A *rōnin* was a samurai without feudal allegiance.

From the 16th century, commoners were not allowed to carry swords, whereas samurai had two swords, and the higher class of samurai were permitted to fight on horseback. It is estimated that 8% of the population belonged to samurai families. A financial depression from about 1700 caused serious hardship to the samurai, beginning a gradual disintegration of their traditions and prestige, accelerated by the fall of the Tokugawa shogunate 1868, in which they had assisted. Under the new Meiji emperor they were stripped of their role, and many rebelled. Their last uprising was the *Satsuma Rebellion* 1877–78, in which 40,000 samurai took part.

Sanatana Dharma the preferred Hindu name for Hinduism. Hence Sanatana Dharma can be roughly translated as the eternal essence of life, which unites all beings, and the teaching which leads one to realize that essence.

sanction economic or military measure taken by a state or number of states to enforce international law. The first use of sanctions was the attempted economic boycott of Italy (1935–36) during the Abyssinian War by the League of Nations.

Other examples of sanctions are the economic boycott of Rhodesia, after its unilateral declaration of independence 1965, by the United Nations; the call for measures against South Africa on human-rights grounds by the UN and other organizations from 1985; and the economic boycott of Iraq 1990 in protest over its invasion of Kuwait, following resolutions passed by the UN.

sanctuary the holiest area of a place of worship; also, a place of refuge from persecution or prosecution, usually in or near a place of worship.

The custom of offering sanctuary in specific places goes back to ancient times and was widespread in Europe in the Middle Ages.

The ancient Hebrews established six separate towns of refuge, and the Greek temple of Diana at Ephesus provided sanctuary within a radius of two stadia (about 434 m/475 yd). In Roman temples the sanctuary was the *cella* (inner room), in which stood the statue of the god worshipped there.

In the Middle Ages a person who crossed the threshold of a church was under the protection of God. The right to sanctuary was generally honoured by the church and endured by the state. In legend and medieval art, hunted stags took sanctuary in church porticoes. At Beverley Minster in E Yorkshire, England, the privilege extended a mile and a half around the church; the closer to the centre of this zone the fugitives got, the more sinful it was to remove them. Beverley accumulated numbers of permanent sanctuary claimants, and they were absorbed into the life of the minster. A similar process took place at Westminster Abbey, London. The sanctuary there, next to the cloisters, developed into a small town, with shops and workshops, bringing in useful revenue.

In England the right of a criminal to seek sanctuary was removed by legislation 1623 and again 1697, though for civil offenders it remained until 1723. Immunity was valid for 40 days only, after which the claimant must either surrender, become an outlaw, or go into permanent exile. Viraj Mendis, a Sri Lankan illegal immigrant, claimed sanctuary for two years until Jan 1989, before police stormed the church in Manchester where he was living and he was deported.

Sanger Frederick 1918– . English biochemist, the first person to win a Nobel Prize for Chemistry twice: the first in 1958 for determining the structure of insulin, and the second in 1980 for work on the chemical structure of genes.

Sanger worked throughout his life at Cambridge University. His second Nobel prize was shared with two US scientists, Paul Berg and Walter Gilbert, for establishing methods of determining the sequence of nucleotides strung together along strands of DNA.

Sangha in Buddhism, the monastic orders, one of the Three Treasures of Buddhism (the other two are Buddha and the law, or dharma).

The term Sangha is sometimes used more generally by Mahāyāna Buddhists to include all believers.

Sanhedrin (2nd century BC–1st century AD) ancient supreme court in Jerusalem headed by the Jewish high priest. Its functions were judicial, administrative, and religious. The Great Sanhedrin was purely religious and continued in Europe until c. 450 as the rabbinic patriarchate.

sannyasa the formal renunciation of worldly life, traditionally adopted only by men as the final stage in the Hindu social cycle. The sannyasin wears saffron cloth and is forbidden the company of women, particularly his former wife. He may travel as a teacher, or train his disciples in his ashram or monastic hermitage. He is expected to live an ascetic life studying the scriptures.

Those who cannot remember the past are condemned to repeat it.

George Santayana
The Life of Reason

Santayana George 1863–1952. Spanish-born US philosopher and critic. He developed his philosophy based on naturalism and taught that everything has a natural basis.

Born in Madrid, Santayana grew up in Spain and the USA and graduated from Harvard University. He taught at Harvard 1889–1912. His books include *The Life of Reason* 1905–06, *Skepticism and Animal Faith* 1923, *The Realm of Truth* 1937, *Background of My Life* 1945; volumes of poetry; and the best-selling novel *The Last Puritan* 1935.

Sapir Edward 1881–1939. German-born US language scholar and anthropologist who initially studied the Germanic languages but later, under the influence of Franz Boas, investigated native American languages. He is noted for the view now known as *linguistic relativity*: that people's ways of thinking are significantly shaped (and even limited) by the language(s) they use. His main work is *Language: An Introduction to the Study of Speech* 1921.

Sartre Jean-Paul 1905–1980. French author and philosopher, a leading proponent of ◊existentialism. He published his first novel, *La Nausée/Nausea*, 1937, followed by the trilogy *Les Chemins de la Liberté/Roads to Freedom* 1944–45 and many plays, including *Huis Clos/In Camera* 1944. *L'Etre et le néant/Being and Nothingness* 1943, his first major philosophical work, sets out a radical doctrine of human freedom. In the later work *Critique de la* *raison dialectique/Critique of Dialectical Reason* 1960 he tried to produce a fusion of existentialism and Marxism.

I am condemned to be free.

Jean-Paul Sartre
Being and Nothingness

Sartre was born in Paris, and was the longtime companion of the feminist writer Simone de Beauvoir. During World War II he was a prisoner for nine months, and on his return from Germany joined the Resistance. As a founder of existentialism, he edited its journal *Les Temps modernes/Modern Times*, and expressed its tenets in his novels and plays. According to Sartre, people's awareness of their own freedom takes the form of anxiety, and they therefore attempt to flee from this awareness into what he terms *mauvaise foi* ('bad faith'); this is the theory he put forward in *L'Etre et le néant/Being and Nothingness*. In *Crime passionel/Crime of Passion* 1948 he attacked aspects of communism while remaining generally sympathetic. In his later work Sartre became more sensitive to the social constraints on people's actions. He refused the Nobel Prize for Literature 1964 for 'personal reasons', but allegedly changed his mind later, saying he wanted it for the money.

Satan a name for the ◊devil.

Satanism worship of the devil (Satan) instead of God, and the belief that doing so can bind a person to his power. Accusations of Satanism are common in times of social and religious upheaval – such as the late 15th to late 17th centuries in Europe when the authority of first the Roman Catholic Church and then of the various major Protestant churches was questioned. There is little evidence that Satanism was ever actually practised, though in the 20th century Churches of Satan have emerged in the USA, which tend to be anti-Christian rather than overtly concerned with the propagation of evil. The high point of Satanism is believed to be the Black Mass, a parody of the Christian Mass or Eucharist.

satire poem or piece of prose that uses wit, humour, or irony, often through ◊allegory or extended metaphor, to ridicule human pretensions or expose social evils. Satire is related to *parody* in its intention to mock, but satire tends to be more subtle and to mock an attitude or a belief, whereas parody tends to mock a particular work (such as a poem) by imitating its style, often with purely comic intent.

The Roman poets Juvenal and Horace wrote *Satires*, and the form became popular in Europe in the 17th and 18th centuries, used by Voltaire in France and by Alexander Pope and Jonathan Swift in England. Both satire and parody are designed to appeal to the intellect rather than the emotions and both, to be effective, require a knowledge of the original attitude, person, or work that is being mocked (although much satire, such as *Gulliver's Travels* by Swift, can also be enjoyed simply on a literal level).

Satire is a sort of glass, wherein beholders do generally discover everybody's face but their own.

satire
Jonathan Swift, 1667–1745, Irish satirist.
The Battle of the Books

---

satori in Zen Buddhism, awakening, the experience of sudden ◊enlightenment.

Saturn in Roman mythology, the god of agriculture, identified by the Romans with the Greek god ◊Kronos. His period of rule was the ancient Golden Age. Saturn was dethroned by his sons Jupiter, Neptune, and Dis. At his festival, the Saturnalia in Dec, gifts were exchanged, and slaves were briefly treated as their masters' equals.

satyagraha nonviolent resistance to British rule in India, as employed by Mahatma ◊Gandhi from 1918 to press for political reform; the idea owes much to the Russian writer Leo ◊Tolstoy.

satyr in Greek mythology, a lustful, drunken woodland creature characterized by pointed ears, two horns on the forehead, and a tail. Satyrs attended the god of wine, ◊Dionysus. Roman writers confused satyrs with goat-footed fauns.

Saul in the Old Testament, the first king of Israel. He was anointed by Samuel and warred successfully against the neighbouring Ammonites and Philistines, but fell from God's favour in his battle against the Amalekites. He became jealous and suspicious of David and turned against him and Samuel. After being wounded in battle with the Philistines, in which his three sons died, he committed suicide.

Saussure Ferdinand de 1857–1913. Swiss language scholar, a pioneer of modern linguistics and the originator of the concept of

◊structuralism as used in linguistics, anthropology, and literary theory.

He taught at the universities of Paris and Geneva. His early work, on the Indo-European language family, led to a major treatise on its vowel system. He is best known for *Cours de linguistique générale/Course in General Linguistics* 1916, a posthumous work derived mainly from his lecture notes by his students Charles Bally and Albert Séchehaye. Saussurean concepts include: (1) language seen as both a unified and shared social system (*langue*) and as individual and idiosyncratic speech (*parole*); (2) language described in **synchronic** terms (as a system at a particular time) and in **diachronic** terms (as changing through time).

savings unspent income, after deduction of tax. In economics a distinction is made between ◊investment, involving the purchase of capital goods, such as buying a house, and saving (where capital goods are not directly purchased; for example, buying shares).

Savonarola Girolamo 1452–1498. Italian reformer, a Dominican friar and an eloquent preacher. His crusade against political and religious corruption won him popular support, and in 1494 he led a revolt in Florence that expelled the ruling Medici family and established a democratic republic. His denunciations of Pope Alexander VI led to his excommunication in 1497, and in 1498 he was arrested, tortured, hanged, and burned for heresy.

Say's law in economics, the 'law of markets' formulated by Jean-Baptiste Say (1767–1832) to the effect that supply creates its own demand and that resources can never be underused.

Widely accepted by classical economists, the 'law' was regarded as erroneous by J M Keynes in his analysis of the depression in Britain during the 1920s and 1930s.

scapegoat the Hebrew Bible (Leviticus 16) describes how a goat was loaded with the sins of the people and then sent out into the wilderness as a way of removing the sins of the people. The goat was sent to Azazel, who is variously understood to be a demon of the desert and of disorder. In contemporary language, a scapegoat is someone, usually relatively minor, who is caught up in a scandal and then dismissed or prosecuted while those higher up who were also involved are left untouched.

scarcity in economics, insufficient availabilty of resources to satisfy wants. The use of scarce resources has an ◊opportunity cost.

scepticism ancient philosophical view that absolute knowledge of things is ultimately unobtainable, hence the only proper attitude is to suspend judgement. Its origins lay in the teachings of the Greek philosopher Pyrrho, who maintained that peace of mind lay in renouncing all claims to knowledge.

It was taken up in a less extreme form by the Greek ◊Academy in the 3rd and 2nd centuries BC. Academic sceptics claimed that although truth is finally unknowable, a balance of probabilities can be used for coming to decisions. The most radical form of scepticism is known as ◊solipsism, which maintains that the self is the only thing that can be known to exist.

Schadenfreude (German) malicious enjoyment at the misfortunes of others.

Scheele Karl Wilhelm 1742–1786. Swedish chemist and pharmacist. In the book *Experiments on Air and Fire* 1777, he argued that the atmosphere was composed of two gases. One, which supported combustion (oxygen), he called 'fire air', and the other, which inhibited combustion (nitrogen), he called 'vitiated air'. He thus anticipated Joseph ◊Priestley's discovery of oxygen by two years.

Schelling Friedrich Wilhelm Joseph 1775–1854. German philosopher who began as a follower of Fichte, but moved away from subjective ◊idealism, which treats the external world as essentially immaterial, toward a 'philosophy of identity' (*Identitätsphilosophie*), in which subject and object are seen as united in the absolute. His early philosophy influenced ◊Hegel, but his later work criticizes Hegel, arguing that being necessarily precedes thought.

Schiaparelli Giovanni (Virginio) 1835–1910. Italian astronomer who discovered the so-called 'Martian canals'. He studied ancient and medieval astronomy, discovered the asteroid 69 (Hesperia) April 1861, observed double stars, and revealed the connection between comets and meteors. In 1877 he was the first to draw attention to the linear markings on Mars, which gave rise to the 'Martian canal' controversy. These markings are now known to be optical effects and not real lines.

Schillebeeckx Edward 1914– . Catholic theologian, born in Belgium. His most significant area of work has been to accept and explore the meaning of modern Biblical scholarship and to engage with secular philosophy. His book *Jesus: An Experiment in Christology* is the first major Catholic book to explore Jesus in the light of these studies, rather than from a doctrinal perspective.

schism formal split over a doctrinal difference between religious believers, as in the ◊Great Schism in the Roman Catholic Church; over the doctrine of papal infallibility, as with the Old Catholics in 1879; and over the use of the Latin Tridentine mass 1988.

schizophrenia mental disorder, a psychosis of unknown origin, which can lead to profound changes in personality and behaviour including paranoia and hallucinations. Contrary to popular belief, it does not involve a split personality. Modern treatment approaches include drugs, family therapy, stress reduction, and rehabilitation.

Schizophrenia implies a severe divorce from reality in the patient's thinking. Although the exact cause is unknown, circumstantial evidence points to overactivity in the brain of those nerve cells that have dopamine as their transmitter substance. Drugs that interfere with the action of dopamine, such as chlorpromazine, may be of benefit.

The prevalence of schizophrenia in Europe is about two to five cases per 1,000 population.

Schlick (Friedrich Albert) Moritz 1882–1936. German philosopher, physicist, and founder of the ◊Vienna Circle. Under the influence of the early Ludwig ◊Wittgenstein and of the ◊logical positivism of Rudolf Carnap (1891–1970), he concluded that all philosophical problems arise from the inadequacy of language. The task of philosophy is to clarify the question in dispute. If the question cannot be ascertained in principle by scientific methods, then the question is meaningless. He based ◊meaning on the possibility of immediate sense-experience. The inaccessibility of this private experience of meaning led Wittgenstein to his 'use' theory of meaning.

Born in Berlin, he became professor of the philosophy of the inductive sciences in Vienna in 1922. He was assassinated in 1936 by a demented student, an event which hastened the impending break-up of the Vienna Circle. His publications include *Allgemeine Erkenntnislehre/ General Theory of Knowledge* 1918.

Schoenberg Arnold (Franz Walter) 1874–1951. Austro-Hungarian composer, a US citizen from 1941. After Romantic early works such as *Verklärte Nacht/Transfigured Night* 1899 and the *Gurrelieder/Songs of Gurra* 1900–11, he experimented with atonality (absence of key), producing works such as *Pierrot Lunaire* 1912 for chamber ensemble and voice, before developing the 12-tone system of musical composition. This was further

developed by his pupils Alban Berg and Anton Webern.

After World War I he wrote several Neo-Classical works for chamber ensembles. He taught at the Berlin State Academy 1925–33. Driven from Germany by the Nazis, he settled in the USA 1933, where he influenced music scoring for films. Later works include the opera *Moses und Aron* 1932–51.

scholasticism the theological and philosophical systems and methods taught in the schools of medieval Europe, especially in the 12th–14th centuries. Scholasticism tried to integrate orthodox Christian teaching with Aristotelian and some Platonic philosophy. The scholastic method involved surveying different opinions and the reasons given for them, and then attempting solutions of the problems raised using logic and dialectic.

The 9th-century neo-Platonist Johannes Scotus Erigena is sometimes regarded as an early scholastic. But scholasticism began at the end of the 11th century, when Roscellinus, a supporter of nominalism, and Anselm, a supporter of realism, disputed the nature of ◊universals. In the 12th century, the foundation of universities in Bologna, Paris, Oxford, and Cambridge, and the recovery of Greek philosophical texts, stimulated scholasticism. Notable scholastic philosophers, or 'schoolmen', as they were called, are William of Champeaux, Abelard, the English monk Alexander of Hales (died 1222), Albertus Magnus, and Peter Lombard. The most important are, in the 13th century, Thomas Aquinas, whose works have become classic texts of Catholic doctrine, and Duns Scotus, and, in the 14th century, William of Occam, who was the last major scholastic philosopher.

In the 20th century there has been a revival of interest in scholasticism, particularly in the writings of Catholic scholars like Jacques Maritian (1882–1973).

Schopenhauer Arthur 1788–1860. German philosopher whose influential *The World as Will and Idea* 1818, inspired by Kant and ancient Hindu philosophy, expounded an atheistic and pessimistic world view: an irrational will is considered as the inner principle of the world, producing an ever-frustrated cycle of desire, of which the only escape is aesthetic contemplation or absorption into nothingness.

Having postulated a world of suffering and disappointment, he based his ethics on compassion. His notion of an irrational force at work in man strongly influenced both Nietzsche and Freud. This theory also struck a responsive chord in the composer Wagner, the German novelist Thomas Mann, and the English writer Thomas Hardy.

Schrödinger Erwin 1887–1961. Austrian physicist who advanced the study of wave mechanics (see ◊quantum theory). Born in Vienna, he became senior professor at the Dublin Institute for Advanced Studies 1940. He shared (with Paul Dirac) a Nobel prize 1933.

Schultz Theodore William 1902– . US economist, a specialist in agricultural economics. He shared the 1979 Nobel prize with W Arthur Lewis for his work on the problems of developing countries.

Small Is Beautiful.

Fritz Schumacher
Book title

Schumacher Fritz (Ernst Friedrich) 1911–1977. German economist who believed that the increasing size of institutions, coupled with unchecked economic growth, created a range of social and environmental problems. He argued his case in books like *Small is Beautiful* 1973, and tested it practically through establishing the Intermediate Technology Development Group.

Schuman Robert 1886–1963. French politician. He was prime minister 1947–48, and as foreign minister 1948–53 he proposed in May 1950 a common market for coal and steel (the *Schuman Plan*), which was established as the European Coal and Steel Community 1952, the basis of the European Community.

Schumpeter Joseph A(lois) 1883–1950. US economist and sociologist. In *Capitalism, Socialism and Democracy* 1942 he contended that Western capitalism, impelled by its very success, was evolving into a form of socialism because firms would become increasingly large and their managements increasingly divorced from ownership, while social trends were undermining the traditional motives for entrepreneurial accumulation of wealth.

Schumpeter was born in Moravia, now the Czech Republic, and migrated to the USA 1932. He was deeply interested in mathematics, and he took part in the founding of the Econometric Society 1930. His writings established him as an authority on economic theory as well as the history of economic thought. Among other standard reference works, he wrote the *History of Economic Analysis* 1954, published posthumously.

Schweitzer Albert 1875–1965. French Protestant theologian, organist, and missionary surgeon. He founded the hospital at Lambaréné in Gabon in 1913, giving organ recitals to support his work there. He wrote a life of Bach and *Von Reimarus zu Wrede/The Quest for the Historical Jesus* 1906 and was awarded the Nobel Peace Prize in 1952 for his teaching of 'reverence for life'.

'Reverence for Life'.

Albert Schweitzer
My Life and Thought ch 13

Schwinger Julian 1918– . US quantum physicist. His research concerned the behaviour of charged particles in electrical fields. This work, expressed entirely through mathematics, combines elements from quantum theory and relativity theory. Schwinger shared the Nobel Prize for Physics 1963 with Richard ◊Feynman and Sin-Itiro Tomonaga (1906–1979).

Described as the 'physicist in knee pants', he entered college in New York at the age of 15, transferred to Columbia University and graduated at 17. At the age of 29 he became Harvard University's youngest full professor.

That is the essence of science: ask an impertinent question, and you are on the way to a pertinent answer.

science
Jacob Bronowski, 1908–1974, US historian and mathematician.
The Ascent of Man

science any systematic field of study or body of knowledge that aims, through experiment, observation, and deduction, to produce reliable explanation of phenomena, with reference to the material and physical world.

Activities such as healing, star-watching, and engineering have been practised in many societies since ancient times. Pure science, especially ◊physics (formerly called natural philosophy), had traditionally been the main area of study for philosophers. The European scientific revolution between about 1650 and 1800 replaced speculative philosophy with a new combination of observation, experimentation, and rationality.

Today, scientific research involves an interaction among tradition, experiment and observation, and deduction. The subject area called **philosophy of science** investigates the nature of this complex interaction, and the extent of its ability to gain access to the truth about the material world. It has long been recognized that induction from observation cannot give explanations based on logic. In the 20th century Karl ◊Popper has described ◊scientific method as a rigorous experimental testing of a scientist's ideas or hypotheses (see ◊hypothesis). The origin and role of these ideas, and their interdependence with observation, have been examined, for example, by the US thinker Thomas S ◊Kuhn, who places them in a historical and sociological setting. The **sociology of science** investigates how scientific theories and laws are produced, and questions the possibility of objectivity in any scientific endeavour. One controversial point of view is the replacement of scientific realism with scientific relativism, as proposed by Paul K ◊Feyerabend. Questions concerning the proper use of science and the role of science education are also restructuring this field of study.

For him [the scientist], truth is so seldom the sudden light that shows new order and beauty; more often, truth is the uncharted rock that sinks his ship in the dark.

science
John Warcup Cornforth, 1917,
Australian chemist.
Nobel prize address 1975

Science is divided into separate areas of study, such as astronomy, biology, geology, chemistry, physics, and mathematics, although more recently attempts have been made to combine traditionally separate disciplines under such headings as ◊life sciences and ◊earth sciences. These areas are usually jointly referred to as the **natural sciences**. The **physical sciences** comprise mathematics, physics, and chemistry. The application of science for practical purposes is called **technology**. **Social science** is the systematic study of human behaviour, and includes such areas as anthropology, economics, psychology, and sociology. One area of contemporary debate is whether the social-science disciplines are actually sciences; that is, whether the study of human beings is capable of scientific precision or prediction in the same way as natural science is seen to be.

Science is all those things which are confirmed to such a degree that it would be unreasonable to withhold one's provisional consent.

science
Stephen Jay Gould, 1941– , US
palaeontologist and author.
Lecture on Evolution

science fiction or **speculative fiction** (also known as **SF** or **sci-fi**) genre of fiction and film with an imaginary scientific, technological, or futuristic basis. It is sometimes held to have its roots in the works of Mary Shelley, notably *Frankenstein* 1818. Often taking its ideas and concerns from current ideas in science and the social sciences, science fiction aims to shake up standard perceptions of reality.

SF works often deal with alternative realities, future histories, robots, aliens, utopias and dystopias (often satiric), space and time-travel, natural or human-made disasters, and psychic powers. Early practitioners were Jules Verne and H G Wells. In the 20th century the US pulp-magazine tradition of SF produced such writers as Arthur C Clarke, Isaac Asimov, Robert Heinlein, and Frank Herbert; a consensus of 'pure storytelling' and traditional values was disrupted by writers associated with the British magazine *New Worlds* (Brian Aldiss, Michael Moorcock, J G Ballard) and by younger US writers (Joanna Russ, Ursula Le Guin, Thomas Disch, Gene Wolfe) who used the form for serious literary purposes and for political and sexual radicalism. Thriving SF traditions, only partly influenced by the Anglo-American one, exist in France, Germany, and E Europe. In the 1980s the cyberpunk school spread from the USA, spearheaded by William Gibson and Bruce Sterling (1954–).

Science-fiction writers include James Tiptree Jr (Alice Sheldon 1915–1987, USA), Philip K Dick (USA), John Brunner (1934– , UK), Samuel Delany (1942– , USA), Stanislaw Lem (1921– , Poland), Boris and Arkady Strugatsky (1931– and 1925–1991, USSR), Harlan Ellison (1934–), Damon Knight (1922–), John Campbell (1910–1971), and Frederik Pohl (1919–) – the last four all US editors and anthologists.

Many mainstream writers have written SF, including Aldous Huxley (*Brave New World* 1932), George Orwell (*Nineteen Eighty-Four* 1949), and Doris Lessing (series of five books *Canopus in Argos: Archives* 1979–83).

The term was coined 1926 by Hugo Gernsback (1884–1967), editor of the US science-fiction magazine *Amazing Stories*.

science, philosophy of systematic study of how science works (or should work) and of the concepts used in scientific enquiry, such as a ◊law of nature, causation, probability, explanation, and ◊induction (reasoning from the particular to the general). Philosophers of science also consider the nature of scientific systems.

Some hold that scientific systems are abstract systems that we fit to the world, as we might choose between Euclidean and non-Euclidean geometries. In addition, these philosophers consider in what sense theoretical entities like electrons can be said to exist.

scientific method in science, the belief that experimentation and observation, properly understood and applied, can avoid the influence of cultural and social values and so build up a picture of a reality independent of the observer.

Improved techniques and mechanical devices, which improve the reliability of measurements, may seem to support this theory; but the realization that observations of subatomic particles influence their behaviour has undermined the view that objectivity is possible in science (see ◊uncertainty principle).

Scientology 'applied religious philosophy' based on ◊dianetics, founded in California in 1954 by L Ron ◊Hubbard as the *Church of Scientology*. It claims to 'increase man's spiritual awareness', but its methods of recruiting and retaining converts have been criticized. Its headquarters from 1959 have been in Sussex, England.

Scribe member of an ancient Jewish group of Biblical scholars, both priests and laypersons, who studied the books of Moses and sat in the ◊Sanhedrin (supreme court). In the New Testament they are associated with the ◊Pharisees. Later, they are the copyists of Hebrew scripture.

scruple in theology, the fear of sin when none has been committed. Generally, thoughts characterized by uncertainty or hesitation in relation to right and wrong moral conduct. Scruples may be condemned as indecision; the classic case is that of Hamlet.

Scruton Roger (Vernon) 1944– . British philosopher and right-wing social critic, professor of aesthetics at Birkbeck College, London, from 1985. Advocating the political theories of Edmund ◊Burke in such books as *The Meaning of Conservatism* 1980, he influenced the free-market movements in E Europe.

Hospitality is the only form of gift that imposes itself as an obligation.

Roger Scruton
The Meaning of Conservatism

Seaborg Glenn Theodore 1912– . US nuclear chemist. He was awarded a Nobel prize in 1951 for his discoveries of transuranic elements (with atomic numbers greater than that of uranium), and for production of the radioisotope uranium-233.

seasonal adjustment in statistics, an adjustment of figures designed to take into account influences that are purely seasonal, and relevant only for a short time. The resulting figures are then thought to reflect long-term trends more accurately.

Sebastian, St Roman soldier, traditionally a member of Emperor Diocletian's bodyguard until his Christian faith was discovered. He was condemned to be killed by arrows (the manner in which he is usually depicted) but he survived and was finally beaten to death with clubs. Feast day 20 Jan.

He has been regarded since the 4th century as a protector against plague. A large number of images of him occur during the Renaissance, which may be explained as an opportunity for depicting the male nude.

Secchi Pietro Angelo 1818–1878. Italian astronomer and astrophysicist, who classified stellar spectra into four classes based on their colour and spectral characteristics. He was the first to classify solar prominences, huge jets of gas projecting from the Sun's surface.

secession (Latin *secessio*) in politics, the withdrawal from a federation of states by one or more of its members, as in the secession of the Confederate states from the Union in the USA 1860.

secondary data information which has been collected by another agency. Examples of secondary data include government reports and statistics, company reports and accounts, and trade association statistics.

secret police any state security force that operates internally, against political dissenters or subversives; for example, the US Federal Bureau of Investigation, the UK Special Branch, and the former Soviet KGB (see ◊intelligence services).

secret society society with membership by invitation only, often involving initiation rites, secret rituals, and dire punishments for those who break the code. Often founded for religious reasons or mutual benefit, some have become the province of corrupt politicians or gangsters, like the ◊Mafia, ◊Ku Klux Klan, and the ◊Triad. See also ◊Freemasonry.

sect small ideological group, usually religious in nature, that may have moved away from a main group, often claiming a monopoly of access to truth or salvation. Sects are usually highly exclusive. They demand strict conformity, total commitment to their code of behaviour, and complete personal involvement, sometimes to the point of rejecting mainstream society altogether in terms of attachments, names, possessions, and family.

Most sects are short-lived, either because their appeal dies out and their members return to mainstream society, or because their appeal spreads and they become part of mainstream society (for example, Christianity began as a small sect in Roman-ruled Palestine).

sector theory model of urban land use in which the various land-use zones are shaped like wedges radiating from the central business district. According to sector theory, the highest prices for land are found along transport routes (especially roads), and once an area has gained a reputation for a particular type of land use (such as industry), it will attract the same land users as the city expands outwards over time.

secularization the process through which religious thinking, practice, and institutions lose their religious and/or social significance. The concept is based on the theory, held by some sociologists, that as societies become industrialized their religious morals, values, and institutions give way to secular ones and some religious traits become common secular practices.

seder meal that forms part of the Jewish festival of ◊Passover, which celebrates the ◊Exodus.

Segrè Emilio 1905–1989. Italian physicist settled in the USA, who in 1955 discovered the antiproton, a new form of ◊antimatter. He shared the 1959 Nobel Prize for Physics with Owen Chamberlain. Segrè had earlier discovered the first synthetic element, technetium (atomic number 43), in 1937.

Sekhmet ancient Egyptian goddess of heat and fire. She was represented with the head of a lioness, and worshipped at Memphis as the wife of ◊Ptah.

self the individual as an experiencing being, the subject of contemplation, the object of ◊introspection, and the agent of thought and action. ◊Personality and ◊ego are commonly used synonyms, though they do not have exactly the same meaning. The personality is more outwardly observable (by others, that is), and the ego, as a psychoanalytical term at least, contains unconscious elements that the self does not recognize.

self-help project any scheme for a community to help itself under official guidance. The most popular self-help projects in the developing world are aimed at improving conditions in shanty towns. Organized building lots are commonly provided, together with properly laid-out drains, water supplies, roads, and lighting. ◊Squatters are expected to build their own homes on the prepared sites, perhaps with loans provided by the government or other agencies. An example is the Arumbakkam scheme in Madras, India, begun 1977. Alternatively, 'basic shell' housing may be provided, as in parts of São Paulo, Brazil, and Salop in W Colombia.

self-sufficiency situation where an individual or group does not rely on outsiders. Economic self-sufficiency means that no trade takes place between the individual or group and others. If an economy were self-sufficient, it would not export or import. For a family to be self-sufficient, for example, it would have to grow all its own food, make its own clothes, and provide all its own services. In a modern economy, there is very little self-sufficiency because ◊specialization enables individuals to enjoy a much higher standard of living then if they were self-sufficient.

semantics the branch of ◊linguistics dealing with the meaning of words.

Semenov Nikoly 1896–1986. Russian physical chemist who made significant contributions to the study of chemical chain reactions. Working mainly in Leningrad at the Institute for Chemical Physics, in 1956 he became the first Russian to gain the Nobel Prize for Chemistry, which he shared with Cyril ◊Hinshelwood.

Senate in ancient Rome, the 'council of elders'. Originally consisting of the heads of patrician families, it was recruited from ex-magistrates and persons who had rendered notable public service, but was periodically purged by the censors. Although nominally advisory, it controlled finance and foreign policy.

Seneca Lucius Annaeus c. 4 BC–65 AD. Roman stoic playwright, author of essays and nine tragedies. He was tutor to the future emperor Nero but lost favour after the latter's accession to the throne and was ordered to commit suicide. His tragedies were accepted as classical models by 16th-century dramatists.

sensationalism or *sensationism* in philosophy, the doctrine that all our knowledge rests ultimately on sense data, or sensations, which are received by us free from any element of interpretation or judgement. The theory originated with English philosopher John ◊Locke, but the term comes from his French follower Etienne de ◊Condillac.

sensibility 18th-century term meaning the capacity to identify with and feel sympathy for the suffering of others. It was a quality extolled by the philosopher the 3rd Earl of Shaftesbury as well as by writers of fiction.

In Jane Austen's novel *Sense and Sensibility* 1811 the good sense of Elinor Dashwood is contrasted with the extreme sensibility of her sister Marianne, to the latter's disadvantage.

separation of powers an approach to limiting the powers of government by separating governmental functions into the executive, legislative, and judiciary. The concept has its fullest practical expression in the the US constitution (see ◊federalism).

separatist one who wants to separate or withdraw from an alliance or association. In 19th century Australian separatists were those who campaigned for the separation from Britain of the administrative and judicial functions of the Australian colonies and for their independence from each other.

Sephardi (plural *Sephardim*) Jew descended from those expelled from Spain and Portugal in the 15th century, or from those forcibly converted during the Inquisition to Christianity (◊Marranos). Many settled in N Africa and in the Mediterranean countries, as well as in the Netherlands, England, and Dutch colonies in the New World. Sephardim speak Ladino, a 15th-century Romance dialect, as well as the language of their nation.

Septuagint the oldest Greek version of the Old Testament or Hebrew Bible, traditionally made by 70 scholars.

seraph (plural *seraphim*) in Christian and Judaic belief, an ◊angel of the highest order. They are mentioned in the book of Isaiah in the Old Testament.

Serapis ancient Graeco-Egyptian god, a combination of Apis and Osiris, invented by the Ptolemies; his finest temple was the Serapeum in Alexandria.

serendipity the ability to make happy discoveries by accident. The word was coined by Horace Walpole 1754, after the fairytale *The Three Princes of Serendip*. Serendip is an archaic name for modern Sri Lanka.

serfdom the legal and economic status of peasants under ◊feudalism. Serfs could not be sold like slaves, but they were not free to leave their master's estate without his permission. They had to work the lord's land without pay for a number of days every week and pay a percentage of their produce to the lord every year. They also served as soldiers in the event of conflict. Serfs also had to perform extra labour at harvest time and other busy seasons; in return they were allowed to cultivate a portion of the estate for their own benefit.

In England serfdom died out between the 14th and 17th centuries, but it lasted in France until 1789, in Russia until 1861, and in most other European countries until the early 19th century.

Sergius, St of Radonezh 1314–1392. Russian monastic reformer and mystic, the patron saint of Russia, who founded the Orthodox monastery of the Blessed Trinity near Moscow 1334. Mediator among Russian feudal princes, he inspired the victory of Dmitri, Grand Duke of Moscow, over the Tatar khan Mamai at Kulikovo, on the upper Don, 1380.

serialism in music, an alternative name for the ◊twelve-tone system of composition.

It usually refers to post-1950 compositions in which further aspects such as dynamics, durations, and attacks are brought under serial control. These other series may consist of fewer than 12 degrees while some pitch series can go higher.

sermon a spoken or written discourse on a religious subject. The Sermon on the Mount is the name given to the teachings of Jesus recorded in Matthew 5:7. This is a summary of Jesus' teaching and formed the core of subsequent Christian teaching on discipleship. The ◊Buddha's first sermon was preached in a deer-park soon after he had reached enlightenment. In it he described the Middle Way, which avoids extremes of asceticism or pleasure-seeking.

Servetus Michael (Miguel Serveto) 1511–1553. Spanish Christian Anabaptist theologian and physician. He was a pioneer in the study of the circulation of the blood and found that it circulates to the lungs from the right chamber of the heart. He was burned alive by the church reformer Calvin in Geneva, Switzerland, for publishing attacks on the doctrine of the Trinity.

Seven against Thebes in Greek legend, the attack of seven captains led by Adrastus, king of Argos, on the seven gates of ancient Thebes, prompted by the rivalry between the two sons of Oedipus, Polynices and Eteocles, for the kingship of Thebes. In the event, the two brothers died by each other's hands. The subject of tragedies by Aeschylus and Euripides (*The Phoenician Women*), and of the epic *Thebaid* by the Roman poet Statius, it forms the background to other Greek tragedies by Sophocles (*Antigone, Oedipus at Colonus*) and Euripides (*Suppliant Women*).

seven deadly sins in Christian theology, the vices that are considered fundamental to all other sins:

Anger	Pride
Avarice	Sloth or Dejection
Envy	Lust
Gluttony.	

Evagrius Ponticus (c. 346–399 AD), a deacon of Constantinople, maintained, in his treatise *On the Eight Evil Thoughts*, that the root or principal sins were: gluttony; fornication; avarice; dejection, or lack of pleasure; anger; weariness, or accidie; vain glory; and pride. The monk, John Cassian, c. 360–435, follows Evagrius. Gregory the Great (c. 540–604 AD), who was Pope from 590–604, was the first to formulate the seven deadly sins more or less as we know them today.

Seventh-Day Adventist or ◊*Adventist* member of a Protestant church of the same name. It originated in the USA in the fervent expectation of Christ's Second Coming, or advent, that swept across New York State following William fundamental ◊Miller's prophecy that Christ would return on 22 Oct 1844. When this failed to come to pass, a number of Millerites, as his followers were called, reinterpreted his prophetic speculations and continued to maintain that the millennium was imminent. Adventists observe Saturday as the Sabbath and emphasize healing and diet; many are vegetarians. The Seventh-Day Adventists have about five million members worldwide, of which 500,000 are in the USA.

Severus of Antioch 467–538. Christian bishop, one of the originators of the ◊Monophysite heresy. As patriarch of Antioch (from 512), Severus was the leader of opposition to the Council of Chalcedon 451, an attempt to unite factions of the early church, by insisting that Christ existed in one nature only. He was condemned by the emperor Justin I in 518, and left Antioch for Alexandria, never to return.

sexism belief in (or set of implicit assumptions about) the superiority of one's own sex, often accompanied by a ◊stereotype or preconceived idea about the opposite sex. Sexism may also be accompanied by ◊discrimination on the basis of sex, generally as practised by men against women.

So this gentleman said a girl with brains ought to do something with them besides think.

sexism
Anita Loos, 1893–1981, US humorous writer.
Gentlemen Prefer Blondes

The term, coined by analogy with racism, was first used in the 1960s by feminist writers to describe language or behaviour that implied women's inferiority. Examples include the contentious use of male pronouns to describe both men and women, and the assumption that some jobs are typically performed only by one sex.

Sextus Empiricus c 160–210 AD. Greek physician and philosopher. He was an exponent of scepticism of an agnostic, not a dogmatic, kind – that is, he rejected the view that knowledge was demonstrably impossible, and he insisted on keeping an open mind on this as on other questions. His most important work is the *Outlines of Pyrrhonism* – a summary of the scepticism of ◊Pyrrho of Elis and his successors. His other surviving works are *Against the Learned* and *Against the Dogmatists*. Sextus' work is a valuable source for the history of philosophy, because of his impartiality in presenting the arguments of his opponents. Little is known of his life.

sexuality the attribute or characteristic of being male or female, usually taken to involve more than the ability or disposition to play the appropriate role in sexual reproduction. Today, as much emphasis is placed on an individual's awareness of and response to culturally and socially derived ◊gender differences as on biological factors in the development of sexuality.

For lust is not easily restrained, when it has no fear.

sexuality
Clement of Alexandria, c.150 AD–c.215 AD,
Greek theologian and philosopher.
Exhortation to the Greeks ch iv.

Sexuality has been an important topic in ◊developmental psychology. In psychoanalysis, in particular, ◊Freud's ideas on infantile sexuality have been immensely influential. Recent years have seen a growth of interest in sexuality and gender differences in such varied fields of study as sociology, social historical and cultural studies, and politics.

Bibl. Weeks, Jeffrey *Sexuality* (London, 1989)

Shafi'i Muhammad ibn Idris al-Shafi'i 767–820 AD. Muslim jurist, founder of one of the four main schools of Sunni Islamic Law. He based the law on four points: the ◊Qur'an, the sayings of ◊Muhammad, *ijma* (the consensus of the whole Muslim community, and analogical reasoning.

Born in Palestine, a descendant of Muhammad's grandfather Abd al-Muttalib. He grew up and was educated in Gaza and Mecca. He wrote his first book *Al-Usul/The Foundations* in Baghdad. He then returned to Mecca and travelled to Egypt where he met Imam ◊Malik. He died in Cairo, where his tomb is still a place of pilgrimage. His publications were numerous.

Shaivism in Hinduism, worship of the god ◊Shiva. It is an important part of the Hindu tradition, particularly in S India, where Shiva temples are the most numerous. The Shiva temple at Ramesvaram is the largest temple in India. Shaivite ascetics often smear their bodies with ashes and carry a trident, keeping their hair uncut. Shaivism stresses asceticism and meditation.

Shaker popular name for a member of the Christian group of the United Society of Believers in Christ's Second Appearing (an offshoot of the ◊Quakers). This was founded by James and Jane Wardley in England about 1747 and taken to North America 1774 by Ann Lee (1736–84), the wife of a Manchester blacksmith, known as Mother Ann. She founded a colony in New York, and eventually 18 colonies existed in several states. Separation from the world in self-regulating farm communities, prescribed modes of simple dress and living conditions, celibacy, and faith healing characterized their way of life. The name was applied because of their ecstatic trembling and shaking during worship.

Mrs Lee held that God had appeared in his masculine aspect as Jesus and would appear a second time in a female aspect, which her followers identified with her. She held that sex is inherently sinful, and Shakers were forbidden to marry. New members were supplied to the colonies through conversion and adopting orphans, but by the 20th century their numbers steadily declined, and today there are only a few Shakers left. Shaker design became renowned for pleasing but austere simplicity.

Shakti in Hinduism, shakti is the female attribute of *purusha* (the Cosmic Self), as light and heat are the shakti of the Sun. Those who worship the goddess ◊Durga or Parvati, consort of Shiva, are called Shaktas. The material world, being made up of shakti, is the realm of the goddess Durga, who is the personification of the shakti of Shiva.

shaman ritual leader who acts as intermediary between society and the supernatural world in many indigenous cultures of Asia, Africa, and the Americas. Also known as a *medicine man*, *seer*, or *sorcerer*, the shaman is expected to use special powers to cure illness and control good and evil spirits. The term is used for any tribal sorcerer or medicine man regardless of geography.

Shamans also use local medicines and curative techniques. Scientists and pharmaceutical companies have begun to take an interest in traditional knowledge systems, which puts the intellectual rights of shamans at issue.

shamanism perhaps the oldest world religion, originating among the Tungus peoples of Siberia over 8,000 years ago and spreading into China and Southeast Asia and across into Russia and into North and Central America via the land bridge which then existed between Siberia and Alaska. The core belief is in two worlds: the spiritual world and the material world.

Shamans are people who are able to be possessed by spirits and who can then be called upon for help or forgiveness in the curing of illness or the remedying of ill fortune. Shamans are usually associated with the ability to turn into animals, of which the bear is the most revered and popular. Shamanism is still practised in China, Japan, Siberia, and in many areas of North and Central America. It has recently undergone a revival of interest especially in the West, where its links with nature have struck a chord with many seeking a more ecological spirituality and world view.

shame emotion or feeling of embarrassment or humiliation when previously concealed shortcomings become known either to oneself or to others. Shame involves one's fundamental sense of ◊self, and the capacity for shame is part of almost everyone's make-up. It is believed to have its origins in early psychosexual development, emerging in the second or third year of life when a child's sense of self is developing.

Shame can become pathological, to the extent that every little rebuke or admission of failure results in distress. It is often a cause of irrational outbursts of rage and probably an important factor in family violence.

Shankara 799–833. Hindu philosopher who wrote commentaries on some of the major Hindu scriptures, as well as hymns and essays on religious ideas. Shankara was responsible for the final form of the ◊Advaita Vedanta school of Hindu philosophy, which teaches that Brahman, the supreme being, is all that exists in the universe, everything else is illusion. Shankara was fiercely opposed to Buddhism and may have influenced its decline in India.

Shannon Claude Elwood 1916– . US mathematician whose paper *The Mathematical Theory of Communication* 1948 marks the beginning of the science of information theory. He argued that information data and ◊entropy are analogous, and obtained a quantitative measure of the amount of information in a given message.

He wrote the first effective program for a chess-playing computer.

Shapley Harlow 1885–1972. US astronomer, whose study of globular clusters showed that they were arranged in a halo around the Galaxy, and that the Galaxy was much larger than previously thought. He realized that the Sun was not at the centre of the Galaxy as then assumed, but two-thirds of the way out to the rim.

Shari'a the law of ◊Islam believed by Muslims to be based on divine revelation, and drawn from a number of sources, including the Qur'an, the Hadith, and the consensus of the Muslim community.

Under this law, **qisās**, or retribution, allows a family to exact equal punishment on an accused; **diyat**, or blood money, is payable to a dead person's family as compensation.

From the latter part of the 19th century, the role of the Shari'a courts in the majority of Muslim countries began to be taken over by secular courts, and the Shari'a to be largely restricted to family law. Modifications of Qur'anic maxims have resulted from the introduction of Western law; for example, compensation can now be claimed only after a conviction by a criminal court.

Anarchism is a game at which the Police can beat you.

George Bernard Shaw
Misalliance

Shaw George Bernard 1856–1950. Irish dramatist. He was also a critic and novelist, and an early member of the socialist ◊Fabian Society. His plays combine comedy with political, philosophical, and polemic aspects, aiming to make an impact on his audience's social conscience as well as their emotions. They include *Arms and the Man* 1894, *Devil's Disciple* 1897, *Man and Superman* 1905, *Pygmalion* 1913, and *St Joan* 1924. Nobel prize 1925.

Shema in Judaism, prayer from the Torah, recited by orthodox men every morning and evening, which affirms the special relationship of the Jews with God. It begins with the Hebrew for 'Hear, O Israel, the Lord our God, the Lord is One.'

Sheol in the Hebrew Bible, the place of the dead. The word also suggests the grave, the underworld, and the state of death. ◊Yahweh was the ruler of Sheol, and in some writings premature committal to Sheol was seen as a form of punishment In later Jewish literature Sheol is divided into areas for the wicked and the righteous.

Shiah or ◊*Shi'ite* member of one of the two main branches of ◊Islam.

shift in demand or supply curve in economics, a shift in the demand or supply curve to the left or right on a price–quantity diagram. A shift in the ◊demand curve can arise because of a change in the income of buyers, a change in the price of other goods, or a change in tastes for the product. A shift in the ◊supply curve can arise because of change in the costs of production, a change in technology, or a change in price of other goods.

An increase in demand caused by an increase in consumer incomes shifts the demand curve to the right; as a result, the equilibrium quantity bought increases, but the equilibrium price also rises. A rise in labour costs leading to a fall in supply shifts the supply curve to the left; as a result, the equilibrium quantity sold falls while the equilibrium price rises.

Shi'ite or **Shiah** member of an Islamic group who believe that ◊Ali was ◊Muhammad's first true successor. They are doctrinally opposed to the ◊Sunni Muslims.

They developed their own law differing only in minor directions, such as inheritance and the status of women. Holy men have greater authority among the Shi'ites than among the Sunnis. They are prominent in Iran, the Lebanon, and Indo-Pakistan, and are also found in Iraq and Bahrain.

Breakaway sub-groups include the **Alawite**s, to which the ruling party in Syria belongs; and the **Ismaili**s, with the Aga Khan IV (1936–   ) as their spiritual head. The term Shi'ite originally referred to shi'a ('the partisans') of Ali.

In the aftermath of the Gulf War 1991, many thousands of Shi'ites in Iraq were forced to take refuge in the marshes of S Iraq, after unsuccessfully rebelling against Saddam Hussein. Shi'ite sacred shrines were desecrated and atrocities committed by the armed forces on civilians.

shila or **sila** Buddhist term for ethical living. This includes the ethical component of the Eightfold Path: right speech, right action, and the right means of making a living. In addition, Buddhist monks have ten *shilas* or moral rules, including not killing, and abstaining from alcohol.

Shingon Japanese school of esoteric Buddhism, one of the main Buddhist traditions of Japan. It emphasizes the gradual path to enlightenment through meditation and reflection, culminating in Shingon. ◊Mandalas (symbolic representations of the universe) are important aids to meditation, as words are thought to be insufficient to convey the true meaning of the Shingon teachings. It was introduced to Japan from China by Kobo Daishi (774–835 AD).

Shinto the indigenous religion of Japan. It combines an empathetic oneness with natural forces and loyalty to the reigning dynasty as descendants of the Sun goddess, Amaterasu-Omikami. Traditional Shinto followers stressed obedience and devotion to the emperor, and an aggressive nationalistic aspect was developed by the Meiji rulers. Today Shinto has discarded these aspects.

Shinto is the Chinese transliteration of the Japanese *Kami-no-Michi*. Shinto ceremonies appeal to the kami, the mysterious forces of nature manifest in topographical features such as mountains, trees, stones, springs, and caves. Shinto focuses on purity, devotion, and sincerity; aberrations can be cleansed through purification rituals. In addition, purification procedures make the worshipper presentable and acceptable when making requests before the kami.

Shinto's holiest shrine is at Ise, near Kyoto, where in the temple of the Sun goddess is preserved the mirror that she is supposed to have given to Jimmu, the legendary first emperor, in the 7th century BC. Sectarian Shinto consists of 130 sects; the sects are officially recognized but not state-supported (as was state Shinto until its disestablishment after World War II and Emperor Hirohito's disavowal of his divinity 1946). The priesthood became hereditary in the 6th–8th centuries; before this, religious functions were performed by the clan chiefs, of which the emperor was the most important.

There is no Shinto philosophical literature, though there are texts on mythologies, ceremonial and administrative procedures, religious laws, and chronicles of ruling families and temple construction. Shinto has no doctrine and no fixed system of ethics. Believers made no images of gods until the introduction of ◊Buddhism, with which Shintoism has co-existed in a syncretic relatironship since the 8th century.

Shiva or **Siva** in Hinduism, the third chief god (with Brahma and Vishnu). As Mahadeva (great lord), he is the creator, symbolized by the phallic lingam, who restores what as Mahakala he destroys. He is often sculpted as Nataraja, performing his fruitful cosmic dance. His consort or female principle (Sakti) is Parvati, otherwise known as Durga or Kali.

Shockley William 1910–1989. US physicist and amateur geneticist who worked with John Bardeen and Walter Brattain on the invention of the transistor. They were jointly awarded a Nobel prize 1956. During the 1970s Shockley was criticized for his claim that blacks were genetically inferior to whites in terms of intelligence.

He donated his sperm to the bank in S California established by the plastic-lens millionaire Robert Graham for the passing on of the genetic code of geniuses.

shofar in Judaism, a ram's horn blown in the synagogue as a call to repentance at the new-year festivals of Rosh Hashanah and Yom Kippur.

Shrove Tuesday in the Christian calendar, the day before the beginning of Lent. It is also known as *Mardi Gras*.

In the UK, it is called *Pancake day*, after the custom of eating rich food before the Lenten fast.

shuttle diplomacy in international relations, the efforts of an independent mediator to achieve a compromise solution between belligerent parties, travelling back and forth from one to the other.

The term came into use in the 1970s. In 1990–91 shuttle diplomacy was practised by US secretary of state James Baker in the period leading up to, and following, the Gulf War.

Sibyl in Roman legend, one of many prophetic priestesses, notably one from Cumae near Naples. She offered to sell Tarquinius Superbus nine collections of prophecies, the *Sibylline Books*, but the price was too high. When she had destroyed all but three, he bought those for the identical price, and these were kept for consultation in emergency at Rome.

Siegfried legendary Germanic and Norse hero. His story, which may contain some historical elements, occurs in the German ◊*Nibelungenlied/Song of the Nibelung* and in the Norse *Elder* or *Poetic Edda* and the prose *Völsunga Saga* (in the last two works, the hero is known as Sigurd). Siegfried wins Brunhild for his liege lord and marries his sister, but is eventually killed in the intrigues that follow.

Siger of Brabant 1240–1282. Medieval philosopher, a follower of ◊Averroës, who taught at the University of Paris, and whose distinguishing between reason and Christian faith led to his works being condemned as heretical 1270. He refused to recant and was imprisoned. He was murdered while in prison.

Sigurd hero of Norse legend; see ◊Siegfried.

Sikhism religion professed by 14 million Indians, living mainly in the Punjab; there are 18 million Sikhs worldwide, with communities in the UK, Canada, and the USA. Sikhism was founded by Nanak (1469–c. 1539). Sikhs believe in a single God who is the immortal creator of the universe and who has never been incarnate in any form, and in the equality of all

human beings; Sikhism is strongly opposed to caste divisions.

Their holy book is the ◊*Guru Granth Sahib*. Guru Gobind Singh (1666–1708) instituted the *Khanda-di-Pahul*, the baptism of the sword, and established the Khalsa ('pure'), the company of the faithful. The Khalsa wear the five Ks: *kes*, long hair; *kangha*, a comb; *kirpan*, a sword; *kachh*, short trousers; and *kara*, a steel bracelet. Sikh men take the last name 'Singh' ('lion') and women 'Kaur' ('princess').

beliefs Human beings can make themselves ready to find God by prayer and meditation but can achieve closeness to God only as a result of God's *nadar* (grace). Sikhs believe in ◊reincarnation and that the ten human gurus were teachers through whom the spirit of Guru Nanak was passed on to live today in the *Guru Granth Sahib* and the Khalsa.

practice Sikhs do not have a specific holy day, but hold their main services on the day of rest of the country in which they are living. Daily prayer is important in Sikhism, and the gurdwara functions as a social as well as religious centre; it contains a kitchen, the *langar*, where all, male and female, Sikh and non-Sikh, may eat together as equals. Sikh women take the same role as men in religious observances, for example, in reading from the *Guru Granth Sahib* at the gurdwara. Festivals in honour of the ten human gurus include a complete reading of the *Guru Granth Sahib*; Sikhs also celebrate at the time of some of the major Hindu festivals, but their emphasis is on aspects of Sikh belief and the example of the gurus. Sikhs avoid the use of all nonmedicinal drugs and, in particular, tobacco.

history On Nanak's death he was followed as guru by a succession of leaders who converted the Sikhs (the word means 'disciple') into a military confraternity which established itself as a political power. The last of the gurus, Guru Gobind Singh (1666–1708), instituted the *Khanda-di-Pahul* and established the Khalsa. Gobind Singh was assassinated 1708, and since then the *Guru Granth Sahib* has taken the place of a leader.

Upon the partition of India many Sikhs migrated from W to E Punjab, and in 1966 the efforts of Sant Fateh Singh (c. 1911–72) led to the creation of a Sikh state within India by partition of the Punjab. However, the Akali separatist movement agitates for a completely independent Sikh state, Khalistan, and a revival of fundamentalist belief, and was headed from 1978 by Sant Jarnail Singh Bhindranwale (1947–84), killed in the siege of the Golden Temple, Amritsar. In retaliation for this, the Indian prime minister Indira Gandhi was assassinated in Oct of the same year by her Sikh bodyguards. Heavy rioting followed, in which 1,000 Sikhs were killed. Mrs Gandhi's successor, Rajiv Gandhi, reached an agreement for the election of a popular government in the Punjab and for state representatives to the Indian parliament with the moderate Sikh leader Sant Harchand Singh Longowal, who was himself killed 1985 by Sikh extremists.

Simeon Stylites, St c. 390–459. Syrian Christian ascetic who practised his ideal of self-denial by living for 37 years on a platform on top of a high pillar (*stylos*). Feast day 5 Jan.

Simmel Georg 1858–1918. German sociologist and professor at Strasburg university from 1914–18.

Simmel attempted to construct a formal system of sociology, 'abstracted' from history and the detail of human experience, in *Soziologie, Untersuchungen über die Formen der Vergesellschaftung/Sociology, Investigations into the Forms of Socialization* 1908. In *Die Philospohie des Geldes/The Philosophy of Money* 1900, he explored the effects of the money economy on human behaviour. He also wrote several brilliant essays on aspects of culture and society.

Simon Herbert 1916– . US social scientist. He researched decision-making in business corporations and argued that maximum profit was seldom the chief motive. He attempted to examine the psychological factors involved in decision-making and created the concept of 'satisfying behaviour' as motivation for some decisions. He also was deeply involved in the effort to create artificial intelligence technology capable of analysing the factors that influence human problem-solving processes. He was awarded the Nobel Prize for Economics 1978.

simony in the Christian church, the buying and selling of church preferments, now usually regarded as a sin. First condemned 451, it remained widespread until the Reformation.

The term is derived from *Simon Magus* (Acts 8) who offered money to the Apostles for the power of the Holy Ghost.

sin transgression of the will of God or the gods, as revealed in the moral code laid down by a particular religion. In Roman Catholic theology, a distinction is made between *mortal sins*, which, if unforgiven, result in damnation, and *venial sins*, which are less serious. In Islam, the one unforgivable sin is *shirk*, denial that Allah is the only god.

The wages of sin is death.

sin
Bible, the sacred book of the
Jewish and Christian religions.
Romans 6:23

In Christian belief, humanity is in a state of *original sin* and therefore in need of redemption through the crucifixion of Jesus. The sacrament of ◊penance is seen by Roman Catholics as an earthly means of atonement for sin.

To err is human, to forgive, divine.

sin
Alexander Pope, 1688–1744,
English poet and satirist.
Essay on Criticism

siren in Greek legend, a sea nymph who lured sailors to their deaths along rocky coasts by her singing. Odysseus, in order to hear the sirens safely, tied himself to the mast of his ship and stuffed his crew's ears with wax.

The Argonauts escaped them because the singing of Orpheus surpassed that of the sirens.

Sisyphus in Greek mythology, a king of Corinth who, as punishment for his evil life, was condemned in the underworld to roll a huge stone uphill; it always fell back before he could reach the top.

Sita in Hinduism, the wife of Rama, an avatar (manifestation) of the god Vishnu; a character in the ◊*Rāmāyana* epic, characterized by chastity and kindness.

situationism in ethics, the doctrine that any action may be good or bad depending on its context or situation. Situationists argue that no moral rule can apply in all situations and that what may be wrong in most cases may be right if the end is sufficiently good. In general, situationists believe moral attitudes are more important than moral rules.

One of the central books of situationism was Joseph Fletcher's *Situation Ethics* 1966. Situationism has been most influential in Christian moral theology, where its proponents have argued that an intensely thankful and loving attitude will result in good actions.

Siva alternative spelling of ◊Shiva, Hindu god.

Skinner B(urrhus) F(rederic) 1904–1990. US psychologist, a radical behaviourist who rejected the study of mental concepts, seeing the organism as a 'black box' where internal processes are not significant in predicting behaviour. He studied operant ◊conditioning and argued that behaviour is shaped and maintained by its consequences, a view summarized in *The Behavior of Organisms* 1938.

He invented the 'Skinner box', an enclosed environment in which the process of learned behaviour can be observed. In it, a rat presses a lever, and learns to repeat the behaviour because it is rewarded by food. Skinner also designed the air crib, a controlled environment for infants. His own daughter was partially reared in such a crib until the age of two.

His radical approach rejected almost all previous psychology; his text *Science and Human Behavior* 1953 contains no references and no bibliography. His other works include *Walden Two* 1948 and *Beyond Freedom and Dignity* 1971.

Skinner's achievement was to create a science of behaviour in its own right. His influential work in the theoretical validation of behavioral conditioning attempted to explain even complex human behavior as a series of conditioned responses to outside stimuli. Skinner opposed the use of punishment, arguing that it did not effectively control behaviour and had unfavourable side effects. However, his vision of a well-ordered, free society, functioning in the absence of punishment, was one that failed to have much appeal. His research and writings had great influence, attracting both converts and critics. He taught at Harvard University from 1947 to 1974, and was active in research until his death.

slavery the enforced servitude of one person (a slave) to another or one group to another. A slave has no personal rights and is the property of another person through birth, purchase, or capture. Slavery goes back to prehistoric times but declined in Europe after the fall of the Roman Empire. During the imperialism of Spain, Portugal, and Britain in the 16th–18th centuries and in the American South in the 17th–19th centuries, slavery became a mainstay of an agricultural factory economy, with millions of Africans sold to work on plantations in North and South America. Millions more died in the process, but the profits from this trade were enormous. Slavery was abolished in the British Empire 1833 and in the USA at the end of the Civil War 1863–65, but continues illegally in some countries.

The 1926 League of Nations Slavery Convention was adopted by the UN 1953.

Slavery was officially abolished in Saudi Arabia 1963, and in Mauritania not until 1980. It was reported Dec 1988 that slaves were being sold for £30 in Sudan. In 1989 China launched a national campaign against the abduction and sale of women and children. In Shaanxi province 2,000 cases were uncovered 1989 and in Sichuan 7,000 cases 1990. In 1990 teenagers from Mozambique were reported as being sold into slavery in South Africa.

Slavophile intellectual and political group in 19th-century Russia that promoted the idea of an Eastern orientation for the empire in opposition to those who wanted the country to adopt Western methods and ideas of development.

Small Is Beautiful book by E F ◊Schumacher, published 1973, which argues that the increasing scale of corporations and institutions, concentration of power in fewer hands, and the overwhelming priority being given to economic growth are both unsustainable and disastrous to environment and society.

The shortest way to do many things is to do only one thing at once.

Samuel Smiles
Self Help

Smiles Samuel 1812–1904. Scottish writer, author of the popular Victorian didactic work *Self Help* 1859. Here, as in *Character* 1871, *Thrift* 1875, and *Duty* 1880, he energetically advocated self-improvement, largely through emulation of the successful. His works were the embodiment of Victorian values, such as diligence, thrift, honesty, sobriety, and independence.

Smith Adam 1723–1790. Scottish economist and philosopher, often regarded as the founder of political economy. His *The Wealth of Nations* 1776 defined national wealth in terms of consumable goods and the labour that produces them, rather than in terms of bullion, as prevailing economic theories assumed. The ultimate cause of economic growth is explained by the division of labour – dividing a production process into several repetitive operations, each carried out by different workers is more efficient. Smith advocated the free working of individual enterprise, and the necessity of 'free trade'. In his *Theory of Moral Sentiments*, 1759, he argued that the correct way to discern the morally right is to ask what a hypothetical impartial spectator would regard as fitting or proper.

He was born in Kirkcaldy, and was professor of moral philosophy at Glasgow 1752–63.

To found a great empire for the sole purpose of raising up a people of customers, may at first sight appear a project fit only for a nation of shopkeepers. It is, however, a project altogether unfit for a nation of shopkeepers; but extremely fit for a nation that is governed by shopkeepers.

Adam Smith
Wealth of Nations

Smith Joseph 1805–1844. US founder of the ◊Mormon religious group.

Born in Vermont, he received his first religious call in 1820, and in 1827 claimed to have been granted the revelation of the *Book of Mormon* (an ancient American prophet), inscribed on gold plates and concealed a thousand years before in a hill near Palmyra, New York. He founded the Church of Jesus Christ of Latter-day Saints in Fayette, New York, 1830. The headquarters of the church was moved to Kirkland, Ohio, 1831; to Missouri 1838; and to Nauvoo, Illinois, 1840. Smith began the construction of a Mormon temple at Nauvoo, organized a private army to defend the group from its enemies, and declared his candidacy for president. Hostility to Smith intensified when rumors that he had taken several wives began to circulate; Smith publicly opposed polygamy and acknowledged only one wife. He was jailed after some of his followers destroyed the printing press of a newspaper that had attacked him, and a mob stormed the jail and killed him.

Smith William 1769–1839. British geologist, the founder of stratigraphy. Working as a canal engineer, he observed while supervising excavations that different beds of rock could be identified by their fossils, and so established the basis of stratigraphy. He also produced the first geological maps of England and Wales.

Smithson Alison (1928–1993) and Peter 1923– . English architects, teachers, and theorists, known for their development in the 1950s and 1960s of the style known as ◊Brutalism, for example, Hunstanton School, Norfolk 1954. Notable among their other designs are the Economist Building, London 1964, and Robin Hood Gardens, London 1968–72.

Snell Willebrord 1581–1626. Dutch mathematician and physicist who devised the basic law of refraction, known as *Snell's law*, in 1621. This states that the ratio between the sine of the angle of incidence and the sine of the angle of refraction is constant.

The laws describing the reflection of light were well known in antiquity, but the principles governing the refraction of light were little understood. Snell's law was published by French mathematician ◊Descartes in 1637.

social behaviour in zoology, behaviour concerned with altering the behaviour of other individuals of the same species. Social behaviour allows animals to live harmoniously in groups by establishing hierarchies of dominance to discourage disabling fighting. It may be aggressive or submissive (for example, cowering and other signals of appeasement), or designed to establish bonds (such as social grooming or preening).

The social behaviour of mammals and birds is generally more complex than that of lower organisms, and involves relationships with individually recognized animals. Thus, courtship displays allow individuals to choose appropriate mates and form the bonds necessary for successful reproduction. In the social systems of bees, wasps, ants, and termites, an individual's status and relationships with others are largely determined by its biological form, as a member of a caste of workers, soldiers, or reproductives; see ◊eusociality.

social contract the idea that government authority derives originally from an agreement between ruler and ruled in which the former agrees to provide order in return for obedience from the latter. It has been used to support both absolutism (◊Hobbes) and democracy (◊Locke, ◊Rousseau).

The term was revived in the UK in 1974 when a head-on clash between the Conservative government and the trade unions resulted in a general election which enabled a Labour government to take power. It now denotes an unofficial agreement (hence also called 'social compact') between a government and organized labour that, in return for control of prices, rents, and so on, the unions would refrain from economically disruptive wage demands.

social costs and benefits in economics, the costs and benefits to society as a whole that result from economic decisions. These include private costs (the financial cost of production incurred by firms) and benefits (the profits made by firms and the value to people of consuming goods and services) and external costs and benefits (affecting those not directly involved in production or consumption); pollution is one of the external costs.

For example, a chemical plant installs machinery that increases output and reduces employment. The private costs of the extra output are the price of the new machinery. The private benefits are the increases in the chemical firm's profits and in consumption. The external costs include the effects of any increased pollution as a result of the increased output, and the effects of increased unemployment, such as higher expenditure on unemployment benefits. The external benefits include any improvements in technology that other firms can benefit from.

Transport policy provides another clear example of the need to take external costs and benefits into account, where increases in the demand for private road transport generate considerable external costs in the form of pollution, road repairs, and extra costs to firms using transport networks and to medical services as a result of traffic congestion.

social credit theory, put forward by Canadian C H Douglas (1879–1952), that economic crises are caused by bank control of money, which leads to shortage of purchasing power. His remedy was payment of a 'social dividend'. There have been provincial social-credit governments in Canada, but the central government has always vetoed the plan.

social democracy political ideology or belief in the gradual evolution of a democratic ◊socialism within existing political structures. The earliest was the German Sozialdemokratische Partei (SPD), today one of the two main German parties, created in 1875 from August Bebel's earlier German Social Democratic Workers' Party, founded 1869. Parties along the lines of the German model were founded in the last two decades of the 19th century in a number of countries, including Austria, Belgium, the Netherlands, Hungary, Poland, and Russia. The British Labour Party is in the social democratic tradition.

social history branch of history that documents the living and working conditions of people rather than affairs of state. In recent years television programmes, books, and museums have helped to give social history a wide appeal.

History became a serious branch of study in the 18th century, but was confined to ancient civilizations and to recent political and religious history. Only in the early 20th century did historians begin to study how people lived and worked in the past.

Letting a hundred flowers blossom and a hundred schools of thought contend is the policy for promoting progress in the arts and the sciences and a flourishing socialist culture in our land.

socialism
Mao Zedong or Mao Tse-tung, 1893–1976,
Chinese Marxist leader and theoretician.
Speech in Peking 27 Feb 1957

---

socialism movement aiming to establish a classless society by substituting public for private ownership of the means of production, distribution, and exchange. The term has been used to describe positions as widely apart as anarchism and social democracy. Socialist ideas appeared in classical times; in early Christianity; among later Christian sects such as the ◊Anabaptists and ◊Diggers; and, in the 18th and early 19th centuries, were put forward as systematic political aims by Jean-Jacques Rousseau, Claude Saint-Simon, François Fourier, and Robert Owen, among others. See also Karl ◊Marx and Friedrich ◊Engels.

The late 19th and early 20th centuries saw a division between those who reacted against Marxism leading to social-democratic parties and those who emphasized the original revolutionary significance of Marx's teachings. Weakened by these divisions, the second ◊International (founded in 1889) collapsed in 1914, right-wing socialists in all countries supporting participation in World War I while the left opposed it. The Russian Revolution took socialism from the sphere of theory to that of practice, and was followed in 1919 by the foundation of the Third International, which completed the division between right and left. This lack of unity, in spite of the temporary successes of the popular fronts in France and Spain in 1936–38, facilitated the rise of fascism and Nazism.

After World War II socialist and communist parties tended to formal union in Eastern Europe, although the rigid communist control that ensued was later modified in some respects in, for example, Poland, Romania, and Yugoslavia. Subsequent tendencies to broaden communism were suppressed in Hungary (1956) and Czechoslovakia (1968). In 1989, however, revolutionary change throughout Eastern Europe ended this rigid control; this was followed in 1991 by the disbanding of the Soviet Communist Party and the ensuing disintegration of the Soviet Union. In Western Europe a communist takeover of the Portuguese revolution failed 1975–76, and elsewhere, as in France under François Mitterrand, attempts at socialist-communist cooperation petered out. Most countries in W Europe have a strong socialist party; for example, in Germany the Social Democratic Party and in Britain the ◊Labour Party.

In the later 19th century socialist parties arose in most European countries; for example, in Britain the ◊Independent Labour Party. This period, when in Russia the Bolsheviks were reviving, witnessed a reaction against Marxism, typified by the ◊Fabian Society in Britain and the German Revisionists, which appealed to popular nationalism and solved economic problems by similar means of state control of the economy, but in the general interests of private capital.

'socialism in one country' concept proposed by ◊Stalin in 1924. In contrast to ◊Trotsky's theory of the permanent revolution, Stalin suggested that the emphasis be changed away from promoting revolutions abroad to the idea of building socialism, economically and politically, in the USSR without help from other countries.

Socialist Realism artistic doctrine set up by the USSR during the 1930s setting out the optimistic, socialist terms in which society should be portrayed in works of art. It applied to music and the visual arts as well as writing.

The policy was used as a means of censoring artists whose work, it was felt, did not follow the approved Stalinist party line, or was too 'Modern'. The policy was relaxed after Stalin's death but remained somewhat in force until the dissolution of the USSR 1991. Artists whose work was censured in this way included the composer Shostakovich and the writers Solzhenitsyn and Sholokhov.

socialization process, beginning in childhood, by which a person becomes a member of a society, learning its norms, customs, laws, and ways of living. The main agents of socialization are the family, school, peer groups, work, religion, and the mass media. The main methods of socialization are direct instruction, rewards and punishment, imitation, experimentation, role play, and interaction.

Some agents of socialization, such as the family and the peer group, may conflict with each other, offering alternative goals, values, and styles of behaviour. Socialization is of particular interest to psychologists, anthropologists, and sociologists, but there are diverse opinions about its methods and effects.

social mobility movement of groups and individuals up and down the social scale in a classed society. The extent or range of social mobility varies in different societies. Individual social mobility may occur through education, marriage, talent, and so on; group mobility usually occurs through change in the occupational structure caused by new technological or economic developments.

The caste system of India and the feudalism of medieval Europe are cited as examples of closed societies, where little social mobility was possible; the class system of Western industrial societies is considered relatively open and flexible.

social psychology branch of ◊psychology concerned with the behaviour of individuals in groups and the ways in which they relate to one another and to the societies of which they are a part.

Different kinds of social act are studied, as are the attitudes and assumptions that lie behind them and make them meaningful. There are two main approaches. One considers individuals as viewers, or perceivers, of the social environment, learning about it and forming judgments and attitudes, and so links up with general experimental psychology and other biological sciences. The other views individuals as participants in the social environment, influencing it and being influenced by it, and thus overlaps with sociology and other social sciences.

Bibl. Eiser, J Richard *Social Psychology: Attitudes, Cognition and Social Behaviour* (1986)

Social Realism in the visual arts and literature, work that realistically depicts subjects of social concern, such as poverty and deprivation, usually from a left-wing standpoint.

The term dates from the end of the Second World War, although the 19th-century French painter Courbet provides an early example with his painting *The Stonebreakers* 1850 (now destroyed). Those painters described as Social Realists may practice in a variety of styles, which are rarely 'realistic' in the sense of creating an exact likeness. They include the Italian painter Guttoso and the American Ashcan School. (See ◊Realism).

social science the group of academic disciplines that investigate how and why people behave the way they do, as individuals and in groups. The term originated with the 19th-century French thinker Auguste ◊Comte. The academic social sciences are generally listed as sociology, economics, anthropology, political science, and psychology.

Western thought about society has been influenced by the ideas and insights of such great theorists as Plato, Aristotle, Machiavelli, Rousseau, Hobbes, and Locke. The study of society, however, can be traced to the great intellectual period of the 18th century called the Enlightenment, and to the industrial and political revolutions of the 18th and 19th centuries, to the moral philosophy of ◊positivism. Comte attempted to establish the study of society as a scientific discipline, capable of precision and prediction in the same way as natural science, but it overlaps extensively with such subject areas as history, geography, law, philosophy, and even biology. Although some thinkers – such as Marx – have attempted to synthesize the study of society within one theory, none has yet achieved what Einstein did for physics or Charles Darwin for biology. A current debate is whether the study of people can or should be a science.

No one can be perfectly free till all are free; no one can be perfectly moral till all are moral; no one can be perfectly happy till all are happy.

society
Herbert Spencer, 1820–1903,
British philosopher.
Social Statics 4, ch 30

---

society the organization of people into communities or groups. Social science, in particular sociology, is the study of human behaviour in a social context. Various aspects of society are discussed under ◊class, ◊community, ◊culture, ◊kinship, ◊norms, ◊role, ◊socialization, and ◊status.

Society of Friends official name of the Quakers; see ◊Friends, Society of.

Society of Jesus official name of the Roman Catholic order commonly known as the ◊Jesuits.

Socinianism 17th-century Christian belief that rejects such traditional doctrines as the Trinity and original sin, named after *Socinus*, the Latinized name of Lelio Francesco Maria

---

There is no such thing as Society. There are individual men and women, and there are families.

society
Margaret Thatcher, Baroness
Thatcher of Kesteven
Woman's Own 31 Oct 1987

Sozzini (1525–1562), Italian Protestant theologian. It is an early form of ◊Unitarianism.

His views on the nature of Christ were developed by his nephew, Fausto Paolo Sozzini (1539–1604), who also taught pacifist and anarchist doctrines akin to those of the 19th-century Russian novelist Tolstoy. Socinianism denies the divinity of Jesus but emphasizes his virtues.

sociobiology study of the biological basis of all social behaviour, including the application of population genetics to the evolution of behaviour. It builds on the concept of inclusive fitness, contained in the notion of the 'selfish gene'. Contrary to some popular interpretations, it does not assume that all behaviour is genetically determined.

The New Zealand biologist W D Hamilton introduced the concept of inclusive fitness, which emphasizes that the evolutionary function of behaviour is to allow an organism to contribute as many of its own alleles as it can to future generations: this idea is encapsulated in the British zoologist Richard Dawkins's notion of the 'selfish gene'.

sociolinguistics the study of language and its relationship to society. Sociolinguists analyse how outside factors – class, gender, ethnicity, and so on – influence the acquisition and development of language in particular groups.

sociology systematic study of society, in particular of social order and social change, social conflict and social problems. It studies institutions such as the family, law, and the church, as well as concepts such as norm, role, and culture. Sociology attempts to study people in their social environment according to certain underlying moral, philosophical, and political codes of behaviour.

Sociology today reflects a variety of perspectives and traditions. Its focus tends to be on contemporary industrial society, sometimes comparing it with pre-industrial society, and occasionally drawing on such related disciplines as history, geography, politics, economics, psychology, and anthropology. Its concerns range from theories of social order and change to detailed analyses of small groups, individuals, and the routines of daily life. The relation between theory and method is one part of the current debate about whether sociology is or should be a science, and whether it can or should be free of ideology.

Nothing can harm a good man, either in life or after death.

Socrates
Plato's *Apology* 42

Socrates c. 469–399 BC. Athenian philosopher. He wrote nothing but was immortalized in the dialogues of his pupil Plato. In his desire to combat the scepticism of the ◊sophists, Socrates asserted the possibility of genuine knowledge. In ethics, he put forward the view that the good person never knowingly does wrong. True knowledge emerges through dialogue and systematic questioning and an abandoning of uncritical claims to knowledge. The effect of Socrates' teaching was disruptive since he opposed tyranny.

Accused in 399 on charges of impiety and corruption of youth, he was condemned by the Athenian authorities to die by drinking hemlock.

Socratic method method of teaching used by Socrates, in which he aimed to guide pupils to clear thinking on ethics and politics by asking questions and then exposing their inconsistencies in cross-examination. This method was effective against the ◊sophists.

Soddy Frederick 1877–1956. English physical chemist who pioneered research into atomic disintegration and coined the term isotope. He was awarded a Nobel prize 1921 for investigating the origin and nature of isotopes.

His works include *Chemistry of the Radio-Elements* 1912–14, *The Interpretation of the Atom* 1932, and *The Story of Atomic Energy* 1949. After his chemical discoveries, Soddy spent some 40 years developing a theory of 'energy economics', which he called 'Cartesian economics'. He argued for the abolition of debt and compound interest, the nationalization of credit, and a new theory of value based on the quantity of energy contained in a thing, believing that as a scientist he was able to see through the errors of economists.

Sodom and Gomorrah two ancient cities in the Dead Sea area of the Middle East, recorded in the Old Testament (Genesis) as being destroyed by fire and brimstone for their wickedness.

software a computer program needed to make computer hardware function. A word-processing program or a ◊spreadsheet are examples of software packages.

Solander Daniel Carl 1736–1772. Swedish botanist. In 1768, as assistant to Joseph Banks, he accompanied the explorer James Cook on his first voyage to the S Pacific, during which he made extensive collections of plants.

Solander was born in Norrland, Sweden, and studied under the botanist Linnaeus. In 1771 he became secretary and librarian to Banks and in 1773 became keeper of the natural history department of the British Museum. Named after him are a genus of Australian plants and a cape at the entrance to Botany Bay.

solipsism in philosophy, a view that maintains that the self is the only thing that can be known to exist. It is an extreme form of ◊scepticism. The solipsist sees himself or herself as the only individual in existence, assuming other people to be a reflection of his or her own consciousness.

Solomon c. 974–c. 937 BC. In the Old Testament, third king of Israel, son of David by Bathsheba. During a peaceful reign, he was famed for his wisdom and his alliances with Egypt and Phoenicia. The much later biblical Proverbs, Ecclesiastes, and Song of Songs are attributed to him. He built the temple in Jerusalem with the aid of heavy taxation and forced labour, resulting in the revolt of N Israel.

The so-called *King Solomon's Mines* at Aqaba, Jordan (copper and iron), are of later date.

soma intoxicating drink made from the fermented sap of the *Asclepias acida* plant, used in Indian religious ritual as a sacrifice to the gods. As *haoma*, its consumption also constituted the central rite in Zoroastrian ritual. Some have argued that the plant was in fact a hallucinogenic mushroom.

Somerville Mary (born Fairfax) 1780–1872. Scottish scientific writer who produced several widely used textbooks, despite having just one year of formal education. Somerville College, Oxford, is named after her.

Her main works were *Mechanism of the Heavens* 1831 (a translation of ◊Laplace's treatise on celestial mechanics), *On the Connexion of Physical Sciences* 1834, *Physical Geography* 1848, and *On Molecular and Microscopic Science* 1869.

Sommerfeld Arnold 1868–1951. German physicist, who demonstrated that difficulties with Niels ◊Bohr's model of the atom, in which electrons move around a central nucleus in circular orbits, could be overcome by supposing that electrons adopt elliptical orbits.

sophist one of a group of 5th-century BC itinerant lecturers on culture, rhetoric, and politics. Sceptical about the possibility of achieving genuine knowledge, they applied bogus reasoning and were concerned with winning arguments rather than establishing the truth. ◊Plato regarded them as dishonest and *sophistry* came to mean fallacious reasoning.

Sorby Henry Clifton 1826–1908. British geologist who made huge advances in the field of petrology. Sorby's interest in studying meteorites led him in 1863 to discover the crystalline nature of steel, thus instituting the study of metallography. Sorby used the thin-slicing of hard minerals in the microscopic study of rocks, enabling the constituent minerals to be scrutinized in transmitted light. He later employed the same techniques in the study of iron and steel under stress.

Sorel Georges 1847–1922. French philosopher who believed that socialism could only come about through a general strike; his theory of the need for a 'myth' to sway the body of the people was used by fascists.

Sørensen Søren 1868–1939. Danish chemist who in 1909 introduced the concept of using the pH scale as a measure of the acidity of a solution. On Sørensen's scale, still used today, a pH of 7 is neutral; higher numbers represent alkalinity, and lower numbers acidity.

Sorokhin Pitirim Alexandrovich 1889–1968. Russian-born sociologist who worked in the USA. His detailed knowledge of history, including first-hand experience of the Russian Revolutions of 1917, led him to make an analysis of macro social change.

In his major work *Social and Cultural Dynamics* 1937–41 he perceived recurring patterns of change within the history of civilization. He saw the current age as being in a crisis of hedonism and violence which could only be cured by altruism.

soteriology study of the way to ◊salvation.

What is a man profited, if he shall gain the whole world, and lose his own soul.

soul
Bible, the sacred book of the Jewish and Christian religions. Matthew 16:26

---

soul according to many religions, the intangible and immortal part of a human being that survives the death of the physical body. Judaism, Christianity, and Islam all teach that at the end of the world each soul will be judged and assigned to heaven or hell on its merits.

According to orthodox Jewish doctrine, most souls first spend time in purgatory to be purged of their sins, and are then removed to paradise. In Christianity the soul is that part of the person that can be redeemed from sin through divine grace. In other religions, such as Hinduism, the soul is thought to undergo ◊reincarnation until the individual reaches enlightenment and is freed from the cycle of rebirth. According to the teachings of Buddhism, no permanent self or soul exists.

In his 1990 New Year's message, the Pope appeared to agree that animals have souls by stating, 'animals possess a soul and that man must love and feel solidarity with our smaller brethren.' This statement is still a source of considerable debate within the Roman Catholic Church.

South American indigenous religions beliefs and myths of the South American Indians. Many have the concept of a supreme force or god, but this force is often so remote or great that it is not worshipped directly. There are many powerful spirits, including souls of the ancestors, that inhabit and influence the natural environment and the lives of humans. To maintain harmony with the forest, rivers, and animals, these spirits are respected. Animals associated with creation myths or seen as harbingers of good or ill luck are not hunted; for example, the anaconda snake among the Sarema people of the Amazon rainforest.

sovereignty absolute authority within a given territory. The possession of sovereignty is taken to be the distinguishing feature of the state, as against other forms of community.

The term has an internal aspect, in that it refers to the ultimate source of authority within a state, such as a parliament or monarch, and an external aspect, where it denotes the independence of the state from any outside authority.

soviet originally a strike committee elected by Russian workers in the 1905 revolution; in 1917 these were set up by peasants, soldiers, and factory workers. The soviets sent delegates to the All-Russian Congress of Soviets to represent their opinions to a future government. They were later taken over by the ◊Bolsheviks.

space–time in physics, combination of space and time used in the theory of ◊relativity. When developing relativity, Albert Einstein showed that time was in many respects like an extra dimension (or direction) to space. Space and time can thus be considered as entwined into a single entity, rather than two separate things.

Space–time is considered to have four dimensions: three of space and one of time. In relativity theory, events are described as occurring at points in space–time. The **general theory of relativity** describes how space–time is distorted by the presence of material bodies, an effect that we observe as gravity.

Spallanzani Lazzaro 1729–1799. Italian priest and biologist. He disproved the theory that microbes spontaneously generate out of rotten food by showing that they would not grow in flasks of broth that had been boiled for 30 minutes and then sealed.

Spartacist member of a group of left-wing radicals in Germany at the end of World War I, founders of the *Spartacus League*, which became the German Communist Party in 1919. The league participated in the Berlin workers' revolt of Jan 1919, which was suppressed by the Freikorps on the orders of the socialist government. The agitation ended with the murder of Spartacist leaders Karl Liebknecht and Rosa Luxemburg.

specialization in economics, a method of organizing production where economic units such as households or nations are not self-sufficient but concentrate on producing certain goods and services and trading the surplus with others. Specialization of workers is known as the ◊division of labour.

Spencer Herbert 1820–1903. British philosopher. He wrote *Social Statics* 1851, expounding his *laissez-faire* views on social and political problems, *Principles of Psychology* 1855, and *Education* 1861. In 1862 he began his ten-volume *System of Synthetic Philosophy*, in which he extended Charles ◊Darwin's theory of evolution to the entire field of human knowledge. The chief of the ten volumes are *First Principles* 1862 and *Principles* of biology, sociology, and ethics. Other works are *The Study of Sociology, Man v. the State, Essays*, and an autobiography.

Science is organized knowledge.

Herbert Spencer
Education

Spengler Oswald 1880–1936. German philosopher whose *Decline of the West* 1918 argued that civilizations go through natural cycles of growth and decay. He was admired by the Nazis.

Christian theology is the grandmother of Bolshevism.

Oswald Spengler
The Hour of Decision

Sphinx mythological creature, represented in Egyptian, Assyrian, and Greek art as a lion with a human head. In Greek myth the Sphinx killed all those who came to her and failed to answer her riddle about what animal went firstly on four legs, then on two, and lastly on three: the answer is humanity (baby, adult, and old person with stick). She committed suicide when ◊Oedipus gave the right answer.

Spinoza Baruch or Benedict 1632–1677. Dutch philosopher of Portuguese–Jewish parentage. In his *Ethics* 1677, he used the geometrical method to demonstrate that there is but one substance, which he pantheistically called 'God or Nature'. This one substance, which exists necessarily, has infinite attributes, of which we know two – extension and thought. Good and evil are realtive. We, as mere modes of God or Nature, do not have any free will. Our true freedom consists in the 'intellectual love of God', or the philosophical understanding of the causes of our actions and of the world.

A Treatise on Religious and Political Philosophy 1670 was the only one of his works published during his life, and was attacked by Christians. He was excommunicated by the Jewish community in Amsterdam on charges of heretical thought and practice 1656 because he deined the existence of a personal deity. He was a lens-grinder by trade.

spiritualism belief in the survival of the human personality and in communication between the living and those who have 'passed on'. The spiritualist movement originated in the USA in 1848. Adherents to this religious denomination practise *mediumship*, which claims to allow clairvoyant knowledge of distant events and spirit healing. The writer Arthur Conan Doyle and the Victorian prime minister Gladstone were converts.

In the UK the Society for Psychical Research was founded in 1882 by W H Myers and Henry Sidgwick (1838–1900) to investigate the claims of spiritualism. Spiritualists include Daniel Home, the scientists Oliver Lodge and William Crookes, and Air Marshal Lord Dowding.

spreadsheet in computing, a program that mimics a sheet of ruled paper, divided into columns and rows. The user enters values in the sheet, then instructs the program to perform some operation on them, such as totalling a column or finding the average of a series of numbers. Highly complex numerical analyses may be built up from these simple steps.

Spreadsheets are widely used in business for forecasting and financial control. The first spreadsheet program, Software Arts' VisiCalc, appeared 1979. The best known include Lotus 1–2–3 and Microsoft Excel.

Sprengel Christian Konrad 1750–1816. German botanist. Writing in 1793 he described the phenomenon of dichogamy, the process whereby stigma and anthers on the same flower ripen at different times and so guarantee cross-fertilization.

Sraffa Piero 1898– . Italian-born economist, living in England since 1927. Sraffa was a critic of orthodox neoclassical ◊economics. In *The Laws of Returns under Competitive Conditions* (*Economic Journal* Dec 1926) he suggested that, contrary to orthodox theory, firms could influence the price of the product even if there were a large number of firms competing against each other. He also pointed out the difficulties of applying supply and demand analysis to capital in his book *Production of Commodities by Means of Commodities* 1960. He suggested that these difficulties, related to the problem of defining ◊capital precisely, meant that the idea that prices are wholly determined by the interaction of supply and demand was flawed.

stagflation economic condition (experienced in Europe in the 1970s) in which rapid inflation is accompanied by stagnating, even declining, output and by increasing unemployment. Its cause is often sharp increases in costs of raw materials and/or labour.

Stahl Georg Ernst 1660–1734. German chemist who produced a fallacious theory of combustion.

He was professor of medicine at Halle, and physician to the king of Prussia. He argued that objects burn because they contain a combustible substance, phlogiston. Substances rich in phlogiston, such as wood, burn almost completely away. Metals, which are low in phlogiston, burn less well. Chemists spent much of the 18th century evaluating Stahl's theories before these were finally proved false by Antoine ◊Lavoisier.

Stalin Joseph. Adopted name (Russian 'steel') of Joseph Vissarionovich Djugashvili 1879–1953. Soviet politician. A member of the October Revolution Committee 1917, Stalin became general secretary of the Communist Party 1922. After ◊Lenin's death 1924, Stalin sought to create 'socialism in one country' and clashed with ◊Trotsky, who denied the possibility of socialism inside Russia until revolution had occurred in W Europe. Stalin won this ideological struggle by 1927, and a series of five-year plans was launched to collectivize industry and agriculture from 1928. All opposition was eliminated in the Great Purge 1936–38. During World War II, Stalin intervened in the military direction of the campaigns against Nazi Germany. His role was denounced after his death by Khrushchev and other members of the Soviet regime.

Born in Georgia, the son of a shoemaker, Stalin was educated for the priesthood but was expelled from his seminary for Marxist propaganda. He became a member of the Social Democratic Party 1898, and joined Lenin and the Bolsheviks 1903. He was repeatedly exiled to Siberia 1903–13. He then became a member of the Communist Party's Politburo, and sat on the October Revolution committee. Stalin rapidly consolidated a powerful following (including Molotov); in 1921 he became commissar for nationalities in the Soviet government, responsible for the decree granting equal rights to all peoples of the Russian Empire, and was appointed general secretary of the Communist Party 1922. As dictator in the 1930s, he disposed of all real and imagined enemies. In recent years increasing evidence has been uncovered revealing Stalin's anti-Semitism, for example, the execution of

19 Jewish activists in 1952 for a 'Zionist conspiracy'.

He met Churchill and Roosevelt at Tehran 1943 and at Yalta 1945, and took part in the Potsdam conference. After the war, Stalin maintained an autocratic rule.

Stalinism totalitarian communism based on the political methods of Joseph ◊Stalin. Power is exclusively in the hands of the Communist Party which is organized on rigidly hierarchical lines. The leader is presented, by state propaganda, as the selfless and benevolent father of the nation. Economic policy is based on enforced industrialization and the collectivization of agriculture. The general population is controlled by a vast bureaucracy and all opposition and internal debate is ruthlessly repressed by the secret police.

standard of living in economics, the measure of consumption and welfare of a country, community, class, or person. Individual standard-of-living expectations are heavily influenced by the income and consumption of other people in similar jobs.

Universal measures of standards of living cannot be applied to individuals. National income and gross national product, which measure a country's wealth, do not take into account unpaid work (housework and family labour) or quality of life and do not show the distribution of wealth or reflect the particular national or individual aspirations, duties, or responsibilities, which differ widely from person to person, class to class, and country to country.

Stanislavsky Konstantin Sergeivich 1863–1938. Russian actor, director, and teacher of acting. He rejected the declamatory style of acting in favour of a more realistic approach, concentrating on the psychological basis for the development of character. The Actors Studio is based on his methods. As a director, he is acclaimed for his productions of the great plays of Chekhov.

Stanislavsky cofounded the Moscow Art Theatre 1898 and directed productions of Chekhov and Gorky. His ideas, which he described in *My Life in Art* 1924 and other works, had considerable influence on acting techniques in Europe and the USA.

Stanley Wendell 1904–1971. US biochemist who crystallized the tobacco mosaic virus (TMV) in 1935. He demonstrated that, despite its crystalline state, TMV remained infectious. Together with John Northrop and James Sumner, Stanley received the 1946 Nobel Prize for Chemistry.

Stanton Elizabeth Cady 1815–1902. US feminist who, with Susan B ◊Anthony, founded the National Woman Suffrage Association 1869, the first women's movement in the USA and was its first president. She and Anthony wrote and compiled the *History of Woman Suffrage* 1881–86. Stanton also worked for the abolition of slavery.

She organized the International Council of Women in Washington DC. Her publications include *Degradation of Disenfranchisement* and *Solitude of Self* 1892, and in 1885 and 1898 she published a two-part feminist critique of the Bible: *The Woman's Bible*.

Stark Johannes 1874–1957. German physicist. In 1902 he predicted, correctly, that high-velocity rays of positive ions (canal rays) would demonstrate the ◊Doppler effect, and in 1913 showed that a strong electric field can alter the wavelength of light emitted by atoms (the *Stark effect*). He was awarded the Nobel Prize for Physics 1919.

Star of David or *Magen David* six-pointed star (made with two equilateral triangles), a symbol of Judaism since the 17th century. It is the central motif on the flag of Israel, and, since 1897, the emblem of Zionism.

state territory that forms its own domestic and foreign policy, acting through laws that are typically decided by a government and carried out, by force if necessary, by agents of that government. It can be argued that growth of regional international bodies such as the European Community means that states no longer enjoy absolute sovereignty.

Although most states are members of the United Nations, this is not a completely reliable criterion: some are not members by choice, like Switzerland; some have been deliberately excluded, like Taiwan; and some are members but do not enjoy complete national sovereignty. The classic definition of a state is given by R M MacIver (*The Modern State* 1926): 'An association which, acting through law as promulgated by a government endowed to this end with coercive power, maintains within a community territorially demarcated the universal external conditions of social order.' There are four essential elements in this definition: that people have formed an association to create and preserve social order; that the community comprising the state is clearly defined in territorial terms; that the government representing the people acts according to promulgated laws; and that it has power to enforce these laws.

Today, the state is seen as the nation state so that any community that has absolute sovereignty over a specific area is a state. Thus the so-called states of the USA, which are to some degree subject to the will of the federal government, are not states in international terms, nor are colonial or similar possessions, which, too, are subject to an overriding authority.

States General former French parliament that consisted of three estates: nobility, clergy, and commons. First summoned 1302, it declined in importance as the power of the crown grew. It was not called at all 1614–1789 when the crown needed to institute fiscal reforms to avoid financial collapse. Once called, the demands made by the States General formed the first phase in the ◊French Revolution. States General is also the name of the Dutch parliament.

stations of the Cross in the Christian church, a series of 14 crosses, usually each with a picture or image, depicting the 14 stages in Jesus' journey to the Crucifixion. They are commonly found on the walls of churches.

statistics branch of mathematics concerned with the collection and interpretation of data. For example, to determine the mean age of the children in a school, a statistically acceptable answer might be obtained by calculating an average based on the ages of a representative sample, consisting, for example, of a random tenth of the pupils from each class. ◊Probability is the branch of statistics dealing with predictions of events.

status in the social sciences, an individual's social position, or the esteem in which he or she is held by others in society. Both within and between most occupations or social positions there is a status hierarchy. *Status symbols*, such as insignia of office or an expensive car, often accompany high status.

The two forms of social prestige may be separate or interlinked. Formal social status is attached to a certain social position, occupation, role, or office. Informal social status is based on an individual's own personal talents, skills, or personality. Sociologists distinguish between *ascribed status*, which is bestowed by birth, and *achieved status*, the result of one's own efforts.

The German sociologist Max Weber analysed social stratification in terms of three separate but interlinked dimensions: class, status, and power. Status is seen as a key influence on human behaviour, on the way people evaluate themselves and others.

status symbol object which symbolizes the status of an individual. Common status symbols are company cars, individual offices, name plates on the door, and personal assistants.

Staudinger Hermann 1881–1965. German organic chemist, founder of macromolecular chemistry, who carried out pioneering research into the structure of albumen and cellulose. Nobel prize 1953.

steady-state theory in astronomy, a rival theory to that of the ◊Big Bang, which claims that the universe has no origin but is expanding because new matter is being created continuously throughout the universe. The theory was proposed 1948 by Hermann ◊Bondi, Thomas Gold (1920–   ), and Fred ◊Hoyle, but was dealt a severe blow in 1965 by the discovery of cosmic background radiation (radiation left over from the formation of the universe) and is now largely rejected.

Stefan Joseph 1835–1893. Austrian physicist who established one of the basic laws of heat radiation in 1874, since known as the *Stefan–Boltzmann law*. This states that the heat radiated by a hot body is proportional to the fourth power of its absolute temperature.

A woman without a man is like a fish without a bicycle.

> **Gloria Steinem**
> Attributed remark

Steinem Gloria 1934–   . US journalist and liberal feminist who emerged as a leading figure in the US women's movement in the late 1960s. She was also involved in radical protest campaigns against racism and the Vietnam War. She co-founded the Women's Action Alliance 1970 and *Ms* magazine. In 1983 a collection of her articles was published as *Outrageous Acts and Everyday Rebellions*.

Steiner Rudolf 1861–1925. German philosopher, occultist, and educationist who, after a detailed study of ◊Goethe's thought turned to ◊theosophy before formulating his own mystic and spiritual teaching which he called ◊anthroposophy.

This rejected materialism and aimed to develop the whole human being, intellectually, socially, and, above all, spiritually. He believed that people are reincarnated several times before attaining complete self-consciousness.

The many subjects on which he lectured include the arts, medicine, where he reintroduced the concept of the ◊humours, and agriculture, where his theory of bio-dynamics suggested that plants germinate better at different points in the lunar cycle. He also designed and built a cultural centre, the Goethanum, at Dornach in Switzerland in a unique geometrical/expressionist style. It became the world centre of anthroposophy.

Steiner school school committed to the educational philosophy of Rudolf ◊Steiner, who developed a curriculum for children from the nursery-school stage to the age of 17.

The curriculum lays a strong emphasis on artistic creativity and intuitive thinking but permits pupils to take state exams in traditional academic subjects. Steiner's pioneer school established in Stuttgart, Germany, 1919, inspired other countries to adopt his ideas. Waldorf school is an alternative name.

In the UK, Steiner methods have been used very successfully in schools and communities for mentally handicapped children and young people, but there are also Steiner schools for children of the whole ability range.

Steinmetz Charles 1865–1923. US engineer who formulated the **Steinmetz hysteresis law** in 1891, which describes the dissipation of energy that occurs when a system is subject to an alternating magnetic force.

stereotype in sociology, a fixed, exaggerated, and preconceived description about a certain type of person, group, or society. It is based on prejudice rather than fact, but by repetition and with time, stereotypes become fixed in people's minds, resistant to change or factual evidence to the contrary.

The term, originally used for a method of duplicate printing, was adopted in a social sense by the US journalist Walter Lippman in 1922. Stereotypes can prove dangerous when used to justify persecution and discrimination. Some sociologists believe that stereotyping reflects a power structure in which one group in society uses labelling to keep another group 'in its place'.

Stern Otto 1888–1969. German physicist. Stern studied with Einstein in Prague and Zürich, where he became a lecturer in 1914. After World War I he demonstrated by means of the **Stern–Gerlach apparatus** that elementary particles have wavelike properties as well as the properties of matter that had been demonstrated. He left Germany for the USA in 1933. He was awarded the Nobel Prize for Physics in 1943.

stigmata impressions or marks corresponding to the five wounds Jesus received at his crucifixion, which are said to have appeared spontaneously on St Francis and other saints.

Stijl, De group of 20th-century Dutch artists and architects led by Mondrian from 1917. They believed in the concept of the 'designer'; that all life, work, and leisure should be surrounded by art; and that everything functional should also be aesthetic. The group had a strong influence on the ◊Bauhaus school.

The name came from a magazine, *De Stijl*, founded 1917 by Mondrian and Theo van Doesburg (1883–1931).

Stirner Max. Pseudonym of Johannes Kasper Schmidt 1806–1856. German anarchist thinker who argued that the state, class, and humanity were meaningless abstractions, and that only individuals mattered. In his extreme form of ◊egoism, the aim of human life is the fulfilment of one's own will. His main work is *Der Einzige und sein Eigentum/The Ego and his Own* 1845.

Adapt thyself to the things amidst which thy lot has been cast and love in sincerity the fellow-creatures with whom destiny has ordained thou shalt live.

stoicism

Marcus Aurelius Antoninus, 121–180, Roman emperor and stoic philosopher.
The Meditations VI. 39

---

stoicism Greek school of philosophy, founded about 300 BC by Zeno of Citium. The stoics were pantheistic materialists who believed that happiness lay in accepting the law of the universe. They emphasized human brotherhood, denounced slavery, and were internationalist. The name is derived from the porch on which Zeno taught.

In the 3rd and 2nd centuries BC, stoics took a prominent part in Greek and Roman revolutionary movements. After the 1st century BC stoicism became the philosophy of the Roman ruling class and lost its revolutionary significance; outstanding stoics of this period were Seneca, Epictetus, and Marcus Aurelius Antoninus.

Stokes George Gabriel 1819–1903. Irish physicist. During the late 1840s, he studied the viscosity (resistance to relative motion) of fluids. This culminated in **Stokes' law**, $F = 6\pi\varepsilon rv$, which applies to a force acting on a sphere falling through a liquid, where ϵ is the liquid's viscosity and r and v are the radius and velocity of the sphere.

Stone (John) Richard (Nicholas) 1913– . British economist, a statistics expert whose system of 'national income accounting' has been adopted in many countries. Nobel Prize for Economics 1984.

Stone Lucy 1818–1893. US feminist orator and editor. Married to the radical Henry Blackwell in 1855, she gained wide publicity when, after a mutual declaration rejecting the legal superiority of the man in marriage, she chose to retain her own surname despite her marriage. The term 'Lucy Stoner' was coined to mean a woman who advocated doing the same.

In the 1860s she helped to establish the American Woman Suffrage Association and founded and edited the Boston *Woman's Journal*, a suffragist paper that was later edited by her daughter Alice Stone Blackwell (1857–1950).

Stopes Marie (Carmichael) 1880–1958. Scottish birth-control campaigner. With her husband H V Roe (1878–1949), an aircraft manufacturer, she founded a London birth-control clinic 1921. The Well Woman Centre in Marie Stopes House, London, commemorates her work. She wrote plays and verse as well as the best-selling manual *Married Love* 1918.

Stravinsky Igor 1882–1971. Russian composer, later of French (1934) and US (1945) nationality. He studied under Rimsky-Korsakov and wrote the music for the Diaghilev ballets *The Firebird* 1910, *Petrushka* 1911, and *The Rite of Spring* 1913 (controversial at the time for their unorthodox rhythms and harmonies). His versatile work ranges from his Neo-Classical ballet *Pulcinella* 1920 to the choral-orchestral *Symphony of Psalms* 1930. He later made use of serial techniques in such works as the *Canticum Sacrum* 1955 and the ballet *Agon* 1953–57.

Strawson Peter Frederick 1919– . English philosopher who studied the distortions that logical systems impose on ordinary language. He also analysed the ways in which we distinguish individual things, concluding that the location of things in space and time is fundamental to all the various ways in which we distinguish individuals of any kind. He called his approach 'descriptive metaphysics' and he identified Immanuel ◊Kant as a fellow practitioner.

His publications include *Introduction to Logical Theory* 1952, *Individuals: An Essay in Descriptive Metaphysics* 1959, and *The Bounds of Sense* 1966. Born in London, he taught at Oxford from 1948, becoming professor of metaphysics in 1968.

stream of consciousness narrative technique in which a writer presents directly the uninterrupted flow of a character's thoughts, impressions, and feelings, without the conventional devices of dialogue and description. It first came to be widely used in the early 20th century. Leading exponents have included the novelists Virginia Woolf, James Joyce, and William Faulkner.

Molly Bloom's soliloquy in Joyce's *Ulysses* is a good example of the technique. The English writer Dorothy Richardson (1873–1957) is said to have originated the technique in her novel sequence *Pilgrimage*, the first volume of which was published 1915 and the last posthumously. The term 'stream of consciousness' was introduced by the philosopher William James in 1890.

stress in psychology, any event or situation that makes demands on a person's mental or emotional resources. Stress can be caused by overwork, anxiety about exams, money, or job security, unemployment, bereavement, poor relationships, marriage breakdown, sexual difficulties, poor living or working conditions, and constant exposure to loud noise.

Many changes that are apparently 'for the better', such as being promoted at work, going to a new school, moving house, and getting married, can also be a source of stress. Stress can cause, or aggravate, physical illnesses, among them psoriasis, eczema, asthma, and stomach and mouth ulcers. Apart from removing the source of stress, acquiring some control over it and learning to relax when possible are the best treatments.

strike stoppage of work by employees, often as members of a trade union, to obtain or resist change in wages, hours, or conditions. A *lockout* is a weapon of an employer to thwart or enforce such change by preventing employees from working. Another measure is *work to rule*, when production is virtually brought to a halt by strict observance of union rules.

Strikes may be 'official' (union-authorized) or 'wildcat' (undertaken spontaneously), and may be accompanied by a *sit-in* or *work-in*, the one being worker occupation of a factory and the other continuation of work in a plant the employer wishes to close. In a 'sympathetic' strike, action is in support of other workers on strike elsewhere, possibly in a different industry.

In the UK, 1.9 million working days were lost in 1990 through industrial disputes, in contrast to the 1970s, when the average loss was 12.9 million days.

Strindberg August 1849–1912. Swedish dramatist and novelist. His plays are in a variety of styles including historical dramas, symbolic dramas (the two-part *Dödsdansen/ The Dance of Death* 1901) and 'chamber plays' such as *Spöksonaten/The Ghost [Spook] Sonata* 1907. *Fadren/The Father* 1887 and *Fröken Julie/Miss Julie* 1888 are among his most famous works.

Born in Stockholm, he lived mainly abroad after 1883, having been unsuccessfully prosecuted for blasphemy in 1884 following publication of his short stories *Giftas/ Marrying*. His life was stormy and his work has been criticized for its hostile attitude to women, but he is regarded as one of Sweden's greatest writers.

strong nuclear force one of the four fundamental ◊forces of nature, the other three being the electromagnetic force, gravity, and the weak nuclear force. The strong nuclear force was first described by Japanese physicist Hideki Yukawa 1935. It is the strongest of all the forces, acts only over very small distances (within the nucleus of the atom), and is responsible for binding together ◊quarks to form hadrons, and for binding together protons and neutrons in the atomic nucleus. The particle that is the carrier of the strong nuclear force is the gluon, of which there are eight kinds, each with zero mass and zero charge.

structural-functionalism an anthropological theory formulated by ◊Radcliffe-Brown which argued that social structures arose and were maintained in order to facilitate the smooth and harmonious functioning of society as a whole.

structuralism 20th-century philosophical movement that has influenced such areas as linguistics, anthropology, and literary criticism. Inspired by the work of the Swiss linguist Ferdinand de ◊Saussure, structuralists believe that objects should be analysed as systems of relations, rather than as positive entities.

Saussure proposed that language is a system of arbitrary signs, meaning that there is no intrinsic link between the 'signifier' (the sound or mark) and the 'signified' (the concept it represents). Hence any linguistic term can only be defined by its differences from other terms. His ideas were taken further by Roman Jakobson and the Prague school of linguistics, and were extended into a general method for the social sciences by the French anthropologist Claude ◊Lévi-Strauss. The French writer Roland ◊Barthes took the lead in applying the ideas of structuralism to literary criticism, arguing that the critic should identify the structures within a text that determine its possible meanings, independently of any reference to the real. This approach is radicalized in Barthes' later work and in the practice of 'deconstruction', pioneered by the French philosopher Jacques ◊Derrida. Here the text comes to be viewed as a 'decentred' play of structures, lacking any ultimately determinable meaning.

Struve Friedrich Georg Wilhelm 1793–1864. German-born Russian astronomer, a pioneer in the observation of double stars. The founder and first director (from 1839) of Pulkovo Observatory near St Petersburg, he was succeeded by his son *Otto Wilhelm Struve* (1819–1905).

His great-grandson *Otto Struve* (1897–1963) left the USSR in 1921 for the USA, where he became joint director of the Yerkes and McDonald observatories 1932 and championed the notion that planetary systems were common around stars.

style those particular and unique characteristics in the work of an individual artist which enable it to be distinguished from that of another. It is also used to distinguish between periods in music and in ◊art history, for instance the Baroque style.

Style is the man himself.

> **style**
> Comte de Buffon, 1707–1778, French naturalist.
> *Discourse on Style*

A stylus was a sharp instrument used for incising a wax tablet with writing. Style, therefore, originally meant a particular manner of writing. Its meaning was later extended to describe the particular appearance of all artefacts, including changes of fashion and even of behaviour. For an individual to possess style means that he or she has an especially distinguished manner of bearing.

subject in grammar and logic, it refers to that part of a sentence or proposition about which something is predicated, or to which something is attributed. The subject is the noun or noun-equivalent with which the verb and adjective(s) must agree. In philosophy, the term has reversed its meaning over the centuries. For ◊Duns Scotus and ◊Descartes, for example, the object was the thinking subject and the subject the thing itself. With ◊Kant, our modern usage appears – the subject is the centre of awareness, the ego, the mind.

There is only one step from the sublime to the ridiculous.

the sublime
Napoleon
Remark to the Polish ambassador,
after the retreat from Moscow

sublime, the in the arts, the quality of being awe-inspiring or possessing grandeur. Its distinctness as an aesthetic category from the merely beautiful was formulated by Edmund ◊Burke in his *Philosophical Enquiry into the Origin of our Ideas of the Sublime and the Beautiful* 1757.

The search for the sublime was apparent in a predilection for wild landscapes in painting, for example, Philippe-Jacques de Loutherbourg's (1740–1812) *An Avalanche in the Alps* 1803, and in the new genre of the Gothic novel, such as Horace Walpole's *Castle of Otranto* 1764.

The sublime and the ridiculous are often so nearly related, that it is difficult to class them separately.

the sublime
Thomas Paine, 1737–1809, English
left-wing political writer.
Age of Reason

subsidiarity a term widely used by European politicians since the signing of the ◊Maastricht Treaty on European unification. As with many such terms, it means different things to different people, usually depending on the audience being addressed. The most favoured interpretation is that it is a process whereby decision-making within the Community is devolved from the centre to the lowest level possible.

In many continental countries, such as Germany, it is seen as devolution to the regions, but in the United Kingdom it is often claimed to represent the transfer of power from the Brussels Commission to the central government in Westminster and Whitehall.

Succot or **Sukkoth** in Judaism, a harvest festival celebrated in Oct, also known as the **Feast of Booths**, which commemorates the time when the Israelites lived in the wilderness during the ◊Exodus from Egypt. As a reminder of the shelters used in the wilderness, huts are built and used for eating and sleeping during the seven days of the festival.

succubus a female spirit; see ◊incubus.

suffering physical or mental pain, interpreted in different ways in different faiths. In Hinduism, Buddhism and Jainism, suffering arises as a direct result of the actions (◊karma) of this or a previous life. In Chinese religion it arises from an imbalance in ◊yin and yang, the forces of the universe. For Christianity, Islam, and Judaism, there is a problem of how to relate a good, loving God with the seemingly inevitable suffering in the world. In Christianity and Judaism the world is seen as having been created good, but becoming subject to suffering by humanity's disobedience. Both look forward to an age when suffering will no longer exist. Islam sees suffering as a test sent by God.

suffragette or **suffragist** woman fighting for the right to vote. In the UK, women's suffrage bills were repeatedly introduced and defeated in Parliament between 1886 and 1911, and a militant campaign was launched 1906 by Emmeline ◊Pankhurst and her daughters. In 1918 women were granted limited franchise; in 1928 it was extended to all women over 21. In the USA the 19th amendment to the constitution 1920 gave women the vote in federal and state elections.

Suffragettes (the term was coined by a *Daily Mail* reporter) chained themselves to railings, heckled political meetings, refused to pay taxes, and in 1913 bombed the home of Lloyd George, then chancellor of the Exchequer. One woman, Emily Davison, threw herself under the king's horse at the Derby in 1913 and was killed. Many suffragettes were imprisoned and were force-fed when they went on hunger strike; under the notorious 'Cat and Mouse Act' of 1913 they could be repeatedly released to regain their health and then rearrested. The struggle was called off on the outbreak of World War I.

Sufism mystical movement of ◊Islam that originated in the 8th century. Sufis believe that deep intuition is the only real guide to knowledge. The movement has a strong strain of asceticism. There are a number of groups or brotherhoods within Sufism, each with its own method of meditative practice, one of which is the whirling dance of the ◊dervishes. Sufism was originally influenced by the ascetics of the early Christian church, but later developed within the structure of orthodox Islam.

My work is done. Why wait?

suicide

George Eastman, 1854–1932, US entrepreneur and inventor.
Suicide note

---

suicide the act of killing oneself intentionally; a person who does this.

Until the Reformation, suicides were condemned by both the church and the state, and burial in consecrated ground was prohibited. The state confiscated the suicide's possessions. Traditionally, suicides were buried at a crossroads with a stake through their body. Even until 1823 burial was at night, without burial service, and with a stake through the heart. Until 1961 it was a criminal offence in English law, if committed while of sound mind. To aid and abet another's suicide is an offence, and euthanasia or mercy killing may amount to aiding in this context. Where there is a suicide pact and one survives, he or she may be charged with manslaughter. In Japan ◊hara-kiri was considered honourable, as was ◊suttee in India.

What's brave, what's noble, / Let's do it after the high Roman fashion, / And make death proud to take us.

suicide

William Shakespeare, 1564–1616, English dramatist and poet.
Antony and Cleopatra IV. xiii

In 1986, the highest suicide rates per million of the population were 430 for men in Finland and 199 for women in Denmark. In 1988, there were 4,193 suicides in England and Wales, about 83 per million of the population. Four times as many young men kill themselves as women. There are 140,000 suicides a year in China, 70% of whom are women.

Sullivan Harry Stack 1892–1949. US psychoanalyst, the chief exponent of the dynamic–cultural school of psychoanalysis which emphasized the role of on-going interpersonal relationships rather than infantile sexuality in the formation of abnormal behaviour.

Although this view incurred considerable criticism from orthodox Freudian psychoanalysts, Sullivan argued that many psychological afflictions were amenable to this approach, including ◊schizophrenia, with which he claimed to achieve considerable therapeutic success.

Sumerian religion Sumerian civilization flourished c. 3000–2300 BC. It was a society ruled by gods. Everything belonged to the gods and the kings were their representatives. Humanity's role was to serve the gods and to fulfil their will in their eternal struggles with each other. The significance today of Sumerian religion is that it provides the earliest Near Eastern texts of cosmology and also the earliest texts about the ◊Flood – in the *Epic of Gilgamesh*. The similarities and differences between this text and the Hebrew Bible have fascinated scholars for many years and provided a better understanding of the origins of certain Jewish beliefs.

Sumner James 1887–1955. US biochemist. In 1926 he succeeded in crystallizing the enzyme urease and demonstrating its protein nature. For this work Sumner shared the 1946 Nobel Prize for Chemistry with John Northrop and Wendell Stanley.

sumptuary law any law restraining excessive individual consumption, such as expenditure on food and dress, or attempting to control religious or moral conduct.

The Romans had several sumptuary laws; for example, the *lex Orchia* in 181 BC limited the number of dishes at a feast. In England sumptuary laws were introduced by Edward III and Henry VII.

sun dance religious ceremony performed by certain ◊Plains Indians at the time of the summer solstice.

Sunday first day of the week; in Christianity, Sunday is set aside for worship in commemoration of Jesus' resurrection, and in predominantly Christian societies banks, offices, and many shops are generally closed. It replaced the Jewish ◊Sabbath, or day of rest, observed on Saturday.

In the UK activities such as shopping and drinking alcohol have been restricted since medieval times on this day; in 1969 curbs on sports, theatres, and dancing were lifted.

In the EC nine of the twelve countries shut down most industrial and commercial activities, the exceptions being the UK, Denmark, and Portugal. In 1990 Germany proposed to make Sunday an official day of rest throughout the EC as part of the EC Social Charter, and this is now being negotiated.

Sunni member of the larger of the two main divisions of ◊Islam, with about 680 million adherents. Sunni Muslims believe that the first three caliphs were all legitimate successors of the prophet Muhammad, and that guidance on belief and life should come from the Qur'an and the Hadith, and from the Shari'a, not from a human authority or spiritual leader. Imams in Sunni Islam are educated lay teachers of the faith and prayer leaders.

Sun worship the obvious power over life and death exercised by the Sun has meant that it, along with the Moon, has been worshipped for millennia. The ◊megalithic religions seem to have centred upon the Sun, which was worshipped throughout the Near East. The radical Egyptian pharoah Akhenaten (1367–1350 BC) made the Sun god Aten the sole god of the universe in his theology, possibly the first instance of ◊monotheism. In Hinduism, worship of Surya, the Sun god, is an established tradition, as exemplified by the monumental temple to the Sun built in the form of the massive 16-wheeled chariot of Surya at Konarak, on the Bay of Bengal. The Sun was a central feature of the religions of Central American people such as the ◊Maya.

When the Roman emperor Constantine converted to Christianity in 312, he moved from being a worshipper of the Sun god Sol Victus, and the influence of this on his thought is shown in his making Sunday, the sun's day, the legal day of worship for Christians.

superego in Freudian psychology, the element of the human mind concerned with the ideal, responsible for ethics and self-imposed standards of behaviour. It is characterized as a form of conscience, restraining the ◊ego, and responsible for feelings of guilt when the moral code is broken.

superpower term used to describe the USA and the USSR from the end of World War II 1945, when they emerged as significantly stronger than all other countries.

superstition popular belief, concerned with (usually) bad luck, often about the evil consequences of apparently trivial actions. Superstitions may arise in cultures where there is or has been a strong ritual code or belief in spirits, and in those where certain numbers (such as 13 – Christ gathered with the disciples, including Judas Iscariot, at the Last Supper) carry an ominous significance.

Superstition is the religion of feeble minds.
superstition
Edmund Burke, 1729–1797, British Whig politician and political theorist, born in Dublin, Ireland.
Reflections on the Revolution in France

superstring theory in physics, a mathematical theory developed in the 1980s to explain the properties of ◊elementary particles and the forces between them (in particular, gravity and the nuclear forces) in a way that combines ◊relativity and ◊quantum theory. In string theory, the fundamental objects in the universe are not pointlike particles but extremely small stringlike objects. These objects exist in a universe of ten dimensions, although, for reasons not yet understood, only three space dimensions and one dimension of time are discernible.

There are many unresolved difficulties with superstring theory, but some physicists think it may be the ultimate 'theory of everything' that explains all aspects of the universe within one framework.

supersymmetry in physics, a theory that relates the two classes of ◊elementary particle, the fermions and the bosons. According to supersymmetry, each fermion particle has a boson partner particle, and vice versa. It has not been possible to marry up all the known fermions with the known bosons, and so the theory postulates the existence of other, as yet undiscovered fermions, such as the photinos (partners of the photons), gluinos (partners of the gluons), and gravitinos (partners of the gravitons). Using these ideas, it has become possible to develop a theory of gravity – called supergravity – that extends Einstein's work and considers the gravitational, nuclear, and electromagnetic forces to be manifestations of an underlying superforce. Supersymmetry has been incorporated into the ◊superstring theory, and appears to be a crucial ingredient in the 'theory of everything' sought by scientists.

supply in economics, the production of goods or services for a market in anticipation of an expected ◊demand. The level of supply is determined by the price of the product, the cost of production, the level of technology available for production, and the price of other goods. There is no guarantee that supply will match actual demand.

supply and demand one of the fundamental approaches to economics, which examines and compares the supply of a good with its demand (usually in the form of a graph of supply and demand curves plotted against price). For a typical good, the supply curve is upward-sloping (the higher the price, the more the manufacturer is willing to sell), while the demand curve is downward-sloping (the cheaper the good, the more demand there is for it). The point where the curves intersect is the equilibrium price at which supply equals demand.

supply curve diagramatic illustration of the relationship between the price of the good and the quantity that producers will supply at that price. It is said to be upward-sloping because the higher the price, the more profitable existing production becomes, attracting new companies into the industry and thus increasing the quantity supplied.

The supply curve will shift to the right (indicating that firms are prepared to produce the same amount but charge a lower price) if, for example, there is a fall in the cost of production or an advance in technology which increases productivity.

supply-side economics school of economic thought advocating government policies that allow market forces to operate freely, such as privatization, cuts in public spending and income tax, reductions in trade-union power, and cuts in the ratio of unemployment benefits to wages. Supply-side economics developed as part of the monetarist (see ◊monetarism) critique of ◊Keynesian economics.

Supply-siders argue that increases in government expenditure to stimulate demand and reduce unemployment, advocated by Keynesians, are ineffective in the long term because intervention distorts market forces and creates inefficiencies that prevent the 'supply side' of the economy from responding to increases in demand. Critics, however, argue that failure of supply to respond to increases in demand may result from the failure of market forces to take account of ◊social costs and benefits. This may require increased public spending on infrastructure, training, and research and development. It is also suggested that such policies create a more uneven distribution of income and wealth, as happened in the USA and the UK in the 1980s.

Suprematism Russian abstract-art movement developed about 1913 by Kasimir Malevich. Suprematist painting gradually became more severe, until in 1918 it reached a climax with Malevich's *White on White* series showing white geometrical shapes on a white ground.

Suprematism was inspired in part by Futurist and Cubist ideas.

Early paintings such as Malevich's *Black Square* 1915 (Russian Museum, St Petersburg) used purely geometrical shapes in bold dynamic compositions. The aims of the movement were expressed by Malevich as 'the supremacy of pure feeling or perception in the pictorial arts – the expression of non-objectivity'. Suprematism greatly influenced Kandinsky and the Bauhaus.

Surrealism movement in art, literature, and film that developed out of ◊Dada around 1922. Led by André ◊Breton, who produced the *Surrealist Manifesto* 1924, the Surrealists were inspired by the thoughts and visions of the subconscious mind. They explored varied styles and techniques, and the movement became the dominant force in Western art between World Wars I and II.

Surrealism is destructive, but it destroys only what it considers to be shackles limiting our vision.

surrealism
Salvador Dali, 1904–1989, Spanish artist.
Declaration

Surrealism followed Freud's theory of the unconscious and his 'free association' technique for bypassing the conscious mind. In art it encompassed André Masson's automatic drawings, paintings based on emotive semi-abstract forms (Ernst, Miró, Tanguy), and dreamlike images painted in a realistic style (Dalí, Magritte). The poets Aragon and Eluard and the film-maker Buñuel were also part of the movement.

Sūrya in Hindu mythology, the sun god, son of the sky god Indra. His daughter, also named Sūrya, is a female personification of the Sun.

Sutherland Earl Wilbur Jr 1915–1974. US physiologist, discoverer of cyclic AMP, a chemical 'messenger' made by a special enzyme in the wall of living cells. Many hormones operate by means of this messenger. He was awarded the Nobel Prize for Medicine 1971.

sūtra in Buddhism, discourse attributed to the historical Buddha. In Hinduism, the term generally describes any sayings that contain moral instruction.

Sutra-pitaka the second part of the three baskets or collections of Buddhist scriptures in the Pali tradition – the ◊Tripitaka. The Sutra-pitaka consists primarily of discourses by the Buddha, often in response to questions from specific individuals.

suttee Hindu custom whereby a widow committed suicide by joining her husband's funeral pyre, often under public and family pressure. Banned in the 17th century by the Mogul emperors, the custom continued even after it was made illegal under British rule 1829. There continue to be sporadic revivals.

Suzuki D T 1870–1966. Japanese scholar and follower of ◊Zen whose books in English first introduced Zen practices to the general public in the West. While studying in Tokyo, he underwent Zen training and rose to become one of the leading exponents of Buddhist philosophy, being professor of Buddhist philosophy at Otani University from 1921 onward. He spent a lot of time in the USA, from 1897–1908 and 1949 onward, lecturing at many universities, and he was married to an American, which enabled him to explain Japanese Buddhist philosophy and practice of Zen Buddhism in Western terms. His works include *Essays in Zen Buddhism* and *An Introduction to Zen Buddhism*.

Svedberg Theodor 1884–1971. Swedish chemist. In 1924 he constructed the first ultra-centrifuge, a machine that allowed the rapid separation of particles by mass. He was awarded the Nobel Prize for Chemistry 1926.

Svetambara ('white-clad') sect of Jain monks (see ◊Jainism) who wear white loincloths, as opposed to the Digambaras sect which believes that total nudity is correct for the Jain monk.

swami title of respect for a Hindu teacher.

Swarajiya or *Self-Government Party* political party established in India in 1922 as an attempt to reinforce the position of the Congress Party in the Indian legislature. In 1923, it became the largest party in the central assembly and also in some provincial assemblies, but its tactics of obstruction against British colonial rule were only partially successful. Recognized by the Congress Party in 1924, Swarajiya continued until 1929 and was revived to help the Congress Party to contest the 1934 elections.

swastika cross in which the bars are extended at right angles in the same clockwise or anti-clockwise direction. An ancient good-luck symbol in both the New and the Old World and an Aryan and Buddhist mystic sign, it was adopted by Hitler as the emblem of the Nazi Party and incorporated into the German national flag 1935–45.

Swedenborg Emanuel 1688–1772. Swedish scientist and mystic. As assessor to the Swedish Royal College of Mines his scientific researches anticipated many later discoveries in the field of engineering, navigation, and astronomy.

In his *Opera Philosophica et Mineralia/ Philosophical and Logical Works* 1734 he attempted to explain the natural world as having a spiritual foundation. From 1744 he devoted himself exclusively to religious speculation, claiming direct access to God via the angels, and formulating a 'doctrine of correspondence' whereby all things in the material world have spiritual correspondences. This doctrine resembled ◊neo-Platonism and, through the New Church inaugurated by him, influenced the Romantics, notably William Blake, and the French theorists of ◊Symbolism.

syllogism set of philosophical statements devised by Aristotle in his work on logic. It establishes the conditions under which a valid conclusion follows or does not follow by deduction from given premises. The following is an example of a valid syllogism: 'All men are mortal, Socrates is a man, therefore Socrates is mortal.'

symbiosis any close relationship between two organisms of different species, and one where both partners benefit from the association. A well-known example is the pollination relationship between insects and flowers, where the insects feed on nectar and carry pollen from one flower to another. This is sometimes known as mutualism. Symbiosis in a broader sense includes ◊commensalism and parasitism.

symbol in general, something that stands for something else. A symbol may be an aesthetic device or a sign used to convey information visually, thus saving time, eliminating language barriers, or overcoming illiteracy.

Symbols are used in art, mathematics, music, and literature; for practical use in science and medicine; for road signs; and as warnings – for example, a skull and crossbones to indicate dangerous contents.

symbolic interactionism sociological method, founded by the US pragmatist George Mead, that studies the behaviour of individuals and small groups through observation and description, viewing people's appearance, gestures, and language as symbols they use to interact with others in social situations. In contrast to theories such as Marxism or functionalism that attempt to analyse society as a whole through economic or political systems, it takes a perspective of society from within, as created by people themselves.

Symbolism late 19th-century movement in French poetry, which inspired a similar trend in French painting. The Symbolist poets used words for their symbolic rather than concrete meaning. Leading exponents were Paul Verlaine, Stéphane Mallarmé, and Arthur Rimbaud. The Symbolist painters rejected Realism and Impressionism, seeking to express moods and psychological states through colour, line, and form. Their subjects were often mythological, mystical, or fantastic.

Gustave Moreau was a leading Symbolist painter. Other Symbolist painters included Puvis de Chavannes and Odilon Redon in France, Arnold Böcklin in Switzerland, and Edward Burne-Jones in the UK.

synaesthesia the experience of one sense as a result of the stimulation of a different sense; for example, an experience of colour may result from hearing a sound. This experience is sometimes imitated in the arts. The poet Baudelaire used the phrase 'scarlet fanfare', while composers, such as Scriabin and Schoenberg, asked for colours to be projected to accompany their works, for example, Scriabin's *Poem of Fire* 1913.

Other examples are Walt Disney's *Fantasia* 1940 and the psychedelic light show.

synagogue in Judaism, a place of worship, also (in the USA) called a temple. As an institution it dates from the destruction of the Temple in Jerusalem AD 70, though it had been developing from the time of the Babylonian exile as a substitute for the Temple. In antiquity it was a public meeting hall where the Torah was also read, but today it is used primarily for prayer and services. A service requires a quorum (*minyan*) of ten adult Jewish men.

In addition to the ark (the sacred ornamented enclosure that holds the Torah scrolls), the synagogue contains a raised platform (bimah) from which the service is conducted, with pews or seats for the high priests. The rest of the congregation sits or stands facing it. Two tablets above the ark are inscribed with the Ten Commandments. In Orthodox synagogues women sit apart from the men.

synchronicity in parapsychology, the key concept of a theory proposed by ◊Jung, to account for ◊paranormal and other puzzling phenomena, such as omens and prophesies.

According to Jung, there is no causal connexion between, for example, two identical thoughts occurring to two individuals in different places at the same time or between a premonitory dream and the event which is seen to correspond with it (make it come true). Nor are such events due to pure chance. But there is a meaningful coincidence, or synchronicity, between two such more or less simultaneous occurrences in that they represent a manifestation of knowledge associated with archetypal processes in the ◊collective unconscious.

syndicalism political movement in 19th-century Europe that rejected parliamentary activity in favour of direct action, culminating in a revolutionary general strike to secure worker ownership and control of industry. After 1918 syndicalism was absorbed in communism, although it continued to have an independent existence in Spain until the late 1930s.

The idea originated under Robert ◊Owen's influence in the 1830s, acquired its name and its more violent aspects in France from the philosopher Georges ◊Sorel, and also reached the USA.

syndrome in medicine, a set of signs and symptoms that always occur together, thus characterizing a particular condition or disorder.

synergy in medicine, the 'cooperative' action of two or more drugs, muscles, or organs; applied especially to drugs whose combined action is more powerful than their simple effects added together.

Synge Richard 1914–1994. British biochemist who investigated paper chromatography (a means of separating mixtures). By 1940 techniques of chromatography for separating proteins had been devised. Still lacking were comparable techniques for distinguishing the amino acids that constituted the proteins. By 1944, Synge and his colleague Archer Martin had worked out a procedure, known as ascending chromatography, which filled this gap and won them the 1952 Nobel Prize for Chemistry.

synthetic in philosophy, a term employed by ◊Kant to describe a judgement in which the predicate is not contained within the subject; for example, 'The flower is blue' is synthetic, since every flower is not blue. It is the converse of ◊analytic.

systems analysis in computing, the investigation of a business activity or clerical procedure, with a view to deciding if and how it can be computerized. The analyst discusses the existing procedures with the people involved, observes the flow of data through the business, and draws up an outline specification of the required computer system (see also ◊systems design).

Systems in use in the 1990s include Yourdon, SSADM (Structured Systems Analysis and Design Methodology), and Soft Systems Methodology.

systems design in computing, the detailed design of an applications package. The designer breaks the system down into component programs, and designs the required input forms, screen layouts, and printouts. Systems design forms a link between systems analysis and programming.

Szent-Györgyi Albert 1893–1986. Hungarian-born US biochemist who isolated vitamin C and studied the chemistry of muscular activity. He was awarded the Nobel Prize for Medicine 1937.

In 1928 Szent-Györgyi isolated a substance from the adrenal glands that he named hexuronic acid; when he found the same substance in cabbages and oranges, he suspected that he had finally isolated vitamin C.

Szilard Leo 1898–1964. Hungarian-born US physicist who, in 1934, was one of the first scientists to realize that nuclear fission, or atom splitting, could lead to a chain reaction releasing enormous amounts of instantaneous energy. He emigrated to the USA in 1938 and there influenced ◊Einstein to advise President Roosevelt to begin the nuclear arms programme. After World War II he turned his attention to the newly emerging field of molecular biology.

Tabligh missionary movement in Islam, which developed after 1945 to take Islamic revival and reform to the less educated. It is active in Asia, Africa, North America, and Northern Europe.

taboo prohibition applied to magical and religious objects. In psychology and the social sciences the term refers to practices that are generally prohibited because of religious or social pressures; for example, ◊incest is forbidden in most societies.

tabula rasa (Latin 'scraped tablet', from the Romans' use of wax-covered tablets which could be written on with a pointed stick and cleared by smoothing over the surface) a mind without any preconceived ideas.

Tacitus Publius Cornelius c. AD 55–c. 120. Roman historian. A public orator in Rome, he was consul under Nerva 97–98 and proconsul of Asia 112–113. He wrote histories of the Roman Empire, *Annales* and *Historiae*, covering the years AD 14–68 and 69–97 respectively. He also wrote a *Life of Agricola* 97 (he married Agricola's daughter in 77) and a description of the German tribes, *Germania* 98.

The butterfly counts not months but moments, and has time enough.

Rabindranath Tagore
Fireflies

Tagore Rabindranath 1861–1941. Bengali Indian writer, born in Calcutta, who translated into English his own verse *Gitanjali* ('song offerings') 1912 and his verse play *Chitra* 1896. Nobel Prize for Literature 1913.

An ardent nationalist and advocate of social reform, he resigned his knighthood as a gesture of protest against British repression in India.

T'ai Chi series of 108 complex, slow-motion movements, each named (for example, the White Crane Spreads Its Wings) and designed to ensure effective circulation of the *chi*, or intrinsic energy of the universe, through the mind and body. It derives partly from the Shaolin martial arts of China and partly from ◊Taoism.

taille in pre-revolutionary France, either of two forms of taxation. The *personal taille*, levied from the 15th century, was assessed by tax collectors on the individual's personal wealth. Nobles, clerics, and many other groups were exempt from this tax and its burden fell disproportionately on the peasantry. During a similar period the *'real' taille* was levied on common land in central and south-western France and produced more revenue for the crown.

Taine Hippolyte Adolphe 1828–1893. French critic and historian. He analysed literary works as products of period and environment, as in *Histoire de la littérature anglaise/History of English Literature* 1863 and *Philosophie de l'art/Philosophy of Art* 1865–69.

takeover in business, the acquisition by one company of a sufficient number of shares in another company to have effective control of that company – usually 51%, although a controlling stake may be as little as 30%.

Takeovers may be agreed or contested; methods employed include the *dawn raid*, and methods of avoiding an unwelcome takeover include *reverse takeover, poison pills*, or inviting a *white knight* to make a takeover bid.

talaq in Islam, divorce performed by the husband. Talaq takes the form of three repudiations of the wife, preferably separated by a period of reflection. After three statements of divorce the couple cannot remarry unless the wife marries another man and is widowed or divorced again. Divorce is the most despised permitted action of a Muslim. Divorce instigated by the wife is mediated by the court and is known as khul'.

Taliesin lived c. 550. Legendary Welsh poet, a bard at the court of the King of Rheged in Scotland. Taliesin allegedly died at Taliesin (named after him) in Dyfed, Wales.

talisman an object, usually inscribed with letters or symbols believed to have occult power, or signs of certain stars, which protect the wearer from any harm. In many cultures such talismans are tied to babies from birth to protect them, and even an object such as a car may have a talisman tied to it to protect those travelling in it. Famous talismans are the Eye of Horus which is now found throughout both Muslim and Christian Mediterranean countries, and the Hand of Fatima.

tallith four-cornered, fringed shawl worn by Jewish men during morning prayers.

Talmud the two most important works of post-Biblical Jewish literature. The Babylonian and the Palestinian (or Jerusalem) Talmud provide a compilation of ancient Jewish law and tradition. The Babylonian Talmud was edited at the end of the 5th century AD and is the more authoritative version for later Judaism; both Talmuds are written in a mix of Hebrew and Aramaic. They contain the commentary (gemara) on the ◊Mishna (early rabbinical commentaries compiled about AD 200), and the material can be generally divided into Halakhah, consisting of legal and ritual matters, and ◊Haggadah, concerned with ethical, theological, and folklorist matters.

Tamil Hinduism traditional form of Hinduism found in S India, particularly in Tamil Nadu, where the invasions and political upheavals of North India had little influence. The important centres of Tamil Hinduism are Rameshvaram, dedicated to Shiva; Shrirangam, dedicated to Vishnu; and Madurai, dedicated to Meenakshi, the wife of Shiva. The unique style of Tamil temple architecture, with its towering *gopurams*, or temple gateways, is famous all over the world. Many of the important teachers of Hinduism in ancient times, such as Shankara, Ramanuja, and Madhva, came from S India.

Tammuz in Sumerian legend, a vegetation god, who died at midsummer and was brought back from the underworld in spring by his lover Ishtar. His cult spread over Babylonia, Syria, Phoenicia, and Palestine. In Greek mythology Tammuz appears as ◊Adonis.

Tanabata festival celebrated annually on 7 July, introduced to Japan from China in the 8th century. It is dedicated to Altair and Vega, two stars in the constellation Aquila, which are united once yearly in the Milky Way. According to legend they represent two star-crossed lovers allowed by the gods to meet on that night.

Tantrism forms of Hinduism and Buddhism that emphasize the division of the universe into male and female forces that maintain its unity by their interaction; this gives women equal status with men. Tantric Hinduism is associated with magical and sexual yoga practices that imitate the union of Siva and Sakti, as described in religious books known as the Tantras. In Buddhism, the Tantras are texts attributed to the Buddha, describing methods of attaining enlightenment.

Tantric Buddhism, practised in medieval India, depended on the tuition of teachers and the use of yoga, mantras, and meditation to enable its followers to master themselves and gain oneness with the universe.

Taoism Chinese philosophical system, traditionally founded by Chinese philosopher Lao Zi 6th century BC. He is also attributed authorship of the scriptures, *Tao Te Ching*, although these were apparently compiled 3rd century BC. The 'tao' or 'way' denotes the hidden principle of the universe, and less stress is laid on good deeds than on harmonious interaction with the environment, which automatically ensures right behaviour. The magical side of Taoism is illustrated by the *I Ching* or *Book of Changes*, a book of divination.

beliefs The universe is believed to be kept in balance by the opposing forces of ◊yin and yang that operate in dynamic tension between themselves. Yin is female and watery: the force in the moon and rain which reaches its peak in the winter; yang is masculine and solid: the force in the sun and earth which reaches its peak in the summer. The interaction of yin and yang is believed to shape all life.

This magical, ritualistic aspect of Taoism developed from the 2nd century AD and was largely responsible for its popular growth; it stresses physical immortality, and this was attempted by means ranging from dietary regulation and fasting to alchemy. By the 3rd century, worship of gods had begun to appear, including that of the stove god Tsao Chun. From the 4th century, rivalry between Taoists and Mahāyāna Buddhists was strong in China, leading to persecution of one religion by the other; this was resolved by mutual assimilation, and Taoism developed monastic communities similar to those of the Buddhists.

Taoist texts record the tradition of mental and physical discipline, and methods to use in healing, exorcism, and the quest for immortality. The second major work is that of Zhuangzi (c. 389–286 BC), *The Way of Zhuangzi*.

Tao Te Ching the most influential Taoist book (5th century BC), reputedly written down in one night by the sage Lao Zi as he left China for the West. The short book is divided into 81 chapters which contain oracle sayings or proverbs with commentary.

The texts are ancient and seem to have collected around the name of a sage, Lao Zi (the name simply means the Old Master). The text is terse and thought-provoking and is something of a handbook of statecraft as well as of wisdom in general. It is probably the best-known Chinese text in the West.

tariff tax or duty placed on goods when they are imported into a country or trading bloc (such as the European Community) from outside. The aim of tariffs is to reduce imports by making them more expensive.

Organizations such as the EC, the European Free Trade Association (EFTA), and the General Agreement on Tariffs and Trade (GATT) have worked towards mutual lowering of tariffs among countries. Tariffs have generally been used by governments to protect home industries from lower-priced foreign goods, and have been opposed by supporters of free trade. For a tariff to be successful, it must not provoke retaliatory tariffs from other countries.

tarot cards fortune-telling aid consisting of 78 cards: the *minor arcana* in four suits (resembling playing cards) and the *major arcana*, 22 cards with densely symbolic illustrations that have links with astrology and the ◊kabbala.

history The earliest known reference to tarot cards is from 1392. The pack is of unknown (probably medieval) origin and may have been designed in Europe in the early 14th century as a repository of Gnostic ideas then being suppressed by the Christian church. Since the 18th century the tarot has interested occult scholars.

taste the ability to judge the quality of a work of art. A person who consistently enjoys the tawdry and the second-rate is said to have bad taste whereas those who admire only the best display good taste. Since taste is nowadays regarded as essentially subjective, the term is only useful as a means of instigating critical debate.

One half of the world cannot understand the pleasures of the other.

taste
Jane Austen, 1775–1817, English novelist.
Emma

Tatum Edward Lawrie 1909–1975. US microbiologist. For his work on biochemical genetics, he shared the 1958 Nobel Prize for Medicine with George Beadle and Joshua Lederberg.

tautology repetition of the same thing in different words. For example, it is tautologous to say that something is *most unique*, since something unique cannot, by definition, be comparative.

Tawney Richard Henry 1880–1962. British economic historian and social critic and reformer who had a great influence on the Labour Party, especially during the 1930s, although he never became an MP. His *Labour and the Nation* was the party's manifesto for the 1931 general election.

As a committed Christian, Tawney based his socialism on moral values. His classic *Religion and the Rise of Capitalism* 1926 examined morals and economic practice in England 1588–1640, his special period. One of his most widely-read books is *The Acquisitive Society* 1921 (later abridged as *Labour and the Nation*), in which he criticized capitalism because it encourages acquisitiveness and so corrupts everyone. In *Equality* 1931, he argued for urgent improvements in social services to deal with some of the glaring inequities of the class system. He helped found the Economic History Society 1926 and became the joint editor of its journal, the *Economic History Review*. After leaving Oxford University, he taught for the Workers' Educational Association while working on *The Agrarian Problem in the 16th Century* 1912.

To tax and to please, no more than to love and to be wise, is not given to men.

taxation
Edmund Burke, 1729–1797, British Whig politician and political theorist, born in Dublin, Ireland.
Speech on American Taxation 1774

---

taxation raising of money from individuals and organizations by the state in order to pay for the goods and services it provides. Taxation can be *direct* (a deduction from income) or *indirect* (added to the purchase price of goods or services, that is, a tax on consumption). The standard form of indirect taxation in Europe is *value-added tax (VAT)*. *Income tax* is the most common form of direct taxation.

The proportions of direct and indirect taxation in the total tax revenue vary widely from country to country. By varying the effect of a tax on the richer and poorer members of society, a government can attempt to redistribute wealth from the richer to the poorer, both by taxing the rich more severely and by returning some of the collected wealth in the form of *benefits*. A *progressive* tax is one that falls proportionally more on the rich; most income taxes, for example, have higher rates for those with higher incomes. A *regressive* tax, on the other hand, affects the poor proportionally more than the rich.

All taxes must, at last, fall upon agriculture.

taxation
Edward Gibbon, 1737–1794, British historian.
Decline and Fall of the Roman Empire ch 8

Taylor Frederick Winslow 1856–1915. US engineer and management consultant, the founder of scientific management. His ideas, published in *Principles of Scientific Management* 1911, were based on the breakdown of work to the simplest tasks, the separation of planning from execution of tasks, and the introduction of time-and-motion studies. His methods were clearly expressed in assembly-line factories, but have been criticized for degrading and alienating workers and producing managerial dictatorship.

technocracy society controlled by technical experts such as scientists and engineers. The term was invented by US engineer W H Smyth (1855–1940) 1919 to describe his proposed 'rule by technicians', and was popularized by James Burham (1905-1987) in *Managerial Revolution* 1941.

Man will never be enslaved by machinery if the man tending the machine be paid enough.

technology
Capek
News Chronicle

---

technology the use of tools, power, and materials, generally for the purposes of production. Almost every human process for getting food and shelter depends on complex technological systems, which have been developed over a 3-million-year period. Significant milestones include the advent of the steam engine 1712, the introduction of electricity and the internal combustion engine in the mid-1800s, and recent developments in ◊communications, electronics, and the nuclear and space industries. The *advanced technology* (highly automated and specialized) on which modern industrialized society depends is frequently contrasted with the *low technology* (labour-intensive and unspecialized) that characterizes some developing countries. *Intermediate technology* is an attempt to adapt scientifically advanced inventions to less developed areas by using local materials and methods of manufacture.

Any sufficiently advanced technology is indistinguishable from magic.

technology
Arthur C(harles) Clarke, 1917, English science-fiction and nonfiction writer.
The Lost Worlds of 2001

---

tefillin or *phylacteries* in Judaism, two small leather boxes containing the ◊shema (prayer from the Torah) written on scrolls, that are strapped to the left arm and the forehead by Jewish men for daily prayer. The tefillin are worn in obedience to the command found in Deuteronomy 6 to bind the words of the shema 'as a sign upon your hands and a frontlet between your eyes'. Most Jews regard them as a God-given symbolic reminder to love God in all one thinks, feels, and does.

Teh Bahadur 1621–1675. Indian religious leader, ninth guru (teacher) of Sikhism 1664–75, executed for refusing to renounce his faith.

Teilhard de Chardin Pierre 1881–1955. French Jesuit theologian, palaeontologist, and philosopher. He developed a creative synthesis of nature and religion, based on his fieldwork and fossil studies. Publication of his *Le Phénomène humain/The Phenomenon of Man*, written 1938–40, was delayed (due to his unorthodox views) until after his death by the embargo of his superiors. He saw humanity as being in a constant process of evolution, moving towards a perfect spiritual state.

Born in the Puy-de-Dôme, he entered the Society of Jesus 1899, was ordained 1911, and during World War I was a stretcher bearer, taking his final vows 1918. From 1951 until his death he lived in the USA.

teleology the view that developments and changes in organisms or systems are due to the purposes, goals, ends, or design served by them (see ◊argument from design).

This belief that all evolution is purposive has been very influential in metaphysical thought from Aristotle and the stoics in ancient Greece to G W F Hegel in the 19th century. Teleology has been opposed by, among others, Epicurus, Lucretius, René Descartes, Thomas Hobbes, and Francis Bacon, all of whom argued that evolution and change are purposeless.

telepathy communication, or 'mind-to-mind' contact, between two, or more, persons not involving any of the known channels of sense; or the alleged ability for such communication. The term was coined in 1882 by F W H ◊Myers.

Teller Edward 1908– . Hungarian-born US physicist known as the father of the hydrogen bomb, which he worked upon, after taking part in the atom bomb project, at the Los Alamos research centre, New Mexico, 1946–52. He was a key witness against his colleague Robert ◊Oppenheimer at the security hearings 1954. He was widely believed to be the model for the leading character in Stanley Kubrick's 1964 film *Dr Strangelove*. More recently he has been one of the leading supporters of the Star Wars programme (Strategic Defense Initiative).

Tel Quel French literary magazine founded 1960 by the critic Philippe Sollers. Its aims were originally aesthetic but became increasingly ideological. It promoted the writings of the Marquis de Sade, Mallarmé, Lautréamont, and ◊Artaud as a revolutionary force that could change society.

Templars or *Knights Templar* or *Order of Poor Knights of Christ and of the Temple of Solomon* military religious order founded in Jerusalem 1119–20 to protect pilgrims travelling to the Holy Land. They played an important part in the ◊Crusades of the 12th and 13th centuries. Innocent II placed them under direct papal authority 1139, and their international links allowed them to adapt to the 13th-century decline of the Crusader states by becoming Europe's bankers. The Templars' independence, power, and wealth, rather than their alleged heresy, probably motivated Philip IV of France, helped by the Avignon Pope Clement V, to suppress the order 1307–14.

temple place of religious worship. In US usage, temple is another name for ◊synagogue.

Temple centre of Jewish national worship in Jerusalem in both ancient and modern days. The Western or *Wailing Wall* is the surviving part of the western wall of the enclosure of Herod's Temple. Since the destruction of the Temple AD 70, Jews have gone there to pray and to mourn their dispersion and the loss of their homeland.

Three temples have occupied the site: *Solomon's Temple*, built about 950 BC, which was destroyed by the Babylonian king Nebuchadnezzar 586 BC; *Zerubbabel's Temple*, built after the return of the Jews from Babylonian captivity 536 BC; and *Herod's Temple*, which was destroyed by the Romans. The Mosque of Omar now stands on the site. Under Jordanian rule Jews had no access to the site, but the Israelis regained this part of the city in the 1967 war.

Temple William 1881–1944. Archbishop of Canterbury 1942–44. A major ecumenical figure who strove to achieve church unity. His theological writings constantly sought to apply Christian teachings to contemporary social conditions as in his *Christianity and the Social Order* 1942.

Ten Commandments in the Old Testament, the laws given by God to the Hebrew leader Moses on Mount Sinai, engraved on two tablets of stone. They are: to have no other gods besides Jehovah; to make no idols; not to misuse the name of God; to keep the sabbath holy; to honour one's parents; not to commit murder, adultery, or theft; not to give false evidence; not to be covetous. They form the basis of Jewish and Christian moral codes; the 'tablets of the Law' given to Moses are also mentioned in the Qur'an. The giving of the Ten Commandments is celebrated in the Jewish festival of Shavuot (see ◊Pentecost).

Tendai Japanese form of the Chinese ◊T'ien-T'ai school of Buddhism, introduced to Japan by Saicho in the 9th century AD. It struggled to become established and later became very militant, with warrior monks engaged in warfare. Tendai teaches of the Buddha-nature within everyone which can be individually realized through ethical behaviour and discipline.

Teresa Mother. Born Agnes Bojaxhiu 1910– . Roman Catholic nun. She was born in Skopje, Macedonia, of Albanian parents, and at 18 entered a Calcutta convent and became a teacher. In 1948 she became an Indian citizen and founded the Missionaries of Charity, an order for men and women based in Calcutta that helps abandoned children and the dying. She was awarded the Nobel peace prize 1979.

Teresa of Avila, St 1515–1582. Spanish mystic who founded an order of nuns (the Discalced Carmelites) 1562.

She wrote *The Way to Perfection* 1583 and an autobiography, *Life of the Mother Theresa of Jesus*, 1611. In 1622 she was canonized.

Born in Avila, she entered the Carmelite monastery there 1535. From 1555 she was subject to fainting fits, during which she saw visions, leading to her founding of the first reformed Carmelite house. In 1970 she was made the first female Doctor of the Church.

terms of trade in international trade, the ratio of export prices to import prices:

$$\frac{\text{export prices}}{\text{import prices}}$$

An improvement in the terms of trade (there is an increase in the value of the ratio) should mean that the country is better off, having to give foreigners fewer exports for the same number of imports as before. ◊Devaluation of the currency will lead to a deterioration of the terms of trade.

Terpsichore in Greek mythology, one of the ◊Muses, of dance and choral song.

territorial behaviour in biology, any behaviour that serves to exclude other members of the same species from a fixed area or territory. It may involve aggressively driving out intruders, marking the boundary (with dung piles or secretions from special scent glands), conspicuous visual displays, characteristic songs, or loud calls.

terrorism systematic violence in the furtherance of political aims, often by small ◊guerrilla groups. Terrorist groups may be motivated by a variety of different ideologies, including religion and nationalism. Often these are combined, as evidenced by the Muslim extremists in the Middle East and the Irish Republican Army (IRA) in the United Kingdom. Some terrorist groups – such as the Italian Red Brigades and the German Baader Meinhoff gang – seek to change a country's political system.

The methods terrorists employ include kidnapping, such as the taking of Western hostages in Lebanon, hijacking of aircraft or ships, and the use of bombs on both military and civilian targets. Because terrorists, by their nature, ignore normal humanitarian principles and social conventions, legitimate governments will always be at a disadvantage in their attempts to combat them. That is why they sometimes use covert methods, or units such

as the SAS in Britain, to 'beat the terrorists at their own game'.

In English law, under the Prevention of Terrorism Act 1984, people arrested may be detained for 48 hours. The secretary of state can extend the period of detention for a maximum of five further days. By 1991, 18,000 people had been detained but only 250 were charged with offences.

tertiary in the Roman Catholic Church, a member of a 'third order' (see under ◊holy orders); a lay person who, while marrying and following a normal employment, attempts to live in accordance with a modified version of the rule of one of the religious orders. The first such order was founded by St ◊Francis 1221.

Tertullian Quintus Septimius Florens AD 155–222. Carthaginian Father of the Church, the first major Christian writer in Latin; he became a leading exponent of ◊Montanism.

textual criticism the attempt, through scholarship, to establish the most accurate and authentic version of a literary text when several different versions exist.

Thales 640–546 BC. Greek philosopher and scientist. He made advances in geometry, predicted an eclipse of the Sun 585 BC, and, as a philosophical materialist, theorized that water was the first principle of all things, that the Earth floated on water, and so proposed an explanation for earthquakes. He lived in Miletus in Asia Minor.

Thalia in Greek mythology, one of the ◊Muses, of comedy and pastoral poetry.

thanatology study of the psychological aspects of the experiences of death and dying and its application in counselling and assisting the terminally ill. It was pioneered by US psychiatrist Elizabeth Kübler-Ross in the 1970s.

Thanksgiving (Day) national holiday in the US (fourth Thursday in Nov) and Canada (second Monday in Oct), first celebrated by the Pilgrim settlers in Massachusetts after their first harvest 1621.

Thatcherism political outlook comprising a belief in the efficacy of market forces, the need for strong central government, and a conviction that self-help is preferable to reliance on the state, combined with a strong element of ◊nationalism. The ideology is associated with Margaret Thatcher but stems from an individualist view found in Britain's 19th-century Liberal and 20th-century Conservative parties. It is no longer confined to Britain, but is also found in the USA, France, Italy, and New Zealand.

No one would remember the Good Samaritan if he'd only had good intentions. He had money as well.

Margaret Thatcher, Baroness Thatcher of Kesteven
Television interview 6 Jan 1986

---

theatre performance by actors for an audience; it may include drama, dancing, music, mime, and puppets. The term is also used for the place or building in which dramatic performances take place. Theatre history can be traced to Egyptian religious ritualistic drama as long ago as 3200 BC. The first known European theatres were in Greece from about 600 BC.

history The earliest Greek theatres were open spaces, possibly associated with the worship of the god Dionysus. The great theatre of Dionysus at Athens provided for an audience of 15,000–20,000 people sitting in tiers on the surrounding slopes. Facing this banked auditorium was a scene-building, built originally of wood and then reconstructed in stone c. 340 BC. The design served as a model for the theatres that were erected in all the main cities of the Graeco-Roman world. Examples of Roman theatres exist at Orange, France, St Albans, England, and elsewhere. But after the collapse of the Roman Empire the theatres fell into disuse.

In medieval times, temporary stages of wood and canvas, some mounted on pageant wagons, were set up side by side in fairgrounds and market squares for the performance of mimes and miracle plays. Small enclosed theatres were built in the 16th century, for example in Vicenza, Italy (by the architect Palladio). The first London theatre was built in Shoreditch 1576 by James Burbage, who also opened the first covered theatre in London, the Blackfriars 1596. His son was responsible for building the Globe Theatre, the venue for Shakespeare's plays. The tradition of open-air performances were continued in the Italian commedia dell'arte, originating in the 16th century. In the 17th and 18th centuries most theatrical productions were performed indoors under license, until the greater commercialization of the 19th century.

In the USA the centre of commercial theatre in the 20th century has been New York City, with numerous theatres on or near Broadway, although Williamsburg, Virginia (1716), and Philadelphia (1766) had the first known American theatres. The 'little theatres', off-Broadway, developed to present less commercial productions, often by new dramatists, and of these the first was the Theater Guild (1919); off-off-Broadway then developed as fringe theatre (alternative theatre).

In Britain repertory theatres (theatres running a different play every few weeks) proliferated until World War II, for example the Old Vic; and in Ireland the Abbey Theatre became the first state-subsidized theatre 1924. The Comédie Française in Paris (founded by Louis XIV 1680 and given a permanent home 1792) was the first national theatre. In Britain the National Theatre company was established 1963; other national theatres exist in Stockholm, Moscow, Athens, Copenhagen, Vienna, Warsaw, and elsewhere. Although the repertory movement declined from the 1950s with the spread of cinema and television, a number of regional community theatres developed. Recently established theatres are often associated with a university or are part of a larger cultural centre.

Historic London theatres include the Haymarket (1720, rebuilt 1821), Drury Lane (1663), and Her Majesty's (1705), both rebuilt several times. The English Stage Company was established at the Royal Court Theatre 1956 to provide a platform for new works.

theism belief in the existence of gods, but more specifically in that of a single personal God, at once immanent (active) in the created world and transcendent (separate) from it.

theocracy political system run by priests, as was once found in Tibet. In practical terms it means a system where religious values determine political decisions. The closest modern example was Iran during the period when Ayatollah Khomeini was its religious leader, 1979–89. The term was coined by the historian Josephus in the 1st century AD.

Theodoric of Freiburg c. 1250–1310. German scientist and monk. He studied in Paris 1275–77. In his work *De Iride/On the Rainbow* he describes how he used a water-filled sphere to simulate a raindrop, and determined that colours are formed in the raindrops and that light is reflected within the drop and can be reflected again, which explains secondary rainbows.

theogony (Greek 'birth of the gods') in Greek mythology, an account of the origin of the gods, conceived largely in terms of human reproduction. The Greek poet ◊Hesiod wrote a *Theogony*, which was in effect a genealogy of the Greek pantheon.

theology study of God or gods, either that which is known by reasoned deduction from the natural world (natural theology) or known only through divine revelation (revealed theology), as in the scriptures of Christianity, Islam, or other religions.

Other branches of theology include comparative theology (the study of the similarities and differences between faiths), and eschatology (the study of the end of the world and afterlife).

Theological attitudes towards other faiths range from exclusivism (that one's own religion is correct and all the others wrong) to the more modern dialogue theology (promoting awareness of other religions) and relativism (arguing that different religions are separate paths to a similar goal).

Theophrastus of Lesbos c. 370–c. 286 BC. Greek philosopher who also laid the foundations of scientific botany in his work *On Plants*. His *Characters*, a series of 30 character sketches, has had a persistent influence on European literature.

Theophrastus was born in Eresus on Lesbos and studied in Athens, at first under Plato and then under Aristotle. He was Aristotle's favourite pupil, and succeeded him as head of the Lyceum. Comic poet Menander was a pupil of Theophrastus.

theory in science, a set of ideas, concepts, principles, or methods used to explain a wide set of observed facts. Among the major theories of science are ◊relativity, ◊quantum theory, ◊evolution, and plate tectonics.

Theory of Everything (ToE) another name for ◊grand unified theory.

theory of three worlds view expounded by Chinese Communist statesman Deng Xiaoping at the United Nations Organization (UNO) General Assembly 1974 that the two superpowers – the USA and the Soviet Union – were seeking world hegemony and that China as a developing socialist country should oppose this by making firmer links with other ◊Third World countries.

theosophy any religious or philosophical system based on intuitive insight into the nature of the divine, but especially that of the Theosophical Society, founded in New York 1875 by Madame Blavatsky and H S Olcott. It was based on Hindu ideas of ◊karma and ◊reincarnation, with ◊nirvana as the eventual aim.

Theravāda one of the two major forms of ◊Buddhism, common in S Asia (Sri Lanka, Thailand, Cambodia, and Myanmar); the other is the later Mahāyāna.

thermodynamics branch of physics dealing with the transformation of heat into and from other forms of energy. It is the basis of the study of the efficient working of engines, such as the steam and internal-combustion engines. The three laws of thermodynamics are (1) energy can be neither created nor destroyed, heat and mechanical work being mutually convertible; (2) it is impossible for an unaided self-acting machine to convey heat from one body to another at a higher temperature; and (3) it is impossible by any procedure, no matter how idealized, to reduce any system to the absolute zero of temperature (0K/–273°C) in a finite number of operations. Put into mathematical form, these laws have widespread applications in physics and chemistry.

Theseus in Greek legend, a hero of Attica, supposed to have united the states of the area under a constitutional government in Athens. Ariadne, whom he later abandoned on Naxos, helped him find his way through the Labyrinth to kill the ◊Minotaur. He also fought the Amazons and was one of the Argonauts.

thing-in-itself technical term in the philosophy of ◊Kant, employed to denote the unknowable source of the sensory component of our experience. Later thinkers, including ◊Fichte and ◊Hegel, denied the coherence of this concept.

think tank popular name for research foundations, generally private, that gather experts to study policy questions and make recommendations. There are think tanks representing positions across the political spectrum, and they are sometimes funded according to the viewpoints they represent.

In the UK the *Central Policy Review Staff*, a consultative body to the government 1970–83, was known as the Think Tank. It was set up to provide cabinet ministers with informed background advice on major policy decisions.

Third Age in education, late middle age and older. A Université du Troisième Age was established in France 1972 to offer people over 50 the opportunity to continue their education. In the UK, the University of the Third Age established 1982 has no teachers and no qualifications for entry, but aims to help its 120 local groups to pursue any topics that interest them.

third estate or *tiers état* in pre-revolutionary France, the order of society comprising the common people as distinct from members of the first (noble) or the second (clerical) estates. All three met collectively as the ◊States General.

Third Reich (Third Empire) term used by the Nazis to describe Germany during the years of Hitler's dictatorship after 1933. The idea of the Third Reich was based on the existence of two previous German empires, the medieval Holy Roman Empire and the second empire 1871–1918.

The term was coined by the German writer Moeller van den Bruck (1876–1925) in the 1920s.

Third World or *developing world* those countries that are less developed than the industrialized free-market countries of the West (First World) and the industrialized former Communist countries (Second World). Third World countries are the poorest, as measured by their income per head of population, and are concentrated in Asia, Africa, and Latin America.

The Third World is divided into low-income countries, including China and India; middle-income countries, such as Nigeria, Indonesia, and Bolivia; and upper-middle-income countries, such as Brazil, Algeria, and Malaysia. The Third World has 75% of the world's population but consumes only 20% of its resources. In 1990 the average income per head of population in the northern hemisphere was $12,500, which is 18 times higher than that in the southern hemisphere.

Problems associated with developing countries include high population growth and mortality rates; poor educational and health facilities; heavy dependence on agriculture and commodities for which prices and demand fluctuate; high levels of underemployment, and, in some cases, political instability. Third World countries, led by the Arab oil-exporting countries, account for over 75% of all arms imports. The economic performance of developing countries in recent years has been mixed, with sub-Saharan Africa remaining in serious difficulties and others, as in Asia, making significant progress. Failure by many developing countries to meet their enormous foreign debt obligations has led to stringent terms being imposed on loans by industrialized countries, as well as rescheduling of loans (deferring payment).

Thirty-Nine Articles set of articles of faith defining the doctrine of the Anglican church; see under ◊Anglican Communion.

Thomas à Kempis 1380–1471. German Augustinian monk who lived at the monastery of Zwolle. He took his name from his birthplace Kempen; his real surname was Hammerken. He wrote hymns, sermons, and biographies but is remembered for his *De Imitatio Christi/Imitation of Christ* which is probably the most widely known devotional work ever written. The work was an expression of the strain of pious devotion known as ◊*devotio moderna*.

Thomas Aquinas medieval philosopher; see ◊Aquinas, St Thomas.

Thomas, St in the New Testament, one of the 12 Apostles, said to have preached in S India, hence the ancient churches there were referred to as the 'Christians of St Thomas'. The Gospel of St Thomas, the Gnostic collection of Jesus' sayings, is falsely attributed to him.

Thomism the philosophy founded by Thomas ◊Aquinas. Neo-Thomists apply it to contemporary problems. It is a form of ◊scholasticism.

Thomson George Paget 1892–1975. English physicist whose work on interference phenomena in the scattering of electrons by crystals helped to confirm the wavelike nature of particles. He shared a Nobel prize with C J ◊Davisson 1937.

He was the son of J J ◊Thomson.

Thomson J(oseph) J(ohn) 1856–1940. English physicist who discovered the electron. He was responsible for organizing the Cavendish atomic research laboratory at Cambridge University. His work inaugurated the electrical theory of the atom, and his elucidation of positive rays and their application to an analysis of neon led to Frederick ◊Aston's discovery of isotopes. Nobel prize 1906.

Thor in Norse mythology, the god of thunder (his hammer), and represented as a man of enormous strength defending humanity against demons. He was the son of Odin and Freya, and Thursday is named after him.

*The mass of men lead lives
of quiet desperation.*

Henry David Thoreau
Walden, 'Economy'

Thoreau Henry David 1817–1862. US author and naturalist. His work *Walden, or Life in the Woods* 1854 stimulated the back-to-nature movement, and he completed some 30 volumes based on his daily nature walks. His essay 'Civil Disobedience' 1849, prompted by his refusal to pay taxes, advocated peaceful resistance to unjust laws and had a wide impact, even in the 20th century.

His other works include *A Week on the Concord and Merrimack Rivers* 1849 and, published posthumously, *Excursions* 1863, *The Maine Woods* 1864, *Cape Cod* 1865, and *A Yankee in Canada* 1866.

It takes two to speak the truth – one to speak, and another to hear.

Henry David Thoreau
A Week on the Concord and Merrimack Rivers

Thorndike Edward Lee 1874–1949. US educational psychologist whose experiments in behaviour of cats and dogs in a 'puzzle box' brought him to the conclusion that learning was improved when it achieved a pleasurable result, which he termed the *law of effect*. He extended this theory to human learning and found that students were encouraged by good results, but that being wrong did not teach them to correct their errors.

Thoth in Egyptian mythology, the god of wisdom and learning. He was represented as a scribe with the head of an ibis, the bird sacred to him.

Three Age System the division of ◊prehistory into the Stone Age, Bronze Age, and Iron Age, proposed by Danish archaeologist Christian Thomsen (1788–1865) between 1816 and 1819. Subsequently, the Stone Age was subdivided into the Old and the New (the Palaeolithic and Neolithic); the Middle (Mesolithic) Stone Age was added later, as well as the Copper Age (inserted between the New Stone Age and Bronze Age). While providing a valuable and valid classification system for prehistoric material, the Three Age System did not provide dates but only a sequence of developmental stages, which, furthermore, were not necessarily followed in that order by different societies.

thug originally a member of a Hindu sect who strangled travellers as sacrifices to ◊Kali, the goddess of destruction. The sect was suppressed about 1830.

Thule Greek and Roman name for the northernmost land known. It was applied to the Shetlands, the Orkneys, and Iceland, and, by later writers, to Scandinavia.

Thunderbird legendary bird of the North American Indians, the creator of storms. It is said to produce thunder by flapping its wings; lightning by opening and closing its eyes.

Thünen Johann von 1785–1850. German economist and geographer who believed that the success of a state depends on the well-being of its farmers. His book *The Isolated State* 1820, a pioneering study of land use, includes the earliest example of *marginal productivity theory*, a theory that he developed to calculate the natural wage for a farmworker. He has been described as the first modern economist.

T'ien-T'ai branch of Chinese Buddhism founded by Hui Ssu (515–577 AD) and based upon the Lotus Sutra, commentaries on the Sutra, and Hui Ssu's own teachings. T'ien-T'ai teaches the Threefold Truth which states that the ◊dharma (the essence of a thing) is nothingness because it has no self or real being, that self only seems to exist because of certain causes and conditions; that it is in an intermediate state of both nothingness (void) and yet also existing. The Japanese school of T'ien-T'ai is ◊Tendai.

Tillich Paul Johannes 1886–1965. Prussianborn US theologian, best remembered for his *Systematic Theology* 1951–63. Fleeing the Nazis, he arrived in the USA 1933 and served as professor of theology at the Union Theological Seminary 1933–55, Harvard University 1955–62, and the University of Chicago 1962–65.

Born in Prussia, Tillich received his PhD from the University of Breslau 1911. Ordained a pastor in the Evangelical Lutheran Church 1912, he served as a chaplain during World War I. Appointed to a professorship at the University of Frankfurt he was removed by the Nazis and fled to the USA.

Time is a great teacher, but unfortunately it kills all its pupils.

time
(Louis) Hector Berlioz, 1803–1869, French Romantic composer.
Almanach des lettres françaises

---

time continuous passage of existence, recorded by division into hours, minutes, and seconds. Formerly the measurement of time was based on the Earth's rotation on its axis, but this was found to be irregular. Therefore the second, the standard SI unit of time, was redefined 1956 in terms of the Earth's annual orbit of the Sun, and 1967 in terms of a radiation pattern of the element caesium.

Universal time (UT), based on the Earth's actual rotation, was replaced by coordinated universal time (UTC) 1972, the difference between the two involving the addition (or subtraction) of leap seconds on the last day of June or Dec. National observatories (in the UK until 1990 the Royal Greenwich Observatory) make standard time available, and the BBC broadcasts six pips at certain hours (five short, from second 55 to second 59, and one long, the start of which indicates the precise minute). Its computerized clock has an accuracy greater than 1 second in 4,000 years. From 1986 the term Greenwich Mean Time was replaced by UTC. However, the Greenwich meridian, adopted 1884, remains that from which all longitudes are measured, and the world's standard time zones are calculated from it.

Time, which is the author of authors.

time
Francis Bacon, 1561–1626, English
politician, philosopher, and essayist.
Advancement of Learning bk I

---

time and motion study process of analysis applied to a job or number of jobs to check the efficiency of the work method, equipment used, and the worker. Its findings are used to improve performance.

Time and motion studies were introduced in the USA by Frederick Taylor (1856–1915) at the beginning of the 20th century. Since then, the practice has spread throughout the industrialized world.

Tinbergen Jan 1903–1988. Dutch economist. He shared a Nobel prize 1969 with Ragnar Frisch for his work on ◊econometrics (the mathematical-statistical expression of economic theory).

Tinbergen Niko(laas) 1907– . Dutch zoologist. He was one of the founders of ◊ethology, the scientific study of animal behaviour in natural surroundings. Specializing in the study of instinctive behaviour, he shared a Nobel prize with Konrad ◊Lorenz and Karl von ◊Frisch 1973. He is the brother of Jan Tinbergen.

Ting Samuel 1936– . US physicist. In 1974 he and his team at the Brookhaven National Laboratory, New York, detected a new subatomic particle, which he named the J particle. It was found to be identical to the ψ particle

discovered in the same year by Burton ◊Richter and his team at the Stanford Linear Accelerator Center, California. Ting and Richter shared the Nobel Prize for Physics 1976.

Titan in Greek mythology, any of the giant children of Uranus and Gaia, who included Kronos, Rhea, Themis, and Oceanus. Kronos and Rhea were in turn the parents of Zeus, who ousted Kronos as the ruler of the world.

tithe formerly, payment exacted from the inhabitants of a parish for the maintenance of the church and its incumbent; some religious groups continue the practice by giving 10% of members' incomes to charity.

It was originally the grant of a tenth of all agricultural produce made to priests in Hebrew society. In the Middle Ages the tithe was adopted as a tax in kind paid to the local parish church, usually for the support of the incumbent, and stored in a special tithe barn; as such, it survived into contemporary times in Europe and Britain. In Protestant countries, these payments were often appropriated by lay landlords.

In the 19th century a rent charge was substituted. By the Tithe Commutation Act 1836, tithes were abolished and replaced by 'redemption annuities' payable to the crown, government stock being issued to tithe-owners.

Tlingit member of a North American Indian people of the NW coast, living in S Alaska and N British Columbia. They used to carve wooden poles representing their family crests, showing such animals as the raven, whale, octopus, beaver, bear, wolf, and the mythical ◊thunderbird. Their language is related to the Athabaskan languages.

Tobin James 1918– . US Keynesian economist. He was awarded a Nobel prize 1981 for his 'general equilibrium' theory, which states that other criteria than monetary considerations are applied by households and firms when making decisions on consumption and investment.

---

*Americans are so enamored of equality
that they would rather be equal in slavery
than unequal in freedom.*

Alexis de Tocqueville
Democracy in America

Tocqueville Alexis de 1805–1859. French politician, sociologist, and historian, author of the first analytical study of the strengths and weaknesses of US society, *De la Démocratie en Amérique/Democracy in America* 1835, and of a penetrating description of France before the Revolution, *L'Ancien Régime et la Révolution/ The Old Regime and the Revolution* 1856. No other 19th-century liberal thinker saw the problems of contemporary democratic society quite so clearly.

Elected to the Chamber of Deputies 1839, Tocqueville became vice president of the Constituent Assembly and minister of foreign affairs 1849. He retired after Napoleon III's coup 1851.

Tolstoy Leo Nikolaievich 1828–1910. Russian novelist who wrote *War and Peace* 1863–69 and *Anna Karenina* 1873–77. From 1880 Tolstoy underwent a profound spiritual crisis and took up various moral positions, including passive resistance to evil, rejection of authority (religious or civil) and private ownership, and a return to basic mystical Christianity. He was excommunicated by the Orthodox Church, and his later works were banned.

Tolstoy was born of noble family at Yasnaya Polyana, near Tula, and fought in the Crimean War. His first published work was *Childhood* 1852, the first part of the trilogy that was completed with *Boyhood* 1854 and *Youth* 1857. *Tales from Sebastopol* was published 1856; later books include *What I Believe* 1883 and *The Kreutzer Sonata* 1889, and the novel *Resurrection* 1900. His desire to give up his property and live as a peasant disrupted his family life, and he finally fled his home and died of pneumonia at the railway station in Astapovo.

Tombaugh Clyde (William) 1906– . US astronomer who discovered the planet Pluto 1930.

Tombaugh, born in Streator, Illinois, became an assistant at the Lowell Observatory in Flagstaff, Arizona, in 1929, and photographed the sky in search of an undiscovered remote planet as predicted by the observatory's founder, Percival ◊Lowell. Tombaugh found Pluto on 18 Feb 1930, from plates taken three weeks earlier. He continued his search for new planets across the entire sky; his failure to find any placed strict limits on the possible existence of planets beyond Pluto.

Tönnies Ferdinand 1855–1936. German social theorist and philosopher, one of the founders of the sociological tradition of community studies and urban sociology through his key work, *Gemeinschaft–Gesellschaft* 1887.

Tönnies contrasted the nature of social relationships in traditional societies and small organizations (◊*Gemeinschaft*, 'community') with those in industrial societies and large organizations (*Gesellschaft*, 'association'). He was pessimistic about the effect of industrialization and urbanization on the social and moral order, seeing them as a threat to traditional society's sense of community.

topography the surface shape and aspect of the land, and its study. Topography deals with relief and contours, the distribution of mountains and valleys, the patterns of rivers, and all other features, natural and artificial, that produce the landscape.

Such features are shown on *topographical maps* (for example, those produced by the Ordnance Survey).

Torah in ◊Judaism, the first five books of the Hebrew Bible (Christian Old Testament); also, more loosely, the whole Hebrew Bible. It contains a traditional history of the world from the Creation to the death of Moses; it also includes the Hebrew people's covenant with their one God, rules for religious observance, and guidelines for social conduct, including the Ten Commandments.

Scrolls on which the Torah is hand-written in the original Hebrew are housed in a sacred enclosure, the ark, in every synagogue, and are treated with great respect. Jews believe that by observing the guidelines laid down in the Torah, they fulfil their part of their covenant with God.

tort in law, a wrongful act for which someone can be sued for damages in a civil court. It includes such acts as libel, trespass, injury done to someone (whether intentionally or by negligence), and inducement to break a contract (although breach of contract itself is not a tort).

In general a tort is distinguished from a crime in that it affects the interests of an individual rather than of society at large, but some crimes can also be torts (for example, assault).

torture infliction of bodily pain to extort evidence or confession. Legally abolished in England about 1640, torture was allowed in Scotland until 1708 and until 1789 in France. In the 20th century torture is widely (though, in most countries, unofficially) used.

The human-rights organization ◊Amnesty International investigates and publicizes the use of torture on prisoners of conscience, and there is now a centre in Copenhagen, Denmark, where torture victims are rehabilitated and studies are carried out into the effects of torture.

Physical torture in the Middle Ages employed devices such as the rack (to stretch the victim's joints to breaking point), the thumbscrew, the boot (which crushed the foot), heavy weights that crushed the whole body, the iron maiden (cage shaped like a human being with interior spikes to spear the occupant), and so on. While similar methods survive today, electric shocks and sexual assault are also common.

Brainwashing was developed in both the communist and the Western bloc in the 1950s, often using drugs. From the early 1960s a method used in the West replaced isolation by severe sensory deprivation; for example, IRA guerrillas were prevented from seeing by a hood, from feeling by being swathed in a loose-fitting garment, and from hearing by a continuous loud noise at about 85 decibels, while being forced to maintain themselves in a 'search' position against a wall by their fingertips. The European Commission on Human Rights found Britain guilty of torture, although the European Court of Human Rights classed it only as 'inhuman and degrading treatment'.

Tory Party the forerunner of the British ◊Conservative Party about 1680–1830. It was the party of the squire and parson, as opposed to the Whigs (supported by the trading classes and Nonconformists). The name is still applied colloquially to the Conservative Party. In the USA a Tory was an opponent of the break with Britain in the War of American Independence 1775–83.

The original Tories were Irish guerrillas who attacked the English, and the name was applied (at first insultingly) to royalists who opposed the Exclusion Bill.

Although largely supporting the 1688 revolution, the Tories were suspected of Jacobite sympathies, and were kept from power 1714–60, but then held office almost continuously until 1830.

If you want a picture of the future, imagine a boot stamping on a human face – for ever.

totalitarianism
Orwell. Pen name of Eric Arthur Blair George, 1903–1950, English author.
Nineteen Eighty-Four pt 3, ch 3

---

totalitarianism government control of all activities within a country, overtly political or otherwise, as in fascist or communist dictatorships. Examples of totalitarian regimes are

Italy under Benito Mussolini 1922–45; Germany under Adolf ◊Hitler 1933–45; the USSR under Joseph ◊Stalin from the 1930s until his death in 1953; more recently Romania under Nicolae Ceausescu 1974–89.

totemism the belief in individual or clan kinship with an animal, plant, or object. This totem is sacred to those concerned, and they are forbidden to eat or desecrate it; marriage within the clan is usually forbidden. Totemism occurs among Pacific Islanders and Australian Aborigines, and was formerly prevalent throughout Europe, Africa, and Asia. Most North and South American Indian societies had totems as well.

Totem poles are carved by Native Americans of the NW coast of North America and incorporate totem objects (carved and painted) as a symbol of the people or to commemorate the dead.

town planning the design of buildings or groups of buildings in a physical and social context, concentrating on the relationship between various buildings and their environment, as well as on their uses.

God made the country, and man made the town.

town
William Cowper, 1731–1800, English poet.
The Task bk 1

An urgent need for town planning emerged in the 19th century with the rapid growth of urban industrial centres. Reformists saw the crowded industrial city as the root of social evil, and various attempts were made to integrate industry with the pastoral vision of the village, culminating in the English town planner Ebenezer ◊Howard's proposal for the ◊garden city. This was first realized at Letchworth in Hertfordshire (begun 1903) and followed in 1946 by the first generation of publicly financed ◊new towns, each with its own civic amenities and industries.

In post-war continental Europe, CIAM, a loose association of Modernist architects and planners, took responsibility for much of the rebuilding and planning of European cities, advocating functional zoning and high-rise mass housing as the only viable solution to urban growth. CIAM remained the dominant force in town planning until the mid 1950s when the concepts of multi-layered, mixed-use city centres were re-evaluated. Since the 1970s

Urban Design in the Twentieth Century: the City of Tomorrow?

At the end of the twentieth century architects were engaged in a battle of styles which precluded the possibility of thinking about utopia. The classicists saw the landscape dotted with very small Vitruvian cities while high-tech designers seemed obsessed with skeletal building forms and transport system diagrams. The more pervasive and believable view of the future city had no form beyond the telecommunications grid and no structure other than that of the software program.

While architects and planners fiddled with components – individual buildings, transport systems, and enterprise zones – the software programmers, science-fiction writers, film makers, and theorists deconstructed what was left of coherent city life. The Los Angeles in the film *Blade Runner* (Ridley Scott, 1982), partly based on present-day Tokyo, was dystopia made visible. There was nothing behind the signs and constant rain, and night obscured the city's detail while the nightmarish possibilities of technology emerged into solid form.

Visions of utopia

At the end of the nineteenth century there was a more optimistic view of the city's future in the work of Ebenezer Howard (1850–1928). His book *Garden Cities of Tomorrow* (1902) was based on the idea of the twin magnets of city and countryside and had its roots in the utopian socialist visions of William Morris (1834–1896). Howard conceived of cities with easy access to green spaces through a hierarchy of gardens, parks, and countryside. Urban centres necessary, but would be ringed by open space. His views belonged to a tradition of geometrical solutions to urban problems, though they addressed the real problem of suburban sprawl and explored the possibilities of the railway.

This fascination with the geometrical plan and the park was taken up in the pioneering years of Modern Movement architecture by Le Corbusier (1887–1965) in his scheme for the 'Ville Radieuse', 1931. Here urban functions were strictly zoned and the vast communal parkland of the city stretched continuously under buildings raised on concrete legs. This vision was to inform Le Corbusier's architecture throughout his career. It was also to appear, designed by others, in various, often degraded, forms around the world in the aftermath of the Second World War. In many cases the tower block was set in wasteland rather than the idyllic landscape envisaged by Le Corbusier.

American visions

In the USA, Frank Lloyd Wright (1867–1959), while embracing technology, rejected the strictly urban in favour of his 'Broadacre City' project of 1932. This had many references to the ideas of self-sufficiency expounded by the anarchist Peter Kropotkin (1842–

1921). In his book *The Disappearing City* 1932, Wright described how each man would be allowed an acre of land on which to live and from which to provide his own food. Wright's ideas, though unrealistic in terms of their denial of industrialization, are linked in diverse ways to American culture: they refer to the pioneering spirit of the nineteenth century, to the supremacy of the automobile and to independence from the weight of history as manifest in the European city. Buckminster Fuller (1895–1983) took up some of these ideas but developed them along strictly technological lines. His futuristic prefabricated Dymaxion House and geodesic structures were based on a conviction that technology could be a powerful agent of social change.

The high-tech dream – or nightmare

Fuller's work inspired many designers in the 1960s, from the visionary architect Paolo Soleri (1920–) who designed and was still building his city Arcosanti in the Arizona desert in the 1990s, to the British group Archigram. The ideas of Archigram ranged across a wide spectrum and were expressed almost exclusively through drawings. Schemes such as 'Walking City' (1964) which were a celebration of fictional technology appear to be, looking back from the environmentally aware 1990s, a horrifying vision of the power of the machine. The leap from drawn designs to the *mises-en-scène* of science-fiction films is relatively easy to make. The film *2001: A Space Odyssey* (Stanley Kubrick, 1968) borrowed not only from existing space technology but also from the plug-in, clip-on fantasies of Archigram and others. Many of the images created in the 1960s anticipated the disintegration of urban patterns which was clearly in sight by the end of the century. This disintegration was approached in a positive way by the British architectural team NATO (Narrative Architecture Today). Their work in the 1980s made use of the chaos of urban life and constructed elaborate narratives around building types and lifestyles. This world of infinite possibility through the invention of stories or through the mobility of the 'Walking City' is not far removed from the no-need-for-mobility of the microchip. The 'cities of tomorrow' of the 1960s still used architecture as part of a future language and were born in a spirit of optimism. The culture which created virtual reality as a replacement for experience need no longer deal with this. The past and the future have equal value in the post-modern present. The past is there to be plundered and it will fill the future. The ghost of Modernist planning still runs amok both in poverty-stricken Third World capitals and in boom-and-bust Western cities but ultimately it is destined to take its place in the network of possibilities scrolling up the computer screen.

Calum Storrie

there has been renewed interest in urban design, with architects and planners working together in search of solutions. Robert Krier (1938–) and Leon Krier have argued eloquently in favour of the pre-industrial European city with its fabric of clearly defined urban spaces, and Aldo Rossi has also emphasized the importance of traditional urban architecture. In the UK Terry Farrell and Richard Rogers have campaigned for an urgent review of planning policy in London.

Toynbee Arnold 1852–1883. English economic historian who coined the term 'industrial revolution' in his *Lectures on the Industrial Revolution*, published 1884.

Toynbee Hall, an education settlement in the east end of London, was named after him.

Tractarianism another name for the ◊Oxford Movement, 19th-century movement for Catholic revival within the Church of England.

trade exchange of commodities between groups or individuals. Direct trade is usually known as barter, whereas indirect trade is carried out through a medium such as money.

In the 17th and 18th centuries, for example, barter between Europeans and West Africans was based on units of value called sortings. A sorting might consist of a quantity of cloth or oil. The amount of goods in each sorting varied according to supply and demand.

No nation was ever ruined by trade.

trade
Benjamin Franklin, 1706–1790, US printer, publisher, author, scientist, and statesman.
'Thoughts on Commercial Subjects'

---

trade cycle or *business cycle* period of time that includes a peak and trough of economic activity, as measured by a country's national income. In Keynesian economics, one of the main roles of the government is to smooth out the peaks and troughs of the trade cycle by intervening in the economy, thus minimizing 'overheating' and 'stagnation'. This is accomplished by regulating interest rates and government spending.

trade union organization of employed workers formed to undertake collective bargaining with employers and to try to achieve improved working conditions for its members. Attitudes of government to unions and of unions to management vary greatly from country to country. Probably the most effective trade-union system

is that of Sweden, and the most internationally known is the Polish Solidarity.

trade unionism, international worldwide cooperation between unions. In 1973 a European Trade Union Confederation was established, membership 29 million, and there is an International Labour Organization, established 1919 and affiliated to the United Nations from 1945, which formulates standards for labour and social conditions. Other organizations are the International Confederation of Free Trade Unions (1949) – which includes the American Federation of Labor and Congress of Industrial Organizations and the UK Trades Union Congress – and the World Federation of Trade Unions (1945).

Though I am native here, / And to the manner born, – it is a custom / More honour'd in the breach than the observance.

tradition
William Shakespeare, 1564–1616, English dramatist and poet.
Hamlet I. iv

---

tradition the passing down of a body of established practices, customs, and beliefs from one generation to the next.

The term was originally applied by early Christian theologians to those central beliefs that were to be handed down through instruction. A tradition often commands respect simply through the authority of long usage. It usually represents the norm and is therefore especially admired by the conservative, while being reviled by the radical as inimical to change. In fact only the strictest beliefs fail to see tradition as a growing and cumulative process and only the most extreme revolutions have attempted to sever all connections with the past.

traditional economy economy based on subsistence agriculture where small family groups or tribes produce nearly all of what they need themselves. There is therefore very little trade, and barter rather than money is used for any trade that does take place. In a traditional economy, people are generally averse to risk, preferring to keep to traditional modes of production and avoid change.

tragedy in the theatre, a play dealing with a serious theme, traditionally one in which a character meets disaster as a result either of personal failings or circumstances beyond his or her control. Historically the classical view of tragedy, as expressed by the Greek tragedians Aeschylus, Euripides, and Sophocles, and the Roman tragedian Seneca, has been predominant in the Western tradition. In the 20th century tragedies dealing with exalted or heroic figures in an elevated manner have virtually died out. Tragedy has been replaced by dramas with 'tragic' implications or overtones, as in the work of Ibsen, O'Neill, Tennessee Williams, and Osborne, for example, or by the problem plays of Pirandello, Brecht, and Beckett.

The Greek view of tragedy was developed by the philosohper Aristotle, but it was the Roman Seneca (whose works were probably intended to be read rather than acted) who influenced the Elizabethan tragedies of Marlowe and Shakespeare. French classical tragedy developed under the influence of both Seneca and an interpretation of Aristotle which gave rise to the theory of ◊unities of time, place, and action, as observed by Racine, one of its greatest exponents. In Germany the tragedies of Goethe and Schiller led to the exaggerated melodrama, which replaced pure tragedy. In the 18th century attempts were made to 'domesticate' tragedy, notably by Lessing, but it was the realistic dramas of Ibsen that confirmed the transformation of serious drama.

trance mental state in which the subject loses the ordinary perceptions of time and space, and even of his or her own body.

In this highly aroused state, often induced by rhythmic music, 'speaking in tongues' (glossolalia) may occur (see ◊Pentecostal Movement); this usually consists of the rhythmic repetition of apparently meaningless syllables, with a euphoric return to consciousness. It is also practised by native American and Australian Aboriginal healers, Afro-Brazilian spirit mediums, and Siberian shamans.

transcendentalism US mystical and literary movement 1840–60 that, influenced by European Romanticism, saw God as immanent in nature and the human soul. It had moral, religious, and political implications, shaping American social attitudes to self-reliance, the abolition of slavery, feminism, and utopian idealism. With its stress on the need for an original US literature, the movement stimulated Ralph Waldo Emerson's essays and poems, Henry Thoreau's *Walden* 1854, and also influenced the novels and stories of Nathaniel Hawthorne, and Walt Whitman's *Leaves of Grass* 1855.

The transcendentalist movement set up an experimental socialist community at Brook Farm near Boston, Massachusetts. Among those associated with it were the feminist Margaret Fuller (1810–1850) and the lecturer and social reformer Orestes Brownson.

transcendental meditation (TM) technique of focusing the mind, based in part on Hindu meditation. Meditators are given a mantra (a special word or phrase) to repeat over and over to themselves; such meditation is believed to benefit the practitioner by relieving stress and inducing a feeling of well-being and relaxation. It was introduced to the West by Maharishi Mahesh Yogi and popularized by the Beatles in the late 1960s.

Practitioners claim that if even as few as 1% of the population meditated in this way, society would see much less stress.

transcription in living cells, the process by which the information for the synthesis of a protein is transferred from the ◊DNA strand on which it is carried to the messenger ◊RNA strand involved in the actual synthesis.

It occurs by the formation of base pairs when a single strand of unwound DNA serves as a template for assembling the complementary nucleotides that make up the new RNA strand.

transference in psychoanalysis, the patient's transfer of feelings and wishes experienced in earlier relationships into the relationship with the analyst.

First described by Freud 1895, the transference relationship is often viewed as taking a positive or negative form. In *positive transference* the patient is compliant or unrealistically overvalues the analyst. In *negative transference* the patient is defiant or dislikes the analyst. When positive, transference can be used as a means of overcoming resistance to the recall of unpleasant material but, when negative, often endangers the continuum of treatment and so is generally isolated. Freud regarded the transference relationship as an essential tool in analysis, but some subsequent schools regard it as a side-effect to be countered early in treatment.

transformation in mathematics, a mapping or function, especially one which causes a change of shape or position in a geometric figure. Reflection, rotation, enlargement, and translation are the main geometrical transformations.

transformational grammar theory of language structure initiated by Noam ◊Chomsky, which proposes that below the actual phrases and sentences of a language (its *surface*

Translation: chronology

3rd century BC–1st century AD	Septuagint: Greek translation from Hebrew of the Old Testament and Apocrypha.
4th century	Vulgate: Latin translation of the Bible by St Jerome, the first complete translation direct from Hebrew.
8th–9th centuries	Translations of many of the Greek classics into Arabic by Arabic scholars, mostly based in Baghdad.
12th century	Translations from Arabic to Latin, centred in Toledo, Spain (school of translators founded by Archbishop Raymund 1,1126–51); translations of Aristotle and Avicenna, by, for example, Gerard of Cremona, John of Seville, and Adelard of Bath.
1382	John Wycliffe's first translation of the Bible into English.
1522	Martin Luther's translation of the New Testament into German.
1525	William Tyndale: English translation of the New Testament.
1537	Miles Coverdale: English translation of the Bible.
1579	Thomas North: the ancient Greek biographer Plutarch's *Parallel Lives* (from French).
1598–1616	George Chapman: the *Iliad* and the *Odyssey* of Homer.
1603	Giovanni Florio: the French writer Montaigne's *Essays*.
1603–11	Authorized Version of the Bible (the King James Bible).
1693	John Dryden: the Roman poet Juvenal.
1697	Dryden: Virgil's *Aeneid*.
1715–26	Alexander Pope: the *Iliad* and the *Odyssey*.
1859	Edward Fitzgerald: (from Persian) the *Rubáiyat of Omar Khayyám*.
1966	The Jerusalem Bible (from the original languages).

---

structure) there lies a more basic layer (its *deep structure*), which is processed by various transformational rules when we speak and write.

Below the surface structure 'the girl opened the door' would lie the deep structure 'the girl open + (past tense) the door'. Note that there is usually more than one way in which a deep structure can be realized; in this case, 'the door was opened by the girl'.

transgenic organism plant, animal, bacterium, or other living organism which has had a foreign gene added to it by means of ◊genetic engineering.

translation in literature, the rendering of words from one language to another. The first recorded named translator was Livius Andronicus, who translated Homer's *Odyssey* from Greek to Latin in 240 BC.

transmigration of souls another name for ◊reincarnation.

transsexual person who identifies himself or herself completely with the opposite sex, believing that the wrong sex was assigned at birth. Unlike *transvestites*, who desire to dress in clothes traditionally worn by the opposite sex, transsexuals think and feel emotionally in a way typically considered appropriate to members of the opposite sex, and may undergo surgery to modify external sexual characteristics.

transubstantiation in Christian theology, the doctrine that the whole substance of the bread and wine changes into the substance of the

body and blood of Jesus when consecrated in the ◊Eucharist.

Trappist member of a Roman Catholic order of monks and nuns, renowned for the strictness of their rule, which includes the maintenance of silence, manual labour, and a vegetarian diet. The order was founded 1664 at La Trappe, in Normandy, France, by Armand de Rancé (1626–1700) as a reformed version of the ◊Cistercian order. In 1792 the monks were expelled (during the French Revolution) but the community remained together until it could return in 1817.

trauma in psychiatry, a painful emotional experience or shock with lasting psychic consequences; in medicine, any physical damage or injury.

In psychiatric terms a trauma may have long-lasting effects, during which an insignificant event triggers the original distress. A person then may have difficulties in normal life, such as in establishing relationships or sleeping. In psychological terms this is known as *post-traumatic stress disorder*. It can be treated by ◊psychotherapy.

treason act of betrayal, in particular against the sovereign or the state to which the offender owes allegiance.

In the USA, treason is defined in the constitution as the crime of 'levying war against [the United States], or adhering to their enemies, giving them aid and comfort'. Congress has the power to declare the punishment for treason.

Treason is punishable in Britain by death. It includes: plotting the wounding or death of the sovereign or his or her spouse or heir; levying war against the sovereign in his or her realm; and giving aid or comfort to the sovereign's enemies in wartime. During World War II, treachery (aiding enemy forces or impeding the crown) was punishable by death, whether or not the offender owed allegiance to the crown. Sixteen spies (not normally capable of treason, though liable to be shot in the field) were convicted under these provisions. William Joyce (Lord Haw-Haw), although a US citizen, was executed for treason because he carried a British passport when he went to Germany in 1939.

Treason doth never prosper: what's the reason? / For if it prosper, none dare call it treason.

treason
John Harington, 1561–1612,
English translator and author.
'Of Treason'

Trent, Council of conference held 1545–63 by the Roman Catholic Church at Trento, N Italy initiating the ◊Counter-Reformation; see also ◊Reformation.

Triad secret society, founded in China as a Buddhist cult AD 36. It became known as the Triad because the triangle played a significant part in the initiation ceremony. Today it is reputed to be involved in organized crime (drugs, gambling, prostitution) among overseas Chinese. Its headquarters are alleged to be in Hong Kong.

In the 18th century the Triad became political, aiming at the overthrow of the Manchu dynasty, and backed the Taiping Rebellion 1851 and Sun Yat-sen's establishment of a republic 1912.

trial in law, the determination of an accused person's innocence or guilt by means of the judicial examination of the issues of the case in accordance with the law of the land. The two parties in a trial, the defendant and plaintiff, or their counsels, put forward their cases and question the witnesses; on the basis of this evidence the jury or other tribunal body decide on the innocence or guilt of the defendant.

tribal society way of life in which people govern their own affairs as independent local communities of families and clans without central government organizations or states. They are found in parts of SE Asia, New Guinea, South America, and Africa.

As the world economy expands, natural resources belonging to tribal peoples are coveted and exploited for farming or industrial use and the people are frequently dispossessed. Pressure groups such as Survival International and Cultural Survival have been established in some Western countries to support the struggle of tribal peoples for property rights as well as civil rights within the borders of the countries of which they are technically a part.

trigonometry branch of mathematics that solves problems relating to plane and spherical triangles. Its principles are based on the fixed proportions of sides for a particular angle in a right-angled triangle, the simplest of which are known as the sine, cosine, and tangent (socalled trigonometrical ratios). It is of practical importance in navigation, surveying, and simple harmonic motion in physics.

Invented by ◊Hipparchus, trigonometry was developed by ◊Ptolemy of Alexandria and was known to early Hindu and Arab mathematicians.

Trimurti the Hindu triad of gods, representing the Absolute Spirit in its three aspects: Brahma, personifying creation; Vishnu, preservation; and Shiva, destruction.

Trinitarianism belief in the Christian Trinity.

Trinity in Christianity, the union of three persons – Father, Son, and Holy Ghost/Spirit – in one godhead. The precise meaning of the doctrine has been the cause of unending dispute, and was the chief cause of the split between the Orthodox and Roman Catholic churches. *Trinity Sunday* occurs on the Sunday after Pentecost.

Tripitaka the canonical texts of Theravāda Buddhism, divided into three parts: the *Vinaya-pitaka*, containing the early history of Buddhism; the *Sutra-pitaka*, a collection of sayings of Buddha; and *Abhidharma-pitaka*, a collection of Buddhist philosophical writings.

Tristan legendary Celtic hero who fell in love with Isolde, the bride he was sent to win for his uncle King Mark of Cornwall; the story became part of the Arthurian cycle and is the subject of Wagner's opera *Tristan und Isolde*.

trivium in medieval European education, the three lower liberal arts (grammar, rhetoric, and logic) studied before the ◊quadrivium.

Trotsky Leon. Adopted name of Lev Davidovitch Bronstein 1879–1940. Russian revolutionary. He joined the Bolshevik party and took a leading part in the seizure of power

1917 and raising the Red Army that fought the Civil War 1918–20. In the struggle for power that followed ◊Lenin's death 1924, ◊Stalin defeated Trotsky, and this and other differences with the Communist Party led to his exile 1929. He settled in Mexico, where he was assassinated with an ice pick at Stalin's instigation. Trotsky believed in world revolution and in permanent revolution, and was an uncompromising, if liberal, idealist.

> Old age is the most unexpected of all
> things that happen to a man.
>
> **Leon Trotsky. Adopted name of Lev
> Davidovitch Bronstein**
>
> *Diary in Exile*

Trotsky became a Marxist in the 1890s and was imprisoned and exiled for opposition to the tsarist regime. He lived in W Europe from 1902 until the 1905 revolution, when he was again imprisoned but escaped to live in exile until 1917. Although as a young man Trotsky admired Lenin, when he worked with him organizing the revolution of 1917, he objected to Lenin's dictatorial ways. He was second in command until Lenin's death. Trotsky's later works are critical of the Soviet regime; for example, *The Revolution Betrayed* 1937. His greatest work is his magisterial *History of the Russian Revolution* 1932–33. Official Soviet recognition of responsibility for his assassination through the secret service came in 1989.

Trotskyism form of Marxism advocated by Leon Trotsky. Its central concept is that of ***permanent revolution***. In his view a proletarian revolution, leading to a socialist society, could not be achieved in isolation, so it would be necessary to spark off further revolutions throughout Europe and ultimately worldwide. This was in direct opposition to the Stalinist view that socialism should be built and consolidated within individual countries.

Trotskyism developed in an attempt to reconcile Marxist theory with actual conditions in Russia in the early 20th century, but it was never officially accepted within the USSR. Instead, it found much support worldwide, primarily in Third World countries, and the Fourth ◊International, which Trotsky founded 1937, has sections in over 60 countries.

True Cross the instrument of Jesus' crucifixion, supposedly found by St Helena, the mother of the emperor Constantine, on the hill of the ◊Calvary 326.

She is reputed to have placed most of it in a church built on the site and to have taken the rest to Constantinople. During the Middle Ages, a large number of relics were claimed to be fragments of the True Cross and were preserved and exhibited in churches and cathedrals.

Truman Doctrine US president Harry Truman's 1947 dictum that the USA would 'support free peoples who are resisting attempted subjugation by armed minorities or by outside pressures'. It was used to justify sending a counterinsurgency military mission to Greece after World War II and sending US troops abroad (for example, to Korea).

Turing Alan Mathison 1912–1954. English mathematician and logician. In 1936 he described a 'universal computing machine' that could theoretically be programmed to solve any problem capable of solution by a specially designed machine. This concept, now called the ***Turing machine***, foreshadowed the digital computer.

During World War II Turing worked on the Ultra project in the team that cracked the German Enigma secret cipher code, and was subsequently involved in the pioneering computer developed at Manchester University from 1948. He is believed to have been the first to suggest the possibility of machine learning and ◊artificial intelligence. His test for distinguishing between real (human) and simulated (computer) thought is known as the ***Turing test***: with a person in one room and the machine in another, an interrogator in a third room asks questions of both to try to identify them. When the interrogator cannot distinguish between them by questioning, the machine will have reached a state of humanlike intelligence.

Turner Victor Witter 1920– . US social anthropologist, although British-born. Turner's fieldwork among the Ndembu of Zambia provided material for a number of books and articles, most notably *Schism and Continuity in an African Society* 1957, a substantial study of social structure and conflict in certain social relationships giving rise to 'social dramas'.

In *The Forest of Symbols: Aspects of Ndembu Ritual* 1967, *The Ritual Process* 1969, and other works, he explored the complexities of symbolism in ritual and this led on to his developing the concept of 'communitas', a bonding social relationship that occurs in 'liminality'. Liminality occurs during changes in an individual's, or group's, social status and cultural or psychological state, for example, during rites of passage and on pilgrimages. These concepts are further elaborated in important articles collected in *Dramas, Fields, and Metaphors: Symbolic Action in Human Society* 1974.

turnover in finance, the value of sales of a business organization over a period of time. For example, if a shop sells 10,000 items in a week at an average price of £2 each, then its weekly turnover is £20,000. ◊Profit of a company is not only affected by the total turnover but also by the rate of turnover.

Twelfth Day the 12th and final day of the Christmas celebrations, 6 Jan; the feast of the ◊Epiphany.

Twelver member of a Shi'ite Muslim group who believes that the 12th imam (Islamic leader) did not die, but is waiting to return towards the end of the world as the ◊Mahdi, the 'rightly guided one', to establish a reign of peace and justice on Earth.

twelve-tone system or *twelve-note system* system of musical composition in which the 12 notes of the chromatic scale are arranged in a particular order, called a 'series' or 'tone-row'. A work using the system consists of restatements of the series in any of its formations. Arnold ◊Schoenberg and Anton Webern were exponents of this technique.

two cultures, the term devised by English novelist C P Snow (1905–1980) in his lecture *The Two Cultures and the Scientific Revolution* 1959 to describe the unassailable intellectual gulf that, he argued, exists between science and the arts.

Tylor, Edward Bennett 1832–1917. British cultural anthropologist, the first person to be appointed to an academic post in anthropology in Britain when he became reader at Oxford University in 1884. He was made professor in 1896.

Tylor left school at 16 and worked in his father's brass foundry until poor health forced him to leave. In 1856 he joined an ethnographical expedition to Mexico and this led to his first book, *Anahuac, Mexico and the Mexicans* 1859. In his classic *Primitive Culture: Researches into the development of mythology, philosophy, religion, language, art, and custom* 1971, he wrote extensively on religion, particularly on ◊animism, believing that the more erroneous the ideas on which a religion was based the more rudimentary it must be. Employing what he called 'social arithmetic', drawing up tables of customs, he studied correlations between them and thus pioneered the comparative method. His observations on exogamy (marrying outside one's own group) anticipate modern anthropological work. He was the first to realize, for example, that exogamy binds a community together especially since women are sisters to one clan and wives to another.

typology in religious studies, has two meanings. First, it refers to a system of Biblical interpretation in which correspondences are found between characters and events in the Old Testament and those in the New, for example, Jonah's escape from the whale is seen as a prefiguration of Christ's resurrection. Second, it is a way of classifying different religions by type, for instance, Christainity, Judaism, and Islam are all living religions as well as being prophetic. Hinduism and Buddhism are also living religions but are mystical rather than prophetic, and so on.

Tragic Sense of Life 1913, about the conflict of reason and belief in religion.

> *The chiefest sanctity of a temple is that it is a place to which men go to weep in common.*
>
> **Miguel de Unamuno**
> *The Tragic Sense of Life*
> 'The Man of Flesh and Bone'

übermensch in the writings of ◊Nietzsche, the ideal to which humans should aspire, set out in *Thus Spake Zarathustra* 1883–85. The term was popularized in George Bernard Shaw's play *Man and Superman* 1903.

Ubiquitarianism doctrine put forward by Martin ◊Luther to explain his understanding of the ◊Eucharist. Luther did not accept the Catholic idea of transubstantiation, nor was he happy with the idea that the bread and the wine were just memorials of the Last Supper. Instead he claimed that as Christ is present everywhere in his human nature, so he is present in a real sense in the bread and wine of the Eucharist.

ulama the bodies of scholars in Islamic law which form the theocratic element of the government in Muslim countries. The ulama may issue fatwas – injunctions on questions that affect both public and private life.

Ultramontanism in the Roman Catholic Church, the tenets of an Italian movement that stresses papal authority rather than nationalism in the church.

ultra vires any act by a public authority, company, or other agency which goes beyond the limits of its powers. In administrative law, the doctrine of ultra vires governs all delegated legislation. Where an act is found to be ultra vires, it will have no legal effect.

Ulysses Roman name for Odysseus, the Greek mythological hero.

UN abbreviation for the ◊*United Nations*.

Unamuno Miguel de 1864–1936. Spanish writer of Basque origin, exiled 1924–30 for criticism of the military directorate of Primo de Rivera. His works include mystic poems and the study *Del sentimiento trágico de la vida/The*

uncertainty principle or *indeterminacy principle* in quantum mechanics, the principle that it is meaningless to speak of a particle's position, momentum, or other parameters, except as results of measurements; measuring, however, involves an interaction (such as a photon of light bouncing off the particle under scrutiny), which must disturb the particle, though the disturbance is noticeable only at an atomic scale. The principle implies that one cannot, even in theory, predict the moment-to-moment behaviour of such a system.

It was established by German physicist Werner ◊Heisenberg, and gave a theoretical limit to the precision with which a particle's momentum and position can be measured simultaneously: the more accurately the one is determined, the more uncertainty there is in the other.

> *The deep well of unconscious cerebration.*
>
> *unconscious*
> Henry James, 1843–1916, US
> novelist, naturalized British 1915.
> *The American* preface

unconscious in psychoanalysis, part of the personality of which the individual is unaware, and which contains impulses or urges that are held back, or repressed, from conscious awareness.

unction in religion, anointing, either in a physical or a metaphorical sense of being appointed for a purpose. In the Hebrew Bible there are references to kings and priests being anointed as a sign of their position. In Christianity, unction (which may be the substance used or the act of anointing) is given in certain rites, including baptism in some churches, but especially for healing or for the dying.

Uniate Church any of the ◊Orthodox churches that accept the Catholic faith and the supremacy of the pope, and are in full communion with the Roman Catholic

Church, but retain their own liturgy and separate organization.

In Ukraine, despite being proscribed 1946–89, the Uniate Church claimed some 4.5 million adherents when it was once again officially recognized. Its rehabilitation was marked by the return of its spiritual leader, Cardinal Miroslav Lubachivsky, to take up residence in Lvov in W Ukraine after 52 years' exile in Rome.

unicorn mythical animal referred to by classical writers, said to live in India and resembling a horse, but with one spiralled horn growing from the forehead.

unidentified flying object or *UFO* any light or object seen in the sky whose immediate identity is not apparent. Despite unsubstantiated claims, there is no evidence that UFOs are alien spacecraft. On investigation, the vast majority of sightings turn out to have been of natural or identifiable objects, notably bright stars and planets, meteors, aircraft, and satellites, or to have been perpetrated by pranksters. The term *flying saucer* was coined in 1947 and has been in use since.

Unification Church or *Moonies* church founded in Korea 1954 by the Reverend Sun Myung ◊Moon. The number of members (often called 'moonies') is about 200,000 worldwide. The theology unites Christian and Taoist ideas and is based on Moon's book *Divine Principle*, which teaches that the original purpose of creation was to set up a perfect family, in a perfect relationship with God.

This was thwarted by the Fall of Man, and history is seen as a continuous attempt to restore the original plan, now said to have found its fulfilment in Reverend and Mrs Moon. The Unification Church teaches that marriage is essential for spiritual fulfilment, and marriage partners are sometimes chosen for members by Reverend Moon, although individuals are free to reject a chosen partner. Marriage, which takes the form of mass blessings by Reverend and Mrs Moon, is the most important ritual of the church; it is preceded by the wine or engagement ceremony.

In the 1970s, the Unification Church was criticized for its methods of recruitment and alleged 'brainwashing', as well as for its business, far-right political, and journalistic activities.

unified field theory in physics, the theory that attempts to explain the four fundamental ◊forces (strong nuclear, weak nuclear, electromagnetic, and gravity) in terms of a single unified force.

Research was begun by Albert Einstein and, by 1971, a theory developed by US physicists Steven Weinberg and Sheldon Glashow, Pakistani physicist Abdus Salam, and others had demonstrated the link between the weak and electromagnetic forces. The next stage is to develop a theory (called the ◊grand unified theory, or GUT) that combines the strong nuclear force with the electroweak force. The final stage will be to incorporate gravity into the scheme. Work on the ◊superstring theory indicates that this may be the ultimate 'theory of everything'.

uniformitarianism in geology, the principle that processes that can be seen to occur on the Earth's surface today are the same as those that have occurred throughout geological time. For example, desert sandstones containing sand-dune structures must have been formed under conditions similar to those present in deserts today. The principle was formulated by James ◊Hutton and expounded by Charles ◊Lyell.

unilateralism in politics, support for *unilateral nuclear disarmament*: scrapping a country's nuclear weapons without waiting for other countries to agree to do so at the same time.

In the UK this principle was Labour Party policy in the 1980s but was abandoned 1989.

Unitarianism Christian-derived group that rejects the orthodox doctrine of the Trinity, asserts the fatherhood of God and the brotherhood of humanity, and gives a pre-eminent position to Jesus as a religious teacher, while denying his divinity.

Unitarians believe in individual conscience and reason as a guide to right action, rejecting the doctrines of original sin, the atonement, and eternal punishment. Unitarianism is widespread in England and North America. See also ◊Arianism and ◊Socinianism.

United Nations (UN) association of states for international peace, security, and cooperation, with its headquarters in New York. The UN was established 1945 as a successor to the ◊League of Nations, and has played a role in many areas, such as refugees, development assistance, disaster relief, and cultural cooperation. Its total proposed budget for 1992/93 was $2,006 million. Boutros Boutros-Ghali became secretary general 1992.

Members contribute financially according to their resources, an apportionment being made by the General Assembly, with the addition of voluntary contributions from some governments to the funds of the UN. These finance the programme of assistance carried out by the UN intergovernmental agencies, the *United Nations Children's Fund* (UNICEF), the UN refugee organizations, and the *United Nations Special Fund* for developing countries. Total unpaid contributions of about $988 million had by the end of 1991 brought the UN to the brink of insolvency. Fewer than half the members had paid their full contributions. There are six official working languages: English, French, Russian, Spanish, Chinese, and Arabic.

United Reformed Church the name given in 1972 to the united church formed by the union of the Congregational Church in England and Wales and the Presbyterian Church of England. In 1981 the Reformed Association of Churches of Christ also joined the URC.

unities, the rules designed to regulate the structure of classical drama. There were three unities: the unity of time restricted the duration of events to 24 hours; the unity of action specified the use of just one plot with no subplots; and the unity of place limited the site of the action to a single location.

They were formulated by 16th-century critics, interpreting Aristotle, and were intended to make the dramatic action more comprehensible. They were largely ignored except by the 17th-century tragedians Corneille and Racine.

universal in philosophy, a property that is instantiated by all the individual things of a specific class: for example, all red things instantiate 'redness'. Many philosophical debates have centred on the status of universals, including the medieval debate between ◊nominalism and ◊realism.

A horse is simply a horse.

universals
Avicenna, 979–1037, Arabian
philosopher and physician.
Medieval Thought: St Augustine to Ockham
Gordon Leff

---

universe all of space and its contents, the study of which is called cosmology. The universe is thought to be between 10 billion and 20 billion years old, and is mostly empty space, dotted with galaxies for as far as telescopes can see. The most distant detected galaxies and ◊quasars lie 10 billion light years or more from Earth, and are moving farther apart as the universe expands. Several theories attempt to explain how the universe came into being and evolved, for example, the ◊Big Bang theory of an expanding universe originating in a single explosive event, and the contradictory ◊steady-state theory.

The heavens declare the glory of God: and the firmament showeth his handiwork.

universe
Common Prayer
Psalm 19

Apart from those galaxies within the Local Group, all the galaxies we see display red shifts in their spectra, indicating that they are moving away from us. The farther we look into space, the greater are the observed red shifts, which implies that the more distant galaxies are receding at ever greater speeds. This observation led to the theory of an expanding universe, first proposed by Edwin Hubble 1929, and to ◊Hubble's law, which states that the speed with which one galaxy moves away from another is proportional to its distance from it. Current data suggest that the galaxies are moving apart at a rate of 50–100 kps/30–60 mps for every million parsecs of distance.

La fonction essentielle de l'univers, qui est une machine à faire des dieux. / The essential function of the universe, which is a machine for making gods.

universe
Henri Bergson, 1859–1941, French
philosopher.
Les Deux sources de la morale et de la religion

---

university institution of higher learning for those who have completed primary and secondary education.

The first European university was Salerno in Italy, established in the 9th century, followed by Bologna, Paris, Oxford, and Cambridge, and Montpellier in the 12th century, and Toulouse in the 13th century. The universities of Prague, Vienna, Heidelberg, and Cologne were established in the 14th century, as well as many French universities including those at Avignon, Orléans, Cahors, Grenoble, Angers, and Orange. The universities of Aix, Dole, Poitiers, Caen, Nantes, Besançon, Bourges, and Bordeaux were established in the 15th century.

St Andrew's, the first Scottish university, was founded in 1411, and Trinity College, Dublin, in 1591. In the UK, a number of universities were founded in the 19th and earlier 20th centuries mainly in the large cities (London 1836, Manchester 1851, Wales 1893, Liverpool 1903, Bristol 1909, and Reading 1926). These became known as the 'redbrick' universities, as opposed to the ancient stone of Oxford and Cambridge. After World War II, many more universities were founded, among them Nottingham 1948 and Exeter 1955 and were nicknamed, from their ultramodern buildings, the 'plate-glass' universities. In the 1960s seven new universities were established on 'green field sites' including Sussex and York. In 1992, polytechnics and some colleges of higher education became universities. The more generous funding of traditional universities was phased out and a joint funding council established. Research is funded separately from teaching and the new universities have gained access to research funds for the first time.

The USA has both state universities (funded by the individual states) and private universities. The oldest universities in the USA are all private: Harvard 1636, William and Mary 1693, Yale 1701, Pennsylvania 1741, and Princeton 1746. Recent innovations include universities serving international areas, for example, the Middle East Technical University 1961 in Ankara, Turkey, supported by the United Nations; the United Nations University in Tokyo 1974; and the British ◊Open University 1969. The Open University has been widely copied; for example, in the National University Consortium set up in the USA 1980.

untouchable or *harijan* member of the lowest Indian ◊caste, formerly forbidden to be touched by members of the other castes.

Upanishad one of a collection of Hindu sacred treatises, written in Sanskrit, connected with the ◊Vedas but composed later, about 800–200 BC. Metaphysical and ethical, their doctrine equated the atman (self) with the Brahman (supreme spirit) – *'Tat tvam asi'* ('Thou art that') – and developed the theory of ◊reincarnation.

Ur ancient city of the Sumerian civilization, in modern Iraq. Excavations by the British archaeologist Leonard Woolley show that it was inhabited from about 3500 BC. He discovered evidence of a flood that may have inspired the *Epic of ◊Gilgamesh* as well as the biblical account, and remains of ziggurats, or step pyramids.

Urania in Greek mythology, one of the ◊Muses, of astronomy.

Urban VIII Maffeo Barberini 1568–1644. Pope 1623–44. His policies during the Thirty Years' War were designed more to maintain the balance of forces in Europe and prevent one side from dominating the papacy than to further the ◊Counter-Reformation. He extended the papal dominions and improved their defences. During his papacy, ◊Galileo was summoned 1633 to recant the theories that the Vatican condemned as heretical.

urbanization process by which the proportion of a population living in or around towns and cities increases through migration as the agricultural population decreases. The growth of urban concentrations in the USA and Europe is a relatively recent phenomenon, dating back only about 150 years to the beginning of the Industrial Revolution (although the world's first cities were built more than 5,000 years ago).

Urbanization has had a major effect on the social structures of industrial societies, affecting not only where people live but how they live, and urban sociology has emerged as a distinct area of study.

urban land-use model in the social sciences, a simplified pattern of the land use (such as industry, housing, and commercial activity) that may be found in towns and cities. These models are based on an understanding of the way in which these areas have grown. There are three main ways of looking at urban land use: ◊concentric-ring theory, ◊sector theory, and multiple-nuclei theory. Each results in different shapes of land-use areas. In practice, factors such as ◊topography, land fertility, and culture vary from one city to another and affect their final form.

urban legend a largely contemporary mode of folklore thriving in big cities, mainly in the USA in the 20th century, and usually transmitted orally. Some of the stories – hitchhikers that turn out to be ghosts, spiders breeding in elaborate hairstyles – are preindustrial in origin, but transformed to fit new circumstances; others – the pet or baby in the microwave oven, people living in department stores – are of their essence recent inventions.

Urey Harold Clayton 1893–1981. US chemist. In 1932 he isolated heavy water and discovered deuterium, for which he was awarded the 1934 Nobel Prize for Chemistry.

During World War II he was a member of the Manhattan Project that produced the

The City and Utopia

Cities have always existed in the mind as well as in bricks and stone. Early cities were typically seen as representations of something divine, the terrestrial city being a copy of the divine model. Babylonian cities were believed to have their prototypes in the constellations – Nineveh, for instance, in Ursa Major. Plato (c. 428–347 BC) also had a celestial prototype for his 'ideal city'. In various Jewish myths, Jerusalem was created by God before it was erected by men. According to the Revelation of St John (21:2), 'I saw the holy city, new Jerusalem, coming down from God out of heaven, prepared as a bride adorned for her husband.' Distrusting earthly cities, Christian theology has made much of ideal cities, as in the *Civitas Dei* (City of God) of St Augustine (fl. 590): Christian millennialism has always incorporated the notion of building the 'new Jerusalem'.

'Ideal cities' in history

Ideal cities have often been imagined on a grid-iron scheme – though Greek architectural ideas were focused on the individual building. The Romans showed concern for the unity of their cities, which developed mainly from the *castrum* or camp, with a grid-iron pattern subdivided into four parts by two main axes. Partly for reasons of defence, Roman town planning emphasized regularity and clear shaping of space.

Medieval towns tended to grow organically, without any special plan; and it was only with the Renaissance that the ideal, planned, geometrical city once again seized the imagination, particularly amongst Florentine humanists like Leonardo Bruni (1369–1444) and Leon Alberti (1404–1472) who praised the city as the site of justice, learning, virtue, and culture. Antonio Filarete's *Trattato di architettura*, written 1460–64, is the most complete vision of the orderly Renaissance city, shaped as an octagonal star, with a round piazza at its centre from which streets radiate. Leonardo da Vinci's (1452–1519) sketches envisage the ideal city existing on two planes, with patricians above and the poor and traffic below. Around the same time, Thomas More's (1478–1535) *Utopia* pictured a city in which none was exploited and none was poor, because all worked; and Tommaso Campanella's (1568–1639) *City of the Sun* (1623) conjured up another utopian city, presided over by a solar religion with a great solar temple.

City versus country

Traditional thinking idealized rural peace and virtue and censured the town as racked with vice; a view echoed by the eighteenth-century English poet, William Cowper (1731–1800), who wrote that 'God made the country, and man made the town'; Samuel Johnson's poem, *London*, depicted the metropolis as all vice and crime, though he also declared that the man who was tired of London was tired of life. Enlightenment thinkers took a more hopeful view, regarding the countryside as backward and benighted and the city as the cradle of progress, knowledge, industry, liberty, wealth, and politeness. Urban living would create urbanity; civility derived from the city.

Industrial darkness

Enlightenment dreams of healthy, orderly cities, like Bath, Edinburgh New Town, or Washington, were disrupted by the 'shock towns' of the industrial revolution – Manchester, the Ruhr, Pittsburgh – with their slums, smoke, disease, and death. Dickens portrayed London as fog-bound; the 'city of dreadful night' became a nineteenth-century reality and poetic metaphor. The Victorian novel, by such authors as Emile Zola (1840–1902) and George Gissing (1857–1903), anticipated twentieth-century sociology (Durkheim) in seeing the city as atomized – a place of alienation, anomie, and desolation.

Looking for the light

From the late nineteenth century, new town planning movements developed, rejecting slums, sprawl, and overcrowding, and attempting to reinvent the city as a place of peace and pleasure. The 'garden city' movement was associated in the UK particularly with Ebenezer Howard (1850–1928), whose *Garden Cities of Tomorrow* (1902) envisaged a self-contained town of approximately 35,000 inhabitants with a managed balance between the urban area and agricultural land. Howard's city is round, and, in order to combine town and country advantages, houses and factories are placed on tracts of open land. Like most other modern planners, Howard attempted to distinguish clearly between the different functions of the city (living, work, leisure, education, and traffic).

Cities dehumanized – Le Corbusier

The evil genius of modern town planning was Le Corbusier (1887–1965), who, unlike most planners, thought big, planning for cities of several million inhabitants. In contrast to Frank Lloyd Wright (1869–1959), he was opposed to horizontal spreading of the urban complex, believing in building upward. A rationalist strain in Le Corbusier led him to place emphasis on the city's different functions, and the stringent separation of traffic, and living and working zones. Despite Le Corbusier's convictions, many find the spaces he conceived destructive of the close personal contact and human dimensions of the successful town.

With deindustrialization and inner-city poverty and violence, the future of the metropolis (to say nothing of megalopolis) must be in doubt at the close of the twentieth century. The flight to the suburbs has been reinforced by a flight to the country. Perhaps the city will be the mausoleum of a moribund humanism.

Roy Porter

atomic bomb, but after the war he advocated nuclear disarmament and world government.

urim and thummim two objects in the breast-plate of the high priests of the ancient Hebrews, which were used for divination. They are mentioned in the Bible but it is not known what they were.

Ursuline Roman Catholic religious order, founded in Brescia, Italy, by St Angela Merici 1537; it carries out educational work among girls.

Usher James 1581–1656. Irish priest, archbishop of Armagh from 1625. He was responsible for dating the creation to the year 4004 BC, a figure that was inserted in the margin of the Authorized Version of the Bible until the 19th century.

usury former term for charging interest on a loan of money. In medieval times, usury was held to be a sin, and Christians were forbidden to lend (although not to borrow).

The practice of charging interest is still regarded as usury in some Muslim countries.

Under English law, usury remained forbidden until the 13th century, when trade and the need for credit was increased; for example, Jews were absolved from the ban on usury by the Fourth Lateran Council of 1215.

Uthman bin Affan 574–656. Companion of the prophet Muhammad, his third Caliph. He supervised the compilation of the ◊Qur'an and distributed copies to distant parts of the Muslim world.

He succeeded Umar in 643 AD. The first half of his rule was peaceful, but strife arose over the division of conquered territory, and he was assassinated in Medina.

utilitarianism philosophical theory of ethics outlined by the philosopher Jeremy ◊Bentham and developed by John Stuart Mill. According to utilitarianism, an action is morally right if it has consequences that lead to happiness, and wrong if it brings about the reverse. Thus society should aim for the greatest happiness of the greatest number.

Utnapishtim in the *Epic of* ◊*Gilgamesh*, a man granted immortality by the gods. In a story exactly like that of the Biblical Noah, he and his household are the lone survivors in a boat built for the purpose of a flood sent by the gods. He is visited by Gilgamesh in grief at the death of his friend Enkidu.

utopianism belief in ideal and often fanciful social and political reforms or systems. Sir Thomas More's *Utopia* 1516 was about an ideal society on a South Pacific island.

Other notable utopian systems include: Plato's *Republic*, Bacon's *New Atlantis* 1626, James Harrington's *The Commonwealth of Oceana* 1656, Saint-Simon's *New Christianity* 1825 and the cooperative communities of both F M C Fourier (1772–1837) and Robert Owen (1771–1858). Attempts at creating utopian communities have often taken the form of ◊communes. Utopias are a common subject in ◊science fiction.

I have seen the future; and it works.

utopianism

Lincoln Steffens, 1866–1936, US journalist.
Of the newly-formed Soviet Union, in letter
to Marie Howe 3 Apr 1919.

when he returned to Rome as secretary to Pope Nicholas V. He proved some of the most hallowed documents in the papal curia to be forgeries, notably the Donation of Constantine, which purported to give the pope temporal sovereignty over the Roman emperor. Valla criticized Aristotelian logic, and believed that medieval philosophy and logic had had a bad effect on theology.

Valla's works include *Elegantiarum libri/On the Elegancies of the Latin Tongue* 1471, which was the first Latin grammar to be written since the Middle Ages, and *Annotationes in Novum Testamentum/Annotations on the New Testament* 1444.

value judgement subjective assessment involving some moral, aesthetic, ideological, or theoretical interpretation of superiority or inferiority.

In the philosophy of science (see ◊science, philosophy of), discussion continues about whether the social sciences can ever be free of value judgements – and, if so, whether this means that objective truth is impossible in the social sciences.

vampire in Hungarian and Slavonic folklore, an 'undead' corpse that sleeps by day in its native earth, and by night, often in the form of a bat, sucks the blood of the living. Dracula is a vampire in popular fiction.

Van Allen James (Alfred) 1914– . US physicist whose instruments aboard the first US satellite *Explorer 1* 1958 led to the discovery of the Van Allen belts, two zones of intense radiation around the Earth. He pioneered high-altitude research with rockets after World War II.

van der Waals Johannes Diderik 1837–1923. Dutch physicist who was awarded a Nobel prize 1910 for his theoretical study of gases. He emphasized the forces of attraction and repulsion between atoms and molecules in describing the behaviour of real gases, as opposed to the ideal gases dealt with in ◊Boyle's law and Charles's law.

Vane John 1927– . British pharmacologist who discovered the wide role of prostaglandins in the human body, produced in response to illness and stress. He shared the 1982 Nobel Prize for Medicine with Sune Bergström (1916–) and Bengt Samuelson (1934–) of Sweden.

van't Hoff Jacobus Henricus 1852–1911. Dutch physical chemist. He explained the 'asymmetric' carbon atom occurring in optically active compounds. His greatest work – the concept of chemical affinity as the maximum work

Vaishnavism worship of the Hindu god Vishnu, numerically the most widespread faith in Hinduism. The principal forms of Vishnu are Krishna and Rama, whose teachings are summarised in such scriptures as the ◊*Bhagavad-Gītā* and ◊*Rāmāyana*, dedicated to Krishna and Rama respectively. The central theme is ◊bhakti, devotion to a personal form of God, accompanied by singing of devotional songs or *bhajans*.

Valentine, St according to tradition a bishop of Terni martyred at Rome, now omitted from the calendar of saints' days as probably nonexistent. His festival was 14 Feb, but the custom of sending 'valentines' to a loved one on that day seems to have arisen because the day accidentally coincided with the Roman mid-February festival of ◊Lupercalia.

Valhalla in Norse mythology, the hall in ◊Odin's palace where he feasted with the souls of heroes killed in battle.

validity in logic, a property of inferences or arguments, which are valid if the conclusion follows necessarily (by ◊deduction) from the premises, as in a ◊syllogism. The premises may be false, but if they are true the conclusion must be true.

Valkyrie in Norse mythology, any of the female attendants of ◊Odin. They selected the most valiant warriors to die in battle and escorted them to Valhalla.

Valla Lorenzo 1407–1457. Italian philosopher, translator, and historian who attacked ◊scholasticism and promoted classical literature, advocating an alliance between faith and eloquence. He influenced Dutch humanist Erasmus and German Protestant Martin Luther.

Valla, born in Rome, was historian and secretary to King Alfonso of Naples 1435–1448, obtainable from a reaction – was shown with measurements of osmotic and gas pressures, and reversible electrical cells. He was the first recipient of the Nobel Prize for Chemistry, in 1901.

Varanasi or **Benares** holy city of the Hindus in Uttar Pradesh, India, on the river Ganges; population (1981) 794,000. There are 1,500 golden shrines, and a 5 km/3 mi frontage to the Ganges with sacred stairways (ghats) for purification by bathing.

At the burning ghats, the ashes of the dead are scattered on the river to ensure a favourable reincarnation.

Varnashrama Vedic system of social division which characterizes traditional Hindu society. The four *varnas* (orders) are the brahmana or priest, the kshatriya or warrior/ruler, the vaishya or merchant/farmer, and the sudra or labourer/craftsman. The four ashramas, or stages of life, are brahmacari or celibate student, grihastha or householder, varnaprastha or retired person, and sannyasin or renunciate.

Varuna in early Hindu mythology, the sky god and king of the universe.

Vasari Giorgio 1511–1574. Italian art historian, architect, and painter, author of *Lives of the Most Excellent Architects, Painters and Sculptors* 1550 (enlarged and revised 1568), in which he proposed the theory of a Renaissance of the arts beginning with Giotto and culminating with Michelangelo. He designed the Uffizi Palace, Florence, as well as palaces and churches in Pisa and Arezzo.

Vasari was a prolific Mannerist painter. His basic view of the Renaissance has remained unchallenged, despite his prejudices and his delight in often ill-founded, libellous anecdotes.

Vatican Council either of two Roman Catholic ecumenical councils called by Pope Pius IX 1869 (which met 1870) and by Pope John XXIII 1959 (which met 1962). These councils deliberated over elements of church policy.

Veblen Thorstein (Bunde) 1857–1929. US social critic. His insights on culture and economics were expressed in his books *The Theory of the Leisure Class* 1899 and *The Theory of Business Enterprise* 1904. He was a founder of the New School for Social Research in New York 1919.

Born in Cato, Wisconsin, USA, and raised in Minnesota, Veblen was educated at Carleton College and received his PhD from Yale University 1884. He taught at Chicago, Stanford, and Missouri universities and edited the *Journal of Political Economy* 1892–1905.

Conspicuous consumption of valuable goods is a means of reputability to the gentleman of leisure.
Thorstein (Bunde) Veblen
Theory of the Leisure Class

Veda the most sacred of the Hindu scriptures, hymns written in an old form of Sanskrit; the oldest may date from 1500 or 2000 BC. The four main collections are: the *Rigveda* (hymns and praises); *Yajurveda* (prayers and sacrificial formulae); *Sāmaveda* (tunes and chants); and *Atharvaveda*, or Veda of the Atharvans, the officiating priests at the sacrifices.

Vedānta school of Hindu philosophy that developed the teachings of the ◊Upanishads. One of its teachers was Śamkara, who lived in S India in the 8th century AD and is generally regarded as a manifestation of Shiva. He taught that there is only one reality, Brahman, and that knowledge of Brahman leads finally to moksha, or liberation from reincarnation.

Vedic culture the culture and way of life, named after the Vedas, or Sanskrit hymns of ancient India, now commonly but inaccurately referred to as Hinduism.

vegetarian person who eats only foods obtained without slaughter, for humanitarian, aesthetic, political, or health reasons. Vegans abstain from all foods of animal origin.

The number of vegetarians in the UK is increasing; in 1990, they made up 10% of the population.

venial sin in Christianity, a less serious sin, or a sin that causes only a partial loss of grace; as opposed to mortal sin, which brings eternal damnation unless repented and forgiven.

In the early church a distinction was made between mortal sins such as ◊apostasy, murder, and adultery, and less serious, or venial sins. The church drew up a list of mortal sins which had to be confessed before participating in Holy Communion. Current Roman Catholic teaching takes account of the inner attitude of the person committing the offence, when measuring the gravity of sin.

Venn diagram in mathematics, a diagram representing a set or sets and the logical relationships between them. The sets are drawn as circles. An area of overlap between two circles (sets) contains elements that are common to both sets, and thus represents a third set. Circles that do not overlap represent sets with no elements in common (disjoint sets). The method is named after the British logician John Venn (1834–1923).

venture capital or *risk capital* money put up by investors such as merchant banks to fund a new company or expansion of an established company. The organization providing the money receives a share of the company's equity and seeks to make a profit by rapid growth in the value of its stake, as a result of expansion by the start-up company or 'venture'.

Any money invested in a company is, of course, at risk in that the money may be lost if the company goes bankrupt.

Venus in Roman mythology, the goddess of love and beauty, equivalent to the Greek ◊Aphrodite. The patrician Romans believed that they were descended from Aeneas, the son of the goddess, and Anchises, a shepherd. She was venerated as the guardian of the Roman people.

Venusberg cavernous court of Venus in late medieval German legend, supposedly visited by Tannhäuser, who then sought absolution from the pope for his sins.

verifiability in logic and philosophy, the feature of a proposition that enables us to check that it is true. A verifiable proposition has to be contingent; that is, it must be possible that it is false.

Twentieth-century positivists and empiricists, seeking to dismiss metaphysics and theology as nonsense, made verifiability into a theory of meaning that requires meaningful propositions to have a method of verification. Since few statements are conclusively verifiable, English philosopher A J ◊Ayer and others sought to defend 'weak' verifiability in which provision of evidence would suffice.

Vernier Pierre 1580–1637. French mathematician who invented a means of making very precise measurements with what is now called the vernier scale. He was a French government official and in 1631 published *La construction, l'usage, et les propriétez du quadrant nouveau mathématique/The construction, uses and properties of a new mathematical quadrant,* in which he explained his method.

Veronica, St woman of Jerusalem who, according to tradition, lent her veil to Jesus to wipe the sweat from his brow on the road to Calvary, whereupon the image of his face was printed upon it. A relic alleged to be the actual veil is preserved in St Peter's, Rome.

Vesalius Andreas 1514–1564. Belgian physician who revolutionized anatomy. His great innovations were to perform postmortem dissections and to make use of illustrations in teaching anatomy.

The dissections (then illegal) enabled him to discover that ◊Galen's system of medicine was based on fundamental anatomical errors. Vesalius's book *De Humani Corporis Fabrica/ On The Structure of the Human Body* 1543, together with the major work of the astronomer Copernicus, published in the same year, marked the dawn of modern science.

vespers seventh of the eight canonical hours in the Catholic church or, more generally, an evening service.

The phrase *Sicilian Vespers* refers to the massacre of the French rulers in Sicily 1282, signalled by vesper bells on Easter Monday.

Vesta in Roman mythology, the goddess of the hearth, equivalent to the Greek Hestia. In Rome, the sacred flame in her shrine in the Forum was kept constantly lit by the six *Vestal Virgins*.

veto (Latin 'I forbid') exercise by a sovereign, branch of legislature, or other political power, of the right to prevent the enactment or operation of a law, or the taking of some course of action.

In the UK the sovereign has a right to refuse assent to any measure passed by Parliament, but this has not been exercised since the 18th century; the House of Lords also has a suspensory veto on all legislation except finance measures, but this is comparatively seldom exercised. In the USA, the president may veto legislation, but this can be overruled by a two-thirds majority in Congress. At the United Nations, members of the Security Council can exercise a veto on resolutions.

vicar Church of England priest, originally one who acted as deputy to a ◊rector, but now also a parish priest.

Vico Giambattista 1668–1744. Italian philosopher, considered the founder of the modern philosophy of history. He argued that we can understand history more adequately than nature, since it is we who have made it. He believed that the study of language, ritual, and myth was a way of understanding earlier societies. His cyclical theory of history (the birth, development, and decline of human societies) was put forward in *New Science* 1725.

Vico postulated that society passes through a cycle of four phases: the divine, or theocratic, when people are governed by their awe of the supernatural; the aristocratic, or 'heroic' (Homer, *Beowulf*); the democratic and individualistic; and chaos, a fall into confusion that startles people back into supernatural reverence. This is expressed in his dictum *verum et factum convertuntur* ('the true and the made are convertible'). His belief that the study of language and rituals was a better way of understanding early societies was a departure from the traditional ways of writing history either as biographies or as preordained God's will. He was born in Naples and was professor of rhetoric there 1698. He became historiographer to the king of Naples 1735.

Vienna Circle group of philosophers in Vienna, Austria, in the 1920s and 1930s, who advocated ◊logical positivism. The group, which was highly influential, centred on the German Moritz Schlick (1882–1936), professor of philosophy at the University of Vienna, and dispersed after he was assassinated 1936.

Viète François 1540–1603. French mathematician who developed algebra and its notation. He was the first mathematician to use letters of the alphabet to denote both known and unknown quantities.

Vincent de Paul, St c. 1580–1660. French Roman Catholic priest and founder of the two charitable orders of Dazarists 1625 and Sisters of Charity 1634. After being ordained 1600, he was captured by Barbary pirates and held as a slave in Tunis until he escaped 1607. He was canonized 1737; feast day 19 July.

virgin birth the Christian belief in the virginal (or immaculate) conception of Jesus through the power of the Holy Spirit at work in the Virgin Mary. Roman Catholic dogma also accepts the perpetual virginity of Mary, teaching that she bore Jesus in a miraculous way so that she remained a virgin and subsequently had no other children.

Virtanen Artturi Ilmari 1895–1973. Finnish chemist who from 1920 made discoveries in agricultural chemistry. Because green fodder tends to ferment and produce a variety of harmful acids, it cannot be preserved for long. Virtanen prevented the process from starting by acidifying the fodder. In this form it lasted longer and remained nutritious. Nobel Prize for Chemistry 1945.

virtual reality advanced form of ◊computer simulation, in which a participant has the illusion of being part of an artificial environment. The participant views the environment through two tiny television screens (one for each eye) built into a visor. Sensors detect movements of the participant's head or body, causing the apparent viewing position to change. Gloves (datagloves) fitted with sensors may be worn, which allow the participant seemingly to pick up and move objects in the environment.

The technology is still under development but is expected to have widespread applications; for example, in military and surgical training, architecture, and home entertainment.

O infinite virtue! com'st thou smiling from / The world's great snare uncaught?

virtue

William Shakespeare, 1564–1616, English dramatist and poet.
Antony and Cleopatra IV. viii

---

virtue originally, ability or efficiency, often involving moral worth. In classical Greek it is used especially to refer to manly qualities. Christian teaching distinguishes the *cardinal virtues* of prudence, temperance, fortitude, and justice, from the *theological virtues* of faith, hope, and love (or charity) which St Paul gives as the basis of Christian life.

The Seven Virtues are:	
Justice Prudence Temperance Fortitude	which are known as the Four Natural or Cardinal Virtues
Faith Hope Charity	which are known as the Three Theological Virtues

virus in computing, a piece of software that can replicate itself and transfer itself from one computer to another, without the user being aware of it. Some viruses are relatively harmless, but others can damage or destroy data. They are written by anonymous programmers, often maliciously, and are spread along telephone lines or on floppy discs. Antivirus software can be used to detect and destroy well-known viruses, but new viruses continually appear and these may bypass existing antivirus programs.

Computer viruses may be programmed to operate on a particular date, such as the Michelangelo Virus, which was triggered on 6 March 1992 (the anniversary of the birthday of Italian artist Michelangelo) and erased hard discs.

Vishnu in Hinduism, the second in the triad of gods (with Brahma and Siva) representing three aspects of the supreme spirit. He is the **Preserver**, and is believed to have assumed human appearance in nine ◊avatars, or incarnations, in such forms as Rama and Krishna. His worshippers are the Vaishnavas.

visitation in the Christian church, a formal visit by a bishop or church official to examine the churches or abbeys within his jurisdiction. In medieval visitations, records were kept of the *detecta*, matters disclosed to the visitor, and *comperta*, what the visitor found for himself.

visualization use of guided mental imagery to activate and focus the body's natural self-healing processes. When used in the treatment of cancer patients, together with complementary techniques, some remarkable remissions have been attributed to visualization.

vitalism the idea that living organisms derive their characteristic properties from a universal life force. In the present century, this view is associated with the French philosopher Henri ◊Bergson.

Vitruvius (Marcus Vitruvius Pollio) 1st century BC. Roman architect whose ten-volume interpretation of Roman architecture *De architectura* provided an impetus for the Renaissance; it was first printed in Rome 1486. Although often obscure, his writings have had a lasting influence on Western perceptions of Classical architecture, mainly through the work of Leon Battista Alberti, and later Raphael and Palladio.

vivisection literally, cutting into a living animal. Used originally to mean experimental surgery or dissection practised on a live subject, the term is often used by ◊antivivisection campaigners to include any experiment on animals, surgical or otherwise.

Britain's 1876 Cruelty to Animals Act was the world's first legislation specifically to protect laboratory animals.

vocational education education relevant to a specific job or career.

The term refers to medical and legal education in the universities as well as higher and further education courses in professional and craft skills. In the UK, the TVEI (Technical and Vocational Education Initiative) was intended to expand pre-vocational education in schools but was in the early 1990s being run down.

Volcker Paul 1927– . US economist. As chair of the board of governors of the Federal Reserve System 1979–87, he controlled the amount of money in circulation in the USA. He was succeeded by Alan Greenspan.

volition in philosophical psychology and the philosophy of mind, the act of willing. Philosophers who hold that mind and body are different substances (dualists) tend to hold that volitions cause actions, while those who hold that mind and body are fundamentally one substance (monists) tend to hold that volitions are inseparable from actions.

Volta Alessandro 1745–1827. Italian physicist who invented the first electric cell (the voltaic pile), the electrophorus (an early electrostatic generator), and an electroscope.

Born in Como, he was a professor there and at Pavia. The volt is named after him.

Voltaire Pen name of François-Marie Arouet 1694–1778. French writer who believed in ◊deism and devoted himself to tolerance, justice, and humanity. He was threatened with arrest for *Lettres philosophiques sur les Anglais/Philosophical Letters on the English* 1733 (essays in favour of English ways, thought, and political practice) and had to take refuge.

Other writings include *Le Siècle de Louis XIV/The Age of Louis XIV* 1751; *Candide* 1759, a parody on ◊Leibniz's 'best of all possible worlds'; and *Dictionnaire philosophique* 1764.

If we do not find anything pleasant, at least we shall find something new.

Voltaire. Pen name of François-Marie Arouet
Candide ch.17

Voltaire was born in Paris, the son of a notary, and used his pen name from 1718. He was twice imprisoned in the Bastille and exiled from Paris 1716–26 for libellous political verse. *Oedipe/Oedipus*, his first essay in tragedy, was staged 1718. While in England 1726–29 he dedicated an epic poem on Henry IV, *La Henriade/The Henriade*, to Queen Caroline, and on returning to France published the successful *Histoire de Charles XII/History of Charles XII* 1731, and produced the play *Zaïre* 1732. He took refuge with his mistress, the Marquise de Châtelet, at Cirey in Champagne, where he wrote the play *Mérope* 1743 and much of *Le Siècle de Louis XIV*. Among his other works are histories of Peter the Great, Louis XV, and India; the satirical tale *Zadig* 1748; *La Pucelle/The Maid* 1755, on Joan of Arc; and the tragedy *Irène* 1778. From 1751 to 1753 he stayed at the court of Frederick II (the Great) of Prussia, who had long been an admirer, but the association ended in deep enmity. From 1754 he established himself near Geneva, and after 1758 at Ferney, just across the French border. His remains were transferred 1791 to the Panthéon in Paris.

von Gesner Konrad 1516–1565. Swiss naturalist who produced an encyclopedia of the animal world, the *Historia animalium* 1551–58.

Gesner was a victim of the Black Death and could not complete a similar project on plants. He is considered a founder of the science of zoology, but was also an expert in languages and an authority on the Classical writers.

Von Neumann John 1903–1957. Hungarian-born US scientist and mathematician, known for his pioneering work on computer design. He invented his 'rings of] operators' (called Von Neumann algebras) in the late 1930s, and also contributed to set theory, games theory, cybernetics (with his theory of self-reproducing automata, called *Von Neumann machines*), and the development of the atomic and hydrogen bombs.

He was born in Budapest and became an assistant professor of physical mathematics at Berlin University before moving to Princeton, USA, in 1929, where he later became professor of mathematics. In the early 1940s he described a design for a stored-program computer.

voodoo set of magical beliefs and practices, followed in some parts of Africa, South America, and the West Indies, especially Haiti. It arose in the 17th century on slave plantations as a combination of Roman Catholicism and W African religious traditions; believers retain membership in the Roman Catholic Church. Beliefs include the existence of *loa*, spirits who closely involve themselves in human affairs, and some of whose identities mesh with those of Christian saints. The loa are invoked by the priest (*houngan*) or priestess (*manbo*) at ceremonies, during which members of the congregation become possessed by the spirits and go into a trance.

A voodoo temple (*houmfort*) has a central post from which the loa supposedly descend to 'mount' the worshipper. The loa can be identified by the characteristic behaviour of the possessed person. Loa include Baron Samedi, who watches over the land of the dead; Erzulie, the black Virgin or Earth goddess; Ogu, a warrior, corresponding to St James the Great; and Legba, the lord of the road and interpreter between humans and spirits, who corresponds to St Anthony the hermit.

Vorticism short-lived British literary and artistic movement 1912–15, influenced by Cubism and Futurism and led by Wyndham Lewis. Lewis believed that painting should reflect the complexity and rapid change of the modern world; he painted in a harsh, angular, semi-abstract style. The last Vorticist exhibition was held 1915.

Vulgate the Latin translation of the Bible produced by St Jerome in the 4th century.

It became the most popular Latin version from the 7th century (hence its name), and in 1546 was adopted by the Council of Trent as the official Roman Catholic Bible.

Vyasa the mystic author of Vedic literature such as the ◊*Mahābhārata*, Vedanta Sutra, and *Bhāgavat Purana*. He is revered as the original guru and teacher of ◊Vaishnavism and is believed to be of divine origin. His dates are unknown.

Vygotsky Lev Semionovich 1896–1934. Soviet psychologist, best-known for his work on language and linguistic development based on his supposition that higher cognitive processes are a product of social development. From early research into the rules and development of tool-use and sign-use behaviour, Vygotsky turned to symbolic processes in language, focusing on the semantic structure of words and the way in which meanings of words change from emotive to concrete to more abstract designations.

Vygotsky, born in Orsha, Byelorussia (now Belarus), was active in a number of other fields during his brief academic career, notably the psychological analysis of art and fables, child psychology, including the problems of deaf and retarded children, and the psychological analysis of brain-injured adults. His major works include *Thought and Language* 1937, *Selected Psychological Studies* 1956, and *Development of the Higher Mental Processes* 1960.

Wahabi puritanical Saudi Islamic group founded by Muhammad ibn-Abd- al-Wahab (1703–1792), which regards all other groups as heretical. By the early 20th century it had spread throughout the Arabian peninsula; it still remains the official ideology of the Saudi Arabian kingdom.

Wailing Wall or (in Judaism) *Western Wall* the remaining part of the ◊Temple in Jerusalem, a sacred site of pilgrimage and prayer for Jews. There they offer prayers either aloud ('wailing') or on pieces of paper placed between the stones of the wall.

wake watch kept over the body of a dead person during the night before their funeral; it originated in Anglo-Saxon times as the eve before a festival.

In the north of England, *wakes week* is the week when a whole town or city traditionally has its annual holiday, and during that period factories and shops are closed.

Waksman Selman Abraham 1888–1973. US biochemist, born in Ukraine. He coined the word 'antibiotic' for bacteria-killing chemicals derived from microorganisms. Waksman was awarded a Nobel prize in 1952 for the discovery of streptomycin, an antibiotic used against tuberculosis.

Wald George 1906– . US biochemist who explored the chemistry of vision. He found that a crucial role was played by the retinal pigment rhodopsin, derived in part from vitamin A. For this he shared the 1967 Nobel Prize for Physiology or Medicine with Ragnar Granit (1900–) and Haldan Hartline (1903–1983).

Waldenses also known as *Waldensians* or *Vaudois* Protestant religious group, founded *c.* 1170 by Peter Waldo, a merchant of Lyons.

They were allied to the ◊Albigenses. They lived in voluntary poverty, refused to take oaths or take part in war, and later rejected the doctrines of transubstantiation, purgatory, and the invocation of saints. Although subjected to persecution until the 17th century, they spread in France, Germany, and Italy, and still survive in Piedmont.

wali honorific title in Islam, given to a saint or wise and holy person, especially to the Sufi masters. It is also used in ◊Shi'ite teaching to indicate close companionship with Muhammad, as in the case of ◊Ali, his son-in-law. Muhammad, speaking to God, said 'O lord, You are my friend and protector, Wali, and Ali is also my wali, may you support he who supports him and destroy he who stands against him.' Some Islamic groups, such as the ◊Wahabis, reject the notion of sainthood as a contradiction of *tawhid*, or the Oneness of God.

walkabout Australian Aboriginal English for a nomadic ritual excursion into the bush. The term was adopted in 1970, during tours of Australia and New Zealand by Elizabeth II, for informal public-relations walks by politicians and royalty.

Wallace Alfred Russel 1823–1913. English naturalist who collected animal and plant specimens in South America and SE Asia, and independently arrived at a theory of evolution by natural selection similar to that proposed by Charles ◊Darwin.

Wallas Graham 1858–1932. British political scientist, the first professor of political science at the London School of Economics. Wallas was an early member of the ◊Fabian Society and contributed to *Fabian Essays in Socialism* 1888. He left the society 1904 because it had become anti-liberal.

In *Human Nature in Politics* 1908 he argued that certain nonrational factors, such as prejudice, custom, and accident, were more likely to affect politics than rational calculation. *The Great Society* 1914 expressed concern for the individual in modern industrial society which was becoming increasingly centralized.

Walpurga, St English abbess who preached Christianity in Germany. *Walpurgis Night*, the night of 1 May (one of her feast days), became associated with witches' sabbaths and other superstitions. Her feast day is 25 Feb.

Walras Léon 1834–1910. French economist. In his *Eléments d'économie politique pure* 1874–77 he attempted to develop a unified model for general equilibrium theory (a hypothetical situation in which demand equals supply in all markets). He also originated the theory of diminishing marginal utility of a good (the increased value to a person of consuming more of a product).

Walton Ernest 1903– . Irish physicist who, as a young doctoral student at the Cavendish laboratory in Cambridge, England, collaborated with John Cockcroft on investigating the structure of the atom. In 1932 they succeeded in splitting the atom; for this experiment they shared the 1951 Nobel Prize for Physics.

Wandering Jew in medieval legend, a Jew named Ahasuerus, said to have insulted Jesus on his way to Calvary and to have been condemned to wander the world until the Second Coming.

Wang An 1920–1990. Chinese-born US engineer, founder of Wang Laboratories 1951, one of the world's largest computer companies in the 1970s. He emigrated to the USA 1945 and three years later invented the computer memory core, the most common device used for storing computer data before the invention of the integrated circuit (chip).

want in economics, the desire of consumers for material goods and services. Wants are argued to be infinite, meaning that consumers can never be satisfied with their existing standard of living but would always like to consume more goods and services. Infinite wants mean that resources have to be allocated.

Warburg Otto 1878–1976. German biochemist who in 1923 devised a manometer (pressure gauge) sensitive enough to measure oxygen uptake of respiring tissue. By measuring the rate at which cells absorb oxygen under differing conditions, he was able to show that enzymes called cytochromes enable cells to process oxygen. He was awarded the Nobel Prize for Medicine 1931. Warburg also demonstrated that cancerous cells absorb less oxygen than normal cells.

Washington Booker T(aliaferro) 1856–1915. US educationist, pioneer in higher education for black people in the South. He was the founder and first principal of Tuskegee Institute, Alabama, in 1881, originally a training college for blacks, and now an academic institution. He maintained that economic independence was the way to achieve social equality.

WASP acronym for *white Anglo-Saxon Protestant*, common (frequently derogatory)

term to describe the white elite in American society, specifically those educated at Ivy League universities and belonging to the Episcopalian Church.

The term was popularized by US sociologist E Digby Baltzell in his book *The Protestant Establishment* 1964.

Watson James Dewey 1928– . US biologist whose research on the molecular structure of DNA and the genetic code, in collaboration with Francis ◊Crick, earned him a shared Nobel prize in 1962. Based on earlier works, they were able to show that DNA formed a double helix of two spiral strands held together by base pairs.

Watson John Broadus 1878–1958. US psychologist, founder of ◊behaviourism. He rejected introspection (observation by an individual of his or her own mental processes) and regarded psychology as the study of observable behaviour, within the scientific tradition.

Watts Alan (Witson) 1915–1973. British-born US philosopher. Educated in England, Watts was a longtime student of Eastern religions and published *The Spirit of Zen* 1936. He emigrated to the USA 1939, graduated from the Seabury-Weston Theological Seminary, and was ordained in the Episcopal Church 1944. Briefly serving as chaplain at Northwestern University, he moved to California and taught philosophy at the College of the Pacific 1951–57. As a popular lecturer and author, he became a spiritual leader of the 'beat generation' of the 1950s. His books include *The Way of Zen* 1957.

weak nuclear force or *weak interaction* one of the four fundamental ◊forces of nature, the other three being gravity, the electromagnetic force, and the strong force. It causes radioactive decay and other subatomic reactions. The particles that carry the weak force are called weakons (or intermediate vector bosons) and comprise the positively and negatively charged W particles and the neutral Z particle.

Money speaks in a language all nations understand.

wealth
Aphra Benn, 1640–1689,
English author and adventuress.
The Rover, Part II III.i'

---

wealth in economics, the wealth of a nation is its stock of physical capital, human capital, and net financial capital owned overseas. Physical capital is the stock of buildings, factories, offices, machines, roads, and so on. Human capital is the workforce; not just the number of workers, but also their stock of education and training which makes them productive. Net financial capital is the difference between the money value of assets owned by foreigners in the domestic economy and the assets owned by the country abroad.

For individuals, the most significant wealth they have is themselves and their ability to generate an income by working.

After that, the largest item of wealth is likely to be their house. Possessions, money, and insurance policies are other examples of individual wealth.

Riches are for spending.

wealth

Francis Bacon, 1561–1626, English politician, philosopher, and essayist.
Essays, 'Of Expense'

Webb (Martha) Beatrice (born Potter) 1858–1943 and Sidney (James), Baron Passfield 1859–1947. English social reformers, writers, and founders of the London School of Economics (LSE) 1895. They were early members of the socialist ◊Fabian Society, and were married in 1892. They argued for social insurance in their minority report (1909) of the Poor Law Commission, and wrote many influential books, including *The History of Trade Unionism* 1894, *English Local Government* 1906–29, and *Soviet Communism* 1935.

If I ever felt inclined to be timid as I was going into a room full of people, I would say to myself, 'You're the cleverest member of one of the cleverest families in the cleverest class of the cleverest nation in the world, why should you be frightened?'

Beatrice Webb
Bertrand Russell *Portraits from Memory*

Sidney Webb was professor of public administration at the LSE 1912–27. He was a member of the Labour Party executive 1915–25, entered Parliament 1922, and was president of the Board of Trade 1924, dominions secretary 1929–30, and colonial secretary

1929–31. Beatrice wrote *The Co-operative Movement in Great Britain* 1891, *My Apprenticeship* 1926, and *Our Partnership* 1948.

Weber Ernst Heinrich 1795–1878. German anatomist and physiologist, brother of Wilhelm Weber. He applied hydrodynamics to study blood circulation, and formulated *Weber's law*, relating response to stimulus.

Weber's law (also known as the Weber–Fechner law) states that sensation is proportional to the logarithm of the stimulus. It is the basis of the scales used to measure loudness of sounds.

Weber Max 1864–1920. German sociologist, one of the founders of modern sociology. He emphasized cultural and political factors as key influences on economic development and individual behaviour. Weber wrote on many aspects of political and social thought, but he is best known for his thesis that the Protestant ethic of thrift and hard work encouraged the development of capitalism and for his analysis of bureaucracy, set out in his classic *The Protestant Ethic and the Spirit of Capitalism* 1904–05.

In his inquiries into the nature and role of domination, he distinguished three types of authority: traditional, based on the customs of the past and the authority of elders; charismatic, when authority springs from some remarkable individual's inspirational power; and legal–rational, based on norms and laws. Social change was more likely to occur, he believed, when a charismatic individual appeared who could overthrow the traditional order. After such a revolution, routine and order would eventually re-establish themselves. For Weber, bureaucracies rather than classes were of major importance in politics, and there were three kinds, corresponding to the types of authority: the patriarchal, the patrimonial, and the legal–rational respectively.

Weber introduced the notion of 'rationalization' into sociology, drawing attention to the importance of increasingly large organizations in politics and to bureaucratization as the inevitable result of the rational control of the material world that modern science has brought about.

In *The Protestant Ethic and the Spirit of Capitalism* 1904–05, Weber proposed that the success of capitalism and the economic prosperity of Germany, Switzerland, England, and Holland was due to the 'Protestant ethic', according to which everyone, entrepreneurs and workers alike, had a 'calling'; work was a creditable activity, and thrift and austerity were virtues.

Economy and Society 1922, his *magnum opus*, though unfinished when he died, is his final exposition of his various ideas on economics, politics, and the sociology of religion.

Wegener Alfred Lothar 1880–1930. German meteorologist and geophysicist, whose theory of ◊continental drift, expounded in *Origin of Continents and Oceans* 1915, was originally known as Wegener's hypothesis. His ideas can now be explained in terms of plate tectonics, the idea that the Earth's crust consists of a number of plates, all moving with respect to one another.

Wei Jingsheng 1951– . Chinese pro-democracy activist and essayist, imprisoned from 1979 for attacking the Chinese communist system. He is regarded as one of China's most important political prisoners.

The son of a Communist Party official in Anhui province, Wei joined the Red Guards in the Cultural Revolution 1966. In 1978 he joined the Democracy Movement of reformist dissidents in Beijing and published essays critical of the government in the journal *Explorations*, which he co-founded. In 1979, he was arrested and sentenced to 15 years' imprisonment 'for handing military secrets to foreigners'.

All sins are attempts to fill voids.

Simone Weil
Gravity and Grace

Weil Simone 1909–1943. French writer who became a practising Catholic after a mystical experience in 1938. Apart from essays, her works (advocating political passivity) were published posthumously, including *Waiting for God* 1951, *The Need for Roots* 1952, and *Notebooks* 1956.

Weinberg Steven 1933– . US physicist who in 1967 demonstrated, together with Abdus ◊Salam, that the weak nuclear force and the electromagnetic force (two of the fundamental ◊forces of nature) are variations of a single underlying force, now called the electroweak force. Weinberg and Salam shared a Nobel prize with Sheldon ◊Glashow in 1979.

Weinerg and Salam's theory involved the prediction of a new interaction, the neutral current (discovered in 1973), which required the presence of charm (see ◊quark).

welfare state political system under which the state (rather than the individual or the private sector) has responsibility for the welfare of its citizens. Services such as unemployment and sickness benefits, family allowances and income supplements, pensions, medical care, and education may be provided and financed through state insurance schemes and taxation.

There is no finer investment for any community than putting milk into babies. Healthy citizens are the greatest asset any country can have.

welfare state
Winston Churchill, 1874–1965, British conservative politician and prime minister.
Speech on radio 21 Mar 1943

In Britain, David Lloyd George, as chancellor, introduced a National Insurance Act 1911. The idea of a welfare state developed in the UK from the 1942 Beveridge Report on social security, which committed the government after World War II to the provision of full employment, a free national health service, and a social-security system. The wartime coalition government accepted its main provisions and they were largely put into effect by the Labour government 1945–51. Since then, economic stringencies and changes in political attitudes have done something to erode the original schemes but the concept remains as an ideal.

Internationally, the aim of creating a welfare state has been adopted in several countries, particularly in Scandinavia, but, again, often more as an ideal than a reality. The welfare-state concept was built into the political structures of communist states, led by the USSR, but even here economic realities tempered its practical implementation.

werewolf in folk belief, a human being either turned by spell into a wolf or having the ability to assume a wolf form. The symptoms of porphyria may have fostered the legends.

wergild or *wergeld* in Anglo-Saxon and Germanic law during the Middle Ages, the compensation paid by a murderer to the relatives of the victim, its value dependent on the social rank of the deceased. It originated in European tribal society as a substitute for the blood feud (essentially a form of vendetta), and was replaced by punishments imposed by courts of law during the 10th and 11th centuries.

Werner Abraham Gottlob 1749–1817. German geologist who developed the first influential paradigms of Earth structure and history. Though now judged largely erroneous, Werner's geology was the first to establish a physically based stratigraphy, grounded on precise mineralogical knowledge. He was the most influential instructor in the history of geology – most of the leading students of the next generation learnt their science under him at the Freiberg Akademie.

Werner Alfred 1866–1919. Swiss chemist. He was awarded a Nobel prize in 1913 for his work on valency theory, which gave rise to the concept of coordinate bonds and coordination compounds. He demonstrated that different three-dimensional arrangements of atoms in inorganic compounds give rise to optical isomerism (the rotation of polarized light in opposite directions by molecules that contain the same atoms but are mirror images of each other).

Wernicke Carl 1848–1905. German neurologist and psychiatrist known for his study of ◊aphasia. In *The Aphasic Syndrome* 1874, he described what later became known as sensory aphasia (that is, defects in, or loss of, speech and expression) as distinct from motor aphasia, first described by Paul Pierre Broca (1824–1880).

Although both forms of aphasia result from brain damage, Wernicke found that the locus of the damage differed: sensory aphasia being induced by lesions to the left temporal lobe, motor aphasia by lesions to the left posterior frontal lobe. He used the differential clinical features of the two aphasias to formulate a general theory of the neural bases of language. Wernicke also described a form of encephalopathy induced by thiamine deficiency which bears his name.

Wertheimer Max 1880–1943. Czech-born psychologist and founder, with Kurt Koffka (1880–1943) and Köhler, of ◊gestalt psychology. While travelling on a train 1910 he saw that a light flashing rapidly from two different positions seemed to be one light in motion. This type of perception became the basis for his gestalt concept.

Wesley Charles 1707–1788. English Methodist, brother of John ◊Wesley and one of the original Methodists at Oxford. He became a principal preacher and theologian of the Wesleyan Methodists, and wrote some 6,500 hymns.

Wesley John 1703–1791. English founder of ◊Methodism. When the pulpits of the Church of England were closed to him and his followers, he took the gospel to the people. For 50 years he rode about the country on horseback, preaching daily, largely in the open air. His sermons became the doctrinal standard of the Wesleyan Methodist Church.

He was born at Epworth, Lincolnshire, where his father was the rector, and went to Oxford University together with his brother Charles, where their circle was nicknamed Methodists because of their religious observances. He was ordained in the Church of England 1728 and returned to his Oxford college 1729 as a tutor. In 1735 he went to Georgia, USA, as a missionary. On his return he experienced 'conversion' 1738, and from being rigidly High Church developed into an ardent Evangelical. His *Journal* gives an intimate picture of the man and his work.

Wheatstone Charles 1802–1875. English physicist and inventor. With William Cooke, he patented a railway telegraph in 1837, and, developing an idea of Samuel Christie, devised the *Wheatstone bridge*, an electrical network for measuring resistance. Originally a musical-instrument maker, he invented the harmonica and the concertina.

wheel of law the title of the Buddha's first sermon after achieving enlightenment was 'Setting in motion the wheel of law'. In this address he taught the ◊Four Noble Truths as a set of fundamental statements about the nature of existence.

wheel of life the symbol of life as a wheel is found in many faiths. The wheel can stand for the whole cycle beginning with birth, rising up to the height of a person's power, and then declining again until death is reached. It can also stand for the rise and fall of fortunes at different times in a person's life. The wheel is frequently used in Buddhist and Hindu art to show the various stages of existence through which the average soul or atman has to pass to reach either release or nirvana. In Western religious art, the vicissitudes of life have been the most popular theme.

Whewell William 1794–1866. British physicist and philosopher who coined the term 'scientist' along with such words as 'Eocene' and 'Miocene', 'electrode', 'cathode', and 'anode'. Most of his career was connected with Cambridge University, where he became the Master of Trinity College. His most enduring influence rests on two works of great scholarship, *The History of the Inductive Sciences* 1837 and *The Philosophy of the Inductive Sciences* 1840.

Whig Party in the UK, predecessor of the Liberal Party. The name was first used of rebel ◊Covenanters and then of those who wished to exclude James II from the English succession (as a Roman Catholic). They were in power continuously 1714–60 and pressed for industrial and commercial development, a vigorous foreign policy, and religious toleration. During the French Revolution, the Whigs demanded parliamentary reform in Britain, and from the passing of the Reform Bill in 1832 became known as Liberals.

Whipple Fred Lawrence 1906– . US astronomer whose hypothesis in 1949 that the nucleus of a comet is like a dirty snowball was confirmed 1986 by space-probe studies of ◊Halley's comet.

Whipple George 1878–1976. US physiologist whose research interest concerned the formation of haemoglobin in the blood. He showed that anaemic dogs, kept under restricted diets, responded well to a liver regime, and that their haemoglobin quickly regenerated. This work led to a cure for pernicious anaemia. He shared the 1934 Nobel Prize for Medicine with George Minot (1885–1950) and William Murphy (1892–1987).

Whitby, Synod of council summoned by King Oswy of Northumbria 664, which decided to adopt the Roman rather than the Celtic form of Christianity for Britain.

Whitefield George 1714–1770. British Methodist evangelist. He was a student at Oxford University and took orders 1738, but was suspended for his unorthodox doctrines and methods. For many years he travelled through Britain and America, and by his preaching contributed greatly to the religious revival. Whitefield's Tabernacle was built for him in Tottenham Court Road, London (1756; bombed 1945 but rebuilt).

Whitehead Alfred North 1861–1947. English philosopher and mathematician. In logic, he pursued the suggestion, originating from ◊Frege, that mathematics can be derived from logic and he co-authored with ◊Russell the three volumes of *Principia Mathematica* 1910–13. In his 'philosophy of organism', he tried to contribute logical, mathematical, physical, biological, psychological, aesthetic, and religious notions in a comprehensive scheme. His other works include *The Concept of Nature* 1920, and *Adventures of Ideas* 1933.

He was lecturer in mathematics at Trinity College, Cambridge, for 30 years; then professor of applied mathematics at London University 1914–24, during which time he wrote on education and the philosophy of science; and professor of philosophy at Harvard University, USA, 1924–37. Other works include *Principles of Natural Knowledge* 1919, *Science and the Modern World* 1925, and *Process and Reality* 1929.

A wise Tory and a wise Whig, I believe, will agree. Their principles are the same, though their modes of thinking are different.

Samuel Johnson, known as 'Dr Johnson'
Written statement given to Boswell May 1781

White terror general term used by socialists and Marxists to describe a right-wing counter-revolution: for example, the attempts by the Chinese Guomindang to massacre the communists 1927–31.

Whitleyism the process of ◊collective bargaining in committees where employers and employees are equally represented, under the leadership of an independent chair, with the aim of reaching unanimous agreement, if necessary by compromise on both sides.

It takes its name from the Committee on the Relations between Employers and Employed set up by the government 1916 and chaired by John Whitley. Whitleyism has been most prevalent and successful in the public and quasi-public sectors.

Whit Sunday Christian festival held seven weeks after Easter, commemorating the descent of the Holy Spirit on the Apostles. The name is probably derived from the white garments worn by candidates for baptism at the festival. Whit Sunday is also called Pentecost because the Holy Spirit came at the Jewish festival of Pentecost (Shavuot).

Wien Wilhelm 1864–1928. German physicist who studied radiation and established the principle, since known as Wien's law, that the wavelength at which the radiation from an idealized radiating body is most intense is inversely proportional to the body's absolute temperature. (That is, the hotter the body, the shorter the wavelength.) For this and other work on radiation, he was awarded the 1911 Nobel Prize for Physics.

Wiener Norbert 1894–1964. US mathematician, credited with the establishment of the science of cybernetics in his book *Cybernetics* 1948. In mathematics, he laid the foundation of the study of stochastic processes (those dependent on random events), particularly Brownian movement.

Wigner Eugene Paul 1902– . Hungarian-born US physicist who introduced the notion of parity into nuclear physics with the consequence that all nuclear processes should be indistinguishable from their mirror images. For this, and other work on nuclear structure, he shared the 1963 Nobel Prize for Physics with Maria ◊Goeppert-Mayer and Hans Jensen (1906–1973).

Wilberforce William 1759–1833. English reformer who was instrumental in abolishing slavery in the British Empire. He entered Parliament 1780; in 1807 his bill for the abolition of the slave trade was passed, and in 1833, largely through his efforts, slavery was abolished throughout the empire.

Wilfrid, St 634–709. Northumbrian-born bishop of York from 665. He defended the cause of the Roman Church at the Synod of ◊Whitby 664 against that of Celtic Christianity. Feast day 12 Oct.

Wilkins Maurice Hugh Frederick 1916– . New Zealand-born British scientist. In 1962 he shared the Nobel Prize for Medicine with Francis ◊Crick and James ◊Watson for his work on the molecular structure of nucleic acids, particularly ◊DNA, using X-ray diffraction.

Wilkins began his career as a physicist working on luminescence and phosphorescence, radar, and the separation of uranium isotopes, and worked in the USA during World War II on the development of the atomic bomb. After the war he turned his attention from nuclear physics to biophysics, and studied the genetic effects of ultrasonic waves, nucleic acids, and viruses by using ultraviolet light.

Willard Frances Elizabeth Caroline 1839–1898. US educationalist and campaigner. Committed to the cause of the prohibition of alcohol, culminating in the Prohibition 1920–33, she served as president of the Women's Christian Temperance Union 1879–98. She was also elected president of the National Council of Women 1888.

Born in Churchville, New York, USA, and raised in Wisconsin, Willard was educated at the Northwestern Female College in Evanston, Illinois. After a career as a teacher, she was appointed dean of women at Northwestern University 1873.

Wilson Charles Thomson Rees 1869–1959. British physicist who in 1911 invented the Wilson cloud chamber, an apparatus for studying subatomic particles. He shared a Nobel prize 1927.

Wilson Edward O 1929– . US zoologist whose books have stimulated interest in biogeography, the study of the distribution of species, and sociobiology, the evolution of behaviour. His works include *Sociobiology: The New Synthesis* 1975 and *On Human Nature* 1978.

Winckelmann Johann Joachim 1717–1768. German art historian, who worked in Rome from 1755. His studies of ancient Greece and Rome were an inspiration for the Neo-Classicism movement, provided the basis for modern art history, and influenced the direction of education in Germany. They include *Geschichte der Kunst des Altertums/History of Ancient Art* 1764, in which he defines art as the expression of the spirit of an age.

wine wine is important in the practice of several religions, usually as a source of inspiration or religious ecstasy or, because of the resemblance of red wine to blood, as a sacrificial libation. In classical antiquity wine was sacred to ◊Dionysus (Bacchus at Rome), the god of performance, communal celebration, and riot. For Christians, it is, with bread, one of the foods of the ◊Eucharist which by ◊transubstantiation become the body and blood of Christ. In Judaism its consumption, in moderation, is regarded as beneficial to health and it is used in the ceremonies of *havdalah* and *kiddush*, on the Sabbath, and at festivals. All alcohol is proscribed in Islam, although the Sufis regard wine as a symbol of divine knowledge, and the description of paradise in the Koran mentions rivers of wine.

Winnicott Donald 1896–1971. British psychoanalyst and child psychiatrist. In his early work, Winnicott studied the relationship between mother and child, developing the view that, for the infant, the mother mediates development of the self. His theories were developed in three volumes summarizing his clinical experience, entitled *Collected Papers: Through Paediatrics to Psychoanalysis* 1958, *The Maturational Process and the Facilitating Environment* 1965, and *Playing and Reality* 1971.

Although often regarded as an exponent of ◊object-relations theory, he was a critic of

Kleinian approaches to therapy, arguing that only a technique which could allow regression to early childhood might help individuals for whom premature parental demands had impaired the course of ego development.

Wise Stephen Samuel 1874–1949. Hungarian-born US religious leader. Ordained as a reform rabbi 1893, he served congregations in New York City 1893–1900 and Portland, Oregon, 1900–07, after which he became rabbi of the Free Synagogue in New York. He was president of the American Jewish Congress 1924–49.

Born in Budapest, Wise emmigrated to the USA with his family 1875. Educated at the City College of New York, he received a PhD from Columbia University 1901. An ardent Zionist, he attended the Versailles Peace Conference 1919.

witchcraft the alleged possession and exercise of magical powers – *black magic* if used with evil intent, and *white magic* if benign. Its origins lie in traditional beliefs and religions. Practitioners of witchcraft have often had considerable skill in, for example, herbal medicine and traditional remedies; this prompted the World Health Organization in 1976 to recommended the integration of traditional healers into the health teams of African states.

The Christian church persecuted witches in Europe between the 15th and 17th centuries and in North America. The last official execution of a witch in Europe was that of Anna Goddi, hanged in Switzerland in 1782. ◊*Obi* is the witchcraft of black Africa imported to the West Indies, and includes Christian elements; ◊*voodoo* is a similar cult.

witch-hunt persecution of minority political opponents or socially nonconformist groups without any regard for their guilt or innocence. Witch-hunts are often accompanied by a degree of public hysteria; for example, the anticommunist hearings of ◊McCarthyism during the 1950s in the USA.

The world is everything that is the case.

Ludwig Wittgenstein
Tractatus Logico-Philosophicus

Wittgenstein Ludwig (Josef Johann) 1889–1951. Austrian philosopher. *Tractatus Logico-Philosophicus* 1922 postulated the 'picture theory' of language: that atomic propositions represent atomic facts (◊logical atomism). He subsequently rejected this idea, and developed the idea that the meaning of a word is its use.

The picture theory is highly obscure. Essentially, Wittgenstein said that it must be possible to break down a sentence into 'atomic propositions' whose elements in some way stand for elements of the real world. His later philosophy developed a quite different, anthropological view of language: words are used according to different rules or conventions in a variety of human activities – different 'language games' are played with them. The traditional philosophical problems arise through the assumption that words (like 'exist' in the sentence 'Physical objects do not really exist') carry a fixed meaning with them, independent of context.

He was a fellow of Trinity College, Cambridge 1930–35, and was professor of philosophy there 1939–47. He gained British nationality 1937. *Philosophical Investigations* 1953 and *On Certainty* 1969 were published posthumously.

During World War I he fought with the Austro-Hungarian army and was subsequently imprisoned in Italy to Aug 1919.

Woden or **Wodan** the foremost Anglo-Saxon god, whose Norse counterpart is ◊Odin.

Wöhler Friedrich 1800–1882. German chemist, a student of Jöns ◊Berzelius, who in 1828 was the first person to synthesize an organic compound (urea) from an inorganic compound (ammonium cyanate). He also devised a method 1827 that isolated the metals aluminium, beryllium, yttrium, and titanium from their ores.

Wolff Christian 1679–1754. German philosopher, mathematician, and scientist who invented the terms 'cosmology' and '◊teleology'. He was science adviser to Peter the Great of Russia 1716–25.

Wolff worked in many fields, including theology, psychology, botany, and physics. He was professor of mathematics at Halle 1707–23 and professor of mathematics and philosophy at Marburg 1723–40. His philosophy was influenced by Gottfried Leibniz and ◊scholasticism. His numerous works include *Vernunftige Gedanken von Gott, der Welt und der Seele der Menschen/Rational Ideas on God, the World and the Soul of Man* 1720.

Wölfflin Heinrich 1864–1945. Swiss art historian and writer on aesthetics. His analyses of style in painting, such as *Kunstgeschichtliche Grundbegriffe/Principles of Art History* 1915, were very influential in his time, advocating a formalist approach and the study of concrete properties such as line, colour, and form. His significance is now, however, seen chiefly in his establishing art history as a rigorous intellectual discipline.

Wollaston William 1766–1828. British chemist and physicist. He amassed a large fortune through his discovery in 1804 of how to make malleable platinum. He went on to discover the new elements palladium 1804 and rhodium 1805. He also contributed to optics through the invention of a number of ingenious and still useful measuring instruments.

Wollstonecraft Mary 1759–1797. English writer and feminist. She was a member of a group of radical intellectuals called the English Jacobins. Her book *A Vindication of the Rights of Women* 1792 demanded equal educational opportunities for women. In 1794 she had a daughter, Fanny, by Gilbert Imlay, an American writer she met in Paris. She married William ◊Godwin 1797 and died shortly after giving birth to their daughter, Mary (later Mary Shelley).

Her other works include *Thoughts on the Education of Daughters* 1787 and *A Vindication of the Rights of Men* 1790, which was a defence of the French Revolution.

But if God had wanted us to think just with our wombs, why did He give us a brain?
women
Clare Boothe Luce, 1903–1987, US journalist, playwright, and politician.
Life 16 Oct 1970

---

women's movement the campaign for the rights of women, including social, political, and economic equality with men. Early European campaigners of the 17th–19th centuries fought for women's right to own property, to have access to higher education, and to vote (see ◊suffragette). Once women's suffrage was achieved in the 20th century, the emphasis of the movement shifted to the goals of equal social and economic opportunities for women, including employment. A continuing area of concern in industrialized countries is the contradiction between the now generally accepted principle of equality and the demonstrable inequalities that remain between the sexes in state policies and in everyday life.

Pioneer 19th-century feminists, considered radical for their belief in the equality of the sexes, include Mary ◊Wollstonecraft and Emmeline ◊Pankhurst in the UK, and Susan B ◊Anthony and Elizabeth Cady ◊Stanton in the USA. The women's movement gained worldwide impetus after World War II with such theorists as Simone de ◊Beauvoir, Betty ◊Friedan, Kate ◊Millett, Gloria ◊Steinem, and Germaine ◊Greer, and he founding of the National Organization of Women (NOW) in New York 1966. From the late 1960s the radical and militant wing of the movement argued that women were oppressed by the male-dominated social structure as a whole, which they saw as pervaded by ◊sexism, despite legal concessions towards equality of the sexes. In the USA the Equal Employment Opportunity Commission, a government agency, was formed 1964 to end discrimination (including sex discrimination) in hiring. The Equal Rights Amendment (ERA), a proposed constitutional amendment prohibiting sex discrimination, was passed by Congress 1972 but failed to be ratified by the necessary majority of 38 states.

In the UK since 1975 discrimination against women in employment, education, housing, and provision of goods, facilities, and services to the public has been illegal under the Sex Discrimination and Equal Pay Acts. The economic value of women's unpaid work has been estimated at £2 trillion annually.

I'm not denyin' the women are foolish: God Almighty made 'em to match the men.
women
George Eliot. Pen name of Mary Ann Evans, 1819–1880, English novelist.
Adam Bede, ch. 53

Woodcraft Folk British name for the youth organization founded in the USA as the Woodcraft League by Ernest Thompson Seton 1902, with branches in many countries. Inspired by the ◊Scouts, it differs in that it is for mixed groups and is socialist in outlook.

Woodward Robert 1917–1979. US chemist who worked on synthesizing a large number of complex molecules. These included quinine 1944, cholesterol 1951, chlorophyll 1960, and vitamin B_{12} 1971. Nobel prize 1965.

Woodworth Robert Sessions 1869–1962. US psychologist. He collaborated with E L ◊Thorndike in examining individual learning differences and later attempted to derive objective tests of emotional stability. Although his contributions to research were limited, he published a number of general

Women's Movement: UK chronology

1562	The Statute of Artificers made it illegal to employ men or women in a trade before they had served seven years' apprenticeship. (It was never strictly enforced for women, as many guilds still allowed members to employ their wives and daughters in workshops.)
1753	Lord Hardwick's Marriage Act brought marriage under state control and created a firmer distinction between the married and unmarried.
1803	Abortion was made illegal.
1836	Marriage Act reform permitted civil weddings and enforced the official registration of births, deaths, and marriages.
1839	The Custody of Infants Act allowed mothers to have custody of their children under seven years old.
1840s	A series of factory acts limited the working day and occupations of women and children. A bastardy amendment put all the responsibility for the maintenance of an illegitimate child onto its mother.
1857	The Marriage and Divorce Act enabled a man to obtain divorce if his wife had committed adultery. (Women were only eligible for divorce if their husband's adultery was combined with incest, sodomy, cruelty, etc.)
1857–82	The Married Women's Property Acts allowed them to own possessions of various kinds for the first time.
1861	Abortion became a criminal offence even if performed as a life-saving act or done by the woman herself.
1862–70	The Contagious Diseases Acts introduced compulsory examination of prostitutes for venereal disease.
1860s	Fathers could be named and required to pay maintenance for illegitimate children.
1864	Schools Enquiry Commission recommendations led to the establishment of high schools for girls.
1867	The Second Reform Act enfranchised the majority of male householders. The first women's suffrage committee was formed in Manchester.
1869	Women ratepayers were allowed to vote in municipal (local) elections.
1871	Newham College, Cambridge, was founded for women.
1872	The Elizabeth Garrett Anderson Hospital for women opened in London.
1874	The London School of Medicine for women was founded.
1878	Judicial separation of a married couple became possible. Maintenance orders could be enforced in court.
1880	The Trades Union Congress (TUC) adopted the principle of equal pay for women.
1882	The Married Women's Property Act gave wives legal control over their own earned income.
1883	The Contagious Diseases Acts were repealed.
1885	The age of consent was raised to 16.
1887	The National Union of Women's Suffrage Societies became a nationwide group under Millicent Fawcett.
1903	The Women's Social and Political Union (WSPU) was founded by Emmeline and Christabel Pankhurst.
1905–10	Militant campaigns split the WSPU. Sylvia Pankhurst formed the East London Women's Federation.
1918	The Parliament (Qualification of Women) Act gave the vote to women householders over 30.
1923	Wives were given equal rights to sue for divorce on the grounds of adultery.
1925	The Guardianship of Infants Act gave women equal rights to the guardianship of their children.
1928	The 'Flapper' Vote: all women over 21 were given the vote.
1937	The Matrimonial Causes Act gave new grounds for divorce including desertion for three years and cruelty.
1944	The Butler Education Act introduced free secondary education for all.
1946	A Royal Commission on equal pay was formed.
1948	Cambridge University allowed women candidates to be awarded degrees.
1960	Legal aid became available for divorce cases.
1967	The Abortion Law Reform Act made abortion legal under medical supervision and within certain criteria.
1969	Divorce reform was introduced that reduced the time a petitioner needed to wait before applying for a divorce.
1973	The Matrimonial Causes Act provided legislation to enable financial provision to be granted on divorce.
1975	The Sex Discrimination and Equal Pay Acts were passed. The National and Scottish Women's Aid Federations were formed.
1976	The Domestic Violence and Matrimonial Proceedings Act came into effect. The Sexual Offences (Amendment) Act attempted to limit a man's defence of consent in rape cases.
1977	The employed married women's option to stay partially out of the National Insurance system was phased out. Women qualified for their own pensions.
1980	The Social Security Act allowed a married woman to claim supplementary benefit and family income supplement if she was the main wage earner.
1983	The government was forced to amend the 1975 Equal Pay Act to conform to European Community directives.
1984	The Matrimonial and Family Proceedings Act made it less likely for a woman to be granted maintenance on divorce. It also reduced the number of years a petitioner must wait before applying for a divorce to one.
1986	The granting of invalid-care allowance was successfully challenged in the European Court of Justice. The Sex Discrimination Act (Amendment) allowed women to retire at the same age as men, and lifted legal restrictions preventing women from working night shifts in manufacturing industries. Firms with less than five employees were no longer exempt from the act.
1990	The legal limit for abortion was reduced to 24 weeks.
1991	Rape within marriage became a prosecutable offence in the UK.

texts on psychology including *Experimental Psychology* 1938, *Contemporary Schools of Psychology* 1931, and *Dynamics of Behavior* 1958.

Woodworth studied at Harvard, where he worked with William James, and at the University of Liverpool in the UK, where he was assistant to Charles Sherrington (1857–1952).

Returning to the USA, he became professor of psychology at Cornell University 1909 and in 1914 was elected president of the American Psychological Association. In 1956 he received the first Gold Medal award of the American Psychological Foundation for his exceptional contribution as an integrator and organizer of psychological science.

Woolman John 1720–1772. American Quaker, born in Ancocas (now Rancocas), New Jersey. He was one of the first antislavery agitators and left an important *Journal*. He supported those who refused to pay a tax levied by Pennsylvania, to conduct the French and Indian War, on the grounds that it was inconsistent with pacifist principles.

Workers' Educational Association (WEA) British institution that aims to provide democratically controlled education for working people.

It was founded 1903 and first received grant aid for its classes 1907. Since then it has been funded partly by the government, although jealously guarding its independence. Its activities are split between traditional liberal education and training for trade unionists. Many Labour Party politicians, including Neil Kinnock and Roy Hattersley, have either taught in or been taught in WEA classes.

For men must work, and women must weep, / And there's little to earn, and many to keep.

work
Mary Henrietta Kingsley,
1862–1900, British ethnologist.
'The Three Fishers'

---

working class term applied to those members of an industrial society who earn their living through manual labour, known in the USA as **blue-collar workers**. The cultural and political identity of the working class has been eroded since World War II by the introduction of new technology and the break-up of traditional communities through urban redevelopment.

As a Marxist term, working class is more or less synonymous with proletariat and means those workers (manual or nonmanual) whose labour is bought and exploited by the ◊bourgeoisie in exchange for wages.

Work is love made visible. And if you cannot work with love but only with distaste, it is better that you should leave your work and sit at the gate of the temple and take alms of those who work with joy.

work
Khalil Gibran, 1883–1931, Syrian poet.
The Prophet 'On Work'

---

work to rule industrial action whereby employees work strictly according to the legal terms of their contract of employment, usually resulting in a slowing-down of the work process.

World Bank popular name for the *International Bank for Reconstruction and Development* specialized agency of the United Nations that borrows in the commercial market and lends on commercial terms. It was established 1945 under the 1944 ◊Bretton Woods agreement, which also created the International Monetary Fund. The *International Development Association* is an arm of the World Bank.

The World Bank now earns almost as much money from interest and loan repayments as it hands out in new loans every year. Over 60% of the bank's loans go to suppliers outside the borrower countries for such things as consultancy services, oil, and machinery. Control of the bank is vested in a board of executives representing national governments, whose votes are apportioned according to the amount they have funded the bank. Thus the USA has nearly 20% of the vote and always appoints the board's president.

In 1989 the World Bank made a net transfer of $42.9 billion to developing countries.

World Council of Churches (WCC) international organization aiming to bring together diverse movements within the Christian church. Established 1945, it has a membership of more than 100 countries and more than 300 churches; headquarters in Geneva, Switzerland.

The supreme governing body, the assembly, meets every seven or eight years to frame policy. A 150-member central committee meets once a year and a 22-member executive committee twice a year.

World Health Organization (WHO) agency of the ◊United Nations established 1946 to prevent the spread of diseases and to eradicate them. In 1990–91 it had 4,500 staff and a budget of £843 million. Its headquarters are in Geneva, Switzerland.

worship adoration and service of God or gods. This service involves reverence, awe, and wonder, and may take many different forms.

Worship is rarely an individual act, but usually takes the form of group participation in rituals. In some religious traditions, such as Christianity, the emphasis is on the attitude of the heart as being essential in true worship. In Hinduism, the principle form of worship is the mantra, in which the divine is embodied in sound.

The physician can bury his mistakes, but the architect can only advise his clients to plant vines.

Frank Lloyd Wright
New York Times Magazine

Wright Frank Lloyd 1869–1959. US architect, known for 'organic architecture', in which buildings reflect their natural surroundings. From the 1890s, he developed his celebrated *prairie house* style, a series of low, spreading houses with projecting roofs. He later diversified, employing reinforced concrete to explore a variety of geometric forms. Among his buildings are his Wisconsin home Taliesin East 1925, in prairie-house style; Falling Water, near Pittsburgh, Pennsylvania 1936, a house of cantilevered terraces straddling a waterfall; and the Guggenheim Museum, New York 1959, a spiral ramp rising from a circular plan.

Wright also designed buildings in Japan 1915–22, most notably the Imperial Hotel in Tokyo 1922. In 1938 he built his winter home in the Arizona desert, Taliesin West, and established an architectural community there. He always designed the interiors and furnishings

for his projects, to create a total environment for his patrons.

Wundt Wilhelm Max 1832–1920. German physiologist, physiologist, philosopher, and psychologist who was the first to recognize that psychology is a scientific discipline in his book *Beitrage zur Theorie des Sinneswahrnehmung/ Contributions in Sensory Perception* 1862.

In *Grundzuge der physiologischen Psychologie/ The Essentials of Physiological Psychology* 1874, he laid the foundations of experimental psychology and in 1879 established the world's first psychological institute, at Leipzig University where he was professor of philosophy for most of his career. For Wundt, psychology was the study of inner experience, or consciousness, and its method was carefully controlled ◊introspection. He also wrote extensively on philosophy.

Wycliffe John c. 1320–1384. English religious reformer. Allying himself with the party of John of Gaunt, which was opposed to ecclesiastical influence at court, he attacked abuses in the church, maintaining that the Bible rather than the church was the supreme authority. He criticized such fundamental doctrines as priestly absolution, confession, and indulgences, and set disciples to work on translating the Bible into English.

Having studied at Oxford University, he became Master of Balliol College there, and sent out bands of travelling preachers. He was denounced as a heretic, but died peacefully at Lutterworth.

Wynne-Edwards Vera 1906– . English zoologist who argued that animal behaviour is often altruistic and that animals will behave for the good of the group, even if this entails individual sacrifice. Her study *Animal Dispersal in Relation to Social Behaviour* was published 1962.

The theory that animals are genetically programmed to behave for the good of the species has since fallen into disrepute. From this dispute grew a new interpretation of animal behaviour, seen in the work of biologist E O ◊Wilson.

wrought over all things'. Considerable fragments of his elegies and of his poem *On Nature* have survived.

But Lord! to see the absurd nature of Englishmen, that cannot forbear laughing and jeering at everything that looks strange.

xenophobia
Samuel Pepys, 1633–1703, English diarist.
Diary 27 Nov 1662

---

xenophobia fear (◊phobia) or strong dislike of strangers or anybody foreign or different.

Xavier, St Francis 1506–1552. Spanish Jesuit missionary. He went to the Portuguese colonies in the East Indies, arriving at Goa 1542. He was in Japan 1549–51, establishing a Christian mission that lasted for 100 years. He returned to Goa in 1552, and sailed for China, but died of fever there. He was canonized 1622.

Xenophanes of Colophon c. 570–c. 470 BC. Greek poet and philosopher who attacked the immoral and humanlike gods depicted by the poet Homer, holding that there is only one deity, 'in no way like men in body or in thought'. He speculated that stars were ignited clouds, and that everything was mud since fossils of sea creatures were found inland.

Leaving Ionia at the age of 25, he travelled around the Greek world reciting his philosophical and other poems. His outlook was generally undogmatic, because 'seeming is

Xenophon c. 430–354 BC. Greek historian, philosopher, and soldier. He was a disciple of ◊Socrates (described in Xenophon's *Symposium*). In 401 he joined a Greek mercenary army aiding the Persian prince Cyrus, and on the latter's death took command. His *Anabasis* describes how he led 10,000 Greeks on a 1,600-km/1,000-mile march home across enemy territory. His other works include *Memorabilia*, *Apology*, and *Hellenica/A History of My Times*.

The sea! the sea!

Xenophon
The cry of the Greek mercenaries on reaching safety at the Black Sea, after escaping from the Battle of Cunaxa, 401BC; *Anabasis* IV. vii

---

century). The beliefs of its adherents mingle folk traditions with Islam, also incorporating features of Judaism and Christianity (they practise circumcision and baptism), and include a cult of the Fallen Angel who has been reconciled with God. Their chief centre is near Mosul, Iraq.

Yggdrasil in Scandinavian mythology, the world tree, a sacred ash that spans heaven and hell. It is evergreen and tended by the Norns, goddesses of past, present, and future.

Yggdrasil has three roots with a spring under each one. One root covers Nifelheim, the realm of the dead; another runs under Jotunheim, where the giants live; the third under Asgard, home of the gods. By the Norns' well at the third root, the gods regularly gather to confer. Various animals inhabit and feed off the tree.

yin and yang Chinese for 'dark' and 'bright' respectively, referring to the passive (characterized as feminine, negative, intuitive) and active (characterized as masculine, positive, intellectual) principles of nature. Their interaction is believed to maintain equilibrium and harmony in the universe and to be present in all things. In ◊Taoism and ◊Confucianism they are represented by two interlocked curved shapes within a circle, one white, one black, with a spot of the contrasting colour within the head of each.

Yippie in the USA, a member of the *Youth International Party* (YIP), led by Abbie Hoffmann and Jerry Rubin (1938–), who mocked the US political process during the 1960s.

Ymir in Scandinavian mythology, the first living being, a giant who grew from melting frost. Of his descendants, the god Odin and his two brothers, Vili and Ve, killed Ymir and created heaven and earth from parts of his body.

yoga Hindu philosophical system attributed to Patanjali, who lived about 150 BC at Gonda, Uttar Pradesh, India. He preached mystical union with a personal deity through the practice of self-hypnosis and a rising above the senses by abstract meditation, adoption of special postures, and ascetic practices. As practised in the West, yoga is more a system of mental and physical exercise, and of induced relaxation as a means of relieving stress.

Yom Kippur the Jewish Day of ◊Atonement.

yoni in Hinduism, an image of the female genitalia as an object of worship, a manifestation of ◊Sakti; the male equivalent is the lingam.

Yahweh alternative spelling of ◊Jehovah or Jahweh – 'The Lord' or 'God' of Israel. This spelling derives from the Greek transliteration of the name of God.

Yale School group of literary critics, based at Yale University, Connecticut, USA, who applied the deconstructionist approach of group member Jacques ◊Derrida to literary theory. They tried to show the impossibility of a text possessing a coherent meaning by highlighting its internal contradictions and by denying the relevance of any reference to external reality or to the author's intentions.

Yale University US university, founded 1701 in New Haven, Connecticut. It was named after Elihu Yale (1648–1721), born in Boston, Massachusetts, one-time governor of Fort St George, Madras, India.

Yalta Conference in 1945, a meeting at which the Allied leaders Churchill (UK), Roosevelt (USA), and Stalin (USSR) completed plans for the defeat of Germany in World War II and the foundation of the United Nations. It took place in Yalta, a Soviet holiday resort in the Crimea.

yarmulke or *kippa* skullcap worn by Jewish men.

yashmak traditional Muslim face veil, worn by devout Muslim women in the presence of men.

Yersin Alexandre Emile Jean 1863–1943. Swiss bacteriologist who discovered the bubonic plague bacillus in Hong Kong 1894 and prepared a serum against it.

yeti Tibetan for the ◊abominable snowman.

Yezidi Islamic group originating as disciples of the Sufi saint Sheik Adi ibn Musafir (12th

Young Brigham 1801–1877. US ◊Mormon religious leader, born in Vermont. He joined the Mormon Church, or Church of Jesus Christ of Latter-day Saints, 1832, and three years later was appointed an apostle. After a successful recruiting mission in Liverpool, England, he returned to the USA and, as successor of Joseph Smith (who had been murdered), led the Mormon migration to the Great Salt Lake in Utah 1846, founded Salt Lake City, and headed the colony until his death.

Young Thomas 1773–1829. British physicist who revived the wave theory of light and identified the phenomenon of interference in 1801.

A child prodigy, he had mastered most European languages and many of the Eastern tongues by the age of 20. He had also absorbed the physics of Newton and the chemistry of Lavoisier. He further displayed his versatility by publishing an account of the Rosetta stone; the work played a crucial role in the stone's eventual decipherment by Jean François Champollion.

Youth Culture imprecise term for the variety of subcultural phenomena associated with young people as a social group. These may be oppositional to the norms of adult life and are often symbolized by distinctive styles of clothing and taste in music.

Yuppie acronym for *young urban professional*, a term used, sometimes pejoratively, to describe a social group that emerged in the 1970s. Yuppies are characterized by their ambition and by their conspicuously affluent lifestyle.

zazen formal seated meditation in Zen Buddhism. Correct posture and breathing are necessary.

Zealot member of a Jewish party opposed to Roman rule during the time of Jesus and later. The Zealots were one of the parties responsible for rising against Rome in the rebellion of 67–70 AD. Simon the Zealot, one of Jesus' disciples, may have been a member of this party, or the term may simply have meant he was zealous.

Zedekiah last king of Judah 597–586 BC. Placed on the throne by Nebuchadnezzar, he rebelled, was forced to witness his sons' execution, then was blinded and sent to Babylon. The witness to these events was the prophet Jeremiah, who describes them in the Old Testament.

Zeeman Pieter 1865–1943. Dutch physicist who discovered 1896 that when light from certain elements, such as sodium or lithium (when heated), is passed through a spectroscope in the presence of a strong magnetic field, the spectrum splits into a number of distinct lines. His discovery, known as the *Zeeman effect*, won him a share of the 1902 Nobel Prize for Physics.

Zeitgeist spirit of the age. The term was used as the title of an exhibition of Neo-Expressionist paintings held in Berlin 1982.

Zen form of ◊Buddhism introduced from India to Japan via China in the 12th century. ◊*Kōan* (paradoxical questions), tea-drinking, and sudden enlightenment are elements of Zen practice. Soto Zen was spread by the priest Dōgen (1200–1253), who emphasized work, practice, discipline, and philosophical questions to discover one's Buddha-nature in the 'realization of self'.

Zend-Avesta sacred scriptures of ◊Zoroastrianism, today practised by the Parsees. They comprise the *Avesta* (liturgical books for the priests); the *Gathas* (the discourses and revelations of Zoroaster); and the *Zend* (commentary upon them).

Zeno of Citium c. 335–262 BC. Greek founder of the ◊stoic school of philosophy in Athens, about 300 BC.

Zeno of Elea c. 490–430 BC. Greek philosopher who defended the theory of ◊Parmenides that reality is a single, motionless being by producing arguments to show that plurality and motion entail logically contradictory consequences. These arguments are known as 'Zeno's Paradoxes', perhaps the most famous of which are the 'Arrow' and 'Achilles and the Tortoise'.

The 'Arrow' paradox states that since an arrow must occupy a determinate space at each instant in its flight, it must at that instant be at rest as it flies, and if it is at rest it cannot be in motion. In the 'Achilles and the Tortoise' paradox, Achilles allows the tortoise a head start in a race. However, as the distance between them is infinitely divisible, Achilles can never reach the same position as the tortoise. Whenever he covers a portion of the distance the tortoise has also moved on and there still remains a gap between them which he will have to make up, and so on ad infitum.

The exact solutions to Zeno's paradoxes are still disputed, but Zeno was evidently unaware that the sum of an infinite geometric progression is finite if the common ratio, or constant multiple, is less than 1.

Zernike Frits 1888–1966. Dutch physicist who developed the phase-contrast microscope 1935. Earlier microscopes allowed many specimens to be examined only after they had been transformed by heavy staining and other treatment. The phase-contrast microscope allowed living cells to be directly observed by making use of the difference in refractive indices between specimens and medium. He was awarded the Nobel Prize for Physics 1953.

zero the number (written 0) that when added to any number leaves that number unchanged. It results when any number is subtracted from itself, or when any number is added to its negative. The product of any number with zero is itself zero.

Zeus in Greek mythology, the chief of the gods (Roman Jupiter). He was the son of Kronos, whom he overthrew; his brothers included Pluto and Poseidon, his sisters

Demeter and Hera. As the supreme god he dispensed good and evil and was the father and ruler of all humankind. His emblems are the thunderbolt and aegis (shield), representing the thundercloud. The colossal ivory and gold statue of the seated god, made by Phidias for the temple of Zeus in the Peloponnese, was one of the Seven Wonders of the World.

Zeus ate his pregnant first wife Metis (goddess of wisdom), fearing their child (Athena) would be greater than himself. However, Athena later sprung fully armed from Zeus's head when Hephaestus split it with an axe. His second wife was Hera, but he also fathered children by other women and goddesses. The offspring, either gods and goddesses or godlike humans, included Apollo, Artemis, Castor and Pollux/Polydeuces, Dionysus, Hebe, Heracles, Hermes, Minos, Perseus, and Persephone.

Ziegler Karl 1898–1973. German organic chemist. In 1963 he shared the Nobel Prize for Chemistry with Giulio Natta of Italy for his work on the chemistry and technology of large polymers. He combined simple molecules of the gas ethylene (ethene) into the long-chain plastic polyethylene (polyethene).

ziggurat in ancient Babylonia and Assyria, a step pyramid of sun-baked brick faced with glazed bricks or tiles on which stood a shrine. The Tower of Babel as described in the Bible may have been a ziggurat.

Zinoviev Alexander 1922– . Soviet philosopher whose satire on the USSR, *The Yawning Heights* 1976, led to his exile 1978. *The Reality of Communism* 1984 outlined the argument that communism is the natural consequence of masses of people living under deprived conditions, and thus bound to expand.

Zion Jebusite (Amorites of Canaan) stronghold in Jerusalem captured by King David, and the hill on which he built the Temple, symbol of Jerusalem and of Jewish national life.

Zionism political movement advocating the re-establishment of a Jewish homeland in Palestine, the 'promised land' of the Bible, with its capital Jerusalem, the 'city of Zion'.

Zola Emile Edouard Charles Antoine 1840–1902. French novelist and social reformer. With *La Fortune des Rougon/The Fortune of the Rougons* 1867 he began a series of some 20 naturalistic novels, portraying the fortunes of a French family under the Second Empire. They include *Le Ventre de Paris/The Underbelly of Paris* 1873, *Nana* 1880, and *La Débâcle/The Debacle* 1892. In 1898 he published *J'accuse/I Accuse*, a pamphlet indicting

the persecutors of Dreyfus, for which he was prosecuted for libel but later pardoned.

Born in Paris, Zola was a journalist and clerk until his *Contes à Ninon/Stories for Ninon* 1864 enabled him to devote himself to literature. Some of the titles in La Fortune des Rougon series are *La Faute de l'Abbé Mouret/ The Simple Priest* 1875, *L'Assommoir/Drunkard* 1878, *Germinal* 1885, and *La Terre/Earth* 1888. Among later novels are the trilogy *Trois Villes/Three Cities* 1894–98, and *Fécondité/ Fecundity* 1899.

I accuse.

Emile Zola
Heading of an open letter to the
President of the Republic concerning
the Dreyfus case 1898

zombie corpse believed to be reanimated by a spirit and enslaved. The idea, widespread in Haiti, possibly arose from voodoo priests using the nerve poison tetrodotoxin (from the puffer fish) to produce a semblance of death from which the victim afterwards physically recovers. Those eating incorrectly prepared puffer fish in Japan have been similarly affected.

Zoroaster or **Zarathustra** 6th century BC. Persian prophet and religious teacher, founder of Zoroastrianism. Zoroaster believed that he had seen God, ◊Ahura Mazda, in a vision. His first vision came at the age of 30 and, after initial rejection and violent attack, he converted King Vishtaspa. Subsequently, his teachings spread rapidly, becoming the official religion of the kingdom. According to tradition, Zoroaster was murdered at the age of 70 while praying at the altar.

Zoroastrianism pre-Islamic Persian religion founded by the Persian prophet ◊Zoroaster in the 6th century BC, and still practised by the ◊Parsees in India. The ◊*Zend-Avesta* are the sacred scriptures of the faith. The theology is dualistic, *Ahura Mazda* or *Ormuzd* (the good God) being perpetually in conflict with *Ahriman* (the evil God), but the former is assured of eventual victory. There are approximately 100,000 (1991) Zoroastrians worldwide; membership is restricted to those with both parents belonging to the faith.

beliefs Humanity has been given free will to choose between the two powers, thus rendering believers responsible for their fate after death in heaven or hell. Moral and physical purity is central to all aspects of Zoroastrianism *yasna* or worship: since life and work are part of worship, there should be purity of action. Fire is considered sacred, and Ahura Mazda believed to be present when the ritual flame is worshipped at home or in the temple. It is believed that there will be a second universal judgement at *Frashokereti*, a time when the dead will be raised and the world cleansed of unnatural impurity.

The Parsee community in Bombay is now the main centre of Zoroastrianism, but since conversion is generally considered impossible, the numbers in India have been steadily decreasing at the rate of 10% per decade since 1947. Parsee groups, mainly in Delhi and outside India, have been pushing for the acceptance of converts, but the concern of the majority in Bombay is that their religious and cultural heritage will be lost.

Zsigmondy Richard 1865–1929. Austrian chemist who devised and built an ultramicroscope in 1903. The microscope's illumination was placed at right angles to the axis. (In a conventional microscope the light source is placed parallel to the instrument's axis.)

Zsigmondy's arrangement made it possible to observe gold particles with a diameter of 10-millionth of a millimetre. He received the Nobel Prize for Chemistry 1925.

Zwicky Fritz 1898–1974. Bulgarian-born Swiss astronomer who lived in the USA from 1925. He was professor of physics at the California Institute of Technology (Caltech) from 1927 until his retirement 1968. In 1934, he predicted the existence of neutron stars and, together with Walter Baade, named supernovae. He discovered 18 supernovae in total, and determined that cosmic rays originated in them.

Zwingli Ulrich 1484–1531. Swiss Protestant, born in St Gallen. He was ordained a Roman Catholic priest 1506, but by 1519 was a Reformer and led the ◊Reformation in Switzerland with his insistence on the sole authority of the Scriptures. He was killed in a skirmish at Kappel during a war against the cantons that had not accepted the Reformation.

INDEX
Contents

INDEX OF SUBJECTS

Arts and Leisure

Architecture
baroque
Bauhaus
Brutalism
community architecture
Deconstructionism
Functionalism
garden city
Gothic Revival
High Tech
international style
mihrab
Stijl
town planning

Literature
allegory
ambiguity
angry young men
anthology
anthropomorphism
anti-hero
beat generation
bestiary
biography
Bloomsbury group
book
Candide
catharsis
children's literature
Classicism
deconstruction
disassociation of senses
doppelganger
dystopia
epic
feminist criticism
Futurism
Gilgamesh
Harlem renaissance
imagism
irony
literary criticism
Modernism
New Criticism
new wave (nouvelle vague)
Nibelungenlied
Nobel prize
noble savage
nouveau roman
novel
objective correlative

pensée
reader-response theory
reception theory
saga
satire
science fiction
social realism
stream of consciousness
symbolism
taliesin
Tel Quel
textual criticism
übermensch
Yale school

The Performing Arts
absolute music
absurd, theatre of the
alternative theatre
catharsis
choreography
comedy
corroboree
cruelty, theatre of
dance
drama, religious
Feldenkrais method
Mudra
music
programme music
Romanticism
serialism
tragedy
twelve-tone system

The Visual Arts
abstract art
Abstract Expressionism
action painting
aestheticism
Aesthetic Movement
aesthetics
aleatory
anti-art
archetype
art
art for art's sake
art history
Art Nouveau
arts and crafts movement
avant-garde
Baroque
camp

cinema verité
conceptual art
connoisseur
Constructivism
Cubism
dada (dadaism)
dance of death
decadence
decorum
degenerate art
design
eclecticism
Expressionism
Fauvism
fine arts
formalism
found object
Futurism
golden section
humanism
icon
iconography
iconology
Impressionism
kitsch
liberal arts
mannerism
Marxist aesthetic theory
Metaphysical Painting
Minimalism
Modernism
morphing
Naturalism
negritude
Neo-Classicism
non-objective art
Orphism
pastoral
pathetic fallacy
plastic arts
Pop art
Post-Impressionism
Post-Modernism
Primitivism
Realism
Rococo
romanticism
sensibility
socialist realism
Stijl
style
sublime, the
Suprematism

apartheid
authoritarianism
autocracy
autonomy
back to the land
black nationalism
black power
bloc
bolshevik
Bonapartism
Butskellism
Caesarism
capitalism
Christian Democracy
Christian Socialism
citizenship
civil rights
collective responsibility
collectivism
colonialism
communism
concordat
conservatism
constitution
cooperative movement
corporatism
corporative state
Declaration of Independence
democracy
despotism
détente
devolution
dictatorship
dictatorship of the proletariat
dissident
distributism
divine right of kings
dominant ideology
dove
egalitarianism
emancipation
equal opportunities
Eurocommunism
fascism
federalism
federalist
force majeure
government
green movement
guild socialism
hawk
hegemony
historical materialism
human rights
ideology
imperialism
individualism
isolationism
judiciary

junta
justice
left wing
Leninism
liberalism
libertarianism
Little Red Book
lumpenproletariat
manifesto
Maoism
Marxism
Marxism–Leninism
menshevik
meritocracy
nationalism
national socialism
nazism
neocolonialism
neoconservatism
neutrality
new left
nihilist
nonviolence
oligarchy
pacifism
peace
personality cult
pluralism
political party
political science
political theory
politics
privacy
privatization
propaganda
radical
reactionary
red
reformism
republic
revisionism
rights
right wing
rule of law
separation of powers
Slavophile
social contract
social credit
social democracy
socialism
'socialism in one country'
society
sovereignty
Soviet
Spartacist
Stalinism
state
strike
subsidiarity

syndicalism
theocracy
theory of three worlds
totalitarianism
trade unionism, international
Trotskyism
unilateralism
Zionism

Psychology
abnormality
androgyny
angst ('anxiety')
animism
anorexia
anti-psychiatry
anxiety
aphasia
automatic writing
automatism
autosuggestion
behaviourism
behaviour therapy
body language
bulimia
castration anxiety
censor
clinical psychology
cognition
cognitive dissonance
cognitive psychology
cognitive therapy
collective unconscious
comparative psychology
complex
conditioning
consciousness
counselling
delusion
depression
developmental psychology
displacement
dream
dyslexia
educational psychology
ego
electroconvulsive therapy
Emmert's Law
emotion
experimental psychology
extrasensory perception
extroversion
fetishism
free association
friendship
fugue
gender differences
genius
gestalt

Physics and Chemistry
anthropic principle
antimatter
atomic mass unit
Bell's theorem
biochemistry
Boyle's law
Cavendish experiment
chemistry
colour vision
critical mass
Doppler effect
efficiency
elementary particle
entropy
ether
Fermat's principle

fission
forces, fundamental
fusion
Grand Unified Theory
gravity
Hooke's law
Mach number
mass
matter
mean life
mechanics
molecule
Newtonian physics
Ohm's law
optics
perpetual motion
physics

quantum chromodynamics
quantum mechanics
quantum number
quantum theory (quantum
　mechanics)
quark
relativity
Reynolds number
space–time
superstring theory
supersymmetry
theory
Theory of Everything
thermodynamics
uncertainty principle
unified field theory

INDEX OF PEOPLE

Mind and Belief

*Religious Figures: Buddhists, Hindus, Sikhs,
and Other Religions*

The Natural World